# MyMISLab™: Improves Student Engagement Before, During, and After Class

- **NEW! VIDEO LIBRARY –** Robust video library with over 100 new book-specific videos that include easy-to-assign assessments, the ability for instructors to add YouTube or other sources, the ability for students to upload video submissions, and the ability for polling and teamwork.
- **Decision-making simulations – NEW and improved feedback for students.** Place your students in the role of a key decision-maker! Simulations branch based on the decisions students make, providing a variation of scenario paths. Upon completion students receive a grade, as well as a detailed report of the choices and the associated consequences of those decisions.
- **Video exercises – UPDATED with new exercises.** Engaging videos that bring business concepts to life and explore business topics related to the theory students are learning in class. Quizzes then assess students' comprehension of the concepts covered in each video.
- **Learning Catalytics –** A "bring your own device" student engagement, assessment, and classroom intelligence system helps instructors analyze students' critical-thinking skills during lecture.
- **Dynamic Study Modules (DSMs) – UPDATED with additional questions.** Through adaptive learning, students get personalized guidance where and when they need it most, creating greater engagement, improving knowledge retention, and supporting subject-matter mastery. Also available on mobile devices.

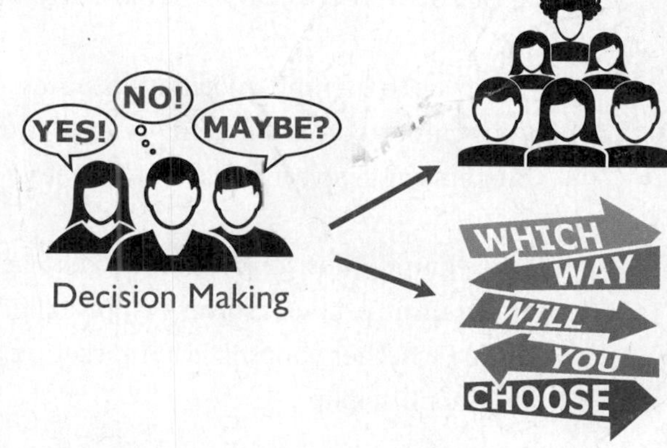


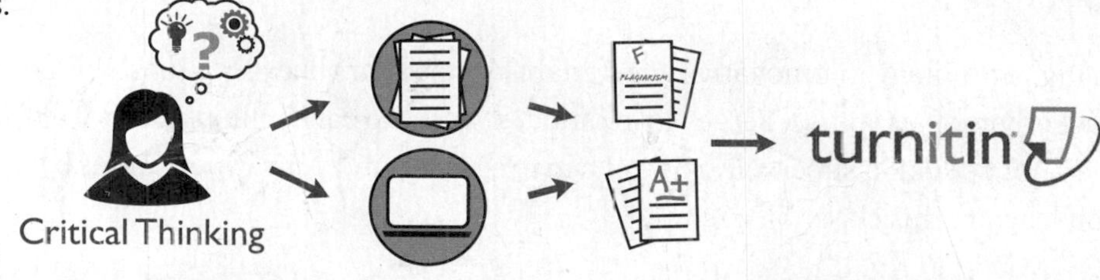


- **Writing Space – UPDATED with new commenting tabs, new prompts, and a new tool for students called Pearson Writer.** A single location to develop and assess concept mastery and critical thinking, the Writing Space offers automatic graded, assisted graded, and create your own writing assignments, allowing you to exchange personalized feedback with students quickly and easily.

  Writing Space can also check students' work for improper citation or plagiarism by comparing it against the world's most accurate text comparison database available from **Turnitin**.

- **Additional Features –** Included with the MyLab are a powerful homework and test manager, robust gradebook tracking, Reporting Dashboard, comprehensive online course content, and easily scalable and shareable content.

http://www.pearsonmylabandmastering.com

*Dear Student,*

College is a fun time in your life. You've experienced the freedom of living on your own, made new friends, and enjoyed once-in-a-lifetime experiences. However, at this point in your college career you've begun to realize that a life transition is on your horizon. You will graduate and you will need to find a career, not just another job. Now is the time to start thinking about that career and how you prepare for it.

Most students say they want a successful career. But defining *successful* is different for each. Most students want an exciting, stable, well-paying job. You owe it to yourself to think about what that job is and how you're going to get it. Which jobs pay the salary you want? Are some jobs more stable than others? What type of work do you want to do for the next 40 years?

This MIS course is important for answering those questions. Over time, technology creates new jobs . . . examples today are mobile application developers, social media analysts, information security specialists, business intelligence analysts, and data architects, to consider just a few jobs that didn't exist 20, even 10, years ago. Similarly, the best jobs 20 years from now probably don't currently exist.

The trick to turning information systems to your advantage is getting ahead of their effect. During your career, you will find many opportunities for the innovative application of information systems in business and government, but only if you know how to look for them.

Once found, those opportunities become your opportunities when you—as a skilled, creative, nonroutine problem solver—apply emerging technology to facilitate your organization's strategy. This is true whether your job is in marketing, operations, sales, accounting, finance, entrepreneurship or another discipline.

Using technology in innovative ways enabled superstars like Steve Jobs, Bill Gates, Larry Ellison, Mark Zuckerberg, Larry Page, Sergey Brin, and Jeff Bezos to earn billions and revolutionize commerce. You may not be such a superstar, but you can exceed beyond your expectations by applying the knowledge you learn in this class.

Congratulations on deciding to study business. Use this course to help you obtain and then thrive in an interesting and rewarding career. Learn more than just the MIS terminology; understand the ways information systems are transforming business and the many, many ways you can participate in that transformation.

In this endeavor, we wish you, a future business professional, the very best success!

*David Kroenke & Randy Boyle*

# The Guides

Each chapter includes two unique guides that focus on current issues in information systems. In each chapter, one of the guides focuses on an ethical issue in business. The other guide focuses on the application of the chapter's contents to some other dimension of business. The content of each guide is designed to stimulate thought, discussion, and active participation in order to help *you* develop your problem-solving skills and become a better business professional.

# LEARNING AIDS FOR STUDENTS

We have structured this book so you can maximize the benefit from the time you spend reading it. As shown in the table below, each chapter includes a series of learning aids to help you succeed in this course.

| Resource | Description | Benefit | Example |
|---|---|---|---|
| **Question-Driven Chapter Learning Objectives** | These queries, and the subsequent chapter sections written around them, focus your attention and make your reading more efficient. | Identify the main point of the section. When you can answer each question, you've learned the main point of the section. | Chapter 6, Q6-1: Why Is the Cloud the Future for Most Organizations? |
| **Guides** | Each chapter includes two guides that focus on current issues relating to information systems. One addresses ethics, and the other addresses other business topics. | Stimulate thought and discussion. Help develop your problem-solving skills. Help you learn to respond to ethical dilemmas in business. | Chapter 5 *Ethics Guide:* Querying Inequality?<br><br>Chapter Extension 12 *Guide:* Data Mining in the Real World |
| **So What?** | Each chapter of this text includes a feature called So What? This feature presents a current issue in IS that is relevant to the chapter content and asks you to consider why that issue matters to you as a future business professional. | Understand how the material in the chapter applies to everyday situations. | Chapter 2 So What?: Augmented Collaboration |
| **How Does the Knowledge in This Chapter Help You?** (near the end of each chapter) | This section revisits the opening scenario and discusses what the chapter taught you about it. | Summarizes the "takeaway" points from the chapter as they apply to the company or person in the story and to you. | Chapter 11 How Does the Knowledge in This Chapter Help You? |
| **Active Review** | Each chapter concludes with a summary-and-review section, organized around the chapter's study questions. | Offers a review of important points in the chapter. If you can answer the questions posed, you understand the material. | Chapter 9 Active Review |
| **Key Terms and Concepts** | Highlight the major terms and concepts with their appropriate page references. | Provide a summary of key terms for review before exams. | Chapter 6 Key Terms and Concepts |

| Resource | Description | Benefit | Example |
|---|---|---|---|
| **Using Your Knowledge** | These exercises ask you to take your new knowledge one step further by applying it to a practice problem. | Tests your critical-thinking skills and keeps reminding you that you are learning material that applies to the real world. | Chapter 4 Using Your Knowledge |
| **Collaboration Exercise** | A team exercise that focuses on the chapter's topic. | Use Google Drive, Windows OneDrive, Microsoft SharePoint, or some other tool to collaborate on team answers. | Collaboration Exercise 3, which explores the use of information systems at a high-value bike rental service |
| **Case Study** | A case study closes each chapter. You will reflect on real organizations' use of the technology or systems presented in the chapter and recommend solutions to business problems. | Requires you to apply newly acquired knowledge to real situations. | Case Study 6: FinQloud Forever... Well, at Least for the Required Interval... |
| **Application Exercises** (at the end of the book) | These exercises ask you to solve business situations using spreadsheet (Excel) or database (Access) applications and other Office applications. | Help develop your computer skills. | 6-2, which builds on your knowledge from Chapter 6 by asking you to import spreadsheet data into Access and produce cost reports |
| **SharePoint Hosting** | Pearson will host Microsoft SharePoint site collections for your university. Students need access to MyMISLab and a browser to participate. | Enables students to collaborate using the world's most popular collaboration software. | |

# Experiencing MIS

## Seventh Edition


**David M. Kroenke**

**Randall J. Boyle**



PEARSON

Boston Columbus Indianapolis New York San Francisco Amsterdam
Cape Town Dubai London Madrid Milan Munich Paris Montréal Toronto
Delhi Mexico City São Paulo Sydney Hong Kong Seoul Singapore Taipei Tokyo

Vice President, Business Publishing: Donna Battista
Editor-in-Chief: Stephanie Wall
Acquisitions Editor: Nicole Sam
Development Editor: Laura Town
Program Management Team Lead: Ashley Santora
Program Manager: Denise Weiss
Editorial Assistant: Olivia Vignone
Vice President, Product Marketing: Maggie Moylan
Director of Marketing, Digital Services and Products: Jeanette Koskinas
Executive Field Marketing Manager: Adam Goldstein
Field Marketing Manager: Lenny Ann Raper
Product Marketing Assistant: Jessica Quazza
Project Management Team Lead: Jeff Holcomb
Project Manager: Karalyn Holland
Operations Specialist: Carol Melville
Creative Director: Blair Brown
Senior Art Director: Janet Slowik
Interior and Cover Designer: Karen Quigley
Interior Illustrations: Simon Alicea
Cover Images: tiero/Fotolia, VIGE.CO/Shutterstock, Mr Aesthetics/Shutterstock
Vice President, Director of Digital Strategy & Assessment: Paul Gentile
Manager of Learning Applications: Paul Deluca
Digital Editor: Brian Surette
Director, Digital Studio: Sacha Laustsen
Digital Studio Manager: Diane Lombardo
Digital Studio Project Manager: Robin Lazrus
Digital Studio Project Manager: Alana Coles
Digital Studio Project Manager: Monique Lawrence
Digital Studio Project Manager: Regina DaSilva
Full-Service Project Management and Composition: Integra Software Services Pvt, Ltd.
Printer/Binder: RR Donnelley/Kendallville
Cover Printer: Phoenix Color/Hagerstown
Text Font: 9.5/13 Photina MT Pro



**Library of Congress Cataloging-in-Publication Data**
Kroenke, David M.
Experiencing MIS.—Seventh edition.
pages cm
Includes bibliographical references and index.
ISBN 978-0-13-431906-3—ISBN 0-13-431906-0
1. Management information systems. 2. Business—Data processing. I. Title.
T58.6.K767 2015
658.4'038011—dc23

2015030049

10 9 8 7 6 5 4 3 2 1
V011

PEARSON

ISBN 10: 0-13-431906-0
ISBN 13: 978-0-13-431906-3

*To C. J., Carter, and Charlotte*
*—David Kroenke*

*To Courtney, Noah, Fiona, and Layla*
*—Randy Boyle*

# CONTENTS OVERVIEW

*Experiencing MIS* offers basic topic coverage of MIS in its 12 chapters and more in-depth, expanded coverage in its chapter extensions. This modular organization allows you to pick and choose among those topics. Here chapter extensions are shown below the chapters to which they are related. You will preserve continuity if you use each of the 12 chapters in sequence. In most cases, a chapter extension can be covered any time in the course after its related chapter. You need not use any of the chapter extensions if time is short.

# CONTENTS

# CHAPTER EXTENSIONS

## CHAPTER EXTENSION 1: COLLABORATION INFORMATION SYSTEMS FOR DECISION MAKING, PROBLEM SOLVING, AND PROJECT MANAGEMENT P. 367



## CHAPTER EXTENSION 2: COLLABORATIVE INFORMATION SYSTEMS FOR STUDENT PROJECTS P. 380



## CHAPTER EXTENSION 3: MOBILE SYSTEMS P. 401

## CHAPTER EXTENSION 4: INTRODUCTION TO MICROSOFT EXCEL 2013 P. 417



## CHAPTER EXTENSION 5: DATABASE DESIGN P. 435



## CHAPTER EXTENSION 6: USING MICROSOFT ACCESS 2013 P. 449



## CHAPTER EXTENSION 7: USING EXCEL AND ACCESS TOGETHER P. 469



## CHAPTER EXTENSION 8: NETWORK AND CLOUD TECHNOLOGY P. 497



## CHAPTER EXTENSION 9: ENTERPRISE RESOURCE PLANNING (ERP) SYSTEMS P. 512

## CHAPTER EXTENSION 10: SUPPLY CHAIN MANAGEMENT P. 527



## CHAPTER EXTENSION 11: ENTERPRISE SOCIAL NETWORKS AND KNOWLEDGE MANAGEMENT P. 535



## CHAPTER EXTENSION 12: DATABASE MARKETING P. 550



## CHAPTER EXTENSION 13: REPORTING SYSTEMS AND OLAP P. 561



## CHAPTER EXTENSION 14: DATA BREACHES P. 573



## CHAPTER EXTENSION 15: INTERNATIONAL MIS P. 584

## CHAPTER EXTENSION 16: SYSTEMS DEVELOPMENT PROJECT MANAGEMENT P. 601



## CHAPTER EXTENSION 17: AGILE DEVELOPMENT P. 614



## CHAPTER EXTENSION 18: BUSINESS PROCESS MANAGEMENT P. 623

# PREFACE

In Chapter 1, we claim that MIS is the most important class in the business curriculum. That's a bold statement, and every year we ask whether it remains true. Is there any discipline having a greater impact on contemporary business and government than IS? We continue to doubt there is. Every year brings important new technology to organizations, and many of these organizations respond by creating innovative applications that increase productivity and otherwise help them accomplish their strategies.

Over the past year, we've seen the largest IPO in history ($25 billion) come from e-commerce giant Alibaba. Amazon revealed that it's using an army of Kiva robots to increase productivity in its fulfillment centers by 50 percent. And we've seen an unprecedented flurry of IoT smart devices aimed at personal, home, and automobile automation services hit the market. It seems like every industry is running full tilt toward the smart door. Technology is fundamentally changing the way organizations operate. It's forcing them to be more productive, innovative, and adaptable.

Even innovations we've known about for several years took big leaps forward this year. MakerBot made huge strides in 3D printing by introducing new composite filaments that can print materials that look just like wood, metal, and stone—not just plastics. Mercedes-Benz was the hit of CES 2015 when it debuted its new driverless F 015 car with saloon-style doors, complete touch-screen interface, and front-room seating. And Google announced it was deploying 25 of its driverless cars around Mountain View, California, starting summer 2015.

Large-scale data breaches were a major problem again this year. eBay, Home Depot, JP Morgan Chase, and Anthem all suffered enormous data losses. Sony Pictures lost more than 100 TB of confidential corporate data, and Apple lost hundreds of explicit celebrity photos to hackers. And these are just a fraction of the total number of organizations affected this year.

In addition, normal revisions were needed to address emergent technologies such as cloud-based services, mobile devices, innovative IS-based business models like that at zulily, changes in organizations' use of social media, and so on.

More sophisticated and demanding users push organizations into a rapidly changing future, one that requires continual adjustments in business planning. To participate, our graduates need to know how to apply emerging technologies to better achieve their organizations' strategies. Knowledge of MIS is critical. And this pace continues to remind us of Carrie Fisher's statement "The problem with instantaneous gratification is that it's just not fast enough."

## WHY THIS SEVENTH EDITION?

The changes in this seventh edition are listed in Table 1. Substantial changes were made in Chapter 1 to strengthen the argument for MIS being the most important course in the business curriculum. The chapter now looks at the Digital Revolution and the exponential change happening to technology. It discusses how digital devices are changing due to increased processing power (Moore's Law), connectivity (Metcalfe's Law), network speed (Nielsen's Law), and storage capacity (Kryder's Law). It then gives examples of how new technology creates entirely new types of businesses and forces existing businesses to change the way they operate.

Chapter 1 also includes new salary data projections from the Bureau of Labor Statistics through 2022. These salary projections cover pay ranges from typical information systems jobs, general business occupations, and managerial-level positions.

Chapters 1 through 6 begin with a new discussion of Falcon Security, a privately owned company that provides surveillance and inspection services for companies using flying drones.

**Table 1** Changes in the Seventh Edition

| Chapter | Change |
|---|---|
| 1 | New Falcon Security Part 1 Introduction |
| 1 | New Falcon Security chapter introduction |
| 1 | New So What? Feature: Biggest IPO Ever: Alibaba |
| 1 | Updated industry statistics throughout the chapter |
| 1 | New Q1-1 covering the Information Age, Digital Revolution, and power of exponential change |
| 1 | New discussion about forces pushing digital change: Bell's Law, Moore's Law, Metcalfe's Law, Nielsen's Law, and Kryder's Law |
| 1 | New Q1-2 looking at how changes in technology will affect students' future job security |
| 1 | New statistics about projected technology job growth from BLS |
| 1 | Combined discussion about MIS, IS, and IT |
| 2 | New Falcon Security chapter introduction |
| 2 | New So What? Feature: Augmented Collaboration |
| 2 | New Guide: Egocentric Versus Empathetic Thinking |
| 2 | Updated Q2-1 for Falcon Security |
| 2 | Updated Q2-2 for Best Bikes example |
| 2 | Updated SharePoint images |
| 3 | New Falcon Security chapter introduction |
| 3 | New So What? Feature: Driving Strategy |
| 3 | Updated Q3-1 focusing on organizational strategy and systems structure |
| 3 | Revised Q3-2 five forces examples using Falcon Security |
| 3 | Updated statistics in the chapter and Amazon case study |
| 4 | New Falcon Security chapter introduction |
| 4 | New So What? Feature: New From CES 2015 |
| 4 | New Ethics Guide: Free Apps for Data |
| 4 | Updated industry statistics throughout |
| 4 | New discussion about augmented reality hardware |
| 4 | Updated developments in 3D printing, self-driving cars, and IoT |
| 4 | Updated terms: *Internet Explorer* to *Edge*, *Windows 8* to *Windows 10* |
| 5 | New Falcon Security chapter introduction |
| 5 | New justification for learning database technology |
| 5 | New Q5-5 on Falcon Security maintaining video metadata in a database |
| 5 | New discussion of NewSQL and in-memory DBMS |
| 6 | New Falcon Security chapter introduction |
| 6 | New So What? Feature: Net Neutrality Enabled |
| 6 | New Guide: From Anthem to Anathema |
| 6 | Updated statistics and AWS offerings |
| 7 | Added new technology as a fifth implementation challenge |
| 8 | New Ethics Guide: Synthetic Friends |
| 8 | New Guide: Digital Is Forever |
| 8 | New discussion about the use of social media in recruiting |
| 8 | Expanded discussion of social capital using a YouTube channels example |
| 8 | Expanded discussion of mobile ad spending |
| 8 | Updated social media statistics throughout the chapter |

| Chapter | Change |
|---|---|
| 9 | Replaced predictive policing example with reporting application in medicine |
| 9 | Updated parts analysis example to remove AllRoad Parts and keep the example anonymous |
| 9 | New So What? Feature: BI for Securities Trading |
| 9 | Updated WebTrends and HDInsight decription |
| 9 | Included latest CEO surveys on the importance of BI |
| 10 | New So What? Feature: New from Black Hat 2014 |
| 10 | New Guide: EMV to the Rescue |
| 10 | New Ethics Guide: Hacking Smart Things |
| 10 | New discussion of notable APTs |
| 10 | Updated security statistics and figures throughout the chapter |
| 10 | New discussion of ransomware |
| 10 | Added discussion of recent large-scale data breaches |
| 11 | New Ethics Guide: Privacy Versus Productivity: The BYOD Dilemma |
| 11 | Updated IS jobs, descriptions, and salary data |
| 12 | New So What? Feature: Using This Knowledge for Your Number-One Priority |
| 12 | Rewrote explanation of why systems development is important to all business professionals today |

| Chapter Extension | Change |
|---|---|
| All CEs | Added new auto-graded questions |
| CE 2 | Changed *Microsoft Lync* to *Skype for Business* and *Google Grid* to *Google Drive* |
| CE 2 | Updated images for Skype for Business, SharePoint, and Google Drive |
| CE 3 | Updated statistics about mobile adoption and use |
| CE 3 | Updated *Windows 8* to *Windows 10* and *Internet Explorer* to *Microsoft Edge* |
| CE 5 | Updated E-R notation for minimum cardinality to conform to contemporary usage |
| CE 8 | Added discussion of new net neutrality regulations |
| CE 8 | Added discussion about personal area networks (PANs) and Bluetooth |
| CE 9 | Defined hybrid-model |
| CE 9 | Updated ERP vendor rankings and comments; replaced Epicor with Sage |
| CE 9 | Discussed the effect of mobility, security threats, and the Internet of Things on enterprise applications |
| CE 11 | Updated social media statistics |
| CE 14 | Updated data breach statistics and trends |
| CE 14 | Added new figures with updated major data breaches |
| CE 14 | Updated QCE14-2 related to the Target data breach |
| CE 15 | Added new discussion of localization using IBM's Watson |
| CE 15 | Expanded discussion of EU's "right to be forgotten" law |
| Appl Ex | Added new data files and updated images |
| Appl Ex | Added new exercise using open source software (LibreOffice) |
| Appl Ex | Added new exercise using software to compress and encrypt files (7-Zip) |
| Appl Ex | Added new exercise related to social media policy |

Chapters 7–12 continue to be introduced by PRIDE Systems, a cloud-based virtual exercise competition and healthcare startup. In addition to motivating the chapter material, both case scenarios provide numerous opportunities for students to practice one of Chapter 1's key skills: "Assess, evaluate, and apply emerging technology to business."

This edition continues to have a focus on teaching ethics. Every Ethics Guide asks students to apply Immanuel Kant's categorical imperative, Bentham and Mill's utilitarianism, or both to the business situation described in the guide. We hope you find the ethical considerations richer and deeper with these exercises. The categorical imperative is introduced in the Ethics Guide in Chapter 1 (pages 20–21) and utilitarianism is introduced in the Ethics Guide in Chapter 2 (pages 46–47).

As shown in Table 1, additional changes were made to every chapter, including eight new So What? Features, four new Ethics Guides, and updates to chapter cases. Additional figures, like one showing mobile ad spending in Chapter 8, were added to make the text more accessible. Numerous changes were made throughout the chapters in an attempt to keep them up to date. MIS moves fast, and to keep the text current, we checked every fact, data point, sentence, and industry reference for obsolescence and replaced them as necessary.

To reiterate the preface of earlier editions, we believe it is exceedingly important to make these frequent adaptations because of the delays associated with a 2-year revision cycle. Text materials that we develop starting in April of one year are published in January of the next year and are first used by students in September—a minimum 17-month delay.

For some areas of study, a year and a half may not seem like a long time because little changes in that amount of time. But in MIS, entire companies can be founded and then sold for billions of dollars in just a few years. YouTube, for example, was founded in February 2005 and then sold in November 2006 to Google for $1.65 billion (21 months). Facebook started in 2004 and currently (2015) has a market capitalization exceeding $212 billion. MIS changes fast—very fast. We hope this new edition is the most up-to-date MIS textbook available.

## STRUCTURE, ORGANIZATION, AND APPEARANCE OF THIS TEXT

Teaching today is a very different endeavor than it was years ago. Students have many more distractions and demands on their time. They are quick to tune in and quick to tune out, so much so that someone compared their attention spans to those of Labrador Retriever puppies. We can lament that fact, but we can't change it. What we can do is to meet students where they are and creatively attempt to obtain their engagement.

We designed this text with that hope and goal in mind. Every feature of this book is designed to make it easy for students to engage with the content, not by watering it down but rather, we hope, by making it interesting and relevant to them. This text is not an encyclopedia; it attempts to teach essential topics well. It does so by providing opportunities for students to actively engage with the content, by providing features to help students better manage their study time, and with an appearance that makes it easy for students to pick up and start.

## ACTIVE ENGAGEMENT

The structure of this edition of *Experiencing MIS* provides many opportunities for active engagement. Each chapter includes a So What? feature that contains exercises and questions for students to answer to demonstrate the relevancy of the chapter's material to them. As with earlier editions, each chapter contains two guides that describe practical implications of the chapter contents that can be used for small in-class exercises. Finally, this edition contains 41 application exercises (see page 637).

## FACILITATE STUDENT STUDY

Today's students were reared in an environment of constant stimulation and channel surfing, and it seems nearly impossible for many students to focus on a single topic for more than a few minutes. Again, we can wish it otherwise, but short attention spans are students' and our reality. And recent research does seem to substantiate students' claim that, except for texting in class, students can multitask in class without problem.[1]

This text is structured to accommodate today's students' learning styles. First, to help students manage their time, it is organized around questions. Each chapter or chapter extension starts with a list of questions. Each major heading of the material is one of those questions, and the end of the chapter or extension includes an Active Review in which students are asked to demonstrate their learning of the answer to each question. Students should study until they can answer the questions; that may be 5 minutes or 5 hours, but their job is to answer those questions. This technique, from Marilla Svinicki's research, vastly helps students manage their study time.[2]

You can also use the questions to structure class sessions or at least parts of those sessions.

You can open class by asking students to "do the questions." Go around the room and call on someone to answer a question or part of one.

Second, students learn more when they are emotionally engaged in the material. The purpose of the vignettes that introduce each chapter is to raise student emotion; their purpose is to cause students to care about the chapter material.

Third, 82 percent of students in the business school prefer visual learning to auditory (voice or word) learning.[3] To make it easier for students to open this book and continue to read it, interesting and engaging art and photos have been used. *In every instance, however, we have insisted that the photo or art be related to the topic under discussion; these photos are not simply eye candy.* Pearson allows us to personally review and approve every photo and art exhibit in this text. We believe a good book does not have to appear boring, but all art must be relevant.

## FEATURES FOR ENGAGING THE STUDENT

*Experiencing MIS* was written to make it impossible for readers of this text to miss the importance of MIS in business. The text is designed to be approachable, easy to use, sometimes humorous, with an upbeat and in-your-face attitude, but always with the goal of underlining the importance of MIS to all businesspeople in the 21st century.

An important part of making the text approachable was choosing a modular design. The text consists of 12 short chapters along with 18 supplemental discussions, called chapter extensions.

The modular nature of this text is discussed in more detail later in this preface.

### Emphasis on Collaboration

As with prior editions, this text emphasizes collaboration. It is one of Reich's key skills for the 21st-century professional, as described in Chapter 1. We believe we need not only to require our students to collaborate but also to teach them key skills for doing so. The first two chapter extensions present collaboration techniques and collaboration information systems, respectively. Each chapter also includes a collaboration exercise at the end of the chapter.

Additionally, Pearson Education is sponsoring Microsoft SharePoint for student use. At your request, Pearson will set up a SharePoint site collection that your students can use when responding to the collaboration exercises at the end of each chapter. Students need nothing more than a browser to participate. See your Pearson sales representative for more information.

### Opening Scenarios for Parts and Chapters

Each part and each chapter opens with a scenario intended to get students involved emotionally. We want students to mentally place themselves in the situation and to realize that this situation—or something like it—could happen to them. Each scenario sets up the chapter's content and provides an obvious example of why the chapter is relevant to them. These scenarios help support the goals of student motivation and learning transfer.

Furthermore, both of these introductory cases involve the application of new technology to existing businesses. Our goal is to provide opportunities for students to see and understand how businesses are affected by new technology and how they need to adapt while, we hope, providing numerous avenues for you to explore such adaptation with your students.

In developing these scenarios, we endeavor to create business situations rich enough to realistically carry the discussions of information systems while at the same time simple enough that students with little business knowledge and even less business experience can understand. We also attempt to create scenarios that will be interesting to teach. This edition introduces the new Falcon Security case and continues the PRIDE Systems case from the sixth edition.

## Falcon Security

The chapters in Parts 1 and 2 are introduced with dialogue from key players at Falcon Security, a privately owned company that provides surveillance and inspection services for companies using flying drones. We wanted to develop the case around an interesting business model that students would want to learn more about. Drones get a lot of attention in the press, but students may not know a lot about how they're used in business. Drones are getting cheaper and easier to fly and have a lot more functionality than they did just a few years ago. It's likely that students will see drones deployed widely during their careers.

Falcon Security is considering strengthening its competitive advantage by 3D printing its own drones. Buying fleets of drones is expensive, and they become outdated quickly. However, were the company to do so, it would be changing its fundamental business model, or at least adding to it. Making drones would require Falcon Security to hire new employees, develop new business processes, and potentially develop a new IS to support the custom-built drones. All of this is good fodder for Chapter 3 and for underlining the importance of the ways IS needs to support evolving business strategy.

Ultimately, Falcon Security determines that it does not want to become a drone manufacturer. It could print some drone parts, but not enough to make it cost effective. They'd still have to buy a lot of expensive component parts to assemble an airworthy drone, something they're not sure they can do consistently. Falcon decides to focus on its core strength of providing integrated security services.

Students may object that, in studying Falcon Security, they devoted considerable time to an opportunity that ultimately didn't make business sense and was rejected. But this outcome is at least as informative as a successful outcome. The example uses knowledge of processes as well as application of business intelligence to avoid making a serious blunder and wasting substantial money. Falcon Security didn't have to open a factory and 3D-print a fleet of custom-built drones just to find out it would be a mistake. It could make a prototype, *analyze* the costs and benefits, and then avoid making the mistake in the first place. The very best way to solve a problem is not to have it!

## PRIDE Systems

The Performance Recording, Integration, Delivery, and Evaluation (PRIDE) system was first developed for the fourth edition. In that version it was an embryonic, entrepreneurial opportunity that used mobile devices, data-gathering exercise equipment, and the cloud to share integrated data among healthcare providers, heart surgery patients, health clubs, health insurance companies, and employers.

PRIDE is a real-world prototype developed for the owner of a health club who wanted to connect the workout data of his club members to their workout data at home and to their employers, insurance companies, and healthcare professionals. PRIDE is written in C#, and the code runs against an Azure database in the cloud. The PRIDE system uses the Windows Phone emulator that is part of Visual Studio. PRIDE was going to be ported to iOS and Android devices after demonstrating feasibility and after the club owner obtained financing. Unfortunately, before the prototype reached that point, the sponsor of the project lost interest.

As reflected in the PRIDE case, the developers realized that it was unlikely to succeed because, as Zev says in Chapter 7, "Doctors don't care about exercise." Dr. Flores was too busy as a cardiac surgeon to make his startup a success. Therefore, he sold it to a successful businessman who changed the staff and the strategy and repurposed the software. All of this is described at the start of Chapter 7.

## Use of the Categorical Imperative and Utilitarianism in Ethics Guides

Since the introduction of the Ethics Guides into the first edition of this text, we believe there was a shift in students' attitudes about ethics. Students seem, at least many of them, to be more cynical and callous about ethical issues.

As a result, in the fifth edition, we began to use Kant's categorical imperative and Bentham and Mill's utilitarianism to ask students, whose ethical standards are often immature, to adopt the categorical imperative and utilitarian perspectives rather than their own perspectives and, in some cases, in addition to their own perspectives. By doing so, the students are asked to "try on" those criteria, and we hope in the process they think more deeply about ethical principles than they do when we allow them simply to apply their personal biases.

The Ethics Guide in Chapter 1 introduces the categorical imperative, and the guide in Chapter 2 introduces utilitarianism. If you choose to use these perspectives, you will need to assign both of those guides.

## Modular Design

Not every MIS class is the same, and even though most MIS professors would agree on the basic content of this class, each professor has his or her own interests, expertise, and emphasis. Further, courses differ not only because of student and professor interests, but also because of the local employment environment, the grade level at which the class is taught, the background and educational maturity of students, and so on.

To support such specialization, the text is organized into short chapters and optional chapter extensions. Each of the 12 short chapters describes the minimum essentials of a topic. Additional material is then presented in 18 optional chapter extensions. Thus, for example, Chapter 9 addresses the basic ideas and purpose of business intelligence. That chapter is then supported by two chapter extensions: one on data mining and one on reporting and OLAP.

You can pick the extensions that relate to your class's interests and needs, or you can use just the chapter itself and skip the extensions without loss of continuity. For a more specific description of how the book is organized, see the section titled "How Is the Content Organized?"

## Guides

This book contains boxed essays called "guides" that amplify each chapter's core material. These features are intended to force students to grapple with some intriguing aspect of the core material, to think about its relevance to them and their future needs as businesspeople, and to discuss that material in small groups or as a class.

Each chapter in this book contains two guides—one of which addresses ethics and one on some other topic. Guides appear in some of the chapter extensions as well. Use of the Ethics Guides will expose students to some of the fundamental principles relating to ethics, information systems, and business in general. The other guides present a variety of ideas: some from cognitive science that will help students become better problem solvers; some that show "contrarian" opinions that have been commonly voiced in business settings; and some that state our personal opinions. All of the guides encourage students to grapple with some idea and its application to them either now or as future business professionals. Working with the guides should help students transfer knowledge from their MIS class to other classes and eventually to their business careers.

## Integration of Excel and Access

Most MIS courses today include some use of Microsoft Office. Usually, professors adopt a main MIS book and then select another book for Office instruction. The result is an expensive package for the student to buy and a schizophrenic break between the "principles" text and the "applications" text.

To eliminate these problems, this text includes four chapter extensions on Microsoft Excel and Access 2013. Chapter Extension 4 teaches the fundamentals of Excel. Chapter Extension 5 teaches database design, and Chapter Extension 6 shows how to apply the principles of database design using Microsoft Access. Finally, Chapter Extension 7 discusses the use of Excel and Access together. Data are passed back and forth between those products so that students can compare and contrast Excel and Access features and strengths. Also, students learn practical skills for managing real data.

Most students should be able to learn (or review) fundamental Excel and Access skills with no supplemental text. Students who need extra instruction can, of course, find it in one of the many excellent tutorials. But having that material in this text means that most students need not buy another book. Those exercises are consolidated into one list, starting on page 640.

## HOW IS THE CONTENT ORGANIZED?

The text is organized into four parts. See the graphic outline on pages x–xi of the front matter for a visual presentation of the parts and chapters and of the relationship of the chapter extensions to the parts and chapters.

Part 1, "Why MIS?," introduces MIS and explains why and how it is important for business students. The three chapters in Part 1 address basic MIS definitions and the five-component framework, show how information and information systems relate to business processes, and explain the role of IS in support of organizational strategy and competitive advantage. Chapter extensions for Part 1 concern collaboration techniques and collaboration IS.

Part 2, "Information Technology," addresses fundamental IT concepts. The three chapters in Part 2 discuss hardware and software, database processing, and data communication. Chapter Extension 3 describes the development of Web and native mobile applications and describes an array of bring your own device (BYOD) policies. The next four chapter extensions teach the basics of Excel and Access, describe database design techniques, and show how to use Excel and Access together. Finally, Chapter Extension 8 discusses data communication technology that supports the cloud with particular focus on SOA and Web service standards.

Part 3 is titled "Using IS for Competitive Advantage." The three chapters in this part consider organization and systems, social media, and business intelligence systems. Part 3 chapter extensions present information on systems for ERP and supply chain management. Chapter Extensions 12 and 13 discuss database marketing and reporting systems and OLAP.

Part 4, "Information Systems Management," concludes the text with three chapters that address information systems security, IS management including outsourcing, and systems development. Note that due to the increased importance of security, that chapter is the first chapter in this part. Part 4 chapter extensions include a detailed description of data breaches, discussions of international MIS, systems development project management, agile systems development with scrum, and business process management.

Again, the goal of the modular organization of this text is to allow you to pick and choose among those topics that best fit your needs. You will preserve continuity if you use each of the 12 chapters in sequence, but you need not use any of the chapter extensions if time is short.

## INSTRUCTOR RESOURCES

At the Instructor Resource Center, *www.pearsonhighered.com/irc*, instructors can easily register to gain access to a variety of instructor resources available with this text in downloadable format. If assistance is needed, our dedicated technical support team is ready to help with the media supplements that accompany this text. Visit *http://247.pearsoned.com* for answers to frequently asked questions and toll-free user support phone numbers.

The following supplements are available with this text:

- Test Bank
- TestGen® Computerized Test Bank
- PowerPoint Presentation

## ACKNOWLEDGMENTS

First, we wish to thank Earl McKinney, professor of information systems at Bowling Green University and author of *Processes, Systems, and Information*, for many hours of insightful conversation about the role of processes in this MIS course as well as for his deep insights into the theory of information. We also thank David Auer of Western Washington University for help with data communications technology and Jeffrey Proudfoot of Bentley University for his insights on information security.

Many thanks as well to Jeff Gains of San Jose State University for helpful feedback about prior editions of this text; Jeff's comments have strongly influenced revisions for years. Also, a special thanks to Harry Reif at James Madison University for most insightful observations about ways to improve this text.

At Microsoft, we are grateful for the help of Randy Guthrie, who supports MIS professors in many ways, including facilitating use of DreamSpark as well as giving many presentations to students. Also, we thank Rob Howard for conversations and consulting about SharePoint and SharePoint Designer and Steve Fox for helpful conversations about both SharePoint and Microsoft Azure. Regarding our SharePoint program, a very special thanks to David Auer of Western Washington University and Laura Atkins of James Madison University, who serve as the community proctors for our SharePoint MIS community site, which enables dozens of professors and hundreds of students to learn how to use SharePoint. Our SharePoint solution is hosted by NSPI in Atlanta, Georgia.

Thanks to Neil Miyamoto, co-owner of The Firm (*http://thefirmmpls.com/*), for the ideas behind the PRIDE case. Additionally, we thank Don Nilson, a certified scrum master, for essential ideas and guidance on the new material on agile development and scrum.

Laura Town is the development editor on all of our MIS books, and we continue to be grateful for her support, knowledge, expertise, and great attitude through thick and thin! The textbook industry is undergoing dramatic changes at this time, and Laura's knowledge, guidance, and wisdom on the textbook production process is most appreciated.

We would like to thank those who contributed to the development of our excellent Instructor Resources: Instructor's Manual, Roberta M. Roth; PowerPoints, Steve Loy; and Test Bank, Katie Trotta/ANSR Source. We would also like to express our thanks to the following authors for creating a superb set of resources for our MyLab: John Hupp, Columbus State University; Timothy P. O'Keefe, University of North Dakota; Roberta M. Roth, University of Northern Iowa; J. K. Sinclaire, Arkansas State University; and Melody White, University of North Texas.

Pearson Education is a great publishing company, chock-full of dedicated, talented, and creative people. We thank Judy Leale and Karalyn Holland for taking over production management of a complex set of texts and doing it so efficiently and willingly. We also thank Janet Slowik, art director, and her team for redesigning this book so beautifully. Finally, we thank Sue Nodine of Integra-Chicago for managing the production of the book.

No textbook makes its way into the hands of students without the active involvement of a dedicated and professional sales force. We thank the Pearson sales team and especially Anne Fahlgren, the marketing manager for this text.

Thanks also goes to our former, and now happily retired, editor Bob Horan for his years of friendship, support, and wise counsel. Finally, like so many authors in college publishing, we owe tremendous thanks to our current editor Nicole Sam. Nicole continues to provide us with the skilled guidance necessary to make these texts a great success.

**David Kroenke**
**Randy Boyle**

## THANKS TO OUR REVIEWERS

The following people deserve special recognition for their work on this seventh edition and previous editions of *Experiencing MIS*. Their feedback is truly appreciated.

**Hans-Joachim Adler**, *The University of Texas at Dallas*
**Ihssan Alkadi**, *University of Louisiana at Lafayette*
**Michel Avital**, *Case Western Reserve University*
**Nick Ball**, *Brigham Young University*
**Hellene Bankowski**, *Philadelphia University*
**Hooshang M. Beheshti**, *Radford University*
**Ernst Bekkering**, *Northeastern State University*
**Meral Binbasioglu**, *Hofstra University*
**Carolyn Borne**, *Louisiana State University, Baton Rouge*
**Uptal Bose**, *University of Houston—Downtown*
**Charles Butler**, *Colorado State University*
**Teuta Cata**, *Northern Kentucky University*
**Joni M. Catanzaro**, *Louisiana State University, Baton Rouge*
**Joseph Cazier**, *Appalachian State University*
**Nettie M. Chaffee**, *Kent State University*
**Nancy Chase**, *Gonzaga University*
**Leida Chen**, *Creighton University*
**Robert Chi**, *California State University, Long Beach*
**Izic Chon**, *University of Washington*
**Anne Cohen**, *University of St. Thomas, Minneapolis*
**John Cole**, *Portland State University*
**Charles Cowell**, *Tyler Junior College*
**Martin B. Dumas**, *Baruch College—The City University of New York*
**Nellis L Freeman, Jr.**, *Notre Dame de Namur University*
**Al Fundaburk**, *Bloomsburg University*
**Jeffrey Gaines**, *San Jose State University*
**Russell Ginnings**, *East Tennessee State University*
**Bonnie C. Glassberg**, *Miami University*
**Sam Goh**, *The University of Tennessee at Chattanooga*
**Richard Grenci**, *John Carroll University*
**Kenneth Griggs**, *California Polytechnic State University, San Luis Obispo*
**Sandra Gustavson**, *Kent State University*
**Bomi Hang**, *Coastal Carolina University*
**Albert L. Harris**, *Appalachian State University*
**Rosie Hauck**, *Illinois State University*
**Richard Herschel**, *Saint Joseph's University*
**Bonnie Homan**, *San Francisco State University*
**C. Steven Hunt**, *Morehead State University*
**John Hupp**, *Columbus State University*
**Mark Hwang**, *Central Michigan University*
**Abdou Illia**, *Eastern Illinois University*
**'Jon (Sean) Jasperson**, *Texas A&M University*
**Ken Jones**, *Northeastern State University*
**Bomi Kang**, *Coastal Carolina University*
**Karthik Kannan**, *Purdue University*
**Pairin Katerattanakul**, *Western Michigan University*
**Bob Keim**, *Arizona State University*
**George Kelley**, *Erie Community College—City Campus*
**Mark Kesh**, *The University of Texas at El Paso*
**Sang Hyun Kim**, *Kyungpook National University*
**David Kitlan**, *Penn State University at Harrisburg*
**Ronald J. Kizior**, *Loyola University Chicago*
**Michael Knight**, *Appalachian State University*
**Parag Kosalge**, *Grand Valley State University*
**Brian Kovar**, *Kansas State University*
**Ram Kumar**, *The University of North Carolina at Charlotte*
**Subodha Kumar**, *University of Washington*
**Terry F. Landry**, *Louisiana State University, Baton Rouge*
**David Lewis**, *University of Massachusetts, Lowell*
**Paul Licker**, *Oakland University School of Business Administration*
**Maurie Lockley**, *The University of North Carolina at Greensboro*
**Steve Loy**, *Eastern Kentucky University*
**Jane Mackay**, *Texas Christian University*
**Mary Malliaris**, *Loyola University Chicago*
**Byron Marshall**, *Oregon State University*
**Sue A. McCrory**, *Missouri State University*
**Don McCubbrey**, *University of Denver*
**William McHenry**, *University of Akron*
**Earl McKinney**, *Bowling Green State University*
**Patricia McQuaid**, *California Polytechnic State University, San Luis Obispo*
**Rayman Meservy**, *Brigham Young University*
**Richard Mickool**, *Northeastern University*
**Robert J. Mills**, *Utah State University*
**Mike Mitri**, *James Madison University*
**Jennifer P. Nightingale**, *Duquesne University*
**Timothy O'Keefe**, *University of North Dakota*
**Michael Pangburn**, *University of Oregon*
**Manimoy Paul**, *Siena College*
**Sharma Pillutla**, *Towson University*
**Taner Pirim**, *The University of Mississippi*
**Jim Quan**, *Salisbury University*
**R. A. Rademacher**, *Colorado State University*
**Madhav Raghunathan**, *Bowling Green State University*
**Betsy Ratchford**, *University of Northern Iowa*
**Muhammad Razi**, *Western Michigan University*
**Shaunda Roach**, *Oakwood University*
**Roberta M. Roth**, *University of Northern Iowa*
**Cynthia Ruppel**, *Nova Southeastern University*
**Bruce Saulnier**, *Quinnipiac University*
**Werner Schenk**, *University of Rochester*
**Andrew Schwarz**, *Louisiana State University, Baton Rouge*
**Tod Sedbrook**, *University of Northern Colorado*
**Jaymeen Shah**, *Texas State University*

**Ganesan Shankaranarayanan**, *Boston University School of Management*
**Mahmudul Sheikh**, *The University of Mississippi*
**Emily Shepard**, *Central Carolina Community College*
**Gurmukh Singh**, *SUNY Fredonia*
**Rod Sink**, *Northern Illinois University*
**Elliot Sloane**, *Villanova University*
**Michael Smith**, *SUNY Oswego*
**Robert St. Louis**, *Arizona State University*
**John Storck**, *Boston University*
**Nathan Stout**, *University of Oklahoma*
**Robert Szymanski**, *Georgia Southern University*
**A. Ross Taylor**, *University of Nebraska at Kearney*
**Lou Thompson**, *The University of Texas at Dallas*
**Michael W. Totaro**, *University of Louisiana at Lafayette*
**Cherie Trumbach**, *The University of New Orleans*
**Emmanuelle Vaast**, *Long Island University*
**Barbara Warner**, *University of South Florida*
**Dwayne Whitten**, *Texas A&M University*
**Rosemary Wild**, *California Polytechnic State University, San Luis Obispo*
**Elaine Winston**, *Hofstra University*
**Michael Zack**, *Northeastern University*
**John A. Zarb**, *The University of Toledo*
**Guoying Zhang**, *University of Washington*
**Zhiwei Zhu**, *University of Louisiana at Lafayette*

## ENDNOTES

1. James M. Kraushaar and David C. Novak, "Examining the Effects of Student Multitasking with Laptops During the Lecture," *Journal of Information Systems Education*, June 2010.
2. Marilla Svinicki, *Learning and Motivation in the Postsecondary Classroom* (New York: Anker Publishing), 2004.
3. Thomas E. Sandman, "Gaining Insight into Business Telecommunications Students Through the Assessment of Learning Styles," *DSI Journal of Innovative Education*, January 2009, pp. 295–320.

# ABOUT THE AUTHORS

**David Kroenke** has many years of teaching experience at Colorado State University, Seattle University, and the University of Washington. He has led dozens of seminars for college professors on the teaching of information systems and technology; in 1991, the International Association of Information Systems named him Computer Educator of the Year. In 2009, David was named Educator of the Year by the Association of Information Technology Professionals-Education Special Interest Group (AITP-EDSIG).

David worked for the U.S. Air Force and Boeing Computer Services. He was a principal in the startup of three companies, serving as the vice president of product marketing and development for the Microrim Corporation and as chief of database technologies for Wall Data, Inc. He is the father of the semantic object data model. David's consulting clients have included IBM, Microsoft, and Computer Sciences Corporation, as well as numerous smaller companies. Recently, David has focused on using information systems for teaching collaboration and teamwork.

His text *Database Processing* was first published in 1977 and is now in its 14th edition. He has authored and coauthored many other textbooks, including *Database Concepts*, 7th ed. (2015), *Using MIS*, 9th ed. (2017), *SharePoint for Students* (2012), *Office 365 in Business* (2012), and *Processes, Systems, and Information: An Introduction to MIS*, 2nd ed. (2015).

**Randall J. Boyle** received his Ph.D. in Management Information Systems from Florida State University in 2003. He also has a master's degree in Public Administration and a B.S. in Finance. He has received university teaching awards at Longwood University, the University of Utah, and the University of Alabama in Huntsville. He has taught a wide variety of classes, including Introduction to MIS, Cyber Security, Networking & Servers, System Analysis and Design, Telecommunications, Advanced Cyber Security, Decision Support Systems, and Web Servers.

His research areas include deception detection in computer-mediated environments, secure information systems, the effects of IT on cognitive biases, the effects of IT on knowledge workers, and e-commerce. He has published in several academic journals and has authored additional textbooks, including *Using MIS*, 7th ed., *Corporate Computer and Network Security*, 4th ed., *Applied Information Security*, 2nd ed., and *Applied Networking Labs*, 2nd ed.

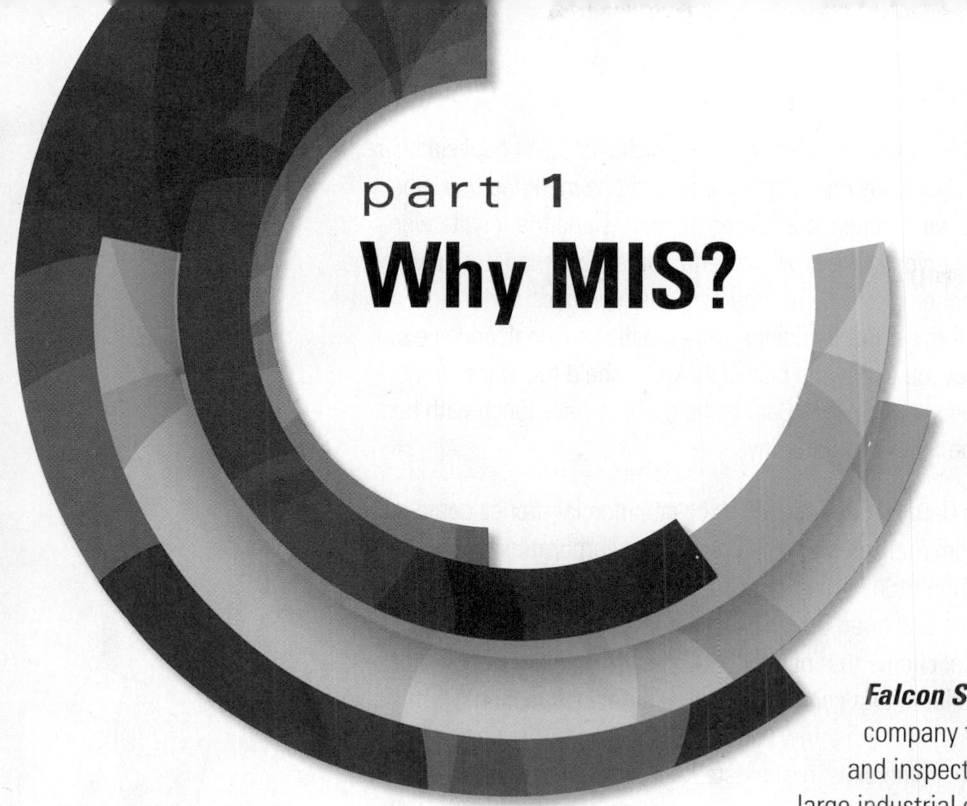

# part 1
# Why MIS?

***Falcon Security*** is a 5-year-old, privately owned company that uses aerial drones to provide surveillance and inspection services for customers. Its customers are large industrial companies that want to reduce their physical security labor costs or need periodic inspection services for industrial sites. Falcon has contracts with several large oil refineries in Texas to provide real-time video surveillance of their sizable industrial facilities. It also does occasional safety inspections on critical infrastructure components (e.g., flare stacks), which would be difficult and dangerous to do in person.

**This could happen to you**

Falcon Security's CEO and cofounder is Mateo Thomas. In the early part of his career, Mateo was a major in the United States Army in charge of physical security at a large military base in the Middle East. After retiring from the Army, Mateo went to work as the director of security at a large Texas-based industrial manufacturer. While serving on a security policy steering committee with business unit managers, he met the young and ambitious Joni Campbell. He told Joni that the company was paying way too much for physical security. He thought the company could buy a few drones to do the work of several physical security guards at a fraction of the cost. From his time in the military, he'd seen how drones could be used successfully to improve security with much less time and effort. The problem was that he didn't know much about actually operating the drones. Neither did Joni.

A week later, Joni was at a friend's wedding and saw a wedding video that included amazing aerial shots of the bride and groom on the beach, driving, and walking in the park. Curious, she approached the photographer, Camillia (Cam) Forset, and asked her how she produced those stunning videos. Turns out that Cam did weddings part-time

*Source:* Top: Julia Tim/Fotolia; Bottom: VIGE.CO/Shutterstock

during the summer months. Her day job, which she didn't especially like, was as a regional sales representative for a drone manufacturer. She experimented with drones at a few photo shoots and the results were spectacular. Everyone who saw the aerial footage wanted it. She was the only photographer in the metro area who could produce aerial video, and her business thrived. But weddings were mostly seasonal, and she still needed her day job to pay the bills. Joni knew she'd found the drone expert she needed and asked Cam if she'd like to have lunch with her and Mateo the following Saturday.

After hearing Cam talk about everything commercial drones could do, Mateo and Joni realized that using drones for corporate security was a much bigger opportunity than they had thought. Mateo and Joni founded Falcon Security and hired Cam. Five years later, Falcon Security has 15 large industrial clients that pay for daily security surveillance and dozens of industrial clients that contract for aerial safety inspections. It has also recently contracted with a few clients asking for one-time aerial land survey, videography (commercials, real estate, etc.), and agricultural monitoring.

Falcon Security has revenues of about $14M a year, most of which comes from providing physical security to its large industrial clients. Mateo wants to grow Falcon Security nationally. He knows there are plenty of industrial clients outside of Texas that would pay for Falcon's services, possibly even a lucrative contract with the federal government. Joni is worried that Falcon is not ready. It's been a bumpy ride. Buying fleets of drones (planes and helicopters) has been expensive and, at times, frustrating. People have to be trained to operate the drones, the drones seem to break frequently, and newer models are always coming out. Then there's the hugely expensive systems development project that's currently underway to automate the collection, storage, and analysis of the data from the drones.

Mateo has also been exploring 3D printing as a way to reduce the costs of the drones. Cam's team was able to rapidly create an innovative prototype of a new passive recharging platform using a 3D printer. Now Falcon's drones can land, charge, and take off again without any human intervention. This has saved countless hours managing the drones and has increased the overall effective range of the drones. Fleets of autonomous drones can now be deployed across long distances by stopping every 10 to 15 miles at a recharging station.

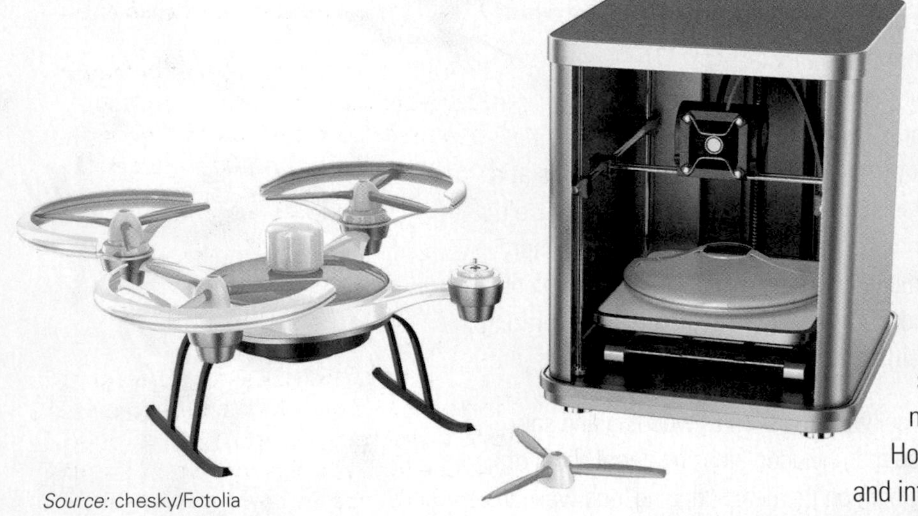

*Source:* chesky/Fotolia

Mateo hopes the company can have the same success in making its own drones. But he's not sure he wants to manufacture drones. How many new employees will he need to hire and train? How much will it cost to buy additional equipment and information systems to support the manufacturing process? Will these new drones be compatible with their existing data collection and processing system? Mateo asks Joni and Cam to figure out if manufacturing drones is the right move for Falcon Security.

# The Importance of MIS

"Fired? You're firing me?"

"Well, *fired* is a harsh word, but ..well, Falcon Security has no further need for your services."

"But, Joni, I don't get it. I really don't. I worked hard, and I did everything you told me to do."

"Jennifer, that's just it. You did everything *I* told you to do."

"I put in so many hours. How could you fire me?"

"Your job was to find ways to reduce our fleet costs using 3D printing."

"Right! And I did that."

## This could happen to you

"No, you didn't. You followed up on ideas *that I gave you*. But we don't need someone who can follow up on my plans. We need someone who can figure out what we need to do, create her own plans, and bring them back to me.... and others."

"How could you expect me to do that? I've only been here 6 months!"

"It's called teamwork. Sure, you're just learning our business, but I made sure all of our senior staff would be available to you ... "

"I didn't want to bother them."

"Well, you succeeded. I asked Cam what she thought of the plans you're working on. 'Who's Jennifer?' she asked."

"But doesn't she work down at the hangar?"

"Right. She's the operations manager... and it would seem to be worth talking to her."

"I'll go do that!"

"Jennifer, do you see what just happened? I gave you an idea and you said you'd do it. That's not what I need. I need you to find solutions on your own."

"I worked really hard. I put in a lot of hours. I've got all these reports written."

"Has anyone seen them?"

"I talked to you about some of them. But I was waiting until I was satisfied with them."

"Right. That's not how we do things here. We develop ideas and then kick them around with each other. Nobody has all the smarts. Our plans get better when we comment and rework them... I think I told you that."

"Maybe you did. But I'm just not comfortable with that."

"Well, it's a key skill here."

"I know I can do this job."

"Jennifer, you've been here almost 6 months; you have a degree in business. Several weeks ago, I asked you for your first idea for a process that would identify potential drones, or drone parts, that could be 3D-printed. Do you remember what you said?"

# STUDY QUESTIONS

**Q1-1 WHY IS INTRODUCTION TO MIS THE MOST IMPORTANT CLASS IN THE BUSINESS SCHOOL?**

**Q1-2 HOW WILL MIS AFFECT ME?**

**Q1-3 WHY ARE MIS-RELATED JOBS IN HIGH DEMAND?**

**Q1-4 WHAT IS MIS?**

**Q1-5 WHAT IS YOUR ROLE IN IS SECURITY?**

## How does the **knowledge** in this chapter help **you?**

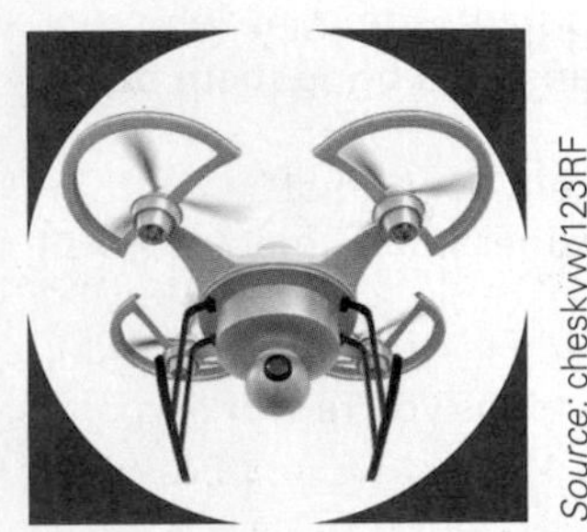

*Source:* cheskyw/123RF

**"But today, they're not enough."**

"Yes, I wasn't sure how to proceed. I didn't want to just throw something out that might not work."

"But how would you find out if it would work?"

"I don't want to waste money . . . "

"No, you don't. So, when you didn't get very far with that task, I backed up and asked you to send me a list of parts that could be printed based on our existing drones, a list of replacement repair parts we buy on a regular basis, the specifications for future drones that we might buy, and a description of how existing 3D-printed drones are made. Not details, just an overview."

"Yes, I sent you those part lists and specifications."

"Jennifer, they made no sense. Your lists included parts that can't be 3D-printed, and your list of potential future drones included models that can't even carry cameras."

"I know which parts can be printed, I just wasn't sure which ones to include. But I'll try again!"

"Well, I appreciate that attitude, but we're a small company, really still a startup in many ways. Everyone needs to pull more than their own weight here. Maybe if we were a bigger company, I'd be able to find a spot for you, see if we could bring you along. But we can't afford to do that now."

"What about my references?"

"I'll be happy to tell anyone that you're reliable, that you work 40 to 45 hours a week, and that you're honest and have integrity."

"Those are important!"

"Yes, they are. But today, they're not enough."

**Optional Extension for this chapter is CE1: Collaboration Information Systems for Decision Making, Problem Solving, and Project Management 367**

## Q1-1 WHY IS INTRODUCTION TO MIS THE MOST IMPORTANT CLASS IN THE BUSINESS SCHOOL?

Introduction to MIS is the most important class in the business school. This wasn't always the case. A couple decades ago, majoring in "computers" was considered a nerdy thing do to. But things have changed—a lot. Now the hottest jobs are found in tech companies. People brag about working for tech startups. Apple Inc. is the largest corporation in the world with a market cap of $740B. The largest IPO offering in history ($25B) came from the online ecommerce giant Alibaba (Alibaba Holdings Group) in 2014.

But why? Why has information technology changed from a minor corporate support function to a primary driver of corporate profitability? Why are tech jobs some of the highest paid? Why is working for a tech company considered über cool?

The answer has to do with the way technology is fundamentally changing business.

### THE DIGITAL REVOLUTION

You've probably heard that we live in the **Information Age**, or a period in history where the production, distribution, and control of information is the primary driver of the economy. The Information Age started in the 1970s with the **Digital Revolution**, or the conversion from mechanical and analog devices to digital devices. This shift to digital devices meant monumental changes for companies, individuals, and our society as a whole.

The problem was, people couldn't really understand how, or even why, this shift was going to affect them. Much like people today, they based their future projections on past events. They knew factories, bureaucracies, mass production, and operational efficiency. But this knowledge didn't prepare them for the changes that were coming.

The Digital Revolution didn't just mean that new "digital" equipment was replacing old mechanical, or analog, equipment. These new digital devices could now be connected to other digital devices and share data among themselves. They could also work faster as processor speed increased. This was ground breaking. In 1972, computer scientist Gordon Bell recognized that these digital devices would change the world as they evolved and became widely used. He formulated **Bell's Law**, which states that "a new computer class forms roughly each decade establishing a new industry."[1] In other words, digital devices will evolve so quickly that they will enable new platforms, programming environments, industries, networks, and information systems every 10 years.

And it has happened just as Bell predicted. About every 10 years since 1970, entirely new classes of digital devices have emerged. They have created entirely new industries, companies, and platforms. In the 1980s, we saw the rise of the personal computer (PC) and small local networks. In the 1990s, we saw the rise of the Internet and widespread adoption of cellular phones. In the 2000s, we saw a push toward making all "things" network-enabled. Social networking and cloud-based services really took off creating a flurry of new companies.

The evolution of digital technology has fundamentally altered businesses and become a primary driver of corporate profitability. And it will probably continue to do so for at least the next few decades. The key to understanding how businesses will be affected by this digital evolution is understanding the forces pushing the evolution of these new digital devices.

### EVOLVING CAPABILITIES

To understand the fundamental forces pushing the evolution of digital devices, let's imagine your body is evolving at the same rate as digital devices. Suppose you can run 8 miles per hour today. That's about average. Now suppose, hypothetically, that your body is changing so quickly that you can run twice as fast every 18 months. In 18 months, you'd be able to run 16 mph. In another 18 months, you'd be at 32 mph. Then 64, 128, 256, and 512. Then, after 10 1/2 years of growth, you'd be running 1,024 mph—on foot! How would this change your life?

Well, you'd certainly give up your car. It would be much too slow. Air travel would also probably be a thing of the past. You could start a very profitable package delivery business and quickly corner the market. You could live outside of the city because your commute would be shorter. You'd also need new clothes and some really tough shoes! And this is the key point—not only would *you* change, but *what* you do and *how* you do it would also change. This is Bell's Law. This same thing is happening to digital devices.

This example may seem silly at first, but it helps you understand how exponential change is affecting digital devices. Processing power, interconnectivity of devices, storage capacity, and bandwidth are all increasing extremely rapidly—so rapidly that it's changing how these devices are used. Let's explore some of these forces by looking at the laws that describe them.

## MOORE'S LAW

In 1965, Gordon Moore, cofounder of Intel Corporation, stated that because of technology improvements in electronic chip design and manufacturing, "The number of transistors per square inch on an integrated chip doubles every 18 months." This became known as **Moore's Law**. His statement has been commonly misunderstood to be "The speed of a computer doubles every 18 months," which is incorrect but captures the sense of his principle.

Because of Moore's Law, the ratio of price to performance of computers has fallen from something like $4,000 for a standard computing device to a fraction of a penny for that same computing device.[2] See Figure 1-1. Increasing processing power has had a greater impact on the global economy in the past 30 years than any other single factor. It has enabled new devices, applications, companies, and platforms. In fact, most tech companies would not exist today if processing power hadn't increased exponentially.

As a future business professional, however, you needn't care how fast of a computer your company can buy for $1,000. That's not the point. The point is, because of Moore's Law, the cost of data processing is approaching zero. Current applications like new drug development, artificial intelligence, and molecular modeling require massive amounts of processing power. Innovations in these areas are being held back because the cost of buying sufficient processing power is so high. But the good news is that the cost of processing is dropping—rapidly.

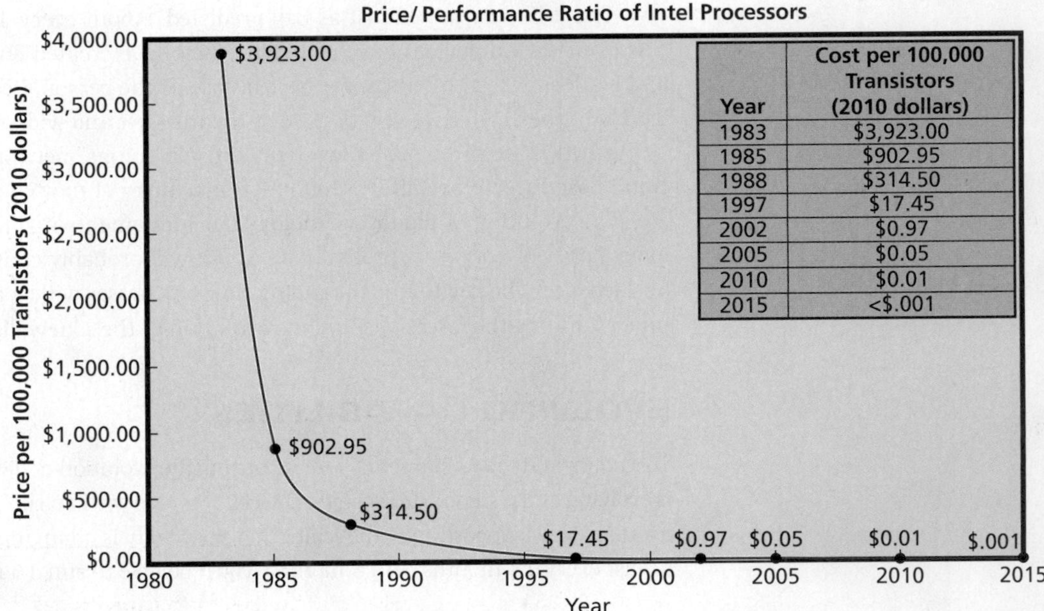


| Year | Cost per 100,000 Transistors (2010 dollars) |
|---|---|
| 1983 | $3,923.00 |
| 1985 | $902.95 |
| 1988 | $314.50 |
| 1997 | $17.45 |
| 2002 | $0.97 |
| 2005 | $0.05 |
| 2010 | $0.01 |
| 2015 | <$.001 |

**Figure 1-1**
Computer Price/Performance Ratio Decreases

## METCALFE'S LAW

Another fundamental force that is changing digital devices is Metcalfe's Law, named after Robert Metcalfe the inventor of Ethernet. **Metcalfe's Law** states that the value of a network is equal to the square of the number of users connected to it. In other words, as more digital devices are connected together, the value of that network will increase.[3] See Figure 1-2. Metcalfe's Law can be clearly seen in the dramatic rise of the Internet in the 1990s. As more users gained access to the Internet, it became more valuable. The dot-com boom ushered in tech giants like Google, Amazon, and eBay. None of these companies would have existed without large numbers of users connected to the Internet.

Metcalfe's Law isn't lost on tech companies, either. Google's Project Loon is a major effort to bring Internet access to everyone on the planet using a network of inflated balloons floating around the world. One of the primary metrics for social media companies is the number of monthly active users (MAU) using their social network. The more people they can get in their network, the more their company will be worth. And look at the network effects of using products like Microsoft Word. Why do you pay for Microsoft Word when you could use a free word processor like LibreOffice Writer? You pay for Microsoft Word because everyone else uses it.

## OTHER FORCES PUSHING DIGITAL CHANGE

And it's not just the number of users on the network that's changing the way we use digital devices—it's the *speed* of the network. **Nielsen's Law**, named after Jakob Nielsen, says that network connection speeds for high-end users will increase by 50 percent per year. As networks become faster, new companies, new products, and new platforms will emerge.

YouTube, for example, started in February 2005 when there wasn't a lot of video shared over the Internet. But average Internet speeds were increasing to the point where a typical Internet connection could handle a stream of YouTube videos. By November 2006, the company was bought by Google for $1.65B. If you're counting, that's less than 2 years to create a billion-dollar company. Network speed matters. The question is, why didn't Google, Microsoft, IBM, or Apple think of video sharing before the YouTube founders?

There are other forces changing digital devices beyond Nielsen's Law, Metcalfe's Law, and Moore's Law (See Figure 1-3). **Kryder's Law**, named after Mark Kryder, the former chief technology officer of Seagate Corp., says that the storage density on magnetic disks is increasing at

**Figure 1-2**
Increasing Value of Networks

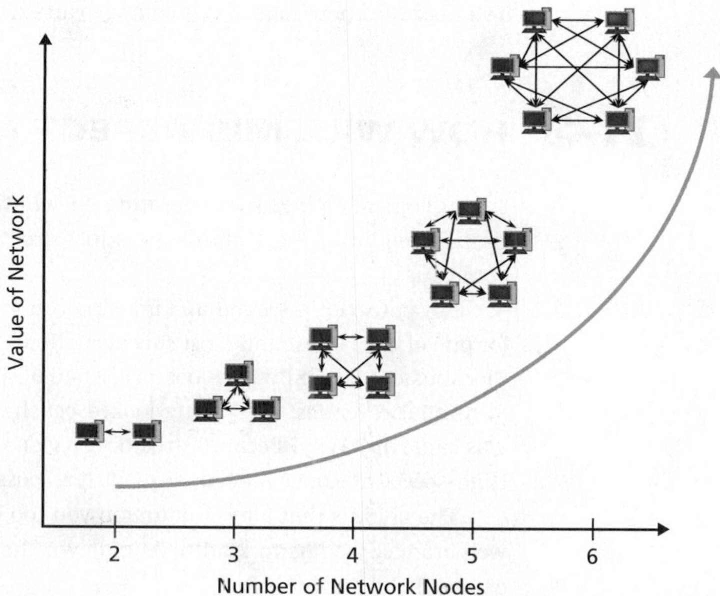

| Law | Meaning | Implications |
|---|---|---|
| Moore's Law | The number of transistors per square inch on an integrated chip doubles every 18 months. | Computers are getting exponentially faster. The cost of data processing is approaching zero. |
| Metcalfe's Law | The value of a network is equal to the square of the number of users connected to it. | More digital devices are connected together. The value of digital and social networks is increasing exponentially. |
| Nielsen's Law | Network connection speeds for high-end users will increase by 50 percent per year. | Network speed is increasing. Higher speeds enable new products, platforms, and companies. |
| Kryder's Law | The storage density on magnetic disks is increasing at an exponential rate. | Storage capacity is increasing exponentially. The cost of storing data is approaching zero. |

**Figure 1-3**
Fundamental Forces Changing Technology

an exponential rate. Digital storage is so important that it's typically the first question you ask when you buy a new computer, smartphone, or tablet. There's also power consumption, image resolution, and interconnectivity between devices all of which are changing, too. And this isn't a complete list.

## THIS IS THE MOST IMPORTANT CLASS IN THE SCHOOL OF BUSINESS

This takes us back to our original statement that Introduction to MIS is the most important class you will take in the school of business. Why? Because this class will show you how technology is fundamentally changing businesses. You'll learn why executives are constantly trying to find ways to use new technology to create a sustainable competitive advantage. This leads us to the first reason Introduction to MIS is the most important course in the business school today:

**Future business professionals need to be able to assess, evaluate, and apply emerging information technology to business.**

You need the knowledge of this course to attain that skill.

# Q1-2 HOW WILL MIS AFFECT ME?

Technological change is accelerating. So what? How is this going to affect you? You may think that the evolution of technology is just great. You can hardly wait for the next i-Gadget to come out.

But pause for a second and imagine you graduated from college in 2004 and went to work for one of the largest and most successful home entertainment companies in the United States—Blockbuster LLC. In 2004, Blockbuster had 60,000 employees and 9,000-plus stores with $5.9B in annual revenues. Everything looked peachy. Fast-forward 6 years to 2010 and Blockbuster was bankrupt! Why? Because streaming a video over the Internet is easier than driving to a store. High-speed Internet connections made it all possible.

The point is that after graduation you too may choose to go to work for a large, successful, well-branded company. And 6 years down the road, it could be bankrupt because technology changed and it didn't.

## HOW CAN I ATTAIN JOB SECURITY?

Many years ago, I had a wise and experienced mentor. One day I asked him about job security, and he told me that the only job security that exists is "a marketable skill and the courage to use it." He continued, "There is no security in our company, there is no security in any government program, there is no security in your investments, and there is no security in Social Security." Alas, how right he turned out to be.

So, what is a marketable skill? It used to be that one could name particular skills, such as computer programming, tax accounting, or marketing. But today, because of Moore's Law, Metcalfe's Law, and Kryder's Law, the cost of data processing, storage, and communications is essentially zero. Any routine skill can and will be outsourced to the lowest bidder. And if you live in the United States, Canada, Australia, Europe, or another advanced economy, the lowest bidder is unlikely to be you.

Numerous organizations and experts have studied the question of what skills will be marketable during your career. Consider two of them. First, the RAND Corporation, a think tank located in Santa Monica, California, has published innovative and groundbreaking ideas for more than 60 years, including the initial design for the Internet. In 2004, RAND published a description of the skills that workers in the 21st century will need:

> Rapid technological change and increased international competition place the spotlight on the skills and preparation of the workforce, particularly the ability to adapt to changing technology and shifting demand. Shifts in the nature of organizations . . . favor strong nonroutine cognitive skills.[4]

Whether you're majoring in accounting, marketing, finance, or information systems, you need to develop strong nonroutine cognitive skills.

What are such skills? Robert Reich, former Secretary of Labor, enumerates four:[5]

- Abstract reasoning
- Systems thinking
- Collaboration
- Ability to experiment

Figure 1-4 shows an example of each. Reread the Falcon Security case that started this chapter, and you'll see that Jennifer lost her job because of her inability to practice these key skills. Even though Reich's book was written in the early 1990's the cognitive skills he mentions are still relevant today because humans, unlike technology, aren't changing that rapidly.[6]

**Figure 1-4**
Examples of Critical Skills for Nonroutine Cognition

| Skill | Example | Jennifer's Problem at Falcon Security |
|---|---|---|
| Abstract Reasoning | Construct a model or representation. | Hesitancy and uncertainty when conceptualizing a method for identifying 3D-printable drone parts. |
| Systems Thinking | Model system components and show how components' inputs and outputs relate to one another. | Inability to model Falcon Security's operational needs. |
| Collaboration | Develop ideas and plans with others. Provide and receive critical feedback. | Unwilling to work with others on work-in-progress. |
| Ability to Experiment | Create and test promising new alternatives, consistent with available resources. | Fear of failure prohibited discussion of new ideas. |

## HOW CAN INTRO TO MIS HELP YOU LEARN NONROUTINE SKILLS?

Introduction to MIS is the best course in the business school for learning Reich's four key skills because every topic requires you to apply and practice them. Here's how.

### Abstract Reasoning

**Abstract reasoning** is the ability to make and manipulate models. You will work with one or more models in every course topic and book chapter. For example, later in this chapter you will learn about a *model* of the five components of an information system. This chapter will describe how to use this model to assess the scope of any new information system project; other chapters will build upon this model.

In this course, you will not just manipulate models that we have developed, you will also be asked to construct models of your own. In Chapter 5, for example, you'll learn how to create data models, and in Chapter 12 you'll learn to make process models.

### Systems Thinking

Can you go to a grocery store, look at a can of green beans, and connect that can to U.S. immigration policy? Can you watch tractors dig up a forest of pulpwood trees and connect that woody trash to Moore's Law? Do you know why Cisco Systems is one of the major beneficiaries of YouTube? Answers to all of these questions require systems thinking. **Systems thinking** is the ability to model the components of the system to connect the inputs and outputs among those components into a sensible whole that reflects the structure and dynamics of the phenomenon observed.

As you are about to learn, this class is about information *systems*. We will discuss and illustrate systems; you will be asked to critique systems; you will be asked to compare alternative systems; you will be asked to apply different systems to different situations. All of those tasks will prepare you for systems thinking as a professional.

### Collaboration

**The first two chapter extensions on pages 367–400 discuss collaboration in detail and guide you in how to collaborate with your peers.**

**Collaboration** is the activity of two or more people working together to achieve a common goal, result, or work product. Chapter Extensions 1 and 2 will teach you collaboration skills and illustrate several sample collaboration information systems. Every chapter of this book includes collaboration exercises that you may be assigned in class or as homework.

Here's a fact that surprises many students: Effective collaboration isn't about being nice. In fact, surveys indicate the single most important skill for effective collaboration is to give and receive critical feedback. Advance a proposal in business that challenges the cherished program of the VP of marketing, and you'll quickly learn that effective collaboration skills differ from party manners at the neighborhood barbeque. So, how do you advance your idea in the face of the VP's resistance? And without losing your job? In this course, you can learn both skills and information systems for such collaboration. Even better, you will have many opportunities to practice them.

### Ability to Experiment

"I've never done this before."
"I don't know how to do it."
"But will it work?"
"Is it too weird for the market?"

Fear of failure: the fear that paralyzes so many good people and so many good ideas. In the days when business was stable, when new ideas were just different verses of the same song, professionals could allow themselves to be limited by fear of failure.

Let's look at an example of the application of social networking to the oil change business. Is there a legitimate application of social networking there? If so, has anyone ever done it? Is there anyone in the world who can tell you what to do? How to proceed? No. As Reich says, professionals in the 21st century need to be able to experiment.

Successful experimentation is not throwing buckets of money at every crazy idea that enters your head. Instead, **experimentation** is making a reasoned analysis of an opportunity, envisioning potential solutions, evaluating those possibilities, and developing the most promising ones, consistent with the resources you have.

In this course, you will be asked to use products with which you have no familiarity. Those products might be Microsoft Excel or Access, or they might be features and functions of Blackboard that you have not used. Or you may be asked to collaborate using OneDrive or SharePoint or Google Drive. Will your instructor explain and show every feature of those products that you'll need? You should hope not. You should hope your instructor will leave it up to you to experiment, to envision new possibilities on your own, and to experiment with those possibilities, consistent with the time you have available.

# Q1-3 WHY ARE MIS-RELATED JOBS IN HIGH DEMAND?

Employment is another factor that makes the Introduction to MIS course vitally important to you. Accenture, a technology consulting and outsourcing company, conducted a survey of college graduates in 2014. It found that 69 percent of 2014 college graduates say they will need additional training or education before they get their desired job. Further, 46 percent of recent graduates were working in jobs that did not require their degree or were otherwise underemployed.[7] But this is not the case in job categories related to information systems.

Spence and Hlatshwayo studied employment in the United States from 1990 to 2008.[8] They defined a *tradable job* as one that was not dependent on a particular location; this distinction is important because such jobs can be outsourced overseas. As shown in Figure 1-5, computer

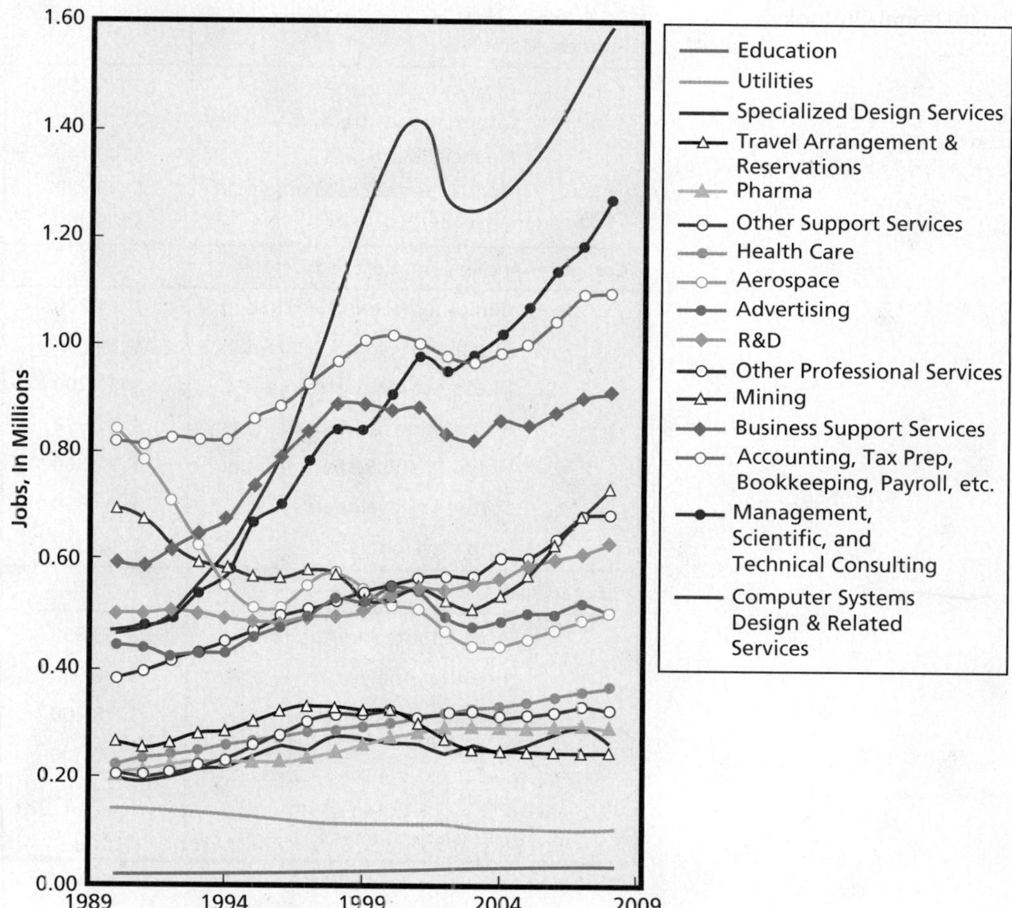


**Figure 1-5**
Growth of Jobs by Sector from 1989 to 2009

*Source:* From *The Evolving Structure of the American Economy* and the *Employment Challenge* by Michael Spence and Sandile Hlatshwayo. Copyright © 2011 by The Council on Foreign Relations Press. Reprinted with permission.

systems design and related services had the strongest growth of any job type in that category. The number of jobs dipped substantially after the dot-com bust in 2000; since 2003, however, job growth has not only recovered but accelerated dramatically. While this category includes technical positions such as computer programmer and database administrator, it includes non-technical sales, support, and business management jobs as well. By the way, because Figure 1-5 shows tradable jobs, it puts an end to the myth that all the good computer jobs have gone overseas. According to their data analysis, sourced from the U.S. Bureau of Labor Statistics, that simply has not happened.

The data in Figure 1-5 stops at 2009 and, unfortunately, Spence and Hlatshwayo have not updated their study. However, Figure 1-6 shows the U.S. Bureau of Labor Statistics recent job projections for business managers, computer and information technology, and other business occupations for the years 2012 to 2022.[9] Growth rates of all information systems related jobs are above the 11 percent average for all occupations.

Information systems and computer technology provide job and wage benefits beyond just IS professionals. Acemoglu and Autor published an impressive empirical study of jobs and wages in the United States and parts of Europe from the 1960s to 2010. They found that early in this period, education and industry were the strongest determinants of employment and salary. However, since 1990, the most significant determinant of employment and salary is the nature of work performed. In short, as the price of computer technology plummets, the value of jobs that benefit from it increases dramatically.[10] For example, plentiful, high-paying jobs are available to business professionals who know how to use information systems to improve business

**Figure 1-6**
Bureau of Labor Statistics Occupational Outlook 2012–22

| | 2012 Median Pay | Job Growth (%) 2012–22 | Job Growth (N) 2012–22 |
|---|---|---|---|
| Business Managers | | | |
| Marketing Managers | $115,750 | 12% | 25,400 |
| Information Systems Managers | $120,950 | 15% | 50,900 |
| Financial Managers | $109,740 | 9% | 47,100 |
| Human Resources Managers | $ 99,720 | 13% | 13,600 |
| Sales Managers | $105,260 | 8% | 29,800 |
| Computer and Information Technology | | | |
| Computer Network Architects | $ 91,000 | 15% | 20,900 |
| Computer Systems Analysts | $ 79,680 | 25% | 127,700 |
| Database Administrators | $118,700 | 15% | 17,900 |
| Information Security Analysts | $ 87,170 | 37% | 27,400 |
| Network and Systems Admin. | $ 72,560 | 12% | 42,900 |
| Software Developers | $ 93,350 | 22% | 222,600 |
| Web Developers | $ 62,500 | 20% | 28,500 |
| Business Occupations | | | |
| Accountants and Auditors | $ 63,550 | 13% | 166,700 |
| Financial Analysts | $ 76,950 | 16% | 39,300 |
| Management Analysts | $ 78,600 | 19% | 133,800 |
| Market Research Analysts | $ 60,300 | 32% | 131,500 |
| Logisticians | $ 72,780 | 22% | 27,600 |
| Human Resources Specialists | $ 55,640 | 7% | 32,500 |

# Biggest IPO Ever: Alibaba

Have you ever thought about starting your own business? It's not easy to turn a new idea into a profitable company. But the Information Age has created an environment in which anyone can grow a small business with minimal investment and marginal risk. Sometimes even technical requirements can be outsourced.

For example, companies like Squarespace.com allow entrepreneurs lacking Web development skills to create dynamic, visually appealing platforms to sell their goods or services. And if you don't want to sit around packing and shipping your products to customers, let Fulfillment by Amazon (FBA) do it for you!

But fledgling entrepreneurs aren't the only ones benefiting from the resources provided by a growing digital economy; companies of all sizes dealing in business-to-business (B2B), business-to-consumer (B2C), and consumer-to-consumer (C2C) commerce are also profiting from new opportunities to find cheaper raw materials, higher quality trading goods, and most importantly, customers.

## What is Alibaba.com?

Founded by Jack Ma in 1999, Alibaba.com started out as an e-commerce portal for buying and selling goods and has since grown to include a variety of financial, auction, and commerce services. Alibaba's mission is to connect suppliers and buyers around the globe.[11]

Alibaba boasts millions of products, dozens of product categories, and thousands of messages exchanged daily between buyers and sellers. While this may be the first time you have heard of Alibaba.com, it has become a major product and information interchange for buying and selling wholesale goods.

The influence Alibaba.com has on global commerce is even more evident when you consider the size of its IPO in the fall of 2014 (NYSE: BABA). BABA broke the record for biggest-ever IPO by roughly $3B with an IPO of $25B.[12] By comparison, Facebook raised $16B in its 2012 IPO, and General Motors' IPO raised $15.7B after emerging from bankruptcy in 2010. Interestingly, Ma started Alibaba.com with less than $70,000 in 1999 and is now the richest man in China.

## Growing Pains

Alibaba rapidly evolved from a "new idea" to a leading global retailer and supplier with the biggest IPO of all time. Given the company's meteoric rise, it might be tempting to assume that Alibaba.com is going to be the dominant worldwide retailer and supplier. But this may not be the case. The site has been mired with suppliers selling counterfeit products despite roughly $16M invested annually to combat the sale of fraudulent goods.[13]

*Source:* Yeong-Ung Yang/Corbis

Alibaba.com has sought to combat counterfeit goods by allowing suppliers to obtain "Gold Supplier" status, a vetting process including site visits by verification services. However, you can imagine the logistical complexities associated with vetting global suppliers and responding to fraud claims by global buyers.

## What Can Alibaba.com Do for You?

If you are thinking of importing wholesale goods and selling them on your own e-commerce site, or in your flagship brick-and-mortar location, then Alibaba.com might end up being a great supplier for you. Even if you don't end up buying products from Alibaba, lessons can be learned from Alibaba's success.

First, Alibaba.com is a perfect example of how managing information can be as profitable as selling a high-quality product. Consider the fact that Alibaba may be the largest retailer in the world, but it has little or no inventory at all.

Second, Alibaba.com demonstrates the complexities associated with operating in a global economy. Managing customer relationships can be more difficult when buyers and sellers are located around the world.

Finally, the story of Alibaba.com illustrates what can be accomplished in a relatively short period of time with a laptop, a good idea, and a lot of hard work. So stop checking your friends' status updates and get to work on your idea for the next great tech company!

## QUESTIONS

1. Take a few minutes to browse Alibaba.com and look at some examples of products for sale on the site. What are some of the logistical differences between buying something on Alibaba.com and buying something on Amazon.com?
2. How has reading this article changed your perception of the difficulty associated with starting a new business?
3. Think about companies that currently have high stock prices. Do these companies sell a product or service or do they offer something else? How is Alibaba.com similar to or different from these companies?
4. What are some of the challenges associated with operating an international business not discussed in this article?
5. Think about your own purchasing habits and the buying habits of your friends/coworkers. Can you identify a product people need that is available on Alibaba.com? Is there a different Web site on which you could purchase this product for wholesale prices and sell it to customers for a profit?

process quality, or those who know how to interpret data mining results for improved marketing, or those who know how to use emerging technology like 3D printing to create new products and address new markets. See the Guide on pages 22–23 for more thoughts on why you might consider an IS-related job.

**The Ethics Guide in each chapter of this book considers the ethics of information system use. The guides challenge you to think deeply about how to apply ethical standards to unfamiliar situations. The Ethics Guide on pages 20–21 considers the ethics of using information that deceives the viewer.**

### WHAT IS THE BOTTOM LINE?

The bottom line? This course is the most important course in the business school because:

1. **It will give you the background you need to assess, evaluate, and apply emerging information systems technology to business.**
2. **It can give you the ultimate in job security—marketable skills—by helping you learn abstraction, systems thinking, collaboration, and experimentation.**
3. **Many well-paid MIS-related jobs are in high demand.**

## Q1-4 WHAT IS MIS?

We've used the term *MIS* several times, and you may be wondering exactly what it is. **MIS** stands for **management information systems**, which we define as *the management and use of information systems that help organizations achieve their strategies*. MIS is often confused with the closely related terms information technology and information systems. An **information system (IS)** is an assembly of hardware, software, data, procedures, and people that produces information. In contrast, **information technology (IT)** refers to the products, methods, inventions, and standards used for the purpose of producing information.

How are MIS, IS, and IT different? You cannot buy an IS. But you can buy IT; you can buy or lease hardware, you can license programs and databases, and you can even obtain predesigned procedures. Ultimately, however, it is *your* people who will assemble the IT you purchase and execute those procedures to employ that new IT. Information technology drives the development of new information systems.

For any new system, you will always have training tasks (and costs), you will always have the need to overcome employees' resistance to change, and you will always need to manage the employees as they use the new system. Hence, you can buy IT, but you cannot buy IS. Once your new information system is up and running, it must be managed and used effectively in order to achieve the organization's overall strategy. This is MIS.

Consider a simple example. Suppose your organization decides to develop a Facebook page. Facebook provides the IT. It provides the hardware and programs, the database structures, and standard procedures. You, however, must create the IS. You have to provide the data to fill your portion of its database, and you must extend its standard procedures with your own procedures for keeping that data current. Those procedures need to provide, for example, a means to review your page's content regularly and a means to remove content that is judged inappropriate. Furthermore, you need to train employees on how to follow those procedures and manage those employees to ensure that they do. MIS is the management of your Facebook page to achieve your overall organization's strategy. Managing your own Facebook page is as simple an IS as exists. Larger, more comprehensive IS that involve many, even dozens, of departments and thousands of employees require considerable work.

The definition of MIS has three key elements: *management and use, information systems*, and *strategies*. Let's consider each, starting first with information systems and their components.

## COMPONENTS OF AN INFORMATION SYSTEM

A **system** is a group of components that interact to achieve some purpose. As you might guess, an *information system (IS)* is a group of components that interacts to produce information. That sentence, although true, raises another question: What are these components that interact to produce information?

Figure 1-7 shows the **five-component framework**—a model of the components of an information system: **computer hardware**, **software**, **data**, **procedures**, and **people**. These five components are present in every information system, from the simplest to the most complex. For example, when you use a computer to write a class report, you are using hardware (the computer, storage disk, keyboard, and monitor), software (Word, WordPerfect, or some other word-processing program), data (the words, sentences, and paragraphs in your report), procedures (the methods you use to start the program, enter your report, print it, and save and back up your file), and people (you).

Consider a more complex example, say, an airline reservation system. It, too, consists of these five components, even though each one is far more complicated. The hardware consists of thousands of computers linked together by data communications hardware. Hundreds of different programs coordinate communications among the computers, and still other programs perform the reservations and related services. Additionally, the system must store millions upon millions of characters of data about flights, customers, reservations, and other facts. Hundreds of different procedures are followed by airline personnel, travel agents, and customers. Finally, the information system includes people, not only the users of the system but also those who operate and service the computers, those who maintain the data, and those who support the networks of computers.

**These five components also mean that building information systems requires many different skills besides those of hardware technicians or computer programmers.** **See the Guide on pages 22–23 for more.**

The important point here is that the five components in Figure 1-7 are common to all information systems, from the smallest to the largest. As you think about any information system, including a new one like social networking, learn to look for these five components. Realize, too, that an information system is not just a computer and a program, but rather an assembly of computers, programs, data, procedures, and people.

**Figure 1-7**
Five Components of an Information System

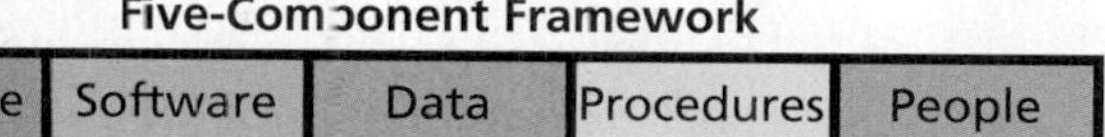

Before we move forward, note that we have defined an information system to include a computer. Some people would say that such a system is a **computer-based information system**. They would note that there are information systems that do not include computers, such as a calendar hanging on the wall outside of a conference room that is used to schedule the room's use. Such systems have been used by businesses for centuries. Although this point is true, in this book we focus on computer-based information systems. To simplify and shorten the book, we will use the term *information system* as a synonym for *computer-based information system*.

## MANAGEMENT AND USE OF INFORMATION SYSTEMS

The next element in our definition of MIS is the *management and use* of information systems. Here we define management to mean develop, maintain, and adapt. Information systems do not pop up like mushrooms after a hard rain; they must be developed. They must also be maintained, and, because business is dynamic, they must be adapted to new requirements.

You may be saying, "Wait a minute, I'm a finance (or accounting or management) major, not an information systems major. I don't need to know how to manage information systems." If you are saying that, you are like a lamb headed for shearing. Throughout your career, in whatever field you choose, information systems will be built for your use and sometimes under your direction. To create an information system that meets your needs, you need to take an *active role* in that system's development. Even if you are not a programmer or a database designer or some other IS professional, you must take an active role in specifying the system's requirements and in managing the system's development project. You will also have an important role in testing the new system. Without active involvement on your part, it will only be good luck that causes the new system to meet your needs.

As a business professional, you are the person who understands business needs and requirements. If you want to apply social networking to your products, you are the one who knows how best to obtain customer responses. The technical people who build networks, the database designers who create the database, the IT people who configure the computers—none of these people know what is needed and whether the system you have is sufficient or whether it needs to be adapted to new requirements. You do!

In addition to management tasks, you will also have important roles to play in the *use* of information systems. Of course, you will need to learn how to employ the system to accomplish your job tasks. But you will also have important ancillary functions as well. For example, when using an information system, you will have responsibilities for protecting the security of the system and its data. You may also have tasks for backing up data. When the system fails (all do, at some point), you will have tasks to perform while the system is down as well as tasks to accomplish to help recover the system correctly and quickly.

## ACHIEVING STRATEGIES

The last part of the definition of MIS is that information systems exist to help organizations *achieve their strategies*. First, realize that this statement hides an important fact: Organizations themselves do not "do" anything. An organization is not alive, and it cannot act. It is the people within a business who sell, buy, design, produce, finance, market, account, and manage. So, information systems exist to help people who work in an organization to achieve the strategies of that business.

Information systems are not created for the sheer joy of exploring technology. They are not created so the company can be "modern" or so the company can show it has a social networking presence on the Web. They are not created because the information systems department thinks it needs to be created or because the company is "falling behind the technology curve."

This point may seem so obvious that you might wonder why we mention it. Every day, however, some business somewhere is developing an information system for the wrong reasons. Right now, somewhere in the world, a company is deciding to create a Facebook presence for the sole reason that "every other business has one." This company is not asking questions such as:

- "What is the purpose of our Facebook page?"
- "What is it going to do for us?"
- "What is our policy for employees' contributions?"
- "What should we do about critical customer reviews?"
- "Are the costs of maintaining the page sufficiently offset by the benefits?"

But that company should ask those questions! Chapter 3 addresses the relationship between information systems and strategy in more depth. Chapter 8 addresses social media and strategy specifically.

Again, MIS is the development and use of information systems that help businesses achieve their strategies. You should already be realizing that there is much more to this class than buying a computer, working with a spreadsheet, or creating a Web page.

## Q1-5 WHAT IS YOUR ROLE IN IS SECURITY?

As you have learned, information systems create value. However, they also create risk. For example, Amazon.com maintains credit card data on millions of customers and has the responsibility to protect that data. If Amazon.com's security system was breached and that credit card data stolen, Amazon.com would incur serious losses—not only lost business, but also potentially staggering liability losses. Because of the importance of information security, we will consider it throughout this textbook. Additionally, Chapter 10 is devoted to security.

However, you have a role in security that is too important for us to wait until you read that chapter. Like all information systems, security systems have the five components, including people. Thus, every security system ultimately depends on the behavior of its users. If the users do not take security seriously, if they do not follow security procedures, then the hardware, software, and data components of the security system are wasted expenses. So, before we proceed further, we will address how you should create and use a strong password, which is an essential component of computer security.

Almost all security systems use usernames and passwords. As a user of information systems in a business organization, you will be instructed to create a strong password and to protect it. *It is vitally important for you to do so.* You should already be using such passwords at your university. (According to an article in *The New York Times*,[14] 20 percent of people use an easily guessed password like "12345." Don't be part of that 20 percent!)

### STRONG PASSWORDS

So what is a strong password, and how do you create one? Microsoft, a company that has many reasons to promote effective security, defines a **strong password** as one with the following characteristics:

- Has 10 or more characters, 12 is even better
- Does not contain your username, real name, or company name
- Does not contain a complete dictionary word in any language

- Is different from previous passwords you have used
- Contains both upper- and lowercase letters, numbers, and special characters (such as ˜! @; # $ % ^; &; * () _ +; – =; {} | [] \: “;’ <; >;?, . /)

Examples of good passwords are:

- Qw37^T1bb?at
- 3B47qq5!7b

The problem with such passwords is that they are nearly impossible to remember. And the last thing you want to do is write your password on a piece of paper and keep it near the workstation where you use it. Never do that!

One technique for creating memorable, strong passwords is to base them on the first letter of the words in a phrase. The phrase could be the title of a song or the first line of a poem or one based on some fact about your life. For example, you might take the phrase “I was born in Rome, New York, before 1990.” Using the first letters from that phrase and substituting the character < for the word *before*, you create the password *IwbiR,NY<1990*. That's an acceptable password, but it would be better if all of the numbers were not placed on the end. So, you might try the phrase, “I was born at 3:00 AM in Rome, New York.” That phrase yields the password *Iwba3:00AMiR,NY*, which is a strong password that is easily remembered.

## PASSWORD ETIQUETTE

Once you have created a strong password, you need to protect it with proper behavior. Proper password etiquette is one of the marks of a business professional. Never write down your password, and do not share it with others. Never ask others for their passwords, and never give your password to someone else.

But what if you need someone else's password? Suppose, for example, you ask someone to help you with a problem on your computer. You sign on to an information system, and for some reason you need to enter that other person's password. In this case, say to the other person, “We need your password,” and then get out of your chair, offer your keyboard to the other person, and look away while he or she enters the password. Among professionals working in organizations that take security seriously, this little “do-si-do” move—one person getting out of the way so that another person can enter a password—is common and accepted.

If someone asks for your password, do not give it out. Instead, get up, go over to that person's machine, and enter your password yourself. Stay present while your password is in use, and ensure that your account is logged out at the end of the activity. No one should mind or be offended in any way when you do this. It is the mark of a professional.

## How does the **knowledge** in this chapter help **you?**

It's too late for Jennifer, at least at Falcon Security. However, it's not too late for you, and it's not too late for Jennifer at her next job. So, what are the takeaways from this chapter?

First, realize that the future belongs to businesspeople who can creatively envision new applications of information systems and technology. You don't have to be an IS major (though it is a very good major with excellent job prospects), but you should be able to innovate the use of MIS into the discipline in which you do major. How can management, marketing, accounting, production, and so on, take advantage of the benefits of Bell's Law, Moore's Law, and Metcalfe's Law?

Second, learn Reich's four key skills: abstract thinking, systems thinking, experimentation, and collaboration. And practice, practice, practice them. This class is the best one in the b-school for teaching those skills, so engage in it. As you study and perform assignments, ask yourself how your activity relates to those four abilities and endeavor to improve your proficiency at them.

Next, learn the components of an IS and understand that every business professional needs to take an active role in new information systems development. Such systems are created for your needs and require your involvement. Know the difference between IT, IS, and MIS. Finally, learn, now, how to create a strong password and begin using such passwords and proper password etiquette.

We're just getting started: there's lots more to come that can benefit Jennifer (in her next job) and you!

# Ethics and Professional Responsibility

Suppose you're a young marketing professional who has just taken a new promotional campaign to market. The executive committee asks you to present a summary of the sales effect of the campaign, and you produce the graph shown in Figure 1. As shown, your campaign was just in the nick of time; sales were starting to fall the moment your campaign kicked in. After that, sales boomed.

But note the vertical axis has no quantitative labels. If you add quantities, as shown in Figure 2, the performance is less impressive. It appears that the substantial growth amounts to less than 20 units. Still, the curve of the graph is impressive, and if no one does the arithmetic, your campaign will appear successful.

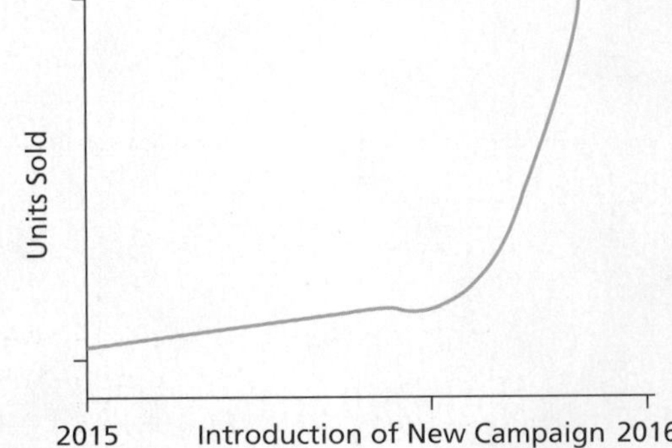


**Figure 1**

This impressive shape is only possible, however, because Figure 2 is not drawn to scale. If you draw it to scale, as shown in Figure 3, your campaign's success is, well, problematic, at least for you.

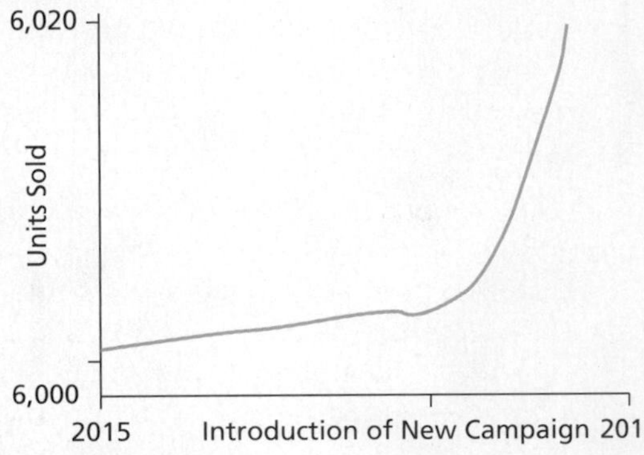


**Figure 2**

Which of these graphs do you present to the committee?

Each chapter of this text includes an Ethics Guide that explores ethical and responsible behavior in a variety of MIS-related contexts. In this chapter, we'll examine the ethics of data and information.

Centuries of philosophical thought have addressed the question "What is right behavior?" and we can't begin to discuss all of it here. You will learn much of it, however, in your business ethics class. For our purposes, we'll use two of the major pillars in the philosophy of ethics. We introduce the first one here and the second in Chapter 2.

6,020
Scale Drawing
Growth rate since 2013 = 0.0025
Units Sold
0
2015 Introduction of New Campaign 2016

**Figure 3**

The German philosopher Immanuel Kant defined the *categorical imperative* as the principle that *one should behave only in a way that one would want the behavior to be a universal law.* Stealing is not such behavior because if everyone steals, nothing can be owned. Stealing cannot be a universal law. Similarly, lying cannot be consistent with the categorical imperative because if everyone lies, words are useless.

When you ask whether a behavior is consistent with this principle, a good litmus test is "Are you willing to publish your behavior to the world? Are you willing to put it on your Facebook page? Are you willing to say what you've done to all the players involved?" If not, your behavior is not ethical, at least not in the sense of Kant's categorical imperative.

Kant defined *duty* as the necessity to act in accordance with the categorical imperative. *Perfect duty* is behavior that must always be met. Not lying is a perfect duty. *Imperfect duty* is action that is praiseworthy but not required according to the categorical imperative. Giving to charity is an example of an imperfect duty.

Kant used the example of cultivating one's own talent as an imperfect duty, and we can use that example as a way of defining professional responsibility. Business professionals have an imperfect duty to obtain the skills necessary to accomplish their jobs. We also have an imperfect duty to continue to develop our business skills and abilities throughout our careers.

We will apply these principles in the chapters that follow. For now, use them to assess your beliefs about Figures 1 through 3 by answering the following questions.

## DISCUSSION QUESTIONS

**1.** Restate Kant's categorical imperative using your own words. Explain why cheating on exams is not consistent with the categorical imperative.

**2.** While there is some difference of opinion, most scholars believe that the Golden Rule ("Do unto others as you would have them do unto you.") is not equivalent to Kant's categorical imperative. Justify this belief.

**3.** Suppose you created Figure 1 using Microsoft Excel. To do so, you keyed the data into Excel and clicked the Make Graph button (there is one, though it's not called that). Voilà, Excel created Figure 1 without any labels and drawn out of scale as shown. Without further consideration, you put the result into your presentation.

**a.** Is your behavior consistent with Kant's categorical imperative? Why or why not?

**b.** If Excel automatically produces graphs like Figure 1, is Microsoft's behavior consistent with Kant's categorical imperative? Why or why not?

**4.** Change roles. Assume now you are a member of the executive committee. A junior marketing professional presents Figure 1 to the committee, and you object to the lack of labels and the scale. In response, the junior marketing professional says, "Sorry, I didn't know. I just put the data into Excel and copied the resulting graph." What conclusions do you, as an executive, make about the junior marketing professional in response to this statement?

**5.** Is the junior marketing person's response in question 4 a violation of a perfect duty? Of an imperfect duty? Of any duty? Explain your response.

**6.** If you were the junior marketing professional, which graph would you present to the committee?

**7.** According to Kant, lying is not consistent with the categorical imperative. Suppose you are invited to a seasonal BBQ at the department chair's house. You are served a steak that is tough, overcooked, and so barely edible that you secretly feed it to the department chair's dog (who appears to enjoy it). The chairperson asks you, "How is your steak?" and you respond, "Excellent, thank you."

**a.** Is your behavior consistent with Kant's categorical imperative?

**b.** The steak seemed to be excellent to the dog. Does that fact change your answer to part a?

**c.** What conclusions do you draw from this example?

# Guide

## Five-Component Careers

Some years, even some decades, students can wait until their last semester to think seriously about jobs. They can pick a major, take the required classes, and prepare to graduate, all the while assuming that job recruiters will be on campus, loaded with good jobs, sometime during their senior year. *Alas, today is not one of those periods.*

In the current employment situation, you need to be proactive and aggressive in your job search. Think about it: You will be spending one-third of your waking life in your job. One of the best things you can do for yourself is to begin thinking seriously about your career prospects now. You don't want to find yourself working as a barista after 4 years of business school, unless, of course, you're planning on starting the next Starbucks.

So, start here. Are you interested in a career in MIS? At this point, you don't know enough to know but Figure 1-5 and Figure 1-6 should catch your attention. With job growth like that, in a category of jobs that is net of outsourcing, you should at least ponder whether there is a career for you in IS and related services.

But what does that mean? If you go to the U.S. Bureau of Labor Statistics, you can find that there are more than a million computer programmers in the United States today and more than 600,000 systems analysts. You probably have some notion of what a programmer does, but you don't yet know what a system analyst is. Examine the five components in Figure 1-7, however, and you can glean some idea. Programmers work primarily with the software component, and system analysts work with the entire system, with all five components. So, as a systems analyst, you work with system users to determine what the organizational requirements are and then with technical people (and others) to help develop that system. You work as a cultural broker: translating the culture of technology into the culture of business, and the reverse.

Fortunately for you, many interesting jobs are not captured by the bureau's data. Why fortunate? Because you can use what you're learning in this course to identify and obtain jobs that other students may not think about or even know about. If so, you've gained a competitive advantage.

The figure on the next page provides a framework for thinking about careers in an unconventional way. As you can see, there are technical jobs in MIS but fascinating, challenging, and high-paying, nontechnical ones as well. Consider, for example, professional sales. Suppose you have the job of selling enterprise-class software to the Mayo Clinic. You will sell to intelligent, highly motivated professionals with tens of millions of dollars to spend. Or suppose you are working for the Mayo Clinic on the receiving end of that sales pitch. How will you spend your tens of millions? You will need knowledge of your business, and you will need to understand enough technology to ask intelligent questions and interpret the responses.

Give this some thought by answering the discussion questions, even if they aren't assigned for a grade!

|  | Hardware | Software | Data | Procedures | People |
|---|---|---|---|---|---|
| Sales & Marketing | Vendors (IBM Cisco, etc.) | Vendors (Microsoft, Oracle, etc.) | Vendors (Acxiom, Google, etc.) | Vendors (SAP, Infor, Oracle) | Recruiters (Robert Half, Lucas Group) |
| Support | Vendors Internal MIS | Vendors Internal MIS | Database administration Security | Vendor and internal customer support | Customer support Training |
| Development | Computer engineering Internal MIS | Application programmer Quality test engineer | Data modeler Database design | Business process management Process re-engineering | Training, Internal MIS recruiting |
| Management | Internal MIS | Internal MIS | Data administration | Project management | Technical management |
| Consulting and Training | Pre- and postsale support. Development and project management. Training for users and developers. |  |  |  |  |

## DISCUSSION QUESTIONS

**1.** What does the phrase *in a category of jobs that is net of outsourcing* mean? Reread the discussion of Figure 1-5 if you're not certain. Why is this important to you?

**2.** Examine the five-component careers figure on this page and choose the row that seems most relevant to your interests and abilities. Describe a job in each component column of that row. If you are uncertain, Google the terms in the cells of that row.

**3.** For each job in your answer to question 2, describe what you think are the three most important skills and abilities for that job.

**4.** For each job in your answer to question 2, describe one innovative action that you can take this year to increase your employment prospects.

*Source:* Tyler Olson/Fotolia

# ACTIVE REVIEW

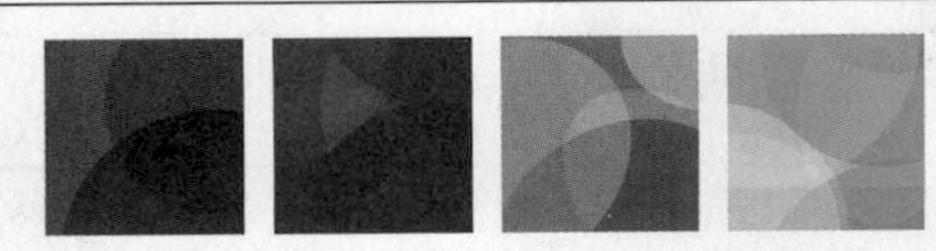

Use this Active Review to verify that you understand the ideas and concepts that answer the chapter's study questions.

## Q1-1 WHY IS INTRODUCTION TO MIS THE MOST IMPORTANT CLASS IN THE BUSINESS SCHOOL?

Define *Bell's Law* and explain why its consequences are important to business professionals today. Describe how *Moore's Law, Metcalfe's Law, Nielsen's Law*, and *Kryder's Law* are changing how digital devices are used. State how business professionals should relate to emerging information technology.

## Q1-2 HOW WILL MIS AFFECT ME?

Define Reich's four key nonroutine cognitive skills. Give the text's definition of *job security* and use Reich's list to explain how this course will help you attain that security. Explain why systems thinking is important to businesses.

## Q1-3 WHY ARE MIS-RELATED JOBS IN HIGH DEMAND?

Summarize IS-related job opportunities. According to the Bureau of Labor Statistics how does the growth rate of IS-related jobs compare to the average growth rate of all jobs nationally? Describe why innovations in technology, or relative drops in the cost of technology, increase the value of IS-related job opportunities.

## Q1-4 WHAT IS MIS?

Identify the three important phrases in the definition of *MIS*. Explain why you can buy IT, but you can never buy IS. What does that mean to you, as a potential future business manager? Name and define each of the five components of an information system. Using the five-component model, explain the difference between IT and IS. Explain why end users need to be involved in the management of information systems. Explain why it is a misconception to say that organizations do something.

## Q1-5 WHAT IS YOUR ROLE IN IS SECURITY?

Summarize the importance of security to corporations such as Amazon.com. Define *strong password*. Explain an easy way to create and remember a strong password. Under what circumstances should you give someone else your password?

## How does the **knowledge** in this chapter help **you?**

Summarize how mastery of Reich's four skills will serve you in your career. Explain why every business professional needs to learn the basics of IS.

## KEY TERMS AND CONCEPTS

Abstract reasoning 10
Bell's Law 5
Collaboration 10
Computer hardware 15
Computer-based information system 15
Data 15
Digital Revolution 5
Experimentation 10
Five-component framework 15
Information Age 5
Information system (IS) 14
Information technology (IT) 14
Kryder's Law 7
Management information systems (MIS) 14
Metcalfe's Law 7
Moore's Law 6
Nielsen's Law 7
People 15
Procedures 15
Software 15
Strong password 17
System 15
Systems thinking 10

MyMISLab™

To complete the problems with the ✪, go to EOC Discussion Questions in the MyLab.

## USING YOUR KNOWLEDGE

✪ **1-1.** Do you agree that this course is the most important course in the business school? Isn't accounting more important? No business can exist without accounting. Or isn't management more important? After all, if you can manage people, why do you need to know how to innovate with technology? You can hire others to think innovatively for you.

On the other hand, what single factor will affect all business more than IS? And aren't knowledge of and proficiency with IS and IT key to future employment and success?

Give serious thought to this question and write a single-page argument as to why you agree or disagree.

✪ **1-2.** Describe three to five personal goals for this class. None of these goals should include anything about your GPA. Be as specific as possible, and make the goals personal to your major, interests, and career aspirations. Assume that you are going to evaluate yourself on these goals at the end of the quarter or semester. The more specific you make these goals, the easier it will be to perform the evaluation.

✪ **1-3.** Consider costs of a system in light of the five components: costs to buy and maintain the hardware; costs to develop or acquire licenses to the software programs and costs to maintain them; costs to design databases and fill them with data; costs of developing procedures and keeping them current; and, finally, human costs to both develop and use the system.

**a.** Over the lifetime of a system, many experts believe that the single most expensive component is people. Does this belief seem logical to you? Explain why you agree or disagree.

**b.** Consider a poorly developed system that does not meet its defined requirements. The needs of the business do not go away, but they do not conform themselves to the characteristics of the poorly built system. Therefore, something must give. Which component picks up the slack when the hardware and software programs do not work correctly? What does this say about the cost of a poorly designed system? Consider both direct money costs as well as intangible personnel costs.

**c.** What implications do you, as a future business manager, recognize after answering parts a and b? What does this say about the need for your involvement in requirements and other aspects of systems development? Who eventually will pay the costs of a poorly developed system? Against which budget will those costs accrue?

## COLLABORATION EXERCISE 1

*Before you start this exercise, read Chapter Extensions 1 and 2, which describe collaboration techniques as well as tools for managing collaboration tasks. In particular, consider using Google Drive, Dropbox, Microsoft OneDrive, Microsoft SharePoint, or some other collaboration tool.*

*Collaborate with a group of fellow students to answer the following questions. For this exercise, do not meet face to face. Coordinate all of your work using email and email attachments only. Your answers should reflect the thinking of the entire group, not just one or two individuals.*

**1-4.** Abstract reasoning.

**a.** Define *abstract reasoning*, and explain why it is an important skill for business professionals.

**b.** Explain how a list of items in inventory and their quantity on hand is an abstraction of a physical inventory.

**c.** Give three other examples of abstractions commonly used in business.

**d.** Explain how Jennifer failed to demonstrate effective abstract reasoning skills.

**e.** Can people increase their abstract reasoning skills? If so, how? If not, why not?

**1-5.** Systems thinking.

**a.** Define *systems thinking*, and explain why it is an important skill for business professionals.

**b.** Explain how you would use systems thinking to explain why Moore's Law caused a farmer to dig up a field of pulpwood trees. Name each of the elements in the system and explain their relationships to each other.

**c.** Give three other examples of the use of systems thinking with regard to consequences of Bell's Law, Moore's Law, and Metcalfe's Law.

**d.** Explain how Jennifer failed to demonstrate effective systems-thinking skills.

**e.** Can people improve their systems-thinking skills? If so, how? If not, why not?

**1-6.** Collaboration.

**a.** Define *collaboration*, and explain why it is an important skill for business professionals.

**b.** Explain how you are using collaboration to answer these questions. Describe what is working with regard to your group's process and what is not working.

**c.** Is the work product of your team better than any one of you could have done separately? If not, your collaboration is ineffective. If that is the case, explain why.

**d.** Does the fact that you cannot meet face to face hamper your ability to collaborate? If so, how?

**e.** Explain how Jennifer failed to demonstrate effective collaboration skills.

**f.** Can people increase their collaboration skills? If so, how? If not, why not?

**1-7.** Experimentation.

**a.** Define *experimentation*, and explain why it is an important skill for business professionals.

**b.** Explain several creative ways you could use experimentation to answer this question.

**c.** How does the fear of failure influence your willingness to engage in any of the ideas you identified in part b?

**d.** Explain how Jennifer failed to demonstrate effective experimentation skills.

**e.** Can people increase their willingness to take risks? If so, how? If not, why not?

**1-8.** Job security.

**a.** State the text's definition of *job security*.

**b.** Evaluate the text's definition of job security. Is it effective? If you think not, offer a better definition of job security.

**c.** As a team, do you agree that improving your skills on the four dimensions in Collaboration Exercises 1-4 through 1-7 will increase your job security?

**d.** Do you think technical skills (accounting proficiency, financial analysis proficiency, etc.) provide job security? Why or why not? Do you think students in 1995 would have answered this differently? Why or why not?

# CASE STUDY 1

## zulily

On November 15, 2013, zulily, a Seattle corporation, issued its initial stock (i.e., went public) at $22 a share. By the end of the day, the stock was trading at $38, and 4 months later it reached $62, nearly tripling its initial price. At $62, the holdings of the company's chairman, Mark Vadon totaled more than $2B.

Before dismissing this as just another successful public offering, consider the company. What is its business model? A high-tech company offering the latest gee-whiz technology? A new tablet? A new Facebook competitor? Another way of sharing pictures? No, no, no, and no. zulily sells to mothers: primarily children's clothes and toys, but also women's clothes, accessories, and décor items. The oldest and most traditional forms of retail. So what is the excitement? Cofounders Mark Vadon and Darrell Cavens found a way to harness information technology to provide an entertaining shopping experience to mothers, one that offers name-brand goods as well as unique and difficult-to-find off-brands and often sells them at substantial discounts. According to the zulily prospectus, 45 percent of its sales occur over mobile devices, as mothers churn through the day's specials while they sit in playgrounds, in cars waiting for kids at soccer practice, or anywhere else young mothers have a break long enough to shop on their mobile devices.

One of your goals for this class should be to learn *to assess, evaluate, and apply emerging information technology to business.* Seem like an empty platitude? Not to Mr. Vadon, who turned that exact principle into $2B... so far.

### The zulily Business Model

zulily conducts flash sales of children's and women's clothing and other items of interest to women. Sales open at 6 AM Pacific time each day and last 72 hours. Customers find brand-name merchandise intermingled with hard-to-find boutique products. zulily uses the term *curated sale* to mean the sale of items specifically selected and grouped by its shopping experts to be exciting to

**Figure 1-8**
zulily Merchandise Variety

*Source:* Retrieved from *www.zulily.com.*

women. Because these curated sales provide interesting variety, women enjoy the thrill of discovery while shopping. zulily thus provides entertainment as well as well as a rewarding shopping experience. And those low prices, some as low as 70 percent off retail, are available for only 72 hours. So, shop and buy now, ladies!

Does it work? Apparently so. As shown in Figure 1-9, in 4 years zulily increased the number of its active customers by 3,121 percent while increasing revenue per active customer by 209 percent. That combination resulted in revenue growth from $18M to $1.2B; that's a 185 percent annual growth rate!

## How zulily Did it

The sales process begins when zulily buyers identify goods to be sold. Buyers negotiate with vendors to establish both wholesale and retail prices, terms, and maximum quantities by size. zulily then obtains sample merchandise and, if necessary, photographs it in-house. It also writes ad copy to be displayed along with the photos during the sale. By taking photos when needed and writing its own ad copy, zulily ensures a consistent quality of presentation on its site. zulily also adds considerable value to smaller vendors who do not otherwise have access to such high-quality expertise.

Items are then grouped together into 3-day sales events. zulily accepts orders for items up to the maximum quantity negotiated with the vendor. At that point, the item (or a particular size of an item) is marked as no longer available, thus increasing pressure to buy remaining items *now*. After the event closes, zulily orders the items from the vendor, receives them, packages them, and then ships the items to customers. zulily thus maintains almost no inventory. Customers receive their items in zulily packaging, thus reinforcing the zulily brand.

zulily is subject to errors and mistakes from vendors. If, for example, the vendor promises to ship 1,000 pairs of shoes of a particular size and zulily sells all 1,000 pairs, but later the vendor delivers only, say, 900 pairs in that size, some customers will be disappointed. And those customers will hold zulily, not the vendor responsible for their disappointment.

## Use of Technology

zulily's business model would be infeasible without information systems. For one, it needs the Internet to reach customers, and it needs mobile technology to do so on phones and other mobile devices. Further, zulily buyers use the Internet to find vendors and items to sell. But what else?

**Figure 1-9**
zulily Performance

| | 2010 | 2011 | 2012 | 2013 | 2014 |
|---|---|---|---|---|---|
| Number of active customers (thousands) | 157 | 791 | 1,580 | 3,200 | 4,900 |
| Revenue (millions) | $18 | $143 | $331 | $696 | $1,200 |
| Sales per active customer | $117 | $180 | $210 | $218 | $245 |

In the prospectus for its initial public offering, zulily stated, "Continual innovation through investment in technology is core to our business."[15] It states that it developed a proprietary technology platform to manage the enormous spikes in Web processing demand that occur due to the nature of flash sales. Reflect on the challenges of such development: In 2010, zulily's platform supported $18M in sales; 4 years later, it supported $1.2B in sales, a 66-fold increase in demand. You will learn some of the ways that such enormous growth can be accommodated in Chapter 6. For now, understand that such growth would be impossible in a world without information systems.

But there's more. In that same prospectus, zulily stated that it has developed "extensive data collection and analytics capabilities" that enable it to anticipate its customers' shopping preferences and to tailor the customers' shopping experiences accordingly. So, as with any good salesperson, what you see and how it is shown to you depend on what you've purchased in the past. That same data can also be analyzed to help buyers determine the items customers are most likely to purchase. You will learn about data analytics in Chapter 9.

## Growth-Management Problems

Such spectacular growth does not come without problems. According to its 2014 annual report (SEC Form 10-K), zulily increased its headcount from 329 at the end of 2011 to 2,907 at the end of 2014. That's an 884 percent increase in zulily's workforce in 3 years. That rate of growth is exceedingly difficult to manage, a fact the company recognized:

> To support continued growth, we must effectively integrate, develop and motivate a large number of new employees, while maintaining our corporate culture. In particular, we intend to continue to make substantial investments to expand our merchandising and technology personnel.[16]

Unfortunately, zulily is located just down the street from Amazon and Nordstrom and just across a lake from Microsoft. Finding (and retaining) those merchandising and technology personnel in Seattle will be difficult. In its annual report, zulily mentioned particularly the need to hire mid-level managers.

## Learning from zulily

zulily is remarkable for its spectacular growth, but it's even more remarkable because that growth occurred in a very traditional market. What's more basic than selling clothes to women? Who would think that the founder of a company in that market could turn his holdings into $1.7B in 5 years? Or that the company could increase its workforce by 884 percent in 3 years?

In the final analysis, zulily succeeded because its founders developed an innovative application of information systems technology. As you will learn, the technology zulily uses is not groundbreaking. All that technology was described in the fourth edition of this textbook in 2009 when zulily was founded. The creative genius was finding a way to apply that technology to a business opportunity and then to have the managerial skill to develop that idea into a thriving business. Without doubt, dozens of such opportunities lie in front of you. You just need to recognize and build on them.

## QUESTIONS

**1-9.** Go to zulily.com and register. Identify features of the site that make shopping entertaining to mothers and explain why those features entertain. Explain why this is important to the zulily business model.

**1-10.** Go to Nordstrom.com and shop for children's clothes. How does the zulily shopping experience differ from that at Nordstrom? Briefly describe the advantages and disadvantages of each type of experience.

**1-11.** If you were a buyer for zulily, what data would you like to have about customer purchase habits?

**1-12.** If you were a buyer for zulily, what data would you like to have about past vendor performance?

**1-13.** In the general course of life, 2-year-old boys become 3-year-old boys, 4-year-old girls become 5-year-old girls, and so on. How can zulily use this not-so-remarkable phenomenon to customize a customer's shopping experience? What data would you need to do this?

**1-14.** As a business professional, it is likely information systems professionals will ask you data questions like those in questions 1-11 to 1-13 above. What is the best way for you to respond? Verbally in a meeting? With a written document? With a sketch or diagram? How will you know if you have been understood?

**1-15.** At the April 2015 stock price of $14.59, the market values zulily at $1.86B. This is a big drop from the February 2014 high of $68.39 a share price. Describe zulily's principle assets. Does a $1.86B valuation seem appropriate, given your description of the company's assets? Justify your answer

## MyMISLab™

Go to the Assignments section of your MyLab to complete these writing exercises.

**1-16.** The text argues that this course is the most important course in the business school because (1) it will give you the background you need to assess, evaluate, and apply emerging information systems technology to business, (2) it can help you develop marketable skills by teaching you abstraction, systems thinking, collaboration, and experimentation, and (3) many well-paid MIS-related jobs are in high demand. Do you agree with this argument? Why or why not?

**1-17.** The U.S. Department of Labor publishes descriptions of jobs, educational requirements, and the outlook for many jobs and professions. Go to its site at *www.bls.gov* and answer the following questions:

**a.** Search for the job title *systems analyst*. Describe what such people do. Is this a job that interests you? Why or why not? What education do you need? What is the median pay and job growth projection?

**b.** Click the Similar Occupations link at the bottom of the page. Find another job that you might want. Describe that job, median salary, and educational requirements.

**c.** The BLS data is comprehensive, but it is not up to date for fast-changing disciplines such as IS. For example, one very promising career today is social media marketing, a job that does not appear in the BLS data. Describe one way that you might learn about employment prospects for such emerging job categories.

**d.** Considering your answer to part c, describe an IS-related job that would be the best match for your skills and interests. Describe how you can learn if that job exists.

## ENDNOTES

1. *http://research.microsoft.com/pubs/64155/tr-2007-146.pdf*
2. These figures represent the cost of 100,000 transistors, which can roughly be translated into a unit of a computing device. If you doubt any of this, just look at your $139 Kindle Fire and realize that you pay nothing for its wireless access. Geoff Colvin claims the cost of 125,000 transistors is less than the cost of a grain of rice. See: *http://chowtimes.com/2010/09/11/food-for-though/food-for-thought*.
3. Zipf's Law is a more accurate, though less easily understood, way of explaining how the value of a network increases as additional network nodes are added. See Briscoe, Odlyzko, and Tilly's 2006 article "Metcalfe's Law Is Wrong" for a better explanation. *http://spectrum.ieee.org/computing/networks/metcalfes-law-is-wrong*.
4. Lynn A. Kaoly and Constantijn W. A. Panis, *The 21st Century at Work* (Santa Monica, CA: RAND Corporation, 2004), p. xiv.
5. Robert B. Reich, *The Work of Nations* (New York: Alfred A. Knopf, 1991), p. 229.
6. In the 2011 book "Literacy Is NOT Enough: 21st Century Fluencies for the Digital Age," Lee Crockett, Ian Jukes, and Andrew Churches list problem solving, creativity, analytical thinking, collaboration, communication, and ethics, action, and accountability as key skills workers need for the 21st century.
7. Accenture, "Accenture 2014 College Graduate Employment Survey," last modified April 16, 2014, *www.accenture.com/sitecollectiondocuments/pdf/accenture-2014-college-graduates-survey.pdf*.
8. Michael Spence and Sandile Hlatshwayo, *The Evolving Structure of the American Economy and the Employment Challenge* (New York: Council on Foreign Relations, 2011).
9. Bureau of Labor Statistics, "Computer Systems Analysts," *Occupational Outlook Handbook*, accessed April 16, 2015, *www.bls.gov/ooh*.
10. Daron Acemoglu and David Autor, "Skills, Tasks, and Technologies: Implications for Employment and Earnings" (working paper, National Bureau of Economic Research, June 2010), *www.nber.org/papers/w16082*.
11. Alibaba.com, "About Alibaba.com," accessed April 6, 2015, *http://activities.alibaba.com/alibaba/following-about-alibaba.php*.
12. Leslie Picker and Lulu Yilun Chen, "Alibaba's Banks Boost IPO Size to Record of $25 Billion," September 22, 2014, accessed April 4, 2015, from *www.bloomberg.com/news/articles/2014-09-22/alibaba-s-banks-said-to-increase-ipo-size-to-record-25-billion*.
13. Carlos Tejada, "China Raps Alibaba for Fakes," January 28, 2015, accessed April 6, 2015, from *www.wsj.com/articles/chinas-saic-criticizes-alibaba-over-fake-goods-1422425378*.
14. Ashley Vance, "If Your Password Is 123456, Just Make It HackMe," *The New York Times*, last modified January 21, 2010. Available at *www.nytimes.com/2010/01/21/technology/21password.html?hp*.
15. zulily Prospectus, *www.sec.gov/Archives/edgar/data/1478484/000119312513443794/d552850d424b4.htm*.
16. zulily, Inc. (2014). Form 10-K 2014. Retrieved from zulily.com. *http://investor.zulily.com/secfiling.cfm?filingid=1478484-15-18*.

# Business Processes, Information Systems, and Information

**This could happen to you**

"No, Felix! Not again! Over, and over, and over! We decide something one meeting and then go over it again the next meeting and again the next. What a waste!"

"What do you mean, Cam?" asks Felix, Falcon Security's customer service manager. "I think it's important we get this right."

"Well, Felix, if that's the case, why don't you come to the meetings?"

"I just missed a couple."

"Right. Last week we met here for, oh, 2, maybe 3 hours, and we decided to print and assemble a new prototype quadcopter using as many 3D-printed parts as possible."

"But Cam, 3D printing a stationary recharging platform is a lot different than 3D printing a complex machine like a drone. What difference does it make if we print a drone that can't fly?"

"Felix! We discussed that last week. We found some existing drone plans that we can use for free. They've already been tested and they do work. We're going to see if we can use existing internal components from an existing quadcopter in the new 3D-printed quadcopter. It might even be possible to use generic parts to reduce costs even more."

"Look, Cam, Joni just wants something reasonable to tell Mateo. If we tell her these new 3D-printed quadcopters can't fly, which they probably won't, Mateo will cancel this project and we can get back to work...flying high-quality drones manufactured by those who know what they're doing!"

"Felix, you're driving me nuts. We discussed this *ad nauseam* last week. Let's make some progress. Why don't some of you other guys help me? Alexis, what do you think?"

"Felix, Cam is right," Alexis, Falcon Security's head of sales, chimes in. "We did have a long discussion on how to go about this—and we did agree to focus first on building a functional drone that might reduce our costs. This could save us a lot of money and give us a more customizable drone platform."

"Well, Alexis, I think it's a mistake. Why didn't anyone tell me? I put in a lot of time looking into flight performance of these 3D-printed drones."

"Did you read the email?" Alexis asks tentatively.

"What email?"

"The meeting summary email that I send out each week," Alexis says with a sigh.

# STUDY QUESTIONS

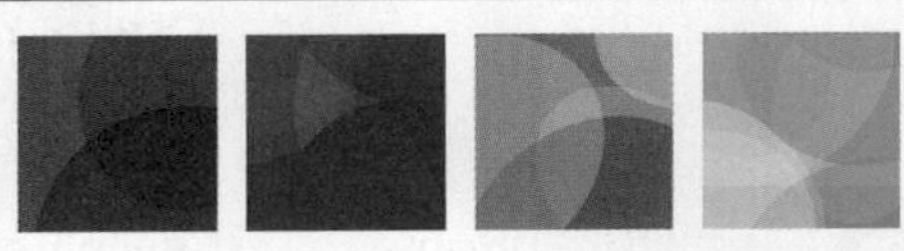

**Q2-1** **WHY DOES THE FALCON SECURITY TEAM NEED TO UNDERSTAND BUSINESS PROCESSES?**

**Q2-2** **HOW CAN BUSINESS PROCESS MODELING HELP ORGANIZATIONS?**

**Q2-3** **HOW CAN INFORMATION SYSTEMS IMPROVE PROCESS QUALITY?**

**Q2-4** **WHAT IS INFORMATION?**

**Q2-5** **WHAT DATA CHARACTERISTICS ARE NECESSARY FOR QUALITY INFORMATION?**

## How does the **knowledge** in this chapter help **you?**

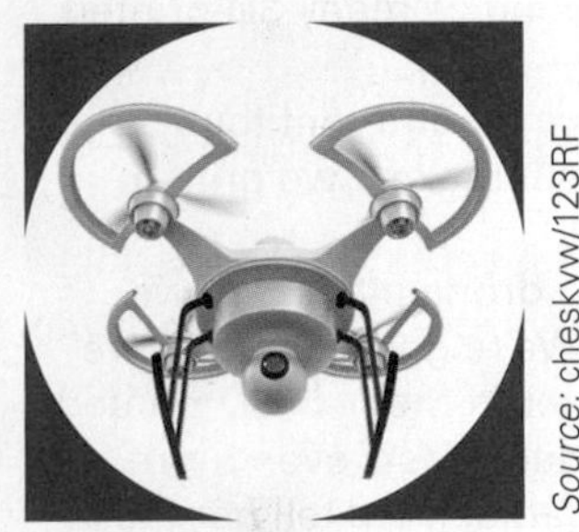

Source: cheskyw/123RF

**"I got the email, but I couldn't download the attachment."**

"I got the email but I couldn't download the attachment. Something weird about a virus checker couldn't access a gizmo or something like that..." Felix trails off.

Cam can't stand that excuse. "Here, Felix, take a look at mine. I'll underline the part where we concluded that we'd focus on building the prototype first so you can be sure to see it."

"Cam, there's no reason to get snippy about this. I thought I had a good idea," Felix says, sounding hurt.

"OK, so we're agreed—*again this week*—that we're going to make the prototype drone using 3D-printed parts based off the free plans. Now, we've wasted enough time covering old ground. Let's get some new thinking on how we're going to do that."

Felix slumps back into his chair and looks down at his cell phone.

"Oh, no, I missed a call from Mapplethorpe. Ahhhh."

"Felix, what are you talking about?" asks Cam.

"Mapplethorpe, my contact at Gulf Oil. He wants to know how to read the new multispectral images of his flare stacks. I'm sorry, but I've got to call him. I'll be back in a few minutes."

Felix leaves the room.

Cam looks at the two team members who are left.

"Now what?" she asks. "If we go forward we'll have to rediscuss everything when Felix comes back. Maybe we should just take a break?"

Alexis shakes her head. "Cam, let's not. It's tough for me to get to these meetings. I don't have to work until tonight, so I drove down here just for this. I've got to pick up Simone from day care. We haven't done anything yet. Let's just ignore Felix."

"OK, Alexis, but it isn't easy to ignore Felix."

The door opens and Joni walks in.

"Hi everyone! How's it going?" she asks brightly. "Is it OK if I sit in on your meeting?"

Optional Extension for this chapter is • CE2: Collaborative Information Systems for Student Projects 380

## Q2-1 WHY DOES THE FALCON SECURITY TEAM NEED TO UNDERSTAND BUSINESS PROCESSES?

**For more information about how to use technology to improve workgroup collaboration, see Chapter Extension 2, Collaborative Information Systems for Student Projects.**

Mateo, Joni, Cam, Toshio, and others at Falcon Security need to understand business processes, not just to evaluate the 3D printing opportunity but because such processes are key to every business's success. Business professionals need to answer questions like:

- Can we change the way we work to better achieve our goals?
- Can we do our work with less cost?
- How can we eliminate special cases?
- Why is it so hard to get something done?
- Why do we have so many forms to fill out?
- Can we improve processes by using information systems?
- Do our information systems need to be changed to more closely fit our processes?

**In all meetings, it is important to remember that not everyone holds the same viewpoint as you. Depending on your actions in these situations, ethical challenges can arise. The Ethics Guide on pages 46–47 explores this issue.**

The abilities to create process models, discuss changes to processes, and know how information systems can support processes are key parts of every business professional's skillset.

In the case at hand, the Falcon Security team needs to understand business processes in order to evaluate the 3D printing opportunity. As Mateo says, if the team decides to print its own drones, it may need to develop new business processes and possibly information systems to support that activity.

Mateo's concerns are legitimate. Changing Falcon Security from a company that *buys* drones to a company that *makes* drones would be a big change. It would change not only *what* the company does but *how* the company does it, too.

To have an informed and effective discussion about how 3D printing its own drones might affect business processes at Falcon Security, Cam's team would need to first create an abstraction or model of Falcon's current processes. The team would then need to use that model to demonstrate how those processes would be altered to support 3D drone manufacturing.

Even if 3D drone manufacturing were able to lower the costs associated with new drones, it's possible that the change to Falcon's business processes may prove too costly. If Cam's team finds substantial cost savings from 3D printing drones, Mateo and Joni will need to see if the savings justify changing business processes.

**See the Guide on pages 48–49 later in the chapter to learn one technique that business professionals use to obtain a common definition of a problem. That technique requires effective communication.**

Further, the Falcon Security team needs to understand the roles that information systems play in supporting business processes. If the company decides to pursue 3D printing its own drones and develops the processes needed to support that activity, can it effectively use existing information systems? If so, how? Would the benefits of developing the new systems justify the costs? We will address these questions throughout this text; by the time you finish reading it, you should be well on your way to effectively participating with a team like that at Falcon.

## Q2-2 HOW CAN BUSINESS PROCESS MODELING HELP ORGANIZATIONS?

In this question, we will look at the business model of a hypothetical online bicycle part retailer named Best Bikes. We will show how to create an abstraction of Best Bikes' basic business processes and then how these processes could be modified if the company decided to 3D-print its own parts rather than buy them from its parts suppliers.

### HOW BEST BIKES WORKS

Best Bikes negotiates with vendors to supply parts at given prices and under certain terms. Once it has a commitment from a vendor to provide parts, it places the parts' descriptions, photos, prices, and related sales data on its Web site. Best Bikes then orders an initial quantity of parts, receives them from the vendor, and places them in inventory. When customers order parts, operations personnel remove items from inventory and ship them to the customers. From time to time, parts need to be ordered to restock inventory, but we will not consider the reorder process in this example. Of course, Best Bikes must keep records of all these activities in order to pay vendors, bill customers, check inventory levels, pay taxes, and so forth.

Best Bikes' business activities are typical of a small online retailer with a relatively simple inventory. Even so, you will see there are ways for Best Bikes to improve what it's doing, even if it doesn't pursue 3D printing.

## THE EXISTING BEST BIKES PROCESS

A **business process** is a network of activities for accomplishing a business function. Figure 2-1 shows a diagram of the existing Best Bikes process. This diagram, which is a model, or an abstraction, of Best Bikes's activities, is constructed using the symbols of **Business Process Modeling Notation**, or BPMN. This notation is an international standard for creating business process diagrams.[1] A key to these symbols is shown in Figure 2-2.

Figure 2-1 is organized in what is called **swimlane format**, which is a graphical arrangement in which all of the activities for a given role (job type) are shown in a single vertical lane.

**Figure 2-1**
Existing Best Bikes Business Process Using BPMN

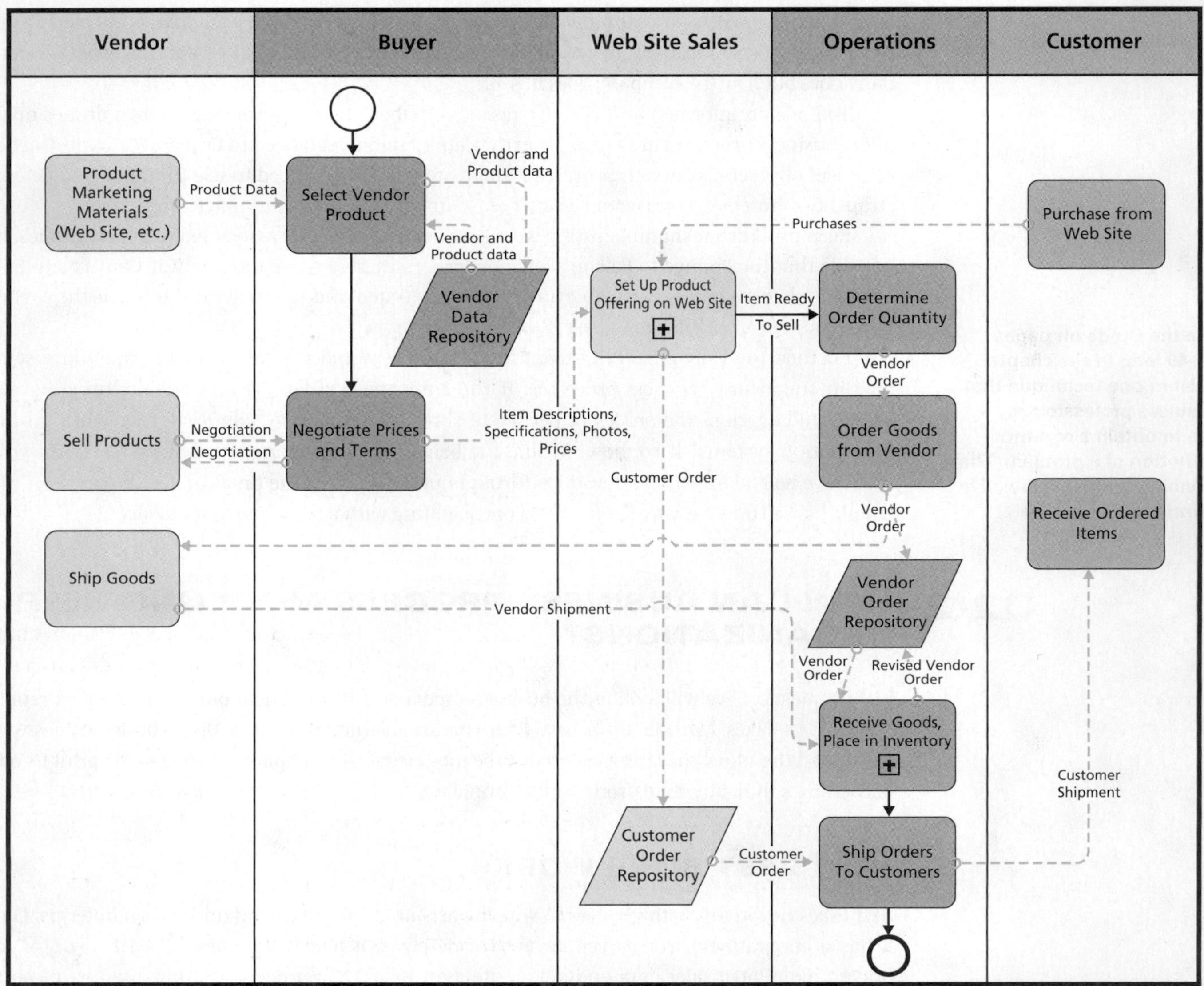

**Figure 2-2**
Process Symbols (BPMN Standard)

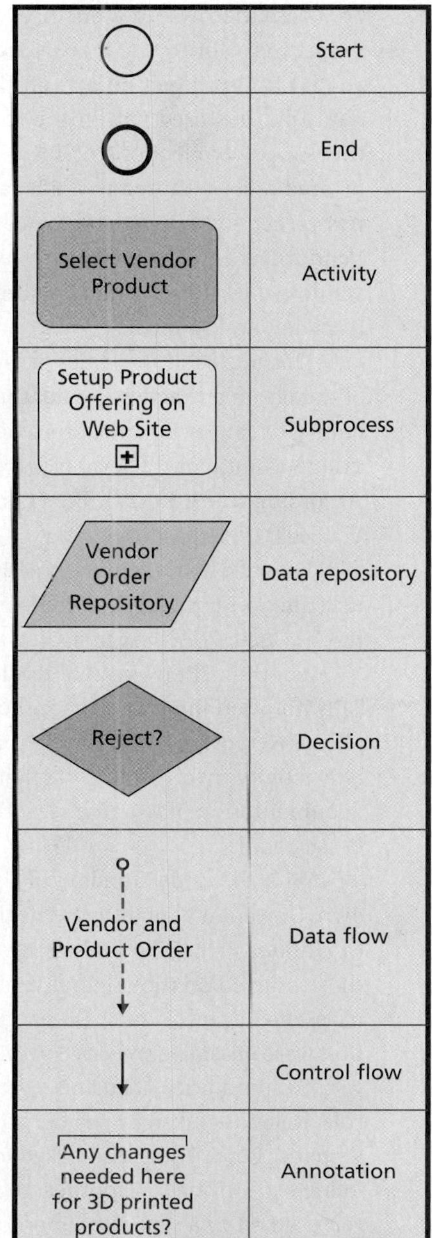


Each swimlane has **activities**, which are specific tasks that need to be accomplished as part of the process. A **role** is a subset of the activities in a business process that is performed by an **actor**, which is a person, group, department, organization, or information system. Figure 2-1 shows the roles of Vendor, Buyer, Web Site Sales, Operations, and Customer.

Notice that we do not write people's names at the top of a swimlane, but rather we write the name of the role. This is because a given role may be fulfilled by many people and because a given employee may play many roles. Furthermore, over time, the organization may change the people who are assigned given roles. In some cases, a role can be fulfilled by an information system.

According to the BPMN standard, the start of a business process is symbolized by a circle having a narrow border. The end of a business process is symbolized by a circle having a thick border. So, in Figure 2-1, the process starts with the Buyer role, or we can also say that a Buyer starts the process.

Activities within a business process are shown in rectangles with rounded corners. The first activity for the Buyer role is *Select Vendor Product*. According to Figure 2-1, buyers obtain vendor and product data from the Vendor Data Repository. A **repository** is a collection of data that is stored within the business process. Repositories can be computer databases, or they can be collections of files in the cloud (think *on the Internet* for now), or they can be printed records stored in a file cabinet or a shoebox. For the purpose of documenting a business process, the particular medium in which repository data is stored is unimportant. The Vendor Data Repository contains not only data from prior purchases but also the results of vendor sales calls, vendor mailings, prior Buyer searches of vendor and product data on the Internet, and so forth.

The labeled dashed lines in Figure 2-1 are called **data flows**. They represent the movement of data from one activity to another. The data can be delivered via email or text message, over the phone, by fax, or by some other means. In a BPMN diagram, the medium of data delivery is also unimportant. For the level of our discussion, the format of the data item is also not important. According to Figure 2-1, Buyers both read and write Vendor and Product data from and to the Vendor Data Repository.

The solid line between the activities *Select Vendor Product* and *Negotiate Prices and Terms* means that after a Buyer finishes the *Select Vendor Product* activity, the Buyer's next action is to perform the *Negotiate Prices and Terms* activity. Such solid lines are called **sequence flows**.

Another BPMN symbol used in Figure 2-1 is an activity with a boxed plus sign inside it. This notation indicates a subprocess and is used when the work to be done is sufficiently complex as to require a process diagram of its own. In Figure 2-1, the *Setup Product Offering on Web Site* activity involves many activities and several different roles. In the complete set of process documentation, it would have a BPMN diagram of its own. Here we will not be concerned with those details.

With the understanding of these symbols, you can interpret the rest of Figure 2-1 on your own. One point to note concerns the *Receive Goods, Place in Inventory* subprocess performed by the Operations Role. When Best Bikes receives a Vendor Shipment, it compares the goods received to those ordered on the original Vendor Order. It will notate that order with the items received and place the Revised Vendor Order back into the Vendor Order Repository. It will also note the items that were missing or received in damaged condition.

To summarize, a business process is a network of activities. Each activity is performed by a role. Roles are taken by people, groups, departments, organizations, and sometimes information systems. Repositories are collections of data. Data flows between activities; when one activity follows directly after another, the flow is shown with a sequence flow. Complex activities are represented by a separate subprocess diagram and denoted by a boxed plus sign in the activity.

## HOW BEST BIKES PROCESSES MUST CHANGE TO SUPPORT 3D PRINTING

Best Bikes was considering 3D printing its own parts in an effort to reduce costs and carry a large selection of parts. The process diagram in Figure 2-3 shows the existing process, but with a new role for 3D printing. The diamond in this diagram represents a decision. For example, when stocking a part, operations will need to decide whether the part is manufactured in-house using 3D printing. Figure 2-3 also includes annotations, which are just comments that Best Bikes' operations manager had about the diagram.

The diagram in Figure 2-3 provides a basis for discussions with others. Best Bikes' operations manager can use it to document where the existing processes need to be altered and to demonstrate the need for additional personnel. If Best Bikes proceeds with 3D printing, it will need to further define the subprocesses *Make the Product* and *Check Product Quality.* From this example, though, you can see how process diagrams provide a means to communicate with others about process structure and possible changes.

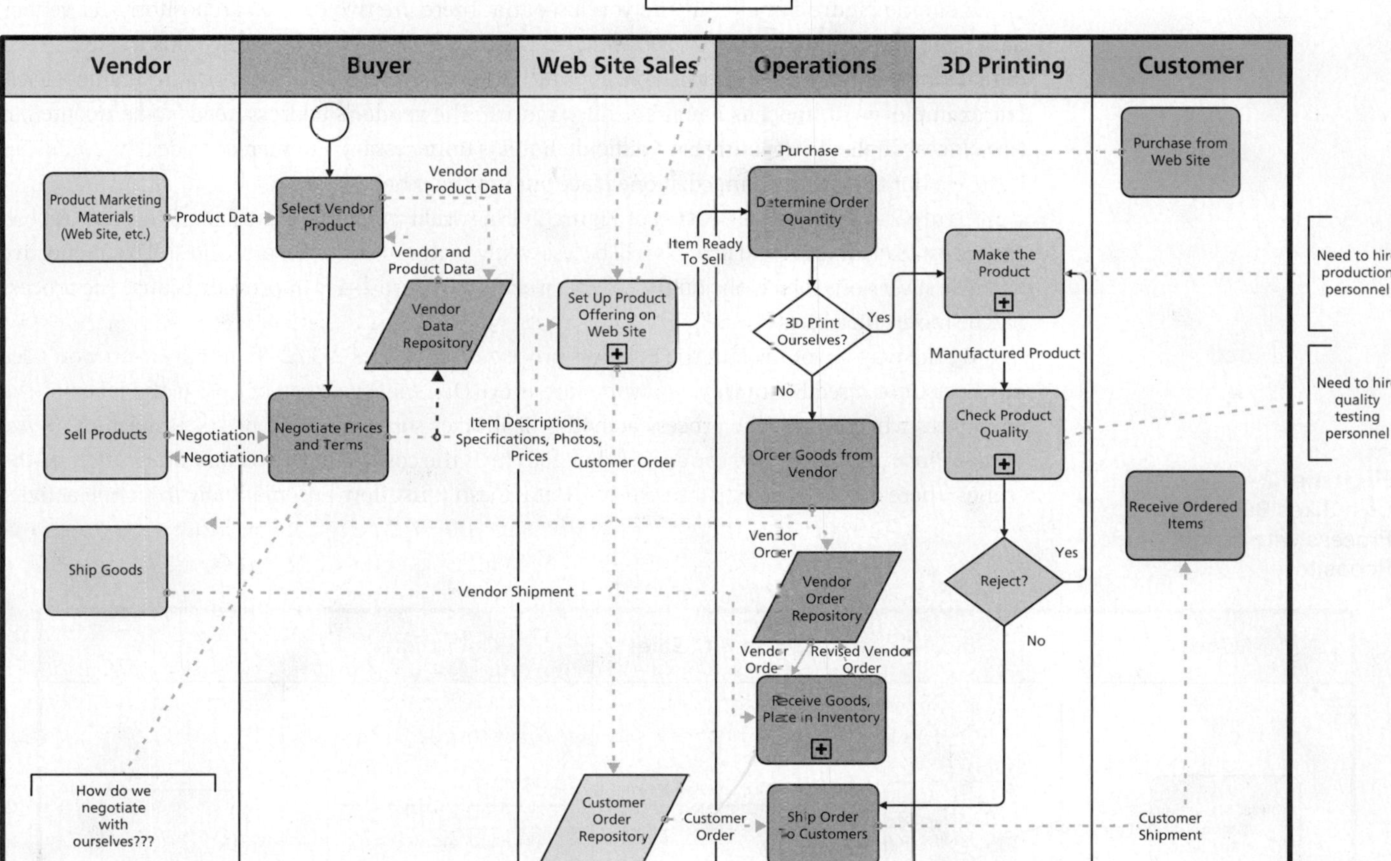


**Figure 2-3**
Revised Best Bikes Process Using BPMN

# Q2-3 HOW CAN INFORMATION SYSTEMS IMPROVE PROCESS QUALITY?

Information systems benefit business processes in many ways. For our purposes, the most succinct summary is to say that *information systems improve process quality.* To understand why that is so, you first need to understand process quality.

## WHAT IS PROCESS QUALITY?

Process quality can be measured in two dimensions: process *effectiveness* and process *efficiency*. An **effective business process** is one that enables the organization to accomplish its strategy. One element of Best Bikes' strategy is to have the largest selection of parts in the industry. It is investigating whether 3D printing will help accomplish that strategy. If so, its current processes are ineffective because they do not support 3D printing. It will need to implement processes like those called for in Figure 2-3 instead.

The second dimension of process quality is efficiency. **Efficiency** is the ratio of benefits to costs. Consider two versions of a business process for accomplishing some function. If both versions create the same benefit, but one costs more than the other does, then the higher-cost version is less efficient than the lower-cost version. Or if both versions cost the same, but one generates less benefit than the other, then the lower-benefit one is less efficient.

Examine Figure 2-1 closely and you'll see that there are two different repositories of vendor data. One is used by Buyers to select vendors, and another is used by Operations to store order data. Such separated data may be appropriate, but more likely it is creating process inefficiencies. For example, what happens when a vendor moves? The vendor's address needs to be updated in two places; duplicate updating isn't difficult, but it is unnecessary. Further, consider the confusion if the vendor address is changed in one place but not the other.

Figure 2-4 shows an alteration of Figure 2-1 in which vendor data is stored in a single repository. Most likely this second process will be less costly, generate fewer errors, and still be as effective as the first version. Hence, the quality of the process in Figure 2-4 is improved because the process will be more efficient.

By the way, if you look at the business processes in Figures 2-1, 2-3, and 2-4, you won't see any costs, not directly anyway. So, where are they? One major source of cost is the labor of the employees who perform the process activities. If it takes someone 10 hours to perform the *Select Vendor Product* activity, then the cost of that activity is the cost of those 10 labor hours. Behind the scenes, there are also infrastructure costs. Data doesn't just flow automatically from one activity

**Figure 2-4**
Best Bikes Business Process with Single Vendor Repository

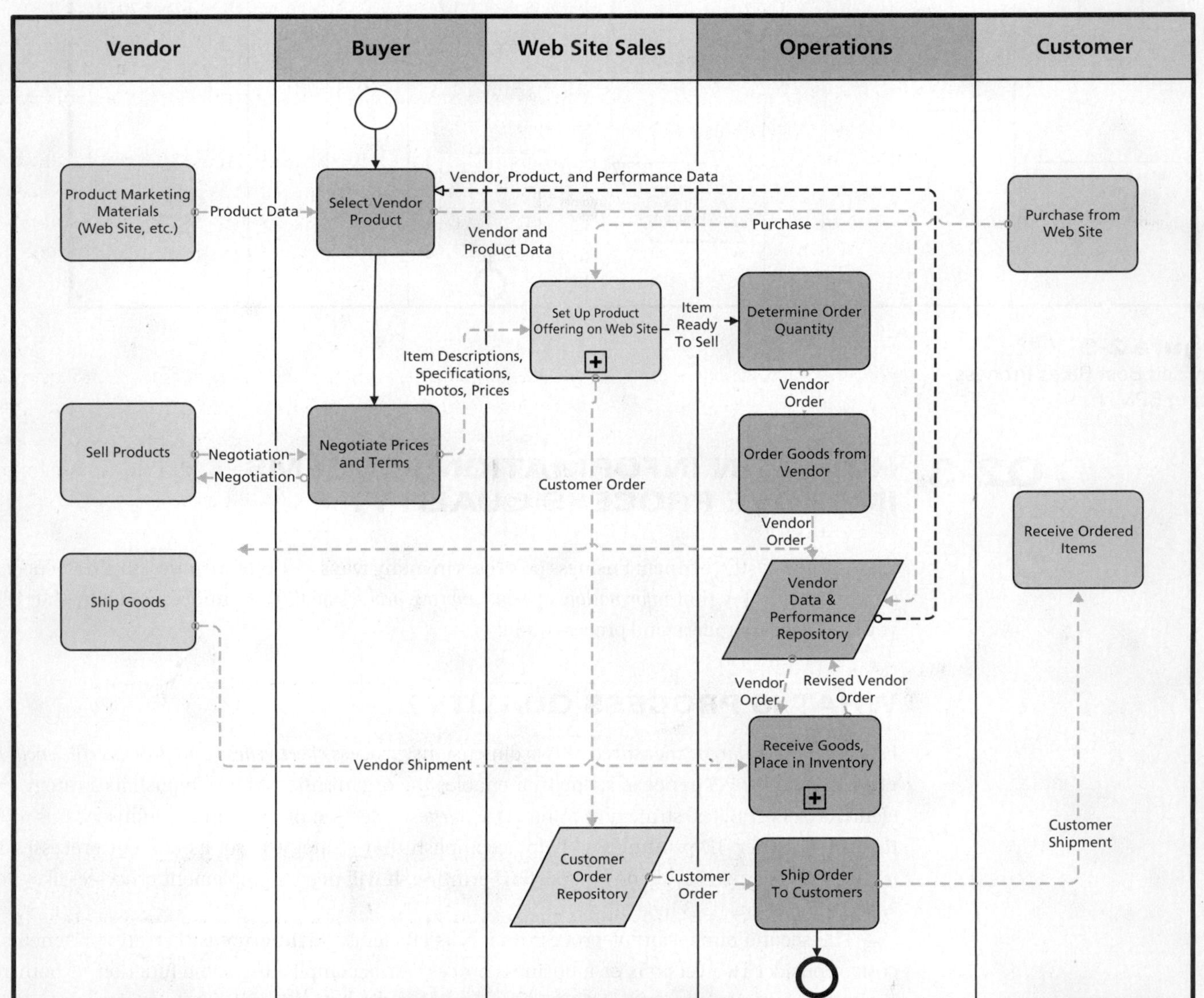

to another. Some type of computer network, email, or other system needs to exist to support those data flows. The cost of that infrastructure is part of the costs of the business process.

## USING INFORMATION SYSTEMS TO IMPROVE PROCESS QUALITY

To understand how information systems improve process quality, consider Figure 2-5, which shows the five components of an information system. Notice the symmetry of these components; the outermost components, hardware and people, are both actors—they take action. The software and procedure components are both sets of instructions. Software is instructions for hardware, and procedures are instructions for people. Finally, data is the bridge between the computer side on the left and the human side on the right.

When an activity in a business process is automated, activities formerly done by people following procedures are moved to computers that perform the work by following instructions in software. Thus, the automation of a process activity consists of moving work from the right-hand side of Figure 2-5 to the left.

### Use an Information System to Store Vendor Data

To understand this, consider the *Select Vendor Product* activity in Figure 2-1. That process could be entirely manual. The buyer could use the Internet (for this example, ignore the fact that she is using a computer system to access the Internet), gather data about vendors and products, make analyses of costs and margins by hand, and store the results of those analyses on paper in a file folder in her desk. When she wants to access past records for a particular vendor, she would manually search through her desk to find those records.

One way to use information systems in this process would be for buyers to store the results of vendor analyses in an Excel file. If this were done, the buyer would have a faster and more reliable means of finding relevant data. The time required to perform the analysis and locate past analyses would be reduced, the cost of the process would decrease, the process would be more efficient, and hence process quality would increase.

### Store Vendor Product and Performance Data in a Database

For another example, suppose Best Bikes implements the improved process shown in Figure 2-4 and stores the Vendor Data Repository in a computer database that combines both product specifications as well as vendor performance data. Now buyers can not only use their own data about vendors and products, but they also can view past vendor performance data to choose among vendors when parts are available from several vendors. Figure 2-6 shows an example display of such performance data.

A process that uses this new information system saves buyer labor and, on the surface, is more efficient. But the new information system will cost something to develop and operate. Those

**Figure 2-5**
Characteristics of the Five Components

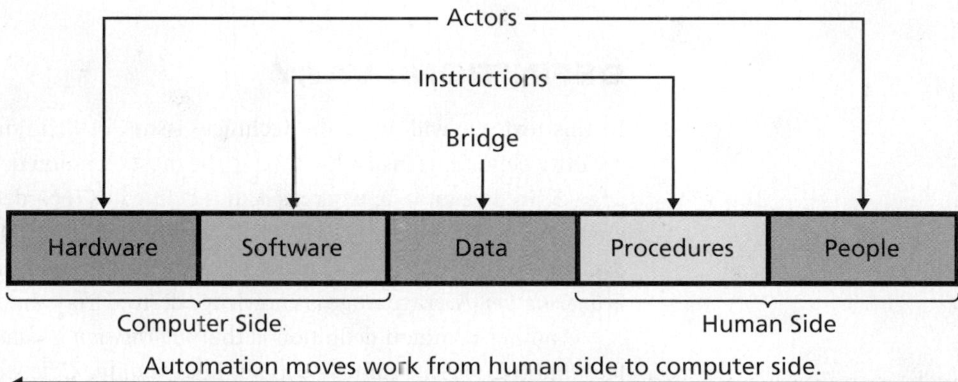

**Figure 2-6**
Best Bikes Data on General Sports

Vendor

VendorName: General Sports
City: Los Angeles
State: CA
ContactName: Maria Jepperson
ContactEmail: MJ@GenSports.com
ContactPhone: (212) 722-5555
OrderHistory

| OrderDate | BuyerName | RecievedBy | ItemName | QuantityOrdered | QuantityReceived | QuantityDamaged | NetSellable |
|---|---|---|---|---|---|---|---|
| 4/10/2016 | Addison | Drew | Deluxe Suspension | 50 | 35 | 2 | 33 |
| 7/15/2016 | Addison | Drew | Over the Edge Suspension | 65 | 65 | 3 | 62 |
| 1/14/2017 | Addison | Drew | Suspension Maintenance Kit | 300 | 350 | 0 | 350 |
| 3/17/2017 | Sarah | Jackson | Deep Valley Trail Tires | 25 | 22 | 0 | 22 |
| 5/19/2013 | Addison | Drew | Over the Edge Sprocket Set | 15 | 15 | 4 | 11 |
| * | | | | 0 | 0 | 0 | 0 |

Record: 1 of 5 No Filter Search

costs must also be considered before the organization can decide if making such a change makes the process more efficient. By the way, you can see from this simple example why it is vital that business professionals be involved in the development of information systems. If systems development is left solely to technical personnel, they may develop a system that is technically elegant but with costs that cannot be justified.

In addition to improving process efficiency, information systems can also improve process effectiveness. If the buyers, for example, share vendor data, they may be able to identify new parts for Best Bikes to carry. By doing so, they are helping achieve the goal of having the largest availability of bicycle parts in the industry.

Furthermore, consider the performance data in Figure 2-6. General Sports frequently ships fewer items (Quantity Received) than were requested (Quantity Ordered), and in one case, it shipped too many parts. In addition, Best Bikes received many items in damaged condition. If Best Bikes can find another vendor to supply these or equivalent parts, its parts availability will increase and it will better achieve its strategy. Therefore, the information system that produces the display in Figure 2-6 makes Best Bikes' buying process more effective.

Of course, we are assuming that the data in Figure 2-6 is correct. But is it? Before we close this chapter, you need to understand the factors that lead to quality information; to do that, you first need to understand the difference between information and data. We discuss that topic next.

# Q2-4 WHAT IS INFORMATION?

*Information* is one of those fundamental terms that we use every day but that turns out to be surprisingly difficult to define. Defining *information* is like defining words such as *alive* and *truth.* We know what those words mean, we use them with each other without confusion, but they are nonetheless difficult to define.

## DEFINITIONS VARY

In this text, we will avoid the technical issues of defining information and will use common, intuitive definitions instead. Probably the most common definition is that **information** is knowledge derived from data, whereas *data* is defined as recorded facts or figures. Thus, the facts that employee James Smith earns $70.00 per hour and that Mary Jones earns $50.00 per hour are *data.* The statement that the average hourly wage of all the graphic designers is $60.00 per hour is *information.* Average wage is knowledge derived from the data of individual wages.

Another common definition is that *information is data presented in a meaningful context.* The fact that Jeff Parks earns $30.00 per hour is data.[2] The statement that Jeff Parks earns half the average hourly wage of the graphic designers, however, is information. It is data presented in a meaningful context.

Another definition of information that you will hear is that *information is processed data* or, sometimes, *information is data processed by summing, ordering, averaging, grouping, comparing, or other similar operations.* The fundamental idea of this definition is that we do something to data to produce information.

There is yet a fourth definition of information, which was set out by the great research psychologist Gregory Bateson. He defined information as a *difference that makes a difference.*

For the purposes of this text, any of these definitions of information will do. Choose the definition that makes sense to you for the purpose you have at hand. The important point is that you discriminate between data and information. You also may find that different definitions work better in different situations.

## WHERE IS INFORMATION?

Suppose you create a graph of Amazon.com's stock price and net income over its history, like that shown in Figure 2-7. Does that graph contain information? Well, if it presents data in a meaningful context or if it shows a difference that makes a difference, then it fits two of the definitions of information, and it's tempting to say that the graph contains information.

However, show that graph to your family dog. Does your dog find information in that graph? Well, nothing about Amazon.com, anyway. The dog might learn what you had for lunch, but it won't obtain any information about Amazon.com's stock price over time.

Reflect on this experiment and you will realize that the graph is not, itself, information. The graph is data that you and other humans *perceive*, and from that perception you *conceive* information. In short, if it's on a piece of paper or on a digital screen, it's data. If it's in the mind of a human, it's information.

Why, you're asking yourself, do I care? Well, for one, it explains why you, as a human, are the most important part of any information system you use. The quality of your thinking, of your ability to conceive information from data, is determined by your cognitive skills. *The data is just the data; the information you conceive from it is the value you add to the information system.*

Furthermore, people have different perceptions and points of view. Not surprisingly, then, they will perceive different information from the same data. You cannot say to someone, "Look,

**Figure 2-7**
Amazon.com Stock Price and Net Income

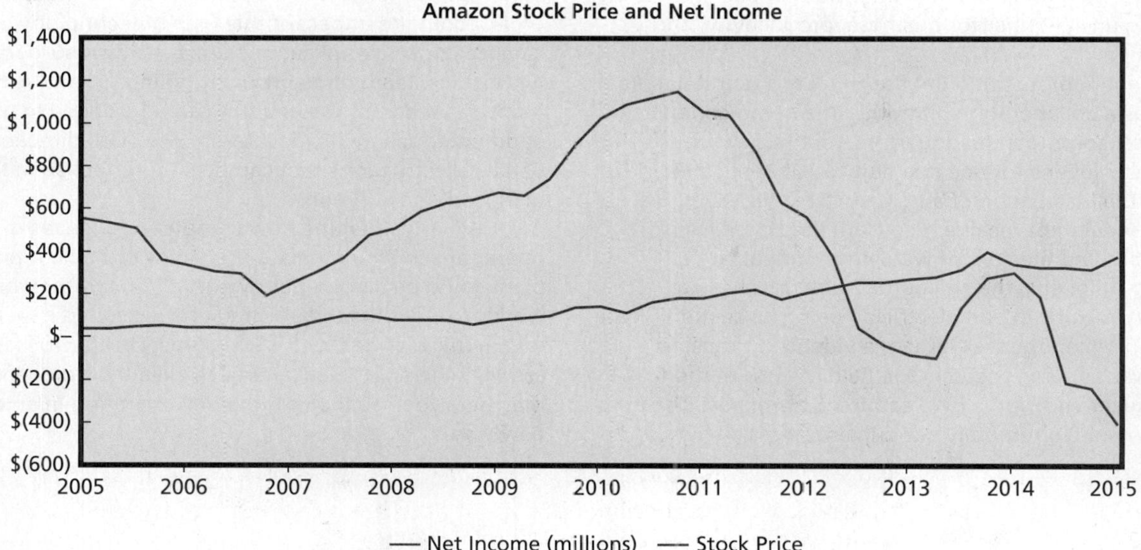

# Augmented Collaboration

When was the last time you turned to the Internet for help in solving a problem? Only a decade or two ago, the world was a very different place. If you wanted to learn something new, you had to make a considerable effort—like checking out a book from the library or using a landline phone to call a friend.

Today, there are limitless resources for you to draw from that are only a mouse click away. These include high-definition videos, message boards, interactive Web sites, collaboration tools, and more! Every day people are turning to sites like YouTube to learn how to do things like change a car tire, write a new programming script, or better manage a supply chain.

But you may be wondering what's next? Will there ever be a *better* approach to learning besides simply reading a message board or watching a video? If you look at new innovations currently under development by Facebook, Google, and Microsoft, the answer to that question is a resounding "yes!"

*Source:* Corbis

## What Is Microsoft HoloLens (aka "Project Baraboo")?

You may have heard about Oculus Rift or Google Glass, but do you know the difference? Oculus Rift, with its development now under Facebook's control, is a virtual reality headset geared to 3D gaming and new forms of social media. Google Glass was designed to provide augmented reality, meaning that the real world is still visible but with the Glass interface superimposed on top of it. As a new entrant to this market, Microsoft recently announced the HoloLens, which is also an augmented reality headset.[3] Recent reviews of the HoloLens indicate that this innovation may be a game changer for business, productivity, and collaboration.

A recent demonstration of the HoloLens pointed to its usability as a collaboration platform. In a demo conducted at Microsoft corporate headquarters, reporters were allowed to test the HoloLens for use in a number of applications, including the installation of a light switch.[4] However, the evaluator would not receive help from the HoloLens by simply searching the Web or watching a video.

Using HoloLens, the evaluator would receive live instruction from an expert electrician using its custom Skype application. When the task began, a videoconferencing window was superimposed in the field of view of the HoloLens user showing a live feed from the expert. The expert was able to remotely see a live feed of the field of view of the user. The expert could draw directions on his or her own device, which would then appear superimposed in the field of view of the user wearing the HoloLens. Within 5 minutes, a number of complicated steps were completed and the switch was properly installed and tested. The expert was then free to move on to the "next call."

## How Can HoloLens Change Collaboration and Business?

Installing a light switch may be a relatively simple task for some people. But what does this basic demonstration mean for the future of collaboration? HoloLens, and other types of headsets, can create new interaction and collaboration opportunities for countless businesses and industries. Think about the impact of this type of technology on health care. Suppose complications arise during a surgery and the medical team on hand is struggling to resolve them. A specialist across the country can be patched in using an augmented reality headset to provide both direction and detailed instructions that can be superimposed in the field of view of the surgeon.

Similarly, imagine how complex sequences of operations in a manufacturing facility or nuclear power plant could be carried out by a novice operator who is working under the supervision of a seasoned expert communicating through a HoloLens. These two examples are only the tip of the iceberg, but like the HoloLens, they may help you see the future of collaboration in an entirely new way!

## QUESTIONS

1. This feature provides two examples of possible business uses for the HoloLens. Think about the future impact of this innovation by identifying other industries that may benefit from the development of augmented reality technology.
2. What is the difference between the Oculus Rift and the Microsoft HoloLens?
3. How could this type of technology benefit your collaborations as a student? Think about how you interact with tutors and fellow students on group projects and how you seek and receive help from your instructor.
4. Privacy concerns are one of the factors that prompted Google to delay a full release of the Google Glass. What are the security and privacy implications of releasing a product like the HoloLens?
5. Virtual reality and augmented reality headsets are currently a novelty, but that will change over the coming years. How might these new innovations affect collaboration and business 10 or 20 years from now?

it's right there in front of you, in the data" because it's not right there in the data. Rather, it's in your head, and your job is to explain what you have conceived so that others can understand it.

Finally, once you understand this, you'll understand that all kinds of common sentences make no sense. "I sent you that information" cannot be true. "I sent you the data, from which you conceived the information" is the most we can say. During your business career, this observation will save you untold frustration if you remember to apply it.

# Q2-5 WHAT DATA CHARACTERISTICS ARE NECESSARY FOR QUALITY INFORMATION?

You have just learned that humans conceive information from data. As stated, the quality of the information that you can create depends, in part, on your thinking skills. It also depends, however, on the quality of the data you are given. Figure 2-8 summarizes critical data characteristics.

## ACCURATE

First, good information is conceived from accurate, correct, and complete data that has been processed correctly as expected. Accuracy is crucial; business professionals must be able to rely on the results of their information systems. The IS function can develop a bad reputation in the organization if a system is known to produce inaccurate data. In such a case, the information system becomes a waste of time and money as users develop work-arounds to avoid the inaccurate data.

A corollary to this discussion is that you, a future user of information systems, ought not to rely on data just because it appears in the context of a Web page, a well-formatted report, or a fancy query. It is sometimes hard to be skeptical of data delivered with beautiful, active graphics. Do not be misled. When you begin to use a new information system, be skeptical. Cross-check the data you are receiving. After weeks or months of using a system, you may relax. Begin, however, with skepticism. Again, you cannot conceive accurate information from inaccurate data.

**Figure 2-8**
Characteristics of Good Data

- Accurate
- Timely
- Relevant
  - To context
  - To subject
- Just barely sufficient
- Worth its cost

## TIMELY

Good information requires that data be timely—available in time for its intended use. A monthly report that arrives 6 weeks late is most likely useless. The data arrives long after the decisions that needed your information have been made. An information system that sends you a poor customer credit report after you have shipped the goods is unhelpful and frustrating. Notice that timeliness can be measured against a calendar (6 weeks late) or against events (before we ship).

When you participate in the development of an IS, timeliness will be part of the requirements you specify. You need to give appropriate and realistic timeliness needs. In some cases, developing systems that provide data in near real time is much more difficult and expensive than producing data a few hours later. If you can get by with data that is a few hours old, say so during the requirements specification phase.

Consider an example. Suppose you work in marketing and you need to be able to assess the effectiveness of new online ad programs. You want an information system that not only will deliver ads over the Web, but that also will enable you to determine how frequently customers click on those ads. Determining click ratios in near real time will be very expensive; saving the data in a batch and processing it some hours later will be much easier and cheaper. If you can live with data that is a day or two old, the system will be easier and cheaper to implement.

## RELEVANT

Data should be relevant both to the context and to the subject. Considering context, you, the CEO, need data that is summarized to an appropriate level for your job. A list of the hourly wage of every employee in the company is unlikely to be useful. More likely, you need average wage information by department or division. A list of all employee wages is irrelevant in your context.

Data should also be relevant to the subject at hand. If you want data about short-term interest rates for a possible line of credit, then a report that shows 15-year mortgage interest rates is irrelevant. Similarly, a report that buries the data you need in pages and pages of results is also irrelevant to your purposes.

## JUST BARELY SUFFICIENT

Data needs to be sufficient for the purpose for which it is generated, but just barely so. We are inundated with data; one of the critical decisions that each of us has to make each day is what data to ignore. The higher you rise into management, the more data you will be given, and, because there is only so much time, the more data you will need to ignore. So, data should be sufficient, but just barely.

## WORTH ITS COST

Data is not free. There are costs for developing an information system, costs of operating and maintaining that system, and costs of your time and salary for reading and processing the data the system produces. For data to be worth its cost, an appropriate relationship must exist between the cost of data and its value.

Consider an example. What is the value of a daily report of the names of the occupants of a full graveyard? Zero, unless grave robbery is a problem for the cemetery. The report is not worth the time required to read it. It is easy to see the importance of economics for this silly example. It will be more difficult, however, when someone proposes new technology to you. You need to be ready to ask, "What's the value of the information that I can conceive from this data?" "What is the cost?" "Is there an appropriate relationship between value and cost?" Information systems should be subject to the same financial analyses to which other assets are subjected.

## How does the knowledge in this chapter help you?

Mateo and the others at Falcon Security know they need to assess business processes if they are going to start 3D printing their own drones. They do not know, however, how to go about making this assessment. With the knowledge of this chapter, they would be able to document Falcon's business processes and explain in a professional way how they think 3D printing would affect Falcon. In doing so, they would demonstrate, using the terms from Chapter 1, their ability to engage in systems thinking, abstraction, collaboration, and experimentation. Hence, this knowledge would not only help Falcon; it would help the career prospects of the team members as well.

If Falcon Security were to move forward with 3D drone printing, the next steps would likely involve hiring new employees to print the drones and working with IS professionals—either in-house or as outside contractors to make sure the new drones are able to integrate with their existing systems. The knowledge of this chapter would help Mateo, Joni, Cam, and the others communicate effectively with those professionals as well. Such communication not only results in a better solution; it also enables the IS professionals to understand more quickly what the business needs, hence reducing Falcon's costs. Think about how Falcon's experience can help you, as you will likely encounter similar issues in your career.

# Ethics Guide

## I Know What's Better, Really

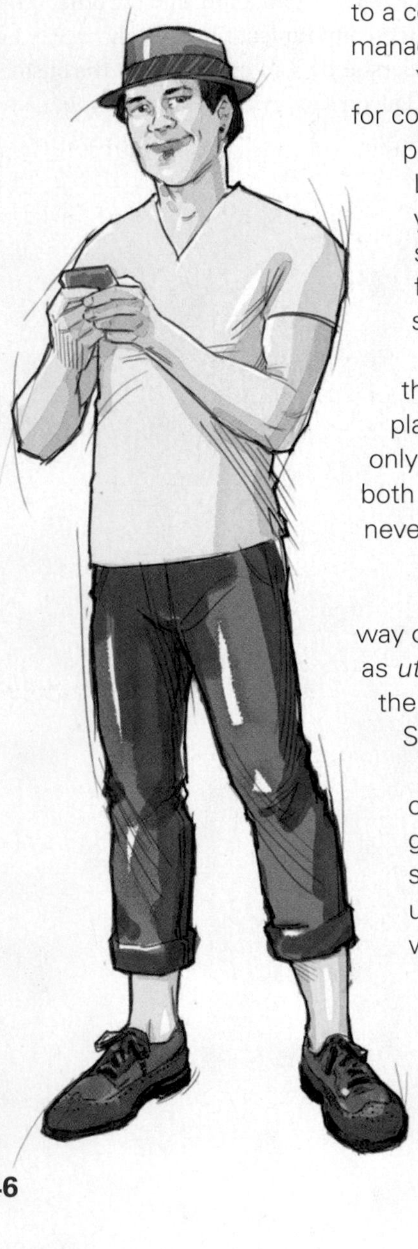

Suppose you work for a small startup company involved in the innovative application of 3D printing technology, like Falcon Security. Your company is 2 years old, employs 50 people, and, like many startup companies, is short of money. Even though you're relatively junior, you've impressed the company's founders, and they have asked you to take a leadership role on a number of special projects. Recently, the company has been investigating developing an information system to store 3D printing designs and make them available to customers for purchase. You've been assigned to a committee that is developing alternative IS solutions for consideration by senior management.

You and a coworker, Leslie Johnson, have developed two different alternatives for consideration by the committee. You believe that Alternative Two is vastly preferable to Alternative One, but Leslie believes just the opposite. You think if Leslie's alternative is chosen, the result will be a major financial loss, one that your young startup company is unlikely to survive. Even if that does not occur, so much time will be lost pursuing Leslie's alternative that your company will fall behind the competition in your dynamic, developing market and will lose substantial market share to the competition as a result.

Unfortunately, Leslie is called away due to a family emergency on the day the two of you are to present your alternatives. You so strongly believe that Leslie's plan is likely to cause irreparable harm to the company that you decide to present only your plan. While you never lie outright, you lead the committee to believe that both of you strongly support your plan. The committee adopts your plan and Leslie never learns that the committee saw only one alternative.

Is your behavior ethical?

The Ethics Guide in Chapter 1 introduced Kant's categorical imperative as one way of assessing ethical conduct. This guide introduces a second way, one known as *utilitarianism.* The basis of this theory goes back to early Greek philosophers, but the founders of the modern theory are considered to be Jeremy Bentham and John Stuart Mill, as you will learn in your business ethics class.

According to utilitarianism, the morality of an act is determined by its outcome. Acts are judged to be moral if they result in the greatest good to the greatest number or if they maximize happiness and reduce suffering. The prior sentence contains a great deal of subtlety that has led to numerous flavors of utilitarianism—flavors that are beyond the scope of this text. Here we will work with the gist of those statements.

Using utilitarianism as a guide, killing can be moral if it results in the greatest good to the greatest number. Killing Adolf Hitler would have been moral if it stopped the Holocaust. Similarly, utilitarianism can assess lying or other forms of deception as moral if the act results in the greatest good to the greatest number. Lying by telling someone with a fatal illness that you're certain he or she will recover is moral if it increases that person's happiness and decreases his or her suffering.

## DISCUSSION QUESTIONS

**1.** According to Kant's categorical imperative, is your action not to present Leslie's alternative ethical?

**2.** According to utilitarianism, is your action not to present Leslie's alternative ethical?

**3.** Assume:

**a.** You were right. Had the company embarked on Leslie's alternative, it would have driven the company into bankruptcy. Does this fact make your actions more ethical? Explain your answer.

**b.** You were wrong. Leslie's alternative would have been far superior to yours for the company's future. Does this fact make your actions less ethical? Explain your answer.

**4.** In your opinion, do the intended consequences or the actual consequences have more bearing when assessing ethics from a utilitarian perspective?

**5.** You could postpone the meeting until Leslie is able to attend and thus allow Leslie to present the alternative to yours. Doing so, however, increases the likelihood that the committee selects Leslie's alternative, and you firmly believe that decision will be fatal to the company.

**a.** According to Kant's categorical imperative, is a decision not to postpone ethical?

**b.** According to utilitarianism, is a decision not to postpone ethical?

**6.** Suppose Leslie learns you presented only your alternative, and you two become arch enemies. To the company's disadvantage, the two of you are never able to work together again. According to utilitarianism, does this outcome change the ethics of your behavior?

**7.** Suppose that instead of not presenting Leslie's alternative at all, you present it, but in a very negative light. You are honest when you focus the bulk of your description of it on disadvantages, because that's what you believe. However, you also know that Leslie does not agree with the way you see the situation. Given your biased presentation, the committee selects your alternative.

**a.** According to Kant's categorical imperative, is your behavior ethical?

**b.** According to utilitarianism, is your behavior ethical?

**8.** What would you do in this circumstance? Justify the ethics of your decision.

**~~Our~~ Recommended Alternative~~s~~**

**~~Alternative One~~**
- ~~In-house stores 3D diagrams~~
- ~~Direct connect to e-commerce server~~

**~~Alternative Two~~ Use the Cloud**
- 3D Diagrams stored on elastic cloud servers
- Use MongoDB on AWS
- SOA connections to e-commerce server

## Egocentric Versus Empathetic Thinking

As stated earlier, a problem is a perceived difference between what is and what ought to be. When developing information systems, it is critical for the development team to have a common definition and understanding of the problem. This common understanding can be difficult to achieve, however.

Cognitive scientists distinguish between egocentric and empathetic thinking. Egocentric thinking centers on the self; someone who engages in egocentric thinking considers his or her view as "the real view" or "what really is." In contrast, those who engage in empathetic thinking consider their view as one possible interpretation of the situation and actively work to learn what other people are thinking.

Different experts recommend empathetic thinking for different reasons. Religious leaders say that such thinking is morally superior; psychologists say that empathetic thinking leads to richer, more fulfilling relationships. In business, empathetic thinking is recommended because it is smart. Business is a social endeavor, and those who can understand others' points of view are always more effective. Even if you do not agree with others' perspectives, you will be much better able to work with them if you understand their views.

Consider an example. Suppose you say to your MIS professor, "Professor Jones, I couldn't come to class last Monday. Did we do anything important?" Such a statement is a prime example of egocentric thinking. It takes no account of your professor's point of view and implies that your professor talked about nothing important. As a professor, it is tempting to say, "No, when I noticed you weren't there, I took out all the important material."

To engage in empathetic thinking, consider this situation from the professor's point of view. Students who do not come to class cause extra work for their professors. It does not matter how valid your reason for not attending class; you may actually have been contagious with a fever of 102. But, no matter what, your not coming to class is more work for your professor. He or she must do something extra to help you recover from the lost class time.

Using empathetic thinking, you would do all you can to minimize the impact of your absence on your professor. For example, you could say, "I couldn't come to class, but I got the class notes from Mary. I read through them, and I have a question about establishing alliances as competitive advantage.... Oh, by the way, I'm sorry to trouble you with my problem."

Before we go on, let's consider a corollary to this scenario: Never, ever, send an email to your boss that says, "I couldn't come to the staff meeting on Wednesday. Did we do anything important?" Avoid this for the same reasons as those for missing class. Instead, find a way to minimize the impact of your absence on your boss.

Now, what does all of this have to do with MIS? Consider the Falcon Security team at the start of this chapter. What is the problem? Cam thinks a big problem is that Felix doesn't come to meetings. Felix thinks the team is focused on the flight performance of the drones. Alexis thinks the team should determine which drone parts could be 3D-printed. Joni, once she understands what is going on, is likely to be focused on wasted employee time and the lack of consensus among team members.

Now imagine yourself in that meeting. If everyone engages in egocentric thinking, what will happen? The meeting will be argumentative and acrimonious and likely will end with nothing accomplished.

Suppose, instead, that the attendees think empathetically. In this case, Cam may make an effort to find out why Felix is missing meetings. Felix would make an effort to understand why his behavior is a problem to the team. The team would make a concerted effort to address the different points of view, and the outcome will be much more positive—possibly a recognition that the team should be meeting virtually and asynchronously. Either way, the attendees have the same information; the difference in outcomes results from the thinking style of the attendees.

Empathetic thinking is an important skill in all business activities. Skilled negotiators always know what the other side wants; effective salespeople understand their customers' needs. Buyers who understand the problems of their vendors get better service. And students who understand the perspective of their professors get better...

## DISCUSSION QUESTIONS

**1.** In your own words, explain how egocentric and empathetic thinking differ.

**2.** Suppose you miss a staff meeting. Using empathetic thinking, explain how you can get needed information about what took place in the meeting.

**3.** How does empathetic thinking relate to problem definition?

**4.** Suppose you and another person differ substantially on a problem definition. Suppose she says to you, "No, the real problem is that..." followed by her definition of the problem. How do you respond?

**5.** Again, suppose you and another person differ substantially on a problem definition. Assume you understand his definition. How can you make that fact clear?

**6.** Explain the following statement: "In business, empathetic thinking is smart." Do you agree?

*Source:* BlueSkyImages/Fotolia

# ACTIVE REVIEW

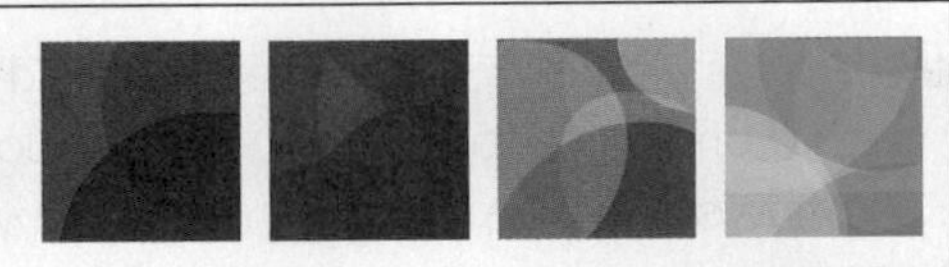

Use this Active Review to verify that you understand the ideas and concepts that answer the chapter's study questions.

## Q2-1 WHY DOES THE FALCON SECURITY TEAM NEED TO UNDERSTAND BUSINESS PROCESSES?

Summarize the reasons that Mateo, Cam, and the Falcon Security team need to understand business processes. Explain how process abstractions make the team more effective. Explain why knowledge of the role of information systems is also important.

## Q2-2 HOW CAN BUSINESS PROCESS MODELING HELP ORGANIZATIONS?

Summarize Best Bike's business operations. Define *business process* and give three examples. Define *BPMN, swimlane format, activity, role, actor, repository, data flow, sequence flow*, and *subprocess*. Describe the BPMN symbols used for each. Review Figure 2-1 and ensure you can explain how this business process works. Explain differences between the processes in Figures 2-1 and 2-3 and relate those differences to the 3D printing opportunity.

## Q2-3 HOW CAN INFORMATION SYSTEMS IMPROVE PROCESS QUALITY?

Define two dimensions of process quality. Explain how information systems can improve both of these dimensions. Summarize the ways that information systems can improve the process quality of the processes in Figures 2-1 and 2-4. Explain how automation relates to the five components in Figure 2-5. Describe uses that buyers can make of the data in Figure 2-6.

## Q2-4 WHAT IS INFORMATION?

Give four definitions of *information.* Using your own experience and judgment, rank those definitions in the order of usefulness in business. Justify your ranking. Describe where both data and information are located.

## Q2-5 WHAT DATA CHARACTERISTICS ARE NECESSARY FOR QUALITY INFORMATION?

Name and describe five data characteristics that are needed to produce quality information. Explain why each is required.

## How does the **knowledge** in this chapter help **you?**

Summarize how knowledge and consideration of business processes will enable the Falcon Security team to accomplish its goal. Describe how you can use process models like Figure 2-3 when investigating opportunities. Explain the differences between Figures 2-1 and 2-4. State two dimensions of process quality and give examples of how information systems can improve both. Describe how you can use your knowledge of process quality, the role of information systems, and process abstractions during your career.

# KEY TERMS AND CONCEPTS

Activities 35
Actor 35
Business process 34
Business Process Modeling Notation (BPMN) 34
Data flows 36
Effective business process 37
Efficiency 37
Information 40
Repository 36
Role 35
Sequence flows 36
Swimlane format 34

MyMISLab™

To complete the problems with the ✪, go to EOC Discussion Questions in the MyLab.

## USING YOUR KNOWLEDGE

✪ **2-1.** Suppose you are discussing 3D printing with the owners of Best Bikes mentioned in Q2-2. Assume you do not have a process abstraction like those shown in Q2-2. Describe how you would explain your concerns about 3D printing at Best Bikes. Now, assume you do have a process abstraction. Again, describe how you would explain your concerns. How do you think Best Bikes will perceive these differences? How do you think other employees at Best Bikes would perceive these differences?

✪ **2-2.** Suppose you manage the buyers at Best Bikes and you have been asked to help determine the requirements for a new vendor selection information system. As you think about those requirements, you wonder how much autonomy you want your employees to have in selecting the vendors and products to sell. You can develop a system that will make the vendor/product selection automatically, or you can build one that allows employees to make that selection. Explain how this characteristic will affect:

**a.** The skill level required for your employees
**b.** The number of employees you will need
**c.** Your criteria for hiring employees
**d.** Your management practices
**e.** The degree of autonomy for your employees
**f.** Your flexibility in managing your department

✪ **2-3.** Suppose management has left you out of the requirements definition process for the development of the system in question 2-2. Explain how you could use the knowledge you developed in answering this question to justify your need to be involved in the requirements definition.

## COLLABORATION EXERCISE 2

*Before you start this exercise, read Chapter Extensions 1 and 2, which describe collaboration techniques as well as tools for managing collaboration tasks. In particular, consider using Google Drive, Google+, Windows OneDrive, Microsoft SharePoint, or some other collaboration tool.*

Many students, especially those with limited business experience, have difficulty understanding how important business processes are and how complex even simple processes can become. The following business situation and exercises will help you understand the need for business processes, the importance of process design, and the role that information systems play in support of such processes.

Suppose you work for a supplier of electric and plumbing supplies, equipment, and tools. Your customers are home builders and construction companies that are accustomed to buying on credit. When you receive an order, you need to evaluate it and approve any special terms before you start removing items from inventory and packaging them for shipment. Accordingly, you have developed the order-approval process shown in Figure 2-9. (In this figure, the diamond represents a decision. Flow out of the diamond depends on the answer that is labeled on the arrow.)

As you can see, your order-approval process consists of several stages: prepare quotation, adjust quotation for requested terms, check inventory, check credit, and evaluate special terms. You check inventory and credit on every order, but you need to approve special terms only if the customer asks for something special, such as free shipping, an extra discount, or unusually fast service and delivery.

As you will see, even a business process this simple has unexpected complexity. For one, are the checks in the proper order? This business process checks inventory before it checks credit. Does it make sense to check inventory before you check credit? Would checking credit first make more sense? And, if it turns out that you are going to reject the special terms of an order, would it make sense to check them first, before evaluating inventory and credit?

Notice that if sufficient inventory does exist, the needed inventory is allocated to that order. But, if the customer's credit or special terms are rejected, that inventory is not released. In that case, you or one of your employees will need to remember to free the allocated inventory.

We can't tell this from Figure 2-9, but if customer credit is increased if credit checking is approved, then a similar

**Figure 2-9**
Existing Order Process

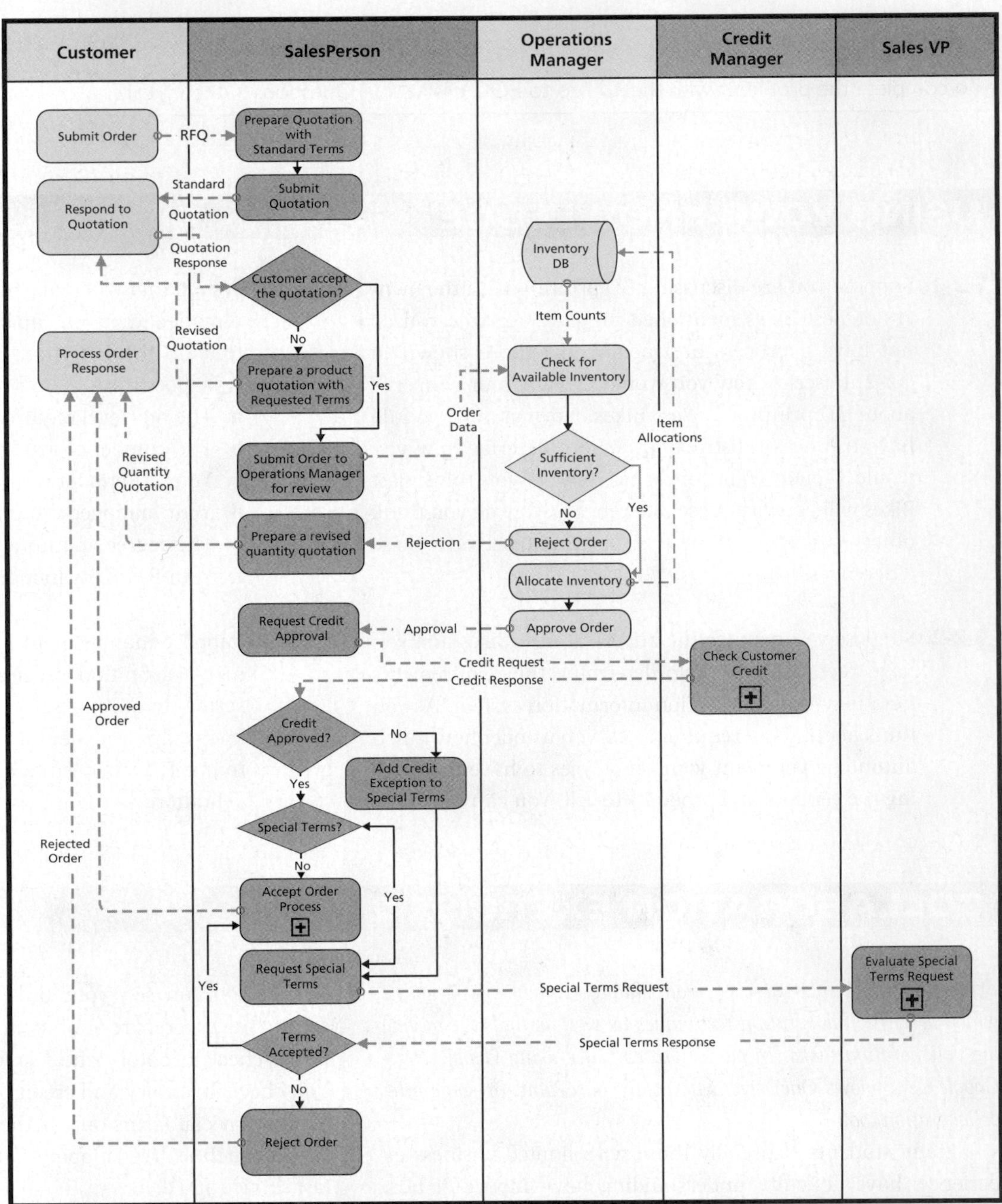


comment pertains to credit. If special terms are not approved, the allocated credit needs to be returned to the customer somehow.

Other problems occur because you are most likely processing many orders at the same time. Suppose two orders include one Kohler Supreme kitchen sink, but you have just one in inventory. You want to sell the sink to the first customer, but that means you must allocate that sink to it. Otherwise, both orders will be processed for the same sink. But suppose that the special terms of the order to which you've allocated the sink are disapproved. You would like to reassign the sink to the second order if it is still around to be processed. How can you accomplish that?

This scenario ignores another possibility. Suppose you have two order requests for the same sink; one is from a retail customer who wants it for her mountain home, and the second is from Big Sky Construction, a customer that buys 500 sinks a year from you. To which customer do you want to allocate that single sink? And how do you know how to do that?

Working with your team, answer the following questions:

**2-4.** In Figure 2-9, explain why inventory must be allocated.

**2-5.** Using Figure 2-9, explain why credit must be allocated to customers. What is the business consequence if these allocations are not adjusted when special terms are not approved?

**2-6.** Recommend a process for adjusting credit for orders for which credit or special terms are not approved. Indicate which role makes the adjustment and how they receive the data for doing so.

**2-7.** Change the process in Figure 2-9 so that allocated inventory is returned when credit or special terms are not approved. Indicate which role makes the adjustment and how they obtain the data for doing so.

**2-8.** There are six different sequences for the three approval tasks in Figure 2-9. Name each and select what your team considers to be the most promising three.

**2-9.** Evaluate each of the three sequences that you selected in question 2-9. Identify which sequence you think is best.

**2-10.** State the criteria that you used for making your selections in questions 2-8 and 2-9.

**2-11.** So far, we haven't considered the impact of this process on the salesperson. What information do salespeople need to maintain good relationships with their customers?

**2-12.** *Optional extension.* Download the Visio diagram version of Figure 2-9 from this book's: Web site, *www.pearsonhighered.com/kroenke*. Modify the diagram to illustrate the sequence of tasks you chose as best in your answer to question 2-9.

# CASE STUDY 2

## Eating Our Own Dog Food

*Dogfooding* is the process of using a product or idea that you develop or promote. The term arose in the 1980s in the software industry when someone observed that the company wasn't using the product it developed. Or "they weren't eating their own dog food." Wikipedia attributes the term to Brian Valentine, test manager for Microsoft LAN Manager in 1988, but I recall using the term before that date. Whatever its origin, if, of their own accord, employees choose to dogfood their own product or idea, many believe that product or idea is likely to succeed.

You may be asking, "So what?" Well, this text was developed by a collaborative team, using Office 365 Professional and many of the techniques described in this chapter. We dogfooded the ideas and products in this chapter.

Figure 2-10 shows a diagram of the process that transforms a draft chapter in Word, PowerPoint, and PNG image format into PDF pages. You will learn more about process diagrams like this in Chapter 12. For now, just realize that each column represents the activities taken by a role, which in this case is a particular person. The process starts with the thin-lined circle in the top left and ends with the thick-lined circle near the bottom right. The dashed lines represent the flow of data from one activity to another.

As shown in Figure 2-10, the authors work closely with the developmental editor, who ensures that the text is complete and complies with the market requirements, as specified by the acquisitions editor. We need not delve into this process in detail here; just observe that many different versions of chapter text and chapter art are created as people playing the various roles edit and approve and adjust edits.

Face-to-face meetings are impossible because the people fulfilling the roles in Figure 2-10 live in different geographic locations. In the past, the developmental process was conducted using the phone, email, and a file server. As you can imagine, considerable confusion can ensue with the hundreds of documents, art exhibits, and multiple reviewed copies of each. Furthermore, task requests delivered via email are easily lost. Dropped tasks and incorrect versions of documents and art are not common, but they do occur.

When we decided to begin publishing a new edition every year, we knew we needed to find some way of increasing our productivity. Consequently, our development team decided to eat its own dog food and use Office 365 Professional. During this process, the author, the developmental editor Laura Town, and the production editors met frequently using Google Hangouts (we couldn't use Skype for Business because Pearson would not allow its employees to install it). Figure 2-11 shows a typical hangout. Notice that the three actors in this process are sharing a common whiteboard. Each can write or draw on that whiteboard. At the end of the meeting, the whiteboards were saved and placed on the team's SharePoint site to be used as minutes of the meeting.

Figure 2-12 shows the team's top-level SharePoint site. The Quick Launch (left-side vertical menu) has links to important content on the site. The center portion has tasks that have a value other than "Completed" for Status.

The team set up alerts so that when new tasks were created in the Tasks list, SharePoint would send an email to the person who had been assigned that task. As shown in Figure 2-13, emails were also sent to a task's creator when that task status was changed by others.

All documents and figures were stored and managed in SharePoint libraries. Figure 2-14 shows the contents of the Draft Documents Chapter 2 library at the time this chapter was written. By storing documents in SharePoint, the team took advantage of library version tracking. Figure 2-15 shows a portion of the version history of one of the documents in this library.

When it is completed, Laura will need to review the final chapter version, so a task should be created asking her to do so. That new task will spawn an email to her like the email in Figure 2-13. I will create that task just as soon as I finish this sentence! That's dogfooding!

## QUESTIONS

**2-13.** In your own words, define *dogfooding*. Do you think dogfooding is likely to predict product success? Why or why not? When would dogfooding not predict product success?

**2-14.** Explain how this team uses the shared whiteboard to generate minutes. What are the advantages of this technique?

**2-15.** Explain how this team uses alerts. Summarize the advantages to this team of using alerts.

**2-16.** Explain why this team does not use Skype for Business.

**2-17.** Summarize the advantages to this team of using SharePoint.

**2-18.** Explain how you think Office 365 Professional contributes to the efficiency of the development team. How might it contribute to the quality of this text?

**2-19.** Which aspects of Office 365 Professional described here could have value to you when accomplishing student team projects? Explain why they add value compared to what you are currently doing.

**Figure 2-10**
Chapter Development Process

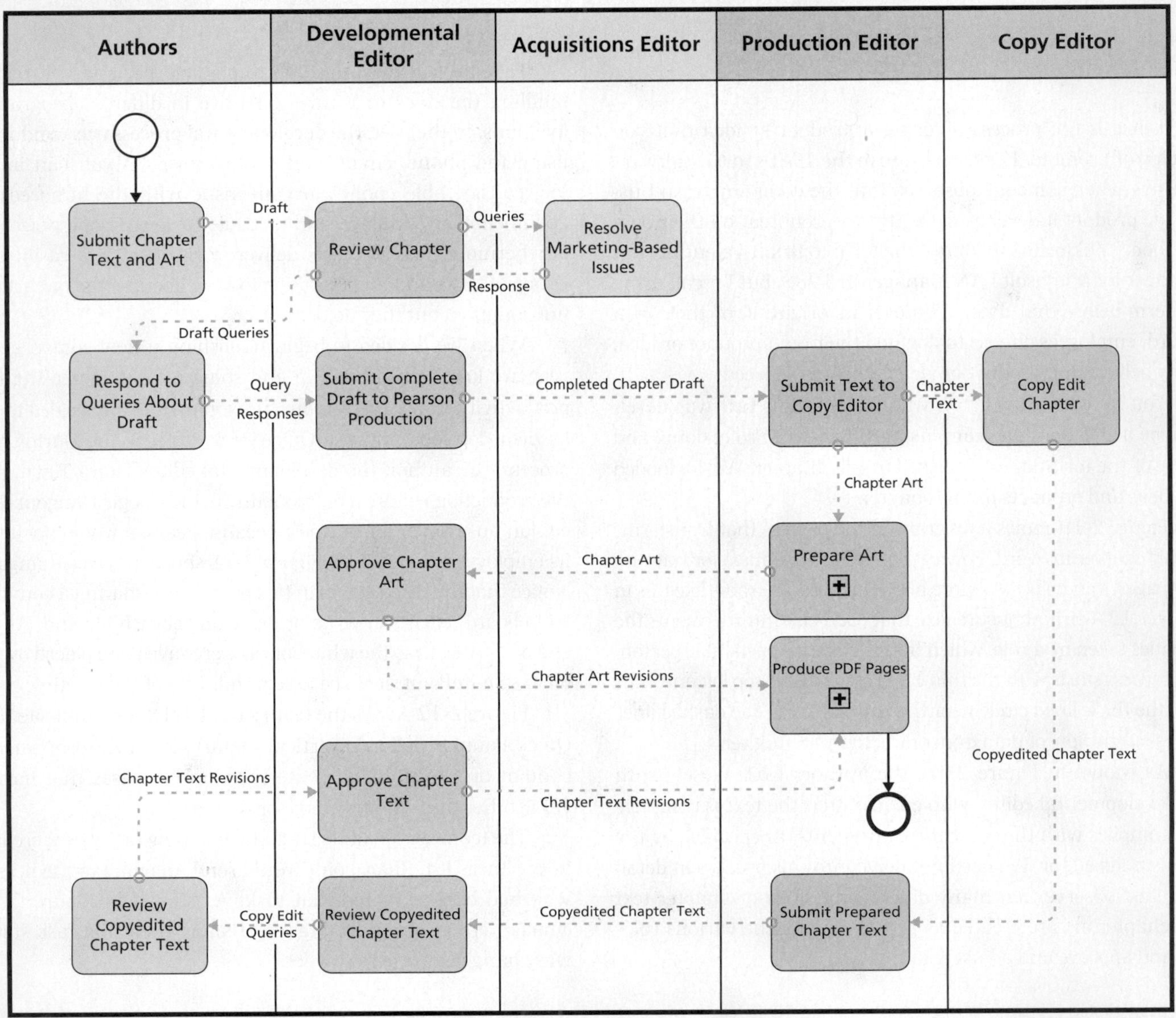

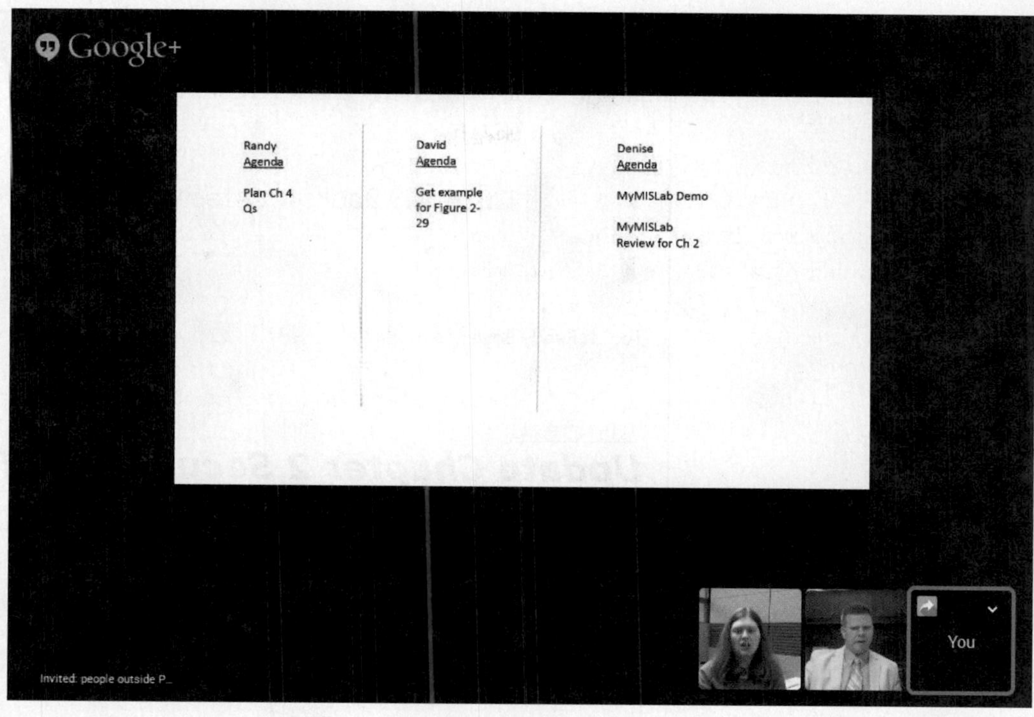


**Figure 2-11**
Google Hangout Group Conversation

*Source:* Google Corporation

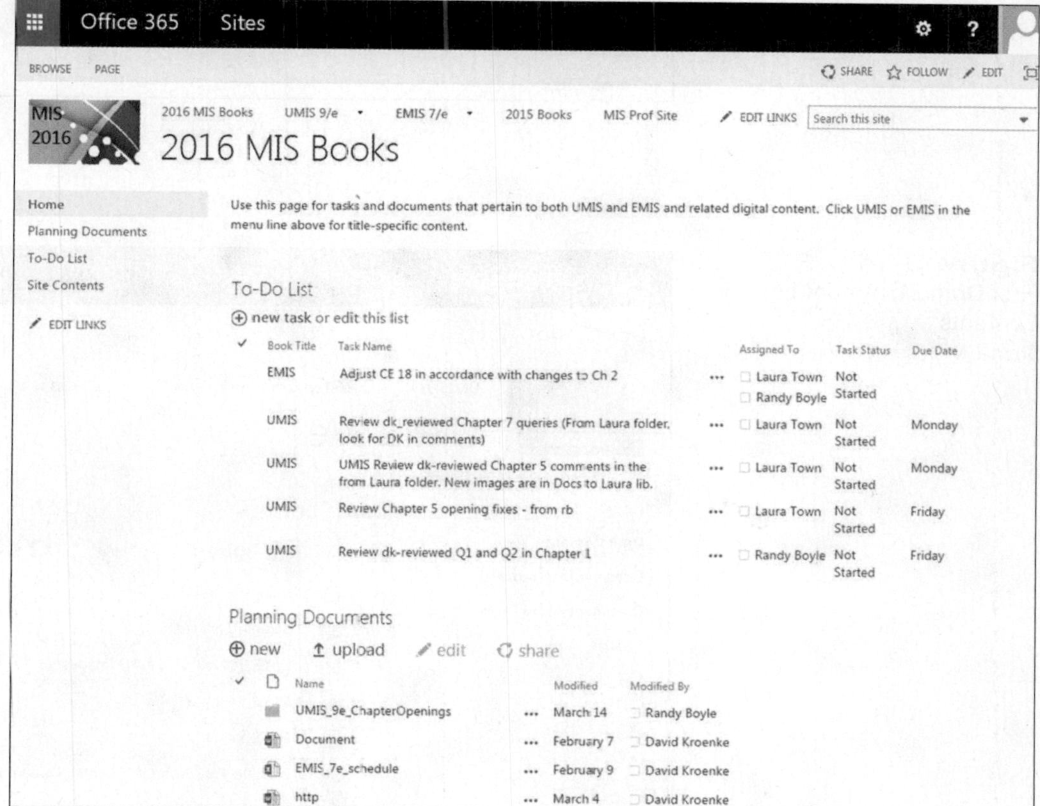


**Figure 2-12**
SharePoint Development Site

*Source:* Microsoft Corporation

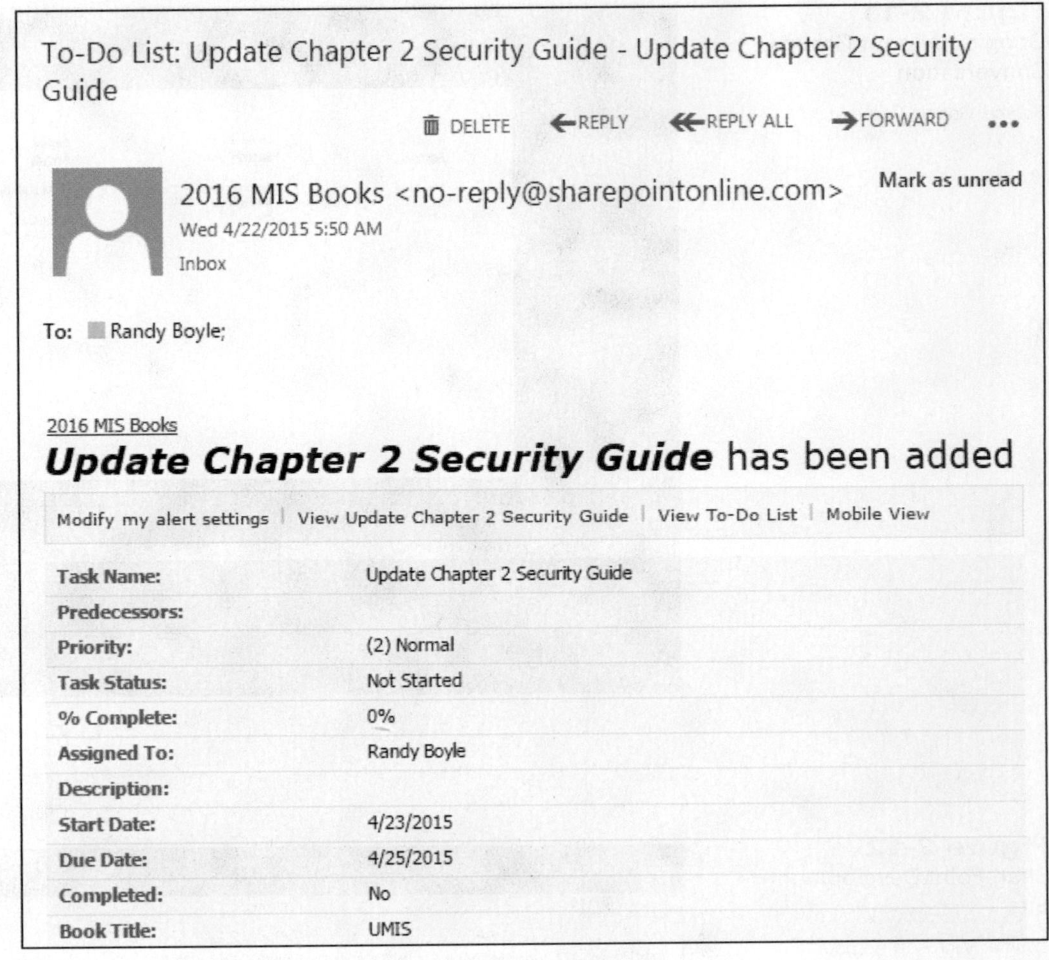


**Figure 2-13**
Example Email from SharePoint
*Source:* Microsoft Corporation

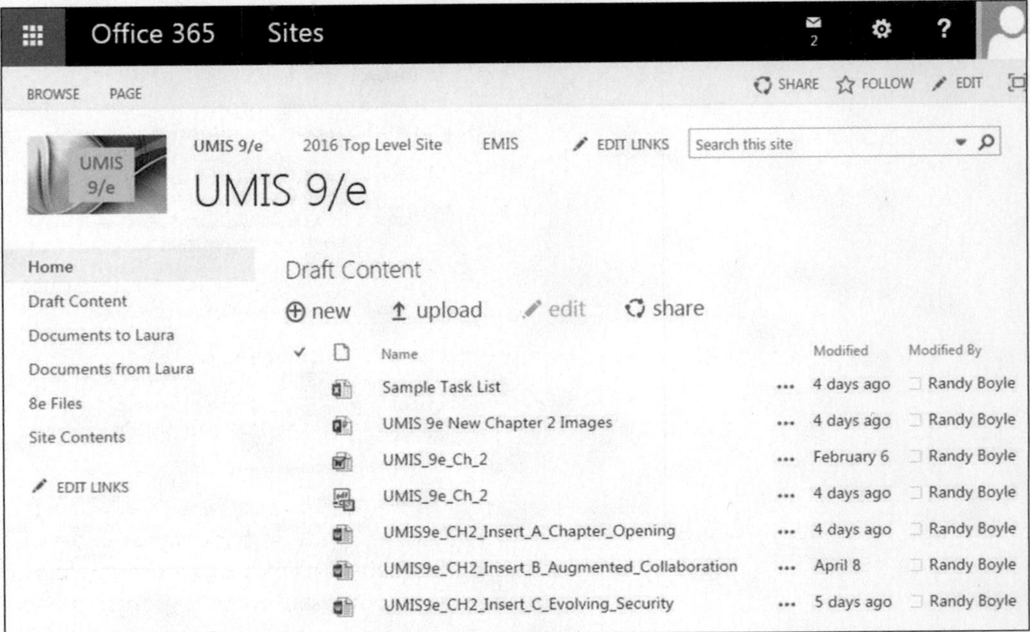


**Figure 2-14**
First Draft Document Library Contents
*Source:* Microsoft Corporation

Version History

Delete All Versions

| No. ↓ | Modified | Modified By | Size | Comments |
|---|---|---|---|---|
| 7.0 | 4/18/2015 7:49 AM | Randy Boyle | 1.7 MB | |
| 6.0 | 4/18/2015 7:00 AM | Randy Boyle | 1.5 MB | |
| 5.0 | 4/18/2015 6:25 AM | Randy Boyle | 1008.7 KB | |
| 4.0 | 4/18/2015 5:57 AM | Randy Boyle | 824.8 KB | |
| 3.0 | 4/18/2015 4:53 AM | Randy Boyle | 199.7 KB | |
| 2.0 | 4/18/2015 3:52 AM | Randy Boyle | 85 KB | |
| 1.0 | 4/18/2015 1:32 AM | Randy Boyle | 97.4 KB | |

**Figure 2-15**
Chapter 6 Version History
*Source:* Microsoft Corporation

## MyMISLab™

Go to the Assignments section of your MyLab to complete these writing exercises.

**2-20.** Consider the four definitions of *information* presented in this chapter. The problem with the first definition, "knowledge derived from data," is that it merely substitutes one word we don't know the meaning of (*information*) for a second word we don't know the meaning of (*knowledge*). The problem with the second definition, "data presented in a meaningful context," is that it is too subjective. Whose context? What makes a context meaningful? The third definition, "data processed by summing, ordering, averaging, etc.," is too mechanical. It tells us what to do, but it doesn't tell us what information is. The fourth definition, "a difference that makes a difference," is vague and unhelpful.

Also, none of these definitions helps us to quantify the amount of information we receive. What is the information content of the statement that every human being has a navel? Zero—you already know that. However, the statement that someone has just deposited $50,000 into your checking account is chock-full of information. So, good information has an element of surprise.

Considering these points, answer the following questions:

**a.** What is information made of?

**b.** If you have more information, do you weigh more? Why or why not?

**c.** If you give a copy of your transcript to a prospective employer, is that information? If you show that same transcript to your dog, is it still information? Where is the information?

**d.** Give your own best definition of *information.*

**e.** Explain how you think it is possible that we have an industry called the *information technology industry*, but we have great difficulty defining the word *information.*

**2-21.** Suppose you work at a large regional health care provider. The CIO of the company has asked you to gather data about the organization's operations. More specifically, the CIO wants to more carefully track supplies and equipment at hospitals and clinics within the organization. The problem is, few of the health care workers are interested in giving you that information. They don't want management interfering with their patient care. They worry that management will start reducing their supplies if they think they have too many of certain items. Then, when they need these items the most, they'll run short of essential supplies!

**a.** Describe why it's important in this case to gather *accurate* information.

**b.** Describe why it's important in this case to gather *timely* information.

**c.** Describe why it's important in this case to gather *relevant* information.

**d.** Describe why it's important in this case to gather information *worth its cost.*

## ENDNOTES

1. These symbols are included with Microsoft's Visio 2013 Professional edition. If your university is a member of Microsoft DreamSpark, you can obtain a license-free copy of Visio and use it to make your own BPMN diagrams.
2. Actually, the word *data* is plural; to be correct, we should use the singular form *datum* and say, "The fact that Jeff Parks earns $30.00 per hour is a datum." The word *datum*, however, sounds pedantic and fussy, and we will avoid it in this text.
3. Jessi Hempel, "Project HoloLens: Our Exclusive Hands-On with Microsoft's Holographic Goggles." *Wired.com*, January 21, 2015, accessed on April 5, 2015, *www.wired.com/2015/01/microsoft-hands-on.*
4. Matt Rosoff, "I Just Tried Microsoft's Remarkable Holographic Headset—Here's What It's Like," *BusinessInsider.com*, January 21, 2015, accessed April 5, 2015, *www.businessinsider.com/microsoft-hololens-hands-on-2015-1.*

chapter 3

# Organizational Strategy, Information Systems, and Competitive Advantage

This could happen to you

"Hey Cam, let's get some lunch. I need to hear more about the new LiDAR imaging we're going to start offering," says a well-dressed Alexis as she pops into the development lab where Cam is closely watching an employee testing a large quadcopter.

"Yeah, sure, I could use the break."

"What's that? Are you testing a new quad?"

"Um, well... yes. Mateo wanted to see if we could 3D-print our own drones. We're testing a new prototype we just finished building. It might be a lot cheaper than buying them. But I've never *built* a drone before."

"Wow. So, we've decided to get into the drone-making business?"

Cam motions to Alexis to move out into the hall so they can talk privately.

"Honestly, I hope not. But we'll see how this turns out. We're still trying to figure out if it will save us enough money to make it worth our while."

"Well, better you than me. They've got the right woman for the job!" Alexis smiles and tries to keep the conversation light.

"Yeah, well, this project is the least of my worries." Cam rolls her eyes and looks sincerely frustrated.

"What do you mean?"

"Who are we?"

"What do you mean?" Alexis is a little taken aback.

"Well, as a company, who are we? We've always been known as a company that provides security monitoring and we've got some big contracts. I get that. But... there's a lot of money we could be making in agricultural survey, industrial inspection, real estate videos, and wedding videos. I think we're really missing out."

"Have you talked with Mateo about this?"

"Yes, he agreed that these are all good ideas, but he wants to stay focused on big security contracts. He's even talking about contracting with law enforcement agencies, search and rescue, and the federal government."

"And... what's the downside?" Alexis asks. "It sounds like if I could close a few big sales we'd be sittin' pretty. From the sales side I'd be doing less work for more money."

# STUDY QUESTIONS

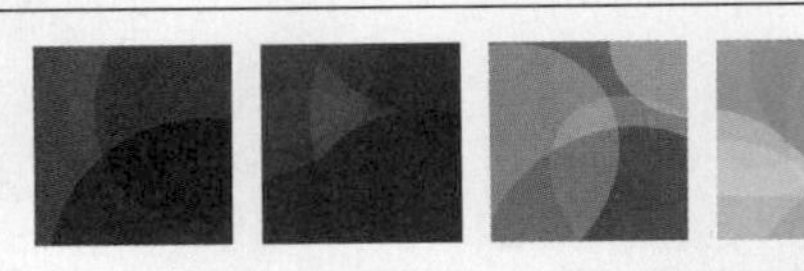

**Q3-1 HOW DOES ORGANIZATIONAL STRATEGY DETERMINE INFORMATION SYSTEMS STRUCTURE?**

**Q3-2 WHAT FIVE FORCES DETERMINE INDUSTRY STRUCTURE?**

**Q3-3 WHAT IS COMPETITIVE STRATEGY?**

**Q3-4 HOW DOES COMPETITIVE STRATEGY DETERMINE VALUE CHAIN STRUCTURE?**

**Q3-5 HOW DO VALUE CHAINS DETERMINE BUSINESS PROCESSES AND INFORMATION SYSTEMS?**

**Q3-6 HOW DO INFORMATION SYSTEMS PROVIDE COMPETITIVE ADVANTAGES?**

## How does the knowledge in this chapter help you?

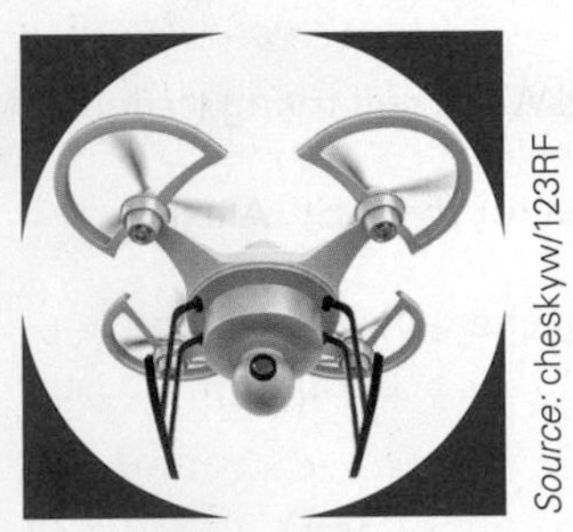

Source: cheskyw/123RF

**"We can't be everything to everybody."**

"Yeah, but that's a big 'if.' What if we can't sign them? What if the funding dries up? What if the public doesn't like the idea of the U.S. federal government using drones to video its citizens?"

"I don't know. If the money's as good as Mateo thinks it is, it might be worth a shot."

"Yes, but we could be spending our time and money developing accounts that we already know are profitable and will be for a long time. People are always getting married. It just seems like a no-brainer to think of Falcon Security as more than just a 'security' company. There's so much money on the table." Cam is clearly frustrated and shakes her head.

"Cam, I completely agree. The side projects we've done have been profitable. There's no arguing that."

"Well?"

"Well, it comes down to focus. We can't be everything to everybody. Providing long-term security monitoring for a chemical company is very different from doing a weekend wedding photo shoot."

"But what about all the money we could be making right now? If we don't earn it, somebody else will."

Alexis starts to smile and says, "Hey, let's grab Joni on the way out to lunch. She's the one who really needs to hear this. You two can talk strategy while I get some of those tasty fish tacos!"

# Q3-1 HOW DOES ORGANIZATIONAL STRATEGY DETERMINE INFORMATION SYSTEMS STRUCTURE?

According to the definition of MIS, information systems exist to help organizations achieve their strategies. As you will learn in your business strategy class, an organization's goals and objectives are determined by its *competitive strategy*. Thus, ultimately, competitive strategy determines the structure, features, and functions of every information system.

Figure 3-1 summarizes this situation. In short, organizations examine the structure of their industry and determine a competitive strategy. That strategy determines value chains, which, in turn, determine business processes. The structure of business processes determines the design of supporting information systems.

Michael Porter, one of the key researchers and thinkers in competitive analysis, developed three different models that help us understand the elements of Figure 3-1. We begin with his five forces model.

# Q3-2 WHAT FIVE FORCES DETERMINE INDUSTRY STRUCTURE?

Organizational strategy begins with an assessment of the fundamental characteristics and structure of an industry. One model used to assess an industry structure is Porter's **five forces model**,[1] summarized in Figure 3-2. According to this model, five competitive forces determine industry profitability: bargaining power of customers, threat of substitutions, bargaining power of suppliers, threat of new entrants, and rivalry among existing firms. The intensity of each of the five forces determines the characteristics of the industry, how profitable it is, and how sustainable that profitability will be.

To understand this model, consider the strong and weak examples for each of the forces in Figure 3-3. A good check on your understanding is to see if you can think of different forces of each category in Figure 3-3. Also, take a particular industry—say, auto repair—and consider how these five forces determine the competitive landscape of that industry.

**Figure 3-1**
Organizational Strategy Determines Information Systems

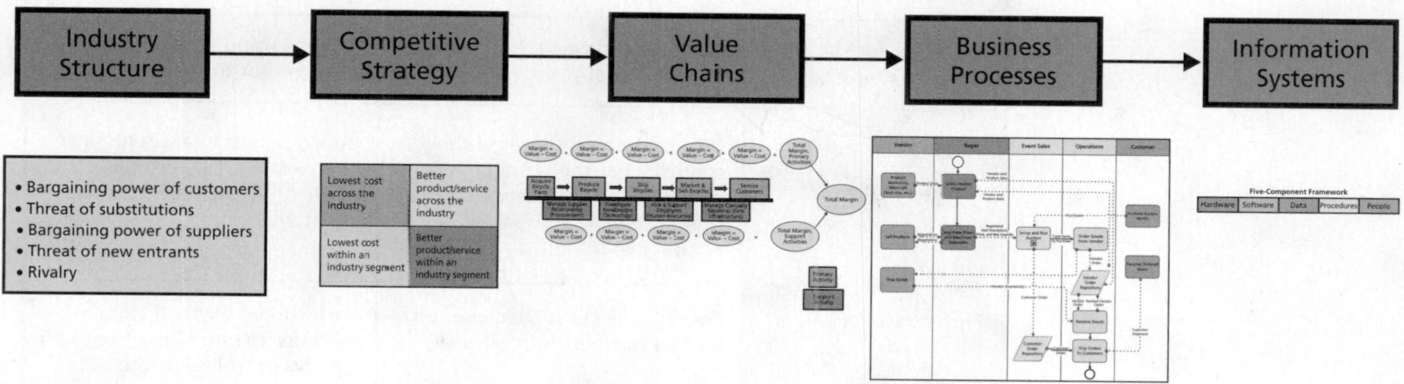

- Bargaining power of customers
- Threat of substitutions
- Bargaining power of suppliers
- Threat of new entrants
- Rivalry

**Figure 3-2**
Porter's Five Forces Model of Industry Structure

*Source:* Based on Michael E. Porter, *Competitive Advantage: Creating and Sustaining Superior Performance* (The Free Press, a Division of Simon & Schuster Adult Publishing Group).

In the opening vignette of this chapter, Cam is concerned that focusing only on physical security may place Falcon Security at a competitive disadvantage. She thinks the company could expand into agricultural survey, industrial inspection, real estate videos, and wedding videos. She's also worried about being financially dependent on a few large industrial accounts. Figure 3-4 shows an analysis of the competitive landscape Falcon Security faces.

The large industrial accounts that Falcon Security serves could demand more services or lower prices because they account for a large percentage of Falcon Security's revenue. The threat of substitutions, like customers choosing to install wireless digital Web cameras, is somewhat strong. But these substitutions may not be viable options for some of the industrial clients due to the lack of internal technical expertise or physical distance limitations. A new entrant, like Amazon starting to offer surveillance service using its delivery drones, could be a substantial threat. But Falcon Security could respond to this by offering additional services, like real-time 3D mapping. Or it could enter new markets like agricultural survey and industrial inspection.

The other forces are not as worrisome to Falcon Security. The bargaining power of drone suppliers is weak because there are lots of drone manufacturers to choose from. And the company always has the option of 3D printing its own drones. The threat from rivals isn't strong because Falcon Security has developed a self-charging drone platform and an integrated video processing system that wouldn't be easy for rivals to replicate.

Like Falcon Security, organizations examine these five forces and determine how they intend to respond to them. That examination leads to competitive strategy.

**Figure 3-3**
Examples of Five Forces

| Force | Example of Strong Force | Example of Weak Force |
|---|---|---|
| **Bargaining power of customer** | Toyota's purchase of auto paint (because Toyota is a huge customer that will purchase paint in large volume) | Your power over the procedures and policies of your university |
| **Threat of substitutions** | Frequent traveler's choice of auto rental | Patients using the only drug effective for their type of cancer |
| **Bargaining power of suppliers** | New car dealers (because they control what the "true price"of a vehicle is and the customer cannot reliably verify the accuracy of that price) | Grain farmers in a surplus year (an oversupply makes the product less valuable and less profitable) |
| **Threat of new entrants** | Corner latte stand (because it is an easy business to replicate) | Professional football team (because the number of teams is tightly controlled by the NFL) |
| **Rivalry** | Used car dealers (because there are many to choose from) | Google or Bing (expensive to develop and market a search engine) |

**Figure 3-4**
Five Forces at Falcon Security

| Force | Falcon Security Example | Force Strength | Falcon Security's Response |
|---|---|---|---|
| Bargaining power of customers | A large account wants more services at a lower price | Strong | Lower prices or diversify into other markets |
| Threat of substitutions | Replace drones with wireless IP Web cameras | Medium | Offer differentiating services, like LiDAR, that cameras can't provide |
| Bargaining power of suppliers | We're increasing the cost of the drones we sell | Weak | We'll make our own drones |
| Threat of new entrants | Amazon begins offering package delivery and surveillance via drones | Medium | Offer differentiating services and enter other markets |
| Rivalry | A new drone company expands its operations into the state | Weak | Offer additional features like direct streaming video to the customer |

## Q3-3 WHAT IS COMPETITIVE STRATEGY?

An organization responds to the structure of its industry by choosing a competitive strategy. As shown in Figure 3-5, Porter defined four fundamental competitive strategies.[2] An organization can be the cost leader and provide products at the lowest prices, or it can focus on adding value to its products or services to differentiate them from those of the competition. Further, the organization can employ the cost or differentiation strategy across an industry, or it can focus its strategy on a particular industry segment. In this text, we define **competitive strategy** to be one of the four alternatives shown in Figure 3-5.

Consider the car rental industry, for example. According to the first column of Figure 3-5, a car rental company can strive to provide the lowest-cost car rentals across the industry, or it can seek to provide the lowest-cost car rentals to a "focused" industry segment—say, U.S. domestic business travelers.

As shown in the second column, a car rental company can seek to differentiate its products from the competition. It can do so in various ways—for example, by providing a wide range of high-quality cars, by providing the best reservation system, by having the cleanest cars or the fastest check-in, or by some other means. The company can strive to provide product differentiation across the industry or within particular segments of the industry, such as U.S. domestic business travelers.

According to Porter, to be effective the organization's goals, objectives, culture, and activities must be consistent with the organization's strategy. To those in the MIS field, this means that all information systems in the organization must facilitate the organization's competitive strategy.

**Figure 3-5**
Porter's Four Competitive Strategies

*Source:* Based on "How Competitive Forces Shape Strategy" by Michael Porter, *Harvard Business Review*, July–August 1997.

| | Cost | Differentiation |
|---|---|---|
| **Industry-wide** | Lowest cost across the industry | Better product/service across the industry |
| **Focus** | Lowest cost within an industry segment | Better product/service within an industry segment |

# Q3-4 HOW DOES COMPETITIVE STRATEGY DETERMINE VALUE CHAIN STRUCTURE?

Organizations analyze the structure of their industry, and, using that analysis, they formulate a competitive strategy. They then need to organize and structure the organization to implement that strategy. If, for example, the competitive strategy is to be a *cost leader*, then business activities need to be developed to provide essential functions at the lowest possible cost.

A business that selects a *differentiation* strategy would not necessarily structure itself around least-cost activities. Instead, such a business might choose to develop more costly systems, but it would do so only if those systems provided benefits to their differentiation strategy that outweighed their costs. Joni at Falcon Security knows that buying the best commercial drones is expensive, and she judges the costs worthwhile. She may find that 3D printing Falcon's own custom drones to be worthwhile, too.

Porter defined **value** as the amount of money that a customer is willing to pay for a resource, product, or service. The difference between the value that an activity generates and the cost of the activity is called the **margin**. A business with a differentiation strategy will add cost to an activity only as long as the activity has a positive margin.

A **value chain** is a network of value-creating activities. That generic chain consists of five primary activities and four support activities. **Primary activities** are business functions that relate directly to the production of the organization's products or services. **Support activities** are business functions that assist and facilitate the primary activities.

## PRIMARY ACTIVITIES IN THE VALUE CHAIN

To understand the essence of the value chain, consider one of Falcon Security's suppliers, a medium-sized drone manufacturer (see Figure 3-6). First, the manufacturer acquires raw materials using the inbound logistics activity. This activity concerns the receiving and handling of raw materials and other inputs. The accumulation of those materials adds value in the sense

**Figure 3-6**
Drone Manufacturer's Value Chain

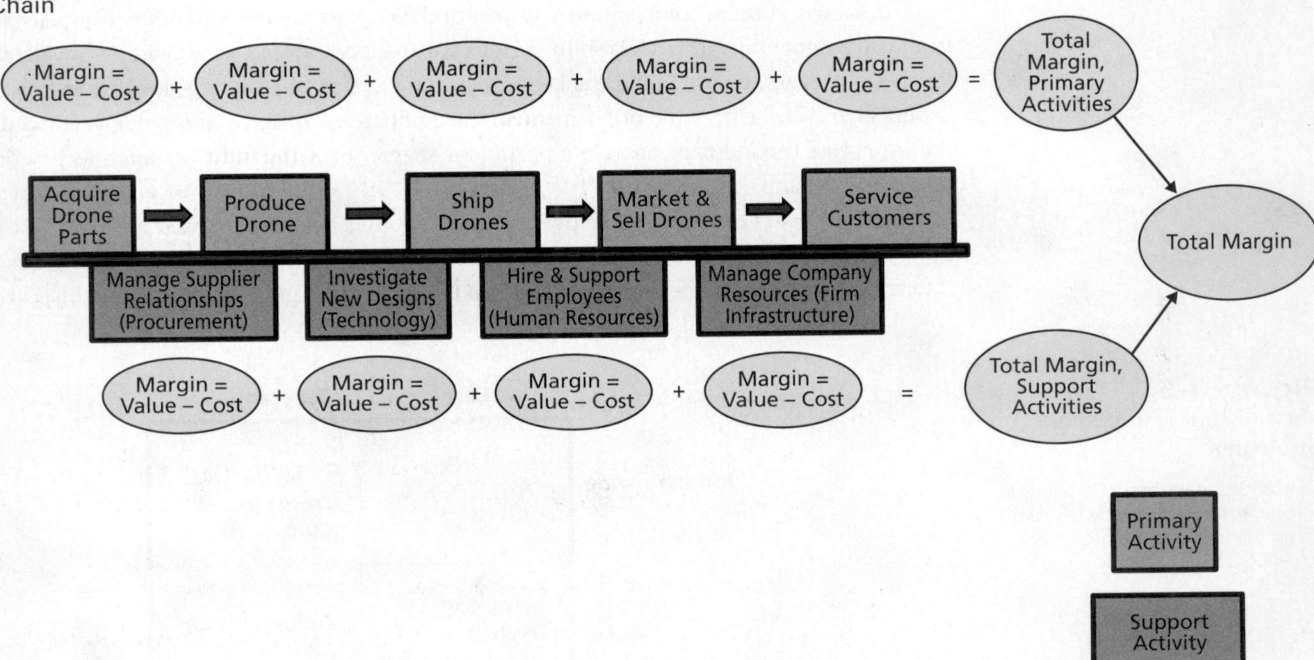

**Figure 3-7**
Task Descriptions for Primary Activities of the Value Chain

| Primary Activity | Description |
|---|---|
| Inbound Logistics | Receiving, storing, and disseminating inputs to the product |
| Operations/Manufacturing | Transforming inputs into the final product |
| Outbound Logistics | Collecting, storing, and physically distributing the product to buyers |
| Sales and Marketing | Inducing buyers to purchase the product and providing a means for them to do so |
| Customer Service | Assisting customer's use of the product and thus maintaining and enhancing the product's value |

that even a pile of unassembled parts is worth something to some customer. A collection of the parts needed to build a drone is worth more than an empty space on a shelf. The value is not only the parts themselves, but also the time required to contact vendors for those parts, to maintain business relationships with those vendors, to order the parts, to receive the shipment, and so forth.

In the operations activity, the drone maker transforms raw materials into a finished drone, a process that adds more value. Next, the company uses the outbound logistics activity to deliver the finished drone to a customer. Of course, there is no customer to send the drone to without the marketing and sales value activity. Finally, the service activity provides customer support to the drone users.

Each stage of this generic chain accumulates costs and adds value to the product. The net result is the total margin of the chain, which is the difference between the total value added and the total costs incurred. Figure 3-7 summarizes the primary activities of the value chain.

## SUPPORT ACTIVITIES IN THE VALUE CHAIN

The support activities in the generic value chain facilitate the primary activities and contribute only indirectly to the production, sale, and service of the product. They include procurement, which consists of the processes of finding vendors, setting up contractual arrangements, and negotiating prices. (This differs from inbound logistics, which is concerned with ordering and receiving in accordance with agreements set up by procurement.)

Porter defined technology broadly. It includes research and development, but it also includes other activities within the firm for developing new techniques, methods, and procedures. He defined human resources as recruiting, compensation, evaluation, and training of full-time and part-time employees. Finally, firm infrastructure includes general management, finance, accounting, legal, and government affairs.

Supporting functions add value, albeit indirectly, and they also have costs. Hence, as shown in Figure 3-6, supporting activities contribute to a margin. In the case of supporting activities, it would be difficult to calculate the margin because the specific value added of, say, the manufacturer's lobbyists in Washington, DC, is difficult to know. But there is a value added, there are costs, and there is a margin—even if it is only in concept.

## VALUE CHAIN LINKAGES

Porter's model of business activities includes **linkages**, which are interactions across value activities. For example, manufacturing systems use linkages to reduce inventory costs. Such a system uses sales forecasts to plan production; it then uses the production plan to determine raw material needs and then uses the material needs to schedule purchases. The end result is just-in-time inventory, which reduces inventory sizes and costs.

Value chain analysis has a direct application to manufacturing businesses like the drone manufacturer. However, value chains also exist in service-oriented companies. The difference is that most of the value in a service company is generated by the operations, marketing and sales, and service activities. Inbound and outbound logistics are not typically as important.

## Q3-5 HOW DO VALUE CHAINS DETERMINE BUSINESS PROCESSES AND INFORMATION SYSTEMS?

**See the Ethics Guide on pages 74–75 to learn how a change in strategy can greatly affect a company's culture.**

As you learned in the last chapter, a business process is a network of activities, resources, facilities, and information that accomplish a business function. Now we can be more specific and say that business processes implement value chains or portions of value chains. Thus, each value chain is supported by one or more business processes.

For example, Figure 3-8 shows a business process for renting bicycles. The top part of this figure shows how a company having a competitive strategy of providing low-cost rentals to college students might implement this portion of its operations value chain. The bottom part shows how a company with a competitive strategy of providing high-quality rentals to business executives at a conference resort might implement this portion of that same value chain.

Note that the value chain activities are the same for both companies. Both greet the customer, determine the customer's needs, rent a bike, and return the bike. However, each company implements these activities in ways that are consistent with its competitive strategy.

The low-cost vendor has created bare-bones, minimal processes to support its value chain. The high-service vendor has created more elaborate business processes (supported by information systems) that are necessary to differentiate its service from that of other vendors. As Porter says, however, these processes and systems must create sufficient value so that they will more than cover their costs. If not, the margin of those systems will be negative.

If a value chain's margin is negative, the company must make some change. Either the value must be increased or the costs of the value chain need to be reduced. To investigate this principle further, consider Collaboration Exercise 3 at the end of this chapter.

Before we continue, review Figure 3-1 again. The material in these first three chapters is presented from the right to the left in this figure. We began with the components of an information system in Chapter 1. We then considered business processes in Chapter 2. In this chapter, we have considered value chains, competitive strategy, and industry structure.

## Q3-6 HOW DO INFORMATION SYSTEMS PROVIDE COMPETITIVE ADVANTAGES?

In your business strategy class, you will study the Porter models in greater detail than we have discussed here. When you do so, you will learn numerous ways that organizations respond to the five competitive forces. For our purposes, we can distill those ways into the list of principles shown in Figure 3-9. Keep in mind that we must apply these principles within the context of the organization's competitive strategy.

Some of these competitive techniques are created via products and services, and some are created via the development of business processes. Consider each.

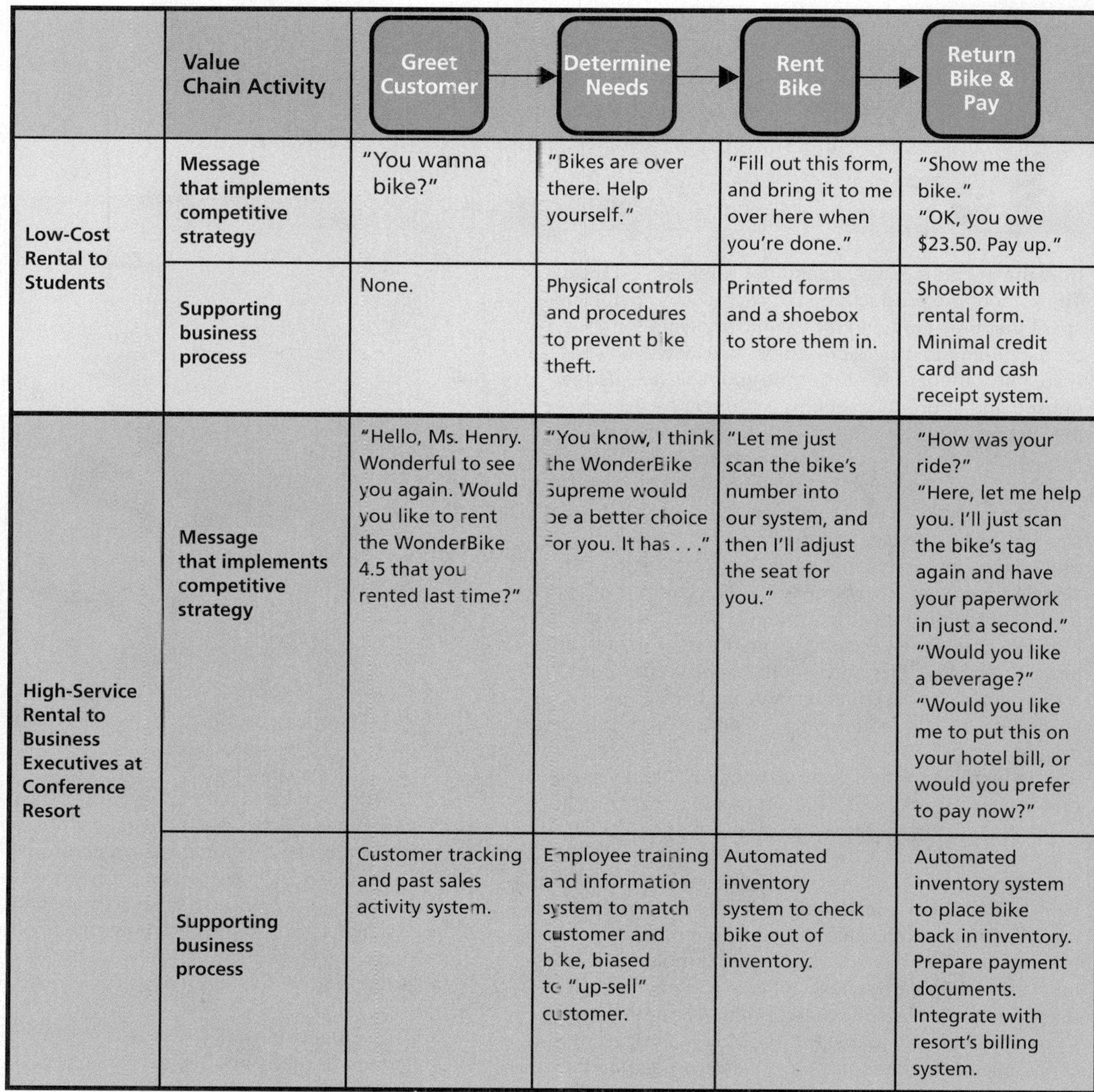

| | Value Chain Activity | Greet Customer → | Determine Needs → | Rent Bike → | Return Bike & Pay |
|---|---|---|---|---|---|
| Low-Cost Rental to Students | Message that implements competitive strategy | "You wanna bike?" | "Bikes are over there. Help yourself." | "Fill out this form, and bring it to me over here when you're done." | "Show me the bike." "OK, you owe $23.50. Pay up." |
| | Supporting business process | None. | Physical controls and procedures to prevent bike theft. | Printed forms and a shoebox to store them in. | Shoebox with rental form. Minimal credit card and cash receipt system. |
| High-Service Rental to Business Executives at Conference Resort | Message that implements competitive strategy | "Hello, Ms. Henry. Wonderful to see you again. Would you like to rent the WonderBike 4.5 that you rented last time?" | "You know, I think the WonderBike Supreme would be a better choice for you. It has . . ." | "Let me just scan the bike's number into our system, and then I'll adjust the seat for you." | "How was your ride?" "Here, let me help you. I'll just scan the bike's tag again and have your paperwork in just a second." "Would you like a beverage?" "Would you like me to put this on your hotel bill, or would you prefer to pay now?" |
| | Supporting business process | Customer tracking and past sales activity system. | Employee training and information system to match customer and bike, biased to "up-sell" customer. | Automated inventory system to check bike out of inventory. | Automated inventory system to place bike back in inventory. Prepare payment documents. Integrate with resort's billing system. |

**Figure 3-8**
Operations Value Chains for Bicycle Rental Companies

**Product Implementations**
1. Create a new product or service
2. Enhance products or services
3. Differentiate products or services

**Process Implementations**

4. Lock in customers and buyers
5. Lock in suppliers
6. Raise barriers to market entry
7. Establish alliances
8. Reduce costs

**Figure 3-9**
Principles of Competitive Advantage

# Driving Strategy

How many hours do you spend per week driving a car? Think about the productivity boost you could get if you spent that time studying for exams, applying for a job, or responding to orders placed on your new Web site. Also, think about how much time your car just sits there—unused and unproductive. Could your car be used more productively if it was shared with a friend, sibling, or spouse? Maybe a driverless car, like those mentioned in Chapter 4, could drop you off at school and then return home to be used by someone else?

Businesses can also recognize gains in efficiency, productivity, and sales that will come from using driverless vehicles. For example, Mercedes is developing a driverless truck that can operate autonomously once it is on the highway (a driver is required to get the truck on and off of the interstate).[3] Not only can this vehicle transport a shipment to its destination faster, it can also make roads safer by eliminating fatigued drivers and distracted driving.

To identify another potential business application of driverless vehicles, take a look at one of Amazon's new projects. Amazon recently filed a patent application for a delivery truck that is outfitted with 3D printers.[4] The purpose of these vehicles is to rapidly respond to orders by manufacturing goods while the vehicle is en route to the delivery location. You may be wondering what this has to do with a driverless car, but if you combine Amazon's innovation *with* a driverless vehicle, you now have an autonomous factory on wheels! Think about the strategic value of being able to instantly deploy manufacturing capabilities to any geographic location on demand.

## Driving Existing Markets to Change

Businesses are constantly fine-tuning and adapting their business strategies to create and maintain competitive advantages. Markets are sometimes disrupted by new entrants, substitute products, or new innovations. It is clear that Über is revolutionizing transportation services around the world. In a few short years, it has become a major player in the transportation industry with a $40B valuation.[5] But is Über invincible to new forms of competition?

Could a new entrant start a transportation company using only driverless vehicles? One of the biggest concerns consumers have with Über is the lack of background checks and other vetting processes required of its drivers. What if you removed drivers from the business model entirely?

*Source:* chombosan/Fotolia

This driverless taxi company would have other benefits as well. Passengers wouldn't have to worry about safety. Profit margins for the company would probably increase due to reduced labor costs, healthcare costs, and accidents. Vehicles would never have to stop for rest, food, bathroom breaks, and so on, so the company could continuously make money (except for vehicle maintenance and filling gas tanks, but both of these activities occur even with human operators).

The implications of driverless vehicles are not just limited to the transportation sector. They could also influence industries like shipping, aviation, and law enforcement. If you still think new innovations cannot take down juggernaut companies, just ask Polaroid!

## QUESTIONS

1. One mechanism that could help (1) inform the navigation of driverless cars and (2) update the vehicle with current road conditions is Internet connectivity to other autonomous vehicles operating in the area. What vulnerabilities could be exploited by equipping one of these vehicles with Internet access?
2. The feature describes a scenario in which Amazon's mobile manufacturing vehicles could be operated autonomously. What are some logistical issues that could arise from a delivery vehicle functioning without a human operator?

3. Creating driverless vehicles that can operate safely is clearly a complex problem. Based on the promising results found in this domain, what other complex tasks exist that may prove feasible for automation?
4. New innovations often disrupt existing markets and force them to adapt or be eliminated (e.g., look at how iTunes and Apple devices have reshaped the music industry). How might the proliferation of driverless cars influence the automotive insurance industry?
5. How would you feel riding in a car that is changing lanes and swerving to avoid debris or poor road conditions all without your control? Do you think that a driverless vehicle is something that everyone would want to own, even if it is sold at an affordable price?

## COMPETITIVE ADVANTAGE VIA PRODUCTS

The first three principles in Figure 3-9 concern products or services. Organizations gain a competitive advantage by creating *new* products or services, by *enhancing* existing products or services, and by *differentiating* their products and services from those of their competitors. As you think about these three principles, realize that an information system can be part of a product or it can provide support for a product or service.

Consider, for example, a car rental agency like Hertz or Avis. An information system that produces information about the car's location and provides driving instructions to destinations is part of the car rental and thus is part of the product itself (see Figure 3-10a). In contrast, an information system that schedules car maintenance is not part of the product but instead supports the product (Figure 3-10b). Either way, information systems can achieve the first three objectives in Figure 3-9.

**Figure 3-10**
Two Roles for Information Systems Regarding Products

**a. Information System as Part of a Car Rental Product**

**b. Information System That Supports a Car Rental Product**

**Daily Service Schedule – November 17, 2017**

**StationID** 22
**StationName** Lubrication

| ServiceDate | ServiceTime | VehicleID | Make | Model | Mileage | ServiceDescription |
|---|---|---|---|---|---|---|
| 11/17/2017 | 12:00 AM | 155890 | Ford | Explorer | 2244 | Std. Lube |
| 11/17/2017 | 11:00 AM | 12448 | Toyota | Tacoma | 7558 | Std. Lube |

**StationID** 26
**StationName** Alignment

| ServiceDate | ServiceTime | VehicleID | Make | Model | Mileage | ServiceDescription |
|---|---|---|---|---|---|---|
| 11/17/2017 | 9:00 AM | 12448 | Toyota | Tacoma | 7558 | Front end alignment inspect |

**StationID** 28
**StationName** Transmission

| ServiceDate | ServiceTime | VehicleID | Make | Model | Mileage | ServiceDescription |
|---|---|---|---|---|---|---|
| 11/17/2017 | 11:00 AM | 155890 | Ford | Explorer | 2244 | Transmission oil change |

The remaining five principles in Figure 3-9 concern competitive advantage created by the implementation of business processes.

## COMPETITIVE ADVANTAGE VIA BUSINESS PROCESSES

Organizations can *lock in customers* by making it difficult or expensive for customers to switch to another product. This strategy is sometimes called establishing high **switching costs**. Organizations can *lock in suppliers* by making it difficult to switch to another organization or, stated positively, by making it easy to connect to and work with the organization. Competitive advantage can be gained by *creating entry barriers* that make it difficult and expensive for new competition to enter the market.

Another means to gain competitive advantage is to *establish alliances* with other organizations. Such alliances establish standards, promote product awareness and needs, develop market size, reduce purchasing costs, and provide other benefits. Finally, by creating better business processes, organizations can gain competitive advantage by *reducing costs*. Such reductions enable the organization to reduce prices and/or to increase profitability. Increased profitability means not just greater shareholder value, but also more cash, which can fund further infrastructure development for even greater competitive advantage.

All of these principles of competitive advantage make sense, but the question you may be asking is "How do information systems help to create competitive advantage?" To answer that question, consider a sample information system.

## HOW CAN AN ORGANIZATION USE IS TO CREATE COMPETITIVE ADVANTAGES?

To help you understand how IS can facilitate competitive advantages, consider the example of a worldwide shipping company. Call it ABC.

ABC maintains customer account data that include not only the customer's name, address, and billing information but also data about the identity of that customer and the locations to which the customer ships. Figure 3-11 shows a Web form that an ABC customer is using to schedule a shipment. When the ABC system creates the form, it fills the Company name drop-down list with the names of companies that the customer has shipped to in the past. Here the user is selecting Pearson Education.

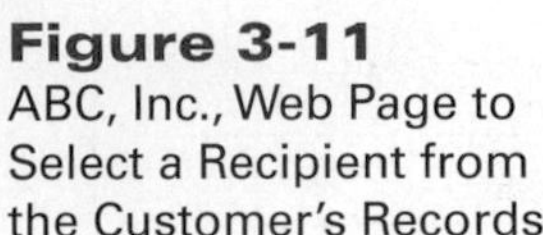

**Figure 3-11**
ABC, Inc., Web Page to Select a Recipient from the Customer's Records

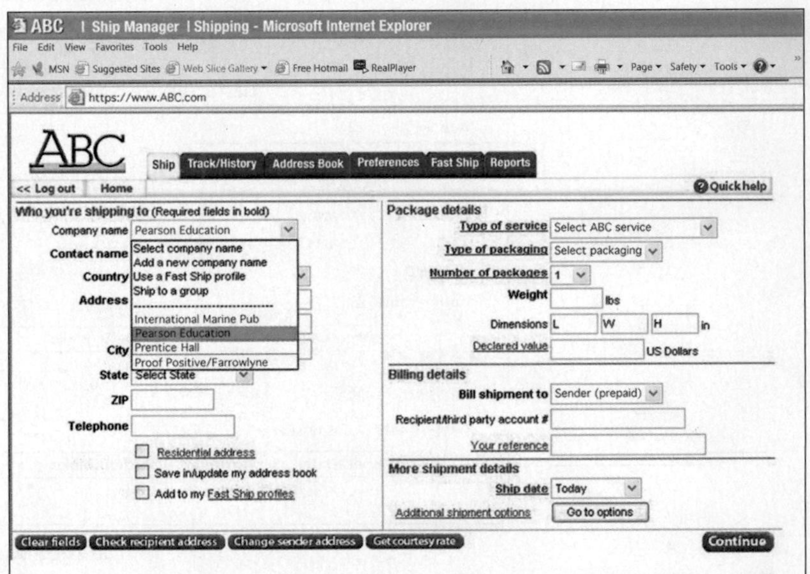

**Figure 3-12**
ABC, Inc., Web Page to Select a Contact from the Customer's Records

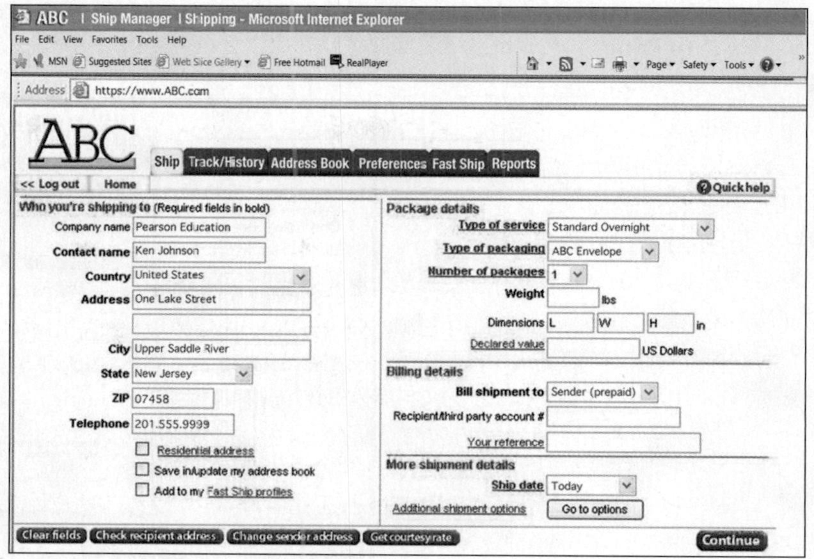


When the user clicks the Company name, the underlying ABC information system reads the customer's contact data from a database. The data consist of names, addresses, and phone numbers of recipients from past shipments. The user then selects a Contact name, and the system inserts that contact's address and other data into the form using data from the database, as shown in Figure 3-12. Thus, the system saves customers from having to reenter data for people to whom they have shipped in the past. Providing the data in this way also reduces data entry errors.

Figure 3-13 shows another feature of this system. On the right-hand side of this form, the customer can request that ABC send email messages to the sender (the customer), the recipient, and others as well. The customer can choose for ABC to send an email when the shipment is created and when it has been delivered. In Figure 3-13, the user has provided three email addresses. The customer wants all three addresses to receive delivery notification, but only the sender will receive shipment notification. The customer can add a personal message as well. By adding this capability to the shipment-scheduling system, ABC has extended its product from a package-delivery service to a package- *and* information-delivery service.

**Figure 3-13**
ABC, Inc., Web Page to Specify Email Notification

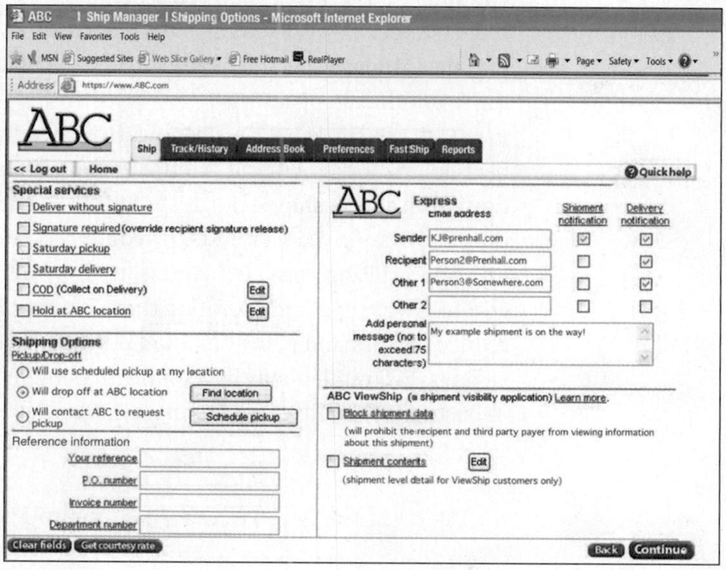

**Figure 3-14**
ABC, Inc., Web Page to Print a Shipping Label

Figure 3-14 shows one other capability of this information system. It has generated a shipping label, complete with bar code, for the user to print. By doing this, the company not only reduces errors in the preparation of shipping labels, but it also causes the customer to provide the paper and ink for document printing! Millions of such documents are printed every day, resulting in a considerable savings to the company.

## HOW DOES THIS SYSTEM CREATE A COMPETITIVE ADVANTAGE?

Now consider the ABC shipping information system in light of the competitive advantage factors in Figure 3-9. This information system *enhances* an existing product because it eases the effort of creating a shipment to the customer while reducing errors. The information system also helps to *differentiate* the ABC package delivery product from competitors that do not have a similar system. Further, the generation of email messages when ABC picks up and delivers a package could be considered to be a *new* product.

Because this information system captures and stores data about recipients, it reduces the amount of customer work when scheduling a shipment. Customers will be *locked in* by this system: If a customer wants to change to a different shipper, he or she will need to rekey recipient data for that new shipper. The disadvantage of rekeying data may well outweigh any advantage of switching to another shipper.

This system achieves a competitive advantage in two other ways as well. First, it raises the barriers to market entry. If another company wants to develop a shipping service, it will not only have to be able to ship packages, but it will also need to have a similar information system. In addition, the system reduces costs. It reduces errors in shipping documents, and it saves ABC paper, ink, and printing costs. (Of course, to determine if this system delivers a *net savings* in cost, the cost of developing and operating the information system will need to be offset against the gains in reduced errors and paper, ink, and printing costs. It may be that the system costs more than the savings. Even still, it may be a sound investment if the value of intangible benefits, such as locking in customers and raising entry barriers, exceeds the net cost.)

Before continuing, review Figure 3-9. Make sure that you understand each of the principles of competitive advantage and how information systems can help achieve them. In fact, the list in Figure 3-9 probably is important enough to memorize because you can also use it for non-IS applications. You can consider any business project or initiative in light of competitive advantage.

## How does the **knowledge** in this chapter help **you?**

Reread the opening dialogue of this chapter. Explain why Cam's concerns about relying on a few large security contracts might be a valid strategic issue. Identify the key points Falcon Security must address in deciding whether to expand its business beyond security services.

**The Guide on pages 76–77 helps you understand how to use the principles of competitive advantage in a personal way.**

Develop guidance for yourself about the relationship between competitive strategy and information systems requirements. Summarize what you have learned from this example in a statement you could make in a job interview. Ensure your statement demonstrates your understanding of the relationship of business strategy and the use of information technology and systems.

# Ethics Guide

## Yikes! Bikes

Suppose you are an operations manager for Yikes! Bikes, a manufacturer of high-end mountain bicycles. Yikes! has been in business more than 25 years and has an annual revenue of $35M. The founder and sole owner recently sold the business to an investment group, Major Capital. You know nothing about the sale until your boss introduces you to Andrea Parks, a partner at Major Capital, who is in charge of the acquisition. Andrea explains to you that Yikes! has been sold to Major Capital and that she will be the temporary general manager. She explains that the new owners see great potential in you and want to enlist your cooperation during the transition. She hints that if your potential is what she thinks it is, you will be made general manager of Yikes!

Andrea explains that the new owners decided there are too many players in the high-end mountain bike business, and they plan to change the competitive strategy of Yikes! from high-end differentiation to lowest-cost vendor. Accordingly, they will eliminate local manufacturing, fire most of the manufacturing department, and import bikes from China. Further, Major Capital sees a need to reduce expenses and plans a 10 percent across-the-board staff reduction and a cut of two-thirds of the customer support department. The new bikes will be of lesser quality than current Yikes! bikes, but the price will be substantially less. The new ownership group believes it will take a few years for the market to realize that Yikes! bikes are not the same quality as they were. Finally, Andrea asks you to attend an all-employee meeting with her and the founder.

At the meeting, the founder explains that due to his age and personal situation, he decided to sell Yikes! to Major Capital and that starting today Andrea Parks is the general manager. He thanks the employees for their many years of service, wishes them well, and leaves the building. Andrea introduces herself to the employees and states that Major Capital is very excited to own such a great company with a strong, quality brand. She says she will take a few weeks to orient herself to the business and its environment and plans no major changes to the company.

You are reeling from all this news when Andrea calls you into her office and explains that she needs you to prepare two reports. In one, she wants a list of all the employees in the manufacturing department, sorted by their salary (or wage for hourly employees). She explains that she intends to cut the most costly employees first. "I don't want to be inflexible about this, though," she says. "If there is someone whom you think we should keep, let me know, and we can talk about it."

She also wants a list of the employees in the customer support department, sorted by the average amount of time each support rep spends with customers. She explains, "I'm not so concerned with payroll expense in customer support. It's not how much we're paying someone; it's how much time they're wasting with customers. We're going to have a bare-bones support department, and we want to get rid of the gabby chatters first."

*Source:* PSD Photography/Shutterstock

You are, understandably, shocked and surprised... not only at the speed with which the transition has occurred, but also because you don't think the founder would do this to the employees. You call him at home and tell him what is going on.

"Look," he explains, "when I sold the company, I asked them to be sure to take care of the employees. They said they would. I'll call Andrea, but there's really nothing I can do at this point; they own the show."

In a black mood of depression, you realize you don't want to work for Yikes! anymore, but your wife is 6 months pregnant with your first child. You need medical insurance for her at least until the baby is born. But what miserable tasks are you going to be asked to do before then? And you suspect that if you balk at any task, Andrea won't hesitate to fire you, too.

As you leave that night, you run into Lori, the most popular customer support representative and one of your favorite employees. "Hey," Lori asks you, "what did you think of that meeting? Do you believe Andrea? Do you think they'll let us continue to make great bikes?"

## DISCUSSION QUESTIONS

**1.** In your opinion, did the new owners take any illegal action? Is there evidence of a crime in this scenario?

**2.** Consider the ethics of the statement that Andrea made to all of the employees. Using both the categorical imperative (pages 20–21) and utilitarianism (pages 46–47), assess the ethics of that statement. If you were to question her about the ethics of her statement, how do you think she would justify herself?

**3.** What do you think Andrea will tell the founder if he calls as a result of your conversation with him? Does he have any legal recourse? Is Major Capital's behavior toward him unethical? Why or why not?

**4.** Andrea is going to use data to perform staff cuts. What do you think about her criteria? Ethically, should she consider other factors, such as number of years of service, past employee reviews, or other criteria?

**5.** How do you respond to Lori? What are the consequences if you tell her what you know? What are the consequences of lying to her? What are the consequences of saying something noncommittal? Consider both the categorical imperative and utilitarian perspectives in your response.

**6.** If you actually were in this situation, would you leave the company? Why or why not?

**7.** In business school, we talk of principles like competitive strategy as interesting academic topics. But, as you can see from the Yikes! case, competitive strategy decisions have human consequences. How do you plan to resolve conflicts between human needs and tough business decisions?

**8.** How do you define *job security*?

*Source:* Claudiu Paizan/Shutterstock

# Guide

## Your Personal Competitive Advantage

Consider the following possibility: After working hard to earn your degree in business, you graduate, only to discover that you cannot find a job in your area of study. You look for 6 weeks or so, but then you run out of money. In desperation, you take a job waiting tables at a local restaurant. Two years go by, the economy picks up, and the jobs you had been looking for become available. Unfortunately, your degree is now 2 years old; you are competing with students who have just graduated with fresh degrees (and fresh knowledge). Two years of waiting tables, good as you are at it, does not appear to be good experience for the job you want. You're stuck in a nightmare that will be hard to get out of—and one that you cannot allow to happen.

Examine Figure 3-9 again, but this time consider those elements of competitive advantage as they apply to you personally. As an employee, the skills and abilities you offer are your personal product. Examine the first three items in the list and ask yourself, "How can I use my time in school—and in this MIS class, in particular—to create new skills, to enhance those I already have, and to differentiate my skills from the competition?" (By the way, you will enter a national/international market. Your competition is not just the students in your class; it's also students in classes in Ohio, California, British Columbia, Singapore, Sydney, and everywhere else they're teaching MIS today.)

Suppose you are interested in a sales job. Perhaps you want to sell in the pharmaceutical industry. What skills can you learn from your MIS class that will make you more competitive as a future salesperson? Ask yourself, "How does the pharmaceutical industry use MIS to gain competitive advantage?" Use the Internet to find examples of the use of information systems in the pharmaceutical industry. How does Pfizer, for example, use a customer information system to sell to doctors? How can your knowledge of such systems differentiate you from your competition for a job there? How does Pfizer use a knowledge management system? How does the firm keep track of drugs that have an adverse effect on each other?

The fourth and fifth items in Figure 3-9 concern locking in customers, buyers, and suppliers. How can you interpret those elements in terms of your personal competitive advantage? Well, to lock in a relationship, you first have to have one. So do you have an internship? If not, can you get one? And once you have an internship, how can you use your knowledge of MIS to lock in your job so that you get a job offer? Does the company you are interning for have an information system for managing customers (or any other information system that is important to the company)? If users are happy with the system, what characteristics make it worthwhile? Can you lock in a job by becoming an expert user of this system? Becoming an expert user not only locks you into your job, but it also raises barriers to entry for others who might be competing for the job. Also, can you suggest ways to improve the system, thus using your knowledge of the company and the system to lock in an extension of your job?

Human resources personnel say that networking is one of the most effective ways of finding a job. How can you use this class to establish alliances with other students? Does your class have a Web site? Is there an email list server for the students in your class? How about a Facebook group? How can you use these to develop job-seeking alliances with other students? Who in your class already has a job or an internship? Can any of those people provide hints or opportunities for finding a job?

Don't restrict your job search to your local area. Are there regions of your country where jobs are more plentiful? How can you find out about student organizations in those regions? Search the Web for MIS classes in other cities, and make contact with students there. Find out what the hot opportunities are in other cities.

Finally, as you study MIS, think about how the knowledge you gain can help you save costs for your employers. Even more, see if you can build a case that an employer would actually save money by hiring you. The line of reasoning might be that because of your knowledge of IS, you will be able to facilitate cost savings that more than compensate for your salary.

In truth, few of the ideas that you generate for a potential employer will be feasible or pragmatically useful. The fact that you are thinking creatively, however, will indicate to a potential employer that you have initiative and are grappling with the problems that real businesses have. As this course progresses, keep thinking about competitive advantage, and strive to understand how the topics you study can help you to accomplish, personally, one or more of the principles in Figure 3-9.

## DISCUSSION QUESTIONS

**1.** Summarize the efforts you have taken thus far to build an employment record that will lead to job offers after graduation.

**2.** Considering the first three principles in Figure 3-9, describe one way in which you have a competitive advantage over your classmates. If you do not have such a competitive advantage, describe actions you can take to obtain one.

**3.** In order to build your network, you can use your status as a student to approach business professionals. Namely, you can contact them for help with an assignment or for career guidance. For example, suppose you want to work in banking and you know that your local bank has a customer information system. You could call the manager of that bank and ask him or her how that system creates a competitive advantage for the bank. You also could ask to interview other employees and go armed with the list in Figure 3-9. Describe two specific ways in which you can use your status as a student and the list in Figure 3-9 to build your network in this way.

**4.** Describe two ways that you can use student alliances to obtain a job. How can you use information systems to build, maintain, and operate such alliances?

*Source:* Brigida Soriano/Fotolia

# ACTIVE REVIEW

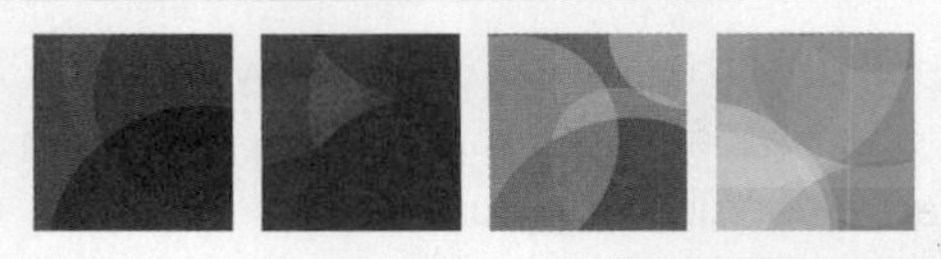

Use this Active Review to verify that you understand the ideas and concepts that answer the chapter's study questions.

## Q3-1 HOW DOES ORGANIZATIONAL STRATEGY DETERMINE INFORMATION SYSTEMS STRUCTURE?

Diagram and explain the relationship among industry structure, competitive strategy, value chains, business processes, and information systems. Working from the bottom up, explain how the knowledge you've gained in these first three chapters pertains to that diagram.

## Q3-2 WHAT FIVE FORCES DETERMINE INDUSTRY STRUCTURE?

Describe the original purpose of the five forces model and the different purpose for which it is used in this chapter. Name two types of forces and describe the strength factors for each. Name three competitive forces and describe the strength factors for each. Name two bargaining power forces. Summarize the five forces operating on Falcon Security.

## Q3-3 WHAT IS COMPETITIVE STRATEGY?

Describe four different strategies, as defined by Porter. For each strategy, offer an example of a company that uses that strategy. Describe Falcon Security's competitive strategy and justify it.

## Q3-4 HOW DOES COMPETITIVE STRATEGY DETERMINE VALUE CHAIN STRUCTURE?

Define the terms *value, margin,* and *value chain.* Explain why organizations that choose a differentiation strategy can use value to determine a limit on the amount of extra cost to pay for differentiation. Name the primary and support activities in the value chain and explain the purpose of each. Explain the concept of linkages.

## Q3-5 HOW DO VALUE CHAINS DETERMINE BUSINESS PROCESSES AND INFORMATION SYSTEMS?

What is the relationship between a value chain and a business process? How do business processes relate to competitive strategy? How do information systems relate to competitive strategy? Justify the comments in the two rows labeled "Supporting business process" in Figure 3-8.

## Q3-6 HOW DO INFORMATION SYSTEMS PROVIDE COMPETITIVE ADVANTAGES?

List and briefly describe eight principles of competitive advantage. Consider your college bookstore, and list one application of each of the eight principles. Strive to include examples that involve information systems.

## How does the **knowledge** in this chapter help **you?**

Explain in your own words how Falcon Security's competitive strategy is threatened by relying on a few large industrial accounts. Describe Falcon Security's planned response and summarize the problems Cam perceives with that response. Recommend a course of action for Falcon Security. Use Cam's idea of diversifying the type of work the company does to illustrate your answer.

## KEY TERMS AND CONCEPTS

MyMISLab™

To complete the problems with the ✪, go to EOC Discussion Questions in the MyLab.

## USING YOUR KNOWLEDGE

✪ **3-1.** Suppose you decide to start a business that recruits students for summer jobs. You will match available students with available jobs. You need to learn what positions are available and which students are available for filling those positions. In starting your business, you know you will be competing with local newspapers, Craigslist (*www.craigslist.org*), and your college. You will probably have other local competitors as well.

**a.** Analyze the structure of this industry according to Porter's five forces model.

**b.** Given your analysis in part a, recommend a competitive strategy.

**c.** Describe the primary value chain activities as they apply to this business.

**d.** Describe a business process for recruiting students.

**e.** Describe information systems that could be used to support the business process in part d.

**f.** Explain how the process you described in part d and the system you described in part e reflect your competitive strategy.

✪ **3-2.** Consider the two different bike rental companies in Q3-4. Think about the bikes that they rent. Clearly, the student bikes will be just about anything that can be ridden out of the shop. The bikes for the business executives, however, must be new, shiny, clean, and in tip-top shape.

**a.** Compare and contrast the operations value chains of these two businesses as they pertain to the management of bicycles.

**b.** Describe a business process for maintaining bicycles for both businesses.

**c.** Describe a business process for acquiring bicycles for both businesses.

**d.** Describe a business process for disposing of bicycles for both businesses.

**e.** What roles do you see for information systems in your answers to the earlier questions? The information systems can be those you develop within your company or they can be those developed by others, such as Craigslist.

✪ **3-3.** Samantha Green owns and operates Twigs Tree Trimming Service. Samantha graduated from the forestry program of a nearby university and worked for a large landscape design firm, performing tree trimming and removal. After several years of experience, she bought her own truck, stump grinder, and other equipment and opened her own business in St. Louis, Missouri.

Although many of her jobs are one-time operations to remove a tree or stump, others are recurring, such as trimming a tree or groups of trees every year or every other year. When business is slow, she calls former clients to remind them of her services and of the need to trim their trees on a regular basis.

Samantha has never heard of Michael Porter or any of his theories. She operates her business "by the seat of her pants."

**a.** Explain how an analysis of the five competitive forces could help Samantha.

**b.** Do you think Samantha has a competitive strategy? What competitive strategy would seem to make sense for her?

**c.** How would knowledge of her competitive strategy help her sales and marketing efforts?

**d.** Describe, in general terms, the kind of information system that she needs to support sales and marketing efforts.

## COLLABORATION EXERCISE 3

*Read Chapter Extensions 1 and 2 if you have not already done so. Meet with your team and build a collaboration IS that uses tools like Google Docs, SharePoint, or other collaboration tools. Do not forget the need for procedures and team training. Now, using that IS, answer the questions below.*

Figure 3-15 shows the business process and related information systems for the high-value bike rental company described in Figure 3-8. The small cylinders (⛁) represent a computer database, the most common type of repository.

In terms of Porter's value chain model, this process involves both the sales and operations activities. The bike rental company uses information systems to maintain customer data in the Customer database and bike inventory data in the Bike Inventory database and to transmit hotel charge data to the Hotel Billing system.

Each information system consists of all five IS components. Consider, for example, the information system for processing the Bike Inventory database. With regard to hardware, the database itself will be stored on a computer, and it will be accessed from other computers or computing devices, such as cash registers or handheld scanning devices (possibly used to check bikes in). Computer programs will provide forms for the system users to query and update the database. Other computer programs will be used to manage the database. (You will learn about such programs in Chapter 5.) Data, the third component of an information system, will be stored in the database. Each employee will be trained on procedures for using the system. For example, the sales clerk will learn how to query the database to determine what bikes are available and how to determine promising up-sell candidates. Finally, the people component will consist of the clerks in the rental shop as well as any support personnel for maintaining the inventory system.

Information systems that support the Customer database and those that interface with the Hotel Billing system will also have the five IS components. (By the way, whenever you consider the development or use of an information system, it is good practice to think about these five components.)

As stated in this chapter, business processes must generate more value than their cost. If they do not—if the margin of a business process is negative—then either costs must be reduced or the value increased. Considering the business process in Figure 3-15, one possibility for reducing costs is to eliminate rental personnel. Bicycles could be placed on racks having locks that customers can open with their hotel room keys; the bike would be rented until the customer places the bike back on the rack. Another possibility is to increase the value of the process. The rental agency could decide to rent additional types of equipment or perhaps to sell clothing or food and beverages.

Using your collaboration IS, work with your team to answer the following questions.

**3-4.** Explain the relationship between value and cost according to the Porter model. When does it make sense to add cost to a business process?

**3-5.** Suppose you are told that the business process in Figure 3-15 has a negative margin. Explain what that means. Suppose the margin of some business process is a negative \$1 million. If costs are reduced by \$1.2 million, will the margin necessarily be positive? Explain why or why not.

**Figure 3-15**
Rental Process for High-Value Bike Rental

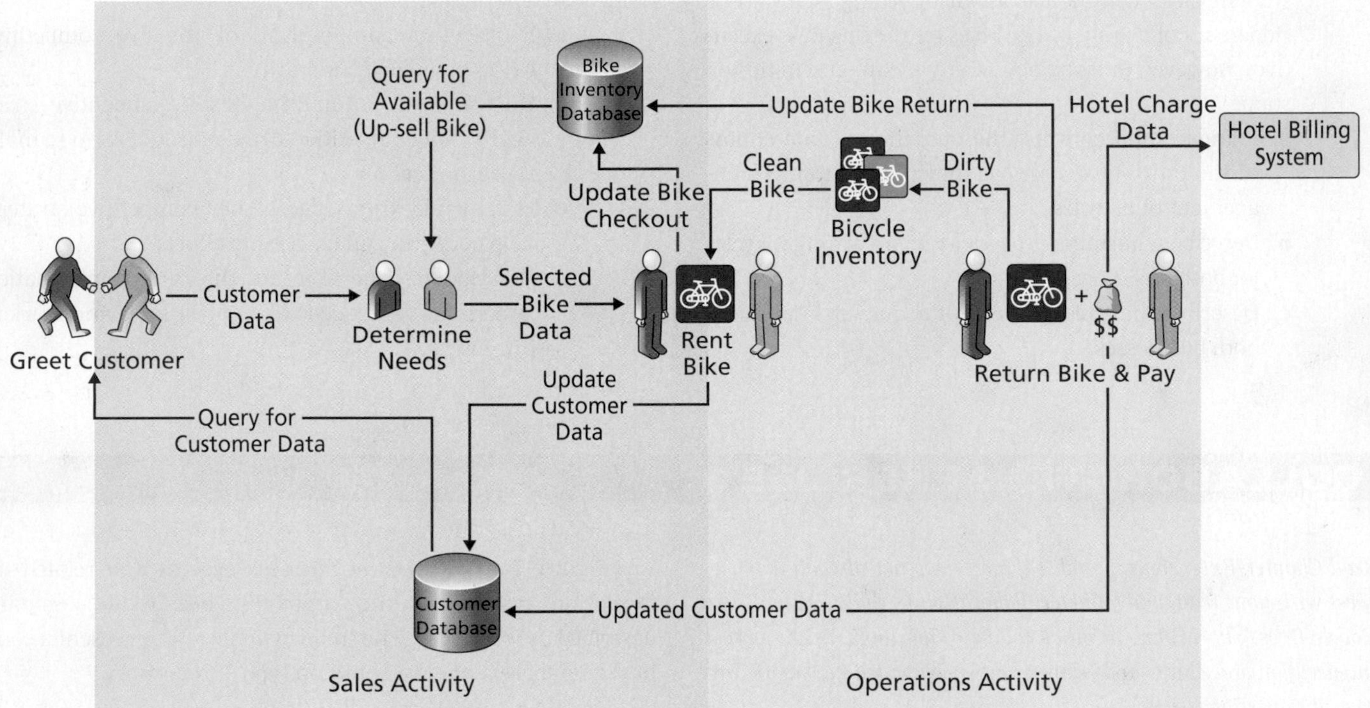

**3-6.** Consider the alternative of replacing the rental personnel from the business process in Figure 3-15.

**a.** Describe changes that will need to be made to the process documented in Figure 3-15. You can download a copy of this Visio diagram from this text's Web site at *www.pearsonhighered.com/kroenke*.

**b.** Would eliminating the rental personnel change the competitive strategy of this company? Is it possible to be a high-value company with no rental personnel? Explain why or why not.

**c.** Would eliminating the rental personnel necessarily reduce costs? What costs would increase as a result of this change?

**3-7.** Consider the alternative of increasing the value delivered by existing rental personnel. The text suggests possibly renting more kinds of equipment or selling items of use to guests who are renting bicycles, but consider other options as well.

**a.** Describe five ways that you think the existing personnel could increase the value of this business process.

**b.** For the five alternatives you developed in part a, name and describe criteria for selecting among them.

**c.** Using your criteria in part b, evaluate the alternatives you identified in part a and select the best one. Explain your selection.

**d.** Redraw Figure 3-15 for the alternative you selected in part c.

## CASE STUDY 3

### The Amazon of Innovation

On Cyber Monday, December 1, 2014, Amazon.com customers ordered more than 18 toys per *second*. And almost 60 percent of Amazon's holiday shoppers bought gifts using a mobile device. This contributed to a 20 percent increase in Amazon's total annual sales of $89B. Amazon's last order for the holiday season was placed on December 24 at 10:24 PM and was delivered at 11:06 PM just in time for Christmas.

You may think of Amazon as simply an online retailer, and that is indeed where the company has achieved most of its success. To do this, Amazon had to build an enormous supporting infrastructure—just imagine the information systems and fulfillment facilities needed to ship 36.8 million items on a single day. That infrastructure, however, is needed only during the busy holiday season. Most of the year, Amazon is left with excess infrastructure capacity. Starting in 2000, Amazon began to lease some of that capacity to other companies. In the process, it played a key role in the creation of what are termed *cloud services*, which you will learn about in Chapter 6. For now, just think of cloud services as computer resources somewhere out in the Internet that are leased on flexible terms.

Today, Amazon's business lines can be grouped into three major categories:

- Online retailing
- Order fulfillment
- Cloud services

Consider each.

Amazon created the business model for online retailing. It began as an online bookstore, but every year since 1998 it has added new product categories. The company is involved in all aspects of online retailing. It sells its own inventory. It incentivizes you, via the Associates program, to sell its inventory as well. Or it will help you sell your inventory within its product pages or via one of its consignment venues. Online auctions are the major aspect of online sales in which Amazon does not participate. It tried auctions in 1999, but it could never make inroads against eBay.[6]

Today, it's hard to remember how much of what we take for granted was pioneered by Amazon. "Customers who bought this, also bought that"; online customer reviews; customer ranking of customer reviews; books lists; Look Inside the Book; automatic free shipping for certain orders or frequent customers; and Kindle books and devices were all novel concepts when Amazon introduced them (Figure 3-16).

Amazon's retailing business operates on very thin margins. Products are usually sold at a discount from the stated retail price, and 2-day shipping is free for Amazon Prime members (who pay an annual fee of $99). How does it do it? For one, Amazon drives its employees incredibly hard. Former employees claim the hours are long, the pressure is severe, and the workload is heavy. But what else? It comes down to Moore's Law and the innovative use of nearly free data processing, storage, and communication.

In addition to online retailing, Amazon also sells order fulfillment services. You can ship your inventory to an Amazon warehouse and access Amazon's information systems just as if they were yours. Using technology known as Web services, your order processing information systems can directly integrate, over the Web, with Amazon's inventory, fulfillment, and shipping applications. Your customers need not know that Amazon played any role at all. You can also sell that same inventory using Amazon's retail sales applications.

Amazon Web Services (AWS) allow organizations to lease time on computer equipment in very flexible ways. Amazon's

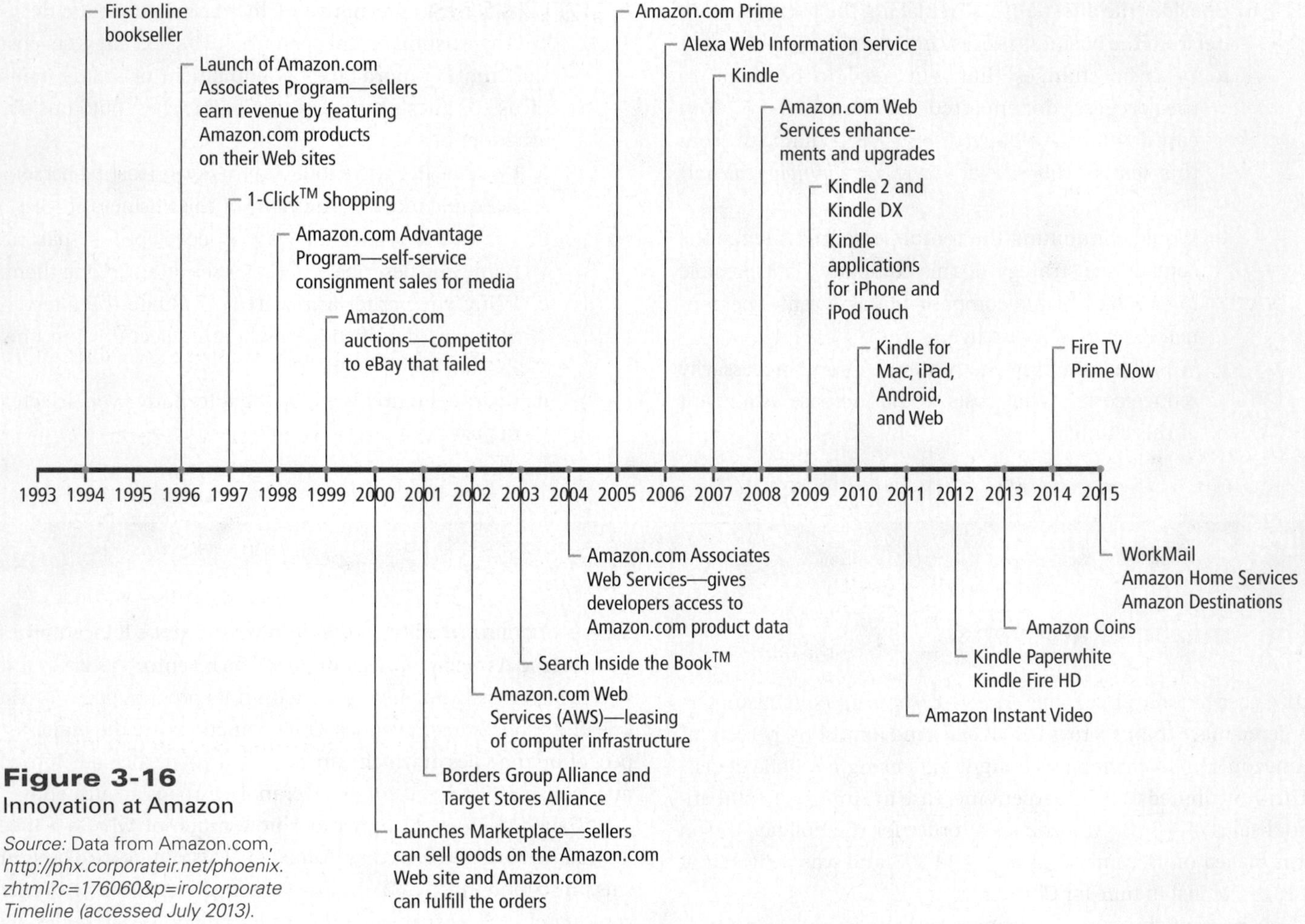


**Figure 3-16**
Innovation at Amazon
*Source:* Data from Amazon.com, *http://phx.corporateir.net/phoenix.zhtml?c=176060&p=irolcorporate Timeline (accessed July 2013).*

Elastic Cloud 2 (EC2) enables organizations to expand and contract the computer resources they need within minutes. Amazon has a variety of payment plans, and it is possible to buy computer time for less than a penny an hour. Key to this capability is the ability for the leasing organization's computer programs to interface with Amazon's to automatically scale up and scale down the resources leased. For example, if a news site publishes a story that causes a rapid ramp-up of traffic, that news site can, programmatically, request, configure, and use more computing resources for an hour, a day, a month, whatever.

With its Kindle devices, Amazon has become both a vendor of tablets and, even more importantly in the long term, a vendor of online music and video. And to induce customers to buy Kindle apps, in 2013 Amazon introduced its own currency, Amazon Coins. In 2014, Amazon opened a 3D printing store from which customers can customize their own toys, jewelry, dog bones, and dozens of other products. It also made a push to provide video services by introducing Fire TV.[7]

In 2015, Amazon introduced WorkMail, a potential cloud-based replacement for Microsoft Exchange. It also introduced Amazon Home Services (local professional services), Amazon Destinations (travel site), and Amazon Dash (a one-button reordering device).[8]

Finally, Jeff Bezos announced in 2014 that Amazon was experimenting with package delivery using drones, a service called Prime Air.[9] In March 2015, the U.S. Federal Aviation Administration gave Amazon permission to start testing its drones in the United States.[10] But drone delivery is something that will happen in the future; consider a business service that Amazon.com is offering right now.

## Fulfillment by Amazon (FBA)

Fulfillment by Amazon (FBA) is an Amazon service by which other sellers can ship goods to Amazon warehouses for stocking, order packaging, and shipment. FBA customers pay a fee for the service as well as for inventory space. Amazon uses its own inventory management and order fulfillment business processes and information systems to fulfill the FBA customers' orders.

FBA customers can sell their goods on Amazon.com, sell them via their own sales channels, or both. If the FBA

| | FBA Costs[11] |
|---|---|
| Order handling (per order) | $1.00 |
| Pick & pack (per item) | $1.04 |
| Weight handling (per pound) | Between $0.50 for less than 1 pound, to $1.59 plus $0.39 per pound for items over 2 pounds |
| Storage (cubic foot per month) | $0.51 between January and September and $0.68 from October to December |

customer sells on Amazon.com, Amazon will provide customer service for order processing (handling returns, fixing erroneously packed orders, answering customer order queries, and the like).

The costs for Fulfillment by Amazon depend on the type and size of the goods to be processed. The FBA fees for standard-size products as of February 2015 are shown in the table.

If goods are sold via Amazon.com, Amazon uses its own information systems to drive the order fulfillment process. However, if the goods are sold via an FBA customer's sales channel, then the FBA customer must connect its own information systems with those at Amazon. Amazon provides a standardized interface by which this is done called Amazon Marketplace Web Service (MWS). Using Web-standard technology (see Chapter 6), FBA customers' order and payment data are directly linked to Amazon's information systems.

FBA enables companies to outsource order fulfillment to Amazon, thus avoiding the cost of developing their own processes, facilities, and information systems for this purpose.

## QUESTIONS

**3-8.** Based on the facts presented in this case, what do you think is Amazon.com's competitive strategy? Justify your answer.

**3-9.** Jeff Bezos, CEO of Amazon.com, has stated that the best customer support is none. What does that mean?

**3-10.** Suppose you work for Amazon or a company that takes innovation as seriously as Amazon does. What do you suppose is the likely reaction to an employee who says to his or her boss, "But, I don't know how to do that!"?

**3-11.** Using your own words and your own experience, what skills and abilities do you think you need to have to thrive at an organization like Amazon?

**3-12.** What should UPS and FedEx be doing in response to Amazon.com's interest in drone delivery?

**3-13.** Summarize the advantages and disadvantages for brick-and-mortar retailers to sell items via Amazon.com. Would you recommend that they do so?

**3-14.** If a brick-and-mortar retailer were to use FBA, what business processes would it not need to develop? What costs would it save?

**3-15.** If a brick-and-mortar retailer were to use FBA, what information systems would it not need to develop? What costs would it save?

**3-16.** If a brick-and-mortar retailer were to use FBA, how would it integrate its information systems with Amazon's? (To add depth to your answer, Google the term *Amazon MWS.*)

## MyMISLab™

Go to the Assignments section of your MyLab to complete these writing exercises.

**3-17.** YourFire, Inc., is a small business owned by Curt and Julie Robards. Based in Brisbane, Australia, YourFire manufactures and sells a lightweight camping stove called the YourFire. Curt, who previously worked as an aerospace engineer, invented and patented a burning nozzle that enables the stove to stay lit in very high winds—up to 90 miles per hour. Julie, an industrial designer by training, developed an elegant folding design that is small, lightweight, easy to set up, and very stable. Curt and Julie manufacture the stove in their garage, and they sell it directly to their customers over the Internet and via phone.

**a.** Explain how an analysis of the five competitive forces could help YourFire.

**b.** What does YourFire's competitive strategy seem to be?

**c.** Briefly summarize how the primary value chain activities pertain to YourFire. How should the company design these value chains to conform to its competitive strategy?

**d.** Describe business processes that YourFire needs in order to implement its marketing and sales and also its service value chain activities.

**e.** Describe, in general terms, information systems to support your answer to part d.

**3-18.** A friend of yours from college, who you haven't talked to in three years, sends you an email asking you to meet him for lunch. He says he's got a great idea for a business and wants to run it by you. At first you're hesitant because your friend, while obviously intelligent, doesn't always think things though. You agree to meet for lunch and talk about the idea. At lunch he explains that he's been developing new flexible screens for his employer that are incredibly tough, waterproof, and use very little energy. His idea is to use these new flexible screens to create wearable computing clothing that can connect directly to smartphones and push ads, promotions, and video. His only problem is that he knows nothing about business. He's not sure where to start.

**a.** Explain how you could use the five forces model to help your friend understand the potential success of his wearable flex screens.

**b.** How might understanding the unique forces affecting this industry determine the competitive advantage for your friend's new company?

# ENDNOTES

1. Michael Porter, *Competitive Strategy: Techniques for Analyzing Industries and Competitors* (New York: Free Press, 1980).
2. Michael Porter, *Competitive Strategy* (New York: Free Press, 1980).
3. Chris Welch, "Mercedes Built a Self-Driving Truck That Could Save Thousands of Lives Every Year," *The Verge*, October 7, 2014, accessed April 10, 2015, *www.theverge.com/2014/10/7/6939809/mercedes-self-driving-truck-could-save-thousands-lives-each-year*.
4. Lee Matthews, "Amazon Files Patent for 3D Printing Delivery Trucks," *Geek.com*, February 25, 2015, accessed April 10, 2015, *www.geek.com/news/amazon-files-patent-for-3d-printing-delivery-trucks-1616525*.
5. Maxwell Wessel, "Making Sense of Uber's $40 Billion Valuation," *HBR.org*, December 10, 2014, accessed April 10, 2015, *https://hbr.org/2014/12/making-sense-of-ubers-40-billion-valuation*.
6. For a fascinating glimpse of this story from someone inside the company, see "Early Amazon: Auctions" at *http://glinden.blogspot.com/2006/04/early-amazon-auctions.html*, accessed August 2012.
7. *www.amazon.com/b?ie=UTF8&node=8323871011*
8. Andy Meek, "Amazon's Roadmap for 2015: Move Fast, Launch as Much as Possible," *BGR Media*, April 24, 2015, accessed May 16, 2015, *https://bgr.com/2015/04/24/amazon-earnings-q1-2015-analysis-roadmap*.
9. Marcus Wholsen, "Jeff Bezos Says Amazon Is Seriously Serious About Drone Deliveries," *Wired*, accessed May 22, 2014, *www.wired.com/2014/04/amazon-delivery-drones*.
10. Bart Jansen, "FAA Approves Amazon Drone Research Again," *USA Today*, accessed April 30, 2015, *www.usatoday.com/story/money/2015/04/09/faa-amazon-drone-approval-prime-air/25534485*.
11. Fulfillment by Amazon Fee Changes 2015," Amazon.com, accessed April 30, 2015, *www.amazon.com/gp/help/customer/display.html/?nodeId=201119410*.

# part 2
# Information Technology

***The next three*** chapters address the technology that underlies information systems. You may think that such technology is unimportant to you as a business professional. However, as you will see, today's managers and business professionals work with information technology all the time, as consumers, if not in a more involved way.

This could happen to you

Chapter 4 discusses hardware, software, and open source alternatives and defines basic terms and fundamental computing concepts. It briefly touches on new developments in self-driving cars, 3D printing, and the Internet of Things.

Chapter 5 addresses the data component of information systems by describing database processing. You will learn essential database terminology and be introduced to techniques for processing databases. We will also introduce data modeling because you may be required to evaluate data models for databases that others develop for you.

Chapter 6 continues the discussion of computing devices begun in Chapter 4 and describes data communications, Internet technologies, and the cloud. It also addresses potential security problems that may come from using the cloud.

The purpose of these three chapters is to teach you technology sufficient for you to be an effective IT consumer, like Mateo, Joni, Cam, and Alexis at Falcon Security. You will learn basic terms, fundamental

*Source*: Top: Julia Tim/Fotolia; Bottom: VIGE.CO/Shutterstock

concepts, and useful frameworks so that you will have the knowledge to ask good questions and make appropriate requests of the information systems professionals who will serve you.

It's difficult to stay up to date on the latest technology changes because things are changing so quickly. Every year a slew of new innovations come out. Some of them may represent real threats to your organization's strategy. Others may represent potential new opportunities for growth. It's important to be able to understand the strategic implications these new technologies represent. You need to be able to ask the right questions.

The concepts and frameworks presented in these chapters will be far more useful to you than learning the latest technology trends. Trends come and go. The technology you're using now will be outdated in 10 years. Understanding how to assess the business implications behind any new innovation will be a benefit to you throughout your entire career.

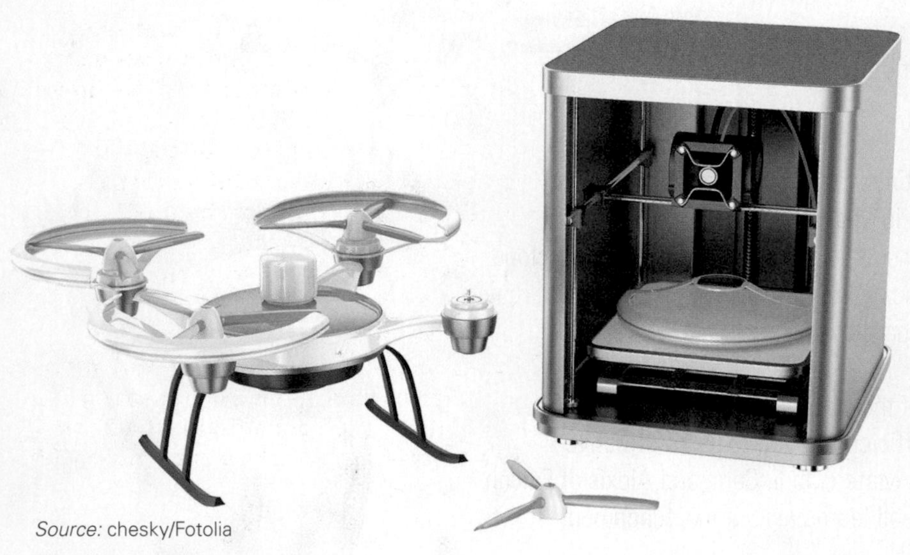

*Source:* chesky/Fotolia

# Hardware and Software

**This could happen to you**

Cam Forset, the operations manager of Falcon Security, asked Mateo Thomas, CEO, Joni Campbell, CFO, and Alexis Moore, head of sales, to come down to the small hangar bay to see how the testing of the new 3D-printed drone is coming along. Mateo asked Cam to investigate the possibility of using 3D-printed parts to make drones in-house rather than buy them from vendors. This could be a tremendous cost-savings opportunity and give the company greater flexibility in updating its current fleet of drones.

Cam waves to Mateo and Joni to come over and look at the screen that she and Alexis are looking at. The screen is showing a live video feed from the new drone as it flies around the perimeter of the building.

"Well, it works—sort of." Cam says to Mateo and Joni with a forced smile. "It's *pretty* stable, and we can get streaming video. I just wish it hadn't taken 2 weeks to get it running." Cam's voice has an undeniably displeased tone.

"That's OK. What was the total cost to make it?" Mateo asks.

"Well, this specific quad cost nearly nothing. We harvested all of the internals from a couple broken quads we had lying around. Everything else we printed." Cam points to a rack of dismantled quadcopters. "We found some free designs on the Web, but we had to make some changes so they would work with our internals."

"Well that's good news, isn't it?" Mateo asks.

"Well, not really," Cam says with a skeptical tone. "If we wanted to build more drones, we'd need to harvest more parts from existing drones or buy generic parts and try to see if they'll work together."

Joni and Mateo both look confused. Mateo shakes his head and asks, "Well, why didn't you build it with generic parts in the first place?"

"Well, honestly, we weren't sure we could make it work even if we used existing internal components. I've never *made* a quadcopter before," Cam says flatly. "We ended up printing about 20 parts, but we still needed motors, a speed controller, a flight control board, a radio transmitter and receiver, propellers, batteries, and a charger."

"We also needed to make sure it could integrate with our internal systems. We didn't want to start experimenting with generic components until we knew we could actually make a quad that could fly," she adds.

# STUDY QUESTIONS

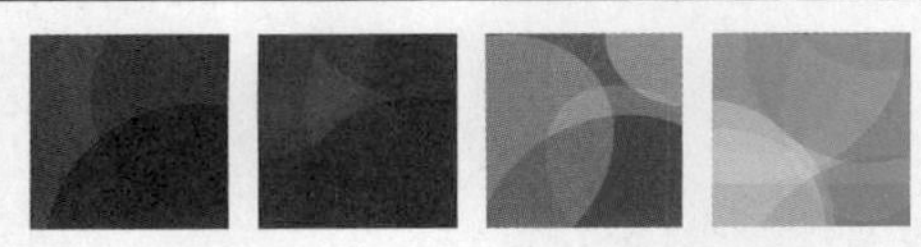

**Q4-1 WHAT DO BUSINESS PROFESSIONALS NEED TO KNOW ABOUT COMPUTER HARDWARE?**

**Q4-2 HOW CAN NEW HARDWARE AFFECT COMPETITIVE STRATEGIES?**

**Q4-4 WHAT DO BUSINESS PROFESSIONALS NEED TO KNOW ABOUT SOFTWARE?**

**Q4-5 IS OPEN SOURCE SOFTWARE A VIABLE ALTERNATIVE?**

## How does the **knowledge** in this chapter help **you?**

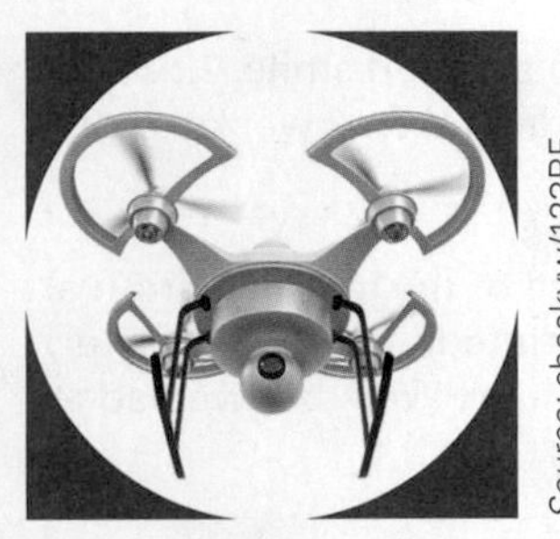

Source: cheskyw/123RF

**"3D printing our own drones isn't going to save us enough money."**

"So your next step is to take out the existing internal components and replace them with generic parts to see if they will work, right?" Mateo asks.

"Well..." Cam starts to say.

Joni interrupts, "It probably won't matter if the generic components work or not. Essentially we've just replaced the frame, skids, and a few other parts to hold the camera. We still have to buy the other nonprintable component parts. Those won't be cheap. Add in the additional labor costs to assemble and test each quad..." she trails off.

"Plus the time and labor to integrate them with our internal systems," Alexis picks up her train of thought. "That won't be easy or cheap."

"Exactly," Cam says. "3D printing our own drones isn't going to save us enough money. There aren't enough parts that can be replaced. Yes, the passive recharging platform we developed using 3D-printed parts was a huge success. It has allowed us to automate the recharging process and extend the reach of our drones. But I just don't think 3D printing our own drones is going reduce our hardware costs enough to justify us becoming a drone manufacturer."

Mateo looks disappointed. "Well, maybe you're right. I really wish there was some way to make it work. It just seems like we keep burning through cash buying dozens of drones that become obsolete in a few years. It's really frustrating being on the cutting edge."

"You mean the bleeding edge... right?" Joni says with a smirk.

**Optional Extensions for this chapter are • CE3: Mobile Systems 401 • CE4: Introduction to Microsoft Excel 2013 417**

## Q4-1 WHAT DO BUSINESS PROFESSIONALS NEED TO KNOW ABOUT COMPUTER HARDWARE?

**Business professionals need to be aware of the latest hardware developments. For more information, see the Guide on pages 112–113.**

Most people think of computer hardware as a laptop, a desktop, a server, or maybe even a tablet. As time passes, however, the way we envision computer hardware is changing. Take phones as an example. Twenty-five years ago, phones were strictly used for voice communication. No one would have considered a phone a piece of computer hardware.

Fast-forward to today. Smartphones have substantial processing power, the ability to connect to networks, internal memory, and virtual keyboards and can interconnect with other devices. Now a "phone" is essentially a powerful piece of computing hardware. Computing hardware is also being integrated into other devices, such as watches, glasses, TVs, cars, and even toothbrushes.

**Computer hardware** consists of electronic components and related gadgetry that input, process, output, and store data according to instructions encoded in computer programs or software. All hardware today has more or less the same components, at least to the level that is important to us. We'll begin with a look at those components, and then we'll quickly survey basic types of hardware and the capacity of these devices.

### HARDWARE COMPONENTS

Every computer has a **central processing unit (CPU)**, which is sometimes called "the brain" of the computer. Although the design of the CPU has nothing in common with the anatomy of animal brains, this description is helpful because the CPU does have the "smarts" of the machine. The CPU selects instructions, processes them, performs arithmetic and logical comparisons, and stores results of operations in memory. Some computers have two or more CPUs. A computer with two CPUs is called a **dual-processor** computer. **Quad-processor** computers have four CPUs. Some high-end computers have 16 or more CPUs.

CPUs vary in speed, function, and cost. Hardware vendors such as Intel, Advanced Micro Devices, and National Semiconductor continually improve CPU speed and capabilities while reducing CPU costs (as discussed under Moore's Law in Chapter 1). Whether you or your department needs the latest, greatest CPU depends on the nature of your work.

The CPU works in conjunction with **main memory**. The CPU reads data and instructions from memory and then stores the results of computations in main memory. Main memory is sometimes called **RAM,** for random access memory.

In addition to RAM and one or more CPUs, all computers also include **storage hardware**, which is used to save data and programs. Magnetic disks (also called hard disks) are the most common storage device. Solid-state storage (also known as an SSD drive) is much faster than a hard drive and gaining in popularity, but is several times more expensive. USB flash drives are small, portable solid-state storage devices that can be used to back up data and transfer it from one computer to another. Optical disks such as CDs and DVDs are also popular portable storage media.

### TYPES OF HARDWARE

Figure 4-1 lists the basic types of hardware. **Personal computers (PCs)** are classic computing devices that are used by individuals. In the past, PCs were the primary computer type used in business. Today, they are gradually being supplanted by tablets and other mobile devices, although many PC users still exist. The Mac Pro is an example of a modern PC. Apple brought **tablets** to prominence with the iPad. In 2012, Microsoft announced Surface and Google announced the Nexus series, all tablets.

Moving down the list of hardware, a mobile device called a phablet combines the functionality of a smartphone with the larger screen of a tablet. Devices like Samsung's Galaxy Note or Apple's iPhone 6 Plus would fall into this crossover category. Smartphones are cell phones with

**Figure 4-1**
Basic Types of Hardware

| Hardware Type | Example(s) |
|---|---|
| Personal computer (PC)<br>*Including desktops and laptops* | Apple Mac Pro |
| Tablet<br>*Including e-book readers* | iPad, Microsoft Surface, Google Nexus, Kindle Fire |
| Phablet | Samsung Galaxy Note, iPhone 6 Plus |
| Smartphone | Samsung Galaxy, iPhone |
| Server | Dell PowerEdge 12G server |
| Server farm | Racks of servers (Figure 4-2) |

processing capability; the Samsung Galaxy S6, or iPhone 6 are good examples. Today, because it's hard to find a cell phone that isn't "smart," people often just call them phones.

A **server** is a computer that is designed to support processing requests from many remote computers and users. A server is essentially a PC on steroids, and it differs from a PC principally because of what it does. The relationship between PCs and servers is similar to the relationship between clients and servers at a typical restaurant: In short, servers take requests from clients and then bring them things. In restaurants, these things are food, drinks, and silverware. Similarly, in computing environments, servers can send Web pages, email, files, or data to PCs or other devices. PCs, tablets, and smartphones that access servers are called **clients**. As of 2015, one good example of a server is the Dell PowerEdge server.

Finally, a **server farm** is a collection of, typically, thousands of servers. (See Figure 4-2.) Server farms are often placed in large truck trailers that hold 5,000 servers or more. Typically a trailer has two large cables coming out of it; one is for power, and the other is for data communications. The operator of the farm backs a trailer into a pre-prepared slab (in a warehouse or sometimes out in the open air), plugs in the power and communications cables, and, voilà, thousands of servers are up and running!

Increasingly, server infrastructure is delivered as a service via the Internet, which is often referred to as *the cloud*. We will discuss cloud computing in Chapter 6, after you have some knowledge of data communications.

**Figure 4-2**
Server Farm
*Source:* © Andrew Twort/Alamy

**Figure 4-3**
Bits Are Easy to Represent Physically

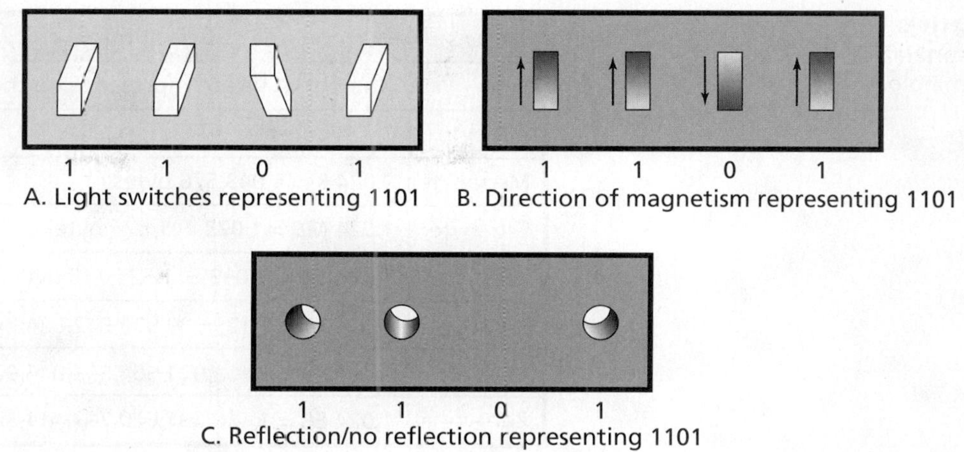


The capacities of each type of computer hardware are specified according to data units, as you'll see in the section that follows.

## COMPUTER DATA

Computers represent data using **binary digits**, also called **bits**. A bit is either a zero or a one. Bits are used for computer data because they are easy to represent physically, as illustrated in Figure 4-3. A switch can be either closed or open. A computer can be designed so that an open switch represents zero and a closed switch represents one. Or the orientation of a magnetic field can represent a bit: magnetism in one direction represents a zero, while magnetism in the opposite direction represents a one. Alternatively, with optical media, small pits are burned onto the surface of the disk so that they will reflect light. In a given spot, a reflection indicates a one, whereas no reflection indicates a zero.

### Computer Data Sizes

All forms of computer data are represented by bits. The data can be numbers, characters, currency amounts, photos, recordings, or whatever—all are simply a string of bits. For reasons that interest many but are irrelevant for future managers, bits are grouped into 8-bit chunks called **bytes**. For character data, such as the letters in a person's name, one character will fit into one byte. Thus, when you read a specification stating that a computing device has 100 million bytes of memory, you know that the device can hold up to 100 million characters.

Bytes are used to measure sizes of noncharacter data as well. Someone might say, for example, that a given picture is 100,000 bytes in size. This statement means the length of the bit string that represents the picture is 100,000 bytes or 800,000 bits (because there are 8 bits per byte).

The specifications for the data storage capacity of main memory, disks, and other computer devices are expressed in bytes. Figure 4-4 shows the set of abbreviations that are used to represent data storage capacity. A **kilobyte**, abbreviated **KB**, is a collection of 1,024 bytes. A **megabyte**, or **MB**, consists of 1,024 kilobytes. A **gigabyte**, or **GB**, is 1,024 megabytes; a **terabyte**, or **TB**, is 1,024 gigabytes; a **petabyte**, or **PB**, is 1,024 terabytes; an **exabyte**, or **EB**, is 1,024 petabytes; and a **zettabyte**, or **ZB**, is 1,024 exabytes. Sometimes you will see these definitions simplified to say that 1KB equals 1,000 bytes, 1MB equals 1,000KB, and so on. Such simplifications are incorrect, but they do ease the math.

To put these sizes in perspective, as of 2014, consider that Walmart stores about 2.5 PB worth of customer data.[1] Facebook processes about 600 TB each day, in a 300PB data warehouse.[2] The super-secret NSA data center in Utah is estimated to hold about 12 EB of data.[3] And Cisco estimates that annual global Internet traffic volume will exceed 1.6 ZB by the end of 2018.[4]

**Figure 4-4**
Important Storage-Capacity Terminology

| Term | Definition | Abbreviation |
|---|---|---|
| Byte | Number of bits to represent one character | |
| Kilobyte | 1,024 bytes | KB |
| Megabyte | 1,024 K = 1,048,576 bytes | MB |
| Gigabyte | 1,024 MB = 1,073,741,824 bytes | GB |
| Terabyte | 1,024 GB = 1,099,511,627,776 bytes | TB |
| Petabyte | 1,024 TB = 1,125,899,906,842,624 bytes | PB |
| Exabyte | 1,024 PB = 1,152,921,504,606,846,976 bytes | EB |
| Zettabyte | 1,024 EB = 1,180,591,620,717,411,303,424 bytes | ZB |

### Specifying Hardware with Computer Data Sizes and Processing Speeds

Computer disk capacities are specified according to the amount of data they can contain. Thus, a 500GB disk can contain up to 500GB of data and programs. There is some overhead, so the actual available storage capacity is not quite 500GB, but it's close enough.

Storage capacity isn't the only thing to consider when selecting a device; you can also purchase computers with CPUs of different speeds. CPU speed is expressed in cycles called **hertz**. In 2015, a slow personal computer had a speed of 3.0 Gigahertz, whereas a fast personal computer had a speed of 3.5+ Gigahertz, with dual processors. As predicted by Moore's Law, CPU speeds continually increase.

An employee who does only simple tasks such as word processing does not need a fast CPU; a 2.0 Gigahertz CPU will be fine. However, an employee who processes large, complicated spreadsheets; manipulates large database files; or edits large picture, sound, or video files needs a fast computer like a dual processor with 3.5 Gigahertz or more. Similarly, when it comes to data storage, employees whose work requires them to use many large applications at the same time need 12 GB or more of RAM. Others can do with less.

One last comment: A device's cache and main memory are **volatile**, meaning their contents are lost when power is off. In contrast, magnetic and optical disks are **nonvolatile**, meaning their contents survive when power is off. Thus, if you suddenly lose power, the contents of unsaved memory—say, documents that have been altered—will be lost. To better protect your data, get into the habit of frequently (every few minutes or so) saving documents or files that you are changing. Save your documents before your roommate trips over your power cord!

## Q4-2 HOW CAN NEW HARDWARE AFFECT COMPETITIVE STRATEGIES?

Organizations are interested in new hardware because they represent potential opportunities, or threats, to their ability to generate revenue. It's important to keep an eye on new tech hardware for the same reason you watch the weather forecast: You care about how the future will affect you. In the following sections, we'll look at three new hardware developments that have the potential to disrupt existing organizations: the Internet of Things, self-driving cars, and 3D printing.

### THE INTERNET OF THINGS

The first disruptive force that has the power to change business is the **Internet of Things (IoT)**. This is the idea that objects are becoming connected to the Internet so that they can interact with other devices, applications, or services. In other words, everyday objects are increasingly being embedded with hardware capable of sensing, processing, and transmitting data. These objects can then connect to a network and share data with any other application, service, or device.

Take your mobile phone, for example. It's probably a smartphone, but it wasn't always "smart." It started out as a simple device that just handled voice calls. Over time it became a **smart device** by adding more processing power, more memory, Internet access, Wi-Fi connectivity, and the ability to interconnect with other devices and applications (Figure 4-5). People thus began to use their mobile phones much differently than before. This shift also changed the way businesses operate. In 2014, for example, *Amazon.com* reported that more than 60 percent of its customers shopped using a mobile device.[5]

What happens when other devices become smart? How would your life change if you had access to a smart car, smart home appliances, or an entire smart building? Within a few short decades, it's possible that you could interact with nearly every object around you from your smartphone. In fact, your devices will be able to talk to other devices, anticipate your actions, make changes, and configure themselves.

This shift away from "dumb" devices to interconnected smart devices is not lost on businesses. Consumers like smart devices and are willing to pay more for them. Accordingly, businesses want to improve the existing devices they manufacture into smart devices and then sell them for twice as much. If they don't, someone else will.

The iPhone, for example, was introduced by Apple Inc. in 2007 when it was considered primarily a computing hardware and software company. When the iPhone was first released, the mobile phone market was already mature. Industry leaders could have created a smartphone, but they didn't. Apple's success with the iPhone was a shot across the bow of other phone manufacturers, and it fundamentally altered how people use their mobile phones and what sorts of devices they want to purchase. Just as the iPhone revolutionized the mobile phone industry, a wave of other smart devices is sure to revolutionize other industries as well.

**Figure 4-5**
Smartphone Development

*Source:* Grgroup/Fotolia

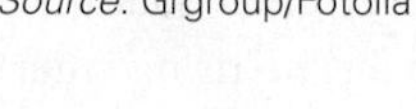

**Figure 4-6**
Microsoft's Redmond, WA, Campus
*Source:* Ian Dagnall/Alamy

### Impact of the Internet of Things

In the years to come, the impact of IoT will be felt by many different high-tech industries. Smart devices need microprocessors, memory, wireless network connections, power sources, and new software. These devices will also need new protocols, more bandwidth, and tighter security, and they will consume more energy.

A good example of this push toward smart devices is General Electric's (GE) Industrial Internet.[6] The Industrial Internet is a broad program focused on creating smart devices, analyzing data from these devices, and then making changes that increase efficiencies, reduce waste, and improve decision making. GE sees the greatest potential for smart devices in hospitals, power grids, manufacturing plants, and transportation. For instance, GE estimates that an average airline using smart devices in its jet aircraft could save an average of 2 percent in fuel consumption. The resulting fuel and carbon dioxide savings would be the equivalent of removing 10,000 cars from the road.[7]

Microsoft has also made tremendous gains using smart devices. The company has created a network of 125 smart buildings spread over 500 acres in Redmond, Washington (Figure 4-6).[8] This campus's operations center processes 500 million data transactions every day from 30,000 devices, including heaters, air conditioners, lights, fans, and doors. Thanks to this network, Microsoft engineers were able to reduce energy costs by 6 percent to 10 percent a year by identifying problems like wasteful lighting, competing heating and cooling systems, and rogue fans. For Microsoft, that's millions of dollars in savings.

What if every corporate building were a smart building? When you consider that 40 percent of the world's energy is consumed in corporate buildings, you can start to get an idea of the potentially immense cost savings.

## SELF-DRIVING CARS

The second disruptive force that could change the way businesses operate is self-driving cars. A **self-driving car** (also known as a driverless car) will use a variety of sensors to navigate like a traditional car but without human intervention. It will be full of advanced hardware and integrated software, and it will be the epitome of a mobile system. In fact, it will be so mobile that it will be able to move without anyone being inside (Figure 4-7).

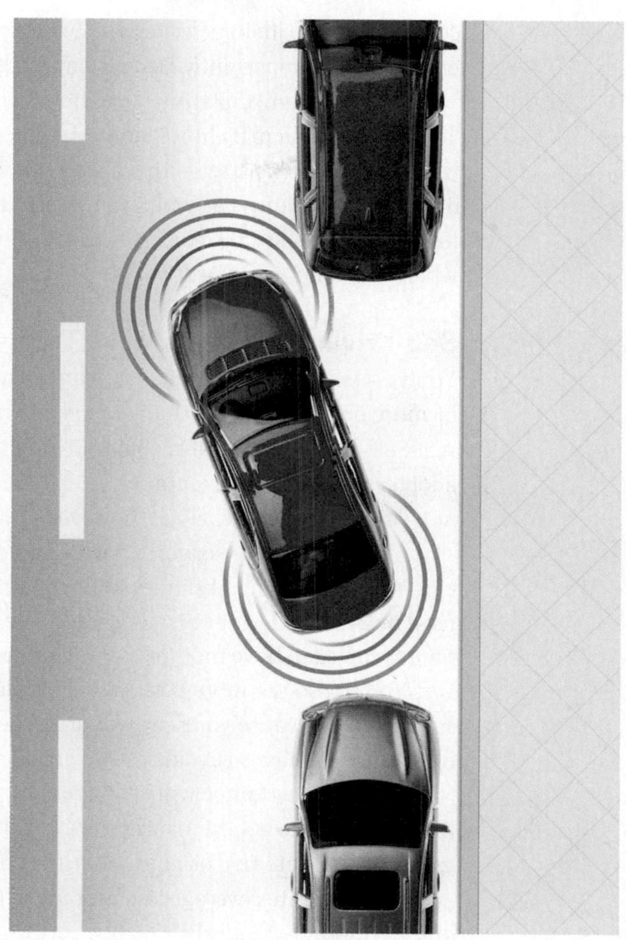

**Figure 4-7**
Future Cars Will Drive Themselves

*Source:* Dan Race/Fotolia

Believe it or not, self-driving cars are in your very near future. A recent report by KPMG and the Center for Automotive Research indicates that self-driving cars will be a reality as soon as 2019.[9] Google is shooting for 2018, and most auto manufacturers (Mercedes-Benz, Nissan, Audi, and BMW) say they will have self-driving cars by 2020.[10] As of 2014, Google's latest self-driving car is a two-seater with no steering wheel, brake pedals, or accelerator.[11] Google's prototype cars have logged more than 700,000 miles without a single accident. The Mercedes-Benz F 015 was the hit of the CES 2015 show when it drove itself on stage and opened its saloon-style doors revealing passenger seats facing each other. It looks like the race to develop self-driving cars is heating up. The competition will be fierce.

As we'll see in the following sections, self-driving cars will make things easier, cheaper, and safer. They'll also disrupt well-established industries.

## Self-driving Cars Will Make Things Easier

Imagine how a self-driving car will change the life of a typical family. For example, a self-driving car could allow Dad to review sales reports while "driving" to work. As a result, he'll be much less stressed out—and much more productive—during his commute than he was with his old car. The self-driving car could then drop off the kids at school—without Dad in the car—and return home to take Mom to work.

After work, the family could go shopping and be dropped off curbside at the store. No need to park anymore. Getting around town would be safer, too. While shopping, Dad might even get a message from his college-aged daughter saying that she needs him to send the car to pick her up at the airport. Dad will certainly be glad he doesn't have to drive all the way out there himself!

As Dad thinks about his new car, he might remember the days when he had to drive himself. It was a long and painful process. Now, the car plans the route for him, fills itself up with gas, communicates with intersections so he never gets a red light, and reroutes itself if there's an accident or traffic. Most importantly, Dad no longer gets mad at other drivers. Traveling is just easier now.

Later, the family plans a vacation to a distant locale. Taking the self-driving car is the way to go. No airport security lines; family members don't have to get frisked by overzealous TSA agents; they get comfortable seats that face each other; they don't have to pay for their bags; and they don't have to rent a car when they get to their destination. Plus, they can leave anytime they'd like. Sometimes, it's nice to leave for vacation at night and sleep while "driving." Driving isn't bad when you don't actually drive!

### Self-driving Cars Will Make Things Cheaper

You've seen how a self-driving car can make life easier. But what about cost? Will a self-driving car be more or less expensive than the car you have now?

Self-driving cars will probably be much less expensive over time than your current car. Early adopters will pay a premium when self-driving cars first hit the market, but that's true of most new products. As time passes, however, cost savings will show up in several ways.

In the preceding scenario, for example, you may have noticed that the family had only one car. This reflects the likelihood that self-driving cars will be used more effectively than cars are used now. Today, most cars sit dormant for 22 hours a day. Sharing a self-driving car could eliminate the need to have multiple cars. That's a big cost savings.

You'll also see more cost savings because self-driving cars will drive better than you. You'll save on fuel because your car will drive more efficiently (less braking, engine revving, and street racing!). You will also avoid costly traffic tickets, parking tickets, and DUI citations.

Your car insurance will drop dramatically. It may be so low that you won't even need it anymore. One of the largest insurers in the United States, Travelers, said, "Driverless cars or technologies that facilitate ride or home sharing, could disrupt the demand for our products from current customers, create coverage issues or impact the frequency or severity of losses, and we may not be able to respond effectively."[12]

They're probably right. Self-driving cars will probably take a big chunk out of the $100B paid each year in car insurance premiums. And they should. Your future self-driving car will be safer because its crash avoidance systems will apply the brakes before you're even aware of a problem. It will be able to know the exact locations, velocities, and routes of all cars within the vicinity. Automobile accidents may become a thing of the past.

### Self-driving Cars Will Make Things Safer

Yes, you read that right—safer. Currently, 90 percent of motor vehicle crashes are caused by human error.[13] Motor vehicle crashes are the leading cause of death for people ages 3 to 33. In fact, spending time driving may be the most dangerous thing you do all day.

In the future, however, your car will be able to see better than you, react more quickly than you, and have better information about your driving environment. It will be able to communicate with other cars around it, dynamically analyze traffic patterns, avoid construction sites, and contact emergency services if needed.

Self-driving cars will mean safer driving, fewer accidents, fewer drunk drivers, fewer road-rage incidents, and fewer auto–pedestrian accidents. Cars will be able to go faster with fewer crashes. In the future, "manual" driving may be a risky and expensive hobby.

### Self-driving Cars Will Disrupt Businesses

As the preceding discussion suggests, self-driving cars have the potential to disrupt several well-established industries. Self-driving cars may mean fewer cars on the road. Fewer cars on the road may mean fewer cars sold (affecting the transportation industry), fewer auto loans written (affecting the finance industry), fewer automobile insurance policies underwritten (affecting the insurance industry), fewer auto parts sold due to fewer accidents (manufacturing), and fewer parking lots (affecting the real estate industry). Also, if they didn't have to drive, consumers might take more trips by car than by plane or train (again affecting the transportation industry).

## New from CES 2015

What's new in hardware? It's the Consumer Electronics Show (CES) held in Las Vegas every January: 3,600 exhibitors and 170,000-plus hardware-gawking attendees whipped to frenzy by loud music, screaming video, and hyperventilating media. It's a show that only Las Vegas can do!

What's hot this year? How about:

1. **Mercedes-Benz F 015:** At the top of everyone's list of must-see innovations at CES 2015 was the new driverless Mercedes-Benz F 015. This isn't just a driverless car. It's one of the first cars designed specifically as a driverless vehicle, not just an adaptation of a traditional driver-centric vehicle. It's more like a futuristic silver carriage with saloon-style doors. Inside the F 015, passengers sit facing each other, chatting while the car does the driving. They are surrounded by interactive touch screens that can control the entire vehicle. Passengers can even control the car using hand gestures and eye movements.

   The F 015 is a fuel-cell plug-in hybrid with a range of about 680 miles. Those aren't stressful driving miles either. Passengers can chat, work, or even sleep the whole way. The Mercedes-Benz F 015 will likely change the way people think about travel.

   Oh, and the F 015 can talk too. Pedestrians walking in front of the F 015's hear its voice telling them that it's safe to cross in front of it. The F 015 then projects a crosswalk in front of the car to guide pedestrians across the street. If you want to see what cars will look like in 10 to 15 years from now, check out the F 015.

2. **Works with Nest:** Nest Labs made big strides over the past year after being acquired by Google in 2014 for $3.2B. Nest Labs is best known for its smart thermostat and smart smoke detector. But Nest Labs is quickly becoming known more broadly as a home automation company. Network-enabled smart devices using Nest standards can be controlled remotely and interact with other devices and applications.

   At the CES 2015 show, the list of "Works with Nest" partners grew beyond Whirlpool, LG, Mercedes-Benz, Logitech, and August Smart Lock. New companies included Pebble (smartwatch), Rachio (sprinklers), Interactive Voice (voice-activated alarm clock), and Life360 (smartphone tracking app). Nest Labs is positioning itself to be the leader in home automation services.

   As more IoT devices come online, expect to see them get the Works with Nest label. This will allow devices to dynamically communicate with each other to create new synergies that didn't exist before. Imagine your car telling your thermostat that you're 20 minutes away and that it should start warming the house up. Your bread maker is nearly done with a fresh loaf of bread, your lights are ready to turn on the instant you pull in the drive, and you're getting live streaming video of your dog playing in the backyard.

   The convergence between home automation and IoT is going to produce some really interesting products over the next couple of years. Watch for new announcements from Nest Labs at CES 2016.

*Source:* VECTORWORKS_ENTERPRISE/Shutterstock

3. **Composite Filaments:** MakerBot really pushed 3D printing ahead this year when it introduced several new *composite* filaments. These composite filaments combine traditional PLA (polylactic acid) thermoplastic with materials like wood, bronze, iron, and limestone. They can be used to 3D-print objects that look and behave like their real-world counterparts.

   Wood furniture can be printed, sanded, and stained just like real wood. And it feels like wood too. Metal objects like jewelry, tools, and parts can be printed and polished and look just like their pure-metal cousins. Even the limestone composite filament produces objects that look and feel like real limestone.

   MakerBot's new composite filaments are important because they make it economical to now print in metal, wood, and stone. In the past it was possible to 3D-print in metal, but metal laser sintering was expensive. These new composite filaments make it possible to print objects like a hammer that have both metal and wood parts. The downside is that printing with these new composite filaments requires a unique print head for each type of filament. For most consumers, the cost of an additional print head to print in each additional material will probably be a minor issue.

MakerBot's introduction of new composite filaments has the potential to push 3D printing beyond the use of hobbyists, inventors, and manufacturers. A reasonably priced 3D printer that can print more than 50 percent of the objects in a typical household could be a valuable home appliance.

## QUESTIONS

1. What would be the benefits of Mercedes-Benz's new "carriage"-type driverless car over a traditional car that has been converted to be driverless?
2. Why would Mercedes-Benz want its new driverless cars to talk to pedestrians?
3. How could a Nest thermostat save you money?
4. What advantages would a Nest-compliant washing machine have over a traditional one?
5. Why are 3D printers a potentially disruptive technology to manufacturing?
6. How could new composite filaments affect innovation, prototyping, and new product development?

On the other side of the coin, the production of self-driving cars will mean more jobs for engineers, programmers, and systems designers. There will be more computer hardware, sensors, and cameras in these vehicles.

Corporations may not completely see the far-reaching effects of self-driving cars on existing industries—but what about you? How will self-driving cars disrupt your personal life? Suppose you get married in a few years and have a child. Will your child ever drive a car? Will driving a "manual" car be too costly? Your potential offspring may never learn how to drive a car, but that may not be so strange after all. Do you know how to ride a horse? Your ancestors did.

## 3D PRINTING

The third disruptive force that has the power to change businesses is 3D printing. As you learned in Chapter 3, 3D printing alters the competitive landscape. Moreover, it may change the nature of businesses themselves. Think back to the Falcon Security case at the start of this chapter. The Falcon Security team chose to not make its own drones because doing so wasn't going to save the company enough money. It didn't want to use 3D printing to become a drone manufacturer.

While manufacturing wasn't right for Falcon, it is a viable option for some companies. Consider how Nike has used 3D printing to improve the way it designs and creates shoes. It recently used a 3D printer to create the world's first 3D-printed cleat plate for a shoe called the Nike Vapor Laser Talon.[14] Nike chose to use a 3D printer to produce the cleat because it could create the optimal geometric shape for optimal traction. Thus, using a 3D printer, Nike could design and produce a lighter, stronger cleat much more quickly than before.

3D printers have the potential to affect a broad array of industries beyond sporting equipment. You can get an idea of the scope of change when you realize that 3D printers can print in more than just plastics (Figure 4-8). They can print in metals, ceramics, foods, and biological material too.

At CES 2015, industry leader MakerBot announced it will begin selling composite filaments that can be used in its 3D printers. These new composite filaments combine traditional PLA (polylactic acid) thermoplastic with materials like wood, bronze, iron, and limestone. While each type of composite filament will require new 3D print head, the printed objects will look and behave like their real-world counterparts.

Take the ability to 3D-print in a variety of materials and look for opportunities across the aerospace, defense, automotive, entertainment, and healthcare industries. What happens

**Figure 4-8**
3D Printer
*Source:* Seraficus/Getty Images

when it becomes feasible to 3D-print extra-large objects like cars,[15] planes, boats, houses, and drones?

Below are three examples of nontraditional 3D printing (i.e., they do not use plastics). Consider how disruptive each one would be to its respective industry:

- 3D Systems new ChefJet^tm Pro can print complex sugary structures in flavors like chocolate, vanilla, mint, cherry, sour apple, and watermelon.[16] With a ChefJet, even a culinary novice could produce intricate, beautiful, and fully customized deserts.
- Researchers at the Harvard School of Engineering and Applied Sciences were able to print a 3D biological structure with blood vessels that could deliver nutrients and remove waste.[17] This development means doctors may someday be able to print fully functional replacements for damaged tissues by simply pressing print. Not only could this save lives, but it could also lower insurance premiums and the overall cost of health care.
- Professor Behrokh Khoshnevis of the University of Southern California has built a large-scale 3D printer that can print an entire house in 24 hours.[18] This 3D home printer would create more stable and better insulated structures, use fewer materials, reduce workplace injuries, and automatically install heating and plumbing, all while producing homes at a fraction of the usual cost.

## Q4-3 WHAT DO BUSINESS PROFESSIONALS NEED TO KNOW ABOUT SOFTWARE?

As a future manager or business professional, you need to know the essential terminology and software concepts that will enable you to be an intelligent software consumer. To begin, consider the basic categories of software shown in Figure 4-9.

Every computer has an **operating system (OS)**, which is a program that controls that computer's resources. Some of the functions of an operating system are to read and write data, allocate main memory, perform memory swapping, start and stop programs, respond to error

**Figure 4-9**
Categories of Computer Software

| | Operating Systems | Application Programs |
|---|---|---|
| Client | Programs that control the client computer's resources | Applications that are processed on client computers |
| Server | Programs that control the server computer's resources | Applications that are processed on server computers |

conditions, and facilitate backup and recovery. In addition, the operating system creates and manages the user interface, including the display, keyboard, mouse, and other devices.

Although the operating system makes the computer usable, it does little application-specific work. If you want to check the weather or access a database, for example, you need application programs, such as an iPad weather application or Oracle's customer relationship management (CRM) software.

Both client and server computers need an operating system, though they need not be the same. Further, both clients and servers can process application programs. The application's design determines whether the client, the server, or both process it.

To be an educated computer consumer, you also need to understand two important software-related constraints. First, remember that particular versions of an operating system are written for particular types of hardware. For example, Microsoft Windows works only on processors from Intel and from companies that make processors that conform to the Intel instruction set (i.e., the commands that a CPU can process). With other operating systems, such as Linux, many versions exist for many different instruction sets.

Second, be aware that two types of application programs exist: native and Web. **Native applications** are programs that are written to use a particular operating system. Microsoft Access, for example, will only run on the Windows operating system. Some applications come in multiple versions; for example, there are Windows and Macintosh versions of Microsoft Word. But unless you are informed otherwise, assume that a native application runs on just one operating system. Native applications are sometimes called **thick-client applications**.

A **Web application** (also known as a **thin-client application**) is designed to run within a computer browser such as Firefox, Chrome, Opera, or Edge (formerly Internet Explorer). Web applications run within the browser and can therefore run on any type of computer. Ideally, a Web application can also run within any browser, although this isn't always true (as you will learn).

## WHAT ARE THE MAJOR OPERATING SYSTEMS?

Every business professional needs to know the three major types of operating systems listed in Figure 4-10. Each is also discussed in more detail in the sections that follow.

### Nonmobile Client Operating Systems

Nonmobile client operating systems are used on personal computers. The most popular is **Microsoft Windows**. Some version of Windows resides on more than 85 percent of the world's desktops, and, if we consider just business users, the figure is more than 95 percent. As of the time of this writing, the most recent version of Windows is Windows 10. Net Applications estimates that overall market share of Windows as of 2015 is Windows 10 at 0.1 percent, Windows 8.1 at 11.2 percent, Windows 8 at 3.5 percent, Windows 7 at 58.4 percent, Windows Vista at 2.0 percent, and Windows XP at 16.0 percent.[19] It's interesting to note that Microsoft dropped support for Windows XP in 2014 despite the fact that it is still more popular than Windows Vista, Windows 8, Windows 8.1, and Windows 10.

**For more on modern-style interfaces, see Chapter Extension 3, Mobile Systems.**

Windows 8 was a major rewrite of prior versions of the Windows operating system. Windows 8 was distinguished by its ability to run what Microsoft calls **modern-style applications**.[20] These

| Category | Operating System | Used for | Remarks |
|---|---|---|---|
| Nonmobile Clients | Windows | Personal computer clients | Most widely used operating system in business. Current version is Windows 10. Includes a touch interface. |
| | Mac OS | Macintosh clients | First used by graphic artists and others in arts community; now used more widely. First desktop OS to provide a touch interface. Current version is the Mac OS X El Capitan. |
| | Unix | Workstation clients | Popular on powerful client computers used in engineering, computer-assisted design, architecture. Difficult for the nontechnical user. Almost never used by business clients. |
| | Linux | Just about anything | Open-source variant of Unix. Adapted to almost every type of computing device. On a PC, used with LibreOffice application software. Rarely used by business clients. |
| Mobile Clients | Symbian | Nokia, Samsung, and other phones | Popular worldwide, but less so in North America. |
| | BlackBerry OS | Research in Motion Blackberries | Device and OS developed for use by business. Very popular in beginning, but losing market share to iOS and Android. |
| | iOS | iPhone, iPod Touch, iPad | Rapidly increasing installed base with success of the iPhone and iPad. Based on Mac OS X. |
| | Android | Samsung, Google, HTC, and Sony smartphones and tablets | Linux-based phone/tablet operating system from Google. Rapidly increasing market share. |
| | Windows 10 | Nokia and Microsoft Surface | Windows 10 tailored specifically for mobile devices. Full Windows 10 on Surface Pro. |
| Servers | Windows Server | Servers | Used by businesses with a strong commitment to Microsoft. |
| | Unix | Servers | Fading from use. Replaced by Linux. |
| | Linux | Servers | Very popular. Aggressively pushed by IBM. |

**Figure 4-10**
Major Operating Systems

applications, now carried over into Windows 10, are touch-screen oriented and provide context-sensitive, pop-up menus. They can also be used with a mouse and keyboard. Microsoft claims that modern-style applications work just as well on portable, mobile devices, such as tablet computers, as they do on desktop computers. One key feature of modern-style applications is the minimization of menu bars, status lines, and other visual overhead. Figure 4-11 shows an example of a modern-style version of searching for images in Windows Explorer.

Not all computers use Windows, however. For example, Apple Computer, Inc., developed its own operating system for the Macintosh, **Mac OS**. The current version is Mac OS X El Capitan. Apple touts Mac OS as the world's most advanced desktop operating system, and until Windows 8 was released, this claim was without doubt. Windows 10 now gives Mac OS a run for the money in terms of that title.

Until recently, Mac OS was used primarily by graphic artists and workers in the arts community. But for many reasons, Mac OS has made headway into the traditional Windows market. According to NetApplications, as of 2015, desktop operating system market share was divided between versions of Windows (91 percent), Mac OS X (5.8 percent), and Linux (1.5 percent).[21]

Mac OS was designed originally to run the line of CPU processors from Motorola, but today a Macintosh with an Intel processor is able to run both Windows and the Mac OS.

The two other nonmobile client operating systems mentioned in Figure 4-10 are Unix and Linux. **Unix** is an operating system that was developed at Bell Labs in the 1970s. It has

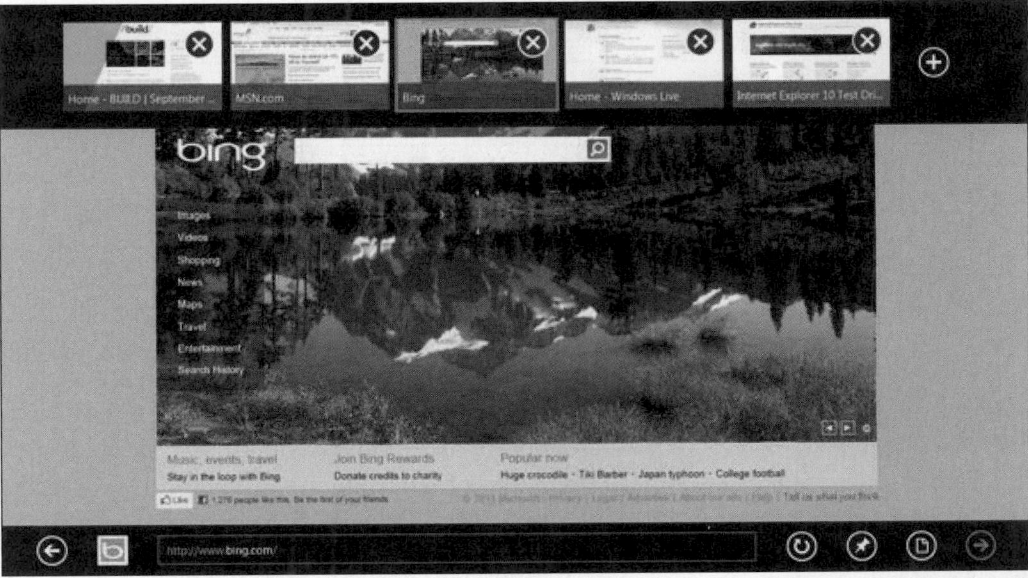


**Figure 4-11**
Example of the Modern-Style Interface

*Source:* Microsoft Corporation

been the workhorse of the scientific and engineering communities since then. Unix is seldom used in business.

**Linux** is a version of Unix that was developed by the open source community. This community is a loosely coupled group of programmers who mostly volunteer their time to contribute code to develop and maintain Linux. The open source community owns Linux, and there is no fee to use it. Linux can run on client computers, but usually only when budget is of paramount concern. By far, Linux is most popular as a server OS. According to *DistroWatch.com*, the five most popular versions of Linux as of 2015 were Linux Mint, Ubuntu, Debian GNU/Linux, openSUSE, and Fedora.[22]

## Mobile Client Operating Systems

Figure 4-10 also lists the five principal mobile operating systems in use in 2014. **Symbian** is popular on phones in Europe and the Far East, but less so in North America. **BlackBerry OS** was one of the most successful early mobile operating systems and was used primarily by business users on BlackBerry devices. In recent years, it has lost market share to iOS, Android, and Windows 10.

**iOS** is the operating system used on the iPhone, iPod Touch, and iPad. When first released, it broke new ground with its ease of use and compelling display, features that are now being copied by the BlackBerry OS and Android. With the popularity of the iPhone and iPad, Apple has seen iOS's market share increase. According to Net Applications, as of 2014, iOS is used on 39 percent of mobile devices.[23] The current version of iOS is iOS 8.

Most industry observers would agree that Apple has led the way, both with the Mac OS and the iOS, in creating easy-to-use interfaces. Certainly, many innovative ideas have first appeared in a Macintosh or iSomething and then later were added, in one form or another, to the Android and Windows operating systems.

Speaking of these OS, **Android** is a mobile operating system licensed by Google. Android devices have a very loyal following, especially among technical users. Net Applications estimates Android's market share to be nearly 52 percent.[24]

Users who want Windows 10 on mobile devices will get either **Windows 10 (mobile)** on smartphones or a full version of Windows 10 on Surface Pro devices. Windows garners about 2 percent of the mobile OS market share.

The smartphone market has always been huge, but recently, e-book readers and tablets have substantially increased the market for mobile client operating systems. As of April 2015, 64 percent of Americans owned a smartphone, and 53 percent owned a tablet in addition to their smartphone.[25]

### Server Operating Systems

The last three rows of Figure 4-10 show the three most popular server operating systems. **Windows Server** is a version of Windows that has been specially designed and configured for server use. It has much more stringent and restrictive security features than other versions of Windows and is popular on servers in organizations that have made a strong commitment to Microsoft.

Unix can also be used on servers, but it is gradually being replaced by Linux.

Linux is frequently used on servers by organizations that want, for whatever reason, to avoid a server commitment to Microsoft. IBM is the primary proponent of Linux and in the past has used it as a means to better compete against Microsoft. Although IBM does not own Linux, IBM has developed many business systems solutions that employ Linux. By using Linux, neither IBM nor its customers have to pay a licensing fee to Microsoft.

## VIRTUALIZATION

**Virtualization** is the process by which one physical computer hosts many different virtual (not literal) computers within it. One operating system, called the **host operating system**, runs one or more operating systems as applications. Those hosted operating systems are called **virtual machines (vm)**. Each virtual machine has disk space and other resources allocated to it. The host operating system controls the activities of the virtual machines it hosts to prevent them from interfering with one another. With virtualization, each vm is able to operate exactly the same as it would if it were operating in a stand-alone, nonvirtual environment.

Three types of virtualization exist:

- PC virtualization
- Server virtualization
- Desktop virtualization

With **PC virtualization**, a personal computer, such as a desktop or laptop, hosts several different operating systems. Say a user needs to have both Linux and Windows 10 running on a computer for training or a development project. In that circumstance, the user can load software like Oracle VirtualBox or VMWare Workstation on the host operating system in order to create Linux and Windows 10 virtual machines. The user can run both systems on the same hardware at the same time if the host operating system has sufficient resources (i.e., memory and CPU power), as shown in Figure 4-12.

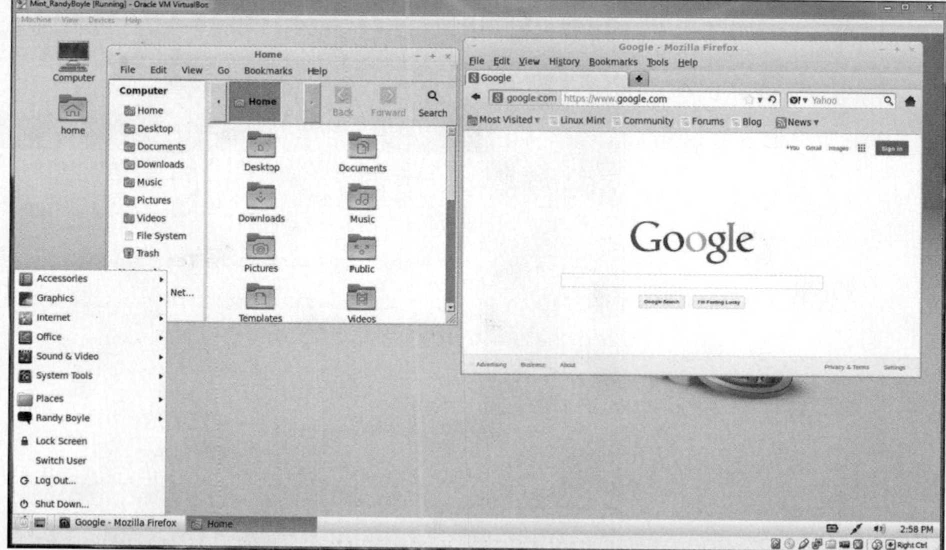


**Figure 4-12**
Linux Mint Virtual Machine Running in Microsoft Windows 7 Professional

*Source:* Microsoft Corporation

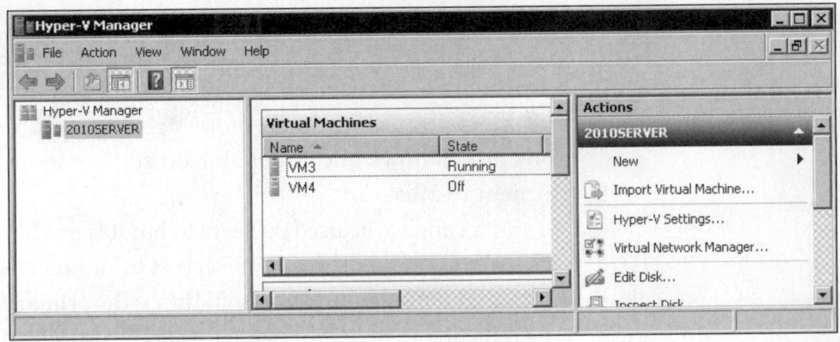


**Figure 4-13**
Windows Server Computer Hosting Two Virtual Machines
*Source:* Microsoft Corporation

With **server virtualization**, a server computer hosts one or more other server computers. In Figure 4-13, for instance, a Windows Server computer is hosting two virtual machines. Users can log on to either of those virtual machines, and they will appear as normal servers. Figure 4-14 shows how virtual machine VM3 appears to a user of that server. Notice that a user of VM3 is running a browser that is accessing SharePoint. In fact, this virtual machine was used to generate many of the SharePoint figures in Chapter 2. Server virtualization plays a key role for cloud vendors, as you'll learn in Chapter 6.

PC virtualization is interesting as well as quite useful, as described in Chapter 6. Desktop virtualization, on the other hand, has the potential to be revolutionary. With **desktop virtualization**, a server hosts many versions of desktop operating systems. Each of those desktops has a complete user environment and appears to the user to be just another PC. However, the desktop can be accessed from any computer to which the user has access. Thus, you could be at an airport and go to a terminal computer from which you can access your virtualized desktop. To you, it would appear as if that airport computer is your own personal computer. Using a virtual desktop also means that you won't have to worry about losing a corporate laptop or confidential internal data. In addition, it means that many different users could access their own "personal" computers using only a single terminal, like the one in the airport example. IBM offers PC virtualization for as low as $12 a month per PC.

Desktop virtualization is in its infancy, but it might have a major impact during the early years of your career.

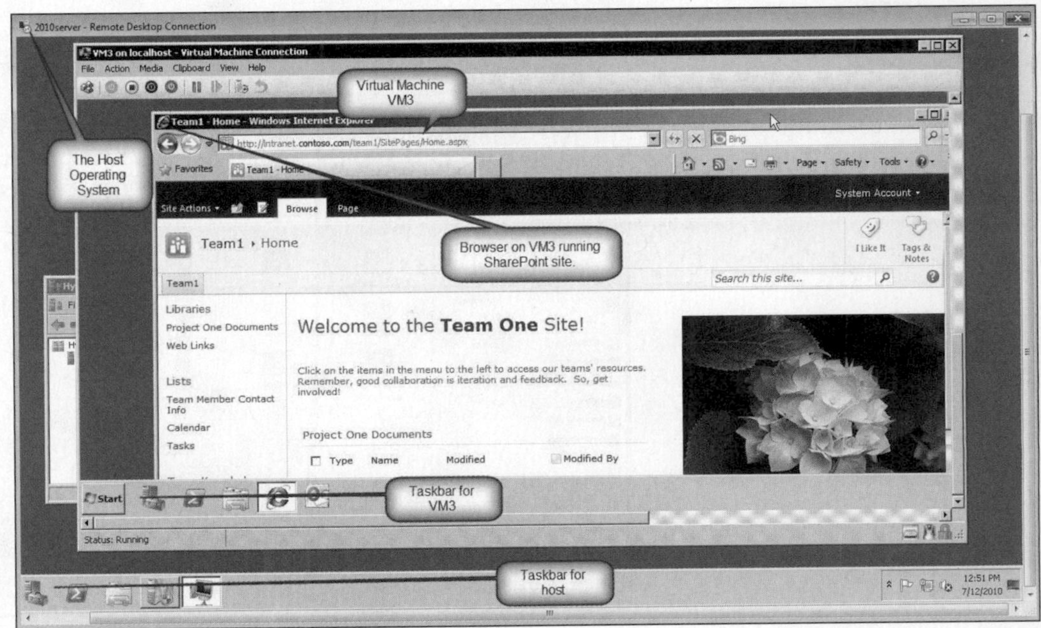


**Figure 4-14**
Virtual Machine Example
*Source:* Microsoft Corporation

## OWNING VERSUS LICENSING

Note that when you buy a computer program, you are not actually buying that program. Instead, you are buying a **license** to use that program. For example, when you buy a Mac OS license, Apple is selling you the right to use Mac OS; Apple itself continues to own the Mac OS program. Unlike individuals, large organizations do not buy a license for each computer user. Instead, they negotiate a **site license**, which is a flat fee that authorizes the organization to install the product (operating system or application) on all of that organization's computers or on all of its computers at a specific site.

In the case of Linux, no company can sell you a license to use it. That's because Linux is owned by the open source community, which states that Linux has no licensing fee (with certain reasonable restrictions). Large companies such as IBM and smaller companies such as RedHat can make money by *supporting* Linux, but no company makes money selling Linux licenses.

## WHAT TYPES OF APPLICATIONS EXIST, AND HOW DO ORGANIZATIONS OBTAIN THEM?

As previously mentioned, **application software** performs a service or function. Some application programs are general purpose, such as Microsoft Excel or Word. Other application programs provide specific functions. QuickBooks, for example, is an application program that provides general ledger and other accounting functions. In the following sections, we begin by describing categories of application programs and then describe sources for them.

**To learn more about Microsoft Excel, see Chapter Extension 4.**

### Horizontal Applications

**Horizontal-market application** software provides capabilities common across all organizations and industries. Word processors, graphics programs, spreadsheets, and presentation programs are all horizontal-market application software.

**Some applications are designed to be free but gather data about the people that use them. Read the Ethics Guide on pages 110–111 about how this is done.**

Some well-known examples of horizontal applications are Microsoft Word, Excel, and PowerPoint. Examples from other vendors include Adobe's Acrobat, Photoshop, and PageMaker and Jasc Corporation's Paint Shop Pro. These applications are used in a wide variety of businesses across all industries. They are purchased off the shelf, and little customization of features is necessary (or even possible). These applications are the automobile equivalent of a sedan: Everybody buys them and then uses them for different purposes.

### Vertical Applications

**Vertical-market application** software serves the needs of a specific industry. Examples of such programs include those used by dental offices to schedule appointments and bill patients, those used by auto mechanics to keep track of customer data and repairs, and those used by parts warehouses to track inventory, purchases, and sales. If horizontal-market applications are sedans, then vertical-market applications would be construction vehicles, like an excavator, because they are specialized for use in a particular field.

Vertical applications usually can be altered or customized. Typically, the company that sold the application software will provide such services or offer referrals to qualified consultants who can provide this service.

### One-of-a-Kind Applications

**One-of-a-kind application** software is developed for a specific, unique need. The U.S. Department of Defense develops such software, for example, because it has needs that no other organization has.

You can think of one-of-a-kind application software as the automotive equivalent of a military tank. Tanks are developed for a very specific and unique need. Tanks cost more to manufacture than sedans, and cost overruns are common. They take longer to make and require unique hardware components. However, tanks are highly customizable and fit the requirements of a heavy-duty battle vehicle very well.

**Figure 4-15**
Software Sources and Types

| | | Software Source | | |
|---|---|---|---|---|
| | | Off-the-shelf | Off-the-shelf and then customized | Custom-developed |
| Software Type | Horizontal applications | | | |
| | Vertical applications | | | |
| | One-of-a-kind applications | | | |

### Selecting an Application Type

If you're headed into battle, you wouldn't want to be driving a four-door sedan. Sometimes paying for a custom vehicle, while expensive, is warranted. It all depends on what you're doing. Militaries, for example, purchase sedans, construction vehicles, and tanks. Each vehicle fills its own need. You can buy computer software in exactly the same ways: as **off-the-shelf software**, as **off-the-shelf with alterations software**, or as **custom-developed software**.

Organizations develop custom application software themselves or hire a development vendor. Like buying a tank, such development is done in situations where the needs of the organization are so unique that no horizontal or vertical applications are available. By developing custom software, the organization can tailor its application to fit its requirements.

Custom development is difficult and risky. Staffing and managing teams of software developers is challenging. Managing software projects can be daunting. Many organizations have embarked on application development projects only to find that the projects take twice as long—or longer—to finish than planned. Cost overruns of 200 percent and 300 percent are not uncommon. We will discuss such risks further in Chapter 12.

In addition, every application program needs to be adapted to changing needs and changing technologies. The adaptation costs of horizontal and vertical software are amortized over all the users of that software, perhaps thousands or millions of customers. For custom-developed software, however, the using organization must pay all of the adaptation costs itself. Over time, this cost burden is heavy.

Because of the risk and expense, custom development is the last-choice alternative, used only when there is no other option. Figure 4-15 summarizes software sources and types.

## WHAT IS FIRMWARE?

**Firmware** is computer software that is installed into devices such as printers, print servers, and various types of communication devices. This software is coded just like other software, but it is installed into special, read-only memory in the printer or other device. In this way, the program becomes part of the device's memory; it is as if the program's logic is designed into the device's circuitry. Therefore, users do not need to load firmware into the device's memory. Firmware can be changed or upgraded, but this is normally a task for IS professionals.

# Q4-4 IS OPEN SOURCE SOFTWARE A VIABLE ALTERNATIVE?

Today, business leaders are increasingly asking whether open source software is a reasonable, cost-effective alternative to more expensive, commercially sold or custom designed software. To answer this question, you first need to know something about the open source movement and process. Most computer historians would agree that Richard Matthew Stallman is the father of the movement. In 1983, he developed a set of tools called **GNU** (a self-referential acronym meaning *GNU Not Unix*) for creating a free Unix-like operating system. Stallman made many other contributions to open source, including the **GNU general public license (GPL) agreement**, one of the standard license agreements for open source software. Stallman was unable to attract enough developers to finish the free Unix system, but he continued making other contributions to the open source movement.

In 1991, Linus Torvalds, working in Helsinki, began work on another version of Unix, using some of Stallman's tools. That version eventually became Linux, the high-quality and very popular operating system discussed previously.

The Internet proved to be a great enabler for the open source movement and the software it created. **Open source** software is typically free and modifiable, and its source code is publicly available. **Source code** is computer code as written by humans and understandable by humans. Many open source projects became successful, including:

- LibreOffice (the default office suite in Linux distributions)
- Firefox (a browser)
- MySQL (a DBMS, see Chapter 5)
- Apache (a Web server, see Chapter 6)
- Ubuntu (a Windows-like desktop operating system)
- Android (a mobile-device operating system, described earlier)
- Cassandra (a NoSQL DBMS, see Chapter 5)
- Hadoop (a BigData processing system, see Chapter 9)

## WHY DO PROGRAMMERS VOLUNTEER THEIR SERVICES?

To a person who has never enjoyed writing computer programs, it is difficult to understand why anyone would donate his or her time and skills to contribute to open source projects. Programming is, however, an intense combination of art and logic, and designing and writing a complicated computer program can be exceedingly pleasurable (and addictive). Many programmers joyfully write computer programs—day after day. If you have an artistic and logical mind, you ought to try it.

Thus, the first reason why people contribute to open source projects is that it is great fun! Also, some people contribute to open source because it gives them the freedom to choose the projects they work on. They may have a programming day job that is not terribly interesting—say, writing a program to manage a computer printer. Their job pays the bills, but it's not fulfilling, so they turn to another outlet.

To better understand the allure of open source projects, consider an example. In the 1950s, Hollywood studio musicians suffered as they recorded the same style of music over and over for a long string of uninteresting movies. To keep their sanity, those musicians would gather on Sundays to play jazz, and a number of high-quality jazz clubs resulted. That's what open source is to programmers: a place where they can exercise their creativity while working on projects they find interesting and fulfilling.

Another reason for contributing to open source is to exhibit one's skill, both for pride and to find a job or consulting employment. A final reason is to start a business selling services that support an open source product.

## HOW DOES OPEN SOURCE WORK?

Source code is compiled into **machine code** that is processed by a computer. Figure 4-16, for instance, shows a portion of the computer code written for the PRIDE project (see start of Chapter 7). Machine code is, in general, not understandable by humans and cannot be modified.

**Figure 4-16**
Source Code Sample

```
/// <summary>
/// Allows the page to draw itself.
/// </summary>
private void OnDraw(object sender, GameTimerEventArgs e)
{
    SharedGraphicsDeviceManager.Current.GraphicsDevice.Clear(Color.CornflowerBlue);

    SharedGraphicsDeviceManager.Current.GraphicsDevice.Clear(Color.Black);

    // Render the Silverlight controls using the UIElementRenderer.
    elementRenderer.Render();

    // Draw the sprite
    spriteBatch.Begin();

    // Draw the rectangle in its new position
    for (int i = 0; i < 3; i++)
    {
        spriteBatch.Draw(texture[i], bikeSpritePosition[i], Color.White);
    }

    // Using the texture from the UIElementRenderer,
```

For example, when a user accesses a Web site, the machine code version of the program runs on the user's computer. We do not show machine code in a figure because it would look like this:

1101001010010111111001110111100100011100000111111011101111100111...

In a **closed source** project, say, Microsoft Office, the source code is highly protected and only available to trusted employees and carefully vetted contractors. The source code is protected like gold in a vault. Only those trusted programmers can make changes to a closed source project.

With open source, however, anyone can obtain the source code from the open source project's Web site. Programmers can then alter or add to this code depending on their interests and goals. In most cases, programmers incorporate code they find into their own projects. Later, they may be able to resell those projects depending on the type of license agreement the project uses.

Open source succeeds because of collaboration. A programmer examines the source code and identifies a need or project that seems interesting. He or she then creates a new feature, redesigns or reprograms an existing feature, or fixes a known problem. That code is then sent to others in the open source project who evaluate the quality and merits of the work and add it to the product, if appropriate.

Typically, there is a lot of give and take within the open source community. Or, as described in Chapter 2, there are many cycles of iteration and feedback. Because of this iteration, a well-managed project with strong peer reviews can result in very high quality code, like that in Linux.

## SO, IS OPEN SOURCE VIABLE?

The answer to this question depends on to whom and for what. Open source has certainly become legitimate. According to *The Economist*, "It is now generally accepted that the future will involve a blend of both proprietary and open-source software."[26] During your career, open source will likely take a greater and greater role in software. However, whether open source works for a particular situation depends on the requirements and constraints of that situation. You will learn more about matching requirements and programs in Chapter 12.

In some cases, companies choose open source software simply because it is "free." It turns out that this advantage may be less important than you'd think, because in many cases, the support and operational costs related to an open source application swamp the initial licensing fee for an existing proprietary application that meets a company's needs.

## How does the **knowledge** in this chapter help **you?**

In the world of today's commerce, you will be involved with the use of technology in business. You have no real choice; the only choice you do have is whether to be a passive participant or to become actively involved. The knowledge of this chapter will help you choose the latter. From it, you know enough about hardware and software to ask good questions and to avoid embarrassing gaffes. You also now know sources of application software and the reasons for choosing one source over another. Finally, you know that open source is not just a "bunch of amateurs" but a movement that has created numerous quality software products and is a viable alternative for many situations. However, all of this knowledge is perishable, just like tomatoes at the farmers' market. You'll need to continually refresh your knowledge.

# Ethics Guide

## Free Apps For Data

You're sitting in your Introduction to MIS class, and the professor starts talking about how profitable software development can be. He points out that billionaires like Bill Gates (Microsoft), Larry Ellison (Oracle), Larry Page (Google), and Mark Zuckerberg (Facebook) all made their fortunes by developing useful software. But a vocal classmate jumps in and points out that he's never paid any of those people a penny. He uses Google Search, Gmail, and Facebook all for free. Yes, he uses Microsoft Office, but it's the free online version through OneDrive. Even the apps on his smartphone are free.

Then comes the perennial question, which also happens to be a major point of frustration for the tech industry: How do you make money from free apps? The professor says something about capturing market share, potential income, and future innovation. You're not buying it. You're interested in *real* income, not *potential* income.

### Nick the Data Broker

The person sitting next to you, Nick, starts smiling broadly and nods his head. He's in your group for your big class project. He leans over and whispers, "If you're not paying for it, *you* are the product. Data is where you make money, not software. Give them the software, take the data, and make the money. It's simple."

You're a little confused at first. But then you think back to last Wednesday when you first met Nick. He said he was coming back to school to get a degree in MIS because he needed the technical knowledge for his new job with his brother's company. He explained that his brother was a data broker (sometimes called an information broker). He buys data about individuals from companies and then sells it to other companies for a profit. It sounded like they were doing really well. Before you could even ask if it was legal or ethical, Nick quipped, "Yes, of course it's legal. Everyone does it." He had obviously gotten this question before.

But was Nick right? He isn't a billionaire like Bill Gates. Nick was only concerned with buying and selling data. He wasn't interested in application development. But he did make a good point, and it got you thinking. What if you started a business that made applications that were designed to collect individual data? You could make dozens of useful apps, collect individual data, and then sell it to Nick.

But what data would Nick pay for? How much of it could you get? He wouldn't care about gaming data. But he would pay for data about user behavior like which Web sites they visit, where they're located, who their friends are, and what they purchase.

### Flashlight Apps

At lunch, you do a few searches about how mobile applications can access data on smartphones. It turns out that users just have to grant the application permission(s), and it can access *any* data on the phone. Could that be right? *Any* data? This could be a gold mine. You get excited at the prospect of harvesting thousands of terabytes of data and selling them to Nick.

But then you find a threat report by SnoopWall looking at the permissions required by the top 10 flashlight apps for Android smartphones.[27] The results were shocking. All of these apps did more than just turn a light on and off. The table below lists the permissions required by each app. Why would your flashlight need your GPS coordinates?

Who was getting this data? What were they using it for? All of a sudden, these free apps don't look as attractive to you—as a consumer. Someone already stole your idea—and your data.

| Permissions | 1 Super-Bright LED Flashlight | 2 Tiny Flashlight + LED | 3 Brightest LED Flashlight | 4 Flashlight | 5 Brightest Flashlight Free | 6 Color Flashlight | 7 High-Powered Flashlight | 8 Super Bright Flashlight |
|---|---|---|---|---|---|---|---|---|
| Take pictures and videos | X | X | X | X | X | X | X | X |
| Receive data from Internet | X | | X | | | | X | |
| Control flashlight | X | X | X | | X | X | X | |
| Change system display settings | X | | X | | | | X | |
| Modify system settings | X | | X | | | | X | |
| Prevent device from sleeping | X | X | X | X | X | | X | |
| View network connections | X | X | X | X | X | X | X | X |
| Full network access | X | X | X | X | X | X | X | X |
| Run at startup | | X | | | | | | |
| Control vibration | | X | | | | | | |
| Retrieve running apps | | | X | | | | X | |
| Modify or delete the contents of your USB storage | | | X | | X | | X | |
| Read the contents of your USB storage | | | X | | X | | X | |
| View Wi-Fi connections | | | X | | X | | X | |
| Read phone status and identity | | | X | | X | | X | |
| Read Home settings and shortcuts | | | | X | X | | | |
| Write Home settings and shortcuts | | | | X | | | | |
| Disable your screen lock | | | | X | | | | |
| Install shortcuts | | | | X | X | | | |
| Uninstall shortcuts | | | | X | X | | | |
| Approximate location | | | | | X | | X | |
| Precise location | | | | | X | | X | |
| Disable or modify status bar | | | | | X | | | |

*Source:* SnoopWall, SnoopWall Flashlight Apps Threat Assessment Report.

## DISCUSSION QUESTIONS

**1.** Consider the decision to create a free application designed to harvest individual data.

**a.** Is this decision ethical according to the categorical imperative (pages 20–21)?

**b.** Is this decision ethical according to the utilitarian perspective (pages 46–47)?

**c.** How would users react if they knew their data was being harvested in exchange for a free app?

**2.** Suppose Google becomes aware that apps in the Google Play store are harvesting user data unrelated to the function of the application.

**a.** Does it have a *legal* obligation to find out which apps are harvesting data inappropriately?

**b.** Does it have an *ethical* obligation to find out which apps are harvesting data inappropriately?

**c.** Does Google provide free apps in exchange for individual data? Why?

**3.** How hard should Google work at curating apps in Google Play to ensure that appropriate permissions are set?

**4.** In 2014, Symantec found that 17 percent of all Android apps were malware in disguise.[28] But a report by Google found that less than 1 percent of all Android devices had a potentially harmful application installed.[29]

**a.** Is it ethical for Google to remove applications it considers inappropriate? Consider both the categorical imperative and utilitarian perspectives.

**b.** Is it ethical for Google to limit permissions for certain applications? Consider both the categorical imperative and utilitarian perspectives.

# Guide

## Keeping Up to Speed

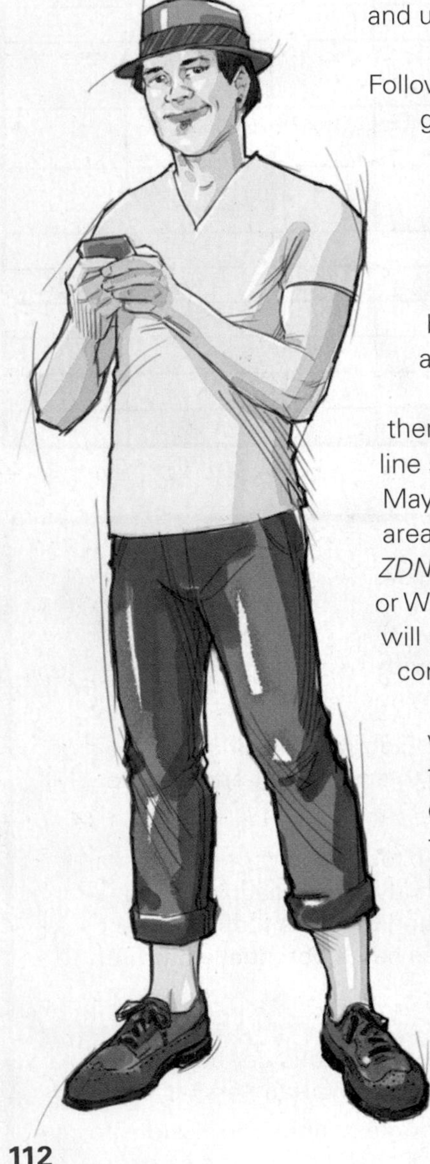

Have you ever been to a cafeteria where you put your lunch tray on a conveyor belt that carries the dirty dishes into the kitchen? That conveyor belt is reminiscent of technology. Like the conveyor, technology just moves along, and all of us run on top of the technology conveyor, trying to keep up. We hope to keep up with the relentless change of technology for an entire career without ending up in the techno-trash.

Technology change is a fact, and the only appropriate question is, "What am I going to do about it?" One strategy you can take is to bury your head in the sand: "Look, I'm not a technology person. I'll leave it to the pros. As long as I can send email and use the Internet, I'm happy. If I have a problem, I'll call someone to fix it."

That strategy is fine, as far as it goes, and many businesspeople have used it. Following that strategy won't give you a competitive advantage over anyone, and it will give someone else a competitive advantage over you, but as long as you develop your advantage elsewhere, you'll be OK—at least for yourself.

What about your department, though? If an expert says, "You should be buying your employees Windows 10 tablet devices," are you going to nod your head and say, "Great. Sell'em to me!"? Or are you going to know enough to realize that it may be too early to know what the success of Windows 10 will be? Or to know that maybe you'll have problems getting homegrown, in-house applications down from whatever stores Microsoft sets up?

At the other end of the spectrum are those who love technology. You'll find them everywhere—they may be accountants, marketing professionals, or production-line supervisors who not only know their field but also enjoy information technology. Maybe they were IS majors or had double majors that combined IS with another area of expertise (e.g., IS with accounting). These people read *CNET News* and *ZDNet* most days, and they can tell you the latest on desktop virtualization or html5 or Windows 10. Those people are sprinting along the technology conveyor belt; they will never end up in the techno-trash, and they will use their knowledge of IT to gain competitive advantage throughout their careers.

Many business professionals fall in between these extremes. They don't want to bury their heads, but they don't have the desire or interest to become technophiles (lovers of technology), either. What should you do if you fall into this category? There are a couple of strategies. For one, don't allow yourself to ignore technology. When you see a technology article in *The Wall Street Journal*, read it. Don't just skip it because it's about technology. Read the technology ads too. Many vendors invest heavily in ads that instruct without seeming to. Another option is to take a seminar or pay attention to professional events that combine your specialty with technology. For example, when you go to the bankers' convention, attend a panel or two on "Mobile Device Use at Banks." There are always sessions like that, and you might make a contact with similar problems and concerns in another company.

Probably the best option, if you have the time for it, is to get involved as a user representative on technology committees in your organization.

Or, if your company is doing a review of its bring your own device (BYOD) policy, see if you can get on the review committee. Alternatively, when there's a need for a representative from your department to discuss needs for the next-generation helpline system, sign up. Or, later in your career, become a member of the business practice technology committee or whatever it is called at your organization.

Just working with such groups will add to your knowledge of technology. Presentations made to such groups, discussions about uses of technology, and ideas about using IT for competitive advantage will all add to your IT knowledge. You'll gain important contacts and exposure to leaders in your organization as well.

It's up to you. You get to choose how you relate to technology. But be sure you choose; don't let your head get stuck in the sand without thinking about it.

## DISCUSSION QUESTIONS

**1.** Do you agree that the change of technology is relentless? What do you think that means to most business professionals? To most organizations?

**2.** Think about the three postures toward technology presented here. Which camp will you join? Why?

**3.** Write a two-paragraph memo to yourself justifying your choice in question 2. If you chose to ignore technology, explain how you will compensate for the loss of competitive advantage. If you're going to join one of the other two groups, explain why, and describe how you're going to accomplish your goal.

**4.** Given your answer to question 2, assume that you're in a job interview and the interviewer asks about your interest in and knowledge of technology. Write a three-sentence response to the interviewer's question.

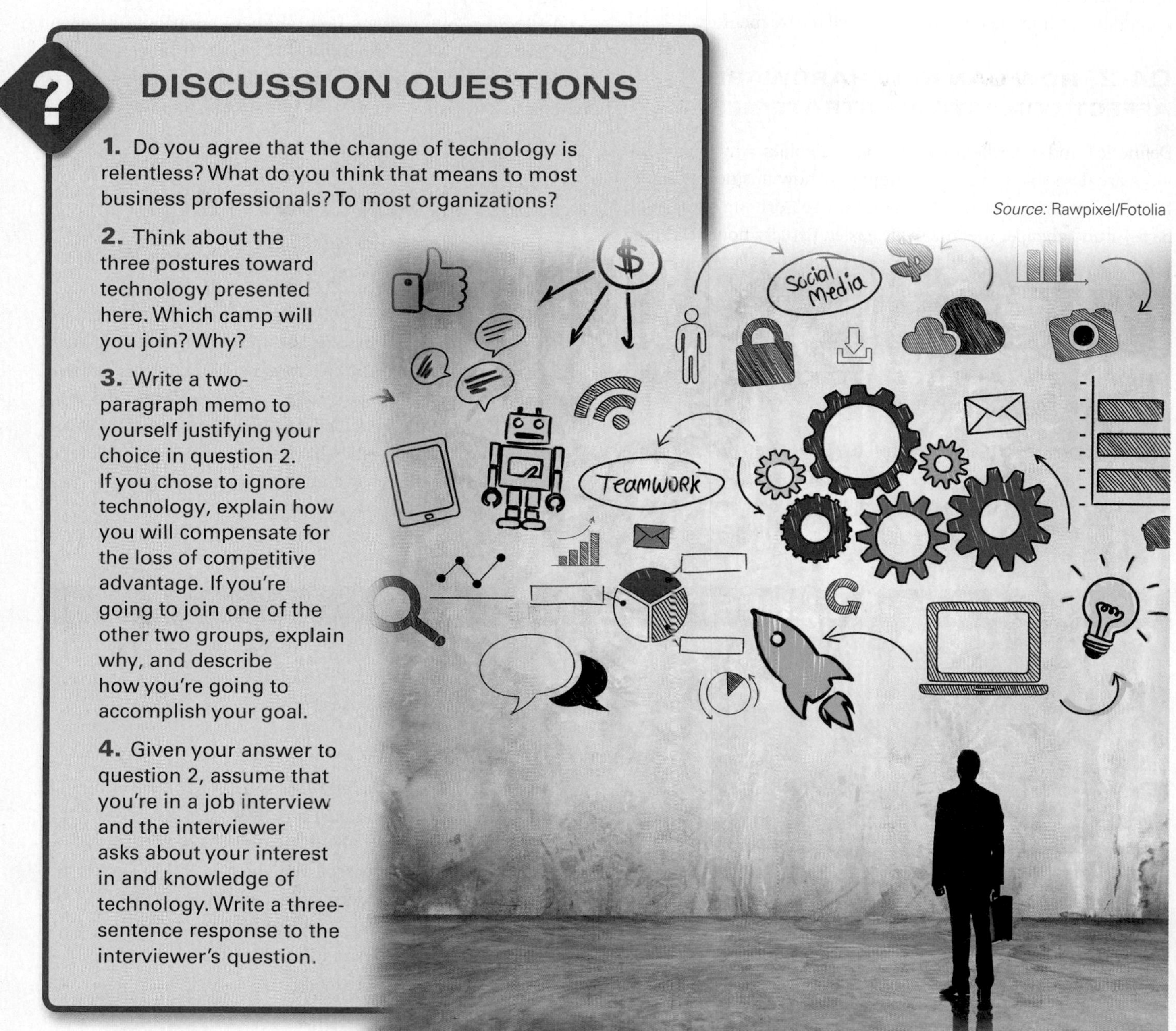


*Source:* Rawpixel/Fotolia

# ACTIVE REVIEW

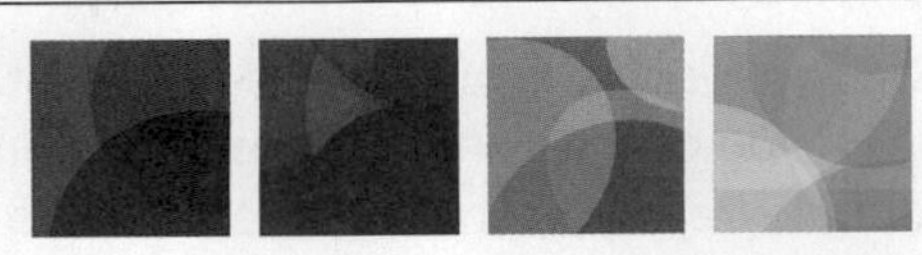

Use this Active Review to verify that you understand the ideas and concepts that answer the chapter's study questions.

## Q4-1 WHAT DO BUSINESS PROFESSIONALS NEED TO KNOW ABOUT COMPUTER HARDWARE?

List categories of hardware and explain the purpose of each. Define *bit* and *byte*. Explain why bits are used to represent computer data. Define the units of bytes used to size memory.

## Q4-2 HOW CAN NEW HARDWARE AFFECT COMPETITIVE STRATEGIES?

Define *IoT* and describe a smart device. Explain why smart devices are desirable. Give two examples of how businesses could benefit from smart devices. Describe how self-driving cars could be safer and cheaper and make life easier. Explain how 3D printing works and how it could affect new product design, manufacturing, distribution, and consumer purchasing.

## Q4-3 WHAT DO BUSINESS PROFESSIONALS NEED TO KNOW ABOUT SOFTWARE?

Review Figure 4-10 and explain the meaning of each cell in this table. Describe three kinds of virtualization and explain the use of each. Explain the difference between software ownership and software licenses. Explain the differences among horizontal-market, vertical-market, and one-of-a-kind applications. Describe the three ways that organizations can acquire software.

## Q4-4 IS OPEN SOURCE SOFTWARE A VIABLE ALTERNATIVE?

Define *GNU* and *GPL*. Name three successful open source projects. Describe four reasons programmers contribute to open source projects. Define *open source, closed source, source code,* and *machine code.* In your own words, explain why open source is a legitimate alternative but may or may not be appropriate for a given application.

## How does the **knowledge** in this chapter help **you?**

State the choice you have with regard to your involvement with technology in commerce. List the topics that you have learned about hardware and software. Explain how you can use knowledge of application software sources. Briefly describe open source software and explain why it is sometimes, but not always, a viable option. Explain why this knowledge is perishable and state what you can do about that fact.

## KEY TERMS AND CONCEPTS

MyMISLab™

To complete the problems with the ✪, go to EOC Discussion Questions in the MyLab.

## USING YOUR KNOWLEDGE

✪ **4-1.** Suppose your roommate, a political science major, asks you to help her purchase a new laptop computer. She wants to use the computer for email, Internet access, and note taking in class. She wants to spend less than $1,000.

**a.** What CPU, memory, and disk specifications would you recommend?

**b.** What software does she need?

**c.** Shop *www.dell.com*, *www.hp.com*, and *www.lenovo.com* for the best computer deal.

**d.** Which computer would you recommend, and why?

✪ **4-2.** Microsoft offers free licenses of certain software products to students at colleges and universities that participate in its DreamSpark program (formerly known as the Microsoft Developer Network [MSDN] Academic Alliance [AA]). If your college or university participates in this program, you have the opportunity to obtain hundreds of dollars of software for free. Here is a partial list of the software you can obtain:

- Microsoft Access 2013
- OneNote 2013
- Windows 2012 Server
- Microsoft Project 2013
- Visual Studio Developer
- SQL Server 2014
- Visio 2013

**a.** Search *www.microsoft.com*, *www.google.com*, or *www.bing.com* and determine the function of each of these software products.

**b.** Which of these software products are operating systems, and which are application programs?

**c.** Which of these programs are DBMS products (the subject of the next chapter)?

**d.** Which of these programs should you download and install tonight?

**e.** Either (1) download and install the programs in your answer to part d or (2) explain why you would choose not to do so.

**f.** Does DreamSpark provide an unfair advantage to Microsoft? Why or why not?

✪ **4-3.** Visit the Open Source Initiative's Web site at *www.opensource.org*. Summarize the mission of this foundation. Find the definition of *open source* on this site, and summarize that definition in your own words. Explain this foundation's role with regard to open source licenses. Summarize the process for having a license approved by the foundation. Describe the advantage of having the foundation's approval.

## COLLABORATION EXERCISE 4

*Read Chapter Extensions 1 and 2 if you have not already done so. Meet with your team and build a collaboration IS that uses tools like Google Docs, SharePoint, or other collaboration tools. Do not forget the need for procedures and team training. Now, using that IS, answer the questions below.*

In the past few years, Microsoft has been promoting **PixelSense**, a hardware–software product that enables people to interact with data on the top of a table. PixelSense initiates a new product category, and the best way to understand it is to view one of Microsoft's promotional videos at *www.microsoft.com/en-us/pixelsense/default.aspx*.

PixelSense paints the top of the 30-inch table with invisible, near-infrared light to detect the presence of objects. It can respond to as many as 52 different touches at the same time. According to Microsoft, this means that four people sitting around the PixelSense table could use all 10 of their fingers to manipulate up to 12 objects, simultaneously.

PixelSense uses wireless and other communications technologies to connect to devices that are placed on it, such as cameras or cell phones. When a camera is placed on PixelSense, pictures "spill" out of it, and users can manipulate those pictures with their hands. Products can be placed on PixelSense, and their product specifications are displayed. Credit cards can be placed on PixelSense, and items to be purchased can be dragged or dropped onto the credit card. Currently, Microsoft PixelSense is marketed and sold to large-scale commercial organizations in the financial services, healthcare, hospitality, retail, and public service business sectors.

One of the first implementers of PixelSense was the iBar lounge at Harrah's Rio All-Suite Hotel and Casino in Las Vegas, Nevada. The subtitle for the press release announcing iBar's system read, "Harrah's Reinvents Flirting and Offers New Uninhibited Fun and Play to iBar Patrons."[30]

The potential uses for PixelSense are staggering. Maps can display local events, and consumers can purchase tickets to those events by just using their fingers. PixelSense can also be used for new computer games and gambling devices. Children can paint on PixelSense with virtual paintbrushes. Numerous other applications are possible. Microsoft envisions PixelSense as a ubiquitous billion dollar technology that will find its way to tabletops, countertops, and mirrors.[31]

As you can see at the PixelSense Web site, this product can be used for many different purposes in many different places, such as restaurants, retail kiosks, and eventually at home. Probably most of the eventual applications for PixelSense have not yet been envisioned. One clear application, however, is in the gambling and gaming industry. Imagine placing your credit card on a PixelSense gambling device and playing the night away. Every time you lose, a charge is made against your credit card. Soon, before you know it, you've run up $15,000 in debt, which you learn when PixelSense tells you you've reached the maximum credit limit on your card.

Recall the RAND study cited in Chapter 1 that stated there will be increased worldwide demand for workers who can apply new technology and products to solve business problems in innovative ways. PixelSense is an excellent example of a new technology that will be applied innovatively.

**4-4.** Consider uses for PixelSense at your university. How might PixelSense be used in architecture, chemistry, law, medicine, business, geography, political science, art, music, or any other discipline in which your team has interest? Describe one potential application for PixelSense for five different disciplines.

**4-5.** List specific features and benefits for each of the five applications you selected in question 4-4.

**4-6.** Describe, in general terms, the work that needs to be accomplished to create the applications you identified in question 4-4.

**4-7.** Until June 2012, PixelSense was called Surface. At that time, Microsoft repurposed the name to use on its tablet devices. Surface was changed to PixelSense. What conclusions do you draw from these naming decisions?

**4-8.** You will sometimes hear the expression "Emerging technology is constantly leveling the playing field," meaning that technology eliminates competitive advantages of existing companies and enables opportunities for new companies. How does this statement pertain to PixelSense, Surface, Windows 10, Apple, and Google?

## CASE STUDY 4

### The Apple of Your i

A quick glance at Apple's stock history in Figure 4-17 will tell you that Apple is an incredibly successful and dramatic company, having peaks around the turn of the century, in 2007–2008, 2012, and again in 2015. At its high, it had the highest market value of any public company worldwide. Apple has been so successful that the NASDAQ stock exchange concluded Apple's price was skewing the price of the NASDAQ 100 Index and reduced Apple's weight in that index from 20 percent

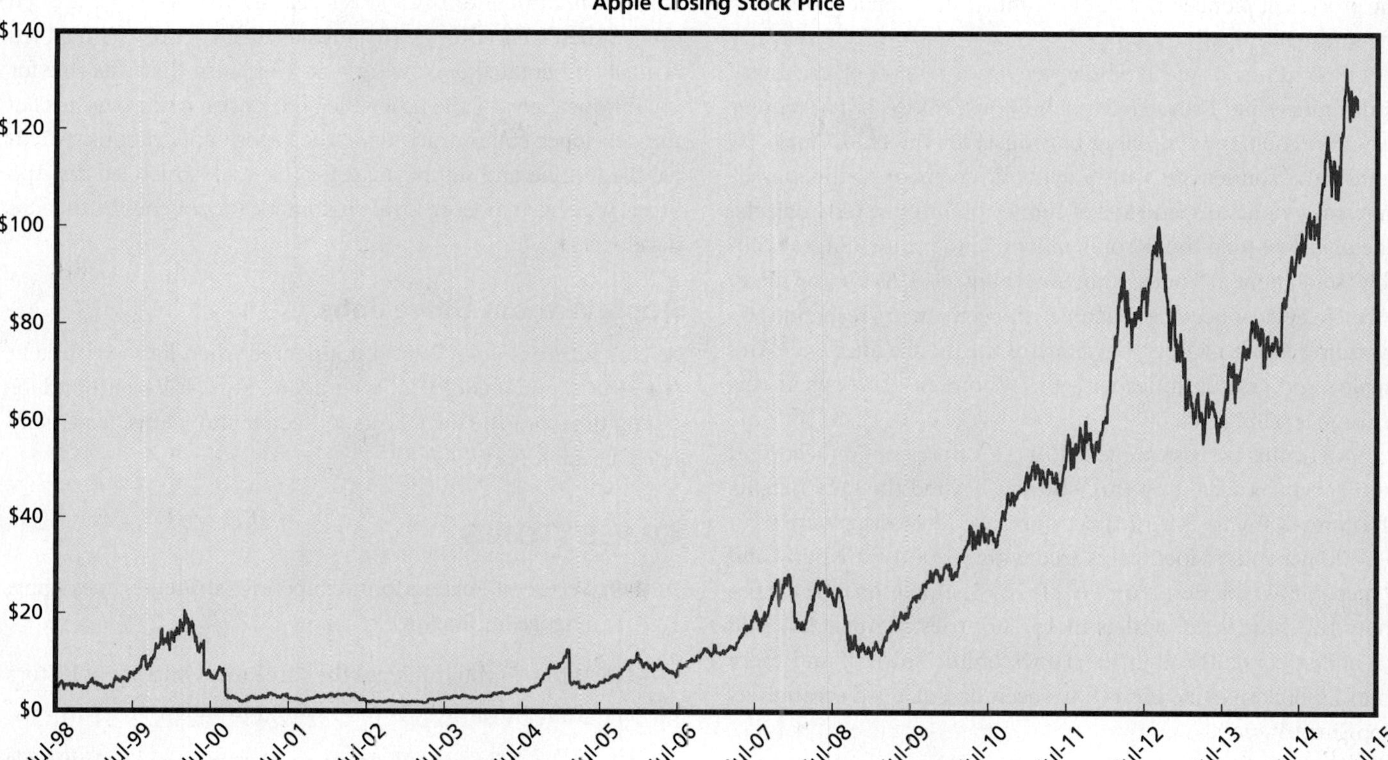


**Figure 4-17**
Growth in Apple Stock Price

to 12 percent. As of this writing, Apple stock is trading at $128 after hitting a recent low of $56 in 2013.

But since Steve Jobs's death (October 5, 2011), there haven't been any groundbreaking products like the iPod, iPhone, and iPad. Yes, iWatch was released in 2015, but many initial reviews were tepid at best.[32] There were already several smartwatches on the market that had similar functionality, and it had performance issues. Most importantly, it wasn't clear if the iWatch provided enough value over the iPhone that was already in users' pockets. In short, it wasn't an immediate hit. So, what does the future look like for Apple and its shareholders? Uncertain, especially if you consider its past history without Jobs.

## Early Success and Downfall

At the dawn of the personal computer age, in the early 1980s, Apple pioneered well-engineered home computers and innovative interfaces with its Apple II PC for the home and its Macintosh computer for students and knowledge workers. At one point, Apple owned more than 20 percent of the PC market, competing against many other PC vendors, most of which are no longer relevant (or in business).

However, Apple lost its way. In 1985, Steve Jobs, Apple's chief innovator, lost a fight with the Apple board and was forced out. He founded another PC company, NeXT, which developed and sold a groundbreaking PC product that was too innovative to sell well in that era. Meanwhile, Apple employed a succession of CEOs, starting with John Sculley, who was hired away from Pepsi-Cola where he'd enjoyed considerable success. Sculley's knowledge and experience did not transfer well to the PC business, however, and the company went downhill so fast that CNBC named him the 14th worst American CEO of all time.[33] Two other CEOs followed in Sculley's footsteps.

During this period, Apple made numerous mistakes, among them not rewarding innovative engineering, creating too many products for too many market segments, and losing the respect of retail computer stores. Apple's PC market share plummeted.

## Steve Jobs, Second Verse

In 1996, Apple bought Jobs's NeXT computing and gained technology that became the foundation of Mac OS X, today's Macintosh operating system. The true asset it acquired, however, was Steve Jobs. Even he, however, couldn't create an overnight miracle. It is exceedingly difficult to regain lost market share and even more difficult to regain the respect of the retail channel that had come to view Apple's products with disdain. Even by 2011, Apple's PC market share was in the range of 10 percent to 12 percent, down from a high of 20 percent in the 1980s.

In response to these problems, Apple broke away from the PC and created new markets with its iPod, iPhone, and iPad. It also countered retailer problems by opening its own stores. In the process, it pioneered the sale of music and applications over the Internet.

iPod, iPhone, and iPad devices are a marvel of creativity and engineering. They exude not only ease of use, but also now/wow/fun coolness. By selling hot music for the iPod, Apple established a connection with a dynamic segment of the market that was willing to spend lots of money on bright, shiny objects. The ability to turn the iPhone on its side to rotate images probably sold more iPhones than anything else. With the iPad, portable devices became readable, and consumers responded by awarding Apple a 44 percent share of the mobile market.[34] And Apple's success continues with the iPhone 6, which as of this writing, is selling well.

All of this success propelled Apple's stores not only beyond vanilla retailers like Best Buy but also beyond the lofty heights of Tiffany & Co. In 2011, Apple stores were grossing more than $4,000 per square foot, compared with $3,000 for Tiffany and a mere $880 for Best Buy. As of 2015, Apple operates more than 447 such retail outlets in 15 countries.[35] Apple has sold 25 billion songs through its iTunes online store,[36] and more than 75 billion applications have been downloaded through its App Store.[37]

Apple encourages customer visits and loyalty with its open and inviting sales floor, its Genius Bar help desk, and its incredibly well-trained and disciplined sales force. Salespeople, who are not commissioned, are taught to be consultants who help customers solve problems. Even some vocabulary is standardized. When an employee cannot solve a customer's problem, the word *unfortunately* is to be avoided; employees are taught to use the phrase *as it turns out*, instead.[38] Try that on your next exam!

To encourage the development of iPhone and iPad apps, Apple shares its revenue with application developers. That would be more than $25B paid to developers over the years![39] Developers responded by creating 1,000,000 iOS applications, and an army of developers are at work building thousands more while you read this.

By the way, if you want to build an iOS application, what's the first thing you need to do? Buy a Macintosh. Apple closed its development to any other development method. Adobe Flash? No way. Apple claims that Flash has too many bugs, and perhaps so. Thus, Flash developers are excluded. Microsoft Silverlight? Nope. Microsoft developers are out in the cold too. The non-Apple development community was furious, and Apple's response was, in essence, "Fine, we'll pay our $2.5B to someone else."

The bottom line? Until Jobs's death, every sales success fed every other sales success. Hot music fed the iPod. The iPod fed iTunes and created a growing customer base that was ripe for the iPhone. Sales of the iPhone fed the stores, whose success fed the developer community, which fed more applications, which fed the iPhone and set the stage for the iPad, which fed the App Store, which led to more loyal customers and, of course, to more developers.

### Apple Without Steve Jobs

Apple's future is uncertain. It floundered when Jobs was fired in the 1990s, and it could flounder again. Sure, it'll be around for a long time, but the days of its incredible innovative leadership could be, alas, over.

## QUESTIONS

**4-9.** Which of Porter's four competitive strategies does Apple engage in? Explain.

**4-10.** What do you think are the three most important factors in Apple's past success? Justify your answer.

**4-11.** Steve Jobs passed away in October 2011. Until his death, he had been the heart and soul of Apple's innovation. Today, 93,000 Apple employees continue onward in his absence. A huge question for many investors is whether the company can be successful without him. What do you think? What role did Jobs play? How can Apple respond to his loss? Would you be willing to invest in Apple without his leadership? Why or why not?

**4-12.** Microsoft took an early lead in the development of tablet devices (like the iPad), and it had the world's leading operating system and applications for more than 20 years. Provide five reasons why Microsoft has not been able to achieve the same success that Apple has. Most industry analysts would agree that the skills and abilities of Microsoft's 128,000 employees are as good, on average, as Apple's.

**4-13.** Considering your answers to the four preceding questions, if you had a spare $5,000 in your portfolio and wanted to buy an equity stock with it, would you buy AAPL (Apple)? Why or why not?

MyMISLab™

Go to the Assignments section of your MyLab to complete these writing exercises.

**4-14.** Suppose your first job out after graduating from college is working at a large insurance company. Your boss asks you to analyze the impact self-driving cars will have on revenues from car insurance policies. List four ways self-driving cars could affect the insurance industry. Justify your answers.

**4-15.** Visit *www.distrowatch.com*. Click on one of the top five listed Linux distributions (like Mint, Ubuntu, Debian, Fedora, or OpenSUSE). Click on the Screenshots link for that distribution. List some similarities between this operating system and your current operating system. Summarize the advantages and disadvantages of switching from your current operating system to a Linux distribution.

## ENDNOTES

1. SAS Institute Inc., "Big Data Meets Big Data Analytics," SAS.com, accessed May 14, 2014, *www.sas.com/resources/whitepaper/wp_46345.pdf*.
2. Pamela Vagata and Kevin Wilfong, "Scaling the Facebook Data Warehouse to 300 PB," Facebook.com, May 2014, accessed May 14, 2014, *https://code.facebook.com/posts/229861827208629/scaling-the-facebook-data-warehouse-to-300-pb*.
3. Kashmir Hill, "Blueprints of NSA's Ridiculously Expensive Data Center in Utah Suggest It Holds Less Info than Thought," *Forbes.com*, July 24, 2013, accessed May 14, 2014, *www.forbes.com/sites/kashmirhill/2013/07/24/blueprints-of-nsa-data-center-in-utah-suggest-its-storage-capacity-is-less-impressive-than-thought*.
4. Cisco Systems, Inc., "VNI Forecast Highlights," Cisco.com, accessed April 30, 2015, *www.cisco.com/web/solutions/sp/vni/vni_forecast_highlights/index.html*.
5. Jillian D'Onfro, "Amazon: Here's the Final Tally for All the Insane Shopping Everyone Did This Holiday Season," Business Insider, December 26, 2014, accessed May 1, 2015, *www.businessinsider.com/amazon-christmas-shopping-release-2014–12*.
6. Peter C. Evans and Marco Annunziata, "Industrial Internet: Pushing the Boundaries of Minds and Machines," General Electric, November 26, 2012, accessed May 21, 2014, *www.ge.com/docs/chapters/Industrial_Internet.pdf*.
7. Ibid.
8. Jennifer Warnick, "88 Acres: How Microsoft Quietly Built the City of the Future," Microsoft Corp., April 15, 2013, accessed May 21, 2014, *www.microsoft.com/en-us/news/stories/88acres/88-acres-how-microsoft-quietly-built-the-city-of-the-future-chapter-1.aspx*.
9. KPMG and the Center for Automotive Research, "Self-Driving Cars: Are We Ready," 2013, accessed May 1, 2015, *www.kpmg.com/US/en/IssuesAndInsights/ArticlesPublications/Documents/self-driving-cars-are-we-ready.pdf*.
10. Glenn Garvin, "Automakers Say Self-driving Cars Are on the Horizon," *Miami Herald*, March 21, 2014, accessed May 22, 2014, *www.tampabay.com/news/business/autos/automakers-say-self-driving-cars-are-on-the-horizon/2171386*.
11. Steven Musil, "Google Unveils Self-driving Car, Sans Steering Wheel," CNET, May 27, 2014, accessed May 28, 2014, *www.cnet.com/news/google-unveils-self-driving-car-sans-steering-wheel*.
12. The Travelers Indemnity Company, "2014 Annual Report," Travelers .com, December 31, 2014, accessed May 1, 2015, *http://investor.travelers.com/corporateprofile.aspx*.
13. Network of Employers for Traffic Safety, "10 Facts Employers Must Know," accessed May 1, 2015, *http://trafficsafety.org/safety/fleet-safety/10-facts-employers-must-know*.
14. Liz Stinson, "For Super Bowl, Nike Uses 3-D Printing to Create a Faster Football Cleat," *Wired*, January 10, 2014, accessed May 23, 2014, *www.wired.com/2014/01/nike-designed-fastest-cleat-history*.
15. See EDAG's GENESIS prototype car at *http://www.EDAG.de*.
16. Vanessa Wong, "A Guide to All the Food That's Fit to 3D Print (So Far)," *BusinessWeek*, January 28, 2014, accessed May 23, 2014, *www.businessweek.com/articles/2014-01-28/all-the-food-thats-fit-to-3d-print-from-chocolates-to-pizza*.
17. Dan Ferber, "An Essential Step Toward Printing Living Tissues," Harvard School of Engineering and Applied Sciences, February 19, 2014, accessed May 23, 2014, *www.seas.harvard.edu/news/2014/02/essential-step-toward-printing-living-tissues*.
18. Ryan Bushey, "Researchers Are Making a 3D Printer That Can Build a House in 24 Hours," *Business Insider*, January 9, 2014, accessed May 23, 2014, *www.businessinsider.com/3d-printer-builds-house-in-24-hours-2014-1*.
19. "Net Applications," April, 2014, accessed May 15, 2015, *www.netapplications.com*.
20. Previously called metro-style. Name change by Microsoft, reputedly because of a trademark lawsuit from Europe.
21. "Net Applications," April, 2014, accessed May 15, 2015, *www.netapplications.com*.
22. DistroWatch.com, accessed May 15, 2015, *www.distrowatch.com*.
23. "Net Applications," accessed July 15, 2013, *www.netapplications.com*.
24. Ibid.
25. Pew Research Center, "U.S. Smartphone Use in 2015," PewInternet .org, accessed May 2015, *www.pewinternet.org/files/2015/03/PI_Smartphones_0401151.pdf*.
26. "Unlocking the Cloud," *The Economist*, May 28, 2009, accessed August 9, 2014, *www.economist.com/node/13740181*.
27. SnoopWall, "SnoopWall Flashlight Apps Threat Assessment Report," October 1, 2014, SnoopWall.com, accessed April 27, 2015, *www.snoopwall.com/threat-reports-10-01-2014*.
28. Symantec Corporation, "Internet Security Report," Symantec.com, Volume 20, April 2015, accessed April 27, 2015, *www4.symantec.com/mktginfo/whitepaper/ISTR/21347932_GA-internet-security-threat-report-volume-20-2015-social_v2.pdf*.

29. Google, "Android Security 2014 Year in Review," *GoogleUserContent.com*, accessed April 27, 2015, *http://static.googleusercontent.com/media/source.android.com/en/us/devices/tech/security/reports/Google_Android_Security_2014_Report_Final.pdf.*
30. Microsoft envisions PixelSense as a ubiquitous billion dollar technology that will find its way to tabletops, countertops, and mirrors.
31. Microsoft press release, May 29, 2007, accessed August 9, 2014, *www.microsoft.com/en-us/news/press/2007/may07/05-29mssurfacepr.aspx.*
32. Will Shanklin, "Apple Watch Review: Elegant, Delightful . . . and Completely Optional," April 29, 2015, *Gizmag.com*, accessed May 22, 2015, *www.gizmag.com/apple-watch-review-iwatch-review/37244.*
33. "Portfolio's Worst American CEOs of All Time," *CNBC.com*, April 30, 2009, accessed August 9, 2014, *www.cnbc.com/id/30502091.*
34. Net Applications, "Mobile/Tablet Operating System Market Share," July 2014, accessed August 9, 2014, *www.netmarketshare.com/mobile-market-share.*
35. The Street Transcripts, "Apple (AAPL) Earnings Report: Q1 2015 Conference Call Transcript," TheStreet.com, January 28, 2015, accessed May 2, 2015, *www.thestreet.com/story/13025362/4/apple-aapl-earnings-report-q1-2015-conference-call-transcript.html.*
36. Alex Pham, "iTunes Crosses 25 Billion Songs Sold, Now Sells 21 Million Songs a Day," *Billboard.com*, February 6, 2013, accessed August 9, 2014, *www.billboard.com/biz/articles/news/1538108/itunes-crosses-25-billion-songs-sold-now-sells-21-million-songs-a-day.*
37. Sarah Perez, "iTunes App Store Now Has 1.2 Million Apps, Has Seen 75 Billion Downloads To Date," TechCrunch, June2, 2014, accessed August 9, 2014, *http://techcrunch.com/2014/06/02/itunes-app-store-now-has-1-2-million-apps-has-seen-75-billion-downloads-to-date/.*
38. Yukari Iwatani Kane and Ian Sherr, "Secrets from Apple's Genius Bar: Full Loyalty, No Negativity," *Wall Street Journal*, last modified June 15, 2011, *online.wsj.com/article/SB10001424052702304563104576364071955678908.html.*
39. The Street Transcripts, "Apple (AAPL) Earnings Report: Q1 2015 Conference Call Transcript."

chapter 5

# Database Processing

This could happen to you

It's Friday night, and Camillia (Cam) Forset is on her way to an art show opening. She gets an urgent call from Jess Denkar, the head of security at PetroTex. PetroTex is a large oil refinery based in Texas and one of Falcon Security's biggest industrial clients. Jess is looking for information that could help him find out who stole almost $75,000 worth of custom piping and copper wiring.

Cam made sure Jess had her personal cell phone number and told him to call her anytime—day or night. She knows it's important to show Jess that the money PetroTex spends on Falcon's services is worth it. She immediately calls Toshio Sato, director of IT Services, and tells him to come back into the office. She also sends a text message to CEO Mateo Thomas and CFO Joni Campbell.

"Have you found anything yet?" Joni asks. She quickly sets down her purse at a nearby workstation and begins hovering behind Toshio.

"Not yet—we're working as fast as we can," Cam replies tersely. Cam wants to focus on helping Toshio find the correct security footage, not discuss the importance of the PetroTex account to Falcon Security.

"Is there anything I can do to help?" Joni wonders.

"No, we're just trying to find the right footage. There's a lot of it to review," Cam sighs.

"What's the problem? Why do we have to look through so much footage?"

Toshio is tempted to tell Joni that "we" aren't looking through anything. He's the one doing the searching. But he holds his tongue. "Well, the problem is we have footage of dozens of different buildings at PetroTex, from several different drones, over about a 2-week period. Tracking down the footage of exactly when the equipment was stolen means we have to search through hundreds of different video files. This could take all night," he answers matter-of-factly.

"There's got to be a faster way to do this. Can't we just search for the footage somehow?" Joni says.

"No," Toshio says calmly. "We don't have a way to track the data about the videos. The video files are sequentially numbered and stored in directories for a specific company. We can also see the date and time the video file was created, but there are several different drones. It's just . . . "

Cam interrupts Toshio to try to keep him from getting distracted. "Toshio and I have talked about creating a database to track all of our video files. We've just been busy trying to automate the data collection and storage process."

"Well, how long would it take to make it? How much would it cost?" Joni asks.

# STUDY QUESTIONS

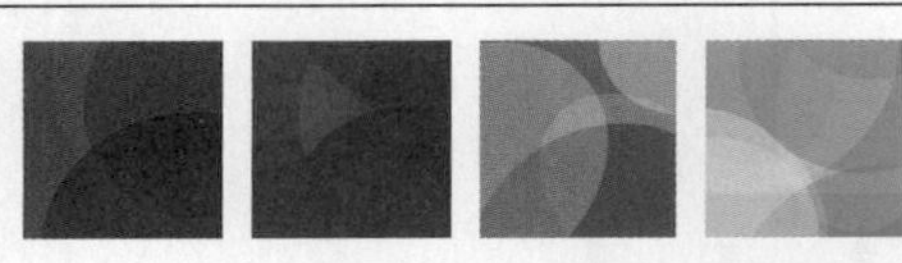

**Q5-1 WHY DO YOU NEED TO KNOW ABOUT DATABASES?**

**Q5-2 WHAT IS A DATABASE?**

**Q5-3 WHAT IS A DATABASE MANAGEMENT SYSTEM (DBMS)?**

**Q5-4 HOW DO DATABASE APPLICATIONS MAKE DATABASES MORE USEFUL?**

**Q5-5 HOW CAN FALCON SECURITY BENEFIT FROM A DATABASE SYSTEM?**

**Q5-6 WHAT ARE NONTRADITIONAL DBMS PRODUCTS?**

## How does the **knowledge** in this chapter help **you?**

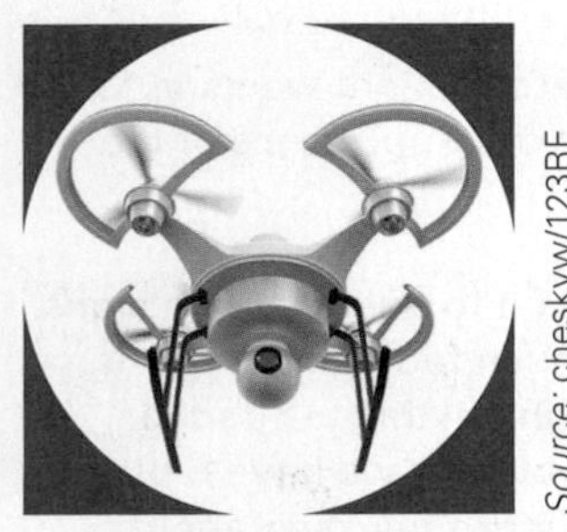

*Source:* cheskyw/123RF

**"We don't have a way to track the data about the videos."**

"We're not sure. We don't even know which database management system we'd use. Toshio and I have both used Microsoft Access, but Toshio mentioned something called MongoDB that might be better for tracking video files."

Toshio pauses the video he's reviewing and starts pointing at a listing of video files in a directory. "Instead of searching through all of these manually, I could just specify characteristics about each video like company name, building name, date, time, and elevation. It would return the URLs for videos matching those characteristics. We'd know right where they are on our file server."

"Sounds good to me. Anything to keep us from spending our Friday nights looking through video footage. Let's do it," Joni quips.

Cam tries to get things back on track. "OK, great, we'll put it on our list. There's no doubt that a database will keep us from having to search through all this footage. For now, though, we should probably focus on finding the footage for Jess. We've got a lot to go through tonight."

CE

Optional Extensions for this chapter are • CE5: Database Design 435 • CE6: Using Microsoft Access 2013 449 • CE7: Using Excel and Access Together 469

# Q5-1 WHY DO YOU NEED TO KNOW ABOUT DATABASES?

This chapter and its related chapter extensions introduce you to database technology. This knowledge is important to you as a future business professional. For one, databases are everywhere. Although you may not realize it, you access dozens, if not hundreds, of databases every day. Every time you make a cell phone call, log on to the Internet, or buy something online using a credit card, applications behind the scenes are processing numerous databases. Use Snapchat, Facebook, Twitter, or LinkedIn, and again applications are processing databases on your behalf. Google something, and yet again dozens of databases are processed to obtain the search results.

## REASONS FOR LEARNING DATABASE TECHNOLOGY

As a user, you need know nothing about the underlying technology. From your perspective, "it just works," to quote the late Steve Jobs. However, as a business professional in the 21st century, it's a different story. You need the knowledge of this chapter and the related extensions for four principal reasons:

1. When you participate in the development of any new business initiative, you need to know if database technology can facilitate your project goals. If so, you need sufficient knowledge to assess whether building that database is akin to building a small shed or is closer to building a skyscraper. Joni, in the opening vignette of this chapter, needs to have some knowledge to assess how hard (and thus how expensive) building that new database will be.
2. Because databases are ubiquitous in commerce, billions of bytes of data are stored every day. You need to know how to turn that data into a format from which you can construct useful information. To that end, you might use one of many different graphical tools to query that data. Or, to become truly proficient, you might learn SQL, an international standard language for querying databases. Many business professionals have done just that. See the So What? feature of this chapter on page 129.
3. Business is dynamic, and information systems must adapt. Often, such adaptation means that the structure of the database needs to be changed. Sometimes, it means that entirely new databases must be created. As you will learn in this chapter, only the users, such as yourself, know what and how details should be stored. You may be asked to evaluate a data model like those described in Chapter Extension 5.
4. Finally, you might someday find yourself or your department in a material mess. Maybe you don't know who has which equipment, or where certain tools are located, or what's really in your supply closet. In that case, you might choose to build your own database. Unless you're an IS professional, that database will be small and relatively simple, but it can still be very useful to you and your colleagues. Case Study 5 on page 147 illustrates one such example.

So let's get started by discussing the purpose of a database.

## WHAT IS THE PURPOSE OF A DATABASE?

The purpose of a database is to help people keep track of things. When most students learn that, they wonder why we need a special technology for such a simple task. Why not just use a list? If the list is long, put it into a spreadsheet.

In fact, many professionals do keep track of things using spreadsheets. If the structure of the list is simple enough, there is no need to use database technology. The list of student grades in Figure 5-1, for example, works perfectly well in a spreadsheet.

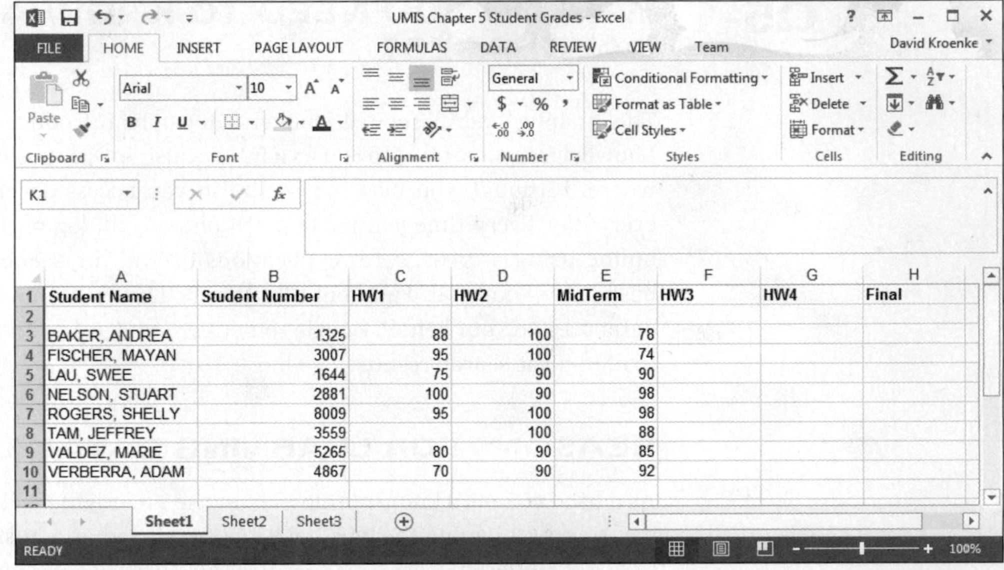

| | A | B | C | D | E | F | G | H |
|---|---|---|---|---|---|---|---|---|
| 1 | Student Name | Student Number | HW1 | HW2 | MidTerm | HW3 | HW4 | Final |
| 2 | | | | | | | | |
| 3 | BAKER, ANDREA | 1325 | 88 | 100 | 78 | | | |
| 4 | FISCHER, MAYAN | 3007 | 95 | 100 | 74 | | | |
| 5 | LAU, SWEE | 1644 | 75 | 90 | 90 | | | |
| 6 | NELSON, STUART | 2881 | 100 | 90 | 98 | | | |
| 7 | ROGERS, SHELLY | 8009 | 95 | 100 | 98 | | | |
| 8 | TAM, JEFFREY | 3559 | | 100 | 88 | | | |
| 9 | VALDEZ, MARIE | 5265 | 80 | 90 | 85 | | | |
| 10 | VERBERRA, ADAM | 4867 | 70 | 90 | 92 | | | |
| 11 | | | | | | | | |

**Figure 5-1**
A List of Student Grades Presented in a Spreadsheet

*Source:* Microsoft Excel 2013

Suppose, however, that the professor wants to track more than just grades. Say that the professor wants to record email messages as well. Or perhaps the professor wants to record both email messages and office visits. There is no place in Figure 5-1 to record that additional data. Of course, the professor could set up a separate spreadsheet for email messages and another one for office visits, but that awkward solution would be difficult to use because it does not provide all of the data in one place.

Instead, the professor wants a form like that in Figure 5-2. With it, the professor can record student grades, emails, and office visits all in one place. A form like the one in Figure 5-2 is difficult, if not impossible, to produce from a spreadsheet. Such a form is easily produced, however, from a database.

**Chapter Extension 5 explains how to apply this general rule using a design process called normalization.**

The key distinction between Figures 5-1 and 5-2 is that the data in Figure 5-1 is about a single theme or concept. It is about student grades only. The data in Figure 5-2 has multiple themes;

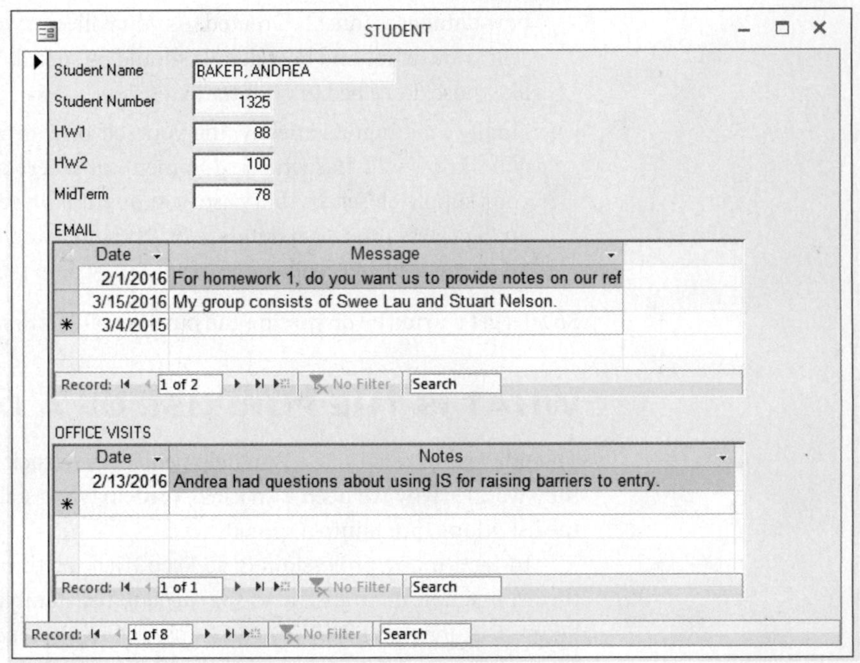

STUDENT

Student Name: BAKER, ANDREA
Student Number: 1325
HW1: 88
HW2: 100
MidTerm: 78

EMAIL

| Date | Message |
|---|---|
| 2/1/2016 | For homework 1, do you want us to provide notes on our ref |
| 3/15/2016 | My group consists of Swee Lau and Stuart Nelson. |
| * 3/4/2015 | |

Record: 1 of 2 No Filter Search

OFFICE VISITS

| Date | Notes |
|---|---|
| 2/13/2016 | Andrea had questions about using IS for raising barriers to entry. |
| * | |

Record: 1 of 1 No Filter Search

Record: 1 of 8 No Filter Search

**Figure 5-2**
Student Data Shown in a Form from a Database

*Source:* Microsoft Access 2013

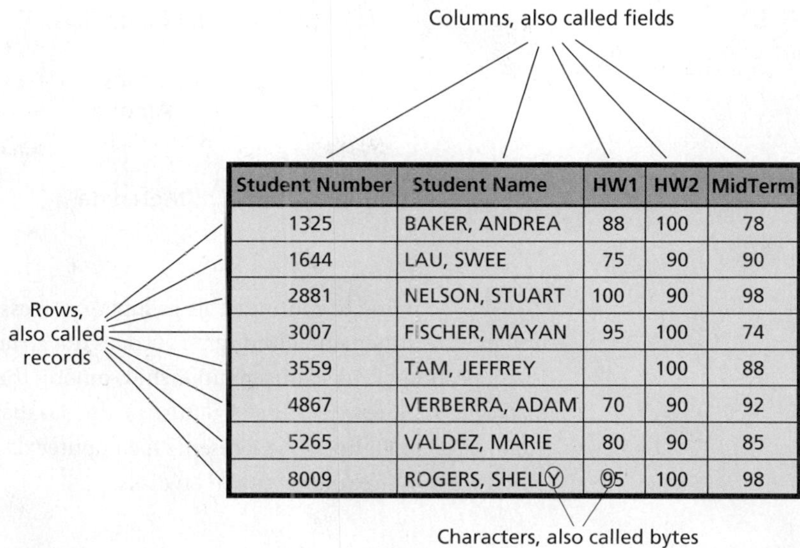


| Student Number | Student Name | HW1 | HW2 | MidTerm |
|---|---|---|---|---|
| 1325 | BAKER, ANDREA | 88 | 100 | 78 |
| 1644 | LAU, SWEE | 75 | 90 | 90 |
| 2881 | NELSON, STUART | 100 | 90 | 98 |
| 3007 | FISCHER, MAYAN | 95 | 100 | 74 |
| 3559 | TAM, JEFFREY | | 100 | 88 |
| 4867 | VERBERRA, ADAM | 70 | 90 | 92 |
| 5265 | VALDEZ, MARIE | 80 | 90 | 85 |
| 8009 | ROGERS, SHELLY | 95 | 100 | 98 |

**Figure 5-3**
Student Table (also called a file)

it shows student grades, student emails, and student office visits. We can make a general rule from these examples: Lists of data involving a single theme can be stored in a spreadsheet; lists that involve data with multiple themes require a database.

## Q5-2 WHAT IS A DATABASE?

A **database** is a self-describing collection of integrated records. To understand the terms in this definition, you first need to understand the terms illustrated in Figure 5-3. As you learned in Chapter 4, a **byte** is a character of data. In databases, bytes are grouped into **columns**, such as *Student Number* and *Student Name*. Columns are also called **fields**. Columns or fields, in turn, are grouped into **rows**, which are also called **records**. In Figure 5-3, the collection of data for all columns (*Student Number, Student Name, HW1, HW2*, and *MidTerm*) is called a *row* or a *record*. Finally, a group of similar rows or records is called a **table** or a **file**. From these definitions, you can see that there is a hierarchy of data elements, as shown in Figure 5-4.

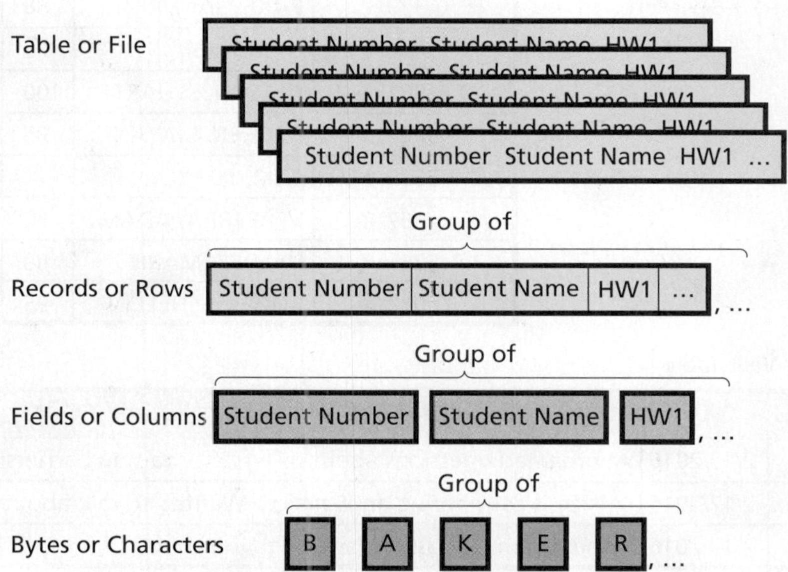


**Figure 5-4**
Hierarchy of Data Elements

**Figure 5-5**
Components of a Database

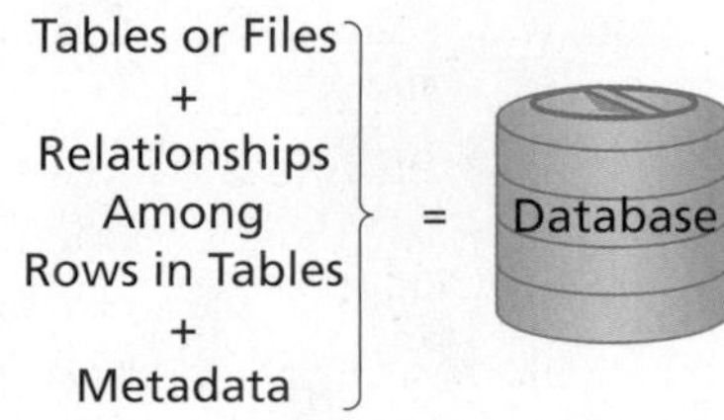


It is tempting to continue this grouping process by saying that a database is a group of tables or files. This statement, although true, does not go far enough. As shown in Figure 5-5, a database is a collection of tables *plus* relationships among the rows in those tables, *plus* special data, called *metadata*, that describes the structure of the database. By the way, the cylindrical symbol labeled "database" in Figure 5-5 represents a computer disk drive. It represents databases because databases are most frequently stored on disks.

**Access is a common database. For more information on Access, see Chapter Extensions 6 and 7. Chapter Extension 7 covers Excel as well.**

## RELATIONSHIPS AMONG ROWS

Consider the terms on the left-hand side of Figure 5-5. You know what tables are. To understand what is meant by *relationships among rows in tables*, examine Figure 5-6. It shows sample data from the three tables *Email*, *Student*, and *Office_Visit*. Notice the column named *Student Number* in the *Email* table. That column indicates the row in *Student* to which a row of *Email* is connected. In the first row of *Email*, the *Student Number* value is 1325. This indicates that this particular email was received from the student whose *Student Number* is 1325. If you examine the *Student* table,

**Figure 5-6**
Example of Relationships Among Rows

**Email Table**

| EmailNum | Date | Message | Student Number |
|---|---|---|---|
| 1 | 2/1/2016 | For homework 1, do you want us to provide notes on our references? | 1325 |
| 2 | 3/15/2016 | My group consists of Swee Lau and Stuart Nelson. | 1325 |
| 3 | 3/15/2016 | Could you please assign me to a group? | 1644 |

**Student Table**

| Student Number | Student Name | HW1 | HW2 | MidTerm |
|---|---|---|---|---|
| 1325 | BAKER, ANDREA | 88 | 100 | 78 |
| 1644 | LAU, SWEE | 75 | 90 | 90 |
| 2881 | NELSON, STUART | 100 | 90 | 98 |
| 3007 | FISCHER, MAYAN | 95 | 100 | 74 |
| 3559 | TAM, JEFFREY | | 100 | 88 |
| 4867 | VERBERRA, ADAM | 70 | 90 | 92 |
| 5265 | VALDEZ, MARIE | 80 | 90 | 85 |
| 8009 | ROGERS, SHELLY | 95 | 100 | 98 |

**Office_Visit Table**

| VisitID | Date | Notes | Student Number |
|---|---|---|---|
| 2 | 2/13/2016 | Andrea had questions about using IS for raising barriers to entry. | 1325 |
| 3 | 2/17/2016 | Jeffrey is considering an IS major. Wanted to talk about career opportunities. | 3559 |
| 4 | 2/17/2016 | Adam will miss class Friday due to job conflict. | 4867 |

you will see that the row for Andrea Baker has this value. Thus, the first row of the *Email* table is related to Andrea Baker.

Now consider the last row of the *Office_Visit* table at the bottom of Figure 5-6. The value of *Student Number* in that row is 4867. This value indicates that the last row in *Office_Visit* belongs to Adam Verberra.

From these examples, you can see that values in one table relate rows of that table to rows in a second table. Several special terms are used to express these ideas. A **key** (also called a **primary key**) is a column or group of columns that identifies a unique row in a table. *Student Number* is the key of the *Student* table. Given a value of *Student Number*, you can determine one and only one row in *Student*. Only one student has the number 1325, for example.

Every table must have a key. The key of the *Email* table is *EmailNum*, and the key of the *Office_Visit* table is *VisitID*. Sometimes more than one column is needed to form a unique identifier. In a table called *City*, for example, the key would consist of the combination of columns (*City, State*) because a given city name can appear in more than one state.

*Student Number* is not the key of the *Email* or the *Office_Visit* tables. We know that about *Email* because there are two rows in *Email* that have the *Student Number* value 1325. The value 1325 does not identify a unique row, therefore *Student Number* cannot be the key of *Email*.

Nor is *Student Number* a key of *Office_Visit*, although you cannot tell that from the data in Figure 5-6. If you think about it, however, there is nothing to prevent a student from visiting a professor more than once. If that were to happen, there would be two rows in *Office_Visit* with the same value of *Student Number*. It just happens that no student has visited twice in the limited data in Figure 5-6.

In both *Email* and *Office_Visit*, *Student Number* is a key, but it is a key of a different table, namely *Student*. Hence, the columns that fulfill a role like that of *Student Number* in the *Email* and *Office_Visit* tables are called **foreign keys**. This term is used because such columns are keys, but they are keys of a different (foreign) table than the one in which they reside.

Before we go on, databases that carry their data in the form of tables and that represent relationships using foreign keys are called **relational databases**. (The term *relational* is used because another, more formal name for a table like those we're discussing is **relation**.) You'll learn about another kind of database in Q5-5.

## METADATA

Recall the definition of database: A database is a self-describing collection of integrated records. The records are integrated because, as you just learned, rows can be linked together by their key/foreign key relationships. Thus, relationships among rows are represented in the database. But what does *self-describing* mean?

It means that a database contains, within itself, a description of its contents. Think of a library. A library is a self-describing collection of books and other materials. It is self-describing because the library contains a catalog that describes the library's contents. The same idea also pertains to a database. Databases are self-describing because they contain not only data, but also data about the data in the database.

**Metadata** are data that describe data. Figure 5-7 shows metadata for the *Email* table. The format of metadata depends on the software product that is processing the database. Figure 5-7 shows the metadata as it appears in Microsoft Access. Each row of the top part of this form describes a column of the *Email* table. The columns of these descriptions are *Field Name, Data Type*, and *Description. Field Name* contains the name of the column, *Data Type* shows the type of data the column may hold, and *Description* contains notes that explain the source or use of the column. As you can see, there is one row of metadata for each of the four columns of the *Email* table: *EmailNum, Date, Message*, and *Student Number*.

The bottom part of this form provides more metadata, which Access calls *Field Properties*, for each column. In Figure 5-7, the focus is on the *Date* column. (Note the light rectangle drawn

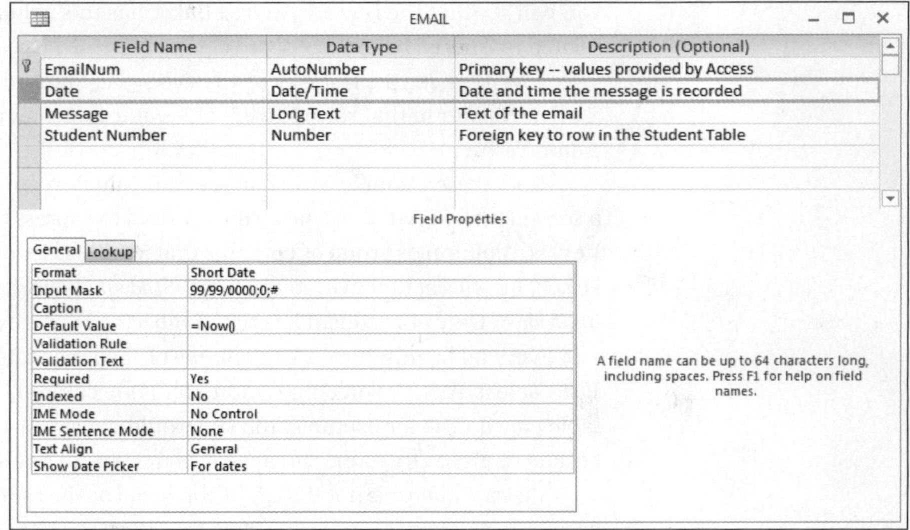


**Figure 5-7**
Sample Metadata (in Access)

*Source:* Microsoft Access 2013

around the *Date* row.) Because the focus is on *Date* in the top pane, the details in the bottom pane pertain to the *Date* column. The Field Properties describe formats, a default value for Access to supply when a new row is created, and the constraint that a value is required for this column. It is not important for you to remember these details. Instead, just understand that metadata are data about data and that such metadata are always a part of a database.

The presence of metadata makes databases much more useful. Because of metadata, no one needs to guess, remember, or even record what is in the database. To find out what a database contains, we just look at the metadata inside the database.

# Q5-3 WHAT IS A DATABASE MANAGEMENT SYSTEM (DBMS)?

A **database management system (DBMS)** is a program used to create, process, and administer a database. As with operating systems, almost no organization develops its own DBMS. Instead, companies license DBMS products from vendors such as IBM, Microsoft, Oracle, and others. Popular DBMS products are **DB2** from IBM, **Access** and **SQL Server** from Microsoft, and **Oracle Database** from the Oracle Corporation. Another popular DBMS is **MySQL**, an open source DBMS product that is license-free for most applications.[1] Other DBMS products are available, but these five process the great bulk of databases today.

Note that a DBMS and a database are two different things. For some reason, the trade press and even some books confuse the two. A DBMS is a software program; a database is a collection of tables, relationships, and metadata. The two are very different concepts.

## Creating the Database and Its Structures

Database developers use the DBMS to create tables, relationships, and other structures in the database. The form in Figure 5-7 can be used to define a new table or to modify an existing one. To create a new table, the developer just fills the new table's metadata into the form.

To modify an existing table—say, to add a new column—the developer opens the metadata form for that table and adds a new row of metadata. For example, in Figure 5-8 the developer has added a new column called *Response?*. This new column has the data type *Yes/No*, which means that the column can contain only one value—*Yes* or *No*. The professor will use this column to

# Not What the Data Says...

Two product managers, Jeremey Will and Neil Town, are arguing about the effectiveness of a September product sales promotion in front of their boss, Sarah Murphy.

SARAH: "So, should we repeat that promotion in October?"

JEREMEY: "No way. It was expensive, and there was no increase in sales."

NEIL: "I disagree. Well, wait, I agree there was no increase in sales from August, but if you look at sales history, we have a substantial increase over past Septembers."

JEREMEY: "Where'd you get that data?"

NEIL: "Extract from the sales database. Anyway, on average, our sales are up 11 percent from past years. And, even better, most of that increase is from new customers."

JEREMEY: "I don't think so. I called four different sales reps, and they said they can't get any prospects to bite."

NEIL: "Not what the data says. I put it into Access and then did a series of queries. Nineteen percent of sales in September were from new customers."

SARAH: "Amazing. But can you relate that to the campaign?"

NEIL: "Yes, strongly. Turns out of the new customers' sales, almost two-thirds used a coupon."

SARAH: "Neil, put this into a report for me. I want to take it to the executive meeting tomorrow."

*Source:* StockLite/Shutterstock

## QUESTIONS

1. Do you want to be Jeremey or Neil? Justify your answer.
2. What skills and abilities will you need to be Neil?
3. List specific sales data you need to provide answers as Neil does.
4. In words, describe how that data needs to be processed in order to produce Neil's responses.
5. All of the results that Neil provides are readily produced by Access or by any SQL-processing DBMS. With a basic understanding of SQL, you could write the queries in 5 minutes or less. However, this chapter will give you necessary background, but it won't teach you SQL queries. Consult your university's course catalog and find a course that would teach you the necessary skills. Name that course and explain why you will (or will not) take it.

indicate whether he has responded to the student's email. A column can be removed by deleting its row in this table, though doing so will cause any existing data to be lost.

### Processing the Database

The second function of the DBMS is to process the database. Such processing can be quite complex, but, fundamentally, the DBMS provides applications for four processing operations: to read, insert, modify, or delete data. These operations are requested in application calls upon the DBMS. From a form, when the user enters new or changed data, a computer

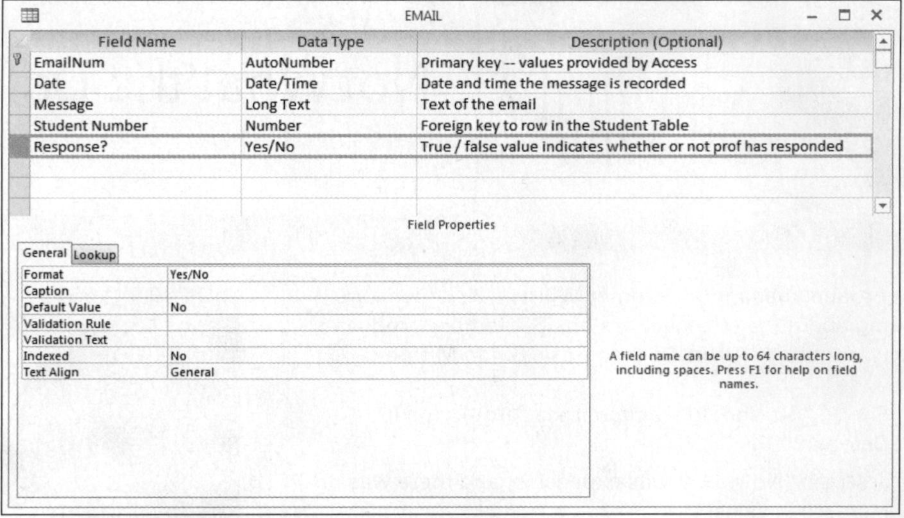


**Figure 5-8**
Adding a New Column to a Table (in Access)
*Source:* Microsoft Access 2013

program behind the form calls the DBMS to make the necessary database changes. From a Web application, a program on the client or on the server application program calls the DBMS to make the change.

**SQL is essential for processing a database, but it can be misused by criminals to steal data. This kind of SQL injection attack is described in the Guide on pages 142–143.**

**Structured Query Language (SQL)** is an international standard language for processing a database. All five of the DBMS products mentioned earlier accept and process SQL (pronounced "see-quell") statements. As an example, the following SQL statement inserts a new row into the *Student* table:

```
INSERT INTO Student
([Student Number], [Student Name], HW1, HW2, MidTerm)
VALUES (1000, 'Franklin, Benjamin', 90, 95, 100);
```

As stated, statements like this one are issued "behind the scenes" by programs that process forms. Alternatively, they can be issued directly to the DBMS by an application program.

You do not need to understand or remember SQL language syntax. Instead, just realize that SQL is an international standard for processing a database. SQL can also be used to create databases and database structures. You will learn more about SQL if you take a database management class.

## Administering the Database

A third DBMS function is to provide tools to assist in the administration of the database. **Database administration** involves a wide variety of activities. For example, the DBMS can be used to set up a security system involving user accounts, passwords, permissions, and limits for processing the database. To provide database security, a user must sign on using a valid user account before she can process the database.

Permissions can be limited in very specific ways. In the Student database example, it is possible to limit a particular user to reading only *Student Name* from the *Student* table. A different user could be given permission to read the entire *Student* table, but limited to update only the *HW1*, *HW2*, and *MidTerm* columns. Other users can be given still other permissions.

In addition to security, DBMS administrative functions include backing up database data, adding structures to improve the performance of database applications, removing data that are no longer wanted or needed, and similar tasks.

**Figure 5-9**
Summary of Database Administration (DBA) Tasks

| Category | Database Administration Task | Description |
|---|---|---|
| Development | Create and staff DBA function | Size of DBA group depends on size and complexity of database. Groups range from one part-time person to small group. |
| | Form steering committee | Consists of representatives of all user groups. Forum for community-wide discussions and decisions. |
| | Specify requirements | Ensure that all appropriate user input is considered. |
| | Validate data model | Check data model for accuracy and completeness. |
| | Evaluate application design | Verify that all necessary forms, reports, queries, and applications are developed. Validate design and usability of application components. |
| Operation | Manage processing rights and responsibilities | Determine processing rights/restrictions on each table and column. |
| | Manage security | Add and delete users and user groups as necessary; ensure that security system works. |
| | Track problems and manage resolution | Develop system to record and manage resolution of problems. |
| | Monitor database performance | Provide expertise/solutions for performance improvements. |
| | Manage DBMS | Evaluate new features and functions. |
| Backup and Recovery | Monitor backup procedures | Verify that database backup procedures are followed. |
| | Conduct training | Ensure that users and operations personnel know and understand recovery procedures. |
| | Manage recovery | Manage recovery process. |
| Adaptation | Set up request tracking system | Develop system to record and prioritize requests for change. |
| | Manage configuration change | Manage impact of database structure changes on applications and users. |

For important databases, most organizations dedicate one or more employees to the role of database administration. Figure 5-9 summarizes the major responsibilities for this function. You will learn more about this topic if you take a database management course.

## Q5-4 HOW DO DATABASE APPLICATIONS MAKE DATABASES MORE USEFUL?

A set of database tables, by itself, is not very useful; the tables in Figure 5-6 contain the data the professor wants, but the format is awkward at best. The data in database tables can be made more useful, or more available for the conception of information, when it is placed into forms like that in Figure 5-2 or other formats.

A **database application** is a collection of **forms**, **reports**, **queries**, and application programs[2] that serves as an intermediary between users and database data. Database applications reformat database table data to make it more informative and more easily updated. Application programs also have features that provide security, maintain data consistency, and handle special cases.

The specific purposes of the four elements of a database application are:

| | |
|---|---|
| **Forms** | View data; insert new, update existing, and delete existing data. |
| **Reports** | Structured presentation of data using sorting, grouping, filtering, and other operations. |
| **Queries** | Search based on data values provided by the user. |
| **Application programs** | Provide security, data consistency, and special-purpose processing, e.g., handle out-of-stock situations. |

Database applications came into prominence in the 1990s and were based on the technology that was available at that time. Many existing systems today are long-lived extensions to those applications; the ERP system SAP (discussed in Chapter 7) is a good example of this concept. You should expect to see these kinds of applications during the early years of your career.

Today, however, many database applications are based on newer technology that employs browsers, the Web, and related standards. These browser-based applications can do everything the older ones do, but they are more dynamic and better suited to today's world. To see why, consider each type.

## TRADITIONAL FORMS, QUERIES, REPORTS, AND APPLICATIONS

**Database technology puts unprecedented ability to conceive information into the hands of users. But what do you do with that information when you find something objectionable? See the Ethics Guide on pages 140–141 for an example case.**

In most cases, a traditional database is shared among many users. In that case, the application shown in Figure 5-10 resides on the users' computers and the DBMS and database reside on a server computer. A network, in most cases *not* the Internet, is used to transmit traffic back and forth between the users' computers and the DBMS server computer.

Single-user databases like those in Microsoft Access are an exception. With such databases, the application, the DBMS, and the database all reside on the user's computer.

Traditional forms appeared in windows-like displays like that in Figure 5-2. They serve their purpose; users can view, insert, modify, and delete data with them, but by today's standards, they look clunky. They are certainly a far cry from the modern interface discussed in Chapter 4.

Figure 5-11 shows a traditional report, which is a static display of data, placed into a format that is meaningful to the user. In this report, each of the emails for a particular student is shown after the students' name and grade data. Figure 5-12 shows a traditional query. The user specifies query criteria in a window-like box (Figure 5-12a), and the application responds with data that fit those criteria (Figure 5-12b).

Traditional database applications programs are written in object-oriented languages such as C++ and VisualBasic (and even in earlier languages like COBOL). They are thick applications that

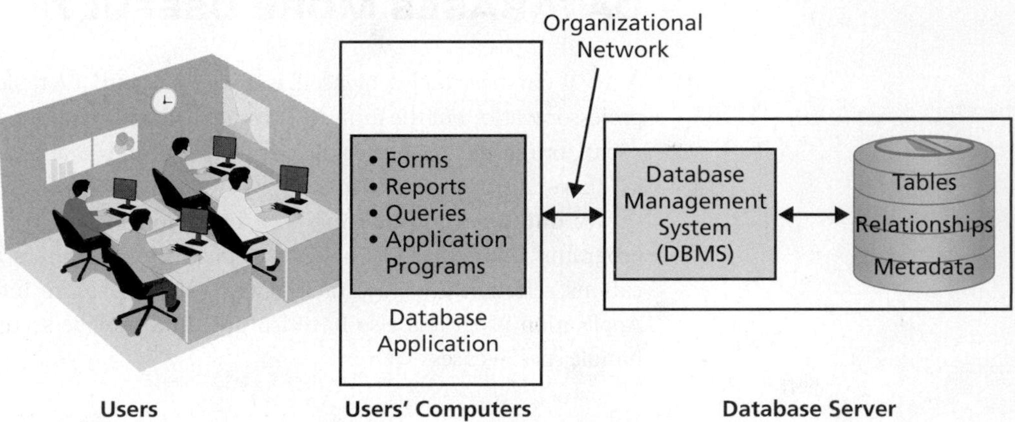


**Figure 5-10**
Processing Environment of a Traditional Database Application

**Figure 5-11**
Example of a Student Report

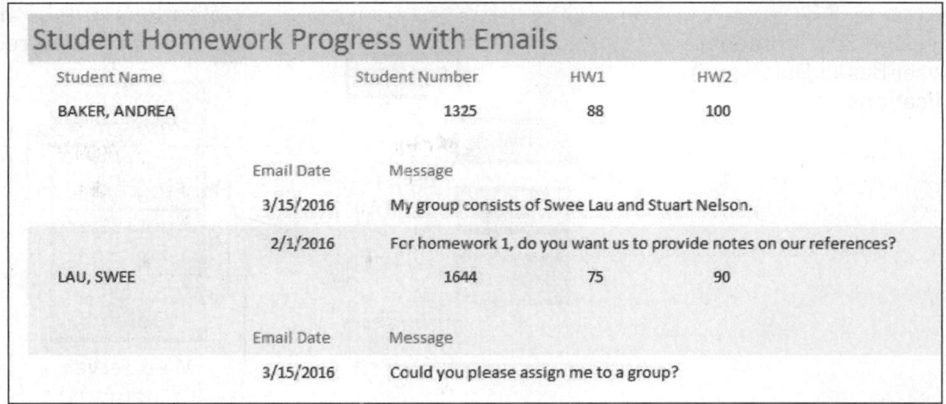

Student Homework Progress with Emails

| Student Name | Student Number | HW1 | HW2 |
|---|---|---|---|
| BAKER, ANDREA | 1325 | 88 | 100 |

| Email Date | Message |
|---|---|
| 3/15/2016 | My group consists of Swee Lau and Stuart Nelson. |
| 2/1/2016 | For homework 1, do you want us to provide notes on our references? |

| Student Name | Student Number | HW1 | HW2 |
|---|---|---|---|
| LAU, SWEE | 1644 | 75 | 90 |

| Email Date | Message |
|---|---|
| 3/15/2016 | Could you please assign me to a group? |

need to be installed on users' computers. In some cases, all of the application logic is contained in a program on users' computers and the server does nothing except run the DBMS and serve up data. In other cases, some application code is placed on both the users' computers and the database server computer.

As stated, in the early years of your career, you will still see traditional applications, especially for enterprise-wide applications like ERP and CRM (discussed in Chapter 7). Most likely, you will also be concerned, as a user if not in a more involved way, with the transition from such traditional applications into thin-client applications.

## THIN-CLIENT FORMS, REPORTS, QUERIES, AND APPLICATIONS

The databases in thin-client applications are nearly always shared among many users. As shown in Figure 5-13, the users' browsers connect over the Internet to a Web server computer, which in turn connects to a database server computer. (Often many computers are involved on the server side of the Internet, as you will learn in Chapter 6.)

As you know, thin-client applications run in a browser and need not be preinstalled on the users' computers. In most cases, all of the code for generating and processing the application elements is shared between the users' computers and the server. JavaScript is the standard language for user-side processing. Languages like C# and Java are used for server-side code, though JavaScript is starting to be used on the server with an open source product named Node.js. (All of this is discussed further in Chapter 6.)

Browser database application forms, reports, and queries are displayed and processed using html and, most recently, using html5, css3, and JavaScript, as you learned in Chapter 4. Figure 5-14 shows a browser form that is used to create a new user account in Office 365. The form's content is dynamic; the user can click on the blue arrow next to *Additional Details* to see more data. Also, notice

**Figure 5-12a**
Sample Query Form Used to Enter Phrase for Search

*Source:* Microsoft Corporation

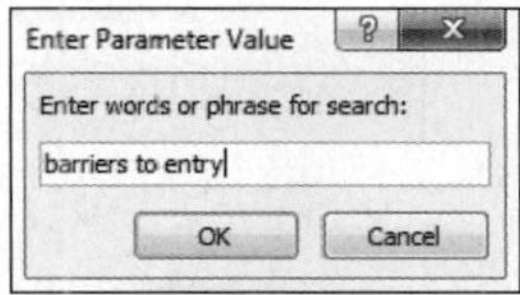


**Figure 5-12b**
Sample Query Results of Query Operation

*Source:* Microsoft Access 2013

Office Visits Keyword Query

| Student Name | Date | Notes |
|---|---|---|
| BAKER, ANDREA | 2/13/2016 | Andrea had questions about using IS for raising barriers to entry. |
| * | | |

**Figure 5-13**
Processing Environment of Browser-Based Database Applications

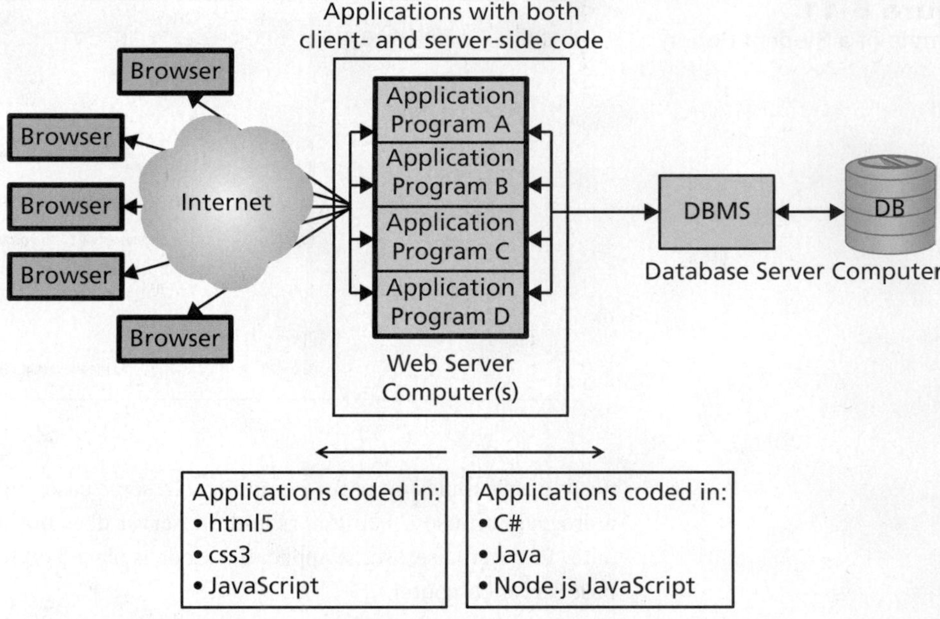


the steps in the left-hand side that outline the process that administrators will follow when creating the new account. The current step is shown in color. Compare and contrast this form with that in Figure 5-2; it is cleaner, with much less chrome.

Figure 5-15 illustrates a browser report that shows the content of a SharePoint site. The content is dynamic; almost all of the items can be clicked to produce other reports or take other actions. The user can search in the box in the upper-right-hand corner to find specific items.

Browser-based applications can support traditional queries, but more exciting are **graphical queries** in which query criteria are created when the user clicks on a graphic. Figure 5-16 shows a map of one of the facilities protected by Falcon Security. The user can click on any one of the video icons on the map, and that click will initiate a query to return a list of all the videos available from that location.

Security requirements are more stringent for thin-client applications than for traditional ones. Most traditional applications run within a corporate network that is protected from the

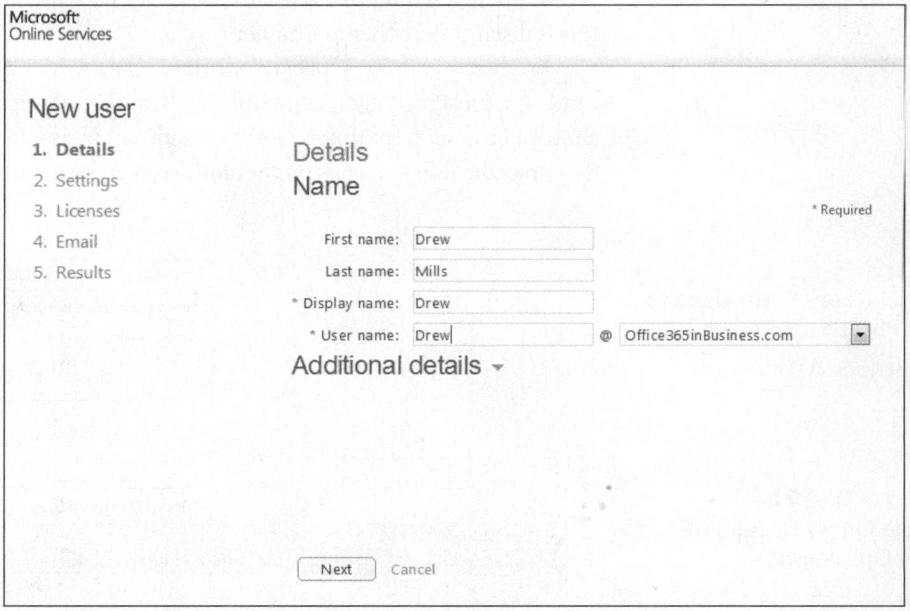

**Figure 5-14**
Microsoft Office 365 User Account Form

*Source:* Microsoft Corporation

Microsoft Online Services

New user

1. Details
2. Settings
3. Licenses
4. Email
5. Results

Details
Name

* Required

First name: Drew
Last name: Mills
* Display name: Drew
* User name: Drew @ Office365inBusiness.com

Additional details

Next Cancel

**Figure 5-15**
Browser Report for SharePoint Site
*Source:* Microsoft Corporation

threats common on the Internet. Browser-based applications that are open to the public, over the Internet, are far more vulnerable. Thus, protecting security is a major function for thin-client application programs. Like traditional database application programs, they need to provide for data consistency and to handle special conditions as well. As an example of the need for data consistency, consider the problems introduced by multiuser processing.

## MULTIUSER PROCESSING

Most traditional and thin-client applications involve multiple users processing the same database. While such **multiuser processing** is common, it does pose unique problems that you, as a future

**Figure 5-16**
Graphical Query: User Clicks on Video Icon to Find All Videos from That Location

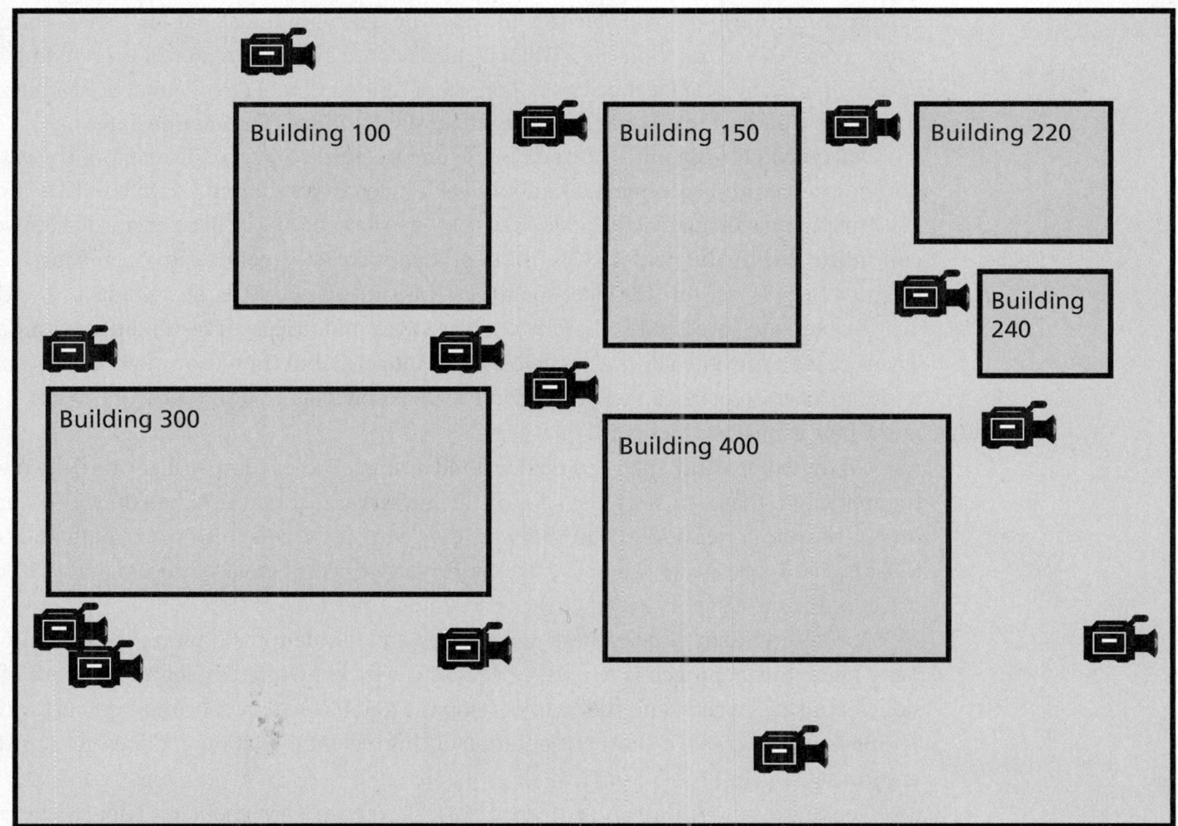

manager, should know about. To understand the nature of those problems, consider the following scenario, which could occur on either type of application.

At a ticket vendor's Web site, two customers, Andrea and Jeffrey, are both attempting to buy the last two tickets to a popular event. Andrea uses her browser to access the site and finds that two are available. She places both of them in her shopping cart. She doesn't know it, but when she opened the order form, she invoked an application program on the vendor's servers that read a database to find that two are available. Before she checks out, she takes a moment to verify with her friend that they still want to go.

Meanwhile, Jeffrey uses his browser and also finds that two tickets are available because his browser activates that same application that reads the database and finds (because Andrea has not yet checked out) that two are available. He places both in his cart and checks out.

Meanwhile, Andrea and her friend decide to go, so she checks out. Clearly, we have a problem. Both Andrea and Jeffrey have purchased the same two tickets. One of them is going to be disappointed.

This problem, known as the **lost-update problem**, exemplifies one of the special characteristics of multiuser database processing. To prevent this problem, some type of locking must be used to coordinate the activities of users who know nothing about one another. Locking brings its own set of problems, however, and those problems must be addressed as well. We will not delve further into this topic here, however.

Be aware of possible data conflicts when you manage business activities that involve multiuser processing. If you find inaccurate results that seem not to have a cause, you may be experiencing multiuser data conflicts. Contact your IS department for assistance.

## Q5-5 HOW CAN FALCON SECURITY BENEFIT FROM A DATABASE SYSTEM?

Falcon Security wants to be able to find videos by querying their characteristics. For example, it wants responses to questions like "Which videos do we have of the Beresford Building in October 2015, shot from 3,000 feet or less?" And, from time to time, Falcon employees analyze some of the videos and want to record comments about their analyses for potential later use.

Falcon can choose one of two database architectures. For one, it can store the video footage on a file server and keep metadata about each video in a relational database that it can query. That metadata will include the address of the video footage on the file server. Alternatively, Falcon can utilize one of the new NoSQL DBMS products like **MongoDB**—an open source document-oriented DBMS—to store the video footage in the same database as the metadata. (See Q5-6.)

Toshio Sato investigates these two alternatives and discusses his findings with Cam Forset. They are both intrigued by the possible use of MongoDB, but they know their interest is, in part, a desire to learn something new. They don't really know how well that product works, nor do they know how robust the MongoDB query facility will be.

On the other hand, they can readily build a simple Access database to store the metadata. In the metadata, they can store the URL of the file server location that has the video (for example, *https://abc.Falcon.com/Video1*). In this way, they can use Access to store the data and then query it using the Access graphical query facility. Because Access can also process native SQL, they can use it for the most sophisticated query operations, if needed.

Toshio and Cam discuss these alternatives and decide to use Access to store the metadata. They know this approach is less risky because it uses known technology. Also, both of them are skilled at using Access, and they can develop the database and application quickly with less risk. Toshio and Cam create a short presentation of this recommendation and present it to Mateo, who approves it.

Their next step is to create a data model, a task you can learn about in Chapter Extension 5.

# Q5-6 WHAT ARE NONTRADITIONAL DBMS PRODUCTS?

The relational model was the single, standard way of processing databases for more than 30 years. Recently, however, that has started to change. Part of the reason is that the major principles of the relational model—fixed-sized tables, representing relationships with foreign keys, and the theory of normalization—came about because of limited storage space and limited processing speeds back in the 1960s and early 1970s.[3] At some point, maybe the mid-1990s, these limitations were removed by improved storage and processing technology, and today they do not exist. In other words, the relational model is not needed today.

Furthermore, the relational model was never a natural fit with business documents. For example, users want to store sales orders; they do not want to break up sales orders via normalization and store the data in separate tables. It's like taking your car into a parking garage and having the attendant break it up into pieces, store the pieces in separate piles, and then reassemble the pieces when you come back to get your car. And why? For the efficiency and convenience of the parking garage management. Thus, the primary reason for the relational model's existence is gone, and document piece-making via normalization is no longer necessary.

## NEED TO STORE NEW DATA TYPES DIFFERENTLY

There are other reasons for the appearance of new styles of database processing. For one, many organizations, like Falcon Security, want to store new types of data such as images, audio, and videos. Those files are large collections of bits, and they don't fit into relational structures. As you learned in Q5-5, collections of such files still need metadata; we need such data to record when, where, how, and for what purpose the files exist, but we don't need to put them into relational databases just to obtain metadata.

Also, many Internet applications process many, many more transactions against much simpler data than traditional applications do. A tweet has a trivial data structure when compared to the configuration of a Kenworth truck, but there are so many more tweets than truck configurations.

Even more important, traditional relational DBMS products devote considerable code and processing power to support what are termed **ACID** (atomic, consistent, isolated, durable) transactions. In essence, this acronym means that either all of a transaction is processed or none of it is (atomic), that transactions are processed in the same manner (consistent) whether processed alone or in the presence of millions of other transactions (isolated), and that once a transaction is stored, it never goes away—even in the presence of failure (durable).

ACID transactions are critical to traditional commercial applications. Even in the presence of machine failure, Vanguard must process both the sell and the buy sides of a transaction: It cannot process part of a transaction. Also, what it stores today must be stored tomorrow. But, many new Internet applications don't need ACID. Who cares if, one time out of 1 million, only half of your tweet is stored? Or if it's stored today and disappears tomorrow?

## NEED FOR FASTER PROCESSING USING MANY SERVERS

Another reason for the development of nonrelational databases is the need to gain faster performance using many servers. A few years ago, Amazon.com determined that relational database technology wouldn't meet its processing needs, and it developed a nonrelational data store called **Dynamo**.[4] Meanwhile, for many of the same reasons, Google developed a nonrelational data store called **Bigtable**.[5] Facebook took concepts from both of these systems and developed a third nonrelational data store called **Cassandra**.[6] In 2008, Facebook turned Cassandra over to the open source community, and now Apache has dubbed it a Top-Level Project (TLP), which is the height of respectability among open source projects.

## NONTRADITIONAL DBMS TYPES

These new requirements have led to three new categories of DBMS:

1. **NoSQL DBMS.** This acronym is misleading. It really should be NotRelational DBMS. It refers to new DBMS products that support very high transaction rates processing relatively simple data structures, replicated on many servers in the cloud, without **ACID** transaction support. MongoDB, Cassandra, Bigtable, and Dynamo are NoSQL products.
2. **NewSQL DBMS.** These DBMS products process very high levels of transactions, like the NoSQL DBMS, but provide ACID support. They may or may not support the relational model. Such products are a hotbed of development with new vendors popping up nearly every day. Leading products are yet unknown.
3. **In-memory DBMS.** This category consists of DBMS products that process databases in main memory. This technique has become possible because today's computer memories can be enormous and can hold an entire database at one time, or at least very large chunks of it. Usually, these products support or extend the relational model. SAP HANA is a computer with an in-memory DBMS that provides high-volume ACID transaction support simultaneously with complex relational query processing. Tableau Software's reporting products are supported by a proprietary in-memory DBMS using an extension to SQL.

## WILL THESE NEW PRODUCTS REPLACE THE RELATIONAL MODEL?

Does the emergence of these new products mean the death knell for relational databases? It seems unlikely because organizations have created thousands of traditional relational databases with millions of lines of application code that process SQL statements against relational data structures. No organization wants to endure the expense and effort of converting those databases and code to something else. There is also a strong social trend among older technologists to hang onto the relational model. However, these new products are loosening the stronghold that relational technology has enjoyed for decades, and in the future it is likely that many NoSQL, NewSQL, and in-memory databases will exist in commerce.

Furthermore, existing DBMS vendors like Oracle, Microsoft, and IBM will not sit still. With substantial cash and highly skilled developers, they will likely incorporate features of these new categories of DBMS into their existing or new products. Acquisitions of some of the NewSQL startups, in particular, are likely.

Using the vocabulary of Chapter 3, for the first time in more than 20 years, the database software market experienced viable new entrants. So, will Microsoft and Oracle and other DBMS vendors lose some of their market to nontraditional products and vendors? Or will they follow IBM's path? Become less of a vendor of software and more a seller of services supporting open source software such as Cassandra? Or will we soon see companies like Oracle, which is rich with cash, purchasing one of these new companies? Indeed, that may have happened by the time you read this.

## WHAT DO NONRELATIONAL DBMS MEAN FOR YOU?

During the early years of your career, many nontraditional databases will be developed, and not just by leading-edge companies like Amazon.com, Google, and Facebook. So, what does that mean to you as a business professional? First, such knowledge is useful; stay abreast of developments in this area. If you were a junior person at Falcon and you went to a meeting today with Toshio and said something like, "Have you thought about using MongoDB for storing our videos?" you would gain his attention and admiration immediately. You'd likely find yourself on Falcon's key users' committee (or whatever Falcon calls it), and that would be a great career opportunity for you. Also, watch nonrelational DBMS product developments from an investor's perspective. Not all such products will be open source; even if they are, there will be companies that integrate them into their product or service offerings, and those companies may well be good investment opportunities.

If you're interested in IS as a discipline or as a second major, pay attention to these products. You still need to learn the relational model and the processing of relational databases; they will be the bread-and-butter of the industry for many more years. But exciting new opportunities and career paths will also develop around nonrelational databases. Learn about them as well, and use that knowledge to separate yourself from the competition when it comes to job interviews.

Lots of interesting, promising developments are under way!

## How does the **knowledge** in this chapter help **you?**

You now understand the purpose of a database and have an introduction to the ways that databases are processed. You also know about new categories of nontraditional DBMS. This knowledge will enable you to be an effective team member when your organization has needs like those at Falcon Security. You can add substantial value to this knowledge by studying Chapter Extensions 5, 6, and 7.

# Ethics Guide

## Querying Inequality?

MaryAnn Baker works as a data analyst in human relations at a large, multinational corporation. As part of its compensation program, her company defines job categories and assigns salary ranges to each category. For example, the category M1 is used for first-line managers and is assigned the salary range of $75,000 to $95,000. Every job description is assigned to one of these categories, depending on the knowledge and skills required to do that job. Thus, the job titles Manager of Customer Support, Manager of Technical Writing, and Manager of Product Quality Assurance are all judged to involve about the same level of management expertise and are all assigned to category M1.

One of MaryAnn's tasks is to analyze company salary data and determine how well actual salaries conform to established ranges. When discrepancies are noted, human relations managers meet to determine whether the discrepancy indicates a need to:

- Adjust the category's salary range;
- Move the job title to a different category;
- Define a new category; or
- Train the manager of the employee with the discrepancy on the use of salary ranges in setting employee compensation.

MaryAnn is an expert in creating database queries. Initially she used Microsoft Access to produce reports, but much of the salary data she needs resides in the organization's Oracle database. At first she would ask the IS Department to extract certain data and move it into Access, but over time she learned that it was faster to ask IS to move all employee data from the operational Oracle database into another Oracle database created just for HR data analysis. Although Oracle provides a graphical query interface like that in Access, she found it easier to compose complex queries directly in SQL, so she learned it and, within a few months, was a SQL expert.

"I never thought I'd be doing this," she said. "But it turns out to be quite fun, like solving a puzzle, and apparently I'm good at it."

One day, after a break, MaryAnn signed into her computer and happened to glance at the results of a query that she'd left running while she was gone. "That's odd," she thought. "All the people with Hispanic surnames have lower salaries than the others." She wasn't looking for that pattern; it just happened to jump out at her as she glanced at the screen.

As she examined the data, she began to wonder if she was seeing a coincidence or if there was a discriminatory pattern within the organization. Unfortunately for MaryAnn's purposes, the organization did not track employee race in its database, so she had no easy way of identifying employees of Hispanic heritage other than reading through the list of surnames. But, as a skilled problem solver, that didn't stop MaryAnn. She realized that many employees having Hispanic origins were born in certain cities in Texas, New Mexico, Arizona, and California. Of course, this wasn't true for all employees; many non-Hispanic employees were born in those cities, too, and many Hispanic employees were born in other cities. This data was still useful, however, because MaryAnn's sample queries revealed that the proportion of employees with Hispanic surnames who were also born in those cities was very high. "OK," she thought, "I'll use those cities as a rough surrogate."

Using birth city as a query criterion, MaryAnn created queries that determined employees who were born in the selected cities earned, on average, 23 percent less than those who were not. "Well, that could be because they work in lower-pay-grade jobs." After giving it a bit of thought, MaryAnn realized that she needed to examine wages and salaries within job categories. "Where," she wondered, "do people born in those cities fall in the ranges of their job categories?" So, she constructed SQL to determine where within a job category the compensation for people born in the selected cities fell. "Wow!" she said to herself. "Almost 80 percent of the employees born in those cities fall into the bottom half of their salary ranges."

MaryAnn scheduled an appointment with her manager for the next day.

## DISCUSSION QUESTIONS

When answering the following questions, suppose that you are MaryAnn:

**1.** Given these query results, do you have an ethical responsibility to do something? Consider both the categorical imperative (pages 20–21) and the utilitarian (pages 46–47) perspectives.

**2.** Given these query results, do you have a personal or social responsibility to do something?

**3.** What is your response if your manager says, "You don't know anything; it could be that starting salaries are lower in those cities. Forget about it."

**4.** What is your response if your manager says, "Don't be a troublemaker; pushing this issue will hurt your career."

**5.** What is your response if your manager says, "Right. We already know that. Get back to the tasks that I've assigned you."

**6.** Suppose your manager gives you funding to follow up with a more accurate analysis, and, indeed, there is a pattern of underpayment to people with Hispanic surnames. What should the organization do? For each choice below, indicate likely outcomes:

**a.** Correct the imbalances immediately.

**b.** Gradually correct the imbalances at future pay raises.

**c.** Do nothing about the imbalances, but train managers not to discriminate in the future.

**d.** Do nothing.

**7.** Suppose you hire a part-time person to help with the more accurate analysis, and that person is so outraged at the outcome that he quits and notifies newspapers in all the affected cities of the organization's discrimination.

**a.** How should the organization respond?

**b.** How should you respond?

**8.** Consider the adage "Never ask a question for which you do not want the answer."

**a.** Is following that adage ethical? Consider both the categorical imperative and utilitarian perspectives.

**b.** Is following that adage socially responsible?

**c.** How does that adage relate to you, as MaryAnn?

**d.** How does that adage relate to you, as a future business professional?

**e.** With regard to employee compensation, how does that adage relate to organizations?

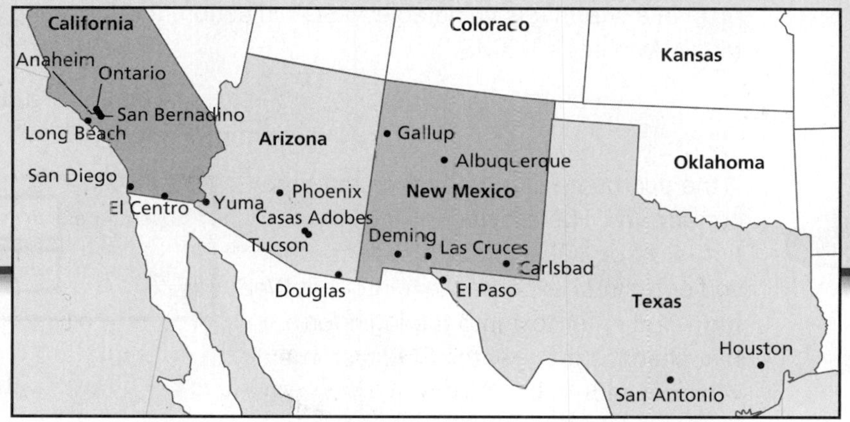

# Guide

## Theft by SQL Injection

**Warning** You are about to learn a technique for compromising an information system called *SQL injection.* Do not try it on existing systems. SQL injection attacks leave log entries with your IP address attached. Attempting SQL injection on a system without permission is illegal. You can be identified, tracked, and charged. Felony hacking convictions are not resume builders.

SQL injection is a popular way to steal data because it can be done from anywhere in the world. You don't even need to physically enter the target country. You need some smart people with time to invest and a couple modest computers. From a criminal's point of view it's a low-risk and high-reward proposition.

SQL injection is a criminal attack on an information system to illegally extract data from a database. It can add or delete data, drop tables and their data, and even shut down an information system. And, because it can be done from anywhere in the world, criminals can rob from countries that don't extradite criminals, such as Russia, China, North Korea, and others.

Criminals have caught on to theft-by-SQL-injection. Imperva®, an enterprise data security firm, listed the following key findings in its 2013 Imperva Web Application Attack Report:[7]

1. Retailers suffer two times as many SQL injection attacks as other industries.
2. Most Web applications receive four or more Web attack campaigns per month, and others are constantly under attack (176 out of 180 days).
3. One Web site received 94,057 SQL injection attack requests in one day.

Let those numbers sink in: Your corporate Web site is likely being attacked on a regular basis.

### How Does SQL Injection Work?

SQL injection, as it sounds, is a way of inserting your own SQL code into someone else's information system. To understand this, consider what happens when you normally log in to a Web site. You enter your username (**JohnDoe001**) and a password (**password1234**) and then press the Enter key.

In a site that is vulnerable to SQL injection, the following SQL statement is sent to the Web site's DBMS:

```
SELECT * FROM Users WHERE username='JohnDoe001'
        AND password='password1234';
```

If the username and password are both correct, you'll be allowed in. The "injection" part of SQL injection happens when you enter in *unexpected* text into that Web form. You enter text into the login form that changes the way the SQL statement is processed.

Instead of entering a real username and password, put in a random username (in this case, we kept it **JohnDoe001**), and a malformed, but tricky, statement into the password field (**anything' or 1=1 --**).

Note that the single quote (') in the password changes the SQL statement by enclosing the word "anything" and allowing 1=1 to be included. (The double hyphen indicates the rest of the SQL statement, which is not shown because it's not relevant to this guide.)

```
SELECT * FROM Users WHERE username='JohnDoe001'
AND password='anything' or 1=1 --';
```

| Username: | JohnDoe001 |
|---|---|
| Password: | anything' or 1=1 -- |

The word "anything" will *not* match the correct password in the database, but because "or 1=1" was included the resulting comparison will always be "true." This is because 1=1 is true, and only one side of the comparison needs to be true if "or" is included. This SQL statement will enable you to bypass the login screen and gain access to the system. Similar malformed SQL statements can be used to extract, add, or delete data. There is even software available that largely automates the SQL injection process.

SQL injection can readily be prevented. The particular techniques are beyond the scope of this text, but they come down to never writing computer programs to append user-entered data to a SQL statement. Instead, the users' data is passed to a program controlled by the DBMS that inspects that user-entered data and then uses it without changing any SQL code.[8]

Unfortunately, not all companies take the time to protect themselves from SQL injection. Sony Corp. lost more than 100 million accounts to SQL injection attacks in 2011. In 2014, two U.S. Navy systems administrators on a nuclear aircraft carrier used SQL injection to get the private data of 220,000 sailors. They said they did it out of "boredom."

## DISCUSSION QUESTIONS

1. Why is data theft attractive to criminals?
2. How common is SQL injection?
3. How does SQL injection work?
4. What can an attacker do to a database using SQL injection?
5. How can organizations prevent SQL injection attacks from being successful?
6. If you were a senior manager at an organization that had serious losses due to SQL injection, what would you do about it?
7. Suppose an organization not only prevents SQL injection from success, but also tracks the identity of sites that attempt such attacks. What should the organization do with that attack data?

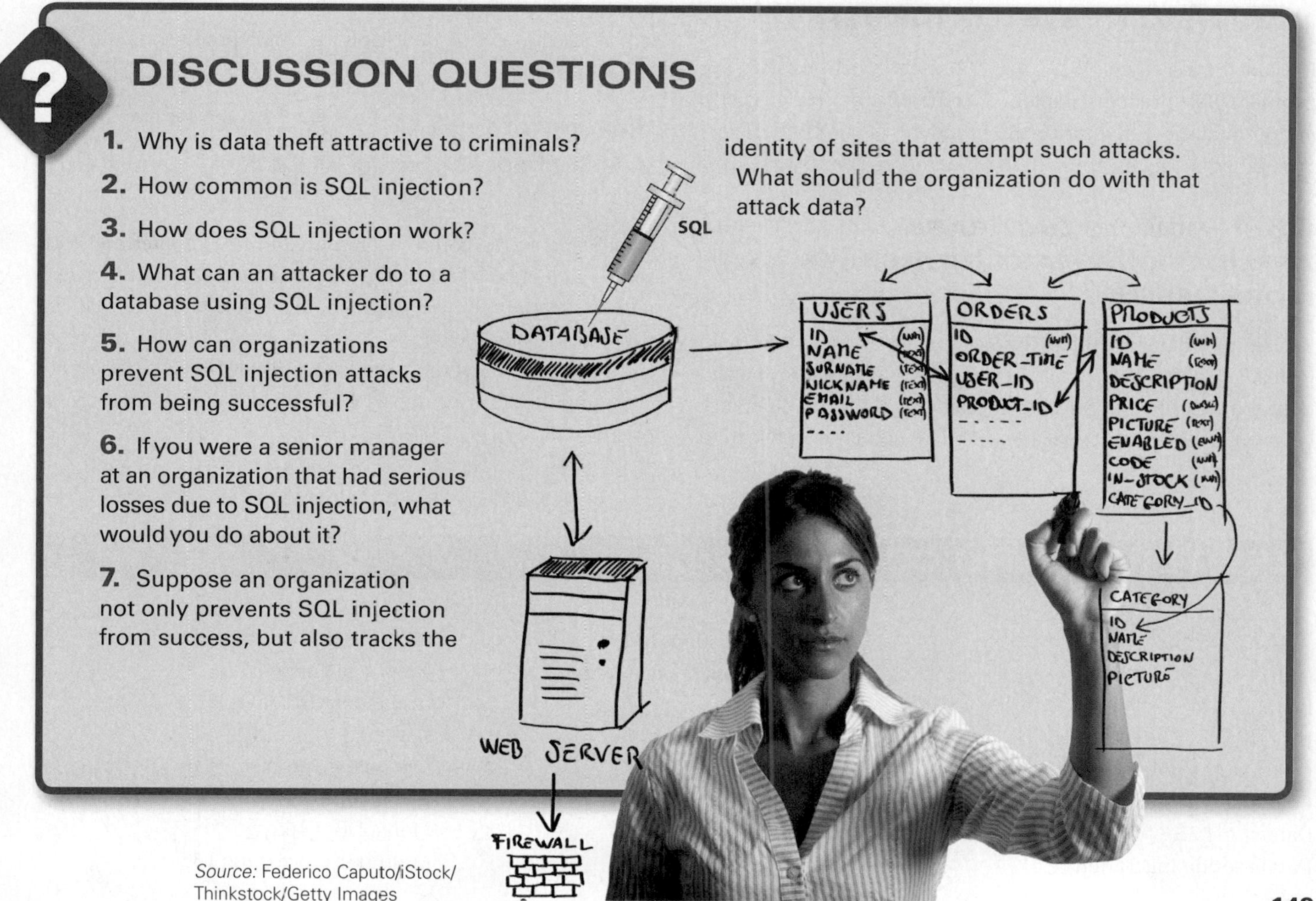


*Source:* Federico Caputo/iStock/Thinkstock/Getty Images

# ACTIVE REVIEW

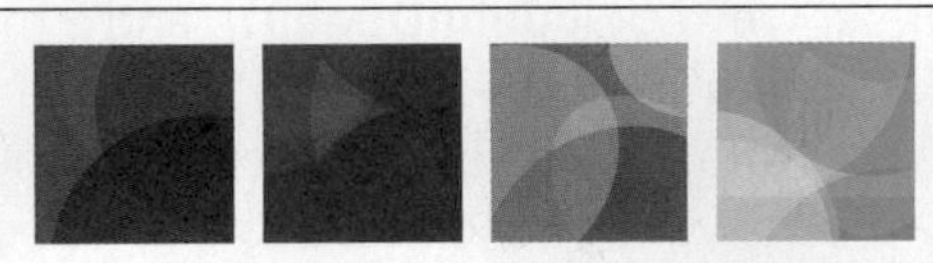

Use this Active Review to verify that you understand the ideas and concepts that answer the chapter's study questions.

## Q5-1 WHAT DO YOU NEED TO KNOW ABOUT DATABASES?

Explain three ways in which you interact with a database each day, even though that database is not directly apparent. Summarize four reasons why a business professional should learn database technology.

## Q5-2 WHAT IS A DATABASE?

Define the term *database*. Explain the hierarchy of data and name three elements of a database. Define *metadata*. Using the example of *Student* and *Office_Visit* tables, show how relationships among rows are represented in a database. Define the terms *primary key*, *foreign key*, and *relational database*.

## Q5-3 WHAT IS A DATABASE MANAGEMENT SYSTEM (DBMS)?

Explain the acronym DBMS and name its functions. List five popular DBMS products. Explain the difference between a DBMS and a database. Summarize the functions of a DBMS. Define *SQL*. Describe the major functions of database administration.

## Q5-4 HOW DO DATABASE APPLICATIONS MAKE DATABASES MORE USEFUL?

Explain why database tables, by themselves, are not very useful to business users. Name the four elements of a database application and describe the purpose of each. Explain the difference between a database application and a database application program. Describe the nature of traditional database applications. Explain why browser-based applications are better than traditional ones. Name the primary technologies used to support browser-based applications.

## Q5-5 HOW CAN FALCON SECURITY BENEFIT FROM A DATABASE SYSTEM?

Describe the two system architecture alternatives available to Falcon Security. Explain the advantages and disadvantages of each. State the alternative they chose and explain why they chose it.

## Q5-6 WHAT ARE NONTRADITIONAL DBMS PRODUCTS?

Define *NoSQL data store* and give three examples. Explain how NoSQL will likely be used in organizations and state why learning Microsoft Access is still important to you. Explain what is unusual about the development of these systems. Describe possible consequences of NoSQL on the DBMS product market.

## How does the **knowledge** in this chapter help **you?**

After learning the concepts presented in this chapter and with some rudimentary knowledge of Access, you'll be able to query and extract data to help you solve the problems your organization faces... or at least you will be able to pinpoint the problems. You also know that new categories of DBMS products are emerging that may be important to the database needs of your organization.

## KEY TERMS AND CONCEPTS

Access 128
ACID 138
Bigtable 137
Byte 125
Cassandra 137
Columns 125
Database 125
Database administration 130
Database application 131
Database management system (DBMS) 128
DB2 128
Dynamo 137
Fields 125
File 125
Foreign keys 127
Form 131
Graphical queries 134
In-memory DBMS 138
Key 127
Lost-update problem 136
Metadata 127
MongoDB 136
Multiuser processing 135

MyMISLab™

To complete the problems with the ✪, go to EOC Discussion Questions in the MyLab.

## USING YOUR KNOWLEDGE

✪ **5-1.** Suppose you are a marketing assistant for a consumer electronics company and are in charge of setting up your company's booth at trade shows. Weeks before the shows, you meet with the marketing managers and determine what displays and equipment they want to display. Then you identify each of the components that needs to be shipped and schedule a shipper to deliver them to the trade show site. You then supervise convention personnel as they set up the booths and equipment. Once the show is over, you supervise the packing of the booth and all equipment as well as schedule its shipment back to your home office. When the equipment arrives, you check it into your warehouse to ensure that all pieces of the booth and all equipment are returned. If there are problems due to shipping damage or loss, you handle those problems. Your job is important; at a typical show, you are responsible for more than a quarter of a million dollars' worth of equipment.

**a.** You will need to track data about booth components, equipment, shippers, and shipments. List typical fields for each type of data.

**b.** Could you use a spreadsheet to keep track of this data? What would be the advantages and disadvantages of doing so?

**c.** Using your answer to part a, give an example of two relationships that you need to track. Show the keys and foreign keys for each.

**d.** Which of the following components of a database application are you likely to need: data entry forms, reports, queries, or application program? Explain one use for each that you will need.

**e.** Will your application be for one user or for multiple users? Will you need a personal DBMS or an enterprise DBMS? If a personal DBMS, which product will you use?

✪ **5-2.** Samantha Green (the same Samantha we met at the end of Chapter 3, page 79) owns and operates Twigs Tree Trimming Service. Recall that Samantha has a degree from a forestry program and recently opened her business in St. Louis, Missouri. Her business consists of many one-time operations (e.g., removing a tree or stump), as well as recurring services (e.g., trimming customers' trees every year or two). When business is slow, Samantha calls former clients to remind them of her services and of the need to trim their trees on a regular basis.

**a.** Name and describe tables of data that Samantha will need to run her business. Indicate possible fields for each table.

**b.** Could Samantha use a spreadsheet to keep track of this data? What would be the advantages and disadvantages of doing so?

**c.** Using your answer to part a, give an example of two relationships that Samantha needs to track. Show the keys and foreign keys for each.

**d.** Which of the following components of a database application is Samantha likely to need: data entry forms, reports, queries, or application program? Explain one use for each that she needs.

**e.** Will this application be for one user or for multiple users? Will she need a personal DBMS or an enterprise DBMS? If a personal DBMS, which product will she use?

✪ **5-3.** YourFire Inc. (the same YourFire we met at the end of Chapter 3, page 83) is a small business owned by Curt and Julie Robards. Based in Brisbane, Australia, YourFire manufactures and sells the YourFire, a lightweight camping stove. Recall that Curt used his previous experience as an aerospace engineer to invent a burning nozzle that enables the stove to stay lit in very high winds. Using her industrial design training, Julie designed the stove so that it is small, lightweight, easy to set up, and very stable. Curt and Julie sell the stove directly to their customers over the Internet and via phone. The warranty on the stove covers 5 years of cost-free repair for stoves used for recreational purposes.

YourFire wants to track every stove and the customer who purchased it. They want to know which customers own which stoves in case they need to notify customers of safety problems or need to order a stove recall. Curt and Julie also want to keep track of any repairs they have performed.

**a.** Name and describe tables of data that YourFire will need. Indicate possible fields for each table.

**b.** Could YourFire use a spreadsheet to keep track of this data? What would be the advantages and disadvantages of doing so?

**c.** Using your answer to part a, give an example of two relationships that YourFire needs to track. Show the keys and foreign keys for each.

**d.** Which of the following components of a database application is YourFire likely to need: data entry forms, reports, queries, or application program? Explain one use for each needed component.

**e.** Will this application be for one user or for multiple users? Will YourFire need a personal DBMS or an enterprise DBMS? If a personal DBMS, which product will it use? If an enterprise DBMS, which product can it obtain license-free?

## COLLABORATION EXERCISE 5

*The Falcon Security problem is an excellent example of the use of a small database in business. It is also within reach for you to develop as a practice exercise. To do so, work with your team to answer the following questions:*

**5-4.** Study Figure 5-17 to understand the entities and their relationships. Justify each of the cardinalities in this model.

**5-5.** Working with your team, develop a list of seven queries that together use all of the entities in Figure 5-17.

**5-6.** Modify the E-R model in Figure 5-17 to include a Contact entity that is related to the Facility entity. Create the relationship, and specify and justify the relationship's cardinalities.

**5-7.** Discuss the advantages and disadvantages of the model you created in your answer to question 5-6 and the model in Figure 5-17.

**5-8.** Transform the data model in Figure 5-17 into a relational database design. *Hint:* Create a table for each entity and relate those tables.

**5-9.** Create an Access database for your design in question 5-8.

**5-10.** Fill your database with sample data. Because you do not have files on a server, leave the URL column blank.

**5-11.** Using the Access query facility, process each of the seven queries you created in your answer to question 5-5.

**Figure 5-17**
E-R Diagram for Falcon Security's Database

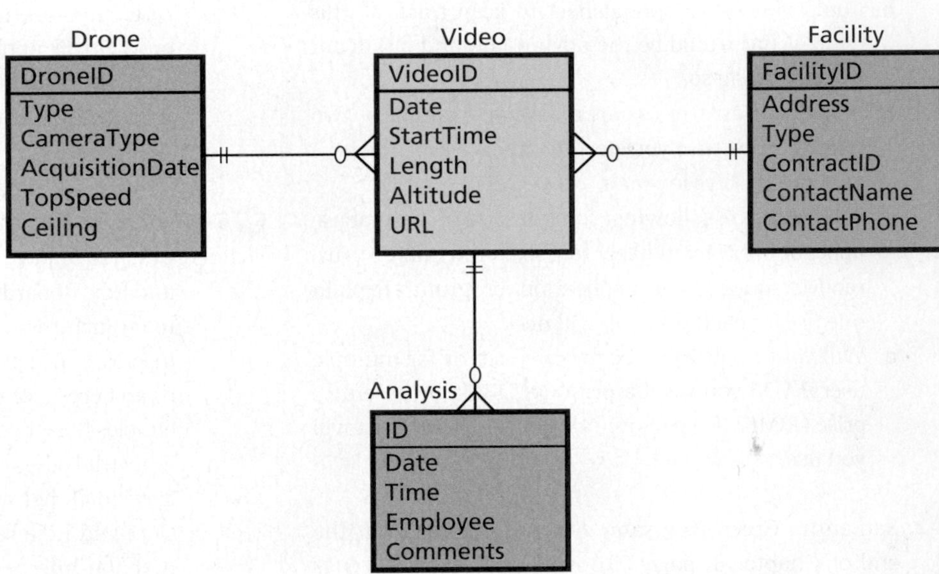

# CASE STUDY 5

## Searching for Pianos...

Figure 5-18
Deano the Clown

*Source:* Dean Petrich

Dean Petrich is a certified piano tuner and technician who has been repairing and restoring pianos since 1973. He also has a career as Deano the Clown, a clown entertainer who performs children's parties in the Seattle, WA, metro area (see Figure 5-18, *http://deanotheclown.com/*). The schedule of his two businesses balance each other: He's busy as a clown in the late spring, summer, and fall, and during the rest of the year, he repairs and restores pianos.

Over the past 20 years, the demand for pianos has dramatically declined. When Grandma dies, or the kids move out, or some other life change occurs, families have no further use for their piano, and when they find there is no market for it, they call Dean, who picks up that piano for a modest fee. For a number of years, Dean restored those pianos and either resold or rented them. Since the turn of the century, however, the decreasing demand for pianos has affected him as well, and over time, he's accumulated far too many pianos. Even discarding the worst of them, he has, today, nearly 100.

As you can imagine, 100 pianos consume considerable storage. At first, Dean stored them in his workshop. When he ran out of room in his workshop, he built and stored them in a large metal shed (Figure 5-19). When the shed overflowed with

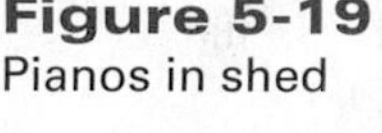

Figure 5-19
Pianos in shed

*Source:* David Kroenke

pianos, he moved them to plastic tents in a meadow on his property (Figure 5-20). Unfortunately, the plastic tents are prone to rips and tears, and because Dean lives in the Pacific Northwest, many pianos have been ruined by rain, even when he covers them with plastic tarps inside the plastic tents.

Two years ago, sinking in his steadily increasing piano inventory, Dean began to offer pianos for free. Not the very best pianos—those he hopes to sell—but he offers many quality pianos for free. However, Dean has two problems. First, he doesn't know which pianos are best and where they are located in the shop, shed, or tents. Second, few people are willing to crawl over the tops of the pianos in the large shed and tents (through refuse of squirrels, rats, and mice) looking for their perfect piano.

To resolve this issue, Dean created a Microsoft Access database with only one table: Piano. To fill the database with data, Dean had to first take an inventory of all the pianos and record the data shown in the columns of Figure 5-21.

As you know, a one-table database could just as easily have been stored in Excel, but Dean used Access because he wants to query his data in a variety of ways. He wants to know, for example, all of the pianos located in a tent that have a sound quality of 4 or higher. And he wants to know which pianos have a sound quality of 1 or less so he can dispose of them. Further, customers have particular needs. One might, for example, want a Baldwin spinet (a brand and type of piano); without a database he has no idea whether he has one or where. Or, when he needs a replacement key top, he might want to know the location of all the pianos in the workshop that have ivory keys and a sound quality of 2 or less, and so on.

Because of the dynamic nature of his needs, Dean uses the Access query facility. Figure 5-22 shows an example query that returns all of the pianos of a sound quality higher than 4 that are located in a tent, and Figure 5-23 shows the result of that query. Dean also suspects that the quality deteriorates faster in the tents than in the shed or the shop. To determine if this is the case, he created the report shown in Figure 5-24.

**Figure 5-20**
Pianos in tents

*Source:* David Kroenke

**Figure 5-21**
Columns in the Piano Table
*Source:* Microsoft Corporation

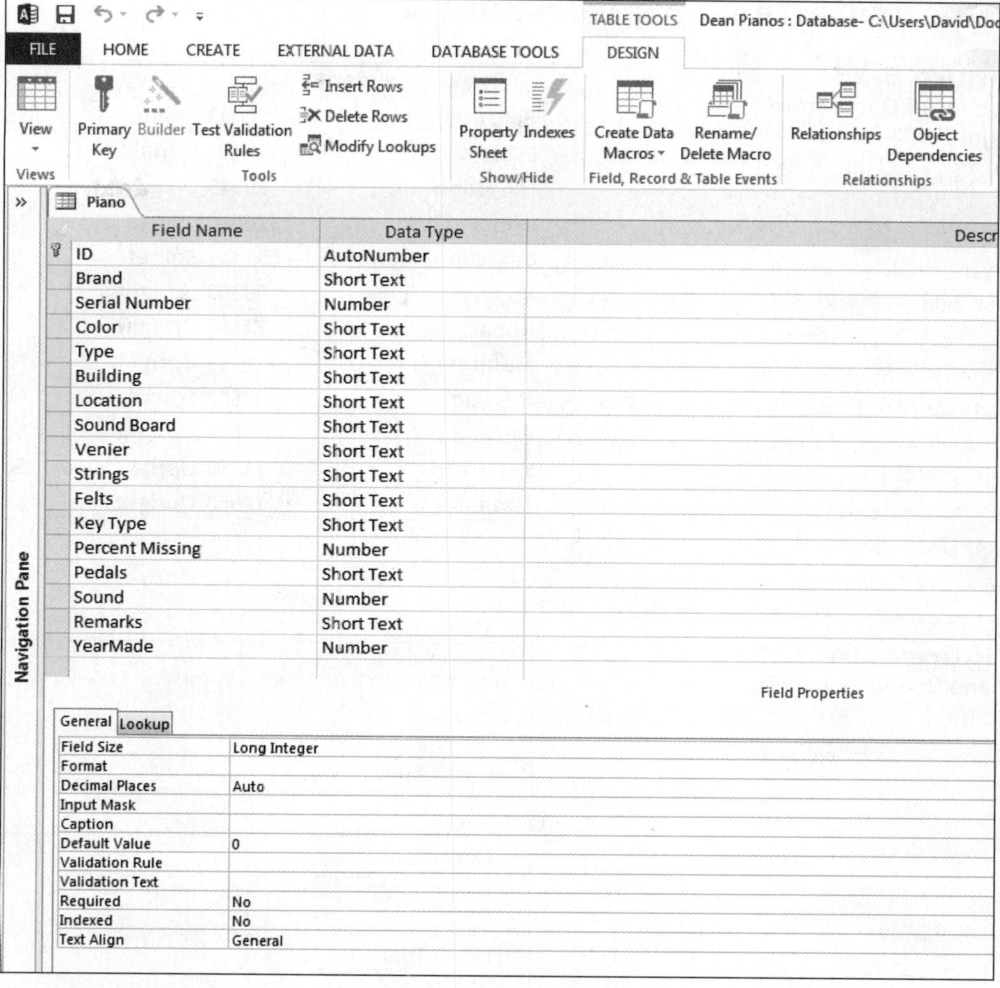


**Figure 5-22**
Example of Access Query
*Source:* Microsoft Corporation

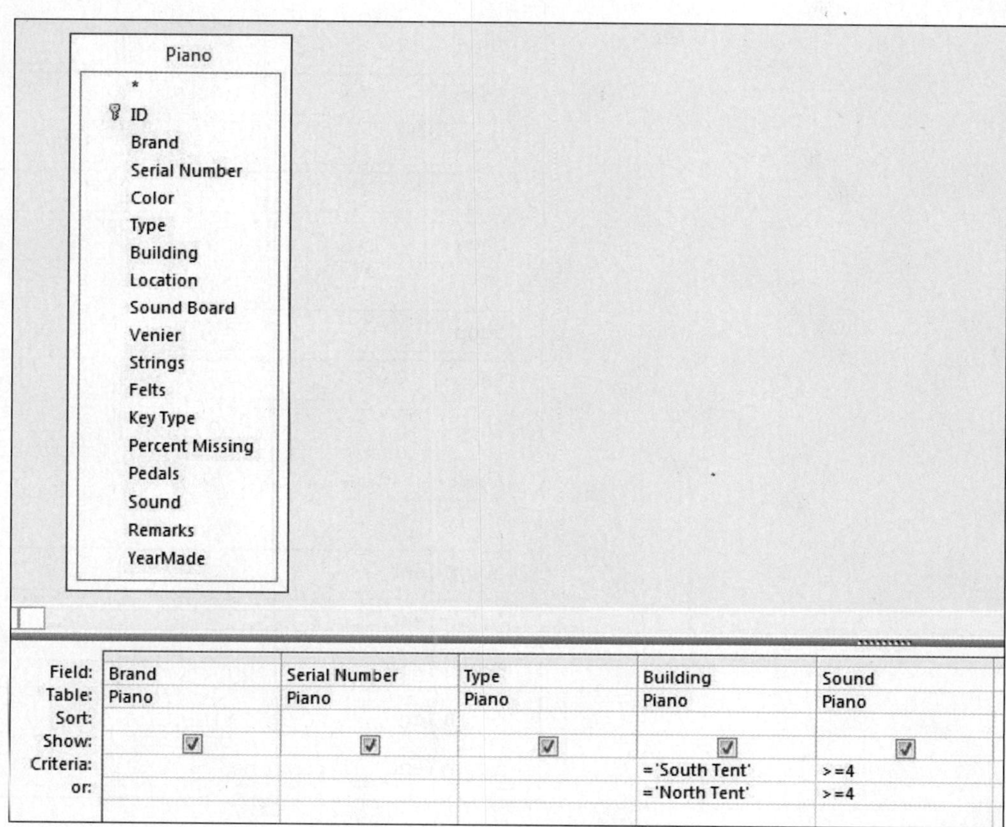

**Figure 5-23**
Results of Query from Figure 5-22
*Source:* Microsoft Corporation

| Brand | Serial Numb | Type | Building | Sound |
|---|---|---|---|---|
| Baldwin | 70452 | Spinet | South Tent | 4 |
| Esteu | 20158 | Upright | North Tent | 4 |
| H.G. Johnson | 10749 | Upright | North Tent | 4 |
| Winter ??? | 326493 | Spinet | North Tent | 4 |
| Baldwin | 637957 | Spinet | North Tent | 4 |
| Briggs | 80360 | Upright | North Tent | 4 |
| Hobart Cable | 77182 | Upright | North Tent | 4 |
| Mehlin | 28733 | Upright | North Tent | 4 |
| Aeolian | 182562 | Spinet | North Tent | 4 |
| Farrand | 27631 | Upright | South Tent | 4 |
| Kurtzman | 21398 | Upright | South Tent | 5 |
| Mathushek | 12963 | Upright | South Tent | 4 |

**Figure 5-24**
Piano Sound Quality by Building
*Source:* Microsoft Corporation

Piano Sound Quality by Building

| Building | Sound Quality | Number Pianos |
|---|---|---|
| North Tent | 1 | 1 |
| North Tent | 3 | 3 |
| North Tent | 4 | 8 |
| Shed | 0 | 10 |
| Shed | 1 | 1 |
| Shed | 2 | 7 |
| Shed | 3 | 13 |
| Shed | 4 | 12 |
| Shop | 0 | 2 |
| Shop | 1 | 2 |
| Shop | 3 | 5 |
| Shop | 4 | 2 |
| South Tent | 0 | 6 |
| South Tent | 2 | 3 |
| South Tent | 3 | 2 |
| South Tent | 4 | 3 |
| South Tent | 5 | 1 |

## QUESTIONS

**5-12.** Explain why a one-table database could be stored just as readily in Excel as in Access.

**5-13.** Justify the decision to use Access to store the piano database.

**5-14.** Examine the columns in Figure 5-21. Name three characteristics of pianos that are not represented in this table.

**a.** If you were a consultant advising Dean, what criteria should you and he use in deciding whether to include that additional data?

**b.** Is this database a model of an inventory of pianos, or is it a model of Dean's model of an inventory of pianos? Explain the difference.

**c.** How does your answer to question 5-14b influence your answer to question 5-14a?

**5-15.** Suppose, in addition to the data about pianos, Dean wants to store data about the manufacturer such as its address (or last known address), its years of operation, and general comments about that manufacturer.

**a.** Design a Manufacturer table.

**b.** Alter the design of the Piano table (Figure 5-21) to represent the relationship between Piano and Manufacturer. State and justify any assumptions.

**5-16.** Using the data in Figure 5-24, draw conclusions about the effect of location on piano sound quality. Justify your statements using this data.

**5-17.** Explain the statement "A database is an abstraction of some aspect of a business." Using this example, explain the ways that processing an abstraction is more effective than examining pianos. Explain the ways that processing an abstraction is more efficient that examining pianos. Generalize your observation to databases for business in general.

**5-18.** This database will soon become useless if it is not kept up to date. List procedures that Dean needs to create and follow to keep his database current.

MyMISLab™

Go to the Assignments section of your MyLab to complete these writing exercises.

**5-19.** Go to *http://aws.amazon.com* and search for AWS database offerings. Explain the differences among Amazon's RDS, DynamoDB, ElastiCache, and Redshift services. Which of these three would you recommend for storing Falcon Security's data? (By the way, whenever you query the Internet for any AWS product, be sure to include the keyword *AWS* in your search. Otherwise, your search will result in Amazon's lists of book about the item you're searching for.)

**5-20.** Suppose you have just been hired by a tech startup that focuses on helping small businesses in South America market their handmade products to consumers around the world. They store a large amount of images and video of the products they sell. In addition, videos of the craftsmen making their products and talking about new products are very popular with customers. The CEO has asked you to look at the potential benefits of using a NoSQL DBMS like MongoDB or Cassandra for these images and videos. Describe the benefits of using a NoSQL DBMS to store this type of data. Would a relational database be a good option? Why?

## ENDNOTES

1. MySQL was supported by the MySQL company. In 2008, that company was acquired by Sun Microsystems, which was, in turn, acquired by Oracle later that year. However, because MySQL is open source, Oracle does not own the source code.
2. Watch out for confusion between a *database application* and a *database application program*. A database application includes forms, reports, queries, and database application programs.
3. For a summary of this early history and an amplification of these ideas, see David Kroenke, "Beyond the Relational Model," *IEEE Computer*, June 2005.
4. Werner Vogel, "Amazon's Dynamo," All Things Distributed blog, last modified October 2, 2007, *www.allthingsdistributed.com/2007/10/amazons_dynamo.html*.
5. Fay Chang, Jeffrey Dean, Sanjay Ghemawat, Wilson C. Hsieh, Deborah A. Wallach, Mike Burrows, Tushar Chandra, Andrew Fikes, and Robert E. Gruber, "Bigtable: A Distributed Storage System for Structured Data," OSDI 2006, Seventh Symposium on Operating System Design and Implementation, Seattle, WA, last modified November 2006, *http://labs.google.com/papers/bigtable.html*.
6. Jonathan Ellis, "Cassandra: Open Source Bigtable + Dynamo," accessed June 2011, *www.slideshare.net/jbellis/cassandra-open-source-bigtable-dynamo*.
7. Imperva, "Imperva Web Application Attack Report," July 2013, accessed May 19, 2014, *www.imperva.com/docs/HII_Web_Application_Attack_Report_Ed4.pdf*.
8. To learn more about how to prevent SQL injection you can visit OWASP.org. It has a helpful SQL Injection Prevention Cheat Sheet that explains how to parameterize queries and use stored procedures to stop SQL injection. See *www.owasp.org/index.php/SQL_Injection_Prevention_Cheat_Sheet*.

chapter

6

# The Cloud

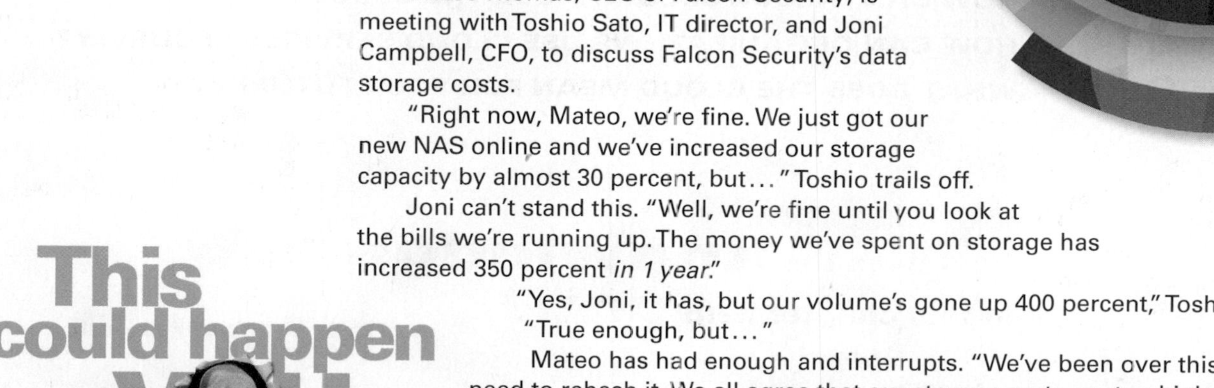


"What's your plan, Toshio?"

Mateo Thomas, CEO of Falcon Security, is meeting with Toshio Sato, IT director, and Joni Campbell, CFO, to discuss Falcon Security's data storage costs.

"Right now, Mateo, we're fine. We just got our new NAS online and we've increased our storage capacity by almost 30 percent, but..." Toshio trails off.

Joni can't stand this. "Well, we're fine until you look at the bills we're running up. The money we've spent on storage has increased 350 percent *in 1 year*."

"Yes, Joni, it has, but our volume's gone up 400 percent," Toshio replies.

"True enough, but..."

Mateo has had enough and interrupts. "We've been over this before. No need to rehash it. We all agree that our storage costs are too high. Toshio, I'd asked you to look into alternatives. What have you got?"

"The cloud."

"The *what?*" Joni hopes he's not losing it.

"The cloud," Toshio repeats. "We move all of our video to the cloud."

Mateo is curious. "OK, Toshio, I'll bite. What's the cloud?"

"It's a movement—I'd call it a fad, except I think it's here to stay."

"So how does it help us?" Mateo asks.

"We lease storage capacity from a third party."

Joni's confused. "You mean we'd lease hard drives rather than buy them?"

"Well, not exactly," Toshio explains. "We wouldn't be installing any more hard drives in our datacenter. We can lease online storage on very, very flexible, pay-as-you-go terms. If we get a large new client, we can acquire more storage and scale it to meet our needs."

"You mean each day? We can change the terms of our lease on a daily basis?" Joni thinks that's not possible. "OK, so how much does it cost? This can't be cheap."

"How about $10 per terabyte?"

Mateo's puzzled at that. "What do you mean $10 per terabyte?"

"I mean we can get 1 terabyte of online storage for about $10 per month." Toshio grins as he says this.

"*What?*" Joni's dumbfounded.

"Yeah, that's it. We can get as much storage as we want, and our systems automatically upload all incoming data from our drones. The net difference would be that our average monthly storage costs would be at least

# STUDY QUESTIONS

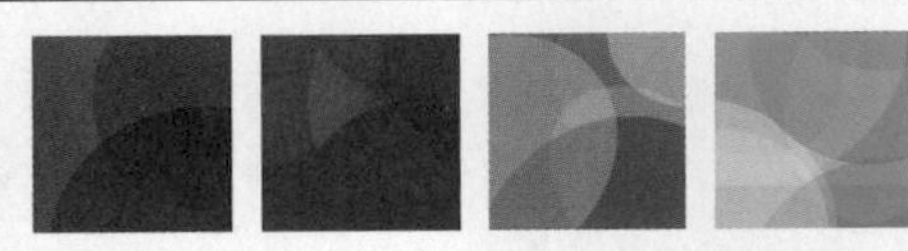

**Q6-1 WHY IS THE CLOUD THE FUTURE FOR MOST ORGANIZATIONS?**

**Q6-2 HOW DO ORGANIZATIONS USE THE CLOUD?**

**Q6-3 HOW CAN FALCON SECURITY USE THE CLOUD?**

**Q6-4 HOW CAN ORGANIZATIONS USE CLOUD SERVICES SECURELY?**

**Q6-5 WHAT DOES THE CLOUD MEAN FOR YOUR FUTURE?**

## How does the **knowledge** in this chapter help **you?**

Source: cheskyw/123RF

**"How about $10 per terabyte?"**

50 percent less than they are now. And that's not counting the power savings, the time saved doing backups, or the fact that we wouldn't have to configure any more new hardware." Toshio isn't quite sure, but he thinks the actual storage costs could be less.

"Toshio, you've got to be kidding. We can save tens of thousands of dollars in storage costs. This is *huge*." As Joni says this, in the back of her mind she's thinking, "If it's true."

"Well, it's good; I don't know about huge. We'd have additional development costs to set up our systems, and that will take some time."

"Toshio, give me a plan. I want a plan." Mateo's thinking what these savings could mean to their next two quarters... and beyond.

"I'll give you something next week," Toshio says.

"I want it by Friday, Toshio."

Optional Extension for this chapter is CE8: Network and Cloud Technology 497

# Q6-1 WHY IS THE CLOUD THE FUTURE FOR MOST ORGANIZATIONS?

Until 2010 or so, most organizations constructed and maintained their own computing infrastructure. Organizations purchased or leased hardware, installed it on their premises, and used it to support organizational email, Web sites, e-commerce sites, and in-house applications such as accounting and operations systems (you'll learn about those in the next chapter). After about 2010, however, organizations began to move their computing infrastructure to the cloud, and it is likely that in the future all, or nearly all, computing infrastructure will be leased from the cloud. So, just what is the cloud, and why is it the future?

## WHAT IS THE CLOUD?

We define the **cloud** as the *elastic* leasing of *pooled* computer resources *over the Internet*. The term *cloud* is used because most early diagrams of three-tier and other Internet-based systems used a cloud symbol to represent the Internet (see Figure 5-13 for an example), and organizations came to view their infrastructure as being "somewhere in the cloud."

### Elastic

Consider each of the italicized terms in the definition. The term **elastic**, which was first used this way by Amazon.com, means that the computing resources leased can be increased or decreased dynamically, programmatically, in a short span of time and that organizations pay for just the resources they use.

Suppose that a car manufacturer creates an ad to run during the Academy Awards. It believes it has a fantastic ad that will result in millions of hits on its Web site. However, it doesn't know ahead of time if there will be a thousand, or a million, or 10 million, or even more site visits. Further, the ad may appeal more to one nationality than to another. Will 70 percent of those visits arise in the United States and the rest in Europe? Or will there be millions from Japan? Or Australia? Given this uncertainty, how does the car manufacturer prepare its computing infrastructure? The car manufacturer knows that if it cannot provide very short response time (say, a fraction of a second) it will lose the benefit of an incredibly expensive ad. On the other hand, if the ad is a flop, preprovisioning of thousands of servers will add to the accumulation of wasted money.

Figure 6-1 shows an example of this situation, based on a real case supported by Amazon.com's CloudFront. Suppose this figure shows the processing on the car manufacturer's Web site on the day of the Academy Awards. During most of the day, the car manufacturer is delivering less than 10 Gbps of its content to users. However, as soon as its ad runs (2 PM in the Hawaii-Aleutian time zone

**Figure 6-1**
Example of a Video Banner Ad Customer

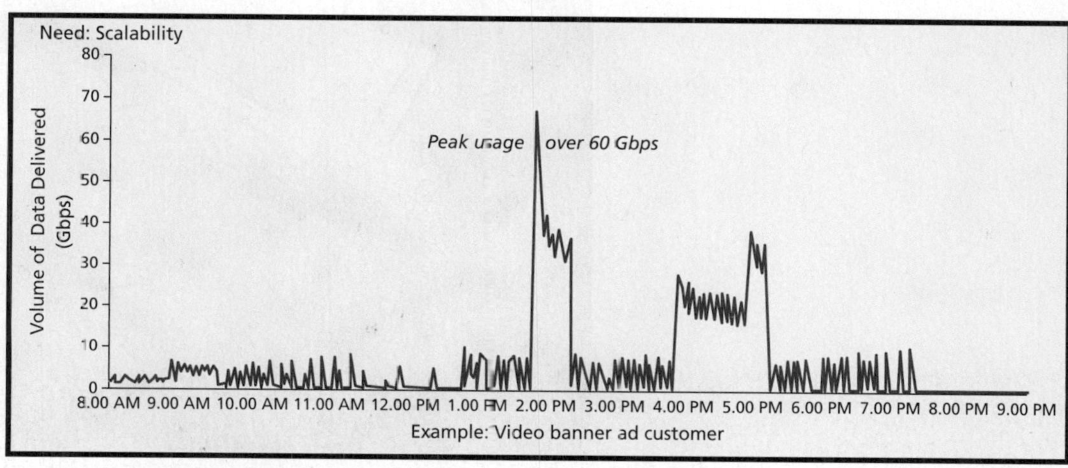

where the data was collected), demand increases seven-fold and stays high for half an hour. After the announcement of Best Picture, when the ad runs again, demand again increases to between 30 and 40 Gpbs for an hour and then returns to its base level.

Without an increase in servers, response time will be 3 or 5 seconds or more, which is far too long to maintain the attention of an Academy Awards viewer. However, the car manufacturer has contracted with its cloud vendor to add servers, wherever needed worldwide, to keep response time to less than 0.5 seconds. Using cloud technology, the cloud vendor will programmatically increase its servers to keep response time below the 0.5-second threshold. As demand falls after the ad's first run, it will release the excess servers and reallocate them after the Best Picture announcement.

In this way, the car manufacturer need not build or contract for infrastructure that supports maximum demand. Had it done so, the vast majority of its servers would have been idle most of the day. And, as you'll learn, the cloud vendor can provision servers worldwide using the cloud; if a good portion of the excess demand is in Singapore, for example, it can provision extra servers in Asia and reduce wait time due to global transmission delays.

## Pooled

The second key in the definition of cloud is *pooled*. Cloud resources are **pooled** because many different organizations use the same physical hardware; they share that hardware through virtualization. Cloud vendors dynamically allocate virtual machines to physical hardware as customer needs increase or decrease. Thus, servers that advertisers need for the Academy Awards can be reallocated to CPA firms that need them later that same day, to textbook publishers who need them for online student activity on Monday, or to the hotel industry that needs them later the next week.

An easy way to understand the essence of this development is to consider electrical power. In the very earliest days of electric power generation, organizations operated their own generators to create power for their company's needs. Over time, as the power grid expanded, it became possible to centralize power generation so that organizations could purchase just the electricity they needed from an electric utility.

Both cloud vendors and electrical utilities benefit from *economies of scale*. According to this principle, the average cost of production decreases as the size of the operation increases. Major cloud vendors operate enormous Web farms. Figure 6-2 shows the building that contains the computers

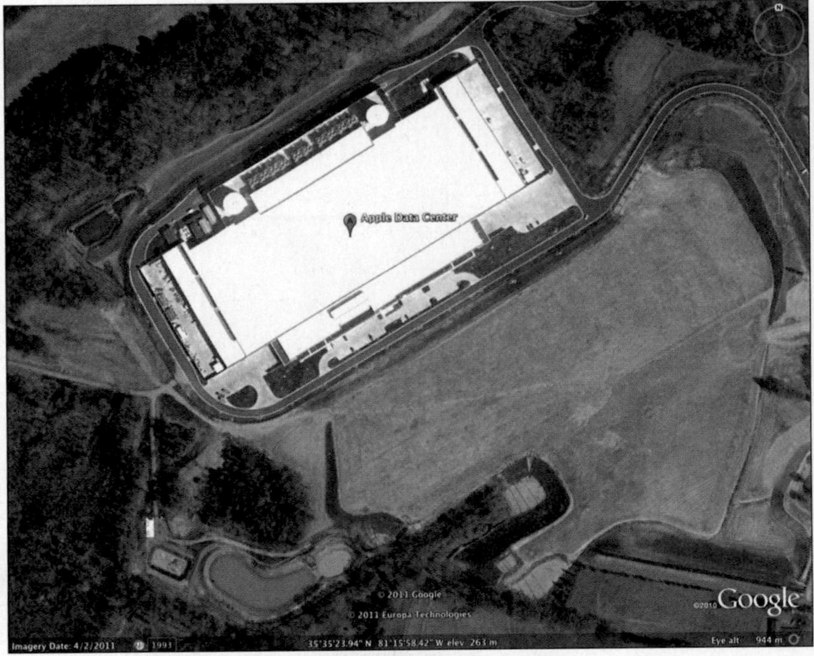


**Figure 6-2**
Apple Data Center in Maiden, NC
*Source:* Google Inc.

in the Web farm that Apple constructed in 2011 to support its iCloud offering. This billion-dollar facility contains more than 500,000 square feet.[1] Amazon.com, IBM, Google, Microsoft, Oracle, and other large companies each operate several or many similar farms worldwide.

### Over the Internet

Finally, with the cloud, resources are accessed **over the Internet**. "Big deal," you're saying. "I use the Internet all the time." Well, think about that for a minute. The car manufacturer in the previous example has contracted with the cloud vendor for a maximum response time; the cloud vendor adds servers as needed to meet that requirement. As stated, the cloud vendor may be provisioning, nearly instantaneously, servers all over the world. How does it do that? And not for just one customer, like the car manufacturer, but for thousands?

In the old days, for such interorganizational processing to occur, developers from the car manufacturer had to meet with developers from the cloud vendor and design an interface. "Our programs will do this, providing this data, and we want your programs to do that, in response, sending us this other data back." Such meetings took days and were expensive and error-prone. Given the design, the developers then returned home to write code to meet the agreed-on interface design, which may not have been understood in the same way by all.

It was a long, slow, and expensive process prone to failure, and it had to be repeated for every pair of communicating companies. If organizations had to do that today, cloud provisioning would be unaffordable and infeasible.

Instead, the computer industry settled on a set of standard ways of requesting and receiving services over the Internet. **Service-oriented architecture (SOA)** is a way of designing computer programs so they can be flexibly combined, like Lego blocks, for cloud processing. Using SOA, programs formally define the services they perform, the data they expect, and the results they produce. **Web service standards** are worldwide standards that programs use to declare what they do, the structure of the data they process, and the ways they will communicate. SOA-designed programs that comply with Web service standards are called **Web services**. These standards enable computers that have never "met" before to organize a dizzying, worldwide dance to deliver and process content to users on PCs, iPads, smartphones, Xboxes, and even exercise equipment in a tenth of a second or less. It is absolutely fascinating and gorgeous technology!

## WHY IS THE CLOUD PREFERRED TO IN-HOUSE HOSTING?

Figure 6-3 compares and contrasts cloud-based and in-house hosting. As you can see, the positives are heavily tilted toward cloud-based computing. The cloud vendor Rackspace will lease you one medium server for less than a penny per hour. You can obtain and access that server today, actually within a few minutes. Tomorrow, if you need thousands of servers, you can readily scale up to obtain them. Furthermore, you know the cost structure; although you might have a surprise in regard to how many customers want to access your Web site, you won't have any surprises as to how much it will cost.

Another positive is that as long as you're dealing with large, reputable organizations, you'll be receiving best-of-breed security and disaster recovery (discussed in Chapter 10). In addition, you need not worry that you're investing in technology that will soon be obsolete; the cloud vendor is taking that risk. All of this is possible because the cloud vendor is gaining economies of scale by selling to an entire industry, not just to you.

The negatives of cloud computing involve loss of control. You're dependent on a vendor; changes in the vendor's management, policy, and prices are beyond your control. Further, you don't know where your data—which may be a large part of your organization's value—is located. Nor do you know how many copies of your data there are or even if they're located in the same country you are. Finally, you have no visibility into the security and disaster preparedness that is actually in place. Your competition could be stealing your data and you don't know it.

| Cloud-Based Hosting | In-House Hosting |
|---|---|
| **Positive:** | |
| Small capital requirements | Control of data location |
| Speedy development | In-depth visibility of security and disaster preparedness |
| Superior flexibility and adaptability to growing or fluctuating demand | |
| Known cost structure | |
| Possibly best-of-breed security/disaster preparedness | |
| No obsolescence | |
| Industry-wide economies of scale, hence cheaper | |
| **Negative:** | |
| Dependency on vendor | Significant capital required |
| Loss of control over data location | Significant development effort |
| Little visibility into true security and disaster preparedness capabilities | Annual maintenance costs |
| | Ongoing support costs |
| | Staff and train personnel |
| | Increased management requirements |
| | Difficult (impossible?) to accommodate fluctuating demand |
| | Cost uncertainties |
| | Obsolescence |

**Figure 6-3**
Comparison of Cloud-Based Hosting and In-House Hosting

The positives and negatives of in-house hosting are shown in the second column of Figure 6-3. For the most part, they are the opposite of those for cloud-based computing; note, however, the need for personnel and management. With in-house hosting, not only will you have to construct your own data center, you'll also need to acquire and train the personnel to run it and then manage those personnel and your facility.

## WHY NOW?

A skeptic might respond to Figure 6-3 by saying, "If it's so great, why hasn't cloud hosting been used for years? Why now?"

**For an example of how one hypothetical company profited from the cloud—and how it spent those profits—read the Ethics Guide on pages 170–171**

In fact, cloud-based hosting (or a version of it under a different name) has been around since the 1960s. Long before the creation of the personal computer and networks, time-sharing vendors provided slices of computer time on a use-fee basis. However, the technology of that time, continuing up until the first decade of this century, did not favor the construction and use of enormous data centers, nor did the necessary standards exist.

Three factors have made cloud-based hosting advantageous today. First, processors, data communication, and data storage are nearly free. At the scale of a Web farm of hundreds of thousands of processors, providing a virtual machine for an hour costs essentially nothing, as suggested by the 1.5 cent-per-hour price. Because data communication is so cheap, getting the data to and from that processor is also nearly free.

Second, virtualization technology enables the near instantaneous creation of a new virtual machine. The customer provides (or creates in the cloud) a disk image of the data and programs of the machine it wants to provision. Virtualization software takes it from there. Finally, as stated, Internet-based standards enable cloud-hosting vendors to provide processing capabilities in flexible yet standardized ways.

### WHEN DOES THE CLOUD NOT MAKE SENSE?

Cloud-based hosting makes sense for most organizations. The only organizations for which it may not make sense are those required by law or by industry standard practice to have physical control over their data. Such organizations might be forced to create and maintain their own hosting infrastructure. A financial institution, for example, might be legally required to maintain physical control over its data. Even in this circumstance, however, it is possible to gain many of the benefits of cloud computing using private clouds and virtual private clouds, possibilities we consider in Q6-4.

## Q6-2 HOW DO ORGANIZATIONS USE THE CLOUD?

Organizations can use the cloud in several different ways. The first, and by far most popular, is to obtain cloud services from cloud service vendors.

### CLOUD SERVICES FROM CLOUD VENDORS

In general, cloud-based service offerings can be organized into the three categories shown in Figure 6-4. An organization that provides **software as a service (SaaS)** provides not only hardware infrastructure, but also an operating system and application programs as well. For example, Salesforce.com provides hardware and programs for customer and sales tracking as a service. Similarly, Google provides Google Drive and Microsoft provides OneDrive as a service. With Office 365, Exchange, Skype for Business and SharePoint applications are provided as services "in the cloud."

You've probably heard of, or used, Apple's iCloud. It's a cloud service that Apple uses to sync all of its customers' iOS devices. As of 2015, Apple provides 10 free applications in the iCloud. Calendar is a good example. When a customer enters an appointment in her iPhone, Apple automatically pushes that appointment into the calendars on all of that customer's iOS devices. Further, customers can share calendars with others that will be synchronized as well. Mail, pictures, applications, and other resources are also synched via iCloud.

**Figure 6-4**
Three Fundamental Cloud Types

| Cloud Category | Examples |
|---|---|
| SaaS (software as a service) | Salesforce.com<br>Google Grid<br>Microsoft OneDrive and Office 365<br>Apple iCloud |
| PaaS (platform as a service) | Microsoft Azure<br>Oracle on Demand |
| IaaS (infrastructure as a service) | Amazon EC2 (Elastic Cloud 2)<br>Amazon S3 (Simple Storage Service) |

An organization can move to SaaS simply by signing up and learning how to use it. In Apple's case, there's nothing to learn. To quote the late Steve Jobs, "It just works."

The second category of cloud hosting is **platform as a service (PaaS)**, whereby vendors provide hosted computers, an operating system, and possibly a DBMS. Microsoft Windows Azure, for example, provides servers installed with Windows Server. Customers of Windows Azure then add their own applications on top of the hosted platform. Microsoft SQL Azure provides a host with Windows Server and SQL Server. Oracle On Demand provides a hosted server with Oracle Database. Again, for PaaS, organizations add their own applications to the host. Amazon EC2 provides servers with Windows Server or Linux installed.

The most basic cloud offering is **infrastructure as a service (IaaS)**, which is the cloud hosting of a bare server computer or data storage. Rackspace provides hardware for customers to load whatever operating system they want and Amazon.com licenses S3 (Simple Storage Server), which provides unlimited, reliable data storage in the cloud.

## CONTENT DELIVERY NETWORKS

A second major use of the cloud is to deliver content from servers placed around the world. A **content delivery network (CDN)** is an information system that stores user data in many different geographical locations and makes that data available on demand. A CDN provides a specialized type of PaaS but is usually considered in its own category, as it is here.

Consider CDN applications. A news organization could use a CDN to store copies of its news articles. The CDN vendor replicates articles on servers, possibly worldwide, so as to minimize latency. When a news reader accesses an article, her request is transmitted to a routing server that determines which CDN server is likely to deliver the article to her the fastest. Because traffic changes rapidly, especially for popular sites, such calculations are made in real time. A request for content at one moment in time could be served by a computer in, say, San Diego, and a few moments later, that same request from that same user might be served by a computer in Salt Lake City.

In addition to news articles, CDNs are often used to store and deliver content that seldom changes. For example, the company banner on an organization's Web page might be stored on many CDN servers. Various pieces of the Web page could be obtained from different servers on the CDN; all such decisions are made in real time to provide the fastest content delivery possible.

Figure 6-5 summarizes CDN benefits. The first two are self-explanatory. Reliability is increased because data is stored on many servers. If one server fails, any of a potentially large number of other servers can deliver the content. You will learn about denial-of-service (DoS) attacks in Chapter 10. For now, just understand that such security threats send so much data to a given server that the server's performance for legitimate traffic becomes unacceptable. By having multiple servers, CDNs help to protect against such attacks.

In some cases, CDNs reduce access costs for mobile users (those who do have a limited data account). By delivering the data faster, site connection charges can be reduced. Finally, many (but not all) CDN services are offered on a flexible, pay-as-you-go basis. Customers need not contract for fixed services and payments; they pay only for what they use, when they use it. Figure 6-6 shows an example of how CDN servers might be distributed. A number of vendors offer CDN.

**Figure 6-5**
Benefits of Content Delivery Networks

| Benefits of Content Delivery Networks |
| --- |
| • Decreased, even guaranteed load time<br>• Reduced load on origin server<br>• Increased reliability<br>• Protection from DoS attacks<br>• Reduced delivery costs for mobile users<br>• Pay-as-you-go |

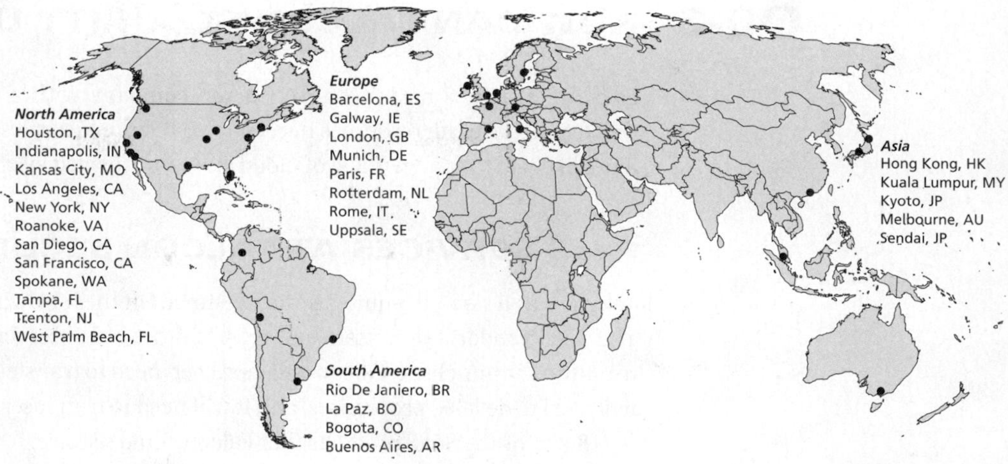


**Figure 6-6**
Servers Used in a Typical CDN Service

## USE WEB SERVICES INTERNALLY

The third way that organizations can use cloud technology is to build internal information systems using Web services. Strictly speaking, this is not using the cloud because it does not provide elasticity nor the advantages of pooled resources. It does advantageously use cloud standards, however, so we include it here.

Figure 6-7 shows a Web services inventory application at a hypothetical online bicycle part retailer named Best Bikes. In this example, Best Bikes is running its own servers on its own infrastructure. To do so, Best Bikes sets up a private internet within the company—an internet that is generally not reachable from outside the company. Best Bikes writes the applications for processing inventory using Web services standards; application users access the inventory Web services using JavaScript that is sent down to the users' browsers.

Users of the inventory Web services include Sales, Shipping, Customer Service, Accounting, and other departments. Internal applications can use the inventory Web services like building blocks. They can use the services they need—and no more. Because the Web services are encapsulated, the inventory system can be altered without affecting other applications. In this way, systems development is more flexible, and it will be faster and hence less costly.

As stated, however, this is not a cloud. In this example, Best Bikes has a fixed number of servers; no attempt is made to make them elastic. Also, the servers are dedicated to inventory. During idle periods, they are not dynamically reused for other purposes. Some organizations remove this limit by creating a private cloud, as discussed in Q6-4.

**To learn more about Web services and encapsulation, read Chapter Extension 8.**

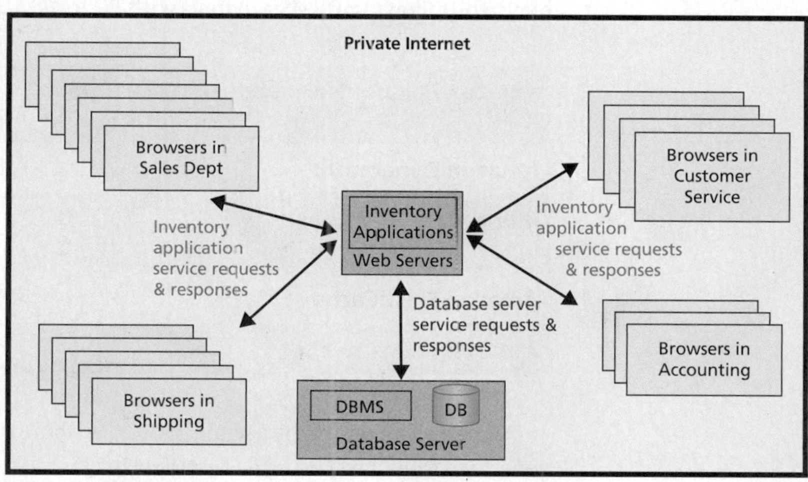


**Figure 6-7**
Web Services Principles Applied to Inventory Applications

# Q6-3 HOW CAN FALCON SECURITY USE THE CLOUD?

Falcon Security is an innovative startup company with a small IT department. As such, it is unlikely to have the resources necessary to develop a large server infrastructure. Instead, it is far more likely to take advantage of cloud services provided by cloud vendors.

## SaaS SERVICES AT FALCON SECURITY

Software as a service requires little investment in the hardware and software system components. The SaaS vendor administers and manages the cloud servers and makes the software available, usually as a thin-client. Falcon will, however, need to transfer existing data and create new data, it will need to develop procedures, and it will need to train users.

Some of the SaaS products that Falcon could use are:

- Google Mail
- Google Drive
- Office 365
- Salesforce.com
- Microsoft CRM OnLine
- And many others...

You already know what the first three SaaS offerings are. Salesforce.com and Microsoft's CRM OnLine are customer relationship management systems, which you will learn about in Chapter 7.

## PaaS SERVICES AT FALCON SECURITY

With PaaS, Falcon leases hardware and operating systems in the cloud from the cloud vendor. For example, it can lease EC2 (Elastic Cloud 2, a PaaS product offered by Amazon.com), and Amazon.com will preinstall either Linux or Windows Server on the cloud hardware. Given that basic capability, Falcon installs its own software. For example, it could install its own, in-house developed applications, or it could install other applications licensed from a software vendor. It could also license a DBMS, say, SQL Server from Microsoft, and place it on an EC2 Windows Server instance. In the case of software licensed from others, Falcon must purchase licenses that permit replication because Amazon.com will replicate software when it increases servers.

Some cloud vendors include DBMS products in their PaaS services. Thus, Falcon could obtain Windows Servers with SQL Server already installed from the Microsoft Azure cloud offerings. That option is likely what Toshio was considering when he mentioned the $10 per TB per month.

DBMS are also included in other vendors' cloud offerings. As of May 2015, Amazon.com offers the following DBMS products with EC2:

| | |
|---|---|
| **Amazon Relational Database Service (RDS)** | A relational database service supporting MySQL, Oracle, SQL Server, or PostgreSQL |
| **Amazon DynamoDB** | A fast and scalable NoSQL database service |
| **MongoDB** | A NoSQL DBMS product that stores objects in JSON format |
| **Amazon ElastiCache** | A very fast in-memory cache database service |
| **Amazon Redshift** | A petabyte-scale data warehouse |

Finally, Falcon might use a CDN to distribute its content worldwide and to respond to leads generated from advertising as described in Q6-1.

## IaaS SERVICES AT FALCON SECURITY

As stated, IaaS provides basic hardware in the cloud. Some companies acquire servers this way and then load operating systems onto them. Doing so requires considerable technical expertise and management, and hence a company like Falcon is unlikely to do so.

Falcon might, however, obtain data storage services in the cloud. Amazon.com, for example, offers data storage with its S3 product. Using it, organizations can place data in the cloud and even have that data be made elastically available. Again, however, an organization like Falcon would more likely use SaaS and PaaS because of the added value they provide.

# Q6-4 HOW CAN ORGANIZATIONS USE CLOUD SERVICES SECURELY?

The Internet and cloud services based on Internet infrastructure provide powerful processing and storage services at a fraction of the cost of private data centers. However, the Internet is a jungle of threats to data and computing infrastructure, as discussed in Chapter 10. How can organizations realize the benefits of cloud technology without succumbing to those threats?

The answer involves a combination of technologies that we will address, at a very high level, in this question. As you read, realize that no security story is ever over; attackers constantly strive to find ways around security safeguards, and occasionally they succeed. Thus, you can expect that cloud security will evolve beyond that described here throughout your career. We begin with a discussion of VPNs, a technology used to provide secure communication over the Internet.

## VIRTUAL PRIVATE NETWORK (VPN)

A **virtual private network (VPN)** uses the Internet to create the appearance of private, secure connections. In the IT world, the term *virtual* means something that appears to exist but in fact does not. Here a VPN uses the public Internet to create the appearance of a private connection on a secure network.

### A Typical VPN

Figure 6-8 shows one way to create a VPN to connect a remote computer, perhaps an employee working at a hotel in Miami, to a LAN at a Chicago site. The remote user is the VPN client. That client first establishes a public connection to the Internet. The connection can be obtained by accessing a local ISP, as shown in Figure 6-8, or, in some cases, the hotel itself provides a direct Internet connection.

In either case, once the Internet connection is made, VPN software on the remote user's computer establishes a connection with the VPN server in Chicago. The VPN client and VPN server then have a secure connection. That connection, called a **tunnel**, is a virtual, private pathway

**Figure 6-8**
Remote Access Using VPN; Actual Connections

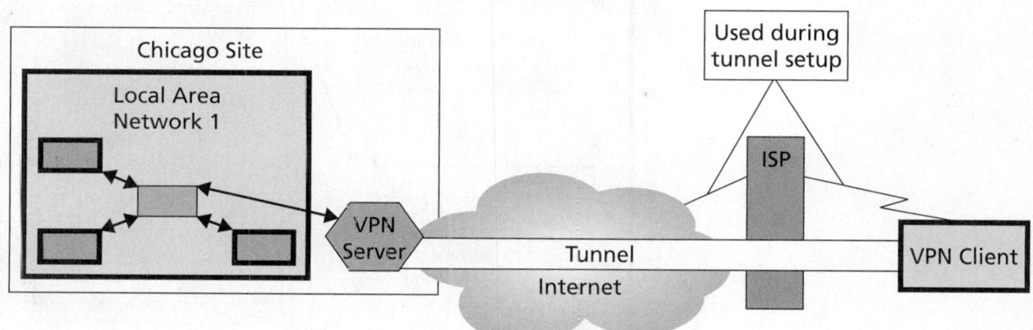

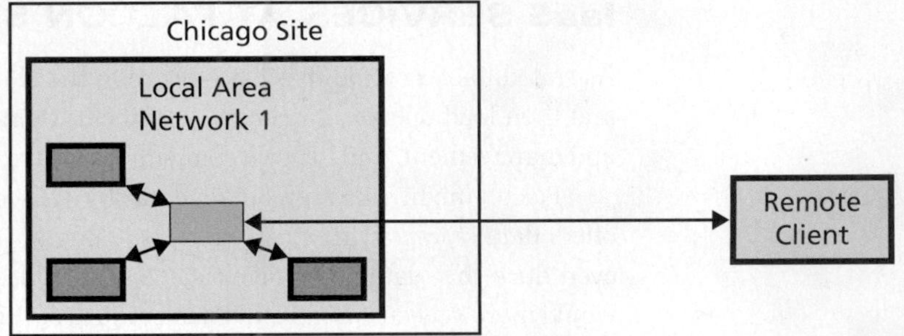


**Figure 6-9**
Remote Access Using VPN; Apparent Connection

over a public or shared network from the VPN client to the VPN server. Figure 6-9 illustrates the connection as it appears to the remote user.

To secure VPN communications over the public Internet, the VPN client software *encrypts*, or codes (see Chapter 10, page 275), messages so their contents are protected from snooping. Then the VPN client appends the Internet address of the VPN server to the message and sends that package over the Internet to the VPN server. When the VPN server receives the message, it strips its address off the front of the message, *decrypts* the coded message, and sends the plain text message to the original address inside the LAN. In this way, secure private messages are delivered over the public Internet.

## USING A PRIVATE CLOUD

A **private cloud** is a cloud owned and operated by an organization for its own benefit. To create a private cloud, the organization creates a *private* internet and designs applications using Web services standards just as shown in Figure 6-7 (page 161). The organization then creates a farm of servers and manages those servers with elastic load balancing just as the cloud service vendors do. Because of the complexity of managing multiple database servers, most organizations choose not to replicate database servers. Figure 6-10 illustrates this possibility.

Private clouds provide security *within* the organizational infrastructure but do not provide secure access from outside that infrastructure. To provide such access, organizations set up a VPN and users employ it to securely access the private cloud as shown in Figure 6-11.

Private clouds provide the advantages of elasticity, but to questionable benefit. What can organizations do with their idle servers? They could realize some cost savings by shutting down idle servers. But unlike cloud vendors, they cannot repurpose them for use by other companies.

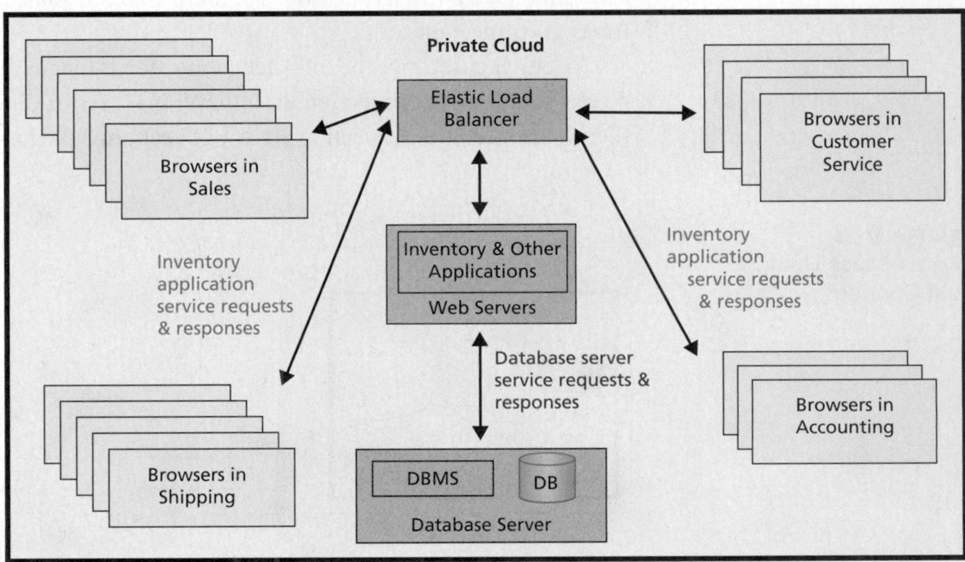


**Figure 6-10**
Private Cloud for Inventory and Other Applications

**Figure 6-11**
Accessing Private Cloud over a Virtual Private Network

Possibly a large conglomerate or major international company could balance processing loads across subsidiary business units and across different geographical regions. 3M, for example, might balance processing for its different product groups and on different continents, but it is difficult to imagine that, in doing so, it would save money or time. A company like Falcon Security is very unlikely to develop a private cloud.

Microsoft, Amazon.com, Oracle, IBM, and other major cloud service vendors employ thousands of highly trained, very highly skilled personnel to create, manage, administer, and improve their cloud services. It is unimaginable that any noncloud company, even large ones like 3M, could build and operate a cloud service facility that competes. The only situation in which this might make sense is if the organization is required by law or business custom to maintain physical control over its stored data. Even in that case, however, the organization is unlikely to be required to maintain physical control over all data, so it might keep critically sensitive data on the premises and place the rest of the data and related applications into the facilities of a public cloud vendor. It might also use a virtual private cloud, which we consider next.

## USING A VIRTUAL PRIVATE CLOUD

A **virtual private cloud (VPC)** is a subset of a public cloud that has highly restricted, secure access. An organization can build its own VPC on top of public cloud infrastructure like AWS or that provided by other cloud vendors. The means by which this is done are beyond the scope of this text, but think of it as VPN tunneling on steroids.

Using a VPC, an organization can store its most sensitive data on its own infrastructure, and store the less sensitive data on the VPC. In this way, organizations that are required to have physical control over some of their data can place that data on their own servers and locate the rest of their data on the VPC as shown in Figure 6-12. By doing so, the organization gains the advantages of cloud storage and possibly cloud processing for that portion of its data that it need not physically control.

In some cases, organizations have obtained permission from regulating bodies to store even their very sensitive data on a VPC. For example, Case Study 6 (pages 176–178) discusses FinQloud, a VPC setup and managed by NASDAQ OMX, the owner of the NASDAQ and other financial exchanges.

# Net Neutrality Enabled

Have you ever wondered what it would have been like to live during the time of the Wild West? Outlaws were abundant, and early settlers were free to stake claim to land with minimal response or oversight from the government. If you stop and think about it, the spread of Internet-connected devices has, in many ways, created a similar environment—a digital Wild West.

The digital Wild West has many parallels to the old American frontier. Modern-day cyberspace bandits can commit deviant or criminal acts (e.g., cyberbullying, stealing data, denial-of-service attacks, cybervandalism, cyberwarfare) and are rarely caught or prosecuted. This lack of legal response to criminal acts is often due to an absence of existing laws needed to convict such offenders. Cybercriminals are also difficult to physically track down.

In the old American frontier, land was "up for grabs" and people rushed to stake claim to valuable land. Similarly, today's digital resources are up for grabs. Companies are trying to stake claim to intellectual property, data streams, and bandwidth. Internet service providers (ISPs), for example, have little control over the amount, type, or origin of the content they deliver. Why is this a problem? Consider the fact that in roughly the past 5 years, Netflix's streaming services have grown so rapidly that 30 percent of all Internet traffic in the United States during peak hours is associated with people watching movies and TV shows using Netflix.[2]

As an ISP, you may feel that Netflix should pay you a fee for clogging up your fiber lines with the release of a new season of a popular TV show. On the other hand, consumers and content providers want net neutrality. This would mean that all users and content providers would be treated equally. There wouldn't be "fast" and "slow" lanes on the Internet. ISPs wouldn't be allowed to block, or even slow, content associated with competing ISPs. They also couldn't charge heavy Internet users additional fees or taxes.

To address these issues, the Federal Communications Commission (FCC) recently made an important ruling on net neutrality and became the new sheriff in town!

## Neutralizing Innovation?

In early 2015, the FCC approved new regulations to ensure that ISPs cannot discriminate between different types of Internet traffic. In short, all consumers will have access to content on an equal basis.[3] This ruling in many ways renders the Internet a utility. It would be governed much like standard utilities (e.g., water and electricity) are by comparable regulations. Many people applauded this ruling. They pointed to the benefits of an Internet free of "fast"

*Source:* bakhtiarzein/Fotolia

lanes and "slow" lanes. However, while on its surface it would seem that this ruling can only be a good thing, there may be downsides to net neutrality.

People against net neutrality argue that it is yet another instance of the government interfering with free markets. This argument is based on laissez-faire economics, which advocates for a marketplace in which government intervention is not allowed. According to this principle, if a company is going to fail, it should fail and the marketplace will correct itself.

In the case of net neutrality, ISPs want to have the freedom to oversee Internet traffic flowing through their infrastructure. They want to be able to throttle it up or down based on whether content providers are paying them for better access. Because this capability has been ruled out by the FCC, ISPs are arguing that the loss of this potential revenue stream will inhibit infrastructure development, limit growth, and stifle new innovation.

Will we ever know if this claim by the ISPs is true? Maybe or maybe not. ISPs are working on finding ways to overturn this ruling. So while this battle is over, the larger war on net neutrality may have only just begun!

## QUESTIONS

1. The article states that access to the Internet can be compared to other utilities due to the regulations that government agencies are beginning to enforce. Do you

agree or disagree with the notion that the Internet is a utility? Explain your reasoning.

2. Imagine if the Internet was not protected by net neutrality. If you were an entrepreneur starting a new e-commerce company, how could your business be hurt by ISPs creating "fast" and "slow" lanes on the Internet?
3. The Internet is a resource used by governments, universities, businesses, and people all around the world. Do you think any one country or organization should be in charge of it?
4. Some economists may frown on the FCC getting involved in the operations of telecommunications companies and ISPs. Think of some examples of other potential harmful effects of net neutrality (besides the potential of lost revenue and stifled innovation)?
5. Netflix was used as an example of a company that is instigating large volumes of Internet traffic. In what ways will the enforcement of net neutrality benefit Netflix?

**Figure 6-12**
Using a Virtual Private Cloud (VPC)

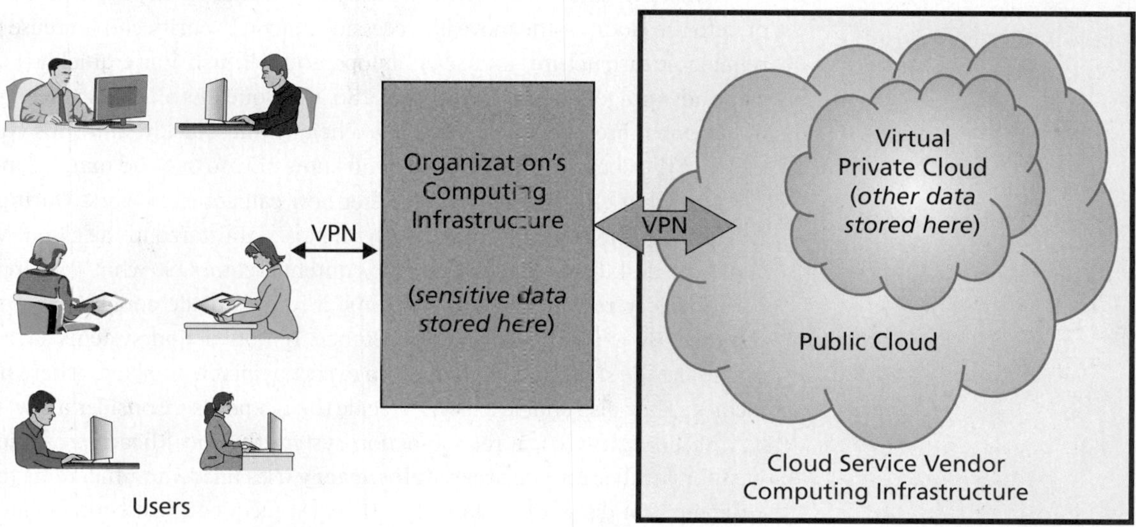


## Q6-5 WHAT DOES THE CLOUD MEAN FOR YOUR FUTURE?

So where does the cloud go during the early years of your career? Absent some unknown factor such as a federal tax on Internet traffic or a consumer push-back to governmental mining of Internet traffic, cloud services will become faster, more secure, easier to use, and cheaper. Fewer and fewer organizations will set up their own computing infrastructure; instead they will benefit from the pooling of servers across organizations and from the economies of scale produced by cloud vendors.

But, looking a bit deeper, the cloud brings both good and bad news. The good news is that organizations can readily obtain elastic resources at very low cost. This trend will benefit everyone from individuals on the iCloud or Google Drive, to small groups using Office 365, to companies like Falcon Security using PaaS, to huge organizations like NASDAQ OMX (Case Study 6) using IaaS.

The overall size of the cloud is getting bigger too. Google's Project Loon looks to seed the atmosphere with high-altitude balloons capable of providing Internet access to previously unreachable parts of the planet. Google isn't stopping there. They're making the cloud faster too. Google Fiber aims to offer users 1 Gbps connections to the Internet. That's 100 times faster than the average broadband connection. Comcast responded to Google's plans by announcing its own gigabit-per-second service.

So what's the bad news? That 500,000-square-foot Apple Web farm in Figure 6-2? Note the size of the parking lot. That tiny lot accommodates the entire operations staff. According to *Computerworld*, that building employs an operations staff of 50 people, which, spread over three shifts, 24/7, means that not many more than eight people will be running that center at any one time. Seems impossible, but is it? Again, look at the size of the parking lot.

And it's not just large companies like Apple. In 2015, every city of almost any size still supports small companies that install and maintain in-house email Exchange and other servers. If SaaS products like Google Drive or Office 365 replace those servers, what happens to those local jobs? They're gone! See Collaboration Exercise 6, page 175, for more on this topic.

But, with computing infrastructure so much cheaper, there have to be new jobs somewhere. Where will they be? For one, there will be more tech-based startups. Cheap and elastic cloud services enable small startups like the football player evaluation company Hudl (*www.hudl.com*) to access CDN and other cloud services for next to nothing, a capability that would have taken years and thousands of dollars in the past. Go to its site to check its response time; it's fast!

An organization like Falcon Security can reduce its storage costs by 50 percent if it moves its data to the cloud. If the move is successful, Falcon Security can increase profitability, have a more reliable infrastructure, and scale its operations much more quickly. Large companies gain the same advantages but on a larger scale. So, the cloud lifts all boats and should enable organizations to develop more information systems, cheaply and quickly, and thus (you knew it was coming!) increase the demand for employees who know how to use and manage information systems![4]

But what else? The cloud will foster new categories of work. During your career, everything will be connected to everything else, with most data stored in the cloud. Mobile systems will be the standard; desktops will be relegated to content creators. So what new opportunities might arise?

Consider **remote action systems**, IS that provide computer-based activity or action at a distance. By enabling action at a distance, remote action systems save time and travel expense and make the skills and abilities of an expert available in places where he or she is not physically located. They also enable experts to scale their expertise. Consider a few examples.

**Telediagnosis** is a remote action system that healthcare professionals use to diagnose illness for rural or remote areas. **Telesurgery** uses telecommunications to link surgeons to robotic equipment at distant locations. In 2001, Dr. Jacques Marescaux, located in New York City, performed the first trans-Atlantic surgery when he successfully operated on a patient in Strasbourg, France. Such examples, which are still rare, will become common during your lifetime.[5]

Other uses for remote systems include **telelaw enforcement**, such as the RedFlex system that uses cameras and motion-sensing equipment to issue tickets for red-light and speeding violations. The RedFlex Group, headquartered in South Melbourne, Victoria, Australia, earns 87 percent of its revenue from traffic violations in the United States. It offers a turn-key traffic citation information system that includes all five components.[6]

Many remote systems are designed to provide services in dangerous locations, such as robots that clean nuclear reactors or biologically contaminated sites. Drones and other unoccupied military equipment are examples of remote systems used in war zones. Private security and law enforcement will increasingly take advantage of remotely controlled flying drones and robots. You may see an upgraded form of Knightscope's 300-pound robot, named K5, patrolling your neighborhood in 10 years.

But, even with these new opportunities, the news isn't all good. New York's Metropolitan Opera is arguably the finest opera company in the world. To see a live performance, you can drive to Manhattan, park your car, taxi to Lincoln Center, and pay $300 per seat. Or you can watch the same opera, remotely broadcasted via Met Live, at a local movie theater, park your car for free, pay $12, and take a seat in the fourth row, where via the magic of digital broadcasting you can see details like the stitching on the singers' costumes, details you just can't see from the $300 seats at the Met. And the sound quality is better. Wonderful, but now, who will go to a local opera performance?

Teleaction reduces the value of local mediocrity. The claim "Well, I'm not the best, but at least I'm here" loses value in a teleaction world. In 1990, when former Secretary of Labor Robert Reich wrote *The Work of Nations*,[7] he could sensibly claim that those who provide routine face-to-face services are exempt from the dangers of offshoring. That claim loses validity in the teleaction world.

In this era, the value of the top-notch performers increases, possibly exponentially. Four million people watch the average Met Live broadcast; agents for the artists who perform at that venue will negotiate a sizable part of that $120 million gate. A famous surgeon or skating coach can reach a bigger market, faster and better, and be much better paid. So, if you can be the world's best at something, do it!

But what about the rest of us? If you're not the world's expert at something, then find a way to be indispensable to someone who is. Own the theaters that broadcast Met Live. Own the skating rink for the remote figure skating coach. Be the vendor of the food at some teleaction event.

Or become essential to the development, use, and management of information systems that support these new opportunities. A business background with IS expertise will serve you very well. The next six chapters discuss many existing and new IS applications. Keep reading!

## How does the **knowledge** in this chapter help **you?**

The cloud is the future of computing. Knowing what the cloud is, how organizations can benefit from it, and understanding the important security issues when using the cloud will be key knowledge for all business professionals in the early years of your career. Knowledge of the cloud will also help you anticipate new categories of jobs that you might find rewarding. Finally, cloud knowledge might also help you save your organization considerable money, and who knows, you too might be sitting on the private island as discussed in the Ethics Guide on pages 170–171.

# Ethics Guide

## Cloudy Profit?

Alliance Partners (a fictitious name) is a data broker. You'll learn about data brokers in Chapter 9, but for now, just know that such companies acquire and buy consumer and other data from retailers, other data brokers, governmental agencies, and public sources and aggregate it into data profiles of individuals. Alliance specializes in acquiring and analyzing market, buyer, and seller data for real estate agents. Alliance sells an individual profile to qualified real estate agents for $100 to $1,500, depending on the amount of data and type of analysis requested.

Alliance is owned by three partners who started the business in 1999. They endured tough times during the dot-com collapse at the turn of the century, but crawled out of that hole and were doing well until they encountered severe revenue shortfalls in the 2008 real estate collapse. In late 2008, in order to reduce operational costs to survive the downturn, Alliance transitioned its data storage and processing from its own Web farm to the cloud. The elastic flexibility of the cloud enables Alliance to improve the speed and quality of its data services at a fraction of prior costs. Furthermore, using the cloud enabled it to reduce the in-house hardware support staff by 65 percent.

The partners meet twice a year to review their financial performance, evaluate strategy, and plan for both the next 6 months and the longer term. In 2008, in the midst of their revenue shortfalls, they met in a small suite in the local Hamilton Inn, ate stale doughnuts, and drank watery orange juice. This year, they've rented a facility in the British Virgin Islands in the Caribbean. The following conversation occurred between two of the partners at the onset of this year's meeting:

"Bart, what are we doing here?" Shelly, the partner in charge of sales and marketing, is challenging Bart Johnson, Alliance's managing partner.

"What do you mean, Shelly? Don't you like it here?"

"I *love* it here. So does my husband. But I also know we're paying $15,000 a night to rent this island!" Shelly rubs sunscreen on her hands as she talks.

"Well, we don't have the entire island." Bart sounds defensive.

"No, I guess not," she says. "They have to let some of the staff stay here. We're the only paying customers . . . the only non-locals.

"But," Shelly continues, "that's not my point. My point is how can we afford this level of expense? We'll pay nearly $200,000 for this meeting alone. Where will we meet next? Some five-star resort on the moon?"

"Look, Shelly, as you're about to hear, our gross margin last year was 74 percent. We're a money machine! We're swimming in profit! We can't spend money fast enough. One of the items on our agenda is whether we want to issue a $1 million, a $3 million, or a $5 million partners' distribution."

"No!" Shelly sounds stunned.

"Yup. Using the cloud, we've reduced our operational expense from 62 percent of our revenue to 9 percent. I'm plowing money back into R&D as fast as I can, but there's only so much that Jacob and his crew can absorb. Meanwhile, order the lobster and wait until you taste tonight's wines."

"That's disgusting."

"OK," Bart says. "Don't drink the wine. Do you want your distribution?"
"No; I mean yes, but this is crazy. It can't last."
"Probably not. But it's what we've got right now."

## DISCUSSION QUESTIONS

When answering the following questions, assume that Alliance has done nothing illegal, including paying all federal, state, and local taxes on a timely basis.

**1.** From the perspective of Kant's categorical imperative (pages 20–21), are Alliance's partners' meeting expense and intended partner distribution unethical?

**2.** From the utilitarian perspective (pages 46–47), are Alliance's partners' meeting expense and intended partner distribution unethical?

**3.** Milton Friedman, world-renowned economist at the University of Chicago, stated that corporate executives have a responsibility to make as much money as possible as long as they don't violate rules embodied in law and in ethical custom.[8]

**a.** Do you agree with his statement? Why or why not?

**b.** Friedman defined *ethical custom* narrowly to mean no *fraud* or *deception*. Using his definition, has Alliance acted ethically?

**c.** Define, using your own words, *ethical custom*.

**d.** Using your definition of *ethical custom*, has Alliance acted ethically?

**4.** Do you find any of the following excessive? Explain your answers:

**a.** Spending nearly $200,000 on a 5-day partners' meeting for three partners and their spouses?

**b.** Earning a 74 percent gross profit?

**c.** Paying a semiannual distribution of $1M, $3M, or $5M? If so, which level is excessive to you?

**5.** Describe the primary driver in Alliance's current profitability.

**6.** From the data presented, what else might Alliance have done with its excess profits?

**7.** Do you think profitable companies, especially very profitable companies, have an ethical obligation to:

**a.** Contribute to charity?

**b.** Lower prices when it is possible to do so and continue to earn a reasonable profit?

**c.** Contribute to environmental causes?

**d.** When possible, pay large bonuses to all employees, not just senior management?

**8.** To most students, someone who earns $500,000 a year in income is rich. To someone who makes $500,000 a year, partners that pay themselves $1M to $5M every 6 months are rich. To someone making $2M to $10M a year, billionaires are rich. What do you think classifies someone as rich?

**9.** Do you think rich people have an ethical obligation to:

**a.** Contribute to charity?

**b.** Contribute to environmental causes?

**c.** Forego governmental benefits to which they are entitled, for example, not take Social Security that they don't need?

Source: Pierre-Yves Babelon/Fotolia

# Guide

## From Anthem to Anathema

Have you ever lost your smartphone, even just for an hour or two? If so, you probably recall the wave of panic that sets in when you thought it might be gone forever. Losing any digital device can be extremely troubling for a number of reasons. First, mobile devices and laptops are not cheap. The thought of spending hundreds of dollars, or even a couple thousand dollars in the case of a laptop, to replace the lost device is distressing. However, what often creates the most panic is the thought of the person now possessing your device finding a way to access all of your data.

If you were to lose a digital device, what data would you be most concerned about—banking data, email archives, social media accounts, your collection of photos, or something else? There is no right or wrong answer to this question as responses will vary from person to person. However, what is constant is the likelihood that in the future someone will access your personal data. The frustrating part is that in most cases, the culprits will not even need physical access to your smartphone or laptop. Your data can be stolen just as easily from a company storing it in the cloud. Don't believe it? Just ask anyone covered by Anthem health care in February 2015.

### Cloudy with a Chance of Theft

More and more data are being stored in the cloud. Why? Because data storage costs have plummeted and Internet access has become faster and cheaper. In 1990, 1 million transistors cost $527, a gigabyte of storage cost $569, and a gigabit per second of bandwidth cost $1,245.[9] But today 1 million transistors cost $0.05, a gigabyte of storage costs $0.02, and a gigabit per second of bandwidth costs $16.

Internet users want easy access to more and more data. Unfortunately, the downside to greater accessibility is that it becomes more accessible to hackers too.

In early 2015, Anthem Insurance Companies, Inc. reported a security breach resulting in the loss of roughly 80 million customer accounts.[10] Hackers stole sensitive account data like names, addresses, social security numbers, and salaries. While any nationally publicized security breach will cause concern, especially in light of the recent trend in breaches with the Target and Home Depot incidents, Anthem customers became more and more irate as details about the nature of the breach were reported. Anthem eventually disclosed that the account data stolen had been stored in plain text—not encrypted. This meant that hackers could immediately begin selling the data on the black market or using it for other nefarious purposes.

Security experts criticized Anthem for not encrypting sensitive customer account data. Numerous clients considered Anthem's failure to encrypt account records negligent, and they subsequently filed lawsuits.

### Bad for Business or Business as Usual?

How would you feel if your account data had been part of the Anthem breach? Would this incident make you want to switch to a different healthcare provider, or would you recognize that large corporate data breaches are just a fact of life in a digital world and that your new healthcare provider could be equally vulnerable? The reality is that data breaches are so pervasive that it is not a matter of if, but when, a company holding data about you will be hacked. In fact, about a month after the Anthem data breach, Premera Blue Cross announced the loss of 11 million customer records. The lost customer records were even more sensitive because they included bank-account and medical data.[11]

Despite these threats, it is highly unlikely that companies will begin pulling data from the cloud. Consumers clearly want the ease of use that Web-based services provide. However, it is possible that corporations' security practices could evolve from being a necessary evil to becoming a competitive advantage. In fact, there could come a time when a company's reputation for information security could be more valuable than the very products or services it sells!

## DISCUSSION QUESTIONS

**1.** Think about all of the cloud services that you use. How vulnerable are you right now to having your data stolen?

**2.** What are some of the ways you can lower the chances of your personal data being stolen?

**3.** The article explains how Anthem failed to encrypt sensitive account data. Why would encrypting account data make it more secure?

**4.** Have prior data breaches, like those at Home Depot or Target, affected your behavior as a consumer? How?

**5.** How can a greater awareness of security best practices help you in your current job?

*Source:* BillionPhotos.com/Fotolia

# ACTIVE REVIEW

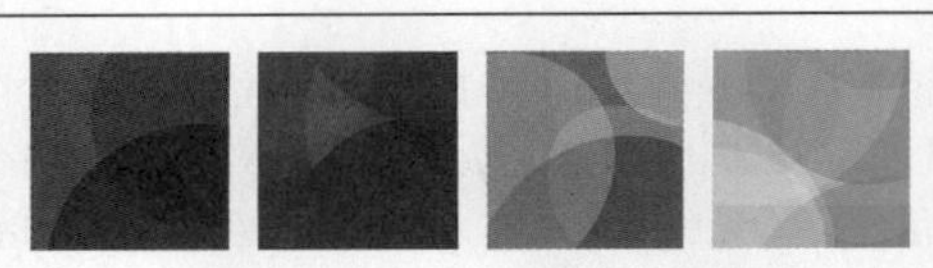

Use this Active Review to verify that you understand the ideas and concepts that answer the chapter's study questions.

## Q6-1 WHY IS THE CLOUD THE FUTURE FOR MOST ORGANIZATIONS?

Define *cloud* and explain the three key terms in your definition. Using Figure 6-3 as a guide, compare and contrast cloud-based and in-house hosting. Explain three factors that make cloud computing possible today. Explain the meaning of the terms *SOA, Web service standards,* and *Web services.* When does it not make sense to use a cloud-based infrastructure?

## Q6-2 HOW DO ORGANIZATIONS USE THE CLOUD?

Define *SaaS, PaaS,* and *IaaS*. Provide an example of each. For each, describe the business situation in which it would be the most appropriate option. Define *CDN* and explain the purpose and advantages of a CDN. Explain how Web services can be used internally.

## Q6-3 HOW CAN FALCON SECURITY USE THE CLOUD?

Name and describe SaaS products that Falcon could use. Explain several ways that Falcon could use PaaS offerings. Summarize why it is unlikely that Falcon would use IaaS. How would Falcon use a CDN?

## Q6-4 HOW CAN ORGANIZATIONS USE CLOUD SERVICES SECURELY?

Explain the purpose of a VPN and describe, in broad terms, how a VPN works. Define the term *virtual* and explain how it relates to VPN. Define *private cloud.* Summarize why the benefits of a private cloud are questionable. What kind of organization might benefit from such a cloud? Explain why it is unlikely that even very large organizations can create private clouds that compete with public cloud utilities. Under what circumstance might a private cloud make sense for an organization? Define *VPC* and explain how and why an organization might use one.

## Q6-5 WHAT DOES THE CLOUD MEAN FOR YOUR FUTURE?

What is the likely future of the cloud? Summarize the good and bad news that the cloud brings. Explain why the photo in Figure 6-2 is disturbing. Explain the statement "The cloud lifts all boats." Describe three categories of remote action systems. Explain how remote systems will increase the value of super-experts but diminish local mediocrity. What can other-than-super-experts do?

## How does the **knowledge** in this chapter help **you?**

The cloud is a fundamental shift in the way that organizations acquire computing infrastructure. It enables organizations to share in the benefits of near-zero costs of data processing, storage, and communication. As shown in the Falcon Security opening story as well as in the Ethics Guide, the cloud can have a dramatic effect on profitability.

So, this chapter helps you be better informed as a business professional, helps you anticipate new, possibly exciting jobs for yourself, and may help you save your organization considerable money. A fundamental shift is afoot; take advantage of it!

## KEY TERMS AND CONCEPTS

MyMISLab™

To complete the problems with the ✪, go to EOC Discussion Questions in the MyLab.

## USING YOUR KNOWLEDGE

✪ **6-1.** Define *cloud* and explain the three key terms in your definition. Compare and contrast cloud-based and in-house hosting using the comparison presented in Q6-1 as a guide. In your opinion, explain the three most important factors that make cloud-based hosting preferable to in-house hosting.

✪ **6-2.** Apple invested more than $1B in the North Carolina data center mentioned in Q6-1. For Apple to spend such a sum, it must perceive the iCloud as being a key component of its future. Using the principles discussed in Q3-2 of Chapter 3, explain all the ways that you believe the iCloud will give Apple a competitive advantage over other mobile device vendors.

✪ **6-3.** Suppose you work at Falcon Security and Joni tells you she doesn't believe that cheap, elastic data storage is possible. "There has to be a catch somewhere," she says. Write a one-page memo to her explaining how the cloud works. In your memo, include the role of standards for cloud processing.

## COLLABORATION EXERCISE 6

*Read Chapter Extensions 1 and 2 if you have not already done so. Meet with your team and build a collaboration IS that uses tools like Google Docs, Dropbox, SharePoint, or other collaboration tools. Do not forget the need for procedures and team training. Now, using that IS, answer the questions below.*

The cloud is causing monumental changes in the information systems services industry. In every city, you will still see the trucks of local independent software vendors (ISVs) driving to their clients to set up and maintain local area networks, servers, and software. You'll know the trucks by the Microsoft, Oracle, and Cisco logos on their sides. For years, those small, local companies have survived, some very profitably, on their ability to set up and maintain LANs, connect user computers to the Internet, set up servers, sell Microsoft Exchange licenses, and install other software on both servers and user computers.

Once everything is installed, these companies continue to earn revenue by providing maintenance for problems that inevitably develop and support for new versions of software, connecting new user computers, and so forth. Their customers vary, but generally are smaller companies of, say, 3 to 50 employees—companies that are large enough to need email, Internet connections, and possibly some entry-level software applications such as QuickBooks.

**6-4.** Using the knowledge of this chapter and the intuition of the members of your team, summarize the threats that cloud services present to such ISVs.

**6-5.** Suppose your team owns and manages one of these ISVs. You learn that more and more of your clients are choosing SaaS cloud services like Google for email, rather than setting up local email servers.

**a.** What, if anything, can you do to prevent the encroachment of SaaS on your business?

**b.** Given your answer to part a, identify three alternative ways you can respond.

**c.** Which of the three responses identified in your answer to part b would you choose? Justify your choice.

**6-6.** Even if SaaS eliminates the need for email and other local servers, there will still remain viable services that you can provide. Name and describe those services.

**6-7.** Suppose instead of attempting to adapt an existing ISV to the threat of cloud services, you and your teammates decide to set up an entirely new business, one that will succeed in the presence of SaaS and other cloud services. Looking at businesses in and around your campus, identify and describe the IS needs those businesses will have in the cloud services world.

**6-8.** Describe the IS services that your new business could provide for the business needs you identified in your answer to question 6-7.

**6-9.** Given your answers to questions 6-4 through 6-8, would you rather be an existing ISV attempting to adapt to this new world or an entirely new company? Compare and contrast the advantages and disadvantages of each alternative.

**6-10.** Changing technology has, for centuries, eliminated the need for certain products and services and created the need for new products and services. What is new, today, however, is the rapid pace at which new technology is created and adapted. Using cloud services as an example, create a statement of the posture that business professionals should take with regard to technology in order to thrive in this fast-changing environment. Notice the verb in this assignment is *thrive*, and not just *survive*.

## CASE STUDY 6

### FinQloud Forever...Well, at Least for the Required Interval....

In 1937, the Securities and Exchange Commission (SEC) set out rules that stipulated records retention requirements for securities brokers and dealers. The SEC's concern was (and is) that records of financial transactions not be altered after the fact, that they be retained for a stipulated period of time, and that indexes be created so that the records can be readily searched.

In 1937, the rules assumed that such records were recorded on paper media. With the rise of information systems storage, the SEC updated the rules in 1997 by stating that such records can be kept electronically, provided that the storage devices are write once, read many times (WORM) devices. This rule was readily accepted by the financial services industry because the first CDs and DVDs were WORM devices.

However, as technology developed, broker-dealers and other financial institutions wanted to store records using regular disk storage and petitioned the SEC for guidance on how they might do that. In May 2003, the SEC interpreted the rule to enable the storage of such records on read-write medium, provided that the storage mechanism included software that would prohibit data alternation:

> A broker-dealer would not violate the requirement in paragraph (f)(2)(ii)(A) of the rule if it used an electronic storage system that prevents the overwriting, erasing or otherwise altering of a record during its required retention period through the use of integrated hardware and software control codes. Rule 17a-4 requires broker-dealers to retain records for specified lengths of time. Therefore, it follows that the non-erasable and non-rewriteable aspect of their storage need not continue beyond that period.
>
> The Commission's interpretation does not include storage systems that only mitigate the risk a record will be overwritten or erased. Such systems—which may use software applications to protect electronic records, such as authentication and approval policies, passwords or other extrinsic security controls—do not maintain the records in a manner that is non-rewriteable and non-erasable. The external measures used by these other systems do not prevent a record from being changed or deleted. For example, they might limit access to records through the use of passwords. Additionally, they might create a "finger print" of the record based on its content. If the record is changed, the fingerprint will indicate that it was altered (but the original record would not be preserved). The ability to overwrite or erase records stored on these systems makes them non-compliant with Rule 17a-4(f).[12]

Notice the SEC specifically excludes extrinsic controls such as authentication, passwords, and manual procedures because it believes it would be possible for such systems to be readily misused to overwrite records. The SEC is striking a fine line in this ruling; if, for example, someone were to tamper with the storage systems' software, it would be possible to overwrite data. Apparently, the SEC assumes such tampering would be illegal and so rare as to not be a concern.

Given this ruling, organizations began to develop systems in compliance. The NASDAQ OMX Group, a multinational corporation that owns and operates the NASDAQ stock market as well as eight European exchanges, developed FinQloud, a cloud-based storage system that is compliant with the SEC's (and other regulating organizations') rulings. NASDAQ OMX operates in 70 different markets, in 50 countries worldwide, and claims that it processes one out of 10 stock transactions worldwide.[13]

Figure 6-13 shows the fundamental structure of the FinQloud system. On the back end, it uses Amazon's S3 product to provide scalable, elastic storage. When financial institutions submit records to FinQloud for storage, FinQloud processes the data in such a way that it cannot be updated, encrypts the data, and transmits the processed, encrypted data to AWS, where it is encrypted yet again and stored on S3 devices. Data is indexed on S3 and can be readily read by authorized users. When development was complete, NASDAQ OMS claimed that FinQloud's processing and encryption were done in such a way that the system meets the SEC requirement.

Of course, NASDAQ OMX knew this statement would be perceived as self-serving, so it hired two independent companies to verify it: Jordan & Jordan, a securities industry consulting company, and Cohasset Associates, a document-processing consulting company. According to *The Wall Street Journal*, both organizations concluded that when properly configured, FinQloud meets the

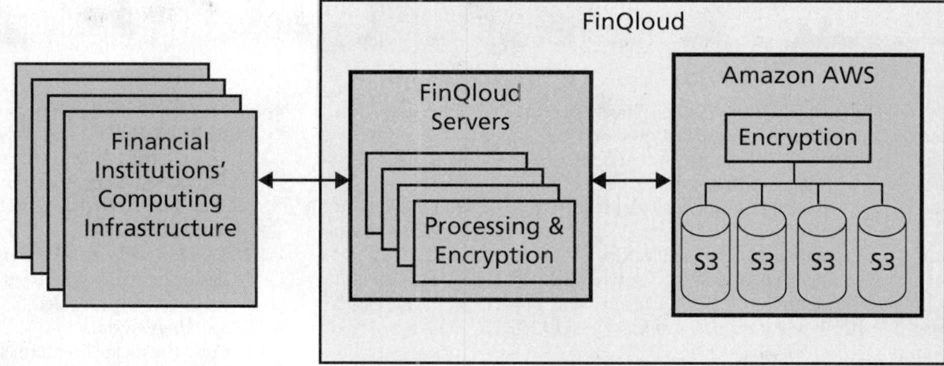


**Figure 6-13**
Components of the FinQloud System

requirements of the SEC's rule (Rule 17a-3) as well as a similar rule set out by the Commodities Futures Trading Commission.[14]

Consequently, NASDAQ OMX customers can use FinQloud; as long as the customers demonstrate that they have properly configured FinQloud, auditors will find it to be in compliance with the SEC rulings.

## QUESTIONS

**6-11.** In your own words, summarize the dealer-broker record retention requirements.

**6-12.** Reread the SEC's 2003 interpretation. In your own words, explain the difference between "integrated hardware and software control codes" and software applications that use "authentication and approval policies, passwords, or other extrinsic controls." Give an example of each.

**6-13.** Clearly, in the view of the SEC, the likelihood of compromise of an integrated system of hardware and software is considerably less than the likelihood of compromise of a system of authentication, passwords, and procedures. Justify this view.

**6-14.** Do you agree with the view in question 6-13? Why or why not?

**6-15.** Investigate Jordan & Jordan (*www.jandj.com/*) and Cohasset Associates (*www.cohasset.com*). If you were a consultant to a financial institution, to what extent would you rely on the statements of these organizations?

**6-16.** If you were a consultant to a financial institution, what else might you do to verify that FinQloud complies with the SEC ruling and its 2003 interpretation?

**6-17.** Explain how the knowledge you have gained so far in this course helps you understand the SEC's 2003 interpretation. Summarize how your knowledge would help you if you worked for a financial institution. Cast your answers to this question in a way that you could use in a job interview.

MyMISLab™

Go to the Assignments section of your MyLab to complete these writing exercises.

**6-18.** Suppose Toshio wants Falcon Security to set up a private internet, and he justifies this request on the basis of better security. Explain why that is not a good decision and rebut his claim about security by suggesting that Falcon Security use a VPC. Justify your suggestion.

**6-19.** Suppose you manage a sales department that uses the SaaS product Salesforce.com. One of your key salespeople refuses to put his data into that system. "I just don't believe that the competition can't steal my data, and I'm not taking that risk." How do you respond to him?

## ENDNOTES


1. Patrick Thibodeau, "Apple, Google, Facebook Turn N.C. into Data Center Hub," *Computerworld*, last modified June 3, 2011, *www.computerworld.com/s/article/9217259/Apple_Google_Facebook_turn_N.C._into_data_center_hub*.
2. M. Prince, "Thoughts on Network Neutrality, the FCC, and the Future of Internet Governance." February 27, 2015, accessed April 10, 2015, *https://blog.cloudflare.com/net-neutrality*.
3. Mike Snider, Roger Yu, and Emily Brown, "What Is Net Neutrality and What Does It Mean for Me?" *USA Today*, February 27, 2015, accessed April 10, 2015, *www.usatoday.com/story/tech/2015/02/24/net-neutrality-what-is-it-guide/23237737*.
4. See, for example, *http://online.wsj.com/article/SB10001424127887323744604578470900844821388.html?mod=itp*, accessed May 2013.
5. Issie Lapowsky, "Video Is About to Become the Way We All Visit the Doctor," *Wired*, April 30, 2015, accessed May 4, 2015, *www.wired.com/2015/04/united-healthcare-telemedicine*.
6. Traffic citation information system is not a commonly accepted term, but providing all five components is essentially IS as a service, or ISaaS.
7. Robert Reich, *The Work of Nations: Preparing Ourselves for Twenty-first Century Capitalism* (New York: Vintage Books, 1992), p. 176.
8. Milton Friedman, "The Social Responsibility of Business Is to Increase Its Profits," *The New York Times Magazine*, September 13, 1970.
9. Gene Marks, "Why the Anthem Breach Just Doesn't Matter Anymore," *Forbes*, February 9, 2015, accessed April 22, 2015, *www.forbes.com/sites/quickerbettertech/2015/02/09/why-the-anthem-breach-just-doesnt-matter-anymore*.
10. Tom Huddleston, "Anthem's Big Data Breach Is Already Sparking Lawsuits," *Fortune*, February 6, 2015, accessed April 22, 2015, *http://fortune.com/2015/02/06/anthems-big-data-breach-is-already-sparking-lawsuits*.
11. Coral Garnick, "Premera Negligent in Data Breach, 5 Lawsuits Claim," *Seattle Times*, March 27, 2015, accessed April 22, 2015, *www.seattletimes.com/seattle-news/premera-negligent-in-data-breach-5-lawsuits-claim*.
12. U.S. Securities and Exchange Commission, "SEC Interpretation: Electronic Storage of Broker-Dealer Records," last modified May 5, 2003, *www.sec.gov/rules/interp/34-47806.htm*.
13. NASDAQ OMX, "NASDAQ OMX FinQloud," accessed May 2013, *www.nasdaqomx.com/technology/yourbusiness/finqloud/*.
14. Greg MacSweeney, "Nasdaq OMX FinQloud R3 Meets SEC/CFTC Regulatory Requirements, Say Consultants," April 15, 2013, *www.wallstreetandtech.com/data-management/nasdaq-omx-finqloud-r3-meets-seccftc-reg/240152909*.

part 3

# Using IS for Competitive Advantage

***In the previous*** six chapters, you gained a foundation of IS fundamentals. In Chapters 7–12, you will apply those fundamentals to learn how organizations use information systems to achieve their strategies. Part 3, Chapters 7–9, focuses on application of IS; Part 4, Chapters 10–12, focuses on management of IS.

## This could happen to you

Chapters 7–12 are introduced using a cloud-based, mobile application for the healthcare industry. To our knowledge, the system described here does not yet exist. However, it is entirely plausible, may be an excellent entrepreneurial opportunity, and features some of today's most exciting emerging technology in one of today's most important industries.

The figure on the next page shows the major actors involved in this system, which we will call Performance Recording, Integration, Delivery, and Evaluation (PRIDE). Using PRIDE, exercise workout data is collected from devices that conform to the ANT[1] protocol, which is a personal network communications protocol implemented by exercise equipment such as treadmills, stationary bikes, heart monitors, footpads, and the like. Using this protocol, data is transmitted from exercise devices to the Internet, either via a local area network or via a cell phone. That exercise data is then stored in a cloud database.

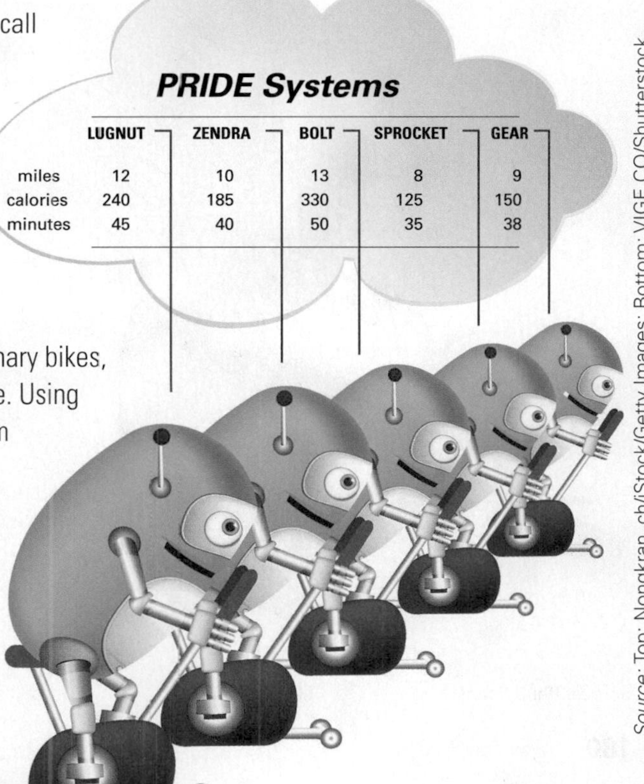


*Source:* Top: Nongkran_ch/iStock/Getty Images; Bottom: VIGE.CO/Shutterstock

Once the data is stored in the cloud, individuals, healthcare professionals, health clubs, insurance companies, and employers can query and obtain exercise reports. Doctors can ensure that their patients are exercising neither too little nor too much; health clubs can integrate exercise class data with personal exercise data; insurance companies can use that data to adjust policy rates for policy holders with healthy lifestyles; and employers can assess the effectiveness of investments they make into improving employee health.

A prototype of this system was developed by a cardiac surgeon, Dr. Romero Flores, for use in his practice. The system was popular and did help patients recover, at least as long as Flores was pushing it in his own practice. Flores had hoped to license this system to other doctors, but he had no success.

Zev Friedman is one of Dr. Flores's patients and was one of the first to benefit from the PRIDE system. Friedman earned considerable wealth starting and selling small businesses over the past 30 years, and he liked what he experienced with PRIDE. So, during an office visit, Friedman asked how the system was being received. Knowing that Flores is a cardiologist and not a business professional, he wasn't surprised to learn that it wasn't getting very far. Friedman thought that with a refocus of its marketing and with experienced management, PRIDE could be a success. Accordingly, he bought the company for a small amount of cash and a royalty agreement with Flores. Using his business contacts, he then found and hired a new general manager, Jared Cooper, and a marketing professional, Nicki Jensen. He kept James Wu, who had been the technology manager under Flores. Jared subsequently hired Michele Russell as sales director.

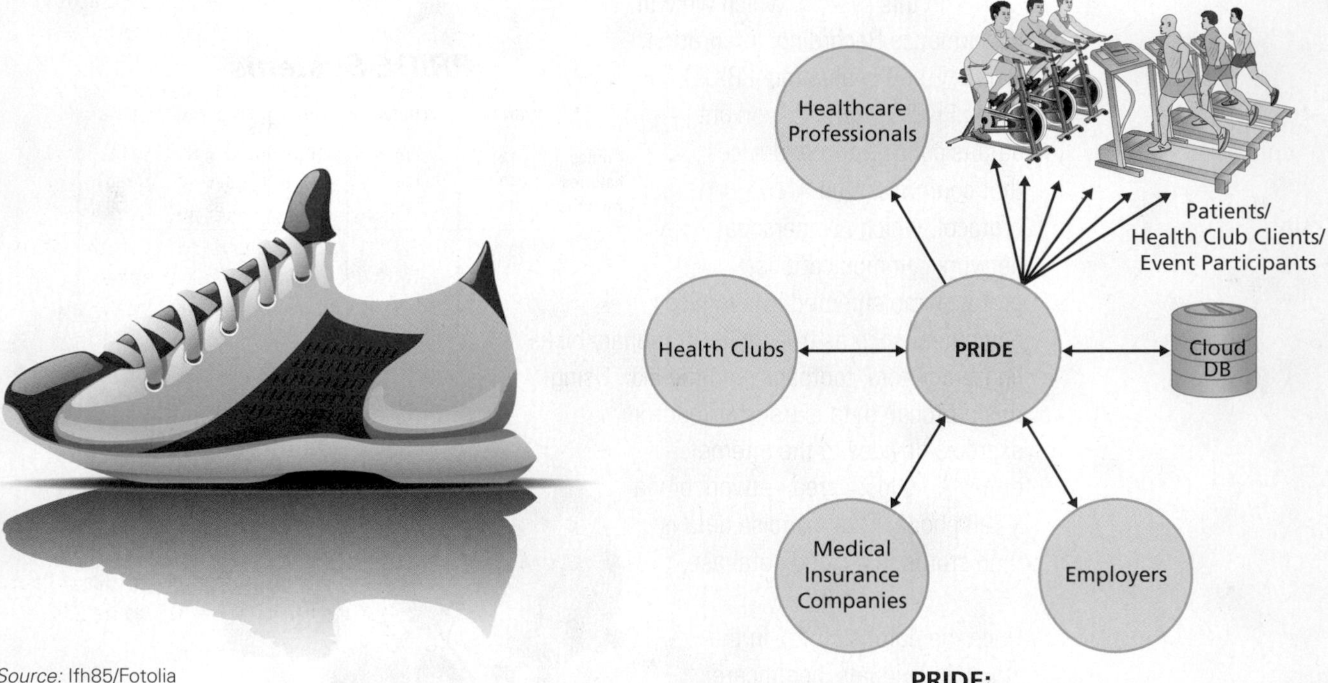


Source: Ifh85/Fotolia

**PRIDE:**
Performance Recording, Integration, Display, and Evaluation

# Organizations and Information Systems

**This could happen to you**

Zev Friedman, the owner of PRIDE Systems, Jared Cooper, general manager, Nicki Jensen, marketing professional, and James Wu, IS professional, are having an introductory meeting at Friedman's luxurious house on a Saturday morning.

After polite conversation, Zev gets down to business.

"Here's where Flores went wrong. Doctors don't care about exercise." Zev looks around the table as he speaks.

"They say they do." Nicki's not sure Zev will tolerate interruption, but it's not her style to sit back and listen.

"What people say and what they do are two different things. Doctors care about medicine, about operations. Some care most about *expensive* operations. If they cared about exercise, they'd own health clubs." Zev's tone is matter of fact; Nicki's interruption didn't bother him at all.

"So we need to figure out who's got the pain and how much they'll pay." Jared, PRIDE Systems' new general manager, likes Zev's forthright manner.

"Right. Flores and his group demonstrated this thing works. You can use the cloud and all this exercise gear and mobile devices to collect, integrate, and report exercise data. So, who do we sell it to, and what do we tell 'em to induce them to buy?"

"I talked to a couple of insurance companies, and they're not promising." Jared looks at Zev.

"No? Why not?" Zev knows the answer, but he wants to see if Jared does.

"They don't like exercise. Exercise doesn't prevent disease. Well, maybe some cardiac diseases, and long term maybe some diabetes, but it doesn't do anything for cancer or Alzheimer's. The insurance companies think exercise just raises claims due to exercise-induced injury."

"You're kidding." Nicki can't believe what's she's hearing.

"Even worse, to them anyway, when you get in good shape you last longer when you do get cancer or whatever. So, you live longer on your way out the door, and their care expenses increase."

"I can't believe I'm hearing this!" Nicki says what she's been thinking.

"So, Zev, I'm wondering, you think there's any government money in this? Obamacare funds we could tap?" Jared's looking right at Zev.

"Maybe. I'll ask some friends. That kind of money is slow to get, and the reporting requirements can be so painful it's not worth it. But I'll find out what I can learn. That won't help us immediately, though."

# STUDY QUESTIONS

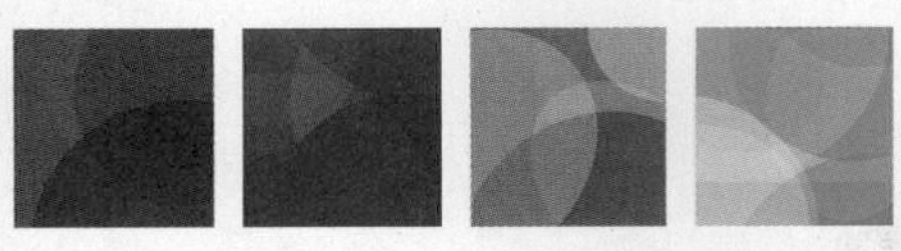

**Q7-1 HOW DO INFORMATION SYSTEMS VARY BY SCOPE?**

**Q7-2 HOW DO ENTERPRISE SYSTEMS SOLVE THE PROBLEMS OF DEPARTMENTAL SILOS?**

**Q7-3 HOW DO CRM, ERP, AND EAI SUPPORT ENTERPRISE SYSTEMS?**

**Q7-4 HOW DO INTER-ENTERPRISE IS SOLVE THE PROBLEMS OF ENTERPRISE SILOS?**

## How does the knowledge in this chapter help you?

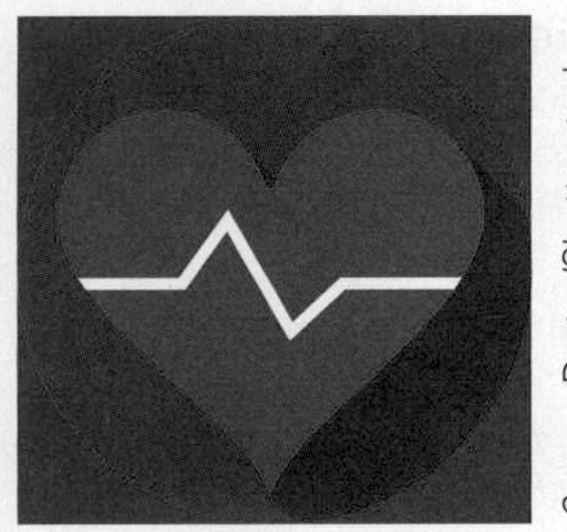

Source: Derter/Shutterstock

**"How much money does a system own?"**

"Well, the real beneficiary of this is the whole system. All the players together." James speaks up for the first time.

"Young man, you may be right. But let me ask you, how much money does a system own?" Zev is gentle, but privately he's amazed at James's naiveté.

"Well, none, Mr. Friedman." James figures out where this is going.

"Then the system can't be a buyer, can it? Saying the system has the benefits might make sense to you techies, but it won't make sense down at the bank." Zev is still gentle, but James is squirming.

"I see. OK." James is embarrassed but has the good sense to shut up.

"Well, besides the medical players, there are employers, health clubs, equipment manufacturers, and people who exercise." Jared is counting on his fingers as he speaks.

"Jared, take a look at those. I suspect employers will respond just as negatively as insurance companies, but maybe not, at least maybe not some. Find out."

"OK."

"You have to show the health clubs how PRIDE adds revenue to them, if it does. Same with the manufacturers." Zev looks at Nicki. "So, Nicki, what have you got to say?"

"Well, I think we should think about selling ads, you know, placing them on our competition sites and clicks."

"Go on."

"Some sort of an ad revenue model based on use. But for that we need to get our numbers up. We have to get people using PRIDE in large groups. Maybe some events, social media–driven."

"I like that, but is it real? Let's find out. Jared, you look into the health clubs and employers. Nicki, you put some meat on your ad revenue idea, and James, you figure out if PRIDE can support, say, 10,000 people spinning at the same time, in the same contest. Questions?"

Everyone looks around the table; no one says a word.

"OK, see you next week."

Optional Extensions for this chapter are • CE9: Enterprise Resource Planning (ERP) Systems 512 • CE10: Supply Chain Management 527

# Q7-1 HOW DO INFORMATION SYSTEMS VARY BY SCOPE?

As shown in Figure 7-1, modern organizations use four types of information systems that vary according to the scope of the organizational unit. We begin by considering each IS type.

## PERSONAL INFORMATION SYSTEMS

**Personal information systems** are information systems used by a single individual. The contact manager in your iPhone or in your email account is an example of a personal information system. Because such systems have only one user, procedures are simple and probably not documented or formalized in any way.

It is easy to manage change to personal information systems. If you switch email from, say, MSN to Google, you'll have to move your contact list from one vendor to the other, and you'll have to inform your correspondents of your new address, but you control the timing of that change. Because you will be the sole user of the new system, if new procedures are required, only you need to adapt. And, if there are problems, you can solve them yourself.

Figure 7-1 uses the example of a drug salesperson. Each person has his or her own personal information systems for managing data about doctors and other customers, appointments, product descriptions and prices, drug companies, and so forth. All of this data exists independently of other salespeople.

## WORKGROUP INFORMATION SYSTEMS

A **workgroup information system** is an information system that facilitates the activities of a group of people. At a physicians' partnership, doctors, nurses, and staff use information systems to manage patient appointments, keep patient records, schedule in-office procedures and equipment, and facilitate other workgroup activities.

Workgroup information systems that support a particular department are sometimes called **departmental information systems**. An example is the accounts payable system that is used by the accounts payable department. Other workgroup information systems support a particular business function and are called **functional information systems**. A prospect tracking application is an example of a functional IS. Finally, the collaboration information systems discussed in Chapter Extension 2 are also workgroup information systems.

Workgroup information systems, whether departmental, functional, or collaborative, share the characteristics shown in Figure 7-1. Typically, workgroup systems support 10 to 100

**Figure 7-1**
Information Systems Scope

| Scope | Example | Characteristics |
|---|---|---|
| Personal | Drug Salesperson | Single user; procedures informal; problems isolated; easy to manage change |
| Workgroup | Physician Partnership | 10–100 users; procedures understood within group; problem solutions within group; somewhat difficult to change |
| Enterprise | Hospital | 100–1,000s users; procedures formalized; problem solutions affect enterprise; difficult to change |
| Inter-enterprise | PRIDE System | 1,000s users; procedures formalized; problem solutions affect multiple organizations; difficult to change |

users. The procedures for using them must be understood by all members of the group. Often, procedures are formalized in documentation, and users are sometimes trained in the use of those procedures.

When problems occur, they almost always can be solved within the group. If accounts payable duplicates the record for a particular supplier, the accounts payable group can make the fix. If the Web storefront has the wrong number of widgets in the inventory database, that count can be fixed within the storefront group.

(Notice, by the way, that the *consequences* of a problem are not isolated to the group. Because the workgroup exists to provide a service to the rest of the organization, its problems have consequences throughout the organization. The *fix* to the problem can usually be obtained within the group, however.)

### ENTERPRISE INFORMATION SYSTEMS

**Enterprise information systems** are information systems that span an organization and support activities of people in multiple departments. At a hospital, doctors, nurses, the pharmacy, the kitchen, and others use information systems to track patients, treatments, medications, diets, room assignments, and so forth.

Enterprise information systems typically have hundreds to thousands of users. Procedures are formalized and extensively documented; users undergo formal procedure training. Sometimes enterprise systems include categories of procedures, and users are defined according to levels of expertise with the system as well as by levels of security authorization.

The solutions to problems in an enterprise system usually involve more than one department. Because enterprise systems span many departments and involve potentially thousands of users, they are very difficult to change. Changes must be carefully planned and cautiously implemented and users given considerable training. Sometimes users are given financial incentives and other inducements to motivate them to change.

### INTER-ENTERPRISE INFORMATION SYSTEMS

**Inter-enterprise information systems** are information systems that are shared by two or more independent organizations. The PRIDE system introduced at the start of this part is an inter-enterprise system that is shared among patients, healthcare providers, health clubs, insurance companies, and employers. All of these organizations have an interest in assigning, recording, or viewing individual performance data.

Such systems involve hundreds to thousands of users, and solutions to problems require cooperation among different, usually independently owned, organizations. Problems are resolved by meeting, by contract, and sometimes by litigation. Because of the wide span, complexity, and multiple companies involved, such systems can be exceedingly difficult to change. The interaction of independently owned and operated information systems is required.

The development of information systems at any level can lead to problems caused by information silos. We turn to those problems and the ways that IS can be used to solve them next.

## Q7-2 HOW DO ENTERPRISE SYSTEMS SOLVE THE PROBLEMS OF DEPARTMENTAL SILOS?

An **information silo** is the condition that exists when data are isolated in separated information systems. Silos come into existence as entities at one organizational level create information systems that meet only their particular needs. For example, Figure 7-2 lists six common departments (workgroups) and several information system applications that support each. Reflect on these

**Figure 7-2**
Common Departmental Information Systems

| Department | Application |
|---|---|
| Sales and marketing | • Lead generation<br>• Lead tracking<br>• Customer management<br>• Sales forecasting<br>• Product and brand management |
| Operations | • Order entry<br>• Order management<br>• Finished-goods inventory management |
| Manufacturing | • Inventory (raw materials, goods-in-process)<br>• Planning<br>• Scheduling<br>• Operations |
| Customer service | • Order tracking<br>• Account tracking<br>• Customer support |
| Human resources | • Recruiting<br>• Compensation<br>• Assessment<br>• HR planning |
| Accounting | • General ledger<br>• Financial reporting<br>• Cost accounting<br>• Accounts receivable<br>• Accounts payable<br>• Cash management<br>• Budgeting<br>• Treasury management |

applications for a moment and you'll realize that each application processes customer, sales, product, and other data, but each uses that data for different purposes and will likely store somewhat different data. Sales, for example, will store contact data for customers' purchasing agents, while Accounting will store contact data for customers' accounts payable personnel.

It's completely natural for a workgroup to develop information systems solely for its own needs, but, over time, the existence of these separate systems will result in information silos that cause numerous problems.

## WHAT ARE THE PROBLEMS OF INFORMATION SILOS?

Figure 7-3 lists the major problems caused by information silos at the department level and illustrates them for a silo between the Sales and Marketing department and the Accounting department. First, data are duplicated. Sales and Marketing and Accounting applications maintain separate databases that store some of the same customer data. As you know, data storage is cheap, so the problem with duplication is not wasted file space. Rather, the problem is data inconsistency. Changes to customer data made in the Sales and Marketing application may take days or weeks to be made to the Accounting application's database. During that period, shipments will reach the customer without delay, but invoices will be sent to the wrong address. When an organization has inconsistent duplicated data, it is said to have a **data integrity** problem.

Additionally, when applications are isolated, business processes are disjointed. Suppose a business has a rule that credit orders over $15,000 must be preapproved by the accounts receivable department. If the supporting applications are separated, it will be difficult for the two activities to reconcile their data, and the approval will be slow to grant and possibly erroneous.

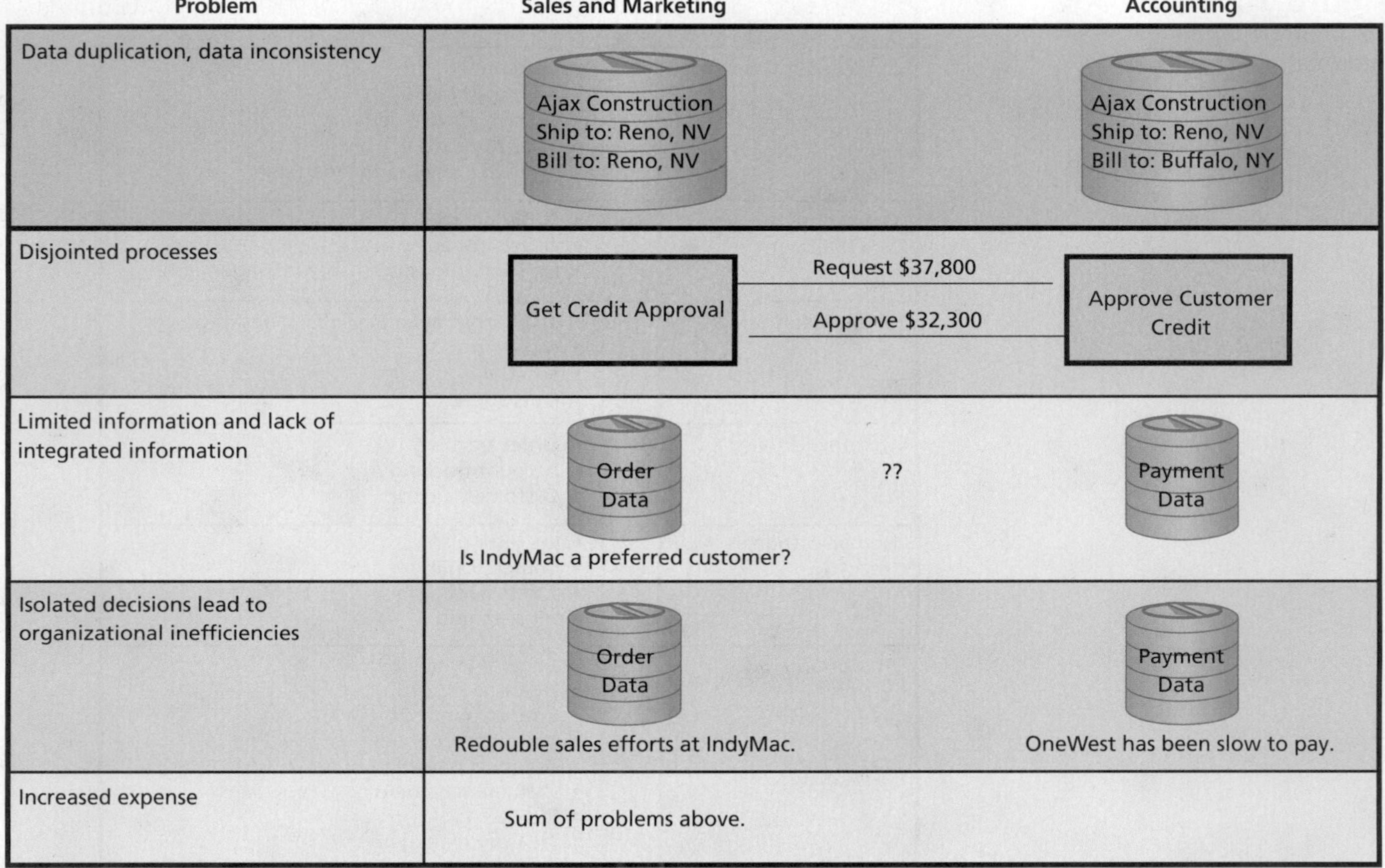


**Figure 7-3**
Problems Created by Information Silos

In the second row of Figure 7-3, Sales and Marketing wants to approve a $20,000 order with Ajax. According to the Sales and Marketing database, Ajax has a current balance of $17,800, so Sales and Marketing requests a total credit amount of $37,800. The Accounting database, however, shows Ajax with a balance of only $12,300 because the accounts receivable application has credited Ajax for a return of $5,500. According to Accounting's records, a total credit authorization of only $32,300 is needed in order to approve the $20,000 order, so that is all it grants.

Sales and Marketing doesn't understand what to do with a credit approval of $32,300. According to its database, Ajax already owes $17,800, so if the total credit authorization is only $32,300, did Accounting approve only $14,500 of the new order? And why that amount? Both departments want to approve the order. It will take numerous emails and phone calls, however, to sort this out. The interacting business processes are disjointed.

A consequence of such disjointed activities is the lack of integrated enterprise information. For example, suppose Sales and Marketing wants to know if IndyMac is still a preferred customer. Assume that determining whether this is so requires a comparison of order history and payment history data. With information silos, that data will reside in two different databases and, in one of them, IndyMac is known by the name of the company that acquired it, OneWest Bank. Data integration will be difficult. Making the determination will require manual processes and days, when it should be readily answered in seconds.

This leads to the fourth consequence: inefficiency. When using isolated functional applications, decisions are made in isolation. As shown in the fourth row of Figure 7-3, Sales and Marketing decided to redouble its sales effort with IndyMac. However, Accounting knows that IndyMac was foreclosed by the FDIC and sold to OneWest and has been slow to pay. There are far better prospects for increased sales attention. Without integration, the left hand of the organization doesn't know what the right hand is doing.

Finally, information silos can result in increased cost for the organization. Duplicated data, disjointed systems, limited information, and inefficiencies all mean higher costs.

## HOW DO ORGANIZATIONS SOLVE THE PROBLEMS OF INFORMATION SILOS?

As defined, an information silo occurs when data is stored in isolated systems. The obvious way to fix such a silo is to integrate the data into a single database and revise applications (and business processes) to use that database. If that is not possible or practical, another remedy is to allow the isolation, but to manage it to avoid problems.

The arrows in Figure 7-4 show this resolution at two levels of organization. First, isolated data created by workgroup information systems are integrated using enterprise-wide applications.

Second, today isolated data created by information systems at the enterprise level are being integrated into inter-enterprise systems using distributed applications (such as PRIDE) that process data in a single cloud database or that connect disparate, independent databases so that those databases appear to be one database. We will discuss inter-enterprise systems further in Q7-4.

For now, to better understand how isolated data problems can be resolved, consider an enterprise system at a hospital.

## AN ENTERPRISE SYSTEM FOR PATIENT DISCHARGE

Figure 7-5 shows some of the hospital departments and a portion of the patient discharge process. A doctor initiates the process by issuing a patient discharge order. That order is delivered to the appropriate nursing staff, who initiates activities at the pharmacy, the patient's family, and the kitchen. Some of those activities initiate activities back at the nursing staff. In Figure 7-5, the enterprise information system (solid red line) supports the discharge process (dashed red line).

Prior to the enterprise system, the hospital had developed procedures for using a paper-based system and informal messaging via the telephone. Each department kept its own records. When

**Figure 7-4**
Information Silos as Drivers

| Scope | Example | Example Information Silo | Enabling Technology |
|---|---|---|---|
| Workgroup | Physician Partnership | Physicians and hospitals store separated data about patients. Unnecessarily duplicate tests and procedures. | Functional applications. |
| | | ⇩ | Enterprise applications (CRM, ERP, EAI) on enterprise networks. |
| Enterprise | Hospital | Hospital and local drug store pharmacy have different prescription data for the same patient. | |
| | | ⇩ | Distributed systems using Web service technologies in the cloud. |
| Inter-enterprise | Inter-agency prescription application | No silo: Doctors, hospitals, pharmacies share patients' prescription and other data. | |

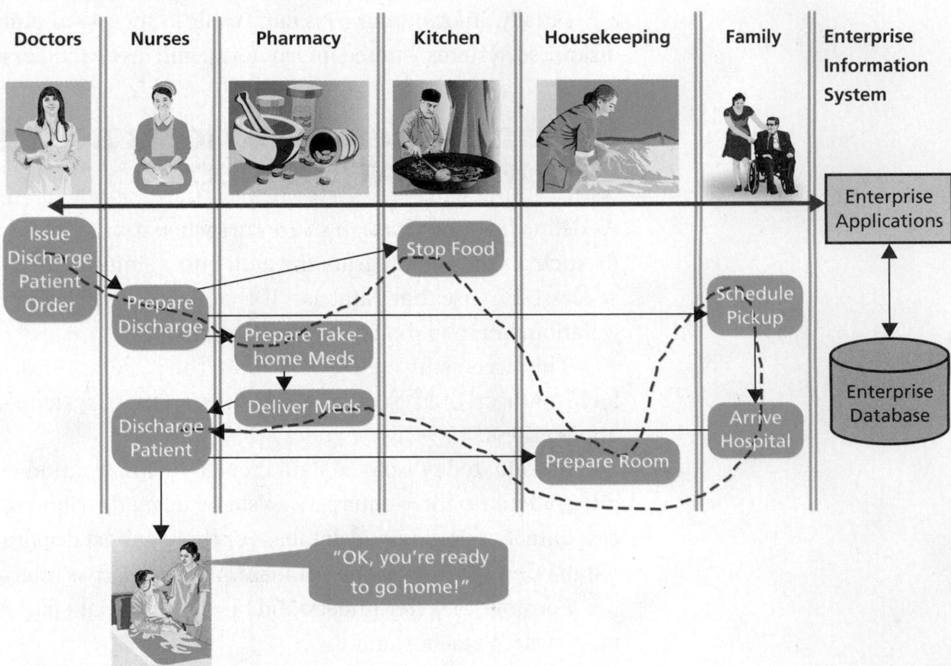


**Figure 7-5** Some of the Departments Involved in Patient Discharge

the new enterprise information system was implemented, not only was the data integrated into a database, but new computer-based forms and reports were created. The staff needed to transition from the paper-based system to the computer-based system. They also needed to stop making phone calls and let the new information system make notifications across departments. These measures involved substantial change, and most organizations experience considerable anguish when undergoing such transitions.

**Eliminating information silos is not without risk; for more information, see the Guide on pages 200–201.**

## BUSINESS PROCESS REENGINEERING

Enterprise systems like the one in Figure 7-5 were not feasible until network, data communication, and database technologies reached a sufficient level of capability and maturity in the late 1980s and early 1990s. At that point, many organizations began to develop enterprise systems.

As they did so, organizations realized that their existing business processes needed to change—partly to use the shared databases and partly to use new computer-based forms and reports. An even more important reason for changing business processes was that integrated data and enterprise systems offered the potential for substantial operational efficiencies. It became possible to do things that had been impossible before. Using Porter's language (Chapter 3, page 65), enterprise systems enabled the creation of stronger, faster, more effective linkages among value chains.

For example, when the hospital used a paper-based system, the kitchen would prepare meals for everyone who was a patient at the hospital as of midnight the night before. It was not possible to obtain data about discharges until the next midnight. Consequently, considerable food was wasted, at substantial cost.

With the enterprise system, the kitchen is notified about patient discharges as they occur throughout the day, resulting in substantial reductions in wasted food. But when should the kitchen be notified? Immediately? And what if the discharge is cancelled before completion? Who will notify the kitchen of the cancelled discharge? Many possibilities and alternatives exist. So, to design its new enterprise system, the hospital needed to determine how best to change its processes to take advantage of the new capability. Such projects came to be known as **business process reengineering**, which is the activity of altering existing and designing new business processes to take advantage of new information systems.

Unfortunately, business process reengineering is difficult, slow, and exceedingly expensive. Business and systems analysts need to interview key personnel throughout the organization to determine how best to use the new technology. Because of the complexity involved, such projects require high-level, expensive skills and considerable time. Many early projects stalled when the enormity of the project became apparent. This left some organizations with partially implemented systems that had disastrous consequences. Personnel didn't know if they were using the new system, the old system, or some hacked-up version of both.

The stage was set for the emergence of the three major enterprise applications, which we discuss next.

## Q7-3 HOW DO CRM, ERP, AND EAI SUPPORT ENTERPRISE SYSTEMS?

When the need for business process reengineering emerged, most organizations were still developing their applications in-house. At the time, organizations perceived their needs as being "too unique" to be satisfied by off-the-shelf or altered applications. However, as applications became more and more complex, in-house development costs became infeasible. As stated in Chapter 4, systems built in-house are expensive, not only because of their initial development but also because of the continuing need to adapt those systems to changing requirements.

In the early 1990s, as the costs of business process reengineering were coupled with the costs of in-house development, organizations began to look more favorably on the idea of licensing preexisting applications. "Maybe we're not so unique, after all."

Some of the vendors who took advantage of this change in attitude were PeopleSoft, which licensed payroll and limited-capability human resources systems; Siebel, which licensed a sales lead tracking and management system; and SAP, which licensed something new, a system called *enterprise resource management*.

These three companies, and ultimately dozens of others like them, offered not just software and database designs. They also offered standardized business processes. These **inherent processes**, which are predesigned procedures for using the software products, saved organizations from expensive and time-consuming business process reengineering. Instead, organizations could license the software and obtain, as part of the deal, prebuilt procedures that the vendors assured them were based upon "industry best practices."

Some parts of that deal were too good to be true because, as you'll learn, inherent processes are almost never a perfect fit. But the offer was too much for many organizations to resist. Over time, three categories of enterprise applications emerged: customer relationship management, enterprise resource planning, and enterprise application integration. Consider each.

### CUSTOMER RELATIONSHIP MANAGEMENT (CRM)

A **customer relationship management (CRM) system** is a suite of applications, a database, and a set of inherent processes for managing all the interactions with the customer, from lead generation to customer service. Every contact and transaction with the customer is recorded in the CRM database. Vendors of CRM software claim using their products makes the organization *customer-centric*. Though that term reeks of sales hyperbole, it does indicate the nature and intent of CRM packages.

Figure 7-6 shows four phases of the **customer life cycle**: marketing, customer acquisition, relationship management, and loss/churn. Marketing sends messages to the target market to attract customer prospects. When prospects order, they become customers who need to be supported. Additionally, relationship management processes increase the value of existing customers by selling them more product. Inevitably, over time the organization loses customers. When this occurs, win-back processes categorize customers according to value and attempt to win back high-value customers.

**Figure 7-6**
The Customer Life Cycle

*Source:* Used with permission of Professor Douglas MacLachlan, Michael G. Foster School of Business, University of Washington.

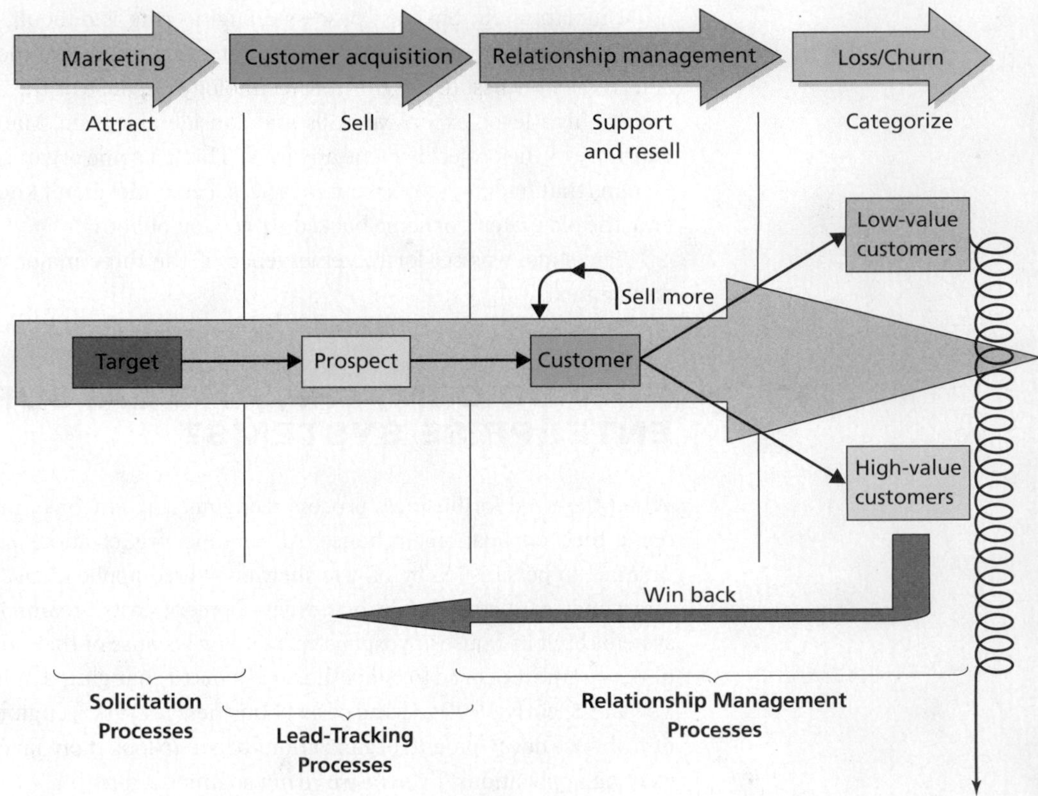


Figure 7-7 illustrates the major components of a CRM application. Notice that components exist for each stage of the customer life cycle. As shown, all applications process a common customer database. This design eliminates duplicated customer data and removes the possibility of inconsistent data. It also means that each department knows what has been happening with the customer at other departments. Customer support, for example, will know not to provide $1,000 worth of support labor to a customer that has generated $300 worth of business over time. They will also know to bend over backward for the customers that have generated hundreds of thousands of dollars of business. The result of this integration to the customer is that he or she feels like he or she is dealing with one entity and not many.

CRM systems vary in the degree of functionality they provide. One of the primary tasks when selecting a CRM package is to determine the features you need and to find a package that meets that set of needs. You might be involved in just such a project during your career.

**Figure 7-7**
CRM Applications

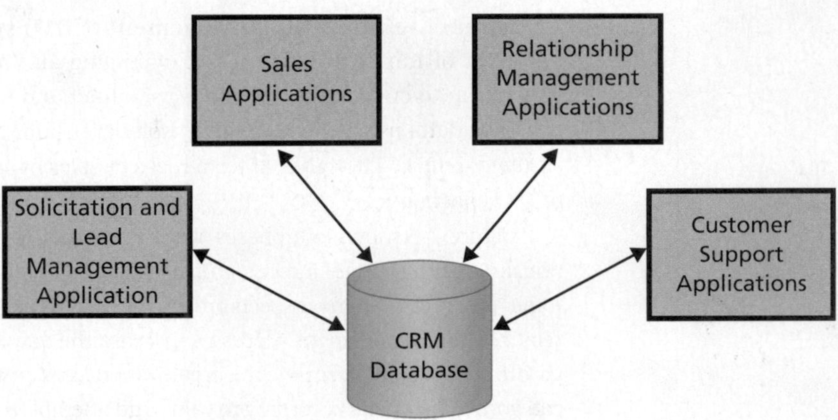

# Workflow Problems

According to John Halamka, CIO of the Harvard Medical School and Group Health System, "Most IT problems are workflow problems, not software problems."[2] Using the knowledge of Chapter 2, you know that workflow problems concern either efficiency (ratio of costs to value delivered is too high) or effectiveness (not contributing to the competitive strategy). So what?

Who fixes a workflow problem? A computer programmer? A network engineer? A database administrator? No, no, and no. So who? Someone with knowledge of the business and, if the workflow involves an information system, someone who is knowledgeable and comfortable working with technical people.

Consider an example close to home. Suppose your university has a limited number of classrooms with sophisticated audiovisual display. And those classrooms are frequently assigned to professors who specialize in old-fashioned lecture and don't use audio/visual display. Meanwhile, professors who want to use, say, Learning Catalytics in their classrooms are making do with poor-quality, hard-to-view computer-based display.

How would you fix that problem? Change the software that allocates classrooms? But how? Who decides what changes need to be made? And does it need to be done in software? Could it be done by fixing a workflow? Is there a convenient point in the professor–class assignment process in which professors (or department chairs) could indicate which professors should teach in which classrooms? Or are classrooms allocated on a university-wide basis? Or maybe the audiovisual system is already generating metadata about its use, and without requiring anyone to provide any extra data, someone in the Assign-Classroom workflow could use these data to allocate those classrooms?

Who develops these alternatives? Who evaluates them? Who implements them with the workflow workers? You! Or it could be you. As you'll learn in Chapter 12, a *business analyst* is someone who knows business, who understands the organization's competitive strategy and ways to implement it, and who knows enough information systems technology to be able to model and design workflow changes and to work with technical personnel, when needed, to effectuate changes to information systems.

Source: Franz Pfluegl/Fotolia

To do this well, you need to know IS_and_something: IS_and_marketing, IS_and_ operations, IS_and_finance.

## QUESTIONS

1. Using your own words, explain the meaning of the statement "Most IT problems are workflow problems, not software problems."
2. Consider the classroom assignment problem. Briefly describe three ways of solving that problem. Which of those three is the most promising? Why?
3. In your opinion, is the demand for professionals who know IS_and_something going to decrease? Increase? Stay about the same? Justify your response; search the Internet for data to support your claim.
4. If you were to become an expert in IS_and_something, what would the *something* be? Search the Internet for employment prospects for that career choice.
5. Examine your current plan of courses before you graduate. What courses do you need to add to your plan to learn IS_and_something? Will you add these courses? Why or why not?

**Figure 7-8**
ERP Applications

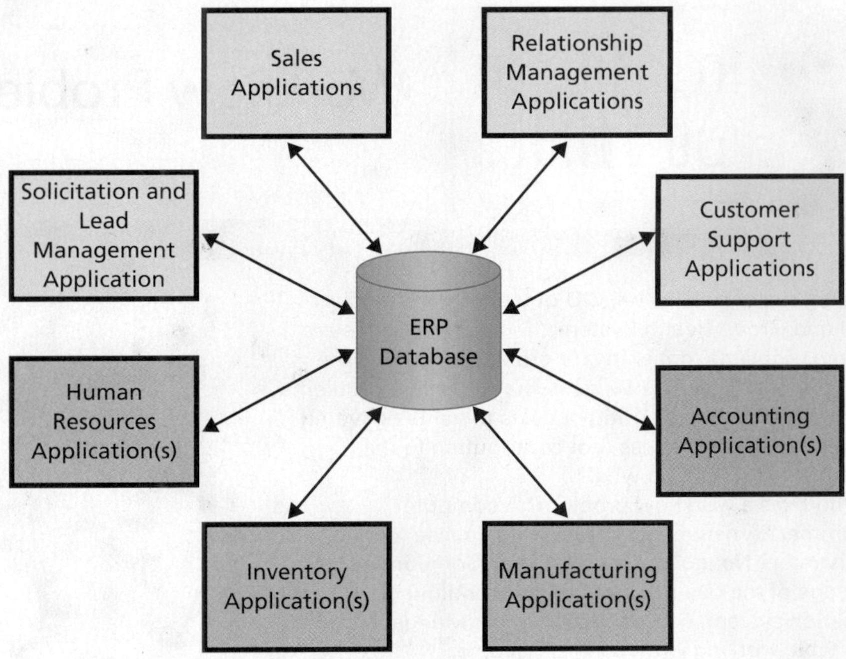


## ENTERPRISE RESOURCE PLANNING (ERP)

**You can learn more about ERP applications in Chapter Extension 9.**

**Enterprise resource planning (ERP)** is a suite of applications, a database, and a set of inherent processes for consolidating business operations into a single, consistent computing platform. As shown in Figure 7-8, ERP includes the functions of CRM but also incorporates accounting, manufacturing, inventory, and human resources application.

**Despite the clear benefits of inherent processes and ERP, there can be an unintended consequence. See the Ethics Guide on pages 198–199 and consider that risk.**

ERP systems are used to forecast sales and to create manufacturing plans and schedules to meet those forecasts. Manufacturing schedules include the use of material, equipment, and personnel and thus need to incorporate inventory and human resources applications. Because ERP includes accounting, all of these activities are automatically posted in the general ledger and other accounting applications.

SAP is the worldwide leader of ERP vendors. In addition to its base ERP offering, SAP offers industry-specific packages that customize its product for particular uses. There is an SAP package for automobile manufacturing, for example, and for many other specialty industries as well.

ERP originated in manufacturing and has a definite manufacturing flavor. However, it has been adapted for use in service organizations such as hospitals as well as many other organizations.

## ENTERPRISE APPLICATION INTEGRATION (EAI)

ERP systems are not for every organization. For example, some nonmanufacturing companies find the manufacturing orientation of ERP inappropriate. Even for manufacturing companies, some find the process of converting from their current system to an ERP system too daunting. Others are quite satisfied with their manufacturing application systems and do not wish to change them.

Companies for which ERP is inappropriate still have the problems of information silos, however, and some choose to use **enterprise application integration (EAI)** to solve those problems. EAI is a suite of software applications that integrates existing systems by providing layers of software that connect applications together. EAI does the following:

- It connects system "islands" via a new layer of software/system.
- It enables existing applications to communicate and share data.
- It provides integrated information.

**Figure 7-9**
Enterprise Application Integration (EAI) Architecture

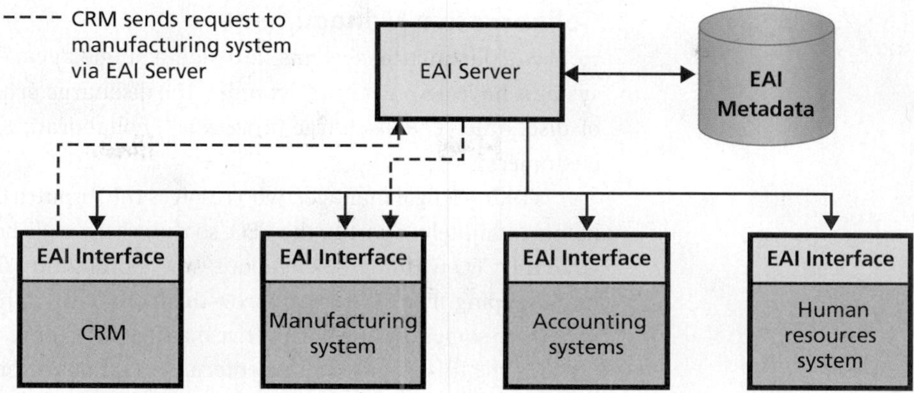


- It leverages existing systems—leaving functional applications as is but providing an integration layer over the top.
- It enables a gradual move to ERP.

The layers of EAI software shown in Figure 7-9 enable existing applications to communicate with each other and to share data. For example, EAI software can be configured to automatically make the conversions needed to share data among different systems. When the CRM applications send data to the manufacturing application system, for example, the CRM system sends its data to an EAI software program. That EAI program makes the conversion and then sends the converted data to the ERP system. The reverse action is taken to send data back from the ERP to the CRM.

Although there is no centralized EAI database, the EAI software keeps files of metadata that describe where data are located. Users can access the EAI system to find the data they need. In some cases, the EAI system provides services that supply a "virtual integrated database" for the user to process.

The major benefit of EAI is that it enables organizations to use existing applications while eliminating many of the serious problems of isolated systems. Converting to an EAI system is not nearly as disruptive as converting to ERP, and it provides many of the benefits of ERP. Some organizations develop EAI applications as a stepping stone to complete ERP systems. Today many EAI systems use Web services standards to define the interactions among EAI components. Some or all of the processing for those components can be moved to the cloud as well.

## WHAT ARE THE CHALLENGES WHEN IMPLEMENTING AND UPGRADING ENTERPRISE SYSTEMS?

Implementing new enterprise systems is challenging, difficult, expensive, and risky. It is not unusual for enterprise systems projects to be well over budget and a year or more late in delivery. In addition to new ERP implementations, numerous organizations implemented ERP 15 or 20 years ago and now need to upgrade their ERP installation to meet new requirements. If you work in an organization that is already using enterprise systems, you may find yourself engaged in a significant upgrade effort. Whether from a new implementation or an upgrade, expense and risks arise from five primary factors:

- Collaborative management
- Requirements gaps
- Transition problems
- Employee resistance
- New technology

## Collaborative Management

Unlike departmental systems in which a single department manager is in charge, enterprise systems have no clear boss. Examine the discharge process in Figure 7-5; there is no manager of discharge. The discharge process is a collaborative effort among many departments (and customers).

With no single manager, who resolves the disputes that inevitably arise? All of these departments ultimately report to the CEO, so there is a single boss over all of them, but employees can't go to the CEO with a problem about, say, coordinating discharge activities between nursing and housekeeping. The CEO would throw them out of his or her office. Instead, the organization needs to develop some sort of collaborative management for resolving process issues.

Usually this means that the enterprise develops committees and steering groups for providing enterprise process management. Although this can be an effective solution, and in fact may be the *only* solution, the work of such groups is both slow and expensive.

## Requirements Gaps

Few organizations today create their own enterprise systems from scratch. Instead, they license an enterprise product that provides specific functions and features and that includes inherent procedures. But such licensed products are never a perfect fit. Almost always there are gaps between the requirements of the organization and the capabilities of the licensed application.

The first challenge is identifying the gaps. To specify a gap, an organization must know both what it needs and what the new product does. However, it can be very difficult for an organization to determine what it needs; that difficulty is one reason organizations choose to license rather than to build. Further, the features and functions of complex products like CRM or ERP are not easy to identify. Thus, gap identification is a major task when implementing enterprise systems.

The second challenge is deciding what to do with gaps once they are identified. Either the organization needs to change the way it does things to adapt to the new application, or the application must be altered to match what the organization does. Either choice is problematic. Employees will resist change, but paying for alterations is expensive, and, as noted in Chapter 4, the organization is committing to maintaining those alterations as the application is changed over time. Here organizations fill gaps by choosing their lesser regret.

## Transition Problems

Transitioning to a new enterprise system is also difficult. The organization must somehow change from using isolated departmental systems to using the new enterprise system, while continuing to run the business. It's like having heart surgery while running a 100-yard dash.

Such transitions require careful planning and substantial training. Inevitably, problems will develop. Knowing this will occur, senior management needs to communicate the need for the change to the employees and then stand behind the new system as the kinks are worked out. It is an incredibly stressful time for all involved employees. We will discuss development techniques and implementation strategies further in Chapter 10.

## Employee Resistance

People resist change. Change requires effort and engenders fear. Considerable research and literature exist about the reasons for change resistance and how organizations can deal with it. Here we will summarize the major principles.

First, senior-level management needs to communicate the need for the change to the organization and must reiterate that need, as necessary, throughout the transition process. Second, employees fear change because it threatens their **self-efficacies**, which is a person's belief that he or she can be successful at his or her job. To enhance confidence, employees need to be trained and coached on the successful use of the new system. Word-of-mouth is a very powerful factor, and, in some cases, key users are trained ahead of time to create positive buzz about the new system. Video demonstrations of employees successfully using the new system are also effective.

Third, in many ways, the primary benefits of a new ERP system accrue to the accounting and finance departments and to senior management. Many of the employees who are asked to change their activities to implement ERP will not receive any direct benefit from it. Therefore, employees may need to be given extra inducement to change to the new system. As one experienced change consultant said, "Nothing succeeds like praise or cash, especially cash." Straight-out pay for change is bribery, but contests with cash prizes among employees or groups can be very effective at inducing change.

Implementing new enterprise systems can solve many problems and bring great efficiency and cost savings to an organization, but it is not for the faint of heart.

### NEW TECHNOLOGY

Emerging, new technology affects all information systems, but it affects enterprise systems particularly because of their importance and their value. Consider, for example, the cloud. Because of the cost savings of cloud-based computing, organizations would like to move their enterprise systems to the cloud. But legal, risk, and business policy factors may make such a move infeasible. The organization may be required to keep physical control over its data. When moving it to the cloud, the cloud vendor controls the physical location of the data, and that location might not even be in the same country as the organization. So, some sort of hybrid model may need to be devised.

Similar comments pertain to mobile technology. Employees want to use mobile devices to access and even modify enterprise system data. But mobile devices are just that—mobile. The enterprise system may be exposed to considerable risk while outside the control of the organization. And ERP data is a juicy target for crime (See "One-Stop Shopping" on pages 200–201.) These factors don't mean organizations cannot use new technology with enterprise systems, but they do add challenges.

## Q7-4 HOW DO INTER-ENTERPRISE IS SOLVE THE PROBLEMS OF ENTERPRISE SILOS?

**Supply chain systems are a common type of inter-enterprise system that you can learn about in Chapter Extension 10.**

The discussions in Q7-2 and Q7-3 have shown you some of the primary ways that enterprise systems solve the problems of workgroup information silos. In this question we will use the PRIDE example to show you how inter-enterprise systems can accomplish the same for enterprise silos. (The transition shown by the lower arrow leading to the bottom row in Figure 7-4, page 187.)

Figure 7-10 shows the information silos that exist among healthcare providers, health clubs, and patients. Providers keep track of patient histories and maintain records of exercise recommendations, called exercise prescriptions in Figure 7-10. Health clubs maintain membership, class, personal trainer, and exercise performance data. At the club, the latter is gathered automatically from exercise equipment and member heart monitors and stored in a club database. At home, individuals generate exercise data on heart monitors and equipment, and those data are recorded in mobile devices using exercise watches.

The isolation of this exercise data causes problems. For example, doctors would like to have reports on exercise data stored on patient devices and in health clubs. Patients would like to have prescription data from their providers as well as exercise data from their time at health clubs. Health clubs would like to have exercise prescriptions and home workout data to integrate with the data they have. All three entities would like to produce reports from the integrated data.

Figure 7-11 shows the structure of an inter-enterprise system that meets the goals of the three types of participant. In this figure, the labeled rectangles inside the cloud represent mobile applications that could be native, thin-client, or both. Some of the application processing might be done on cloud servers as well as on the mobile devices. Those design decisions are not shown.

**Figure 7-10**
Information Silos Without PRIDE

Healthcare Providers
Health Clubs
Patients at Home
Patient history
Exams
Operations
Hospital stays
Medications
Patient progress
Exercise prescriptions
Membership data
Class data
Personal trainer data
Exercise performance data
Heart monitor data
Treadmill, bike exercise data
Watch data recorded in mobile devices
Information Silos

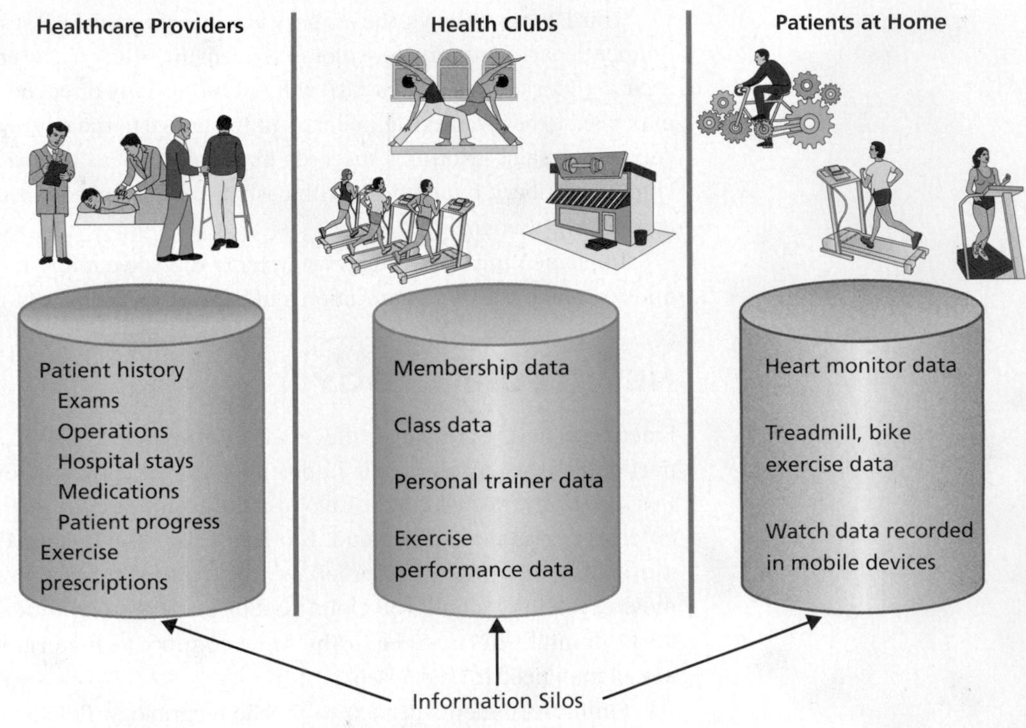

**Figure 7-11**
Inter-enterprise PRIDE system

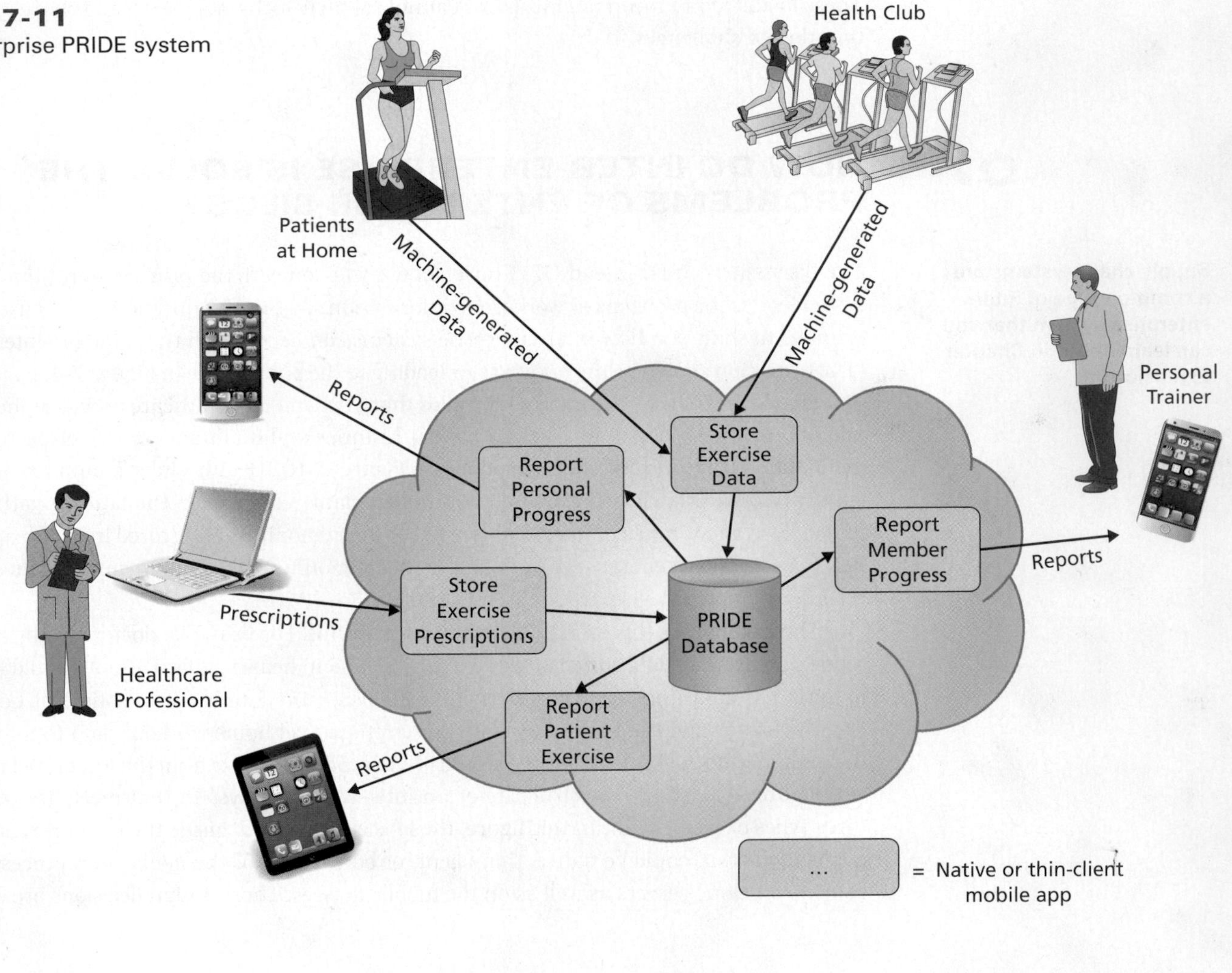

Health Club
Patients at Home
Machine-generated Data
Machine-generated Data
Personal Trainer
Reports
Store Exercise Data
Report Personal Progress
Report Member Progress
Reports
Store Exercise Prescriptions
PRIDE Database
Prescriptions
Healthcare Professional
Report Patient Exercise
Reports
...
= Native or thin-client mobile app

As shown, this system assumes that all users receive reports on mobile devices but, because of the large amount of keying involved, that healthcare providers submit and manage prescriptions using a personal computer.

As you can see, prescription and exercise data is integrated in the PRIDE database; that integrated data is processed by a reporting application (Chapter 9) to create and distribute the reports as shown.

Systems like that shown in Figure 7-11 are referred to as **distributed systems** because processing is distributed across multiple computing devices. Standards such as http, https, html5, css3, JavaScript, and Web services enable programs on varied and disparate devices to flexibly communicate with the cloud servers and database and indirectly communicate with each other.

## How does the **knowledge** in this chapter help **you?**

The knowledge of this chapter will help you understand levels of information systems and the problems that each level can have. It will also help you to put information systems that you use into perspective and to understand how they may or may not be creating information silos. You also know the potential problems of silos and how to resolve them at both the workgroup and enterprise levels. Further, when you encounter CRM, ERP, and EAI applications in your future, you will know what such systems are, what they do, and some of the issues you will run into when using and implementing them. Finally, understanding how PRIDE uses the cloud to support an inter-enterprise system will give you the background for investigating the use of the cloud for other applications as well.

# Ethics Guide

## Dialing for Dollars

Suppose you are a salesperson and your company's CRM forecasts that your quarterly sales will be substantially under quota. You call your best customers to increase sales, but no one is willing to buy more.

Your boss says that it has been a bad quarter for all of the salespeople. It's so bad, in fact, that the vice president of sales has authorized a 20 percent discount on new orders. The only stipulation is that customers must take delivery prior to the end of the quarter so that accounting can book the order. "Start dialing for dollars," she says, "and get what you can. Be creative."

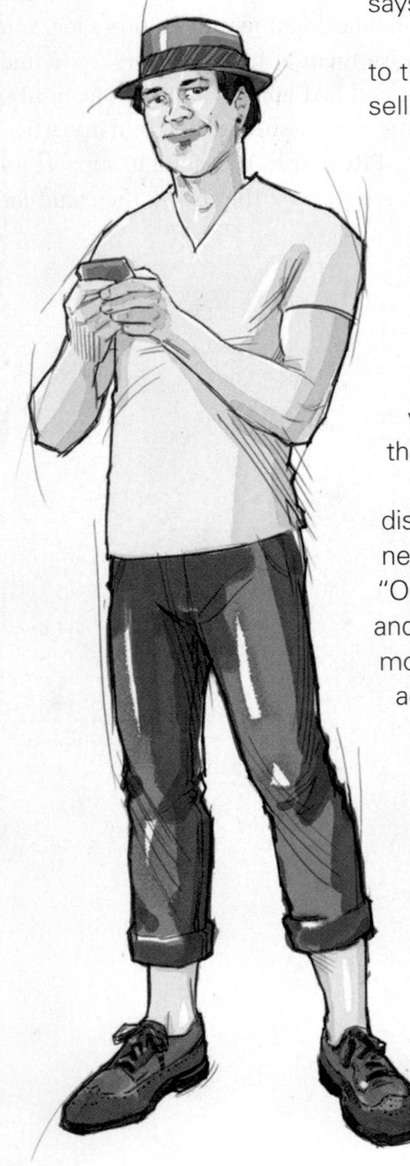

Using your CRM, you identify your top customers and present the discount offer to them. The first customer balks at increasing her inventory: "I just don't think we can sell that much."

"Well," you respond, "how about if we agree to take back any inventory you don't sell next quarter?" (By doing this, you increase your current sales and commission, and you also help your company make its quarterly sales projections. The additional product is likely to be returned next quarter, but you think, "Hey, that's then and this is now.")

"OK," she says, "but I want you to stipulate the return option on the purchase order."

You know that you cannot write that on the purchase order because accounting won't book all of the order if you do. So you tell her that you'll send her an email with that stipulation. She increases her order, and accounting books the full amount.

With another customer, you try a second strategy. Instead of offering the discount, you offer the product at full price but agree to pay a 20 percent credit in the next quarter. That way you can book the full price now. You pitch this offer as follows: "Our marketing department analyzed past sales using our fancy new computer system, and we know that increasing advertising will cause additional sales. So, if you order more product now, next quarter we'll give you 20 percent of the order back to pay for advertising."

In truth, you doubt the customer will spend the money on advertising. Instead, it will just take the credit and sit on a bigger inventory. That will kill your sales to the company next quarter, but you'll solve that problem then.

Even with these additional orders, you're still under quota. In desperation, you decide to sell product to a fictitious company that you say is owned by your brother-in-law. You set up a new account, and when accounting calls your brother-in-law for a credit check, he cooperates with your scheme. You then sell $40,000 of product to the fictitious company and ship the product to your brother-in-law's garage. Accounting books the revenue in the quarter, and you have finally made quota. A week into the next quarter, your brother-in-law returns the merchandise.

Meanwhile, unknown to you, your company's ERP system is scheduling production. The program that creates the production schedule reads the sales from your activities (and those of the other salespeople) and finds a sharp increase in product demand. Accordingly, it generates a schedule that calls for substantial production increases and schedules workers for the production runs. The production system, in turn, schedules the material requirements with the inventory application, which increases raw materials purchases to meet the increased production schedule.

## DISCUSSION QUESTIONS

**1.** Consider the email you write that agrees to take the product back.

**a.** Is your action ethical according to the categorical imperative (pages 20–21) perspective?

**b.** Is your action ethical according to the utilitarian perspective (pages 46–47)?

**c.** If that email comes to light later, what do you think your boss will say?

**2.** Regarding your offer of the "advertising" discount:

**a.** Is your action ethical according to the categorical imperative perspective?

**b.** Is your action ethical according to the utilitarian perspective?

**c.** What effect does that discount have on your company's balance sheet?

**3.** Regarding your shipping to the fictitious company:

**a.** Is your action ethical according to the categorical imperative perspective?

**b.** Is your action ethical according to the utilitarian perspective?

**c.** Is your action legal?

**4.** Describe the effect of your activities on next quarter's inventories.

**5.** Setting aside ethical and legal issues, would you say the enterprise system is more of a help or a hindrance in this example?

*Source:* koya979/Fotolia

# Guide

## One-Stop Shopping

In this chapter, you've learned how the problems of information silos shown in Figure 7-3 can be eliminated by increasing the scope of information systems: Workgroup-induced silos can be eliminated by developing enterprise IS, and enterprise-induced silos can be eliminated by developing inter-enterprise IS. Nowhere in this discussion, however, have we thought about security.

In fact, while removing information silos does have the advantages discussed, moving data into a single, centralized facility creates a potential security problem. Namely, fraudsters can find all the data they want in one convenient location. It's one-stop shopping. So, data integration can make organizations more vulnerable.

On the other hand, centralizing data in one location enables the organization to focus security measures on a single resource. The IS support staff need not manage security over several, possibly many, distributed databases, but rather can focus security management on a single database. So, assuming appropriate security management, the two factors counterbalance one another: Risk of loss is higher, but security against such loss can be focused and ultimately result in less actual risk.

Consider how a large-scale integrated IS like the PRIDE system discussed at the start of this chapter can create unique security concerns. To start, for the purpose of this guide, let's assume that client privacy is appropriately protected. Clients only share the data with each of the PRIDE entities (employers, health clubs, equipment manufacturers, insurance companies, and healthcare providers) that they want to.

Even with that assumption, however, there are significant privacy and security issues. Clients, personal trainers, and healthcare providers need to see a client's complete exercise data. This means, however, that competing personal trainers (and health clubs) view data on their competitors' practices. Is this a problem? It's likely to be perceived as a problem even if there is no real danger, and that perception could limit PRIDE sales and use.

This example underlines some of the management problems of inter-enterprise IS. Unlike an enterprise system, where everyone works for the same employer and, except for inter-departmental rivalry, has the same incentive to protect data, an inter-enterprise system can connect competitors with different incentives and agendas. This fact not only increases security risk, it takes away one of the major ways of dealing with security flaws: procedures. In an enterprise system, it's possible for the organization to set up manual procedures that compensate for security weaknesses in programs or data controls. However, in an inter-enterprise system, if system users compete, they may have an incentive not to follow the compensating procedures.

PRIDE's use of the cloud brings up another important security concern, one that exists at both the enterprise and inter-enterprise levels. How secure is the cloud vendor? The more important the information you store, the more attractive a target you become for attackers. The simplest example of this comes in the form of bitcoins.

In February 2014, Mt. Gox, the largest bitcoin exchange at the time, lost about 850,000 bitcoins valued at $460M.[3] It declared bankruptcy and wouldn't, or couldn't, explain where all the bitcoins and cash had gone. Essentially, bitcoins represented a large cloud-based monetary system that was supposed to replace national currencies. It was, and still could be, a revolutionary idea.

The downside of Mt. Gox was that its very nature made it a perfect target. It was centrally located and accessible from anywhere, and it had a very large sum of money that could be electronically stolen. Hackers from around the world would never stop trying to steal from Mt. Gox. Gold is hard to steal because it's so heavy. But bits are light and easy to transport. Healthcare records, personal identities, financial records, and credit card information are all in digital form now too.

The fall of Mt. Gox should cause one to wonder about the security of cloud storage. Most of the time, we don't even know the physical location of cloud data, let alone how well the data center is secured, who works there, what procedures and policies are in place, and so on. We will return to this question in Chapter 10; for now, understand that this issue exists.

## DISCUSSION QUESTIONS

**1.** Summarize why security risk is higher for integrated databases than for information silos. Describe a factor that can compensate for this increased risk.

**2.** Using PRIDE as an example, explain how users' incentives to protect data differ between an enterprise system and an inter-enterprise system. How does the use of security procedures differ between the two types of system?

**3.** Suppose you are a health club owner and you are approached by a PRIDE salesperson who says, "The PRIDE database is located in an xyz cloud facility," where *xyz* is the name of a large, reputable company such as Amazon.com, Oracle, Microsoft, or IBM. You ask about data security and he says, "You and I don't know anything about their security, but it has to be better than the security you have on that server you're operating in the closet down the hallway." How do you respond?

**4.** If you were a personal trainer at a health club, explain the value to you of having competitors' data about clients you share. Explain the value to you of obtaining, if you can, data about competitors' PRIDE clients who you have never treated.

**5.** Suppose you are a personal trainer at a health club and you are approached by a PRIDE salesperson who says, "Our system's security ensures that no one can see your clients' data." How do you respond?

**6.** Suppose the salesperson in question 5 says, "Only others who are coaching the same clients as you can see your client data." How can you verify the truth of this statement?

**7.** Suppose that a personal trainer at a health club uses a trivial password such as *dog*. One of that health club's members watches the personal trainer sign in, obtains that password, and later steals all of the data on the clients treated by that club.

**a.** Who is responsible for the data theft?

**b.** How do you respond if you are the personal trainer using the trivial password?

**c.** If you are the club owner, how will you likely learn about this theft? How do you respond when you do learn of it?

**d.** If you are a participating healthcare provider, how will you likely learn about this theft? How do you respond when you do learn of it?

**e.** If you are a client who is using this system, whom do you hold accountable, and why?

**8.** Where was Mt. Gox physically located? Is the physical location of where your data is being stored important? Why or why not?

Source: Zentilia/Shutterstock

# ACTIVE REVIEW

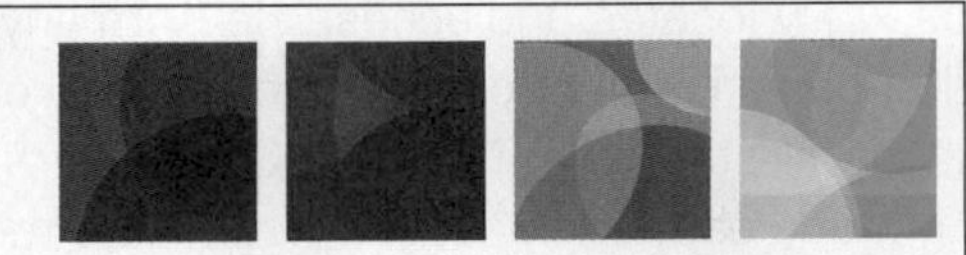

Use this Active Review to verify that you understand the ideas and concepts that answer the chapter's study questions.

## Q7-1 HOW DO INFORMATION SYSTEMS VARY BY SCOPE?

Explain how information systems vary by scope. Provide examples of four levels of information scope other than those in this chapter. Describe characteristics of information systems for each.

## Q7-2 HOW DO ENTERPRISE SYSTEMS SOLVE THE PROBLEMS OF DEPARTMENTAL SILOS?

Define *information silo* and explain how such silos come into existence. When do such silos become a problem? Name and describe five common functional applications. Describe data that are likely duplicated among those five applications. Summarize the problems that information silos cause. Summarize the ways that enterprise systems can be used to solve problems of information silos at both the workgroup and the enterprise level. Define *business process engineering* and explain why it is difficult and expensive.

## Q7-3 HOW DO CRM, ERP, AND EAI SUPPORT ENTERPRISE SYSTEMS?

Explain two major reasons why it is expensive to develop enterprise information systems in-house. Explain the advantages of inherent processes. Define and differentiate among *CRM, ERP,* and *EAI.* Explain how CRM and ERP are more similar to one another than to EAI. Name and describe five sources of challenge when implementing enterprise systems. Describe why enterprise systems management must be collaborative. Explain two major tasks required to identify requirements gaps. Summarize challenges of transitioning to an enterprise system. Explain why employees resist change and describe three ways of responding to that resistance.

## Q7-4 HOW DO INTER-ENTERPRISE IS SOLVE THE PROBLEMS OF ENTERPRISE SILOS?

Describe information silos that exist among healthcare providers, health clubs, and individuals with regard to patient exercise data. Describe problems that those silos create. Explain how the system shown in Figure 7-11 will solve the problems caused by those silos.

## How does the **knowledge** in this chapter help **you?**

Describe how you can benefit from the information in this chapter. Suppose a job interviewer asked you, "What do you know about ERP?" How would you respond? What if the question were "How does the cloud help organizations integrate their activities?"

# KEY TERMS AND CONCEPTS

MyMISLab™

To complete the problems with the ✪, go to EOC Discussion Questions in the MyLab.

## USING YOUR KNOWLEDGE

✪ **7-1.** Using the example of your university, give examples of information systems with personal, workgroup, enterprise, and inter-enterprise scope. Describe three workgroup information systems that are likely to duplicate data. Explain how the characteristics of information systems relate to your examples.

✪ **7-2.** In your answer to question 7-1, explain how the three workgroup information systems create information silos. Describe the kinds of problems that those silos are likely to cause.

✪ **7-3.** Using your answer to question 7-2, describe an enterprise information system that will eliminate the silos. Would the implementation of your system require process reengineering? Explain why or why not.

## COLLABORATION EXERCISE 7

*Read Chapter Extensions 1 and 2 if you have not already done so. Meet with your team and build a collaboration IS that uses tools like Google Docs, SharePoint, or other collaboration tools. Do not forget the need for procedures and team training. Now, using that IS, answer the questions below.*

The county planning office issues building permits, septic system permits, and county road access permits for all building projects in the county. The planning office issues permits to homeowners and builders for the construction of new homes and buildings and for any remodeling projects that involve electrical, gas, plumbing, and other utilities, as well as the conversion of unoccupied spaces such as garages into living or working space. The office also issues permits for new or upgraded septic systems and permits to provide driveway entrances to county roads.

Figure 7-12 shows the permit process that the county used for many years. Contractors and homeowners found this process to be slow and very frustrating. For one, they did not like its sequential nature. Only after a permit had been approved or rejected by the engineering review process would they find out that a health or highway review was also needed. Because each of these reviews could take 3 or 4 weeks, applicants requesting permits wanted the review processes to be concurrent rather than serial. Also, both the permit applicants and county personnel were frustrated because they never knew where a particular application was in the permit process. A contractor would call to ask how much longer, and it might take an hour or more just to find which desk the permits were on.

Accordingly, the county changed the permit process to that shown in Figure 7-13. In this second process, the permit office made three copies of the permit and distributed one to each department. The departments reviewed the permits in parallel; a clerk would analyze the results and, if there were no rejections, approve the permit.

Unfortunately, this process had a number of problems, too. For one, some of the permit applications were lengthy; some included as many as 40 to 50 pages of large architectural drawings. The labor and copy expense to the county was considerable.

Second, in some cases departments reviewed documents unnecessarily. If, for example, the highway department rejected an application, then neither the engineering nor health departments needed to continue their reviews. At first, the county responded to this problem by having the clerk who analyzed results cancel the reviews of other departments when he or she received a rejection. However, that policy was exceedingly unpopular with the permit applicants because once an application was rejected and the problem corrected, the permit had to go back through the other departments. The permit would go to the end of the line and work its way back into the departments from which it had been pulled. Sometimes this resulted in a delay of 5 or 6 weeks.

Cancelling reviews was unpopular with the departments as well because permit-review work had to be repeated. An application might have been nearly completed when it was cancelled due to a rejection in another department. When the application came through again, the partial work results from the earlier review were lost.

**7-4.** Explain why the processes in Figures 7-12 and 7-13 are classified as enterprise processes rather than as departmental processes. Why are these processes not considered to be inter-enterprise processes?

**Figure 7-12**
Sequential Permit Review Process

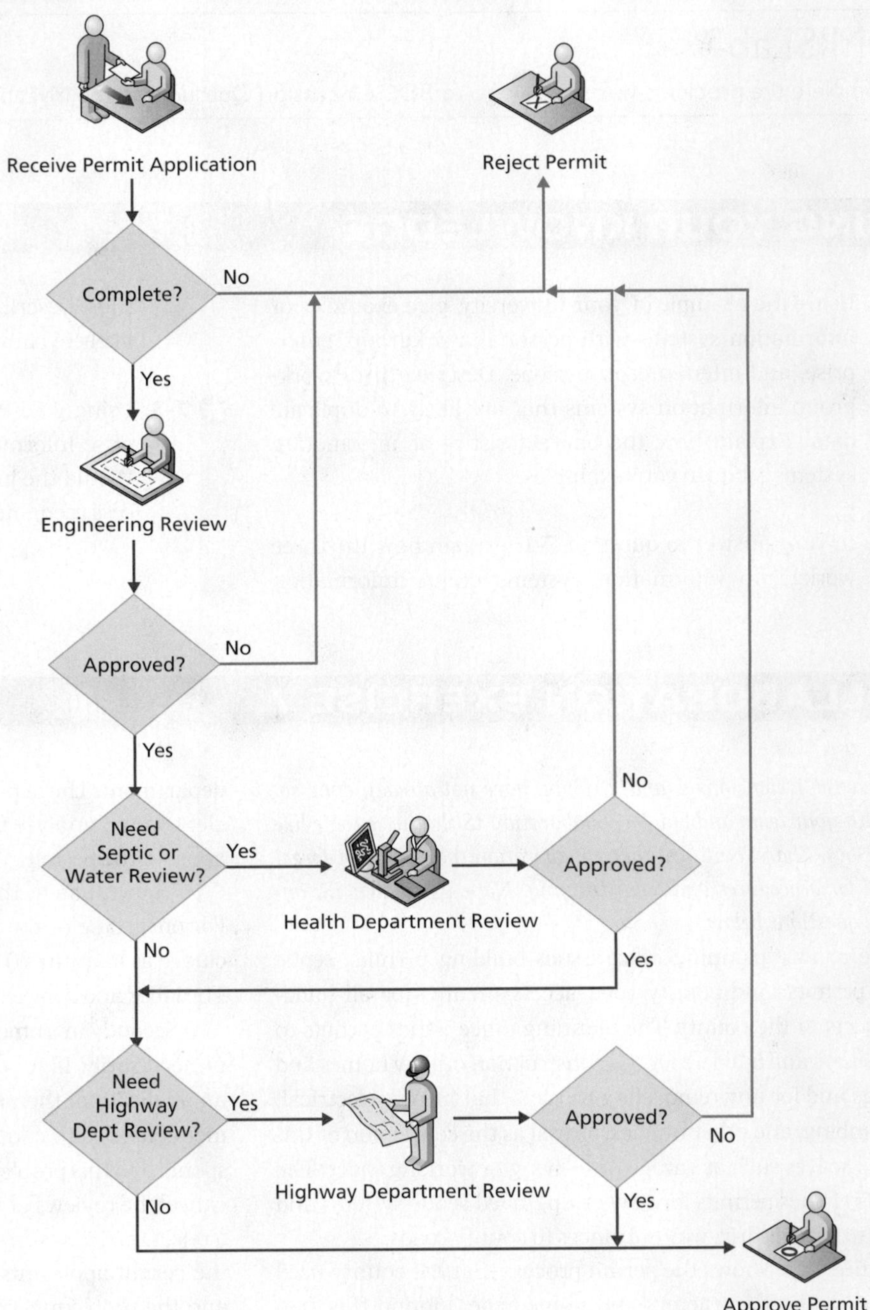


**7-5.** Using Figure 7-5 as an example, redraw Figure 7-12 using an enterprise information system that processes a shared database. Explain the advantages of this system over the paper-based system in Figure 7-12.

**7-6.** Using Figure 7-5 as an example, redraw Figure 7-13 using an enterprise information system that processes a shared database. Explain the advantages of this system over the paper-based system in Figure 7-13.

**7-7.** Assuming that the county has just changed from the system in Figure 7-12 to the one in Figure 7-13, which of your answers in questions 7-5 and 7-6 do you think is better? Justify your answer.

**7-8.** Assume your team is in charge of the implementation of the system you recommend in your answer to question 7-7. Describe how each of the five challenges discussed in Q7-3 pertain to this implementation. Explain how your team will deal with those challenges.

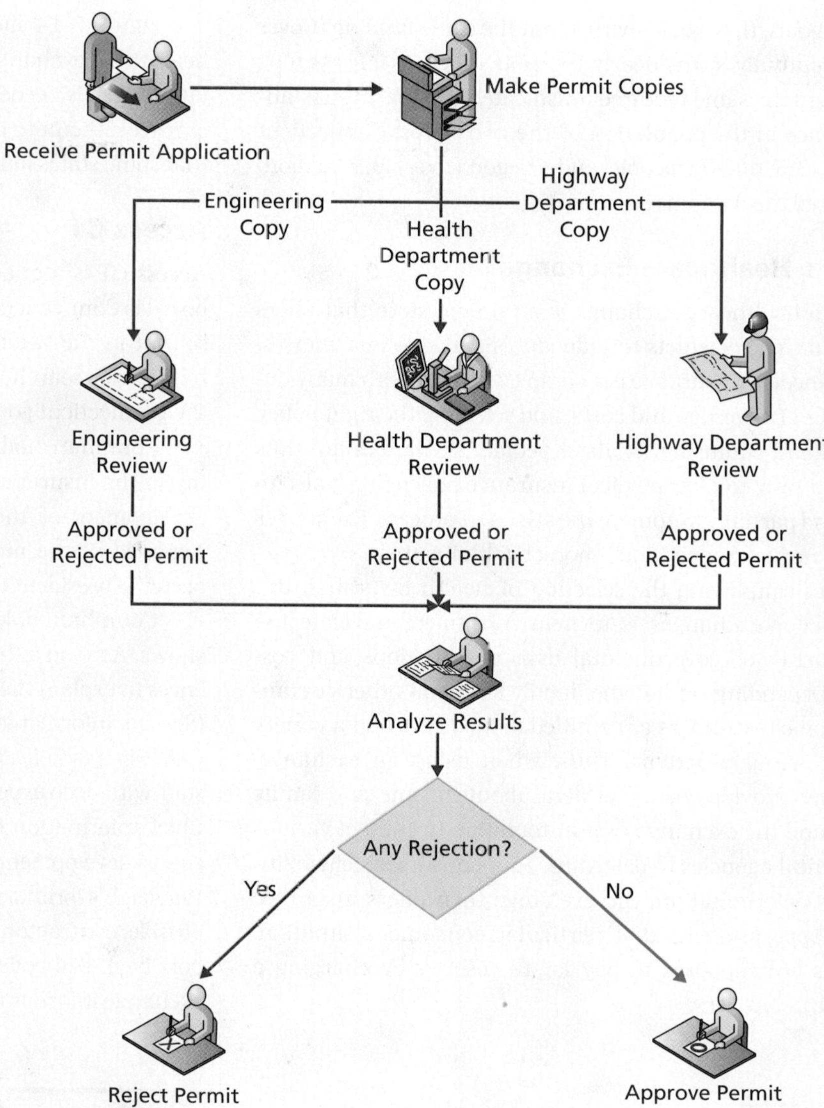


**Figure 7-13**
Parallel Permit-Review Process

## CASE STUDY 7

### A Tale of Two Interorganizational IS

The Affordable Care Act (also known as Obamacare) requires the creation of healthcare exchanges that necessitate the development of interorganizational information systems. States were encouraged to set up exchanges for their own residents, but if they elected not to do so, the states' residents could use an exchange developed by the federal government. About half of the states decided to use the federal exchange. The remainder developed their own exchanges (and supporting information systems). These many parallel development projects give us a unique opportunity to learn from the experience of similar projects that had, in some cases, very different outcomes.

Consider, for example, Connecticut and Oregon. The state of Connecticut created an exchange named *Access CT*. It was delivered on time and on budget and has been such a success that the state of Maryland stopped developing its own system and licensed the Access CT solution instead.[4] Other states are considering licensing Access CT as well. On the other hand, the state of Oregon created an exchange named *Cover Oregon* that was a complete and utter failure. Cover Oregon was never operable in spite of costing more than $248M of U.S. and Oregon tax dollars. In May 2014, the U.S. attorney's office in Portland opened a grand jury investigation into the project.[5]

Why were there such different outcomes? The two states started their projects about the same time, they had the same scope and goals, they began with about the same funding (Cover Oregon eventually spent nearly twice as much as Access CT), and they had the same required finish date. There is no substantial difference in the population of the two states; Connecticut has about 3.5 million people and Oregon about 3.9 million. What caused the different outcomes?

## What Is a Healthcare Exchange?

To begin, a healthcare exchange is an online store that offers health insurance products to individuals and small businesses. Choosing medical insurance is a complex process with many different levels of coverage and costs, and selecting the right policy is difficult and confusing for most people. Exchanges are thus created not only to offer medical insurance policies, but also to simplify and partially automate the selection process. Exchanges also promote fair competition among health insurers.

Besides simplifying the selection of health insurance, another goal for exchanges is to help consumers navigate the complex array of governmental assistance options and possibilities. Depending on income, family size, and other circumstances, some consumers are entitled to Medicare and a variety of governmental programs. Thus, when using an exchange, a consumer provides personal data about income and family situation and the exchange uses automation to contact various governmental agencies to determine that consumer's eligibility. Given this determination, the exchange then offers insurance products appropriate to that particular consumer's situation. Exchanges are supposed to pay for themselves by charging a modest fee to insurers.

Figure 7-14 shows some of the organizations involved in a healthcare exchange. Clearly, an interorganizational information system is needed. As you know from this chapter, such projects are difficult to develop and manage, and it is not surprising that some states failed.

## Access CT

Access CT is a quasi-public corporation. The chairman of the board is Connecticut's lieutenant governor, Nancy Wyman, who set out in the summer of 2012 to find an appropriate CEO. A nationwide searched identified 74 candidates, and in July 2012, the Connecticut governor hired Kevin Counihan.

Counihan had more than 30 years of experience working in the insurance industry and had been a key player in the development of the Massachusetts healthcare system (widely regarded as the model for Obamacare); most recently he had been the president of a private health exchange in California.[6]

Counihan holds a masters degree in marketing, and it shows. As soon as he was hired, he began a series of press conferences to explain the nature and goals of the project to the public. (See an informative interview with him at *www.youtube.com/watch?v=8-w4nilpuiQ*). Within a few months, he hired senior staff with deep experience in insurance, including Jim Wadleigh, Chief Information Officer. Wadleigh had been director of application development for CIGNA, a health services organization.[7] Wadleigh's primary assignment was to hire and manage an outside contractor to develop the exchange website and support back-end code and to manage the implementation of the exchange information system.

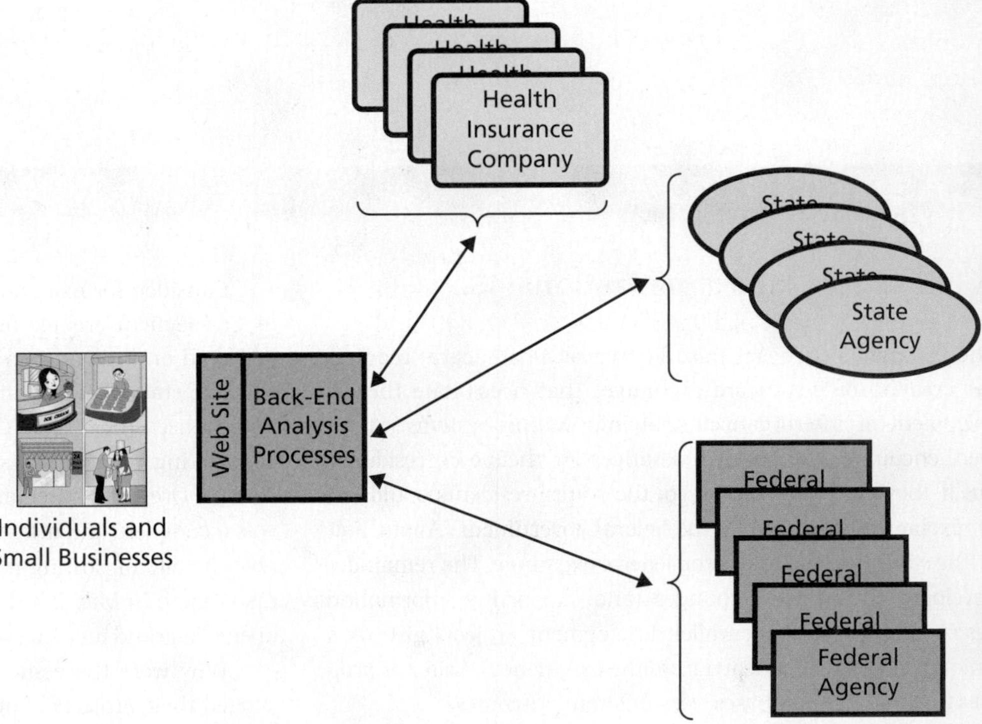


**Figure 7-14**
Healthcare Exchange Interorganizational IS

By June 2012, Access CT had created a project plan and begun a search for the contractor to develop the site. By September 2012, it selected Deloitte Consulting LLP. At the time, Wadleigh stated, "With only 12 months until the Exchange goes live, we look forward to beginning our work with them immediately."[8]

During that summer, in an interview on July 13, a local press reporter asked CEO Counihan, "Can you get it done on time?" His response: "This state's going to get it done in time."[9]

And it did. By the end of the federally mandated deadline, Access CT had enrolled 208,301 Connecticut residents,[10] and Connecticut had become a model for state-run exchanges.

## Cover Oregon

The outcome was not positive in Oregon. After spending nearly $250M, the exchange was clearly inoperable and the exchange's board of directors decided to stop development and utilize the federal exchange instead.[11] After this decision, the Oregon legislature hired an independent company, First Data Corporation, to investigate the causes of this debacle.[12]

Unlike in Connecticut, neither the Oregon governor nor any other elected official was directly involved in the project. In fact, in January 2014, the Oregon governor stated that he'd only become aware of the failure in "late October."[13] The site was to have gone operational on October 1, and it strains credulity to believe that it took 3 weeks for the news of the failure to reach him. In any case, it is safe to assume the governor was not a "hands-on manager" of the project nor did he delegate any senior elected official to take that role.

According to First Data,[14] from the onset, the project suffered from divided direction. Cover Oregon is a quasi-independent corporation, as is Access CT, but the exchange information system was to be developed by a different governmental agency, Oregon Health Authority (OHA). Personnel in the two agencies engaged in turf battles and held deep differences about project requirements. These differences resulted in always-changing, inconsistent direction to software developers.[15]

Further, unlike Access CT, OHA did not hire a supervising contractor for the project, but instead decided itself to take an active role in the software's development. Unfortunately, the agency suffered high employee turnover and had difficulty hiring and keeping qualified personnel. OHA did hire the services of a professional software development company to create major software components. However, of the three finalists for this work, two dropped out at the last minute, and the winner by default, Oracle Corporation, became in essence a sole source vendor. Consequently, Oracle was able to negotiate time and materials contracts rather than contracts for specific deliverables at specific prices. Later, when problems developed, it was paid tens of millions of additional money for "change orders" on that same time and materials basis. OHA also attempted to do much of its own programming, but the team had no experience with Oracle and lacked both developers and managers.[16]

Ironically, because of prior problems with technology projects, the Oregon legislature had required the state to hire a quality assurance contractor, Maximus Corporation, to oversee the project. From the project's start, Maximus reported significant problems involving divided control, lack of clear requirements, inappropriate contracting methodology, lack of project planning, and lack of progress. It is unclear to whom those reports were delivered or what was done with them. In January 2013, when the head of the OHA project received another negative report in a long string of such negative reports, she threatened to withhold Maximus's payment.[17]

Alas, when, in January 2013, *The Oregonian* asked Rocky King, the director of Cover Oregon, whether the system would work, he responded, "I haven't the foggiest idea."[18] Sadly, when the fog cleared, the exchange failed.

# QUESTIONS

**7-9.** Summarize the purpose and intended benefits of a healthcare exchange.

**7-10.** Explain why a healthcare exchange requires an interorganizational information system.

**7-11.** Using knowledge from this chapter, summarize the difficulties and challenges of developing inter-organizational information systems.

**7-12.** Healthcare exchanges must utilize personal and confidential data about their users. Write a one-paragraph policy that stipulates responsible processing and storage of these data.

**7-13.** Explain what you believe are the reasons for the Access CT success.

**7-14.** Read the Executive Summary of the First Data report located at *www.oregon.gov/DAS/docs/co_assessment.pdf*. Summarize those findings.

**7-15.** Using the facts described in this case and your answer to question 7-14, list five key learnings you can take from the Access CT and Cover Oregon projects.

MyMISLab™

Go to the Assignments section of your MyLab to complete these writing exercises.

**7-16.** Using the patient discharge process in Q7-2, explain how the hospital benefits from an ERP solution. Describe why integration of patient records has advantages over separated databases. Explain the value of an industry-specific ERP solution to the hospital.

**7-17.** Explain how the four sources of challenge discussed in Q7-3 would pertain to the implementation of the PRIDE system. Give specific examples of each. In general, do you think these challenges are more difficult to overcome for an inter-enterprise system like PRIDE or for an enterprise system like CRM?

## ENDNOTES

1. See *www.thisisant.com*.
2. D. Peak, "An Interview with John Halamka, MD, Chief Information Officer, Harvard Medical School and CareGroup Health System, USA," *Journal of IT Case and Application Research*, 10, no. 1 (2008): 70.
3. Robert Mcmillian, "The Inside Story of Mt. Gox, Bitcoin's $460 Million Disaster," *Wired*, March 3, 2014, accessed June 2, 2014, *www.wired.com/2014/03/bitcoin-exchange*.
4. Office of Congressman John Delaney, "Delaney Statement on Maryland Adopting Connecticut Health Exchange," April 1, 2014, accessed August 27, 2014, *http://delaney.house.gov/news/press-releases/delaney-statement-on-maryland-adopting-connecticut-health-exchange*.
5. Maeve Reston, "U.S. Prosecutors Investigate Oregon's Failed Health Insurance Exchange," *LA Times*, May 21, 2014, accessed May 25, 2014, *www.latimes.com/nation/nationnow/la-na-us-attorneys-office-probes-oregons-health-insurance-exchange-20140521-story.html*.
6. Matthew Sturdevant, "CT Health Exchange Has A New Chief Executive," *Hartford Courant*, June 21, 2012, accessed May 25, 2014, *http://articles.courant.com/2012-06-21/health/hc-health-exchange-ceo-20120621_1_health-insurance-exchange-health-care-victoria-veltri*.
7. Healthcare IT Connect, "Jim Wadleigh," accessed May 25, 2014, *www.healthcareitconnect.com/jim-wadleigh/*.
8. Office of Lieutenant Governor Nancy Wyman, "Health Insurance Exchange Hires Key Technical Consultant," September 27, 2012, accessed May 25, 2014, *http://ct.gov/hix/lib/hix/HIX-DELOITTE-RELEASE.pdf*.
9. Matthew Sturdevant, "Health Exchange Chief Explains How It Will Work," *Hartford Courant*, July 13, 2012, accessed May 25, 2014, *www.courant.com/health/connecticut/hc-health-exchange-20120712,0,4877364.story*.
10. Arielle Levin Becker, "Obamacare Exchange's Final Tally: 208,301 People Signed Up," *The CT Mirror*, April 17, 2014, accessed May 25, 2014, *http://ctmirror.org/obamacare-exchanges-final-tally-208301-people-signed-up/*.
11. Jeff Manning, "Cover Oregon: State Moves to Federal Exchange, but Oracle Technology Lives On," *The Oregonian*, May 6, 2014, accessed May 25, 2014, *www.oregonlive.com/health/index.ssf/2014/05/cover_oregon_state_moves_to_fe.html*.
12. "Cover Oregon Website Implementation Assessment," April 23, 2014, accessed May 25, 2014, *www.oregon.gov/DAS/docs/co_assessment.pdf*.
13. Dusty Lane, "'We Look Like Fools:' A History of Cover Oregon's Failure," *Katu.com*, January 10, 2014, accessed May 25, 2014, *www.katu.com/news/investigators/We-look-like-fools-A-history-of-Cover-Oregons-failure-239699521.html*.
14. "Cover Oregon Website Implementation Assessment."
15. Nick Budnick, "Cover Oregon: Health Exchange Failure Predicted, but Tech Watchdogs' Warnings Fell on Deaf Ears," *The Oregonian*, January 18, 2014, accessed May 25, 2014, *www.oregonlive.com/health/index.ssf/2014/01/cover_oregon_health_exchange_f.html*.
16. Nick Budnick, "Oregon Health Exchange Technology Troubles Run Deep due to Mismanagement, Early Decisions," *The Oregonian*, December 14, 2013, accessed May 25, 2014, *www.oregonlive.com/health/index.ssf/2013/12/oregon_health_exchange_technol.html*.
17. Budnick, "Cover Oregon: Health Exchange Failure Predicted."
18. Ibid.

# Social Media Information Systems

"It's all about eyeballs." Nicki Jensen is PRIDE Systems' new marketing director, and she's exploring ways to generate revenue from clicks on online ads. Zev Friedman, PRIDE Systems' new owner, told her to do this in their last meeting (page 182).

"What do you mean?" James Wu is PRIDE's manager of information systems. He was with the company when it was owned by Dr. Flores. When Friedman bought the company, he kept James on staff.

**This could happen to you**

"I mean, the number of eyeballs we get to look at our ads," Nicki responds.

"Well, not quite. It's about clicks, too." Michele Wilson is PRIDE Systems' new sales director. Her job is to convince vendors to sign up for ads for display on PRIDE's competitions and events.

Nicki looks at James. "We get as many eyes to look at our ads as we can. Then we motivate them to click."

She continues, "So how many people can we get into a virtual race? When we have the cloud connecting the data, we can get people spinning from their homes, their health clubs, wherever, worldwide, to race against one another."

Michele jumps in, "It could be 10,000 at one time, no?" She's looking for some information to help make her case to vendors.

James shakes his head. "Maybe so, but we're getting way ahead of ourselves. PRIDE was designed to support eight to twelve people in an exercise class. People who were in treatment following a heart attack or something like that. Now you're saying, 'Let's have a class of 10,000.' Whoa. We're not there with our systems."

Nicki's heard this kind of talk in the past. "But we *could* support 10,000 in an event, no?"

"In theory, sure. But the devil's in the details... or in this case, in the requirements. What kind of a user experience do you want? You can't put 10,000 little dots on a cell phone to show people where they are in the race. Well, let me correct myself: Of course we can put 10,000 little dots in the middle of a cell phone screen. We do it all the time, in fact, but what possible meaning would that have to anyone? They would see a blur."

"Well, we can figure that out. Couldn't we just show users the five or so people in front of them?"

"Sure we could. We could do anything. It's just bits. We can build anything you want. How much money and time you got?" James is trying to sound positive.

He pauses to think, then continues, "And, like I said, the devil's in the details. Let's say the person in front of a user is only 0.00000005 seconds ahead. How do we display that? Scale it up so it appears the person is way ahead? Or what if the

# STUDY QUESTIONS

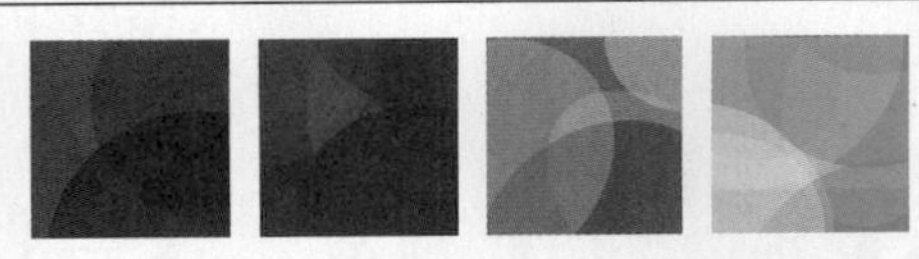

**Q8-1 WHAT IS A SOCIAL MEDIA INFORMATION SYSTEM (SMIS)?**

**Q8-2 HOW DO SMIS ADVANCE ORGANIZATIONAL STRATEGY?**

**Q8-3 HOW DO SMIS INCREASE SOCIAL CAPITAL?**

**Q8-4 HOW DO (SOME) COMPANIES EARN REVENUE FROM SOCIAL MEDIA?**

**Q8-5 HOW CAN ORGANIZATIONS ADDRESS SMIS SECURITY CONCERNS?**

**Q8-6 WHERE IS SOCIAL MEDIA TAKING US?**

## How does the **knowledge** in this chapter help **you?**

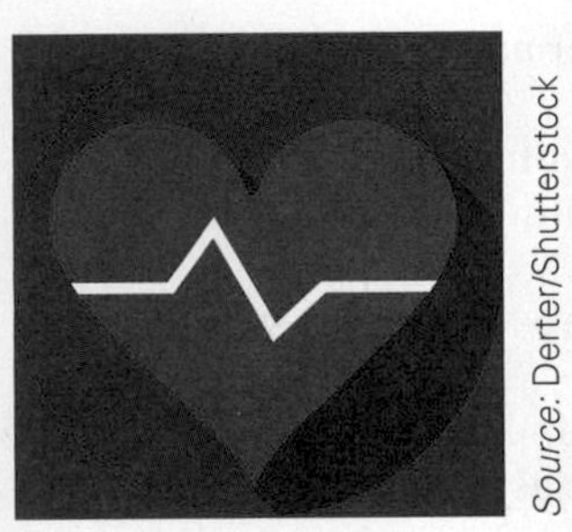

Source: Derter/Shutterstock

**"It's all about eyeballs."**

person in front is 10 minutes ahead, what then? And what if he or she is the leader? What do we show? A blank screen?"

"Ah, we can figure that out. That doesn't seem so hard."

"No, it's not. It's just bits. We can do it, just like we could build a 20-story building to replace this old relic of a warehouse we're in. But we can't do it tomorrow, and it won't be free."

"So, what do you want to tell Zev, James?" Nicki is frustrated.

"I don't want to tell him anything. But he bought a company that had software that supported 10 people in an exercise class, and now he has you two telling me that we should multiply that by 1,000. All doable. Nothing wrong with the idea. But we are not there right now."

"Well," presses Nicki, "how long will it take? And what will it cost?"

"For goodness sake, Nicki! Let me try again. I want you to build a 20-story building to replace this one. How long will it take? How much will it cost?"

"I have no idea. I need an architect and a contractor, and I need to know how much it costs to tear this building down." Nicki smiles at James's analogy.

"OK. You've got it now."

As Michele listens to this, she wishes she hadn't left her last job. "Well, I'm telling you two: I can't sell anything with 10 people at an event. That's crazy."

"Well, what about 1,000 events with 10 people? You'll still get your 20,000 eyes... assuming everyone has two eyes, of course. In reality, you'll probably get a few less than 20,000." James likes accuracy.

"Come on, James. No vendor's gonna ask me how many one-eyed racers we've got."

"Stop it, you two! Michele, James is on to something. Think about it. How many people are there in an online chess game?"

"Two, and let's assume that means four eyes, OK?" Michele is disgusted at James's comment.

"Let it go, Michele. But those online chess vendors make money. What if we did heats of races of 10 people each, then let the winner of each heat compete in the next round? We'd have continuing events, and we'd be able to sell between events... " Nicki trails off as she considers the possibilities.

Optional Extension for this chapter is CE11: Enterprise Social Networks and Knowledge Management 535

# Q8-1 WHAT IS A SOCIAL MEDIA INFORMATION SYSTEM (SMIS)?

Before we address this question, understand that this chapter makes no attempt to discuss the latest features of Facebook, Twitter, LinkedIn, Instagram, Pinterest, or any other social media service. Most likely you know much about these already, and further, they are changing so fast that whatever particulars you learn today will be old when you graduate and obsolete when you begin work. Instead, this chapter focuses on principles, conceptual frameworks, and models that will last rather than changes in social media services and technology and, in this way, will be useful when you address the opportunities and risks of social media systems in the early years of your professional career.

That knowledge will also help you avoid mistakes. Every day, you can hear businesspeople saying, "We're using Twitter" and "We've connected our Facebook page to our Web site." Or creating ads and news releases that say, "Follow us on Twitter." The important question these people should be asking is why are we doing this? To be modern? To be hip? Are these efforts worth their costs? How do they advance the organization's strategy?

**Social media (SM)** is the use of information technology to support the sharing of content among networks of users. Social media enables people to form **communities of practice**, or **communities**, which are groups of people related by a common interest. A **social media information system (SMIS)** is an information system that supports the sharing of content among networks of users.

As illustrated in Figure 8-1, social media is a convergence of many disciplines. In this book, we will focus on the MIS portion of Figure 8-1 by discussing SMIS and how they contribute to organizational strategy. If you decide to work in the SM field as a professional, you will need some knowledge of all these disciplines, except possibly computer science.

## THREE SMIS ROLES

Before discussing the components of an SMIS, we first need to clarify the roles played by the three organizational units of an SMIS:

- Social media providers
- Users
- Communities

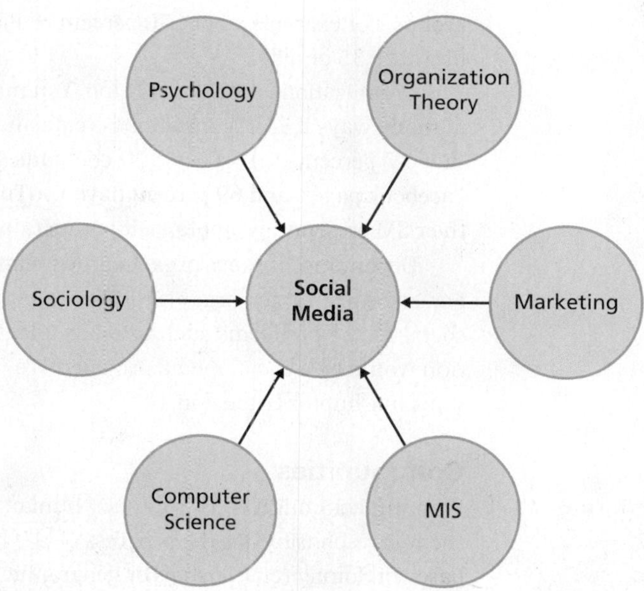


**Figure 8-1**
Social Media Is a Convergence of Disciplines

**Figure 8-2**
Number of Social Media Active Users

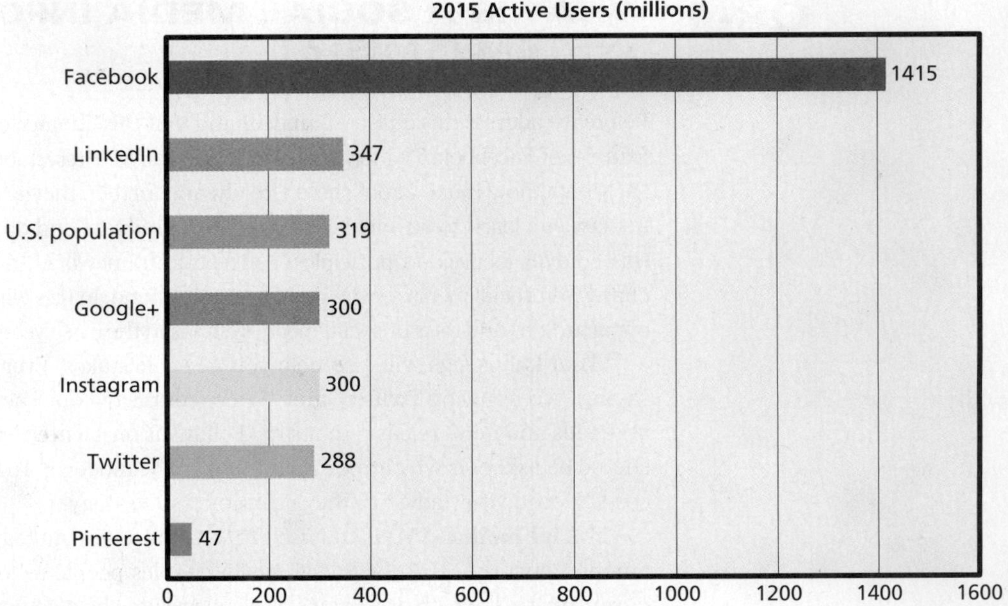


## Social Media Providers

**Social media providers** such as Facebook, Google+, LinkedIn, Twitter, Instagram, and Pinterest provide platforms that enable the creation of **social networks**, or social relationships among people with common interests. The growth of SM providers over the past few years has been tremendous. Figure 8-2 shows the size of some well-known SM providers as of January 2015; collectively, their number of active users exceeds the total population of the United States.[1] The growth of SM has drawn extraordinary interest from businesses, advertisers, and investors. Social media providers compete with one another for the attention of users—and the associated advertising dollars.

## Users

**Users** include both individuals *and* organizations that use SM sites to build social relationships. As previously mentioned, hundreds of millions of individuals visit SM sites on a regular basis, and they do so in several ways. One report from early 2014 indicates that more than 73 percent of people with Internet access use SM, and at least 40 percent of them use SM via their mobile phones.[2] Social media providers frequently attract or target people from certain demographic groups. For example, about 70 percent of Pinterest users are female.[3] On LinkedIn, 80 percent of users are 35 or older.[4]

Organizations are SM users too. You may not think of an organization as a typical user, but in many ways it is. Organizations create and manage SM accounts just like you do. It's estimated that 77 percent of Fortune 500 companies maintain active Twitter accounts; 70 percent have Facebook pages, and 69 percent have YouTube accounts.[5] These companies hire staff to maintain their SM presence, promote their products, build relationships, and manage their images.

Depending on how organizations want to use SM, they can be users, providers, or both. For example, larger organizations are big enough to create and manage their own internal social media platforms such as wikis, blogs, and discussion boards. In this case, the organization would be a social media provider. We'll see how social media can be used within organizations in Chapter Extension 11.

## Communities

Forming communities is a natural human trait; anthropologists claim that the ability to form them is responsible for the progress of the human race. In the past, however, communities were based on family relationships or geographic location. In short, everyone who lived in a particular village formed a community. The key difference with SM communities is that they are formed based on mutual interests and transcend familial, geographic, and organizational boundaries.

Because of this transcendence, most people belong to several, or even many, different SM user communities. Google+ recognized this fact when it created circles that enable users to allocate their connections (*people*, using Google+ terminology) to one or more community groups. Facebook and other SM application providers are adapting in similar ways.

Figure 8-3 shows that, from the point of view of the SM site, Community A is a first-tier community. It consists of users that have a direct relationship to the site. User 1, in turn, belongs to three communities: A, B, and C (these could be, say, classmates, professional contacts, and friends). From the point of view of the SM site, Communities B–E are second-tier communities because the relationships in those communities are intermediated by first-tier users. The number of second- and third-tier community members grows exponentially. If each community had, for example, 100 members, then the SM site would have 100 × 100, or 10,000, second-tier members and 100 × 100 × 100, or 1 million, third-tier members. However, this statement is not quite true because communities often overlap; in Figure 8-3, for example, User 7 belongs to Communities C and E. Thus, these calculations indicate the maximum—but not necessarily the actual—number of users.

How an SM site chooses to relate to these communities depends on its goals. If the site is interested in pure publicity, it will want to relate to as many tiers of communities as it can. If so, it will create a **viral hook**, which is some inducement, such as a prize or other reward, for passing communications along through the tiers. If, however, the purpose of the SM site is to solve an embarrassing problem, say, to fix a product defect, then it would endeavor to constrain, as much as it can, the communications to Community A.

**Figure 8-3**
SM Communities

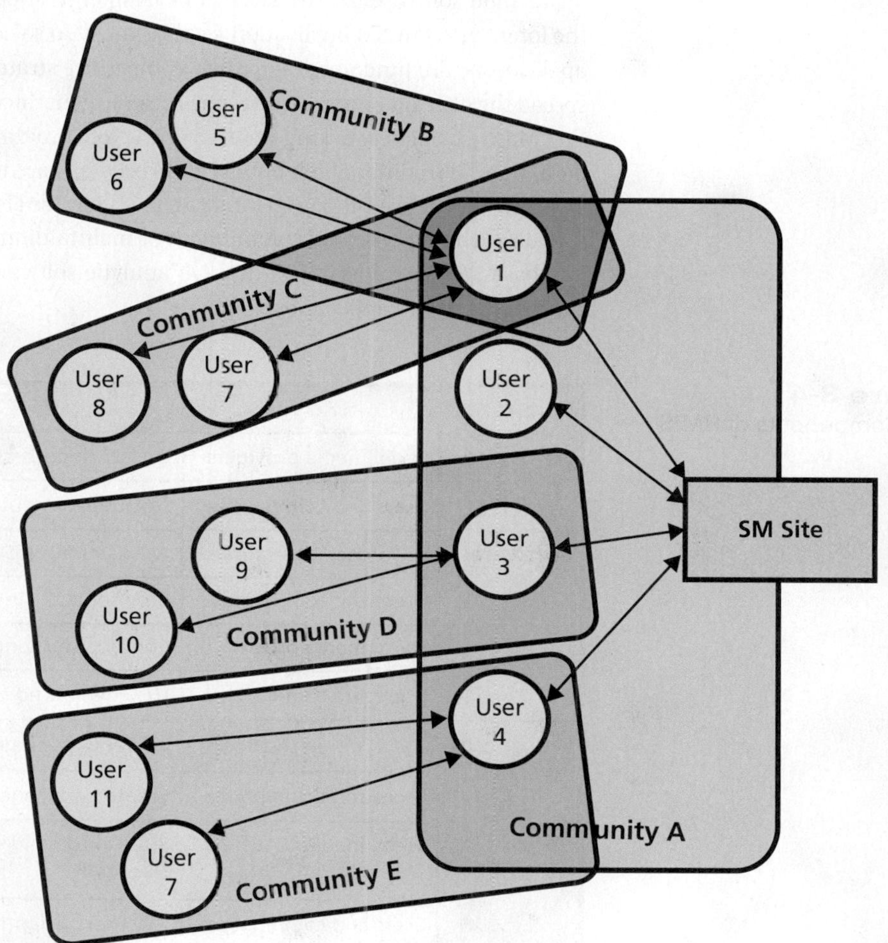

The exponential nature of relationships via community tiers offers organizations both a blessing and a curse. For example, an employee who is a member of Community A can share her sincere and legitimate pride in her organization's latest product or service with hundreds or thousands of people in her communities. However, she can also blast her disappointment at some recent development to that same audience or, worse, inadvertently share private and proprietary organizational data with someone in that audience who works for the competition.

As this example illustrates, social media is a powerful tool. To use it well, organizations must know their goals and plan accordingly.

## SMIS COMPONENTS

Because they are information systems, SMIS have the same five components as all IS: hardware, software, data, procedures, and people. Keeping SMIS in mind, consider each component shown in Figure 8-4.

### Hardware

Both users and organizations process SM sites using desktops, laptops, and mobile devices. In most cases, social media providers host the SM presence using elastic servers in the cloud.

### Software

SM users employ browsers and client applications to communicate with other users, send and receive content, and add and remove connections to communities and other users. These include desktop and mobile applications for a variety of platforms, including iOS, Android, and Windows.

Social media providers develop and operate their own custom, proprietary, social networking application software. As you learned in Chapter 4, supporting custom software is expensive over the long term, but SM application vendors must do so because the features and functions of their applications are fundamental to their competitive strategy. They can afford to do so because they spread the development costs over the revenue generated by millions of users.

Many social networking vendors use a NoSQL database management system to process their data, though traditional relational DBMS products are used as well. Facebook began development of its own in-house DBMS (Cassandra), but later donated it to the open source community when it realized the expense and commitment of maintaining it. In addition to custom applications and databases, SM providers also invest in analytic software to understand how users interact with their site and with application software.

**Figure 8-4**
Five Components of SMIS

| Component | Role | Description |
|---|---|---|
| Hardware | Social media providers | Elastic, cloud-based servers |
| | Users and communities | Any user computing device |
| Software | Social media providers | Application, NoSQL or other DBMS, Analytics |
| | Users and communities | Browser, iOS, Android, Windows 10, and other applications |
| Data | Social media providers | Content and connection data storage for rapid retrieval |
| | Users and communities | User-generated content, connection data |
| Procedures | Social media providers | Run and maintain application (beyond the scope of this text) |
| | Users and communities | Create and manage content, informal, copy each other |
| People | Social media providers | Staff to run and maintain application (beyond the scope of this text) |
| | Users and communities | Key users, adaptive, can be irrational |

### Data

SM data falls into two categories: content and connections. **Content data** is data and responses to data that are contributed by users. For example, you provide the source content data for your Facebook site, and your friends provide response content when they write on your wall, make comments, tag you, or otherwise publish on your site.

**Connection data** is data about relationships. On Facebook, for instance, the relationships to your friends are connection data. The fact that you've liked particular organizations is also connection data. Connection data differentiates SMIS from Web site applications. Both Web sites and social networking sites present user and responder content, but only social networking applications store and process connection data.

SM providers store and retrieve SM data on behalf of users. They must do so in the presence of network and server failures, and they must do so rapidly. The problem is made somewhat easier, however, because SM content and connection data have a relatively simple structure.

### Procedures

For social networking users, procedures are informal, evolving, and socially oriented. You do what your friends do. When the members of your community learn how to do something new and interesting, you copy them. Software is designed to be easy to learn and use.

Such informality makes using SMIS easy; it also means that unintended consequences are common. The most troubling examples concern user privacy. Many people have learned not to post pictures of themselves in front of their house numbers on the same publicly accessible site on which they're describing their new high-definition television. Many others, alas, have not.

For organizations, social networking procedures are more formalized and aligned with the organization's strategy. Organizations develop procedures for creating content, managing user responses, removing obsolete or objectionable content, and extracting value from content. For example, setting up an SMIS to gather data on product problems is a wasted expense unless procedures exist to extract knowledge from that social networking data. Organizations also need to develop procedures to manage SM risk, as described in Q8-5.

Procedures for operating and maintaining an SM application are beyond the scope of this text.

### People

Users of social media do what they want to do depending on their goals and their personalities. They behave in certain ways and observe the consequences. They may or may not change their behavior. By the way, note that SM users aren't necessarily rational, at least not in purely monetary ways. See, for example, the study by Vernon Smith in which people walked away from free money because they thought someone else was getting more![6]

Organizations cannot be so casual. Anyone who uses his or her position in a company to speak for an organization needs to be trained on both SMIS user procedures and the organization's social networking policy. We will discuss such procedures and policies in Q8-5.

Social media is creating new job titles, new responsibilities, and the need for new types of training. For example, what makes a good tweeter? What makes an effective wall writer? What type of people should be hired for such jobs? What education should they have? How does one evaluate candidates for such positions? How do you find these types of people? All of these questions are being asked and answered today.

**Buying automated bot followers is a questionable practice. Read more about it in the Ethics Guide on pages 234–235.**

## Q8-2 HOW DO SMIS ADVANCE ORGANIZATIONAL STRATEGY?

In Chapter 3, Figure 3-1 (page 61), you learned the relationship of information systems to organizational strategy. In brief, strategy determines value chains, which determine business processes, which determine information systems. Insofar as value chains determine *structured* business

**Figure 8-5**
SM in Value Chain Activities

| Activity | Focus | Dynamic process | Risks |
|---|---|---|---|
| Sales and marketing | Outward to prospects | Social CRM; Peer-to-peer sales | Loss of credibility; Bad PR |
| Customer service | Outward to customers | Peer-to-peer support | Loss of control |
| Inbound logistics | Upstream supply chain providers | Problem solving | Privacy |
| Outbound logistics | Downstream supply chain shippers | Problem solving | Privacy |
| Manufacturing and operations | Outward for user design; Inward to operations and manufacturing | User-guided design; Industry relationships; Operational efficiencies | Efficiency/effectiveness |
| Human resources | Employment candidates; Employee communications | Employee prospecting, recruiting, and evaluation SharePoint for employee-to-employee communication | Error; Loss of credibility |

**You can learn more about knowledge management in Chapter Extension 11.**

processes, such as those discussed in Chapter 7, this value chain is straightforward. However, social media is by its very nature *dynamic*; its flow cannot be designed or diagrammed, and, if it were, no sooner would the diagram be finished than the SM process would have changed.

Therefore, we need to back up a step and consider how value chains determine dynamic processes and thus set SMIS requirements. As you will see, social media fundamentally changes the balance of power among users, their communities, and organizations.

Figure 8-5 summarizes how social media contributes to the five primary value chain activities and to the human resources support activity. Consider each row of this table.

## SOCIAL MEDIA AND THE SALES AND MARKETING ACTIVITY

In the past, organizations controlled their relationships with customers using structured processes and related information systems. In fact, the primary purpose of traditional CRM was to manage customer touches. Traditional CRM ensured that the organization spoke to customers with one voice and that it controlled the messages, the offers, and even the support that customers received based on the value of each particular customer. For example, in 1990, if you wanted to know something about an IBM product, you'd contact IBM's local sales office; that office would then classify you as a prospect and use that classification to control the literature and documentation you received and your access to IBM personnel.

As opposed to traditional CRM, **social CRM** is a dynamic, SM-based process. The relationships between organizations and customers emerge in an ever-changing process as both parties create and process content. In addition to the traditional forms of promotion, employees in the organization create wikis, blogs, discussion lists, frequently asked questions, sites for user reviews and commentary, and other dynamic content. Customers then search this content, contribute their own reviews and commentary, ask more questions, create user groups, and so forth. Thus, with social CRM, each customer crafts his or her own relationship with the company.

Social CRM flies in the face of the structured and controlled processes of traditional CRM. Because relationships emerge from joint activity, customers have as much control as companies. This characteristic is anathema to traditional sales managers who want structured processes for controlling what the customer reads, sees, and hears about the company and its products.

Further, traditional CRM is centered on lifetime value; customers that are likely to generate the most business get the most attention and have the most effect on the organization. However, with social CRM, the customer who spends 10 cents but who is an effective reviewer, commentator, or blogger can have more influence than the quiet customer who purchases $10 million a year. Such imbalance is incomprehensible to traditional sales managers.

Nonetheless, traditional sales managers *are* happy to have loyal customers sell their products using peer-to-peer recommendations. A quick look at products and their reviews on Amazon.com will show how frequently customers are willing to write long, thoughtful reviews of products they like or do not like. Amazon.com and other online retailers also allow readers to rate the helpfulness of reviews. In that way, substandard reviews are revealed for the wary.

Today, many organizations are struggling to make the transition from controlled, structured, traditional CRM processes to wide-open, adaptive, dynamic social CRM processes. This struggle represents a significant job opportunity for those interested in IS, sales, and social media.

## SOCIAL MEDIA AND CUSTOMER SERVICE

Product users are amazingly willing to help one another solve problems. Even more, they will do so without pay; in fact, payment can warp and ruin the support experience as customers fight with one another. SAP, for example, learned that it was better to reward its SAP Developer Network with donations to charitable organizations on their behalf than to give them personal rewards.

Not surprisingly, organizations whose business strategy involves selling to or through developer networks have been the earliest and most successful at SM-based customer support. In addition to SAP, Microsoft has long sold through its network of partners. Its MVP (Most Valuable Professional) program is a classic example of giving praise and glory in exchange for customer-provided customer assistance (*http://mvp.support.microsoft.com*). Of course, the developers in Microsoft's networks have a business incentive to participate because that activity helps them sell their services to the communities in which they participate.

However, users with no financial incentive are also willing to help others. Amazon.com supports a program called Vine by which customers can be selected to give prerelease and new product reviews to the buyer community.[7] You'll need your psychology course to explain what drives people to strive for such recognition. MIS just provides the platform!

The primary risk of peer-to-peer support is loss of control. Businesses may not be able to control peer-to-peer content, so negative comments about cherished products and recommendations for competitor's products are a real possibility. We address these risks in Q8-5.

## SOCIAL MEDIA AND INBOUND AND OUTBOUND LOGISTICS

Companies whose profitability depends on the efficiency of their supply chain have long used information systems to improve both the effectiveness and the efficiency of structured supply chain processes. Because supply chains are tightly integrated into structured manufacturing processes, there is less tolerance for the unpredictability of dynamic, adaptive processes. Solving problems is an exception; social media can be used to provide numerous solution ideas and rapid evaluation thereof. For instance, the Japanese earthquake in the spring of 2011 created havoc in the automotive supply chain when major Japanese manufacturers lacked power and, in some cases, facilities to operate. Social media was thus used to dispense news, allay fears of radioactive products, and address ever-changing needs and problems.

As this example illustrates, SM communities may provide better and faster solutions to complex supply chain problems. Social media is designed to foster content creation and feedback among networks of users, and that characteristic facilitates the iteration and feedback needed for problem solving, as described in Chapter 2.

Loss of privacy is, however, a significant risk. Problem solving requires the open discussion of problem definitions, causes, and solution constraints. Because suppliers and shippers work with many companies, supply chain problem solving via social media may be problem solving in front of your competitors.

## SOCIAL MEDIA AND MANUFACTURING AND OPERATIONS

Operations and manufacturing activities are dominated by structured processes. The flexibility and adaptive nature of social media would result in chaos if applied to the manufacturing line or to the warehouse. However, social media does play a role in product design, developing supplier relationships, and improving operational efficiencies.

**Crowdsourcing** is the dynamic social media process of employing users to participate in product design or product redesign. For example, eBay often solicits customers to provide feedback on their eBay experience. As its site says, "There's no better group of advisors than our customers." Similarly, user-guided design has been used in the creation of video games, shoes, and many other products.

Since its inception, social media has been widely used in **business-to-consumer (B2C)** relationships to market products to end users. Now manufacturers are starting to use social media to become industry leaders, promote brand awareness, and generate new **business-to-business (B2B)** leads to retailers. For instance, a manufacturer might start a blog that discusses the latest industry-related news, posts interviews with experts, and comments on new product innovations. It could also create a YouTube channel and post videos of product reviews and testing and factory walk-throughs. Similarly, Facebook and Twitter accounts may be useful for promoting positive consumer stories, announcing new products, and following competitors. Retailers will view manufacturers who engage in these SM efforts as industry leaders.

Operations can use social media to improve communication channels within the organization as well as externally with consumers. For example, an enterprise social networking service like Yammer can be used to provide managers with real-time feedback about how to resolve internal operational inefficiencies. Externally, a retailer could monitor its corporate Twitter account and respond to product shortages or spikes in demand for new products around holidays.

## SOCIAL MEDIA AND HUMAN RESOURCES

**Social media is increasingly used to recruit and evaluate employees.** **See the Guide on pages 236–237.**

The last row in Figure 8-5 concerns the use of social media and human resources. As previously mentioned, social media is increasingly used for finding employee prospects, for recruiting candidates, and—in some organizations—for candidate evaluation.

Organizations use social media sites like LinkedIn to hire the best people more quickly and at a lower cost. For about $750 a month, recruiters can search through 350 million LinkedIn members to find the perfect candidate.[8] That $750 a month may sound like a lot to you, but to corporate customers, it's peanuts. The cost of hiring just one new employee runs around $4,000.[9] If an independent recruiting company is involved, that cost can be as high as 10 percent of the new employee's salary. LinkedIn also gives employers access to *passive* candidates who might not be looking for a job but are a perfect fit for a particular position. Once hired, the employer can leverage that new employee's social network to hire more candidates just like him or her.

Reppler, a social networking image management company, reports that 93 percent of employers it surveyed used social media to screen candidates. Furthermore, 55 percent of survey respondents reported that they had reconsidered a candidate because of what he or she had on social media sites. The good news is that 39 percent of those were positive reconsiderations. The bad news is that 61 percent were negative reconsiderations based on finding profanity; spelling or grammar mistakes; and references to sex, drugs, alcohol, or guns.[10]

Social media is also used for employee communications, often via internal personnel sites such as MySite and MyProfile in SharePoint or other similar enterprise systems. SharePoint provides a place for employees to post their expertise in the form of "Ask me about" questions. When

# Facebook for Organizations... and Machines?

Social media is fun and entertaining for individuals, but what about for commerce?

For example, what would happen if you took Facebook functionality and created an enterprise social network? How would the organization change if everyone was talking with everyone? That's exactly what Salesforce.com did when it created Chatter.

Chatter can be used to connect employees and customers via social media. For example, retail salespeople can communicate directly with managers to give instant feedback about a new sales promotion. Chatter can also connect salespeople with presale support personnel or customer service personnel with customers.

With Chatter or its rival Yammer, organizational communities of practice identify and solve problems more quickly and more effectively than before. These communities readily find needed experts within the organization and recruit them to help solve problems. Organizations thus become more responsive because of faster project collaboration. Indeed, internal-facing communities of practice use all the things you like about your personal social media to make their organizations better.

Enterprise social media is taking off, and consumer social media is an established success. But what's next? Where will social media be applied next? Well, there's one player that's been left out of this scenario so far: the machines.

For years, machines have helped facilitate communication, but they haven't really been treated as communication partners. Recently, however, we've begun to see human-to-computer communication in applications like Apple's Siri and IBM's Watson, which allow humans to naturally interact with machines. The potential here is tremendous. But what about machine-to-machine communication?

A startling—and potentially groundbreaking—application is mentioned in a video featuring Beth Comstock, Chief Marketing Officer for General Electric, who says, "We want to use Chatter to connect our employees, our customers, and our machines." (Listen for yourself at *www.youtube.com/watch?v=nHaBCcn-9BU*.) Does Comstock mean that GE jet engines are going to be social media users? Will these engines share their flight data (weather, air speed, chop, pilot effectiveness, etc.) with other planes that fly their same routes? Will they be submitting reviews on mechanics, as in "Don't accept maintenance from Charlie Smith; he's too rough with his tools"? Will GE's jet engines chat with GE's servers about their performance and need for scheduled maintenance?

*Source:* Tuomas Kujansuu/istock/Getty Images

From a consumer perspective, social media among machines might have distinct advantages. For example, your car could communicate with each traffic light along your route to work to speed up your commute. No more sitting at red lights! Your car could also communicate with your phone, watch, tablet, and home (appliances, lights, doors, etc.) to solve problems you didn't think were solvable. For instance, once self-driving cars become widely used, they will likely be able to interact with a host of different devices. Thus, your self-driving car might get information from your health monitor indicating that you haven't eaten in 5 hours. Your car might also know, via your online calendar, that you have a meeting across town in an hour. Your car could then map out a route with a stop at your favorite bistro, pick up an electronic coupon, call in your order, and send the dietary information to your health monitor, all while getting you to your meeting on time.

Although this example may seem far-fetched, there is no doubt that social machines will change the way organizations operate as well as the way people live their lives. Embrace the change.

## QUESTIONS

1. Visit *www.salesforce.com/chatter* to learn about Chatter's features and applications. How could Chatter affect value chain activities?
2. How might Chatter help Apple, Inc. create better products?
3. Why would employees, managers, and owners want to use Chatter? Consider each group individually.
4. One example of social media and machines involves having machines report operational status data (say, speed, temperature, fuel usage, and so on, depending on the type of machine) to a Chatter or other SM site. How can an organization use such reporting in the context of machine, customer, and employee social media?
5. How might machines use foursquare (location-based social networking)? Consider machine-to-machine interactions, as well as human-to-machine interactions.
6. Could machine-to-machine social interactions lead to security or privacy concerns? If so, how?

employees are looking for an internal expert, they can search SharePoint for people who have posted the desired expertise. SharePoint 2013 greatly extends support for social media beyond that in earlier SharePoint versions.

The risks of social media in human resources concern the possibility of error when using sites such as Facebook to form conclusions about employees and job applicants. A second risk is that the SM site becomes too defensive or is obviously promulgating an unpopular management message. Again, study Figure 8-5 to understand the general framework by which organizations can accomplish their strategy via dynamic processes supported by SMIS. We will now turn to an economic perspective on the value and use of SMIS.

# Q8-3 HOW DO SMIS INCREASE SOCIAL CAPITAL?

Business literature describes three types of capital: traditional, human, and social. Karl Marx defined **capital** as the investment of resources for future profit. This traditional definition refers to investments into resources such as factories, machines, manufacturing equipment, and the like. In comparison, **human capital** is the investment in human knowledge and skills for future profit. By taking this class, you are investing in your own human capital. In other words, you are investing your money and time to obtain knowledge that you hope will differentiate you from other workers and ultimately give you a wage premium in the workforce.

According to Nan Lin, **social capital** is investment in social relations with the expectation of returns in the marketplace.[11] You can see social capital at work in your personal life. You strengthen your social relationships when you help someone get a job, set a friend up on a date, or introduce a friend to someone famous. You weaken your social relationships by continually free-loading, declining requests for help, or failing to spend time with friends.

In your professional life, you are investing in your social capital when you attend a business function for the purpose of meeting people and reinforcing relationships. Similarly, you can use social media to increase your social capital by recommending or endorsing someone on LinkedIn, liking a picture on Facebook, retweeting a tweet, or commenting on an Instagram picture.

## WHAT IS THE VALUE OF SOCIAL CAPITAL?

According to Nan Lin, people benefit from social capital in four ways:

- Information
- Influence
- Social credentials
- Personal reinforcement

First, relationships in social networks can provide *information* about opportunities, alternatives, problems, and other factors important to business professionals. On a personal level, this could come in the form of a friend telling you about a new job posting or recommending which teacher to take for Business Law. As a business professional, this could involve a friend introducing you to a potential new supplier or letting you know about the opening of a new sales territory.

Second, social networks provide an opportunity to *influence* decision makers at one's employer or in other organizations that are critical to your success. For example, playing golf every Saturday with the CEO of the company you work for could increase your chances of being promoted. Such influence cuts across formal organizational structures, such as reporting relationships.

Third, being linked to a network of highly regarded contacts is a form of *social credential*. You can bask in the glory of those with whom you are connected. Others will be more inclined to work with you if they believe critical personnel are standing with you and may provide resources to support you.

Finally, being linked into social networks *reinforces* a professional's identity, image, and position in an organization or industry. It reinforces the way you define yourself to the world (and to yourself). For example, being friends with bankers, financial planners, and investors may reinforce your identity as a financial professional.

As mentioned earlier, a social network is a network of social relationships among individuals with a common interest. Each social network differs in value. The social network you maintain with your high school friends probably has less value than the network you have with your business associates, but not necessarily so. According to Henk Flap, the **value of social capital** is determined by the number of relationships in a social network, by the strength of those relationships, and by the resources controlled by those related.[12] So, if your high school friends happened to have been Mark Zuckerberg or Cameron and Tyler Winklevoss and if you still maintain strong relations with them via your high school network, then the value of that social network far exceeds the value of any network you'll have at work. For most of us, however, our network of current professional contacts provides the most social capital.

So, when you use social networking professionally, consider these guidelines. You gain social capital by adding more friends and by strengthening the relationships you have with existing friends. Further, you gain more social capital by adding friends and strengthening relationships with people who control resources that are important to you. Such calculations may seem cold, impersonal, and possibly even phony. When applied to the recreational use of social networking, they may be. But when you use social networking for professional purposes, keep them in mind.

One way to measure the success of your social networking efforts is through an online service like Klout.com. Klout.com searches social media activity on Facebook, Twitter, and other sites and then creates what it calls a Klout score, which is a measure of an individual's social capital. Klout scores vary from 0 to 100; the more that others respond to your content, the higher your score. Also, responses from people who seldom respond are valued more than responses from those who respond frequently.[13] As a business professional, it's important to understand what social capital is, why it's valuable, and how you can benefit from it.

## HOW DO SOCIAL NETWORKS ADD VALUE TO BUSINESSES?

Organizations have social capital just as humans do. Historically, organizations created social capital via salespeople, customer support, and public relations. Endorsements by high-profile people are a traditional way of increasing social capital.

Today, progressive organizations maintain a presence on Facebook, LinkedIn, Twitter, and possibly other sites. They include links to their social networking presence on their Web sites and make it easy for customers and interested parties to leave comments.

To understand how social networks add value to businesses, consider each of the elements of social capital: number of relationships, strength of relationships, and resources controlled by "friends."

## USING SOCIAL NETWORKING TO INCREASE THE NUMBER OF RELATIONSHIPS

In a traditional business relationship, a client (you) has some experience with a business, such as a restaurant or resort. Traditionally, you may express your opinions about that experience by word of mouth to your social network. If you are an **influencer** in your social network, your opinion may force a change in others' behavior and beliefs.

However, such communication is unreliable and brief: You are more likely to say something to your friends if the experience was particularly good or bad—but even then, you are likely only to say something to those friends whom you encounter while the experience is still recent. And once you have said something, that's it; your words don't live on for days or weeks.

However, consider what would happen if you used SM to instantly communicate your experience using text, pictures, and video to everyone in your social network. For example, suppose you're a wedding photographer who uses social media to promote your business by asking a recent client (user 1) to "like" your Facebook page as well as the wedding photos you took (Figure 8-6). You also tag people in the client's pictures on Facebook. You may even ask the client to tweet about her experience.

All of the people in the client's social network (users 4–6) see the likes, tags, and tweets. If user 6 likes the pictures, they might be seen by users 10–12—and it's possible that one of those users may be looking for a wedding photographer. Using social media, you have grown your social network to reach potential clients who you wouldn't have otherwise had access to. You also used SM to grow the number of relationships you have with clients. Depending on the number, strength, and value of those relationships, your social capital within those networks would substantially increase.

Such relationship sales have been going on by word of mouth for centuries; the difference here is that SMIS allow such sales to scale to levels not possible in the past. In fact, the

**Figure 8-6**
Growing Social Networks

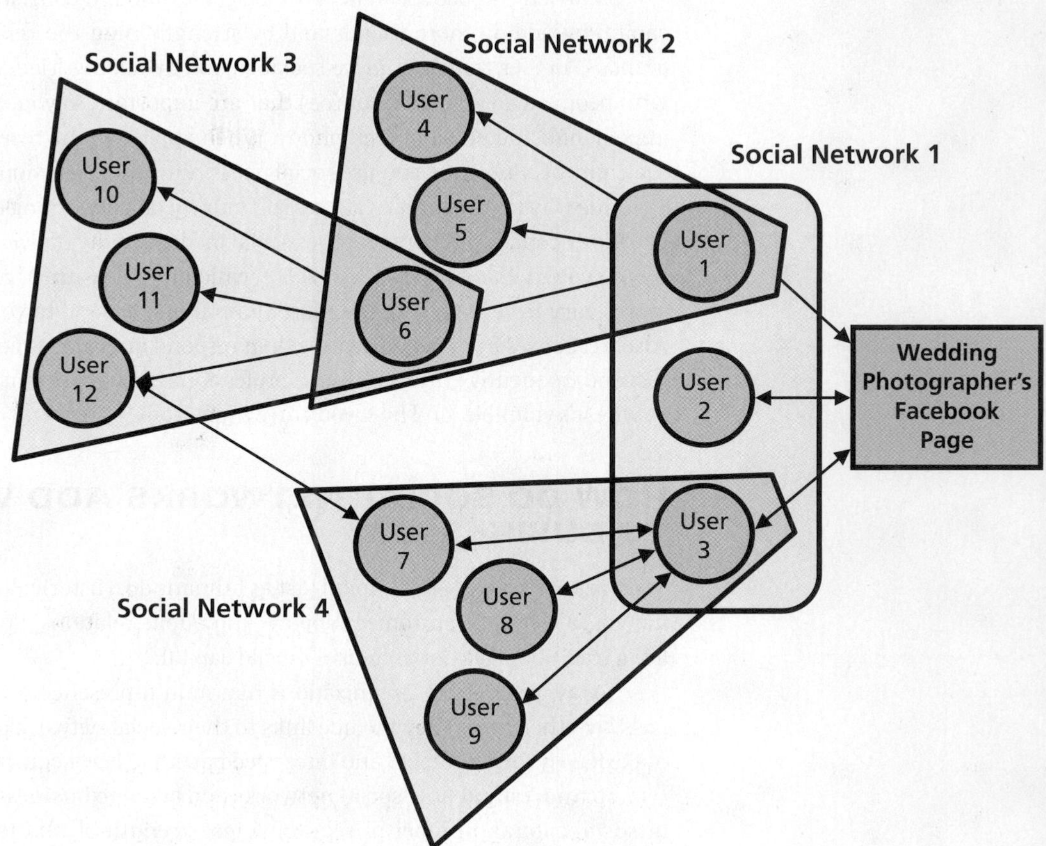

photographer in our example (you) might even consider *paying* the client for the opportunity to take the wedding pictures if the client were a famous celebrity with hundreds of thousands of followers. In this way, social media may allow users to convert social capital into financial capital. In fact, some famous celebrities get paid more than $10,000 for a single 140-character tweet![14]

## USING SOCIAL NETWORKS TO INCREASE THE STRENGTH OF RELATIONSHIPS

To an organization, the **strength of a relationship** is the likelihood that the other entity (person or other organization) in the relationship will do something that benefits the organization. For example, an organization may have a strong relationship with you if you write positive reviews about it, post pictures of yourself using the organization's products or services, tweet about upcoming product releases, and so on.

In the previous scenario, the photographer asked a client to like her Facebook page and wedding photos. To the photographer, the number of friends the client has in her social network is important, but equally important is the strength of the relationships. Will the client's friends like the photographer's page and photos? Will they retweet the client's success story? If none of the client's friends like the photographer's page and photos, then the strength of the relationships is weak. If, however, all of the client's friends like the photographer's page and photos, then the strength of the relationships in the client's social network is strong.

In his autobiography, Benjamin Franklin provided a key insight.[15] He said that if you want to strengthen your relationship with someone in power, ask him to do you a favor. Before Franklin invented the public library system, he would ask powerful strangers to lend him their expensive books. In that same sense, organizations have learned that they can strengthen their relationships with you by asking you to do them a favor. When you provide that favor, it strengthens your relationship with the organization.

Of course, traditional capital depreciates. Machines wear out, factories get old, technology and computers become obsolete, and so forth. Does social capital also depreciate? Do relationships wear out from use? So far, the answer seems to be both yes and no.

Clearly, there are only so many favors you can ask of someone in power. Similarly, there are only so many times a company can ask you to review a product, post pictures, or provide connections to your friends. At some point, the relationship deteriorates due to overuse. So, yes, social capital can be spent.

However, frequent interactions strengthen relationships and hence increase social capital. The more you interact with a company, the stronger your commitment and allegiance—but continued frequent interactions occur only when both parties see value in continuing the relationship. Thus, at some point, the organization must provide an incentive for you to continue to do it a favor.

So, social capital can be spent, but it can also be earned by adding something of value to the interaction. If an organization can induce the other parties in its relationships to provide more influence, information, social credentials, or personal reinforcement, it has strengthened those relationships. And continuing successful relationships over time substantially increases the strength of those relationships.

## USING SOCIAL NETWORKS TO CONNECT TO THOSE WITH MORE RESOURCES

The third measure of the value of social capital is the value of the resources controlled by the parties in the relationships. An organization's social capital is thus partly a function of the social capital of those to whom it relates. The most visible measure is the number of relationships. Someone with 1,000 loyal Twitter followers is usually more valuable than someone with 10—but the actual calculation is more subtle than that. For instance, if those 1,000 followers are college

**Figure 8-7**
Top YouTube Channels

*Source:* Adapted from Nat Ives, "What a YouTube Celeb Pulls In," Adage.com, April 15, 2015, accessed May 5, 2015, *http://adage.com/article/news/a-youtube-celeb-pulls/298015.*

| Top 5 Beauty and Style Channels | Monthy Views (millions) | Est. Monthly Earnings |
|---|---|---|
| Yuya | 35.8 | $41,476 |
| grav3yardgirl | 27.7 | $32,292 |
| Zoella | 23.5 | $27,375 |
| Cute Girls Hairstyles | 18.3 | $21,078 |
| Rclbeauty101 | 17.8 | $20,960 |

| Top 5 Food and Cooking Channels | Monthy Views (millions) | Est. Monthly Earnings |
|---|---|---|
| CharlisCraftyKitchen | 29.1 | $127,777 |
| Mosogourmet | 22.9 | $100,031 |
| CookiesCupcakesandCardio | 17.1 | $ 79,309 |
| How To Cook That | 16.4 | $ 77,773 |
| MyCupcakeAddiction | 13.5 | $ 64,268 |

students and the organization's product is adult diapers, then the value of the relationship to the followers is low. A relationship with 10 Twitter followers who are in retirement homes would be much more valuable.

To illustrate this point, Figure 8-7 shows the top five most popular YouTube channels in the beauty and style category and the food and cooking category.[16] In general, the more views a channel gets, the more the content creator gets paid. However, notice that the food and cooking channels have higher earnings than the beauty and style channels. The number of views is not the only factor influencing earnings. The resources (money) controlled by the viewers of the food and cooking channels may be higher than the viewers of the beauty and style channels.

There is no formula for computing social capital, but the three factors would seem to be more multiplicative than additive. Or, stated in other terms, the value of social capital is more in the form of

$$\textit{Social Capital} = \textit{Number of Relationships} \times \textit{Relationship Strength} \times \textit{Entity Resources}$$

than it is in the form of

$$\textit{Social Capital} = \textit{Number of Relationships} + \textit{Relationship Strength} + \textit{Entity Resources}$$

Again, do not take these equations literally; take them in the sense of the multiplicative interaction of the three factors. This multiplicative nature of social capital means that a huge network of relationships with people who have few resources may ultimately be of less value than a smaller network of relationships with people who have substantial resources. Furthermore, those resources must be relevant to the organization. Students with pocket change are relevant to Pizza Hut; they are irrelevant to a BMW dealership.

This discussion brings us to the brink of social networking practice. Most organizations today ignore the value of entity assets and simply try to connect to more people with stronger relationships. This area is ripe for innovation. Data aggregators such as ChoicePoint and Acxiom maintain detailed data about people worldwide. It would seem that such data could be used by information systems to calculate the potential value of a relationship to a particular individual. This possibility would enable organizations to better understand the value of their social networks as well as guide their behavior with regard to particular individuals.

Stay tuned; many possibilities exist, and some ideas—maybe yours!—will be very successful.

# Q8-4 HOW DO (SOME) COMPANIES EARN REVENUE FROM SOCIAL MEDIA?

Having a large social network with strong relationships may not be enough to guarantee profitability. Facebook, for example, has more than 1.4 billion active users that generate 4.5 billion likes each day.[17] YouTube has more than 1 billion active users that watch more than 6 billion hours of video each month.[18] Both companies thus have extremely large numbers of active users. The only problem is that they give their services away for free. Billions of anything multiplied by zero is, well, zero. Do all those users really matter if a company can't make a single penny off of them?

As a business student, you know that nothing is free, even in the world of social media. Processing time, data communication, and data storage may be cheap, but they still cost something. Who pays for the hardware required by SMIS? Social media companies like Facebook, Twitter, and LinkedIn also need to pay people to develop, implement, and manage the SMIS. And where does Web content come from? *Fortune* pays authors for the content that it offers for free. Who is paying those authors? And from what revenue?

## YOU ARE THE PRODUCT

Social media has evolved in such a way that users expect to use SM applications without paying for them. SM companies want to build up a large network of users quickly, but they have to offer a free product in order to attract users. The dilemma then becomes how do the companies **monetize**, or make money from, their application, service, or content?

The answer is by making *users* the product. That may sound strange at first, and you probably don't want to think of yourself as a product. But try to look at the situation from the company's point of view. When a company runs an advertisement, it's essentially being paid to put the ad in front of its users. So, in a way, the company is renting your eyeballs to an advertiser for a short period of time. Google, for example, is paid to target users with ads based on their search terms, the sites they visit, and "scans" of their emails. In essence, then, users are the product being sold to advertisers. As the old saying says, "If you're not paying, you're the product."

## REVENUE MODELS FOR SOCIAL MEDIA

The two most common ways SM companies generate revenue are by advertising and by charging for premium services. On Facebook, for example, creating a company page is free, but Facebook charges a fee to advertise to communities that "like" that page.

### Advertising

Most SM companies earn revenue through advertising. For example, Facebook made 94 percent of its 2015 first quarter earnings ($3.5B) from advertising.[19] About 90 percent of Twitter's $436M first quarter earnings came from advertising as well.[20] Advertising in SM can come in the form of paid search, display or banner ads, mobile ads, classifieds, or digital video ads.

Google led the way in making digital advertising revenue with paid search results, followed by Gmail and then YouTube. Today, it doesn't seem like any great insight to realize that if someone is searching an Audi A5 Cabriolet, that person may be interested in ads from local Audi dealers and BMW and Mercedes dealers as well. Or if someone is watching a soccer game on YouTube, it seems sensible to assume that he or she may like soccer. Although not mind-boggling to imagine, Google was the first to realize substantial revenue streams from targeted ads based on user content. Other tech companies soon followed.

Advertisers like digital ads because, unlike with traditional media such as newspapers, users can respond directly to these ads by clicking on them. Run an ad in the print version of *The Wall Street Journal*, and you have no idea of who responds to that ad and how strongly. But place an ad for that same product in the newspaper's online version, and you'll soon know the percentage of viewers who clicked that ad and what action they took next. The ability to track these statistics led to development of the **pay-per-click** revenue model, in which advertisers display ads to potential customers for free and then get paid when the customer clicks on the ad.

Another way to grow ad revenue is to increase site value with user contributions. The phrase *use increases value* means that the more people use a site, the more value the site has, and the more people that visit it. Furthermore, the more value a site has, the more its existing users will return. This phenomenon led to the rise of user comments and reviews, blogging, and, within a few years, social media. Ad revenue, as a result, increased because more people were seeing, and clicking on, more ads on their favorite sites.

### Freemium

The **freemium** revenue model offers users a basic service for free and then charges a premium for upgrades or advanced features. For example, LinkedIn earns part of its revenue by selling upgrades to its standard SaaS (software as a service) product. As of May 2015, regular users can access LinkedIn for free; individual upgrades range from $29 to $79 a month and offer advanced search capabilities, greater visibility of user profiles, and more direct email messages to LinkedIn users outside one's network. Similarly, businesses that want to use LinkedIn for recruiting can purchase a Recruiter Corporate account for $120 to $750 a month. About 19 percent of LinkedIn's revenue comes from premium subscriptions, 62 percent from online recruitment, and 19 percent from advertising.[21]

By diversifying its revenue streams, LinkedIn has reduced its dependence on fluctuating ad revenue and ad-blocking software. A recent report by PageFair indicated that 27.6 percent of Web surfers use **ad-blocking software** to filter out advertising content and rarely, if ever, see Internet ads.[22] The report also stated that use of ad-blocking software grew by 69 percent over the past year. SM companies that rely solely on ad revenue may therefore see their share prices plummet if the use of ad-blocking software becomes widespread.

Other ways of generating revenue on SM sites include the sale of apps and virtual goods; donations; and affiliate commissions, or revenue paid as the result of referring paying customers. In 2012, Facebook generated more than $810M in revenue from virtual goods.[23] Wikipedia took in about $52.8M in donations during 2014.[24] Interestingly, some SM companies, like Pinterest, don't generate any revenue at all. They just focus on building a large network of users now and then figuring out how to make money later.

As these examples illustrate, social media is perhaps the ultimate expression of use increasing value. The more communities of practice a site connects with, the more people use the site, and the more incentive people will have to come back again and again. So, social media would seem to be the next great revenue generator, except, possibly, for the movement from PCs to mobile devices.

## DOES MOBILITY REDUCE ONLINE AD REVENUE?

The transition from PCs to mobile devices presents another interesting question related to social media. Specifically, the ad click revenue model described in the previous section emerged on PC devices where there is plenty of space for lots of ads. But now, as users increasingly move from PCs to mobile devices, particularly small-screen smartphones, there is much less ad space available. Does this mean a reduction in ad revenue?

On the surface, the answer is yes. According to eMarketer, mobile ad spending increased more than 100 percent in 2014 to $42B, accounting for 29 percent of total digital ad spending.[25] By 2019, as shown in Figure 8-8, mobile ad spending should reach $195B and account for 70 percent of total digital ad spending. However, growth in the number of mobile devices far exceeds PC growth. In 2014, for example, global mobile data traffic increased by 69 percent, and the number of mobile devices worldwide exceeded 7 billion. By 2019, the number of mobile devices is expected to reach 10 billion, which will exceed the world's population.[26] Cisco predicts that by 2019, smartphones will account for 75 percent of total global mobile traffic.[27] So, even though

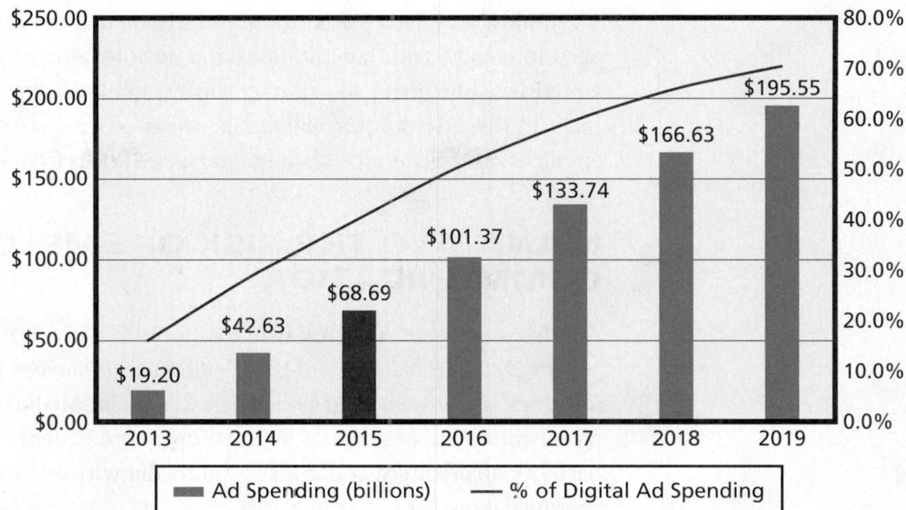


**Figure 8-8**
Mobile Ad Spending

the revenue per device may be lower for mobile devices than PCs, the sheer number of mobile devices in use may swamp the difference in revenue.

Furthermore, the number of devices is not the whole story. According to Marin Software, the average click-through rate of smartphones is 3.75 percent, while that same rate on PCs is 2.29 percent.[28] So, mobile users click ads more often and hence generate more revenue. This is especially true in Facebook's case. In the first quarter of 2015, 87 percent of Facebook users visited from a mobile device, and 73 percent of their total ad revenue came from mobile ads.[29]

However, clicks aren't the final story. Because ads take up so much more space on mobile devices than they do on PCs, many of the mobile clicks could have been accidental. **Conversion rate** measures the frequency that someone who clicks on an ad makes a purchase, "likes" a site, or takes some other action desired by the advertiser. According to Monetate, conversion rates for PCs (3.41 percent) are higher than those for tablets (2.86 percent) or smartphones (0.92 percent). So, on average, PC ad clicks are more effective than mobile clicks.[30]

Clickstream data is easy to gather, and as we have seen, analyses of it are widespread. It's possible, for example, to measure click and conversion rates by type of mobile device. According to Moovweb, iOS users have higher conversion rates than Android users, 1.18 percent versus 1.04 percent.[31] But why? Is it the device? Is it the way the ads are integrated into the user experience? Is it the user? Are iOS users more curious than Android users? Or do they have more spendable income? We do not know for sure.

What we can conclude from this morass of confusing data, however, is that mobile devices are unlikely to spell the death of the Web/social media revenue model. The users are there, the interest is there, and what remains is a design problem: how best to configure the mobile experience to obtain legitimate clicks and conversions. The computer industry is superb at solving design problems; given the current dynamic evolution of mobile interfaces and USX, active, interesting, and compelling ways of presenting ads in iOS/Android/Windows 10 environments are just around the corner.

## Q8-5 HOW CAN ORGANIZATIONS ADDRESS SMIS SECURITY CONCERNS?

Twenty years ago, most organizations managed all public and internal messaging with the highest degree of control. Every press conference, press release, public interview, presentation, and even academic paper needed to be preapproved by both the legal and marketing departments. Such approval could take weeks or months.

Today, progressive organizations have turned that model on its head. Employees are encouraged to engage with communities and, in most organizations, to identify themselves with their employer while doing so. All of this participation, all of this engagement, however, comes with risks. In this question, we will discuss the need for a social media policy, consider risks from non-employee user-generated content, and look at risks from employee use of social media.

## MANAGING THE RISK OF EMPLOYEE COMMUNICATION

The first step that any organization should take is to develop and publicize a **social media policy**, which is a statement that delineates employees' rights and responsibilities. You can find an index to 100 different policies at the Social Media Today Web site.[32] In general, the more technical the organization, the more open and lenient the social policies. The U.S. military has, perhaps surprisingly, endorsed social media with enthusiasm, tempered by the need to protect classified data.

Intel Corporation has pioneered open and employee-trusting SM policies, policies that continue to evolve as they gain more experience with employee-written social media. The three key pillars of its policy in 2015 are:

- Disclose
- Protect
- Use Common Sense[33]

Those policies are further developed as shown in Figure 8-9. Visit *www.intel.com/content/www/us/en/legal/intel-social-media-guidelines.html*. Read this policy carefully; it contains great advice and considerable wisdom.

Two elements in this list are particularly noteworthy. The first is the call for transparency and truth. As an experienced and wise business professional once told me, "Nothing is more serviceable than the truth." It may not be convenient, but it is serviceable, long term. Second, SM contributors and their employers should be open and candid. If you make a mistake, don't obfuscate; instead, correct it, apologize, and make amends. The SM world is too open, too broad, and too powerful to fool.

In 2013, Justine Sacco, a PR executive at IAC, was boarding a plane headed to South Africa and tweeted, "Going to Africa. Hope I don't get AIDS. Just kidding. I'm white." When she landed, she found out that she had been fired in flight and had elicited thousands of hostile posts.

The best way to avoid these types of missteps is to include an SM awareness module in users' annual security training. Social media is still new to many users. Honestly, they may be unaware a policy even exists. When cell phones first became popular they were constantly ringing in movie theaters. Over time, people learned to mute their phones before entering a crowded theater. It just takes time for society to catch up to technology. Training helps.

**Figure 8-9**
Intel's Rules of Social Media Engagement

*Source:* Intel Social Media Guidelines, Intel, accessed May 7, 2015, *www.intel.com/content/www/us/en/legal/intel-social-media-guidelines.html*.

| | |
|---|---|
| Disclose | Be transparent—use your real name and employer<br>Be truthful—point out if you have a vested interest<br>Be yourself—stick to your expertise and write what you know |
| Protect | Don't tell secrets<br>Don't slam the competition<br>Don't overshare |
| Use Common Sense | Add value—make your contribution worthwhile<br>Keep it cool—don't inflame or respond to every criticism<br>Admit mistakes—be upfront and quick with corrections |

## MANAGING THE RISK OF INAPPROPRIATE CONTENT

As with any relationship, comments can be inappropriate in content, excessively negative in tone, or otherwise problematic. Organizations need to determine how they will deal with such issues before engaging in social media. This is done by designating a single individual to be responsible for official organizational SM interactions and by creating a process to monitor and manage SM interactions. This allows the organization to have a clear, coordinated, and consistent message.

**User-generated content (UGC)**, which simply means content on your SM site that is contributed by users, is the essence of SM relationships. Below are a few examples of inappropriate UGC that can negatively affect organizations.

### Problems from External Sources

The major sources of UGC problems are:

- Junk and crackpot contributions
- Inappropriate content
- Unfavorable reviews
- Mutinous movements

When a business participates in a social network or opens its site to UGC, it opens itself to misguided people who post junk unrelated to the site's purpose. Crackpots may also use the network or UGC site as a way of expressing passionately held views about unrelated topics, such as UFOs, government cover-ups, fantastic conspiracy theories, and so forth. Because of the possibility of such content, organizations should regularly monitor the site and remove objectionable material immediately. Monitoring can be done by employees or companies such as Bazaarvoice that offer services not only to collect and manage ratings and reviews but also to monitor the site for irrelevant content.

Unfavorable reviews are another risk. Research indicates that customers are sophisticated enough to know that few, if any, products are perfect. Most customers want to know the disadvantages of a product before purchasing it so they can determine if those disadvantages are important for their application. However, if every review is bad, if the product is rated 1 star out of 5, then the company is using social media to publish its problems. In this case, some action must be taken, as described next.

Mutinous movements are an extension of bad reviews. In January 2012, McDonald's opened a Twitter campaign to promote customer stories. Within a few hours, it was clear that disgruntled customers were hijacking the campaign. McDonald's pulled the Twitter hashtag, and within a few hours negative conversations stopped. To be able to respond promptly, McDonald's created a contingency plan for dealing with unwanted results in all of its social media marketing.[34]

### Responding to Social Networking Problems

Part of managing social networking risk is to know the sources of potential problems and to monitor sites for problematic content. Once such content is found, however, organizations needs to respond appropriately. Three possibilities are:

- Leave it
- Respond to it
- Delete it

If the problematic content represents reasonable criticism of the organization's products or services, the best response may be to leave it where it is. Such criticism indicates that the site is not just a shill for the organization but contains legitimate user content. Such criticism also serves as a free source of product reviews, which can be useful for product development. For the criticism to be useful, the development team needs to know about it, so, as stated, processes to ensure the criticism is found and communicated to the team are necessary.

A second alternative is to respond to the problematic content. However, this alternative is dangerous. If the response can be construed in any way as patronizing or insulting to the content contributor, it can enrage the community and generate a strong backlash. Also, if the response appears defensive, it can become a public relations negative.

In most cases, responses are best reserved for when the problematic content has caused the organization to do something positive as a result. For example, suppose a user publishes that he or she was required to hold for customer support for 45 minutes. If the organization has done something to reduce wait times, then an effective response to the criticism is to recognize it as valid and state, nondefensively, what has been done to reduce wait times.

If a reasoned, nondefensive response generates continued and unreasonable UGC from that same source, it is best for the organization to do nothing. Never wrestle with a pig; you'll get dirty and the pig will enjoy it. Instead, allow the community to constrain the user. It will.

Deleting content should be reserved for contributions that are inappropriate because they are contributed by crackpots, they have nothing to do with the site, or they contain obscene or otherwise inappropriate content. However, deleting legitimate negative comments can result in a strong user backlash. In the early days of social media, Nestlé created a PR nightmare on its Facebook account with its response to criticism it received about its use of palm oil. Someone altered the Nestlé logo, and in response Nestlé decided to delete all Facebook contributions that used that altered logo and did so in an arrogant, heavy-handed way. The result was a negative firestorm on Twitter.[35]

A sound principle in business is to never ask a question to which you do not want the answer. We can extend that principle to social networking; never set up a site that will generate content for which you have no effective response!

## Internal Risks from Social Media

The increased adoption of social media has created new risks within organizations. These risks can be threats to information security, increased organizational liability, and decreased employee productivity.

First, the use of social media can directly affect the ability of the organization to secure their information resources. For example, suppose a senior-level employee tweets, "Married 20 years ago today in Dallas," or "Class of 1984 reunion at Central High School was awesome," or "remembering my honeymoon to Hawaii." All of these tweets provide attackers with the answers to password reset questions. Once attackers reset the user's passwords they could have full access to internal systems. Thus, seemingly innocuous comments can inadvertently leak information used to secure access to organizational resources. Unfortunately, it turns out that it's not a good idea to tell everyone it's your birthday because your date of birth (DOB) can be used to steal your identity.

Employees using social media can unintentionally (or intentionally) leak information about intellectual property, new marketing campaigns, future products, potential layoffs, budget woes, product flaws, or upcoming mergers. It's not just information leakage, either. Employees may install unauthorized apps that deliver content using SM that bypasses existing security measures. Or, worse, they may use their corporate password at less secure SM sites.

Second, employees may inadvertently increase corporate liability when they use social media. For example, suppose a coworker regularly looks at SM content with questionable sexual content on his or her own smartphone. The organization could be slapped with a sexual harassment lawsuit. Other organizations may face legal issues if employees leak information via social media. Schools, healthcare providers, and financial institutions must all follow specific guidelines to protect user data and avoid regulatory compliance violations. Tweeting about students, patients, or customer accounts could have legal consequences.

Finally, the increased use of social media can be a threat to employee productivity. Posts, tweets, pins, likes, comments, and endorsements all take time. This is time employers are paying for, but not benefiting from. Forbes notes that 64 percent of employees visit non-work related Web sites each day. Among the SM sites that are most detrimental to employee productivity include Tumblr (57 percent), Facebook (52 percent), Twitter (17 percent), Instagram (11 percent), and SnapChat (4 percent).[36]

From an employee's point of view, you might think a little lost productivity is OK. But imagine you're the employer or manager, which hopefully you'll be at some point. Would you mind if your employees spend their days using SM to look for another job, chat with friends, or look at vacation pictures when your paycheck is tied to their productivity? What if SM was being used for interoffice gossip that created HR problems, morale issues, and possible lawsuits? Smart managers will understand that, like any technology, SM comes with both benefits and costs.

## Q8-6 WHERE IS SOCIAL MEDIA TAKING US?

So much change is in the air: social media, Web 2.0, Enterprise 2.0. Is there an Enterprise 3.0 around the corner? Will social media become more unified on a single platform, or become more fragmented across many different platforms? We don't know. However, new mobile devices with innovative mobile-device UX, coupled with dynamic and agile information systems based on cloud computing and dynamic virtualization, guarantee that monumental changes will continue to occur over the next 10 years.

Organizations like Harvard, Microsoft, and Starbucks are concerned enough with SM that they have hired Chief Digital Officers (CDOs), a position responsible for developing and managing innovative social media programs.[37]

Advance the clock 10 years. You're now the product marketing manager for an important new product series for your company...the latest in a line of, say, intelligent home appliances. How are you going to promote your products? Will your machines do SM with family members? Will your refrigerators publish what kids are eating after school on the family's social media site? And what even more creative ideas will you need to have by then?

Think about your role as a manager in ten years. Your team has 10 people, three of whom report to you; two report to other managers; and five work for different companies. Your company uses OpenGizmo 2025 with integrated mobile video, augmented by Google/Facebook's Whammo++ Star, all of which have many features that enable employees and teams to instantly publish their ideas in blogs, wikis, videos, and whatever other means have become available. Your employees no longer are assigned computers at work; a liberal, yet secure, BYOD policy enables them to use their own devices, often in their own unique way. Of course, your employees have their own accounts on whatever Facebook, Twitter, LinkedIn, foursquare, and other social networking sites have become popular, and they regularly contribute to them.

How do you manage this team? If "management" means to plan, organize, and control, how can you accomplish any of these functions in this emergent network of employees? If you and your organization follow the lead of tech-savvy companies such as Intel, you'll know you cannot close the door on your employees' SM lives, nor will you want to. Instead, you'll harness the power of the social behavior of your employees and partners to advance your strategy.

In the context of CRM, the vendor might lose control of the customer relationship. Customers use all the vendor's touch points they can find to craft their own relationships. Emergence in the context of management means loss of control of employees. Employees craft their own relationships with their employers, whatever that might mean in ten years. Certainly it means a loss of control, one that is readily made public to the world.

In the 1960s, when someone wanted to send a letter to Don Draper at Sterling Cooper, his or her secretary addressed the envelope to Sterling Cooper and down at the bottom added, "Attention: Don Draper." The letter was to Sterling Cooper and, oh, by the way, also to Don Draper.

Email changed that. Today, someone would send an email to *DonDraper@SterlingCooper.com* or even just to *Don@SterlingCooper.com*. That address is to a person and then to the company.

Social media changes addresses further. When Don Draper creates his own blog, people respond to Don's Blog and only incidentally do they notice in the "About Don" section of the blog that Don works for Sterling Cooper. In short, the focus has moved in 50 years from organizations covering employee names to employees covering organization names.

Does this mean that organizations go away? Hardly. They are needed to raise and conserve capital and to organize vast groups of people and projects. No group of loosely affiliated people can envision, design, develop, manufacture, market, sell, and support an iPad. Organizations are required.

So what, then? Maybe we can take a lesson from biology. Crabs have an external exoskeleton. Deer, much later in the evolutionary chain, have an internal endoskeleton. When crabs grow, they must endure the laborious and biologically expensive process of shedding a small shell and growing a larger one. They are also vulnerable during the transition. When deer grow, the skeleton is inside and it grows with the deer. No need for vulnerable molting. And, considering agility, would you take a crab over a deer?

In the 1960s, organizations were the exoskeleton around employees. In 10 years, organizations will be the endoskeleton, supporting the work of people on the exterior.

Mobility + cloud + social media mean fascinating opportunities for your nonroutine cognitive skills in the next 10 years!

## How does the **knowledge** in this chapter help **you?**

You already know how to use Facebook and Twitter and other social sites for your personal use. This chapter has shown you how to apply some of your knowledge to help organizations. You learned the components of a social media IS and the commitment that an organization makes when it places a Facebook or Twitter icon on its Web page. You also learned how organizations use SMIS to achieve their strategies across the five primary value chain activities and how SMIS can increase social capital. Finally, you learned how revenue can be earned from social media, how organizations need to manage the risks of social media, and how social media will challenge you in the future.

Stay tuned, however; the story is evolving. When you read about social media developments in the future, think about organizations and not just your own use.

# Ethics Guide

## Synthetic Friends

You've just been hired as a marketing manager for a national clothing retailer. Your boss has made it crystal clear that your predecessor was fired because she couldn't get any traction with the company's social media campaign. He wants results—soon. This is your dream job, and you don't want to lose it.

You read an online news article about a person who bought an army of bots that would follow him on Instagram. This could immediately inflate your follower count and show your boss that you're making real progress. Of course, the bots wouldn't be real followers, but if your follower count goes up, it might be easier to attract real human followers. People like popular people.

You do some searching and find an online forum where users are bragging about how realistic their bots are. You even find Web sites (click farms) that advertise Facebook "likes" for sale. You decide to spend $100 and see what happens. You end up getting 15,000 followers that slowly trickle in over the next couple weeks. Not bad. Not bad at all. Real progress that you can show your boss. Well, maybe not "real" progress. But at least it's progress.

You start looking at the profiles of your newly minted synthetic friends and find that they're pretty easy to identify. They only put one word in their name field. But the photos, names, and other content look very believable. You also noticed that you've started to attract annoying spammy accounts that leave URLs and discount codes in their comments. This is buggy, but it helps push up your follower count and that might mean more real followers.

Then comes the purge. Only a few months into your campaign, Instagram starts deleting bots! You lose about 2,000 followers overnight. Ouch. But you still have loads of fictitious followers left. Justin Bieber had the worst hit—3.5 million followers deleted in one day.[38] Other celebrities lost millions of followers as well. You check the news, and it looks like nearly every company, actor, singer, politician, and popular user on Instagram lost followers. You immediately get a sinking feeling in the pit of your stomach. What if you're not the only one who bought followers?

## DISCUSSION QUESTIONS

**1.** Consider your decision to use company funds to buy an army of bot followers.

**a.** Is your action ethical according to the categorical imperative (pages 20–21)?

**b.** Is your action ethical according to the utilitarian perspective (pages 46–47)?

**c.** What would your boss say if he found out that all of their new corporate followers and Facebook likes are fake?

**2.** Consider Instagram's action to purge bot accounts.

**a.** Is it ethical for Instagram to delete followers? Consider both the categorical imperative and utilitarian perspectives.

**b.** Is it ethical for Instagram to allow any bots at all? Consider both the categorical imperative and utilitarian perspectives.

**3.** How hard should Instagram, or any other social media company, work to eliminate bots?

**4.** Suppose a social media startup decides to become a publicly traded company. It hasn't been profitable—yet. The number of average monthly users is one of the primary means of valuing the company.

**a.** Does it have a *legal* obligation to find out how many of its users are bots?

**b.** Does it have an *ethical* obligation to find out how many of its users are bots?

**c.** Is there any way for investors to determine how many users are bots? How?

**5.** Consider the position of an advertising agency, or social media company that sells your firm advertising.

**a.** Suppose your company is charged based on the number of ads shown to users and the number of clicks on those ads. Does the advertising agency have an ethical obligation to find out how many of the ads it sells are seen by actual humans—not bots?

**b.** The advertising agency offers to sell you "likes" for a new product line you're launching. It tells you that buying likes is just like hiring actors for a TV commercial. You're paying them to say they like your product. Is it ethical to buy or sell likes? Consider both the categorical imperative and utilitarian perspectives.

*Source:* gilbertc/Fotolia

# Guide

## Digital Is Forever

Have you ever told a friend something and asked him or her to keep it private? Most people have. Unfortunately, at some point, the person you confided in violated your trust. He or she shared that information with someone else. If so, you can probably recall the horrible feeling that accompanied the thought of other people knowing things you wanted kept private.

This is how several A-list celebrities felt when scores of their personal and highly sensitive photos stored in iCloud were hacked and subsequently plastered all over the Internet. You may be wondering how this could happen—how could cybercriminals access the private data of someone else stored on an iCloud account?

It turns out there was a security vulnerability associated with Apple's Find My iPhone application. Safeguards had not been implemented by Apple to limit the number of login attempts permitted before an account would be locked, a common security practice used to prevent hackers from entering endless combinations of usernames and passwords in an exhaustive attempt to guess the correct set of credentials (referred to as a brute-force attack).[39]

The celebrities affected by these attacks are still trying to remove their private data from the Web. The sad truth is that their private data will never completely be removed. Even more sobering is the fact that anyone who chooses to transmit any personal information using an Internet connection (i.e., send something via email, post something on a social media site, etc.) can become a victim, too.

### Privacy? What's That?

Once you click the button to send an email, post a photo, or share a video, you lose control over that data. It can be copied, shared, and copied again. Your data will travel through numerous servers until it is delivered to the intended recipient. It will also be stored on a data farm owned by the company whose app you're using. You can *never* withdraw this information—and once it is transmitted, it is nearly impossible (and in most cases, impossible) to delete.

Think about it this way. Have you ever heard the saying that "two can keep a secret if one of them is dead"? Well, from a technology perspective, "two *can't* keep a secret if one of them is the Internet." Anything shared over the Internet morphs into a digital zombie, destined to wander the far reaches of cyberspace forever!

You may think that as long as you are sharing messages or photos with a trusted party you have nothing to worry about. Unfortunately, our digital world is rife with cybercriminals who spend countless hours trying to steal data from both companies and everyday citizens (just ask the Apple iCloud victims).

And cybercriminals aren't the only ones trying to take advantage of your personal data. Companies see the value in accessing and running various analyses on everything you digitally say or do. Google, for example, scans the contents of your emails sent through Gmail so it can serve you targeted ads. In fact, Google looks at more than just your emails. Google also looks at your search queries, the sites you visit, and your Google profile in an effort to make its ads more relevant.[40]

## Big Data = Big Money

Taking into account the actions of both cybercriminals and corporations, we can infer one thing—accessing the private data of Internet users equals big money as personal data can be (1) illegally accessed by criminals and sold on the black market to other nefarious actors or (2) legally accessed by companies and sold to other companies. The good news is that high-profile privacy breaches like the iCloud incident raise awareness for everyone concerning the risks of storing or sharing personal information online.

For example, a recent poll conducted by the Pew Research Center found that "86% of Internet users have taken steps online to remove or mask their digital footprints—ranging from clearing cookies to encrypting their email, from avoiding using their name to using virtual networks that mask their internet protocol (IP) address."[41] This is encouraging, but they can do more. Rather than spending time trying to erase their digital footprint, users need to keep from making tracks in the first place. Think before you click, share, or post. Digital is forever.

### DISCUSSION QUESTIONS

**1.** The guide emphasizes that criminals and corporations both seek out the private data of Internet users for their own gains, but they are not the only ones trying to access your data. Why do you think employers might seek out data about applicants when making their hiring decisions?

**2.** You likely heard news reports about the iCloud and Sony breaches, both of which resulted in private photos and emails being shared with the masses on the Internet. But can you recall hearing about the perpetrators being brought to justice? If not, why do you think this is the case?

**3.** Stolen or compromised devices can also be used to access your private data. Even if that data has been deleted. Search the Web for information about software used to recover deleted files. Does normal deletion permanently remove a file from the memory of your device? Can it be recovered? How?

**4.** Take a few minutes to reflect on your online habits. Have you sent emails or posted messages or images that could be perceived as controversial in nature? Are there posts that you wouldn't want a future employer to see? How might your emails or posts affect your career?

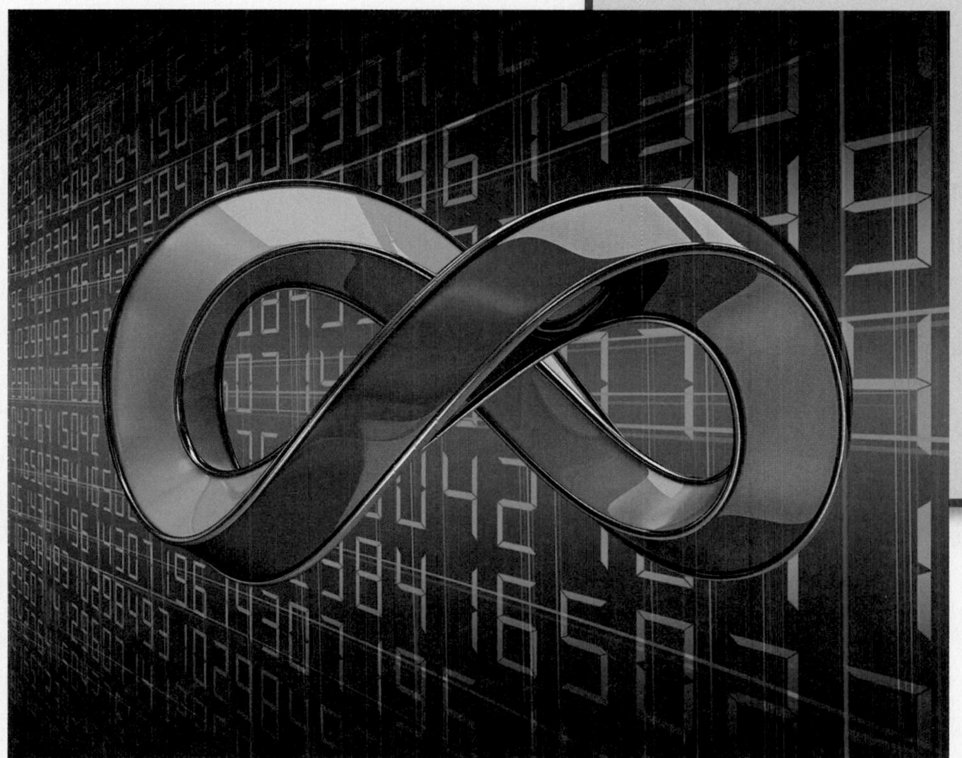

*Source:* valdis torms/Fotolia and vilisov/Fotolia

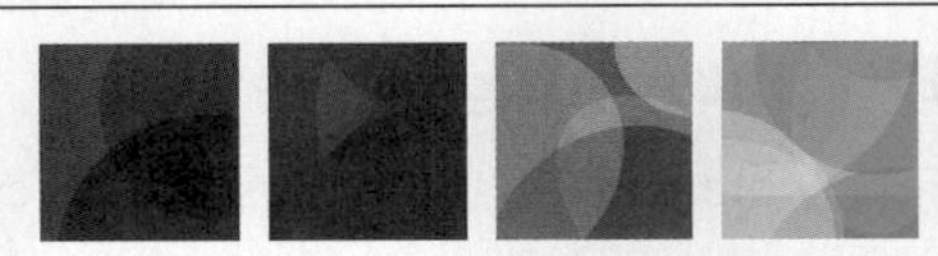

Use this Active Review to verify that you understand the ideas and concepts that answer this chapter's study questions.

## Q8-1 WHAT IS A SOCIAL MEDIA INFORMATION SYSTEM (SMIS)?

Define *social media, communities of practice, social media information systems, social media provider,* and *social networks*. Name and describe three SMIS organizational roles. Explain the elements of Figure 8-3. In your own words, explain the nature of the five components of SMIS for each of the three SMIS organizational roles.

## Q8-2 HOW DO SMIS ADVANCE ORGANIZATIONAL STRATEGY?

Summarize how social media contributes to sales and marketing, customer support, inbound logistics, outbound logistics, manufacturing and operations, and human resources. Name SM risks for each activity. Define *social CRM* and *crowdsourcing*.

## Q8-3 HOW DO SMIS INCREASE SOCIAL CAPITAL?

Define *capital, human capital,* and *social capital*. Explain four ways that social capital adds value. Name three factors that determine social capital and explain how "they are more multiplicative than additive." Define *influencer* and describe how you could use social media to increase the number and strength of your social relationships.

## Q8-4 HOW DO (SOME) COMPANIES EARN REVENUE FROM SOCIAL MEDIA?

Define *monetize* and describe why it's difficult for social media companies to generate revenue. Give examples of how social media companies generate revenue from advertising and charging for premium services. Define *pay-per-click, conversion rate,* and *freemium*. Define *ad blocking* and explain how it hurts online companies' ability to generate revenue. Summarize how growth in mobile devices affected revenue streams. Explain why concerns about mobile devices limiting ad revenue are overreactions.

## Q8-5 HOW CAN ORGANIZATIONS ADDRESS SMIS SECURITY CONCERNS?

Name and describe two sources of SM risk. Describe the purpose of an SM policy, and summarize Intel's guiding principles. Describe an SM mistake, other than one in this text, and explain the wise response to it. Name four sources of problems of user-generated content; name three possible responses and give the advantages and disadvantages of each. Explain how internal use of social media can create risks to information security, organizational liability, and employee productivity.

## Q8-6 WHERE IS SOCIAL MEDIA TAKING US?

Describe ways in which the use of social media is changing today. Summarize possible management challenges when controlling employees 10 years in the future. Describe the text's suggested response. How does the change in forms of address since the 1960s indicate a change in the relationship of employees and organizations to the business world? Explain the relationship of the differences between crab and deer to this change.

## How does the **knowledge** in this chapter help **you?**

You know how to use Facebook and Twitter. Explain how each of the questions addressed in this chapter will help you help your employers to use them as well. Summarize the challenges (and opportunities) that social media will present to you, a future manager.

## KEY TERMS AND CONCEPTS

Ad-blocking software 226
Business-to-business (B2B) 218
Business-to-consumer (B2C) 218
Capital 220
Communities 211
Communities of practice 211
Connection data 215
Content data 215
Conversion rate 227
Crowdsourcing 218
Freemium 226
Human capital 220

MyMISLab™

To complete the problems with the ✪, go to EOC Discussion Questions in the MyLab.

## USING YOUR KNOWLEDGE

✪ **8-1.** Using the Facebook page of a company that you have "liked" (or would choose to), fill out the five components of an SMIS grid shown in Q8-1. Strive to replace the phrases in the description column of that grid with specific statements that pertain to Facebook, the company you like, and you and users whom you know. For example, if you and your friends access Facebook using an Android phone, enter that specific device.

✪ **8-2.** Name a company for which you would like to work. Describe, as specifically as you can, how that company could use social media in each of the areas from Q8-2 listed below. Include community type, specific focus, processes involved, risks, and any other observations.

**a.** Sales and marketing
**b.** Customer service
**c.** Inbound logistics
**d.** Outbound logistics
**e.** Manufacturing and operations
**f.** Human resources

**8-3.** Visit *www.lie-nielsen.com* or *www.sephora.com*. On the site you chose, find links to social networking sites. In what ways are those sites sharing their social capital with you? In what ways are they attempting to cause you to share your social capital with them? Describe the business value of social networking to the business you chose.

## COLLABORATION EXERCISE 8

*Read Chapter Extensions 1 and 2 if you have not already done so. Meet with your team and build a collaboration IS that uses tools like Google Docs, SharePoint, or other collaboration tools. Do not forget the need for procedures and team training. Now, using that IS, answer the questions below.*

Twitter's IPO on November 7, 2013, was one of the biggest tech IPOs in history. The social media giant's stock closed that day at $44.90 a share, making it worth an estimated $25B.[42] Not bad for a company that had never made a profit. In fact, Twitter posted a $70M loss the quarter before listing! How could a company be worth $25B and never have made any money?

Analysts argue that tech companies like those shown in Figure 8-10 should be valued based on growth potential, user base, consumer engagement, and market size. It turns out that Amazon.com, Instagram, and Pinterest weren't profitable when they went public, either.

Traditional IPO valuations focus on measures of profitability. This means investors look at revenues, profits, assets, liabilities, and new products. Figure 8-10 shows price-to-earnings ratios (P/E) for several well-known companies. Using iteration and feedback, answer the following questions:

**8-4.** Compare the tech companies' P/E ratios in Figure 8-10 with the traditional companies' P/E ratios. Note that some of the tech companies have very high P/E ratios (a low P/E is good, a high P/E is bad). Some don't even have a P/E ratio because they didn't turn a profit. As

| Tech Companies | Market Cap ($) | P/E |
|---|---|---|
| Apple | 721.63B | 16.96 |
| Google | 368.92B | 25.82 |
| Facebook | 219.51B | 75.63 |
| Amazon.com | 198.24B | N/A |
| Netflix | 34.20B | 147.31 |
| LinkedIn | 25.35B | N/A |
| Twitter | 24.68B | N/A |

| Traditional Companies | Market Cap ($) | P/E |
|---|---|---|
| General Electric | 272.23B | N/A |
| Wal-Mart Stores | 251.73B | 15.45 |
| Verizon Comm. | 202.80B | 20.88 |
| Toyota | 216.92B | 12.91 |
| BP | 126.88B | 34.17 |
| Johnson & Johnson | 277.11B | 17.48 |
| Ford | 61.65B | 19.44 |

**Figure 8-10**
Tech Company Valuations

a group, list the reasons why the tech companies have such high P/E ratios. Are the prices of these stocks justified given the earnings? Why?

**8-5.** Identify public tech stocks you believe are undervalued (not limited to those shown in Figure 8-10). Design an investment portfolio consisting solely of tech stocks that you believe will be profitable. Justify your decision with regards to risk and return on those stocks.

**8-6.** Create a free online portfolio of these stocks (e.g., via Yahoo! Finance) and track its progress. Report on its performance.

**8-7.** Could overvalued tech stocks lead to a dot-com 2.0 crash like the original in 1999–2001? Discuss why this may or may not happen. Summarize your discussion in a couple of paragraphs.

# CASE STUDY 8

## Sedona Social

Sedona, Arizona, is a small city of 10,000 people that is surrounded by Coconino National Forest. At an elevation of 4,500 feet, it is considerably higher than the valley cities of Phoenix and Tucson, but 2,000 feet below the altitude of Flagstaff. This middle elevation provides a moderate climate that is neither too hot in the summer nor too cold in the winter. Sedona is surrounded by gorgeous sandstone red/orange rocks and stunning red rock canyons, as shown in Figure 8-11.

This beautiful city was the location for more than 60 movies, most of them westerns, between the 1930s and the 1950s. If you've ever watched an old black-and-white western, it could very likely have been situated in Sedona. Among the well-known movies located in Sedona are *Stagecoach, Johnny Guitar, Angel and the Badman,* and *3:10 to Yuma.*

Many who visit Sedona believe there is something peaceful yet energizing about the area, especially in certain locations known as *vortices*, according to VisitSedona.com.

"Vortex sites are enhanced energy locations that facilitate prayer, meditation, mind/body healing, and exploring your relationship with your Soul and the divine. They are neither electric nor magnetic."[43]

Tests with scientific instruments have failed to identify any unusual readings of known energy types, and yet many people, of all religions and religious persuasions, believe there is something about Sedona that facilitates spiritual practice. For a city of its size, Sedona has many more churches than one might expect, including the Catholic Chapel of the Holy Cross (Figure 8-12), Protestant churches of many dominations, the Latter-Day Saints (Mormon) church, the local synagogue, and the new-age Sedona Creative Life Center.

Because it is situated in the middle of a national forest, Sedona is surrounded by hundreds of miles of hiking trails; it is possible to hike every day for a year and not use all the trails. The area was home to Native Americans in the twelfth and thirteenth centuries, and there are numerous cliff dwellings and other native sites nearby.

As a relatively young modern city, Sedona does not have the cultural history of Santa Fe or Taos, New Mexico. Nonetheless, there is a burgeoning arts community centered around Tlaquepaque, a 1980s-built shopping area modeled on a Mexican city of the same name.

As with many tourist destinations, there are tensions. Pink Jeep Tours (see Figure 8-13) runs daily trips of raucous tourists past vortices occupied by meditating spiritual practitioners. With its Hollywood past, Sedona is home to many Los Angeles expatriates, and at the local health food store it's possible to see 50-something blond women wearing tight pants and jewel-studded, fresh-from-Rodeo-Drive sandals fighting for the last pound of organic asparagus with aging male hippies shaking their white-gray ponytails off the shoulders of their tie-dyed shirts.

**Figure 8-11**
Sedona Red Rocks

*Source:* ©David Kroenke

The emerging arts community wants to be serious; the uptown Jeep-riding tourists (see Figure 8-13) want to have fun with four-wheel thrills and margaritas (we hope in that sequence). Hikers want to visit petroglyphs, while nature preservers don't want the locations of those sites to be known. Those seeking spiritual guidance want enlightenment in silence, while the locals want to shut out everyone, just as long, that is, as their property values increase at a steady pace, year by year. Meanwhile, the Lear Jets and Citations fly in and out carrying who-knows-who Hollywood celebrity from her home behind the walls of Seven Canyons Resort. And businesses in town want to have reliable, year-round revenue and not too much competition.

Given all that, let's suppose that the Sedona Chamber of Commerce has just hired you as its first-ever manager of community social media. They want you to provide advice and assistance to local businesses in the development of their social media sites, and they want you to manage their own social media presence as well.

## QUESTIONS

**8-8.** Search Facebook for *Sedona, Arizona*. Examine a variety of Sedona-area pages. Using the knowledge of this chapter and your personal social media experience,

**Figure 8-12**
Chapel of the Holy Cross

*Source:* ©David Kroenke

**Figure 8-13**
Pink Jeep Tours

*Source:* ©David Kroenke

evaluate these pages and list several positive and negative features of each. Make suggestions on ways they could be improved.

**8-9.** Repeat question 8-8 for another social media provider. As of this writing, possibilities are Twitter, LinkedIn, and Pinterest, but choose another social media provider if you wish.

**8-10.** The purpose of a Chamber of Commerce is to foster a healthy business climate for all of the businesses in the community. Given that purpose, your answers to questions 8-8 and 8-9, and the knowledge of this chapter, develop a set of 7 to 10 guidelines for local businesses to consider when developing their social media presence.

**8-11.** Sedona has quite a number of potentially conflicting community groups. Explain three ways the Chamber of Commerce can use social media to help manage conflict so as to maintain a healthy business environment.

**8-12.** Examine Figure 8-5, and state how the focus of each of the primary value chain activities pertains to the Chamber of Commerce. If one does not pertain, explain why. In your answer, be clear about who the Chamber's customers are.

**8-13.** Given your answer to question 8-12 and considering your responsibility to manage the Chamber's social media presences, state how each applicable row of Figure 8-5 guides the social media sites you will create.

**8-14.** Using your answers to these questions, write a job description for yourself.

**8-15.** Write a two-paragraph summary of this exercise that you could use to demonstrate your knowledge of the role of social media in commerce in a future job interview.

## MyMISLab™

Go to the Assignments section of your MyLab to complete these writing exercises.

**8-16.** According to Paul Greenberg, Amazon.com is the master of the 2-minute relationship, and Boeing is the master of the 10-year relationship.[44] Visit *www.boeing.com* and *www.amazon.com*. From Greenberg's statement and from the appearance of these Web sites, it appears that Boeing is committed to traditional CRM and Amazon.com to social CRM. Give evidence from each site that this might be true. Explain why the products and business environment of both companies cause this difference. Is there any justification for traditional CRM at Amazon.com? Why or why not? Is there any justification for social CRM at Boeing? Why or why not? Based on these companies, is it possible that a company might endorse Enterprise Social Networks but not endorse social CRM? Explain.

**8-17.** Suppose you are hired by the Visit California organization to develop a SMIS. The organization wants to promote travel to California, increase awareness about the fun things to do in California, increase traffic to its Web site, and direct visitors to its business partners. Which success metrics would indicate that Visit California has achieved its goals? Who would be the organization's target audience? What value would the SMIS provide to visitors? How could the organization make personal connections with its visitors? Which SM platform(s) would you recommend Visit California use? Justify your recommendation.

## ENDNOTES


1. Shea Bennett, "Pinterest, Twitter, Facebook, Instagram, Google+, LinkedIn—Social Media Stats 2014," All Twitter on MediaBistro.com, January 20, 2014, accessed June 17, 2014, *www.mediabistro.com/alltwitter/social-media-stats-2014_b54243.*
2. Pew Research Internet Project, "Social Networking Fact Sheet," Pew Research, February 27, 2014, accessed May 5, 2015, *www.pewinternet.org/fact-sheets/social-networking-fact-sheet/.*
3. John McDermott, "Pinterest: The No-bro Zone," Digiday.com, February 20, 2014, accessed May 5, 2015, *http://digiday.com/platforms/why-pinterest-is-still-a-predominantly-female-platform/.*
4. Quantcast, LinkedIn.com profile, accessed May 5, 2015, *www.quantcast.com/linkedin.com.*
5. Amy Gesenhues, "Social Media Use Growing Among Fortune 500 List with 77% Tweeting & 70% on Facebook," Marketing Land, July 23, 2013, accessed May 5, 2015, *http://marketingland.com/fortune-500-companys-social-media-use-on-the-rise-52726.*
6. Vernon Smith, *Rationality in Economics: Constructivist and Ecological Forms* (Cambridge, UK: Cambridge University Press, 2007), pp. 247–250.
7. "About Customer Ratings," Amazon.com, accessed July 30, 2013, *www.amazon.com/gp/help/customer/display.html/ref=hp_200791020_vine?nodeId=200791020#vine.*
8. LinkedIn Talent Solutions, "Recruiter," accessed May 5, 2015, *http://business.linkedin.com/talent-solutions/products/recruiter.html.*
9. Erika Welz Prafder, "Hiring Your First Employee," Entrepreneur.com, accessed May 26, 2014, *www.entrepreneur.com/article/83774.*
10. Jobvite Inc., "2014 Social Recruiting Survey," Jobvite.com, August 2014, accessed July 23, 2015, *https://www.jobvite.com/wp-content/uploads/2014/10/Jobvite_SocialRecruiting_Survey2014.pdf.*
11. Nan Lin, *Social Capital: The Theory of Social Structure and Action* (Cambridge, UK: Cambridge University Press, 2002), Kindle location 310.
12. Henk D. Flap, "Social Capital in the Reproduction of Inequality," *Comparative Sociology of Family, Health, and Education*, Vol. 20 (1991), pp. 6179–6202. Cited in Nan Lin, *Social Capital: The Theory of Social Structure and Action* (Cambridge, UK: Cambridge University Press, 2002), Kindle location 345.
13. The Klout Score," *Klout*, accessed May 5, 2015, *http://klout.com/corp/score.*
14. SponsoredTweets.com maintains a list of celebrities, number of their followers, and their price for a sponsored tweet (*https://app.sponsoredtweets.com/tweeters*).
15. Founding father of the United States. Author of *Poor Richard's Almanac.* Successful businessman; owner of a chain of print shops. Discoverer of groundbreaking principles in the theory of electricity. Inventor of bifocals, the potbelly stove, the lightning rod, and much more. Founder of the public library system and the U.S. postal service. Darling of the French court and salons and, now, contributor to social network theory!
16. Nat Ives, "What a YouTube Celeb Pulls In," Adage.com, April 15, 2015, accessed May 5, 2015, *http://adage.com/article/news/a-youtube-celeb-pulls/298015.*
17. Dan Noyes, "The Top 20 Valuable Facebook Statistics," Zephoria.com, June 13, 2014, accessed July 7, 2014, *http://zephoria.com/social-media/top-15-valuable-facebook-statistics/.*
18. "YouTube Press Statistics," YouTube.com, accessed May 5, 2015, *www.youtube.com/yt/press/statistics.html.*
19. Josh Constine, "Facebook Has Mixed Q1 Earnings with Miss on $3.54B Revenue, Beat on $0.42 EPS, User Growth Up to Hit 1.44B," TechCrunch.com, April 22, 2015, accessed May 5, 2015, *http://techcrunch.com/2015/04/22/facebook-q1-2015-earnings.*
20. Twitter Inc., "Twitter Reports First Quarter 2015 Results," Twitterinc.com, April 28, 2015, accessed May 5, 2015, *https://investor.twitterinc.com/results.cfm.*
21. LinkedIn Corporation, "LinkedIn Announces First Quarter 2015 Results," *LinkedIn Investor Relations*, April 30, 2015, accessed May 5, 2015, *http://investors.linkedin.com.*
22. Sean Blanchfield, "Adblocking Goes Mainstream," *PageFair*, August 2014, accessed May 5, 2015, *http://blog.pagefair.com/2014/adblocking-report.*
23. Brittany Darwell, "27M Users Bought Virtual Goods Using Facebook Payments in 2012; Zynga's Influence on Revenue Further Diminishes," InsideSocialGames.com, February 1, 2013, accessed July 7, 2014, *www.insidesocialgames.com/2013/02/01/27m-users-bought-virtual-goods-using-facebook-payments-in-2012-zyngas-influence-on-revenue-further-diminishes/.*
24. Wikimedia Foundation, "2013–2014 Annual Plan Questions and Answers," WikimediaFoundation.org, accessed June 19, 2014, *https://meta.wikimedia.org/wiki/Wikimedia_Foundation/Annual_Report/2013-2014.*
25. eMarketer, "Mobile Ad Spend to Top $100 Billion Worldwide in 2016, 51% of Digital Market," eMarketer.com, April 2, 2015 accessed May 6, 2015, *www.emarketer.com/Article/Mobile-Ad-Spend-Top-100-Billion-Worldwide-2016-51-of-Digital-Market/1012299.*
26. Cisco, "Cisco Visual Networking Index: Global Mobile Data Traffic Forecast Update, 2013–2018," Cisco.com, February 3, 2015, accessed May 6, 2015, *www.cisco.com/c/en/us/solutions/collateral/service-provider/visual-networking-index-vni/white_paper_c11-520862.pdf.*
27. Ibid.
28. Marin Software, "Mobile Search Advertising Around the Globe: 2014 Annual Report," MarinSoftware.com, March 2014, accessed May 6, 2015, *www.marinsoftware.com/resources/whitepapers.*
29. Facebook Inc., "Facebook Reports First Quarter 2015 Results," Facebook.com, April 22, 2015, accessed May 6, 2015, *http://investor.fb.com/releasedetail.cfm?ReleaseID=908022.*
30. Monetate, "Ecommerce Quarterly EQ4 2014: The Gift of Personalization," Monetate.com, February 2015, accessed May 6, 2015, *www.monetate.com/resources/research/#ufh-i-48179143-ecommerce-quarterly-q4-2014.*

31. Moovweb, "Android vs iOS, Are iOS Shoppers More Valuable than Android Shoppers," Moovweb.com, December 9, 2014, accessed May 6, 2015, *www.moovweb.com/blog/android-vs-ios.*
32. Ralph Paglia, "Social Media Employee Policy Examples from Over 100 Organizations," July 3, 2010, *Social Media Today*, accessed May 7, 2015, *http://socialmediatoday.com/ralphpaglia/141903/social-media-employee-policy-examples-over-100-companies-andorganizations.*
33. Intel Social Media Guidelines," *Intel*, accessed May 7, 2015, *www.intel.com/content/www/us/en/legal/intel-social-media-guidelines.html.*
34. Marissa Brassfield, "McDonald's McDStories Twitter Promotion Sparks Huge Backlash," *Foodista*, last modified January 24, 2012, *www.foodista.com/blog/2012/01/24/mcdonalds-mcdstories-twitter-promotion-sparks-huge-backlash.*
35. Bernhard Warner, "Nestlé's 'No Logo' Policy Triggers Facebook Revolt," *Social Media Influence*, March 19, 2010, accessed August 27, 2014, *http://socialmediainfluence.com/2010/03/19/nestles-no-logo-policy-triggers-facebook-revolt/.*
36. Cheryl Conner, "Who Wastes the Most Time at Work," *Forbes*, September 7, 2014, accessed June 24, 2014, *www.forbes.com/sites/cherylsnappconner/2013/09/07/who-wastes-the-most-time-at-work/.*
37. Jennifer Wolfe, "How Marketers Can Shape the Chief Digital Officer Role," *CMO.com*, March 21, 2013, accessed June 21, 2014, *www.cmo.com/articles/2013/3/20/how_marketers_can_shape.html.*
38. Rex Santus, "Justin Bieber Dethroned as King of Instagram in Massive Follower Purge," *Mashable*, December 19, 2013, accessed April 2, 2015, *http://mashable.com/2014/12/19/instagram-purge.*
39. Mohit Kumar, "Apple Patches 'Find My iPhone' Vulnerability Which May Caused Celebrities Photo Leak," *The Hacker News*, September 4, 2014, accessed April 24, 2015, *http://thehackernews.com/2014/09/apple-patches-find-my-iphone.html.*
40. Google, "Ads in Gmail," *Gmail Help*, accessed April 26, 2015, *https://support.google.com/mail/answer/6603?hl=en.*
41. Lee Rainie, Sara Kiesler, Ruogu Kang, and Mary Madden, "Anonymity, Privacy, and Security Online," September 5, 2013, *The Hacker News*, accessed April 26, 2015, *www.pewinternet.org/2013/09/05/anonymity-privacy-and-security-online.*
42. Olivia Oran and Gerry Shih, "Twitter Shares Soar in Frenzied NYSE Debut," November 7, 2013, *Reuters*, accessed May 28, 2014, *www.reuters.com/article/2013/11/07/us-twitter-ipo-idUSBRE99N1AE20131107.*
43. Sedona Chamber of Commerce, accessed August 19, 2013, *www.visitsedona.com/article/151.*
44. Paul Greenberg, *CRM at the Speed of Light*, 4th ed. (New York: McGraw-Hill, 2010), p. 105.

# Business Intelligence Systems

This could happen to you

"What'd you get for lunch, Nicki?" James asks as they walk back to the office together.

"That five-spice beef thing they do at Hong's. You?"

"Oh, pot stickers and stuff from New China."

"That place has good food; I should have gone there with you. Hey, James, I'm wondering if you can help me with something."

"I'll try. What's up?"

"Well, we're tracking winners and runners-up from each of our spinning events, and we're having unbelievable success selling products to them."

"Ah, competition. Participants want something to gain an advantage in the next heat?"

"Right. But I know there's more we can do if we can link in personal trainers somehow. Maybe go after the losers, the people who didn't win their heats. I'd like to send them to a trainer and earn a referral fee back to us... or maybe take a percent of the training fees."

"OK. Makes sense. So, where do you need my help?"

"Where do they live? The racers, I mean. Where are they? Are they clustered geographically? I mean, we don't want to send the name of a trainer in Minneapolis to someone living in San Diego."

"Well, we could ask them for their address when they sign up for the event?"

"Yeah, maybe, justify it by saying we need it for some sort of map we could display. They might like that. But I hate to ask them for anything that distracts them from the races."

"We could use their connection IP addresses. That would tell us where the bikes are that they're using... might not be where they live, though."

"I don't mean where they sleep; I mean where they work out. That would do."

"What if they're traveling?"

"I don't care... most people won't be. I'm not quite sure what I want, and I know that drives you crazy."

"It does for operational things; it's typical for BI."

"What's BI?"

"Business intelligence. Data analysis, where you don't know the second question to ask until you see the answer to the first one."

"Yeah. That's it exactly! That's where I am right now."

# STUDY QUESTIONS

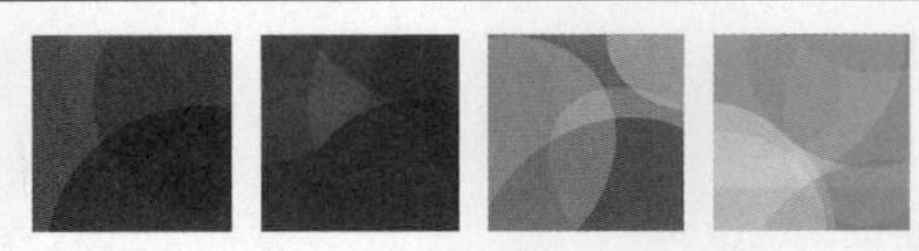

**Q9-1** HOW DO ORGANIZATIONS USE BUSINESS INTELLIGENCE (BI) SYSTEMS?

**Q9-2** WHAT ARE THE THREE PRIMARY ACTIVITIES IN THE BI PROCESS?

**Q9-3** HOW DO ORGANIZATIONS USE DATA WAREHOUSES AND DATA MARTS TO ACQUIRE DATA?

**Q9-4** WHAT ARE THREE TECHNIQUES FOR PROCESSING BI DATA?

**Q9-5** WHAT ARE THE ALTERNATIVES FOR PUBLISHING BI?

## How does the **knowledge** in this chapter help **you?**

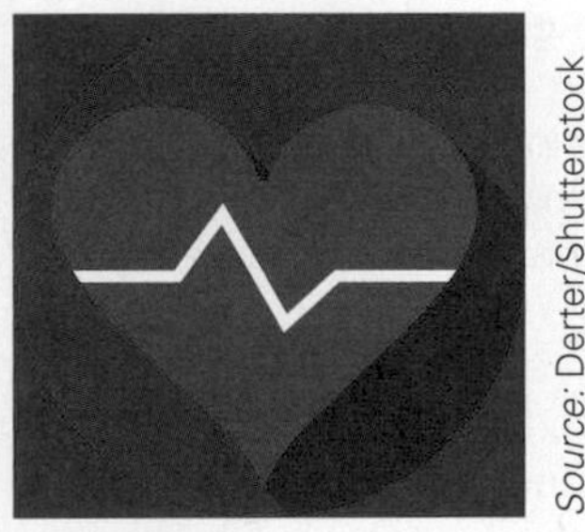

Source: Derter/Shutterstock

**"Data analysis, where you don't know the second question to ask until you see the answer to the first one."**

"Suppose we start with this. I'll sample a bunch of our data, maybe 5,000 racers, and locate them with the connection IP. Then I'll give it to you in an Excel pivot table."

"Yeah, so what?"

"Well, then you can look at it by state, city, and ZIP code and see what we've got."

"How come you're not asking me for budget?"

"I might, but this part is easy. We've got the data, and I can deliver it with Excel. And I've got just one user: *you.* So I don't have to make the UI easy, write documentation, develop procedures, etcetera. Besides, you're a pretty smart user."

"Thanks for the praise..."

"On the other hand, if you take off with this in some crazy way and you want to use it to build something for users or do some serious data mining, set up a data mart, then you'll need to come up with some money for my budget."

"You mean this Excel thing is sort of a taste teaser."

"Yeah, but you've got to like the taste."

"Hope it's better than that five-spice thing."

"See you later."

"When do I get my report?"

"Friday?"

"That soon?"

"It's just a teaser, Nicki."

**Optional Extensions for this chapter are • CE12: Database Marketing 550 CE13: Reporting Systems and OLAP 562**

# Q9-1 HOW DO ORGANIZATIONS USE BUSINESS INTELLIGENCE (BI) SYSTEMS?

**Business intelligence (BI) systems** are information systems that process operational and other data to analyze past performance and to make predictions. The patterns, relationships, and trends identified by BI systems are called **business intelligence**. As information systems, BI systems have the five standard components: hardware, software, data, procedures, and people. The software component of a BI system is called a **BI application**.

In the context of their day-to-day operations, organizations generate enormous amounts of data. AT&T, for example, processes 1.9 trillion call records in its database, and Google stores a database with more than 33 trillion entries.[1] Business intelligence is buried in that data, and the function of a BI system is to extract it and make it available to those who need it.

As shown in Figure 9-1, source data for a BI system can be the organization's own operational databases, it can be social data like that generated by social media IS, it can be data that the organization purchases, and it can be employee knowledge. The BI application processes the data to produce business intelligence for use by knowledge workers. As you will learn, this definition encompasses reporting applications, data mining applications, BigData applications, and knowledge management applications.

## HOW DO ORGANIZATIONS USE BI?

As shown in Figure 9-2, organizations use BI for all four of the collaborative tasks described in Chapter Extension 1. Starting with the last row of this figure, business intelligence is used just for informing. Personal trainers can use PRIDE to learn how clients are using the new system. At the time of the analysis, the staff may not have any particular purpose in mind but are just browsing the BI results for some future, unspecified purpose. At Falcon Security, the company we studied in Chapters 1–6, Mateo may just want to know how Falcon's current sales compare to the forecast; he may have no particular purpose in mind and just want to know "how we're doing."

**Figure 9-1**
Structure of a Business Intelligence System

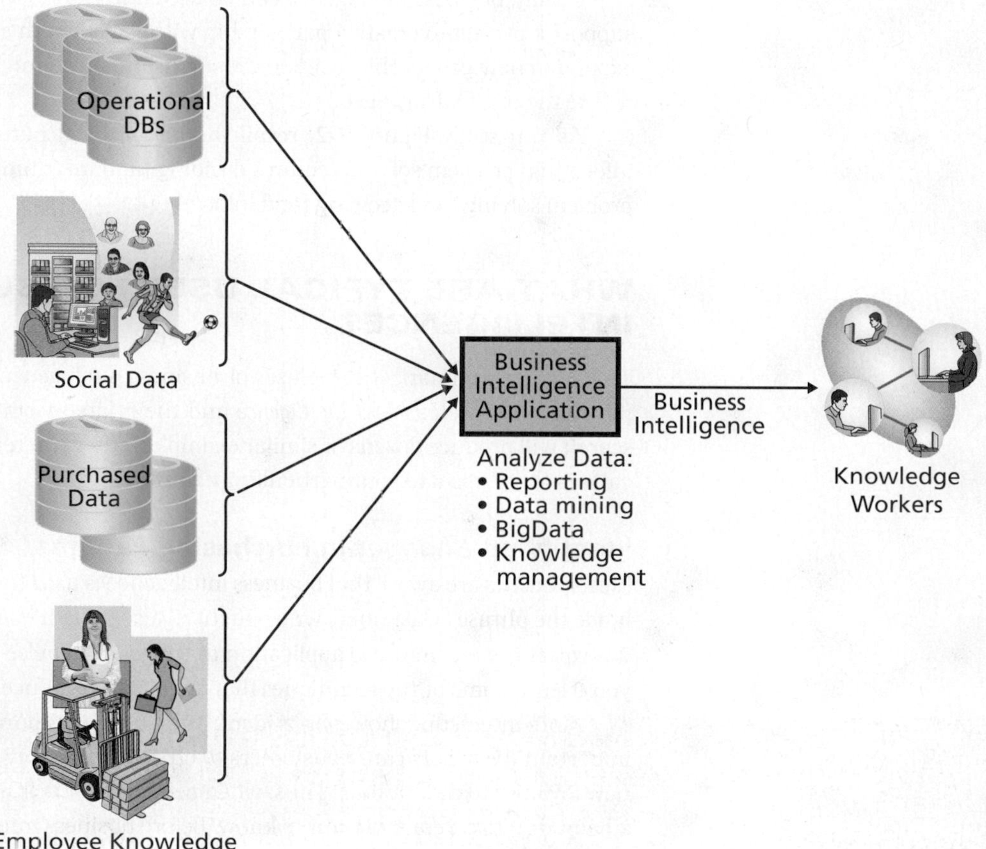

**Figure 9-2**
Example Uses of Business Intelligence

| Task | PRIDE Example | Falcon Security Example |
|---|---|---|
| Project Management | Create a partnership program between PRIDE event clients and local health clubs. | Expand geographically. |
| Problem Solving | How can we increase ad revenue from competitions? | How can we save costs by rerouting drone flights? |
| Deciding | Which competitions generate the most ad revenue? Develop more of the best competitions. | Which drones and equipment are in need of maintenance? |
| Informing | In what ways are clients using the PRIDE system? | How do sales compare to our sales forecast? |

Moving up a row in Figure 9-2, some managers use BI systems for decision making. PRIDE Systems could use BI on its competitive events to determine characteristics of events that generate the most revenue and then conduct more of that type of event. Falcon Security could use a BI analysis of flight failures to decide when it is time to service drones and related camera equipment.

(By the way, some authors define BI systems as supporting decision making only, in which case they use the older term **decision support systems** as a synonym for decision-making BI systems. We take the broader view here to include all four of the tasks in Figure 9-2 and will avoid the term *decision support systems*.)

Problem solving is the next category of business intelligence use. Again, a problem is a perceived difference between what is and what ought to be. Business intelligence can be used for both sides of that definition: determining *what is* as well as *what should be*. If revenue is below expectations, PRIDE Systems can use business intelligence to learn what factors to change to obtain more event attendance and more ad revenue. Falcon Security could use BI to determine whether it could save costs by rerouting its drone flights.

Finally, business intelligence can be used during project management. PRIDE can be used to support a project to create a partnership with local health clubs. When Falcon Security wants to expand to new geographic locations, it can use business intelligence to determine which locations will be the most advantageous.

As you study Figure 9-2, recall the hierarchical nature of these tasks. Deciding requires informing; problem solving requires deciding (and informing); and project management requires problem solving (and deciding [and informing]).

## WHAT ARE TYPICAL USES FOR BUSINESS INTELLIGENCE?

This section summarizes three uses of business intelligence that will give you a flavor of what is possible. Because *business intelligence* and the related term *BigData* are hot topics today, a Web search will produce dozens of similar examples. After you read this chapter, search for more applications that appeal to your particular interests.

### Identifying *Changes* in Purchasing Patterns

Most students are aware that business intelligence is used to predict purchasing patterns. Amazon made the phrase "Customers who bought... also bought" famous; when we buy something today, we expect the e-commerce application to suggest what else we might want. Later in this chapter, you'll learn some of the techniques that are used to produce such recommendations.

More interesting, however, is identifying *changes* in purchasing patterns. Retailers know that important life events cause customers to change what they buy and, for a short interval, to form new loyalties to new brands. Thus, when people start their first professional job, get married, have a baby, or retire, retailers want to know. Before business intelligence, stores would watch the local newspapers for graduation, marriage, and baby announcements and send ads in response. That is a slow, labor-intensive, and expensive process.

Target wanted to get ahead of the newspapers and in 2002 began a project to use purchasing patterns to determine that someone was pregnant. By applying business intelligence techniques to its sales data, Target was able to identify a purchasing pattern of lotions, vitamins, and other products that reliably predicts pregnancy. When Target observed that purchasing pattern, it sent ads for diapers and other baby-related products to those customers.

Its program worked—too well for one teenager who had told no one she was pregnant. When she began receiving ads for baby items, her father complained to the manager of the local Target store, who apologized. It was the father's turn to apologize when he learned that his daughter was, indeed, pregnant.[2]

### Business Intelligence for Entertainment

Amazon, Netflix, Pandora, Spotify, and other media-delivery organizations generate billions of bytes of data on consumer media preferences. Using that data, Amazon has begun to produce its own video and TV shows, basing plots and characters and selecting actors on the results of its BI analysis.[3]

Netflix decided to buy *House of Cards*, starring Kevin Spacey, based on its analysis of customers' viewing patterns. Similarly, Spotify processes data on customers' listening habits to determine locations where particular bands' songs are heard most often. Using that data, it then recommends the best cities for popular bands and other musical groups to perform in.[4]

A popular adage among marketing professionals is that "buyers are liars," meaning they'll say they want one thing but purchase something else. That characteristic reduces the efficacy of marketing focus groups. Business intelligence produced from data on watching, listening, and rental habits, however, determines what people actually want, not what they say. Will this enable data miners like Amazon to become the new Hollywood? We will see.

### Just-in-Time Medical Reporting

Practice Fusion Inc., a medical record startup, provides injection notification services to doctors during exams. As the doctor enters data, the software analyzes patient's records, and if injections are needed, it recommends that the doctor prescribe them as the exam progresses. It seems to work, too. During a 4-month study period, patients whose doctors were using the recommendation service prescribed 73 percent more vaccinations than those in a control group who did not use that service.[5]

The service is free to doctors. Practice Fusion is paid by Merck, a pharmaceutical company. While Practice Fusion's software recommends many products not sold by Merck, it also recommends many that are. Hence, the service stands on the blurry edge of medical ethics. Should a drug company provide software that recommends its products to doctors "for free"? If the injections are truly needed, who could object? On the other hand, how unbiased is the Practice Fusion software?

Setting the ethical issues aside, Practice Fusion provides an excellent example of data mining and reporting in real time. During your career, there likely will be many examples of middle-of-the-sales-call sales assistance.

With the speed at which data is generated today and with the near-zero cost of processing, we can be certain that many even more innovative applications of business intelligence will occur. Watch for them; they will present interesting career opportunities for you.

Given these examples, we next consider the process used to create business intelligence.

## Q9-2 WHAT ARE THE THREE PRIMARY ACTIVITIES IN THE BI PROCESS?

**Data mining and other BI systems are useful, but they are not without problems, as discussed in the Guide on pages 268–269.**

Figure 9-3 shows the three primary activities in the BI process: acquire data, perform analysis, and publish results. These activities directly correspond to the BI elements in Figure 9-1. **Data acquisition** is the process of obtaining, cleaning, organizing, relating, and cataloging source data. We will illustrate a simple data acquisition example later in this question and discuss data acquisition in greater detail in Q9-3.

**Figure 9-3**
Three Primary Activities in the BI Process

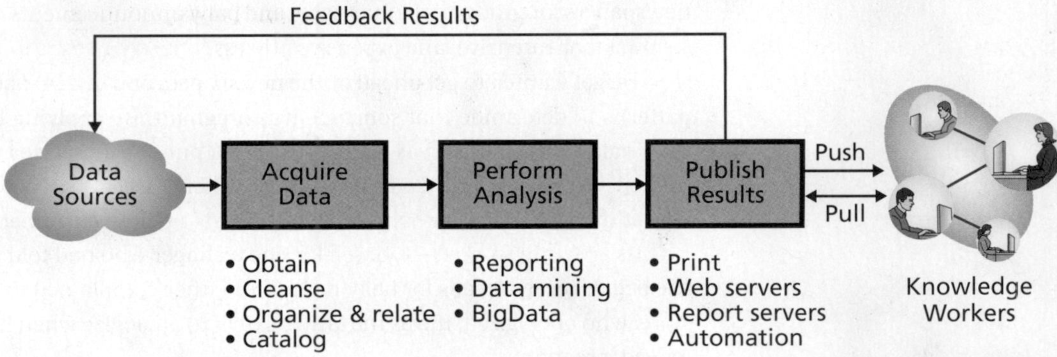


**BI analysis** is the process of creating business intelligence. The three fundamental categories of BI analysis are reporting, data mining, and BigData. We will illustrate a simple example of a reporting system later in this question and describe each of the three categories of BI analysis in greater detail in Q9-4.

**Publish results** is the process of delivering business intelligence to the knowledge workers who need it. **Push publishing** delivers business intelligence to users without any request from the users; the BI results are delivered according to a schedule or as a result of an event or particular data condition. **Pull publishing** requires the user to request BI results. Publishing media include print as well as online content delivered via Web servers, specialized Web servers known as *report servers*, and BI results that are sent via automation to other programs. We will discuss these publishing options further in Q9-5.

For now, to better understand the three phases of BI analysis, consider an example of the use of business intelligence.

## USING BUSINESS INTELLIGENCE TO FIND CANDIDATE PARTS

3D printing offers the possibility for customers to print parts they need rather than order them from a retailer or distributor. One large distributor of bicycle parts wanted to stay on top of this potential change in demand and decided to investigate the possibility of selling the parts' 3D printing files rather than the parts themselves. Accordingly, it created a team to examine past sales data to determine which parts designs it might sell. To do so, the company needed to identify qualifying parts and compute how much revenue potential those parts represent.

To address this problem, the team obtained an extract of sales data from its IS department and stored it in Microsoft Access. It then created five criteria for parts that might quality for this new program. Specifically, it looked for parts that were:

1. Provided by certain vendors (starting with just a few vendors that had already agreed to make part design files available for sale)
2. Purchased by larger customers (individuals and small companies would be unlikely to have 3D printers or the expertise needed to use them)
3. Frequently ordered (popular products)
4. Ordered in small quantities (3D printing is not suited for mass production)
5. Simple in design (easier to 3D print)

The team knew that the fifth criterion would be difficult to evaluate because the company doesn't store data on part complexity per se. After some discussion, the team decided to use part weight and price as surrogates for simplicity, operating under the assumption that "If it doesn't weigh very much or cost very much, it probably isn't complex." At least, it decided to start that way and find out. Accordingly, the team asked the IS department to include part weight in the extract.

## Acquire Data

**To learn more about database marketing, see Chapter Extension 12.**

As shown in Figure 9-3, acquiring data is the first step in the BI process. In response to the team's request for data, the IS department extracted operational data to produce the following two tables:

Sales (CustomerName, Contact, Title, Bill Year, Number Orders, Units, Revenue, Source, PartNumber)

Part (PartNumber, Shipping Weight, Vendor)

Sample data for these two tables are shown in Figure 9-4. As team members examined this data, they concluded they had what they needed and actually wouldn't need all of the data columns in the Sales table. They were surprised that the data was divided into different billing years, but because they planned to sum item sales over those years, that division wouldn't affect their analysis.

**Figure 9-4**
Sample Extracted Data: Order Extract Table and Part Data Table

*Source:* Microsoft Corporation

| | | | | | | | | |
|---|---|---|---|---|---|---|---|---|
| Island Biking | John Steel | Marketing Manager | 2014 | | 14 | 59 | $438.81 | Internet |
| Island Biking | John Steel | Marketing Manager | 2014 | | 21 | 55 | $255.96 | AWS |
| Island Biking | John Steel | Marketing Manager | 2015 | | 4 | 11 | $85.55 | Internet |
| Kona Riders | Renate Messne | Sales Representative | 2012 | | 43 | 54 | $349.27 | Internet |
| Kona Riders | Renate Messne | Sales Representative | 2013 | | 30 | 53 | $362.45 | Internet |
| Kona Riders | Renate Messne | Sales Representative | 2014 | | 1 | 2 | $14.34 | Internet |
| Lone Pine Crafters | Jaime Yorres | Owner | 2015 | | 4 | 14 | $108.89 | Internet |
| Lone Pine Crafters | Jaime Yorres | Owner | 2015 | | 2 | 2 | $15.56 | Internet |
| Lone Pine Crafters | Jaime Yorres | Owner | 2016 | | 2 | 2 | $15.56 | Internet |
| Moab Mauraders | Carlos Gonzále | Accounting Manager | 2015 | | 2 | 4 | $4,106.69 | Internet |
| Moab Mauraders | Carlos Gonzále | Accounting Manager | 2015 | | 3 | 7 | $7,404.18 | Internet |
| Moab Mauraders | Carlos Gonzále | Accounting Manager | 2015 | | 2 | 6 | $6,346.44 | Internet |
| Sedona Mountain Trails | Felipe Izquierd | Owner | 2015 | | 6 | 7 | $73.46 | Internet |
| Sedona Mountain Trails | Felipe Izquierd | Owner | 2015 | | 3 | 7 | $39.14 | Phone |
| Sedona Mountain Trails | Felipe Izquierd | Owner | 2015 | | 3 | 9 | $74.59 | Phone |
| Sedona Mountain Trails | Felipe Izquierd | Owner | 2014 | | 5 | 20 | $153.00 | Phone |
| Sedona Mountain Trails | Felipe Izquierd | Owner | 2012 | | 3 | 8 | $37.14 | Phone |
| Sedona Mountain Trails | Felipe Izquierd | Owner | 2013 | | 1 | 0 | $89.30 | Internet |
| Sedona Mountain Trails | Felipe Izquierd | Owner | 2013 | | 6 | 20 | $73.13 | Phone |
| Sedona Mountain Trails | Felipe Izquierd | Owner | 2012 | | 4 | 8 | $67.41 | Internet |
| Flat Iron Riders | Maria Anders | Sales Representative | 2013 | | 7 | 22 | $11,734.25 | Internet |
| Flat Iron Riders | Maria Anders | Sales Representative | 2015 | | 2 | 1 | $595.00 | Internet |
| Flat Iron Riders | Maria Anders | Sales Representative | 2014 | | 10 | 29 | $16,392.25 | Internet |
| Flat Iron Riders | Maria Anders | Sales Representative | 2015 | | 20 | 32 | $12,688.80 | AWS |

a. Order Extract Table

Part Data

| ID | PartNumber | Shipping Weight | Vendor | Click to Add |
|---|---|---|---|---|
| 9 | 200-219 | 7.28 | DePARTures, Inc. | |
| 22 | 200-225 | 3.61 | DePARTures, Inc. | |
| 23 | 200-227 | 5.14 | DePARTures, Inc. | |
| 11 | 200-207 | 9.23 | DePARTures, Inc. | |
| 28 | 200-205 | 4.11 | DePARTures, Inc. | |
| 29 | 200-211 | 4.57 | DePARTures, Inc. | |
| 10 | 200-213 | 1.09 | DePARTures, Inc. | |
| 37 | 200-223 | 3.61 | DePARTures, Inc. | |
| 45 | 200-217 | 1.98 | DePARTures, Inc. | |
| 2 | 200-209 | 10.41 | DePARTures, Inc. | |
| 3 | 200-215 | 1.55 | DePARTures, Inc. | |
| 47 | 200-221 | 10.85 | DePARTures, Inc. | |
| 42 | 200-203 | 3.20 | DePARTures, Inc. | |
| 17 | 300-1007 | 2.77 | Desert Gear Supply | |
| 13 | 300-1017 | 9.46 | Desert Gear Supply | |
| 50 | 300-1016 | 4.14 | Desert Gear Supply | |
| 27 | 300-1013 | 2.66 | Desert Gear Supply | |
| 8 | 300-1008 | 10.13 | Desert Gear Supply | |
| 30 | 300-1015 | 5.96 | Desert Gear Supply | |
| 15 | 300-1014 | 10.18 | Desert Gear Supply | |
| 7 | 300-1009 | 3.76 | Desert Gear Supply | |
| 6 | 300-1011 | 6.41 | Desert Gear Supply | |
| 43 | 300-1010 | 10.87 | Desert Gear Supply | |
| 31 | 300-1012 | 9.08 | Desert Gear Supply | |
| 1 | 500-2035 | 9.66 | ExtremeGear | |
| 41 | 500-2030 | 4.71 | ExtremeGear | |
| 40 | 500-2040 | 9.92 | ExtremeGear | |

b. Part Data Table

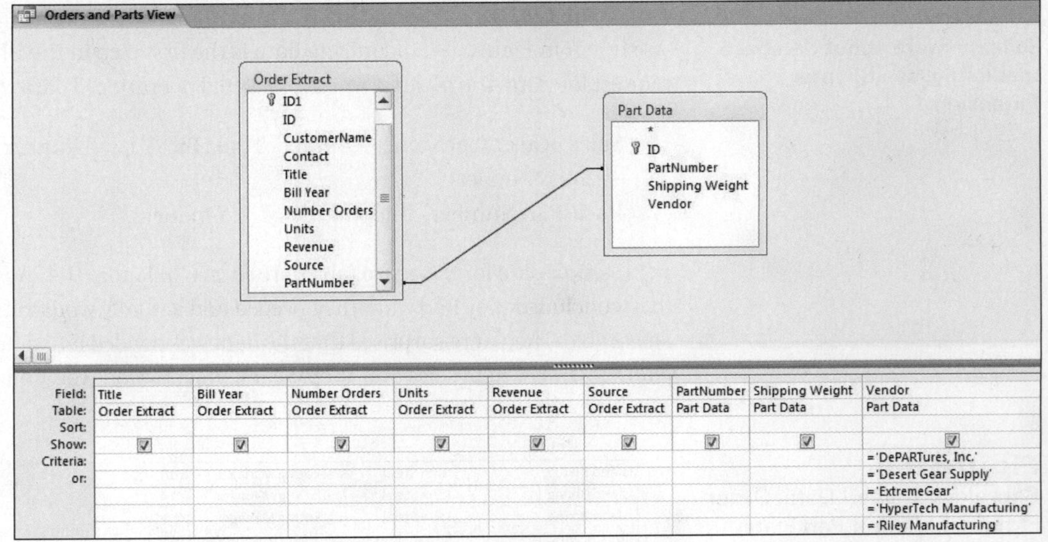


**Figure 9-5**
Joining *Order Extract* and Filtered *Parts* Tables
*Source:* Microsoft Corporation

## Analyze Data

The team's first step was to combine the data in the two tables into a single table that contained both the sales and part data. Also, because the team had already selected certain vendors to work with (those it knew would agree to release design files for 3D printing), it set filtering criteria for those vendor names, as shown in Figure 9-5. In this Access query, the line between PartNumber in Order Extract and PartNumber in Part Data means that rows of the two tables are to be combined if they have matching values of PartNumber.

The result of this query is shown in Figure 9-6. Notice there are some missing and questionable values. Numerous rows have missing values of Contact and Title, and a few of the rows have a value of zero for Units. The missing contact and title data wasn't a problem. Because team members had their own contact data, they didn't need this data. But the values of zero units might be problematic. At some point, the team might need to investigate what these values mean and possibly correct the data or remove those rows from the analysis. In the immediate term, however, the team decided to proceed even with these incorrect values. You will learn in Q9-3 that, for a number of reasons, such problematic data is common in data extracts.

The data in Figure 9-6 have been filtered for their first criterion and the team considers parts only from particular vendors. For their next criterion, team members needed to decide how to

**Figure 9-6**
Sample *Orders and Parts View* Data
*Source:* Microsoft Corporation

Orders and Parts View

| CustomerName | Contact | Title | Bill Year | Number Orders | Units | Revenue | Source | PartNumber | Shipping Weight | Vendor |
|---|---|---|---|---|---|---|---|---|---|---|
| Gordos Dirt Bikes | Sergio Gutiérrez | Sales Represe | 2011 | 43 | 107 | $26,234.12 | Internet | 100-108 | 3.32 | Riley Manufacturing |
| Island Biking | | | 2012 | 59 | 135 | $25,890.62 | Phone | 500-2035 | 9.66 | ExtremeGear |
| Big Bikes | | | 2010 | 29 | 77 | $25,696.00 | AWS | 700-1680 | 6.06 | HyperTech Manufacturing |
| Lazy B Bikes | | | 2009 | 19 | 30 | $25,576.50 | Internet | 700-2280 | 2.70 | HyperTech Manufacturing |
| Lone Pine Crafters | Carlos Hernández | Sales Represe | 2012 | 1 | 0 | $25,171.56 | Internet | 500-2030 | 4.71 | ExtremeGear |
| Seven Lakes Riding | Peter Franken | Marketing Ma | 2009 | 15 | 50 | $25,075.00 | Internet | 500-2020 | 10.07 | ExtremeGear |
| Big Bikes | | | 2012 | 10 | 40 | $24,888.00 | Internet | 500-2025 | 10.49 | ExtremeGear |
| B' Bikes | Georg Pipps | Sales Manage | 2012 | 14 | 23 | $24,328.02 | Internet | 700-1680 | 6.06 | HyperTech Manufacturing |
| Eastern Connection | Isabel de Castro | Sales Represe | 2012 | 48 | 173 | $24,296.17 | AWS | 100-105 | 10.73 | Riley Manufacturing |
| Big Bikes | Carine Schmitt | Marketing Ma | 2009 | 22 | 71 | $23,877.48 | AWS | 500-2035 | 9.66 | ExtremeGear |
| Island Biking | Manuel Pereira | Owner | 2011 | 26 | 45 | $23,588.86 | Internet | 500-2045 | 3.22 | ExtremeGear |
| Mississippi Delta Riding | Rene Phillips | Sales Represe | 2012 | 9 | 33 | $23,550.25 | Internet | 700-2180 | 4.45 | HyperTech Manufacturing |
| Uncle's Upgrades | | | 2012 | 9 | 21 | $22,212.54 | Internet | 700-1680 | 6.06 | HyperTech Manufacturing |
| Big Bikes | | | 2010 | 73 | 80 | $22,063.92 | Phone | 700-1680 | 6.06 | HyperTech Manufacturing |
| Island Biking | | | 2012 | 18 | 59 | $22,025.88 | Internet | 100-108 | 3.32 | Riley Manufacturing |
| Uncle's Upgrades | | | 2011 | 16 | 38 | $21,802.50 | Internet | 500-2035 | 9.66 | ExtremeGear |
| Hard Rock Machines | | | 2012 | 42 | 57 | $21,279.24 | Internet | 100-108 | 3.32 | Riley Manufacturing |
| Kona Riders | | | 2012 | 11 | 20 | $21,154.80 | Internet | 700-1880 | 2.28 | HyperTech Manufacturing |
| Moab Mauraders | | | 2012 | 6 | 20 | $21,154.80 | Internet | 700-2180 | 4.45 | HyperTech Manufacturing |
| Lone Pine Crafters | | | 2012 | 35 | 58 | $21,016.59 | Internet | 100-106 | 6.23 | Riley Manufacturing |
| Big Bikes | Carine Schmitt | Marketing Ma | 2010 | 9 | 36 | $20,655.00 | Internet | 500-2035 | 9.66 | ExtremeGear |
| East/West Enterprises | | | 2011 | 14 | 60 | $20,349.00 | Internet | 100-104 | 5.80 | Riley Manufacturing |
| Jeeps 'n More | Yvonne Moncada | Sales Agent | 2012 | 47 | 50 | $20,230.00 | AWS | 500-2030 | 4.71 | ExtremeGear |
| East/West Enterprises | | | 2009 | 14 | 60 | $20,178.15 | AWS | 500-2035 | 9.66 | ExtremeGear |
| Lone Pine Crafters | | | 2012 | 20 | 54 | $20,159.28 | Internet | 100-106 | 6.23 | Riley Manufacturing |
| Lone Pine Crafters | Carlos Hernández | Sales Represe | 2012 | 1 | 0 | $20,137.27 | Internet | 500-2030 | 4.71 | ExtremeGear |
| Lazy B Bikes | | | 2012 | 21 | 29 | $19,946.78 | AWS | 700-1580 | 7.50 | HyperTech Manufacturing |
| Eastern Connection | Isabel de Castro | Sales Represe | 2012 | 42 | 173 | $19,907.06 | Phone | 100-105 | 10.73 | Riley Manufacturing |
| Lazy B Bikes | | | 2012 | 8 | 30 | $19,724.25 | AWS | 700-1580 | 7.50 | HyperTech Manufacturing |

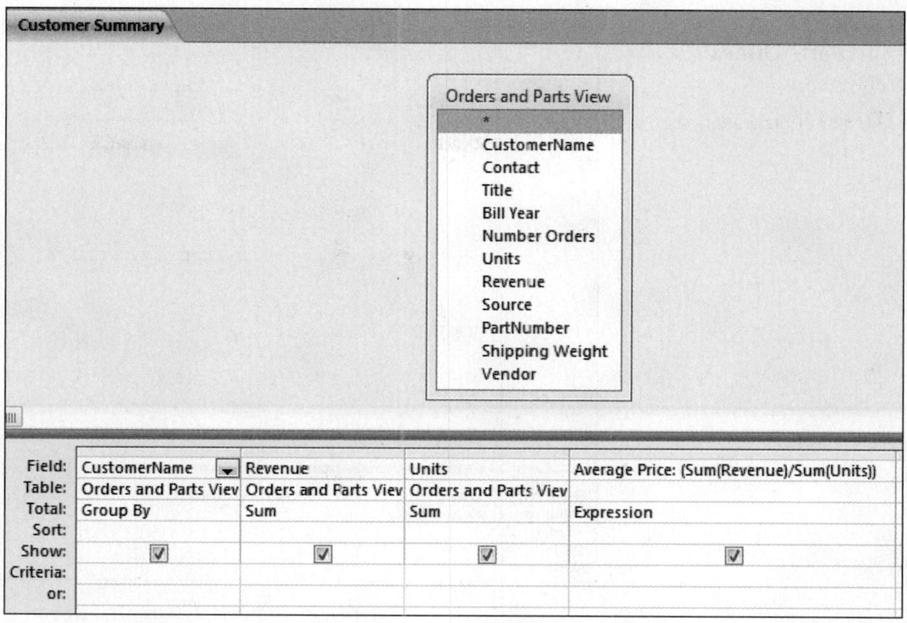


**Figure 9-7**
Creating the Customer Summary Query
*Source:* Microsoft Corporation

identify large customers. To do so, they created the query in Figure 9-7, which sums the revenue, units, and average price for each customer. Looking at the query results in Figure 9-8, they decided to consider only customers having more than $200,000 in total revenue; they changed the query to include just those customers and named that modified query Big Customers.

Next, the team members discussed what they meant by frequent purchase and decided to include items ordered an average of once a week or roughly 50 times per year. You can see that they set that criterion for Number Orders in the query in Figure 9-9. To select only parts that are ordered in small quantities, they first created a column that computes average order size (Units/[Number Orders]) and then set a criterion on that expression that the average must be less than 2.5. Their last two criteria were that the part be relatively inexpensive and that it be lightweight. They decided to select parts with a unit price (computed as Revenue/Units) less than 100 and a shipping weight less than 5 pounds.

**Figure 9-8**
Customer Summary
*Source:* Microsoft Corporation

Customer Summary

| CustomerName | SumOfRevenue | SumOfUnits | Average Price |
|---|---|---|---|
| Great Lakes Machines | $1,760.47 | 142 | 12.3976535211268 |
| Seven Lakes Riding | $288,570.71 | 5848 | 49.3451963919289 |
| Around the Horn | $16,669.48 | 273 | 61.0603611721612 |
| Dewey Riding | $36,467.90 | 424 | 86.0092018867925 |
| Moab Mauraders | $143,409.27 | 1344 | 106.7033234375 |
| Gordos Dirt Bikes | $113,526.88 | 653 | 173.854335068913 |
| Mountain Traders | $687,710.99 | 3332 | 206.395855432173 |
| Hungry Rider Off-road | $108,602.32 | 492 | 220.736416056911 |
| Eastern Connection | $275,092.28 | 1241 | 221.669848186946 |
| Mississippi Delta Riding | $469,932.11 | 1898 | 247.593315542676 |
| Island Biking | $612,072.64 | 2341 | 261.457770098249 |
| Big Bikes | $1,385,867.98 | 4876 | 284.222310233798 |
| Hard Rock Machines | $74,853.22 | 241 | 310.594267219917 |
| Lone Pine Crafters | $732,990.33 | 1816 | 403.629038215859 |
| Sedona Mountain Trails | $481,073.82 | 1104 | 435.755269474638 |
| Flat Iron Riders | $85,469.20 | 183 | 467.044808743169 |
| Bottom-Dollar Bikes | $72,460.85 | 154 | 470.52502012987 |
| Uncle's Upgrades | $947,477.61 | 1999 | 473.975794047024 |
| Ernst Handel Mechanics | $740,951.15 | 1427 | 519.236962438683 |
| Kona Riders | $511,108.05 | 982 | 520.476624439919 |
| Lazy B Bikes | $860,950.72 | 1594 | 540.119648619824 |
| Jeeps 'n More | $404,540.62 | 678 | 596.667583185841 |
| French Riding Masters | $1,037,386.76 | 1657 | 626.063224984912 |
| B' Bikes | $113,427.06 | 159 | 713.377735849057 |
| East/West Enterprises | $2,023,402.09 | 2457 | 823.525474074074 |
| Bon App Riding | $65,848.90 | 60 | 1097.48160833333 |

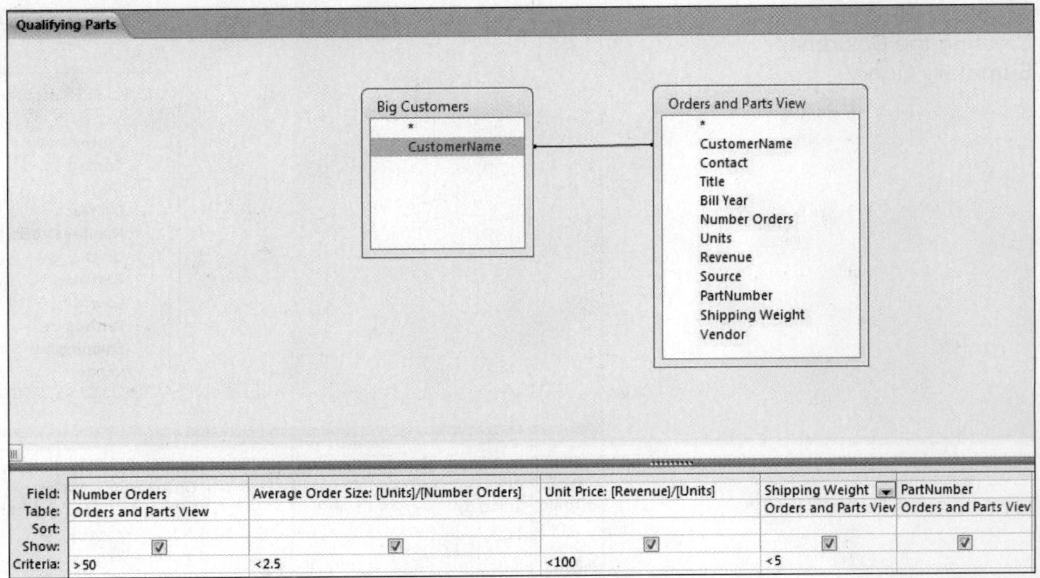


**Figure 9-9**
Qualifying Parts Query Design

*Source:* Microsoft Corporation

The results of this query are shown in Figure 9-10. Of all the parts the company sells, these 12 fit the criteria the team created.

The next question was how much revenue potential these parts represent. Accordingly, team members created a query that connected the selected parts with their past sales data. The results are shown in Figure 9-11.

## Publish Results

Publish results is the last activity in the BI process shown in Figure 9-3. In some cases, this means placing BI results on servers for publication to knowledge workers over the Internet or other networks. In other cases, it means making the results available via a Web service for use by other applications. In still other cases, it means creating PDFs or PowerPoint presentations for communicating to colleagues or management.

In this case, the team members reported these results to their management in a team meeting. Judging just by the results in Figure 9-11, there seems to be little revenue potential in

**Figure 9-10**
Qualifying Parts Query Results

*Source:* Microsoft Corporation

Qualifying Parts

| Number Orders | Average Order Size | Unit Price | Shipping Weight | PartNumber |
|---|---|---|---|---|
| 275 | 1 | 9.14173854545455 | 4.14 | 300-1016 |
| 258 | 1.87596899224806 | 7.41284524793388 | 4.14 | 300-1016 |
| 110 | 1.18181818181818 | 6.46796923076923 | 4.11 | 200-205 |
| 176 | 1.66477272727273 | 12.5887211604096 | 4.14 | 300-1016 |
| 139 | 1.0431654676259 | 6.28248965517241 | 1.98 | 200-217 |
| 56 | 1.83928571428571 | 6.71141553398058 | 1.98 | 200-217 |
| 99 | 1.02020202020202 | 7.7775 | 3.20 | 200-203 |
| 76 | 2.17105263157895 | 12.0252206060606 | 2.66 | 300-1013 |
| 56 | 1.07142857142857 | 5.0575 | 4.57 | 200-211 |
| 73 | 1.15068493150685 | 5.0575 | 4.57 | 200-211 |
| 107 | 2.02803738317757 | 6.01096405529954 | 2.77 | 300-1007 |
| 111 | 2.07207207207207 | 6.01096434782609 | 2.77 | 300-1007 |

**Figure 9-11**
Sales History for Selected Parts

*Source:* Microsoft Corporation

Revenue Potential

| Total Orders | Total Revenue | PartNumber |
|---|---|---|
| 3987 | $84,672.73 | 300-1016 |
| 2158 | $30,912.19 | 200-211 |
| 1074 | $23,773.53 | 200-217 |
| 548 | $7,271.31 | 300-1007 |
| 375 | $5,051.62 | 200-203 |
| 111 | $3,160.86 | 300-1013 |
| 139 | $1,204.50 | 200-205 |

selling designs for these parts. The company would earn minimal revenue from the parts themselves; the designs would have to be priced considerably lower than the parts, and that would mean almost no revenue.

In spite of the low revenue potential, the company might still decide to offer 3D designs to customers. It might decide to give the designs away as a gesture of goodwill to its customers; this analysis indicates it will be sacrificing little revenue to do so. Or it might do it as a PR move intended to show that the company is on top of the latest manufacturing technology. Or it might decide to postpone consideration of 3D printing because it doesn't see that many customers ordering the qualifying parts.

Of course, there is the possibility that the team members chose the wrong criteria. If they have time, it might be tempting for them to change their criteria and repeat the analysis. Such a course is a slippery slope, however. They might find themselves changing criteria until they obtain a result they want, which results in a very biased study.

This possibility points again to the importance of the human component of an IS. The hardware, software, data, and query-generation procedures are of little value if the decisions that the team made when setting and possibly revising criteria are poor. Business intelligence is only as intelligent as the people creating it!

With this example in mind, we will now consider each of the activities in Figure 9-3 in greater detail.

## Q9-3 HOW DO ORGANIZATIONS USE DATA WAREHOUSES AND DATA MARTS TO ACQUIRE DATA?

Although it is possible to create basic reports and perform simple analyses from operational data, this course is not usually recommended. For reasons of security and control, IS professionals do not want data analysts processing operational data. If an analyst makes an error, that error could cause a serious disruption in the company's operations. Also, operational data is structured for fast and reliable transaction processing. It is seldom structured in a way that readily supports BI analysis. Finally, BI analyses can require considerable processing; placing BI applications on operational servers can dramatically reduce system performance.

For these reasons, most organizations extract operational data for BI processing. For small organizations, the extraction may be as simple as an Access database. Larger organizations, however, typically create and staff a group of people who manage and run a **data warehouse**, which is a facility for managing an organization's BI data. The functions of a data warehouse are to:

- Obtain data
- Cleanse data
- Organize and relate data
- Catalog data

Figure 9-12 shows the components of a data warehouse. Programs read operational and other data and extract, clean, and prepare those data for BI processing. The prepared data are stored in a data warehouse database using a data warehouse DBMS, which can be different from the organization's operational DBMS. For example, an organization might use Oracle for its operational processing but use SQL Server for its data warehouse. Other organizations use SQL Server for operational processing but use DBMSs from statistical package vendors such as SAS or SPSS in the data warehouse.

**Collecting and selling data about consumer shopping habits is big business. But what information about you is being collected? And how is it being used? The Ethics Guide on pages 266–267 considers these questions.**

Data warehouses include data that are purchased from outside sources. The purchase of data about other organizations is not unusual or particularly concerning from a privacy standpoint. However, some companies choose to buy personal, consumer data (like marital status) from data

**Figure 9-12**
Components of a Data Warehouse

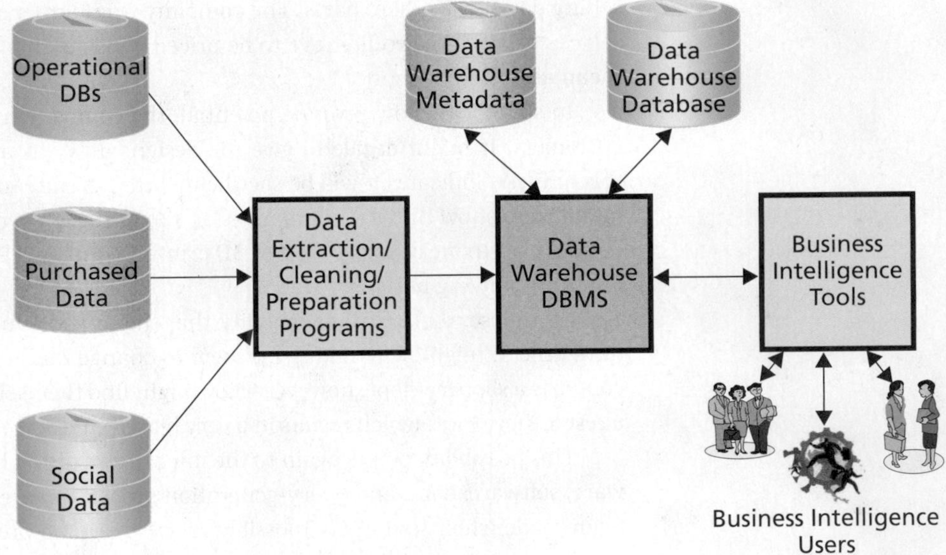


vendors like Acxiom Corporation. Figure 9-13 lists some of the consumer data that can be readily purchased. An amazing (and, from a privacy standpoint, frightening) amount of data is available.

Metadata concerning the data—its source, its format, its assumptions and constraints, and other facts about the data—is kept in a data warehouse metadata database. The data warehouse DBMS extracts and provides data to BI applications.

The term *business intelligence users* is different from *knowledge workers* in Figure 9-1. BI users are generally specialists in data analysis, whereas knowledge workers are often nonspecialist users of BI results. A loan approval officer at a bank is a knowledge worker, but not a BI user.

## PROBLEMS WITH OPERATIONAL DATA

Most operational and purchased data have problems that inhibit their usefulness for business intelligence. Figure 9-14 lists the major problem categories. First, although data that are critical for successful operations must be complete and accurate, data that are only marginally necessary need not be. For example, some systems gather demographic data in the ordering process. But because such data are not needed to fill, ship, and bill orders, their quality suffers.

Problematic data are termed *dirty data*. Examples are a value of B for customer gender and of 213 for customer age. Other examples are a value of 999–999–9999 for a U.S. phone number, a part color of "gren," and an email address of *WhyMe@GuessWhoIAM.org*. The value of zero for Units in Figure 9-6 is dirty data. All of these values can be problematic for BI purposes.

**Figure 9-13**
Examples of Consumer Data That Can Be Purchased

- Name, address, phone
- Age
- Gender
- Ethnicity
- Religion
- Income
- Education
- Voter registration
- Home ownership
- Vehicles
- Magazine subscriptions
- Hobbies
- Catalog orders
- Marital status, life stage
- Height, weight, hair and eye color
- Spouse's name, birth date
- Children's names and birth dates

**Figure 9-14**
Possible Problems with Source Data

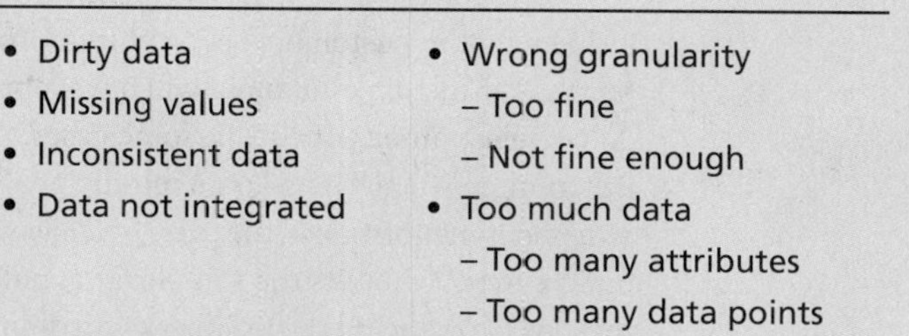
- Dirty data
- Missing values
- Inconsistent data
- Data not integrated
- Wrong granularity
  - Too fine
  - Not fine enough
- Too much data
  - Too many attributes
  - Too many data points

Source data can contain missing elements. The contact data in Figure 9-6 is a typical example. Orders can be shipped without contact data, so its quality is spotty with many missing values. For purchased data, most data vendors state the percentage of missing values for each attribute in the data they sell. An organization buys such data because for some uses, some data are better than no data at all. This is especially true for data items whose values are difficult to obtain, such as Number of Adults in Household, Household Income, Dwelling Type, and Education of Primary Income Earner. However, care is required here because for some BI applications, a few missing or erroneous data points can seriously bias the analysis.

Inconsistent data, the third problem in Figure 9-14, is particularly common for data that have been gathered over time. When an area code changes, for example, the phone number for a given customer before the change will not match the customer's number after the change. Likewise, part codes can change, as can sales territories. Before such data can be used, they must be recoded for consistency over the period of the study.

Some data inconsistencies occur from the nature of the business activity. Consider a Web-based order-entry system used by customers worldwide. When the Web server records the time of order, which time zone does it use? The server's system clock time is irrelevant to an analysis of customer behavior. Coordinated Universal Time (formerly called Greenwich Mean Time) is also meaningless. Somehow, Web server time must be adjusted to the time zone of the customer.

Another problem is nonintegrated data. A particular BI analysis might require data from an ERP system, an e-commerce system, and a social networking application. Analysts may wish to integrate that organizational data with purchased consumer data. Such a data collection will likely have relationships that are not represented in primary key/foreign key relationships. It is the function of personnel in the data warehouse to integrate such data somehow.

Data can also have the wrong **granularity**, a term that refers to the level of detail represented by the data. Granularity can be too fine or too coarse. For the former, suppose we want to analyze the placement of graphics and controls on an order-entry Web page. It is possible to capture the customers' clicking behavior in what is termed *clickstream data*. Those data, however, include everything the customer does at the Web site. In the middle of the order stream are data for clicks on the news, email, instant chat, and a weather check. Although all of that data may be useful for a study of consumer browsing behavior, it will be overwhelming if all we want to know is how customers respond to an ad located differently on the screen. To proceed, the data analysts must throw away millions and millions of clicks.

Data can also be too coarse. For example, a file of regional sales totals cannot be used to investigate the sales in a particular store in a region, and total sales for a store cannot be used to determine the sales of particular items within a store. Instead, we need to obtain data that is fine enough for the lowest-level report we want to produce.

In general, it is better to have too fine a granularity than too coarse. If the granularity is too fine, the data can be made coarser by summing and combining. This is what the team did with the sales data in Figure 9-6. Sales by Bill Year were too fine for its needs, so it summed sales data over those years. If the granularity is too coarse, however, there is no way to separate the data into constituent parts.

The final problem listed in Figure 9-14 is to have too much data. As shown in the figure, we can have either too many attributes or too many data points. Think back to the discussion of tables in Chapter 5. We can have too many columns or too many rows.

Consider the first problem: too many attributes. Suppose we want to know the factors that influence how customers respond to a promotion. If we combine internal customer data with purchased customer data, we will have more than a hundred different attributes to consider. How do we select among them? In some cases, analysts can just ignore the columns they don't need. But in more sophisticated data mining analyses, too many attributes can be problematic. Because of a phenomenon called the *curse of dimensionality*, the more attributes there are, the easier it is to build a model that fits the sample data, but that is worthless as a predictor. There are other good reasons for reducing the number of attributes, and one of the major activities in data mining concerns efficient and effective ways of selecting attributes.

The second way to have too much data is to have too many data points—too many rows of data. Suppose we want to analyze clickstream data on CNN.com. How many clicks does that site receive per month? Millions upon millions! In order to meaningfully analyze such data, we need to reduce the amount of data. One good solution to this problem is statistical sampling. Organizations should not be reluctant to sample data in such situations.

## DATA WAREHOUSES VERSUS DATA MARTS

A **data mart** is a data collection, smaller than the data warehouse, that addresses the needs of a particular department or functional area of the business. To understand the difference between data warehouses and data marts, think of a data warehouse as a distributor in a supply chain. The data warehouse takes data from the data manufacturers (operational systems and other sources), cleans and processes the data, and locates the data on the shelves, so to speak, of the data warehouse. The data analysts who work with a data warehouse are experts at data management, data cleaning, data transformation, data relationships, and the like. However, they are not usually experts in a given business function.

If the data warehouse is the distributor in a supply chain, then a data mart is like a retail store in a supply chain. Users in the data mart obtain data that pertain to a particular business function from the data warehouse. Such users do not have the data management expertise that data warehouse employees have, but they are knowledgeable analysts for a given business function.

Figure 9-15 illustrates these relationships. In this example, the data warehouse takes data from the data producers and distributes the data to three data marts. One data mart is used to analyze clickstream data for the purpose of designing Web pages. A second analyzes store sales

**Figure 9-15**
Data Mart Examples

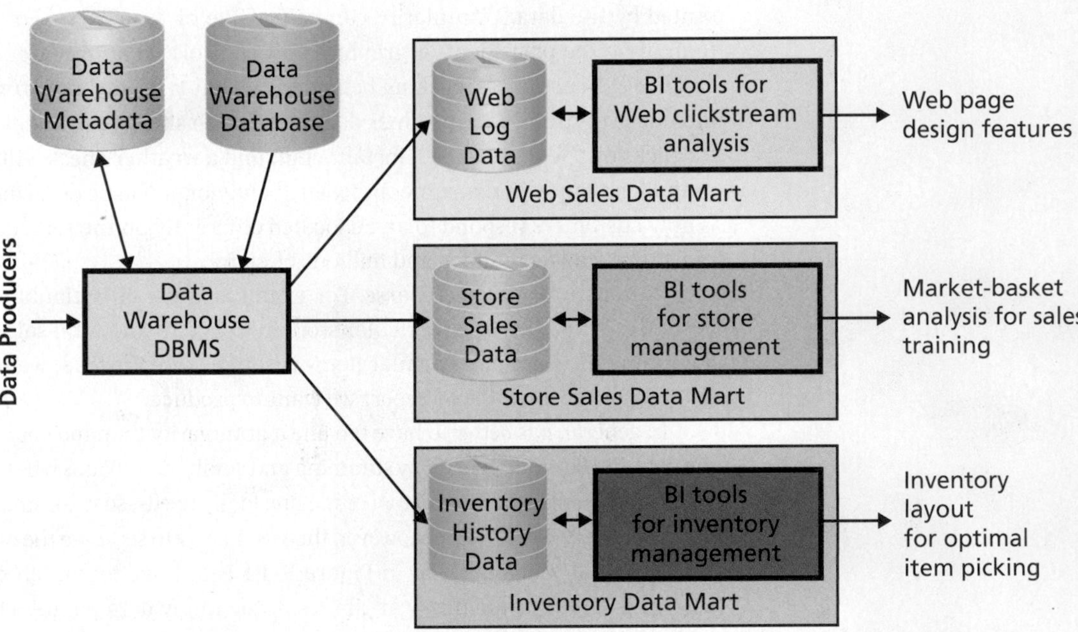

data and determines which products tend to be purchased together. This information is used to train salespeople on the best way to up-sell to customers. The third data mart is used to analyze customer order data for the purpose of reducing labor for item picking from the warehouse. A company like Amazon.com, for example, goes to great lengths to organize its warehouses to reduce picking expenses.

As you can imagine, it is expensive to create, staff, and operate data warehouses and data marts. Only large organizations with deep pockets can afford to operate a system like that shown in Figure 9-12. Smaller organizations operate subsets of this system, but they must find ways to solve the basic problems that data warehouses solve, even if those ways are informal.

## Q9-4 WHAT ARE THREE TECHNIQUES FOR PROCESSING BI DATA?

Figure 9-16 summarizes the goals and characteristics of three fundamental types of BI analysis. In general, reporting analyses are used to create information about past performance, whereas data mining is used primarily for classifying and predicting. There are exceptions, but these statements are reasonable rules of thumb. The goal of BigData analysis is to find patterns and relationships in the enormous amounts of data generated from sources like social media sites or Web server logs. As indicated, BigData data techniques can include reporting and data mining as well. Consider the characteristics of each type.

### REPORTING ANALYSIS

**To learn more about Reporting Systems and OLAP, see Chapter Extension 13.**

**Reporting analysis** is the process of sorting, grouping, summing, filtering, and formatting structured data. **Structured data** is data in the form of rows and columns. Most of the time structured data means tables in a relational database, but it can refer to spreadsheet data as well.

The parts analysis you read in Q9-2 is an example of a reporting analysis. Another type of report, **exception reports** are reports produced when something out of predefined bounds occurs. The just-in-time injection recommendations discussed in Q9-1 are an example of an exception report.

In the past, reports were printed and therefore needed to be static. With the increasing use of mobile systems, however, many reports can be dynamic.

### DATA MINING ANALYSIS

**Data mining** is the application of statistical techniques to find patterns and relationships among data for classification and prediction. Data mining techniques emerged from the combined discipline of statistics, mathematics, artificial intelligence, and machine-learning.

**Figure 9-16**
Three Types of BI Analysis

| BI Analysis Type | Goal | Characteristics |
|---|---|---|
| Reporting | Create information about past performance. | Process structured data by sorting, grouping, summing, filtering, and formatting. |
| Data mining | Classify and predict. | Use sophisticated statistical techniques to find patterns and relationships. |
| BigData | Find patterns and relationships in BigData. | Volume, velocity, and variety force use of MapReduce techniques. Some applications use reporting and data mining as well. |

Most data mining techniques are sophisticated, and many are difficult to use well. Such techniques are valuable to organizations, however, and some business professionals, especially those in finance and marketing, have become expert in their use. Today, in fact, there are many interesting and rewarding careers for business professionals who are knowledgeable about data mining techniques.

Data mining techniques fall into two broad categories: unsupervised and supervised. We explain both types in the following sections.

### Unsupervised Data Mining

With **unsupervised data mining**, analysts do not create a model or hypothesis before running the analysis. Instead, they apply the data mining technique to the data and observe the results. With this method, analysts create hypotheses after the analysis to explain the patterns found.

One common unsupervised technique is **cluster analysis**. With it, statistical techniques identify groups of entities that have similar characteristics. A common use for cluster analysis is to find groups of similar customers from customer order and demographic data.

For example, suppose a cluster analysis finds two very different customer groups: One group has an average age of 33; owns a laptop, two Android phones, an iPad, and a Kindle; drives an expensive SUV; and tends to buy expensive children's play equipment. The second group has an average age of 64, owns vacation property, plays golf, and buys expensive wines. Suppose the analysis also finds that both groups buy designer children's clothing.

These findings are obtained solely by data analysis. There is no prior model about the patterns and relationship that exist. It is up to the analyst to form hypotheses, after the fact, to explain why two such different groups are both buying designer children's clothes.

### Supervised Data Mining

With **supervised data mining**, data miners develop a model prior to the analysis and apply statistical techniques to data to estimate parameters of the model. For example, suppose marketing experts in a communications company believe that cell phone usage on weekends is determined by the age of the customer and the number of months the customer has had the cell phone account. A data mining analyst would then run an analysis that estimates the impact of customer and account age. One such analysis, which measures the impact of a set of variables on another variable, is called a **regression analysis**. A sample result for the cell phone example is:

$$\text{CellPhoneWeekendMinutes} = 12 + (17.5 \times \text{times CustomerAge}) + (23.7 \times \text{times NumberMonthsOfAccount})$$

Using this equation, analysts can predict the number of minutes of weekend cell phone use by summing 12, plus 17.5 times the customer's age, plus 23.7 times the number of months of the account.

As you will learn in your statistics classes, considerable skill is required to interpret the quality of such a model. The regression tool will create an equation, such as the one shown. Whether that equation is a good predictor of future cell phone usage depends on statistical factors such as $t$ values, confidence intervals, and related statistical techniques.

## BIGDATA

**BigData** (also spelled Big Data) is a term used to describe data collections that are characterized by huge *volume*, rapid *velocity*, and great *variety*. Considering volume, BigData refers to data sets that are at least a petabyte in size, and usually larger. A data set containing all Google searches in the United States on a given day is BigData in size. Additionally, BigData has high velocity, meaning that it is generated rapidly. (If you know physics, you know that *speed* would be a more accurate term, but speed doesn't start with a *v*, and the *vvv* description has become a common way to describe BigData.) The Google search data for a given day is generated in, well, just a day. In the past, months or years would have been required to generate so much data.

Finally, BigData is varied. BigData may have structured data, but it also may have free-form text, dozens of different formats of Web server and database log files, streams of data about user responses to page content, and possibly graphics, audio, and video files.

## MapReduce

Because BigData is huge, fast, and varied, it cannot be processed using traditional techniques. **MapReduce** is a technique for harnessing the power of thousands of computers working in parallel. The basic idea is that the BigData collection is broken into pieces, and hundreds or thousands of independent processors search these pieces for something of interest. That process is referred to as the *Map* phase. In Figure 9-17, for example, a data set having the logs of Google searches is broken into pieces, and each independent processor is instructed to search for and count search keywords. This figure, of course, shows just a small portion of the data; here you can see a portion of the keywords that begin with *H*.

As the processors finish, their results are combined in what is referred to as the *Reduce* phase. The result is a list of all the terms searched for on a given day and the count of each. The process is considerably more complex than described here, but this is the gist of the idea.

By the way, you can visit Google Trends to see an application of MapReduce. There you can obtain a trend line of the number of searches for a particular term or terms. Figure 9-18 compares the search trends for the terms *Web 2.0* and *Hadoop*. Go to *www.google.com/trends* and enter the terms *Big Data, BigData,* and *data analytics* to see why it's a good use of your time to learn about them!

## Hadoop

**Hadoop** is an open source program supported by the Apache Foundation[6] that manages thousands of computers and that implements MapReduce. Hadoop could drive the process of finding and counting the Google search terms, but Google uses its own proprietary version of MapReduce to do so instead.

**Figure 9-17**
MapReduce Processing Summary

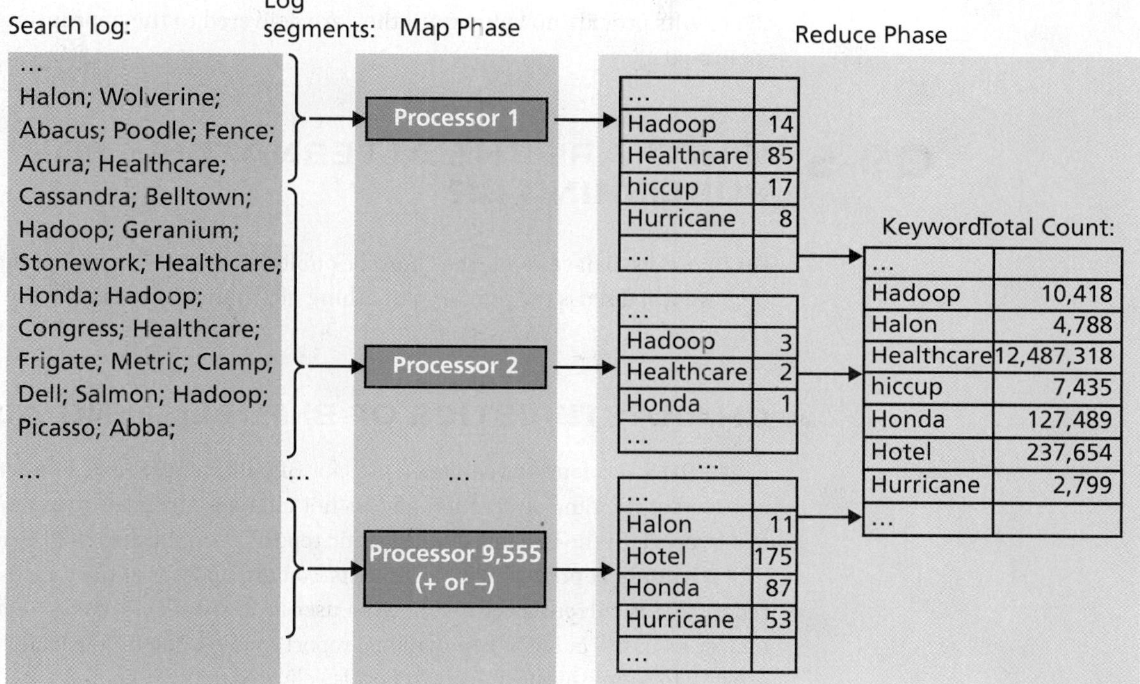

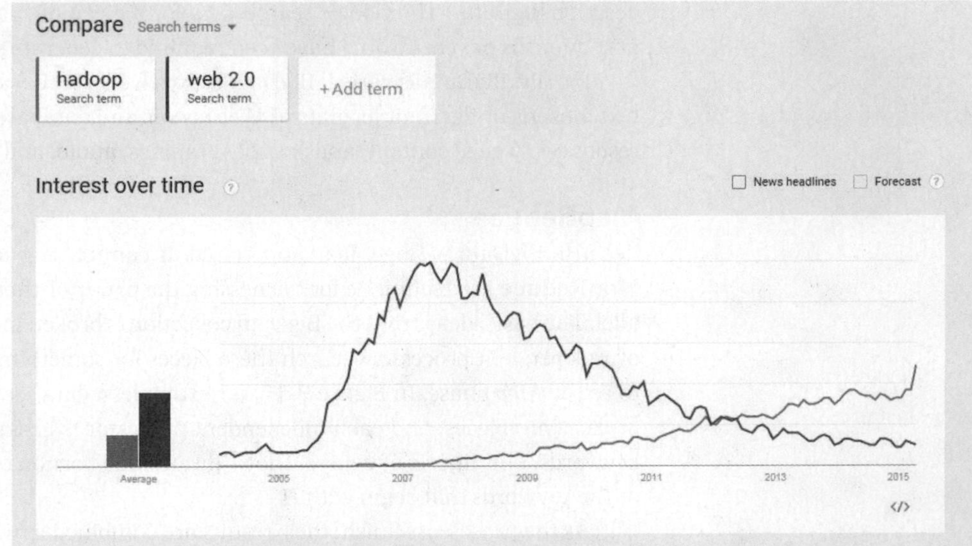


**Figure 9-18**
Google Trends on the Terms *Web 2.0* and *Hadoop*

*Source:* Google and the Google logo are registered trademarks of Google Inc. Used with permission.

Hadoop began as part of Cassandra, but the Apache Foundation split it off to become its own product. Hadoop is written in Java and originally ran on Linux. Some companies implement Hadoop on server farms they manage themselves, and others run Hadoop in the cloud. Amazon.com supports Hadoop as part of its EC3 cloud offering. Microsoft offers Hadoop on its Azure platform as a service named HDInsight. Hadoop includes a query language titled **Pig**.

At present, deep technical skills are needed to run and use Hadoop. Judging by the development of other technologies over the years, it is likely that higher-level, easier-to-use products will be implemented on top of Hadoop. For now, understand that expert programmers are required to use it; you may be involved, however, in planning a BigData study or in interpreting results.

BigData analysis can involve both reporting and data mining techniques. The chief difference is, however, that BigData has volume, velocity, and variation characteristics that far exceed those of traditional reporting and data mining.

Whether an analysis is performed with reporting, data mining, or BigData techniques, the results provide no value until they are delivered to the appropriate users. We turn to that topic next.

# Q9-5 WHAT ARE THE ALTERNATIVES FOR PUBLISHING BI?

For BI results to have value, they must be published to the right user at the right time. In this question, we will discuss the primary publishing alternatives and discuss the functionality of BI servers, a special type of Web server.

## CHARACTERISTICS OF BI PUBLISHING ALTERNATIVES

Figure 9-19 lists four server alternatives for BI publishing. **Static reports** are BI documents that are fixed at the time of creation and do not change. A printed sales analysis is an example of a static report. In the BI context, most static reports are published as PDF documents.

**Dynamic reports** are BI documents that are updated at the time they are requested. A sales report that is current as of the time the user accessed it on a Web server is a dynamic report. In almost all cases, publishing a dynamic report requires the BI application to access a database or other data source at the time the report is delivered to the user.

# BI for Securities Trading?

Since the 1970s there have been rumors of large computers buried in nondescript offices near Wall Street, cranking out analyses for smart stock trading. Do they work? Who knows? If you found a correlation between, say, a decrease in the dollar-to-euro exchange rate that influenced the price of 3M stock, would you publish it? No, you'd trade on it and hope that no one else noticed that correlation. Or if your hedge fund developed a model that failed miserably, would you publish that failure? No. So, due to a lack of data, no controlled study of the success and failure of model-based trading has been done (nor is likely to be done).

Still, it is known that traders such as Alexander Migdal, a former Soviet physicist, made millions of dollars in a high-frequency trading firm[7] that he started. The firm and others like it earn small gains on hundreds of thousands of automated transactions.[8] Unfortunately, such high-frequency trading places severe stresses on the market and was responsible for the near meltdowns in 2007 and 2008.[9] Still such trading continues, if with a bit more control.

Critics say that there is far too much noise in the market for any reliable-over-time predictive analysis to work. Consider, for example, the factors that influence the price of 3M stock: global exchange rates, oil prices, the overall stock market, recent patent filings, patents that are about to expire, employee and customer tweets, product failures—the list goes on and on. No model can account for such complexity.

Or can it?

Today a new class of quantitative applications is using BigData and business intelligence to analyze immense amounts of data over a broad spectrum of sources. These applications both build and evaluate investment strategies. Two Sigma (*www.twosigma.com*) is in the forefront of this new style of quantitative analysis. According to the firm, it analyzes vast amounts of data, including corporate financial statements, developing news, Twitter activity, weather reports, and other data sources. From those analyses, it develops and tests investment strategies.[10] It could, in theory, model all of the factors that influence stocks like 3M.

Two Sigma uses a five-step process:

1. Acquire data
2. Create models
3. Evaluate models
4. Analyze risks
5. Place trades[11]

Does it work? Two Sigma and other firms claim it does. We will see.

*Source:* tonsnoei/Fotolia

We can, however, make one important observation: It has never been easy, some would say never even possible, for regular investors to *time the market* by buying just before an upturn or selling just before a downturn. But today, if you try that, you're not only trying to beat the market, you're competing with Two Sigma, with its hundreds of PhDs and massive computing power, and with a slew of similar companies. For most of us, John Bogle, founder of Vanguard, had it right. Buy an index fund, take your 6 percent, and be happy. And, over 30 years, that 6 percent will net a near sixfold increase.

## QUESTIONS

1. Consider two publicly traded companies: Apple and Alaska Airlines. List 10 factors that influence the price of those two stocks. The factors may be different.
2. Pick one of the two companies in question 1. Briefly explain how each of the 10 factors you chose influences the price of the stock.
3. For the factors in your answer to question 2, list sources of data for measuring each of the 10 factors. What role would BigData play in processing that data?
4. If you had the data in your answer to question 3, how would you go about determining how much each of the factors influences the price of the stock? What kinds of BI techniques would you employ?

5. Assuming you had used BI to answer question 4 and now had a model of how your 10 factors influence the price of that stock, how would you determine how good your model is? How would you know that the 10 factors you chose were the right 10 factors?
6. Suppose it is possible to obtain the data needed and to build a model to predict with 51 percent accuracy the price of a stock. Is that a usable model? What do you need to make such a model effective?
7. Suppose you've misjudged your model and it predicts with only 49 percent accuracy. What is likely to happen?
8. Summarize what you have learned from this exercise.

Pull options for each of the servers in Figure 9-19 are the same. The user goes to the site, clicks a link (or opens an email), and obtains the report. Because they're the same for all four server types, they are not shown in Figure 9-19.

Push options vary by server type. For email or collaboration tools, push is manual; someone, say a manager, an expert, or an administrator, creates an email with the report as an attachment (or URL to the collaboration tool) and sends it to the users known to be interested in that report. For Web servers and SharePoint, users can create alerts and RSS feeds to have the server push content to them when the content is created or changed, with the expiration of a given amount of time, or at particular intervals. SharePoint workflows can also push content.

A BI server extends alert/RSS functionality to support user **subscriptions**, which are user requests for particular BI results on a particular schedule or in response to particular events. For example, a user can subscribe to a daily sales report, requesting that it be delivered each morning. Or the user might request that analyses be delivered whenever a new result is posted on the server or a sales manager might subscribe to receive a sales report whenever sales in his region exceed $1M during the week.

The skills needed to create a publishing application are either low or high. For static content, little skill is needed. The BI author creates the content, and the publisher (usually the same person) attaches it to an email or puts it on the Web or a SharePoint site, and that's it. Publishing dynamic BI is more difficult; it requires the publisher to set up database access when documents are consumed. In the case of a Web server, the publisher will need to develop or have a programmer write code for this purpose. In the case of SharePoint and BI servers, program code is not necessarily needed, but dynamic data connections need to be created, and this task is not for the technically faint of heart. You'll need knowledge beyond the scope of this class to develop dynamic BI solutions. You should be able to do this, however, if you take a few more IS courses or major in IS.

## WHAT ARE THE TWO FUNCTIONS OF A BI SERVER?

A **BI server** is a Web server application that is purpose-built for the publishing of business intelligence. The Microsoft SQL Server Report manager (part of Microsoft SQL Server Reporting Services) is the most popular such product today, but there are other products as well.

**Figure 9-19**
BI Publishing Alternatives

| Server | Report Type | Push Options | Skill Level Needed |
|---|---|---|---|
| Email or collaboration tool | Static | Manual | Low |
| Web server | Static<br>Dynamic | Alert/RSS | Low for static<br>High for dynamic |
| SharePoint | Static<br>Dynamic | Alert/RSS | Low for static<br>High for dynamic |
| BI server | Dynamic | Alert/RSS<br>Subscription | High |

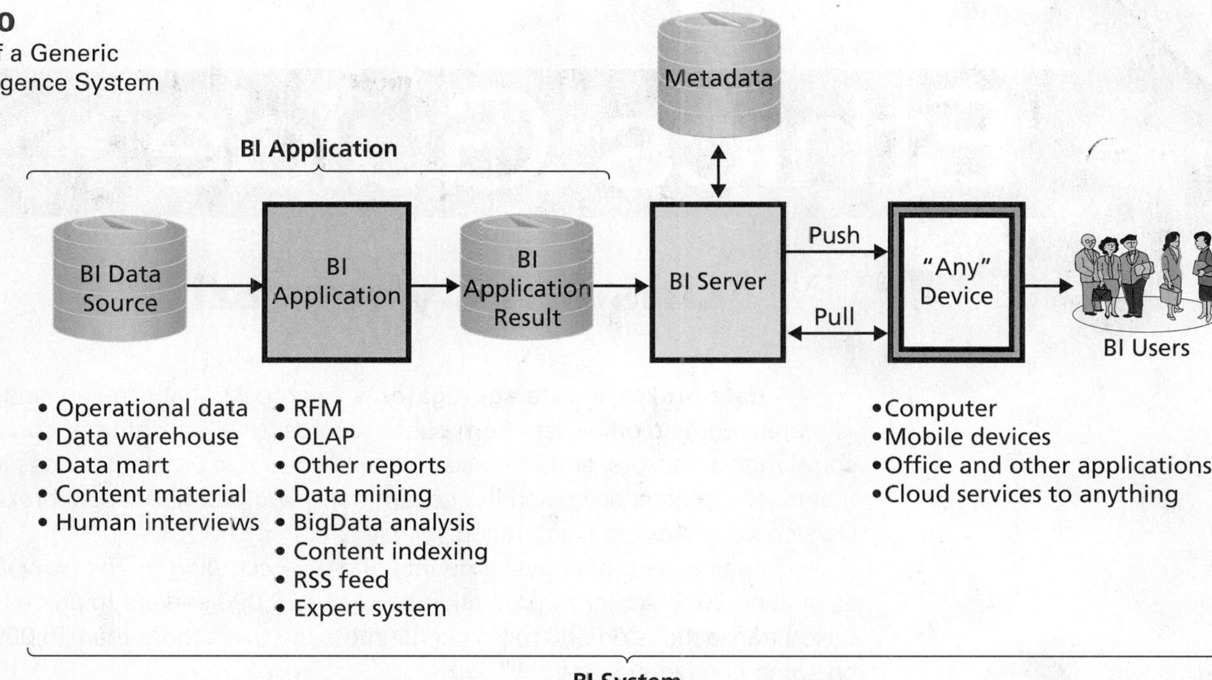


**Figure 9-20**
Components of a Generic Business Intelligence System

BI servers provide two major functions: management and delivery. The management function maintains metadata about the authorized allocation of BI results to users. The BI server tracks what results are available, what users are authorized to view those results, and the schedule upon which the results are provided to the authorized users. It adjusts allocations as available results change and users come and go.

As shown in Figure 9-20, all management data needed by any of the BI servers is stored in metadata. The amount and complexity of such data depend, of course, on the functionality of the BI server.

BI servers use metadata to determine what results to send to which users and, possibly, on which schedule. Today, the expectation is that BI results can be delivered to "any" device. In practice, *any* is interpreted to mean computers, mobile devices, applications such as Microsoft Office, and cloud services.

## How does the **knowledge** in this chapter help **you?**

As a future business professional, you will find that business intelligence is a critical skill. According to a recent survey by Pricewaterhouse Coopers, 50 percent of U.S. CEOs see *very high value* of digital technology in data analytics (business intelligence). Eighty percent reported that data mining and analytics were strategically important to their organizations.[12] In 2014, Gartner found that CEOs believe digital marketing (of which business intelligence is the core) to be the number-one priority for technology investment. Foundation Capital estimates that marketing technology expenditures will grow from $12B in 2014 to $120B by 2026. As you will learn, business intelligence is the key technology supporting such marketing technology.[13]

This chapter has given you the fundamentals of this increasingly important business discipline. You know the three phases of BI analysis, and you have learned common techniques for acquiring, processing, and publishing business intelligence. This knowledge will enable you to imagine innovative uses for data that your employer generates and also to know some of the constraints of such use. At PRIDE, the knowledge of this chapter will help you understand possible uses for the exercise data that is being generated. If PRIDE becomes a successful product, with millions of users, you know that BigData techniques can be used to analyze minute-by-minute exercise data. Finding a valuable use of such BI, however, will be up to you!

# Ethics Guide

## Unseen Cyberazzi

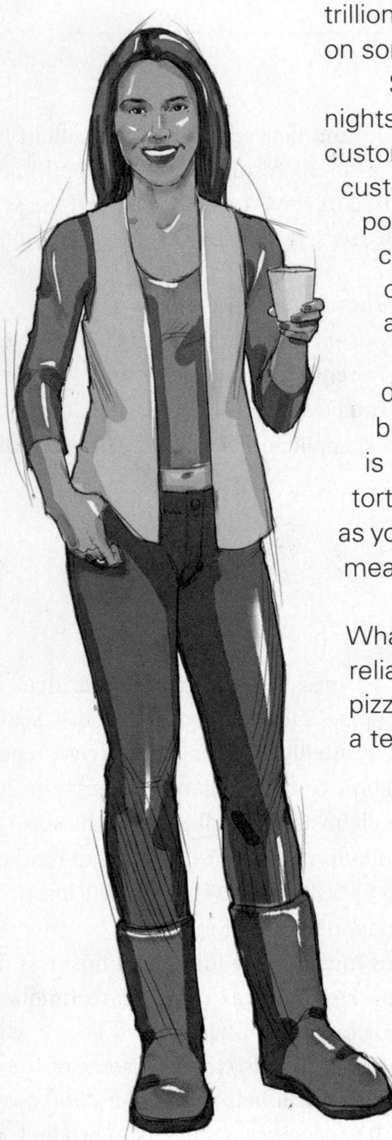

A **data broker** or **data aggregator** is a company that acquires and purchases consumer and other data from public records, retailers, Internet cookie vendors, social media trackers, and other sources and uses it to create business intelligence that it sells to companies and the government. Two prominent data brokers are Datalogix and Acxiom Corporation.

Data brokers gather vast amounts of data. According to *The New York Times*, as of June 2012, Acxiom Corporation had used 23,000 servers to process data of 50 trillion transactions on 500 million consumers. It stores more than 15,000 data points on some consumers.[14]

So, what do data brokers do with all this data? If you buy pizza online on Friday nights only when you receive a substantial discount, a data broker (or the broker's customer) knows to send you a discount pizza coupon Friday morning. If you use a customer loyalty card at your local grocery store and regularly buy, say, large bags of potato chips, the data broker or its customer will send you coupons for more potato chips or for a second snack product that is frequently purchased by potato chip consumers. Or, as discussed in Q9-1, if you suddenly start buying certain lotions and vitamins, the data broker will know you're pregnant.

Federal law provides strict limits on gathering and using medical and credit data. For other data, however, the possibilities are unlimited. In theory, data brokers enable you to view the data that is stored about you, but in practice it is difficult to learn how to request your data. Further, the process for doing so is torturous, and ultimately, the data that is released is limited to innocuous data such as your name, phone numbers, and current and former addresses.[15] Without an easy means for viewing all of your data, it is impossible to verify its accuracy.

Of even greater concern, however, is the unknown processing of such data. What BI techniques are employed by these companies? What are the accuracy and reliability of those techniques? If the data broker errs in predicting that you'll buy a pizza on Friday night, who cares? But if the data broker errs in predicting that you're a terrorist, it matters. Data brokers are silent on these questions.

Source: Sergey Nivens/Shutterstock

## DISCUSSION QUESTIONS

**1.** We've used Kant's categorical imperative for assessing ethical behavior: *Act as if you would have your behavior be a universal law.* As a litmus test, we've said that if you're willing to publish your behavior in *The New York Times*, then your behavior conforms to the categorical imperative.

**a.** Consider the inverse of that litmus test. Is it true that if you're not willing to publish your behavior in *The New York Times*, it is unethical? (Or, in a different but equivalent form: Your behavior is ethical *if and only if* you're willing to publish it in *The New York Times*.)

**b.** Considering your answer to question a, if data brokers are unwilling to say what data they are collecting and how they are processing it, is it reasonable to conclude their behavior is unethical? Explain your answer.

**2.** Using business intelligence on purchasing data for targeted marketing seems innocuous. Is it? Using both the categorical imperative (pages 20–21) and utilitarian (pages 46–47) perspectives, assess the ethics of the following:

**a.** Some people, whether from genetic factors, habit, lack of education, or other factors, are prone to overeating junk food. By focusing junk food sales offers at this market segment, data brokers or their customers are promoting obesity. Is their behavior ethical?

**b.** Data brokers claim they can reliably infer ethnicity from consumer behavior data. Suppose they also determine that one ethnic group is more likely to attend college than others. Accordingly, they focus the marketing for college-prep materials, scholarships, and university admissions applications on this ethnic group. Over time, that group will be guided into positive (assuming you believe college is positive) decisions that other groups will not. Is this behavior different from ethnic profiling? Is it ethical?

**3.** Suppose a data broker correctly identifies that your grandmother is addicted to playing online hearts. From its business intelligence, it knows that frequent hearts players are strong prospects for online gambling. Accordingly, the data broker refers your grandmother's data to an online gambling vendor. Grandma gets hooked and loses all of her savings, including money earmarked for your college tuition.

**a.** Is the data broker's behavior ethical?

**b.** Assume the data broker says, "Look, it's not us, it's our customer, the online gambling vendor, that's causing the problem." Does the broker's posture absolve it of ethical considerations for Grandma's losses?

**c.** Assume the online gambling vendor says, "Look, it's not us; it's Grandma. We provide fair and honest games. If Grandma likes to play games where the odds of winning are low, talk to Grandma." Assume in your answer that the gaming company has gone to great lengths to provide the elderly with an emotionally rewarding user experience for games with low winning odds. Does the vendor's posture absolve it of any ethical considerations for Grandma's losses?

**4.** According to the Privacy Act of 1974, the U.S. government is prohibited from storing many types of data about U.S. citizens. The act does not, however, prohibit it from purchasing business intelligence from data brokers. If the government purchases business intelligence that is based, in part, on data that it is prohibited from storing, is the government's behavior ethical? Use both the categorical imperative and utilitarian perspectives in your answer.

# Guide

## Semantic Security

Security is a very difficult problem—and risks grow larger every year. Not only do we have cheaper, faster computers (remember Moore's Law), we also have more data, more systems for reporting and querying that data, and easier, faster, and broader communication. We have organizational data in the cloud that is not physically under our control. All of these combine to increase the chances that private or proprietary information is inappropriately divulged.

Access security is hard enough: How do we know that the person (or program) who signs on as Megan Cho really is Megan Cho? We use passwords, but files of passwords can be stolen. Setting that issue aside, we need to know that Megan Cho's permissions are set appropriately. Suppose Megan works in the HR department, so she has access to personal and private data of other employees. We need to design the reporting system so that Megan can access all of the data she needs to do her job, and no more.

Also, the delivery system must be secure. A BI server is an obvious and juicy target for any would-be intruder. Someone can break in and change access permissions. Or a hacker could pose as someone else to obtain reports. Application servers help the authorized user, resulting in faster access to more information. But without proper security reporting, servers also ease the intrusion task for unauthorized users.

All of these issues relate to access security. Another dimension to security is equally serious and far more problematic: **semantic security**. Semantic security concerns the unintended release of protected information through the release of a combination of reports or documents that are independently not protected. The term *data triangulation* is also used for this same phenomenon.

Take an example from class. Suppose I assign a group project and I post a list of groups and the names of students assigned to each group. Later, after the assignments have been completed and graded, I post a list of grades on the Web site. Because of university privacy policy, I cannot post the grades by student name or identifier; so, instead, I post the grades for each group. If you want to get the grades for each student, all you have to do is combine the list from Lecture 5 with the list from Lecture 10. You might say that the release of grades in this example does no real harm—after all, it is a list of grades from one assignment.

But go back to Megan Cho in HR. Suppose Megan evaluates the employee compensation program. The COO believes salary offers have been inconsistent over time and that they vary too widely by department. Accordingly, the COO authorizes Megan to receive a report that lists *SalaryOfferAmount* and *OfferDate* and a second report that lists *Department* and *AverageSalary*.

Those reports are relevant to her task and seem innocuous enough. But Megan realizes that she could use the information they contain to determine individual salaries—information she does not have and is not authorized to receive. She proceeds as follows.

Like all employees, Megan has access to the employee directory on the Web portal. Using the directory, she can obtain a list of employees in each department, and using the facilities of her ever-so-helpful report-authoring system she combines that list with the department and average-salary report. Now she has a list of the names of employees in a group and the average salary for that group.

Megan's employer likes to welcome new employees to the company. Accordingly, each week the company publishes an article about new employees who have been hired. The article makes pleasant comments about each person and encourages employees to meet and greet them.

Megan, however, has other ideas. Because the report is published on SharePoint, she can obtain an electronic copy of it. It's an Acrobat report, and using Acrobat's handy Search feature, she soon has a list of employees and the week they were hired.

She now examines the report she received for her study, the one that has *SalaryOfferAmount* and the offer date, and she does some interpretation. During the week of July 21, three offers were extended: one for \$35,000, one for \$53,000, and one for \$110,000. She also notices from the "New Employees" report that a director of marketing programs, a product test engineer, and a receptionist were hired that same week. It's unlikely that they paid the receptionist \$110,000; that sounds more like the director of marketing programs. So, she now "knows" (infers) that person's salary.

Next, going back to the department report and using the employee directory, she sees that the marketing director is in the marketing programs department. There are just three people in that department, and their average salary is \$105,000. Doing the arithmetic, she now knows that the average salary for the other two people is \$102,500. If she can find the hire week for one of those other two people, she can find out both the second and third person's salaries.

You get the idea. Megan was given just two reports to do her job. Yet she combined the information in those reports with publicly available information and was able to deduce salaries, for at least some employees. These salaries are much more than she is supposed to know. This is a semantic security problem.

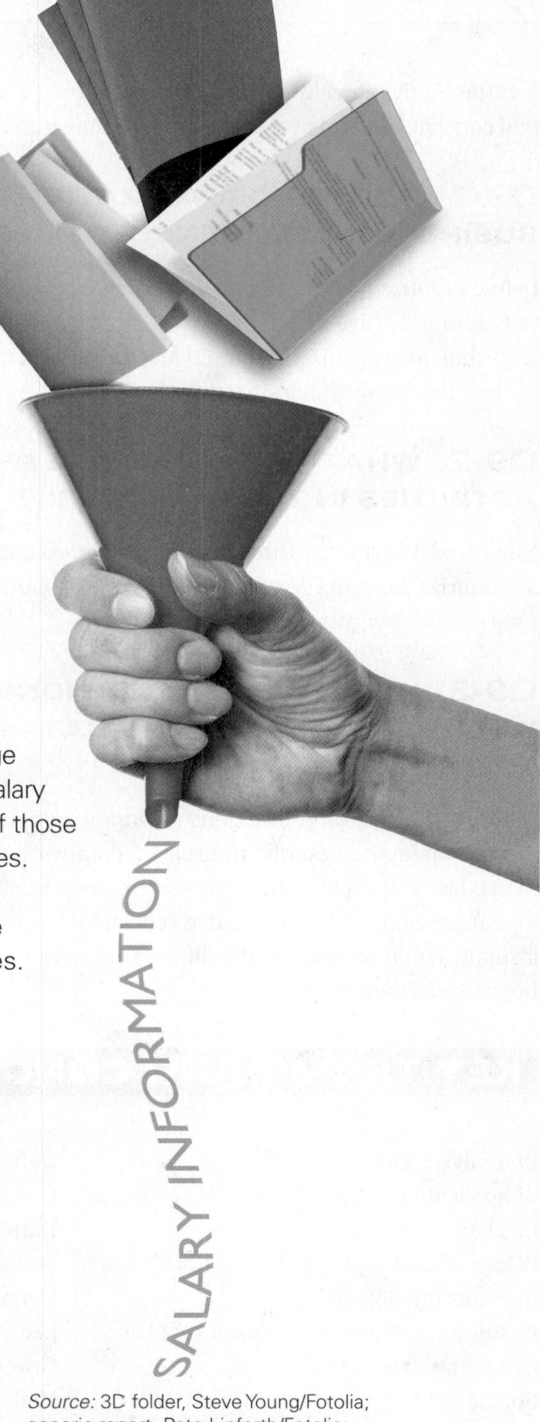


*Source:* 3D folder, Steve Young/Fotolia; generic report, Pete Linforth/Fotolia; document file, kitkana/Fotolia; hand/funnel, viviamo/Shutterstock.

## DISCUSSION QUESTIONS

**1.** In your own words, explain the difference between access security and semantic security.

**2.** Why do reporting systems increase the risk of semantic security problems?

**3.** What can an organization do to protect itself against accidental losses due to semantic security problems?

**4.** What legal responsibility does an organization have to protect against semantic security problems?

**5.** Suppose semantic security problems are inevitable. Do you see an opportunity for new products from insurance companies? If so, describe such an insurance product. If not, explain why not.

# ACTIVE REVIEW

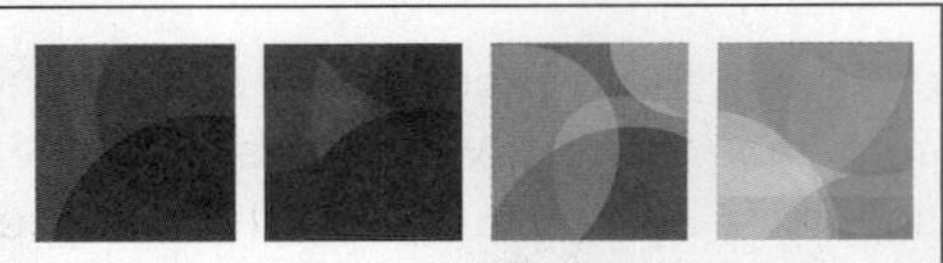

Use this Active Review to verify that you understand the ideas and concepts that answer the chapter's study questions.

## Q9-1 HOW DO ORGANIZATIONS USE BUSINESS INTELLIGENCE (BI) SYSTEMS?

Define *business intelligence* and *BI system*. Explain the elements in Figure 9-1. Give an example, other than in this text, of one way that an organization could use business intelligence for each of the four collaborative tasks in Figure 9-2.

## Q9-2 WHAT ARE THE THREE PRIMARY ACTIVITIES IN THE BI PROCESS?

Name and describe the three primary activities in the BI process. Summarize how the team at the parts distribution company used these activities to produce BI results.

## Q9-3 HOW DO ORGANIZATIONS USE DATA WAREHOUSES AND DATA MARTS TO ACQUIRE DATA?

Describe the need and functions of data warehouses and data marts. Name and describe the role of data warehouse components. List and explain the problems that can exist in data used for data mining and sophisticated reporting. Use the example of a supply chain to describe the differences between a data warehouse and a data mart.

## Q9-4 WHAT ARE THREE TECHNIQUES FOR PROCESSING BI DATA?

Name and describe the three techniques. State the goals and characteristics of each. Summarize reporting analysis. Define *structured data*. Summarize data mining. Explain the difference between supervised and unsupervised data mining. Differentiate between reporting analysis and data mining. Name and explain the three Vs of BigData. Describe how MapReduce works and explain the purpose of Hadoop.

## Q9-5 WHAT ARE THE ALTERNATIVES FOR PUBLISHING BI?

Name four alternative types of servers used for publishing business intelligence. Explain the difference between static and dynamic reports; explain the term *subscription*. Describe why dynamic reports are difficult to create.

## How does the **knowledge** in this chapter help **you?**

Summarize the knowledge you learned in this chapter and explain how you might use it as a future business professional. Explain how your knowledge would benefit the PRIDE project and describe one use of BigData and PRIDE.

## KEY TERMS AND CONCEPTS



MyMISLab™

To complete the problems with the ✪, go to EOC Discussion Questions in the MyLab.

## USING YOUR KNOWLEDGE

**9-1.** Explain in your own words how the sales analysis team in Q9-2 implemented each of the five criteria it developed. Use data and tables shown in Q9-2 in your answer.

**9-2.** In Q9-2, the sales analysis team created a query that connected the selected parts with their past sales data (Sales History for Selected Parts). Explain why the query results do not show promise for the selling of these part designs. In light of these results, should the team look at changing its criteria? If so, how? If not, why not?

**9-3.** Given the results from the Sales History for Selected Parts query, list three actions that the company can take. Recommend one of these actions and justify your recommendation.

## COLLABORATION EXERCISE 9

*Read Chapter Extensions 1 and 2 if you have not already done so. Meet with your team and build a collaboration IS that uses tools like Google Docs, SharePoint, or other collaboration tools. Do not forget the need for procedures and team training. Now, using that IS, answer the questions below.*

Read Case Study 9 (pages 272–273) if you have not already done so. Undeniably, third-party cookies offer advantages to online sellers. They also increase the likelihood that consumers will receive online ads that are close to their interests; thus, third-party cookies can provide a consumer service as well. But at what cost to personal privacy? And what should be done about them? Working with your team, answer the following questions:

**9-4.** Summarize the ways that third-party cookies are created and processed. Even though cookies are not supposed to contain personally identifying data, explain how such data can readily be obtained. (See question 9-14, page 273.)

**9-5.** Numerous browser features, add-ins, and other tools exist for blocking third-party cookies. Search the Web for *block third-party cookies for xxx,* and fill in the *xxx* with the name and version of your browser. Read the instructions and summarize the procedures that you need to take to view the cookies issued from a given site.

**9-6.** In large measure, ads pay for the free use of Web content and even Web sites themselves. If, because of a fear of privacy, many people block third-party cookies, substantial ad revenue will be lost. Discuss with your group how such a movement would affect the valuation of Facebook and other ad-revenue-dependent companies. Discuss how it would affect the delivery of online content like that provided by *Forbes* or other providers of free online content.

**9-7.** Many companies have a conflict of interest with regard to third-party cookies. On the one hand, such cookies help generate revenue and pay for Internet content. On the other hand, trespassing on users' privacy could turn out to be a PR disaster. As you learned in your answer to question 9-5, browsers include options to block third-party cookies. However, in most cases, those options are turned off in the default browser installation. Discuss why that might be so. If sites were required to obtain your permission before installing third-party cookies, how would you determine whether to grant it? List criteria that your team thinks you would actually use (as opposed to what the team thinks you *should* do). Assess the effectiveness of such a policy.

**9-8.** The processing of third-party cookies is hidden; we don't know what is being done behind the scenes with the data about our own behavior. Because there is so much of it and so many parties involved, the possibilities are difficult to comprehend, even if the descriptions were available. And if your privacy is compromised by the interaction of seven different companies working independently, which is to be held accountable? Summarize consequences of these facts for consumers.

**9-9.** Summarize the benefits of third-party cookies to consumers.

**9-10.** Given all you have learned about third-party cookies, what does your team think should be done about them? Possible answers are a) nothing; b) require Web sites to ask users before installing third-party cookies; c) require browsers to block third-party cookies; d) require browsers to block third-party cookies by default, but enable them at the users' option; e) something else. Discuss these alternatives among your team and recommend one. Justify your recommendation.

# CASE STUDY 9

## Hadoop the Cookie Cutter

A **cookie** is data that a Web site stores on your computer to record something about its interaction with you. The cookie might contain data such as the date you last visited, whether you are currently signed in, or something else about your interaction with that site. Cookies can also contain a key value to one or more tables in a database that the server company maintains about your past interactions. In that case, when you access a site, the server uses the value of the cookie to look up your history. Such data could include your past purchases, portions of incomplete transactions, or the data and appearance you want for your Web page. Most of the time cookies ease your interaction with Web sites.

Cookie data include the URL of the Web site of the cookie's owner. Thus, for example, when you go to Amazon, it asks your browser to place a cookie on your computer that includes its name, *www.amazon.com*. Your browser will do so unless you have turned cookies off.

A **third-party cookie** is a cookie created by a site other than the one you visited. Such cookies are generated in several ways, but the most common occurs when a Web page includes content from multiple sources. For example, Amazon designs its pages so that one or more sections contain ads provided by the ad-servicing company DoubleClick. When the browser constructs your Amazon page, it contacts DoubleClick to obtain the content for such sections (in this case, ads). When it responds with the content, DoubleClick instructs your browser to store a DoubleClick cookie. That cookie is a third-party cookie. In general, third-party cookies do not contain the name or any value that identifies a particular user. Instead, they include the IP address to which the content was delivered.

On its own servers, when it creates the cookie, DoubleClick records that data in a log, and if you click on the ad, it will add the fact of that click to the log. This logging is repeated every time DoubleClick shows an ad. Cookies have an expiration date, but that date is set by the cookie creator, and they can last many years. So, over time, DoubleClick and any other third-party cookie owner will have a history of what they've shown, what ads have been clicked, and the intervals between interactions.

But the opportunity is even greater. DoubleClick has agreements not only with Amazon, but also with many others, such as Facebook. If Facebook includes any DoubleClick content on its site, DoubleClick will place another cookie on your computer. This cookie is different from the one that it placed via Amazon, but both cookies have your IP address and other data sufficient to associate the second cookie as originating from the same source as the first. So, DoubleClick now has a record of your ad response data on two sites. Over time, the cookie log will contain data to show not only how you respond to ads, but also your pattern of visiting various Web sites on all those sites on which it places ads.

You might be surprised to learn how many third-party cookies you have. The browser Firefox has an optional feature called *Lightbeam* that tracks and graphs all the cookies on your computer. Figure 9-21 shows the cookies that various Web sites placed on a sample computer as the user moved from site to site. As you can see, in Figure 9-21a, when the browser was started, there were no cookies. The cookies after visiting *www.msn.com* are shown in Figure 9-21b. At this point, there are already eight third-party cookies. After visiting five sites, there were 27 third-party cookies, and after visiting seven sites, there were 69, as shown in Figures 9-21c and d.

Who are these companies that are gathering this browser behavior data? If you hold your mouse over one of the cookies, Lightbeam will highlight it in the data column on the right. As you can see in Figures 9-21d, after visiting seven sites, DoubleClick was connected to a total of 16 other sites, only seven of which can be sites the user visited. So, DoubleClick is connecting to sites the user doesn't know about and on the user's computer. Examine the connection column on the right. The user visited MSN, Amazon, MyNorthwest, and WSJ, but who are BlueKai and Rubiconproject? It is likely the user has never heard of them; they, apparently, know of the user, however!

Third-party cookies generate incredible volumes of log data. For example, suppose a company, such as DoubleClick, shows 100 ads to a given computer in a day. If it is showing ads to 10 million computers (possible), that is a total of one billion log entries per day, or 365 billion a year. Truly this is BigData.

Storage is essentially free, but how can companies possibly process all that data? How do they parse the log to find entries just for your computer? How do they integrate data from different cookies on the same IP address? How do they analyze those entries to determine which ads you clicked on? How do they then characterize differences in ads to determine which characteristics matter most to you? The answer, as you learned in Q9-4, is to use parallel processing. Using a MapReduce algorithm, they distribute the work to thousands of processors that work in parallel. They then aggregate the results of these independent processors and then, possibly, move to a second phase of analysis where they do it again. Hadoop, the open source program that you learned about in Q9-4, is a favorite for this process. No wonder Amazon offers Hadoop MapReduce as part of EC3. Amazon built it for itself and now, given that it has it, why not lease it out?

*(See Collaboration Exercise 9 on page 271 for an additional discussion of the third-party cookie problem. Or is it an opportunity?)*

a. Display on Startup

b. After MSN.com and Gmail

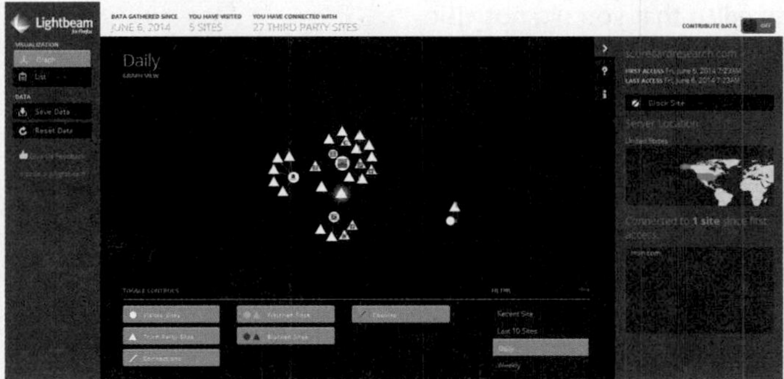


c. Five Sites Visited Yield 27 Third Parties

d. Sites Connected to DoubleClick

**Figure 9-21**
Third-party Cookie Growth

*Source:* Mozilla Foundation

## QUESTIONS

**9-11.** Using your own words, explain how third-party cookies are created.

**9-12.** Suppose you are an ad-serving company and you maintain a log of cookie data for ads you serve to Web pages for a particular vendor (say Amazon).

- **a.** How can you use this data to determine which are the best ads?
- **b.** How can you use this data to determine which are the best ad formats?
- **c.** How could you use records of past ads and ad clicks to determine which ads to send to a given IP address?
- **d.** How could you use this data to determine how well the technique you used in your answer to part c was working?
- **e.** How could you use this data to determine that a given IP address is used by more than one person?
- **f.** How does having this data give you a competitive advantage vis-à-vis other ad-serving companies?

**9-13.** Suppose you are an ad-serving company and you have a log of cookie data for ads served to Web pages of all your customers (Amazon, Facebook, etc.).

- **a.** Describe, in general terms, how you can process the cookie data to associate log entries for a particular IP address.
- **b.** Explain how your answers to question 9-12 change given that you have this additional data.
- **c.** Describe how you can use this log data to determine users who consistently seek the lowest price.
- **d.** Describe how you can use this log data to determine users who consistently seek the latest fashion.
- **e.** Explain why uses like those in parts c and d are only possible with MapReduce or similar technique.

**9-14.** As stated, third-party cookies usually do not contain, in themselves, data that identifies you as a particular person. However, Amazon, Facebook, and other first-party cookie vendors know who you are because you signed in. Only one of them needs to reveal your identity to the ad server and your identity can then be correlated with your IP address. At that point, the ad server and potentially all of its clients know who you are. Are you concerned about the invasion of your privacy that third-party cookies enable? Explain your answer.

MyMISLab™

Go to the Assignments section of your MyLab to complete these writing exercises.

**9-15.** Reflect on the differences between reporting systems and data mining systems. What are their similarities and differences? How do their costs differ? What benefits does each offer? How would an organization choose between these two BI tools?

**9-16.** Install Firefox, if you do not already have it, and then install the Lightbeam add-on. Visit the sites you normally visit first thing in your day.

**a.** How many third-party sites are you connected to?

**b.** Find DoubleClick in the Lightbeam display. List the companies that DoubleClick is connected to that you did not visit.

**c.** Choose one of the companies in your answer to part b. Google it to describe what it does.

**9-17.** Suppose you were hired by the dean of your school to analyze graduation rates. He wants to know if there's anything that can be done to help students graduate faster. He wants to move students through school and into well-paid jobs. What types of data do you think you would need for this project? Would a data mart be helpful to you? Explain why or why not?

**9-18.** Suppose you are the director of student activities at your university. Recently, some students have charged that your department misallocates its resources. They claim the allocation is based on outdated student preferences. Funds are given to activities that few students find attractive, and insufficient funds are allocated to new activities in which students do want to participate. Describe how you could use reporting and/or data mining applications to assess this claim.

## ENDNOTES

1. Nipun Gupta, "Top 10 Databases in the World," May 4, 2014, accessed April 2, 2015, *http://csnipuntech.blogspot.com/2014/05/top-10-largest-databases-in-world.html.*
2. Charles Duhigg, "How Companies Learn Your Secrets," *The New York Times*, last modified February 16, 2012, *http://www.nytimes.com/2012/02/19/magazine/shopping-habits.html?_r=2&hp=&pagewanted=all&.*
3. Alistair Barr, "Crowdsourcing Goes to Hollywood as Amazon Makes Movies," *Reuters*, last modified October 10, 2012, *www.reuters.com/article/2012/10/10/us-amazon-hollywood-crowd-idUSBRE8990JH20121010*
4. Martin U. Müller, Marcel Rosenbach, and Thomas Schulz, "Living by the Numbers: Big Data Knows What Your Future Holds," *Der Spiegel*, accessed July 31, 2013, *www.spiegel.de/international/business/big-data-enables-companies-and-researchers-to-look-into-the-future-a-899964.html.*
5. Elizabeth Dwoskin, "The Next Marketing Frontier: Your Medical Records," *Wall Street Journal*, March 3, 2015, accessed April 3, 2015, *www.wsj.com/articles/the-next-marketing-frontier-your-medical-records-1425408631?mod=WSJ_hpp_MIDDLENexttoWhatsNewsFifthhttp.*
6. A nonprofit corporation that supports open source software projects, originally those for the Apache Web server, but today for a large number of additional major software projects.
7. Bradley Hope, "5 Things to Know about High Frequency Trading," *Wall Street Journal*, April 2, 2014, accessed April 2, 2015, *http://blogs.wsj.com/briefly/2014/04/02/5-things-to-know-about-high-frequency-trading/.*
8. Bradley Hope, "How Computers Troll a Sea of Data for Stock Picks, *Wall Street Journal*, April 2, 2015, accessed April 2, 2015, *www.wsj.com/articles/how-computers-trawl-a-sea-of-data-for-stock-picks-1427941801?mod=WSJ_hp_RightTopStories.*
9. Scott Patterson. *The Quants.* (New York: Crown Business, 2011).
10. *www.twosigma.com/about.html*, accessed April 2, 2015.
11. Bradley Hope, "How Computers Troll a Sea of Data for Stock Picks, *Wall Street Journal*, April 2, 2015, accessed April 2, 2015, *www.wsj.com/articles/how-computers-trawl-a-sea-of-data-for-stock-picks-1427941801?mod=WSJ_hp_RightTopStories.*
12. Pricewaterhouse Coopers. *2015 US CEO Survey*, accessed April 3, 2015, *www.pwc.com/us/en/ceo-survey/index.html.*
13. Mary K Pratt, "Data in a Blender," *CIO*, April 1, 2015, p. 12.
14. Natasha Singer, "Mapping, and Sharing, the Consumer Genome," *The New York Times*, last modified June 16, 2012, *www.nytimes.com/2012/06/17/technology/acxiom-the-quiet-giant-of-consumer-database-marketing.html.*
15. Lois Beckett, "What Data Brokers Know About You," *RealClearTechnology*, last modified March 8, 2013, *www.realcleartechnology.com/articles/2013/03/08/what_data_brokers_know_about_you_326.html.*

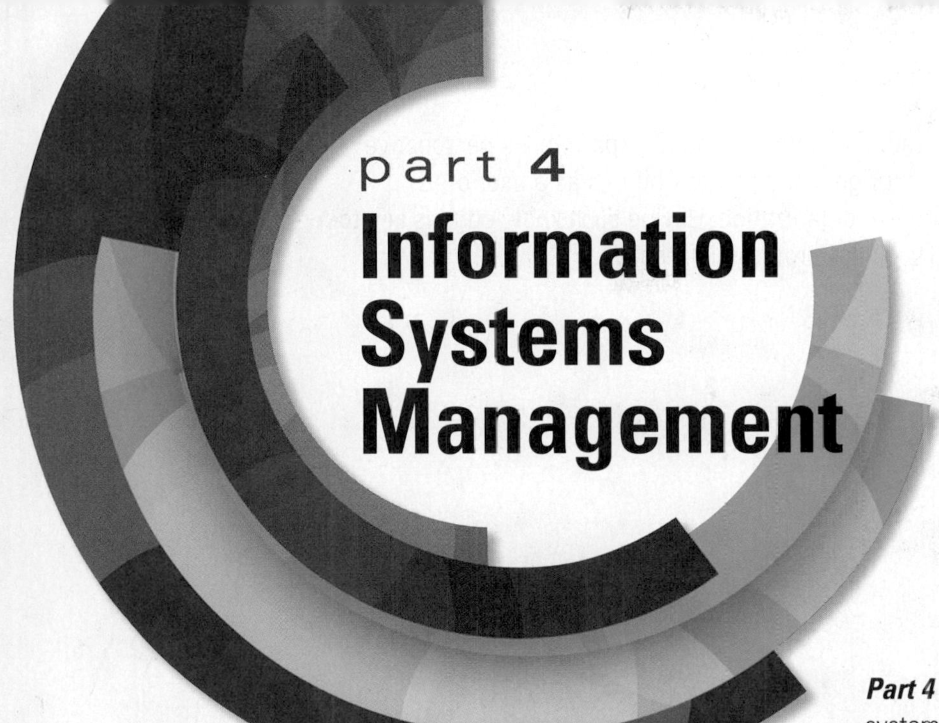

part 4

# Information Systems Management

**_Part 4 addresses_** the management of information systems security, development, and resources. We begin with security because of its great importance today. With the Internet, the interconnectivity of systems, and the rise of interorganizational IS, security problems in one organization become security problems in connected organizations as well. You'll see how that affects PRIDE in the Chapter 10 opener.

This could happen to you

While you can readily understand that IS security is important to you as a future manager, it may be more difficult for you to appreciate why you need to know about IS development. As a business professional, you will be the customer of development projects. You need basic knowledge of development processes to be able to assess the quality of the work being done on your behalf. As a manager, you may allocate budget and release funds for IS development. You need knowledge that allows you to be an active and effective participant in such projects.

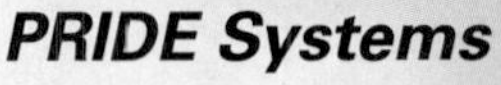


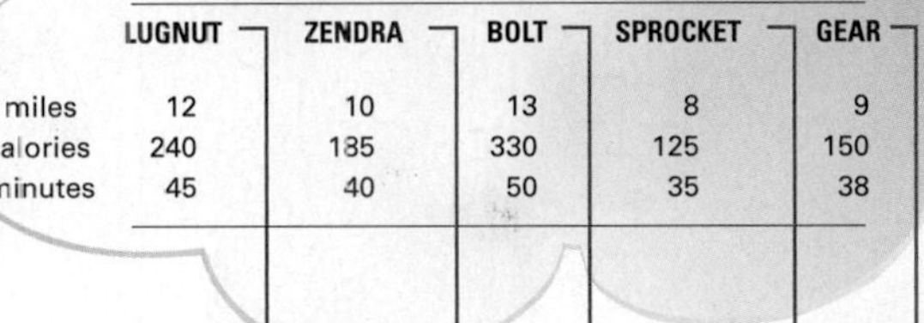

| | LUGNUT | ZENDRA | BOLT | SPROCKET | GEAR |
|---|---|---|---|---|---|
| miles | 12 | 10 | 13 | 8 | 9 |
| calories | 240 | 185 | 330 | 125 | 150 |
| minutes | 45 | 40 | 50 | 35 | 38 |

Finally, you need to know how IS resources are managed so that you can better relate to your IS department. IS managers can sometimes seem rigid and overly protective of IS assets, but usually they have important reasons for their

*Source:* Top: Nongkran_ch/iStock/Getty Images; Bottom: VIGE.CO/Shutterstock

concerns. You need to understand the IS department's perspective and know both your rights and responsibilities as a user of IS resources within your organization. Having such knowledge is key to success for any business professional today.

*Source:* Ifh85/Fotolia

# Information Systems Security

James and Michele are videoconferencing with Sam Ide, the manager of security for San Diego Sports, a large sports equipment vendor that Michele wants to involve in race events. Mr. Ide's job is to determine if PRIDE Systems provides an acceptable level of security. Michele has gone over this several times with San Diego Sports personnel, and they asked to speak with someone outside of sales who has direct knowledge of PRIDE Systems' security. Michele asked James to participate in the videoconference with Mr. Ide.

**This could happen to you**

"Sam, I have James Wu, our IS manager here, on our videoconference line. Why don't I let you explain your concerns and I'll ask James to respond?"

"Sure. James, thanks for taking the time to speak with me."

"Happy to do it."

"OK, we at SDS... that's how we refer to ourselves... we at SDS have always been concerned with security. But, given the recent troubles at Target and Adobe, our senior management team has asked us to be even more careful. It appears that criminals have begun to focus attacks on interorganizational systems, and so we address security with all of our partners."

"I understand, Sam. Although in this case, we're not talking about any connection between your systems and ours. As I understand it, we just want to feature San Diego Sports in a major way in our advertising and promotion of events." James is careful as he gains a sense of his interests.

"Thanks, James, that's my understanding as well. All the same, we don't want to become affiliated in the mind of our market with any company that does have a major security problem, and that's the reason for this call."

"Got it. Do you have specific matters you'd like me to address?"

"Actually, I do. Michele has explained to me the basics of your security program, and she said that, given the fact that your systems were originally designed to store medical data, you have designed security deep into your systems." Sam sounds like he's reading from notes.

"Correct." James nods at Michele as he says this.

"I wonder if you could explain that to me with some specifics."

"Sure, but first, may I ask if you have a technical background?" James isn't sure how much detail to provide him.

"I'm not a developer, not by a long shot, but I was closely involved as a systems analyst in the development of many of our systems." Sam's actually quite a bit more technical than he reveals.

"Great. Let me dive in then, and if the dive is too deep, just let me know." There's not the least bit of condescension in James's voice as he speaks.

# STUDY QUESTIONS

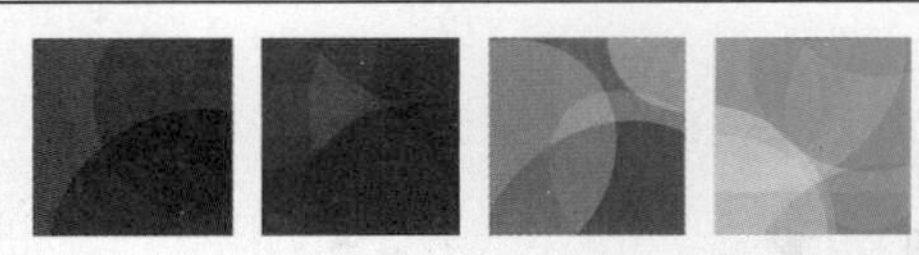

**Q10-1 WHAT IS THE GOAL OF INFORMATION SYSTEMS SECURITY?**

**Q10-2 HOW BIG IS THE COMPUTER SECURITY PROBLEM?**

**Q10-3 HOW SHOULD YOU RESPOND TO SECURITY THREATS?**

**Q10-4 HOW SHOULD ORGANIZATIONS RESPOND TO SECURITY THREATS?**

**Q10-5 HOW CAN TECHNICAL SAFEGUARDS PROTECT AGAINST SECURITY THREATS?**

**Q10-6 HOW CAN DATA SAFEGUARDS PROTECT AGAINST SECURITY THREATS?**

**Q10-7 HOW CAN HUMAN SAFEGUARDS PROTECT AGAINST SECURITY THREATS?**

**Q10-8 HOW SHOULD ORGANIZATIONS RESPOND TO SECURITY INCIDENTS?**

## How does the **knowledge** in this chapter help **you?**

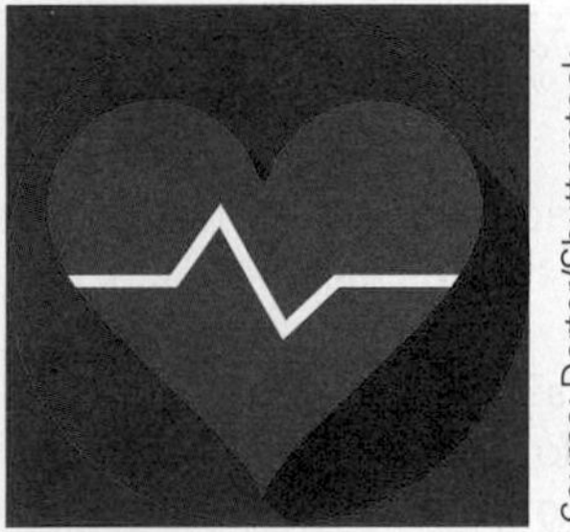

*Source:* Derter/Shutterstock

**"But how do you implement that security?"**

"Will do."

"Each user is in charge of the distribution of his or her data. Initially, users' data is not shared at all. But we provide a simple-to-use UI that allows users to change their security settings."

"OK. Michele told me that. But how do you implement that security?" Sam wants to dive deeper.

"Because we have thousands and thousands of users, we store all privacy settings in a database and we have elaborate security on that database that I can go into later, if you want." James wants to focus on specific PRIDE features.

"Maybe. Just keep explaining."

"It turns out that event participants have a many-to-many relationship with all of our major players. Thus, for example, a participant may belong to several health clubs, and of course a health club has a relationship to many of our participants. Similarly, a participant has a relationship to potentially many insurance companies, and each company can have a relationship to many of our participants. Are you with me?"

"Yes, keep going." Sam sounds curious.

"So, as you know, to represent a many-to-many relationship we create an intersection or bridge table. And we store the security preferences for each person and his or her relationship to the external agent in that intersection table."

Michele jumps in at this point. "Sam, let me see if I can bring up an illustration onto your screen. Do you see the table diagram?"

"Just a second. Something's loading. Ah, yes, there it is."

James continues, "OK, the data for each participant is stored in the Person table in the center. Actually, we store quite a bit more data than shown here, but this will give you the idea of what we do. The security allowed is stored in attributes called *PolicyStatements*

**Optional Extension for this chapter is • CE14: Data Breaches 574**

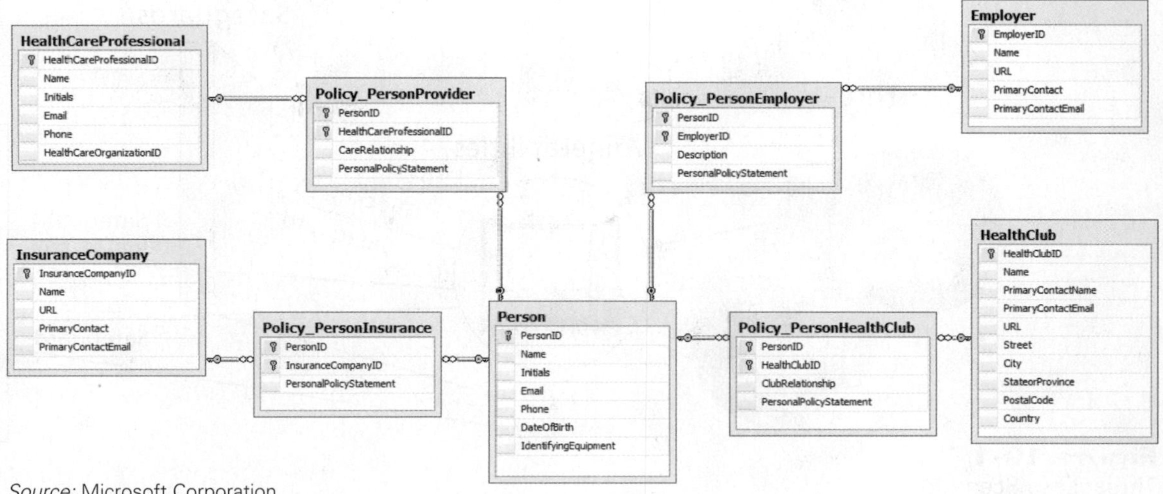


*Source:* Microsoft Corporation

in the intersection tables. By default, the value is 'None.' However, if someone decides to share his or her data with, say, a health club, then he or she uses a form to specify what he or she wants, and we store the result of that decision in the PolicyStatement attribute. All of our code uses the value of that attribute to limit data access."

"That makes sense; it's a clean design. But what about SQL injection?"

"Good question. There are four types of access allowed: None, which is the default; Non-identifying; Summary; and Full Access. The last two include the person's identity. In the form, those four are presented with radio buttons and the user picks. There's no place for SQL injection to occur."

The meeting continues in this vein for another 15 minutes. Sam seems satisfied with James's responses. Afterward, James and Michele walk back to their offices together.

"James, that was the best meeting I've had with him. He is impatient with me, but he related to you really well."

"Michele, I'm glad you're happy with it. I couldn't tell what he thought, but his questions were good and ones that we've thought about a lot."

"Well, James, you're good at explaining things. Ever think about going into sales?"

"Heavens, no, Michele. But I'll take that as a compliment."

"Thanks again."

# Q10-1 WHAT IS THE GOAL OF INFORMATION SYSTEMS SECURITY?

Information systems security is really about trade-offs. In one sense, it's a trade-off between security and freedom. For example, organizations can increase the security of their information systems by taking away users' freedom to choose their own passwords and force them to choose stronger passwords that are difficult for hackers to crack.

Another way to look at information systems security, and the primary focus of this chapter, is that it's a trade-off between cost and risk. To understand the nature of this trade-off, we begin with a description of the security threat/loss scenario and then discuss the sources of security threats. Following that, we'll state the goal of information systems security.

## THE IS SECURITY THREAT/LOSS SCENARIO

Figure 10-1 illustrates the major elements of the security problem that individuals and organizations confront today. A **threat** is a person or organization that seeks to obtain or alter data or other IS assets illegally, without the owner's permission and often without the owner's knowledge.

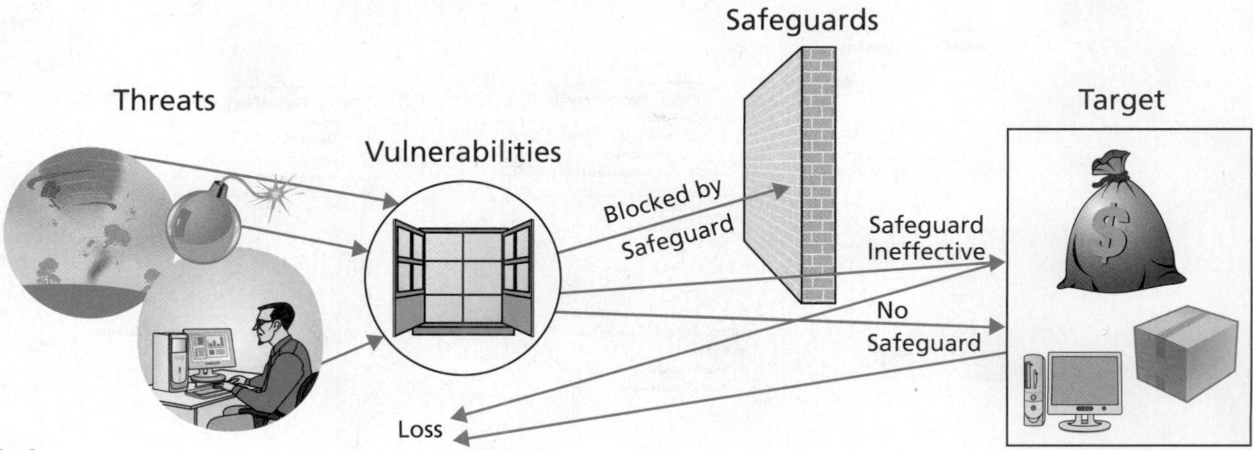


**Figure 10-1**
Threat/Loss Scenario

A **vulnerability** is an opportunity for threats to gain access to individual or organizational assets. For example, when you buy something online, you provide your credit card data; when that data is transmitted over the Internet, it is vulnerable to threats. A **safeguard** is some measure that individuals or organizations take to block the threat from obtaining the asset. Notice in Figure 10-1 that safeguards are not always effective; some threats achieve their goal despite safeguards. Finally, the **target** is the asset that is desired by the threat.

Figure 10-2 shows examples of threats/targets, vulnerabilities, safeguards, and results. In the first two rows, a hacker (the threat) wants your bank login credentials (the target) to access your bank account. If you click on links in emails you can be directed to phishing sites that look identical to your bank's Web site. Phishing sites don't typically use https. If, as shown in the first row of Figure 10-2, you always access your bank's site using https rather than http (discussed in Q10-5), you will be using an effective safeguard, and you will successfully counter the threat.

If, however, as described in the second row of Figure 10-2, you access what appears to be your bank's site without using https (i.e., an unsecured site), you have no safeguard at all. Your login credentials can be quickly recorded and resold to other criminals.

The bottom row of Figure 10-2 shows another situation. Here an employee at work obtains sensitive data and posts it on what he thinks is a work-only Google+ group. However, the employee errs and instead posts it to a public group. The target is the sensitive data, and the vulnerability is public access to the group. In this case, there are several safeguards that should have prevented this loss; the employee needed passwords to obtain the sensitive data and to join the private, work-only group. The employer has procedures that state employees are not to post confidential data to any public site, such as Google+, but these procedures were either unknown or ignored. A third safeguard is the training that all employees are given. Because the employee ignores the procedures, though, all of those safeguards are ineffective and the data is exposed to the public.

**Figure 10-2**
Examples of Threat/Loss

| Threat/Target | Vulnerability | Safeguard | Result | Explanation |
|---|---|---|---|---|
| Hacker wants to steal your bank login credentials | Hacker creates a phishing site nearly identical to your online banking site | Only access sites using https | No loss | Effective safeguard |
| | | None | Loss of login credentials | Ineffective safeguard |
| Employee posts sensitive data to public Google + group | Public access to not-secure group | Passwords Procedures Employee training | Loss of sensitive data | Ineffective safeguard |

**Figure 10-3**
Security Problems and Sources

| | | Threat | | |
|---|---|---|---|---|
| | | Human Error | Computer Crime | Natural Disasters |
| Loss | Unauthorized data disclosure | Procedural mistakes | Pretexting<br>Phishing<br>Spoofing<br>Sniffing<br>Hacking | Disclosure during recovery |
| | Incorrect data modification | Procedural mistakes<br>Incorrect procedures<br>Ineffective accounting controls<br>System errors | Hacking | Incorrect data recovery |
| | Faulty service | Procedural mistakes<br>Development and installation errors | Usurpation | Service improperly restored |
| | Denial of service (DoS) | Accidents | DoS attacks | Service interruption |
| | Loss of infrastructure | Accidents | Theft<br>Terrorist activity | Property loss |

## WHAT ARE THE SOURCES OF THREATS?

Figure 10-3 summarizes the sources of security threats. The type of threat is shown in the columns, and the type of loss is shown in the rows.

### Human Error

*Human errors and mistakes* include accidental problems caused by both employees and nonemployees. An example is an employee who misunderstands operating procedures and accidentally deletes customer records. Another example is an employee who, in the course of backing up a database, inadvertently installs an old database on top of the current one. This category also includes poorly written application programs and poorly designed procedures. Finally, human errors and mistakes include physical accidents, such as driving a forklift through the wall of a computer room.

### Computer Crime

The second threat type is *computer crime*. This threat type includes employees and former employees who intentionally destroy data or other system components. It also includes hackers who break into a system and virus and worm writers who infect computer systems. Computer crime also includes terrorists and those who break into a system to steal for financial gain.

### Natural Events and Disasters

*Natural events and disasters* are the third type of security threat. This category includes fires, floods, hurricanes, earthquakes, tsunamis, avalanches, and other acts of nature. Problems in this category include not only the initial loss of capability and service, but also losses stemming from actions to recover from the initial problem.

## WHAT TYPES OF SECURITY LOSS EXIST?

Five types of security loss exist: unauthorized data disclosure, incorrect data modification, faulty service, denial of service, and loss of infrastructure. Consider each.

## Unauthorized Data Disclosure

*Unauthorized data disclosure* occurs when a threat obtains data that is supposed to be protected. It can occur by human error when someone inadvertently releases data in violation of policy. An example at a university is a department administrator who posts student names, identification numbers, and grades in a public place, when the releasing of names and grades violates state law. Another example is employees who unknowingly or carelessly release proprietary data to competitors or to the media. WikiLeaks is a famous example of unauthorized disclosure; the situation described in the third row of Figure 10-2 is another example.

The popularity and efficacy of search engines have created another source of inadvertent disclosure. Employees who place restricted data on Web sites that can be reached by search engines might mistakenly publish proprietary or restricted data over the Web.

Of course, proprietary and personal data can also be released and obtained maliciously. **Pretexting** occurs when someone deceives by pretending to be someone else. A common scam involves a telephone caller who pretends to be from a credit card company and claims to be checking the validity of credit card numbers: "I'm checking your MasterCard number; it begins with 5491. Can you verify the rest of the number?" Thousands of MasterCard numbers start with 5491; the caller is attempting to steal a valid number.

**Phishing compromises legitimate brands and trademarks. See the Guide on page 306–307 for more.**

**Phishing** is a similar technique for obtaining unauthorized data that uses pretexting via email. The **phisher** pretends to be a legitimate company and sends an email requesting confidential data, such as account numbers, Social Security numbers, account passwords, and so forth.

**Spoofing** is another term for someone pretending to be someone else. If you pretend to be your professor, you are spoofing your professor. **IP spoofing** occurs when an intruder uses another site's IP address to masquerade as that other site. **Email spoofing** is a synonym for phishing.

**Sniffing** is a technique for intercepting computer communications. With wired networks, sniffing requires a physical connection to the network. With wireless networks, no such connection is required: **Wardrivers** simply take computers with wireless connections through an area and search for unprotected wireless networks. They can monitor and intercept traffic on unsecured wireless networks. Even protected wireless networks are vulnerable, as you will learn. Spyware and adware are two other sniffing techniques discussed later in this chapter.

Other forms of computer crime include **hacking**, which is breaking into computers, servers, or networks to steal data such as customer lists, product inventory data, employee data, and other proprietary and confidential data.

Finally, people might inadvertently disclose data during recovery from a natural disaster. During a recovery, everyone is so focused on restoring system capability that they might ignore normal security safeguards. A request such as "I need a copy of the customer database backup" will receive far less scrutiny during disaster recovery than at other times.

## Incorrect Data Modification

The second type of security loss in Figure 10-3 is *incorrect data modification*. Examples include incorrectly increasing a customer's discount or incorrectly modifying an employee's salary, earned days of vacation, or annual bonus. Other examples include placing incorrect information, such as incorrect price changes, on a company's Web site or company portal.

Incorrect data modification can occur through human error when employees follow procedures incorrectly or when procedures have been designed incorrectly. For proper internal control on systems that process financial data or control inventories of assets, such as products and equipment, companies should ensure separation of duties and authorities and have multiple checks and balances in place.

A final type of incorrect data modification caused by human error includes *system errors*. An example is the lost-update problem discussed in Chapter 5 (page 121).

Computer criminals can make unauthorized data modifications by hacking into a computer system. For example, hackers could hack into a system and transfer people's account balances or place orders to ship goods to unauthorized locations and customers.

Finally, faulty recovery actions after a disaster can result in incorrect data changes. The faulty actions can be unintentional or malicious.

### Faulty Service

The third type of security loss, *faulty service*, includes problems that result because of incorrect system operation. Faulty service could include incorrect data modification, as just described. It also could include systems that work incorrectly by sending the wrong goods to a customer or the ordered goods to the wrong customer, inaccurately billing customers, or sending the wrong information to employees. Humans can inadvertently cause faulty service by making procedural mistakes. System developers can write programs incorrectly or make errors during the installation of hardware, software programs, and data.

**Usurpation** occurs when computer criminals invade a computer system and replace legitimate programs with their own, unauthorized ones that shut down legitimate applications and substitute their own processing to spy, steal and manipulate data, or achieve other purposes. Faulty service can also result when service is improperly restored during recovery from natural disasters.

### Denial of Service

Human error in following procedures or a lack of procedures can result in **denial of service (DoS)**, the fourth type of loss. For example, humans can inadvertently shut down a Web server or corporate gateway router by starting a computationally intensive application. An OLAP application that uses the operational DBMS can consume so many DBMS resources that order-entry transactions cannot get through.

Computer criminals can launch an intentional DoS attack in which a malicious hacker floods a Web server, for example, with millions of bogus service requests that so occupy the server that it cannot service legitimate requests. Also, computer worms can infiltrate a network with so much artificial traffic that legitimate traffic cannot get through. Finally, natural disasters may cause systems to fail, resulting in denial of service.

### Loss of Infrastructure

Many times, human accidents cause loss of infrastructure, the last loss type. Examples are a bulldozer cutting a conduit of fiber-optic cables and a floor buffer crashing into a rack of Web servers.

Theft and terrorist events also cause loss of infrastructure. For instance, a disgruntled, terminated employee might walk off with corporate data servers, routers, or other crucial equipment. Terrorist events also can cause the loss of physical plants and equipment.

Natural disasters present the largest risk for infrastructure loss. A fire, flood, earthquake, or similar event can destroy data centers and all they contain.

You may be wondering why Figure 10-3 does not include terms such as viruses, worms, and Trojan horses. The answer is that viruses, worms, and Trojan horses are techniques for causing some of the problems in the figure. They can cause a DoS attack, or they can be used to cause malicious, unauthorized data access or data loss.

Finally, a new threat term has come into recent use. An **Advanced Persistent Threat (APT)** is a sophisticated, possibly long-running computer hack perpetrated by large, well-funded organizations such as governments. APTs can be a means to engage in cyberwarfare and cyber-espionage. An example of an APT is a group called "APT1" based in Shanghai. In 2014, the U.S. Department of Justice indicted five individuals involved with APT1 for theft of intellectual property from U.S. firms. Mandiant, a U.S. security firm, released a detailed report about APT1's attacks on nearly 150 victims over a seven-year period. They provided detailed descriptions of APT1's tools, tactics, and procedures.[1] More recently, an APT group named "Deep Panda" was identified by forensic experts as the group behind the Anthem healthcare data breach that resulted in the loss of sensitive data for 80 million people. If you work in the military or for intelligence agencies, you will certainly be concerned, if not involved, with APTs.

## GOAL OF INFORMATION SYSTEMS SECURITY

As shown in Figure 10-1, threats can be stopped, or if not stopped, the costs of loss can be reduced by creating appropriate safeguards. Safeguards are, however, expensive to create and maintain. They also reduce work efficiency by making common tasks more difficult, adding additional labor expense. The goal of information security is to find an appropriate trade-off between the risk of loss and the cost of implementing safeguards.

Business professionals need to consider that trade-off carefully. In your personal life, you should certainly employ antivirus software. You should probably implement other safeguards that you'll learn about in Q10-3. Some safeguards, such as deleting browser cookies, will make using your computer more difficult. Are such safeguards worth it? You need to assess the risks and benefits for yourself.

Similar comments pertain to organizations, though they need to go about it more systematically. The bottom line is not to let the future unfold without careful analysis and action as indicated by that analysis. Get in front of the security problem by making the appropriate trade-off for your life and your business.

# Q10-2 HOW BIG IS THE COMPUTER SECURITY PROBLEM?

We do not know the full extent of the financial and data losses due to computer security threats. Certainly, the losses due to human error are enormous, but few organizations compute those losses, and even fewer publish them. However, a recent security report by Risk Based Security called 2014 a record-breaking year due to the loss of 1.1 billion personal records in 3,014 security incidents. Some of the more notable data breaches included the loss of user accounts at Home Depot (56 million), JPMorgan (83 million), and eBay (145 million).[2] And that's not even counting the loss of more than 100TB of corporate data from Sony or the loss of hundreds of nude celebrity photos from Apple's iCloud. The majority of user records stolen (83 percent) were taken by external hackers targeting businesses. These are only the companies that made the news and reported estimated losses.

Losses due to natural disasters are also enormous and impossible to compute. The 2011 earthquake in Japan, for example, shut down Japanese manufacturing, and losses rippled through the supply chain from the Far East to Europe and the United States. One can only imagine the enormous expense for Japanese companies as they restored their information systems.

Furthermore, no one knows the cost of computer crime. For one, there are no standards for tallying crime costs. Does the cost of a DoS attack include lost employee time, lost revenue, or long-term revenue losses due to lost customers? Or, if an employee loses a $2,000 laptop, does the cost include the value of the data that was on it? Does it include the cost of the time of replacing it and reinstalling software? Or, if someone steals next year's financial plan, how is the cost of the value that competitors glean determined?

Second, all the studies on the cost of computer crime are based on surveys. Different respondents interpret terms differently, some organizations don't report all their losses, and some won't report computer crime losses at all. Absent standard definitions and a more accurate way of gathering crime data, we cannot rely on the accuracy of any particular estimate. The most we can do is look for trends by comparing year-to-year data, assuming the same methodology is used by the various types of survey respondents.

Figure 10-4 shows the results of a survey done over five years.[3] It was commissioned by Hewlett-Packard and performed by the Ponemon Institute, a consulting group that specializes in computer crime. It shows the average cost and percent of total incidents of the six most expensive types of attack. Without tests of significance, it's difficult to determine if the differences shown are random; they could be. But, taking the data at face value, it appears the source of most of

**Figure 10-4**
Average Computer Crime Cost and Percent of Attacks by Type (Six Most Expensive Types)

*Source:* Based on Ponemon Institute. *2014 Cost of Cyber Crime Study: United States*, October 2014, p. 12.

| | 2010 | 2011 | 2012 | 2013 | 2014 |
|---|---|---|---|---|---|
| Denial of Service | NA | $187,506 (17%) | $172,238 (20%) | $243,913 (21%) | $166,545 (18%) |
| Malicous Insiders | $100,300 (11%) | $105,352 (9%) | $166,251 (8%) | $198,769 (8%) | $213,542 (8%) |
| Web-based Attacks | $143,209 (15%) | $141,647 (12%) | $125,795 (13%) | $125,101 (12%) | $116,424 (14%) |
| Malicous Code | $124,083 (26%) | $126,787 (23%) | $109,533 (26%) | $102,216 (21%) | $ 19,500 (23%) |
| Phishing and Social Engineering | $ 35,514 (12%) | $ 30,397 (9%) | $ 18,040 (7%) | $ 21,094 (11%) | $ 45,959 (13%) |
| Stolen Devices | $ 25,663 (17%) | $ 24,968 (13%) | $ 23,541 (12%) | $ 20,070 (9%) | $ 43,565 (10%) |

the increase in computer crime costs is malicious insiders. The number of attacks of this type is slightly decreasing, but the average cost of such attacks is increasing, possibly dramatically (Figure 10-5). Apparently, insiders are getting better at stealing more. The study, by the way, defined an insider as an employee, temporary employee, contractor, or business partner. The average costs of the remaining categories are slightly decreasing.

In addition to this data, Ponemon also surveyed losses by type of asset compromised. It found that business disruption was the single most expensive consequence of computer crime, accounting for 38 percent of costs in 2014. Information loss was the second highest cost, at 35 percent in 2014. Equipment losses and damages were only 4 percent of the lost value. Clearly, value lies in data and not in hardware!

Looking to the future, in a separate study,[4] Ponemon reported that 78 percent of its respondents believe that negligent or careless employees not following security policies pose a significant risk to their organizations. The next most worrisome concerns were personal devices connected to the corporate network (68 percent) and employee use of commercial cloud-based applications at work (66 percent).

The *2014 Cost of Computer Crime Study* includes an in-depth analysis of the effect of different security policies on the savings in computer crime. The bottom line is that organizations that spend more to create the safeguards discussed in Q10-4 through Q10-7 (later in this chapter) experience less computer crime and suffer smaller losses when they do. Security safeguards do work!

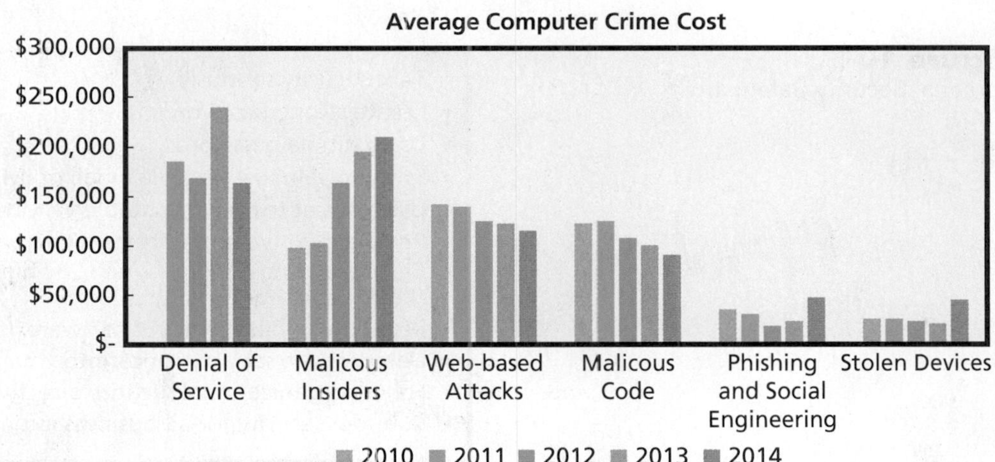


**Figure 10-5**
Computer Crime Costs

*Source:* Based on Ponemon Institute. 2014 Cost of Cyber Crime Study: United States, October 2014, p. 12.

If you search for the term *computer crime statistics* on the Web, you will find numerous similar studies. Some are based on dubious sampling techniques and seem to be written to promote a particular safeguard product or point of view. Be aware of such bias as you read.

Using the Ponemon study, the bottom line, as of 2014, is:

- Malicious insiders are an increasingly serious security threat.
- Business disruption and data loss are the principal costs of computer crime.
- Survey respondents believe negligent employees, personal devices connecting to the corporate network, and the use of commercial cloud-based applications pose a significant security threat.
- Security safeguards work.

## Q10-3 HOW SHOULD YOU RESPOND TO SECURITY THREATS?

As stated at the end of Q10-1, your personal IS security goal should be to find an effective tradeoff between the risk of loss and the cost of safeguards. However, few individuals take security as seriously as they should, and most fail to implement even low-cost safeguards.

Figure 10-6 lists recommended personal security safeguards. The first safeguard is to take security seriously. You cannot see the attempts that are being made, right now, to compromise your computer. However, they are there.

Unfortunately, the first sign you receive that your security has been compromised will be bogus charges on your credit card or messages from friends complaining about the disgusting email they just received from your email account. Computer security professionals run intrusion detection systems to detect attacks. An **intrusion detection system (IDS)** is a computer program that senses when another computer is attempting to scan or access a computer or network. IDS logs can record thousands of attempts each day. If these attempts come from outside the country, there is nothing you can do about them except use reasonable safeguards.

If you decide to take computer security seriously, the single most important safeguard you can implement is to create and use strong passwords. We discussed ways of doing this in Chapter 1 (pages 17–18). To summarize, do not use any word, in any language, as part of your password. Use passwords with a mixture of upper- and lowercase letters and numbers and special characters.

Such nonword passwords are still vulnerable to a **brute force attack** in which the password cracker tries every possible combination of characters. John Pozadzides, a security researcher, estimates that a brute force attack can crack a six-character password of either upper- or lowercase letters in about 5 minutes. However, brute force requires 8.5 days to crack that length password having a mixture of upper- and lowercase letters, numbers, and special characters. A 10-digit password of only upper- and lowercase letters takes 4.5 years to crack, but one using a

**Figure 10-6**
Personal Security Safeguards

- Take security seriously
- Create strong passwords
- Use multiple passwords
- Send no valuable data via email or IM
- Use https at trusted, reputable vendors
- Remove high-value assets from computers
- Clear browsing history, temporary files, and cookies (CCleaner or equivalent)
- Regularly update antivirus software
- Demonstrate security concern to your fellow workers
- Follow organizational security directives and guidelines
- Consider security for all business initiatives

mix of letters, numbers, and special characters requires nearly 2 million years. A 12-digit, letter-only password requires 3 million years, and a 12-digit mixed password will take many, many millions of years.[5] All of these estimates assume, of course, that the password contains no word in any language. The bottom line is this: Use long passwords with no words, 10 or more characters, and a mix of letters, numbers, and special characters.

In addition to using long, complex passwords, you should also use different passwords for different sites. That way, if one of your passwords is compromised, you do not lose control of all of your accounts. Make sure you use very strong passwords for important sites (like your bank's site), and do not reuse those passwords on less important sites (like your social networking sites). Some sites are focused on innovating products and may not allocate the same amount of resources to protect your information. Guard your information with a password it deserves.

Never send passwords, credit card data, or any other valuable data in email or IM. As stated numerous times in this text, most email and IM is not protected by encryption (see Q10-5), and you should assume that anything you write in email or IM could find its way to the front page of *The New York Times* tomorrow.

Buy only from reputable online vendors using a secure https connection. If the vendor does not support https in its transactions (look for https:// in the address line of your browser), do not buy from that vendor.

You can reduce your vulnerability to loss by removing high-value assets from your computers. Now, and especially later as a business professional, make it your practice not to travel out of your office with a laptop or other device that contains any data that you do not need. In general, store proprietary data on servers or removable devices that do not travel with you. (Office 365, by the way, uses https to transfer data to and from SharePoint. You can use it or a similar application for processing documents from public locations such as airports while you are traveling.)

Your browser automatically stores a history of your browsing activities and temporary files that contain sensitive data about where you've visited, what you've purchased, what your account names and passwords are, and so forth. It also stores **cookies**, which are small files that your browser receives when you visit Web sites. Cookies enable you to access Web sites without having to sign in every time, and they speed up processing of some sites. Unfortunately, some cookies also contain sensitive security data. The best safeguard is to remove your browsing history, temporary files, and cookies from your computer and to set your browser to disable history and cookies.

CCleaner is a free, open source product that will do a thorough job of securely removing all such data (*http://download.cnet.com/ccleaner/*). You should make a backup of your computer before using CCleaner, however.

Removing and disabling cookies presents an excellent example of the trade-off between improved security and cost. Your security will be substantially improved, but your computer will be more difficult to use. You decide, but make a conscious decision; do not let ignorance of the vulnerability of such data make the decision for you.

We will address the use of antivirus software in Q10-5. The last three items in Figure 10-6 apply once you become a business professional. With your coworkers, and especially with those whom you manage, you should demonstrate a concern and respect for security. You should also follow all organizational security directives and guidelines. Finally, consider security in all of your business initiatives.

## Q10-4 HOW SHOULD ORGANIZATIONS RESPOND TO SECURITY THREATS?

Q10-3 discussed ways that you as an individual should respond to security threats. In the case of organizations, a broader and more systematic approach needs to be taken. To begin, senior management needs to address two critical security functions: security policy and risk management.

Considering the first, senior management must establish company-wide security policies. Take, for example, a data security policy that states the organization's posture regarding data that it gathers about its customers, suppliers, partners, and employees. At a minimum, the policy should stipulate:

- What sensitive data the organization will store
- How it will process that data
- Whether data will be shared with other organizations
- How employees and others can obtain copies of data stored about them
- How employees and others can request changes to inaccurate data

The specifics of a policy depend on whether the organization is governmental or nongovernmental, on whether it is publically held or private, on the organization's industry, on the relationship of management to employees, and on other factors. As a new hire, seek out your employer's security policy if it is not discussed with you in new-employee training.

The second senior management security function is to manage risk. Risk cannot be eliminated, so *manage risk* means to proactively balance the trade-off between risk and cost. This trade-off varies from industry to industry and from organization to organization. Financial institutions are obvious targets for theft and must invest heavily in security safeguards. On the other hand, a bowling alley is unlikely to be much of a target, unless, of course, it stores credit card data on computers or mobile devices (a decision that would be part of its security policy and that would seem unwise, not only for a bowling alley but also for most small businesses).

To make trade-off decisions, organizations need to create an inventory of the data and hardware they want to protect and then evaluate safeguards relative to the probability of each potential threat. Figure 10-3 is a good source for understanding categories and frequencies of threat. Given this set of inventory and threats, the organization needs to decide how much risk it wishes to take or, stated differently, which security safeguards it wishes to implement.

A good analogy of using safeguards to protect information assets is buying car insurance. Before buying car insurance you determine how much your car is worth, the likelihood of incurring damage to your car, and how much risk you are willing to accept. Then you transfer some of your risk to the insurer by buying a safeguard called an insurance policy. Instead of buying just one insurance policy, organizations implement a variety of safeguards to protect their data and hardware.

An easy way to remember information systems safeguards is to arrange them according to the five components of an information system, as shown in Figure 10-7. Some of the safeguards involve computer hardware and software. Some involve data; others involve procedures and people. We will consider technical, data, and human safeguards in the next three questions.

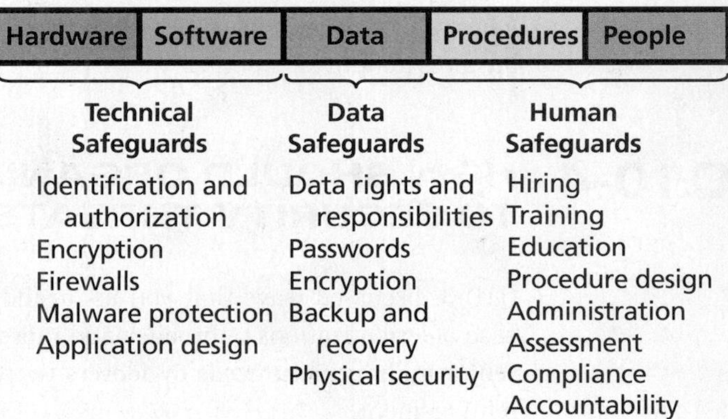


**Figure 10-7**
Security Safeguards as They Relate to the Five Components

# New from Black Hat 2014

Hackers, security professionals, and government agents flock to Las Vegas each year to attend an important security conference: Black Hat. Black Hat caters to hackers, security professionals, corporations, and government entities.

Each year, speakers make briefings on how things can be hacked. Presenters show exactly how to exploit weaknesses in hardware, software, protocols, or systems. One session may show you how to hack your smartphone, while another may show you how to empty the cash out of an ATM.

Presentations encourage companies to fix product vulnerabilities and serve as an educational forum for hackers, developers, manufacturers, and government agencies. The following are highlights from the 2014 Black Hat conference:

*Source:* Rawpixel/Fotolia

**Keynote by Dan Geer:** The most talked-about event at Black Hat was the keynote speech by In-Q-Tel CISO Dan Geer. In-Q-Tel is a venture capital firm that invests in technologies that support the missions of the Central Intelligence Agency and the U.S. Intelligence Community. In his talk, Geer discussed 10 policy proposals he believed would greatly improve information security.[6] Some of his more notable policy proposals included:

1. Mandatory reporting of security vulnerabilities similar to the way disease outbreaks are reported to the Centers for Disease Control and Prevention.
2. Software makers need to be liable for the damage their code may cause after they abandon it or allow users to see their source code and choose to cut out the code they don't want to run.
3. Internet service providers (ISP) need to be liable for harmful content going over their networks if they inspect the data being sent. If they don't inspect users' data, they could still be protected as a common carrier.
4. The European Union's laws that guarantee an individual's "right to be forgotten" are appropriate and advantageous.

**End-to-End Encrypted Email:** Yahoo!'s CISO Alex Stamos revealed that consumers will be able to use end-to-end encrypted email through Yahoo! Mail by 2015.[7] This would mean that only the original sender and final receiver of a message would be able to read it. This announcement was the highlight of the conference for most conference goers who saw it as a first step at bringing back individual privacy. Edward Snowden's revelations about the complicit relationship between government and tech industry giants designed to monitor consumers was still fresh in the minds of security professionals and civil libertarians at the conference.

**Hacking Smart Things:** Some of the more eye-catching briefings at Black Hat were about hacking smart things like smartphones, TVs, webcams, thermostats, and cars. Security researchers Charlie Miller (Twitter©) and Chris Valasek (IOActive©) looked at potential vulnerabilities for 24 different cars.[8] They found that automobiles with wireless features (i.e. Bluetooth, Wi-Fi, and cellular connectivity) and poor internal systems architecture may allow hackers to access automated driving functions through seemingly innocuous features like a car's radio.

Another security researcher, Jesus Molina, talked about security vulnerabilities at the St. Regis Shenzhen hotel in China.[9] On a recent stay at the hotel, Molina discovered that he was able to control the lights, thermostats, televisions, and blinds in more than 200 rooms by reverse-engineering a home automation protocol called KNX/IP. These briefings illustrate the importance of companies developing secure software for IP-enabled smart things. In a recent study looking at vulnerabilities of smart devices HP noted that 70 percent of the smart devices they tested used unencrypted network services, and six out of 10 devices were vulnerable to persistent XSS (cross-site scripting) and weak credentials.[10]

## QUESTIONS

1. How could mandatory reporting of vulnerabilities make systems more secure?
2. Dan Geer suggested that software makers be held liable for damage caused by their software after they abandon it or freed from liability by making the source code open source so it can be "fixed." What impact would this policy have on Microsoft?
3. How would a "right to be forgotten" rule affect online businesses like Google or Facebook?
4. Who might be harmed by end-to-end encrypted email?
5. Why are vulnerabilities in smart devices so important?

# Q10-5 HOW CAN TECHNICAL SAFEGUARDS PROTECT AGAINST SECURITY THREATS?

**Technical safeguards** involve the hardware and software components of an information system. Figure 10-8 lists primary technical safeguards. Consider each.

## IDENTIFICATION AND AUTHENTICATION

Every information system today should require users to sign on with a username and password. The username *identifies* the user (the process of **identification**), and the password *authenticates* that user (the process of **authentication**).

Passwords have important weaknesses. In spite of repeated warnings (don't let this happen to you!), users often share their passwords, and many people choose ineffective, simple passwords. In fact, a 2014 Verizon report states, "Passwords, usernames, emails, credit/debit card and financial account information, and Social Security numbers are being compromised at a staggering rate, endangering the identities of consumers nationwide."[11] Because of these problems, some organizations choose to use smart cards and biometric authentication in addition to passwords.

### Smart Cards

A **smart card** is a plastic card similar to a credit card. Unlike credit, debit, and ATM cards, which have a magnetic strip, smart cards have a microchip. The microchip, which holds far more data than a magnetic strip, is loaded with identifying data. Users of smart cards are required to enter a **personal identification number (PIN)** to be authenticated.

**Figure 10-8**
Technical Safeguards

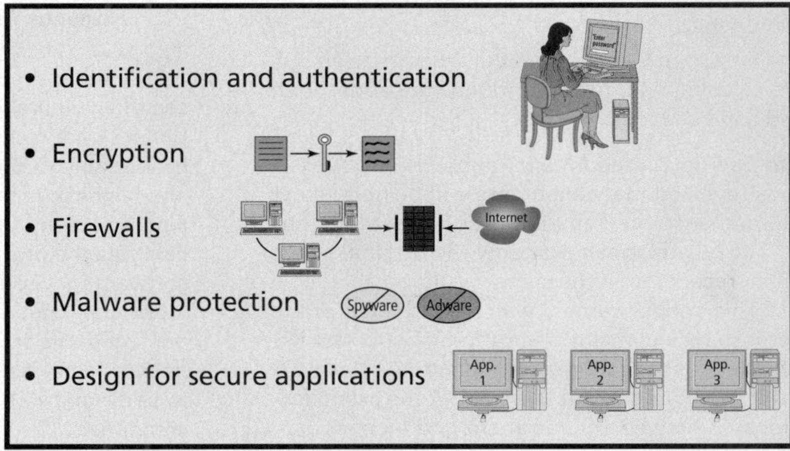

### Biometric Authentication

**Biometric authentication** uses personal physical characteristics such as fingerprints, facial features, and retinal scans to authenticate users. Biometric authentication provides strong authentication, but the required equipment is expensive. Often, too, users resist biometric identification because they feel it is invasive.

Biometric authentication is in the early stages of adoption. Because of its strength, it likely will see increased usage in the future. It is also likely that legislators will pass laws governing the use, storage, and protection requirements for biometric data. For more on biometrics, search for *biometrics* at *http://searchsecurity.techtarget.com*.

Note that authentication methods fall into three categories: what you know (password or PIN), what you have (smart card), and what you are (biometric).

## SINGLE SIGN-ON FOR MULTIPLE SYSTEMS

Information systems often require multiple sources of authentication. For example, when you sign on to your personal computer, you need to be authenticated. When you access the LAN in your department, you need to be authenticated again. When you traverse your organization's WAN, you will need to be authenticated to even more networks. Also, if your request requires database data, the DBMS server that manages that database will authenticate you yet again.

It would be annoying to enter a name and password for every one of these resources. You might have to use and remember five or six different passwords just to access the data you need to perform your job. It would be equally undesirable to send your password across all of these networks. The further your password travels, the greater the risk it can be compromised.

Instead, today's operating systems have the capability to authenticate you to networks and other servers. You sign on to your local computer and provide authentication data; from that point on your operating system authenticates you to another network or server, which can authenticate you to yet another network and server, and so forth. Because this is so, your identity and passwords open many doors beyond those on your local computer; remember this when you choose your passwords!

## ENCRYPTION

**Encryption** is the process of transforming clear text into coded, unintelligible text for secure storage or communication. Considerable research has gone into developing **encryption algorithms** (procedures for encrypting data) that are difficult to break. Commonly used methods are DES, 3DES, and AES; search the Web for these terms if you want to know more about them.

A **key** is a string of bits used to encrypt the data. It is called a *key* because it unlocks a message. But it is actually a string of bits, expressed as numbers or letters, used with an encryption algorithm. It's not a physical thing like the key to your apartment.

To encrypt a message, a computer program uses the encryption method (say, AES) combined with the key (say, the word "key") to convert a plaintext message (in this case, the word "secret") into an encrypted message. The resulting coded message ("U2FsdGVkX1+b637aTP80u+y2WYl UbqUz2XtYcw4E8m4=") looks like gibberish. Decoding (decrypting) a message is similar; a key is applied to the coded message to recover the original text. With **symmetric encryption**, the same key is used to encode and to decode. With **asymmetric encryption**, two keys are used; one key encodes the message, and the other key decodes the message. Symmetric encryption is simpler and much faster than asymmetric encryption.

A special version of asymmetric encryption, **public key encryption**, is used on the Internet. With this method, each site has a *public key* for encoding messages and a *private key* for decoding them. Before we explain how that works, consider the following analogy.

Suppose you send a friend an open combination lock (like you have on your gym locker). Suppose you are the only one who knows the combination to that lock. Now, suppose your friend puts something in a box and locks the lock. Now, neither your friend nor anyone else can open that box. That friend sends the locked box to you, and you apply the combination to open the box.

A *public key* is like the combination lock, and the *private key* is like the combination. Your friend uses the public key to code the message (lock the box), and you use the private key to decode the message (open the lock).

Now, suppose we have two generic computers, A and B. Suppose B wants to send an encrypted message to A. To do so, A sends B its public key (in our analogy, A sends B an open combination lock). Now B applies A's public key to the message and sends the resulting coded message back to A. At that point, neither B nor anyone other than A can decode that message. It is like the box with a locked combination lock. When A receives the coded message, A applies its private key (the combination in our analogy) to unlock or decrypt the message.

Again, public keys are like open combination locks. Computer A will send a lock to anyone who asks for one. But A never sends its private key (the combination) to anyone. Private keys stay private.

Most secure communication over the Internet uses a protocol called **https**. With https, data are encrypted using a protocol called the **Secure Sockets Layer (SSL)**, which is also known as **Transport Layer Security (TLS)**. SSL/TLS uses a combination of public key encryption and symmetric encryption.

The basic idea is this: Symmetric encryption is fast and is preferred. But the two parties (say, you and a Web site) don't share a symmetric key. So, the two of you use public key encryption to share the same symmetric key. Once you both have that key, you use symmetric encryption for the remainder of the communication.

Figure 10-9 summarizes how SSL/TLS works when you communicate securely with a Web site:

1. Your computer obtains the *public* key of the Web site to which it will connect.
2. Your computer generates a key for symmetric encryption.
3. Your computer encodes that key using the Web site's public key. It sends the encrypted symmetric key to the Web site.
4. The Web site then decodes the symmetric key using its *private* key.
5. From that point forward, your computer and the Web site communicate using symmetric encryption.

At the end of the session, your computer and the secure site discard the keys. Using this strategy, the bulk of the secure communication occurs using the faster symmetric encryption. Also, because keys are used for short intervals, there is less likelihood they can be discovered.

Use of SSL/TLS makes it safe to send sensitive data such as credit card numbers and bank balances. Just be certain that you see *https://* in your browser and not just *http://*. Most browsers have additional plug-ins or add-ons (like HTTPS Everywhere) that can force https connections when available.

**Figure 10-9**
The Essence of https (SSL or TLS)

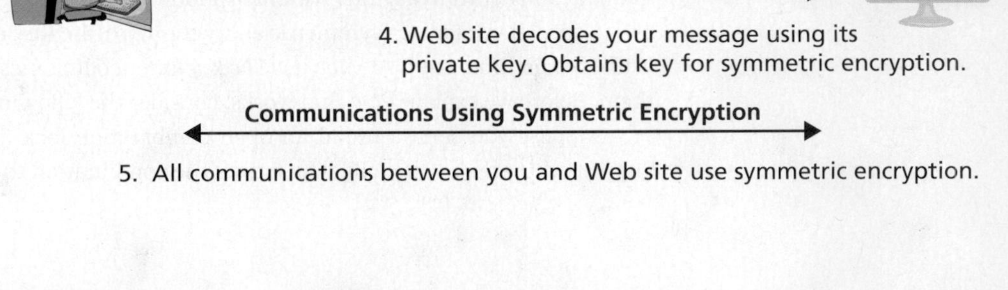

## FIREWALLS

A **firewall** is a computing device that prevents unauthorized network access. A firewall can be a special-purpose computer, or it can be a program on a general-purpose computer or on a router. In essence, a firewall is simply a filter. It can filter traffic in a variety of ways including where network traffic is coming from, what types of packets are being sent, the contents of the packets, and if the packets are part of an authorized connection.

Organizations normally use multiple firewalls. A **perimeter firewall** sits outside the organizational network; it is the first device that Internet traffic encounters. In addition to perimeter firewalls, some organizations employ **internal firewalls** inside the organizational network. Figure 10-10 shows the use of a perimeter firewall that protects all of an organization's computers and a second internal firewall that protects a LAN.

A **packet-filtering firewall** examines each part of a message and determines whether to let that part pass. To make this decision, it examines the source address, the destination address(es), and other data.

Packet-filtering firewalls can prohibit outsiders from starting a session with any user behind the firewall. They can also disallow traffic from particular sites, such as known hacker addresses. They can prohibit traffic from legitimate, but unwanted, addresses, such as competitors' computers, and filter outbound traffic as well. They can keep employees from accessing specific sites, such as competitors' sites, sites with pornographic material, or popular news sites. As a future manager, if you have particular sites with which you do not want your employees to communicate, you can ask your IS department to enforce that limit via the firewall.

Packet-filtering firewalls are the simplest type of firewall. Other firewalls filter on a more sophisticated basis. If you take a data communications class, you will learn about them. For now, just understand that firewalls help to protect organizational computers from unauthorized network access.

No computer should connect to the Internet without firewall protection. Many ISPs provide firewalls for their customers. By nature, these firewalls are generic. Large organizations supplement such generic firewalls with their own. Most home routers include firewalls, and Microsoft Windows has a built-in firewall as well. Third parties also license firewall products.

## MALWARE PROTECTION

The next technical safeguard in our list in Figure 10-8 concerns malware. **Malware** is a broad category of software that includes viruses, spyware, and adware.

A **virus** is a computer program that replicates itself. Unchecked replication is like computer cancer; ultimately, the virus consumes the computer's resources. Furthermore, many viruses also take unwanted and harmful actions. The program code that causes the unwanted

**Figure 10-10**
Use of Multiple Firewalls

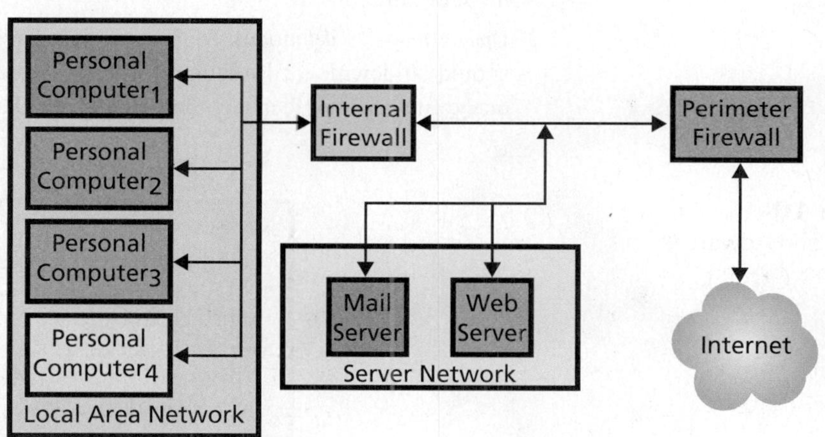

actions is called the payload. The **payload** can delete programs or data—or, even worse, modify data in undetected ways.

**Trojan horses** are viruses that masquerade as useful programs or files. The name refers to the gigantic mock-up of a horse that was filled with soldiers and moved into Troy during the Trojan War. A typical Trojan horse appears to be a computer game, an MP3 music file, or some other useful, innocuous program.

A **worm** is a virus that self-propagates using the Internet or other computer network. Worms spread faster than other virus types because they can replicate by themselves. Unlike nonworm viruses, which must wait for the user to share a file with a second computer, worms actively use the network to spread. Sometimes, worms can propagate so quickly that they overload and crash a network.

**Spyware** programs are installed on the user's computer without the user's knowledge or permission. Spyware resides in the background and, unknown to the user, observes the user's actions and keystrokes, monitors computer activity, and reports the user's activities to sponsoring organizations. Some malicious spyware, called **key loggers**, captures keystrokes to obtain usernames, passwords, account numbers, and other sensitive information. Other spyware supports marketing analyses such as observing what users do, Web sites visited, products examined and purchased, and so forth.

**Adware** is similar to spyware in that it is installed without the user's permission and resides in the background and observes user behavior. Most adware is benign in that it does not perform malicious acts or steal data. It does, however, watch user activity and produce pop-up ads. Adware can also change the user's default window or modify search results and switch the user's search engine.

**Ransomware** is malicious software that blocks access to a system or data until money is paid to the attacker. Some forms of ransomware encrypt your data (CryptoLocker), prevent you from running applications, or even lock you out of your operating system (Reveton).

Figure 10-11 lists some of the symptoms of adware and spyware. Sometimes these symptoms develop slowly over time as more malware components are installed. Should these symptoms occur on your computer, remove the spyware or adware using antimalware programs.

## Malware Safeguards

Fortunately, it is possible to avoid most malware using the following malware safeguards:

1. *Install antivirus and antispyware programs on your computer.* Your IS department will have a list of recommended (perhaps required) programs for this purpose. If you choose a program for yourself, choose one from a reputable vendor. Check reviews of antimalware software on the Web before purchasing.
2. *Set up your antimalware programs to scan your computer frequently.* You should scan your computer at least once a week and possibly more often. When you detect malware code, use the antimalware software to remove it. If the code cannot be removed, contact your IS department or antimalware vendor.
3. *Update malware definitions.* **Malware definitions**—patterns that exist in malware code—should be downloaded frequently. Antimalware vendors update these definitions continuously, and you should install these updates as they become available.

**Figure 10-11**
Spyware and Adware Symptoms

- Slow system startup
- Sluggish system performance
- Many pop-up advertisements
- Suspicious browser homepage changes
- Suspicious changes to the taskbar and other system interfaces
- Unusual hard-disk activity

4. *Open email attachments only from known sources.* Also, even when opening attachments from known sources, do so with great care. With a properly configured firewall, email is the only outside-initiated traffic that can reach user computers.

   Most antimalware programs check email attachments for malware code. However, all users should form the habit of *never* opening an email attachment from an unknown source. Also, if you receive an unexpected email from a known source or an email from a known source that has a suspicious subject, odd spelling, or poor grammar, do not open the attachment without first verifying with the known source that the attachment is legitimate.
5. *Promptly install software updates from legitimate sources.* Unfortunately, all programs are chock full of security holes; vendors are fixing them as rapidly as they are discovered, but the practice is inexact. Install patches to the operating system and application programs promptly.
6. *Browse only reputable Web sites.* It is possible for some malware to install itself when you do nothing more than open a Web page. You can use the Web of Trust (WOT) browser plug-in to help you know which Web sites might be harmful. Recently, malware writers have been paying for banner ads on legitimate sites and embedding malware in the ads. One click and you're infected.

## DESIGN FOR SECURE APPLICATIONS

The final technical safeguard in Figure 10-8 concerns the design of applications. As you learned in the opening vignette, Michele and James are designing PRIDE with security in mind; PRIDE will store users' privacy settings in a database, and it will develop all applications to first read the privacy settings before revealing any data in exercise reports. Most likely, PRIDE will design its programs so that privacy data is processed by programs on servers; that design means that such data need be transmitted over the Internet only when it is created or modified.

By the way, a **SQL injection attack** occurs when users enter a SQL statement into a form in which they are supposed to enter a name or other data. If the program is improperly designed, it will accept this code and make it part of the database command that it issues. Improper data disclosure and data damage and loss are possible consequences. A well-designed application will make such injections ineffective.

As a future IS user, you will not design programs yourself. However, you should ensure that any information system developed for you and your department includes security as one of the application requirements.

# Q10-6 HOW CAN DATA SAFEGUARDS PROTECT AGAINST SECURITY THREATS?

**Data safeguards** protect databases and other organizational data. Two organizational units are responsible for data safeguards. **Data administration** refers to an organization-wide function that is in charge of developing data policies and enforcing data standards.

**Database administration** refers to a function that pertains to a particular database. ERP, CRM, and MRP databases each have a database administration function. Database administration develops procedures and practices to ensure efficient and orderly multiuser processing of the database, to control changes to the database structure, and to protect the database. Database administration was summarized in Chapter 5.

Both data and database administration are involved in establishing the data safeguards in Figure 10-12. First, data administration should define data policies such as "We will not share identifying customer data with any other organization" and the like. Then data administration and database administration(s) work together to specify user data rights and responsibilities. Third, those rights should be enforced by user accounts that are authenticated at least by passwords.

**Figure 10-12**
Data Safeguards

- Define data policies
- Data rights and responsibilities
- Rights enforced by user accounts authenticated by passwords
- Data encryption
- Backup and recovery procedures
- Physical security

The organization should protect sensitive data by storing it in encrypted form. Such encryption uses one or more keys in ways similar to that described for data communication encryption. One potential problem with stored data, however, is that the key might be lost or that disgruntled or terminated employees might destroy it. Because of this possibility, when data are encrypted, a trusted party should have a copy of the encryption key. This safety procedure is sometimes called **key escrow**.

Another data safeguard is to periodically create backup copies of database contents. The organization should store at least some of these backups off premises, possibly in a remote location. Additionally, IT personnel should periodically practice recovery to ensure that the backups are valid and that effective recovery procedures exist. Do not assume that just because a backup is made that the database is protected.

Physical security is another data safeguard. The computers that run the DBMS and all devices that store database data should reside in locked, controlled-access facilities. If not, they are subject not only to theft, but also to damage. For better security, the organization should keep a log showing who entered the facility, when, and for what purpose.

When organizations store databases in the cloud, all of the safeguards in Figure 10-12 should be part of the cloud service contract.

## Q10-7 HOW CAN HUMAN SAFEGUARDS PROTECT AGAINST SECURITY THREATS?

**Read more about how to secure smart things in the Ethics Guide on pages 304–305.**

**Human safeguards** involve the people and procedure components of information systems. In general, human safeguards result when authorized users follow appropriate procedures for system use and recovery. Restricting access to authorized users requires effective authentication methods and careful user account management. In addition, appropriate security procedures must be designed as part of every information system, and users should be trained on the importance and use of those procedures. In this section, we will consider the development of human safeguards for employees. According to the survey of computer crime discussed in Q10-2, crime from malicious insiders is increasing in frequency and cost. This fact makes safeguards even more important.

## HUMAN SAFEGUARDS FOR EMPLOYEES

Figure 10-13 lists security considerations for employees. Consider each.

### Position Definitions

Effective human safeguards begin with definitions of job tasks and responsibilities. In general, job descriptions should provide a separation of duties and authorities. For example, no single individual should be allowed to both approve expenses and write checks. Instead, one person should approve expenses, another pay them, and a third should account for the payment. Similarly, in inventory, no single person should be allowed to authorize an inventory withdrawal and also to remove the items from inventory.

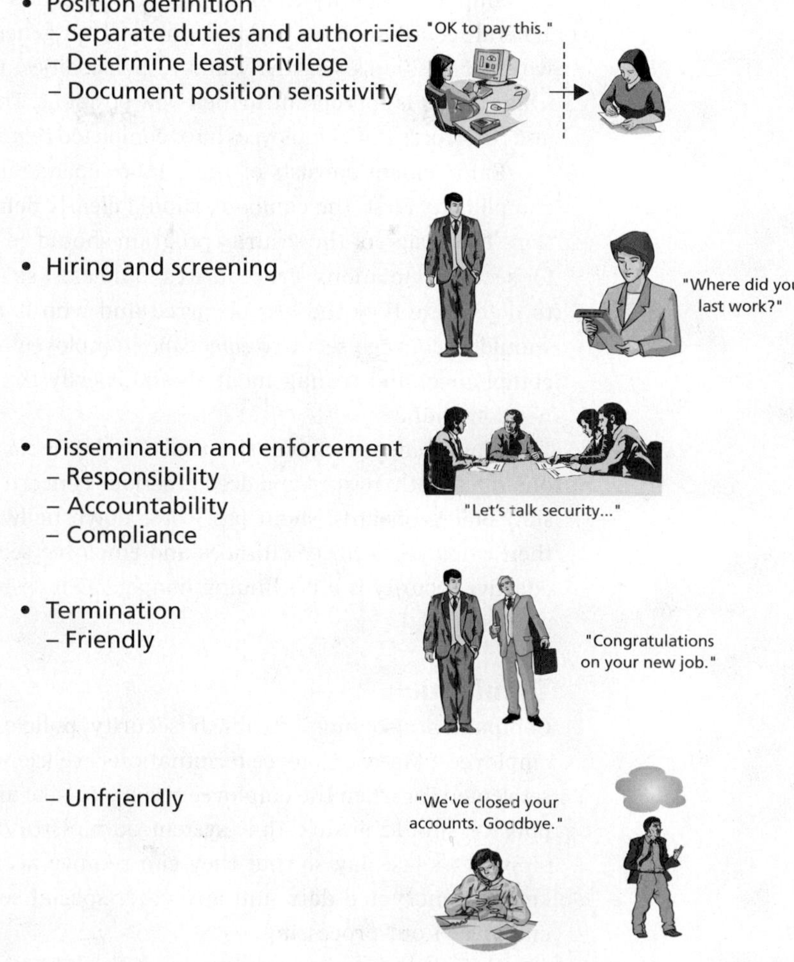


**Figure 10-13**
Security Policy for In-House Staff

Given appropriate job descriptions, user accounts should be defined to give users the *least possible privilege* needed to perform their jobs. For example, users whose job description does not include modifying data should be given accounts with read-only privileges. Similarly, user accounts should prohibit users from accessing data their job description does not require. Because of the problem of semantic security, even access to seemingly innocuous data may need to be limited.

Finally, the security sensitivity should be documented for each position. Some jobs involve highly sensitive data (e.g., employee compensation, salesperson quotas, and proprietary marketing or technical data). Other positions involve no sensitive data. Documenting *position sensitivity* enables security personnel to prioritize their activities in accordance with the possible risk and loss.

## Hiring and Screening

Security considerations should be part of the hiring process. Of course, if the position involves no sensitive data and no access to information systems, then screening for information systems security purposes will be minimal. When hiring for high-sensitivity positions, however, extensive interviews, references, and background investigations are appropriate. Note, too, that security screening applies not only to new employees, but also to employees who are promoted into sensitive positions.

## Dissemination and Enforcement

Employees cannot be expected to follow security policies and procedures that they do not know about. Therefore, employees need to be made aware of the security policies, procedures, and responsibilities they will have.

Employee security training begins during new-employee training, with the explanation of general security policies and procedures. That general training must be amplified in accordance with the position's sensitivity and responsibilities. Promoted employees should receive security training that is appropriate to their new positions. The company should not provide user accounts and passwords until employees have completed required security training.

Enforcement consists of three interdependent factors: responsibility, accountability, and compliance. First, the company should clearly define the security *responsibilities* of each position. The design of the security program should be such that employees can be held *accountable* for security violations. Procedures should exist so that when critical data are lost, it is possible to determine how the loss occurred and who is accountable. Finally, the security program should encourage security *compliance.* Employee activities should regularly be monitored for compliance, and management should specify the disciplinary action to be taken in light of noncompliance.

Management attitude is crucial: Employee compliance is greater when management demonstrates, both in word and deed, a serious concern for security. If managers write passwords on staff bulletin boards, shout passwords down hallways, or ignore physical security procedures, then employee security attitudes and employee security compliance will suffer. Note, too, that effective security is a continuing management responsibility. Regular reminders about security are essential.

### Termination

Companies also must establish security policies and procedures for the termination of employees. Many employee terminations are friendly and occur as the result of promotion or retirement or when the employee resigns to take another position. Standard human resources policies should ensure that system administrators receive notification in advance of the employee's last day so that they can remove accounts and passwords. The need to recover keys for encrypted data and any other special security requirements should be part of the employee's out-processing.

Unfriendly termination is more difficult because employees may be tempted to take malicious or harmful actions. In such a case, system administrators may need to remove user accounts and passwords prior to notifying the employee of his or her termination. Other actions may be needed to protect the company's data assets. A terminated sales employee, for example, may attempt to take the company's confidential customer and sales-prospect data for future use at another company. The terminating employer should take steps to protect those data prior to the termination.

The human resources department should be aware of the importance of giving IS administrators early notification of employee termination. No blanket policy exists; the information systems department must assess each case on an individual basis.

## HUMAN SAFEGUARDS FOR NONEMPLOYEE PERSONNEL

Business requirements may necessitate opening information systems to nonemployee personnel—temporary personnel, vendors, partner personnel (employees of business partners), and the public. Although temporary personnel can be screened, to reduce costs the screening will be abbreviated from that for employees. In most cases, companies cannot screen either vendor or partner personnel. Of course, public users cannot be screened at all. Similar limitations pertain to security training and compliance testing.

In the case of temporary, vendor, and partner personnel, the contracts that govern the activity should call for security measures appropriate to the sensitivity of the data and the IS resources involved. Companies should require vendors and partners to perform appropriate screening and security training. The contract also should mention specific security responsibilities that are particular to the work to be performed. Companies should provide accounts and passwords with the least privilege and remove those accounts as soon as possible.

The situation differs with public users of Web sites and other openly accessible information systems. It is exceedingly difficult and expensive to hold public users accountable for security violations. In general, the best safeguard from threats from public users is to *harden* the Web site or other facility against attack as much as possible. **Hardening** a site means to take extraordinary measures to reduce a system's vulnerability. Hardened sites use special versions of the operating system, and they lock down or eliminate operating systems features and functions that are not required by the application. Hardening is actually a technical safeguard, but we mention it here as the most important safeguard against public users.

Finally, note that the business relationship with the public, and with some partners, differs from that with temporary personnel and vendors. The public and some partners use the information system to receive a benefit. Consequently, safeguards need to protect such users from internal company security problems. A disgruntled employee who maliciously changes prices on a Web site potentially damages both public users and business partners. As one IT manager put it, "Rather than protecting ourselves from them, we need to protect them from us." This is an extension of the fifth guideline in Figure 10-7.

## ACCOUNT ADMINISTRATION

The administration of user accounts, passwords, and help-desk policies and procedures is another important human safeguard.

### Account Management

Account management concerns the creation of new user accounts, the modification of existing account permissions, and the removal of unneeded accounts. Information system administrators perform all of these tasks, but account users have the responsibility to notify the administrators of the need for these actions. The IS department should create standard procedures for this purpose. As a future user, you can improve your relationship with IS personnel by providing early and timely notification of the need for account changes.

The existence of accounts that are no longer necessary is a serious security threat. IS administrators cannot know when an account should be removed; it is up to users and managers to give such notification.

### Password Management

Passwords are the primary means of authentication. They are important not just for access to the user's computer, but also for authentication to other networks and servers to which the user may have access. Because of the importance of passwords, the National Institute of Standards and Technology (NIST) recommends that employees be required to sign statements similar to those shown in Figure 10-14.

**Figure 10-14**
Sample Account Acknowledgment Form

*Source:* National Institute of Standards and Technology, Introduction to Computer Security: The NIST Handbook, Publication 800–812

> I hereby acknowledge personal receipt of the system password(s) associated with the user IDs listed below. I understand that I am responsible for protecting the password(s), will comply with all applicable system security standards, and will not divulge my password(s) to any person. I further understand that I must report to the Information Systems Security Officer any problem I encounter in the use of the password(s) or when I have reason to believe that the private nature of my password(s) has been compromised.

When an account is created, users should immediately change the password they are given to one of their own. In fact, well-constructed systems require the user to change the password on first use.

Additionally, users should change passwords frequently thereafter. Some systems will require a password change every 3 months or perhaps more frequently. Users grumble at the nuisance of making such changes, but frequent password changes reduce not only the risk of password loss, but also the extent of damage if an existing password is compromised.

Some users create two passwords and switch back and forth between those two. This strategy results in poor security, and some password systems do not allow the user to reuse recently used passwords. Again, users may view this policy as a nuisance, but it is important.

### Help-Desk Policies

In the past, help desks have been a serious security risk. A user who had forgotten his password would call the help desk and plead for the help-desk representative to tell him his password or to reset the password to something else. "I can't get this report out without it!" was (and is) a common lament.

The problem for help-desk representatives is, of course, that they have no way of determining that they are talking with the true user and not someone spoofing a true user. But they are in a bind: If they do not help in some way, the help desk is perceived to be the "unhelpful desk."

To resolve such problems, many systems give the help-desk representative a means of authenticating the user. Typically, the help-desk information system has answers to questions that only the true user would know, such as the user's birthplace, mother's maiden name, or last four digits of an important account number. Usually, when a password is changed, notification of that change is sent to the user in an email. Email, as you learned, is sent as plaintext, however, so the new password itself ought not to be emailed. If you ever receive notification that your password was reset when you did not request such a reset, immediately contact IT security. Someone has compromised your account.

All such help-desk measures reduce the strength of the security system, and, if the employee's position is sufficiently sensitive, they may create too large a vulnerability. In such a case, the user may just be out of luck. The account will be deleted, and the user must repeat the account-application process.

## SYSTEMS PROCEDURES

Figure 10-15 shows a grid of procedure types—normal operation, backup, and recovery. Procedures of each type should exist for each information system. For example, the order-entry system will have procedures of each of these types, as will the Web storefront, the inventory

**Figure 10-15**
Systems Procedures

| | System Users | Operations Personnel |
|---|---|---|
| **Normal operation** | Use the system to perform job tasks, with security appropriate to sensitivity. | Operate data center equipment, manage networks, run Web servers, and do related operational tasks. |
| **Backup** | Prepare for loss of system functionality. | Back up Web site resources, databases, administrative data, account and password data, and other data. |
| **Recovery** | Accomplish job tasks during failure. Know tasks to do during system recovery. | Recover systems from backed up data. Perform role of help desk during recovery. |

system, and so forth. The definition and use of standardized procedures reduces the likelihood of computer crime and other malicious activity by insiders. It also ensures that the system's security policy is enforced.

Procedures exist for both users and operations personnel. For each type of user, the company should develop procedures for normal, backup, and recovery operations. As a future user, you will be primarily concerned with user procedures. Normal-use procedures should provide safeguards appropriate to the sensitivity of the information system.

Backup procedures concern the creation of backup data to be used in the event of failure. Whereas operations personnel have the responsibility for backing up system databases and other systems data, departmental personnel have the need to back up data on their own computers. Good questions to ponder are, "What would happen if I lost my computer or mobile device tomorrow?" "What would happen if someone dropped my computer during an airport security inspection?" "What would happen if my computer was stolen?" Employees should ensure that they back up critical business data on their computers. The IS department may help in this effort by designing backup procedures and making backup facilities available.

Finally, systems analysts should develop procedures for system recovery. First, how will the department manage its affairs when a critical system is unavailable? Customers will want to order and manufacturing will want to remove items from inventory even though a critical information system is unavailable. How will the department respond? Once the system is returned to service, how will records of business activities during the outage be entered into the system? How will service be resumed? The system developers should ask and answer these questions and others like them and develop procedures accordingly.

## SECURITY MONITORING

Security monitoring is the last of the human safeguards we will consider. Important monitoring functions are activity log analyses, security testing, and investigating and learning from security incidents.

Many information system programs produce *activity logs.* Firewalls produce logs of their activities, including lists of all dropped packets, infiltration attempts, and unauthorized access attempts from within the firewall. DBMS products produce logs of successful and failed log-ins. Web servers produce voluminous logs of Web activities. The operating systems in personal computers can produce logs of log-ins and firewall activities.

None of these logs adds any value to an organization unless someone looks at them. Accordingly, an important security function is to analyze these logs for threat patterns, successful and unsuccessful attacks, and evidence of security vulnerabilities.

Today, most large organizations actively investigate their security vulnerabilities. They may employ utilities such as Tenable's Nessus or IBM's Security AppScan to assess their vulnerabilities. Many companies create **honeypots**, which are false targets for computer criminals to attack. To an intruder, a honeypot looks like a particularly valuable resource, such as an unprotected Web site, but in actuality the only site content is a program that determines the attacker's IP address. Organizations can then trace the IP address back using free online tools, like DNSstuff, to determine who has attacked them.[12] If you are technically minded, detail-oriented, and curious, a career as a security specialist in this field is almost as exciting as it appears on *CSI*. To learn more, check out DNSstuff, Nessus, or Security AppScan. See also *Applied Information Security*, 2nd ed.[13]

Another important monitoring function is to investigate security incidents. How did the problem occur? Have safeguards been created to prevent a recurrence of such problems? Does the incident indicate vulnerabilities in other portions of the security system? What else can be learned from the incident?

Security systems reside in a dynamic environment. Organization structures change. Companies are acquired or sold; mergers occur. New systems require new security measures. New technology changes the security landscape, and new threats arise. Security personnel must constantly monitor the situation and determine if the existing security policy and safeguards are adequate. If changes are needed, security personnel need to take appropriate action.

Security, like quality, is an ongoing process. There is no final state that represents a secure system or company. Instead, companies must monitor security on a continuing basis.

## Q10-8 HOW SHOULD ORGANIZATIONS RESPOND TO SECURITY INCIDENTS?

The last component of a security plan that we will consider is incident response. Figure 10-16 lists the major factors. First, every organization should have an incident-response plan as part of the security program. No organization should wait until some asset has been lost or compromised before deciding what to do. The plan should include how employees are to respond to security problems, whom they should contact, the reports they should make, and steps they can take to reduce further loss.

Consider, for example, a virus. An incident-response plan will stipulate what an employee should do when he notices the virus. It should specify whom to contact and what to do. It may stipulate that the employee should turn off his computer and physically disconnect from the network. The plan should also indicate what users with wireless computers should do.

The plan should provide centralized reporting of all security incidents. Such reporting will enable an organization to determine if it is under systematic attack or whether an incident is isolated. Centralized reporting also allows the organization to learn about security threats, take consistent actions in response, and apply specialized expertise to all security problems.

When an incident does occur, speed is of the essence. The longer the incident goes on, the greater the cost. Viruses and worms can spread very quickly across an organization's networks, and a fast response will help to mitigate the consequences. Because of the need for speed, preparation pays. The incident-response plan should identify critical personnel and their off-hours contact information. These personnel should be trained on where to go and what to do when they get there. Without adequate preparation, there is substantial risk that the actions of well-meaning people will make the problem worse. Also, the rumor mill will be alive with all sorts of nutty ideas about what to do. A cadre of well-informed, trained personnel will serve to dampen such rumors.

**Figure 10-16**
Factors in Incident Response

- Have plan in place
- Centralized reporting
- Specific responses
  - Speed
  - Preparation pays
  - Don't make problem worse
- Practice

Finally, organizations should periodically practice incident response. Without such practice, personnel will be poorly informed on the response plan, and the plan itself may have flaws that only become apparent during a drill.

## How does the **knowledge** in this chapter help **you?**

The knowledge in this chapter helps you by making you aware of the threats to computer security both for you as an individual and business professional as well as for any organization in which you work. You know that both you and your organization must trade off the risk of loss against the cost of safeguards. You have learned techniques that you can and should employ to protect your own computing devices and your data. You know how organizations should respond to security threats. This chapter introduced you to technical, data, and human safeguards and summarized how organizations should respond to security incidents.

One more time: Above all, create and use strong passwords!

# Ethics Guide

## Hacking Smart Things

You may have noticed a recent trend in TV commercials for cars. Many car manufacturers are focusing on technology-centric special features. One of the most popular add-ons right now is adding the capability to turn your car into an Internet hot spot. Sure, allowing your friends to check their social media updates using your car's Wi-Fi sounds pretty cool. But there may be some unintended risks associated with incorporating this capability into your car—or any device, for that matter. What if one of your passengers used that Wi-Fi connection to access your car's brakes?

**Internet of Things (IoT)**

You may have already heard of the *Internet of Things* (IoT), or the idea that objects are becoming connected to the Internet so they can interact with other devices, applications, or services. Countless companies are working to capitalize on the possibilities of new "smart" products designed to automatically communicate with other devices and exchange data with little or no intervention by the user. The trend of developing new Internet-enabled devices is so widespread that some estimates place the number of IoT devices at roughly 26 billion by 2020.[14]

But what can all of these new smart devices be used for? Take home automation, for example. The home automation market is growing rapidly with new Internet-enabled devices like thermostats, smoke detectors, light bulbs, surveillance cameras, and door locks gaining in popularity.[15] These devices allow a homeowner to remotely monitor the temperature of their home, turn lights on or off, or remotely keep an eye on the family dog by tapping into a webcam feed. While all of these capabilities seem like a great idea and add convenience to daily life, the trend of outfitting every object with Internet access may prove to be a hazardous, even dangerous, proposition.

**Internet of Threats**

You might already be aware of some of the types of security threats on the Internet. If you tune in to the evening news on any given night you will see stories about data being stolen from large corporations, government insiders leaking sensitive information, or cyberattacks being launched from around the globe.

But what about security threats to your personal data? Could hackers target data stored on your Internet-enabled smart devices? Think about the security implications of having to protect 10, 20, or 30 different Internet-enabled devices in your home. Will you have to buy antivirus software for your refrigerator or configure a firewall on your thermostat?

As more and more devices are accessible over some form of network, users will have to weigh the pros and the cons of using them. The same thing that makes these devices great will also make them vulnerable to attack. Yes, of course, a smart thermostat will save you money. But what happens when it gets a virus? Will you be the one running a temperature?

# DISCUSSION QUESTIONS

**1.** Suppose you own a company that makes smart air purifying devices. Your air purifiers can filter and analyze the contents of the air. Then the data is sent back to corporate headquarters and formatted into online reports for users.

**a.** Would it be ethical to sell the data you collect? Assume each user had to accept a "terms and conditions" agreement before using the online reporting application. Consider both the categorical imperative and utilitarian perspectives.

**b.** Suppose an insurance agency wanted to buy data from you that showed which users' air purifiers recorded tobacco smoke. Would it be ethical to sell this type of identifying data? Consider both the categorical imperative and utilitarian perspectives.

**c.** Suppose you've been contacted by law enforcement with a request for data on all homes that report trace amounts of illegal drugs. If you tell your users that you are being forced to hand over their data to the police, you may lose a lot of business. Is it ethical to withhold this information from your users? Consider both the categorical imperative and utilitarian perspectives.

**2.** Suppose you own a company that makes smart refrigerators. Your smart refrigerators can tell you exactly what is in your refrigerator and let you know when you need to buy more of certain items. They also send data back to corporate headquarters to be used in online reports for users.

**a.** Would it be ethical to sell the data you collect about the contents of users' refrigerators? Assume each user had to accept a "terms and conditions" agreement before using the online reporting application. Consider both the categorical imperative and utilitarian perspectives.

**b.** Advertisers want to buy data from you so they can target consumers with ads about the foods they buy. But insurance companies, employers, news reporters, law enforcement, government agencies, and medical offices are also asking for access to the data you're collecting. Would it be ethical to sell your data to everyone? Consider both the categorical imperative and utilitarian perspectives.

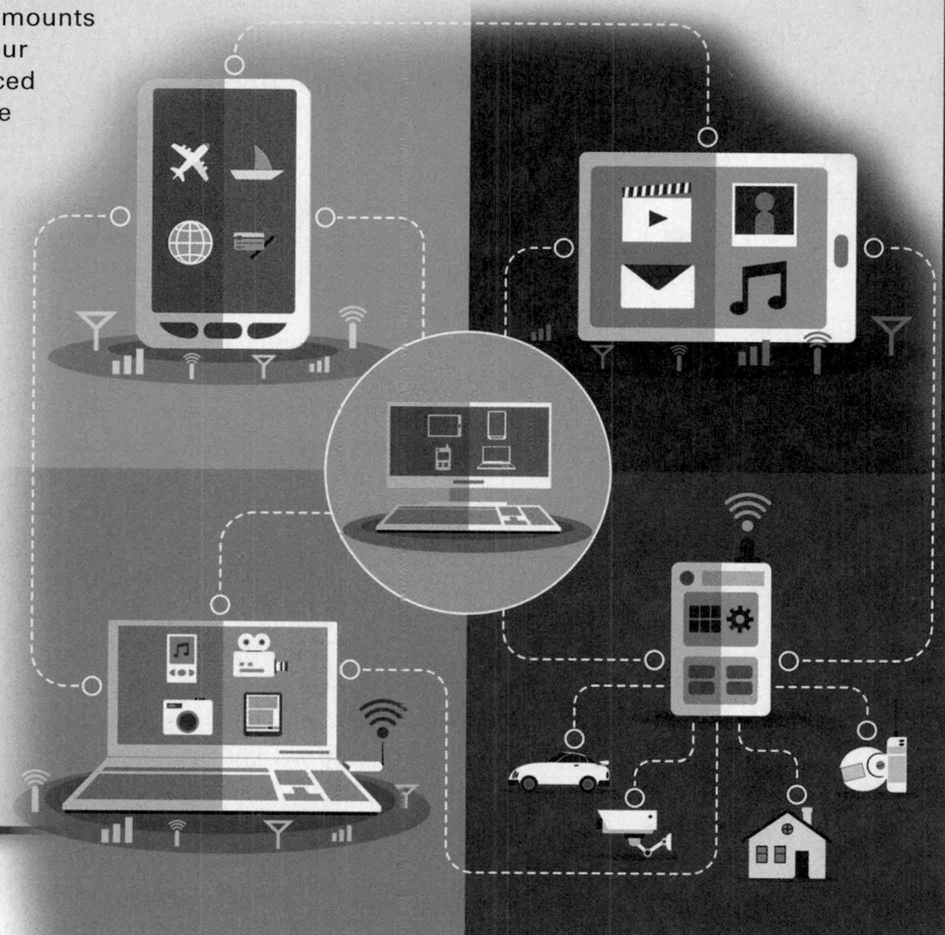

*Source:* macrovector/Fotolia

## EMV to the Rescue

Have you traveled abroad recently? If so, you may have noticed that retailers in foreign countries now prefer, and in many cases require, that you make purchases using EMV chip-and-PIN technology. EMV stands for Europay, MasterCard®, and Visa®, the first three financial institutions involved in developing this technology.[17] If you didn't have an EMV card, you probably had to show your passport or use an alternative method of payment.

EMV has the potential to make companies more secure because it means they won't have to store credit card data that hackers want to steal. EMV changes the way cards are verified. With a traditional magnetic stripe card the *account* associated with that card is verified. With EMV, the chip embedded in the card verifies the authenticity of the physical *card*, and the PIN (or signature) entered by the customer verifies the identity of the *cardholder*. Without the physical card and the associated PIN, stolen account data cannot be used to make purchases. EMV makes credit card fraud much more difficult.

Let's take a look at a recent data breach to see what EMV can do to protect you!

### Data Breach at Home Depot

Home Depot suffered a major data breach in 2014 that resulted in the loss of 56 million customer credit card records and 53 million customer email addresses.[18] When viewed in conjunction with the Target (98 million accounts) and JPMorgan Chase (83 million accounts) data breaches, all three of which occurred within less than a year, these incidents formed a tipping point. The prevalence and severity of cybercrimes occurring in corporate America have become more visible.

Hackers gained access to Home Depot's internal network using stolen credentials from a third-party vendor. They then distributed malware to internal point-of-sale (POS) terminals that would "scrape" credit card data from the random-access memory of the terminals. From there the stolen account data was collected and moved out of Home Depot's network.

After reviewing the details of the data breach, analysts found that Home Depot was using an older version of antivirus software, and lacked encryption between point-of-sale (POS) systems and central servers. However, even though the software wasn't the latest version, the virus signature files (used to identify specific viruses) were up to date. The malware used by the hackers was likely new and undetectable. The lack of encryption didn't directly contribute to the data breach either. The credit card numbers were stolen from the POS systems directly, not hijacked en route to a central server.[19]

The real security weakness was the access to the residual credit card data being stored in the memory of the POS. This could have been prevented through the adoption of EMV chip-and-PIN (or chip-and-signature) technology because the credit card data wouldn't have been stored in memory. Only transaction ID numbers are processed using EMV. Memory scraping malware, like the one used in the Home Depot data breach, wouldn't be able to recover any credit card data at all if Home Depot and its customers used EMV.

**Building Adoption Momentum**

Adoption of EMV chip-and-PIN is widespread in Western Europe (99.9 percent), Canada (84.7 percent), and Asia (71.4 percent).[20] But only 0.3 percent of transactions in the United States are completed using a chip-and-PIN card. Consequently, about 50 percent of credit card fraud worldwide occurs in the United States. This is because the United States is one of the last places that still allows purchases with older magnetic stripe card technology.

But there is good news on the horizon. Major credit card issuers, and some large banks, in the United States have announced adoption deadlines for chip-and-PIN technology by October 2015. At that point, merchants will start to become liable for credit card fraud occurring at their location if their POS terminals do not support EMV. But all benefits come with costs. In this case the cost of the cards themselves will rise from $0.25 per card to between $1.25 and $2.50 per card.[21] And the cost of upgrading each card reader will rise from $20 per card reader to between $40 and $100 per card reader. By the end of 2015, nearly 575 million new credit cards will be reissued to cardholders in the United States.

## DISCUSSION QUESTIONS

**1.** Why would EMV chip-and-PIN cards be more secure than older magnetic stripe cards?

**2.** How have the data breaches discussed in this article (Home Depot, Target, and JPMorgan Chase) influenced your perception of cyberattacks and cybercrimes? Have you changed your behavior to help protect your own systems and data because of these breaches?

**3.** This article discusses how Home Depot's antivirus software program was out of date but that the virus signature files used by the software were current. Explain why security experts would argue that out-of-date antivirus software would not have played a role in the Home Depot breach.

**4.** The cybercriminals responsible for the Home Depot breach stole residual credit card data from self-checkout POS systems. What does it mean to access residual data?

**5.** When a breach of this magnitude is reported there are often lawsuits filed against the company that was attacked. Do you think companies should be legally responsible for securing customer data? Why or why not?

*Source:* nobeastsofierce/Fotolia

# ACTIVE REVIEW

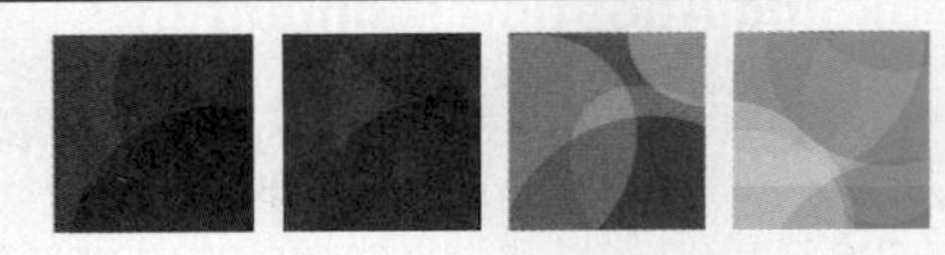

Use this Active Review to verify that you understand the ideas and concepts that answer the chapter's study questions.

## Q10-1 WHAT IS THE GOAL OF INFORMATION SYSTEMS SECURITY?

Define *threat, vulnerability, safeguard,* and *target*. Give an example of each. List three types of threats and five types of security losses. Give different examples for the three rows of Figure 10-2. Summarize each of the elements in the cells of Figure 10-3. Explain why it is difficult to know the true cost of computer crime. Explain the goal of IS security.

## Q10-2 HOW BIG IS THE COMPUTER SECURITY PROBLEM?

Explain why it is difficult to know the true size of the computer security problem in general and of computer crime in particular. List the takeways in this question and explain the meaning of each.

## Q10-3 HOW SHOULD YOU RESPOND TO SECURITY THREATS?

Explain each of the elements in Figure 10-6. Define *IDS* and explain why the use of an IDS program is sobering, to say the least. Define *brute force attack*. Summarize the characteristics of a strong password. Explain how your identity and password do more than just open doors on your computer. Define *cookie* and explain why using a program like CCleaner is a good example of the computer security trade-off.

## Q10-4 HOW SHOULD ORGANIZATIONS RESPOND TO SECURITY THREATS?

Name and describe two security functions that senior management should address. Summarize the contents of a security policy. Explain what it means to manage risk. Summarize the steps that organizations should take when balancing risk and cost.

## Q10-5 HOW CAN TECHNICAL SAFEGUARDS PROTECT AGAINST SECURITY THREATS?

List five technical safeguards. Define *identification* and *authentication*. Describe three types of authentication. Explain how SSL/TLS works. Define *firewall* and explain its purpose. Define *malware* and name six types of malware. Describe six ways to protect against malware. Summarize why malware is a serious problem. Explain how PRIDE is designed for security.

## Q10-6 HOW CAN DATA SAFEGUARDS PROTECT AGAINST SECURITY THREATS?

Define *data administration* and *database administration* and explain their difference. List data safeguards.

## Q10-7 HOW CAN HUMAN SAFEGUARDS PROTECT AGAINST SECURITY THREATS?

Summarize human safeguards for each activity in Figure 10-12. Summarize safeguards that pertain to nonemployee personnel. Describe three dimensions of safeguards for account administration. Explain how system procedures can serve as human safeguards. Describe security monitoring techniques.

## Q10-8 HOW SHOULD ORGANIZATIONS RESPOND TO SECURITY INCIDENTS?

Summarize the actions that an organization should take when dealing with a security incident.

## How does the **knowledge** in this chapter help **you?**

Summarize the knowledge you have learned from this chapter and explain how it helps you be both a better business professional and a better employee. State the one behavior you should choose above all. Do it!

## KEY TERMS AND CONCEPTS

Advanced Persistent Threat (APT) 283
Adware 294
Asymmetric encryption 291
Authentication 290
Biometric authentication 291
Brute force attack 286
Cookies 287
Data administration 295
Data safeguards 295
Database administration 295
Denial of service (DoS) 283
Email spoofing 282
Encryption 291
Encryption algorithms 291
Firewall 293
Hacking 282
Hardening 299
Honeypots 301
https 292
Human safeguards 296
Identification 290
Internal firewalls 293
Intrusion detection system (IDS) 286
IP spoofing 282
Key 291
Key escrow 296
Key loggers 294
Malware 293
Malware definitions 294
Packet-filtering firewall 293
Payload 294
Perimeter firewall 293
Personal identification number (PIN) 290
Phisher 282
Phishing 282
Pretexting 282
Public key encryption 291
Ransomware 294
Safeguard 280
Secure Sockets Layer (SSL) 292
Smart cards 290
Sniffing 282
Spoofing 282
Spyware 294
SQL injection attack 295
Symmetric encryption 291
Target 280
Technical safeguards 290
Threat 279
Transport Layer Security (TLS) 292
Trojan horses 294
Usurpation 283
Virus 293
Vulnerability 280
Wardrivers 294
Worm 294

MyMISLab™
To complete the problems with the ✪, go to EOC Discussion Questions in the MyLab.

## USING YOUR KNOWLEDGE

✪ **10-1.** Credit reporting agencies are required to provide you with a free credit report each year. Most such reports do not include your credit score, but they do provide the details on which your credit score is based. Use one of the following companies to obtain your free report: *www.equifax.com*, *www.experion.com*, and *www.transunion.com*.

**a.** You should review your credit report for obvious errors. However, other checks are appropriate. Search the Web for guidance on how best to review your credit records. Summarize what you learn.

**b.** What actions can you take if you find errors in your credit report?

**c.** Define *identity theft*. Search the Web and determine the best course of action if someone thinks he or she has been the victim of identity theft.

✪ **10-2.** Suppose you lose your company laptop at an airport. What should you do? Does it matter what data are stored on your disk drive? If the computer contained sensitive or proprietary data, are you necessarily in trouble? Under what circumstances should you now focus on updating your resume for your new employer?

✪ **10-3.** Suppose you alert your boss to the security threats discussed in Q10-1 and to the safeguards discussed in Q10-4. Suppose she says, "Very interesting. Tell me more." In preparing for the meeting, you decide to create a list of talking points.

**a.** Write a brief explanation of each threat discussed in Q10-1.

**b.** Explain how the five components relate to safeguards.

**c.** Describe two to three technical, two to three data, and two to three human safeguards.

**d.** Write a brief description about the safeguards discussed in Q10-4.

**e.** List security procedures that pertain to you, a temporary employee.

**f.** List procedures that your department should have with regard to disaster planning.

## COLLABORATION EXERCISE 10

*Read Chapter Extensions 1 and 2 if you have not already done so. Meet with your team and build a collaboration IS that uses tools like Google Docs, SharePoint, or other collaboration tools. Do not forget the need for procedures and team training. Now, using that IS, answer the questions below.*

The purpose of this activity is to assess the current state of computer crime.

**10-4.** Search the Web for the term *computer crime* and any related terms. Identify what you and your teammates think are the five most serious recent examples. Consider no crime that occurred more than 6 months ago. For each crime, summarize the loss that occurred and the circumstances surrounding the loss, and identify safeguards that were not in place or were ineffective in preventing the crime.

**10-5.** Search the Web for the term *computer crime statistics* and find two sources other than the Ponemon surveys cited in Q10-2.

**a.** For each source, explain the methodology used and explain strengths and weaknesses of that methodology.

**b.** Compare the data in the two new sources to that in Q10-2 and describe differences.

**c.** Using your knowledge and intuition, describe why you think those differences occurred.

**10-6.** Go to *www.ponemon.org/blog/ponemon-institute-releases-2014-cost-of-data-breach-global-analysis* and down-load the 2014 report (or a more recent report if one is available).

**a.** Summarize the survey with regard to safeguards and other measures that organizations use.

**b.** Summarize the study's conclusions with regard to the efficacy of organizational security measures.

**c.** Does your team agree with the conclusions in the study? Explain your answer.

**10-7.** Suppose your boss asks for a summary of what your organization should do with regard to computer security. Using the knowledge of this chapter and your answer to questions 10-4 through 10-6, create a PowerPoint presentation for your summary. Your presentation should include, but not be limited to:

**a.** Definition of key terms

**b.** Summary of threats

**c.** Summary of safeguards

**d.** Current trends in computer crime

**e.** What senior managers should do about computer security

**f.** What managers at all levels should do about computer security

## CASE STUDY 10

### Hitting the Target

On December 18, 2013, Target Corporation announced that it had lost 40 million credit and debit card numbers to attackers. Less than a month later Target announced an additional 70 million customer accounts were stolen that included names, emails, addresses, phone numbers, and so on.

After accounting for some overlap between the two data losses, it turns out that about 98 million customers were affected.[22] That's 31 percent of all 318 million people in the United States (including children and those without credit cards). This was one of the largest data breaches in U.S. history.

These records were stolen from point-of-sale (POS) systems at Target retail stores during the holiday shopping season November 27 to December 15, 2013). If you were shopping at a Target during this time, it's likely your data was lost. Below is a short summary of how attackers got away with that much data.

### How Did They Do It?

The attackers first used spear-phishing to infect a Target third-party vendor named Fazio Mechanical Services (refrigeration and HVAC services).[23] Attackers placed a piece of malware called Citadel to gather keystrokes, login credentials, and screenshots from Fazio users.[24] The attackers then used the stolen login credentials from Fazio to access a vendor portal (server) on Target's network. The attackers escalated privileges on that server and gained access to Target's internal network.

Once in, the attackers compromised an internal Windows file server. From this server the attackers used malware named Trojan.POSRAM (a variant of BlackPOS) to extract information from POS terminals. BlackPOS was developed by a 17-year-old from St. Petersburg, Russia, and can be purchased from underground sites for about $2,000.[25]

The customer data was continuously sent from the POS terminals to an extraction server within Target's network. It was

**Figure 10-17**
Target Data Breach

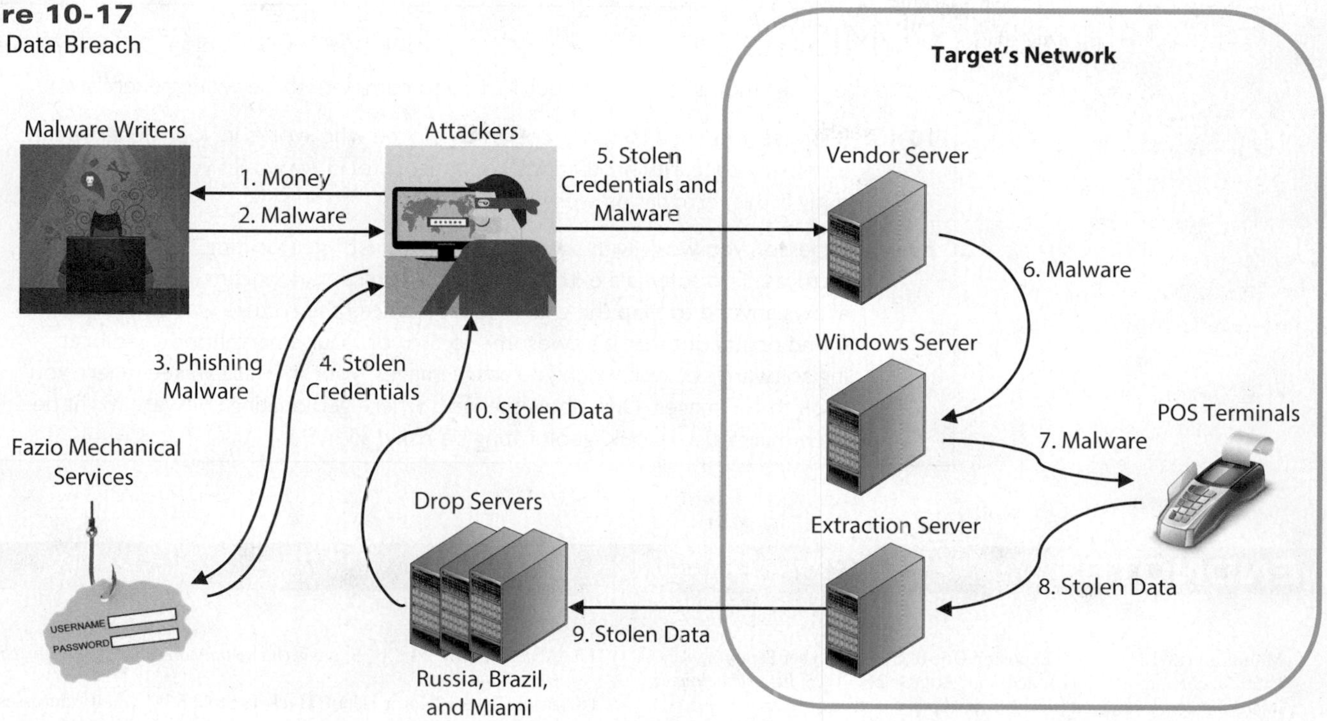

Malware Writers
Attackers
1. Money
2. Malware
5. Stolen Credentials and Malware
Target's Network
Vendor Server
6. Malware
Windows Server
3. Phishing Malware
4. Stolen Credentials
10. Stolen Data
POS Terminals
7. Malware
Fazio Mechanical Services
Drop Servers
Extraction Server
8. Stolen Data
USERNAME
PASSWORD
9. Stolen Data
Russia, Brazil, and Miami

then funneled out of Target's network to drop servers in Russia, Brazil, and Miami. From there the data was taken and sold on the black market.

## The Damage

For the attackers, the "damage" was great. It's estimated that the attackers sold about 2 million credit cards for about $26.85 each for a total profit of $53.7M.[26] Not bad for a few weeks of work. Incentives for this type of criminal activity are substantial. Payoffs like these encourage even more data breaches.

Target, on the other hand, incurred much greater losses than the hacker's gains. It was forced to upgrade its payment terminals to support chip-and-PIN-enabled cards (to prevent cloning cards from stolen information), which cost more than $100M. In 2015, Target lost a legal battle with banks over reimbursement of costs associated with the data breach, which could exceed $160M. It also had to pay increased insurance premiums, pay legal fees, pay for consumer credit monitoring, and pay regulatory fines.

Target faced a loss of customer confidence and a drop in its revenues (a 46 percent loss for that quarter). Analysts put the direct loss to Target as high at $450M.[27] The company lost its CIO Beth Jacob and paid its CEO Gregg Steinhafel $16M to leave.[28]

The data breach affected more than just Target. The amount of media coverage related to the Target data breach likely accelerated the shift from magnetic swipe cards to EMV-compliant smart cards set to happen in 2015. This shift will force the replacement of 800 million payment cards and 14 million POS terminals at a cost of $7B.[29]

The good news is that the adoption of EMV-compliant smart cards will greatly reduce the $10B in credit card fraud that occurs each year. It will also likely reduce the amount of credit card theft by hackers because stolen credit card numbers are of little value without the physical card.

Just like car accidents, data breaches may not be viewed as important until *after* they occur. The data breach affected Target enough that it upgraded its infrastructure, changed internal systems, and hired a Chief Information Security Officer (CISO).[30]

Will there be a more severe data breach in the future? Probably. Are organizations ready for it? Based on past performance, they won't be ready for it until *after* it happens.

## QUESTIONS

**10-8.** Why did the attackers spear-phish a contractor to Target?

**10-9.** Explain how a third-party contractor could weaken an organization's overall security.

**10-10.** Describe how data was stolen from Target.

**10-11.** How might a data loss at one organization affect other organizations?

**10-12.** Explain why large organizations are attractive targets for attackers.

**10-13.** Why might chip-and-pin cards reduce this type of theft?

**10-14.** Why didn't Target have a CISO before the data breach?

MyMISLab™

Go to the Assignments section of your MyLab to complete these writing exercises.

**10-15.** Suppose you need to terminate an employee who works in your department. Summarize security protections you must take. How would you behave differently if this termination were a friendly one?

**10-16.** A person you work with shows you how to use "geolocating" software on pictures. This software extracts embedded information from images and allows anyone to map the exact location where the picture was taken. Your friend points out that it's awesome to turn on your smartphone's geolocating software because when you share images, your friends can see where you took those images. Describe a scenario where geolocating software might be used maliciously. Could geolocating be risky? Why?

## ENDNOTES

1. Mandiant (2013), "APT1: Exposing One of China's Cyber Espionage Units," February 18, 2013, accessed August 26, 2015. *http://intelreport.mandiant.com/Mandiant_APT1_Report.pdf.*
2. Risk Based Security, "2014 Data Breach Trends," February 2015, *RiskedBasedSecurity.com*, accessed May 8, 2015, *www.riskbasedsecurity.com/reports/2014-YEDataBreachQuickView.pdf.*
3. Ponemon Institute, 2014 Cost of Cyber Crime Study: United States. October 2014.
4. Ponemon Institute, "2014 Global Report on the Cost of Cyber Crime," October 2014, accessed August 26, 2015 *http://www.ponemon.org/library/2014-global-report-on-the-cost-of-cyber-crime.*
5. John Pozadzides, "How I'd Hack Your Weak Passwords." One Man's Blog, last modified March 26, 2007, *http://onemansblog.com/2007/03/26/how-id-hack-your-weak-passwords/*. When Pozadzides wrote this in 2007, it was for a personal computer. Using 2013 technology, these times would be half or less. Using a cloud-based network of servers for password cracking would cut these times by 90 percent or more.
6. Dan Geer, "Cybersecurity as Realpolitik," *Black Hat USA 2014*, accessed April 1, 2015, *www.blackhat.com/us-14/video/cybersecurity-as-realpolitik.html.*
7. Violet Blue, "Yahoo CISO: End-to-End Mail Encryption by 2015," *ZDNet.com*, August 7, 2014, accessed April 1, 2015, *www.zdnet.com/article/yahoo-ciso-end-to-end-mail-encryption-by-2015.*
8. Andy Greenberg, "How Hackable Is Your Car?," *Wired.com*, August 6, 2014, accessed April 1, 2015, *www.wired.com/2014/08/car-hacking-chart.*
9. Danielle Walker, "Black Hat: Researcher Demonstrates How He Controlled Room Devices in Luxury Hotel," *SC Magazine*, August 6, 2014, accessed on April 1, 2015, *www.scmagazine.com/black-hat-researcher-demonstrates-how-he-controlled-room-devices-in-luxury-hotel/article/365038.*
10. Hewlett-Packard Development Company, *Internet of Things Research Study*, September 2014, accessed April 1, 2015, *http://h20195.www2.hp.com/V2/GetDocument.aspx?docname=4AA5-4759ENW.*
11. *Verizon 2014 Data Breach Investigations Report*, accessed June 2014, *www.verizonenterprise.com/DBIR/2014/.*
12. For this reason, do *not* attempt to scan servers for fun. It won't take the organization very long to find you, and it will not be amused!
13. Randall Boyle and Jeffrey Proudfoot, *Applied Information Security*, 2nd ed. (Upper Saddle River, NJ: Pearson Education, 2014).
14. P. Middleton, P. Kjeldsen, and J. Tully, J. "Forecast: The Internet of Things, Worldwide, 2013," November 18, 2013, accessed April 18, 2015, *www.gartner.com/doc/2625419/forecast-internet-things-worldwide.*
15. *https://nest.com/works-with-nest/.*
16. J. Markoff, "Researchers Show How a Car's Electronics Can Be Taken Over Remotely," *The New York Times*, March 9, 2011, p. B3.
17. Accessed July 24, 2015, *www.chasepaymentech.com/faq_emv_chip_card_technology.html.*
18. Brian Krebs, "Home Depot: Hackers Stole 53M Email Addresses," *Krebs On Security*, November 7, 2014, accessed April 28, 2015, *http://krebsonsecurity.com/2014/11/home-depot-hackers-stole-53m-email-addreses.*
19. Mathew Schwartz, "Analysis: Home Depot Breach Details: Why Anti-Virus Didn't Stop POS Malware Attack," *Bank Info Security*, September 16, 2014, accessed April 28, 2015, *www.bankinfosecurity.com/analysis-home-depot-breach-details-a-7323/op-1.*
20. Accessed July 24, 2015, *www.paypal.com/webapps/mpp/emv.*
21. Tom Groenfeldt, "American Credit Cards Improving Security with EMV, At Last," *Forbes*, January 28, 2014, accessed April 28, 2015, *http://www.forbes.com/sites/tomgroenfeldt/2014/01/28/american-credit-cards-improving-security-with-emv-at-last.*
22. Ben Elgin, "Three New Details from Target's Credit Card Breach," *Bloomberg Business*, March 26, 2014, accessed June 23, 2015, *www.bloomberg.com/bw/articles/2014-03-26/three-new-details-from-targets-credit-card-breach.*
23. Brian Krebs, "Target Hackers Broke In via HVAC Company," *KrebsonSecurity.com*, February 5, 2014, accessed June 23, 2015, *http://krebsonsecurity.com/2014/02/target-hackers-broke-in-via-hvac-company.*
24. Chris Poulin, "What Retailers Need to Learn from the Target Data Breach to Protect Against Similar Attacks," *Security Intelligence*, January 31, 2014, accessed June 23, 2015, *http://securityintelligence.com/target-breach-protect-against-similar-attacks-retailers/#.VYngl_lVikr.*
25. Swati Khandelwal, "BlackPOS Malware Used in Target Data Breach Developed by 17-Year-Old Russian Hacker," The Hacker News, January 17, 2014, accessed June 23, 2015, *http://thehackernews.com/2014/01/BlackPOS-Malware-russian-hacker-Target.html.*
26. Brian Krebs, "The Target Breach, by the Numbers," *KrebsonSecurity.com*, May 6, 2014, accessed June 23, 2015, *http://krebsonsecurity.com/2014/05/the-target-breach-by-the-numbers.*
27. Bruce Horovitz, "Data Breach Takes Toll on Target Profit," *USA Today*, February 26, 2014, accessed June 23, 2015, *www.usatoday.com/story/money/business/2014/02/26/target-earnings/5829469.*
28. Fred Donovan, "Target Breach: A Timeline," *FierceITSecurity.com*, February 18, 2014, accessed June 23, 2015, *www.fierceitsecurity.com/story/target-breach-timeline/2014-02-18.*
29. Dick Mitchell, "The EMV Migration Will Be a Rough, Risky Ride," *PaymentSource.com*, January 14, 2015, accessed May 23, 2015, *www.paymentssource.com/news/paythink/the-emv-migration-will-be-a-rough-risky-ride-randstad-exec-3020311-1.html.*
30. Dune Lawrence, "Target Taps an Outsider to Revamp IT Security After Massive Hack," *BusinessWeek*, April 29, 2014, accessed June 23, 2015, *www.businessweek.com/articles/2014-04-29/target-turns-to-an-outsider-for-cio-bob-derodes-to-revamp-it-security-after-massive-hack.*

chapter 11

# Information Systems Management

"I've worked with him before, but not on an Android project." James Wu and Jared Cooper are discussing the pros and cons of outsourcing Amazon Fire phone development to India.

"But it was a phone application?" Jared trusts James to do his homework, but he wants to understand his risks in outsourcing.

"Right, and in native iOS. I'm not sure about his skills developing on Android."

"So tell me what you know about this guy."

"His name is Ajit Barid. At least that's the name of his company." James looks a little sheepish.

"That's not his name?"

"I don't know. Maybe. You know what Ajit Barid means?" He starts to smile...

"No. What?"

"Invincible cloud."

"Umm... probably not the name his mother gave him... or she was prophetic. James, this makes me nervous. I don't know anything about doing business in India. The guy takes our money and runs, what do we do?" Jared is down to business now.

"Well, we don't pay him until he delivers... or at least not much. But I've had a positive experience with him, and his references are good on a recent game development project."

"India is a long way away. What if he gives our code to somebody else? Or our ideas? What if we find some horrible bug in his code, and we can't find him to fix it? What if he just disappears? What if he gets two-thirds done and then loses interest... or goes to work on someone else's project?" Jared is on a roll.

"All are risks, I agree. But it will cost you four to six times as much to develop over here." James starts to list risks on the whiteboard.

"Well, it's been my experience that you get what you pay for in this life..."

"You want me to find some local developers we can outsource to?" James thinks local development is a poor choice but wants Jared to feel comfortable with the decision they reach.

"Yes, no, I mean no. I don't think so. How'd you meet him?"

"At a conference when he was working for Microsoft in its Hyderabad facility. He was programming SharePoint cloud features. When the iPad took off, he left Microsoft and started his own company. That's when I hired him to build the iOS app."

"That worked out OK?" Jared wants to be convinced.

"Yes, but it was one of his first jobs... he had to get it right for us."

# STUDY QUESTIONS

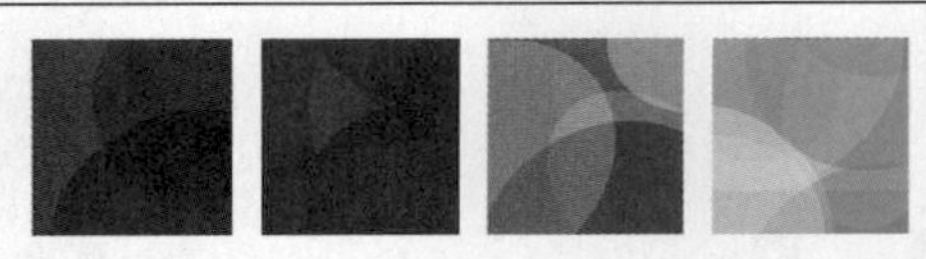



## How does the **knowledge** in this chapter help **you?**

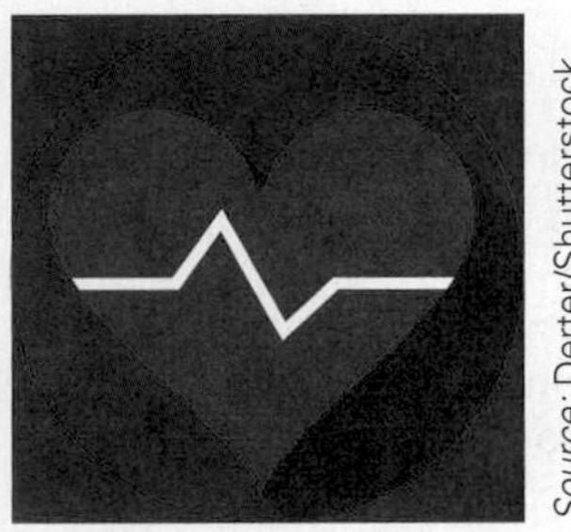

*Source:* Derter/Shutterstock

**"I don't know anything about doing business in India."**

"What do you think? What do you want to do?"

James ponders the questions. "Well, I think the biggest risk is his success. You know, the restaurant that gets the great reviews and then is buried in new customers and the kitchen falls apart."

"Doesn't he have more employees now?"

"Yes, he does, and I know he's a good developer, but I don't know whether he's a good manager."

"OK, what else?" Jared is all business.

"Well, Android development is different from iOS, which is what he used for the iPad. I guess I'd say inexperience with this dev environment would be another risk factor."

"What about money?"

"Well, like I said, we structure the agreement so we don't pay much until we know it all works."

"So what else do you worry about?" Jared wants to get all of James's concerns on the table.

"Loss of time. Maybe he gets distracted, doesn't finish the app, or hires someone else to do it, and they can't. And September rolls around and we find that, while we're not out any real money, we've lost most of a year of time."

"I don't like the sound of that."

"Neither do I," James responds while he adds schedule risk to the list.

"You think maybe we should bite the bullet and hire our own programmers?"

"Good heavens, no! No way! That would be incredibly expensive, we couldn't keep them busy, not yet, anyway, and I don't have the time to manage a software project nor the money to hire someone who does." James is certain about this.

"But what about long term?"

"Long term, maybe. We'll have to see what we have for budget and what our long-term dev needs are. That's a big step. We need to build infrastructure we don't have like testing facilities, hire developers, QA personnel, and managers. If we make PRIDE Systems the success we hope, we'll do that. But not yet."

"So?" Jared's tone shows he wants to wrap up this conversation.

James summarizes, "Let me finish the requirements document and then get a proposal and bid from Ajit as well as a local, domestic developer. We'll look at the proposals and bids and then make a decision. One problem, though . . . "

Optional Extension for this chapter is CE15: International MIS 584

"What's that?"

"The local developer may outsource it anyway."

"You mean we pay the local developer to hire Ajit or his cousin?" Jared shakes his head.

"Something like that."

Jared gets up from the table to show James out of his office. "That's crazy."

"Maybe not. Let's see what we get."

# Q11-1 WHAT ARE THE FUNCTIONS AND ORGANIZATION OF THE IS DEPARTMENT?

The major functions of the information systems department[1] are as follows:

- Plan the use of IS to accomplish organizational goals and strategy.
- Manage outsourcing relationships.
- Protect information assets.
- Develop, operate, and maintain the organization's computing infrastructure.
- Develop, operate, and maintain applications.

We will consider the first two functions in Q11-2 and Q11-3 of this chapter. The protection function is the topic of Chapter 10. The last two functions are important for IS majors, but less so for other business professionals, and we will not consider them in this text. To set the stage, consider the organization of the IS department.

## HOW IS THE IS DEPARTMENT ORGANIZED?

Figure 11-1 shows typical top-level reporting relationships. As you will learn in your management classes, organizational structure varies depending on the organization's size, culture, competitive environment, industry, and other factors. Larger organizations with independent divisions will have a group of senior executives like those shown here for each division. Smaller companies may combine some of these departments. Consider the structure in Figure 11-1 as typical.

**Figure 11-1**
Typical Senior-Level Reporting Relationships

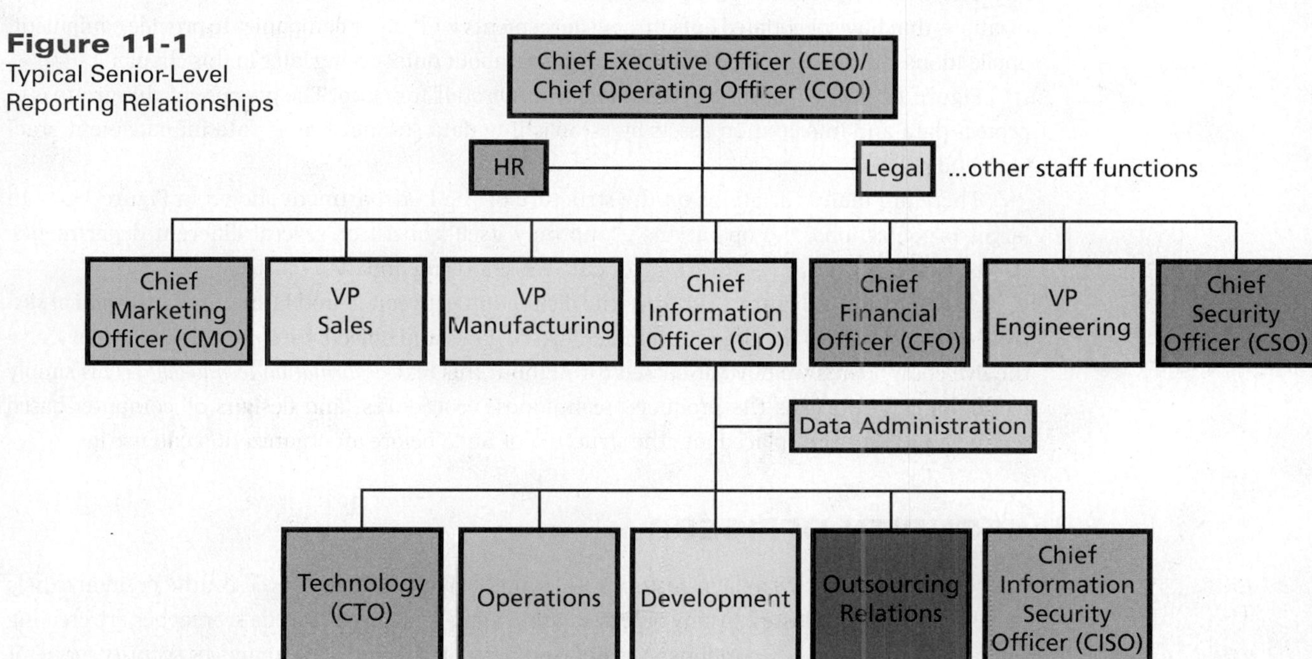

The title of the principal manager of the IS department varies from organization to organization. A common title is **chief information officer**, or **CIO**. Other common titles are *vice president of information services, director of information services*, and, less commonly, *director of computer services*.

In Figure 11-1, the CIO, like other senior executives, reports to the *chief executive officer* (CEO), though sometimes these executives report to the *chief operating officer* (COO), who, in turn, reports to the CEO. In some companies, the CIO reports to the *chief financial officer* (CFO). That reporting arrangement might make sense if the primary information systems support only accounting and finance activities. In organizations such as manufacturers that operate significant nonaccounting information systems, the arrangement shown in Figure 11-1 is more common and effective.

The structure of the IS department also varies among organizations. Figure 11-1 shows a typical IS department with four groups and a data administration staff function.

Most IS departments include a *Technology* office that investigates new information systems technologies and determines how the organization can benefit from them. For example, today many organizations are investigating social media and elastic cloud opportunities and planning how they can use those capabilities to better accomplish their goals and objectives. An individual called the **chief technology officer**, or **CTO**, often heads the technology group. The CTO evaluates new technologies, new ideas, and new capabilities and identifies those that are most relevant to the organization. The CTO's job requires deep knowledge of information technology and the ability to envision and innovate applications for the organization.

The next group in Figure 11-1, *Operations*, manages the computing infrastructure, including individual computers, in-house server farms, networks, and communications media. This group includes system and network administrators. As you will learn, an important function for this group is to monitor the user experience and respond to user problems.

The third group in the IS department in Figure 11-1 is *Development*. This group manages the process of creating new information systems as well as maintaining existing information systems. (We'll learn in Chapter 12 that in the context of information systems *maintenance* means either fixing problems or adapting existing information systems to support new features and functions.)

The size and structure of the development group depend on whether programs are developed in-house. If not, this department will be staffed primarily by business and systems analysts who work with users, operations, and vendors to acquire and install licensed software and to set up the system components around that software. If the organization develops programs in-house, then this department will also include programmers, test engineers, technical writers, and other development personnel.

The last IS department group in Figure 11-1 is *Outsourcing Relations*. This group exists in organizations that have negotiated outsourcing agreements with other companies to provide equipment, applications, or other services. You will learn more about outsourcing later in this chapter.

Figure 11-1 also includes a *Data Administration* staff function. The purpose of this group is to protect data and information assets by establishing data standards and data management practices and policies.

There are many variations on the structure of the IS department shown in Figure 11-1. In larger organizations, the operations group may itself consist of several different departments. Sometimes, there is a separate group for data warehousing and data marts.

As you examine Figure 11-1, keep the distinction between IS and IT in mind. *Information systems (IS)* exist to help the organization achieve its goals and objectives. Information systems have the five components we have discussed throughout this text. *Information technology (IT)* is simply technology. It concerns the products, techniques, procedures, and designs of computer-based technology. IT must be placed into the structure of an IS before an organization can use it.

## SECURITY OFFICERS

After Target Corp. lost 98 million customer accounts, it created a new C-level security position to help prevent these type of losses.[2] Many organizations reeling from large-scale data breaches are creating similar executive security positions. A **chief security officer**, or **CSO**, manages security for all of the organization's assets: physical plant and equipment, employees, intellectual property, and digital. The CSO reports directly to the CEO. A **chief information security officer**, or **CISO**, manages security for the organization's information systems and information. The CISO reports to the CIO.

Both positions involve the management of staff, but they also call for strong diplomatic skills. Neither the CSO nor the CISO has line authority over the management of the activities he or she is to protect and cannot enforce compliance with the organization's security program by direct order. Instead, they need to educate, encourage, even cajole the organization's management into the need for compliance with the security program (discussed in Chapter 10).

## WHAT IS-RELATED JOB POSITIONS EXIST?

IS departments provide a wide range of interesting and well-paying jobs. Many students enter the MIS class thinking that IS departments consist only of programmers and tech support engineers. If you reflect on the five components of an information system, you can understand why this cannot be true. The data, procedures, and people components of an information system require professionals with highly developed interpersonal communications skills.

Figure 11-2 summarizes the major job positions in the IS industry. With the exception of tech support engineers and possibly test QA engineers, all of these positions require a 4-year degree. Furthermore, with the exception of programmer and test QA engineer, all of these positions require business knowledge. In most cases, successful professionals have a degree in business. Note, too, that most positions require good verbal and written communications skills. Business, including information systems, is a social activity.

Median salaries and approximate salary ranges for the positions discussed in Figure 11-2 are shown in Figure 11-3.[3] According to the U.S. Social Security Administration, the median salary in 2013 for the average U.S. worker was $28,031.[4] Salary ranges for CTO, CIO, and CISO are higher than these positions because they require many more years of experience.

Salaries for information systems jobs have a wide range. Higher salaries are for professionals with more experience, working for larger companies, and living in larger cities.[5] Do not expect to begin your career at the high end of these ranges. As noted, all salaries are for positions in the United States and are shown in U.S. dollars.

(By the way, for all but the most technical positions, knowledge of a business specialty can add to your marketability. If you have the time, a dual major can be an excellent choice. Popular and successful dual majors are accounting and information systems, marketing and information systems, and management and information systems.)

# Q11-2 HOW DO ORGANIZATIONS PLAN THE USE OF IS?

We begin our discussion of IS functions with planning. Figure 11-4 lists the major IS planning functions.

## ALIGN INFORMATION SYSTEMS WITH ORGANIZATIONAL STRATEGY

The purpose of an information system is to help the organization accomplish its goals and objectives. In order to do so, all information systems must be aligned with the organization's competitive strategy.

Recall the four competitive strategies from Chapter 3. The first two strategies are that an organization can be a cost leader either across an industry or within an industry segment. Alternatively, for the second two strategies, an organization can differentiate its products or services either across the industry or within a segment. Whatever the organizational strategy, the CIO and the IS department must constantly be vigilant to align IS with it.

**Figure 11-2**
Job Positions in the Information Systems Industry

| Title | Responsibilities | Knowledge, Skill, and Characteristics Requirements |
|---|---|---|
| Business analyst, IT | Work with business leaders and planners to develop processes and systems that implement business strategy and goals. | Knowledge of business planning, strategy, process management, and technology. Can deal with complexity. See big picture but work with details. Strong interpersonal and communications skills needed. |
| Systems analyst | Work with users to determine system requirements, design and develop job descriptions and procedures, help determine system test plans. | Strong interpersonal and communications skills. Knowledge of both business and technology. Adaptable. |
| Programmer | Design and write computer programs. | Logical thinking and design skills, knowledge of one or more programming languages. |
| Test QA engineer | Develop test plans, design and write automated test scripts, perform testing. | Logical thinking, basic programming, superb organizational skills, eye for detail. |
| Technical writer | Write program documentation, help-text, procedures, job descriptions, training materials. | Quick learner, clear writing skills, high verbal communications skills. |
| Tech support engineer | Help users solve problems, provide training. | Communications and people skills. Product knowledge. Patience. |
| Network administrator | Monitor, maintain, fix, and tune computer networks. | Diagnostic skills, in-depth knowledge of communications technologies and products. |
| Consultant, IT | Wide range of activities: programming, testing, database design, communications and networks, project management, security and risk management, social media, strategic planning. | Quick learner, entrepreneurial attitude, communication and people skills. Respond well to pressure. Particular knowledge depends on work. |
| Technical sales | Sell software, network, communications, and consulting services. | Quick learner, knowledge of product, superb professional sales skills. |
| Project manager, IT | Initiate, plan, manage, monitor, and close down projects. | Management and people skills, technology knowledge. Highly organized. |
| Manager, IT | Manage teams of technical workers and manage the implementation of new systems | Management and people skills, critical thinking, very strong technical skills. |
| Database administrator | Manage and protect database. | Diplomatic skills, database technology knowledge. |
| Business intelligence analyst | Collaborate with cross-functional teams on projects, analyze organizational data. | Excellent analytical, presentation, collaboration, database, and decision-making skills. |
| Chief technology officer (CTO) | Advise CIO, executive group, and project managers on emerging technologies. | Quick learner, good communications skills, business background, deep knowledge of IT. |
| Chief information officer (CIO) | Manage IT departments, communicate with executive staff on IT- and IS-related matters. Member of the executive group. | Superb management skills, deep knowledge of business and technology, and good business judgment. Good communicator. Balanced and unflappable. |
| Chief information security officer (CISO) | Manage IS security program, protect the organization's information systems and information, manage IS security personnel. | Deep knowledge of security threats, protections, and emerging security threat trends. Excellent communication and diplomacy skills. Good manager. |

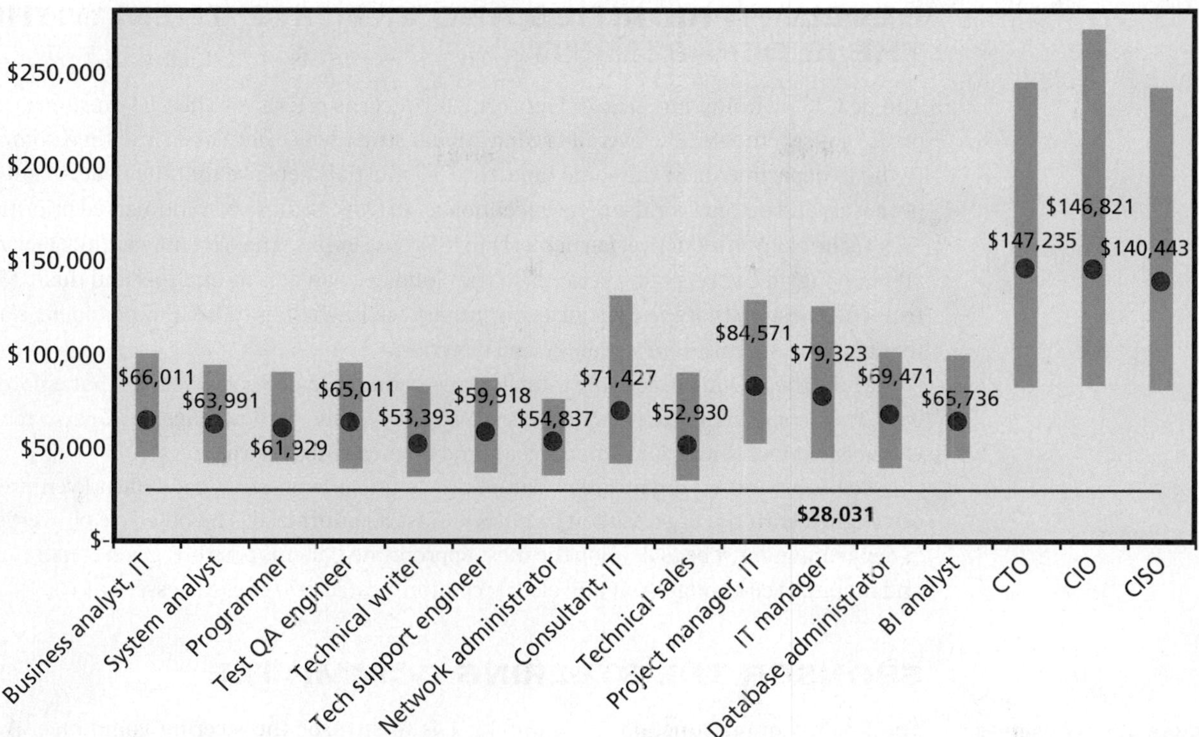


**Figure 11-3**
Salaries for Information Systems Jobs

Maintaining alignment between IS direction and organizational strategy is a continuing process. As strategies change, as the organization merges with other organizations, as divisions are sold, IS must evolve along with the organization.

Unfortunately, however, IS infrastructure is not malleable. Changing a network requires time and resources. Integrating disparate information systems applications is even slower and more expensive. This fact often is not appreciated in the executive suite. Without a persuasive CIO, IS can be perceived as a drag on the organization's opportunities.

## COMMUNICATE IS ISSUES TO THE EXECUTIVE GROUP

This last observation leads to the second IS planning function in Figure 11-4. The CIO is the representative for IS and IT issues within the executive staff. The CIO provides the IS perspective during discussions of problem solutions, proposals, and new initiatives.

For example, when considering a merger, it is important that the company consider integration of information systems in the merged entities. This consideration needs to be addressed during the evaluation of the merger opportunity. Too often, such issues are not considered until after the deal has been signed. Such delayed consideration is a mistake; the costs of the integration need to be factored into the economics of the purchase. Involving the CIO in high-level discussions is the best way to avoid such problems.

**Figure 11-4**
Planning the Use of IS/IT

- Align information systems with organizational strategy; maintain alignment as organization changes.
- Communicate IS/IT issues to executive group.
- Develop/enforce IS priorities within the IS department.
- Sponsor steering committee.

## DEVELOP PRIORITIES AND ENFORCE THEM WITHIN THE IS DEPARTMENT

The next IS planning function in Figure 11-4 concerns priorities. The CIO must ensure that priorities consistent with the overall organizational strategy are developed and then communicated to the IS department. At the same time, the CIO must also ensure that the department evaluates proposals and projects for using new technology in light of those communicated priorities.

Technology is seductive, particularly to IS professionals. The CTO may enthusiastically claim, "By moving all our reporting services to the cloud, we can do this and this and this..." Although true, the question that the CIO must continually ask is whether those new possibilities are consistent with the organization's strategy and direction.

Thus, the CIO must not only establish and communicate such priorities, but enforce them as well. The department must evaluate every proposal, at the earliest stage possible, as to whether it is consistent with the organization's goals and aligned with its strategy.

Furthermore, no organization can afford to implement every good idea. Even projects that are aligned with the organization's strategy must be prioritized. The objective of everyone in the IS department must be to develop the most appropriate systems possible, given constraints on time and money. Well-thought-out and clearly communicated priorities are essential.

## SPONSOR THE STEERING COMMITTEE

**To learn more about business process management, see Chapter Extension 17.**

The final planning function in Figure 11-4 is to sponsor the steering committee. A **steering committee** is a group of senior managers from the major business functions that works with the CIO to set the IS priorities and decide among major IS projects and alternatives.

The steering committee serves an important communication function between IS and the users. In the steering committee, information systems personnel can discuss potential IS initiatives and directions with the user community. At the same time, the steering committee provides a forum for users to express their needs, frustrations, and other issues they have with the IS department.

**One other task related to planning the use of IT is to establish the organization's computer-use policy. For more on computer-use issues, read the Ethics Guide on pages 330–331.**

Typically, the IS department sets up the steering committee's schedule and agenda and conducts the meetings. The CEO and other members of the executive staff determine the membership of the steering committee.

# Q11-3 WHAT ARE THE ADVANTAGES AND DISADVANTAGES OF OUTSOURCING?

**Outsourcing** is the process of hiring another organization to perform a service. Outsourcing is done to save costs, to gain expertise, and to free management time.

The father of modern management, Peter Drucker, is reputed to have said, "Your back room is someone else's front room." For instance, in most companies, running the cafeteria is not an essential function for business success; thus, the employee cafeteria is a "back room." Google wants to be the worldwide leader in search and mobile computing hardware and applications, all supported by ever-increasing ad revenue. It does not want to be known for how well it runs its cafeterias. Using Drucker's sentiment, Google is better off hiring another company, one that specializes in food services, to run its cafeterias.

Because food service is some company's "front room," that company will be better able to provide a quality product at a fair price. Outsourcing to a food vendor will also free Google's management from attention on the cafeteria. Food quality, chef scheduling, plastic fork acquisition, waste disposal, and so on, will all be another company's concern. Google can focus on search, mobile computing, and advertising-revenue growth.

# Is James Right for the Job?

Why do you need to know about IS management? Of course, if you're an IS major, you need to know the responsibilities and organization of your future department. But what if you're an accounting major or a marketing major or a management major? Why do you need to know about IS management?

As a future user of the IS department's services, it will be helpful to you to know the factors that drive standards and policies. And, if you're a manager, this knowledge will help you guide your employees behavior vis-à-vis the IS department. But let's take it a step further. Suppose you work for Zev at PRIDE Systems. Zev brought James over when he bought PRIDE Systems from Dr. Flores. Suppose Zev has some misgivings about James and asks you to help him. Zev would likely say something like "Do you think James knows his job?" or "Is James the right guy for us?"

If you had that assignment, how would you proceed? Answering the following questions will help you.

*Source: Peshkova/Shutterstock*

## QUESTIONS

1. State the major functions of this new IS department. Explain how each of the functions defined in this chapter pertain to PRIDE.
2. Assume James hired Ajit Barid and, so far, he's worked out well. Even still, Zev, as PRIDE Systems' owner, and you, as a key employee, might be nervous about the risks of this decision. Describe those risks. Assess how significant they are. Explain how the decision to use an offshore contractor influences your assessment of James.
3. Assume that James decided to use a cloud vendor to provide PaaS functionality. Explain what this means and how it reflects on James's competence.
4. Given the decisions (in questions 1–3) that James has made,
   - **a.** What will be the function and goals of the Operations group (see Figure 11-1)?
   - **b.** What will be the function and goals of the Development group? What job descriptions will this group need to staff?
   - **c.** What will be the function and goals of the Outsourcing Relations group?
   - **d.** Assume James has not specified the need for a CTO. Is this a mistake?
5. Given your answers to questions 1–4, how would you respond to Zev's question "Is James right for us?"

## OUTSOURCING INFORMATION SYSTEMS

Many companies today have chosen to outsource portions of their information systems activities. Figure 11-5 lists popular reasons for doing so. Consider each major group of reasons.

### Management Advantages

First, outsourcing can be an easy way to gain expertise. As you'll learn in Chapter 12, PRIDE Systems wants to build an Xbox prototype, but no one on their staff knows the particulars of coding for that device. Outsourcing can be an easy and quick way to obtain that expertise.

Another reason for outsourcing is to avoid management problems. At PRIDE Systems, building a large development and test team may be more than the company needs and require

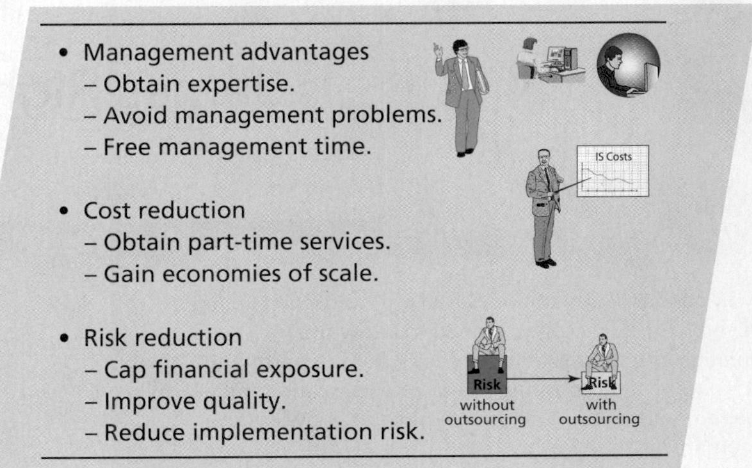


**Figure 11-5**
Popular Reasons for Outsourcing IS Services

management skills that neither James nor Jared have. Outsourcing the development function saves them from needing this expertise.

Similarly, some companies choose to outsource to save management time and attention. Toshio at Falcon Security has the skills to manage a new software development project, but he may choose not to invest the time.

Note, too, that it's not just Toshio's time. It is also time taken from more senior managers who approve the purchase and hiring requisitions for that activity. And those senior managers, like Joni, will need to devote the time necessary to learn enough about cloud alternatives to approve or reject the requisitions. Outsourcing saves both direct and indirect management time.

### Cost Reduction

Other common reasons for choosing to outsource concern cost reductions. With outsourcing, organizations can obtain part-time services. Another benefit of outsourcing is to gain economies of scale. If 25 organizations develop their own payroll applications in-house, then when the tax law changes, 25 different groups will have to learn the new law, change their software to meet the law, test the changes, and write the documentation explaining the changes. However, if those same 25 organizations outsource to the same payroll vendor, then that vendor can make all of the adjustments once, and the cost of the change can be amortized over all of them (thus lowering the cost that the vendor must charge).

### Risk Reduction

Another reason for outsourcing is to reduce risk. First, outsourcing can cap financial risk. In a typical outsourcing contract, the outsource vendor will agree to a fixed price contract for services. This occurs, for example, when companies outsource their hardware to cloud vendors. Another way to cap financial risk is as James recommends: delay paying the bulk of the fee until the work is completed and the software (or other component) is working. In the first case, outsourcing reduces risk by capping the total due; in the second, it ensures that little money is spent until the job is done.

Second, outsourcing can reduce risk by ensuring a certain level of quality or avoiding the risk of having substandard quality. A company that specializes in food service knows what to do to provide a certain level of quality. It has the expertise to ensure, for example, that only healthy food is served. So, too, a company that specializes in, say, cloud-server hosting knows what to do to provide a certain level of reliability and performance for a given workload.

Note that there is no guarantee that outsourcing will provide higher quality than could be achieved in-house. If it doesn't outsource the cafeteria, Google might get lucky and hire only great chefs. James might get lucky and hire the world's best software developer. But, in general, a professional outsourcing firm knows how to avoid giving everyone food poisoning or how to develop new mobile applications. And if that minimum level of quality is not provided, it is easier to hire another vendor than it is to fire and rehire internal staff.

Finally, organizations choose to outsource IS in order to reduce implementation risk. Hiring an outside cloud vendor reduces the risk of picking the wrong brand of hardware or the wrong virtualization software or implementing tax law changes incorrectly. Outsourcing gathers all of these risks into the one risk of choosing the right vendor. Once the company has chosen the vendor, further risk management is up to that vendor.

## INTERNATIONAL OUTSOURCING

Choosing to use an outsourcing developer in India is not unique to PRIDE. Many firms headquartered in the United States have chosen to outsource overseas. Microsoft and Dell, for example, have outsourced major portions of their customer support activities to companies outside the United States. India is a popular choice because it has a large, well-educated, English-speaking population that will work for 20 to 30 percent of the labor cost in the United States. China and other countries are used as well. In fact, with modern telephone technology and Internet-enabled service databases, a single service call can be initiated in the United States, partially processed in India, then Singapore, and finalized by an employee in England. The customer knows only that he has been put on hold for brief periods of time.

International outsourcing is particularly advantageous for customer support and other functions that must be operational 24/7. Amazon.com, for example, operates customer service centers in the United States, Costa Rica, Ireland, Scotland, Germany, Italy, Beijing, Japan, and India. During the evening hours in the United States, customer service reps in India, where it is daytime, can handle the calls. When night falls in India, customer service reps in Ireland or Scotland can handle the early morning calls from the east coast of the United States. In this way, companies can provide 24/7 service without requiring employees to work night shifts.

By the way, as you learned in Chapter 1, the key protection for your job is to become someone who excels at nonroutine symbolic analysis. Someone with the ability to find innovative applications of new technology is also unlikely to lose his or her job to overseas workers.

## WHAT ARE THE OUTSOURCING ALTERNATIVES?

Organizations have found hundreds of different ways to outsource information systems and portions of information systems. Figure 11-6 organizes the major categories of alternatives according to information systems components.

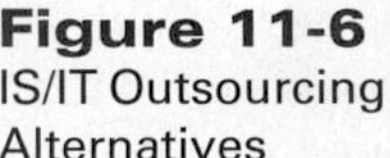

**Figure 11-6**
IS/IT Outsourcing Alternatives

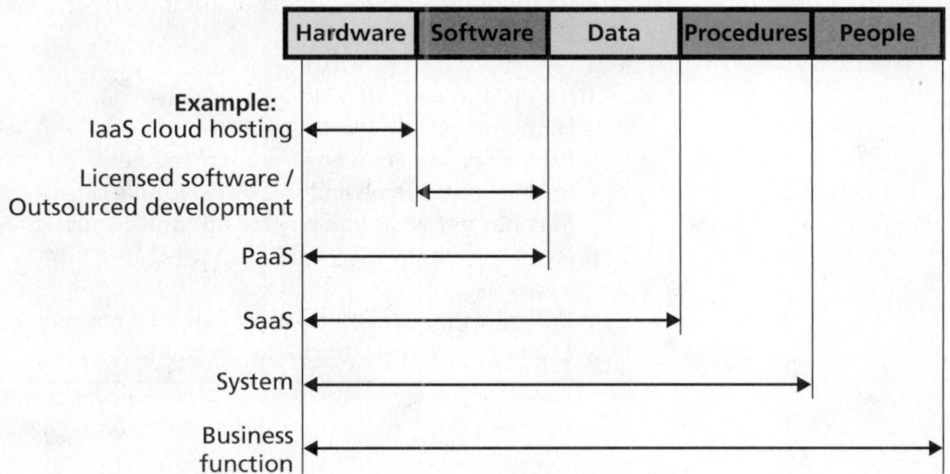

Some organizations outsource the acquisition and operation of computer hardware. Electronic Data Systems (EDS) has been successful for more than 30 years as an outsource vendor of hardware infrastructure. Figure 11-6 shows another alternative: outsourcing the computers in the cloud via IaaS.

Acquiring licensed software, as discussed in Chapters 4 and 12, is a form of outsourcing. Rather than develop the software in-house, an organization licenses it from another vendor. Such licensing allows the software vendor to amortize the cost of software maintenance over all of the users, thus reducing that cost for all users. Another option is Platform as a Service (PaaS), which is the leasing of hardware with preinstalled operating systems as well as possibly DBMS systems. Microsoft's Azure is one such PaaS offering.

Some organizations choose to outsource the development of software. Such outsourcing might be for an entire application, as with PRIDE, or it could also be for making customizations to licensed software, as is frequently done with ERP implementations.

Yet another alternative is Software as a Service (SaaS), in which hardware and both operating system and application software is leased. *Salesforce.com* is a typical example of a company that offers SaaS.

It is also possible to outsource an entire system. PeopleSoft (now owned by Oracle) attained prominence by providing the entire payroll function as an outsourced service. In such a solution, as the arrow in Figure 11-6 implies, the vendor provides hardware, software, data, and some procedures. The company need only provide employee and work information; the payroll outsource vendor does the rest.

Finally, some organizations choose to outsource an entire business function. For years, many companies have outsourced to travel agencies the function of arranging for employee travel. Some of these outsource vendors even operate offices within the company facilities. Such agreements are much broader than outsourcing IS, but information systems are key components of the applications that are outsourced.

## WHAT ARE THE RISKS OF OUTSOURCING?

**Not everyone agrees on the desirability of outsourcing. For potential pitfalls, read the example in the Guide on pages 332–333.**

With so many advantages and with so many different outsourcing alternatives, you might wonder why any company has any in-house IS/IT functions. In fact, outsourcing presents significant risks, as listed in Figure 11-7.

**Figure 11-7**
Outsourcing Risks

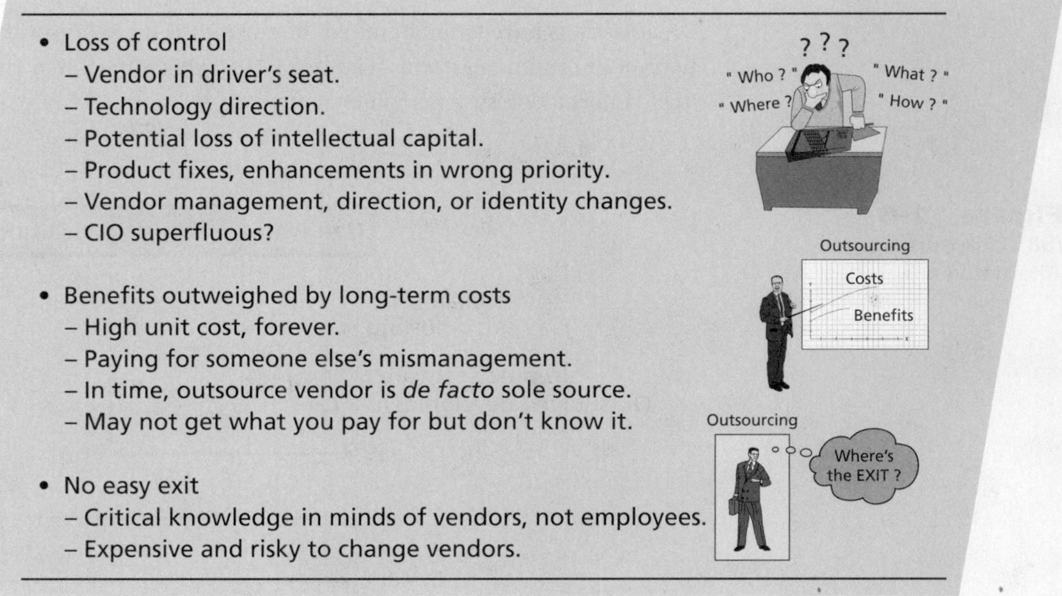

## Loss of Control

The first risk of outsourcing is a loss of control. For PRIDE, once James contracts with Ajit, Ajit is in control. At least for several weeks or months. If he makes PRIDE a priority project and devotes his attention and the attention of his employees as needed, all can work out well. On the other hand, if he obtains a larger, more lucrative contract soon after he starts PRIDE, schedule and quality problems can develop. Neither Jared nor James has any control over this eventuality. If they pay at the end, they may not lose money, but they can lose time.

For service-oriented outsourcing, say, the outsourcing of IT infrastructure, the vendor is in the driver's seat. Each outsource vendor has methods and procedures for its service. The organization and its employees will have to conform to those procedures. For example, a hardware infrastructure vendor will have standard forms and procedures for requesting a computer, for recording and processing a computer problem, or for providing routine maintenance on computers. Once the vendor is in charge, employees must conform.

When outsourcing the cafeteria, employees have only those food choices that the vendor provides. Similarly, when obtaining computer hardware and services, the employees will need to take what the vendor supports. Employees who want equipment that is not on the vendor's list will be out of luck.

Unless the contract requires otherwise, the outsource vendor can choose the technology that it wants to implement. If the vendor, for some reason, is slow to pick up on a significant new technology, then the hiring organization will be slow to attain benefits from that technology. An organization can find itself at a competitive disadvantage because it cannot offer the same IS services as its competitors.

Another concern is a potential loss of intellectual capital. The company may need to reveal proprietary trade secrets, methods, or procedures to the outsource vendor's employees. As part of its normal operations, that vendor may move employees to competing organizations, and the company may lose intellectual capital as that happens. The loss need not be intellectual theft; it could simply be that the vendor's employees learned to work in a new and better way at your company, and then they take that learning to your competitor.

Similarly, all software has failures and problems. Quality vendors track those shortcomings and fix them according to a set of priorities. When a company outsources a system, it no longer has control over prioritizing those fixes. Such control belongs to the vendor. A fix that might be critical to your organization might be of low priority to the outsource vendor.

Other problems are that the outsource vendor may change management, adopt a different strategic direction, or be acquired. When any of those changes occur, priorities may change, and an outsource vendor that was a good choice at one time might be a bad fit after it changes direction. It can be difficult and expensive to change an outsource vendor when this occurs.

The final loss-of-control risk is that the company's CIO can become superfluous. When users need a critical service that is outsourced, the CIO must turn to the vendor for a response. In time, users learn that it is quicker to deal directly with the outsource vendor, and soon the CIO is out of the communication loop. At that point, the vendor has essentially replaced the CIO, who has become a figurehead. However, employees of the outsource vendor work for a different company, with a bias toward their employer. Critical managers will thus not share the same goals and objectives as the rest of the management team. Biased, bad decisions can result.

## Benefits Outweighed by Long-Term Costs

The initial benefits of outsourcing can appear huge. A cap on financial exposure, a reduction of management time and attention, and the release of many management and staffing problems are all possible. (Most likely, outsource vendors promise these very benefits.) Outsourcing can appear too good to be true.

In fact, it *can be* too good to be true. For one, although a fixed cost does indeed cap exposure, it also removes the benefits of economies of scale. The outsourcing vendor obtains them instead. If a cloud vendor can run 20,000 servers almost as cheaply as it can run 2,000, it can get the benefit of the economies of scale. If PRIDE were to run those 20,000 servers in-house, instead, then PRIDE would obtain those benefits. It is unlikely to need that many; however, in most cases, the loss of benefit of economies of scale is more than offset by the benefits of cloud elasticity.

Also, the outsource vendor may change its pricing strategy over time. Initially, an organization obtains a competitive bid from several outsource vendors. However, as the winning vendor learns more about the business and as relationships develop between the organization's employees and those of the vendor, it becomes difficult for other firms to compete for subsequent contracts. The vendor becomes the *de facto* sole source and, with little competitive pressure, might increase its prices.

Another problem is that an organization can find itself paying for another organization's mismanagement, with little knowledge that that is the case. If PRIDE outsources its servers, it is difficult for it to know if the vendor is well managed. The PRIDE investors may be paying for poor management; even worse, PRIDE may suffer the consequences of poor management, such as lost data. It will be very difficult for PRIDE to learn about such mismanagement.

### No Easy Exit

The final category of outsourcing risk concerns ending the agreement. There is no easy exit. For one, the outsource vendor's employees have gained significant knowledge of the company. They know the server requirements in customer support, they know the patterns of usage, and they know the best procedures for downloading operational data into the data warehouse. Consequently, lack of knowledge will make it difficult to bring the outsourced service back in-house.

Also, because the vendor has become so tightly integrated into the business, parting company can be exceedingly risky. Closing down the employee cafeteria for a few weeks while finding another food vendor would be unpopular, but employees would survive. Shutting down the enterprise network for a few weeks would be impossible; the business would not survive. Because of such risk, the company must invest considerable work, duplication of effort, management time, and expense to change to another vendor. In truth, choosing an outsource vendor can be a one-way street.

At PRIDE, if, after the initial application development, the team decides to change development vendors, it may be very difficult to do. The new vendor will not know the application code as well as the current one who created it. It may become cost infeasible to consider moving to another better, lower-cost vendor.

Choosing to outsource is a difficult decision. In fact, the correct decision might not be clear, but time and events could force the company to decide.

## Q11-4 WHAT ARE YOUR USER RIGHTS AND RESPONSIBILITIES?

As a future user of information systems, you have both rights and responsibilities in your relationship with the IS department. The items in Figure 11-8 list what you are entitled to receive and indicate what you are expected to contribute.

### YOUR USER RIGHTS

You have a right to have the computing resources you need to perform your work as proficiently as you want. You have a right to the computer hardware and programs that you need. If you process huge files for data-mining applications, you have a right to the huge disks and the fast processor

| You have a right to: | You have a responsibility to: |
|---|---|
| – Computer hardware and programs that allow you to perform your job proficiently<br>– Reliable network and Internet connections<br>– A secure computing environment<br>– Protection from viruses, worms, and other threats<br>– Contribute to requirements for new system features and functions<br>– Reliable systems development and maintenance<br>– Prompt attention to problems, concerns, and complaints<br>– Properly prioritized problem fixes and resolutions<br>– Effective training | – Learn basic computer skills<br>– Learn standard techniques and procedures for the applications you use<br>– Follow security and backup procedures<br>– Protect your password(s)<br>– Use computers and mobile devices according to your employer's computer-use policy<br>– Make no unauthorized hardware modifications<br>– Install only authorized programs<br>– Apply software patches and fixes when directed to do so<br>– When asked, devote the time required to respond carefully and completely to requests for requirements for new system features and functions<br>– Avoid reporting trivial problems |

**Figure 11-8**
User Information Systems Rights and Responsibilities

that you need. However, if you merely receive email and consult the corporate Web portal, then your right is for more modest requirements (leaving the more powerful resources for those in the organization who need them).

You have a right to reliable network and Internet services. *Reliable* means that you can process without problems almost all of the time. It means that you never go to work wondering, "Will the network be available today?" Network problems should be rare.

You also have a right to a secure computing environment. The organization should protect your computer and its files, and you should not normally even need to think about security. From time to time, the organization might ask you to take particular actions to protect your computer and files, and you should take those actions. But such requests should be rare and related to specific outside threats.

You have a right to participate in requirements meetings for new applications that you will use and for major changes to applications that you currently use. You may choose to delegate this right to others, or your department may delegate that right for you, but if so, you have a right to contribute your thoughts through that representative.

You have a right to reliable systems development and maintenance. Although schedule slippages of a month or 2 are common in many development projects, you should not have to endure schedule slippages of 6 months or more. Such slippages are evidence of incompetent systems development.

Additionally, you have a right to receive prompt attention to your problems, concerns, and complaints about information services. You have a right to have a means to report problems, and you have a right to know that your problem has been received and at least registered with the IS department. You have a right to have your problem resolved, consistent with established priorities. This means that an annoying problem that allows you to conduct your work will be prioritized below another's problem that interferes with his ability to do his job.

Finally, you have a right to effective training. It should be training that you can understand and that enables you to use systems to perform your particular job. The organization should provide training in a format and on a schedule that is convenient to you.

## YOUR USER RESPONSIBILITIES

You also have responsibilities toward the IS department and your organization. Specifically, you have a responsibility to learn basic computer skills and to learn the techniques and procedures for the applications you use. You should not expect hand-holding for basic operations. Nor should you expect to receive repetitive training and support for the same issue.

You have a responsibility to follow security and backup procedures. This is especially important because actions that you fail to take might cause problems for your fellow employees and your organization as well as for you. In particular, you are responsible for protecting your password(s). This is important not only to protect your computer but, because of intersystem authentication, also to protect your organization's networks and databases.

You have a responsibility for using your computer resources in a manner that is consistent with your employer's policy. Many employers allow limited email for critical family matters while at work but discourage frequent and long casual email. You have a responsibility to know your employer's policy and to follow it. Further, if your employer has a policy concerning use of personal mobile devices at work, you have a responsibility to follow it.

You also have a responsibility to make no unauthorized hardware modifications to your computer and to install only authorized programs. One reason for this policy is that your IS department constructs automated maintenance programs for upgrading your computer. Unauthorized hardware and programs might interfere with these programs. Additionally, the installation of unauthorized hardware or programs can cause you problems that the IS department will have to fix.

You have a responsibility to install computer updates and fixes when asked to do so. This is particularly important for patches that concern security, backup, and recovery. When asked for input to requirements for new and adapted systems, you have a responsibility to take the time necessary to provide thoughtful and complete responses. If you do not have that time, you should delegate your input to someone else.

Finally, you have a responsibility to treat information systems professionals professionally. Everyone works for the same company, everyone wants to succeed, and professionalism and courtesy will go a long way on all sides. One form of professional behavior is to learn basic computer skills so that you avoid reporting trivial problems.

## How does the **knowledge** in this chapter help **you?**

You now know the primary responsibilities of the IS department and can understand why that department may implement the standards and policies that it does. You know the planning functions of IS and how they relate to the rest of your organization. You also know the reasons for outsourcing IS services, the most common and popular outsource alternatives, and the outsourcing risks. Finally, you know your rights and responsibilities with regard to services provided by your IS department.

All of this knowledge will help you be a better consumer of the services of your IS department. If you work in a small company, with little or no IS support, you know the kinds of work that must be done and the advantages, disadvantages, and choices for outsourcing that work. If you find yourself in James's position, you know the advantages and disadvantages of outsourcing software development. Finally, knowledge of your rights and responsibilities will enable you to be a more effective business professional by setting reasonable expectations as to what you can expect from the IS department while at the same time knowing what the IS department expects of you.

# Ethics Guide

## Privacy versus Productivity: The BYOD Dilemma?

I'm Justin, I work in operations. My boss asked me to meet with a committee the IS department created. The purpose of the committee is to determine our company's BYOD policy. Well, that's not quite right. The IS department will determine the policy, but they want to hear from active mobile users before they do so.

The first meeting we had was a real eye-opener. I thought we would be discussing which devices we could use and when. I see a few coworkers constantly checking social media, browsing the Web, or messaging their friends. They obviously need some guidance on what is and is not acceptable. No doubt, this needs to be addressed. But on my team, we live on our smartphones. We use them for everything, and they really do make us more productive. We're not giving them up.

I thought the meeting was going to be a discussion about how to restrict these devices to improve productivity. Boy, was I wrong. The IS folks started right into security issues. They worried about how they were going to secure company data from leaking out through new devices. They wanted to discuss the possibility of "configuring" people's personal devices. I was shocked. I get that they want to protect the company's data. I agree with that 100 percent. But, honestly, I thought they were being a little too cynical. From what I've seen, our people may be a little unfocused, but they're not criminal.

Honestly, the more I think about it, mobile devices aren't really a new data security threat. Twenty years ago, you could copy data onto a CD and take it out of the office. Later, you could use a thumb drive or take it home on your laptop and, if you wanted to steal it, copy it onto one of your home computers. Now, we can take data on our own mobile devices if we want.

Maybe it isn't what I'm taking ***out*** that's a threat; maybe it's what I'm bringing ***in***. The IS department doesn't know what apps I've got on my mobile device. That must be why they want to "configure" it. Maybe they want to make sure I'm not using an app to steal data. Or maybe they want to see that I don't have malware that could damage the corporate network. But they did mention that they want to add apps of their own to it as well.

That part makes me nervous. I heard that one company installs *key loggers*, you know, a program that records all the user's keystrokes into a file. The IS department regularly checks what owners are doing with *their own devices*. What prevents them from looking at my personal messages or pictures or seeing whom I talk to? This sounds like a big privacy issue. People won't like this at all.

Plus, on the committee, I've learned one plan is to install a program that IS can use to remotely wipe all the programs off mobile devices at their command. They say they need it in case we lose our devices. OK, I get that. But what if someone makes a mistake? Wipes out my device by accident? Will they wipe all the programs off my mobile device then?

Right now, I'm not sure what to do. I told my boss that our productivity and morale would tank if our personal devices were banned. I also told him that there would be a full-scale revolt if the IS department loaded any type of monitoring software on our devices. Honestly, I doubt they'll be able to get anything loaded onto any personal device. The most talented people we've got might just quit.

But from the IS perspective, they don't trust the programs I put on my mobile device. They've also got some legitimate concerns about data walking out the door. Maybe they should just buy me a smartphone and computer to use at work. Their hardware costs would go up, but they'd be able to control their devices. I'll still bring my mobile device to work, but I'll use my own wireless network, not theirs, and I won't do work with it. Is that why my boss wants me on this committee?

## DISCUSSION QUESTIONS

**1.** Consider the decision to install monitoring software on an employee's personal device.

**a.** Is this decision ethical according to the categorical imperative (pages 20–21)?

**b.** Is this decision ethical according to the utilitarian perspective (pages 46–47)?

**c.** How could monitoring software be used unethically by the IS department?

**d.** How would users react if they found out that the IS department was reading their personal text messages or viewing their browsing history?

**2.** The IS department is concerned about data theft by employees. But employees are concerned about the IS department using monitoring software to violate their privacy.

**a.** Which do you think is more likely to happen?

**b.** Which do you think would cause more harm to the organization? Why?

**3.** In your opinion, which is the greater threat of mobile devices at work: the data the employees take *out* or the programs they bring *in*? Explain your answer.

**4.** Is it ethical for an organization to monitor its employees' behavior if it purchased the devices for them? Consider both the categorical imperative and utilitarian perspectives.

*Source:* Pixsooz/Fotolia

# Guide

## Is Outsourcing Fool's Gold?

"People are kidding themselves. It sounds so good—just pay a fixed, known amount to some vendor for your computer infrastructure, and all your problems go away. Everyone has the computers they need, the network never goes down, and you never have to endure another horrible meeting about network protocols, https, and the latest worm. You're off into information systems nirvana. . . .

"Except it doesn't work that way. You trade one set of problems for another. Consider the outsourcing of computer infrastructure. What's the first thing the outsource vendor does? It hires all of the employees who were doing the work for you. Remember that lazy, incompetent network administrator that the company had—the one who never seemed to get anything done? Well, he's baaaaack, as an employee of your outsource company. Only this time he has an excuse, 'Company policy won't allow me to do it that way.'

"So the outsourcers get their first-level employees by hiring the ones you had. Of course, the outsourcer says it will provide management oversight, and if the employees don't work out, they'll be gone. What you're really outsourcing is middle-level management of the same IT personnel you had. But there's no way of knowing whether the managers they supply are any better than the ones you had.

"Also, you think you had bureaucratic problems before? Every vendor has a set of forms, procedures, committees, reports, and other management 'tools.' They will tell you that you have to do things according to the standard blueprint. They have to say that because if they allowed every company to be different, they'd never be able to gain any leverage themselves, and they'd never be profitable.

"So now you're paying a premium for the services of your former employees, who are now managed by strangers who are paid by the outsource vendor, who evaluates those managers on how well they follow the outsource vendor's profit-generating procedures. How quickly can they turn your operation into a clone of all their other clients? Do you really want to do that?

"Suppose you figure all this out and decide to get out of it. Now what? How do you undo an outsource agreement? All the critical knowledge is in the minds of the outsource vendor's employees, who have no incentive to work for you. In fact, their employment contract probably prohibits it. So now you have to take an existing operation within your own company, hire employees to staff that function, and relearn everything you ought to have learned in the first place.

"Gimme a break. Outsourcing is fool's gold, an expensive leap away from responsibility. It's like saying, 'We can't figure out how to manage an important function in our company, so you do it!' You can't get away from IS problems by hiring someone else to manage them for you. At least you care about *your* bottom line."

*Source:* Barbol/Shutterstock

## ? DISCUSSION QUESTIONS

**1.** Hiring an organization's existing IS staff is common practice when starting a new outsourcing arrangement. What are the advantages of this practice to the outsource vendor? What are the advantages to the organization?

**2.** Suppose you work for an outsource vendor. How do you respond to the charge that your managers care only about how they appear to their employer (the outsource vendor), not how they actually perform for the organization?

**3.** Consider the statement "We can't figure out how to manage an important function in our company, so you do it!" Do you agree with the sentiment of this statement? If this is true, is it necessarily bad? Why or why not?

**4.** Explain how it is possible for an outsource vendor to achieve economies of scale that are not possible for the hiring organization. Does this phenomenon justify outsourcing? Why or why not?

**5.** In what ways is outsourcing IS infrastructure like outsourcing the company cafeteria? In what ways is it different? What general conclusions can you make about infrastructure outsourcing?

**6.** This guide assumes that the outsourcing agreement is for the organization's computing infrastructure. Outsourcing for software development, as PRIDE is doing, involves less direct involvement with the contractor. Explain how your answers to questions 2–5 would be different for software outsourcing.

**7.** How do your answers to questions 2–5 differ if the outsourcing agreement is just for PaaS resources?

# ACTIVE REVIEW

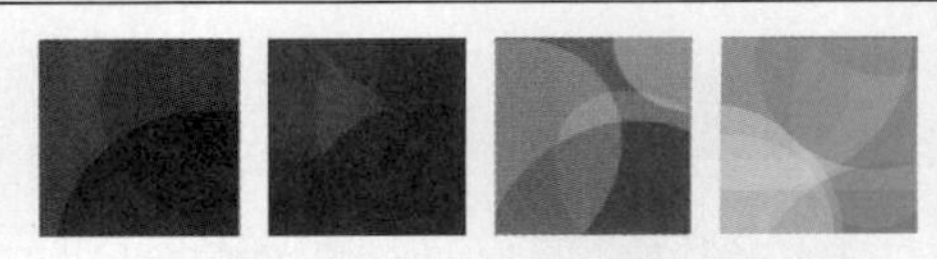

Use this Active Review to verify that you understand the ideas and concepts that answer the chapter's study questions.

## Q11-1 WHAT ARE THE FUNCTIONS AND ORGANIZATION OF THE IS DEPARTMENT?

List the five primary functions of the IS department. Define *CIO* and explain the CIO's typical reporting relationships. Name the four groups found in a typical IS department and explain the major responsibilities of each. Define *CTO* and explain typical CTO responsibilities. Explain the purpose of the data administration function. Define *CSO* and *CISO* and explain the differences in their responsibilities.

## Q11-2 HOW DO ORGANIZATIONS PLAN THE USE OF IS?

Explain the importance of strategic alignment as it pertains to IS planning. Explain why maintaining alignment can be difficult. Describe the CIO's relationship to the rest of the executive staff. Describe the CIO's responsibilities with regard to priorities. Explain challenges to this task. Define *steering committee* and explain the CIO's role with regard to it.

## Q11-3 WHAT ARE THE ADVANTAGES AND DISADVANTAGES OF OUTSOURCING?

Define *outsourcing*. Explain how Drucker's statement "Your back room is someone else's front room" pertains to outsourcing. Summarize the management advantages, cost advantages, and risks of outsourcing. Differentiate among outsourcing of IaaS, PaaS, and SaaS and give an example of each. Explain why international outsourcing can be particularly advantageous. Describe skills you can develop that will protect you from having your job outsourced. Summarize the outsourcing risks concerning control, long-term costs, and exit strategy.

## Q11-4 WHAT ARE YOUR USER RIGHTS AND RESPONSIBILITIES?

Explain in your own words the meaning of each of your user rights as listed in Figure 11-8. Explain in your own words the meaning of each of your user responsibilities in Figure 11-8.

## How does the **knowledge** in this chapter help **you?**

State how the knowledge of this chapter will help you as an employee of a large company. State how it will help you if you work for a small company. Explain how this knowledge will help you should you find yourself in Jared's position. Explain how this knowledge will enable you to be a more effective business professional.

## KEY TERMS AND CONCEPTS

Chief information officer (CIO) 316
Chief information security officer (CISO) 317
Chief security officer (CSO) 316
Chief technology officer (CTO) 316
Green computing 335
Outsourcing 320
Steering committee 320

MyMISLab™

To complete the problems with the ✪, go to EOC Discussion Questions in the MyLab.

## USING YOUR KNOWLEDGE

**11-1.** According to this chapter, information systems, products, and technology are not malleable; they are difficult to change, alter, or bend. How do you think senior executives other than the CIO view this lack of malleability? For example, how do you think IS appears during a corporate merger?

**11-2.** Suppose you represent an investor group that is acquiring hospitals across the nation and integrating them into a unified system. List five potential problems and risks concerning information systems. How do you think IS-related risks compare to other risks in such an acquisition program?

**11-3.** Describe what happens to IS when corporate direction changes rapidly. How does IS appear to other departments? What happens to IS when the corporate strategy changes frequently? Do you think such frequent changes are a greater problem to IS than to other business functions? Why or why not?

## COLLABORATION EXERCISE 11

*Read Chapter Extensions 1 and 2 if you have not already done so. Meet with your team and build a collaboration IS that uses tools like Google Docs, SharePoint, or other collaboration tools. Do not forget the need for procedures and team training. Now, using that IS, answer the questions below.*

**Green computing** is environmentally conscious computing consisting of three major components: power management, virtualization, and e-waste management. In this exercise, we focus on power.

You know, of course, that computers (and related equipment, such as printers) consume electricity. That burden is light for any single computer or printer. But consider all of the computers and printers in the United States that will be running tonight, with no one in the office. Proponents of green computing encourage companies and employees to reduce power and water consumption by turning off devices when not in use.

Is this issue important? Is it just a concession to environmentalists to make computing professionals appear virtuous? Form a team and develop your own, informed opinion by considering computer use at your campus.

**11-4.** Search the Internet to determine the power requirements for typical computing and office equipment. Consider laptop computers, desktop computers, CRT monitors, LCD monitors, and printers. For this exercise, ignore server computers. As you search, be aware that a *watt* is a measure of electrical power. It is *watts* that the green computing movement wants to reduce.

**11-5.** Estimate the number of each type of device in use on your campus. Use your university's Web site to determine the number of colleges, departments, faculty, staff, and students. Make assumptions about the number of computers, copiers, and other types of equipment used by each.

**11-6.** Using the data from questions 11-4 and 11-5, estimate the total power used by computing and related devices on your campus.

**11-7.** A computer that is in screensaver mode uses the same amount of power as one in regular mode. Computers that are in sleep mode, however, use much less power, say, 6 watts per hour. Reflect on computer use on your campus and estimate the amount of time that computing devices are in sleep versus screensaver or use mode. Compute the savings in power that result from sleep mode.

**11-8.** Computers that are automatically updated by the IS department with software upgrades and patches cannot be allowed to go into sleep mode because if they are sleeping they will not be able to receive the upgrade. Hence, some universities prohibit sleep mode on university computers (sleep mode is never used on servers, by the way). Determine the cost, in watts, of such a policy.

**11-9.** Calculate the monthly cost, in watts, if:

**a** All user computers run full time night and day.

**b** All user computers run full time during work hours and in sleep mode during off-hours.

**c** All user computers are shut off during nonwork hours.

**11-10.** Given your answers to questions 11-4 to 11-9, is computer power management during off-hours a significant concern? In comparison to the other costs of running a university, does this issue really matter? Discuss this question among your group and explain your answer.

# CASE STUDY 11

## iApp$$$$ 4 U

Let's suppose that you have a great idea for an iOS application. It doesn't matter what it is; it could be something to make life easier for college students or your parents or something to track healthcare expenses and payments for your grandparents. Whatever it is, let's assume that the idea is a great one.

First, what is the value of that idea? According to Raven Zachary, writing on the O'Reilly blog, it is zero.[6]

*Nada*. According to Zachary, no professional iPhone developer (he wrote this in 2008 about iPhone apps) will take equity or the promise of future revenue sharing in exchange for cash. There is too much cash-paying work. And ideas are only as good as their implementation, a fact that is true for every business project, not just iOS applications.

So, how can you go about getting your iOS application developed? You have three basic choices. You can go to a professional developer, one with a series of successes behind it. It will provide developers, designers, and project management. The cost depends, of course, on the requirements of your app, but according to Ryan Matzner, who manages *fueled.com*, a typical mobile commerce application will cost about $150K.[7]

If that's too high, your choices are either to attempt to do some of the work yourself, perhaps by managing an offshore developer, or to reduce your requirements. If you choose the former, you're engaging in a risky endeavor.

So, what are your options? First, do as much work as you can. Read the stages in the systems development life cycle in Chapter 12. Determine how many of those stages you can do yourself. Unless you are already a skilled object-oriented programmer and comfortable writing in Objective-C or Apple's new language, Swift, you cannot do the coding yourself. You might, however, be able to reduce development costs if you design the user interface and specify the ways that your users will employ it. You can also develop at least the skeleton of a test plan. You might also perform some of the testing tasks yourself.

If you have, let's round up, say, $3,000 that you're willing to invest, then you could outsource the development to a developer in the United States. If not, you have two other possible choices: outsource offshore or hire a computer science student. Elance is a clearinghouse for development experts; it lists developers, their locations, typical costs, and ratings provided by previous customers.[8] As you can see, you can hire developers in India, Russia, the Ukraine, Romania, and other countries. Costs tend start at $2,000 for a simple app, but again, that estimate does not include costs for design, graphics, and project management. Nor the costs you will incur getting your application into the App Store.

What about hiring a local computer science student? The price might be right, certainly far less than a professional developer, but this alternative is fraught with problems. First, good students are in high demand, and, second, good students are still, well, students. They need to study and don't have as much time to devote to your app. And, hard as it is to believe, some students are irresponsible flakes. However, if you have a friend whom you trust, you might make this option work.

One other option is to divide and conquer. Break your really great idea up into smaller apps. Pick one that is sure to be a hit, and sell it cheaply, say, for $.99. Use the money that you earn from that application to fund the next application, one that you might sell for more.

## QUESTIONS

**11-11.** What characteristics make a mobile application great? Describe at least five characteristics that compel you to buy applications. What characteristics would make an application easy and cheap to develop? Difficult and expensive?

**11-12.** Visit *www.elance.com* and identify five potential outsource vendors that you could use to develop an iOS app. Describe criteria you would use for selecting one of these vendors.

**11-13.** Explain how you think Google's purchase of Motorola Mobility changes the opportunity for iOS apps. In theory, does this purchase cause you to believe it would be wiser for you to develop on the Android or on the Windows 10 phone?

**11-14.** Search the Web for "Android developers" and related terms. Does it appear that the process of creating an Android app is easier, cheaper, or more desirable than creating an iOS app?

**11-15.** This case assumes that you have made the decision to develop an iOS application. Take an opposing view that developing a thin-client browser application would be a better decision. Explain how you would justify a thin-client app as a better decision.

**11-16.** Prepare a 1-minute summary of your experience with this exercise that you could use in a job interview to demonstrate innovative thinking. Give your summary to the rest of your class.

MyMISLab™

Go to the Assignments section of your MyLab to complete these writing exercises.

**11-17.** Consider the following statement: "In many ways, choosing an outsource vendor is a one-way street." Explain what this statement means. Do you agree with it? Why or why not? Does your answer change depending on what systems components are being outsourced? Why or why not?

**11-18.** A large multinational corporation experiences a severe data breach that results in the loss of customer data for nearly 250 million customers. The lost data includes names, addresses, email addresses, passwords, credit card numbers, and dates of birth. During the first week the entire company is in damage control mode. About 2 weeks after the data breach, the company's board of directors starts asking who was responsible. Heads are going to roll. They want to show their customers that they are taking steps so this won't happen again. Should they fire the CEO, CIO, CISO, CTO, database administrators, or line workers? Justify your choice.

## ENDNOTES

1. Often, the department we are calling the *IS department* is known in organizations as the *IT department*. That name is a misnomer, however, because the IT department manages systems as well as technology. If you hear the term *IT department* in industry, don't assume that the scope of that department is limited to technology.


2. Kristin Burnham, "Target Hires GM Exec as First CISO," *InformationWeek*, June 11, 2014, accessed May 11, 2015, *www.informationweek.com/strategic-cio/team-building-and-staffing/target-hires-gm-exec-as-first-ciso/d/d-id/1269600*.
3. PayScale Inc., "Salary Data & Career Research Center (United States)," *PayScale.com*, accessed May 12, 2015, *www.payscale.com/research/US/Country=United_States/Salary*.
4. U.S. Social Security Administration, "Measures of Central Tendency for Wage Data," *SSA.gov*, accessed May 12, 2015, *www.ssa.gov/oact/cola/central.html*.
5. DHI Group Inc., "Dice Tech Salary Survey," January 22, 2015, *Dice.com*, accessed May 12, 2015, *http://marketing.dice.com/pdf/Dice_TechSalarySurvey_2015.pdf*.
6. Raven Zachary, "Turning Ideas into iPhone Applications," *O'Reilly Media*, last modified November 21, 2008, *http://blogs.oreilly.com/iphone/2008/11/turning-ideas-into-application.html*.
7. Mary Hurd, "How Much Does It Cost to Develop an App?," *Fueled.com*, February 24, 2015, accessed June 27, 2015, *http://fueled.com/blog/how-much-does-it-cost-to-develop-an-app*.
8. "iPhone Development Experts Group," Elance, accessed June 27, 2015, *www.elance.com/groups/iPhone_Development_Experts/1115*.

chapter 12

# Information Systems Development

"Thanks for coming over on a Saturday morning. I just finished tennis, and the game went on longer than I expected. Anyway, forgive my appearance." Zev Friedman looks around the table.

"You must have won, Mr. Friedman. You look pleased." Michele is just getting to know PRIDE Systems' owner.

"Call me Zev. These other folks do. And yes, we won."

"Yes, sir." Michele is still a bit formal.

## This could happen to you

"OK, so, Jared, I understand you want to spend some real money. This morning you're going to tell me why, right?"

"That's why we're here, Zev. We've got a couple of options for you to consider. Here's a copy. I'm going to let James take you through it."

"I can hardly wait." Zev's mood is upbeat, but his demeanor and sleepy-eyed posture don't fool anyone. They know he's poised to detect errors or poor preparation.

"OK, Zev, you know that we were able to adjust our systems in order to support the new focus on multi-heat races." James is a little nervous as he starts.

"Yes, I do. And I understand that was your idea." Zev wants to make James comfortable with that compliment, and it works.

"It was a team discussion. Anyway, we were able to do that, and thanks to everyone's hard work, we're having success." James looks around the table as he speaks.

"It's a start, anyway." Zev knows they have a long way to go to establish a sustainable business.

"As you know, we only run on Apple and Android devices. We've done OK ignoring Surface and Windows phones."

"Yeah. I just don't understand Microsoft. They've blown every opportunity at mobile devices."

"Except, well, we think we can open the doors to an entirely new market if we start developing for the Xbox."

"The Xbox?"

"Yes, because these contests are very game-like. I'm spinning on my bike in my basement against 10 other players. They happen to be real people, but why don't we push the UI and use the Xbox to make it more visually exciting?"

"Interesting. Could be. So you want funds for Xbox development?"

"Yes, but take a look at the third page of the document we gave you. There are two ways to go. One is to develop using tools and technology specific to the Xbox. That would give us three separate code bases: Apple, Android, and Xbox."

"So?"

"We'll have essentially three different projects under way at the same time, with a lot of duplicated effort." From his voice and expression it's clear James hates the idea of duplicated effort.

# STUDY QUESTIONS

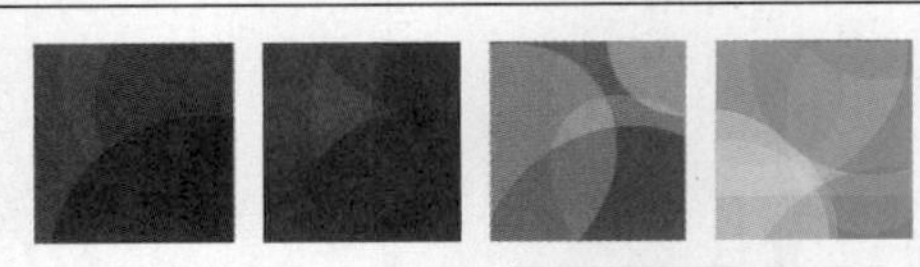

**Q12-1 WHAT IS SYSTEMS DEVELOPMENT?**

**Q12-2 WHY IS SYSTEMS DEVELOPMENT DIFFICULT AND RISKY?**

**Q12-3 WHAT ARE THE FIVE PHASES OF THE SDLC?**

**Q12-4 HOW IS SYSTEM DEFINITION ACCOMPLISHED?**

**Q12-5 WHAT IS THE USERS' ROLE IN THE REQUIREMENTS PHASE?**

**Q12-6 HOW ARE THE FIVE COMPONENTS DESIGNED?**

**Q12-7 HOW IS AN INFORMATION SYSTEM IMPLEMENTED?**

**Q12-8 WHAT ARE THE TASKS FOR SYSTEM MAINTENANCE?**

**Q12-9 WHAT ARE SOME OF THE PROBLEMS WITH THE SDLC?**

## How does the knowledge in this chapter help you?

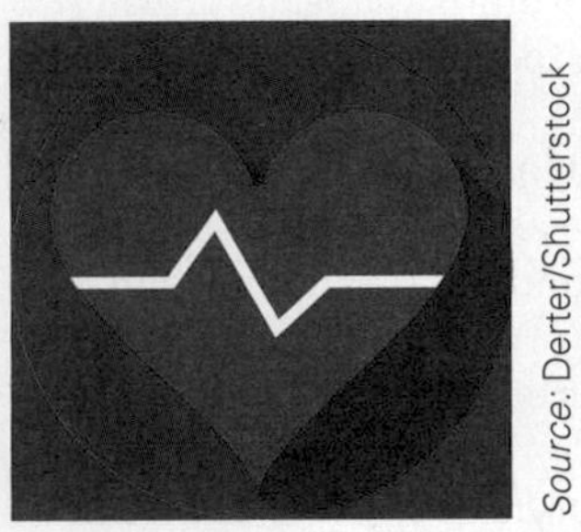

*Source:* Derter/Shutterstock

**"We think we can open the doors to an entirely new market."**

"Hmph."

"But if we use—and I'll spare you the details—but if we use another, more generic type of technology, called *html5* and *css3*, we can have a lot of common code. Not all, but a lot."

"Do spare me the details. I'll let Jared be my guide there. So have you got costs on this?"

"As shown on the third page, for the first—the Xbox only—somewhere between $100K and $175K."

"Big range." Zev sounds dubious.

"And, as shown on the fourth page, for reengineering all of our interfaces for html5, something between $225K and $300K." James sits back to watch Zev's reaction.

"Jared, what do you think?" Zev looks at Jared.

"It's a question of how much we want to spend to position ourselves for the future, Zev." Jared knows its Zev's money and his decision.

"That it is, that it is," Zev ponders.

"Nicki, what's your thinking?" Zev moves in his seat to get a better look at her face.

"Xbox is a big market. No doubt about it. And we'd be the first to really get into that market space."

"Can you sell this, Michele?"

"Without a doubt. It would be huge. It has to be incredibly exciting, though. People expect Wow/Now on game devices."

Zev sits silently for a minute or two. Then he looks back at the group, each person at a time, as he speaks.

"Nope. I don't want to do either one. We're not ready for it. But what I do want to do is develop an Xbox prototype. Use whatever technology will get you there fastest. Then I want to try it out... not with all the bells and whistles, but enough that we can see how well this gamer direction will work. Jared, bring me back a plan to do that. James, I want you there too. Questions?"

Silence around the table until Jared speaks, "Thanks, Zev, we'll do just that."

**Optional Extensions for this chapter are CE16: Systems Development Project Management 601 • CE17: Agile Development 614 • CE18: Business Process Management 623**

## Q12-1 WHAT IS SYSTEMS DEVELOPMENT?

**Systems development**, or systems analysis and design as it is sometimes called, is the process of creating and maintaining information systems. Notice that this process concerns *information systems*, not just computer programs. Developing an *information system* involves all five components: hardware, software, data, procedures, and people. Developing a *computer program* involves software programs, possibly with some focus on data and databases. Figure 12-1 shows that systems development has a broader scope than computer program development.

Because systems development addresses all five components, it requires more than just programming or technical expertise. Establishing the system's goals, setting up the project, and determining requirements necessitate business knowledge and management skill. Tasks such as building computer networks and writing computer programs require technical skills; developing the other components requires nontechnical, human relations skills. Creating data models requires the ability to interview users and understand their view of the business activities. Designing procedures, especially those involving group action, requires business knowledge and an understanding of group dynamics. Developing job descriptions, staffing, and training all require human resource and related expertise.

Therefore, do not suppose that systems development is exclusively a technical task undertaken by programmers and hardware specialists. Rather, it requires coordinated teamwork of both specialists and nonspecialists with business knowledge.

In Chapter 4, you learned that there are three sources for software: off-the-shelf, off-the-shelf with adaptation, and custom-made. Although all three sources pertain to software, only two of them pertain to information systems. Unlike software, *information systems are never off-the-shelf.* Because information systems involve your company's people and procedures, you must construct or adapt procedures to fit your business and people, regardless of how you obtain the computer programs.

As a future business manager, you will have a key role in information systems development. In order to accomplish the goals of your department, you need to ensure that effective procedures exist for using the information system. You need to ensure that personnel are properly trained and are able to use the IS effectively. If your department does not have appropriate procedures and trained personnel, you must take corrective action. Although you might pass off hardware, program, or data problems to the IT department or independent contractor, you cannot pass off procedural or personnel problems to that department. Such problems are your problems. The single most important criterion for information systems success is for users to take ownership of their systems.

## Q12-2 WHY IS SYSTEMS DEVELOPMENT DIFFICULT AND RISKY?

Systems development is difficult and risky. Many projects are never finished. Of those that are finished, some are 200 or 300 percent over budget. Still other projects finish within budget and schedule, but never satisfactorily accomplish their goals.

You may be amazed to learn that systems development failures can be so dramatic. You might suppose that with all the computers and all the systems developed over the years that by now

**Figure 12-1**
Systems Development Versus Program Development

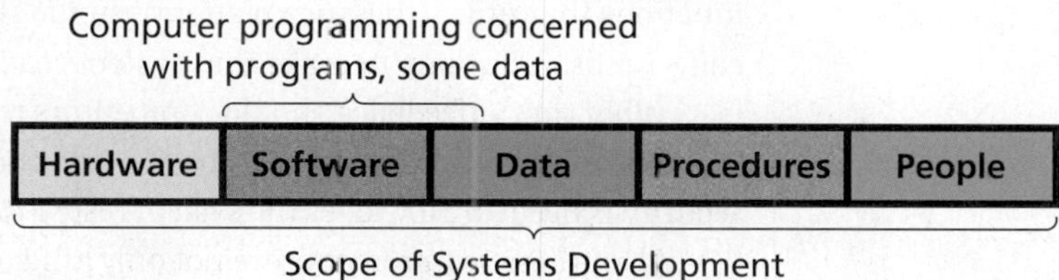

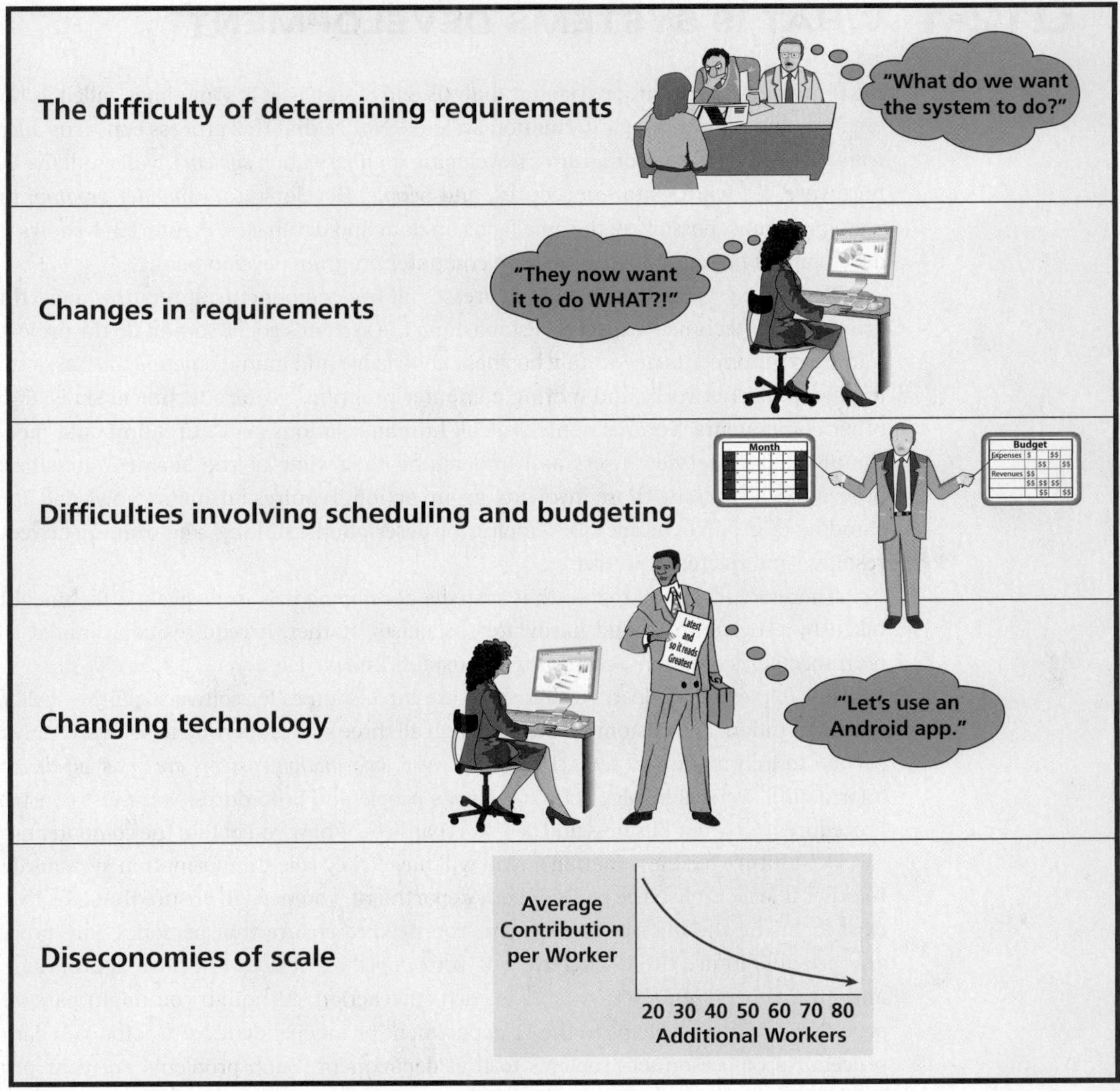


**Figure 12-2**
Major Challenges to Systems Development

there must be some methodology for successful systems development. In fact, there *are* systems development methodologies that can result in success, and we will discuss the primary one in this chapter. But even when competent people follow this or some other accepted methodology, the risk of failure is still high.

In the following sections, we will discuss the five major challenges to systems development displayed in Figure 12-2.

## THE DIFFICULTY OF REQUIREMENTS DETERMINATION

First, requirements are difficult to determine. Zev wants to start the Xbox project with a prototype, which, as you'll learn, is often a good way to begin. But then what? What specific features and functions that utilize the Xbox platform should the new PRIDE system implement? What, specifically, needs to be done to make that system ready for use? What should the screen displays look like? What sort of feedback should competitors receive?

Or consider pragmatic questions. How do competitors get started? How do they sign in? What security is needed? How does the system respond when people forget their password, and so on?

All of these requirements are not only difficult to specify, they are difficult to even know.

As any experienced systems analyst knows, there will be important questions that no one knows to ask. Perhaps the requirements are specified in calendar Q1, and there are year-end reporting needs that no one currently remembers. Once the system is in use, however, the need for any missing features will appear, to the great frustration of users and PRIDE Systems' staff. One of the major purposes of the systems development process is to create an environment in which such questions are both asked and answered.

## CHANGES IN REQUIREMENTS

Even more difficult, systems development aims at a moving target. Requirements change as the system is developed, and the bigger the system and the longer the project, the more the requirements change. For example, midway through the development process, a major health club chain approaches Jared with a lucrative contract proposal. But that proposal necessitates major changes in planned Xbox requirements.

When requirements do change, what should the development team do? Stop work and rebuild the system in accordance with the new requirements? If they do that, the system will develop in fits and starts and may never be completed. Or should the team finish the system, knowing that it will be unsatisfactory the day it is implemented and will, therefore, need immediate maintenance?

## SCHEDULING AND BUDGETING DIFFICULTIES

Other challenges involve scheduling and budgeting. How long will it take to build a system? That question is not easy to answer. Suppose you are developing a new database. You need to create a data model. How long will it take to create? Even if you know how long it takes to create the data model, others may disagree with that model and with each other. How many times will you need to rebuild the data model until everyone agrees? How many labor hours should you plan?

Consider database applications. How long will it take to build the forms, reports, queries, and application programs? How long will it take to test all of them? What about procedures and people? What procedures need to be developed, and how much time should be set aside to create and document them, develop training programs, and train the personnel?

Further, how much will all of this cost? Labor costs are a direct function of labor hours; if you cannot estimate labor hours, you cannot estimate labor costs. Moreover, if you cannot estimate how much a system costs, then how do you perform a financial analysis to determine if the system generates an appropriate rate of return?

## CHANGING TECHNOLOGY

Yet another challenge is that while the project is underway, technology continues to change. For example, say that while you are developing the PRIDE application, Apple, Microsoft, and Google and their business partners all release hot, new mobile devices with vastly improved graphics and animation, much better than any device you now support. You know that with these new devices you can create far better animations for comparative exercise.

Do you want to stop your development to switch to the new technology? Would it be better to finish developing according to the existing plan? Such decisions are tough. Why build an out-of-date system? But can you afford to keep changing the project?

## DISECONOMIES OF SCALE

Unfortunately, as development teams become larger, the average contribution per worker decreases. This is true because as staff size increases, more meetings and other coordinating activities are required to keep everyone in sync. There are economies of scale up to a point, but beyond a workgroup of, say, 20 employees, diseconomies of scale begin to take over.

A famous adage known as **Brooks' Law** points out a related problem: *Adding more people to a late project makes the project later.*[1] Brooks' Law is true not only because a larger staff requires increased coordination, but also because new people need training. The only people who can train the new employees are the existing team members, who are thus taken off productive tasks. The costs of training new people can overwhelm the benefit of their contribution.

In short, managers of software development projects face a dilemma: They can increase work per employee by keeping the team small, but in doing so they extend the project's timeline. Or they can reduce the project's timeline by adding staff, but because of diseconomies of scale they will have to add 150 or 200 hours of labor to gain 100 hours of work. And due to Brooks' Law, once the project is late, both choices are bad.

Furthermore, schedules can be compressed only so far. According to another popular adage, "Nine women cannot make a baby in one month."

### IS IT REALLY SO BLEAK?

Is systems development really as bleak as the list of challenges makes it sound? Yes and no. All of the challenges just described do exist, and they are all significant hurdles that every development project must overcome. As noted previously, once the project is late and over budget, no good choice exists. "I have to pick my regrets," said one beleaguered manager of a late project.

The IT industry has more than 50 years of experience developing information systems; over those years, methodologies have emerged that successfully deal with these problems. In the next study question, we will consider the systems development life cycle (SDLC), the most common process for systems development. Chapter Extension 17 addresses agile *development*, a newer and promising development methodology.

## Q12-3 WHAT ARE THE FIVE PHASES OF THE SDLC?

**You can learn more about project planning by reading Chapter Extension 16, Systems Development Project Management.**

The **systems development life cycle (SDLC)** is the traditional process used to develop information systems. The IT industry developed the SDLC in the "school of hard knocks." Many early projects met with disaster, and companies and systems developers sifted through the ashes of those disasters to determine what went wrong. By the 1970s, most seasoned project managers agreed on the basic tasks that need to be performed to successfully build and maintain information systems. These basic tasks are combined into phases of systems development.

Different authors and organizations package the tasks into different numbers of phases. Some organizations use an eight-phase process, others use a seven-phase process, and still others use a five-phase process. In this book, we will use the following five-phase process:

1. **System definition**
2. **Requirements analysis**
3. **Component design**
4. **Implementation**
5. **Maintenance**

Figure 12-3 shows how these phases are related. Development begins when a business-planning process identifies a need for a new system. We addressed IS planning processes in Chapter 11. For now, suppose that management has determined, in some way, that the organization can best accomplish its goals and objectives by constructing a new information system.

Developers in the first SDLC phase—system definition—use management's statement of the system needs in order to begin to define the new system (for PRIDE, this statement is the need for the prototype). The resulting project plan is the input to the second phase—requirements analysis. Here developers identify the particular features and functions of the new system. The output

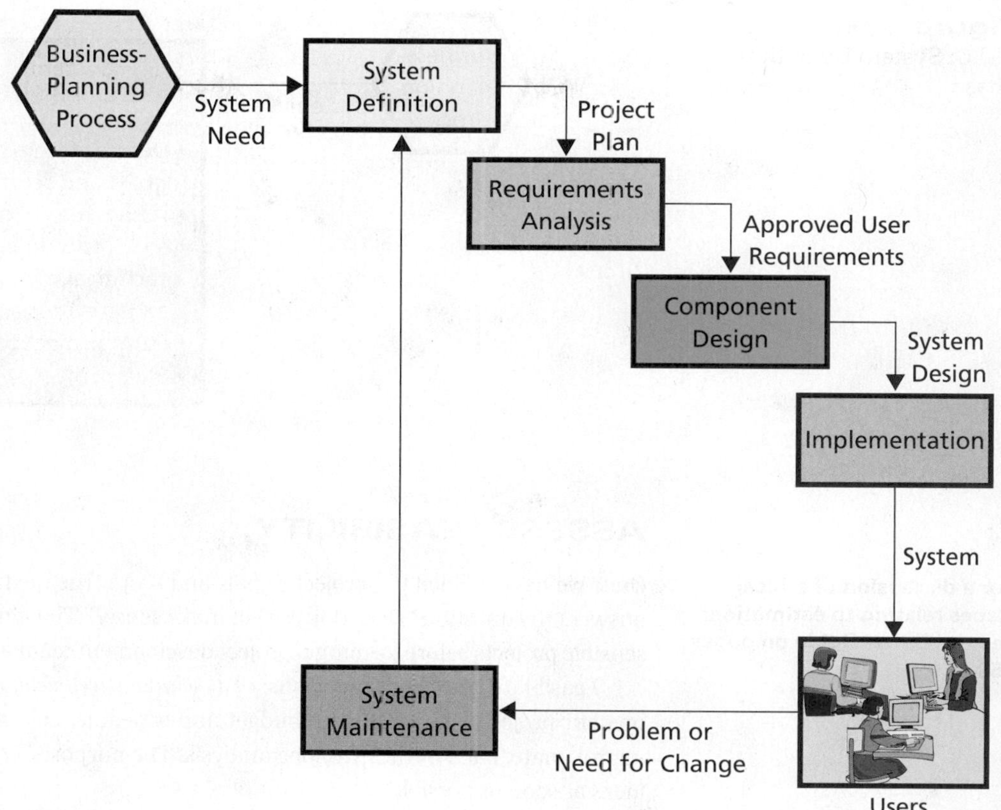


**Figure 12-3**
Phases in the SDLC

of that phase is a set of approved user requirements, which become the primary input used to design system components. In phase 4, developers implement, test, and install the new system.

Over time, users will find errors, mistakes, and problems. They will also develop new requirements. The description of fixes and new requirements is input into a system maintenance phase. The maintenance phase starts the process all over again, which is why the process is considered a cycle.

In the following sections, we will consider each phase of the SDLC in more detail.

# Q12-4 HOW IS SYSTEM DEFINITION ACCOMPLISHED?

In response to the need for the new system, the organization will assign a few employees, possibly on a part-time basis, to define the new system, to assess its feasibility, and to plan the project. Typically, that is someone from the IS department (or a consultant if the company does not have such a department), but the members of that initial team are both users and IS professionals.

## DEFINE SYSTEM GOALS AND SCOPE

As Figure 12-4 shows, the first step is to define the goals and scope of the new information system. Information systems exist to facilitate an organization's competitive strategy. At this step, the development team defines the goal and purpose of the new system in terms of that strategy.

Consider PRIDE. How will the Xbox application contribute to more ad revenue? Will it enable PRIDE Systems to earn more from current clients? Will it attract new clients? What are the major features of the Xbox application that need to be implemented?

In other systems, the scope might be defined by specifying the business activities and users who will be involved, or the business processes that will be involved, or the plants, offices, and factories that will be involved.

**Figure 12-4**
SDLC: System Definition Phase

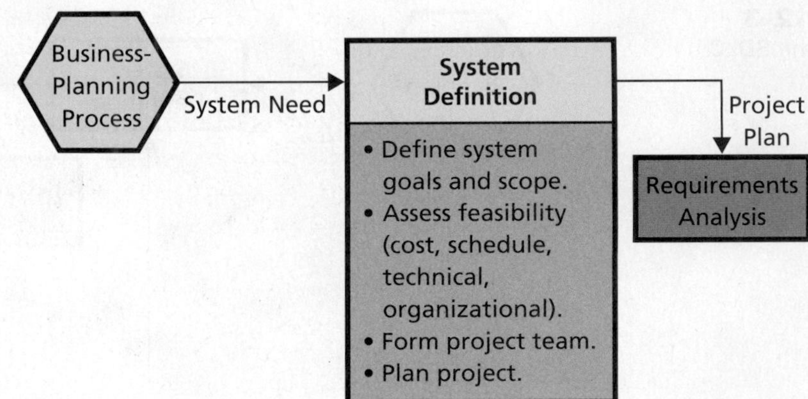


## ASSESS FEASIBILITY

**For a discussion of ethical issues relating to estimation, see the Ethics Guide on pages 358–359.**

Once we have defined the project's goals and scope, the next step is to assess feasibility. This step answers the question "Does this project make sense?" The aim here is to eliminate obviously nonsensible projects before forming a project development team and investing significant labor.

Feasibility has four dimensions: *cost, schedule, technical,* and *organizational.* Because IS development projects are difficult to budget and schedule, cost and schedule feasibility can only be approximate, back-of-the-envelope analysis. The purpose is to eliminate any obviously infeasible ideas as soon as possible.

**Cost feasibility** approximates total costs and compares it to system value. For PRIDE, and almost all new systems, this is a difficult assessment. Clearly, costs depend on the scope of the project, but until requirements are known, the range of potential costs will be large. That is one reason Zev wanted to start with an Xbox prototype. Further, until users employ the prototype, no one on the team knows the value of an Xbox application to the competitive strategy.

At this point, all the team can do is to make estimates. Any potential investor will scrutinize these estimates, and Zev wants to start with a prototype to gain evidence for the costs of developing the full system. Still, at this point, the team doesn't need a precise total; it simply needs a range of costs to compare to value.

Like cost feasibility, **schedule feasibility** is difficult to determine because it is hard to estimate the time it will take to build the system. However, if James determines that it will take, say, no less than 6 months to develop the prototype, Zev, Jared, and the rest of the team can decide if they can accept that minimum schedule. If not, they're wasting their time and money and should do something else. At this stage of the project, the organization should not rely on either cost or schedule estimates; the purpose of these estimates is simply to rule out any obviously unacceptable projects.

**Technical feasibility** refers to whether existing information technology is likely to be able to meet the needs of the new system. Can an Xbox be configured to work with the Ant protocol? Is there a feasible way to integrate the data from simultaneous competitors and display it accurately in many locations? Most likely this will not be a problem, but the team needs to investigate it nonetheless.

Finally, **organizational feasibility** concerns whether the new system fits within the organization's customs, culture, charter, or legal requirements.

## FORM A PROJECT TEAM

If the defined project is determined to be feasible, the next step is to form the project team. Normally the team consists of both IS professionals and user representatives. The project manager and IS professionals can be in-house personnel or outside contractors. In Chapter 11, we described various means of obtaining IT personnel using outside sources and the benefits and risks of outsourcing.

Typical personnel on a development team are a manager (or managers for larger projects), business analysts, systems analysts, programmers, software testers, and users. **Business analysts** specialize in understanding business needs, strategies, and goals and helping businesses implement systems to accomplish their competitive strategies. **Systems analysts** are IT professionals who understand both business and technology.

Systems analysts are closer to IT and are a bit more technical than business analysts, though there is considerable overlap in their duties and responsibilities. Both are active throughout the systems development process and play a key role in moving the project through the systems development process. Business analysts work more with managers and executives; systems analysts integrate the work of the programmers, testers, and users. Depending on the nature of the project, the team may also include hardware and communications specialists, database designers and administrators, and other IT specialists.

The team composition changes over time. During requirements definition, the team will be heavy with business and systems analysts. During design and implementation, it will be heavy with programmers, testers, and database designers. During integrated testing and conversion, the team will be augmented with testers and business users.

User involvement is critical throughout the system development process. Depending on the size and nature of the project, users are assigned to the project either full or part time. Sometimes users are assigned to review and oversight committees that meet periodically, especially at the completion of project phases and other milestones. Users are involved in many different ways. *The important point is for users to have active involvement and to take ownership of the project throughout the entire development process.* (See also Case Study 12 , pages 365–366.)

The first major task for the assembled project team is to plan the project. Members of the project team specify tasks to be accomplished, assign personnel, determine task dependencies, and set schedules.

## Q12-5 WHAT IS THE USERS' ROLE IN THE REQUIREMENTS PHASE?

The primary purpose of the requirements analysis phase is to determine and document the specific features and functions of the new system. For most development projects, this phase requires interviewing dozens of users and documenting potentially hundreds of requirements. Requirements definition is, thus, expensive. It is also difficult, as you will see.

### DETERMINE REQUIREMENTS

Determining the system's requirements is the most important phase in the SDLC. If the requirements are wrong, the system will be wrong. If the requirements are determined completely and correctly, then design and implementation will be easier and more likely to result in success.

Examples of requirements are the contents and the format of Web pages and the functions of buttons on those pages, or the structure and content of a report, or the fields and menu choices in a data entry form. Requirements include not only what is to be produced, but also how frequently and how fast it is to be produced. Some requirements specify the volume of data to be stored and processed.

If you take a course in systems analysis and design, you will spend weeks learning techniques for determining requirements. Here, we will just summarize that process. Typically, systems analysts interview users and record the results in some consistent manner. Good interviewing skills

**Figure 12-5**
SDLC: Requirements Analysis Phase

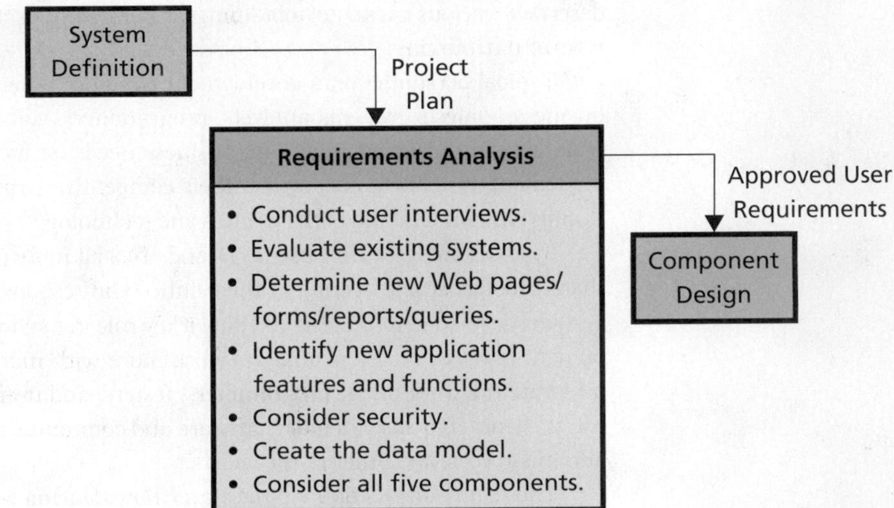


are crucial; users are notorious for being unable to describe what they want and need. Users also tend to focus on the tasks they are performing at the time of the interview. Tasks performed at the end of the quarter or end of the year are forgotten if the interview takes place mid-quarter. Seasoned and experienced systems analysts know how to conduct interviews to bring such requirements to light.

As listed in Figure 12-5, sources of requirements include existing systems as well as the Web pages, forms, reports, queries, and application features and functions desired in the new system. Security is another important category of requirements.

If the new system involves a new database or substantial changes to an existing database, then the development team will create a data model. As you learned in Chapter 5, that model must reflect the users' perspective on their business and business activities. Thus, the data model is constructed on the basis of user interviews and must be validated by those users.

Sometimes, the requirements determination is so focused on the software and data components that other components are forgotten. Experienced project managers ensure consideration of requirements for all five IS components, not just for software and data. Regarding hardware, the team might ask: Are there special needs or restrictions on hardware? Is there an organizational standard governing what kinds of hardware may or may not be used? Must the new system use existing hardware? What requirements are there for communications and network hardware or cloud services?

Similarly, the team should consider requirements for procedures and personnel: Do accounting controls require procedures that separate duties and authorities? Are there restrictions that some actions can be taken only by certain departments or specific personnel? Are there policy requirements or union rules that restrict activities to certain categories of employees? Will the system need to interface with information systems from other companies and organizations? In short, requirements need to be considered for all of the components of the new information system.

These questions are examples of the kinds of questions that must be asked and answered during requirements analysis.

## APPROVE REQUIREMENTS

Once the requirements have been specified, the users must review and approve them before the project continues. The easiest and cheapest time to alter the information system is in the requirements phase. Changing a requirement at this stage is simply a matter of changing a description. Changing a requirement in the implementation phase may require weeks of reworking applications components and the database structure.

### ROLE OF A PROTOTYPE

Because requirements are difficult to specify, building a working prototype, as with the PRIDE system Xbox project, can be quite beneficial. Whereas future systems users often struggle to understand and relate to requirements expressed as word descriptions and sketches, working with a prototype provides direct experience. As they work with a prototype, users will assess usability and remember features and functions they have forgotten to mention. Additionally, prototypes provide evidence to assess the system's technical and organizational feasibility. Further, prototypes create data that can be used to estimate both development and operational costs.

To be useful, a prototype needs to work; mock-ups of forms and reports, while helpful, will not generate the benefits just described. The prototype needs to put the user into the experience of employing the system to do his or her tasks.

Prototypes can be expensive to create; however, this expense is often justified not only for the greater clarity and completeness of requirements, but also because parts of the prototype can often be reused in the operational system. The cloud helps in that hardware and storage can be leased cheaply for a short term and need not be purchased and installed.

Unfortunately, systems developers face a dilemma when funding prototypes; the cost of the prototype occurs early in the process, sometimes well before full project funding is available. "We need the prototype to get the funds, and we need the funds to get the prototype." Unfortunately, no uniform solution to this dilemma exists, except the application of experience guided by intuition. Once again we see the need for nonroutine problem-solving skills.

## Q12-6 HOW ARE THE FIVE COMPONENTS DESIGNED?

Each of the five components is designed in the next stage. Typically, the team designs each component by developing alternatives, evaluating each of those alternatives against the requirements, and then selecting among those alternatives. Accurate requirements are critical here; if they are incomplete or wrong, then they will be poor guides for evaluation. Figure 12-6 shows that design tasks pertain to each of the five IS components.

**Figure 12-6**
SDLC: Component Design Phase

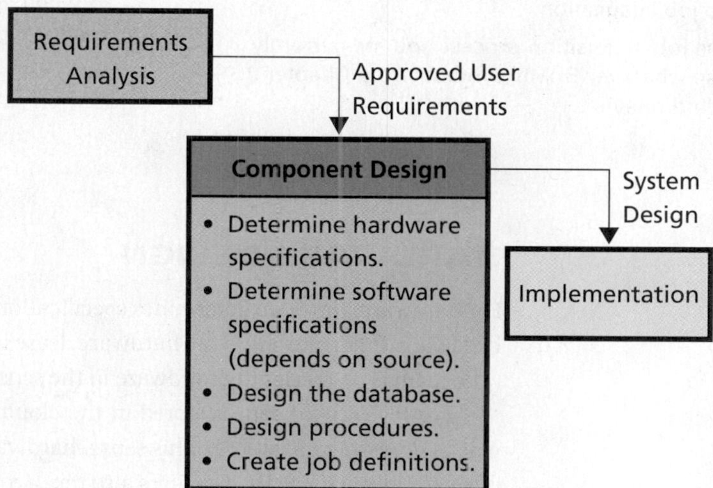

## Using This Knowledge for Your Number-One Priority

Examine the picture of the dog team. Those dogs are starting a 1,049-mile race in which they will sometimes run 20 hours a day. They can't qualify for this race unless they've succeeded at similar events, so they know what they're in for. But, clearly, they like their jobs.

That should be you. No, not a musher on the Iditarod, but that's the way you should feel at the start of your workweek. You will spend at least a third of your life at work; work will be one of the biggest sources of personal satisfaction; and your job will determine the quality of your life in money, in friends and associates, and in interesting experiences. So between now and graduation, finding and getting that job should be the *number-one priority* in your life. Don't wait.

So, how will you do that? Haphazardly sign up for whatever recruiters happen to come to campus? That's one approach, and you can hope that your competitors use it. But what about you? Can you find a way to apply what you've learned in this chapter to finding that job? It's worth taking 20 minutes to think about it, no? And, hey, you might get to wear booties, too!

*Source:* Daniel A. Leifheit/Getty Images

### QUESTIONS

1. Examine Figure 12-3 and the following figures that detail tasks in each of the five phases. Interpret each of the activities in the SDLC not as they pertain to systems development but rather as they could pertain to finding your job. Briefly summarize the tasks you can perform at each stage.
2. Finding a job is a process. Like all processes, job-acquiring processes vary in quality. State two dimensions of process and quality and explain how they pertain to job acquisition.
3. Sketch the job-acquisition process you are currently using. Use whatever BPMN symbols from Chapter 2 that you find relevant.
4. Examine the quality of your current job-acquisition process. Explain two ways you could improve the quality of that process.
5. To answer this question, you'll need to read Chapter Extension 17, particularly QCE17-3 and QCE17-4. Write the requirements for the job-acquisition process using scrum-like requirements statements. Break the requirements into sufficient detail so that you can satisfy each one in 2 hours or less. Rather than start every requirement with "As a student," start them with the role you will use: "As an interviewee, I will" or "As a prospect seeker, I will."
6. Consider your answers to questions 1–5. Explain how those answers inform you about how to obtain that perfect job.
7. Start tonight!

## HARDWARE DESIGN

For hardware, the team determines specifications for the hardware it needs and the source of that hardware. It can purchase the hardware, lease it, or lease time from a hosting service in the cloud. (The team is not designing hardware in the sense of building a CPU or a disk drive.)

For PRIDE, the data is stored in the cloud and perhaps some of the application processing will be done there as well. In this sense, hardware design is a matter of what cloud resources are needed. However, PRIDE designers also need to decide which devices they intend to support. What game consoles will they want to support in addition to Xbox? This decision involves interaction with software design; if PRIDE uses a thin-client application, the project can afford to support more devices than if it must create native applications for every device type.

## SOFTWARE DESIGN

Software design depends on the source of the programs. For off-the-shelf software, the team must determine candidate products and evaluate them against the requirements. For off-the-shelf-with-alteration software, the team identifies products to be acquired off-the-shelf and then determines the alterations required. For custom-developed programs, the team produces design documentation for writing program code.

For a cloud-based system (like PRIDE), one important design decision is where application processing will occur. All can occur on mobile devices, all can occur on cloud servers, or a mixture can be used. Furthermore, for mobile systems projects, like PRIDE, at this stage the team will decide whether it is building a thin-client or native application.

## DATABASE DESIGN

If developers are constructing a database, then during this phase they convert the data model to a database design using techniques such as those described in Chapter 5. If developers are using off-the-shelf programs, then little database design needs to be done; the programs will handle their own database processing.

## PROCEDURE DESIGN

For a business information system, the system developers and the organization must also design procedures for both users and operations personnel. Procedures need to be developed for normal, backup, and failure recovery operations, as summarized in Figure 12-7. Usually, teams of systems analysts and key users design the procedures.

## DESIGN OF JOB DESCRIPTIONS

With regard to people, design involves developing job descriptions for both users and operations personnel. Sometimes new information systems require new jobs. If so, the duties and responsibilities for these jobs need to be defined in accordance with the organization's human resources policies.

**Figure 12-7**
Procedures to Be Designed

| | Users | Operations Personnel |
|---|---|---|
| **Normal processing** | • Procedures for using the system to accomplish business tasks. | • Procedures for starting, stopping, and operating the system. |
| **Backup** | • User procedures for backing up data and other resources. | • Operations procedures for backing up data and other resources. |
| **Failure recovery** | • Procedures to continue operations when the system fails.<br>• Procedures to convert back to the system after recovery. | • Procedures to identify the source of failure and get it fixed.<br>• Procedures to recover and restart the system. |

More often, organizations add new duties and responsibilities to existing jobs. In this case, developers define these new tasks and responsibilities in this phase. Sometimes, the personnel design task is as simple as statements such as "Jason will be in charge of administering passwords." As with procedures, teams of systems analysts and users determine job descriptions and functions.

# Q12-7 HOW IS AN INFORMATION SYSTEM IMPLEMENTED?

Once the design is complete, the next phase in the SDLC is implementation. Tasks in this phase are to build, test, and convert the users to the new system (see Figure 12-8). Developers construct each of the components independently. They obtain, install, and test hardware. They license and install off-the-shelf programs; they write adaptations and custom programs as necessary. They construct a database and fill it with data. They document, review, and test procedures, and they create training programs. Finally, the organization hires and trains needed personnel.

## SYSTEM TESTING

Once developers have constructed and tested all of the components, they integrate the individual components and test the system. So far, we have glossed over testing as if there is nothing to it. In fact, software and system testing are difficult, time-consuming, and complex tasks. Developers need to design and develop test plans and record the results of tests. They need to devise a system to assign fixes to people and to verify that the fixes are correct and complete.

A **test plan** consists of sequences of actions that users will take when using the new system. Test plans include not only the normal actions that users will take, but also incorrect actions. A comprehensive test plan should cause every line of program code to be executed. The test plan should cause every error message to be displayed. Testing, retesting, and re-retesting consume huge amounts of labor. Often, developers can reduce the labor cost of testing by writing programs that invoke system features automatically.

Today, many IT professionals work as testing specialists. Testing, or **product quality assurance (PQA)**, as it is often called, is an important career. PQA personnel usually construct the test plan with the advice and assistance of users. PQA test engineers perform testing, and they also supervise user test activity. Many PQA professionals are programmers who write automated test programs.

**Figure 12-8**
SDLC: Implementation Phase

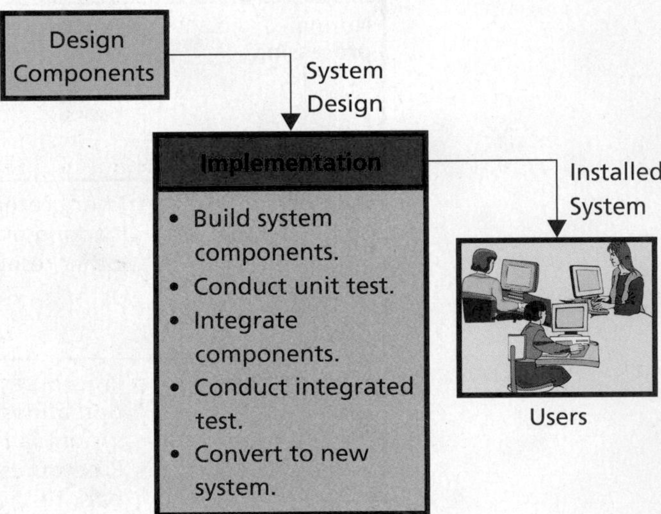

In addition to IT professionals, users should be involved in system testing. Users participate in the development of test plans and test cases. They also can be part of the test team, usually working under the direction of PQA personnel. Users have the final say on whether the system is ready for use. If you are invited to participate as a user tester, take that responsibility seriously. It will become much more difficult to fix problems after you have begun to use the system in production. *For any system on which you will rely, it is important (and wise) to become involved in the development of test cases as well as testing itself.* It is unprofessional, unwise, and unfair to the development team to sit on the sidelines until the system is finished and then complain about missing or misguided features!

**Beta testing** is the process of allowing future system users to try out the new system on their own. Software vendors, such as Microsoft, often release beta versions of their products for users to try and to test. Such users report problems back to the vendor. Beta testing is the last stage of testing. Normally, products in the beta test phase are complete and fully functioning; they typically have few serious errors. Organizations that are developing large new information systems sometimes use a beta-testing process just as software vendors do.

## SYSTEM CONVERSION

Once the system has passed integrated testing, the organization installs the new system. The term **system conversion** is often used for this activity because it implies the process of *converting* business activity from the old system to the new.

Organizations can implement a system conversion in one of four ways:

- Pilot
- Phased
- Parallel
- Plunge

IS professionals recommend any of the first three, depending on the circumstances. In most cases, companies should avoid "taking the plunge"!

With **pilot installation**, the organization implements the entire system on a limited portion of the business. The advantage of pilot implementation is that if the system fails, the failure is contained within a limited boundary. This reduces exposure of the business and also protects the new system from developing a negative reputation throughout the organization.

As the name implies, with **phased installation** the new system is installed in phases across the organization. Once a given piece works, the organization then installs and tests another piece of the system, until the entire system has been installed. Some systems are so tightly integrated that they cannot be set up in phased pieces. Such systems must be installed using one of the other techniques.

With **parallel installation**, the new system runs in parallel with the old one until the new system is tested and fully operational. Parallel installation is expensive because the organization incurs the costs of running both systems. Users must work double time, if you will, to run both systems. Then considerable work is needed to determine if the results of the new system are consistent with those of the old system.

However, some organizations consider the costs of parallel installation to be a form of insurance. It is the slowest and most expensive style of installation, but it does provide an easy fallback position if the new system fails.

The final style of conversion is **plunge installation** (sometimes called *direct installation*). With it, the organization shuts off the old system and starts the new system. If the new system fails, the organization is in trouble: Nothing can be done until either the new system is fixed or the old one is reinstalled. Because of the risk, organizations should avoid this conversion style, if

| | Hardware | Software | Data | Procedures | People |
|---|---|---|---|---|---|
| Design | Determine hardware specifications. | Select off-the-shelf programs. Design alterations and custom programs as necessary. | Design database and related structures. | Design user and operations procedures. | Develop user and operations job descriptions. |
| Implementation | Obtain, install, and test hardware. | License and install off-the-shelf programs. Write alterations and custom programs. Test programs. | Create database. Fill with data. Test data. | Document procedures. Create training programs. Review and test procedures. | Hire and train personnel. |
| | Integrated Test and Conversion | | | | |

(Implementation row: Unit test each component)

**Figure 12-9**
Design and Implementation for the Five Components

possible. The one exception is if the new system is providing a new capability that is not vital to the operation of the organization.

Figure 12-9 summarizes the tasks for each of the five components during the design and implementation phases. Use this figure to test your knowledge of the tasks in each phase.

## Q12-8 WHAT ARE THE TASKS FOR SYSTEM MAINTENANCE?

The last phase of the SDLC is maintenance. Maintenance is a misnomer; the work done during this phase is either to *fix* the system so that it works correctly or to *adapt* it to changes in requirements.

Figure 12-10 shows tasks during the maintenance phase. First, there needs to be a means for tracking both failures[2] and requests for enhancements to meet new requirements. For small

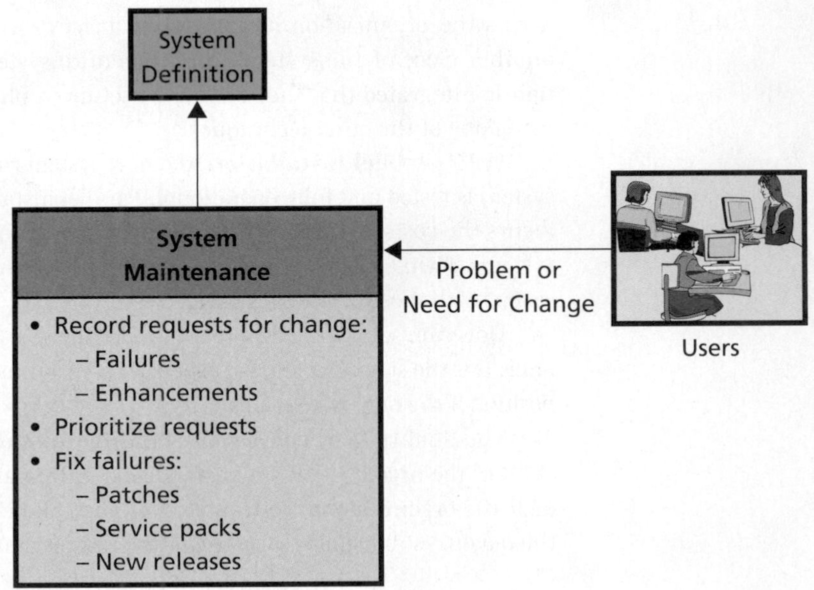


**Figure 12-10**
SDLC: System Maintenance Phase

systems, organizations can track failures and enhancements using word-processing documents. As systems become larger, however, and as the number of failure and enhancement requests increases, many organizations find it necessary to develop a failure-tracking database. Such a database contains a description of each failure or enhancement. It also records who reported the problem, who will make the fix or enhancement, what the status of that work is, and whether the fix or enhancement has been tested and verified by the originator.

Typically, IS personnel prioritize system problems according to their severity. They fix high-priority items as soon as possible, and they fix low-priority items as time and resources become available.

With regard to the software component, software developers group fixes for high-priority failures into a **patch** that can be applied to all copies of a given product. Software vendors supply patches to fix security and other critical problems. They usually bundle fixes of low-priority problems into larger groups called **service packs**. Users apply service packs in much the same way that they apply patches, except that service packs typically involve fixes to hundreds or thousands of problems.

By the way, you may be surprised to learn this, but all commercial software products are shipped with known failures. Usually vendors test their products and remove the most serious problems, but they seldom, if ever, remove all of the defects they know about. Shipping with defects is an industry practice; Microsoft, Apple, Google, Adobe, and many others ship products with known problems.

Because an enhancement is an adaptation to new requirements, developers usually prioritize enhancement requests separate from failures. The decision to make an enhancement includes a business decision that the enhancement will generate an acceptable rate of return. Although minor enhancements are made using service packs, major enhancement requests usually result in a new release of a product.

As you read this, keep in mind that although we usually think of failures and enhancements as applying to software, they can apply to the other components as well. There can be hardware or database failures or enhancements. There can also be failures and enhancements in procedures and people, though the latter is usually expressed in more humane terms than *failure* or *enhancement*. The underlying idea is the same, however.

As stated earlier, note that the maintenance phase starts another cycle of the SDLC process. The decision to enhance a system is a decision to restart the systems development process. Even a simple failure fix goes through all of the phases of the SDLC; if it is a small fix, a single person may work through those phases in an abbreviated form. But each of those phases is repeated, nonetheless.

## Q12-9 WHAT ARE SOME OF THE PROBLEMS WITH THE SDLC?

Although the industry has experienced notable successes with the SDLC process, there have also been many problems with it, as discussed in this section.

### THE SDLC WATERFALL

One of the reasons for SDLC problems is due to the **waterfall** nature of the SDLC. Like a series of waterfalls, the process is supposed to operate in a sequence of nonrepetitive phases. For example, the team completes the requirements phase and goes over the waterfall into the design phase and on through the process (look back to Figure 12-3, page 345).

Unfortunately, systems development seldom works so smoothly. Often, there is a need to crawl back up the waterfall, if you will, and repeat work in a prior phase. Most commonly, when design work begins and the team evaluates alternatives, they learn that some requirements statements are incomplete or missing. At that point, the team needs to do more requirements work, yet that phase is supposedly finished. On some projects, the team goes back and forth between requirements and design so many times that the project seems to be out of control.

**You can learn about another promising development technique called agile development in Chapter Extension 17.**

## REQUIREMENTS DOCUMENTATION DIFFICULTY

Another problem, especially on complicated systems, is the difficulty of documenting requirements in a usable way. I (David Kroenke) once managed the database portion of a software project at Boeing in which we invested more than 70 labor-years into a requirements statement. When printed, the requirements document consisted of 20-some volumes that stood 7 feet tall when stacked on top of one another.

When we entered the design phase, no one really knew all the requirements that concerned a particular feature. We would begin to design a feature only to find that we had not considered a requirement buried somewhere in the documentation. In short, the requirements were so unwieldy as to be nearly useless. Additionally, during the requirements analysis interval, the airplane business moved on. By the time we entered the design phase, many requirements were incomplete, and some were obsolete. Projects that spend so much time documenting requirements are sometimes said to be in **analysis paralysis**.

## SCHEDULING AND BUDGETING DIFFICULTIES

For a new, large-scale system, schedule and budgeting estimates are so approximate as to become nearly laughable. Management attempts to put a serious face on the need for a schedule and a budget, but when you are developing a large, multiyear, multimillion-dollar project, estimates of labor hours and completion dates are approximate and fuzzy. The employees on the project, who are the source for the estimates, know little about how long something will take and about how much they had actually guessed. They know that the total budget and timeline is a summation of everyone's similar guesses. Many large projects live in a fantasy world of budgets and timelines.

In truth, the software community has done much work to improve software development forecasting. But for large projects with large SDLC phases, just too much is unknown for any technique to work well. So, development methodologies other than the SDLC have emerged for developing systems through a series of small, manageable chunks. Agile techniques like scrum, object-oriented development, and extreme programming are three such methodologies.

## How does the **knowledge** in this chapter help **you?**

**That's it! You've reached the end of this text. Take a moment to consider how you will use what you learned, as described in the Guide on pages 360–361.**

At some point in your career, probably within five years, you will need the knowledge of this chapter and its related chapter extensions. To give one example, in the next decade technical marketing expenses are projected to increase tenfold from $12B per year in 2014 to $120B per year.[3] If anything close to that increase occurs, countless new systems will be developed for marketing and sales, and those systems will need to be managed. Given robots, drones, driverless cars, and 3D printing, how will anyone in manufacturing or operations not be involved in systems development? Finance and accounting? Where are the great opportunities? And how are they to be funded? And, of course, all management grads are going to play strong roles in developing new systems strategies and priorities as well as managing the projects.

Your generation, with its experience with mobile devices and applications, is more computer-savvy than any generation before. You won't put up with poorly designed interfaces because you know better. Similarly, you'll expect IS to help you do your job and will not endure ineffective systems. But, to make your voice heard, effectively, you'll need systems development knowledge. You will need to know how to proceed, and the knowledge of this chapter will get you started on the right path and help you manage your way through new development projects.

# Ethics Guide

## Estimation Ethics

A *buy-in* occurs when a company agrees to produce a system or product for less money than it knows the project will require. For example, when a vendor of development services agrees to build a system for, say, $50,000, when good estimating techniques indicate it would take $75,000. If the contract for the system or product is written for "time and materials," the project's sponsors will ultimately pay the $75,000 for the finished system. Or the project will fail once the true cost is known. If the contract for the system or product is written for a fixed cost, then the developer will absorb the extra costs. A vendor would use the latter strategy if the contract opens up other business opportunities that are worth the $25,000 loss.

Buy-ins always involve deceit. Most would agree that buying-in on a time-and-materials project, planning to stick the customer with the full cost later, is wrong. Opinions on buying-in on a fixed-priced contract vary. You know you'll take a loss, but why? To build intellectual capital for sale elsewhere? For a favor down the road? Or for some other unethical reason?

What about in-house projects? Do the ethics change if an in-house development team is building a system for use in-house? If team members know there is only $50,000 in the budget, should they start the project if they believe that its true cost is $75,000? If they do start, at some point senior management will either have to admit a mistake and cancel the project with a loss or find the additional $25,000. Project sponsors can state all sorts of reasons for such buy-ins. For example, "I know the company needs this system. If management doesn't realize it and fund it appropriately, then we'll just force their hand."

These issues become even stickier if team members disagree about how much the project will cost. Suppose one faction of the team believes the project will cost $35,000, another faction estimates $50,000, and a third thinks $65,000. Can the project sponsors justify taking the average? Or should they describe the range of estimates?

Other buy-ins are more subtle. Suppose you are a project manager of an exciting new project that is possibly a career-maker for you. You are incredibly busy, working 6 days a week and long hours each day. Your team has developed an estimate for $50,000 for the project. A little voice in the back of your mind says that maybe not all costs for every aspect of the project are included in that estimate. You mean to follow up on that thought, but more pressing matters in your schedule take precedence. Soon you find yourself in front of management, presenting the $50,000 estimate. You probably should have found the time to investigate the estimate, but you didn't. Is there an ethical issue here?

Or suppose you approach a more senior manager with your dilemma. "I think there may be other costs, but I know that $50,000 is all we've got. What should I do?" Suppose the senior manager says something like, "Well, let's go forward. You don't know of anything else, and we can always find more budget elsewhere if we have to." How do you respond?

You can buy-in on schedule as well as cost. If the marketing department says, "We have to have the new product for the trade show," do you agree, even if you know it's highly unlikely that you'll make the deadline? What if marketing says, "If we don't have it by then, we should just cancel the project." Suppose it's not impossible to make that schedule; it's just highly unlikely. How do you respond?

## DISCUSSION QUESTIONS

**1.** Assess the ethics of buying-in on a cost-and-materials project from both the perspective of the categorical imperative (pages 20–21) and utilitarianism (pages 46–47).

**2.** Are there circumstances in which buying-in on a cost-and-materials contract could be illegal? If so, state them.

**3.** Suppose you learn through the grapevine that your opponents in a competitive bid are buying-in on a time-and-materials contract. Does this change your answer to question 1?

**4.** Suppose you are a project manager who is preparing a request for a proposal on a cost-and-materials systems development project. What can you do to prevent buy-ins?

**5.** Under what circumstances do you think buying-in on a fixed-price contract is ethical? Use either the categorical imperative or utilitarian perspective or both. What are the dangers of this strategy?

**6.** Explain why in-house development projects are always time-and-materials projects.

**7.** Given your answer to question 5, assess the ethics of buying-in on an in-house project from the perspective of the categorical imperative and utilitarianism. Are there circumstances that will change your ethical assessment? If so, state what they are and why.

**8.** Suppose you ask a senior manager for advice as described in the guide. Does the manager's response absolve you of ethical responsibility? Suppose you ask the manager and then do not follow her guidance. What problems could result?

**9.** Explain how you can buy-in on schedule as well as costs.

**10.** For an in-house project, what is an ethical response to the marketing manager who says the project should be canceled if it will not be ready for the trade show? In your answer, suppose that you disagree with this opinion because you know the system has value regardless of whether it is done by the trade show.

*Source:* Antonio Gravante/Fotolia

## The Final, Final Word

Congratulations! You've made it through the entire book. With this knowledge, you are well prepared to be an effective user of information systems. And with work and imagination, you can be much more than that. Many interesting opportunities are available to those who can apply information in innovative ways. Your professor has done what she can do, and the rest, as they say, is up to you.

So what's next? In Chapter 1, we claimed that Introduction to MIS is the most important course in the business curriculum today. That claim was based on the organization's innovative use of nearly free data communications and data storage. By now, you've learned many of the ways that businesses and organizations use these resources and information systems based upon those resources. You've also seen how businesses like Falcon Security use information systems to solve problems and further their competitive strategies. With PRIDE, you've investigated the use of mobile and cloud technology for an inter-enterprise system.

How can you use that knowledge? Chapter 1 claimed that future business professionals must be able "to assess, evaluate, and apply emerging information technology to business." Have you learned how to do that? At least, are you better able to do that than you were before this class? You probably know the meaning of many more terms than you did when you started, and such knowledge is important. But even more important is the ability to use that knowledge to apply MIS to your business interests.

Chapter 1 also reviewed the work of the RAND Corporation and that of Robert Reich on what professional workers in the 21st century need to know. Those sources state that such workers need to know how to innovate the use of technology and how to "collaborate, reason abstractly, think in terms of systems, and experiment." Have you learned those behaviors? Or, at least, are you better at them than you were when you started this course?

Overall, job prospects have been improving in recent years, but good jobs, and the perfect job for you, will not be easy to obtain. You need to apply every asset you have. One of those assets is the knowledge you've gained in this class. Take the time to do the exercises at the end of this guide, and then use the answers in your job interviews!

Look for the job you truly want to do, get that job, and work hard. In the movie *Glass: A Portrait of Philip in Twelve Parts,* the composer Philip Glass claimed he knew the secret to success. It was, he said, "Get up early and work hard all day." That quotation seems obvious and hardly worth stating, except that it has the ring of truth. And, if you can find a job you truly love, it isn't even hard. Actually, it's fun, most of the time. So, use what you've learned in this class to obtain the job you really want!

## DISCUSSION QUESTIONS

**1.** Reflect on what you have learned from this course. Write two paragraphs about how the knowledge you have gained will help you to "assess, evaluate, and apply emerging information technology to business." Shape your writing around the kind of job that you want to obtain upon graduation.

**2.** Write two paragraphs about how the knowledge and experiences you've had in this class will help you "collaborate, reason abstractly, think in terms of systems, and experiment." Again, shape your writing around the kind of job you wish to obtain.

**3.** Using your answer to question 1, extract three or four sentences about yourself that you could use in a job interview.

**4.** Using your answer to question 2, extract three or four sentences about yourself that you could use in a job interview.

**5.** Practice using your answers to questions 3 and 4 in a job interview with a classmate, roommate, or friend.

*Source:* Africa Studio/Fotolia

# ACTIVE REVIEW

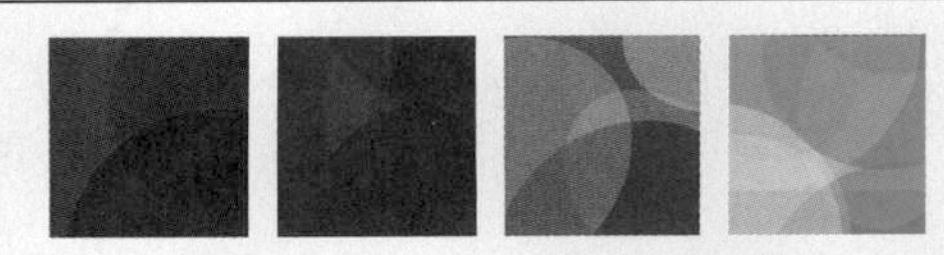

Use this Active Review to verify that you understand the ideas and concepts that answer this chapter's study questions.

## Q12-1 WHAT IS SYSTEMS DEVELOPMENT?

Define *systems development*. Explain how systems development differs from program development. Describe the types of expertise needed for systems development projects. Explain why Zev needs the knowledge in this chapter.

## Q12-2 WHY IS SYSTEMS DEVELOPMENT DIFFICULT AND RISKY?

Describe the risks in systems development. Summarize the difficulties posed by the following: requirements definition, requirements changes, scheduling and budgeting, changing technology, and diseconomies of scale.

## Q12-3 WHAT ARE THE FIVE PHASES OF THE SDLC?

Name the five phases in the systems development life cycle and briefly describe each.

## Q12-4 HOW IS SYSTEM DEFINITION ACCOMPLISHED?

Using Figure 12-4 as a guide, explain how you would describe the systems definition task. Name and describe four elements of feasibility. (*Hint:* The four types of feasibility can be arranged as Cost, Operational, Schedule, Technical; arranged this way, the first letter of each makes the acronym *COST.*)

## Q12-5 WHAT IS THE USERS' ROLE IN THE REQUIREMENTS PHASE?

Summarize the tasks in the requirements phase. Describe the role for users in this phase. Discuss what you believe will happen if users are not involved or if users do not take this work seriously. Describe the role users play in requirements approval.

## Q12-6 HOW ARE THE FIVE COMPONENTS DESIGNED?

Summarize design activities for each of the five components of an information system. Explain six categories of procedure that need to be designed.

## Q12-7 HOW IS AN INFORMATION SYSTEM IMPLEMENTED?

Name the two major tasks in systems implementation. Summarize the system testing process. Describe the difference between system and software testing. Explain testing tasks for each of the five components. Name four types of system conversion. Describe each way and give an example of when each would be effective.

## Q12-8 WHAT ARE THE TASKS FOR SYSTEM MAINTENANCE?

Explain why the term *maintenance* is a misnomer. Summarize tasks in the maintenance phase.

## Q12-9 WHAT ARE SOME OF THE PROBLEMS WITH THE SDLC?

Explain why the SDLC is considered a waterfall process and describe why this characteristic can be a problem. Describe problems that occur when attempting to develop requirements using the SDLC. Summarize scheduling and budgeting difficulties that the SDLC presents.

## How does the **knowledge** in this chapter help **you?**

Describe changes in the business environment that make systems development knowledge important for every business professional. Explain how these changes will affect your major field of study.

## KEY TERMS AND CONCEPTS

Analysis paralysis 356
Beta testing 353
Brooks' Law 344
Business analyst 347
Component design 344
Cost feasibility 346
Implementation 344
Maintenance 344
Organizational feasibility 346
Parallel installation 353
Patch 355
Phased installation 353
Pilot installation 353
Plunge installation 353
Product quality assurance (PQA) 352
Requirements analysis 344
Schedule feasibility 346
Service pack 355
System conversion 353
System definition 344
Systems analyst 347
Systems development 341
Systems development life cycle (SDLC) 344
Technical feasibility 346
Test plan 352
Waterfall 355

MyMISLab™
To complete the problems with the ✪, go to EOC Discussion Questions in the MyLab.

## USING YOUR KNOWLEDGE

✪**12-1.** Assume you are an intern working with Jared and you are present at the meeting at the start of this chapter. Jared asks you to help him investigate this opportunity.

**a.** Develop a plan for this prototype project using the SDLC. Describe, in general terms, the work to be done in each phase.

**b.** Specify in detail the tasks that must be accomplished during the system definition phase.

**c.** Write a memo to Jared explaining how you think he should investigate all four types of feasibility.

✪**12-2.** After answering question 12-1, assume Zev pushes back because he thinks you are making the project overly complicated, possibly to increase the length of your internship. Write a one-page memo explaining to Zev why it is important to follow the SDLC or some similar process.

✪**12-3.** Use Google or Bing to search for the phrase "what is a business analyst?" Investigate several of the links you find and answer the following questions:

**a.** What are the primary job responsibilities of a business analyst?

**b.** What is the difference between a business analyst and a systems analyst?

**c.** What knowledge do business analysts need?

**d.** What skills and personal traits do successful business analysts need?

**e.** Would a career as a business analyst be interesting to you? Explain why or why not.

## COLLABORATION EXERCISE 12

*Read Chapter Extensions 1 and 2 if you have not already done so. Meet with your team and build a collaboration IS that uses tools like Google Docs, SharePoint, or other collaboration tools. Do not forget the need for procedures and team training. Now, using that IS, answer the questions below.*

Wilma Baker, Jerry Barker, and Chris Bickel met in June 2015 at a convention of resort owners and tourism operators. They sat next to each other by chance while waiting for a presentation; after introducing themselves and laughing at the odd sound of their three names, they were surprised to learn that they managed similar businesses. Wilma Baker lives in Santa Fe, New Mexico, and specializes in renting homes and apartments to visitors to Santa Fe. Jerry Barker lives in Whistler Village, British Columbia, and specializes in renting condos to skiers and other visitors to the Whistler/Blackcomb Resort. Chris Bickel lives in Chatham, Massachusetts, and specializes in renting homes and condos to vacationers to Cape Cod.

The three agreed to have lunch after the presentation. During lunch, they shared frustrations about the difficulty of obtaining new customers, given the numerous travel opportunities available via the Internet today. Further, the rise in value of the dollar over the euro has created substantial competition for North American tourism.

As the conversation developed, they began to wonder if there was some way to combine forces (i.e., they were seeking a competitive advantage from an alliance). So, they decided to skip one of the next day's presentations and meet to discuss ways to form an alliance. Ideas they wanted to discuss further were sharing customer data, developing a joint reservation service, and exchanging property listings.

As they talked, it became clear they had no interest in merging their businesses; each wanted to stay independent. They also discovered that each was very concerned, even paranoid, about protecting their existing customer base from poaching. Still, the conflict was not as bad as it first seemed. Barker's business was primarily the ski trade, and winter was his busiest season; Bickel's business was mostly Cape Cod vacations, and she was busiest during the summer. Baker's high season was the summer and fall. So, it seemed there was enough difference in their high seasons that they would not necessarily cannibalize their businesses by selling the others' offerings to their own customers.

The question then became how to proceed. Given their desire to protect their own customers, they did not want to develop a common customer database. The best idea seemed to be to share data about properties. That way they could keep control of their customers but still have an opportunity to sell time at the others' properties.

They discussed several alternatives. Each could develop her or his own property database, and the three could then share those databases over the Internet. Or they could develop a centralized property database that they would all use. Or they could find some other way to share property listings.

Because we do not know Baker, Barker, and Bickel's detailed requirements, you cannot develop a plan for a specific system. In general, however, they first need to decide how elaborate an information system they want to construct. Consider the following two alternatives:

**a.** They could build a simple system centered on email. With it, each company sends property descriptions to the others via email. Each independent company then forwards these descriptions to its own customers, also using email. When a customer makes a reservation for a property, that request is then forwarded back to the property manager via email.

**b.** They could construct a more complex system using a cloud-based, shared database that contains data on all their properties and reservations. Because reservations tracking is a common business task, it is likely that they can license an existing application with this capability.

**12-4.** From the description given, define the scope of the project.

**12.5.** Consider technical feasibility of the two alternatives:

**a.** Name and describe criteria you would use for alternative a.

**b.** Name and describe criteria you would use for alternative b.

**c.** Is it possible to know, without further investigation, whether either alternative is technically feasible? Why or why not?

**12-6.** Consider organizational feasibility:

**a.** Explain what organizational feasibility means in the context of an inter-enterprise system.

**b.** List criteria you would use for assessing organizational feasibility for these alternatives. Differentiate criteria between the two alternatives if you think it is important to do so.

**c.** Is either alternative a or b more likely to be organizationally feasible than the other? Explain your answer.

**12.7.** Consider schedule feasibility:

**a.** List criteria you would use for schedule feasibility for these alternatives. Differentiate criteria between the two alternatives if you think it is important to do so.

**b.** Is either alternative a or b more likely to be schedule feasible than the other? Explain your answer.

**12.8.** Consider cost feasibility:

**a.** List sources of the major development costs for alternative a.

**b.** List sources of the major operational costs for alternative a.

**c.** List sources of the major development costs for alternative b.

**d.** List sources of the major operational costs for alternative b.

**e.** Which alternative is likely to be cheaper to develop?

**f.** List and describe factors that may make alternative a cheaper to operate.

**g.** List and describe factors that may make alternative b cheaper to operate.

**12-9.** Given your answers to questions 12-5 through 12-8, which of the alternatives do you believe is likely to be feasible? It could be both, just one, or neither. Justify your answer.

**12-10.** What would you say if one of the three principals were to ask you at this point, "Is it worthwhile for me to even consider this idea anymore?" Justify your answer. Without more data, you cannot make a true assessment, but apply your knowledge, experience, and intuition to formulate a response to that question.

# CASE STUDY 12

## When Will We Learn?

When David Kroenke, one of the authors of this text, was teaching at Colorado State in 1974, he participated in a study that investigated the primary causes of information systems development failures. The findings? The number one reason for failure was a lack of user involvement in creating and managing system requirements.

Technology has made enormous strides since that study. In 1974, computers consumed large rooms, and neither the minicomputer nor the personal computer had been invented. Alas, the development of information systems has not kept up; in fact, one can argue that nothing has changed.

Consider Case Study 7 (pages 205–207). The state of Oregon wasted more than $248M attempting to develop an information system to support its healthcare exchange. And very early in the project, Maximus Company, an independent consulting firm that had been hired to provide quality assurance, warned that requirements were vague, changing, and inconsistent. Those warnings made no difference. Why?

### Why Are Requirements Not Managed?

In 1974, it might have been that managers were computer illiterate and thus couldn't know how to manage requirements. However, everyone involved in Cover Oregon has a cell phone and probably an iPad or Kindle, so they are hardly computer illiterate. So today, at least, computer literacy isn't the problem.

Does the problem of *managing requirements* lie with *management?* Or with *requirements?* In Case Study 7, you learned that Access CT, the Connecticut healthcare project, succeeded. Was it because the project was closely managed by the lieutenant governor? A woman with future political ambitions? Oregon has no lieutenant governor, but surely there was someone to manage the project. One indication of management problems in Oregon is that the information system was to be used by one healthcare agency (Cover Oregon) but developed by a different healthcare agency (Oregon Health Administration). The two agencies fought battles over requirements. Due to lack of senior-level management, not only were requirements unmanaged, they were fought over by two competing governmental agencies.

That might be the prime cause for Cover Oregon's failure. But is there something else? Even in well-managed organizations, is there something about requirements that makes them hard to manage? Fred Brooks provided one insight when he said that software is logical poetry. It's made of pure thought-stuff. If two governmental agencies were to construct a building and if they fought over, say, how many stories that building was to have, then their disagreement would be visible for all to see. People would notice one group of contractors adding a floor while another group is tearing it down.

So part of the problem is that the requirements are requirements for pure thought-stuff. But what else?

How do you know if the requirements are complete? If the blueprints for a building don't include any provisions for electrical systems, that omission is obvious. Less so with software and systems. For example, what if no one considers the need to do something when a client forgets his username or password and has no record of policy numbers? Software or procedures need to be developed for this situation, but if no one thinks to specify that requirement, then nothing will be done. The system will fail when such a client need appears.

And how do you know the quality of the requirements statements? A requirement like "Select a qualifying insurance policy for this client" is written at such a high level that it is useless. One of the reasons for building a prototype is to flush out missing and incomplete requirements.

### Assess Feasibility and Make Trade-offs

But there's more we can learn from this example. All of the state and federal healthcare exchanges needed to be operating by October 1, 2013. So, the schedule was fixed with no chance for an adjustment. Considering cost, while funds were not fixed, they were not easily changed. The states initially provided some funding, as did the U.S. government. Once those financial allocations were made, it was difficult to obtain more money. Not impossible, but difficult.

Read QCE16-2 of Chapter Extension 16 if you have not already done so. If schedule is fixed and if funding is nearly fixed, what is the one factor that can be traded off to reduce project difficulty and risk? The requirements. Reduce them to the bare minimum and get the system running. Then, after some success, add to the project. That seems to be the strategy that Access CT followed.

But this principle exposes another of the problems in Oregon. It wanted everything. It embarked on a policy called "No Wrong Door,"[4] a policy that would leave no person nor problem behind. Cover Oregon should provide a solution for all. Such statements make wonderful political messaging, but if the schedule is fixed and the funding is nearly so, how are those goals to be accomplished? Tell your roommate that you have 1 week between semesters and nearly no money and you plan to take a first-class, 2-month jungle excursion in Africa. Hello? Anyone home?

Software and systems are made of pure thought-stuff. Easy to imagine a glorious future of amazing capability. But they are constructed by costly human labor, and nine women can't make a baby in 1 month. Remember that sentence when you are asked to help determine requirements for your new information system.

Will this case still be relevant 40 years from now? It's up to you and your classmates.

## QUESTIONS

**12-11.** Describe three reasons why cases like this will remain relevant 40 years from now. Describe three developments that could make these cases obsolete. Which will pertain? Will such cases be relevant 40 years from now? Justify your opinion.

**12-12.** Read the Executive Summary of the First Data report located at *www.oregon.gov/DAS/docs/co_assessment.pdf*. Applying your knowledge about the SDLC, describe what you think are the three major reasons that Cover Oregon failed.

**12-13.** In Case Study 7 (pages 205–207), you learned that three vendors had been considered as outside contractors, but two of them bowed out of the competition. Describe three reasons that they may have done so.

**12-14.** The project was known to be in trouble, but it seemed to have a life of its own. Ying Kwong, a technology analyst at Oregon's Department of Administrative Services, said in May 2013 that the Cover Oregon project reminded him of the science fiction movie *The Blob*: "You simply don't know how to shoot this beast, because it does not have a known anatomy with the normal vital organs that make it tick."[5] Had you been a senior manager at Cover Oregon, what would you have done when the problems became apparent?

**12-15.** In a June 2014 survey, a majority of Oregonians held Governor Kitzhaber responsible. But in that same survey, 48 percent say they would vote for his reelection.[6] Bruce Goldberg, former head of OHA and acting head of Cover Oregon, was fired on March 18, 2014, yet by May 15 was back on full salary with OHA.[7] Given these results, does it seem likely that anyone will bear the consequences for these mistakes? If so, who?

MyMISLab™

Go to the Assignments section of your MyLab to complete these writing exercises.

**12-16.** Suppose you work for the U.S. Postal Service (USPS) and have been told that the organization will be adopting a new information system to run all USPS operations. You were asked about your recommendations for installation. Would you recommend a parallel, phased, pilot, or plunge installation? Justify your answer.

**12-17.** A good friend approaches you about installing a solar array on the roof of your business. He says it will reduce your utility costs and give you a tax deduction at the same time. He shows you a video of a computer monitoring the solar power system and you're interested. But you're worried about the feasibility of the new solar power system. Discuss potential concerns related to cost, schedule, technical, and organizational feasibility related to the success of this project.

## ENDNOTES

1. Fred Brooks was a successful executive at IBM in the 1960s. After retiring from IBM, he wrote a classic book on IT project management called *The Mythical Man-Month*. Published by Addison-Wesley in 1975, the book is still pertinent today and should be read by every IT or IS project manager. It's an enjoyable book, too.
2. A *failure* is a difference between what the system does and what it is supposed to do. Sometimes, you will hear the term *bug* used instead of *failure*. As a future user, call failures *failures*—because that's what they are. Don't have a *bugs list*; have a *failures list*. Don't have an *unresolved bug*; have an *unresolved failure*. A few months of managing an organization that is coping with a serious failure will show you the importance of this difference in terms.
3. Ashu Garg, "MarTech and the Decade of the CMO," accessed July 11, 2015, *https://foundationcapital.com/assets/whitepapers/DotCMO_whitepaper.pdf*.
4. Maria L. La Ganga, "Oregon Dumps Its Broken Healthcare Exchange for Federal Website," *Los Angeles Times*, April 15, 2014, accessed June 14, 2014, *www.latimes.com/nation/politics/politicsnow/la-pn-oregon-drops-broken-healthcare-exchange-20140425-story.html*.
5. Nick Budnick, "Cover Oregon: Health Exchange Failure Predicted, but Tech Watchdogs' Warnings Fell on Deaf Ears," *The Oregonian*, January 18, 2014, accessed June 14, 2014, *www.oregonlive.com/health/index.ssf/2014/01/cover_oregon_health_exchange_f.html*.
6. Hillary Lake, "Exclusive Poll: Majority Holds Kitzhaber Accountable for Cover Oregon Failure," *KATU News*, June 11, 2014, accessed June 14, 2014, *www.katu.com/politics/Exclusive-poll-Majority-holds-Kitzhaber-accountable-for-Cover-Oregon-failure-262818611.html*.
7. Nick Budnick, "Long after Announced 'Resignation,' Ex-Cover Oregon Director Bruce Goldberg Draws $14,425 Monthly Salary," *The Oregonian*, May 21, 2014, accessed June 14, 2014, *www.oregonlive.com/politics/index.ssf/2014/05/long_after_publicized_resignat.html*.

chapter extension **1**

**Chapter 1** provides the background for this extension.

# Collaboration Information Systems for Decision Making, Problem Solving, and Project Management

**STUDY QUESTIONS**

**QCE1-1 WHAT ARE THE TWO KEY CHARACTERISTICS OF COLLABORATION?**

**QCE1-2 WHAT ARE THREE CRITERIA FOR SUCCESSFUL COLLABORATION?**

**QCE1-3 WHAT ARE THE FOUR PRIMARY PURPOSES OF COLLABORATION?**

**QCE1-4 WHAT ARE THE COMPONENTS AND FUNCTIONS OF A COLLABORATION INFORMATION SYSTEM?**

## QCE1-1 WHAT ARE THE TWO KEY CHARACTERISTICS OF COLLABORATION?

To answer this question, we must first distinguish between the terms *cooperation* and *collaboration*. **Cooperation** is a group of people working together, all doing essentially the same type of work, to accomplish a job. A group of four painters, each painting a different wall in the same room, are working cooperatively. Similarly, a group of checkers at the grocery store or clerks at the post office are working cooperatively to service customers. A cooperative group can accomplish a given task faster than an individual working alone can, but the cooperative result is usually not better in quality than the result of someone working alone.

In this text, we define **collaboration** as a group of people working together to achieve a common goal *via a process of feedback and iteration*. Using feedback and iteration, one person will produce something, say, the draft of a document, and a second person will review that draft and provide critical feedback. Given the feedback, the original author or someone else will then revise the first draft to produce a second. The work proceeds in a series of stages, or *iterations*, in which something is produced, members criticize it, and then another version is produced. Using iteration and feedback, the group's result can be better than what any single individual can produce alone. This is possible because different group members provide different perspectives. "Oh, I never thought of it that way" is a typical signal of collaboration success.

Many, perhaps most, student groups incorrectly use cooperation rather than collaboration. Given an assignment, a group of five students will break it up into five pieces, work to accomplish their piece independently, and then merge their independent work for grading by the professor. Such a process will enable the project to be completed more quickly, with less work by any single individual, but it will not be better than the result obtained if the students were to work alone.

In contrast, when students work collaboratively, they set forth an initial idea or work product, provide feedback to one another on those ideas or products, and then revise in accordance with feedback. Such a process can produce a result far superior to that produced by any student working alone.

### IMPORTANCE OF EFFECTIVE CRITICAL FEEDBACK

Given this definition, for collaboration to be successful, members must provide and receive *critical* feedback. A group in which everyone is too polite to say anything critical cannot collaborate. As Darwin John, the world's first chief information officer (CIO), once said, "If two of you have the

CE1

exact same idea, then we have no need for one of you." On the other hand, a group that is so critical and negative that members come to distrust, even hate, one another cannot effectively collaborate either. For most groups, success is achieved between these extremes.

To underline this point, consider the research of Ditkoff, Allen, Moore, and Pollard. They surveyed 108 business professionals to determine the qualities, attitudes, and skills that make a good collaborator.[1] Figure CE1-1 lists the most and least important characteristics reported in the survey. Most students are surprised to learn that 5 of the top 12 characteristics involve disagreement (highlighted in red in Figure CE1-1). Most students believe that "we should all get along" and more or less have the same idea and opinions about team matters. Although it is important for the team to be sociable enough to work together, this research indicates that it is also important for team members to have different ideas and opinions and to express them to each other.

When we think about collaboration as an iterative process in which team members give and receive feedback, these results are not surprising. During collaboration, team members learn from each other, and it will be difficult to learn if no one is willing to express different, or even unpopular, ideas. The respondents also seem to be saying, "You can be negative, as long as you care about what we're doing." These collaboration skills do not come naturally to people who have been taught to "play well with others," but that may be why they were so highly ranked in the survey.

The characteristics rated *not relevant* are also revealing. Experience as a collaborator or in business does not seem to matter. Being popular also is not important. A big surprise, however, is

**Figure CE1-1**
Important Characteristics of a Collaborator

**The Most Important Characteristics for an Effective Collaborator**

1. Is enthusiastic about the subject of our collaboration.
2. Is open-minded and curious.
3. Speaks his or her mind even if it's an unpopular viewpoint.
4. Gets back to me and others in a timely way.
5. Is willing to enter into difficult conversations.
6. Is a perceptive listener.
7. Is skillful at giving/receiving negative feedback.
8. Is willing to put forward unpopular ideas.
9. Is self-managing and requires "low maintenance."
10. Is known for following through on commitments.
11. Is willing to dig into the topic with zeal.
12. Thinks differently than I do/brings different perspectives.

. . .

31. Is well organized.
32. Is someone I immediately liked. The chemistry is good.
33. Has already earned my trust.
34. Has experience as a collaborator.
35. Is a skilled and persuasive presenter.
36. Is gregarious and dynamic.
37. Is someone I knew beforehand.
38. Has an established reputation in field of our collaboration.
39. Is an experienced businessperson.

that being well organized was rated 31st out of 39 characteristics. Perhaps collaboration itself is not a very well organized process?

## GUIDELINES FOR GIVING AND RECEIVING CRITICAL FEEDBACK

Giving and receiving critical feedback is the single most important collaboration skill. So, before we discuss the role that information systems can play for improving collaboration, study the guidelines for giving and receiving critical feedback shown in Figure CE1-2.

Many students have found that when they first form a collaborative group, it's useful to begin with a discussion of critical feedback guidelines like those in Figure CE1-2. Begin with this list, and then, using feedback and iteration, develop your own list. Of course, if a group member does not follow the agreed-upon guidelines, someone will have to provide critical feedback to that effect as well.

## WARNING!

If you are like most undergraduate business students, especially freshmen or sophomores, your life experience is keeping you from understanding the need for collaboration. So far, almost everyone you know has the same experiences as you and, more or less, thinks like you. Your friends and associates have the same educational background, scored more or less the same on standardized tests, and have the same orientation toward success. So, why collaborate? Most of you think the same way anyway: "What does the professor want, and what's the easiest, fastest way to get it to her?"

So, consider this thought experiment. Your company is planning to build a new facility that is critical for the success of a new product line and will create 300 new jobs. The county government won't issue a building permit because the site is prone to landslides. Your engineers believe your design overcomes that hazard, but your chief financial officer (CFO) is concerned about possible litigation in the event there is a problem. Your corporate counsel is investigating the best way to overcome the county's objections while limiting liability. Meanwhile, a local environmental group is protesting your site because they believe it is too close to an eagle's nest. Your public relations director is meeting with those local groups every week.

Do you proceed with the project?

**Figure CE1-2** Guidelines for Providing and Receiving Critical Feedback

| Guideline | Example |
|---|---|
| Be specific. | "I was confused until I got to Section 2" rather than "The whole thing is a disorganized mess." |
| Offer suggestions. | "Consider moving Section 2 to the beginning of the document." |
| Avoid personal comments. | Never: "Only an idiot would miss that point ... or write that document." |
| Strive for balance. | "I thought Section 2 was particularly good. What do you think about moving it to the start of the document?" |
| Question your emotions. | "Why do I feel so angry about the comment he just made? What's going on? Is my anger helping me?" |
| Do not dominate. | If there are five members of the group, unless you have special expertise, you are entitled to just 20 percent of the words/time. |
| Demonstrate a commitment to the group. | "I know this is painful, but if we can make these changes our result will be so much better." or "Ouch. I really didn't want to have to redo that section, but if you all think it's important, I'll do it." |

To decide, you create a working team of the chief engineer, the CFO, your legal counsel, and the PR director. Each of those people has different education and expertise, different life experience, and different values. In fact, the only thing they have in common is that they are paid by your company. That team will participate collaboratively in ways that are far different from your experience so far. Keep this example in mind as you continue to read this chapter extension.

Bottom line: The two key characteristics of collaboration are iteration and feedback.

# QCE1-2 WHAT ARE THREE CRITERIA FOR SUCCESSFUL COLLABORATION?

J. Richard Hackman studied teamwork for many years, and his book *Leading Teams* contains many useful concepts and tips for future managers.[2] According to Hackman, there are three primary criteria for judging team success:

- Successful outcome
- Growth in team capability
- Meaningful and satisfying experience

## SUCCESSFUL OUTCOME

Most students are primarily concerned with the first criterion. They want to achieve a good outcome, measured by their grade, or they want to get the project done with an acceptable grade while minimizing the effort required. For business professionals, teams need to accomplish their goals: make a decision, solve a problem, or manage a project. Whatever the objective is, the first success criterion is "Did we do it?"

Although not as apparent in student teams, most business teams also need to ask, "Did we do it within the time and budget allowed?" Teams that produce a work product too late or far over budget are not successful, even if they did achieve their goal.

## GROWTH IN TEAM CAPABILITY

The other two criteria are surprising to most students, probably because most student teams are short-lived. But, in business, where teams often last months or years, it makes sense to ask, "Did the team get better?" If you're a football fan, you've undoubtedly heard your college's coach say, "We really improved as the season progressed." (Of course, for the team with 2 wins and 12 losses, you didn't hear that.) Football teams last only a season. If the team is permanent, say, a team of customer support personnel, the benefits of team growth are even greater. Over time, the team's process quality increases. It becomes more efficient because it can provide more service for a given cost or the same service for less cost.

With experience, teams can become more effective as well. Activities are combined or eliminated. Linkages are established so that "the left hand knows what the right hand is doing," or needs, or can provide. Teams also get better as individuals improve at their tasks. Part of that improvement is the learning curve; as someone does something over and over, he or she gets better at it. But team members also teach task skills and give knowledge to one another. Team members also provide perspectives that other team members need.

## MEANINGFUL AND SATISFYING EXPERIENCE

The third element of Hackman's definition of team success is that team members have a meaningful and satisfying experience. Of course, the nature of team goals is a major factor in making work meaningful. But few of us have the opportunity to develop a life-saving cancer vaccine or safely land a stricken airliner in the middle of the Hudson River in winter. For most of us, it's a matter of making the product, or creating the shipment, or accounting for the payment, or finding the prospects, and so on.

So, in the more mundane world of most business professionals, what makes work meaningful? Hackman cites numerous studies in his book, and one common thread is that the work is perceived as meaningful *by the team*. Keeping prices up to date in the product database may not be the most exciting work, but if that task is perceived by the team as important, it will become meaningful.

Furthermore, if an individual's work is not only perceived as important, but the person doing that work is also given credit for it, then the experience will be perceived as meaningful. So, recognition for work well done is vitally important for a meaningful work experience.

Another aspect of team satisfaction is camaraderie. Business professionals, just like students, are energized when they have the feeling that they are part of a group, each person doing his or her own job and combining efforts to achieve something worthwhile that is better than any could have done alone.

## QCE1-3 WHAT ARE THE FOUR PRIMARY PURPOSES OF COLLABORATION?

Collaborative teams accomplish four primary purposes:

- Become informed
- Make decisions
- Solve problems
- Manage projects

These four purposes build on each other. For example, making a decision requires that team members be informed. In turn, to solve a problem, the team must have the ability to make decisions (and become informed). Finally, to conduct a project, the team must be able to solve problems (and make decisions and become informed).

Before we continue, understand you can use the hierarchy of these four purposes to build your professional skills. You cannot make good decisions if you do not have the skills to inform yourself. You cannot solve problems if you are unable to make good decisions. And you cannot manage projects if you don't know how to solve problems!

In this question, we will consider the collaborative nature of these four purposes and describe requirements for information systems that support them, starting with the most basic, becoming informed.

### BECOMING INFORMED

Informing is the first and most fundamental collaboration purpose. Two individuals can receive the same data but construct different interpretations or, as stated in the terms of Chapter 2, conceive different information. The goal of the informing is to ensure, as much as possible, that team members are conceiving information in the same way.

For example, the team at Falcon Security has been assigned the task of investigating the 3D printing opportunity. One of the team's first tasks is to ensure that everyone understands that goal and, further, understands the basics of 3D printing technology and what is required to implement it.

Informing, which supports all of the purposes of collaboration, presents several requirements for collaborative information systems. As you would expect, team members need to be able to share data and to communicate with one another to share interpretations. Furthermore, because memories are faulty and team membership can change, it is also necessary to document the team's understanding of the information conceived. To avoid having to go "over and over and over" a topic, a repository of information, such as a wiki, is needed.

# MAKING DECISIONS

Collaboration is used for some types of decision making, but not all. Consequently, to understand the role for collaboration we must begin with an analysis of decision making. Decisions are made at three levels: *operational, managerial,* and *strategic.*

## Operational Decisions

**Operational decisions** are those that support operational, day-to-day activities. Typical operational decisions are: How many widgets should we order from vendor A? Should we extend credit to vendor B? Which invoices should we pay today?

## Managerial Decisions

**Managerial decisions** are decisions about the allocation and utilization of resources. Typical decisions are: How much should we budget for computer hardware and programs for department A next year? How many engineers should we assign to project B? How many square feet of warehouse space do we need for the coming year?

In general, if a managerial decision requires consideration of different perspectives, then it will benefit from collaboration. For example, consider the decision of whether to increase employee pay in the coming year. No single individual has the answer. The decision depends on an analysis of inflation, industry trends, the organization's profitability, the influence of unions, and other factors. Senior managers, accountants, human resources personnel, labor relations managers, and others will each bring a different perspective to the decision. They will produce a work product for the decision, evaluate that product, and make revisions in an iterative fashion—the essence of collaboration.

## Strategic Decisions

**Strategic decisions** are those that support broad-scope, organizational issues. Typical decisions at the strategic level are: Should we start a new product line? Should we open a centralized warehouse in Tennessee? Should we acquire company A?

Strategic decisions are almost always collaborative. Consider a decision about whether to move manufacturing operations back from China. This decision affects every employee in the organization, the organization's suppliers, its customers, and its shareholders. Many factors and many perspectives on each of those factors must be considered.

## The Decision Process

Information systems can be classified based on whether their decision processes are *structured* or *unstructured.* These terms refer to the method or process by which the decision is to be made, not to the nature of the underlying problem. A **structured decision** process is one for which there is an understood and accepted method for making the decision. A formula for computing the reorder quantity of an item in inventory is an example of a structured decision process. A standard method for allocating furniture and equipment to employees is another structured decision process. Structured decisions seldom require collaboration.

An **unstructured decision** process is one for which there is no agreed-on decision-making method. Predicting the future direction of the economy or the stock market is a classic example. The prediction method varies from person to person; it is neither standardized nor broadly accepted. Another example of an unstructured decision process is assessing how well suited an employee is for performing a particular job. Managers vary in the manner in which they make such assessments. Unstructured decisions are often collaborative.

## The Relationship Between Decision Type and Decision Process

The decision type and decision process are loosely related. Decisions at the operational level tend to be structured, and decisions at the strategic level tend to be unstructured. Managerial decisions tend to be both structured and unstructured.

**Figure CE1-3**
Collaboration Needs for Decision Making

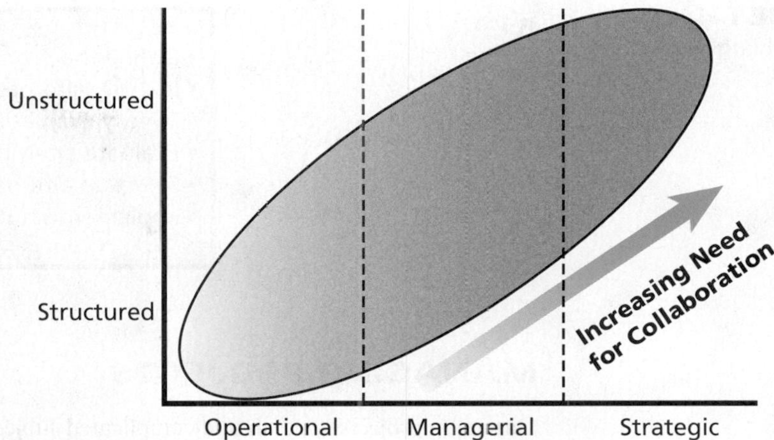


We use the words *tend to be* because there are exceptions to the relationship. Some operational decisions are unstructured (e.g., "How many taxicab drivers do we need on the night before the homecoming game?"), and some strategic decisions can be structured (e.g., "How should we assign sales quotas for a new product?"). In general, however, the relationship holds.

### Decision Making and Collaboration Systems

As stated, few structured decisions involve collaboration. Deciding, for example, how much of product A to order from vendor B does not require the feedback and iteration among members that typify collaboration. Although the process of generating the order might require the coordinated work of people in purchasing, accounting, and manufacturing, there is seldom a need for one person to comment on someone else's work. In fact, involving collaboration in routine, structured decisions is expensive, wasteful, and frustrating. "Do we have to have a meeting about everything?" is a common lament.

The situation is different for unstructured decisions because feedback and iteration are crucial. Members bring different ideas and perspectives about what is to be decided, how the decision will be reached, what criteria are important, and how decision alternatives score against those criteria. The group may make tentative conclusions or discuss potential outcomes of those conclusions, and members will often revise their positions. Figure CE1-3 illustrates the change in the need for collaboration as decision processes become less structured.

## SOLVING PROBLEMS

Solving problems is the third primary reason for collaborating. A **problem** is a perceived difference between what is and what ought to be. Because it is a perception, different people can have different problem definitions.

Therefore, the first and arguably most important task for a problem-solving collaborative group is defining the problem. For example, the Falcon Security team has been assigned the problem of determining whether 3D printing drones is a viable option. As stated as part of the informing purpose, the group needs first to ensure that the team members understand this goal and have a common understanding of what 3D printing entails.

However, because a problem is a difference between what is and what ought to be, the statement "reduce operational expenses" is not specific enough. Is saving one dollar enough of a reduction? Is saving $100,000 enough? Does it take $1,000,000 for the reduction to be enough? A better problem definition would be to reduce operational expenses by 10 percent or by $100,000 or some other more specific statement of what is desired.

Figure CE1-4 lists the principal problem-solving tasks. Because this text is about information systems and not about problem solving per se, we will not delve into those tasks here. Just note the work that needs to be done, and consider the role of feedback and iteration for each of these tasks.

**Figure CE1-4**
Problem-Solving Tasks

- Define the problem.
- Identify alternative solutions.
- Specify evaluation criteria.
- Evaluate alternatives.
- Select an alternative.
- Implement solution.

## MANAGING PROJECTS

Managing projects is a rich and complicated subject, with many theories and methods and techniques. Here we will just touch on the collaborative aspects of four primary project phases.

Projects are formed to create or produce something. The end goal might be a marketing plan, or the design of a new factory, or a new product, or it could be performing the annual audit. Because projects vary so much in nature and size, we will summarize generic project phases here. Figure CE1-5 shows project management with four phases, the major tasks of each, and the kinds of data that collaborative teams need to share.

### Starting Phase

The fundamental purpose of the starting phase is to set the ground rules for the project and the team. In industry, teams need to determine or understand what authority they have. Is the project description given to the team? Or is a part of the team's task to identify what the project is? Is the team free to determine team membership, or is membership given? Can the team devise its own methods for accomplishing the project, or is a particular method required? Student teams differ from those in industry because the team's authority and membership are set by the instructor. However, although student teams do not have the authority to define the project, they do have the authority to determine how that project will be accomplished.

Other tasks during the starting phase are to set the scope of the project and to establish an initial budget. Often this budget is preliminary and is revised after the project has been

**Figure CE1-5**
Project Management Tasks and Data

| Phase | Tasks | Shared Data |
|---|---|---|
| Starting | Set team authority.<br>Set project scope and initial budget.<br>Form team.<br>Establish team roles, responsibilities, and authorities.<br>Establish team rules. | Team member personal data<br>Start-up documents |
| Planning | Determine tasks and dependencies.<br>Assign tasks.<br>Determine schedule.<br>Revise budget. | Project plan, budget, and other documents |
| Doing | Perform project tasks.<br>Manage tasks and budget.<br>Solve problems.<br>Reschedule tasks, as necessary.<br>Document and report progress. | Work in process<br>Updated tasks<br>Updated project schedule<br>Updated project budget<br>Project status documents |
| Finalizing | Determine completion.<br>Prepare archival documents.<br>Disband team. | Archival documents |

planned. An initial team is formed during this phase with the understanding that team membership may change as the project progresses. It is important to set team member expectations at the outset. What role will each team member play, and what responsibilities and authority will he or she have? Team rules are also established as discussed under decision making.

### Planning Phase

The purpose of the planning phase is to determine "who will do what and by when." Work activities are defined, and resources such as personnel, budget, and equipment are assigned to them. Tasks often depend on one other. For example, you cannot evaluate alternatives until you have created a list of alternatives to evaluate. In this case, we say that there is a *task dependency* between the task *Evaluate alternatives* and the task *Create a list of alternatives.* The *Evaluate alternatives* task cannot begin until the completion of the *Create a list of alternatives* task.

Once tasks and resources have been assigned, it is possible to determine the project schedule. If the schedule is unacceptable, more resources can be added to the project, or the project scope can be reduced. Assessing trade-offs among schedule, cost, and scope is one of the most important tasks not only during the planning phase, but throughout the project. The project budget is usually revised during the planning phase as well.

### Doing Phase

Project tasks are accomplished during the doing phase. The key management challenge here is to ensure that tasks are accomplished on time and, if not, to identify schedule problems as early as possible. As work progresses, it is often necessary to add or delete tasks, change task assignments, add or remove task labor or other resources, and so forth. Another important task is to document and report project progress.

### Finalizing Phase

Are we done? This question is an important and sometimes difficult one to answer. If work is not finished, the team needs to define more tasks and continue the doing phase. If the answer is yes, then the team needs to document its results, document information for future teams, close down the project, and disband the team.

Review the third column of Figure CE1-5. All of this project data needs to be stored in a location accessible to the team. Furthermore, all the data is subject to feedback and iteration. That means that there will be hundreds, perhaps thousands, of versions of data items to be managed. We will consider ways that collaboration information systems can facilitate the management of such data in Chapter Extension 2.

## QCE1-4 WHAT ARE THE COMPONENTS AND FUNCTIONS OF A COLLABORATION INFORMATION SYSTEM?

As you would expect, a **collaboration information system** or, more simply, a **collaboration system** is an information system that supports collaboration. Given our discussion in QCE1-1, this means that the system needs to support iteration and feedback among team members. We will discuss specific system features in Chapter Extension 2. For now, consider the components of a collaboration system as well as its basic functions.

### THE FIVE COLLABORATION SYSTEM COMPONENTS

As information systems, collaboration systems have the five components of every information system: hardware, software, data, procedures, and people. Concerning hardware, most collaboration systems are hosted on organizational servers or in what is called *the cloud*, which you will learn about in Chapter 6. We will ignore that component in the discussion in this chapter extension. Just know that the tools you're using and the data you're sharing are supported by computer hardware somewhere. Collaboration programs are applications like email or text messaging that support collaborative work; we will discuss many such programs in the next chapter extension.

Collaboration involves two types of data. **Project data** is data that is part of the collaboration's work product. For example, for a team that is designing a new product, design documents are examples of project data. A document that describes a recommended solution is project data for a problem-solving project. **Project metadata** is data that is used to manage the project. Schedules, tasks, budgets, and other managerial data are examples of project metadata. Both types of data, by the way, are subject to iteration and feedback.

Collaboration information systems procedures specify standards, policies, and techniques for conducting the team's work. An example is procedures for reviewing documents or other work products. To reduce confusion and increase control, the team might establish a procedure that specifies who will review documents and in what sequence. Rules about who can do what to which data are also codified in procedures.

The final component of a collaboration system is, of course, people. We discussed the importance of the ability to give and receive critical feedback in QCE1-1. In addition, team members know how and when to use collaboration applications.

## PRIMARY FUNCTIONS: COMMUNICATION AND CONTENT SHARING

Figure CE1-6 lists the five important collaboration activities discussed in QCE1-1 and QCE1-2 and summarizes the requirements those activities pose for collaboration systems. Notice these requirements fall into two categories: communication and the sharing of content. The second, fourth, and last of these activities concern communication, and the first and third concern tracking and require the storage and sharing of content.

Figure CE1-7 lists the four purposes of collaboration activities discussed in QCE1-3 and summarizes IS requirements for collaboration systems for each purpose. Again, notice that these requirements fall into communication and content-sharing categories. As you think about your

**Figure CE1-6**
Collaboration System Requirements

| Collaborative Activity | Information Systems Requirements |
|---|---|
| Iteration. | Track many versions of many documents and other work products. |
| Feedback. | Provide easy-to-use and readily available multiparty communication. |
| Accomplish task within time and budget. | Track tasks, schedules, budgets, and other project metadata.<br>Account for and report progress and status. |
| Promote team growth. | Provide for intrateam teaching. |
| Increase team satisfaction. | Provide for team and member recognition. |

**Figure CE1-7**
IS Requirements for Different Collaboration Purposes

| Purpose | IS Requirements |
|---|---|
| Become informed. | Share data.<br>Support group communication.<br>Store history. |
| Make decisions. | Share decision criteria, alternative descriptions, evaluation tools, evaluation results, and implementation plan.<br>Support group communication during decision-making process.<br>Publish decision, as needed.<br>Store records of process and results. |
| Solve problems. | Share problem definitions, solution alternatives, costs and benefits, alternative evaluations, and solution implementation plan.<br>Support group communication.<br>Publish problem and solution, as needed.<br>Store problem definition, alternatives, analysis, and plan. |
| Conduct projects. | Support starting, planning, doing, and finalizing project phases. |

own collaboration projects in school, use Figures CE1-6 and CE1-7 as a guide for determining the tools you need for your own collaboration system.

Note the difference between the terms *collaboration system* and *collaboration tool*. A **collaboration tool** is the program component of a collaboration system. For the tool to be useful, it must be surrounded by the other four components of an information system.

# ACTIVE REVIEW

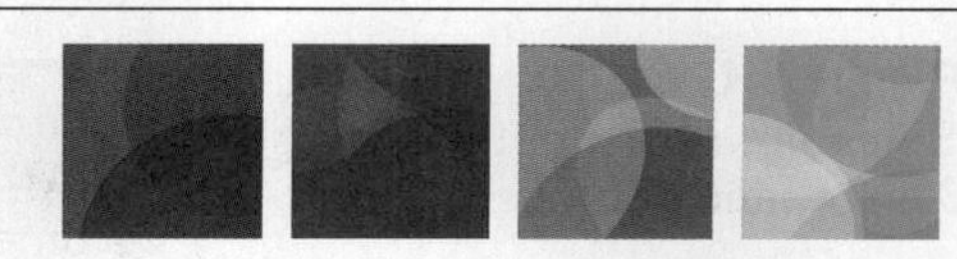

Use this Active Review to verify that you understand the ideas and concepts that answer this chapter extension's study questions.

## QCE1-1 WHAT ARE TWO KEY CHARACTERISTICS OF COLLABORATION?

In your own words, explain the difference between cooperation and collaboration. Name the two key characteristics of collaboration and explain how they improve group work. Summarize important skills for collaborators and list what you believe are the best ways to give and receive critical feedback.

## QCE1-2 WHAT ARE THREE CRITERIA FOR SUCCESSFUL COLLABORATION?

Name and describe three criteria for collaboration success. Summarize how these criteria differ between student and professional teams.

## QCE1-3 WHAT ARE THE FOUR PRIMARY PURPOSES OF COLLABORATION?

Name and describe four primary purposes of collaboration. Explain their relationship. Describe ways that collaboration systems can contribute to each purpose.

## QCE1-4 WHAT ARE THE COMPONENTS AND FUNCTIONS OF A COLLABORATION INFORMATION SYSTEM?

Name and describe the five components of a collaboration information system. Name and describe two key collaboration IS functions.

## KEY TERMS AND CONCEPTS

Collaboration 367
Collaboration information system 375
Collaboration system 375
Collaboration tool 376
Cooperation 367
Managerial decisions 372
Operational decisions 372
Problem 373
Project data 376
Project metadata 376
Strategic decisions 372
Structured decision 372
Unstructured decision 372

MyMISLab™
To complete the problems with the ✪, go to EOC Discussion Questions in the MyLab.

## USING YOUR KNOWLEDGE

✪ **CE1-1.** Give an example of a cooperative team and a collaborative team. Use examples other than those in this book. Explain why iteration and feedback are more important for collaboration than for cooperation. Summarize factors that cause most student teams to be cooperative and not collaborative. What is the disadvantage when student teams are not collaborative? How can information systems be used to make it easier for students to truly collaborate?

✪ **CE1-2.** Using your experience working in past teams, give examples of unhelpful feedback according to the guidelines for providing critical feedback in QCE1-1. Correct your examples to a more productive and helpful comment.

**CE1-3.** Using a past team project from your own experience, summarize how your team conducted the four phases (starting, planning, doing, and finalizing) in QCE1-3. Evaluate how your team conducted problem-solving, decision-making, and informing activities. Rate your past team on Hackman's criteria as discussed in QCE1-2.

MyMISLab™

Go to the Assignments section of your MyLab to complete these writing exercises.

**CE1-4.** Suppose you are the manager of a campaign to elect one of your friends as university student body president.

**a.** Describe why this campaign will be more successful if managed collaboratively rather than cooperatively.

**b.** Explain how each of the criteria for team success pertains to this campaign. Are the second and third criteria important? Explain your answer.

**c.** Describe how each of the four primary purposes of collaboration pertains to this campaign. Explain the hierarchical nature of these four factors.

**d.** Suppose that one of the tasks for the campaign team is to decide how to allocate scarce labor. Would this decision be more operational, managerial, or strategic in nature? Explain your answer.

**CE1-5.** Consider how you may use information technology in group projects for your university classes. Using the discussion of IS requirements for collaboration presented in QCE1-4, answer the following questions.

**a.** Suppose that a group member wants to use nothing other than face-to-face meetings, email, and texting for communication. What problems can you expect if you use only these methods? How might these methods affect group communication and content sharing?

**b.** Assuming you are using only face-to-face meetings, email, texting, PowerPoint, and Excel, how will you share documents? What problems might you expect?

**c.** Consider the four purposes of collaboration activities mentioned in QCE1-3. For which purpose(s) might you use online data storage tools like Google Drive, Dropbox, and OneDrive?

**d.** Describe what you think would be the single most important additional collaboration tool that you could add to your team.

## ENDNOTES

1. Mitch Ditkoff, Tim Moore, Carolyn Allen, and Dave Pollard, "The Ideal Collaborative Team," *Idea Champions*, accessed June 27, 2014, *www.ideachampions.com/downloads/collaborationresults.pdf*.
2. J. Richard Hackman, *Leading Teams: Setting the Stage for Great Performances* (Boston: Harvard Business Press, 2002).

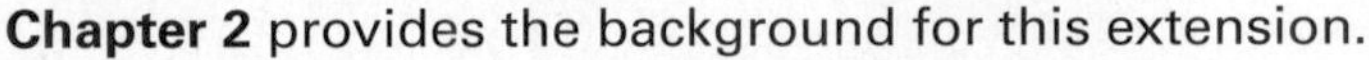

chapter extension **2**

**Chapter 2** provides the background for this extension.

# Collaborative Information Systems for Student Projects

**STUDY QUESTIONS**

**QCE2-1** WHAT ARE THE IS REQUIREMENTS FOR STUDENT PROJECT COLLABORATIONS?

**QCE2-2** HOW CAN YOU USE COLLABORATION TOOLS TO IMPROVE TEAM COMMUNICATION?

**QCE2-3** HOW CAN YOU USE COLLABORATION TOOLS TO SHARE CONTENT?

**QCE2-4** HOW CAN YOU USE COLLABORATION TOOLS TO MANAGE TASKS?

**QCE2-5** WHICH COLLABORATION INFORMATION SYSTEM IS RIGHT FOR YOUR TEAM?

CE2

## QCE2-1 WHAT ARE THE IS REQUIREMENTS FOR STUDENT PROJECT COLLABORATIONS?

Your MIS class will help you gain knowledge and skills that you'll use throughout your business career. But why wait? You can benefit from this knowledge right now and put it to use tonight. Most business courses involve a team project—why not use what you're learning to construct a collaboration IS that will make teamwork easier and help your team achieve a better product? You can use it not only for projects in this class, but with some leadership on your part, for teams in other classes as well.

To begin, read Chapter Extension 1, if you have not already done so. Ensure that you understand the difference between *cooperation* and *collaboration*. Also ensure that any team that will use the system you're building wants to *collaborate*. If team members just want to cooperate, you won't need this system. Finally, make sure you understand the need for and relationships among informing, deciding, solving problems, and managing projects.

Figure CE2-1 summarizes requirements for an IS that supports collaborative student teams. The requirements are divided into three categories as shown.

### REQUIRED FEATURES

A collaborative information system must support the following three categories of requirements:

- Communication
- Content sharing
- Project planning and management

Regarding team communication, if you meet face to face, you most likely will need some medium for sharing ideas. You can use a whiteboard or similar device, but that means in order to have minutes or some other record of the team's work, someone needs to copy the results to paper or a file. Another approach is to use PowerPoint or OneNote and a projector during the meeting. At the end, those files can be shared with all team members to serve as minutes. You'll see other ways of using collaborative tools during meetings later in this chapter extension.

By default, most student teams attempt to meet face to face. But why? Such meetings are difficult to schedule and invariably someone can't be on campus, is stuck in traffic, misses the bus, or whatever. In the next question, you'll see tools for online meetings that make face-to-face meetings less important.

If your team is going to practice feedback and iteration, it needs some way to share content and to track different versions of content items. When team members work on documents at the

**Figure CE2-1**
Student-Project Collaboration IS Requirements Summary

- **Required Features**
  - Communication
  - Content sharing
  - Task management
- **Nice-to-Have Features**
  - Discussion forums
  - Surveys
  - Wikis
  - Blogs
  - Photo/video sharing
- **Collaboration Tool Characteristics**
  - Free/cheap
  - Easy to learn/use
  - Integrated features
  - Provides evidence of versions
  - Used in business

same time, the system should provide a means to ensure that one user's changes don't override another's. Some tools do that automatically; however, if your team does not use such a tool, you must develop procedures to avoid lost work.

As discussed in Chapter Extension 1, project planning and management necessitate the creation of tasks and assigning those tasks to individuals. The fundamental goal is to "decide who's going to do what and by when." When those decisions have been made, the task, person, and date due need to be recorded somewhere so all team members can follow progress (or lack thereof) and so team members can be held accountable for their tasks. Of course, nothing goes as planned, and so this capability needs to allow tasks to be altered when necessary. Teams also need the ability to keep track of events such as intermediate meetings, final reviews, and so on.

## NICE-TO-HAVE FEATURES

The features in the next category are not essential, but they can make teamwork easier and more effective. Also, some of these features might be required for certain types of projects.

Discussion forums are useful when the team needs to meet on some topic but everyone cannot meet at the same time. Surveys obtain team members' opinions outside of team meetings as well. Wikis are useful for documenting team knowledge; blogs enable team members to publish their ideas. Sharing photos and videos can be a great way of building team cohesion.

## COLLABORATION TOOL CHARACTERISTICS

The last category of requirements concerns characteristics of the collaboration tool (the computer program part of the IS). It needs to be free, or at least cheap. It should be easy to learn and use. Feature integration is very useful but rare. An example of such integration occurs when someone changes a task and the collaboration tool automatically sends an email change notification to the person who has that task.

If your professor wants to evaluate your collaboration process, you will want to submit evidence of many versions and contributions from team members as part of your project deliverable. Some collaboration tools automatically generate such data, as you will see. Finally, you will benefit if the tool you use is one that you will likely employ in your professional career. Blackboard, Canvas, and Moodle (course management software) have support for collaboration, but they are nearly unknown in business. Google Drive and SharePoint, on the other hand, are well known. SharePoint skills, in particular, are in great demand in industry, and knowing how to use SharePoint gives you a competitive advantage.

## QCE2-2 HOW CAN YOU USE COLLABORATION TOOLS TO IMPROVE TEAM COMMUNICATION?

Because of the need to provide feedback, team communication is essential to every collaborative project. In addition to feedback, however, communication is important to manage content, project tasks, and other requirements. Developing an effective communication facility is the first thing your team should do, and it is arguably the most important feature of a collaboration IS.

The particular tools used depend on the ways that the team communicates, as summarized in Figure CE2-2. **Synchronous communication** occurs when all team members meet at the same time, such as with conference calls or face-to-face meetings. **Asynchronous communication** occurs when team members do not meet at the same time. Employees who work different shifts at the same location or team members who work in different time zones around the world must meet asynchronously.

As stated in QCE2-1, for most face-to-face meetings, you need little software support; you may want to use PowerPoint, OneNote, or another application and a projector for team discussions. However, *given today's communication technology, most students should forgo face-to-face meetings.* As stated in QCE2-1, they are too difficult to arrange and seldom worth the trouble. Instead, learn to use **virtual meetings** in which participants do not meet in the same place, and possibly not at the same time.

If your virtual meeting is synchronous (all meet at the same time), you can use conference calls, multiparty text chat, screen sharing, Webinars, or videoconferencing. Some students find it weird to use text chat for school projects, but why not? You can attend meetings wherever you are, without using your voice. Google Hangouts support multiparty text chat, as does Microsoft Skype for Business, Google, or Bing "multiparty text chat" to find other, similar products.

**Screen-sharing applications** enable users to view the same whiteboard, application, or other display. Figure CE2-3 shows an example whiteboard for a Falcon Security meeting. This whiteboard, which is part of Skype for Business, allows multiple people to contribute simultaneously. To organize the simultaneous conversation, the whiteboard real estate is divided among the members of the group, as shown. Some groups save their whiteboards as minutes of the meeting.

A **Webinar** is a virtual meeting in which attendees view one of the attendees' computer screens for a more formal and organized presentation. WebEx (*www.webex.com*) is a popular commercial webinar application used in virtual sales presentations.

If everyone on your team has a camera on his or her computer, you can also do **videoconferencing**, like that shown in Figure CE2-4. Skype is a common choice for student videoconferencing, but you can also use Google+ Hangouts, Microsoft Skype for Business, and other tools as well. Search the Internet for *videoconferencing tools*. Videoconferencing is more intrusive than text chat (you have to comb your hair), but it does have a more personal touch.

In some classes and situations, synchronous meetings, even virtual ones, are impossible to arrange. You just cannot get everyone together at the same time. In this circumstance, when the

**Figure CE2-2**
Collaboration Tools for Communication

| Synchronous | | Asynchronous |
|---|---|---|
| Shared calendars<br>Invitation and attendance | | |
| Single location | Multiple locations | Single or multiple locations |
| Office applications such as Word and PowerPoint<br><br>Shared whiteboards | Conference calls<br>Multiparty text chat<br>Screen sharing<br>Webinars<br>Videoconferencing | Email<br>Discussion forums<br>Team surveys |
| | Virtual meetings | Virtual meetings |

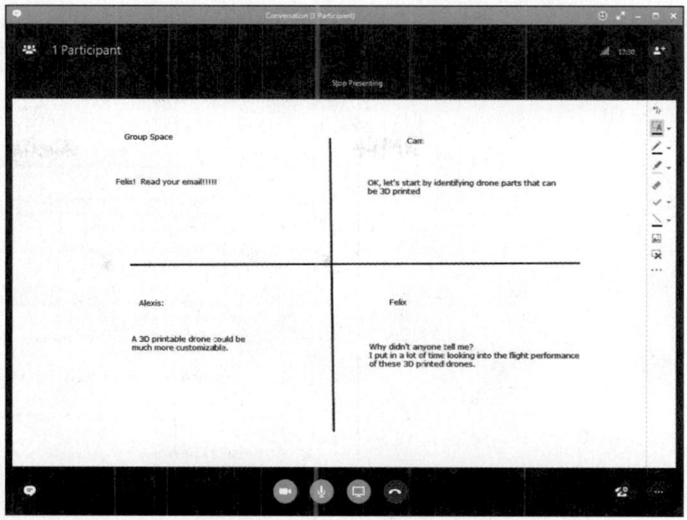


**Figure CE2-3**
Skype for Business Whiteboard Showing Simultaneous Contributions

*Source:* Used by permission from Skype Communications SARL

team must meet asynchronously, most students try to communicate via **email**. The problem with email is that there is too much freedom. Not everyone will participate because it is easy to hide from email. Email threads become disorganized and disconnected. After the fact, it is difficult to find particular emails, comments, or attachments.

**Discussion forums** are an alternative. Here one group member posts an entry, perhaps an idea, a comment, or a question, and other group members respond. Figure CE2-5 shows an example. Such forums are better than email because it is harder for the discussion to get off track. Still, however, it remains easy for some team members not to participate.

**Team surveys** are another form of communication technology. With these, one team member creates a list of questions and other team members respond. Surveys are an effective way to obtain team opinions; they are generally easy to complete, so most team members will participate. Also, it is easy to determine who has not yet responded. Figure CE2-6 shows the results of one team survey. SurveyMonkey (*www.surveymonkey.com*) is one common survey application program. You can find others on the Internet. Microsoft SharePoint has a built-in survey capability, as we discuss in QCE2-5.

**Figure CE2-4**
Videoconferencing Example

*Source:* Tom Merton/OJO Images/Getty Images

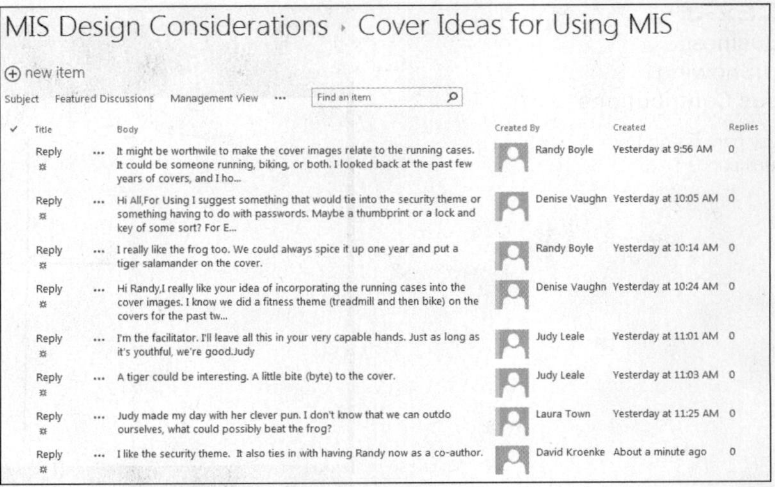


**Figure CE2-5**
Example Discussion Forum

Video and audio recordings are also useful for asynchronous communication. Key presentations or discussions can be recorded and played back for team members at their convenience. Such recordings are also useful for training new employees.

## QCE2-3 HOW CAN YOU USE COLLABORATION TOOLS TO SHARE CONTENT?

Content sharing is the second major function of collaboration systems. To enable iteration and feedback, team members need to share both project data (such as documents, spreadsheets, presentations, and work-product data) as well as project metadata (such as tasks, schedules, calendars, and budgets). The applications that teams use and the means by which they share data depend on the type of content. Figure CE2-7 provides an overview.[1]

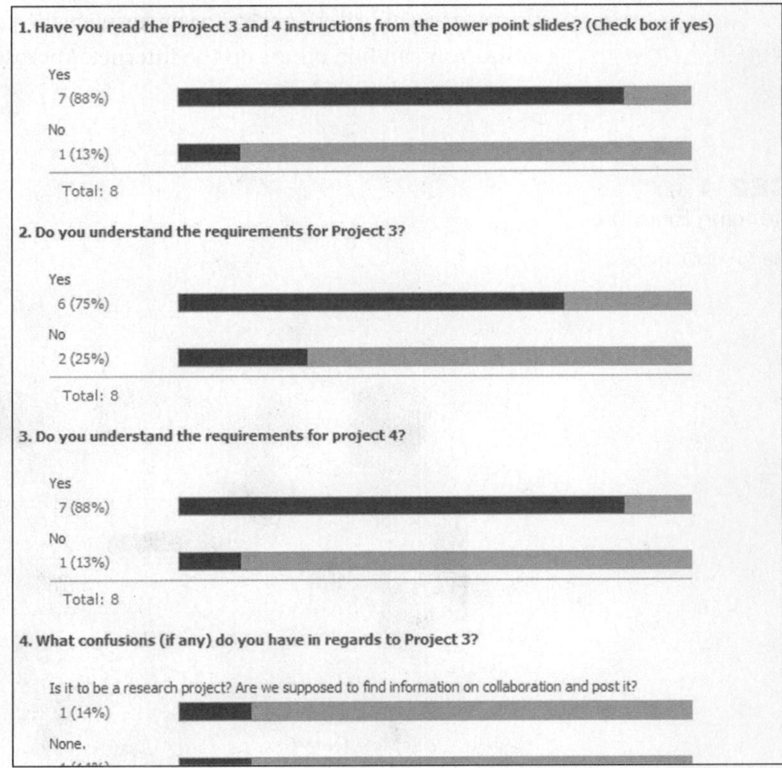


**Figure CE2-6**
Example Survey Report

**Figure CE2-7**
Content Applications and Storage Alternatives

| Content Type | Desktop Application | Web Application | Popular Cloud Drive Alternatives |
|---|---|---|---|
| Office documents (Word, Excel, PowerPoint) | Microsoft Office<br>LibreOffice<br>OpenOffice | Google Docs (Import/Export non-Google Docs)<br>Microsoft Office Online (Microsoft Office only) | Google Drive<br>Microsoft OneDrive<br>Microsoft SharePoint<br>Dropbox |
| PDFs | Adobe Acrobat | Viewers in Google Drive and Microsoft Web OneDrive and SharePoint | Google Drive<br>Microsoft OneDrive<br>Microsoft SharePoint<br>Dropbox |
| Photos, Videos | Adobe Photoshop, Camtasia, and numerous others | Google Picasa | Google Drive<br>Microsoft OneDrive<br>Microsoft SharePoint<br>Apple iCloud<br>Dropbox |
| Other (engineering drawings) | Specific application (Google SketchUp) | Rare | Google Drive<br>Microsoft OneDrive<br>Microsoft SharePoint<br>Dropbox |

For teams that are sharing Office documents such as Word, Excel, and PowerPoint, the gold standard of desktop applications is Microsoft Office. However, it is also the most expensive. To minimize costs, some teams use either LibreOffice (*www.libreoffice.org*) or Apache OpenOffice (*www.openoffice.org*). Both are license-free, open-source products. (You'll learn more about these terms in Chapter 4; for now, think free.) These products have a small subset of the features and functions of Microsoft Office, but they are robust for what they do and are adequate for many businesses and students.

Teams that are sharing documents of other types need to install applications for processing those particular types. For examples, Adobe Acrobat processes pdf files; Photoshop and Google Picasa process photos; and Camtasia and the Mix add-in to PowerPoint produce computer screen videos that are useful for teaching team members how to use computer applications.

In addition to desktop applications, teams can also process some types of content using Web applications inside their browsers (Firefox, Chrome, etc.). Both **Google Docs** and **Microsoft Office Online** can process Word, Excel, and PowerPoint files. However, Google has its own version of these files. Consequently, if the user uploads a Word document that was created using a desktop application and then wishes to edit that document, he or she must convert it into Google Docs format by opening it with Google Docs. After editing the document, if the user wants to place the document back into Word format, he or she will need to specifically save it in Word format. This is not difficult once the user is aware of the need to do so. Of course, if the team never uses a desktop application, and instead uses Google Docs to create and process documents via the Web, then no conversion between the desktop and Google Docs formats is needed. Microsoft Office Online can be used in a similar way, but Office Online will edit only documents that were created using Microsoft Office. Documents created using LibreOffice and OpenOffice cannot always be edited using Microsoft Office Online.

Browser applications require that documents be stored on a cloud server. Google Docs documents must be stored on Google Drive; Microsoft Office Online must be stored on either Microsoft OneDrive or Microsoft SharePoint. We will illustrate the use of Google Drive and Google Grid when we discuss version management later in this chapter extension.

Documents other than Office documents can be stored (but not processed via the browser) on any cloud server. Team members store the documents on the server for other team members

**Figure CE2-8**
Collaboration Tools for Sharing Content

| Alternatives for Sharing Content | | |
|---|---|---|
| No Control | Version Management | Version Control |
| Email with attachments<br>Shared files on a server | Google Docs<br>Windows Office Online<br>Microsoft Office | Microsoft SharePoint |

Increasing degree of content control →

to access. DropBox is one common alternative, but you can use Google Drive, Microsoft OneDrive, and SharePoint as well. You can also store photos and videos on Apple's iCloud.

Figure CE2-8 lists collaboration tools for three categories of content: no control, version management, and version control.

## SHARED CONTENT WITH NO CONTROL

The most primitive way to share content is via email attachments. However, email attachments have numerous problems. For one, there is always the danger that someone does not receive an email, does not notice it in his or her inbox, or does not bother to save the attachments. Then, too, if three users obtain the same document as an email attachment, each changes it, and each sends back the changed document via email, then different, incompatible versions of that document will be floating around. So, although email is simple, easy, and readily available, it will not suffice for collaborations in which there are many document versions or for which there is a desire for content control.

Another way to share content is to place it on a shared **file server**, which is simply a computer that stores files... just like the disk in your local computer. If your team has access to a file server at your university, you can put documents on the server and others can download them, make changes, and upload them back onto the server.

Storing documents on servers is better than using email attachments because documents have a single storage location. They are not scattered in different team members' email boxes, and team members have a known location for finding documents.

However, without any additional control, it is possible for team members to interfere with one another's work. For example, suppose team members A and B download a document and edit it, but without knowing about the other's edits. Person A stores his version back on the server and then person B stores her version back on the server. In this scenario, person A's changes will be lost.

Furthermore, without any version management, it will be impossible to know who changed the document and when. Neither person A nor person B will know whose version of the document is on the server. To avoid such problems, the team will need to develop manual procedures to prevent two people from working on the same document at the same time, or it will need to use a tool that supports version management.

## SHARED CONTENT WITH VERSION MANAGEMENT ON GOOGLE DRIVE

Collaboration tools that provide **version management** track changes to documents and provide features and functions to accommodate concurrent work. For office documents, you can obtain version management services from Google Drive, Microsoft OneDrive, and Microsoft SharePoint. Here we will discuss the use of Google Drive.

**Google Drive** is a free service that provides a virtual drive in the cloud into which you can create folders and store files. You can upload files of any type, but only files that are processed by Google Docs receive version management. We'll restrict the rest of this discussion to files of those types.

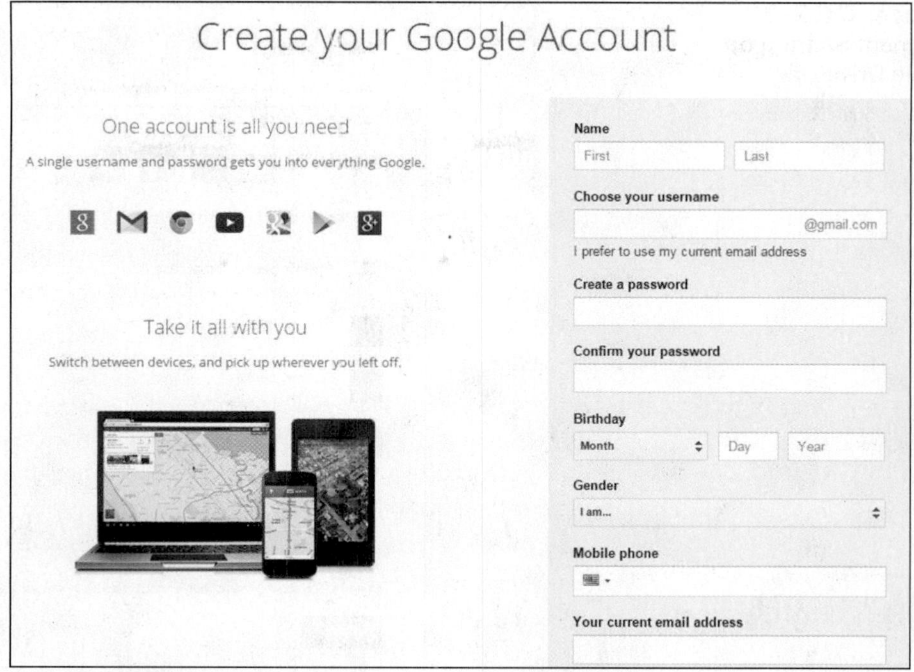


**Figure CE2-9**
Form for Creating a Google Drive Account

*Source:* Google Corporation

To use Google Drive, you need a Google Account, which you obtain by creating a gmail address. (If you already have a gmail address, you already have a Google Account with the same name as your gmail address.) To create a Google account, go to *http://accounts.google.com* (note that there is no www in this address) and fill out the form shown in Figure CE2-9.

In this form, you need not provide a value for your current email address. though it's a good idea to provide one if you can. That address is used by Google in the event you forget your password and for other security backup purposes.

To create a Google document, go to *http://drive.google.com*. Sign in with your Google account. From that point on, you can create, upload, process, save, and download documents. You can also save most of those documents to PDF and Microsoft Office formats, such as Word, Excel, and PowerPoint. (We do not discuss it here, but Microsoft provides a cloud-based service similar to Google Drive named **OneDrive**.)

With Google Drive, you can make documents available to others by entering their email addresses or Google accounts. Those users are notified that the document exists and are given a link by which they can access it. If they have a Google account, they can edit the document; otherwise, they can just view the document. To see who can share one of the documents in Figure CE2-10, right-click on any document on the screen, click Share, and click Advanced. A screen showing those who share the document will appear like that in Figure CE2-11.

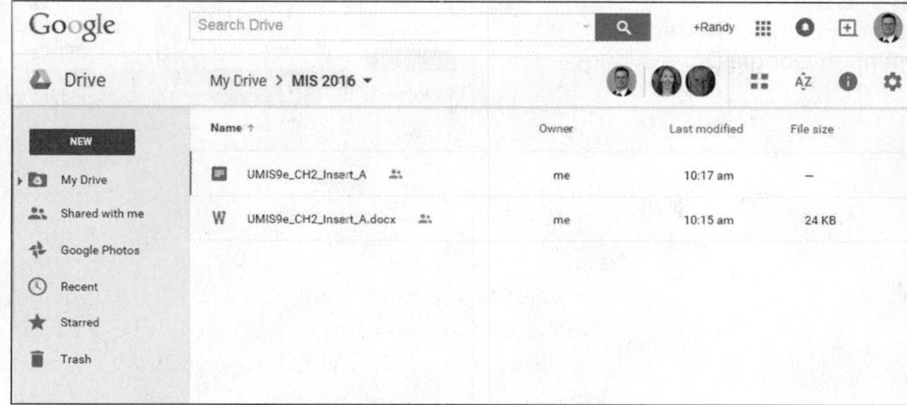


**Figure CE2-10**
Available Types of Documents on Google Drive

*Source:* Google Corporation

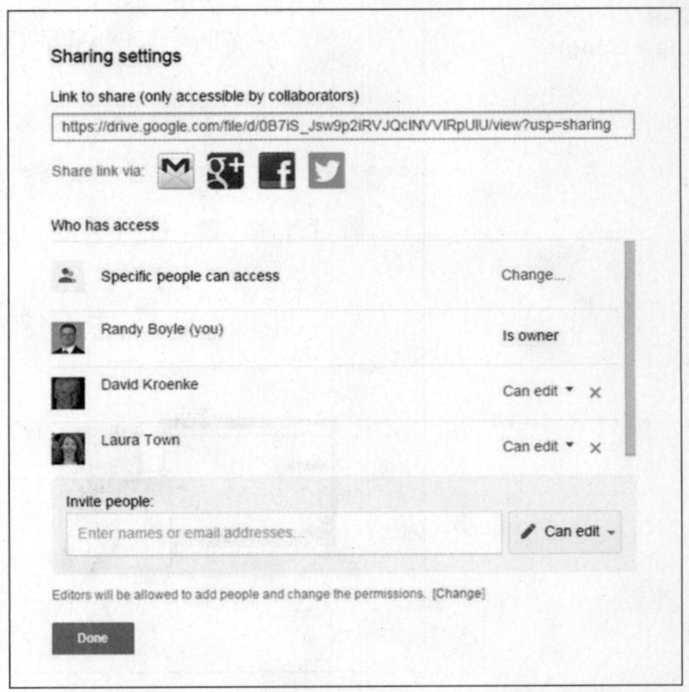


**Figure CE2-11**
Document Sharing on Google Drive

*Source:* Google Corporation

Documents stored on Google Drive can be simultaneously seen and edited by users. In the background, Google Docs merges the users' activities into a single document. You are notified that another user is editing a document at the same time as you are, and you can refresh the document to see that user's latest changes. Google tracks document revisions, with brief summaries of changes made. Figure CE2-12 shows the revision history for a document that has been shared among three users. You can improve your collaboration activity even more by combining Google Drive with Google+.

Google Drive is free and very easy to use. Google Drive, Dropbox, and Microsoft OneDrive are all far superior to exchanging documents via email or via a file server. If you are not using one of these products, you should.

## SHARED CONTENT WITH VERSION CONTROL

Version management systems improve the tracking of shared content and potentially eliminate problems caused by concurrent document access. They do not, however, provide **version control**,

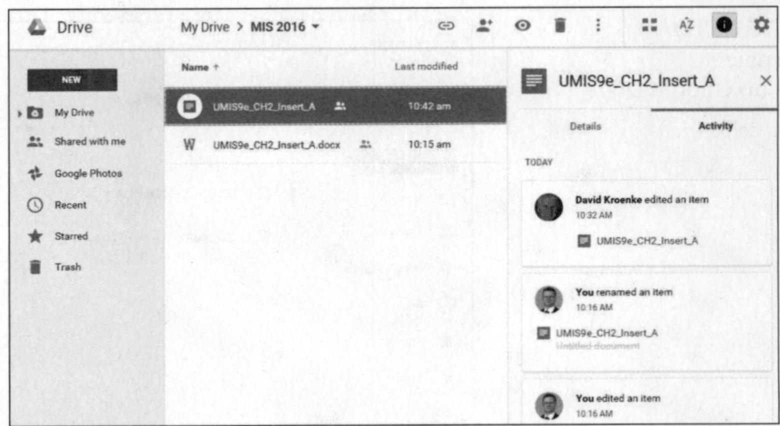


**Figure CE2-12**
Example of Editing a Shared Document on Google Drive

*Source:* Google Corporation

the process that occurs when the collaboration tool limits, and sometimes even directs, user activity. Version control involves one or more of the following capabilities:

- User activity limited by permissions
- Document checkout
- Version histories
- Workflow control

Microsoft SharePoint is a large, complex, and very robust application for all types of collaboration. It has many features and functions, including all of those listed above. It also contains features for managing tasks, sharing non-Office documents, keeping calendars, publishing blogs, and many more capabilities. Some organizations install SharePoint on their own Windows servers; others access it over the Internet using SharePoint OnLine. Office 365 Professional and other versions of Office 365 include SharePoint.

SharePoint is an industrial-strength product, and if you have an opportunity to use it, by all means learn to do so. SharePoint is used by thousands of businesses, and SharePoint skills are in high demand. The latest version is SharePoint 2013; we will illustrate its use here. Consider the SharePoint implementation of the four functions listed above.

## Permission-Limited Activity

With SharePoint (and other version control products), each team member is given an account with a set of permissions. Then shared documents are placed into shared directories, sometimes called **libraries**. For example, on a shared site with four libraries, a particular user might be given read-only permission for library 1; read and edit permission for library 2; read, edit, and delete permission for library 3; and no permission to even see library 4.

## Document Checkout

With version control applications, document directories can be set up so that users are required to check out documents before they can modify them. When a document is checked out, no other user can obtain it for the purpose of editing it. Once the document has been checked in, other users can obtain it for editing.

Figure CE2-13 shows a screen for a user of Microsoft SharePoint 2013. The user is checking out the document UMIS 9e Chapter 2. Once it has been checked out, the user can edit it and return it to this library. While it is checked out, no other user will be able to edit it, and the user's changes will not be visible to others.

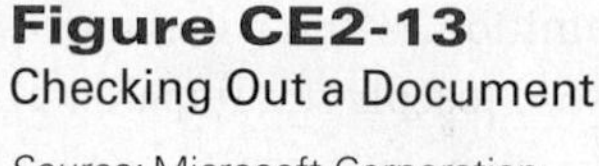

**Figure CE2-13**
Checking Out a Document

*Source:* Microsoft Corporation

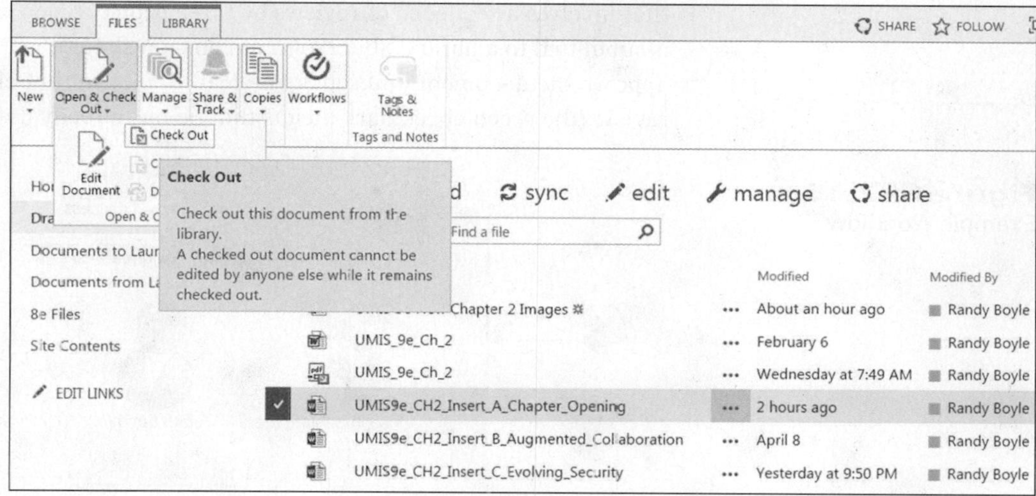

**Figure CE2-14**
Chapter Version History
*Source:* Microsoft Corporation

Version History

Delete All Versions

| No. ↓ | Modified | Modified By | Size | Comments |
|---|---|---|---|---|
| 7.0 | 4/18/2015 7:49 AM | Randy Boyle | 1.7 MB | |
| 6.0 | 4/18/2015 7:00 AM | Randy Boyle | 1.5 MB | |
| 5.0 | 4/18/2015 6:25 AM | Randy Boyle | 1008.7 KB | |
| 4.0 | 4/18/2015 5:57 AM | Randy Boyle | 824.8 KB | |
| 3.0 | 4/18/2015 4:53 AM | Randy Boyle | 199.7 KB | |
| 2.0 | 4/18/2015 3:52 AM | Randy Boyle | 85 KB | |
| 1.0 | 4/18/2015 1:32 AM | Randy Boyle | 97.4 KB | |
| | Title | Figure 4-??? | | |

With SharePoint, Microsoft manages concurrent updates on office documents (Word, Excel, etc.) and documents need not normally be checked out. In Figure CE2-13, the user has checked out an Acrobat PDF, which is not an Office document.

## Version History

Because collaboration involves feedback and iteration, it is inevitable that dozens, or even hundreds, of documents will be created. Imagine, for example, the number of versions of a design document for the Boeing 787. In some cases, collaboration team members attempt to keep track of versions by appending suffixes to file names. The result for a student project is a file name like *Project1_lt_kl_092914_most_recent_draft.docx*, or something similar. Not only are such names ugly and awkward, no team member can tell whether this is the most current version.

Collaboration tools that provide version control maintain metadata to provide histories on behalf of the users. When a document is changed (or checked in), the collaboration tool records the name of the author and the date and time the document is stored. Users also have the option of recording notes about their version. You can see an example of a version history report produced by SharePoint 2013 in Figure CE2-14.

## Workflow Control

Collaboration tools that provide **workflow control** manage activities in a predefined process. If, for example, a group wants documents to be reviewed and approved by team members in a particular sequence, the group would define that workflow for the tool. Then the workflow is started, and the emails to manage the process are sent as defined. For example, Figure CE2-15 shows a SharePoint workflow in which the group defined a document review process that involves a sequence of reviews by three people. Given this definition, when a document is submitted to a library, SharePoint assigns a task to the first person, Joseph Schumpeter, to approve the document and sends an email to him to that effect. Once he has completed his review (the green checkmark means that he has already done so), SharePoint assigns a task

**Figure CE2-15**
Example Workflow

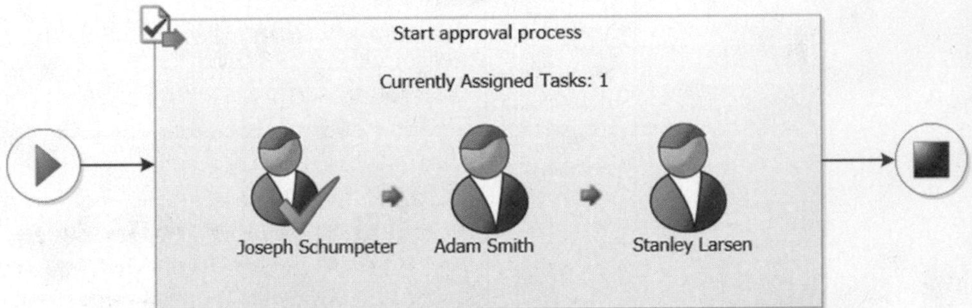

to and sends an email to Adam Smith to approve the document. When all three reviewers have completed their review, SharePoint marks the document as approved. If any disapprove, the document is marked accordingly and the workflow is terminated.

Workflows can be defined for complicated, multistage business processes. See *SharePoint for Students*[2] for more on how to create them.

Numerous version control applications exist. For general business use, SharePoint is the most popular. Other document control systems include MasterControl (*www.mastercontrol.com*) and Document Locator (*www.documentlocator.com*). Software development teams use applications such as CVS (*www.nongnu.org/cvs*) or Subversion (*http://subversion.tigris.org*) to control versions of software code, test plans, and product documentation.

## QCE2-4 HOW CAN YOU USE COLLABORATION TOOLS TO MANAGE TASKS?

As you will learn in project management classes, one of the keys for making team progress is keeping a current task list. Good project managers make sure that every team meeting ends with an updated list of tasks, including who is responsible for getting each task done and the date by which he or she will get it done. We've all been to meetings in which many good ideas were discussed, even agreed upon, but nothing happened after the meeting. When teams create and manage using tasks lists, the risks of such nonaction diminish. Managing with a task list is critical for making progress.

Task descriptions need to be specific and worded so that it is possible to decide whether the task was accomplished. "Create a good requirements document" is not an effective-testable task description, unless all team members already know what is supposed to be in a good requirements document. A better task would be: "Define the contents of the requirements document for the XYZ project."

**We will discuss such task dependencies further in Chapter Extension 15 when we discuss the management of systems development projects.**

In general, one person should be made responsible for accomplishing a task. That does not mean that the assigned person does the task; it means that they are responsible for ensuring that it gets done. Finally, no benefit will come from this list unless every task has a date by which it is to be completed. Further, team leaders need to follow up on tasks to ensure that they are done by that date. Without accountability and follow-up, there is no task management.

As you'll learn in your project management classes, you can add other data to the task list. You might want to add critical resources that are required, and you might want to specify tasks that need to be finished before a given task can be started.

For team members to utilize the task list effectively, they need to share it. In this question, we will consider two options: sharing a task spreadsheet on Google Drive and using the task list feature in Microsoft SharePoint. Google Gmail and calendar also have a task list feature, but as of this writing, it is impossible to share it with others, so it is not useful for collaboration.

### SHARING A TASK LIST ON GOOGLE DRIVE

Sharing a task list on Google Drive is simple. To do so, every team member needs to obtain a Google account. Then one team member can create a team folder and share it with the rest of the team, giving everyone edit permission on documents that it contains. One of the team members then creates a task spreadsheet on that folder.

Figure CE2-16 shows a sample task list containing the name of each task, the name of the person that it is assigned to, the date it is due, the task's status, and remarks. Because every member of the team has edit permission, everyone can contribute to this task list. Google Drive will allow simultaneous edits. Because Google Drive tracks version history, it will be possible, if necessary, to learn who made which changes to the task list.

Setting up such a list is easy and having such a list greatly facilitates project management. They key for success is to keep it current and to use it to hold team members accountable.

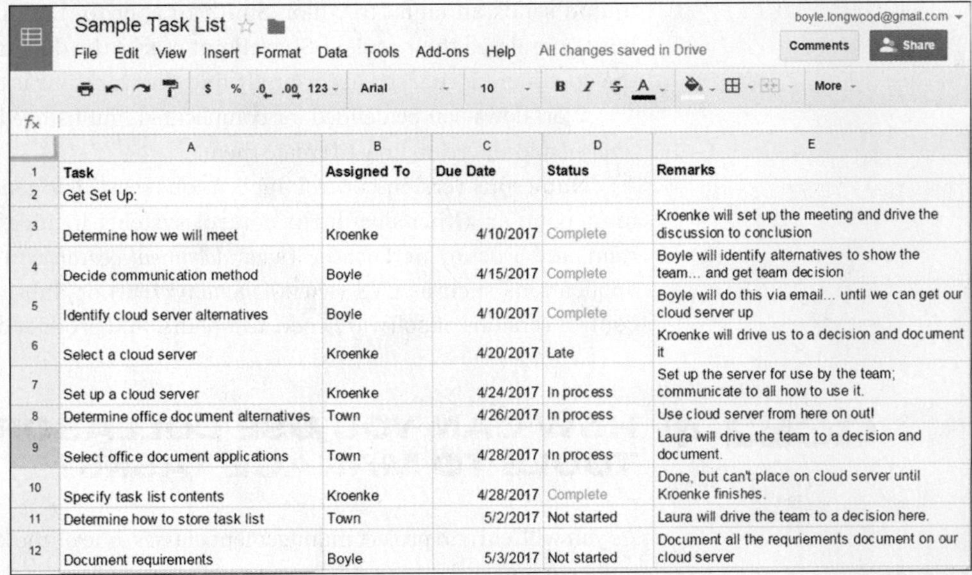

| | Task | Assigned To | Due Date | Status | Remarks |
|---|---|---|---|---|---|
| 1 | **Task** | **Assigned To** | **Due Date** | **Status** | **Remarks** |
| 2 | Get Set Up: | | | | |
| 3 | Determine how we will meet | Kroenke | 4/10/2017 | Complete | Kroenke will set up the meeting and drive the discussion to conclusion |
| 4 | Decide communication method | Boyle | 4/15/2017 | Complete | Boyle will identify alternatives to show the team... and get team decision |
| 5 | Identify cloud server alternatives | Boyle | 4/10/2017 | Complete | Boyle will do this via email... until we can get our cloud server up |
| 6 | Select a cloud server | Kroenke | 4/20/2017 | Late | Kroenke will drive us to a decision and document it |
| 7 | Set up a cloud server | Kroenke | 4/24/2017 | In process | Set up the server for use by the team; communicate to all how to use it. |
| 8 | Determine office document alternatives | Town | 4/26/2017 | In process | Use cloud server from here on out! |
| 9 | Select office document applications | Town | 4/28/2017 | In process | Laura will drive the team to a decision and document. |
| 10 | Specify task list contents | Kroenke | 4/28/2017 | Complete | Done, but can't place on cloud server until Kroenke finishes. |
| 11 | Determine how to store task list | Town | 5/2/2017 | Not started | Laura will drive the team to a decision here. |
| 12 | Document requirements | Boyle | 5/3/2017 | Not started | Document all the requriements document on our cloud server |

**Figure CE2-16**
Sample Task List

*Source:* Google Corporation

## SHARING A TASK LIST USING MICROSOFT SHAREPOINT

SharePoint includes a built-in content type for managing task lists that provides robust and powerful features. The standard task list can readily be modified to include user-customized columns and many different views can be constructed to show the list in different ways for different users. Like the rest of SharePoint, its task lists are industrial-strength.

Figure CE2-17 shows a task list that we used for the production of this text. The first three columns are built-in columns that SharePoint provides. The last column, labeled Book Title, is the book for which the task was assigned. "EMIS" stands for the book titled *Experiencing MIS*. When one of our team members opens this site, the view of the task list shown in Figure CE2-18 is displayed. The tasks in this view are sorted by Due Date value and are filtered on the value of Status so that any task that has been completed is not shown. Hence, this is a to-do list. Another view of this list, shown in Figure CE2-19, includes only those tasks in which Status equals Completed. That view is a "what we've done so far" list.

Alerts are one of the most useful features in SharePoint task lists. Using alerts, team members can request SharePoint to send emails when certain events occur. Our team sets alerts so that SharePoint sends a team member an email whenever a task is created that is assigned to him or

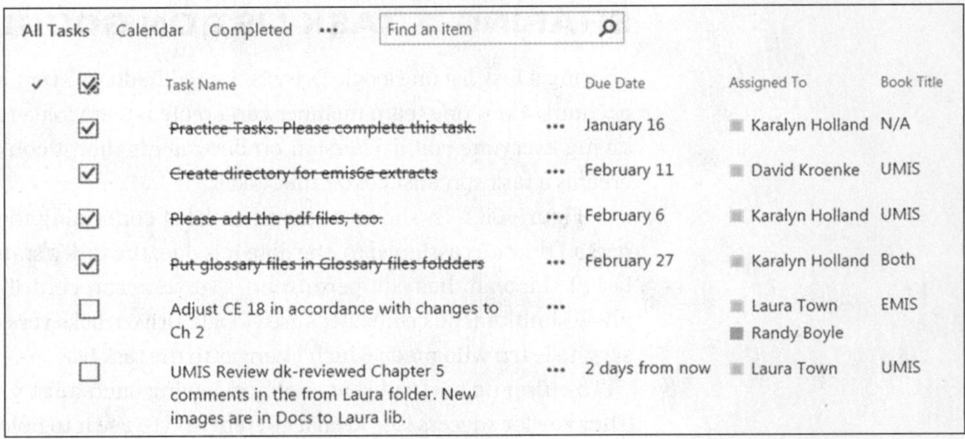


| | Task Name | Due Date | Assigned To | Book Title |
|---|---|---|---|---|
| ☑ | ~~Practice Tasks. Please complete this task.~~ | January 16 | Karalyn Holland | N/A |
| ☑ | ~~Create directory for emis6e extracts~~ | February 11 | David Kroenke | UMIS |
| ☑ | ~~Please add the pdf files, too.~~ | February 6 | Karalyn Holland | UMIS |
| ☑ | ~~Put glossary files in Glossary files foldders~~ | February 27 | Karalyn Holland | Both |
| ☐ | Adjust CE 18 in accordance with changes to Ch 2 | | Laura Town<br>Randy Boyle | EMIS |
| ☐ | UMIS Review dk-reviewed Chapter 5 comments in the from Laura folder. New images are in Docs to Laura lib. | 2 days from now | Laura Town | UMIS |

**Figure CE2-17**
Production Task List

*Source:* Microsoft Corporation

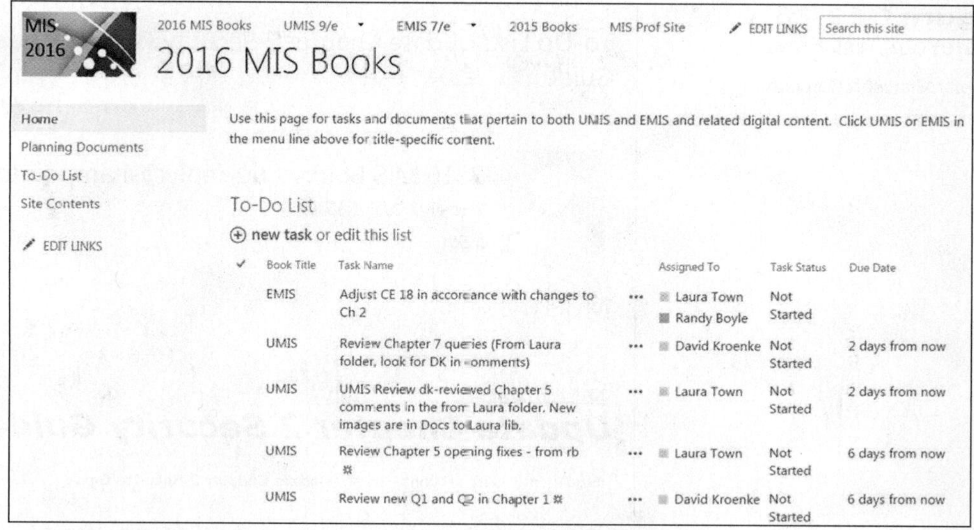


**Figure CE2-18**
To-Do List
*Source:* Microsoft Corporation

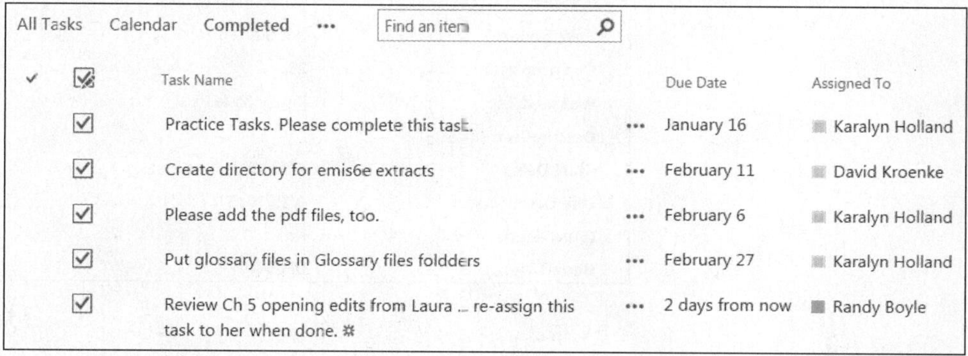


**Figure CE2-19**
What We've Done So Far
*Source:* Microsoft Corporation

her. Figure CE2-20 shows the email that SharePoint sent when Randy Boyle completed a task that had been created for him. Having SharePoint send such alerts means that no team member need continually check the task list for new tasks. They will receive an email when one is created.

SharePoint task lists provide features and functions that are far superior to the Google Drive spreadsheet shown in Figure CE2-16. Again, if you can obtain access to SharePoint, you should strongly consider using it, a possibility we address in the next question.

## QCE2-5 WHICH COLLABORATION INFORMATION SYSTEM IS RIGHT FOR YOUR TEAM?

So far, we have addressed the base requirements of a collaboration IS for a student team, and we've looked at a variety of collaboration tools that support communication, content sharing, and task management. What can you do with this knowledge? What system is right for you and your teams? In this question, we will define and set up your evaluation of three sets of collaboration tools. Figure CE2-21 summarizes three different sets of collaboration tools that you might use.

### THE MINIMAL COLLABORATION TOOL SET

The first, the Minimal set, is shown in the second column of Figure CE2-21. With this set, you will be able to collaborate with your team, though you will get little support from the software. In particular, you will need to manage concurrent access by setting up procedures and agreements

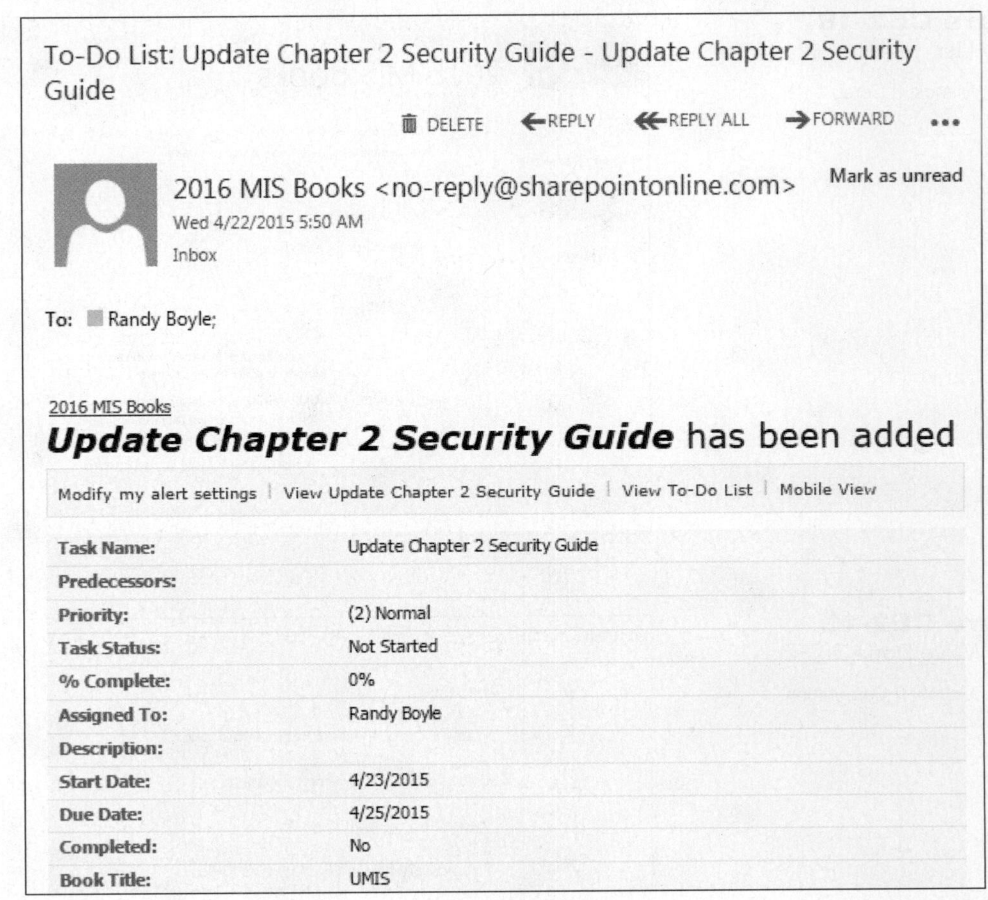
To-Do List: Update Chapter 2 Security Guide - Update Chapter 2 Security Guide

DELETE REPLY REPLY ALL FORWARD

2016 MIS Books <no-reply@sharepointonline.com> Mark as unread
Wed 4/22/2015 5:50 AM
Inbox

To: Randy Boyle;

2016 MIS Books
**Update Chapter 2 Security Guide** has been added

Modify my alert settings | View Update Chapter 2 Security Guide | View To-Do List | Mobile View

| | |
|---|---|
| **Task Name:** | Update Chapter 2 Security Guide |
| **Predecessors:** | |
| **Priority:** | (2) Normal |
| **Task Status:** | Not Started |
| **% Complete:** | 0% |
| **Assigned To:** | Randy Boyle |
| **Description:** | |
| **Start Date:** | 4/23/2015 |
| **Due Date:** | 4/25/2015 |
| **Completed:** | No |
| **Book Title:** | UMIS |

**Figure CE2-20**
SharePoint Task Email
*Source:* Microsoft Corporation

**Figure CE2-21**
Three Collaboration Tool Sets

### Three Collaboration Tool Sets

| | Minimal | Good | Comprehensive |
|---|---|---|---|
| Communication | Email; multiparty text chat | Google+ Hangouts | Microsoft Skype for Business |
| Content Sharing | Email or file server | Google Drive | SharePoint |
| Task Management | Word or Excel files | Google Spreadsheet | SharePoint lists integrated with email |
| Nice-to-Have Features | | Discussion boards, surveys, wikis, blogs, share pictures/videos from third-party tools | Built-in discussion boards, surveys, wikis, blogs, picture/video sharing |
| Cost | Free | Free | $8/month per user or Free |
| Ease of Use (time to learn) | None | 1 hour | 3 hours |
| Value to Future Business Professional | None | Limited | Great |
| Limitations | All text, no voice or video; no tool integration | Tools not integrated, must learn to use several products | Cost, learning curve required |

to ensure that one user's work doesn't conflict with another's. Your collaboration will be with text only; you will not have access to audio or video so you cannot hear or see your collaborators. You also will not be able to view documents or whiteboards during your meeting. This set is probably close to what you're already doing.

## THE GOOD COLLABORATION TOOL SET

The second set, the Good set, shown in the third column of Figure CE2-21, shows a more sophisticated set of collaboration tools. With it, you will have the ability to conduct multiparty audio and video virtual meetings, and you will also have support for concurrent access to document, spreadsheet, and presentation files. Without work on your part, however, you will not have any of the nice-to-have feature requirements discussed in QCE2-1. If you want any of them, you will need to search the Internet to find products that support surveys, wikis, and blogs and share pictures and videos.

## THE COMPREHENSIVE COLLABORATION TOOL SET

The third set of collaboration tools, the Comprehensive set, is shown in the last column of Figure CE2-21. You can obtain this tool set with Office 365 Professional. However, Microsoft continually revises the versions and what's included in them, so you'll need to investigate which version provides the features of the comprehensive tool set. Look for a version (perhaps a free trial) that includes all the products shown in Figure CE2-22. If your school has adopted Office 365 for Education, then you should be able to obtain these features for free.

This set is the best of these three because it includes content management and control, workflow control, and online meetings in which participants can view shared whiteboards, applications, and monitors. Furthermore, this set is integrated; SharePoint alerts can send emails via the Microsoft email server Exchange when tasks or other lists and libraries change. You can click on users' names in emails or in SharePoint, and Office 365 will automatically start a Skype for Business text, audio, or video conversation with that user if he or she is currently available. All text messages you send via Skype for Business are automatically recorded and stored in your email folder.

## CHOOSING THE SET FOR YOUR TEAM

Which set should you choose for your team? Unless your university has already implemented Office 365 Education university-wide, you will have to pay for it. You can obtain a 30-day free trial

**Figure CE2-22**
Office 365 Features You Need for the Comprehensive Tool Set

| Component | Features |
|---|---|
| Skype for Business | Multiparty text chat<br>Audio- and videoconferencing<br>Online content sharing<br>Webinars with PowerPoint |
| SharePoint Online | Content management and control using libraries and lists<br>Discussion forums<br>Surveys<br>Wikis<br>Blogs |
| Exchange | Email integrated with Skype for Business and SharePoint Online |
| Office 2013 | Concurrent editing for Word, Excel, PowerPoint, and OneNote |
| Hosted integration | Infrastructure built, managed, and operated by Microsoft |

**Figure CE2-23**
Product Power Curve

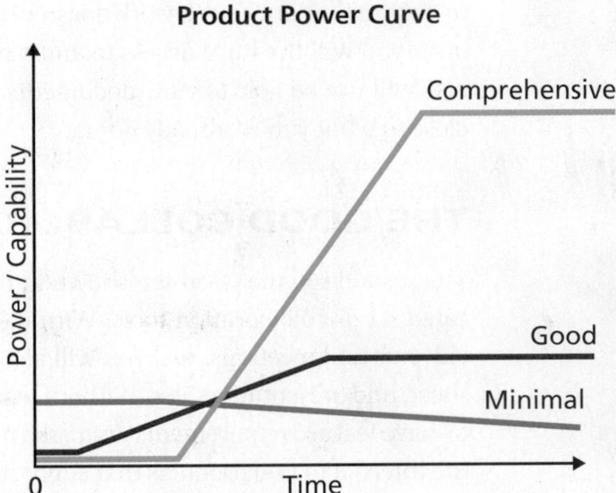


of Office 365 Professional, and if your team can finish its work in that amount of time, you might choose to do so. Otherwise, your team will need to pay a minimum of $8 per month per user. So, if cost is the only factor, you can rule out the comprehensive tool set.

But even if you can afford the most comprehensive, you may not want to use it. As noted in Figure CE2-21, team members need to be willing to invest something on the order of 3 hours to begin to use the basic features. Less time, on the order of an hour, will be required to learn to use the Good tool set, and you most likely already know how to use the Minimal set.

When evaluating learning time consider Figure CE2-23. This diagram is a product **power curve**, which is a graph that shows the relationship of the **power** (the utility that one gains from a software product) as a function of the time using that product. A flat line means you are investing time without any increase in power. The ideal power curve starts at a positive value at time zero and has no flat spots.

The Minimal product set gives you some power at time zero because you already know how to use it. However, as you use it over time, your project will gain complexity, and the problems of controlling concurrent access will actually cause power to decrease. The Good set has a short flat spot as you get to know it. However, your power then increases over time until you reach the most capability your team can do with it. The Comprehensive set has a longer flat spot in the beginning because it will take longer to learn. However, because it has such a rich collaboration feature set, you will be able to gain considerable collaborative power, much more so than the Good set, and the maximum capability is much greater than the Good set.

Finally, consider the next-to-last row in Figure CE2-21. The Minimal set has no value to you as a future professional and contributes nothing to your professional competitive advantage. The Good set has some limited value; there are organizations that use Google Drive and Hangouts. The Comprehensive set has the potential to give you a considerable competitive advantage, particularly because SharePoint skills are highly valued in industry. You can use knowledge of it to demonstrate the currency of your knowledge in job interviews.

So, which is the right set for your team? It's up to you. See Exercise CE2-3 on page 399.

## DON'T FORGET PROCEDURES AND PEOPLE!

One last and very important point: Most of this chapter extension focuses on collaboration tools, the software component of an information system. Regarding the other four components, you need not worry about hardware, at least not for the Good or Comprehensive sets since those tools are hosted on hardware in the cloud. The data component is up to you; it will be your content as well as your metadata for project management and for demonstrating that your team practiced iteration and feedback.

As you evaluate alternatives, however, you need to think seriously about the procedure and people components. How are team members going to use these tools? Your team needs to have agreement on tools usage, even if you do not formally document procedures. As noted, such procedures are especially necessary for controlling concurrent access in the Minimal system. You need to have agreement not only on how to use these tools, but also on what happens when teammates don't use these tools. What will you do, for example, if teammates persist in emailing documents instead of using Google Drive or SharePoint?

Additionally, how will your team train its members in the use of these tools? Will you divvy up responsibility for learning features and then teach the skills to one another? You will find a plethora of training materials on the Web.[3] But who will find them, learn them, and then teach the others?

Finally, does your team need to create any special jobs or roles? Do you want to identify, for example, someone to monitor your shared documents to ensure that deliverables are stored appropriately? Do you want someone identified to store minutes of meetings? Or to remove completed tasks from a task list? Or to keep the task list in agreement with current planning? Consider these and similar needs and, if needed, appoint such a person before problems develop.

Remember this example as a future business professional: In commerce and government, we are never selecting just software; to put that software to use as a system, we need to create all five of the IS components!

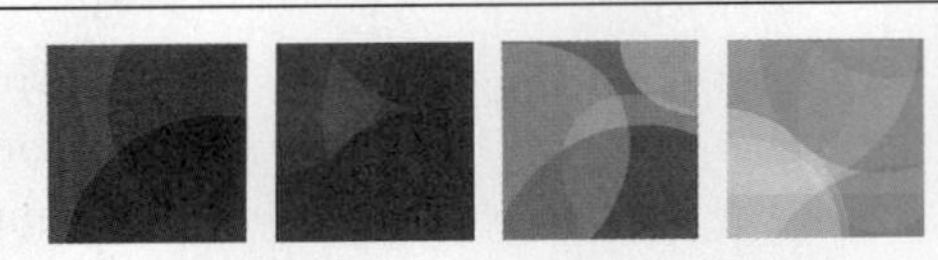

# ACTIVE REVIEW

Use this Active Review to verify that you understand the ideas and concepts that answer this chapter extension's study questions.

## QCE2-1 WHAT ARE THE IS REQUIREMENTS FOR STUDENT PROJECT COLLABORATIONS?

Summarize why you should learn about collaboration IS for today as well as later. Name the three categories of requirements discussed in this chapter extension. Name and describe the three required features. Summarize the other two sets of features.

## QCE2-2 HOW CAN YOU USE COLLABORATION TOOLS TO IMPROVE TEAM COMMUNICATION?

Explain why communication is important to collaboration. Define *synchronous* and *asynchronous communication* and explain when each is used. Name two collaboration tools that can be used to help set up synchronous meetings. Describe collaboration tools that can be used for face-to-face meetings. Describe tools that can be used for virtual, synchronous meetings. Describe tools that can be used for virtual, asynchronous meetings.

## QCE2-3 HOW CAN YOU USE COLLABORATION TOOLS TO SHARE CONTENT?

Summarize alternatives for processing Office documents on the desktop as well as over the Internet. Describe two ways that content is shared with no control and explain the problems that can occur. Explain the difference between version management and version control. Describe how user accounts, passwords, and libraries are used to control user activity. Explain how check in/check out works. Describe workflows and give an example.

## QCE2-4 HOW CAN YOU USE COLLABORATION TOOLS TO MANAGE TASKS?

Explain why managing tasks is important to team progress. Specify how a task should be described. List the minimal content of a task list. Summarize the advantages and disadvantages of using Google Docs and Microsoft SharePoint for managing tasks.

## QCE2-5 WHICH COLLABORATION INFORMATION SYSTEM IS RIGHT FOR YOUR TEAM?

Describe the three collaboration tool sets and indicate how each meets the minimum requirements for collaboration. Explain the differences among them. Summarize the criteria for choosing the right set for your team. Explain the meaning of the power curve and discuss the power curve for each of the three alternatives described.

# KEY TERMS AND CONCEPTS

Asynchronous communication 382
Discussion forums 383
Email 383
File server 386
Google Docs 385
Google Drive 386
Libraries 389
Microsoft Office Online 385
OneDrive 387
Power 396
Power curve 396
Screen-sharing applications 382
Synchronous communication 382
Team surveys 383
Version control 388
Version management 386
Videoconferencing 382
Virtual meetings 382
Webinar 382
Workflow control 390

MyMISLab™

To complete the problems with the ✪, go to EOC Discussion Questions in the MyLab.

## USING YOUR KNOWLEDGE

✪ **CE2-1.** Evaluate QCE2-1. Based on your experience as a team member, do you agree that the three requirements are mandatory for a collaborative team? Justify your answer. Modify those requirements in any way you see fit to better describe your own collaborative team experience. Do you find any of the nice-to-have requirements unnecessary? Would you add any others? Do you think any of the collaboration tool characteristics requirements are unnecessary? Would you add any?

✪ **CE2-2.** Based on your answers to question CE2-1, revise the student-project collaboration IS requirements list in QCE2-1 so that it is appropriate for your team experience. Discuss your revised list with others and describe any changes they would make to it.

✪ **CE2-3.** Choose one of the three alternatives described in QCE2-5 for use by your collaborative team. To do so, answer the following questions (if possible, answer these questions with your team):

**a.** Using your and your teammates' answers to question CE2-2, create your team's list of requirements.

**b.** Create a list of criteria for selecting collaboration tools and creating a collaboration IS. Start with the "minimal" list of items in the collaboration tool sets table in QCE2-5, but add, modify, or delete items depending on your answer to part a.

**c.** Score the three alternatives in QCE2-5 against your requirements and your criteria. If you wish, change any of the elements of those three alternatives to create a fourth alternative. Score it as well.

**d.** Based on your answer to part c, select a collaboration tool set. Explain your selection.

**e.** Given your answer to part d, how will you construct your collaboration IS? Specifically, what procedures will you need to develop and how will your team members obtain training? Will you need to have any special jobs or roles for your team members? If so, describe them.

MyMISLab™

Go to the Assignments section of your MyLab to complete these writing exercises.

**CE2-4.** Suppose you've just been assigned a large semester-long group project. You're given a business case about investing in a tech startup company. You're told your deliverables will include a custom database for the company, several spreadsheets of financial analyses, presentation slides, and a 20-page final report with supporting analysis.

**a.** Describe how the required features of a collaborative information system would help your group produce better deliverables.

**b.** Not all features of a collaborative system are useful for every project. Explain which of the nice-to-have features discussed in QCE2-1 would not be useful for this type of project.

**c.** Which collaboration tools would you use for synchronous and asynchronous communication within your group? Describe a situation in which you'd use each of these tools.

**CE2-5.** Suppose you are consulting for a large law firm that is having issues with sharing documents. Some of the younger lawyers are used to using online services like Google Drive, Dropbox, or OneDrive. The whole firm recently started using an internal file server. But management of the server has been time consuming and increasingly complex. Senior partners want more control over their files, yet realize it's important to give their employees flexible and powerful tools.

**a.** Write a proposal to the senior partners describing document sharing alternatives that would provide them with version management and version control.

**b.** Describe the added capabilities of version control over version management and why these capabilities might be important to the firm.

**c.** Based on the discussion in QCE2-5, explain which collaboration tool set (minimal, good, or comprehensive) might be the best fit for the firm.

## ENDNOTES

1. Warning: The data in this figure is changing rapidly. The features and functions of both Web applications and cloud drives may have been extended from what is described here. Check the vendor's documentation for new capabilities.
2. Carey Cole, Steve Fox, and David Kroenke, *SharePoint for Students* (Upper Saddle River, NJ: Pearson Education, 2012), pp. 116–129.
3. See also David Kroenke and Donald Nilson, *Office 365 in Business* (Indianapolis, IN: John Wiley, 2011).

chapter extension **3**

**Chapter 4** provides the background for this extension.

# Mobile Systems

**STUDY QUESTIONS**

**QCE3-1** WHAT ARE MOBILE SYSTEMS?

**QCE3-2** WHY ARE MOBILE SYSTEMS IMPORTANT?

**QCE3-3** HOW DO NATIVE AND WEB-BASED MOBILE APPLICATIONS COMPARE?

**QCE3-4** WHAT CHARACTERIZES QUALITY MOBILE USER EXPERIENCES?

**QCE3-5** WHAT ARE THE CHALLENGES OF PERSONAL MOBILE DEVICES AT WORK?

## QCE3-1 WHAT ARE MOBILE SYSTEMS?

**Mobile systems** are information systems that support users in motion. Mobile systems users access the system from *any place*—at home, at work, in the car, on the bus, or at the beach—using any smart device, such as a smartphone, tablet, or PC. The possibilities are endless.

Mobile systems users not only move geographically, they also move from device to device. The user who starts reading a book on an iPad on a bus, continues reading that book on a PC at work, and finishes it on a Kindle Fire at home is mobile both geographically and across devices.

As shown in Figure CE3-1, the major elements in a mobile system are *users in motion, mobile devices, wireless connectivity,* and *cloud-based resources*. A **mobile device** is a small, lightweight, power-conserving computing device that is capable of wireless connectivity. Almost all mobile devices have a display and some means for data entry. Mobile devices include smartphones, tablets, smartwatches, and small, light laptops. Desktop computers, Xboxes, and large, heavy, power-hungry laptops are not mobile devices.

You will learn about the cloud in Chapter 6. For now, just assume that the cloud is a group of servers on the other end of a connection with a mobile device. When downloading a book for a Kindle, for example, the cloud is one or more servers on the other end that store that book and download a copy of it to your device.

## QCE3-2 WHY ARE MOBILE SYSTEMS IMPORTANT?

The major reason for the importance of mobile systems is the size of their market. According to Cisco, at the end of 2014 there were 7.4 billion mobile devices generating 2.5 exabytes of traffic per month.[1] By 2019, this will jump to 11.5 billion mobile devices generating more than 24.3 exabytes per month. That's 1.5 devices for every person on the planet. Smartphones will account for nearly 75 percent of global mobile traffic.[2]

It took 7 years after the launch of the first iPhone (2007–2014) for smartphones to achieve mainstream use by 70 percent of the U.S. market.[3] That's faster than any other technology except television in the early 1950s, which tied the smartphone adoption rate.[4] The February 2015 comScore Report shows 182 million people in the United States owned smartphones, which accounted for 74.9 percent of the mobile phone market.[5] The size of the mobile e-commerce, or **m-commerce**, market is expected to exceed $113 billion by 2017.[6]

Additionally, mobile use is favored by the young. According to Nielsen's measures of mobile device use, the younger the age group, the greater the percentage of people with mobile devices. Further, younger people have more devices per capita than older groups.[7] These young cohorts will further increase mobile systems use in the years to come.

Because of this vast and growing market, mobile systems are having a major impact on business and society today—impact that is forcing industry change while creating new career

**Figure CE3-1**
Elements of a Mobile Information System

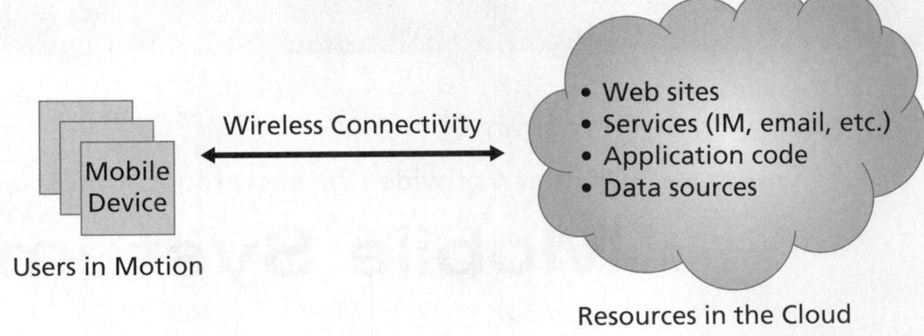


opportunities for mobile-IS-savvy professionals as well as large numbers of new, interesting mobile-IS-related jobs.

Figure CE3-2 summarizes the mobile-system impact for each of the five components of an information system. We will discuss each of the components in this figure, starting with hardware.

## HARDWARE

Clearly, increasing demand for mobile systems means the sales of many more mobile devices, often at the expense of PC sales. Hewlett-Packard, a large PC manufacturer, learned this fact when it didn't respond quickly enough to the onslaught of mobile devices and was forced to eliminate 27,000 jobs in 2012. In the future, there will be high demand for innovative mobile devices as well as cheap copycats.

If you're reading this book, you're unlikely to be a hardware engineer, and if you're not living in Asia, you're also unlikely to be involved in hardware manufacturing. However, any market having 3.9 billion prospects is ripe with opportunities in marketing, sales, logistics, customer support, and related activities.

## SOFTWARE

The reduced size of mobile devices requires the invention of new, innovative interfaces, as we will discuss in QCE3-4. The mobile user is an active user and expects an active screen experience.

**Figure CE3-2**
Five Components of Mobile Change and Opportunity

| | Hardware | Software | Data | Procedures | People |
|---|---|---|---|---|---|
| Impact of mobile systems growth | Many, many more mobile devices will be sold. | Compact interfaces; new technology for active users; application scaling. | More data, but more information? Less device real estate means fewer ads possible. | Always on, always at work. Employee lifestyle becomes hybrid of personal and professional. | Ability to thrive in a dynamic environment more important. |
| Industry changes | PCs less important; high demand (and requirement) for innovative devices as well as cheap copycats. | html5, css3, and JavaScript increase capability of web apps. | Loss of control. Less room for advertisement. | Personal mobile devices at work policy. | More part-time employees and independent contractors. |
| Career opportunities | Jobs for mobile device sales, marketing, support. | New technology levels the playing field for html5, graphics skills. Business expertise needed for mobile requirements. New companies! | Reporting, data mining even more important. Design of effective mobile reports. | Innovative use of just-in-time data. Need for adjusting business processes gives another premium to nonroutine problem solvers. | Independent contractors (and some employees) work where and when they want. What is this new social organism? |

The premium will be for moving graphics, changing Web pages, and animation. Applications will need to scale from the very smallest to the very largest, while providing a user experience appropriate to the device's size.

Rapid technology change in mobile software continually levels the playing field. Today, for example, expert programmers in Objective-C better not relax. html5 and css3 are gaining popularity, and they will reduce the need for Objective-C expertise. Further, while languages like Objective-C are difficult and time-consuming to learn, html5, css3, and JavaScript are less so. With the reduced barrier to entry, hordes of less-experienced and less-educated new entrants will appear as competitors. You might be one of them.

Additionally, continually evolving software means new and exciting entrepreneurial opportunities. Are you sorry that you missed the early days working at Facebook? Right now, somewhere, there is another Mark Zuckerberg starting...well, what? Because of the continually changing software environment, new opportunities abound and will continue to do so for decades.

## DATA

Many more mobile systems mean an incredible amount of new data, data that professionals can use to create much more information. But, as you learned in Chapter 2, more data doesn't necessarily mean more information. In fact, many business professionals believe they're drowning in data while starving for information. What can be done with all of this mobile-systems data to enable humans to conceive information of greater value to them? Data mining and better reporting are possibilities for you that are discussed in Chapter 9 and Chapter Extensions 12 and 13.

On the other hand, not all the news is good, at least not for many organizations. For one, smaller screens mean less room for advertising, a factor that limited the success of the Facebook public offering in May 2012. Also, mobile systems increase the risk of organizations losing control over their data. In the past, employees used only computer equipment provided by the employer and connected only via employer-managed networks. In that situation, it is possible for the organization to control who does what with which data and where. No longer. Employees come to work with their own mobile devices. Data leakage is inevitable.

With more people switching to mobile devices and with less room for ads, online advertising revenue may be sharply reduced, possibly endangering the revenue model that supports most of the Web's free content. If this happens, dramatic change is just around the corner!

## PROCEDURES

Mobile systems are always on. They have no business hours. And people who use mobile systems are equally always on. In the mobile world, we're always open for business. It is impossible to be out of the office. One consequence of always-on is the blending of our personal and professional lives. Such blending means, in part, that business will intrude on your personal life, and your personal life will intrude on your business. This intrusion can be distracting and stressful; on the other hand, it can lead to richer, more complex relationships.

Employees will expect to use their mobile devices at work, but should they? In truth, who can keep them from it? If the organization blocks them from connecting to the work-related networks, they can connect over the wireless networks that they pay for themselves. In this case, the organization is entirely out of the loop. Could employees send confidential corporate information through their personal mobile devices? We will discuss these issues in more detail in QCE3-5.

Mobile systems offer the potential of **just-in-time data**, which is data delivered to the user at the precise time it is needed. A pharmaceutical salesperson uses just-in-time data when she accesses a mobile system to obtain the latest literature on a new drug while waiting for the doctor to whom she will pitch it. She needn't remember the drug's characteristics any longer than it takes her to walk down the hallway and make the sale.

Furthermore, some organizations will passively wait for change to happen, while others will proactively reengineer their processes to incorporate mobile systems for higher process quality. Either way, the need for business process change creates opportunity for creative, nonroutine business problem solvers.

## PEOPLE

Mobile systems change the value of our thinking. For example, just-in-time data removes the premium on the ability to memorize vast quantities of product data, but creates a premium for the ability to access, query, and present that data. Mobile systems increase the speed of business, giving an advantage to those who can nimbly respond to changing conditions and succeed with the unexpected.

With the ability to be connected and always on, organizations may find they can be just as effective with part-time employees and independent contractors. The increasing regulatory complexity and cost of full-time employees will create an incentive for organizations to do just that.

As that occurs, professionals who can thrive in a dynamic environment with little need for direct supervision will find that they can work both where and when they want, at least a good part of the time. Once you're always on and remote, it doesn't matter if you're always on in New Jersey or at a ski area in Vermont. New lifestyle choices become possible for such workers.

These mobile workers can work where they want and for whom they want. There won't be a boss looking over their shoulder. They can work multiple jobs with different companies at the same time! Companies may have to change the way they pay workers. Instead of paying employees by the hour, they would need to focus more on paying for productivity. This shift toward focusing on performance will empower great employees and make it harder for slackers to hide out in an organization. Companies will benefit from mobile workers too. They won't need as much expensive commercial office space. What an incredible time to be starting a business career!

# QCE3-3 HOW DO NATIVE AND WEB-BASED MOBILE APPLICATIONS COMPARE?

There are two primary ways for developing mobile applications. On the one hand, organizations can develop a *native application* (native app), which is a thick-client application designed to work with a particular operating system. It is sometimes even designed to work only with a particular mobile device that runs that operating system. On the other hand, they can develop a *Web application* (Web app) that runs within a browser. In this case, the browser provides a more or less consistent environment for the application. The peculiarities of operating systems and hardware are handled by the browser's code and hidden from the Web application.

Figure CE3-3 contrasts native and Web mobile applications on their important characteristics. Consider the native application column first.

## DEVELOPING NATIVE MOBILE APPLICATIONS

Native mobile applications are developed using serious, heavy-duty, professional programming languages. Mac OS and iOS applications are constructed using Objective-C or the **Swift** programming language. Linux (Android) applications are constructed using Java, and Windows applications are constructed using C#, VB.NET, C++, and others. All of these languages are **object-oriented**, which means they can be used to create difficult, complex

**Figure CE3-3**
Characteristics of Native and Web Applications

| | Native Applications | Web Applications |
|---|---|---|
| Development languages | Objective-C<br>Java<br>C#, C++, VB.NET, Swift<br>(object-oriented languages) | html5<br>css3<br>JavaScript<br>(scripting language) |
| Developed by | Professional programmers, only | Professional programmers and technically oriented Web developers and business professionals |
| Skill level required | High | Low to high |
| Difficulty | High | Easy to hard, depending on application requirements |
| Developer's degree | Computer science | Computer science<br>Information systems<br>Graphics design |
| User experience | Can be superb, depending on programming quality | Simple to sophisticated, depending on program quality |
| Possible applications | Whatever you can pay for... | Some limits prohibit very sophisticated applications |
| Dependency | iOS, Android, Windows | Browser differences, only |
| Cost | High. Difficult work by highly paid employees, multiple versions required. | Low to high ... easier work by lesser-paid employees, only multiple browser files necessary. Sophisticated applications may require high skill and pay. |
| Application distribution | Via application stores (e.g., Apple Store) | Via Web sites |
| Example | Vanguard iPad application (free in Apple's iTunes store) | Seafood Web site: *www.wildrhodyseafood.com*<br>Picozu editor: *www.picozu.com/editor* |

applications and, if used properly, will result in high-performance code that is easy to alter when requirements change. The particular characteristics of object-oriented languages are beyond the scope of this text.

Object-oriented languages can be used only by professional programmers who have devoted years to learning object-oriented design and coding skills. Typically such developers were computer science majors in college.

The benefit of such languages is that they give programmers close control over the assets of the computing device and enable the creation of sophisticated and complex user interfaces. If the programs are well written, they perform fast and use memory efficiently. The limits on native applications are usually budgetary, not technological. As a businessperson, you can get just about any application you can afford.

The downside of native applications is that they are, well, native. They only run on the operating system for which they are programmed. An iOS mobile application must be completely recoded in order to run on Android and recoded again to run on Windows.[8] Thus, to reach all mobile users, an organization will need to support and maintain three separate versions of the same application. It will also have to staff and manage three different development teams with three different skill sets.

As a general rule, the cost of native applications is high. Many organizations reduce that cost by outsourcing development to India and other countries (see the introduction to Chapter 11), but native applications are still expensive relative to Web applications. The standard way for distributing native applications is via a company store, such as iTunes, owned by Apple. An excellent example of a native application is Vanguard's iPad application. It is easy to use, has complex functionality, and is highly secure, as you would expect. Companies such as Vanguard must and can afford to pay for exceedingly high-quality applications.

## DEVELOPING WEB MOBILE APPLICATIONS

The third column in Figure CE3-3 summarizes Web application characteristics. Such applications run inside a browser such as Firefox, Chrome, Opera, or Edge. The browser handles the idiosyncrasies of the operating system and underlying hardware. In theory, an organization should be able to develop a single application and have it run flawlessly on all browsers on all mobile devices. Unfortunately, there are some differences in the way that browsers implement the Web code. This means that some applications won't run correctly in some browsers.

As shown in the first row of Figure CE3-3, Web development languages are html5, css3, and JavaScript. html5 is the latest version of html. The advantages of this version are the support for graphics, animation, 2D animations, and other sophisticated user experiences. css3 is used with html5 to specify the appearance of content coded in html. JavaScript is a programming language that is much easier to learn than native-client languages. It is used to provide the underlying logic of the application.

Web applications can be written by professional programmers, and, indeed, most are. However, it is possible for technically oriented Web developers and business professionals to develop them as well. The entry-level technical skill level required is low, and simple applications are relatively easy to develop. But sophisticated user experiences are difficult. Web application developers may have degrees in computer science, information systems, or graphic design.

The user experience provided by a Web application varies considerably. Some are simply fancy Web-based brochures (*www.wildrhodyseafood.com*); others are quite sophisticated, such as SpiroCanvas in Figure CE3-4 (*www.GetHuGames.in/*) or, even more impressive, *www.biodigital.com* in Figure CE3-5.

Web applications are limited by the capabilities of the browser. While browsers are becoming increasingly sophisticated, they cannot offer the full capabilities of the underlying operating system and hardware. Thus, Web applications are unable to support very specialized and complex applications, though this becomes less true each year.

**Figure CE3-4**
GetHuGames SpiroCanvas

*Source: www.gethugames.in/spirocanvas/.* Reprinted by permission.

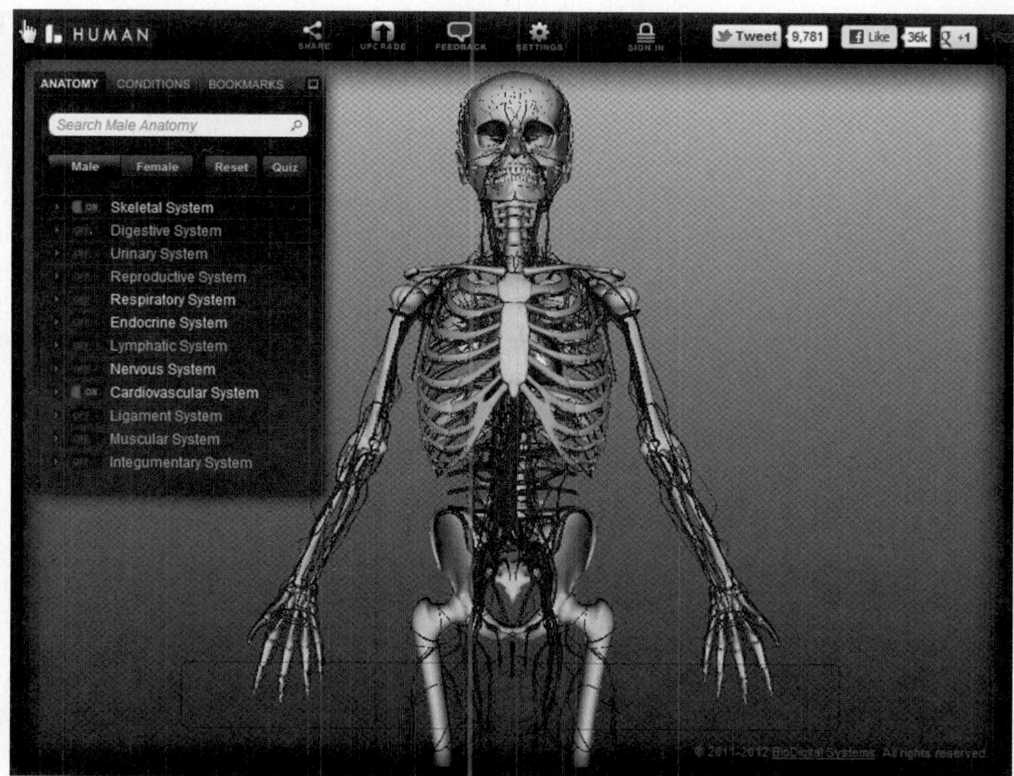


**Figure CE3-5**
Sophisticated html5 Application

*Source:* Image created using the BioDigital Human (*www.biodigitalhuman.com*).

As stated, the major advantage of Web over native applications is that they will run on any operating system and mobile device. There are some browser differences, but these differences are very minor when compared with the differences between iOS, Android, and Windows. In general, unlike native applications, you can assume that a Web application has one code base and one development team.

Because Web applications can be developed by less-skilled, lesser-paid employees and because only one code base and one development team are necessary, they are considerably cheaper to develop than native applications. However, this statement assumes applications of equivalent complexity. A simple native application can be cheaper to develop than a complex Web application.

Users obtain Web applications via the Web. When you go to *www.picozu.com/editor*, the required html5, css3, and JavaScript files are downloaded automatically over the Web. Updates to the application are automatic and seamless. You need not install (or reinstall) anything. This difference is an advantage to the user; it makes it more difficult, however, to earn money from your application. Amazon, for example, will sell your native application and pay you a royalty. However, unless you require users to buy your Web application (which is possible, but rare), you'll have to give it away.

## WHICH IS BETTER?

You know the answer to that question. If it were clear-cut, we'd only be discussing one alternative. It's not. The choice depends on your strategy, your particular goals, the requirements for your application, your budget, your schedule, your tolerance for managing technical projects, your need for application revenue, and other factors. In general, Web native applications are cheaper to develop and maintain, but they may lack the wow factor. You and your organization have to decide for yourselves!

# QCE3-4 WHAT CHARACTERIZES QUALITY MOBILE USER EXPERIENCES?

A **user interface (UI)** is the presentation format of an application. It consists of windows, menus, icons, dialog boxes, toolbars, and so on, as well as user content. A **user experience (UX)** is a newer term that refers not only to the UI, but also to the way that the application affects the user's emotions and motivation to continue to use the interface.

Apple redefined the UX for mobile applications when it introduced the iPhone with touch, gravity-sensing portrait/landscape orientation, and other innovative UX behavior. Since then Microsoft has defined its modern-style application that builds and (possibly) improves upon Apple's UX. Figure CE3-6 lists the primary characteristics of a quality mobile application.[9] Consider each.

## FEATURE CONTENT

First, quality mobile user interfaces should place the primary emphasis on users' content, giving such content as much of the display as possible. Rather than show menus, toolbars, and heavy window borders, the content should be shown cleanly and in center stage. **Chrome** is a term that refers to the visual overhead in a computer display. It is the windows, the menus, and other apparatus that drive the application. Because mobile screen size is often limited, modern mobile applications eliminate it as much as possible. (By the way, do not confuse this use of *chrome* with Google Chrome, the popular browser.)

Figure CE3-7 shows a portion of the chrome-less Start screen on a Windows Surface Pro device. The user doesn't need a toolbar (chrome) for starting a program; the user intuitively knows to click the image to start the application.

Using content to drive application behavior is called **direct interaction**. For another example, when you see blue, underlined type, you know to tap on it to navigate to that Web site. Similarly, if users want to highlight a word, they know to touch it to see what will happen.

## USE CONTEXT-SENSITIVE CHROME

Designing for direct action reduces the need for chrome, but not entirely. In an online store application, once you select the application, say, a game, you'll need controls to play it. For such cases, mobile applications do provide chrome, but it is **context-sensitive chrome**, meaning it pops up in the display when appropriate. Ideally, no button or command name is ever shown in a disabled (grayed-out) state. Instead, if it's disabled, the application doesn't show it, thus simplifying the UI and reserving more of the display for the users' content.

## PROVIDE ANIMATION AND LIVELY BEHAVIOR

Great mobile applications are lively. They capture your attention with motion and sound. If you are not doing something, they are. For example, an icon to play a movie has the movie's preview playing inside it. An unused game displays a sample game underway. When you do act, something happens immediately. The touched word or image changes color, pops up, or does something to give you active feedback that the application is alive and running.

**Figure CE3-6**
Characteristics of a Quality Mobile UX

- Feature content and support direct interaction
- Use context-sensitive chrome when needed
- Provide animation and lively behavior
- Design to scale and share (display and data)
- Use the cloud

**Figure CE3-7**
Chrome-less Interface

*Source:* © Microsoft Corporation.

All of this is easy to comprehend for games and entertainment applications. How these ideas pertain to commercial applications is on the leading edge of commercial UX design. Everyone wants activity, but when you access your mobile Vanguard application, do you really want to watch the application shrink if your portfolio value has diminished? Or watch it crash to the bottom of your display if the market is down substantially? Or hear *Money, Money, Money* every time the market is up? Probably not. Also, rapidly changing screen icons are hard to ignore and therefore are often annoying. What is appropriate is being determined today; there is a lot of opportunity for techno-savvy, marketing-oriented, graphics designers here.

## DESIGN TO SCALE AND SHARE

Mobile applications appear on phones, tablets, PCs, and even large displays. Applications must be designed so that they can scale up and down without appearing awkward or taking over the device. Note the slightly different appearances of the application in the displays in Figure CE3-8.

Modern operating systems (native applications) and browsers (Web applications) are designed to support such scaling. Microsoft Edge, for example, allows applications to provide three sizes and versions of graphics; Edge will choose the version that is appropriate for the size of the device on which it is running.

Mobile applications share their device with other mobile applications. They need to be designed to share the display effectively; applications that aggressively take over the screen are unappreciated by users and other application developers.

Mobile applications also need to be designed to share data. For example, Windows 8 introduced a feature called **charms**, which are icons that slide in from the right of the display. One of the default charms is Share, and it is used to share data from one mobile application to another. In Windows 10, the Share option is located in the menu for each modern Windows app. Microsoft Edge allows Web pages to share thumbnails, descriptions, and links with other applications. If a user wants to email a page, Edge will provide the shared thumbnail, description, and link to the mail application, as shown in Figure CE3-9.

Understand the power of this functionality; the Web application in the Web page has declared the data it will share; here it has provided the thumbnail picture, the description, and the link, as

**Figure CE3-8**
Example of Application Scaling

*Source:* Oleksiy Mark/Fotolia

shown in the right-hand side of Figure CE3-9. Any program can receive that data. The Web page programmer has no idea where that data may go or be displayed. It could be emailed, as shown here, but it could equally go to a graphics application, or a travel planning application, or a social networking application, or an event planning application, and so on.

This example focuses on Windows 10 and Microsoft Edge, but the concepts pertain equally to iOS, Android, and other browsers as well.

## USE THE CLOUD

Figure CE3-10 lists the primary cloud assets that mobile applications use. Web sites and services like IM and email are obvious. Less obvious are the use of services such as Fulfillment by Amazon. By using that service, the developers of the mobile application can harness the power of Amazon's inventory and process management software with very little development work on their own.

Another use of the cloud is to extend the application itself. Mobile devices are frequently (almost always?) running on battery power, and minimizing power use is important. Consequently,

**Figure CE3-9**
Example of Microsoft Edge Charm Sharing

*Source:* Microsoft Corporation: *blogs.msdn.com/b/b8/archive/2012/03/13/web-browsing-in-windows-8-consumer-preview-with-ie10.aspx.*

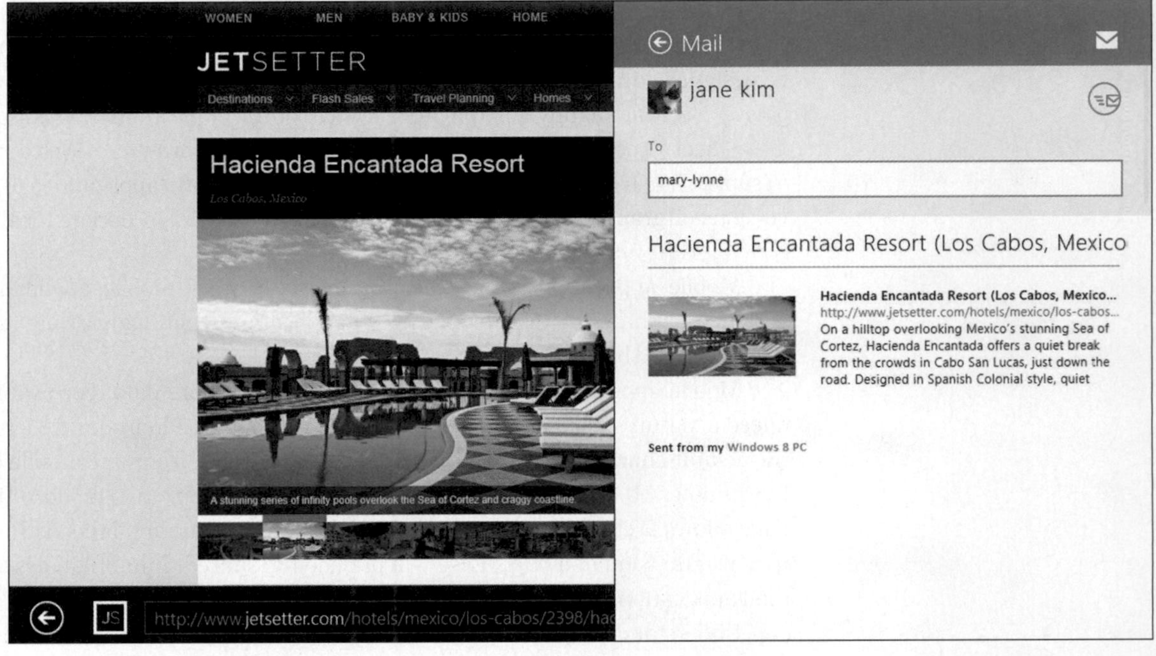

**Figure CE3-10**
Mobile Systems Cloud Use

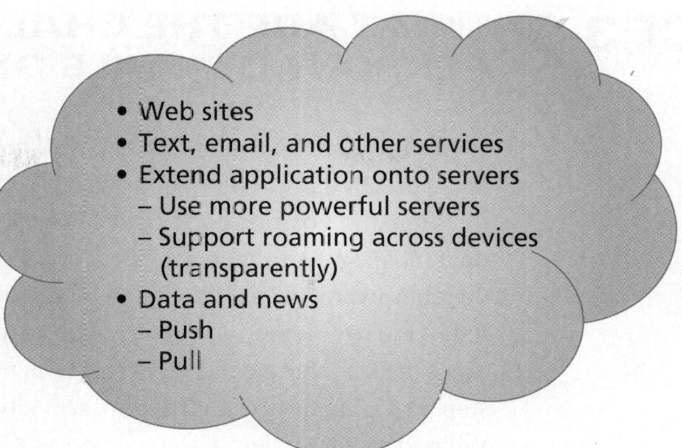


some applications move complex code that requires substantial processing onto powered and powerful cloud servers. Doing so also improves security because data that is used for intermediate calculations need not be transmitted over the Internet.

**Roaming** occurs when users move their activities, especially long-running transactions (reading a book, for example), across devices. The best mobile applications do this transparently; the user need take no action. Figure CE3-11 shows a message created by a Kindle app when a book was opened on an iPad that had previously been read on Kindle device. This tracking and informing were entirely automatic.

Roaming on reading devices is interesting, but even greater power will be achieved when mobile applications allow roaming for other long-running transactions as well; editing a document, spreadsheet, or other Office document is an example. At some point (not yet), applications like CRM and ERP may support roaming as well.

The last cloud use in Figure CE3-10 concerns data. Live, active mobile applications are designed to receive the latest application data and automatically show it to the user, perhaps in a graphically exciting *breaking news* type banner. Such data includes industry or employee news, but it could also be SharePoint alerts, updates to orders, changes in credit ratings or banking accounts, and so forth. **Push data** is data that the server sends to or pushes onto the device. **Pull data** is data that the device requests from the server. (Notice that those terms use the server's perspective.) Of the two types, push data is more impressive to users because they need do nothing to receive it. On the other hand, excessive pushing is annoying.

**Figure CE3-11**
Kindle Roaming Message Displays in Front of Kindle Text

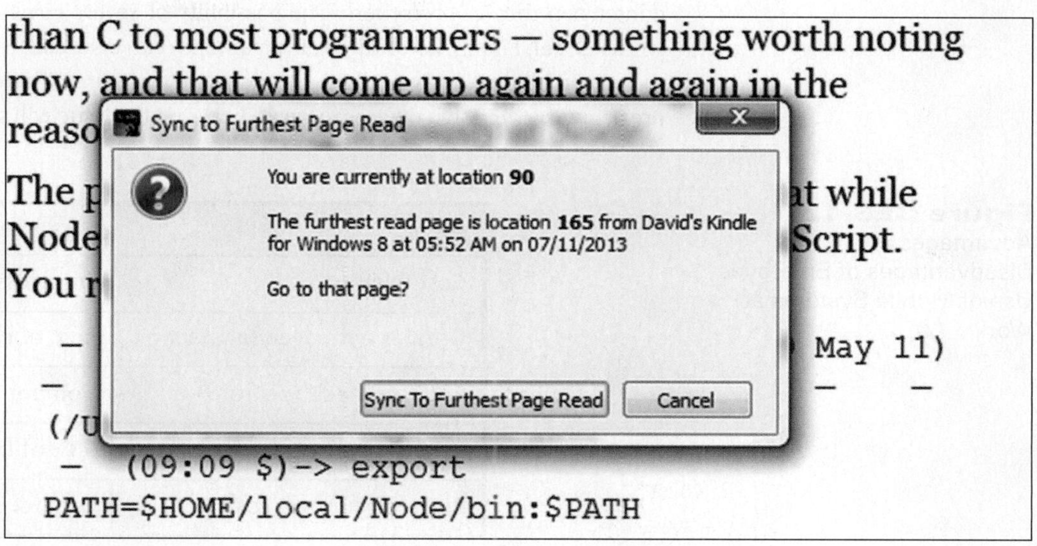

# QCE3-5 WHAT ARE THE CHALLENGES OF PERSONAL MOBILE DEVICES AT WORK?

So far, we've focused on mobile applications that organizations create for their customers and others to use. In this question, we will address the use of mobile systems *within* organizations.

In truth, organizations today have a love/hate relationship with their employees' use of their own mobile devices at work. They love the cost-saving possibility of having employees buy their own hardware, but they hate the increased vulnerability and loss of control. The result, at least today, is a wide array of organizational attitudes.

Consider a recent Gartner report that estimates by 2016, nearly 38 percent of companies will stop providing devices to their workers altogether.[10] You'll have to bring your own device. David Willis, a senior analyst at Gartner, notes, "BYOD Strategies are the most radical change to the economics and the culture of client computing in business in decades."[11] Yet only 43 percent of all organizations have created an official mobile-use policy.[12]

## ADVANTAGES AND DISADVANTAGES OF EMPLOYEE USE OF MOBILE SYSTEMS AT WORK

Figure CE3-12 summarizes the advantages and disadvantages of employee use of mobile systems at work. Advantages include the cost savings just mentioned as well as greater employee satisfaction of using devices that they chose according to their own preferences rather than organization-supplied PCs. Because employees are already using these devices for their own purposes, they need less training and can be more productive. All of this means reduced support costs.

On the other hand, employee use of mobile devices has significant disadvantages. First, there is the real danger of lost or damaged data. When data is brought into employee-owned computing devices, the organization loses control over where it goes or what happens to it. In May 2012, IBM disallowed the use of Apple's voice searching application, Siri, on employees' mobile devices for just that reason.[13] Also, if an employee loses his or her device, the data goes with it, and when employees leave the organization, the data on their personal devices needs to be deleted somehow.

Organizations also lose control over the updating of software and the applications that users employ. This control loss leads to compatibility problems; users can process data, for example edit documents, with software that is incompatible with the organization's standard software. The result to the organization is a mess of inconsistent documents.

Possibly the greatest disadvantage of employee use of their own devices is the risk of infection. The organization cannot know where the users have been with their devices or what they've done when they've been there. The possibility of severe viruses infecting the organization's networks is real. Finally, all of these disadvantages can also lead, ironically, to greater support costs.

Given all that, organizations cannot avoid the issue. Whatever the costs and risks, employees are bringing their own devices to work. Ignoring the issue will simply make matters worse.

**Figure CE3-12**
Advantages and Disadvantages of Employee Use of Mobile Systems at Work

| Advantages | Disadvantages |
|---|---|
| Cost savings | Data loss or damage |
| Greater employee satisfaction | Loss of control |
| Reduced need for training | Compatibility problems |
| Higher productivity | Risk of infection |
| Reduced support costs | Greater support costs |

## SURVEY OF ORGANIZATIONAL BYOD POLICY

A **bring your own device (BYOD) policy** is a statement concerning employees' permissions and responsibilities when they use their own device for organizational business. Figure CE3-13 arranges BYOD policies according to functionality and control. Starting in the lower left-hand corner, the most primitive policy is to ignore mobile use. That posture, which provides neither functionality to the employee nor control to the organization, has no advantages and, as just stated, cannot last.

The next step up in functionality is for the organization to offer its wireless network to mobile devices, as if it were a coffee shop. The advantage to the organization of this policy is that the organization can sniff employees' mobile traffic, thus learning how employees are using their devices (and time) during work.

The next policy provides more functionality and somewhat more control. Here the organization creates secure application services using https that require employee sign-on and can be accessed from any device, mobile or not. Such applications can be used when employees are at work or elsewhere. These services provide controlled access to some organizations' assets.

A fourth policy is more of a strategic maneuver than a policy. The organization tells employees that they can sign on to the organization's network with their mobile devices, but the employee is financially responsible for any damage he or she does. The hope is that this policy discourages employees from bringing their own devices.

A more enlightened policy is to manage the users' devices as if they were owned by the organization. With this policy, employees turn over their mobile devices to the IS department, which cleanses and reloads software and installs programs that enable the IS department to manage the device remotely. Numerous vendors license products called **mobile device management (MDM) software** that assist this process. These products install and update software, back up and restore mobile devices, wipe employer software and data from devices in the event the device is lost or the employee leaves the company, report usage, and provide other mobile device management data.

This policy benefits the organization, but some employees resist turning over the management of their own hardware to the organization. This resistance can be softened if the organization pays at least a portion of the hardware expense.

The most controlling policy is for the organization to declare that it owns any mobile device that employees connect to its network. To be enforceable, this policy must be part of the

**Figure CE3-13**
Six Common BYOD Policies

| Functionality (High → Low) / Control: Low → High | | | | | |
|---|---|---|---|---|---|
| Full VPN Access to Organizational Systems | | | You're responsible for damage | We'll check it out, reload software and data, and manage it remotely | If you connect it, we own it |
| Organizational Services on Public Internet | | We'll offer limited systems you can access from any device | | | |
| Access to Internet | We'll be a coffee shop | | | | |
| None | They don't exist | | | | |

**Figure CE3-14**
Advantages of Example BYOD Policies

| BYOD Policy | Description | Advantage to Organization |
|---|---|---|
| They don't exist. | Organization looks the other way when employees bring mobile devices to work. | None. |
| We'll be a coffee shop. | You'll be able to sign in to our wireless network using your mobile device. | Packet sniffing of employee mobile device use at work. |
| We'll offer limited systems you can access from any device. | Organization creates https:// applications with sign-in and offers access to noncritical business systems. | Employees gain public access from any device, not just mobile devices, without having to use VPN accounts. |
| You're responsible for damage. | Threatening posture to discourage employee use of mobile devices at work. | Appear to be permissive without actually being so. |
| We'll check it out, reload software, then manage remotely. | Employees can use their mobile devices just as if they were computers provided by the corporate IS Department. | Employee buys the hardware (perhaps with an employer's contribution). |
| If you connect it, we own it. | Employees are not to use mobile devices at work. If they do, they lose them. Part of employment agreement. | Ultimate in control for highly secure work situations (intelligence, military). |

employee's contract. It is taken by organizations that manage very secure operations and environments. In some military/intelligence organizations, the policy is that any smart device that ever enters the workplace may never leave it. The advantages of these six policies are summarized in Figure CE3-14.

BYOD policies are rapidly evolving, and many organizations have not yet determined what is best for them. If your employer has a committee to develop such policies, join it if you can. Doing so will provide a great way to gain exposure to the leading technology thinkers at your organization.

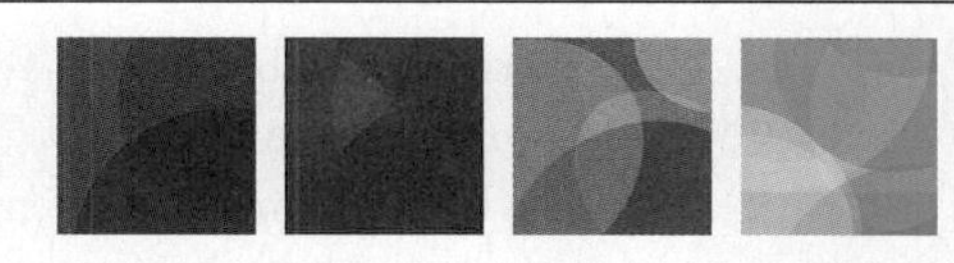

# ACTIVE REVIEW

Use this Active Review to verify that you understand the ideas and concepts that answer this chapter extension's study questions.

## QCE3-1 WHAT ARE MOBILE SYSTEMS?

Define *mobile systems*. Name and describe the four elements of a mobile system.

## QCE3-2 WHY ARE MOBILE SYSTEMS IMPORTANT?

Summarize the size of and opportunities in the mobile market. Explain why the mobile market will become stronger in the future. Explain why a problem for one organization is an opportunity for another. Using the five-component model, describe particular opportunities for each component. Define *just-in-time data* and explain how it changes the value of human thinking.

## QCE3-3 HOW DO NATIVE AND WEB-BASED MOBILE APPLICATIONS COMPARE?

In your own words, summarize the differences between native applications and Web applications. In high-level terms, explain the difference between native application languages and Web languages. Explain each cell of Figure CE3-3. State which is better: native or Web applications.

## QCE3-4 WHAT CHARACTERIZES QUALITY MOBILE USER EXPERIENCES?

Explain the difference between the terms *UI* and *UX*. Describe how each of the following can affect the UX of a mobile application: user content, context-sensitive chrome, animation and lively behavior, scaling and sharing, the cloud. Define *chrome, charms, roaming, push,* and *pull.*

## QCE3-5 WHAT ARE THE CHALLENGES OF PERSONAL MOBILE DEVICES AT WORK?

Summarize the advantages and disadvantages of employees' use of mobile systems at work. Define *BYOD* and *BYOD policy.* Name six possible policies and compare them in terms of functionality and organizational control. Summarize the advantage of each to employers.

## KEY TERMS AND CONCEPTS

Bring your own device (BYOD) policy 413
Charms 409
Chrome 408
Context-sensitive chrome 408
Direct interaction 408
Just-in-time data 403
M-commerce 401
Mobile device 401
Mobile device management (MDM) software 413
Mobile systems 401
Object-oriented 404
Pull data 411
Push data 411
Roaming 411
Swift 404
User experience (UX) 408
User interface (UI) 408

MyMISLab™

To complete the problems with the ✪, go to EOC Discussion Questions in the MyLab.

## USING YOUR KNOWLEDGE

**CE3-1.** Reflect on each of the five components related to changes caused by mobile devices in QCE3-2.

**a.** Describe a job that you would like to have upon graduation.

**b.** Describe how changes in mobile hardware will affect that job.

**c.** Explain how you can use your knowledge of the differences between native and Web mobile application development to help you in that job.

**d.** Explain two ways that just-in-time data will affect that job.

**e.** Describe two ways that mobile systems will change business processes in that job.

**f.** Explain ways that mobile systems will change the premium on the skills necessary for that job.

**g.** Summarize your answers to parts b–f in a two-paragraph statement that you could use in a job interview.

**CE3-2.** Suppose you are Cam at Falcon Security. List five criteria you would use in helping Falcon Security decide whether it should make its own drones. Justify your criteria.

**CE3-3.** Choose a mobile application that you frequently use. It could be Facebook, Twitter, or some other more vertical application. Evaluate that application according to the principles of a quality mobile UX discussed in QCE3-4.

MyMISLab™

Go to the Assignments section of your MyLab to complete these writing exercises.

**CE3-4.** A friend of yours asks you for advice about an idea she has for an application. She wants to create a mobile location sharing app that would allow users to see where food trucks are parked around the city. Users could see which trucks are close and what food those trucks are serving that day.

**a.** Based on the discussion in QCE3-3, explain the advantages and disadvantages of developing native versus web mobile applications.

**b.** Would you recommend that your friend develop a native mobile application or a web mobile application? Justify your recommendation.

**CE3-5.** Judging from your personal experience, describe the BYOD policy that appears to be in place at your university. Explain the advantages and disadvantages of the policy to you as a student and to the organization as a whole. How do you think that BYOD policy will change in the next 5 years? Explain your answer.

## ENDNOTES

1. Cisco Systems Inc., "Cisco Visual Networking Index: Global Mobile Data Traffic Forecast Update, 2014–2019," *Cisco.com*, February 3, 2015, accessed May 22, 2015, *www.cisco.com/c/en/us/solutions/collateral/service-provider/visual-networking-index-vni/white_paper_c11-520862.html*.
2. Ibid.
3. Horace Dediu, "Late Late Majority," *Asymco.com*, July 8, 2014, *www.asymco.com/2014/07/08/late-late-majority*.
4. Michael Degusta, "Are Smart Phones Spreading Faster Than Any Other Technology in Human History?" MIT Technology Review, May 9, 2012, *www.technologyreview.com/business/40321/*.
5. comScore, "comScore Reports March 2015 U.S. Smartphone Subscriber Market Share," February 9, 2015, accessed May 16, 2015, *www.comscore.com/Insights/Market-Rankings/comScore-Reports-December-2014-US-Smartphone-Subscriber-Market-Share*.
6. eMarketer, "Mobile Commerce Roundup," *eMarketer.com*, October 2013, accessed June 10, 2015, *www.emarketer.com/public_media/docs/eMarketer_Mobile_Commerce_Roundup.pdf*.
7. Survey New U.S. Smartphone Growth by Age and Income," accessed May 2015, *http://blog.nielsen.com/nielsenwire/online_mobile/survey-new-u-s-smartphone-growth-by-age-and-income*.
8. Not quite true. Much of the design and possibly some of the code can be reused between native applications. But for your planning, assume that it all must be redone. Not enough will carry over to make it worth considering.
9. See *msdn.microsoft.com/en-us/library/windows/apps/dn958439.aspx* for the source of much of this figure as well as for an extended discussion of modern-style UX. Accessed June 2015.
10. David Willis, "Bring Your Own Device: The Facts and the Future," Gartner Inc., April 11, 2013.
11. Ibid.
12. "CDH," accessed July 15, 2013, *www.cdh.com*.
13. Robert McMillan, "IBM Worries iPhone's Siri Has Loose Lips," last modified May 24, 2012, *www.cnn.com/2012/05/23/tech/mobile/ibm-siri-ban/index.html?iphoneemail*.

chapter extension **4**

**Chapter 4** provides the background for this extension.

# Introduction to Microsoft Excel 2013

**STUDY QUESTIONS**

**QCE4-1 WHAT IS A SPREADSHEET?**

**QCE4-2 HOW DO YOU GET STARTED WITH EXCEL?**

**QCE4-3 HOW CAN YOU ENTER DATA?**

**QCE4-4 HOW CAN YOU INSERT AND DELETE ROWS AND COLUMNS AND CHANGE THEIR SIZE?**

**QCE4-5 HOW CAN YOU FORMAT DATA?**

**QCE4-6 HOW CAN YOU CREATE A (SIMPLE) FORMULA?**

**QCE4-7 HOW CAN YOU PRINT RESULTS?**

This chapter extension teaches basic skills with Microsoft Excel, a product for creating and processing spreadsheets. If you already know how to use Excel, use this chapter extension for review. Otherwise, use this chapter extension to gain essential knowledge that every businessperson needs today.

## QCE4-1 WHAT IS A SPREADSHEET?

A **spreadsheet** is a table of data having rows and columns. Long before the advent of the computer, accountants and financial planners used paper spreadsheets to make financial calculations. Today, the term *spreadsheet* almost always refers to an *electronic* spreadsheet, and most frequently to a spreadsheet that is processed by Microsoft Excel. Electronic spreadsheets provide incredible labor savings over paper spreadsheets and were a major factor in the early adoption of personal computers.

As shown in Figure CE4-1, Excel spreadsheets have rows and columns. The rows are identified by numbers, and the columns are identified by letters. Because there are only 26 letters in the alphabet, the following scheme is used to label columns: The letters A through Z identify the first 26 columns; the letters AA through AZ identify the next 26; BA through BZ the next 26; and so forth.

In Excel, the term **worksheet** refers to a spreadsheet. One or more worksheets are combined to form a **workbook**.

In the lower left-hand corner of Figure CE4-1, notice the tab called Sheet 1. Excel creates just one worksheet when you create a new workbook, but you can create more worksheets if needed.

Figure CE4-1 shows a spreadsheet processed by Excel 2013, the current version of Excel. You can process spreadsheets in earlier versions of Excel, but the structure of commands and menu items will be different from that described here. If you are just starting to learn Excel, learn Excel 2013 rather than an earlier version.

The intersection of a row and a column is called a **cell**. Each cell is identified by the name of its row and column. In Figure CE4-1, the cell named A1 is highlighted. The cell K5 is the cell in the K column, row number 5. The cell AB1207 (not visible in Figure CE4-1) is the cell located in column AB and row 1207.

You may be asking, "Row 1207? How many rows and columns can I have?" Don't bother asking...you can have more than you will ever need or want. And if you should ever run out of rows and columns, you're using the wrong tool. In that case, you probably should be using Microsoft Access or another DBMS (see Chapter 5) instead.

CE4

**Figure CE4-1**
Excel Spreadsheet Showing Rows and Columns

*Source:* Microsoft Excel 2013

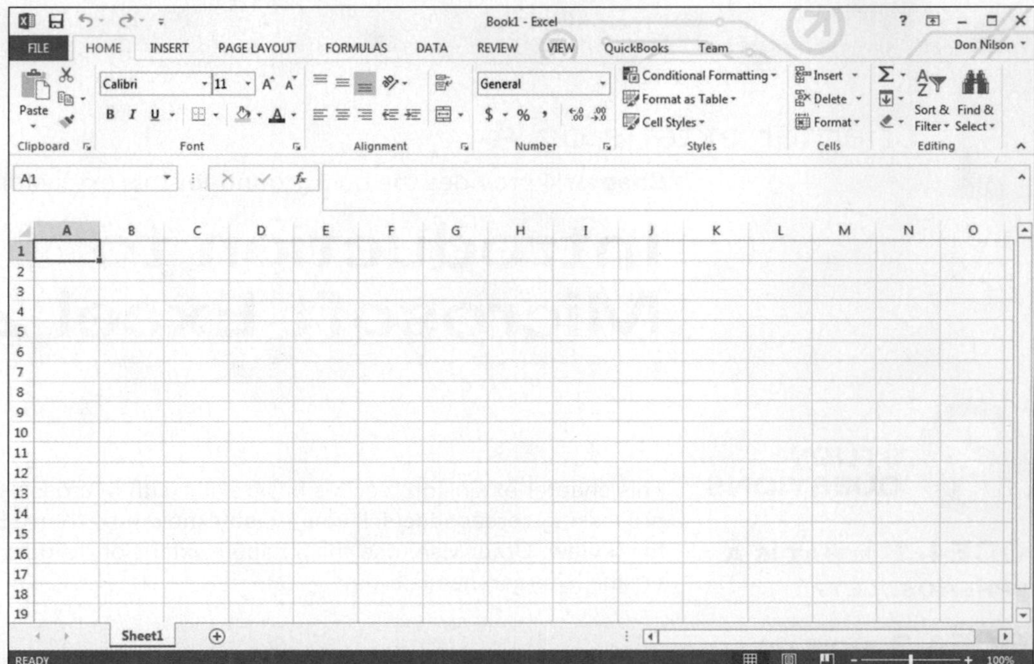


# QCE4-2 HOW DO YOU GET STARTED WITH EXCEL?

When you first start Excel 2013, it will create a workbook exactly like that in Figure CE4-1. Even though you haven't done anything yet, your first task should be to save your workbook under an appropriate name. Life is uncertain; you never know when a computer might fail or power might be cut off or some other unplanned event might occur. Get in the habit of saving your work initially and then frequently after that.

To save your workbook, click *File* with your left mouse button (in the following text, unless otherwise specified, the term *click* means to click with the left mouse button), and click *Save As* as shown in Figure CE4-2. The choices available to you will depend on the license you have and your

**Figure CE4-2**
Saving Your Workbook in Excel

*Source:* Microsoft Excel 2013

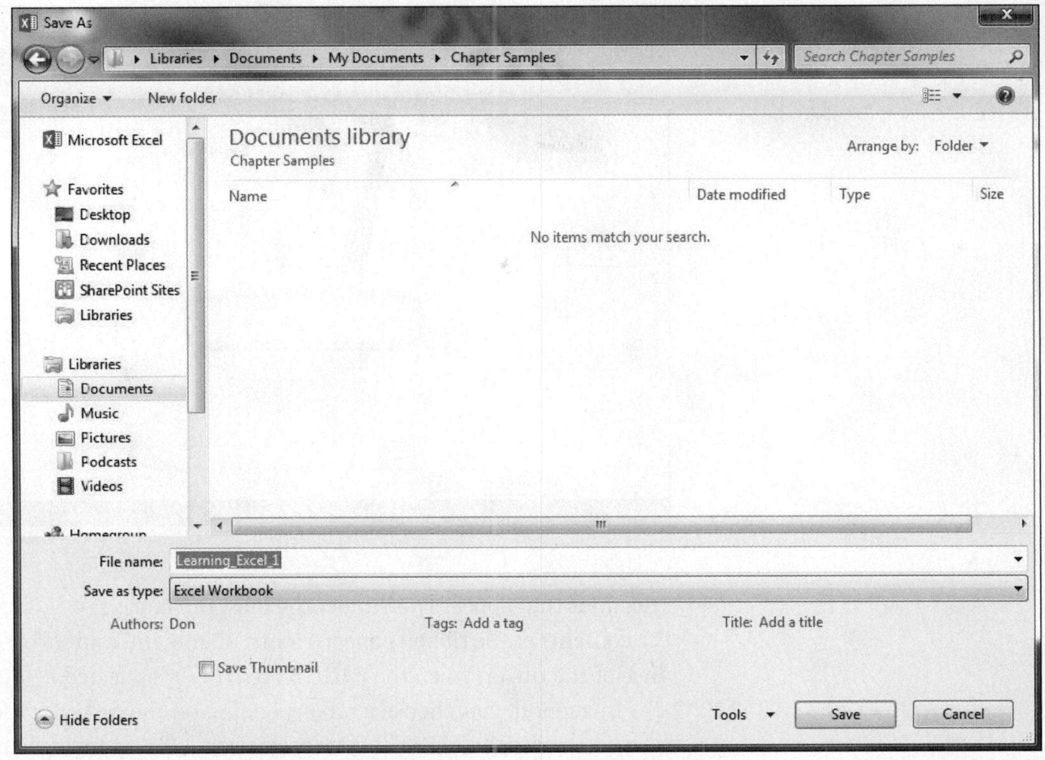


**Figure CE4-3**
Entering a File Name in Excel

*Source:* Microsoft Excel 2013

working environment. In this example, Excel displays a SharePoint site named *David Kroenke*, a Microsoft OneDrive location, Computer, and *Add a Place* where you can define new locations for saving documents. For now, click Computer, then Browse as shown in Figure CE4-2. Navigate to the location on your computer where you want to save your workbook. The display in Figure CE4-3 will appear. In the lower center, find the label *File name:* and to the right of that label enter a name for this file. In Figure CE4-3, I have entered the file name *Learning_Excel_1*. Your instructor may have given you instructions for creating file names; if so, follow them. Otherwise, follow this example or use some other scheme. Click the *Save* button to save your workbook. Once you have saved your workbook, you can perform subsequent saves by clicking the small disk icon located next to the Excel icon at the top left.

Figure CE4-4 shows the workbook. A sequence of tabs appears in a horizontal line, just below the Excel icon. These tabs control the contents of the **ribbon**, which is the wide bar of tools and

**Figure CE4-4**
Excel Menu Tabs and Ribbon Bar

*Source:* Microsoft Excel 2013

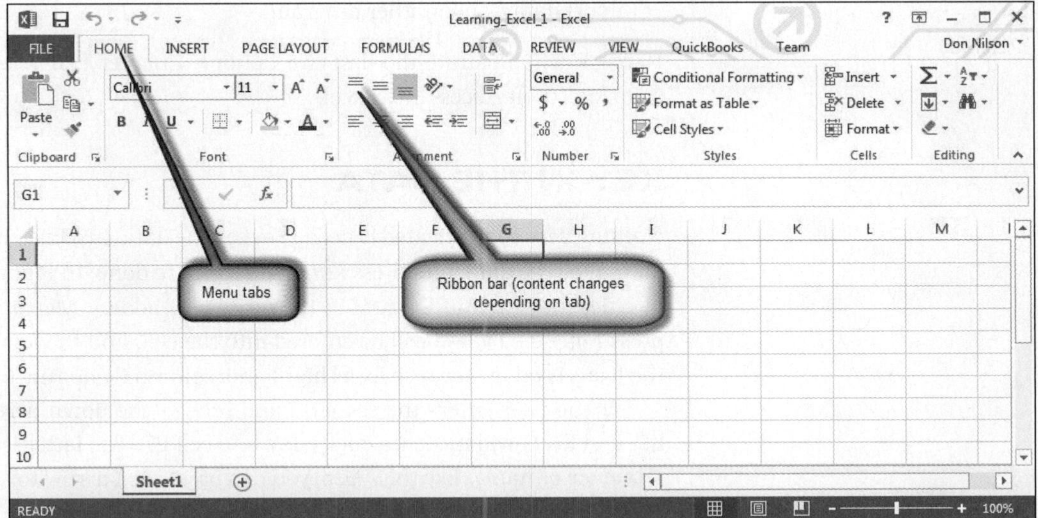

**Figure CE4-5**
Ribbon with Page Layout Tab Selected

*Source:* Microsoft Excel 2013

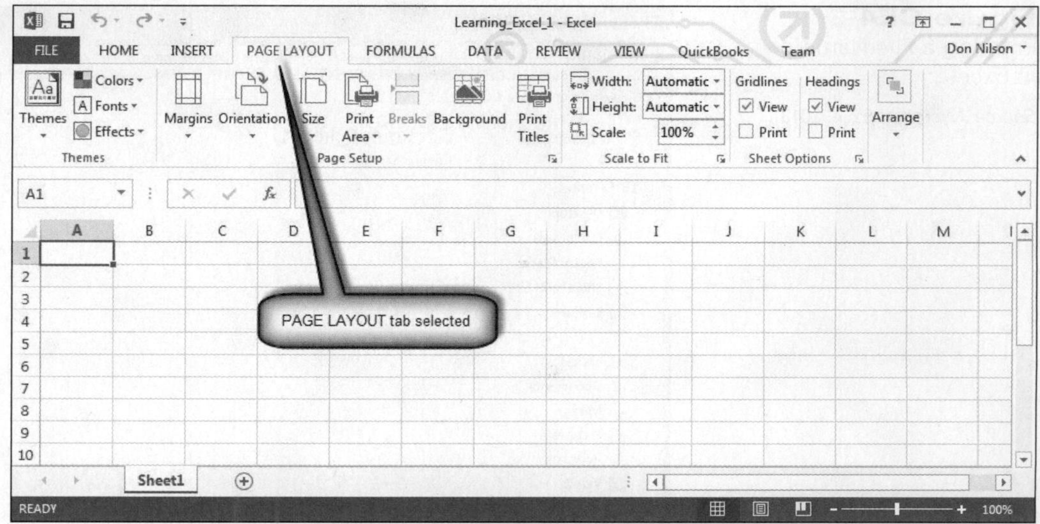


selections that appears just under the tabs. In Figure CE4-4, the *HOME* tab has been selected, and the contents of the ribbon concern fonts, alignment, and so forth. Figure CE4-5 shows the appearance of the ribbon when the *PAGE LAYOUT* tab is selected.

In general, you choose a tab depending on the task at hand. For general work, the tools and selection under the *HOME* tab are most useful. If you are inserting pictures, graphs, hyperlinks, or other items into your spreadsheet, click the *INSERT* tab. You would use *PAGE LAYOUT* to format your page, often for printing. The *FORMULAS* tab is used for creating more complex formulas, the *DATA* tab for filtering and sorting data in your spreadsheet, the *REVIEW* tab for tracking changes and making comments, and the *VIEW* tab for configuring the appearance of Excel.

At this point, don't worry about which tab to choose; just click around to see the tools and selections available. If in doubt, click on the *Home* tab because it holds the most frequently used tools and selections.

# QCE4-3 HOW CAN YOU ENTER DATA?

Data can be entered into an Excel worksheet in three ways:

- Key in the data.
- Let Excel add data based on a pattern.
- Import data from another program.

Here we will illustrate the first two options. Chapter Extension 7 discusses how to import data from Microsoft Access into Excel.

## KEY IN THE DATA

Nothing very sophisticated is needed to key the data. Just click in the cell in which you want to add data, type the data, and press *Enter* when you're done. In Figure CE4-6 the user has keyed names of cities into column E and is in the process of adding *Miami*. After typing the second *i*, she can press *Enter*. The value will be entered into the cell, and the focus will stay on cell E6. You can tell the focus is on E6 because Excel highlights column E and row 6.

If the user enters the second *i* and presses the down arrow, the value will be added to cell E6, and Excel will move the focus down to cell E7. The latter is useful if you are adding a vertical sequence of names like this. Also, you can press a left arrow to add the data and move the focus left or a right or up arrow to move right or up.

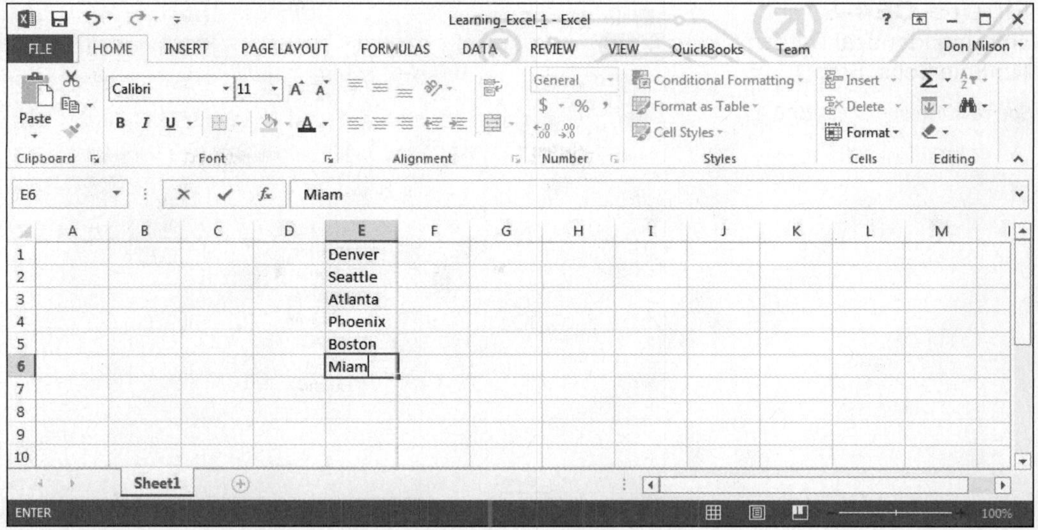


**Figure CE4-6**
Entering City Names in Column E

*Source:* Microsoft Excel 2013

In Figure CE4-6, notice the row just above the spreadsheet, immediately above the names of the columns. In that row, the value E6 indicates that cell E6 has the focus and further to the right the letters *Miam* indicate the current value of that cell.

Figure CE4-7 shows a sequence of seven city names. But notice that the user never entered the second *i* in Miami. To correct this, she can go back to that cell and retype the entire word *Miami* or she can go to the cell and press the <F2> function key. In the latter case, she can just add the missing *i* to the word and press Enter (or down or up, etc.). Using the F2 key is recommended when you have a long value in a cell and you just want to fix a letter or two without retyping the whole entry. (If nothing happens when you press F2, press the F Lock key on your keyboard. Then press F2 again.)

## LET EXCEL ADD THE DATA USING A PATTERN

Suppose that for some reason for each of the cities we want to have the number 100 in column G of the spreadsheet in Figure CE4-7. Another way of saying this is that we want the value 100 to be entered into cells G1 through G7. One way of proceeding is to type the value 100 in each of the seven rows. There's a better way, however.

If our user types the value 100 into cell G1, presses Enter, and then clicks cell G1, a rectangle will be drawn around the cell with a little black box in the lower right-hand corner, as shown in

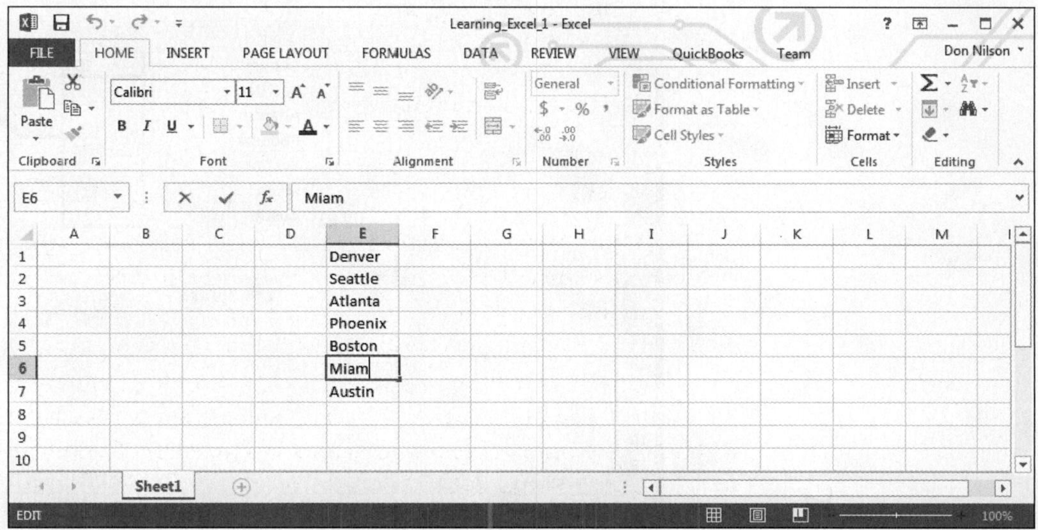


**Figure CE4-7**
Using a Function Key to Make Entry Corrections

*Source:* Microsoft Excel 2013

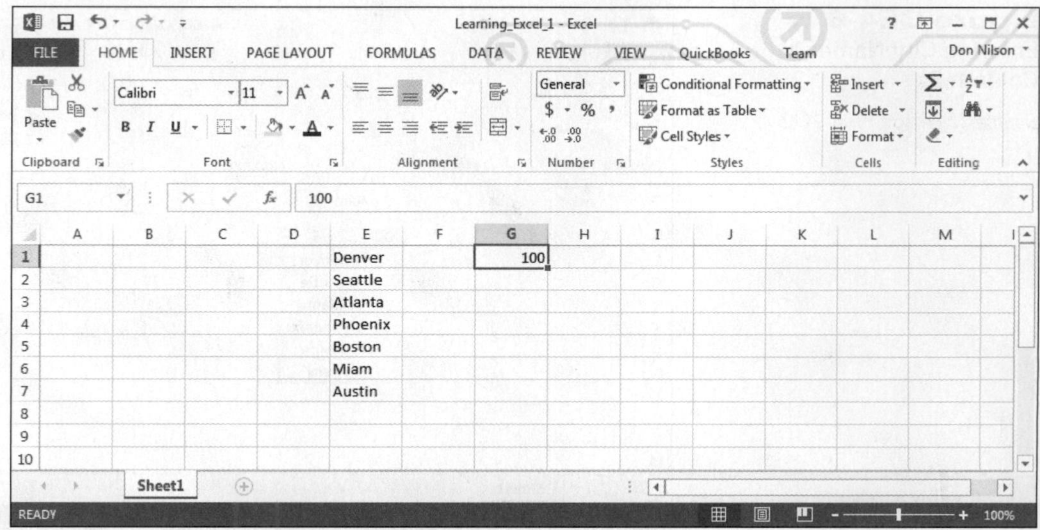

**Figure CE4-8**
Entering Identical Data in Multiple Cells, Step 1
*Source:* Microsoft Excel 2013

Figure CE4-8. Now if the user drags (left-click and hold the mouse button down as you move the mouse) that little black box down to cell G7, Excel will fill in the value 100 into all of those cells. Figure CE4-9 shows the user dragging the cells, and Figure CE4-10 shows the result.

But it gets much better! Suppose we want the numbers in column G to identify the cities. Say we want the first city, Denver, to have the number 100, the second city, Seattle, to have the number 200, the third city, Atlanta, to have the number 300, and so forth.

Excel will fill in the values we want if we give it an indication of the pattern to follow. So, if our user types 100 in cell G1, 200 in cell G2, and then *selects both cells G1 and G2*, Excel will draw a rectangle around the two cells and again show the small black box, as shown in Figure CE4-11. If the user drags the small black box, Excel will fill in the numbers in a sequence, as shown in Figure CE4-12.

Excel is sophisticated in its interpretation of the patterns. If you key *January* and *February* into cells C1 and C2 and then select both cells and drag down, Excel will fill in with March, April, May,

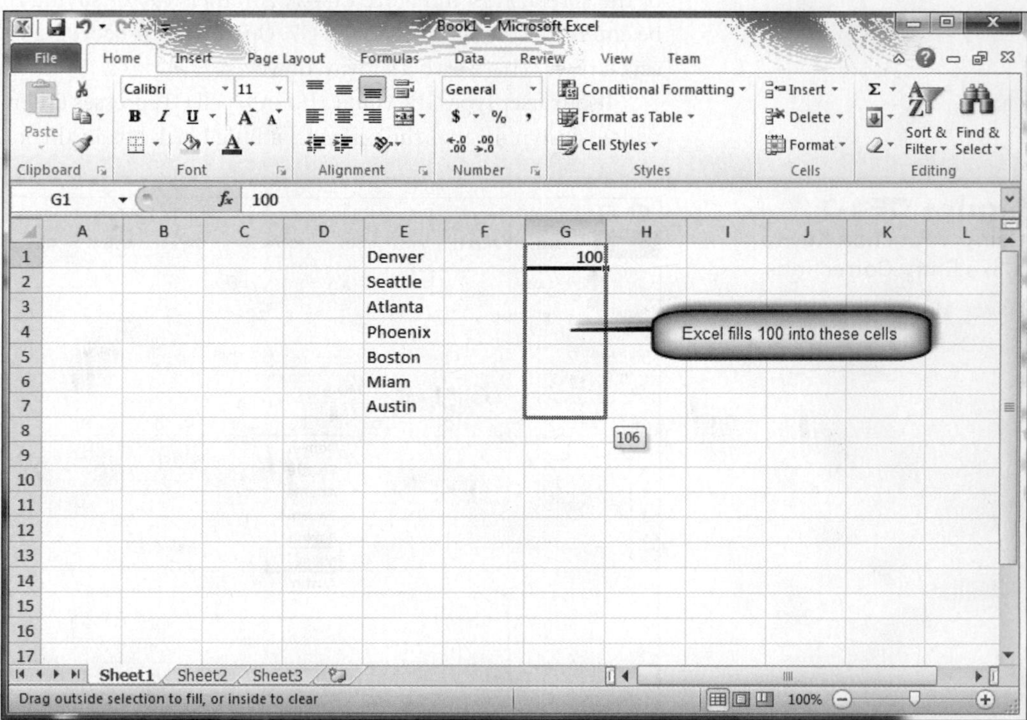


**Figure CE4-9**
Entering Identical Data in Multiple Cells, Step 2
*Source:* Microsoft Excel 2013

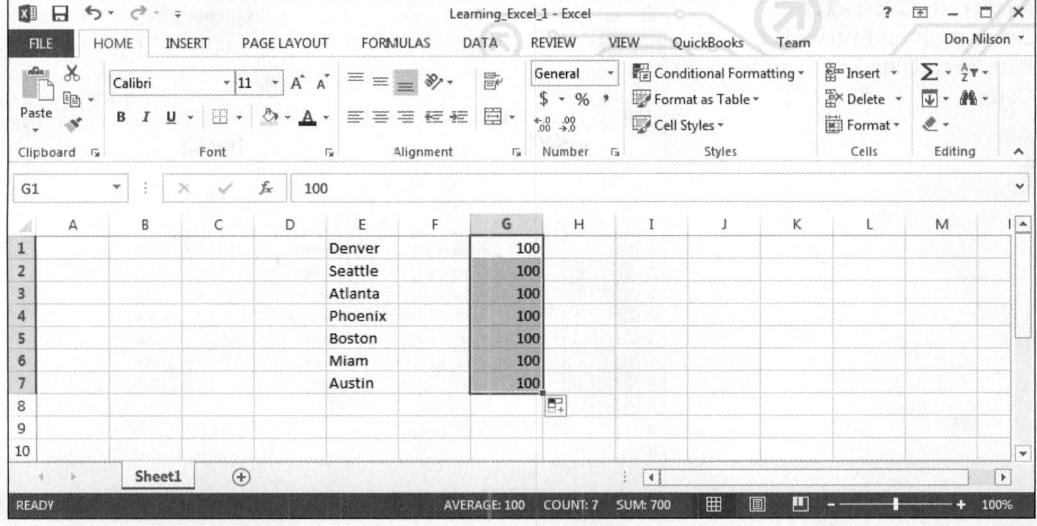


**Figure CE4-10**
Identical Data Entered in Multiple Cells

*Source:* Microsoft Excel 2013

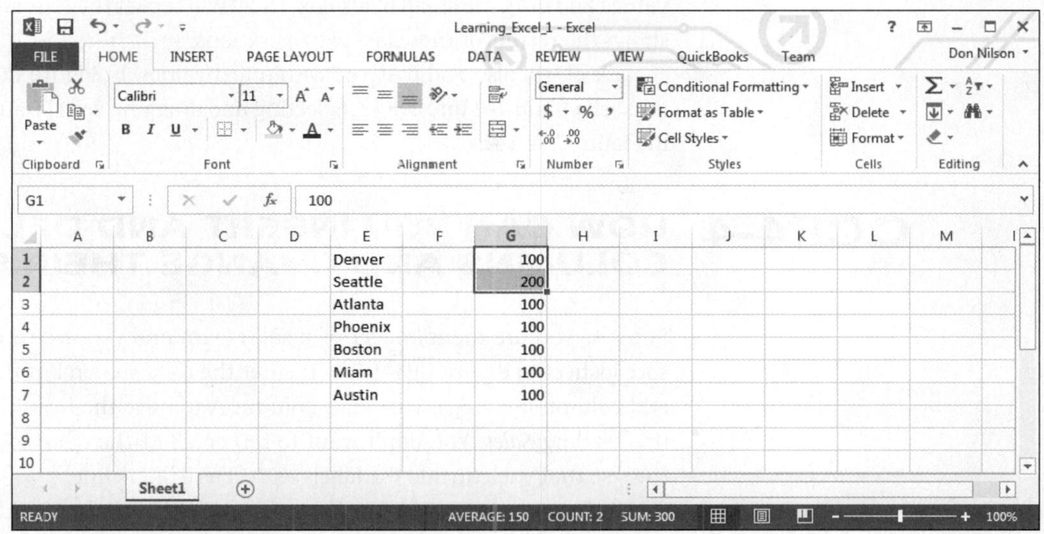


**Figure CE4-11**
Entering Patterned Data in Multiple Cells

*Source:* Microsoft Excel 2013

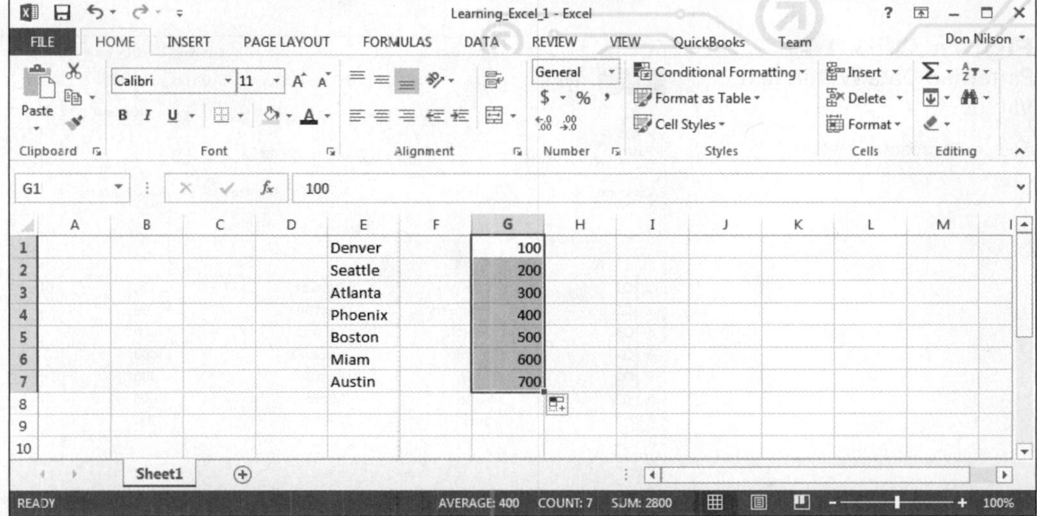


**Figure CE4-12**
Patterned Data Entered in Multiple Cells

*Source:* Microsoft Excel 2013

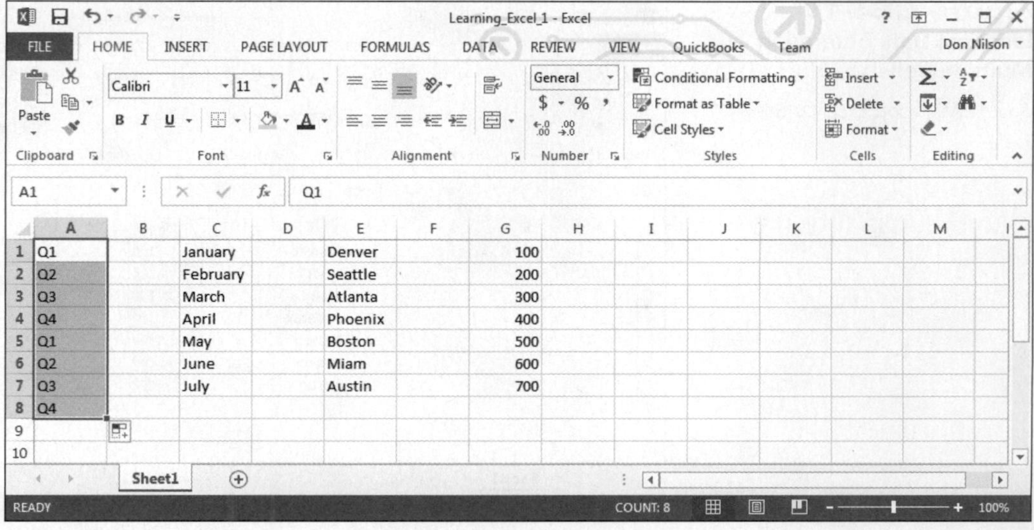

**Figure CE4-13**
Sophisticated Entry of Patterned Data in Multiple Cells

*Source:* Microsoft Excel 2013

and so on. Or, if in column A you key in the sequence *Q1, Q2, Q3,* and *Q4* and then select all four values and drag the small black box, Excel will repeat the sequence Q1 through Q4. Figure CE4-13 shows the results of these last two operations.

Excel will also find patterns within text values. In Figure CE4-14, the user entered Figure 1-1 into cell J1 and 1-2 into cell J2. Selecting and dragging cells J1 and J2 produced the sequence shown in Figure CE4-14.

## QCE4-4 HOW CAN YOU INSERT AND DELETE ROWS AND COLUMNS AND CHANGE THEIR SIZE?

Suppose you are the manager of a sales team and you are recording this month's sales into the spreadsheet in Figure CE4-15. You enter the data shown but then realize that you've forgotten to add column headings. You'd like column A to have the heading *Sales Rep* and column B to have the heading *Sales.* You don't want to retype all of the data; instead, you want to insert two new rows so that you can add the labels as well as a blank line.

To insert new rows, click the number of the row above which you want new rows, and select as many rows as you want to insert. In Figure CE4-16, the user has clicked row 1 and selected two rows. Now, using the right mouse button, click the selection. The menu shown in Figure CE4-16 will appear. Using your mouse, left-click the word *Insert* and two rows will be inserted, as shown

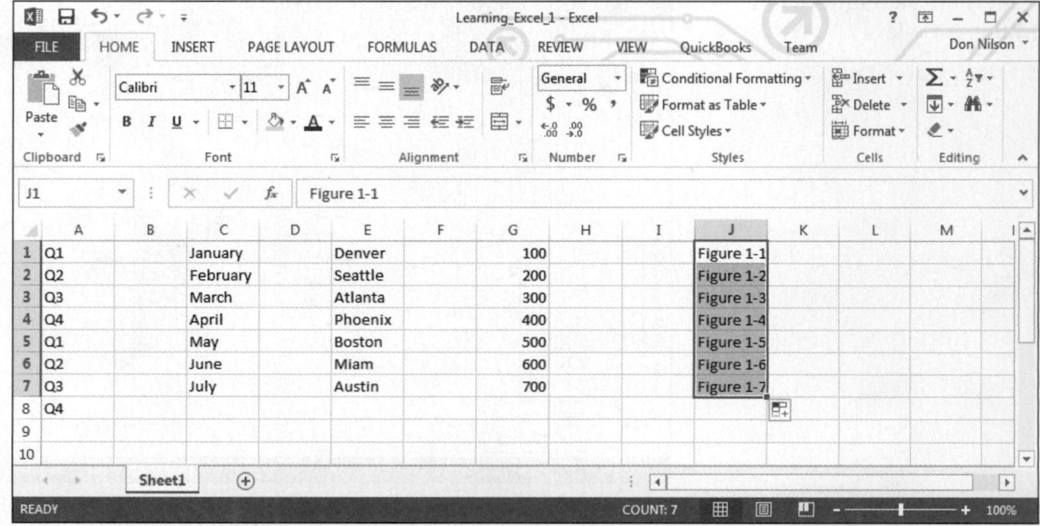

**Figure CE4-14**
Patterned Data Within Text Values

*Source:* Microsoft Excel 2013

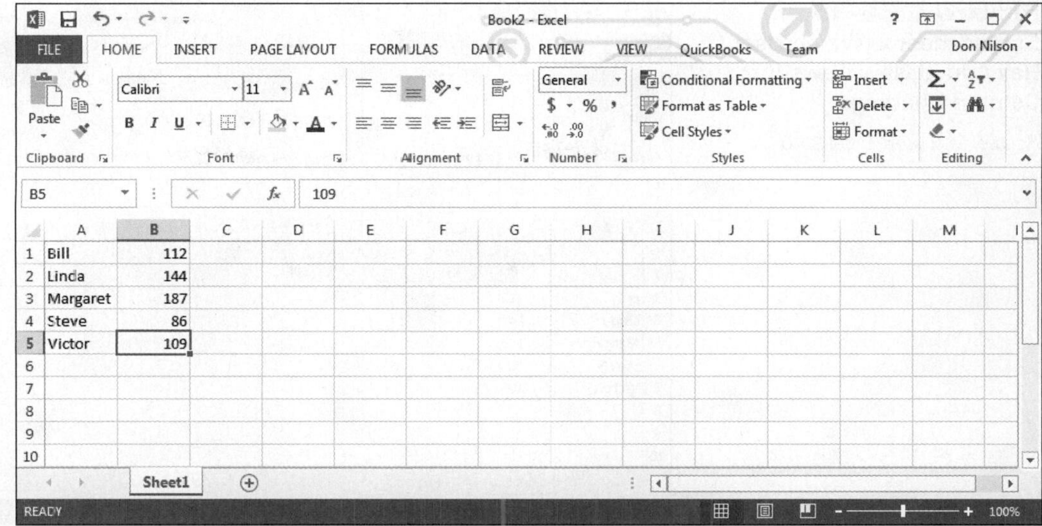

**Figure CE4-15**
Spreadsheet to Which User Wants to Add New Rows for Column Headings

*Source:* Microsoft Excel 2013

in Figure CE4-17. If you had selected only one row, then only one row would be added. If you had selected five rows, then five rows would be added.

Notice that when you click the name of a row (or column) you are selecting the *entire* row (or column). Thus, when you click the 1 of row 1, you are selecting the entire row, even if it has 1,000 or more columns.

You can use a similar approach to delete rows. Click the name of the row (or rows) you want to delete and then right-click. Then left-click the word *Delete.* Those rows will be deleted and any remaining rows moved up.

Adding and deleting columns are similar. To add a column, click the name of the column before which you want to insert columns, select as many columns to the right of that as you want to add, right-click, and then select *Insert.* To delete, click the name of the columns you want to delete, right-click, and then select *Delete.*

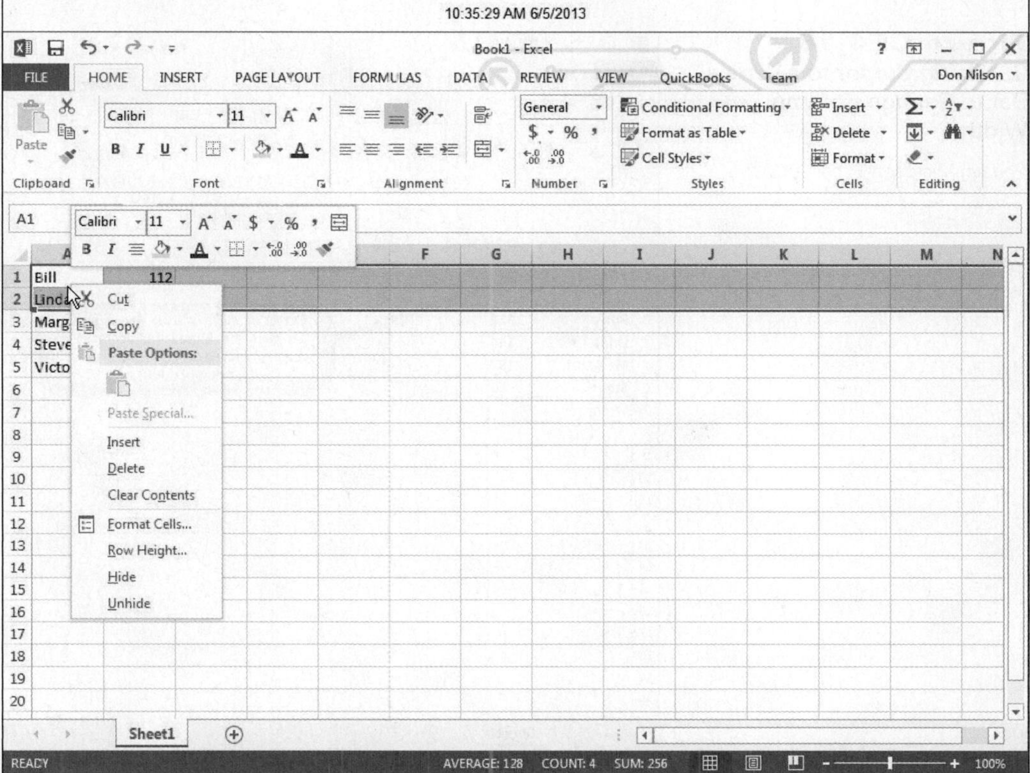

**Figure CE4-16**
Menu for Adding Inserts Such as New Rows

*Source:* Microsoft Excel 2013

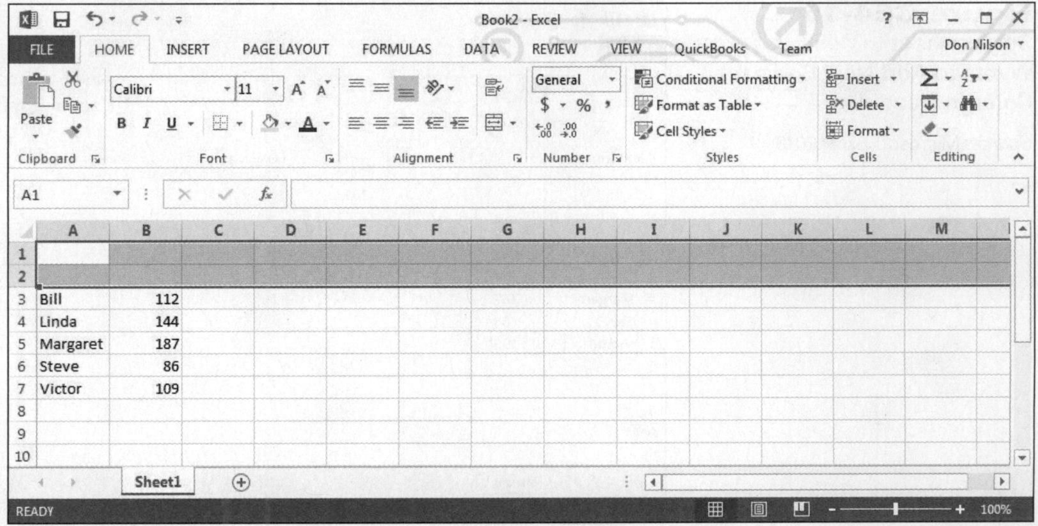


**Figure CE4-17**
Spreadsheet to Which User Has Added New Rows for Column Headings

*Source:* Microsoft Excel 2013

Changing the width of a column or the height of a row is easy. Suppose in Figure CE4-17 that you want to include both first and last names in column A. At present, column A is not large enough to show both names. To make it larger, in the column headings click the line between the A and the B. Your cursor changes to a vertical bar with an arrow on each side, as shown in Figure CE4-18. Move the cursor to the right to increase the size of the column and to the left to decrease it. Similarly, to increase or decrease the height of a row, click the line between the line numbers and drag up to decrease the row height and down to increase it.

Figure CE4-19 shows the spreadsheet after column A has been made wider and row 1 has been increased in height. *Sales Rep* has been entered as the heading for column A, and *Sales* has been entered as the name for column B.

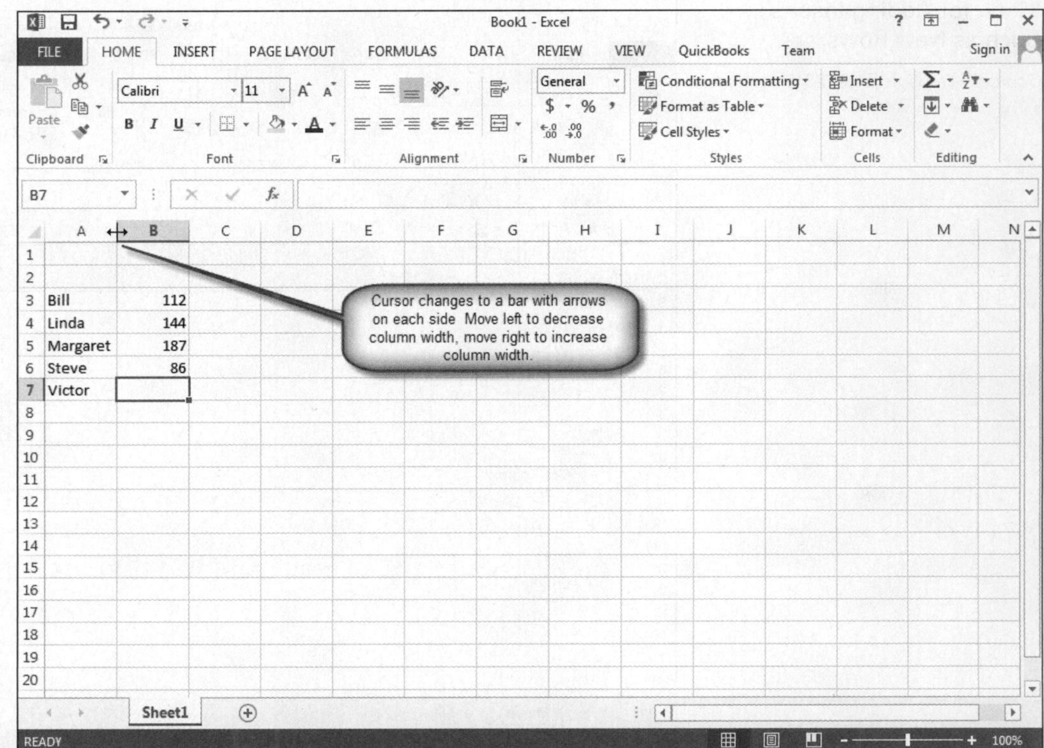


**Figure CE4-18**
Changing Cursor to a Vertical Bar to Change Column Widths

*Source:* Microsoft Excel 2013

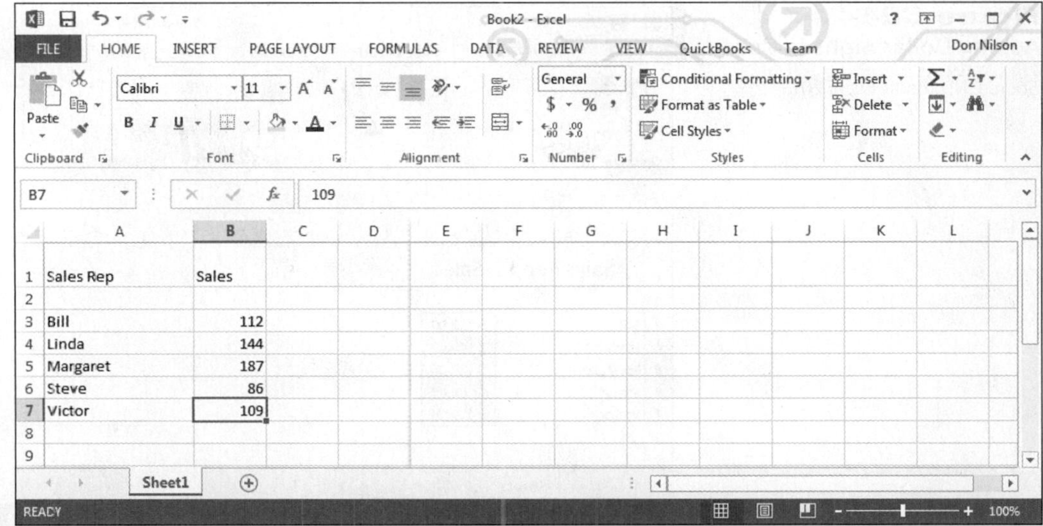


**Figure CE4-19**
Spreadsheet with Rows Added and Sizes of Columns Changed

*Source:* Microsoft Excel 2013

# QCE4-5 HOW CAN YOU FORMAT DATA?

Excel has a powerful and complicated set of tools for formatting spreadsheets. Here we will just scratch the surface with a few of the hundreds of possibilities.

The spreadsheet in Figure CE4-19 is boring and misleading. It would be better if the headings were centered over the columns and if they looked like headings. Also, are the sales in dollars or some other currency? If in dollars, they should have a dollar sign and maybe two decimal places.

To make the headings more interesting, highlight cells A1 and B1 (to do this, click A1 and hold the mouse button down as you move the mouse pointer to B1) and in the *Font* section of the ribbon select 16 rather than 11. This action increases the font size of the labels. In the same *Font* section of the ribbon, with A1 and B1 selected, click the bucket of paint. Select a medium blue. Now, still with cells A1 and B1 selected, in the *Alignment* section of the ribbon click the center icons, as shown in Figure CE4-20. Your labels will appear centered both horizontally and vertically in the cell.

The sales figures are actually in dollars, but they are formatted incorrectly. To place dollar signs in front of them, select cells B3 to B7 and in the *Number* section of the ribbon click the down arrow next to the dollar sign. Select $ English (United States), and your spreadsheet will be formatted like that in Figure CE4-21.

As stated, Excel provides hundreds of options for formatting your spreadsheet. You can add lines and borders, you can change the color of font, and you can even add conditional formatting

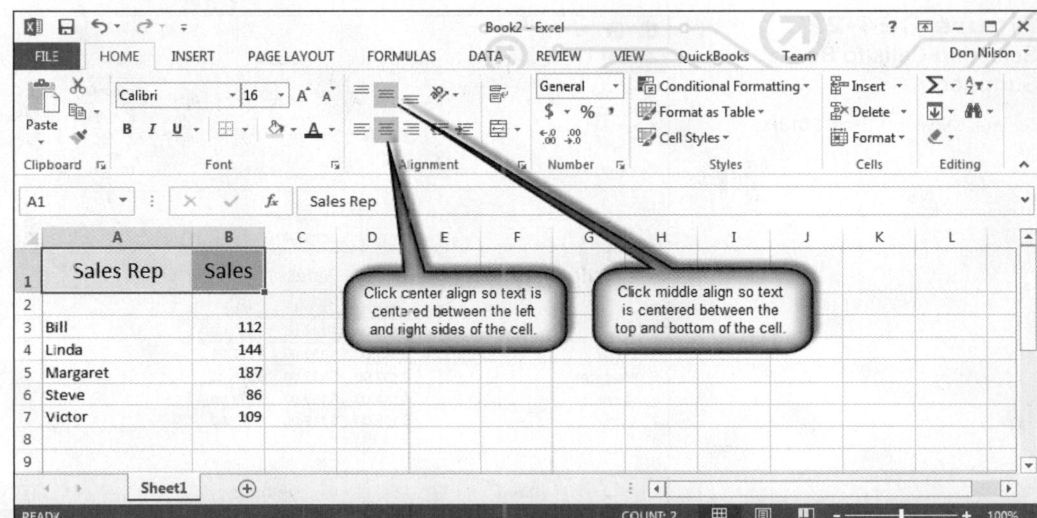


**Figure CE4-20**
Centering Labels in Cells

*Source:* Microsoft Excel 2013

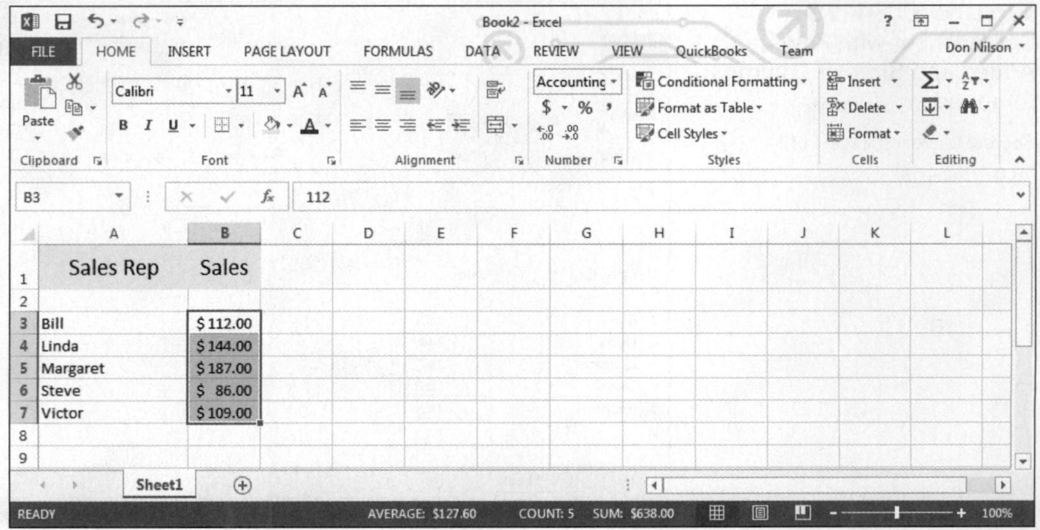

**Figure CE4-21**
Adding Dollar Signs in Cells

*Source:* Microsoft Excel 2013

so that large sales numbers appear in bold, red type. There is insufficient room in this short introduction to explain such capabilities, but explore on your own using Excel Help (the question mark in the upper right-hand corner).

## QCE4-6 HOW CAN YOU CREATE A (SIMPLE) FORMULA?

In spite of how it might appear to you at this point, the power of Excel is not the ease by which you can enter data or change the form of the spreadsheet, nor is it in the flexible ways you can format your data. The real power of Excel lies in its amazing computational capability. In this section, we will introduce a few simple formulas.

Consider the spreadsheet in Figure CE4-22. Suppose that we want to add Bill's sales numbers together to obtain his total sales for the months of March, April, and May. Those sales are located in cells C3, D3, and E3, respectively. A logical way to add the three together is with the following formula: *C3+D3+E3*.

To enter this formula in Excel, first choose the cell into which you want to place the total. For the spreadsheet in Figure CE4-22, suppose that is cell G3. Click that cell and enter the expression *=C3+D3+E3* and then press *Enter.* The result will appear as shown in Figure CE4-23. (Be sure to start with an equal sign. If you omit the equal sign, Excel will think you're attempting to enter a label or text value and will just show the letters *C3+D3+E3* in the cell.)

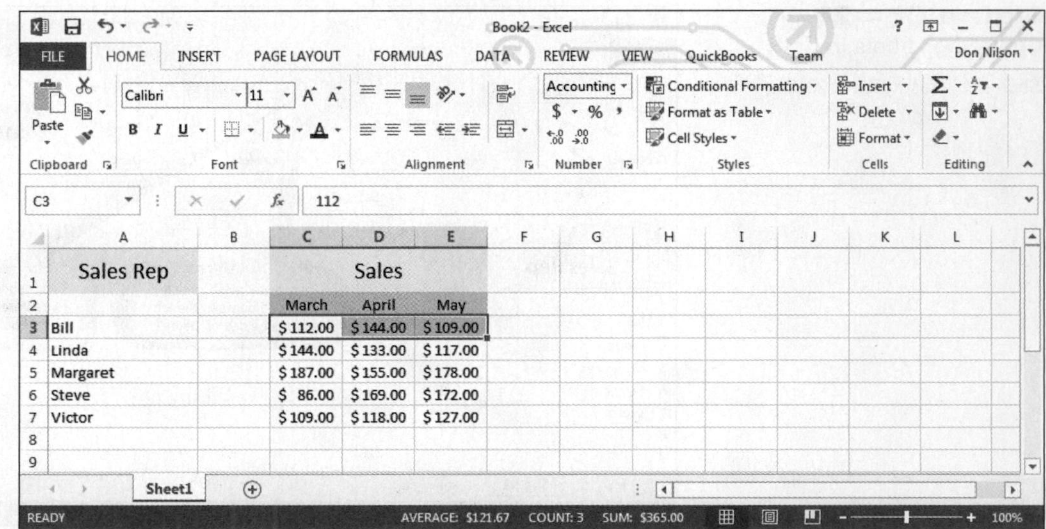

**Figure CE4-22**
Selecting Cells to Be Summed

*Source:* Microsoft Excel 2013

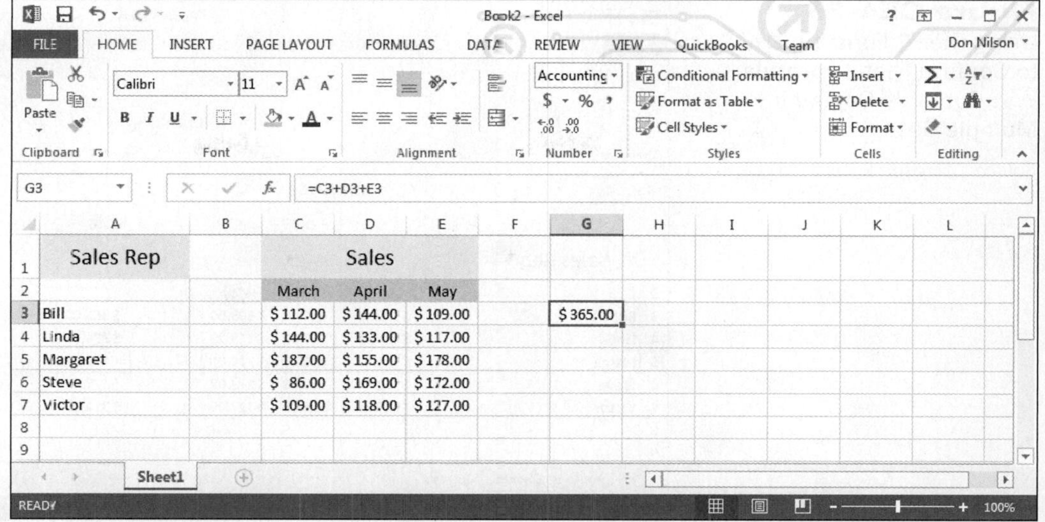


**Figure CE4-23**
The Result of Applying a Formula That Summed Cells C3, D3, and E3

*Source:* Microsoft Excel 2013

Before you go on, select cell G3 and press the F2 function key, as shown in Figure CE4-24. Notice the color coding that Excel presents. The term *C3* is shown in blue text, and the C3 cell is outlined in blue; *D3* and *E3* are shown in other colors. Whenever you have a problem with a calculation, press F2 to have Excel highlight the cells involved in that calculation.

The next operation is actually quite amazing. Suppose that you want to add the 3 months' sales data for all of the salespeople. To do that, right-click cell G3 and select *Copy.* Next, highlight cells G4 through G7, right-click, and select *Paste.* The formula will be copied into each of the cells. The correct totals will appear in each row.

Here's the amazing part: When Excel copied the formula, it did not do so blindly. Instead, it adjusted the terms of the formula so that each would refer to cells in the row to which it was copied. To verify this, highlight cell G5, for example, and press F2, as shown in Figure CE4-25. Notice that the formula in this cell is *=C5−D5+E5.* The formula you copied was *=C3+D3+E3.* Excel adjusted the row numbers when it copied the formula!

Suppose now we want to total the sales for each month. To obtain the total for March, for example, we want to total cells C3+C4+C5+C6+C7. To do so, we could go to an appropriate cell, say, C9, and enter the formula *=C3+C4+C5+C6−C7.* This will work, but there is an easier way to proceed.

Highlight cell C9 and then select the *Formulas* tab at the top of the ribbon. At the top of the tab, click *Auto Sum,* as shown in Figure CE4-26. Press *Enter,* and Excel will total the values in the column. If you click cell C9 and press F2, you will see that Excel entered the formula *=SUM(C3:C8).* This is a shorthand way of summing the values in those cells using a built-in function called **SUM.** To finish

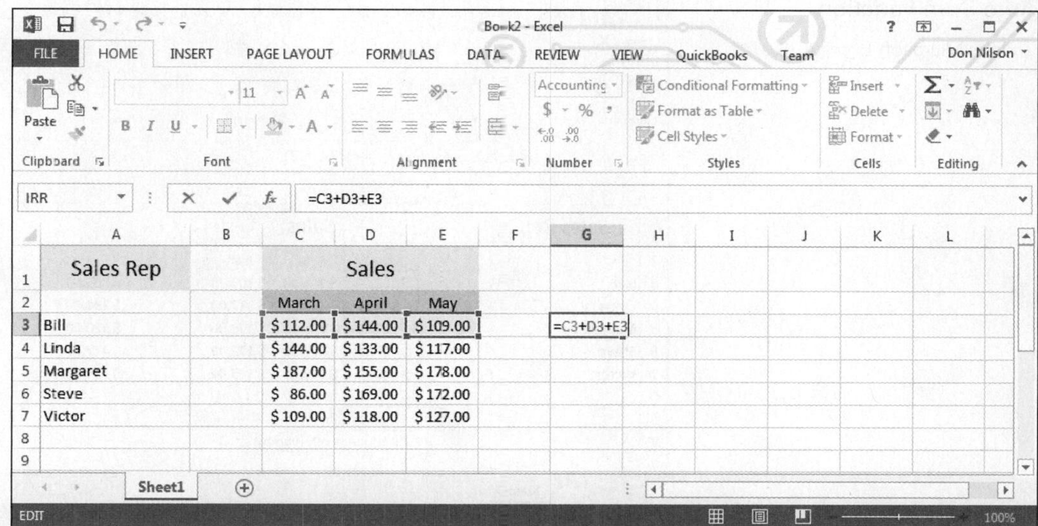


**Figure CE4-24**
Using the F2 Function Key to Show Color Coding of Cells Involved in a Calculation

*Source:* Microsoft Excel 2013

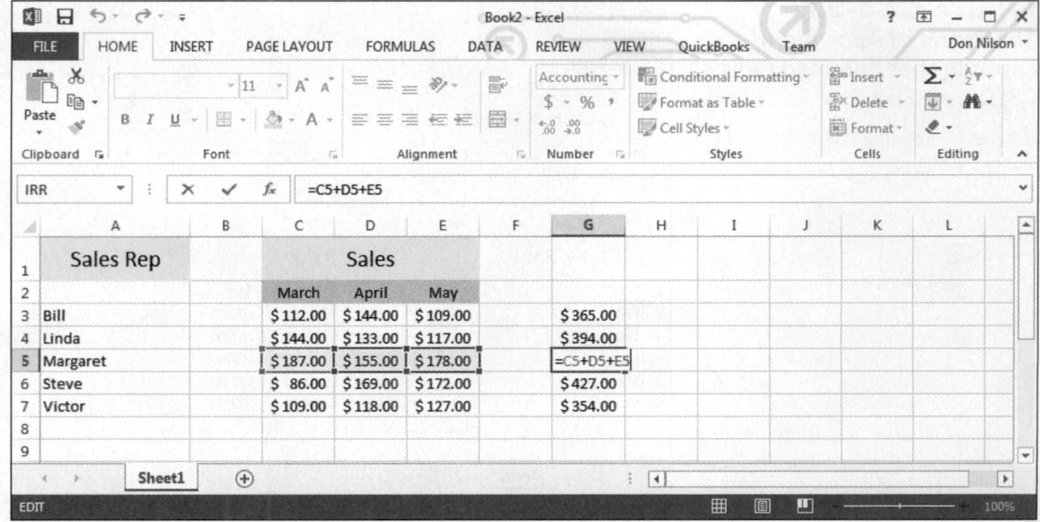


**Figure CE4-25**
Using the F2 Function Key to Confirm That a Formula Was Correctly Copied into Multiple Cells

*Source:* Microsoft Excel 2013

this spreadsheet, copy the formula from cell C9 to cells D9, E9, and G9. The spreadsheet will appear as in Figure CE4-27. Now all that remains to do is to add labels to the *total* row and *total* column.

You can use an Excel formula to create just about any algebraic expression. However, when you create a formula, remember the rules of high school algebra. For example, *=(B2+B3)/7* will add the contents of cell B2 to those of B3 and divide the sum by 7. In contrast, *=B2+B3/7* will first divide B3 by 7 and then add the result to the contents of B2. When in doubt, just key in a formula you think might work and experiment until you get the results you want.

## QCE4-7 HOW CAN YOU PRINT RESULTS?

Excel provides a wide variety of tools and settings for printing worksheets. Here we will illustrate several features that will give you an idea of the possibilities. After you have read this section, you can experiment on your own.

Before you start printing, you can save paper and ink if you make use of Excel's Print Preview feature. To do so, click *FILE* and then *Print*. The result is shown in Figure CE4-28. Before you click the large *Print* button (next to Copies), examine the *Print Preview* thumbnail of your printout to see if you like it. If you do, press *Print*, and Excel will print your document. For now, however, select the *PAGE LAYOUT* tab in the Excel ribbon.

**Figure CE4-26**
Auto Sum Function

*Source:* Microsoft Excel 2013

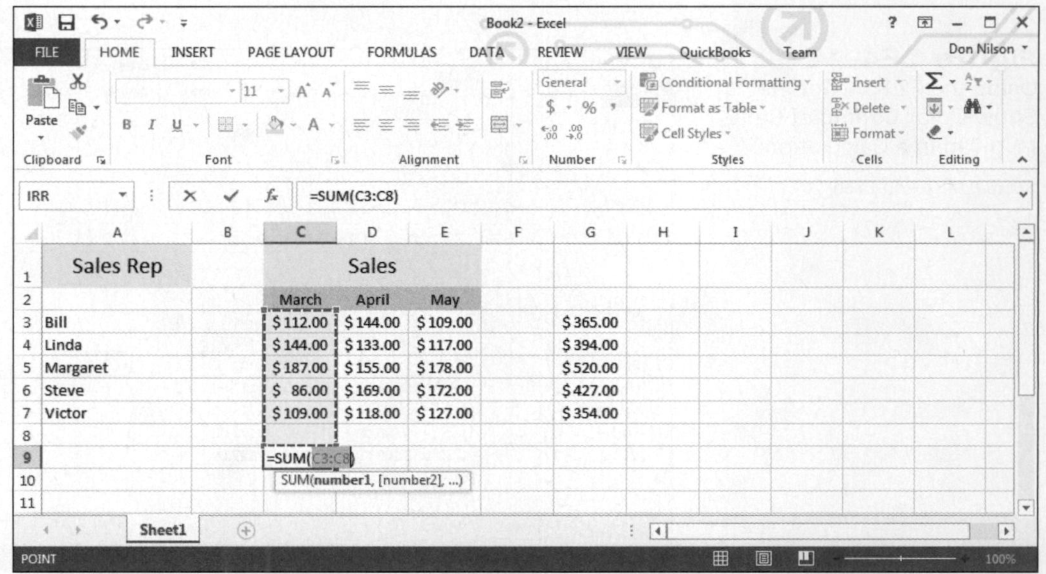

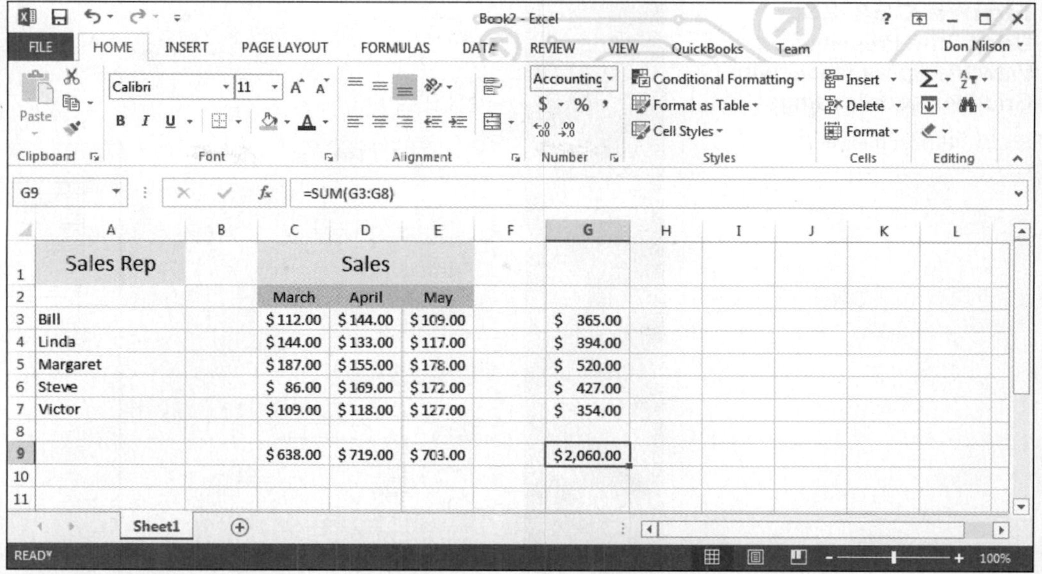


**Figure CE4-27**
Summing Sales by Month
*Source:* Microsoft Excel 2013

The tools and selections in the PAGE LAYOUT ribbon determine how the document will be arranged as a printed document. In this ribbon, the next to last group is *Sheet Options*; in that group, notice that you have the option of viewing and printing gridlines as well as column and row headings.

If you now select *Print* under *Gridlines* and *Headings* and then select *Print Preview*, you can see that your worksheet will be printed with gridlines and headings, as shown in Figure CE4-29. Most people prefer to see gridlines and headings in the screen display but not see them, or at least not see the headings, in the printed display. Click *Close Print Preview* to return to the spreadsheet view. For now, check *View* and *Print Gridlines*, but under *Headings* check only *View*.

As you can see, you have many other options in the PAGE LAYOUT ribbon. Use *Margins* to set the size of the page margins. *Orientation* refers to whether the worksheet is printed normally (upright) on the page (called *Portrait*) or sideways on the page (called *Landscape*). Try each and preview your print to see the impact each has.

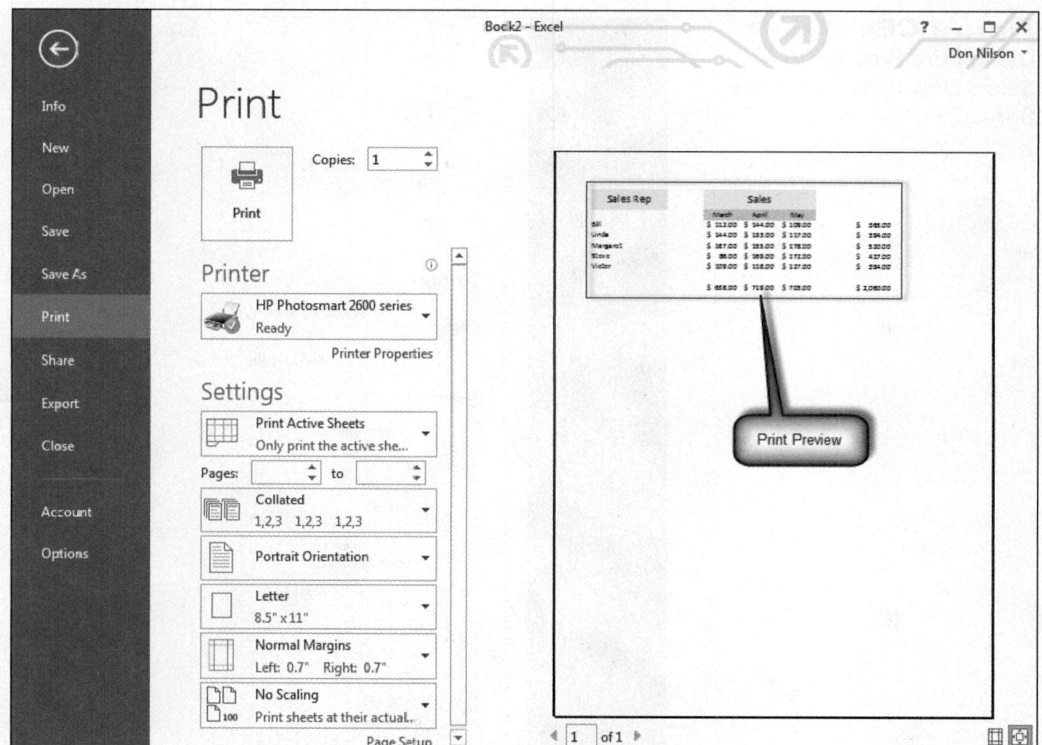


**Figure CE4-28**
The Print Preview Screen in Excel
*Source:* Microsoft Excel 2013

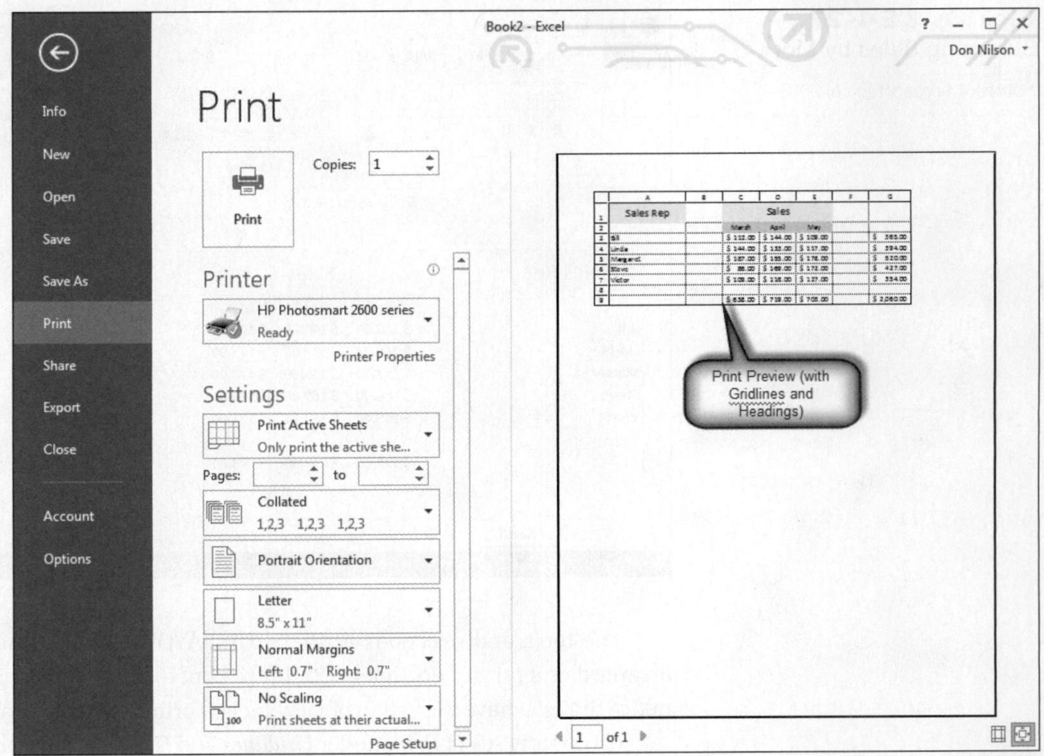


**Figure CE4-29** Using Print Preview to View the Spreadsheet with Gridlines and Headings

*Source:* Microsoft Excel 2013

You can use print area to specify the portion of the spreadsheet that you want to print. If for some reason you want to list only the name of the sales reps, you can highlight cells A1 through A7 and then click *Print Area* and then click *Set Print Area.* If you do this, your print preview will appear as in Figure CE4-30.

These commands should be enough for you to print basic assignments. Of course, Excel offers many more options for you to explore. Experiment with them!

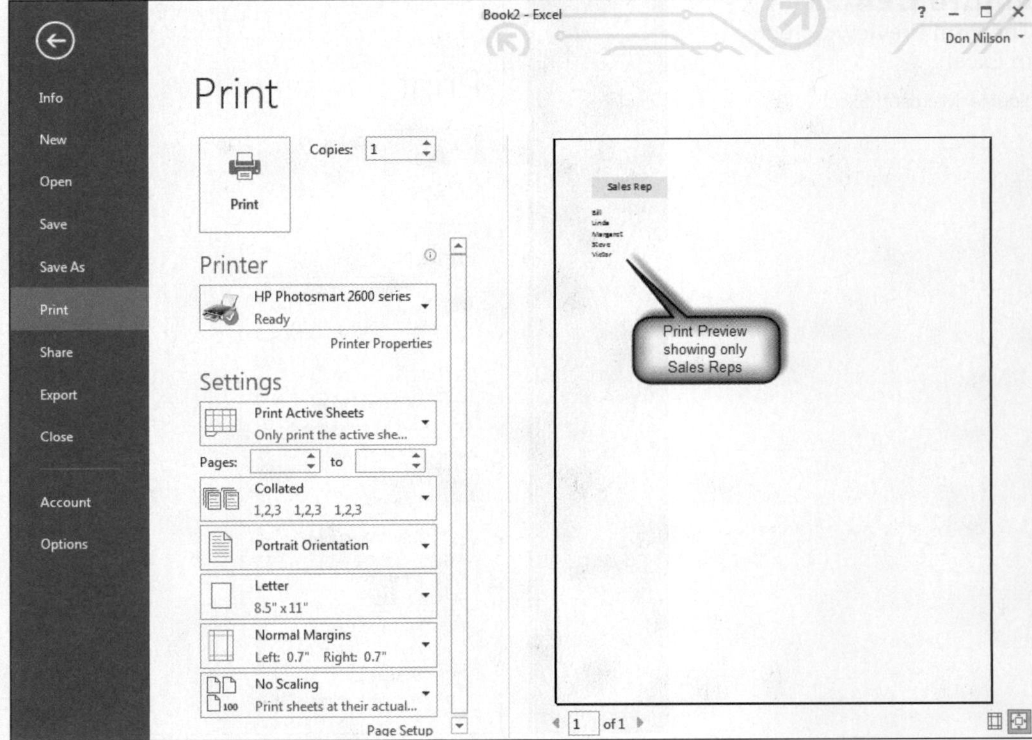


**Figure CE4-30** Using Print Preview to Select Only a Portion of the Spreadsheet

*Source:* Microsoft Excel 2013

# ACTIVE REVIEW

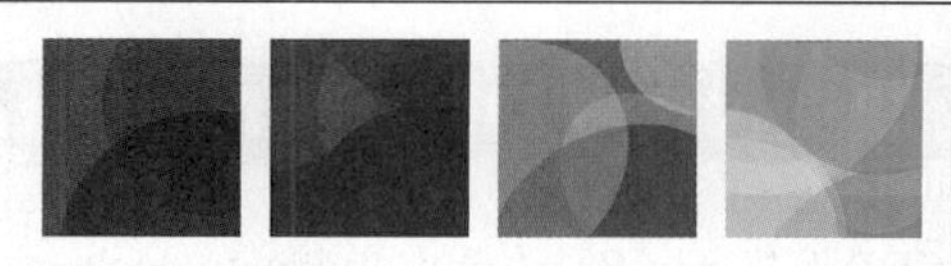

Use this Active Review to verify that you understand the ideas and concepts that answer this chapter extension's study questions.

## QCE4-1 WHAT IS A SPREADSHEET?

Explain how the following terms are related: *spreadsheet, electronic spreadsheet, Microsoft Excel, worksheet,* and *workbook.* Explain how spreadsheet cells are addressed. Where would you find cell Q54?

## QCE4-2 HOW DO YOU GET STARTED WITH EXCEL?

Describe the first task you should do when creating a spreadsheet. Open a new workbook and give it the name *My_Sample_WB.* Explain the relationship of tabs and tools and selections. Which tab is the most likely one to have the tools and selections you need?

## QCE4-3 HOW CAN YOU ENTER DATA?

List three ways of entering data into Excel. Describe the advantage of using the F2 key to edit data. Explain two ways that Excel uses a pattern to enter data.

## QCE4-4 HOW CAN YOU INSERT AND DELETE ROWS AND COLUMNS AND CHANGE THEIR SIZE?

Describe how to insert and delete rows. Describe a circumstance in which you would need to insert rows. Describe how to make a row taller or shorter. Describe how to change the width of a column.

## QCE4-5 HOW CAN YOU FORMAT DATA?

Open Excel and explain the purpose of each of the icons in the *Font* section of the *Home* tab of the ribbon. Explain the purpose of the *Alignment* and *Number* sections.

## QCE4-6 HOW CAN YOU CREATE A (SIMPLE) FORMULA?

Write the expression you would need to add the content of cell B2 to the content of cell B7. Write the expression to multiply the content of cell C4 by 7.3. Write the expression to find the average of the values in cells D7, D8, and D9. Use a built-in formula to total the values in cells E2, E3, E4, E5, E6, and E7.

## QCE4-7 HOW CAN YOU PRINT RESULTS?

Explain the purpose and use of *Print Preview.* Open Excel, go to the *PAGE LAYOUT* tab, and explain the purpose of the *Margins, Orientation,* and *Print Area* tools in the *Page Setup* section. Also, explain the function of the *View* and *Print* checkboxes in the *Gridlines* and *Headings* portion of the *Sheet Options* section.

# KEY TERMS AND CONCEPTS

Cell 417
Ribbon 419
Spreadsheet 417
SUM 429
Workbook 417
Worksheet 417

MyMISLab™

To complete the problems with the ✪, go to EOC Discussion Questions in the MyLab.

## USING YOUR KNOWLEDGE

**CE4-1.** Open Excel and duplicate each of the actions in this chapter extension.

**CE4-2.** Create a new workbook and take the following actions:

**a.** Name and save your workbook using a name of your own choosing.

**b.** Enter the value *This is the content of cell C7* into cell C7.

**c.** Use F2 to change the value in cell C7 to *This is part of the content of cell C7.*

**d.** Add the value *January* to cells B2 through B14. Key the data just once.

**e.** Add the value *January* to cell C2 and the value *February* to cell C3. Highlight both cells C2 and C3 and drag the small black box down to cell C14. Explain what happens.

**f.** Create a list of odd numbers from 1 to 11 in cells C3 through C8. Key only the values 1 and 3.

**g.** Enter the value *MIS-1* in cell D2 and the value *MIS-2* in cell D3. Highlight cells D2 and D3 and drag the small black box down to cell D14. Explain what happens.

**CE4-3.** Click the tab named *Sheet2* in the workbook you used for question 2.

**a.** Place the labels *Part Description, Quantity on Hand, Cost,* and *Total Value* in cells B2, C2, D2, and E2, respectively. Center each label in its cell and make the labels bold. (Do this by highlighting the labels and clicking the bold B in the *Font* section of the *Home* tab.) Make each column large enough to show the entire label after formatting.

**b.** In cells B3, B4, B5, B6, and B7, respectively, enter the following values:

- This is where one would type the description of Part 1
- This is where one would type the description of Part 2
- This is where one would type the description of Part 3
- This is where one would type the description of Part 4
- This is where one would type the description of Part 5

Enter these values using the fewest possible keystrokes.

**c.** Enter the quantity-on-hand values *100, 150, 100, 175,* and *200* in cells C3 through C7, respectively. Enter these values using the fewest possible keystrokes.

**d.** Enter the values *$100, $178, $87, $195,* and *$117* in cells D3 through D7, respectively. Do not enter the dollar signs. Instead, enter only the numbers and then reformat the cells so that Excel will place them.

**e.** In cell E3, enter a formula that will multiply the quantity on hand (C3) by the cost (D3).

**f.** Create the same formula in cells E4 through E7. Use select and copy operations.

**g.** Explain what is magic about the operation in part f.

**h.** Print the result of your activities in parts a–f. Print your document in landscape mode, showing cell boundaries and row and column names.

MyMISLab™

Go to the Assignments section of your MyLab to complete these writing exercises.

**CE4-4.** Explain why spreadsheets are so widely used in business. Why are they so useful to so many different types of business workers? How does their relative ease of use compared to databases affect their use by workers?

**CE4-5.** Explain why knowing how to use spreadsheets effectively could impact your future employment opportunities. How might the ability to create more complex spreadsheets increase your earnings potential? Why is it important to know how to use spreadsheets effectively regardless of the industry you're working in?

chapter extension **5**

**Chapter 5** provides the background for this extension.

# Database Design

**STUDY QUESTIONS**

**QCE5-1 WHO WILL VOLUNTEER?**

**QCE5-2 HOW ARE DATABASE APPLICATION SYSTEMS DEVELOPED?**

**QCE5-3 WHAT ARE THE COMPONENTS OF THE ENTITY-RELATIONSHIP DATA MODEL?**

**QCE5-4 HOW IS A DATA MODEL TRANSFORMED INTO A DATABASE DESIGN?**

**QCE5-5 WHAT IS THE USERS' ROLE?**

**QCE5-6 WHO WILL VOLUNTEER? (CONTINUED)**

In this chapter extension, you will learn about data modeling and how data models are transformed into database designs. You'll also learn the important role that business professionals have in the development of a database application system.

## QCE5-1 WHO WILL VOLUNTEER?

Suppose you are the manager of fund-raising for a local public television station. Twice a year you conduct fund drives during which the station runs commercials that ask viewers to donate. These drives are important; they provide nearly 40 percent of the station's operating budget.

One of your job functions is to find volunteers to staff the phones during these drives. You need 10 volunteers per night for 6 nights, or 60 people, twice per year. The volunteers' job is exhausting, and normally a volunteer will work only one night during a drive.

Finding volunteers for each drive is a perpetual headache. Two months before a drive begins, you and your staff start calling potential volunteers. You first call volunteers from prior drives, using a roster that your administrative assistant prepares for each drive. Some volunteers have been helping for years; you'd like to know that information before you call them so that you can tell them how much you appreciate their continuing support. Unfortunately, the roster does not have that data.

Additionally, some volunteers are more effective than others. Some have a particular knack for increasing the callers' donations. Although those data are available, the information is not in a format that you can use when calling for volunteers. You think you could better staff the fund-raising drives if you had that missing information.

You know that you can use a computer database to keep better track of prior volunteers' service and performance, but you are not sure how to proceed. By the end of this chapter extension, when we return to this fund-raising situation, you will know what to do.

## QCE5-2 HOW ARE DATABASE APPLICATION SYSTEMS DEVELOPED?

You learned in Chapter 5 that a database application system consists of a database, a DBMS, and one or more database applications. A database application, in turn, consists of forms, reports, queries, and possibly application programs. The question then becomes: How are such systems developed? And, even more important to you, what is the users' role? We will address these questions in this chapter extension.

Figure CE5-1 summarizes the database application system development process. First, the developers interview users and develop the requirements for the new system. During this process, the developers analyze existing forms, reports, queries, and other user activities. They also determine the need for new forms, reports, and queries. The requirements for the database are then

CE5

**Figure CE5-1**
Database Development Process

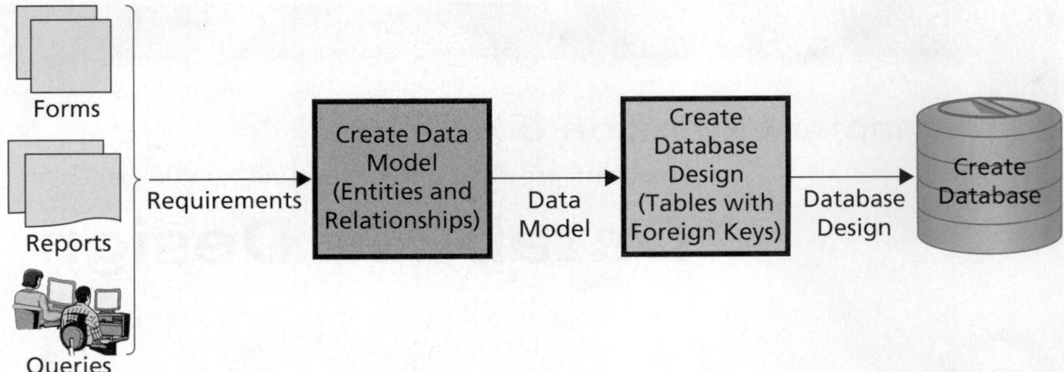


summarized in something called a **data model**, which is a logical representation of the structure of the data. The data model contains a description of both the data and the relationships among the data. It is akin to a blueprint. Just as building architects create a blueprint before they start construction, so, too, database developers create a data model before they start designing the database.

Once the users have validated and approved the data model, it is transformed into a database design. After that, the design is implemented in a database, and that database is then filled with user data.

You will learn much more about systems development in Chapter 12 and its related extensions. We discuss data modeling here because users have a crucial role in the success of any database development: They must validate and approve the data model. Only the users know what should be in the database.

Consider, for example, a database of students that an adviser uses for his or her advisees. What should be in it? Students? Classes? Records of emails from students? Records of meetings with students? Majors? Student organizations? Even when we know what themes should be in the database, we must ask, how detailed should the records be? Should the database include campus addresses? Home addresses? Billing addresses?

In fact, there are many possibilities, and the database developers do not and cannot know what to include. They do know, however, that a database must include all the data necessary for the users to perform their jobs. Ideally, it contains that amount of data and no more. So during database development, the developers must rely on the users to tell them what they need in the database. They will rely on the users to check the data model and to verify it for correctness, completeness, and appropriate level of detail. That verification will be your job. We begin with a discussion of the entity-relationship data model—the most common tool to use to construct data models.

## QCE5-3 WHAT ARE THE COMPONENTS OF THE ENTITY-RELATIONSHIP DATA MODEL?

The most popular technique for creating a data model is the **entity-relationship (E-R) data model**. With it, developers describe the content of a database by defining the things (*entities*) that will be stored in the database and the *relationships* among those entities. A second, less popular tool for data modeling is the **Unified Modeling Language (UML)**. We will not describe that tool here. However, if you learn how to interpret E-R models, with a bit of study you will be able to understand UML models as well.

### ENTITIES

An **entity** is something that the users want to track. Examples of entities are *Order*, *Customer*, *Salesperson*, and *Item*. Some entities represent a physical object, such as *Item* or *Salesperson*; others represent a logical construct or transaction, such as *Order* or *Contract*. For

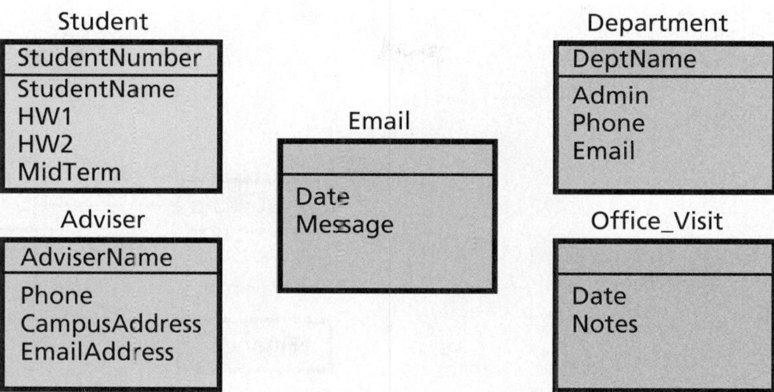


**Figure CE5-2**
Student Data Model Entities

reasons beyond this discussion, entity names are always singular. We use *Order*, not *Orders*; *Salesperson*, not *Salespersons*.

Entities have **attributes** that describe characteristics of the entity. Example attributes of *Order* are *OrderNumber, OrderDate, SubTotal, Tax, Total*, and so forth. Example attributes of *Salesperson* are *SalespersonName, Email, Phone*, and so forth.

Entities have an **identifier**, which is an attribute (or group of attributes) whose value is associated with one and only one entity instance. For example, *OrderNumber* is an identifier of *Order* because only one *Order* instance has a given value of *OrderNumber*. For the same reason, *CustomerNumber* is an identifier of *Customer*. If each member of the sales staff has a unique name, then *SalespersonName* is an identifier of *Salesperson*.

Before we continue, consider that last sentence. Is the salesperson's name unique among the sales staff? Both now and in the future? Who decides the answer to such a question? Only the users know whether this is true; the database developers cannot know. This example underlines why it is important for you to be able to interpret data models because only users like you will know for sure.

Figure CE5-2 shows examples of entities for the Student database. Each entity is shown in a rectangle. The name of the entity is just above the rectangle, and the identifier is shown in a section at the top of the entity. Entity attributes are shown in the remainder of the rectangle. In Figure CE5-2, the *Adviser* entity has an identifier called *AdviserName* and the attributes *Phone, CampusAddress*, and *EmailAddress*.

Observe that the entities *Email* and *Office_Visit* do not have an identifier. Unlike *Student* or *Adviser*, the users do not have an attribute that identifies a particular email. In fact, *Email* and *Office_Visit* are identified, in part, by their relationship to *Student*. For now, we need not worry about that. The data model needs only to show how users view their world. When it comes to database design, the designer will deal with the missing identifiers by adding columns, possibly using hidden identifiers, to implement the users' view. You can learn about the modeling and representation of such entities if you enroll in a database class.

## RELATIONSHIPS

Entities have **relationships** to each other. An *Order*, for example, has a relationship to a *Customer* entity and also to a *Salesperson* entity. In the Student database, a *Student* has a relationship to an *Adviser*, and an *Adviser* has a relationship to a *Department*.

Figure CE5-3 shows sample *Department, Adviser*, and *Student* entities and their relationships. For simplicity, this figure shows just the identifier of the entities and not the other attributes. For this sample data, *Accounting* has three professors, Jones, Wu, and Lopez, and *Finance* has two professors, Smith and Greene.

The relationship between *Advisers* and *Students* is a bit more complicated because in this example an adviser is allowed to advise many students and a student is allowed to have many

**Figure CE5-3**
Example of *Department, Adviser,* and *Student* Entities and Relationships

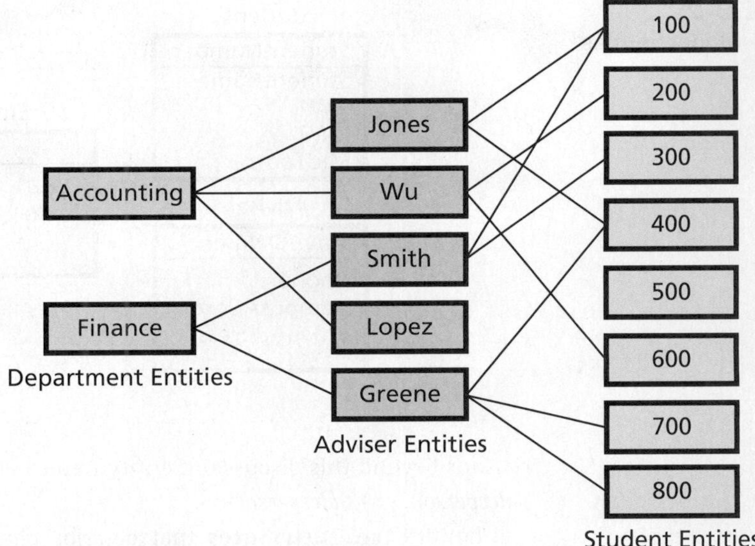


advisers. Perhaps this happens because students can have multiple majors. In any case, note that Professor Jones advises students 100 and 400 and that student 100 is advised by both Professors Jones and Smith.

Diagrams like the one in Figure CE5-3 are too cumbersome for use in database design discussions. Instead, database designers use diagrams called **entity-relationship (E-R) diagrams**. Figure CE5-4 shows an E-R diagram for the data in Figure CE5-3. In this figure, all of the entities of one type are represented by a single rectangle. Thus, there are rectangles for the *Department, Adviser*, and *Student* entities. Attributes are shown as before in Figure CE5-2.

Additionally, a line is used to represent a relationship between two entities. Notice the line between *Department* and *Adviser*, for example. The forked lines on the right side of that line signify that a department may have more than one adviser. The angled lines, which are referred to as a **crow's foot**, are shorthand for the multiple lines between *Department* and *Adviser* in Figure CE5-3. The left end of the line has a single vertical bar, indicating that an adviser works in just one department. Relationships like this one are called **one-to-many (1:N) relationships** because one department can have many advisers.

Now examine the line between *Adviser* and *Student*. Here a crow's foot appears at each end of the line. This notation signifies that an adviser can be related to many students and that a student can be related to many advisers, which is the situation in Figure CE5-3. Relationships like this one are called **many-to-many (N:M) relationships** because one adviser can have many students and one student can have many advisers.

Students sometimes find the notation N:M confusing. Interpret the *N* and *M* to mean that a variable number, greater than one, is allowed on each side of the relationship. Such a relationship is not written *N:N* because that notation would imply that there are the same number of entities on each side of the relationship, which is not necessarily true. *N:M* means that more than one entity is allowed on each side of the relationship and that the number of entities on each side can be different.

**Figure CE5-4**
Example Relationships—Version 1

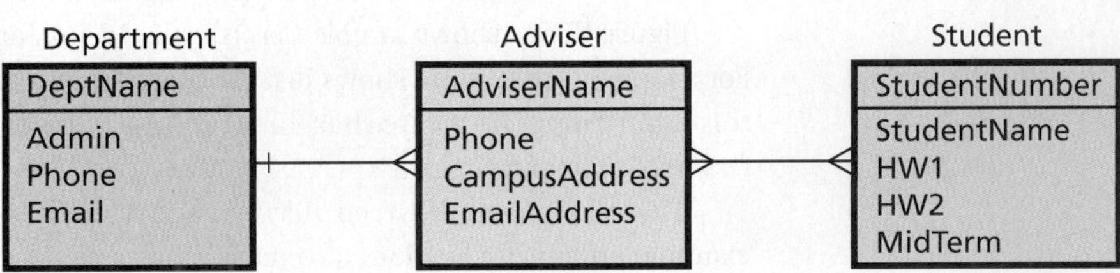

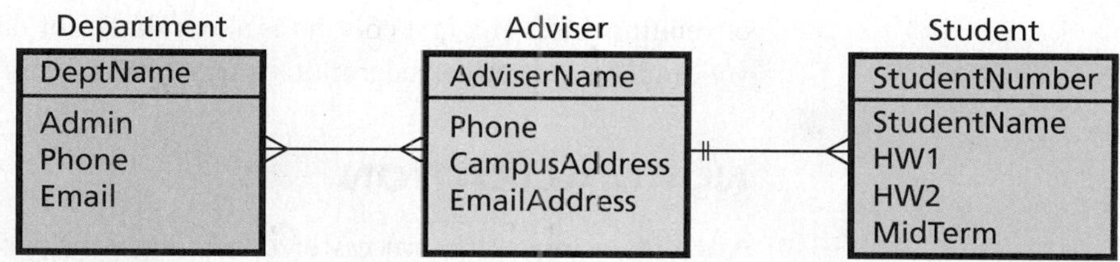


**Figure CE5-5**
Example Relationships—Version 2

Figure CE5-4 is an example of an entity-relationship diagram. Unfortunately, there are several different styles of entity-relationship diagrams. This one is called, not surprisingly, a **crow's-foot diagram** version. You may learn other versions if you take a database management class.

Figure CE5-5 shows the same entities with different assumptions. Here advisers may advise in more than one department, but a student may have only one adviser, representing a policy that students may not have multiple majors.

Which, if either of these versions—Figure CE5-4 or Figure CE5-5—is correct? Only the users know. These alternatives illustrate the kinds of questions you will need to answer when a database designer asks you to check a data model for correctness.

The crow's-foot notation shows the maximum number of entities that can be involved in a relationship. Accordingly, they are called the relationship's **maximum cardinality**. Common examples of maximum cardinality are 1:N, N:M, and 1:1 (not shown).

Another important question is, "What is the minimum number of entities required in the relationship?" Must an adviser have a student to advise, and must a student have an adviser? Constraints on minimum requirements are called **minimum cardinalities**.

Figure CE5-6 presents a third version of this E-R diagram that shows both maximum and minimum cardinalities. The second vertical bar on the lines means that at least one entity of that type is required. The small oval means that the entity is optional; the relationship need not have an entity of that type. Using this notation, if there are two vertical bars, both the minimum and maximum cardinality are one. If there is a vertical bar with a crow's foot, then the minimum cardinality is one and the maximum is many.

Thus, in Figure CE5-6, a department is not required to have a relationship to any adviser, but an adviser is required to belong to a department. Similarly, an adviser is not required to have a relationship to a student, but a student is required to have a relationship to an adviser. Note, also, that the maximum cardinalities in Figure CE5-6 have been changed so that both are 1:N.

Is the model in Figure CE5-6 a good one? It depends on the rules of the university. Again, only the users know for sure.

## QCE5-4 HOW IS A DATA MODEL TRANSFORMED INTO A DATABASE DESIGN?

Database design is the process of converting a data model into tables, relationships, and data constraints. The database design team transforms entities into tables and expresses relationships by defining foreign keys. Database design is a complicated subject; as with data modeling, it occupies weeks in a database management class. In this section, however, we will introduce two important database design concepts: normalization and the representation of two kinds

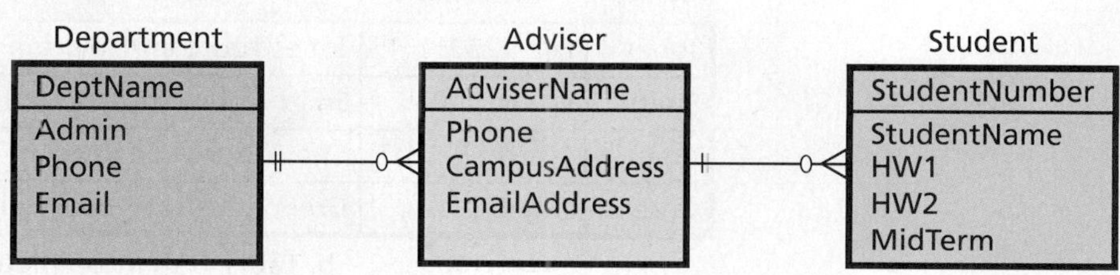


**Figure CE5-6**
Example of Relationships Showing Both Maximum and Minimum Cardinalities

of relationships. The first concept is a foundation of database design, and the second will help you understand key considerations made during design.

## NORMALIZATION

**Normalization** is the process of converting poorly structured tables into two or more well-structured tables. A table is such a simple construct that you may wonder how one could possibly be poorly structured. In truth, there are many ways that tables can be malformed—so many, in fact, that researchers have published hundreds of papers on this topic alone.

Consider the *Employee* table in Figure CE5-7. It lists employee names, hire dates, email addresses, and the name and number of the department in which the employee works. This table seems innocent enough. But consider what happens when the Accounting department changes its name to Accounting and Finance. Because department names are duplicated in this table, every row that has a value of "Accounting" must be changed to "Accounting and Finance."

### Data Integrity Problems

Suppose the Accounting name change is correctly made in two rows, but not in the third. The result is shown in Figure CE5-7b. This table has what is called a **data integrity problem**: Two rows indicate that the name of Department 100 is Accounting and Finance, and another row indicates that the name of Department 100 is Accounting.

This problem is easy to spot in this small table. But consider a table in a large database that has more than 300,000 rows. Once a table that large develops serious data integrity problems, months of labor will be required to remove them.

Data integrity problems are serious. A table that has data integrity problems will produce incorrect and inconsistent information. Users will lose confidence in the information, and the system will develop a poor reputation. Information systems with poor reputations become heavy burdens to the organizations that use them.

### Normalizing for Data Integrity

The data integrity problem can occur only if data are duplicated. Because of this, one easy way to eliminate the problem is to eliminate the duplicated data. We can do this by transforming the table design in Figure CE5-7a into two tables, as shown in Figure CE5-8. Here the name of the department is stored just once; therefore, no data inconsistencies can occur.

**Figure CE5-7**
A Poorly Designed *Employee* Table

**Employee**

| Name | HireDate | Email | DeptNo | DeptName |
|---|---|---|---|---|
| Jones | Feb 1, 2010 | Jones@ourcompany.com | 100 | Accounting |
| Smith | Dec 3, 2007 | Smith@ourcompany.com | 200 | Marketing |
| Chau | March 7, 2007 | Chau@ourcompany.com | 100 | Accounting |
| Greene | July 17, 2010 | Greene@ourcompany.com | 100 | Accounting |

a. Table Before Update

**Employee**

| Name | HireDate | Email | DeptNo | DeptName |
|---|---|---|---|---|
| Jones | Feb 1, 2010 | Jones@ourcompany.com | 100 | Accounting and Finance |
| Smith | Dec 3, 2007 | Smith@ourcompany.com | 200 | Marketing |
| Chau | March 7, 2007 | Chau@ourcompany.com | 100 | Accounting and Finance |
| Greene | July 17, 2010 | Greene@ourcompany.com | 100 | Accounting |

b. Table with Incomplete Update

**Figure CE5-8**
Two Normalized Tables

**Employee**

| Name | HireDate | Email | DeptNo |
|---|---|---|---|
| Jones | Feb 1, 2010 | Jones@ourcompany.com | 100 |
| Smith | Dec 3, 2011 | Smith@ourcompany.com | 200 |
| Chau | March 7, 2007 | Chau@ourcompany.com | 100 |
| Greene | July 17, 2010 | Greene@ourcompany.com | 100 |

**Department**

| DeptNo | DeptName |
|---|---|
| 100 | Accounting |
| 200 | Marketing |
| 300 | Information Systems |

Of course, to produce an employee report that includes the department name, the two tables in Figure CE5-8 will need to be joined back together. Because such joining of tables is common, DBMS products have been programmed to perform it efficiently, but it still requires work. From this example, you can see a trade-off in database design: Normalized tables eliminate data duplication, but they can be slower to process. Dealing with such trade-offs is an important consideration in database design.

The general goal of normalization is to construct tables such that every table has a *single* topic or theme. In good writing, every paragraph should have a single theme. This is true of databases as well: every table should have a single theme. The problem with the table design in Figure CE5-7 is that it has two independent themes: employees and departments. The way to correct the problem is to split the table into two tables, each with its own theme. In this case, we create an *Employee* table and a *Department* table, as shown in Figure CE5-8.

As mentioned, there are dozens of ways that tables can be poorly formed. Database practitioners classify tables into various **normal forms** according to the kinds of problems they have. Transforming a table into a normal form to remove duplicated data and other problems is called *normalizing* the table.[1] Thus, when you hear a database designer say, "Those tables are not normalized," she does not mean that the tables have irregular, not-normal data. Instead, she means that the tables have a format that could cause data integrity problems.

### Summary of Normalization

As a future user of databases, you do not need to know the details of normalization. Instead, understand the general principle that every normalized (well-formed) table has one and only one theme. Further, tables that are not normalized are subject to data integrity problems.

Be aware, too, that normalization is just one criterion for evaluating database designs. Because normalized designs can be slower to process, database designers sometimes choose to accept non-normalized tables. The best design depends on the users' requirements.

## REPRESENTING RELATIONSHIPS

Figure CE5-9 shows the steps involved in transforming a data model into a relational database design. First, the database designer creates a table for each entity. The identifier of the entity becomes the key of the table. Each attribute of the entity becomes a column of the table. Next, the resulting tables are normalized so that each table has a single theme. Once that has been done, the next step is to represent the relationship among those tables.

For example, consider the E-R diagram in Figure CE5-10a. The *Adviser* entity has a 1:N relationship to the *Student* entity. To create the database design, we construct a table for *Adviser* and a

**Figure CE5-9**
Transforming a Data Model into a Database Design

- Represent each entity with a table
  - Entity identifier becomes table key
  - Entity attributes become table columns
- Normalize tables as necessary
- Represent relationships
  - Use foreign keys
  - Add additional tables for N:M relationships

second table for *Student*, as shown in Figure CE5-10b. The key of the *Adviser* table is *AdviserName*, and the key of the *Student* table is *StudentNumber.*

Further, the *EmailAddress* attribute of the *Adviser* entity becomes the *EmailAddress* column of the *Adviser* table, and the *StudentName* and *MidTerm* attributes of the *Student* entity become the *StudentName* and *MidTerm* columns of the *Student* table.

**Figure CE5-10**
Representing a 1:N Relationship

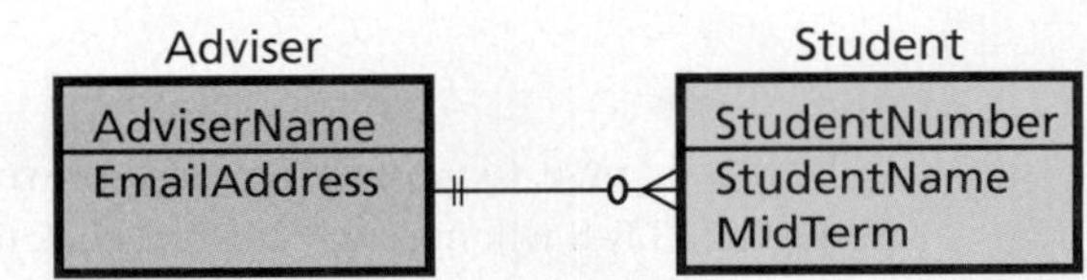


**a. 1: N Relationship Between Adviser and Student Entities**

Adviser Table—Key Is AdviserName

| AdviserName | EmailAddress |
|---|---|
| Jones | Jones@myuniv.edu |
| Choi | Choi@myuniv.edu |
| Jackson | Jackson@myuniv.edu |

Student Table—Key Is StudentNumber

| StudentNumber | StudentName | MidTerm |
|---|---|---|
| 100 | Lisa | 90 |
| 200 | Jennie | 85 |
| 300 | Jason | 82 |
| 400 | Terry | 95 |

**b. Creating a Table for Each Entity**

Adviser Table—Key Is AdviserName

| AdviserName | EmailAddress |
|---|---|
| Jones | Jones@myuniv.edu |
| Choi | Choi@myuniv.edu |
| Jackson | Jackson@myuniv.edu |

Foreign Key Column Represents Relationship

Student—Key Is StudentNumber

| StudentNumber | StudentName | MidTerm | AdviserName |
|---|---|---|---|
| 100 | Lisa | 90 | Jackson |
| 200 | Jennie | 85 | Jackson |
| 300 | Jason | 82 | Choi |
| 400 | Terry | 95 | Jackson |

**c. Using the AdviserName Foreign Key to Represent the 1:N Relationship**

The next task is to represent the relationship. Because we are using the relational model, we know that we must add a foreign key to one of the two tables. The possibilities are: (1) place the foreign key *StudentNumber* in the *Adviser* table or (2) place the foreign key *AdviserName* in the *Student* table.

The correct choice is to place *AdviserName* in the *Student* table, as shown in Figure CE5-10c. To determine a student's adviser, we just look into the *AdviserName* column of that student's row. To determine the adviser's students, we search the *AdviserName* column in the *Student* table to determine which rows have that adviser's name. If a student changes advisers, we simply change the value in the *AdviserName* column. Changing *Jackson* to *Jones* in the first row, for example, will assign student 100 to Professor Jones.

For this data model, placing *StudentNumber* in *Adviser* would be incorrect. If we were to do that, we could assign only one student to an adviser. There is no place to assign a second adviser.

This strategy for placing foreign keys will not work for N:M relationships, however. Consider the data model in Figure CE5-11a (page 444); here there is an N:M relationship between advisers and students. An adviser may have many students, and a student may have multiple advisers (for multiple majors). The strategy we used for the 1:N data model will not work here. To see why, examine Figure CE5-11b. If student 100 has more than one adviser, there is no place to record second or subsequent advisers.

It turns out that to represent an N:M relationship, we need to create a third table, as shown in Figure CE5-11c. The third table has two columns, *AdviserName* and *Student-Number.* Each row of the table means that the given adviser advises the student with the given number.

As you can imagine, there is a great deal more to database design than we have presented here. Still, this section should give you an idea of the tasks that need to be accomplished to create a database. You should also realize that the database design is a direct consequence of decisions made in the data model. If the data model is wrong, the database design will be wrong as well.

## QCE5-5 WHAT IS THE USERS' ROLE?

As stated, a database is a model of how the users view their business world. This means that the users are the final judges of what data the database should contain and how the records in that database should be related to one another.

The easiest time to change the database structure is during the data modeling stage. Changing a relationship from 1:N to N:M in a data model is simply a matter of changing the 1:N notation to N:M. However, once the database has been constructed, and loaded with data and application forms, reports, queries, and application programs have been created, changing a 1:N relationship to N:M means weeks of work.

You can glean some idea of why this might be true by contrasting Figure CE5-10c with Figure CE5-11c. Suppose that instead of having just a few rows, each table has thousands of rows; in that case, transforming the database from one format to the other involves considerable work. Even worse, however, is that application components will need to be changed as well. For example, if students have at most one adviser, then a single text box can be used to enter *AdviserName.* If students can have multiple advisers, then a multiple-row table will need to be used to enter *AdviserName*, and a program will need to be written to store the values of *AdviserName* into the *Adviser_Student_Intersection* table. There are dozens of other consequences as well, consequences that will translate into wasted labor and wasted expense.

The conclusion from this discussion is that user review of a data model is crucial. When a database is developed for your use, you must carefully review the data model. If you do not understand any aspect of it, you should ask for clarification until you do. The data model must accurately reflect your view of the business. If it does not, the database will be designed incorrectly, and the applications will be difficult to use, if not worthless. Do not proceed unless the data model is accurate.

**Figure CE5-11**
Representing an N:M Relationship

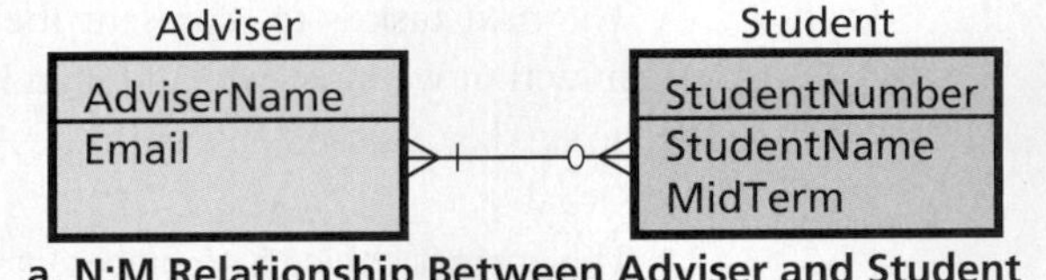


**a. N:M Relationship Between Adviser and Student**

Adviser—Key Is AdviserName

| AdviserName | Email |
|---|---|
| Jones | Jones@myuniv.edu |
| Choi | Choi@myuniv.edu |
| Jackson | Jackson@myuniv.edu |

No room to place second or third AdviserName

Student—Key Is StudentNumber

| StudentNumber | StudentName | MidTerm | AdviserName |
|---|---|---|---|
| 100 | Lisa | 90 | Jackson |
| 200 | Jennie | 85 | Jackson |
| 300 | Jason | 82 | Choi |
| 400 | Terry | 95 | Jackson |

**b. Incorrect Representation of N:M Relationship**

Adviser—Key Is AdviserName

| AdviserName | Email |
|---|---|
| Jones | Jones@myuniv.edu |
| Choi | Choi@myuniv.edu |
| Jackson | Jackson@myuniv.edu |

Student—Key Is StudentNumber

| StudentNumber | StudentName | MidTerm |
|---|---|---|
| 100 | Lisa | 90 |
| 200 | Jennie | 85 |
| 300 | Jason | 82 |
| 400 | Terry | 95 |

Adviser_Student_Intersection

| AdviserName | StudentNumber |
|---|---|
| Jackson | 100 |
| Jackson | 200 |
| Choi | 300 |
| Jackson | 400 |
| Choi | 100 |
| Jones | 100 |

Student 100 has three advisers.

**c. Adviser_Student_Intersection Table Represents the N:M Relationship**

As a corollary, when asked to review a data model, take that review seriously. Devote the time necessary to perform a thorough review. Any mistakes you miss will come back to haunt you, and by then the cost of correction may be very high with regard to both time and expense. This brief introduction to data modeling shows why databases can be more difficult to develop than spreadsheets.

## QCE5-6 WHO WILL VOLUNTEER? (CONTINUED)

Knowing what you know now, if you were the manager of fund-raising at the TV station, you would hire a consultant and expect the consultant to interview all of the key users. From those interviews, the consultant would then construct a data model.

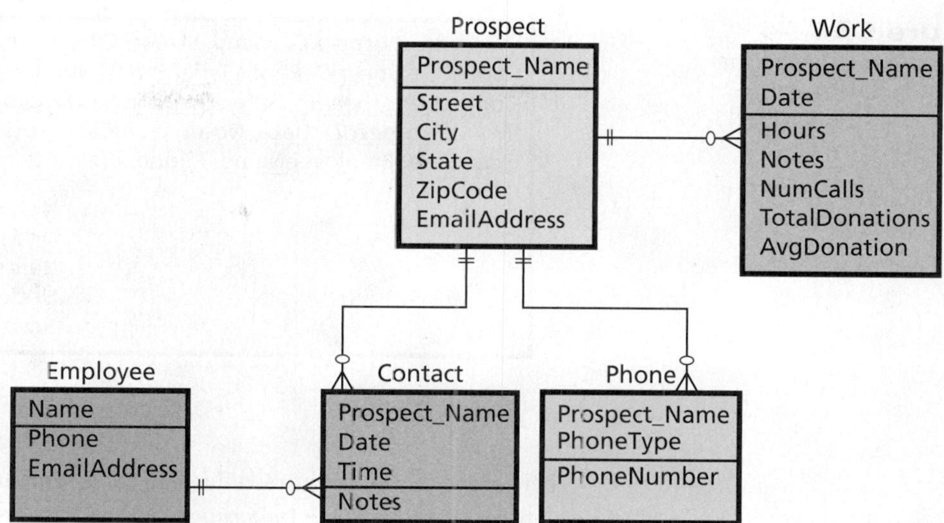


**Figure CE5-12**
Data Model for Volunteer Database

You now know that the structure of the database must reflect the way the users think about their activities. If the consultant did not take the time to interview you and your staff or did not construct a data model and ask you to review it, you would know that you are not receiving good service and would take corrective action.

Suppose you found a consultant who interviewed your staff for several hours and then constructed the data model shown in Figure CE5-12. This data model has an entity for *Prospect*, an entity for *Employee*, and three additional entities for *Contact*, *Phone*, and *Work*. The *Contact* entity records contacts that you or other employees have made with the prospective volunteer. This record is necessary so that you know what has been said to whom. The *Phone* entity is used to record multiple phone numbers for each prospective volunteer, and the *Work* entity records work that the prospect has performed for the station.

After you reviewed and approved this data model, the consultant constructed the database design shown in Figure CE5-13. In this design, table keys are underlined, foreign keys are shown in italics, and columns that are both table and foreign keys are underlined and italicized. Observe that the *Name* column is the table key of *Prospect*, and it is both part of the table key and a foreign key in *Phone*, *Contact*, and *Work*.

The consultant did not like having the *Name* column used as a key or as part of a key in so many tables. Based on her interviews, she suspected that prospect names are fluid—and that sometimes the same prospect name is recorded in different ways (e.g., sometimes with a middle initial and sometimes without). If that were to happen, phone, contact, and work data could be misallocated to prospect names. Accordingly, the consultant added a new column, *ProspectID*, to the prospect table and created the design shown in Figure CE5-14. Values of this ID will have no meaning to the users, but the ID will be used to ensure that each prospect obtains a unique record in the Volunteer database. Because this ID has no meaning to the users, the consultant will hide it on forms and reports that users see.

**Figure CE5-13**
First Table Design for Volunteer Database

Prospect (<u>Name</u>, Street, City, State, Zip, EmailAddress)
Phone (<u>*Name*</u>, <u>PhoneType</u>, PhoneNumber)
Contact (<u>*Name*</u>, <u>Date</u>, <u>Time</u>, Notes, *EmployeeName*)
Work (<u>*Name*</u>, <u>Date</u>, Notes, NumCalls, TotalDonations)
Employee (<u>EmployeeName</u>, Phone, EmailAddress)

Note:
Underline means table key.
Italics means foreign key.
Underline and italics mean both table and foreign key.

**Figure CE5-14**
Second Table Design for Volunteer Database

Prospect (*ProspectID*, Name, Street, City, State, Zip, EmailAddress)
Phone (*ProspectID*, PhoneType, PhoneNumber)
Contact (*ProspectID*, Date, Time, Notes, *EmployeeName*)
Work (*ProspectID*, Date, Notes, NumCalls, TotalDonations)
Employee (EmployeeName, Phone, EmailAddress)

Note:
Underline means table key.
Italics means foreign key.
Underline and italics mean both table and foreign key.

There is one difference between the data model and the table designs. In the data model, the *Work* entity has an attribute, *AvgDonation*, but there is no corresponding *AvgDonation* column in the *Work* table. The consultant decided that there was no need to store this value in the database because it could readily be computed on forms and reports using the values in the *NumCalls* and *TotalDonations* columns.

Once the tables had been designed, the consultant created a Microsoft Access 2013 database. She defined the tables in Access, created relationships among the tables, and constructed forms and reports. Figure CE5-15 shows the primary data entry form used for the Volunteer database. The top portion of the form has contact data, including multiple phone numbers. It is important to know the type of the phone number so that you and your staff know if you're calling someone at work or another setting. The middle and bottom sections of this form have contact and prior work data. Observe that *AvgDonation* has been computed from the *NumCalls* and *TotalDonations* columns.

You were quite pleased with this database application, and you're certain that it helped you to improve the volunteer staffing at the station. Of course, over time, you thought of several new requirements, and you already have changes in mind for next year.

**Figure CE5-15**
Volunteer Prospect Data Entry Form
*Source:* Microsoft Access 2013

Name: Mary Smith
EmailAddress: MaryS@somewhere.com

Phone

| PhoneType | PhoneNumber |
|---|---|
| Mobile | (206)-555-1234 |
| Home | (425)-555-5587 |
| Office | (206)-555-7767 |
| * | |

Record: 1 of 3

Street: 123 Elm Street
City: Bellevue
State: WA
ZipCode: 98050-1234

Contact

| DateOfConta | Notes | EmployeeName |
|---|---|---|
| 3/17/2016 | Not sure about schedule | David |
| 4/2/2016 | Willing to work on Thursdays | Selma |
| * | | |

Record: 1 of 2 No Filter Search

Work

| Date | Notes | NumCa | TotalDonations | AvgDonation |
|---|---|---|---|---|
| 7/10/2016 | Enjoyable Team Member | 37 | $7,350.00 | $198.65 |
| * | | 1 | $0.00 | $0.00 |

Record: 1 of 1 No Filter Search

# ACTIVE REVIEW

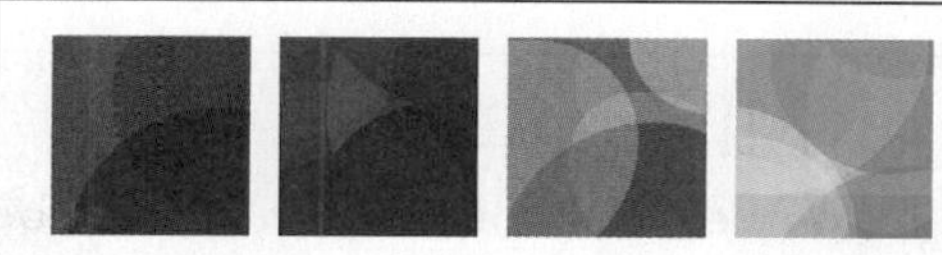

Use this Active Review to verify that you understand the ideas and concepts that answer this chapter extension's study questions.

## QCE5-1 WHO WILL VOLUNTEER?

Summarize the problem that the fund-raising manager must solve. Explain how a database can help solve this problem. Describe the missing information. In your own words, what data must be available to construct the missing information?

## QCE5-2 HOW ARE DATABASE APPLICATION SYSTEMS DEVELOPED?

Name and briefly describe the components of a database application system. Explain the difference between a database application system and a database application program. Using Figure CE5-1 as a guide, describe the major steps in the process of developing a database application system. Explain what role is crucial for users and why that role is so important.

## QCE5-3 WHAT ARE THE COMPONENTS OF THE ENTITY-RELATIONSHIP DATA MODEL?

Define the terms *entity*, *attributes*, and *relationship*. Give an example of two entities (other than those in this book) that have a 1:N relationship. Give an example of two entities that have an N:M relationship. Explain the difference between maximum and minimum cardinality. Show two entities having a 1:N relationship in which one is required and one is optional.

## QCE5-4 HOW IS A DATA MODEL TRANSFORMED INTO A DATABASE DESIGN?

Give an example of a data integrity problem. Describe, in general terms, the process of normalization. Explain how normalizing data prevents data integrity problems. Explain the disadvantage of normalized data. Using your examples from QCE5-3, show how 1:N relationships are expressed in relational database designs. Show how N:M relationships are expressed in relational database designs.

## QCE5-5 WHAT IS THE USERS' ROLE?

Describe the major role for users in the development of a database application system. Explain what is required to change a 1:N relationship to an N:M relationship during the data modeling stage. Explain what is required to make that same change after the database application system has been constructed. Describe how this knowledge impacts your behavior when a database application system is being constructed for your use.

## QCE5-6 WHO WILL VOLUNTEER? (CONTINUED)

Examine Figure CE5-12. Describe the maximum and minimum cardinality for each relationship. Justify these cardinalities. Change the relationship between *Prospect* and *Phone* to N:M, and explain what this means. Change the relationship between *Prospect* and *Work* to 1:1, and explain what this means. Explain how each relationship is represented in the design in Figure CE5-14. Show examples of both primary keys and foreign keys in this figure. In *Contact*, determine whether *EmployeeName* is part of a primary key or part of a foreign key.

Explain what problem the consultant foresaw in the use of the *Name* attribute. Explain how that problem was avoided. The consultant added an attribute to the data model that was not part of the users' world. Explain why that attribute will not add unnecessary complication to the users' work experiences.

## KEY TERMS AND CONCEPTS

MyMISLab™

To complete the problems with the ✪, go to EOC Discussion Questions in the MyLab.

## USING YOUR KNOWLEDGE

✪ **CE5-1.** Explain how you could use a spreadsheet to solve the volunteer problem at the television station. What data would you place in each column and row of your spreadsheet? Name each column and row of your spreadsheet. What advantages does a database have over a spreadsheet for this problem? Compare and contrast your spreadsheet solution to the database solution shown in the text.

✪ **CE5-2.** Suppose you are asked to build a database application for a sports league. Assume that your application is to keep track of teams and equipment that is checked out to teams. Explain the steps that need to be taken to develop this application. Specify entities and their relationships. Build an E-R diagram. Ensure your diagram shows both minimum and maximum cardinalities. Transform your E-R diagram into a relational design.

✪ **CE5-3.** Suppose you are asked to build a database application for a bicycle rental shop. Assume your database is to track customers, bicycles, and rentals. Explain the steps that need to be taken to develop this application. Specify entities and their relationships. Build an E-R diagram. Ensure your diagram shows both minimum and maximum cardinalities. Transform your E-R diagram into a relational design.

MyMISLab™

Go to the Assignments section of your MyLab to complete these writing exercises.

**CE5-4.** Assume you work at the television station and are asked to evaluate the data model shown in QCE5-6. Suppose that you want to differentiate between prospects who have worked in the past and those who have never worked but who are prospects for future work. Say that one of the data modelers tells you, "No problem. We'll know that because any *Prospect* entity that has no relationship to a *Work* entity is a prospect who has never worked." Restate the data modeler's response in your own words. Does this seem like a satisfactory solution? What if you want to keep *Prospect* data that pertains only to prospects who have worked? (No such attributes are shown in *Prospect* in the data model shown in QCE5-6, but say there is an attribute such as *YearFirstVolunteered* or some other attribute that pertains to prospects who have worked in the past.) Show an alternative E-R diagram that would differentiate between prospects who have worked in the past and those who have not. Compare and contrast your alternative to the one shown in the data model in QCE5-6.

**CE5-5.** Suppose you are the accounts manager at a wholesale auto parts distributor. You use spreadsheets to keep track of just about everything. So do your employees. You have hundreds of different spreadsheets to update, back up, and share. Some of them are getting extremely large and unwieldy. You're worried about losing track of them or, worse, having a malicious employee permanently destroy them. A new hire fresh out of college says building a database would solve most of your problems. How would you determine if a database would really solve your problems? If you chose to develop a centralized database, how would you choose the employees to create the database? What criteria would you use to select those employees? How would you justify allocating people and money to developing this database?

## ENDNOTE

1. See David Kroenke and David Auer, *Database Concepts*, 7th ed. (Upper Saddle River, NJ: Pearson Education, 2015) for more information.

chapter extension **6**

**Chapter 5** provides the background for this extension.

# Using Microsoft Access 2013

**STUDY QUESTIONS**

**QCE6-1 HOW DO YOU CREATE TABLES?**

**QCE6-2 HOW DO YOU CREATE RELATIONSHIPS?**

**QCE6-3 HOW DO YOU CREATE A DATA ENTRY FORM?**

**QCE6-4 HOW DO YOU CREATE QUERIES USING THE QUERY DESIGN TOOL?**

**QCE6-5 HOW DO YOU CREATE A REPORT?**

In this chapter extension, you will learn fundamental techniques for creating a database and forms, queries, and reports with Microsoft Access.

## QCE6-1 HOW DO YOU CREATE TABLES?

Before using Access or any other DBMS, you should have created a data model from the users' requirements, and you must transform that data model into a database design. For the purpose of this chapter extension, we will use a portion of the database design created in Chapter Extension 5. Specifically, we will create a database with the following two tables:

PROSPECT (<u>ProspectID</u>, Name, Street, City, State, Zip, Email Address)

and

WORK (<u>*ProspectID*</u>, <u>Date</u>, <u>Hour</u>, NumCalls, TotalDonations)

As in Chapter Extension 5, an underlined attribute is the primary key, and an italicized attribute is a foreign key. Thus, <u>ProspectID</u> is the primary key of PROSPECT, and the combination (<u>ProspectID</u>, <u>Date</u>, <u>Hour</u>) is the primary key of WORK. *ProspectID* is also a foreign key in WORK; hence it is shown both underlined and in italics. The data model and database design in Chapter Extension 5 specified that the key of WORK is the combination (<u>*ProspectID*</u>, <u>Date</u>). Upon review, the users stated that prospects will sometimes work more than one time during the day. For scheduling and other purposes, the users want to record both the date and the hour that someone worked. Accordingly, the database designer added the Hour attribute and made it part of the key of WORK.

The assumption in this design is that each row of WORK represents an hour's work. If a prospect works for consecutive hours, say, from 7 to 9 PM, then he or she would have two rows, one with an Hour value of 1900 and a second with an Hour value of 2000. Figure CE6-1 further documents the attributes of the design. Sample data for this table are shown in Figure CE6-2 on page 451.

Note the ambiguity in the name *PROSPECT.* Before someone has become a volunteer, he is a prospect, and the term is fine. However, once that person has actually done work, he is no longer merely a prospect. This ambiguity occurs because the database is used both for finding volunteers and for recording their experiences once they have joined. We could rename PROSPECT as VOLUNTEER, but then we'd still have a problem. The person is not a volunteer until he has actually agreed to become one. So, for now, just assume that a PROSPECT who has one or more WORK records is no longer a prospect but has become a volunteer.

CE6

| Table | Attribute (Column) | Remarks | Data Type | Example Value |
|---|---|---|---|---|
| PROSPECT | ProspectID | An identifying number provided by Access when a row is created. The value has no meaning to the user. | AutoNumber | 55 |
| PROSPECT | Name | A prospect's name. | Text (50) | Emily Jones |
| PROSPECT | Street | Prospect's contact street address. | Text (50) | 123 West Elm |
| PROSPECT | City | Prospect's contact city. | Text (40) | Miami |
| PROSPECT | State | Prospect's contact state. | Text (2) | FL |
| PROSPECT | Zip | Prospect's contact ZIP code. | Text (10) | 30210-4567 or 30210 |
| PROSPECT | EmailAddress | Prospect's contact email address. | Text (65) | ExamplePerson@somewhere.com |
| WORK | ProspectID | Foreign key to PROSPECT. Value provided when relationship is created. | Number (Long Integer) | 55 |
| WORK | Work Date | The date of work. | Date | 9/15/2014 |
| WORK | Hour | The hour at which work is started. | Number (Integer) | 0800 or 1900 (7 PM) |
| WORK | NumCalls | The number of calls taken. | Number (Integer) | 25 |
| WORK | TotalDonations | The total of donations generated. | Currency | $10,575 |
| WORK | AvgDonations | The average donation. | Currency | To be computed in queries and reports |

**Figure CE6-1**
Attributes of the Database

## STARTING ACCESS

Figure CE6-3 shows the opening screen for Microsoft Access 2013. (If you use another version of Access, your screen will appear differently, but the essentials will be the same.) To create a new database, select Blank desktop database in the templates displayed in the center of the screen, as shown in Figure CE6-4. Then type the name of your new database under *File Name* (here we use *Volunteer*). Access will suggest a directory; change it if you want to use another one, and then click *Create.* You will see the screen shown in Figure CE6-5 on page 452.

## CREATING TABLES

Access opens the new database by creating a default table named Table. We want to modify the design of this table, so in the upper left-hand corner, where you see a pencil and a right angle square, click *View* and select *Design View.* Access will ask you to name your table. Enter *PROSPECT* and click *OK.* Your screen will appear as in Figure CE6-6 on page 452.

The screen shown in Figure CE6-6 has three parts. The left-hand pane lists all of the tables in your database. At this point, you should see only the PROSPECT table in this list. We will use the upper part of the right-hand pane to enter the name of each attribute (which Access calls *Fields*) and its *Data Type.* We can optionally enter a *Description* of that field. The Description is used for documentation; as you will see, Access displays any text you enter as help text on forms. In the bottom part of the screen, we set the properties of each field (or attribute, using our term). To start

**Example of PROSPECT Data**

| Prospect ID | Name | Street | City | State | Zip | EmailAddress |
|---|---|---|---|---|---|---|
| 1 | Carson Wu | 123 Elm | Los Angeles | CA | 98007 | Carson@somewhere.com |
| 2 | Emily Jackson | 2234 17th | Pasadena | CA | 97005 | JacksonE@elsewhere.com |
| 3 | Peter Lopez | 331 Moses Drive | Fullerton | CA | 97330 | PeterL@ourcompany.com |
| 4 | Lynda Dennison | 54 Strand | Manhattan Beach | CA | 97881 | Lynda@somewhere.com |
| 5 | Carter Fillmore III | Restricted | Brentwood | CA | 98220 | Carter@BigBucks.com |
| 6 | CJ Greene | 77 Sunset Strip | Hollywood | CA | 97330 | CJ@HollywoodProducers.com |
| 7 | Jolisa Jackson | 2234 17th | Pasadena | CA | 97005 | JacksonJ@elsewhere.com |

**Example of WORK Data**

| ProspectID | Work Date | Hour | NumCalls | TotalDonations |
|---|---|---|---|---|
| 3 | 9/15/2014 | 1600 | 17 | 8755 |
| 3 | 9/15/2014 | 1700 | 28 | 11578 |
| 5 | 9/15/2014 | 1700 | 25 | 15588 |
| 5 | 9/20/2014 | 1800 | 37 | 29887 |
| 5 | 9/10/2015 | 1700 | 30 | 21440 |
| 5 | 9/10/2015 | 1800 | 39 | 37050 |
| 6 | 9/15/2014 | 1700 | 33 | 21445 |
| 6 | 9/16/2014 | 1700 | 27 | 17558 |
| 6 | 9/10/2015 | 1700 | 31 | 22550 |
| 6 | 9/10/2015 | 1800 | 37 | 36700 |

**Figure CE6-2**
Sample Data

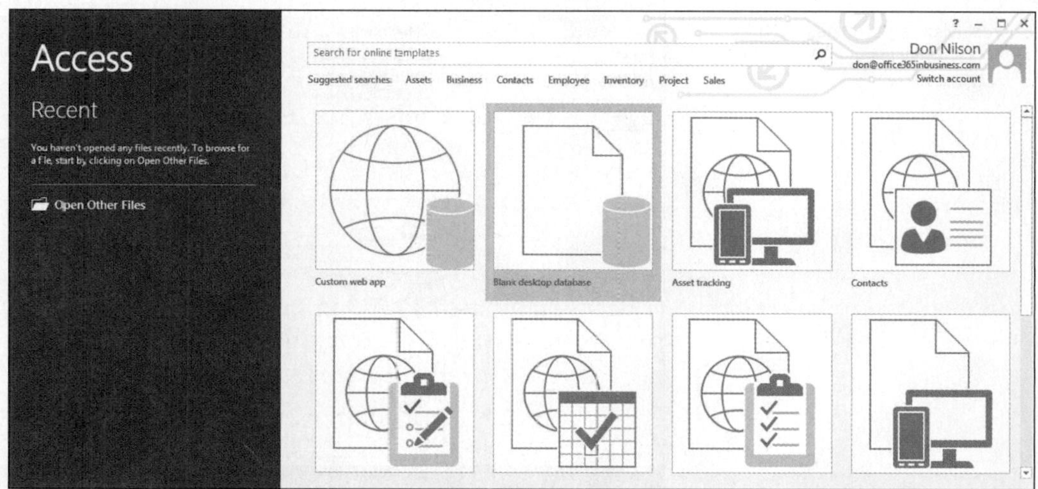


**Figure CE6-3**
Opening Screen for Microsoft Access 2013

*Source:* Microsoft Access 2013

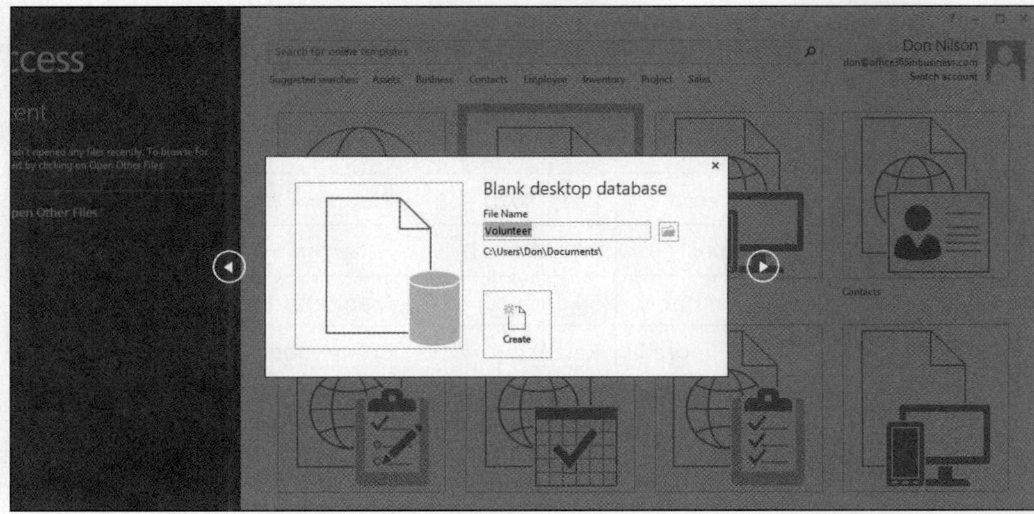


**Figure CE6-4**
Naming a Desktop Database

Source: Microsoft Access 2013

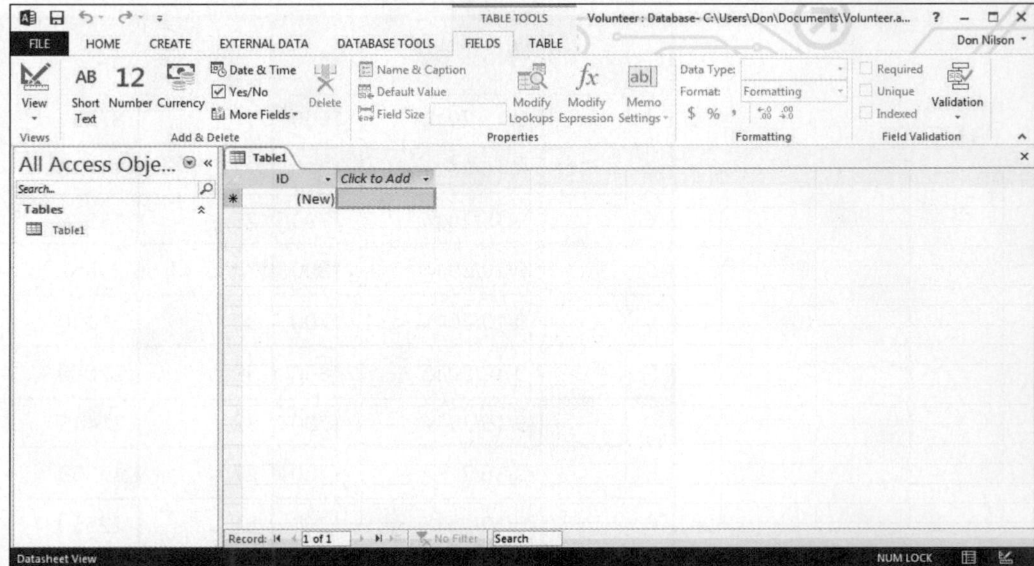


**Figure CE6-5**
Access Opens with an Initial Table Definition

*Source:* Microsoft Access 2013

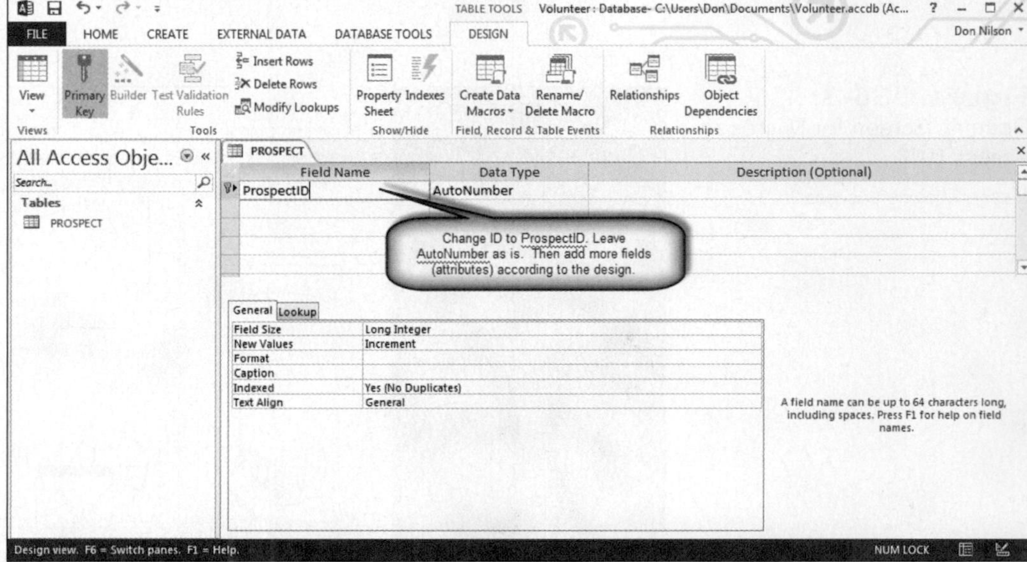


**Figure CE6-6**
Creating Tables in Access, Step 1

*Source:* Microsoft Access 2013

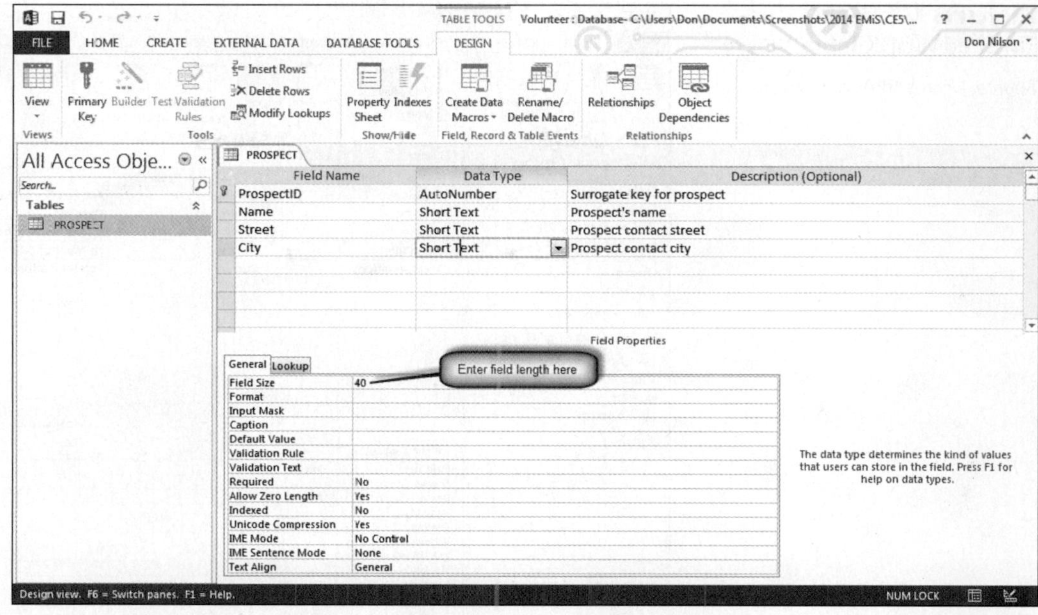


**Figure CE6-7**
Creating Tables in Access, Step 2

*Source:* Microsoft Access 2013

designing the table, replace the *Field Name* ID with *ProspectID.* Access has already set its type to *AutoNumber*, so you can leave that alone.

To create the rest of the table, enter the *Field Names* and *Data Types* according to our design.[1] Figure CE6-7 shows how to set the length of a Short Text Data Type. In this figure, the user has set City to *Text* and then has moved down into the bottom part of this form and entered 40 under *Field Size.* You will do the same thing to set the length of all of the Short Text Field Names. The complete table is shown in Figure CE6-8.

*ProspectID* is the primary key of this table, and the little key icon next to the ProspectID *Field Name* means Access has already made it so. If we wanted to make another field the primary key, we would highlight that field and then click the *Primary Key* icon in the left-hand portion of the *DESIGN* ribbon.

Follow similar steps to create the WORK table. The only difference is that you will need to create a key of the three columns (ProspectID, WorkDate, Hour). To create that key, highlight all three rows by dragging over the three squares to the left of the names of ProspectID,

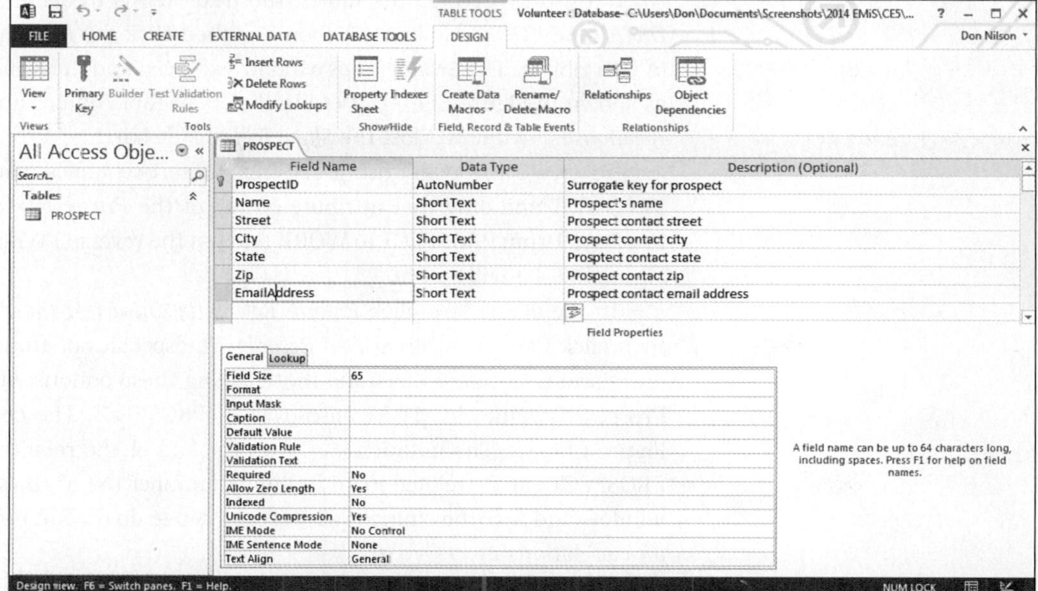


**Figure CE6-8**
Complete Sample PROSPECT Table

*Source:* Microsoft Access 2013

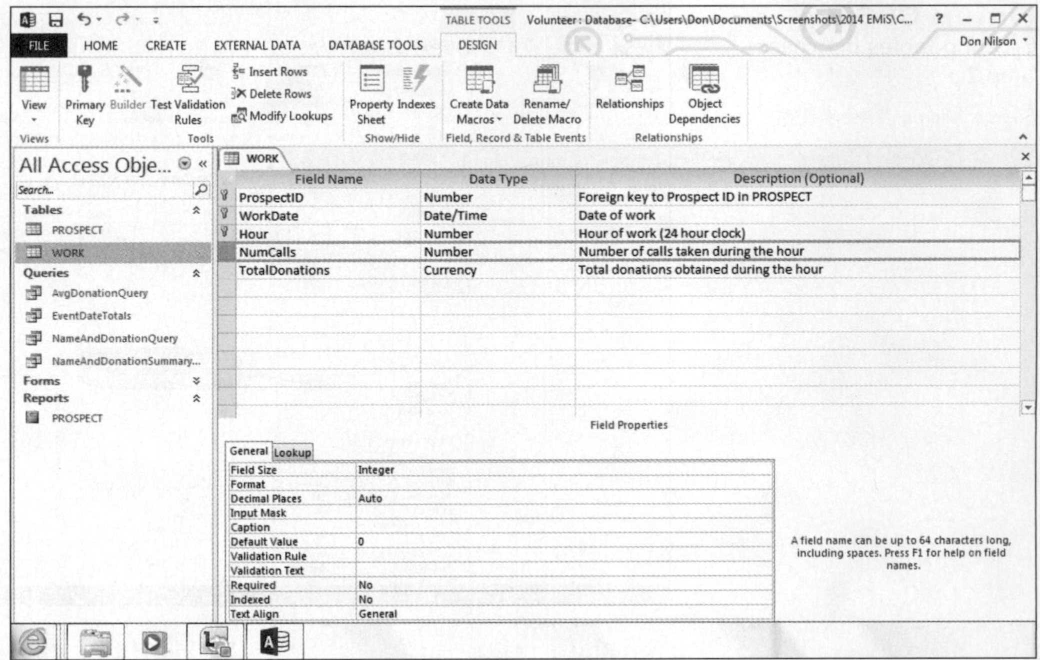

**Figure CE6-9**
Finished WORK Table

*Source:* Microsoft Access 2013

WorkDate, and Hour. Then click the *Key* icon in the *DESIGN* ribbon. Also, change the *Required Field Property* for each of these columns to *Yes*. The finished WORK table is shown in Figure CE6-9. This figure also shows that the user selected *Number* for the *Data Type* of *NumCalls* and then set its *Field Size* (lower pane) to *Integer*. This same technique was used to set the *Data Type* of ProspectID (in WORK) to *Number* (*Field Size* of *Long Integer*) and that of *Hour* to *Number* (*Field Size* of *Integer*).

At this point, close both tables and save your work. You have created your first database!

## QCE6-2 HOW DO YOU CREATE RELATIONSHIPS?

After you have created the tables, the next step is to define relationships. To do so, click the *DATABASE TOOLS* tab in the ribbon and then click the *Relationships* icon near the left-hand side of that ribbon. The *Relationships* window will open and the *Show Table* dialog box will be displayed, as shown in Figure CE6-10. Double-click both table names and both tables will be added to the *Relationships* window. Close the *Show Table* dialog box.

To create the relationship between these two tables, click on the attribute *ProspectID* in PROSPECT and drag that attribute on top of the *ProspectID* in WORK. (It is important to drag *ProspectID* from PROSPECT to WORK and not the reverse.) When you do this, the screen shown in Figure CE6-11 will appear.

In the dialog box, click *Enforce Referential Integrity*, click *Cascade Update Related Fields*, and then click *Cascade Delete Related Records*. The specifics of these actions are beyond the scope of our discussion. Just understand that clicking these options will cause Access to make sure that ProspectID values in WORK also exist in PROSPECT. The completed relationship is shown in Figure CE6-12. The notation $1 \ldots \infty$ at the end of the relationship line means that one row of PROSPECT can be related to an unlimited number (*N*) of rows in WORK. Close the *Relationships* window and save the changes when requested to do so. You now have a database with two tables and a relationship.

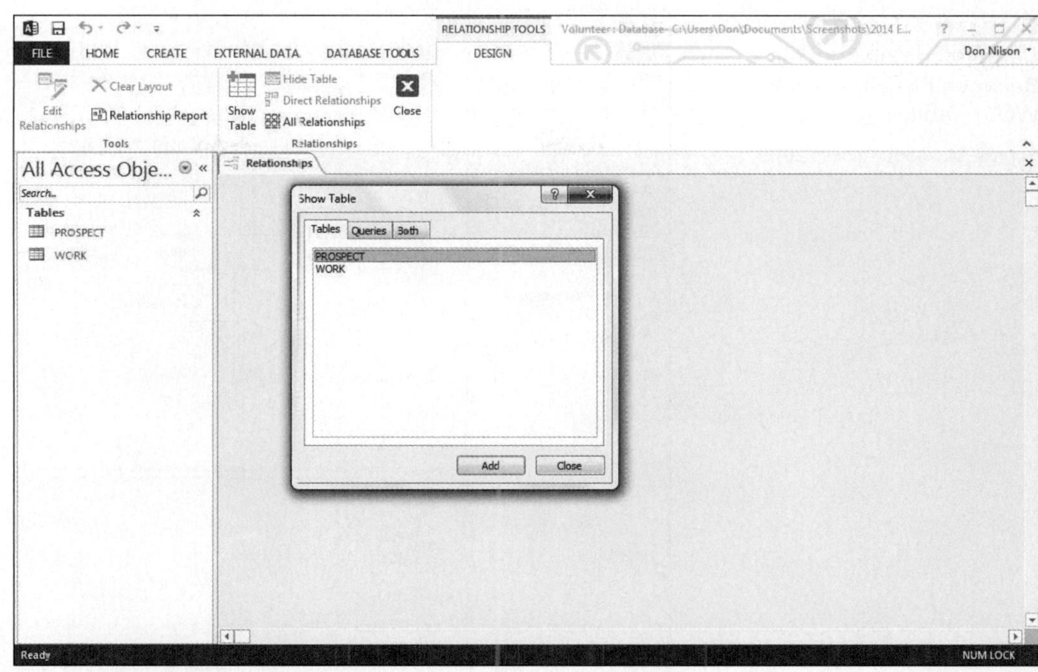


**Figure CE6-10**
The Show Table Dialog Box in Access

*Source:* Microsoft Access 2013

The next step is to enter data. To enter data, double-click the table name in the *left hand* pane. The table will appear, and you can enter values into each cell. You cannot and need not enter values for the *ProspectID* field. Access will create those values for you.

Enter the data in Figure CE6-2 for both PROSPECT and WORK, and you will see a display like that in Figures CE6-13a and CE6-13b. Examine the lower left-hand corner of Figure CE6-13b. The text *Foreign key to ProspectID in PROSPECT* is the Description that you provided when you defined the ProspectID column when the WORK table was created. (You can see this in the ProspectID column in Figure CE6-9.) Access displays this text because the focus is on the ProspectID column in the active table window (WORK). Move your cursor from field to field and watch this text change.

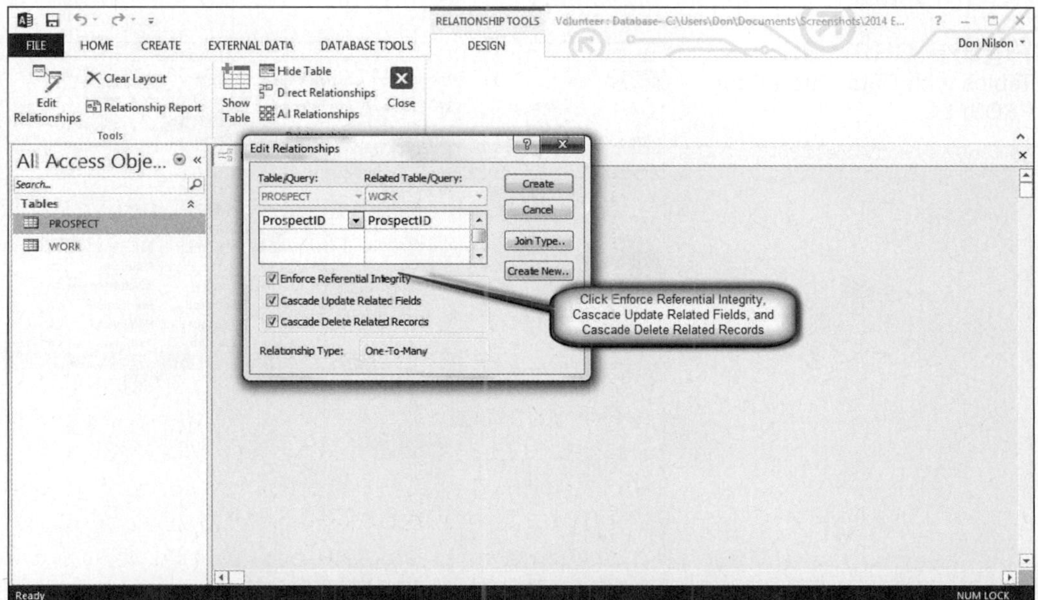


**Figure CE6-11**
Creating a Relationship Between Two Tables

*Source:* Microsoft Access 2013

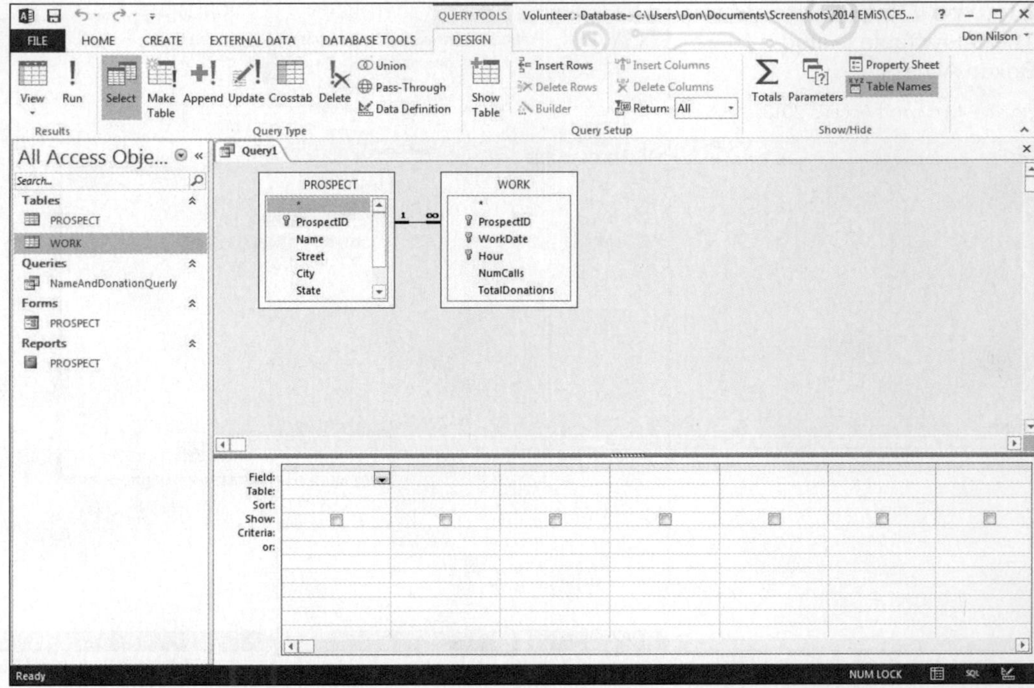

**Figure CE6-12** Completed Relationship Between PROSPECT and WORK Tables

*Source:* Microsoft Access 2013

## QCE6-3 HOW DO YOU CREATE A DATA ENTRY FORM?

Access provides several alternatives for creating a data entry form. The first is to use the default table display, as shown in Figure CE6-13a. Enter data for each row of PROSPECT. As you do so, Access places a plus sign on the left. If you click the plus sign, you will be able to enter data for the WORK rows related to the prospect you are entering. This data entry display, although convenient, is limited in its capability. It also does not provide a very pleasing user interface. For more generality and better design, you can use the Access form generator.

Access can generate a data entry form that is more pleasing to view and easier to use than that in Figure CE6-14. The process is shown in Figure CE6-15. First, click the *CREATE* tab to

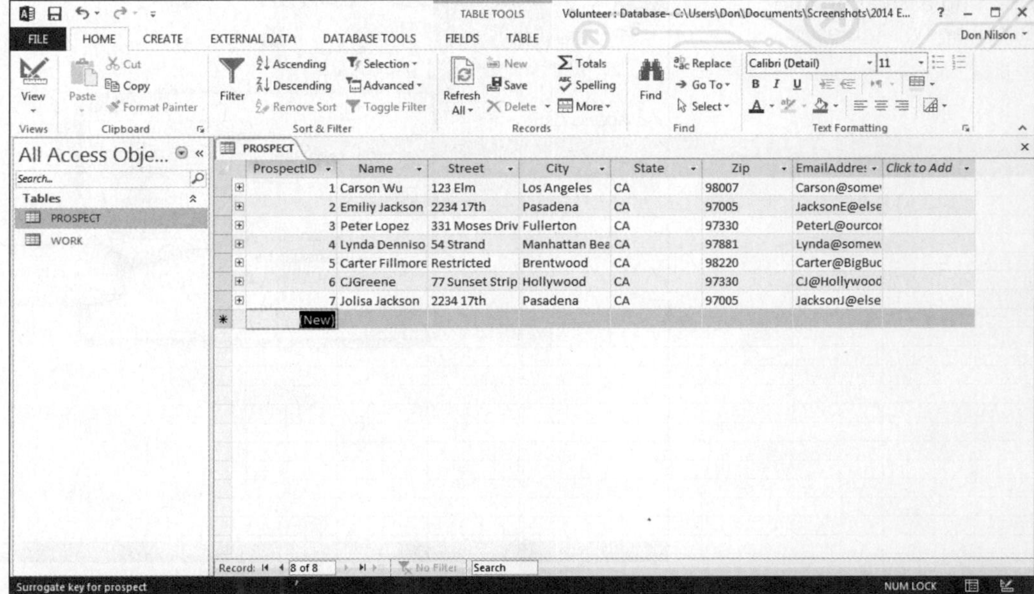

**Figure CE6-13a** Tables with Data Entered for PROSPECT

*Source:* Microsoft Access 2013

**Figure CE6-13b**
Tables with Data Entered for WORK

*Source:* Microsoft Access 2013

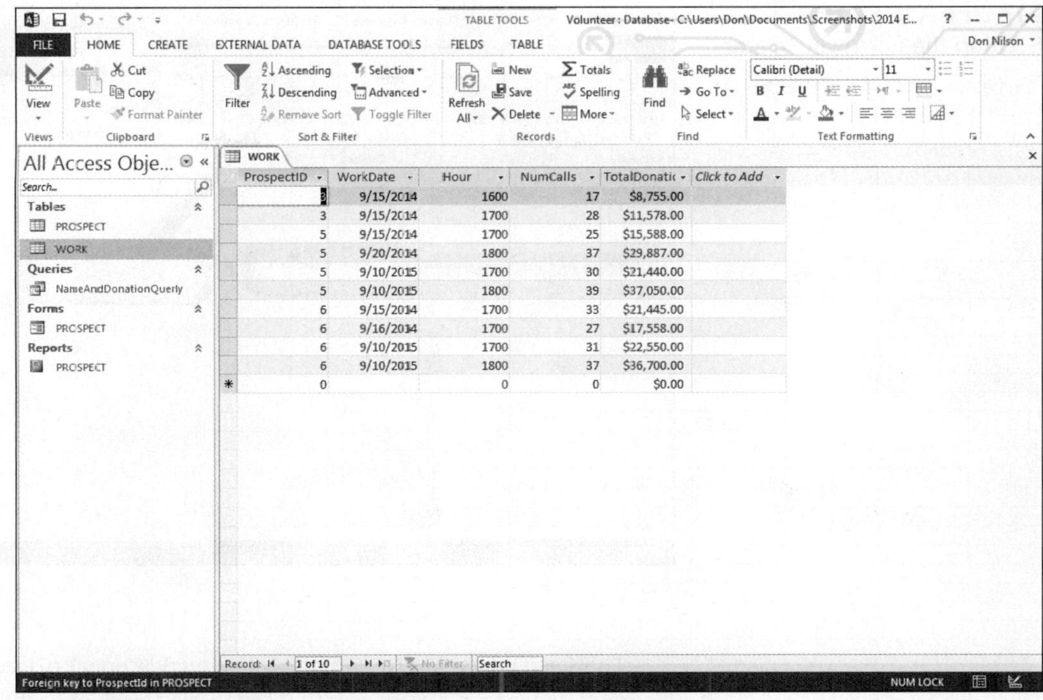

open the *CREATE* ribbon. Next, click the PROSPECT table (this causes Access to create a form for PROSPECT). Finally, click *Form.* Access uses metadata about the tables and their relationship to create the data entry form in Figure CE6-16.

You can use this form to modify data; just type over any data that you wish to change. You can also add data. To add work data, just click in the last row of the work grid; in this case that would be the first row of this grid. To delete a record, click the *HOME* tab, and then in the *Records* section click the down arrow next to *Delete* and select *Delete Record.* This action will delete the prospect data and all related work data (not shown in Figure CE6-16).

**Figure CE6-14**
Default Table Display

*Source:* Microsoft Access 2013

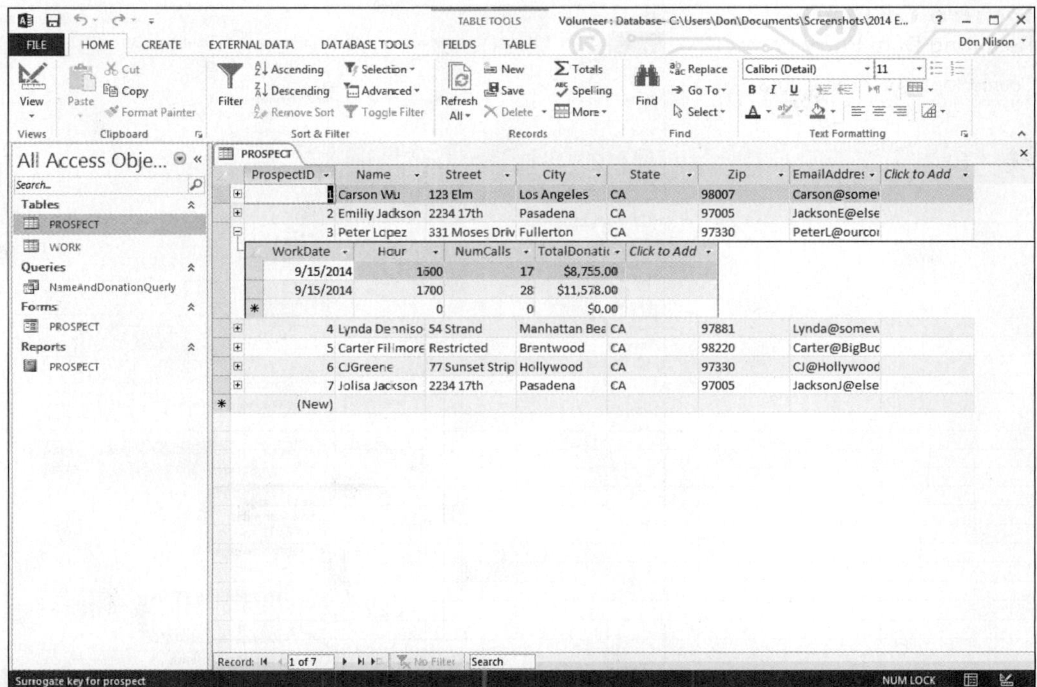

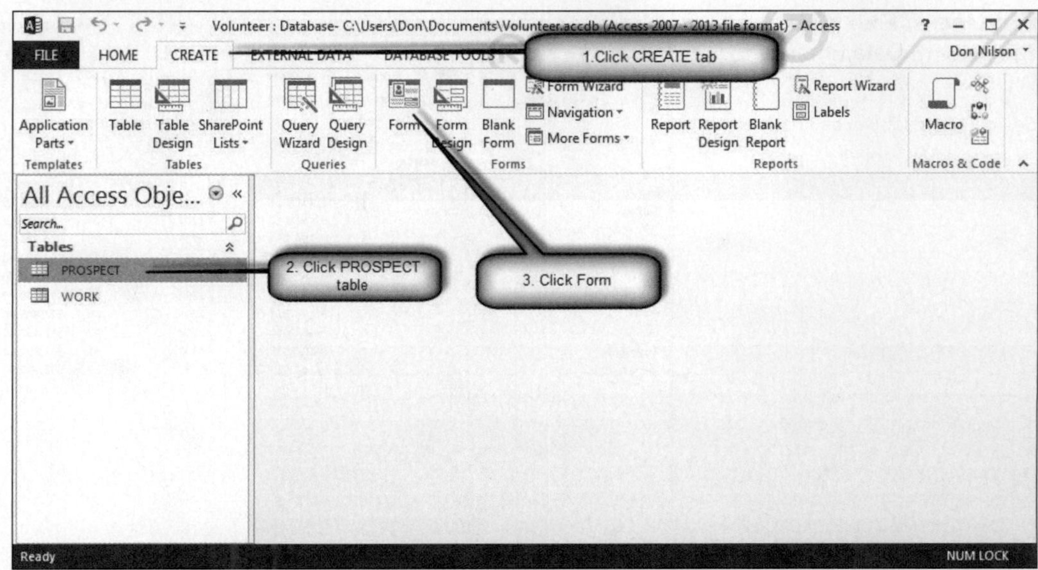


**Figure CE6-15**
Starting the Form Generator
*Source:* Microsoft Access 2013

This form is fine, but we can make it better. For one, ProspectID is a surrogate key and has no meaning to the user. Access uses that key to keep track of each PROSPECT row. Because it has no meaning to the user (in fact, the user cannot change or otherwise modify its value), we should remove it from the form. Also, we might like to reduce the size of the fields as well as reduce the size of the work area and center it on the form. Figure CE6-17 shows the form after these changes. It is smaller and cleaner, and it will be easier to use.

The data about a prospect is shown in the top portion of this form, and data about that person's work sessions is shown in the bottom portion. The user of this form has clicked the arrow at the bottom of the form to bring up the third Prospect record, the one for Peter Lopez. Notice that he has two work sessions. If you click the arrow in the next-to-last row of this form, you will change the focus of the work record. To make the changes shown, see the steps illustrated in Figure CE6-18. First,

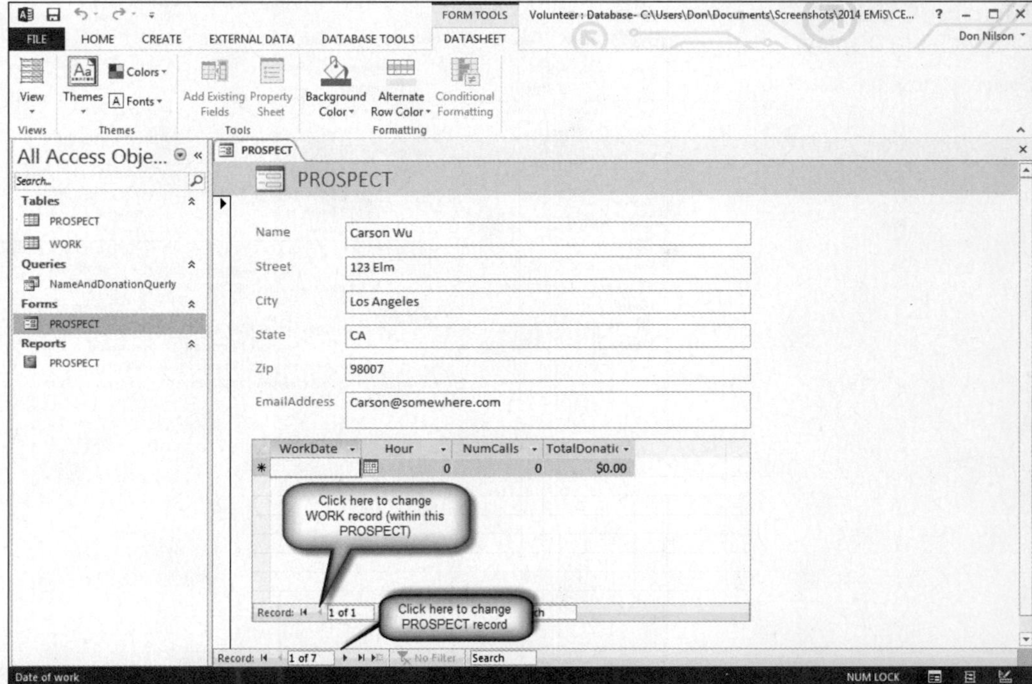


**Figure CE6-16**
Resulting Data Entry Form
*Source:* Microsoft Access 2013

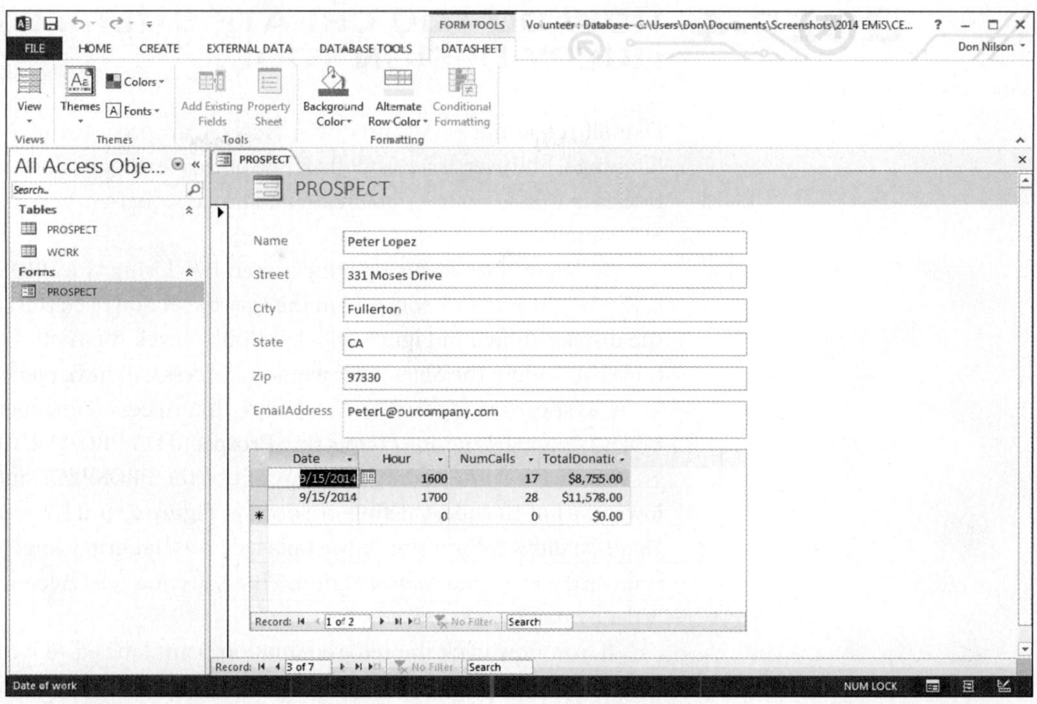


**Figure CE6-17**
Reformatted Data Entry Form

*Source:* Microsoft Access 2013

right-click the PROSPECT tab and then select *Design View.* The form will open in Design mode; click the right edge of the rightmost rectangle and, holding your mouse down, drag to the left. Access will reduce the width of each of these fields as well as the table.

Finally, click *ProspectID,* as shown in step 4. Press the *Delete* key, and the ProspectID field will be removed from the form. Click *View/Form View,* and your form should look like that in Figure CE6-17. You can go back to *Design View* to make more adjustments, if necessary.

To save your form, either close it and Access will give you the chance to save it or click *FILE* and select *Save.* Save with an informative file name, such as PROSPECT Data Entry Form.

There are many options for customizing Access forms. You can learn about them if you take a database processing class after you complete this MIS class.

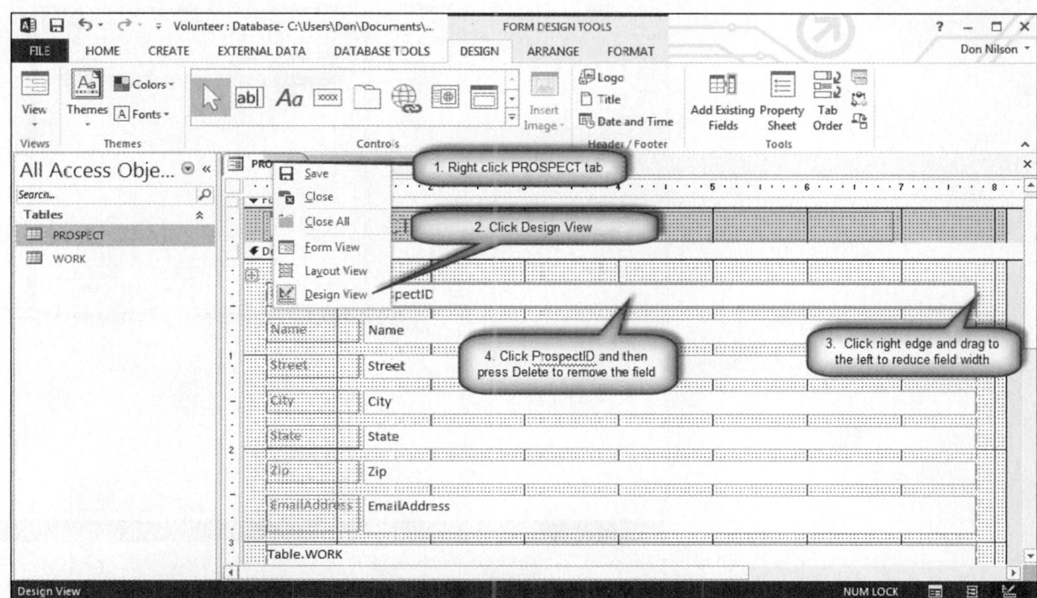


**Figure CE6-18**
Process for Reformatting Data Entry Form

*Source:* Microsoft Access 2013

# QCE6-4 HOW DO YOU CREATE QUERIES USING THE QUERY DESIGN TOOL?

Like all relational DBMS products, Access can process the SQL query language. Learning that language, however, is beyond the scope of this textbook. However, Access does provide a graphical interface that we can use to create and process queries, and that graphical interface will generate SQL statements for us, behind the scenes.

To begin, first clean up your screen by closing the PROSPECT Data Entry Form. Click the *CREATE* tab in the ribbon, and in the *Queries* section click the *Query Design* button. You should see the display shown in Figure CE6-19. Double-click the names of both the PROSPECT and WORK tables, and close the *Show Table* window. Access will have placed both tables into the query design form, as shown in Figure CE6-20. Notice that Access remembers the relationship between the two tables (shown by the line connecting ProspectID in PROSPECT to the same attribute in WORK).

To create a query, drag columns out of the PROSPECT and WORK tables into the grid in the lower part of the query definition form. In Figure CE6-21, the *Name*, *EmailAddress*, *NumCalls*, and *TotalDonations* columns have been placed into that grid. Note, too, that the *Ascending* keyword has been selected for the *Name* column. That selection tells Access to present the data in alphabetical order by name.

If you now click the red exclamation point labeled *Run* in the *Results* section of the ribbon, the result shown in Figure CE6-22 will appear. Notice that only PROSPECT rows that have at least one WORK row are shown. By default, for queries of two or more tables Access (and SQL) shows only those rows that have value matches in both tables. Save the query under the name *NameAndDonationQuery*.

Queries have many useful purposes. For example, suppose we want to see the average dollar value of donations generated per hour of work. This query, which is just slightly beyond the scope of this chapter extension, can readily be created using either the Access graphical tool or SQL. The results of such a query are shown in Figure CE6-23. This query processes the *NameAndDonationQuery* query just created. Again, if you take a database class, you will learn how to create queries like this and others of even greater complexity (and utility).

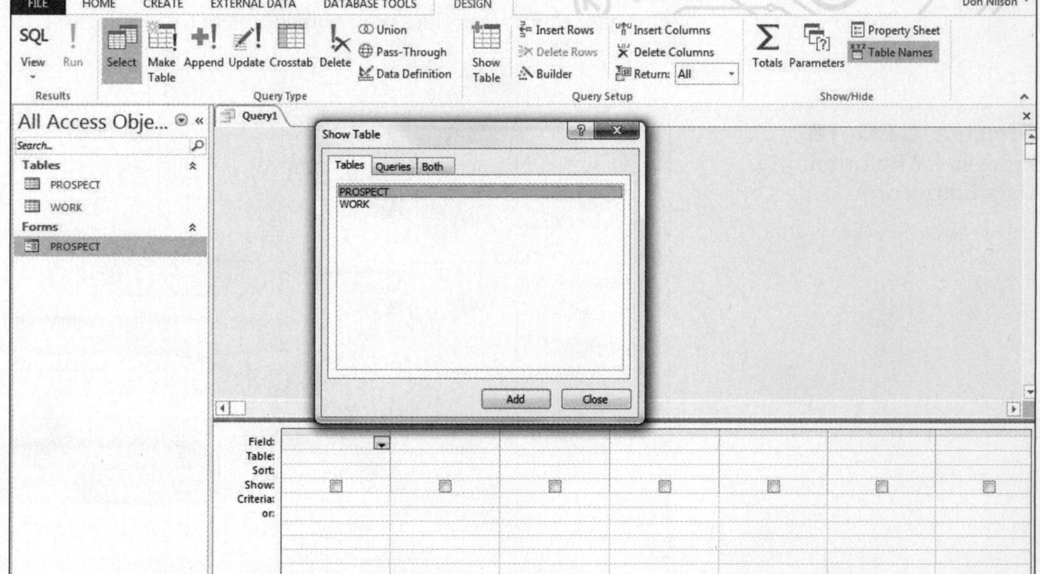


**Figure CE6-19**
Creating a Query, Step 1
*Source:* Microsoft Access 2013

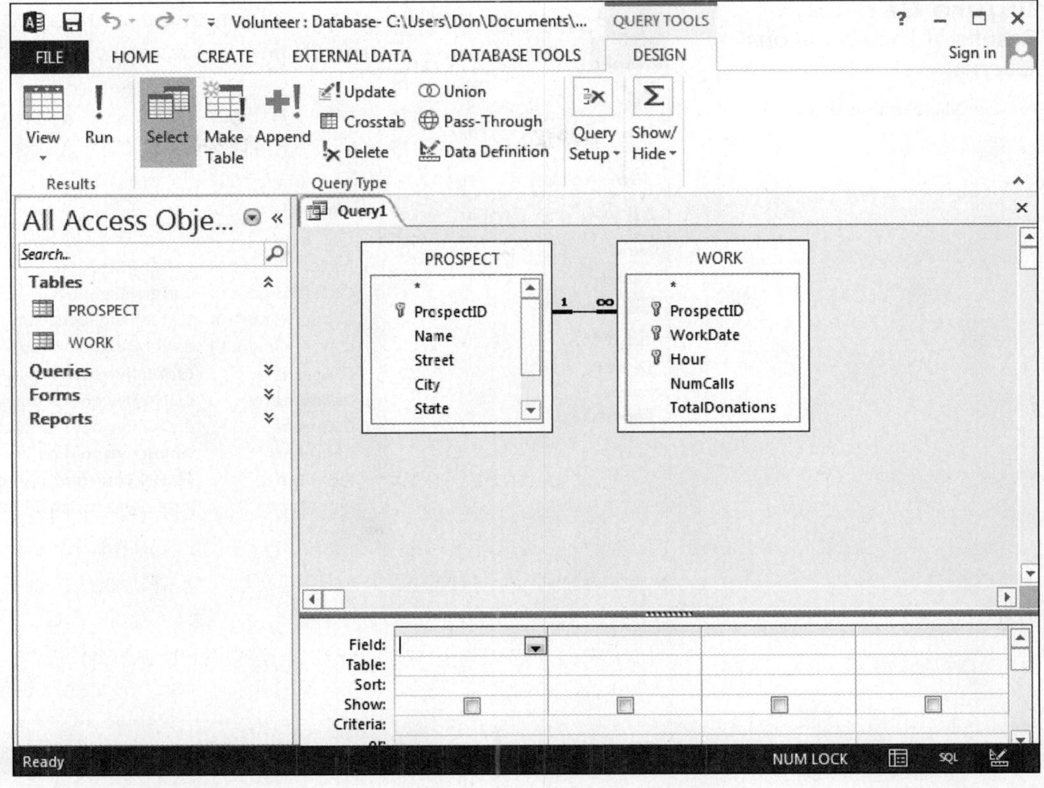


**Figure CE6-20**
Creating a Query, Step 2
*Source:* Microsoft Access 2013

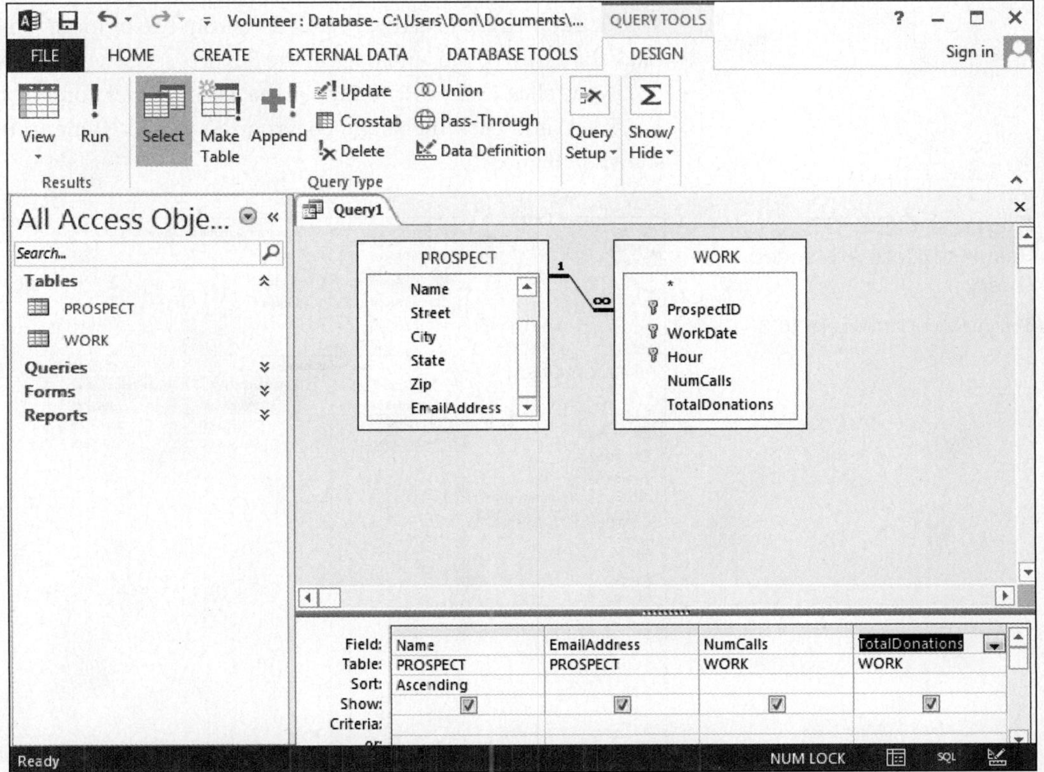


**Figure CE6-21**
Creating a Query, Step 3
*Source:* Microsoft Access 2013

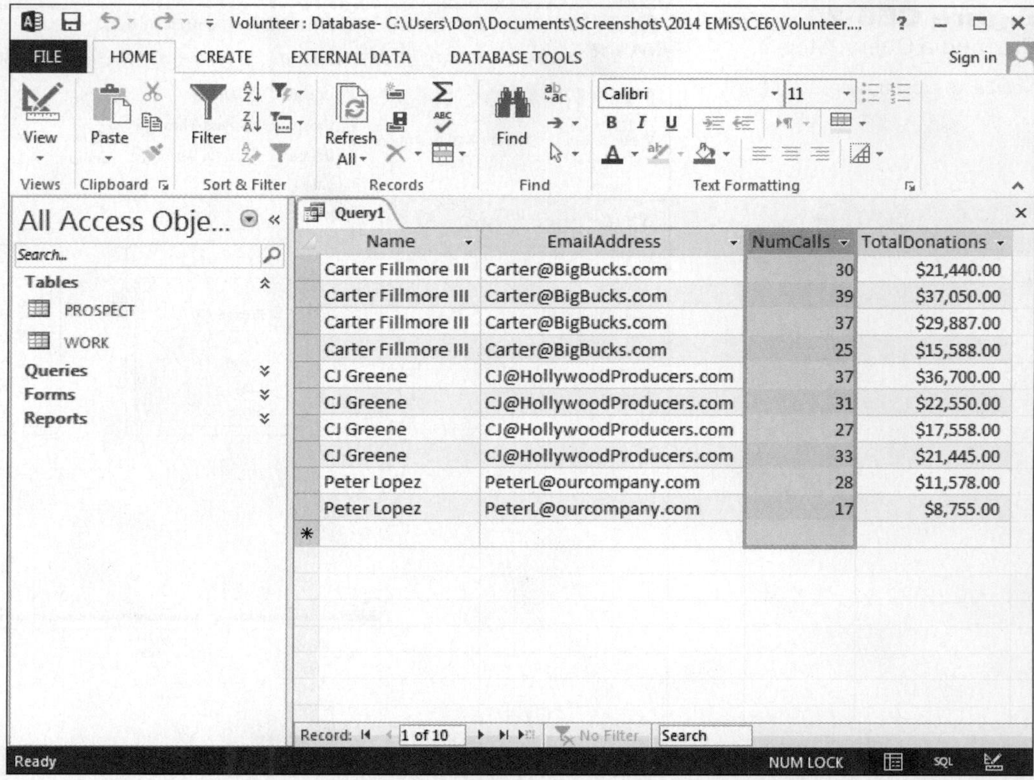

**Figure CE6-22**
Results of *TotalDonations Query*

*Source:* Microsoft Access 2013

## QCE6-5 HOW DO YOU CREATE A REPORT?

You can create a report using a process similar to that for forms, but the report won't include the WORK data. To create a report with data from two or more tables, we must use the Report Wizard. Click the *CREATE* tab, and then in the Reports section click *Report Wizard.*

Now, click *Table: PROSPECT* in the *Table/Queries* combo box, highlight *Name* in the *Available Fields* list, and click the single chevron (>) to add Name to the report. You will see the display shown in Figure CE6-24.

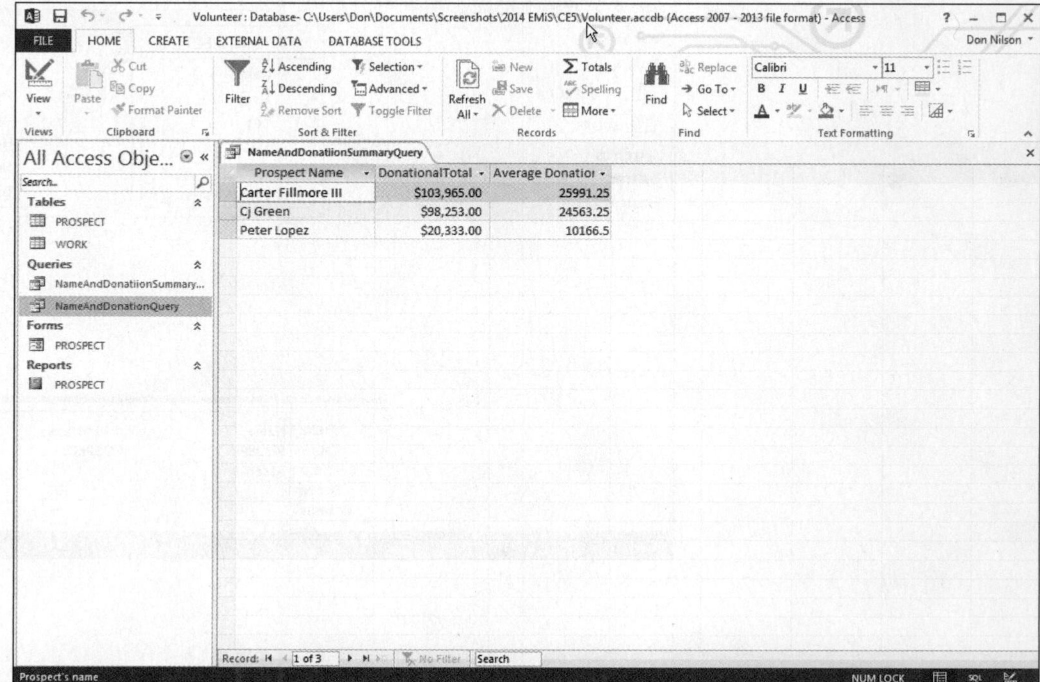

**Figure CE6-23**
Result of More Advanced Query

*Source:* Microsoft Access 2013

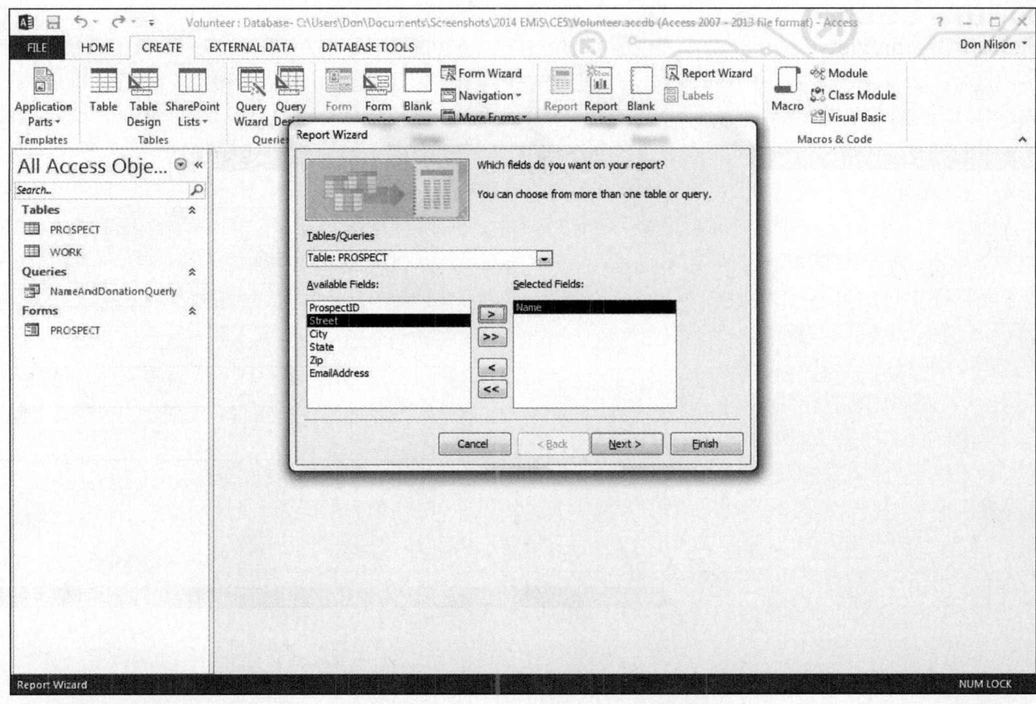


**Figure CE6-24**
Selecting Data to Show in a Report

*Source:* Microsoft Access 2013

Using a similar process, add *EmailAddress.* Then select *Table: WORK* in the *Table/Queries* combo box and add *WorkDate, Hour, NumCalls,* and *TotalDonations.* Click *Finish,* and you will see the report shown in Figure CE6-25. (By the way, we are skipping numerous options that Access provides in creating reports.)

We will consider just one of those options now. Suppose we want to show the total donations that a prospect has obtained, for all hours of his or her work. To do that, right-click the *PROSPECT* tab, and then click *Design View*. Your report will appear as shown in Figure CE6-26. (If it does not appear like this, click *View, Design View* in the ribbon.)

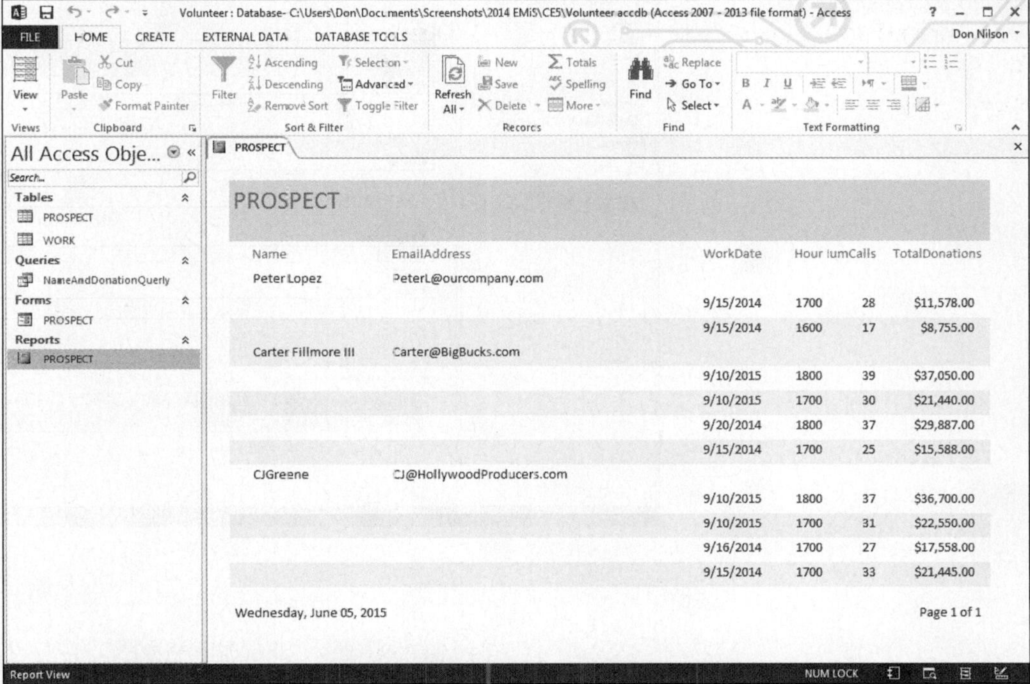


**Figure CE6-25**
Report on Donations, by Prospect

*Source:* Microsoft Access 2013

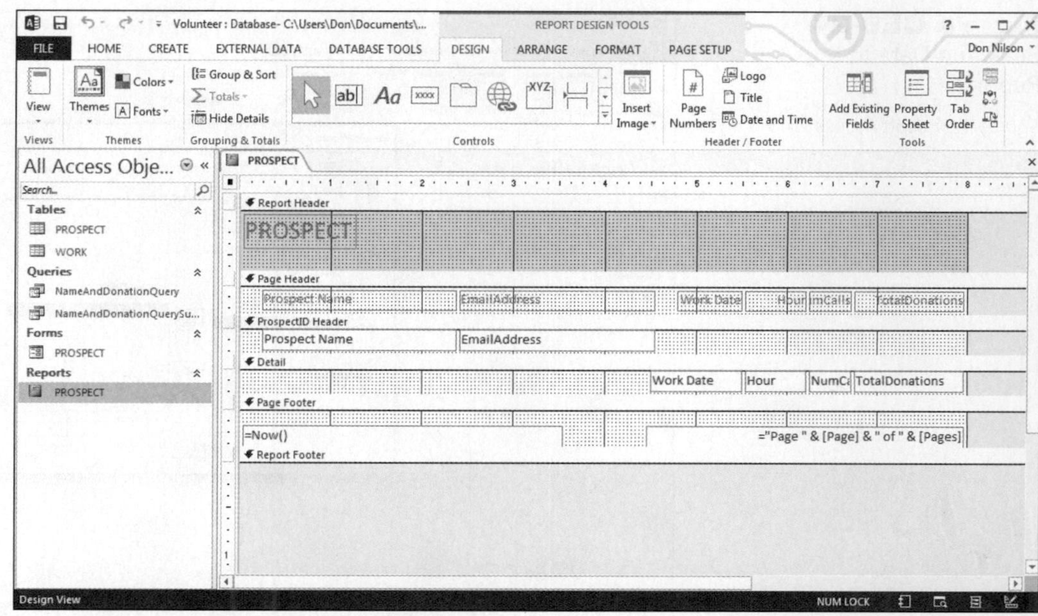

**Figure CE6-26**
Report Design View

*Source:* Microsoft Access 2013

In the ribbon, click *Group & Sort* in the *Grouping & Totals* section. In the bottom of the form, under Group, Sort, and Total click *More*, and then click the down arrow next to the phrase *with no totals*. Next, select *TotalDonations* from the *Total On* box, and then check *Show Grand Total* and *Show subtotal in group footer*, as illustrated in Figure CE6-27.

Click the *Report* icon in the *View* section of the ribbon, and you will see the report shown in Figure CE6-28. The only remaining problem is that the label NumCalls is cut off. We need to

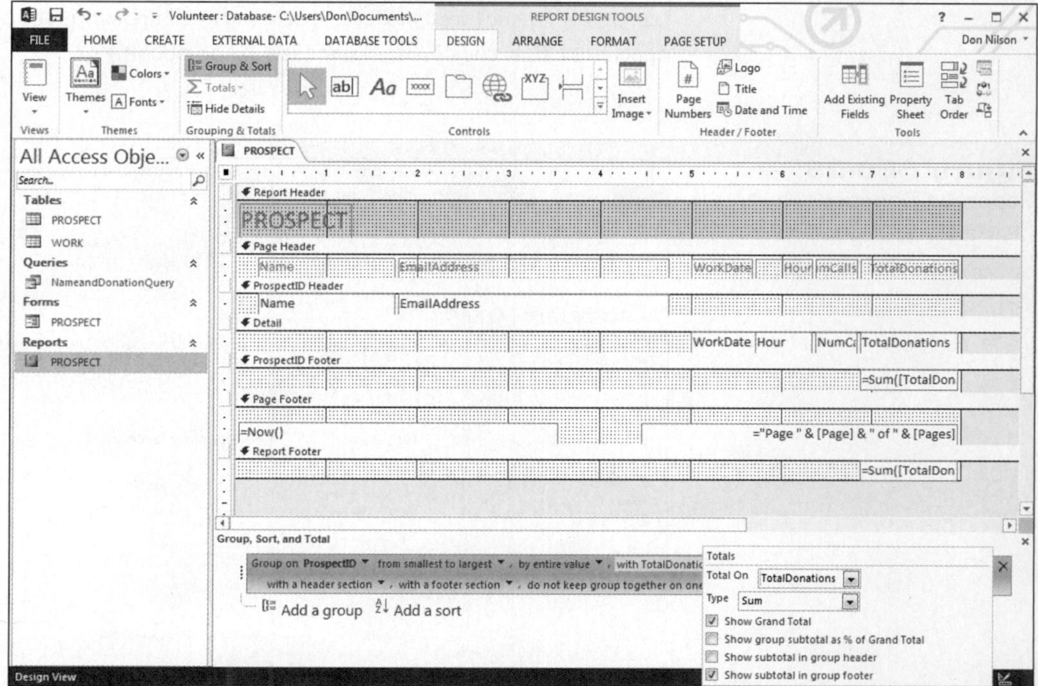

**Figure CE6-27**
Creating a Sum of *TotalDonations* for Each Prospect

*Source:* Microsoft Access 2013

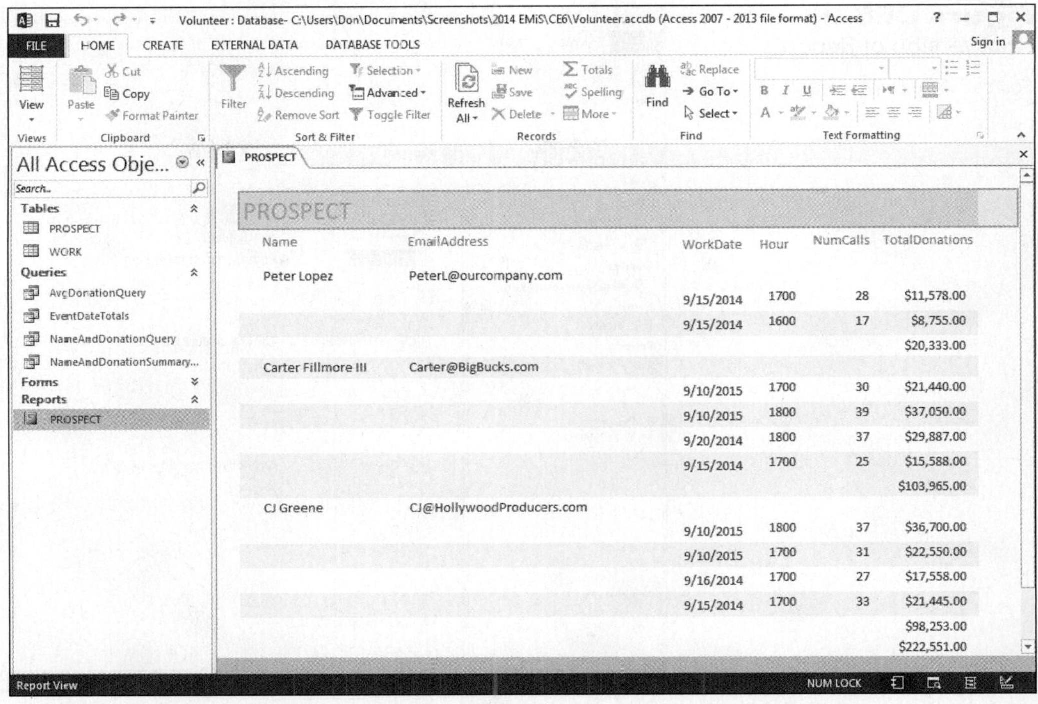


**Figure CE6-28**
Report with Sum of *TotalDonations*

*Source:* Microsoft Access 2013

expand the box that contains this value. To do so, select *Layout View* from *View* in the ribbon, click *Date*, and then slide it slightly to the left. Do the same with Hour. Then expand NumCalls until you can see all of the label, as shown in Figure CE6-29. Click *Report View* in *View*, and your report should appear as shown in Figure CE6-30.

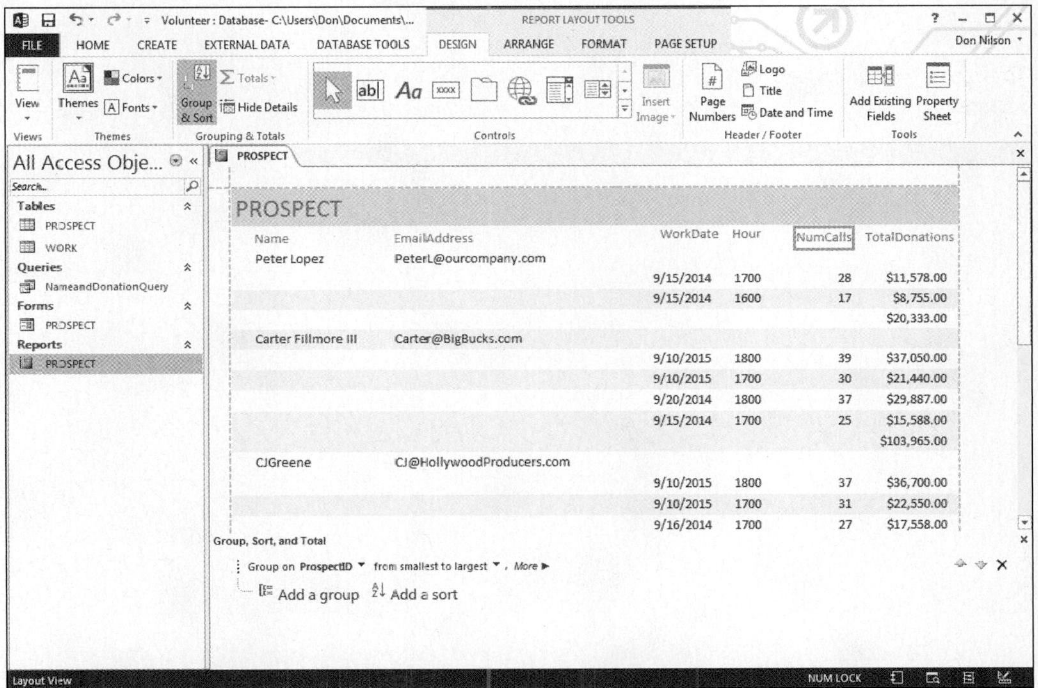


**Figure CE6-29**
Increasing the Size of the *NumCalls* Field

*Source:* Microsoft Access 2013

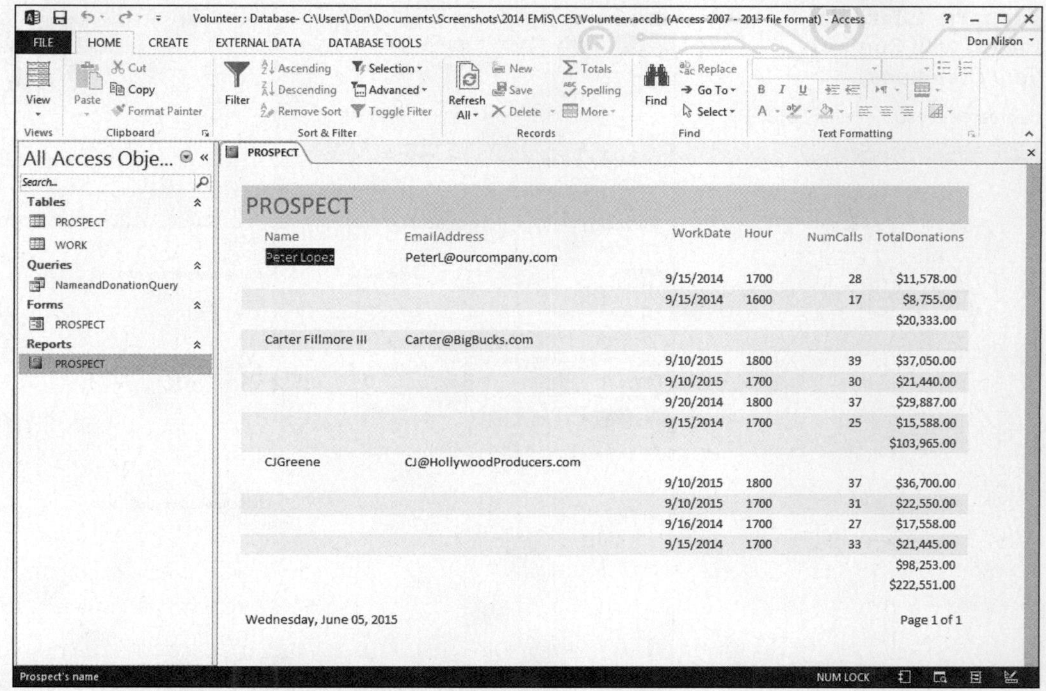


**Figure CE6-30**
Final Version of Report
*Source:* Microsoft Access 2013

# ACTIVE REVIEW

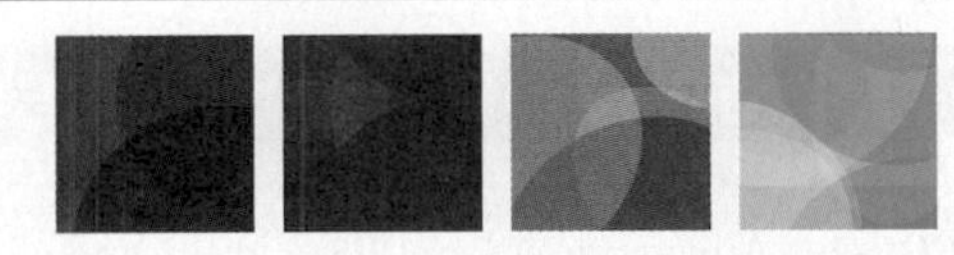

Use this Active Review to verify that you understand the ideas and concepts in this chapter extension's study questions.

For this Active Review, assume that you are creating a database application having the following two tables:

```
CUSTOMER (CustomerID, Name, Email)
CONTACT (CustomerID, Date, Subject)
```

## QCE6-1 HOW DO YOU CREATE TABLES?

Open Access and create a new database having a name of your choosing. Create the CUSTOMER and CONTACT tables. Assume the following data types:

| Attribute (Field) | Data Type |
|---|---|
| CustomerID (in CUSTOMER) | AutoNumber |
| Name | Text (50) |
| Email | Text (75) |
| CustomerID (in CONTACT) | Number (long integer) |
| Date | Date |
| Subject | Text (200) |

Add Description entries to the Field definitions that you think are appropriate.

## QCE6-2 HOW DO YOU CREATE RELATIONSHIPS?

Open the *Relationships* window and create a relationship from CUSTOMER to CONTACT using the CustomerID attribute. Click all of the check boxes. Enter sample data. Add at least five rows to CUSTOMER and at least seven rows to CONTACT. Ensure that some CUSTOMER rows have no matching CONTACT rows.

## QCE6-3 HOW DO YOU CREATE A DATA ENTRY FORM?

Open the default data entry form for the CUSTOMER table. Click the CUSTOMER rows to display the related CONTACT data. Now use the *Form* tool to create a data entry form. Navigate through that form to see that the CONTACT rows are correctly connected to the CUSTOMER rows. Adjust spacing as you deem appropriate; remove the CustomerID field from the CUSTOMER section.

## QCE6-4 HOW DO YOU CREATE QUERIES USING THE QUERY DESIGN TOOL?

Create a query that displays Name, Email, Date, and Subject. Sort the results of Name in alphabetical order.

## QCE6-5 HOW DO YOU CREATE A REPORT?

Use the Report Wizard to create a report that has Name, Email, Date, and Subject. View that report. Add a group total for each CUSTOMER that counts the number of contacts for each customer. Follow the procedure shown, except instead of selecting Sum for Type choose *Count Records* instead.

MyMISLab™

To complete the problems with the ✪, go to EOC Discussion Questions in the MyLab.

## USING YOUR KNOWLEDGE

**CE6-1.** Answer question CE5-2 at the end of Chapter Extension 5 (page 448). Use Access to implement your database design. Create the tables and add sample data. Create a data entry form that shows teams and the equipment they have checked out. Verify that the form correctly processes new checkouts, changes to checkouts, and equipment returns. Create a report that shows each team, the items they have checked out, and the number of items they have checked out. (Use *Count Records* as explained in Active Review QCE6-5.)

**CE6-2.** Answer question CE5-3 at the end of Chapter Extension 5 (page 448). Create an Access database for the CUSTOMER and RENTAL tables only. Create the tables and add sample data. Create a data entry form that shows customers and all of their rentals (assume customers rent bicycles more than once). Verify that the form correctly processes new rentals, changes to rentals, and rental returns. Create a report that shows each customer, the rentals they have made, and the total rental fee for all of their rentals.

### MyMISLab™

Go to the Assignments section of your MyLab to complete these writing exercises.

**CE6-3.** Explain why it is important to have a data model created before you start making tables. Why is it necessary to identify a primary key for each table? Explain why primary keys (not attributes) are used to create relationships between tables.

**CE6-4.** Compare and contrast two different data entry methods: entering data directly into a table versus entering data using a data entry form. When might one be preferred over the other? Why might data entry forms be more appealing to employees entering the data? Similarly, why create reports when you can get the data you need from a set of queries?

## ENDNOTE

1. When you enter the Name field, Access will give you an error message. Ignore the message and click OK. The fact that you are using a reserved word for this example will not be a problem. If you want to be safe, you could enter *PName* or *ProspectName* (rather than *Name*) and avoid this issue. Many people believe that Access is poorly designed in this respect. You ought to be able to enter any value for Field Name the way you want. Access should stay out of your way; you shouldn't have to stay out of its way!

chapter extension 7

**Chapter 5** provides the background for this extension.

# Using Excel and Access Together

**STUDY QUESTIONS**

**QCE7-1 WHY USE EXCEL AND ACCESS TOGETHER?**

**QCE7-2 WHAT IS IMPORT/EXPORT?**

**QCE7-3 HOW CAN YOU CREATE CHARTS WITH EXCEL?**

**QCE7-4 HOW CAN YOU CREATE GROUP TOTALS IN ACCESS?**

**QCE7-5 HOW CAN YOU USE EXCEL TO GRAPH ACCESS DATA?**

**QCE7-6 HOW CAN YOU USE ACCESS TO REPORT EXCEL DATA?**

**QCE7-7 HOW CAN YOU COMBINE EXCEL AND ACCESS TO ANALYZE DATA?**

CE7

Excel and Access are two different products with two different purposes. In this chapter extension, you will learn how to use them together to analyze data in ways that neither can do alone. You will also learn how to create graphs in Excel and group totals in Access queries.

## QCE7-1 WHY USE EXCEL AND ACCESS TOGETHER?

As you learned in Chapter Extension 4, Excel is superb at processing interrelated formulas. Because of this strength, business users often select Excel for processing financial statements, creating budgets, and performing financial analyses. As you will learn in this chapter extension, you can use Excel to create sophisticated and stylish graphics with very little work on your part. (Excel does a lot of work, though!)

Access is a DBMS, and, as you learned in Chapter 5, the primary purpose of a DBMS is to keep track of things. Access is superior for tracking orders, inventory, equipment, people, and so forth. As you learned in Chapter Extension 6, you can readily create data entry forms, queries, and sophisticated and professional reports with Access. In this chapter extension, you will learn how to create more sophisticated queries.

But what if you want to use Excel to process data stored in Access? What if you want, for example, to create graphs of Access data? Or what if you want to include Access data in a financial analysis? You could rekey all of the Access data into Excel, but that process is not only labor-intensive (and therefore expensive), but also error-prone. Similarly, what if you want to use Access to summarize Excel data and produce sophisticated reports? Again, you could rekey the data into Access, but with the same disadvantages.

In both cases, a better approach than rekeying is to import or export the data to or from Excel or Access. We begin with a discussion of import/export in the next question.

## QCE7-2 WHAT IS IMPORT/EXPORT?

**Import/export** is the process of transferring data from one computer system to another. We can say that system A imports data from system B or, equivalently, that system B exports data to system A.

In almost all cases, including Excel and Access, import/export does not maintain an active connection to the source of the data. For example, when you import Access data into Excel, the data are current at the time of the import. If users subsequently change the Access data, the imported data in Excel will be out of date until you reimport it. Because imported data can become out of date, you should develop procedures (either manual or automated) to ensure that data are refreshed on a timely basis.

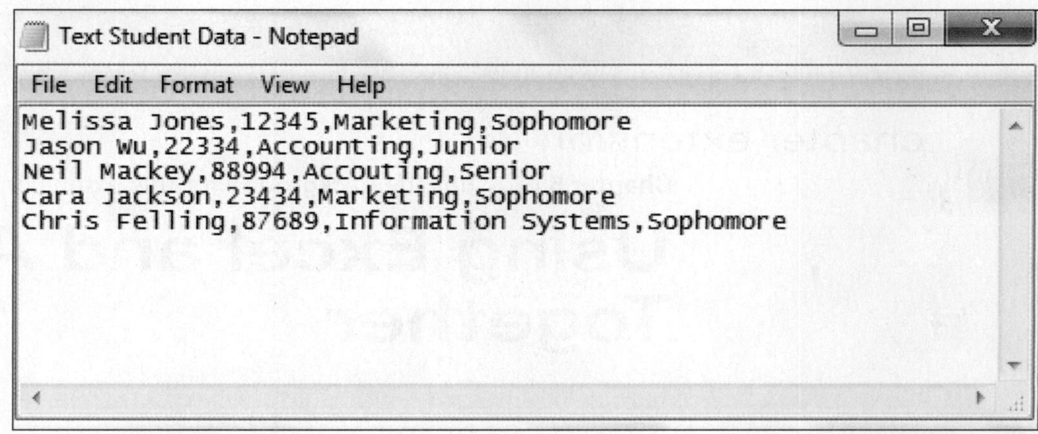


**Figure CE7-1**
Example of Data Exported from University Enrollment System

*Source:* Microsoft Access 2013

## IMPORT/EXPORT OF TEXT DATA

A common way for systems to exchange data is to create files of text. One system will export text data, and another will import it. Consider, for example, a professor who wants to track students' in-class comments using Microsoft Access. Most university enrollment systems can export class enrollment data into text files. Figure CE7-1 shows a typical export.

This file contains students' names, numbers, majors, and grade levels. Notice that the field values are separated by commas. Accordingly, such a file is called a **comma-delimited file**. Sometimes, however, the data itself contains commas, and so commas cannot be used to separate field data. In that case, some other character is used to delimit the fields. The tab character is frequently used, in which case the export file is called a **tab-delimited file**.

Delimited text files are easy to import into either Excel or Access. In Access, just create (or open a database) and click the *EXTERNAL DATA* tab, as shown in Figure CE7-2. Next, as shown in Figure CE7-3, select the file that contains the data and check *Import the source data into a new table in the current database.* (Ignore the other options, as they are beyond the scope of our discussion.) When you click *OK*, a multiple-panel wizard opens.

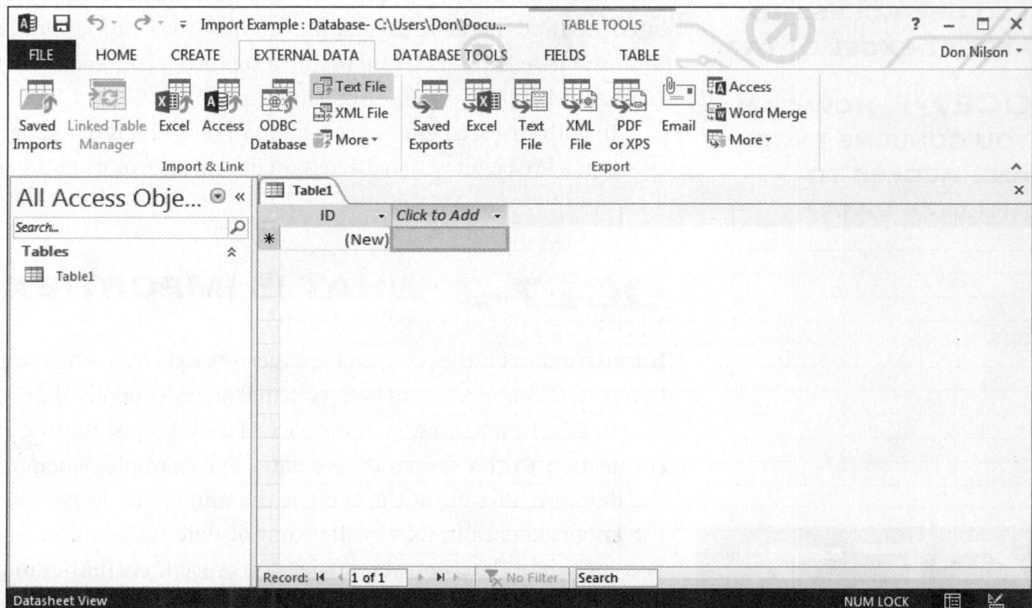


**Figure CE7-2**
*EXTERNAL DATA* Menu Choice

*Source:* Microsoft Access 2013

**Figure CE7-3**
Specifying the Source File and Destination

*Source:* Microsoft Access 2013

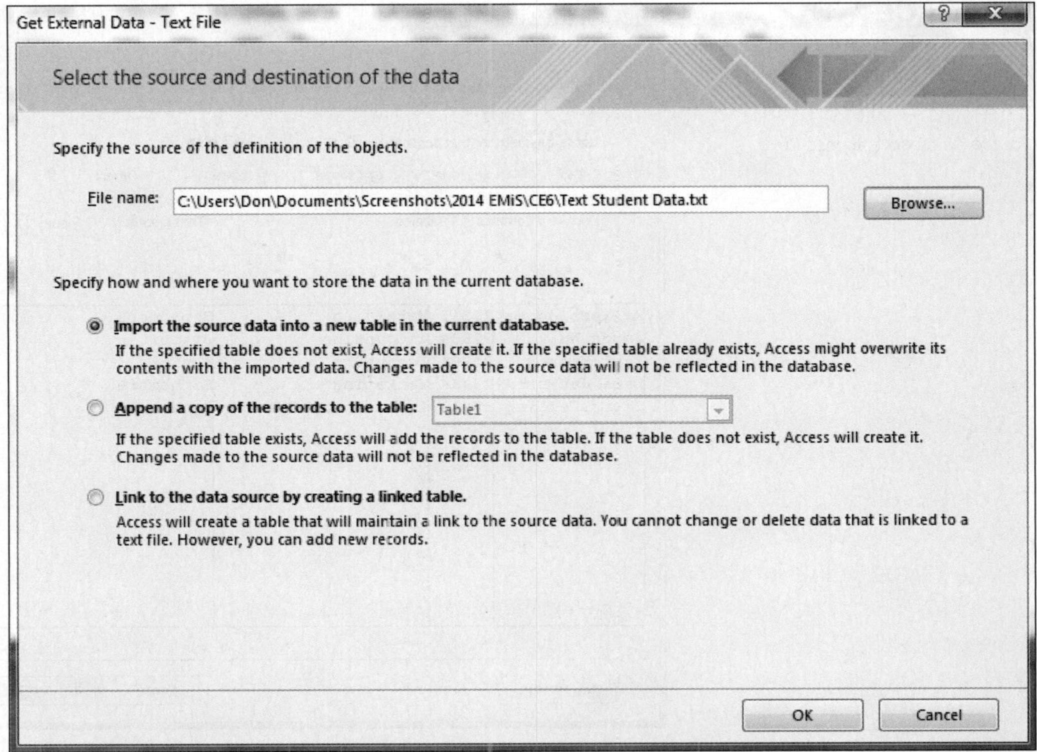


In Figure CE7-4a, you specify that your file is delimited. To assist you, Access shows the first rows of the file. Click *Next* to specify the delimiter; here we are using the comma, as shown in Figure CE7-4b. Click *Next* again and you will be given a chance to name the fields as well as to specify their data type. Ignore Indexed. In Figure CE7-4c, we have renamed the first three columns and are about to rename the fourth. In the next screen (not shown), you have a chance to name

**Figure CE7-4a**
Importing Text Data into Access: Specifying a Delimited File

*Source:* Microsoft Access 2013

Import Text Wizard

Your data seems to be in a 'Delimited' format. If it isn't, choose the format that more correctly describes your data.

Delimited - Characters such as comma or tab separate each field
Fixed Width - Fields are aligned in columns with spaces between each field

Sample data from file: C:\USERS\DON\DOCUMENTS\SCREENSHOTS\2014 EMIS\CE6\TEXT STUDENT DATA.TXT.

```
1 Melissa Jones,12345,Marketing,Sophomore
2 Jason Wu,22334,Accounting,Junior
3 Neil Mackey,88994,Accouting,Senior
4 Cara Jackson,23434,Marketing,Sophomore
5 Chris Felling,87689,Information Systems,Sophomore
```

Advanced... Cancel < Back Next > Finish

**Figure CE7-4b**
Importing Text Data into Access: Specifying a Comma-Delimited File

*Source:* Microsoft Access 2013

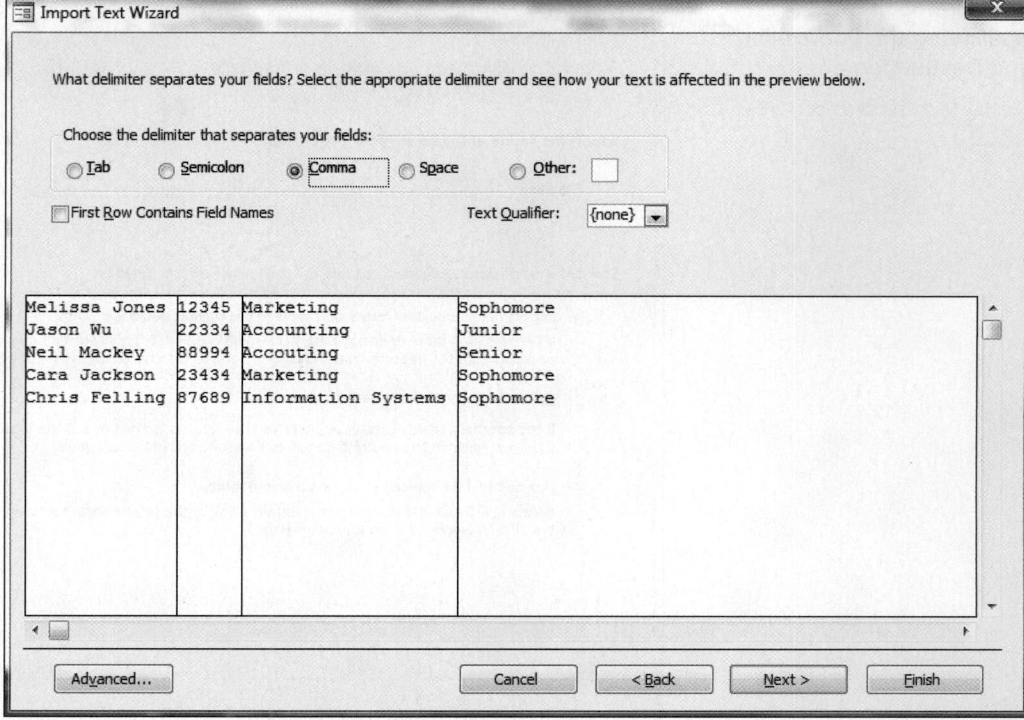


**Figure CE7-4c**
Importing Text Data into Access: Naming and Describing Columns During Import

*Source:* Microsoft Access 2013

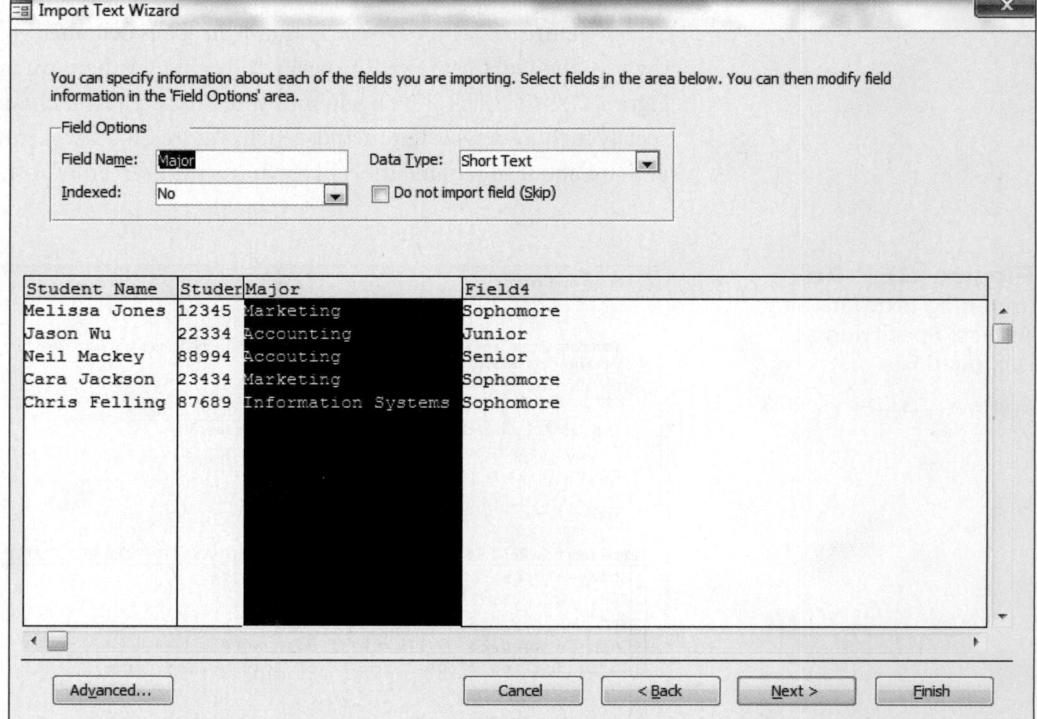


the table into which Access will import the data. At this point, click *Finish*, and Access will import the data into a new table, as shown in Figure CE7-5.

Access will process the new table just like any other table. You can create data entry forms, reports, queries, and even relationships to other tables. Note, too, that although we have imported only five rows in this example, it would be no more work for us to import 50, 5,000, or 50,000 rows.

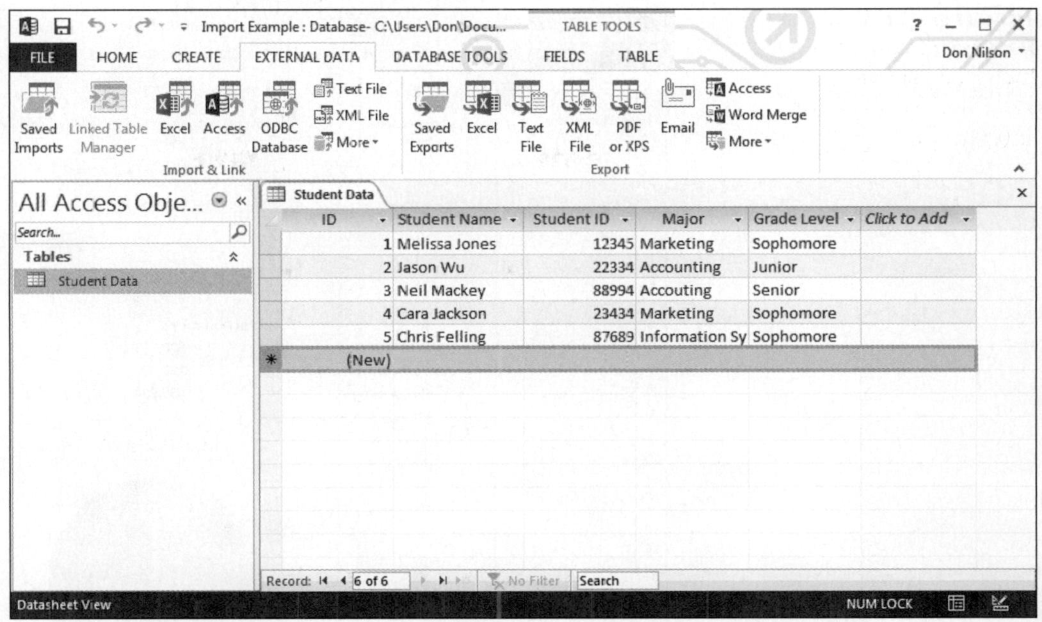


**Figure CE7-5**
Data After Import

*Source:* Microsoft Access 2013

You can follow an almost identical process to import data into Excel. (Memo to Microsoft: Why isn't it *exactly* the same process?) Open Excel, click the *Data* tab, and in the *Get External Data* section of that ribbon click *From Text*. You will need to specify a comma delimiter and indicate where in the worksheet you want the data placed. This process is easy, as you will see when you do Using Your Knowledge question CE7-1 at the end of this extension.

### IMPORT/EXPORT OF EXCEL AND ACCESS DATA

One way you could exchange data between Excel and Access would be to export the data into a text file and then import that text data. However, because many users want to transfer data between Excel and Access, Microsoft has created special tools for that purpose. You can use Access to both export and import data. You can use Excel to import data from Access. You will see examples of the use of the specialized import/export tools in QCE7-5 and QCE7-6. Before we turn to these tools, we will first consider additional features of Excel and Access.

## QCE7-3 HOW CAN YOU CREATE CHARTS WITH EXCEL?

Microsoft Excel includes comprehensive tools for graphing data. You can use it to construct column and bar charts, pie charts, line and scatter plots, and other graphs. Here you will learn how to construct pie and column charts. Follow the discussion in this section to learn the gist of the process, and then learn more by experimenting with Excel. You can make custom charts quite easily; like the rest of Office 2013, however, it's a matter of finding the ribbon that has the tool you want.

In this section, we will construct charts for donations obtained by three volunteers. We won't import this data from Access yet but instead will assume that the names and donation values have been keyed in by hand.

### CREATING A PIE CHART

Figure CE7-6 shows a pie chart of Total Donations for three volunteers. This chart, which is very easy to create, is one example of the kind of graph that Excel can produce. To create this pie chart, we highlight cells D4 through E7, click the *INSERT* tab in the ribbon, and in the *Charts* section of that ribbon select the *Pie* icon (shown in Figure CE7-7). As you can see, Excel can create several different versions of pie charts; here we have selected the first choice.

**Figure CE7-6**
Pie Chart

*Source:* Microsoft Excel 2013

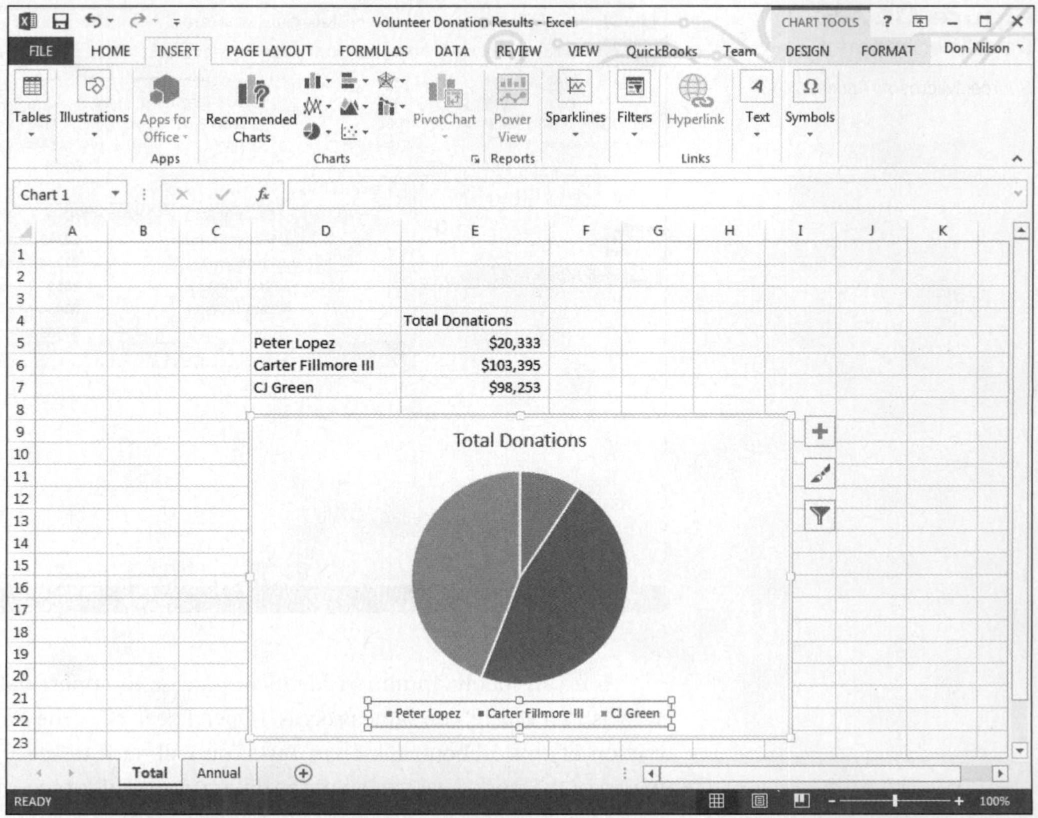


Excel provides many different tools to customize a graph. To access them, click the graph you want to change. Excel will show a special tab called *Chart Tools* at the top of the window. Click *Chart Tools* to make them available, as shown in Figure CE7-8. The discussion of these tools is beyond the scope of this chapter extension. But they are intuitive, and you can learn much about their use by experimenting with them.

**Figure CE7-7**
Creating the Pie Chart

*Source:* Microsoft Excel 2013

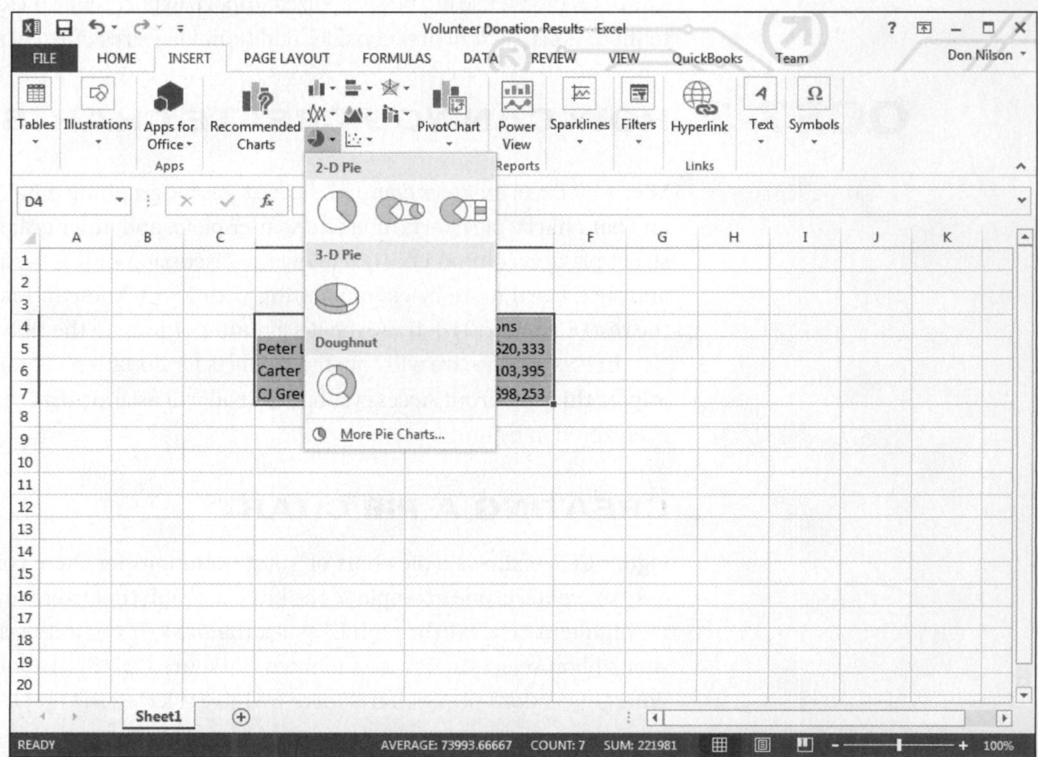

**Figure CE7-8**
Selecting the Chart Tools
*Source:* Microsoft Excel 2013

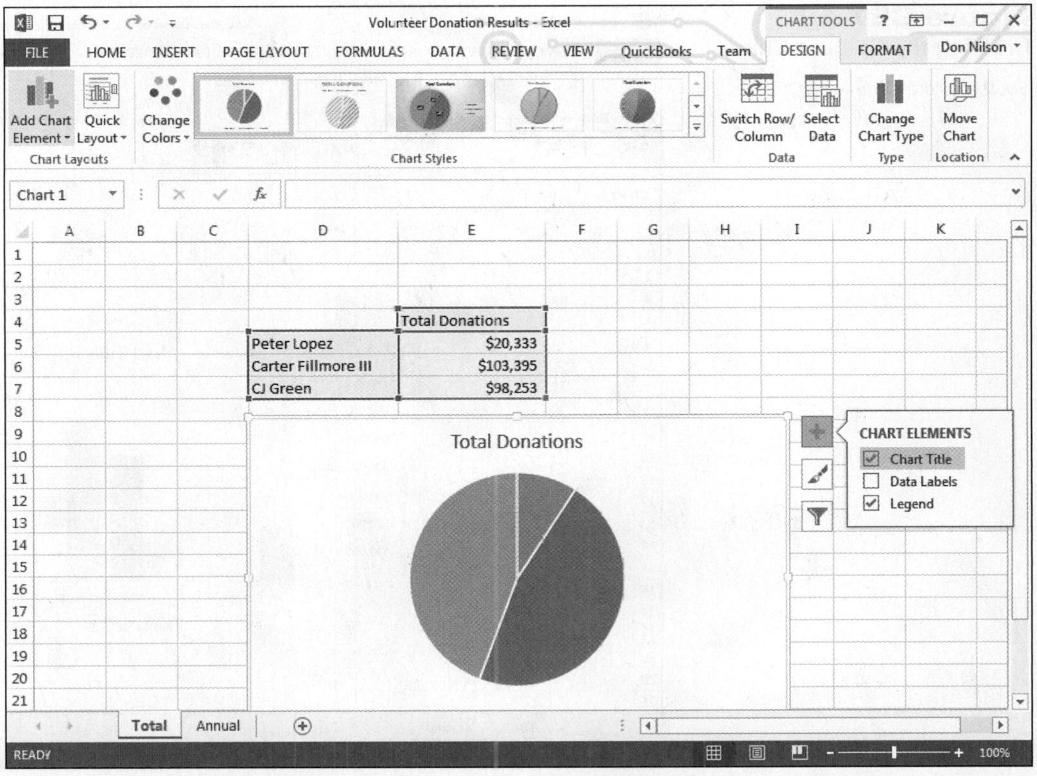


## CREATING A COLUMN CHART

The pie chart in Figure CE7-6 shows only the total data for each volunteer. If we want to compare results for 2 years, we can do so with a column or bar chart. Figure CE7-9 shows a column chart.

To create the column chart, we highlighted the data and selected *Column* in the *Charts* section of the *INSERT* tab, as shown in Figure CE7-10. With one exception, Excel created the chart shown in Figure CE7-9 with no further work on our part.

**Figure CE7-9**
Sample Column Chart
*Source:* Microsoft Excel 2013

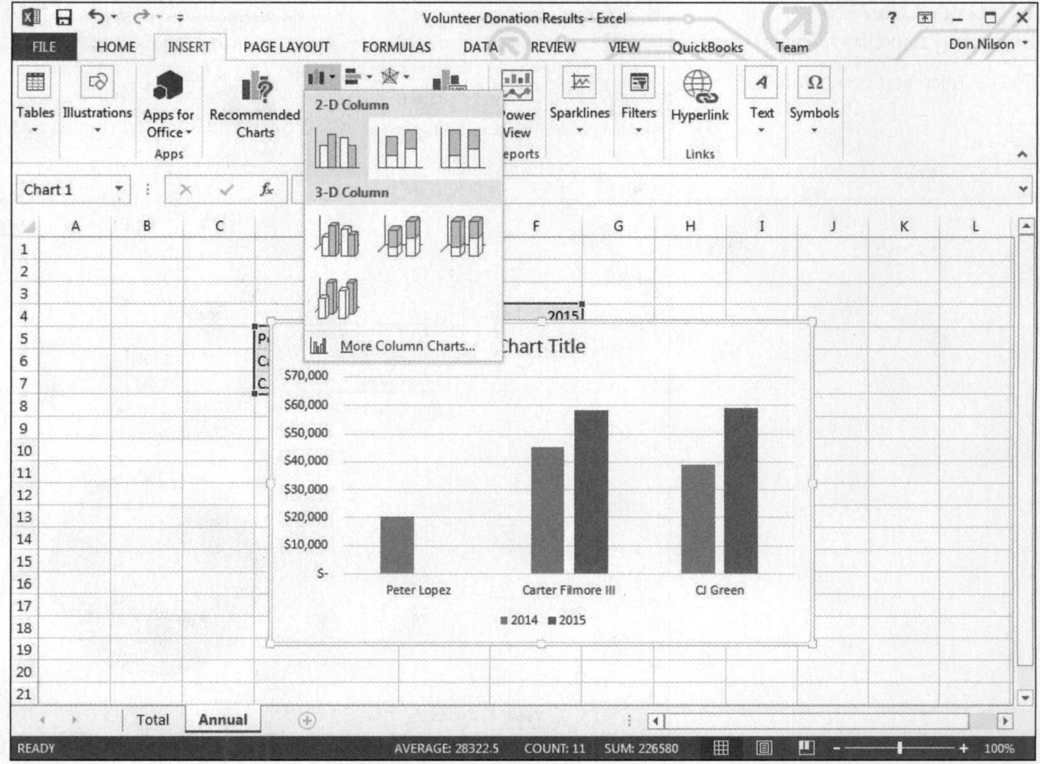


**Figure CE7-10**
Creating the Column Chart

*Source:* Microsoft Excel 2013

The exception concerns the title. Notice that the data on which the graph is based do not include any text that would make a suitable title. Hence, when Excel first produced the graph shown in Figure CE7-9, the graph had a default title, "Chart Title." To change it, you can click in the area and edit the text.

As you can imagine, Excel has many, many options for creating interesting and informative graphs. To see them, click on the column chart. If you want to customize a title, select Chart Title and then choose where you want the title to appear. The Add Chart Element list has numerous other options as you can see in Figure CE7-11. As stated earlier, one good way to learn more is to create some data and experiment. You can also find many resources for learning Excel on the Web.

## QCE7-4 HOW CAN YOU CREATE GROUP TOTALS IN ACCESS?

In Chapter Extension 6, you learned how to create basic queries in Access. With more advanced queries, you can create considerably more information from the same amount of data. To learn some of the possibilities, consider the Volunteer database that we created in Chapter Extension 6.

Suppose a manager of the station wants to know the total of TotalDonations[1] for each date of fund-raising effort. Maybe she thinks that certain dates are more advantageous than others. To create this information, we can query the WORK table, group all donations for a given date, and then sum the TotalDonations for each group.

To do that, open the Volunteer database, click the *CREATE* tab, click *Query Design*, and then, as shown in Figure CE7-12, select the WORK table for the query. After adding that table, click *Close*.

Now, to add *WorkDate* and TotalDonations to the query output, double-click *Date* and *TotalDonations* in the WORK table diagram. Access adds them to the query contents table at the

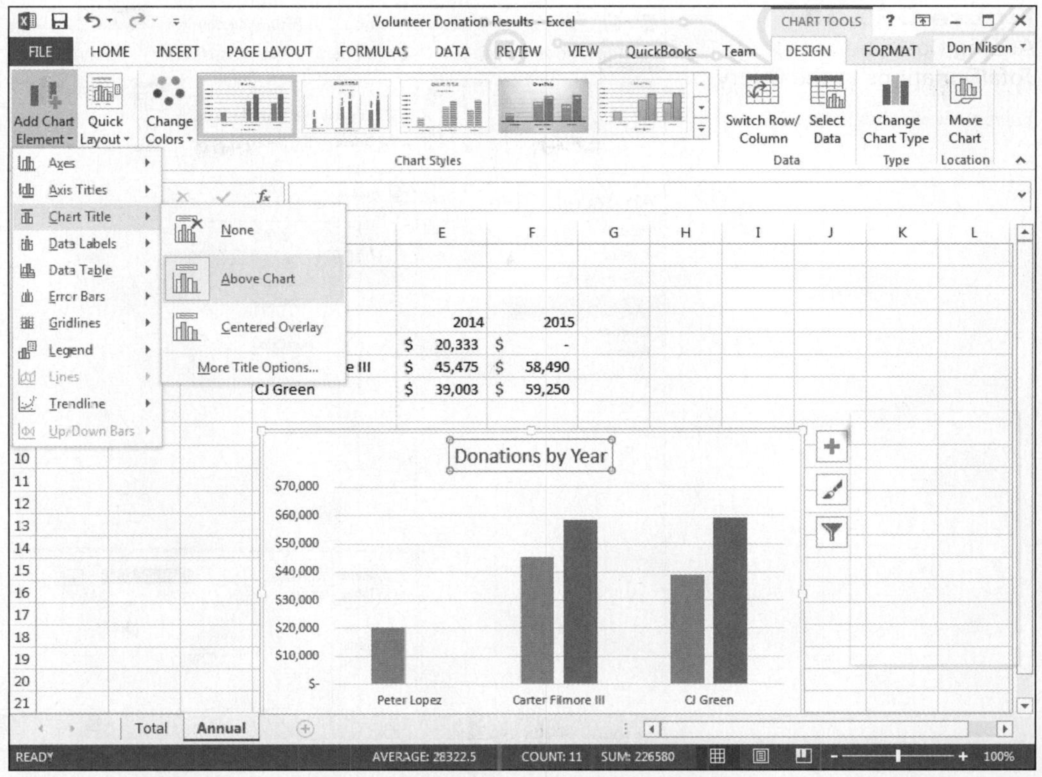


**Figure CE7-11**
Creating the Chart Title
*Source:* Microsoft Excel 2013

bottom of the query, as shown in Figure CE7-13. To group the WORK rows according to date, click the *Totals* button in the *Show/Hide* section of the *DESIGN* tab. In response, Access adds a row labeled *Total* to the query contents table, as shown in Figure CE7-14.

To group the rows by date, select the keyword *Group By* in the Total row under *WorkDate.* To sum TotalDonations for each group, select the keyword *Sum* under the TotalDonations column, in that same Total row. Figure CE7-14 shows this last action.

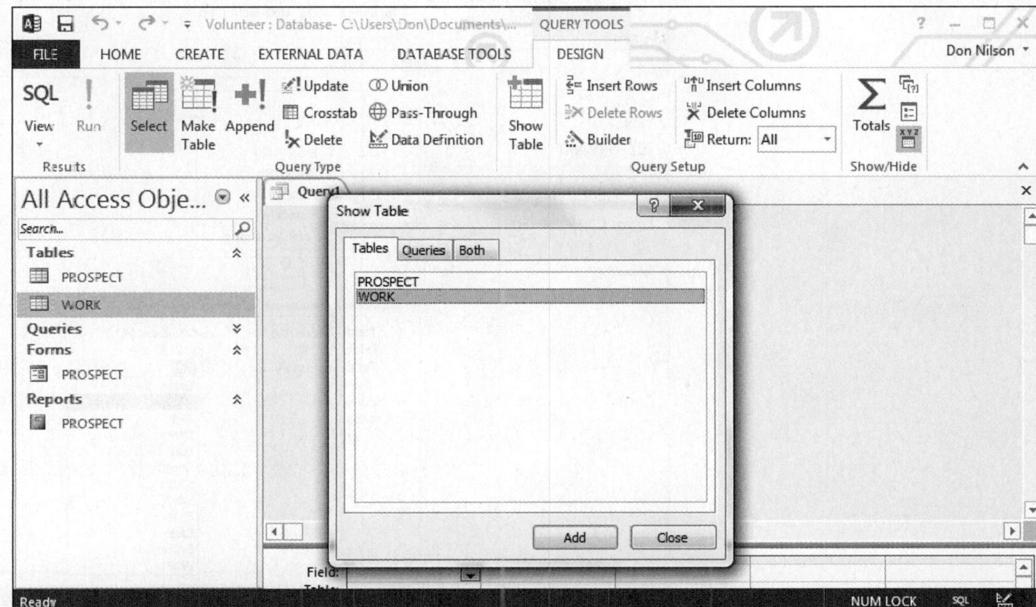


**Figure CE7-12**
Selecting the WORK Table for the Query
*Source:* Microsoft Access 2013

**Figure CE7-13**
Adding Data and TotalDonations to the Query

*Source:* Microsoft Access 2013

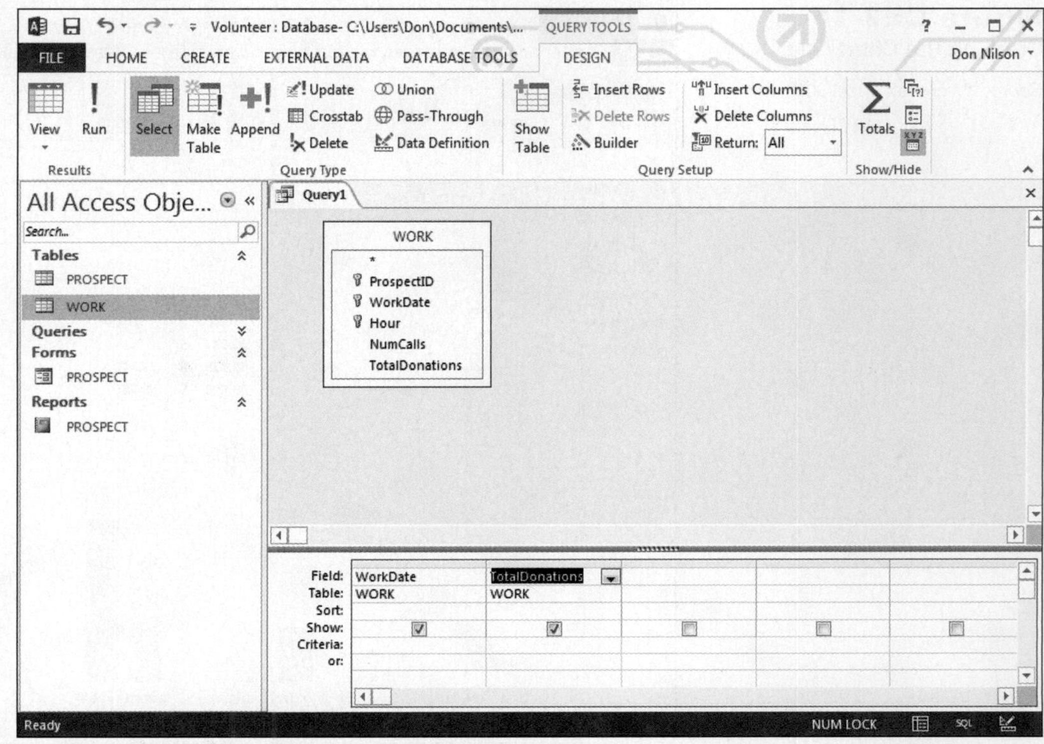

Run the query by clicking the large exclamation point in the *Results* section of the *Design* ribbon, and the results shown in Figure CE7-15 are generated. Access has summed TotalDonations for each Date. Save this query using the name *EventDateTotals.*

Suppose we want to perform another, similar query, but for a more complicated example. Say we want to show the name of each volunteer (called PROSPECT in this database), the total number of hours each has worked, and the total donations obtained. Recall that each row of WORK

**Figure CE7-14**
Selecting Sum in the Total Row for TotalDonations

*Source:* Microsoft Access 2013

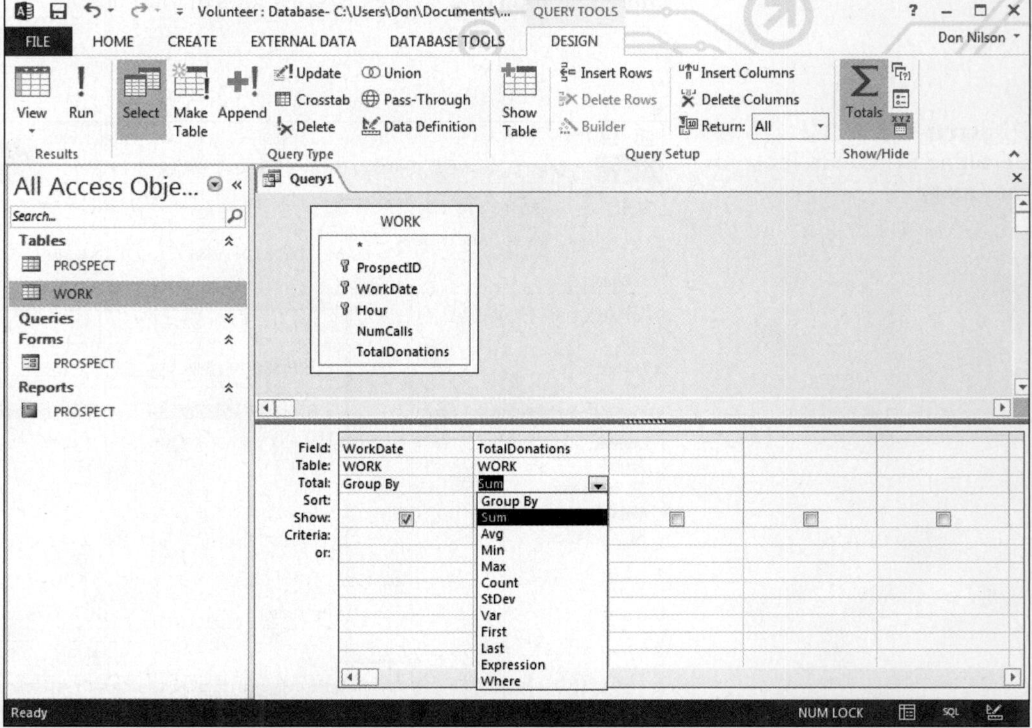

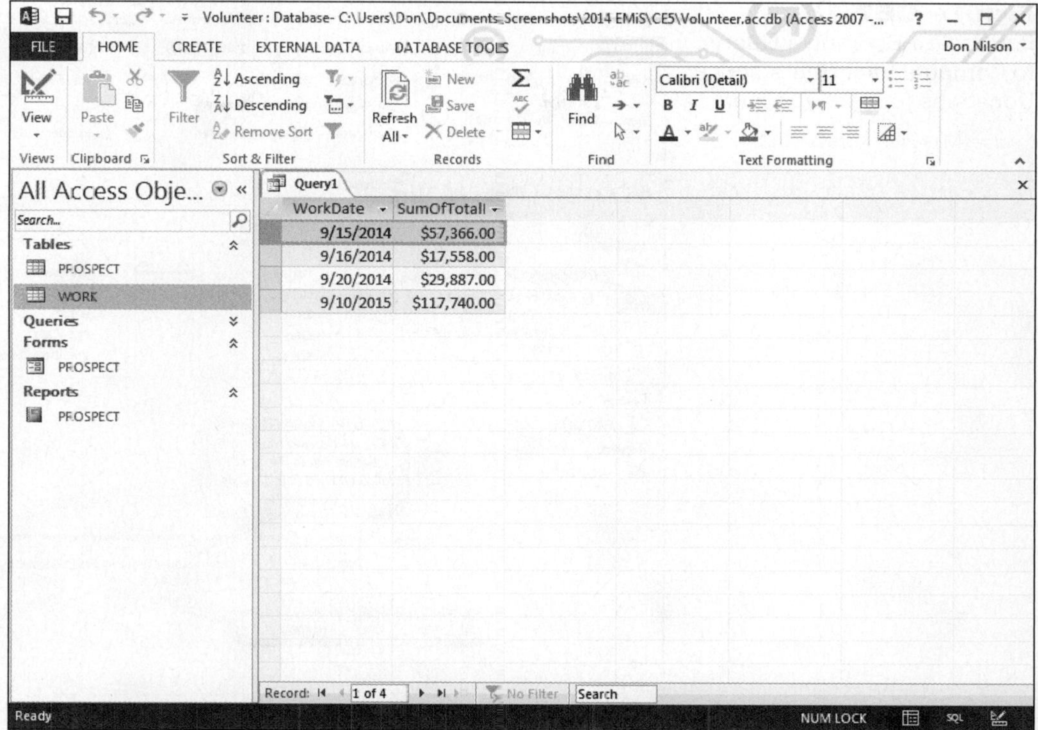


**Figure CE7-15**
Results of Query with Group by Date

*Source:* Microsoft Access 2013

details the results from 1 hour's activity. Therefore, we can compute the total number of hours a prospect worked by counting the number of rows for that prospect's ID.

The process is summarized in Figure CE7-16. To begin, open *Query Design* from the *CREATE* tab and add both the PROSPECT and WORK tables. Now, complete the following seven steps:

1. In the PROSPECT table, double-click *Name* to insert it into the query results.
2. In the WORK table, double-click *ProspectID* and *TotalDonations* to insert them into the query.
3. In the ribbon, click the *Totals* icon to cause Access to insert the Total row into the query contents table.
4. In the *Total* row under ProspectID, select *Count*. This informs Access to count the number of times each value of ProspectID occurred in the table.
5. In the *Total* row under TotalDonations, select *Sum*.
6. Create a column heading for the ProspectID column by typing the heading *Hours Worked*, followed by a colon in front of ProspectID.
7. Create a column heading for the TotalDonations column by typing the heading *Total Obtained*, followed by a colon in front of TotalDonations.

Running the query produces the results shown in Figure CE7-17.

We could use this query to compute the average donation total per hour for each worker. We would just divide Total Obtained by Hours Worked. However, Access provides an average function, and it is easier to use it.

To obtain the average, add TotalDonations again to the query (in column 4 of Figure CE7-18) and, under this copy of TotalDonations, in the *Total* row, select *Avg*. Insert the column heading *Average per Hour*. Running this query generates the results in Figure CE7-19. Use a calculator to verify the averages are what you would expect. Save this query using the name *AvgDonationQuery*.

Again, to learn more about queries and Access, create a table, enter some data, and experiment!

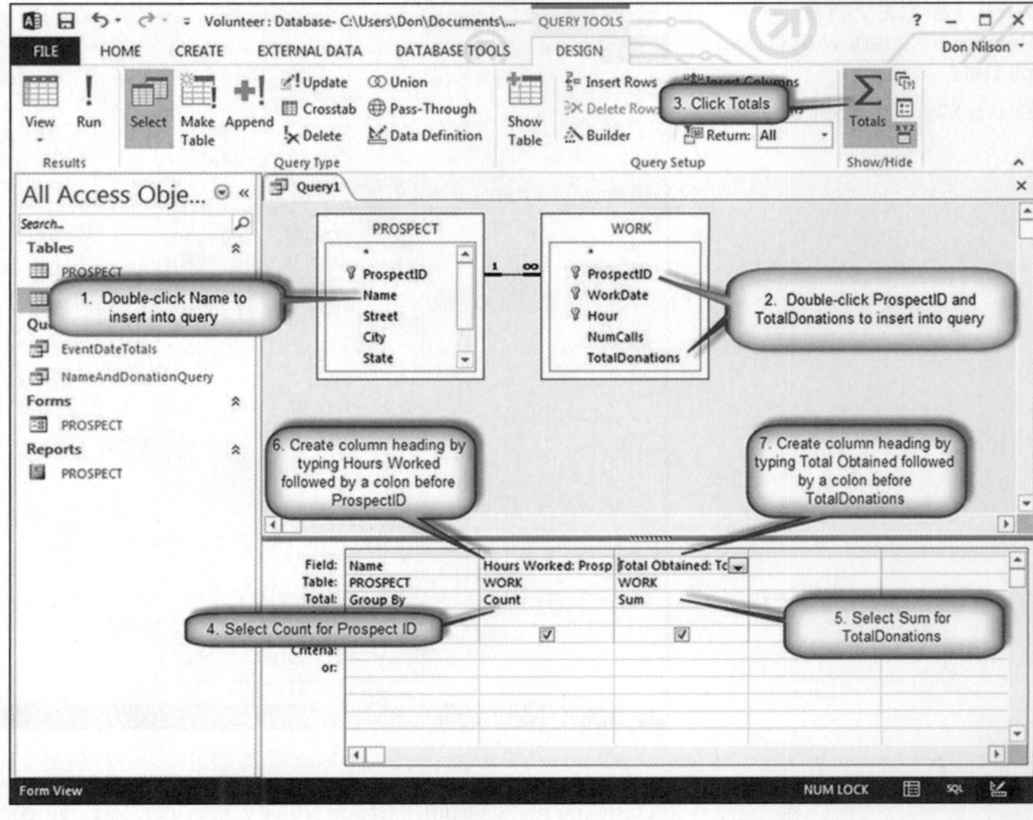


**Figure CE7-16** Process for Creating a Query to Compute Total Hours and Donations for Each Prospect

*Source:* Microsoft Access 2013

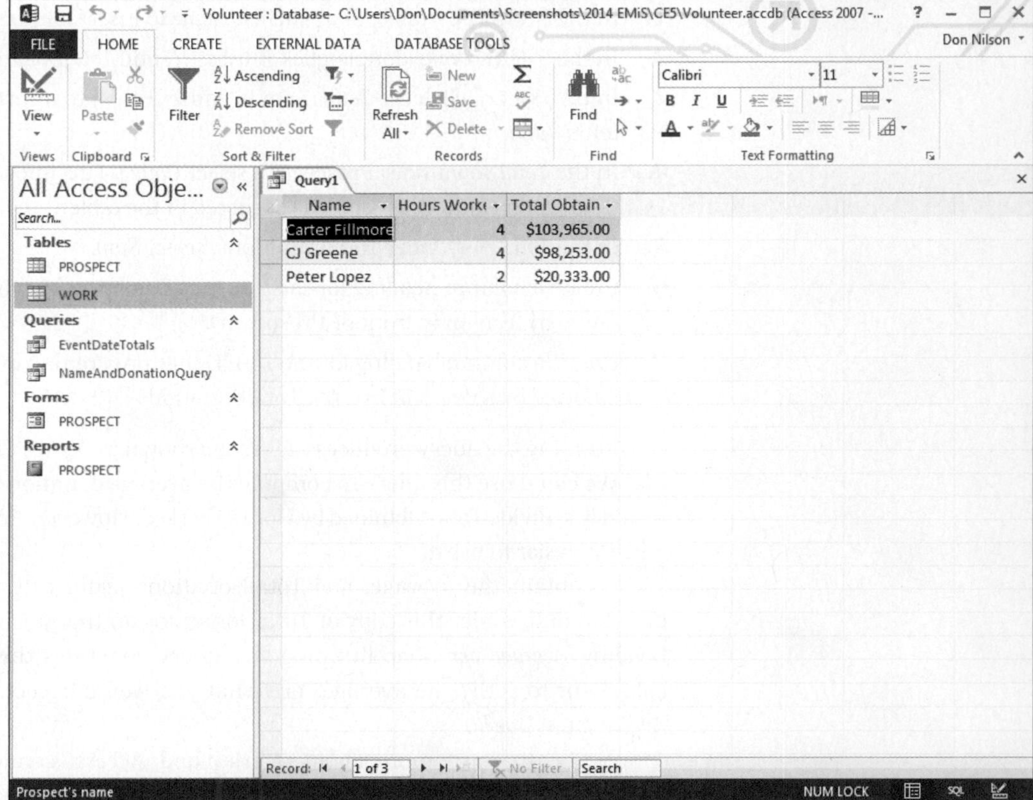


**Figure CE7-17** Results of the Query in Figure CE7-16

*Source:* Microsoft Access 2013

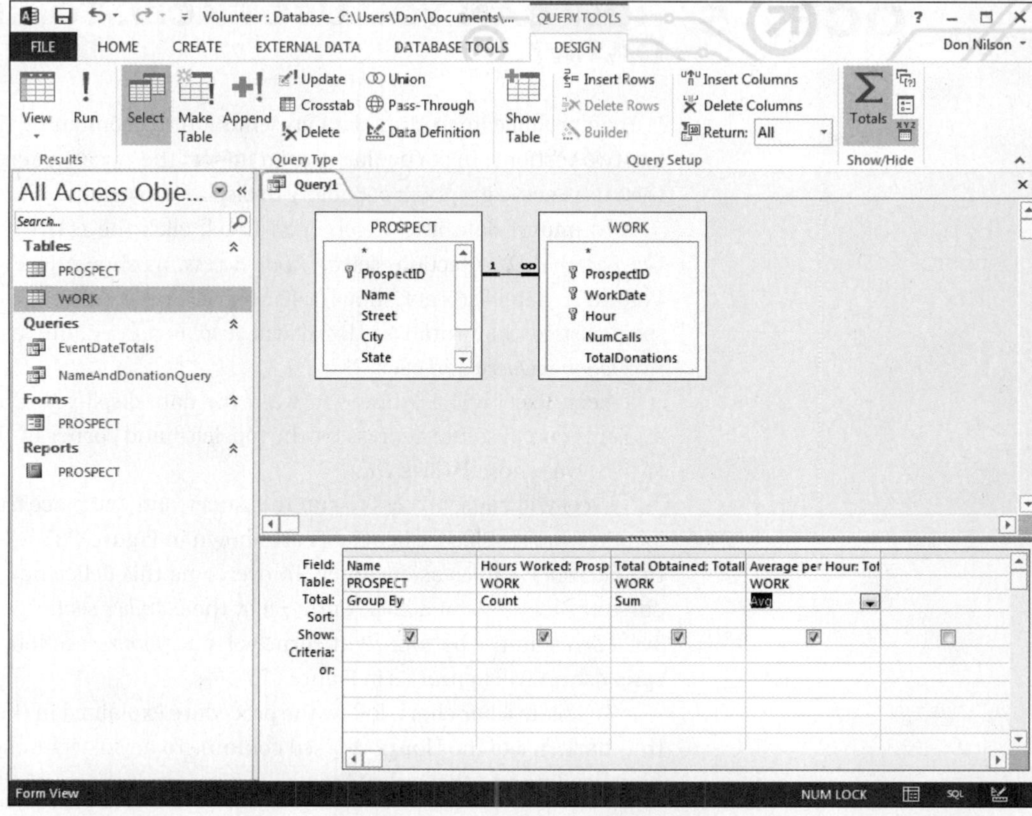


**Figure CE7-18**
Adding Average Donations per Hour

*Source:* Microsoft Access 2013

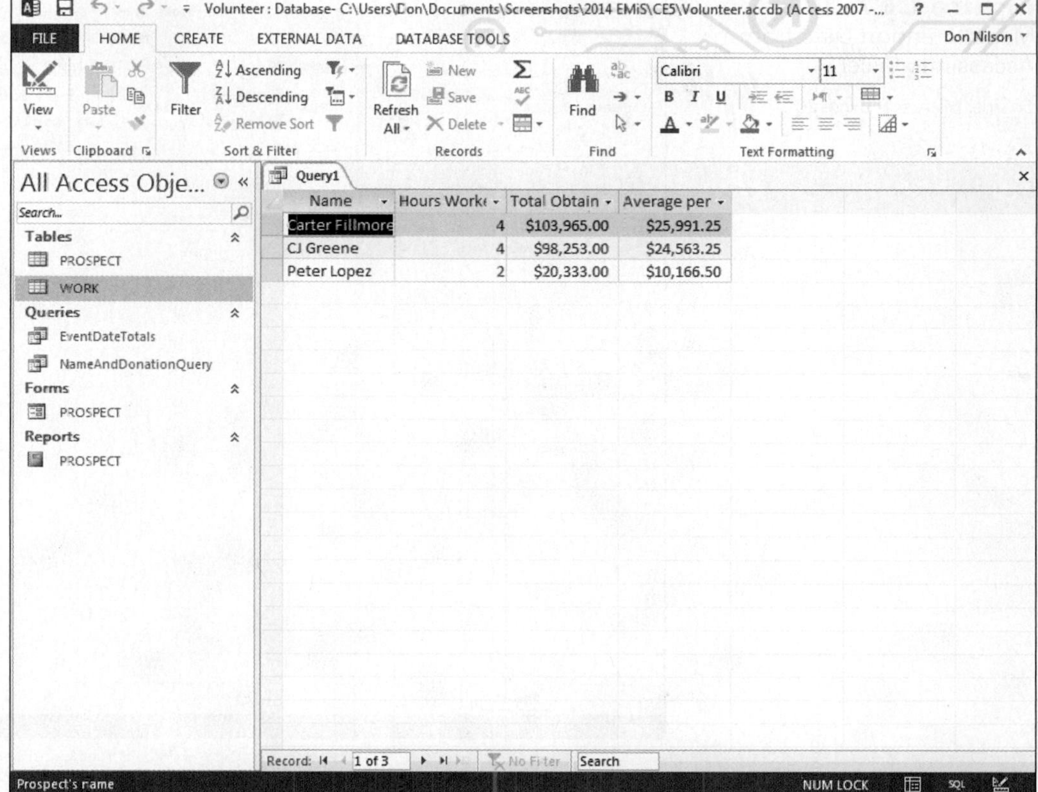


**Figure CE7-19**
Results of the Query in Figure CE7-18

*Source:* Microsoft Access 2013

## QCE7-5 HOW CAN YOU USE EXCEL TO GRAPH ACCESS DATA?

We can produce interesting data presentations by combining the results of the discussions in the last two sections. In particular, we can import the Access query created in QCE7-4 into Excel and then use Excel's graphing capability to display the results.

To import data into Excel, open Excel, click the *DATA* tab in the ribbon, and then, in the *Get External Data* section, select *From Access*, as shown in Figure CE7-20. After you select the Volunteer database (not shown), Excel will query Access to determine the tables and queries that exist in that database. Excel will display the results, as shown in Figure CE7-21. Select *AvgDonationQuery* and click *OK*.

Next, Excel will ask how you want the data displayed. Choose *Table* and *Existing worksheet*, and enter an absolute address for the top, left-hand corner of the table. In Figure CE7-22, cell C3 (*$C$3*) was chosen. Click *OK*.

Excel will cause Access to run this query and will place the results into the worksheet in the location you specified. The results are shown in Figure CE7-23. Notice that Excel does not format the currency values as currency. To overcome this deficiency, highlight the cells containing the currency amounts and click *Currency* in the *Number* section of the *Home* ribbon. Next, click the *small arrow* in the bottom-right corner of the *Number* section, and select *zero decimal points*. The spreadsheet will appear as in Figure CE7-24.

To create a bar chart, follow the procedure explained in the discussion of QCE7-3. To simplify the chart, delete the Hours Worked column. To do so, right-click the *D* in the Hours Worked column heading and then select Delete.

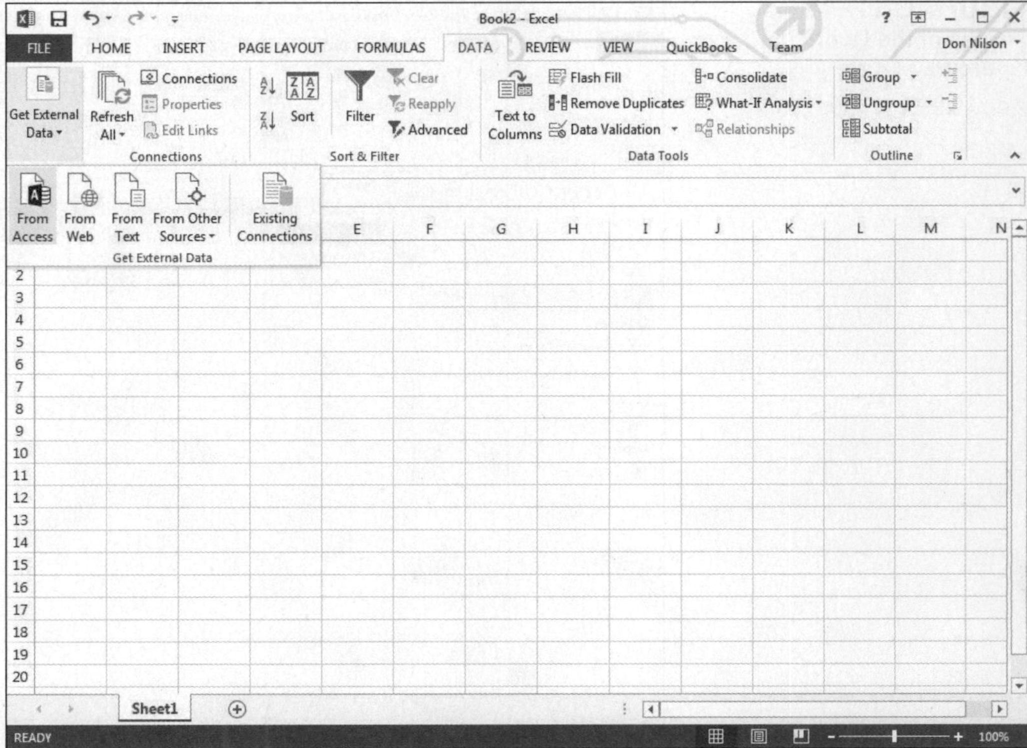


**Figure CE7-20**
Menu to Import Data from Access into Excel

*Source:* Microsoft Excel 2013

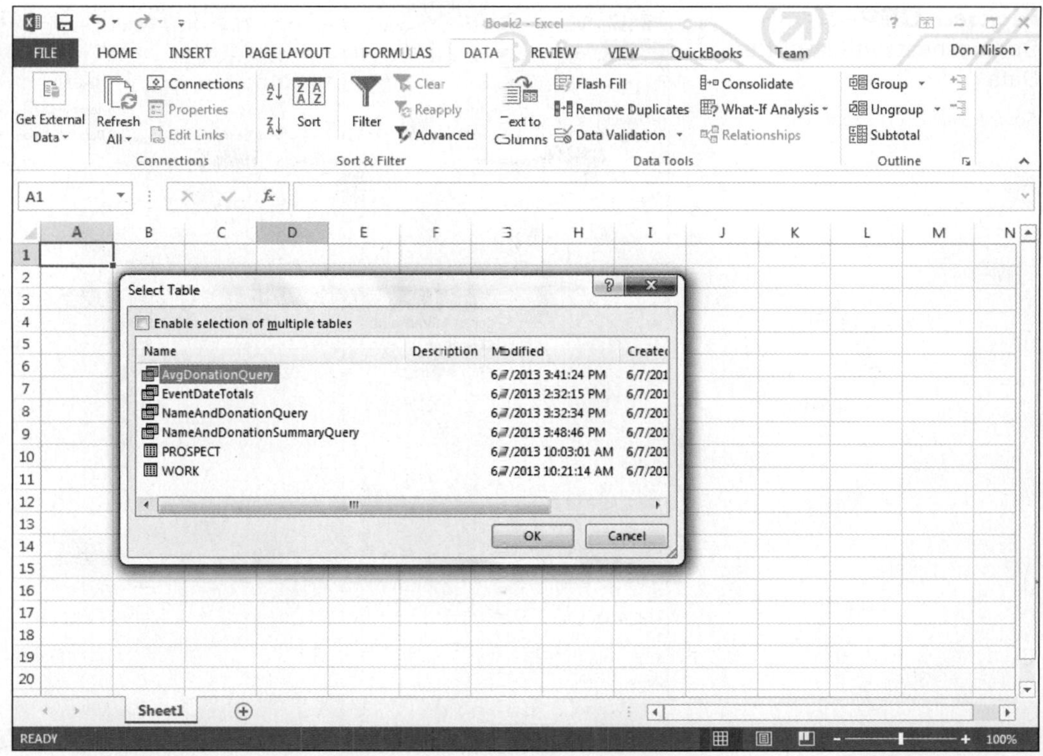


**Figure CE7-21**
Selecting the Query to Import

*Source:* Microsoft Excel 2013

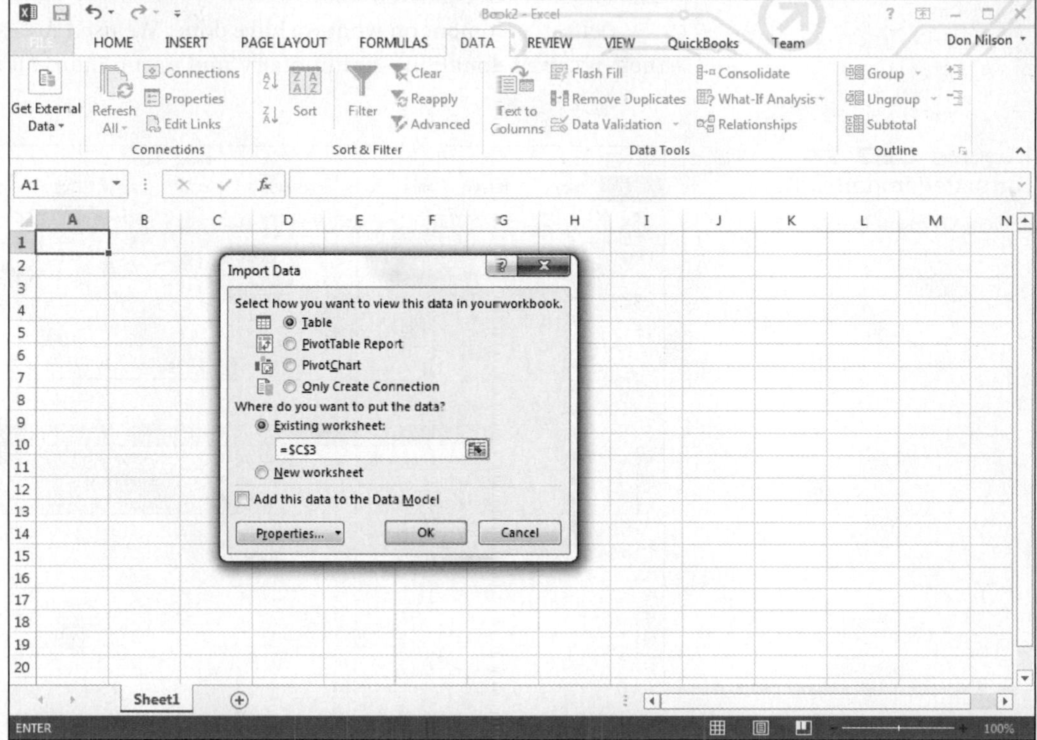


**Figure CE7-22**
Placing the Imported Data in the Spreadsheet

*Source:* Microsoft Excel 2013

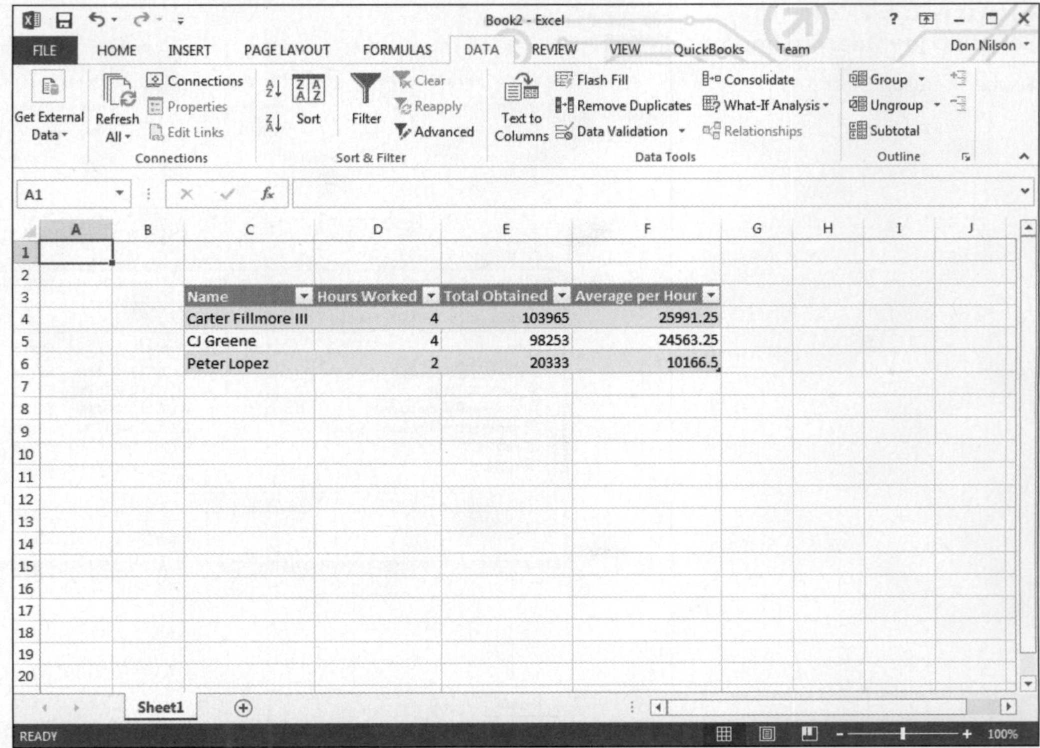


**Figure CE7-23**
Spreadsheet with Imported Data

*Source:* Microsoft Excel 2013

Now, to make the chart, highlight cells C3 through E6, click the *Insert* tab, and select *bar chart*. Next, enter *Donations Collected by Volunteer* in the Chart Title space provided by Excel. The result is shown in Figure CE7-25.

Reflect a moment on what we have done. We used Access to keep track of volunteers and their received donations and to query and group data, all tasks for which Access is ideally

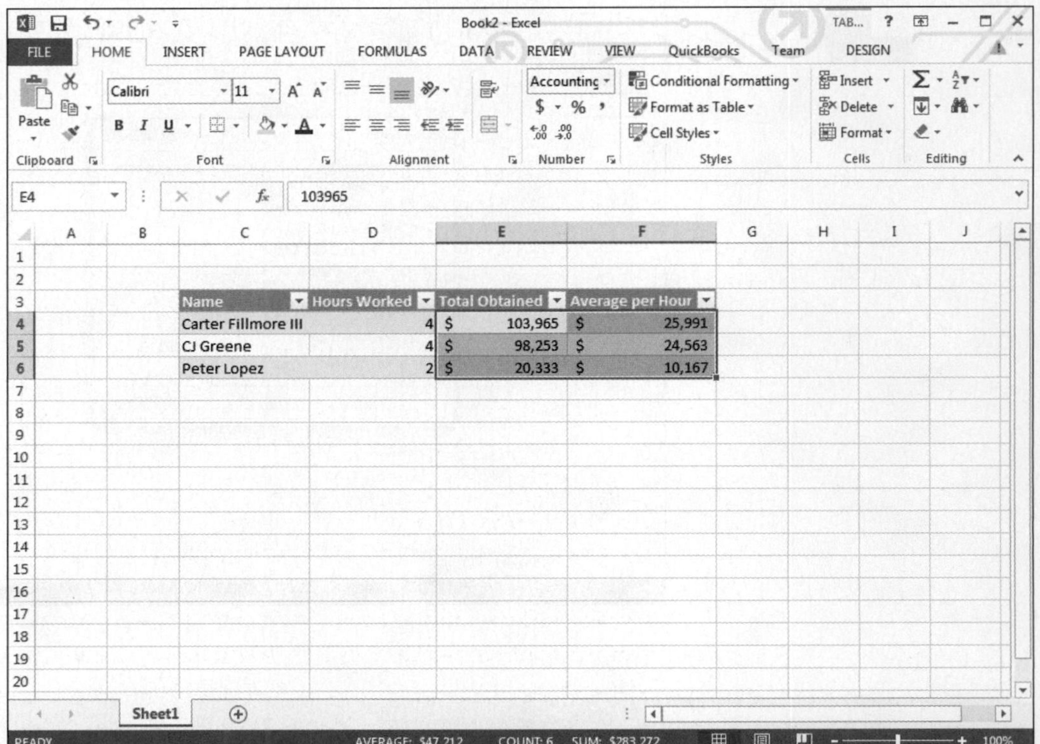


**Figure CE7-24**
Formatted Imported Data

*Source:* Microsoft Excel 2013

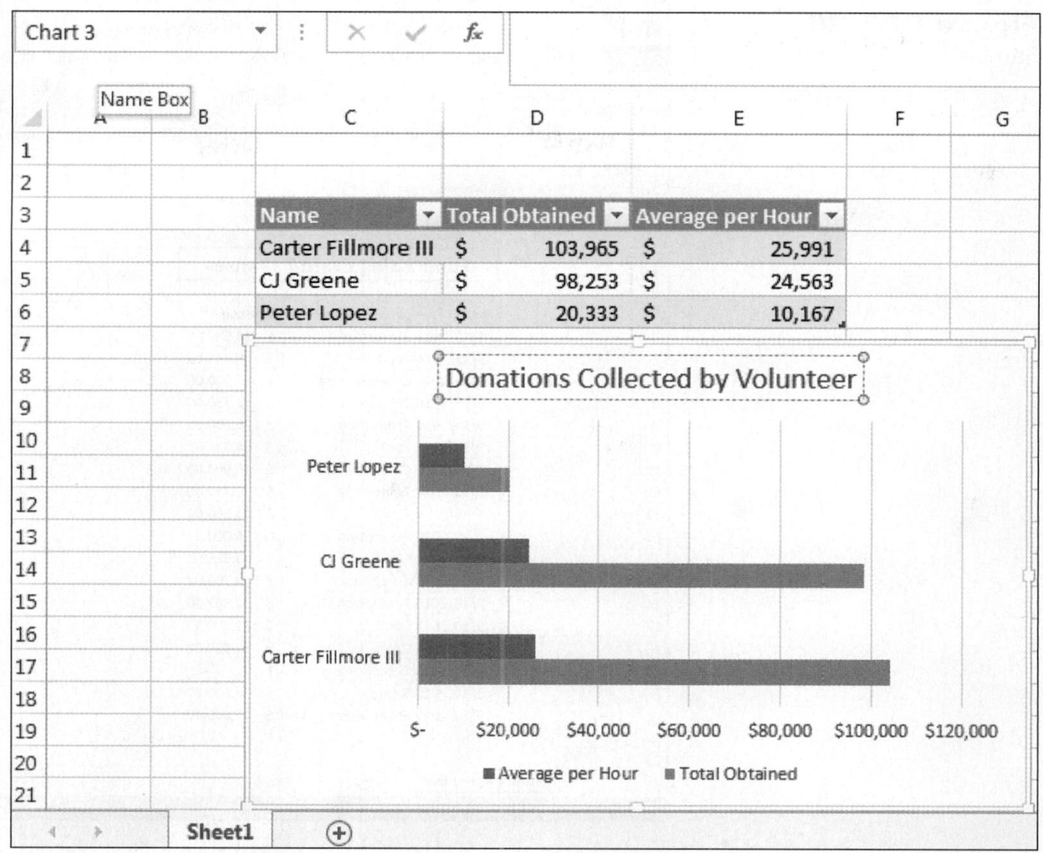


**Figure CE7-25**
A Bar Chart of the Imported Data

*Source:* Microsoft Excel 2013

suited. However, we then imported that data into Excel and used Excel's easy graphing capability to create the bar chart. Cool!

## QCE7-6 HOW CAN YOU USE ACCESS TO REPORT EXCEL DATA?

In Chapter Extension 6, you learned how easy it is to create professional-looking reports in Access. You can sort, group, and format data to present the data in context, creating information. But what if your data doesn't reside in Access? What if it is stored in an Excel worksheet instead?

In QCE7-2, you learned how to import text data into Access. Here you will learn how to use a similar process to import data from Excel.

Consider the event expense data in the Excel worksheet in Figure CE7-26. Suppose that you want to produce two different reports from this data. In one, you want to group all expenses for a given expense category and produce an expense total for that category. In the second, you want to group all the expenses for particular dates and produce an expense total for each date. You can do both of these by importing this Excel data into Access and using the Access report generator.

To begin, you need to identify the data that you want to transfer. An easy way to do this is to create a **named range**, which is a subset of the cells in a worksheet that has a unique name. To create a named range for the expense data, first highlight all of the data (including the column headings) and then click the *FORMULAS* tab. In the *Defined Names* section, click *Define Name* and then enter a suitable name. In Figure CE7-27, we use the name *Event_Expenses.* (Range names cannot contain any spaces, so the underscore character is used to connect the words *Event* and *Expenses.*)

To import the data into Access we will use a process similar to that for importing text data. First, close the workbook that has the data. Then open the Access database into which you want

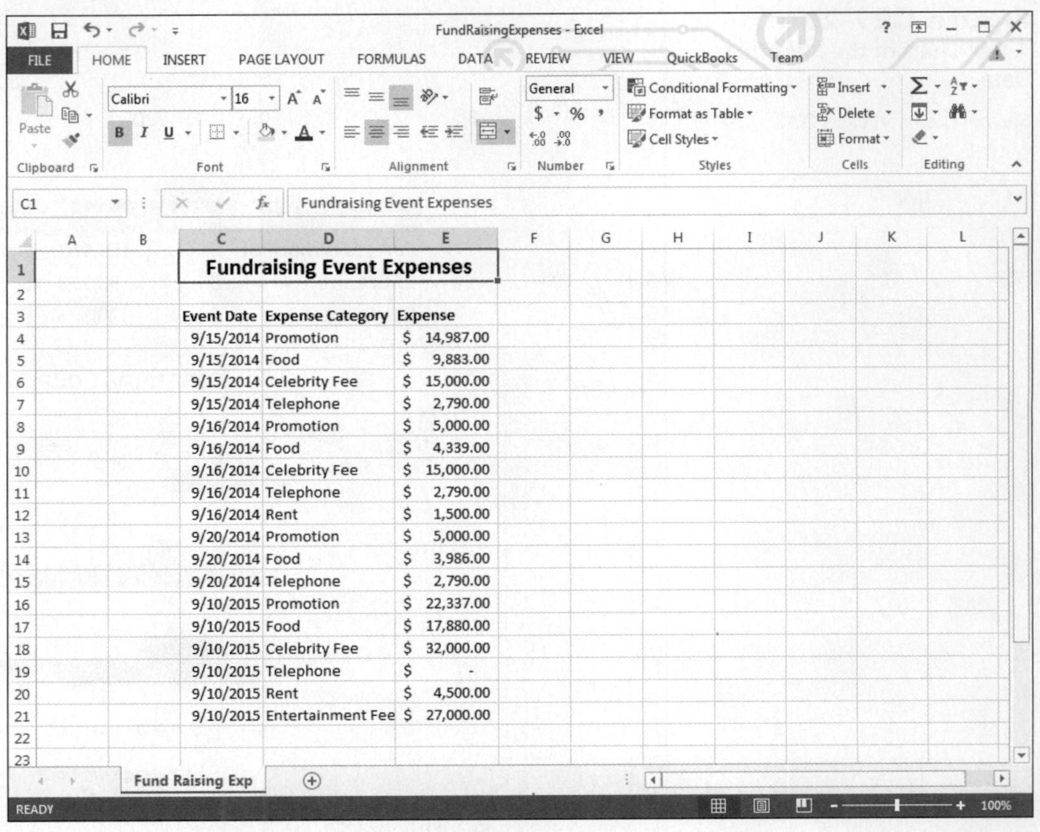


**Figure CE7-26**
Sample Expense Data
*Source:* Microsoft Excel 2013

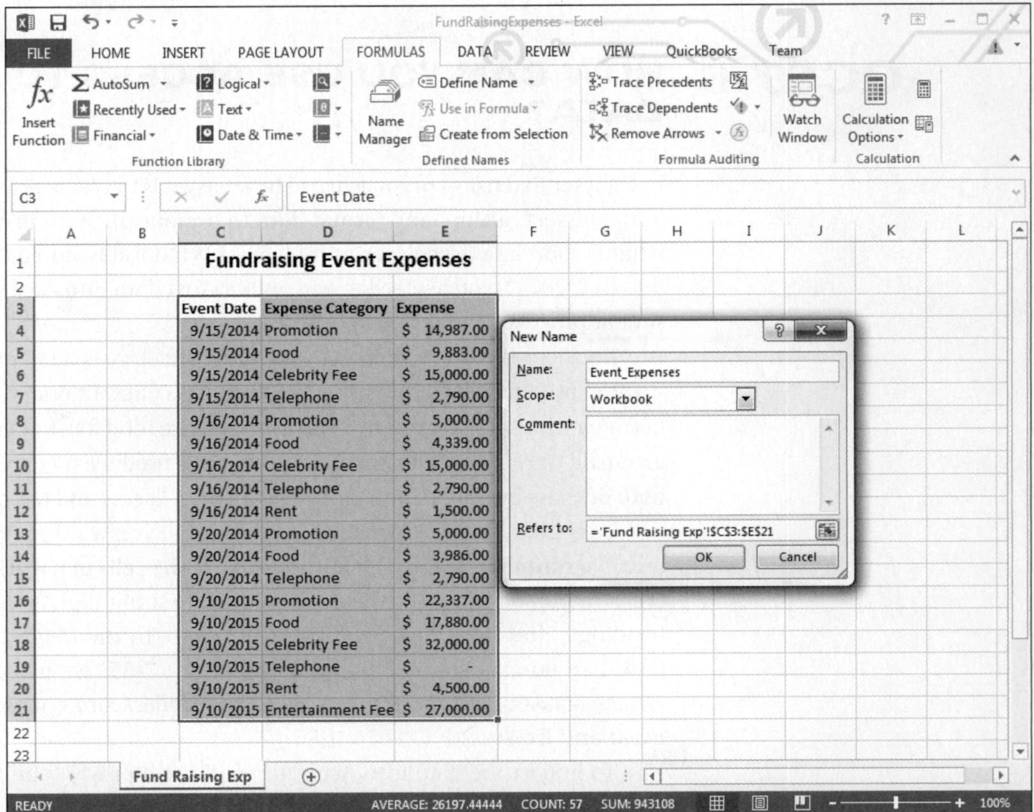


**Figure CE7-27**
Creating a Named Range
*Source:* Microsoft Excel 2013

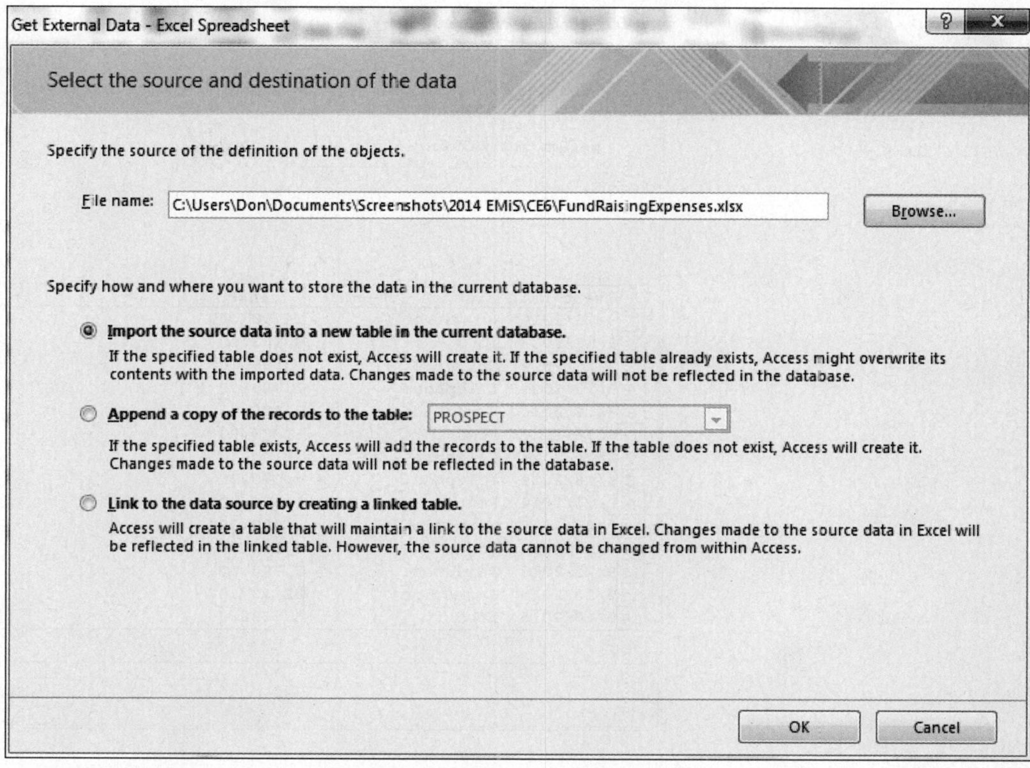


**Figure CE7-28**
Importing an Excel File
*Source:* Microsoft Access 2013

to import the data, click the *EXTERNAL DATA* tab, and, in the *Import* section, click *Excel.* In the screen that appears, select the spreadsheet that has the data and click *Import the source data into a new table in the current database,* as shown in Figure CE7-28. Click *OK* to continue.

In the next form that appears, click *Show Name Ranges* and select the *Event_Expenses* range, as shown in Figure CE7-29a. Click *Next.* Check *First Row Contains Column Names* if it is not already checked. Your screen should look like that in Figure CE7-29b. At this point, Access has

Import Spreadsheet Wizard

Your spreadsheet file contains more than one worksheet or range. Which worksheet or range would you like?

Show Worksheets
Show Named Ranges

Event_Expenses

Sample data for range 'Event_Expenses'.

| 1 | Event Date | Expense Category | Expense |
|---|---|---|---|
| 2 | 9/15/2014 | Promotion | 14,987.00 |
| 3 | 9/15/2014 | Food | 9,883.00 |
| 4 | 9/15/2014 | Celebrity Fee | 15,000.00 |
| 5 | 9/15/2014 | Telephone | 2,790.00 |
| 6 | 9/16/2014 | Promotion | 5,000.00 |
| 7 | 9/16/2014 | Food | 4,339.00 |
| 8 | 9/16/2014 | Celebrity Fee | 15,000.00 |
| 9 | 9/16/2014 | Telephone | 2,790.00 |
| 10 | 9/16/2014 | Rent | 1,500.00 |
| 11 | 9/20/2014 | Promotion | 5,000.00 |
| 12 | 9/20/2014 | Food | 3,986.00 |
| 13 | 9/20/2014 | Telephone | 2,790.00 |
| 14 | 9/10/2015 | Promotion | 22,337.00 |

Cancel | < Back | Next > | Finish

**Figure CE7-29a**
Importing Excel Data into Access: Importing the Data in the Named Range
*Source:* Microsoft Access 2013

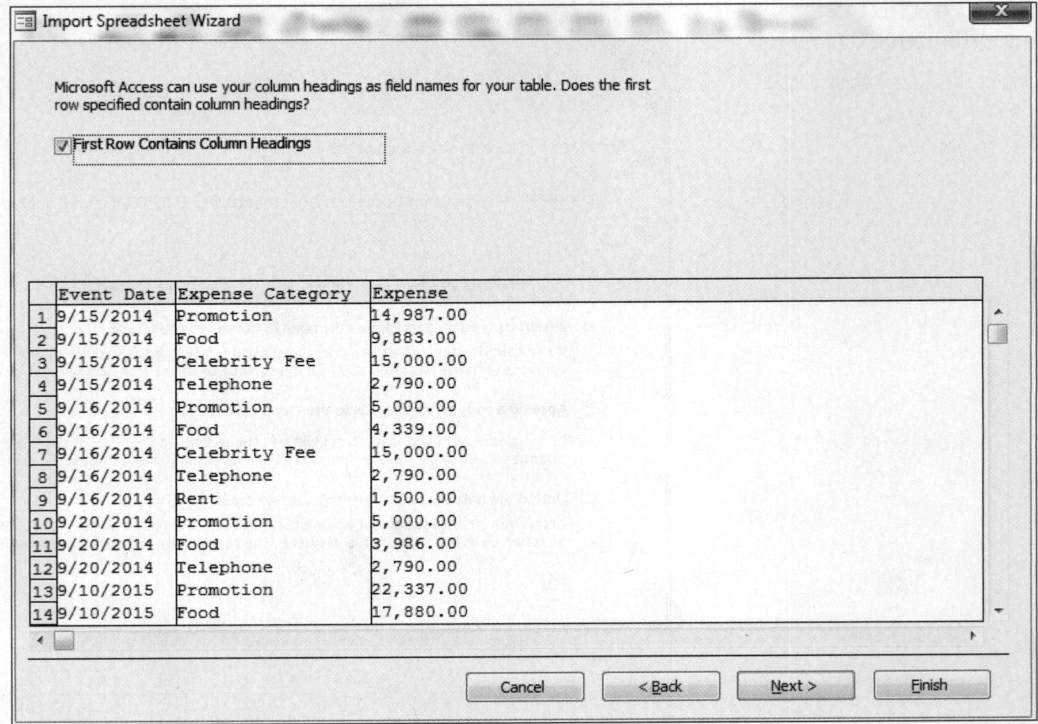


**Figure CE7-29b**
Importing Excel Data into Access: Access Has Metadata to Guide Import

*Source:* Microsoft Access 2013

enough metadata to perform the import correctly, so you can click *Finish.* If you're curious, just click *Next* to see the default import values that Access will use. When asked if you want to save the import steps, ignore the instructions and just click *Close.*

At this point, Access has imported the data and placed it into a table named Event_Expenses. Open that table to ensure that the data has been imported as you would expect. Observe that Access added a surrogate key named ID. We will ignore this field in this example.

With the Event_Expenses table highlighted, click *CREATE*, and, in the *Reports* section of the ribbon, click *Report.* Access creates a report that we will modify to obtain the format we want.

First, in the *View* section, click the down arrow and select *Design View.* Click in an unused part of this screen to deselect all of the columns (those outlined in a heavy yellow/brown line). Once everything has been deselected, click *ID* in the *Page Header* to give it the focus and then press *Delete.* Do the same for ID in the Detail section. The ID column will be removed from the report. (If you don't deselect everything before you press *Delete*, you will delete all of the report's contents. If you do this, just close the report without saving it and start over.)

In the *Grouping & Totals* section of the *Design* ribbon, click *Group & Sort*, if it is not already clicked. Then, at the bottom of the report design window, click *Add a group.* Then click *Expense Category*, as shown in Figure CE7-30. At the bottom of the design window, click *More* and then click *with Expense totaled.* As shown in Figure CE7-31, select *Expense* for *Total On* and click *Show Grand Total* and *Show subtotal in group footer.* At this point your report is finished. In Views, click the report icon and you will see a report like that in Figure CE7-32.

You can perform a similar series of steps to create a report that is grouped by Event Date rather than Expense Category.

# QCE7-7 HOW CAN YOU COMBINE EXCEL AND ACCESS TO ANALYZE DATA?

In QCE7-5, you learned how to use Excel to graph Access data. In this section, you will learn how to use Excel to perform calculations on data imported from Access. We will use the Event_Expenses data imported from Excel in the last section.

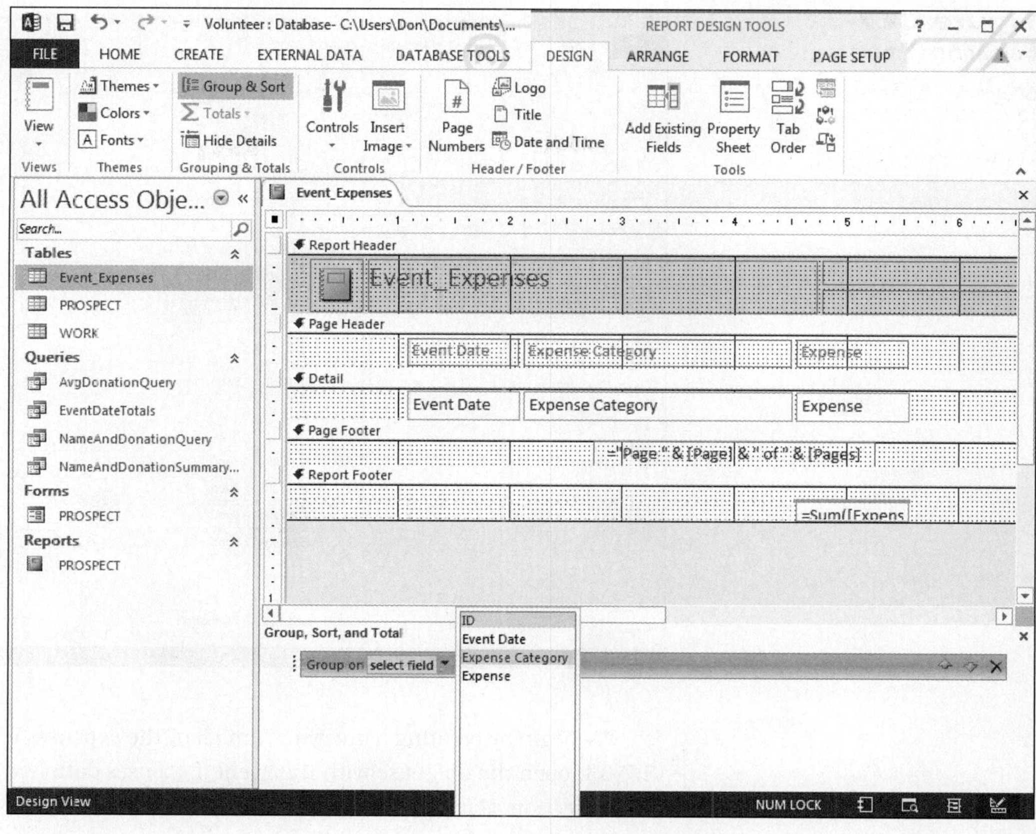

**Figure CE7-30**
Grouping Report Data by Expense Category
*Source:* Microsoft Access 2013

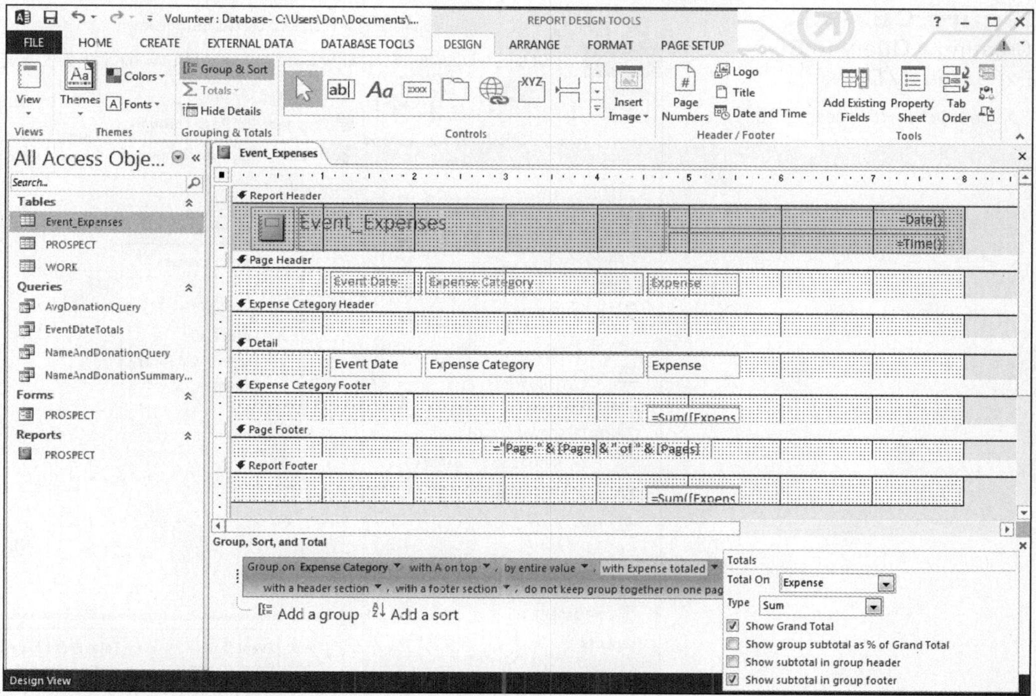

**Figure CE7-31**
Creating Group Totals
*Source:* Microsoft Access 2013

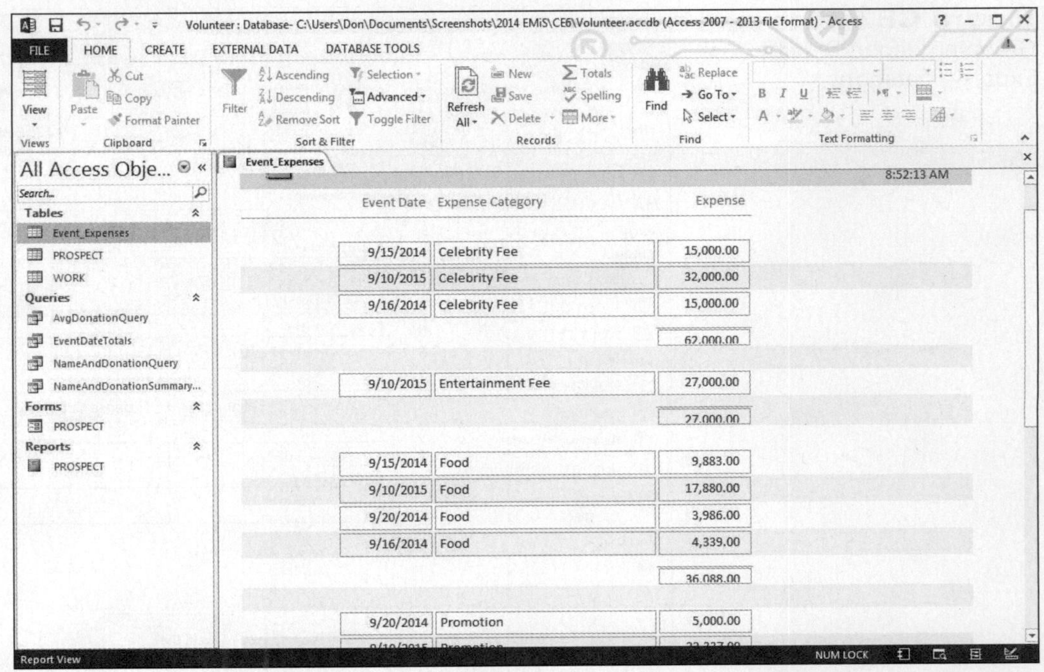


**Figure CE7-32**
Resulting Report

*Source:* Microsoft Access 2013

We begin by creating a query to sum all of the expenses for a given date. As shown in Figure CE7-33, open the database with the Event_Expenses data and click *CREATE/Query Design* in the *Queries* section. Next, click *Event_Expenses* and then *Close*. Now add Event Date and Expense to the query, click *Totals* to create the Total row in the query contents grid, and select *Group By* under *Event Date* and *Sum* under *Expense*. Enter the heading *Total Event Expense* for the Event Expense column as shown in Figure CE7-33. Save this query with the name *EventExpenseTotals.*

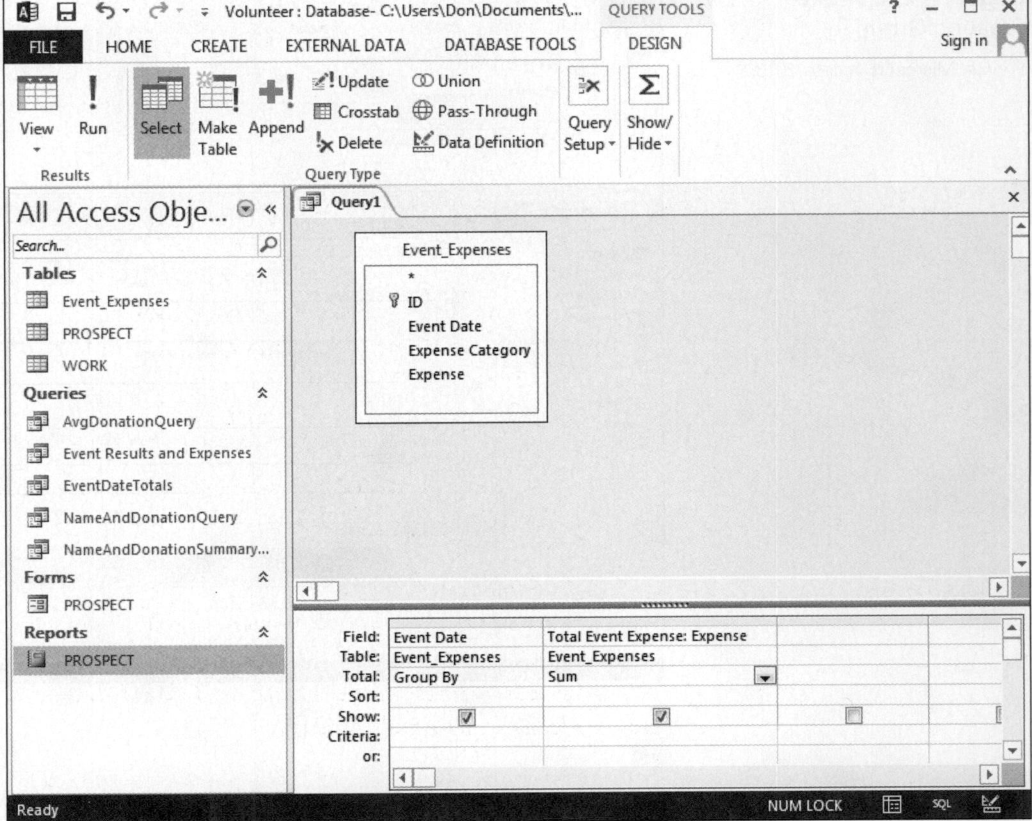


**Figure CE7-33**
Creating a Query to Sum Expenses by Date

*Source:* Microsoft Access 2013

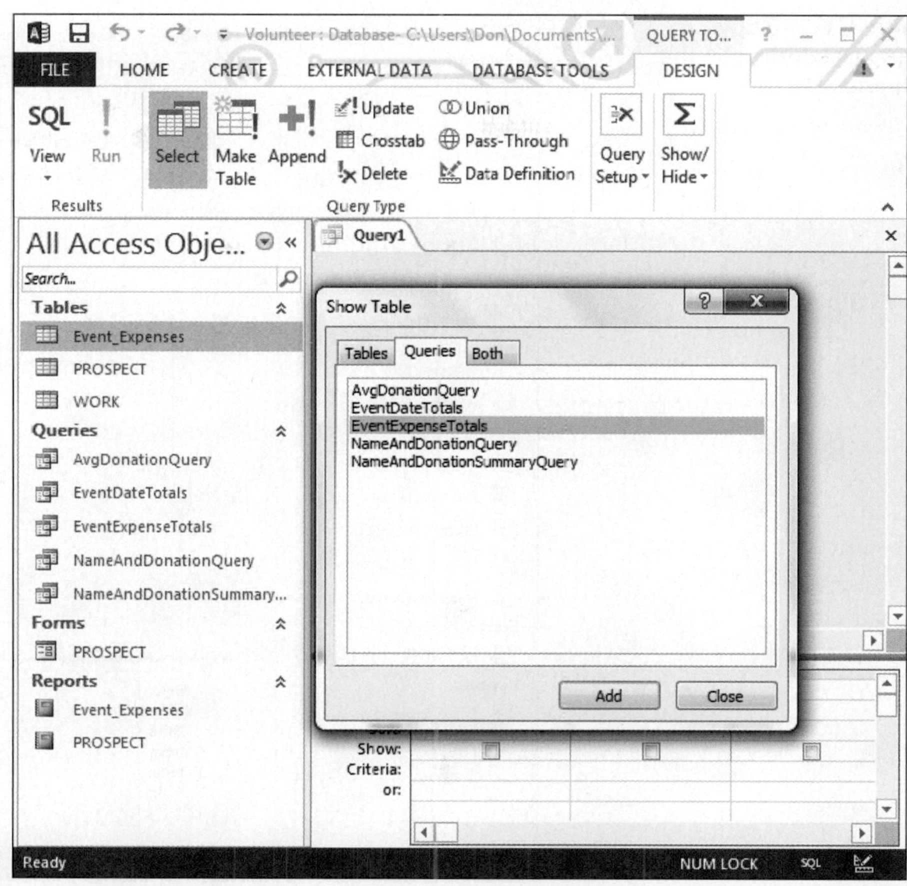


**Figure CE7-34**
Combining the Results of Two Queries

*Source:* Microsoft Access 2013

Now we are going to create a query that combines the results of two other queries. Specifically, we are going to merge EventExpenseTotals (the query we just created) with the EventDateTotals query we created in QCE7-4. To do this, click *CREATE/Query Design*, but this time click the *Queries* tab in the *Show Table* window, as shown in Figure CE7-34. Now add both EventDateTotals and EventExpenseTotals to the query.

We need to inform Access that the date values in the two queries are the same. To do so, drag the WorkDate field in EventDateTotals and drop it on top of Event Date in the EventExpenseTotals query. The result is shown in Figure CE7-35. Now add WorkDate, SumOfTotalDonation, and Total Event Expense to the query, as shown in Figure CE7-36. Run the query, and you will see the result, as shown in Figure CE7-37. Save your query with the name *Event Results and Expenses.*

Now, open a workbook in Excel and import the Event Results and Expenses query. Use the same process used in the discussion of QCE7-5. Click *Data From Access* in the *Get External Data* section of the DATA ribbon. Then select the Access database that has the query, and select *Event Results and Expenses.* In Figure CE7-38, we have placed the upper left-hand corner of the data in cell B2.

Now we can operate on this data just as if we had entered it via the keyboard. We can graph it as described in QCE7-5. Or we can analyze it as shown in Figure CE7-39. Here the user is computing the Net Gain, Net Gain as a Percent of Expense, and Totals for donations and expenses. The focus is on cell F3; notice that this cell contains the formula $=C3-D3$, which computes the difference between two imported numbers.

**Figure CE7-35**
Matching Date Values in the Two Queries

*Source:* Microsoft Access 2013

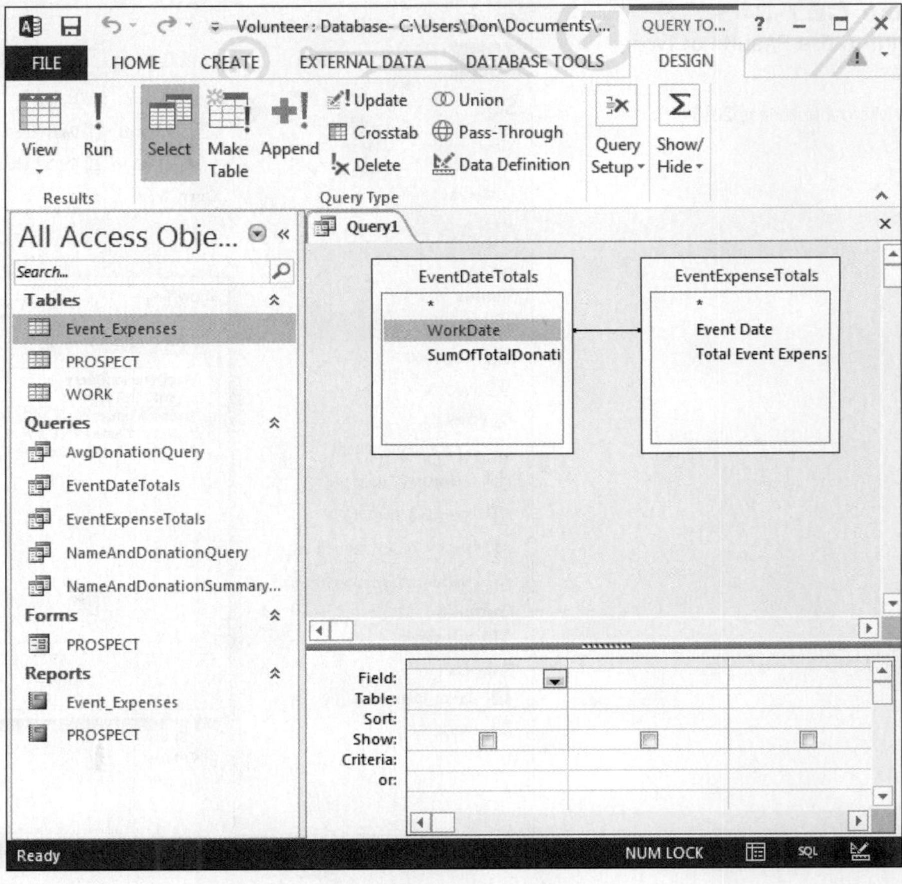

**Figure CE7-36**
Query with Columns Added

*Source:* Microsoft Access 2013

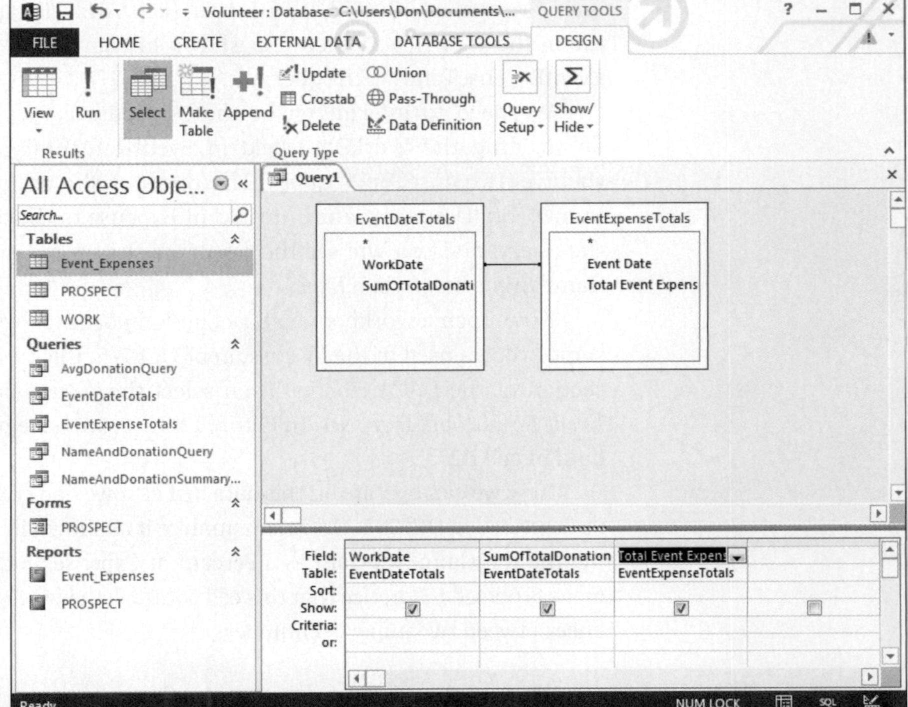

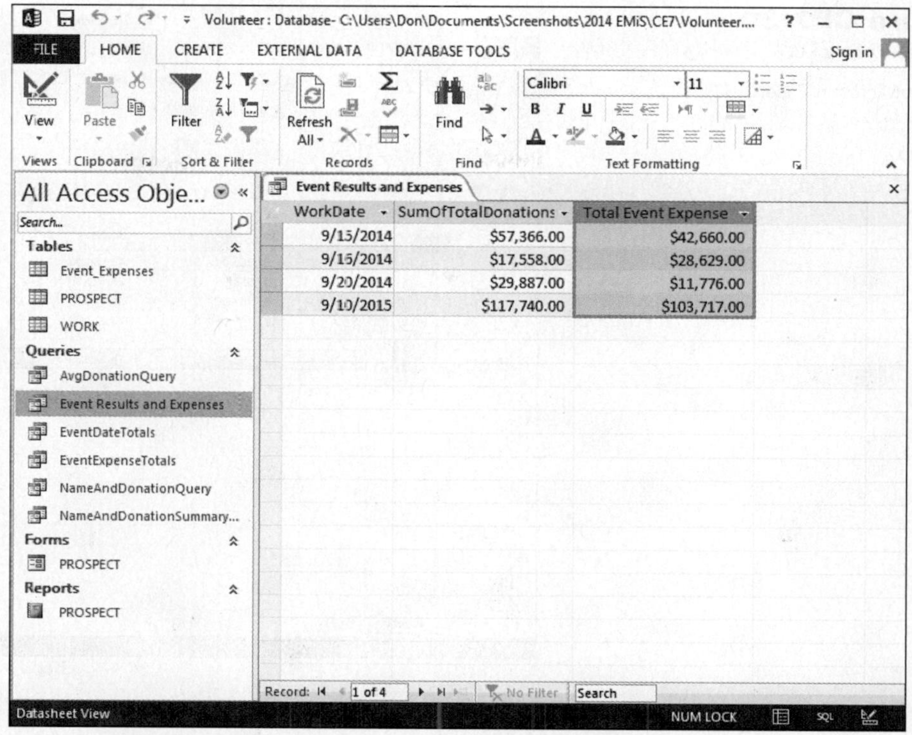

**Figure CE7-37**
Result of Query in Figure CE7-36

*Source:* Microsoft Access 2013

Reflect for a moment on the history of this data. The Total Donation data originated in Access and was summed using an Access query. The expense data began as Excel data in the FundRaising Exp worksheet and was imported into Access, where it was summed. The results of the Total Event Expense query were then imported back to Excel, where they were analyzed as shown in Figure CE7-39!

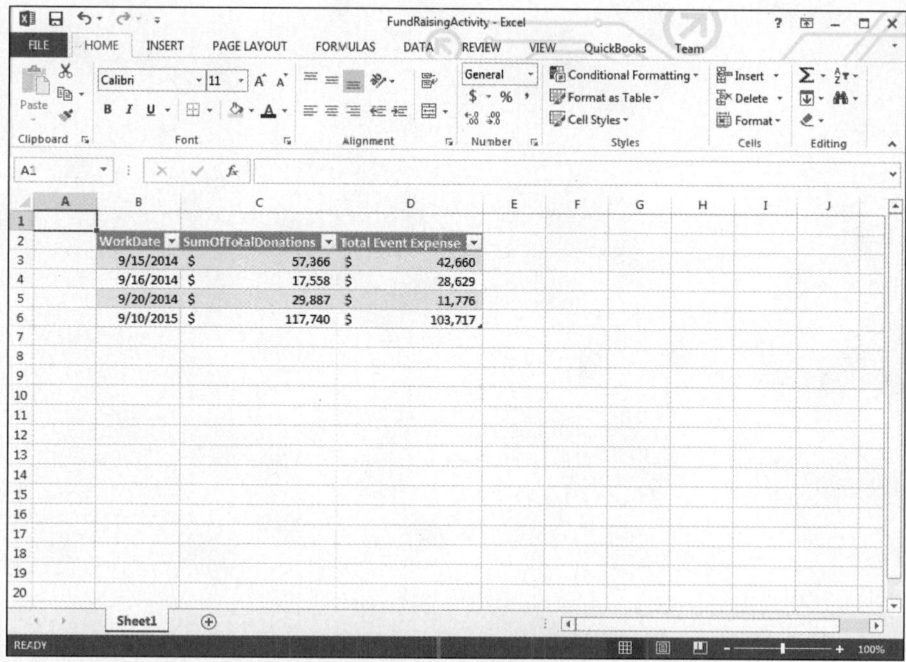

**Figure CE7-38**
Query in Figure CE7-36 Imported to Excel

*Source:* Microsoft Excel 2013

**Figure CE7-39**
Imported to Excel
*Source:* Microsoft Excel 2013

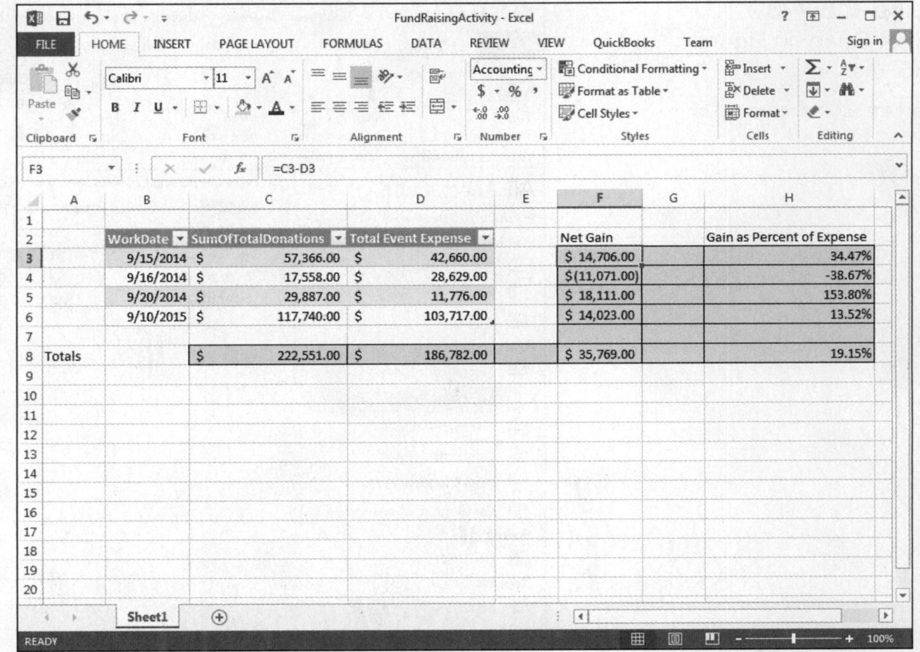

# ACTIVE REVIEW

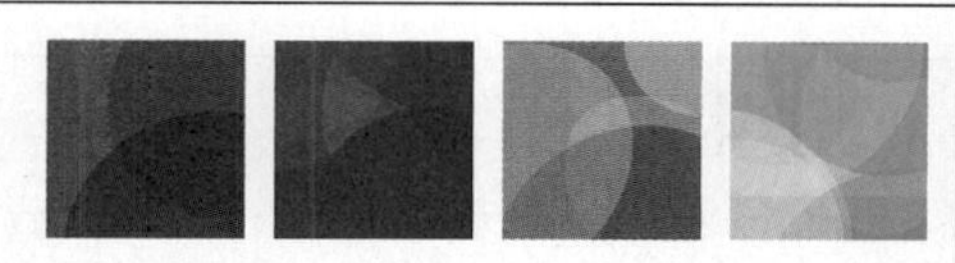

Use this Active Review to verify that you understand the ideas and concepts that answer this chapter extension's study questions.

## QCE7-1 WHY USE EXCEL AND ACCESS TOGETHER?

Describe the chief strengths of both Excel and Access. Summarize the primary purposes of Excel and Access. Give an example of why you might want to process Access data in Excel and another example of why you might want to process Excel data in Access.

## QCE7-2 WHAT IS IMPORT/EXPORT?

Define *import/export.* Explain how data can become out of date when using import/export and describe a solution to this problem. Explain the difference between comma-delimited and tab-delimited data. Go to the text's Web site at *www.pearsonhighered.com/kroenke* and obtain the text file **EMIS CE7 Student Data.txt**. Follow the process described in QCE7-2 to import the data into Access. Explain how you could use a text file to transfer data from Access to Excel. Describe tools that Microsoft provides that make this unnecessary.

## QCE7-3 HOW CAN YOU CREATE CHARTS WITH EXCEL?

Follow the steps explained in QCE7-3 to create the graphics shown in Figures CE7-6 and CE7-9. Enter data manually as described in QCE7-3.

## QCE7-4 HOW CAN YOU CREATE GROUP TOTALS IN ACCESS?

Explain the term *day's total of TotalDonations.* Explain what the *Group By* function does. Go to the text's Web site at *www.pearsonhighered.com/kroenke* and download the Access database file **EMIS Volunteer_CE7**. Follow the instructions in this question to duplicate the query shown in Figures CE7-15, CE7-17, and CE7-19.

## QCE7-5 HOW CAN YOU USE EXCEL TO GRAPH ACCESS DATA?

Follow the instructions in this section to use Excel to graph the results of the query you generated in your review for QCE7-4. Your graph should look like that in Figure CE7-25. Explain how this exercise takes advantage of some of the relative strengths of these two products.

## QCE7-6 HOW CAN YOU USE ACCESS TO REPORT EXCEL DATA?

Explain why you might want to use Access to create reports on Excel data. Go to the text's Web site at *www.pearsonhighered.com/kroenke* and download the Excel file **EMIS CE7 FundRaisingExpenses.xslx**. Follow the instructions in the discussion of this question to create a report like that in Figure CE7-32. Use the same Access database that you used for your review of QCE7-4.

## QCE7-7 HOW CAN YOU COMBINE EXCEL AND ACCESS TO ANALYZE DATA?

Open the database with the Event_Expenses query that you created in your review of QCE7-6. Follow the procedures described in this section to create an Excel worksheet that looks like that shown in Figure CE7-39. Explain how some of this data made a round-trip from Excel to Access and back to Excel. Does this make sense? Why or why not?

# KEY TERMS AND CONCEPTS

Comma-delimited file 470
Import/export 469
Named range 485
Tab-delimited file 470

MyMISLab™

To complete the problems with the ✪, go to EOC Discussion Questions in the MyLab.

## USING YOUR KNOWLEDGE

✪ **CE7-1.** Create a spreadsheet of sample college expenses. Place a grid in your spreadsheet that has three rows—*Rent, Food, Entertainment*—and three columns—*2013, 2014, 2015.* Enter realistic but hypothetical data. Create a pie chart showing the expenses for 2015. Create a column chart for expenses for all 3 years. Create a bar chart for expenses for all 3 years. Do you prefer the column chart or the bar chart? Explain.

✪ **CE7-2.** Create an Access database with a table called *My_Expenses* that has the fields Date, Expense Category, and Amount. Fill the table with 12 rows of hypothetical student expense data. Ensure that you have several expenses for each date and for each expense category. Create a query that shows the total expenses for each date. Create a query that shows the total and average expenses for each category.

✪ **CE7-3.** Export the data that you created in question CE7-2 to an Excel spreadsheet. Create a pie chart of the data for expenses by category. Create a bar chart for expenses by category and date (one bar of each date within a category).

MyMISLab™

Go to the Assignments section of your MyLab to complete these writing exercises.

**CE7-4.** Open the database you created in question CE7-2. Import the data from Excel that you created for question CE7-3 into this database. (Yes, you are reimporting the same data from Excel that you previously exported to Excel. You should have the original copy of the data as well.) Compare the values for the original data to the values of the import/export data. They should be the same. Using the imported data, construct a report similar to that shown in QCE7-7.

**CE7-5.** Using the workbook that you created in your answer to question CE7-3, add a budgeted amount column for each expense category. Enter values for each budgeted amount. Add a column showing the difference between the budgeted amount and the actual amount. Generalize this example. Describe a business scenario in which a financial analyst would obtain data from a database and compare it to data in a spreadsheet.

## ENDNOTE

1. The terminology may be confusing. The value in TotalDonations is the total of all donations received by a particular volunteer in a particular hour on a particular date. Here, the manager wants to know the total of all donations for all volunteers for all hours on a given date.

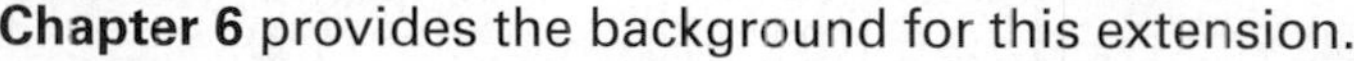

chapter extension **8**

**Chapter 6** provides the background for this extension.

# Network and Cloud Technology

STUDY QUESTIONS

**QCE8-1** WHAT IS A COMPUTER NETWORK?

**QCE8-2** WHAT ARE THE COMPONENTS OF A LAN?

**QCE8-3** HOW DOES THE INTERNET WORK?

**QCE8-4** HOW DOES THE CLOUD WORK?

## QCE8-1 WHAT IS A COMPUTER NETWORK?

Before we can address how the cloud works, we need to discuss computer networks and the technology that underlies them. A computer **network** is a collection of computers that communicate with one another over transmission lines or wirelessly. As shown in Figure CE8-1, the four basic types of networks are personal area networks, local area networks, wide area networks, and internets.

A **personal area network (PAN)** connects devices located around a *single person.* Most PAN devices connect wirelessly to other devices located within 10 meters. A **local area network (LAN)** connects computers that reside in a single geographic location on the premises of the company that operates the LAN. The number of connected computers can range from two to several hundred. The distinguishing characteristic of a LAN is *a single location.* A **wide area network (WAN)** connects computers at different geographic locations. The computers in two separated company sites must be connected using a WAN. To illustrate, a smartwatch or fitness tracker will create a PAN by connecting to a student's smartphone. The computers for a college of business located on a single campus can be connected via a LAN. The computers for a college of business located on multiple campuses must be connected via a WAN.

The single- versus multiple-site distinction between LANs and WANs is important. With a LAN, an organization can place communications lines wherever it wants because all lines reside on its premises. The same is not true for a WAN. A company with offices in Chicago and Atlanta cannot run a wire down the freeway to connect computers in the two cities. Instead, the company contracts with a communications vendor that is licensed by the government and that already has lines or has the authority to run new lines between the two cities.

An **internet** is a network of networks. Internets connect LANs, WANs, and other internets. The most famous internet is "**the Internet**" (with an uppercase letter *I*), the collection of networks that you use when you send email or access a Web site. In addition to the Internet, private networks of networks, called *internets,* also exist. A private internet that is used exclusively within an organization is sometimes called an **intranet**.

The networks that comprise an internet use a large variety of communication methods and conventions, and data must flow seamlessly across them. To provide seamless flow, an elaborate scheme called a *layered protocol* is used. The details of protocols are beyond the scope of this text. Just understand that a **protocol** is a set of rules that programs on two communicating devices follow.

Computers need to use protocols so they can exchange data. People use similar protocols to communicate. People, for example, follow a conversational protocol that says when one person talks, the other person listens. They switch back and forth until they are done communicating. Without a protocol for conversations people would continually talk over each other and nothing would be communicated.

CE8

**Figure CE8-1**
Basic Network Types

| Type | Characteristic |
|---|---|
| Personal Area Network (PAN) | Devices connected around a single person |
| Local area network (LAN) | Computers connected at a single physical site |
| Wide area network (WAN) | Computers connected between two or more separated sites |
| The Internet and internets | Networks of networks |

There are many different protocols; some are used for PANs, some are used for LANs, some are used for WANs, some are used for internets and the Internet, and some are used for all of these. We will identify several common protocols in this chapter extension.

# QCE8-2 WHAT ARE THE COMPONENTS OF A LAN?

As stated, a LAN is a group of computers connected together on a single site. Usually the computers are located within a half-mile or so of each other. The key distinction, however, is that all of the computers are located on property controlled by the organization that operates the LAN. This means that the organization can run cables wherever needed to connect the computers.

Figure CE8-2 shows a LANs typical of those in a **small office or a home office (SOHO)**. Typically, such LANs have fewer than a dozen or so computers and printers. Many businesses, of course, operate LANs much larger than this one. The principles are the same for a larger LAN, but the additional complexity is beyond the scope of this text.

**Figure CE8-2**
Typical Small Office/Home Office

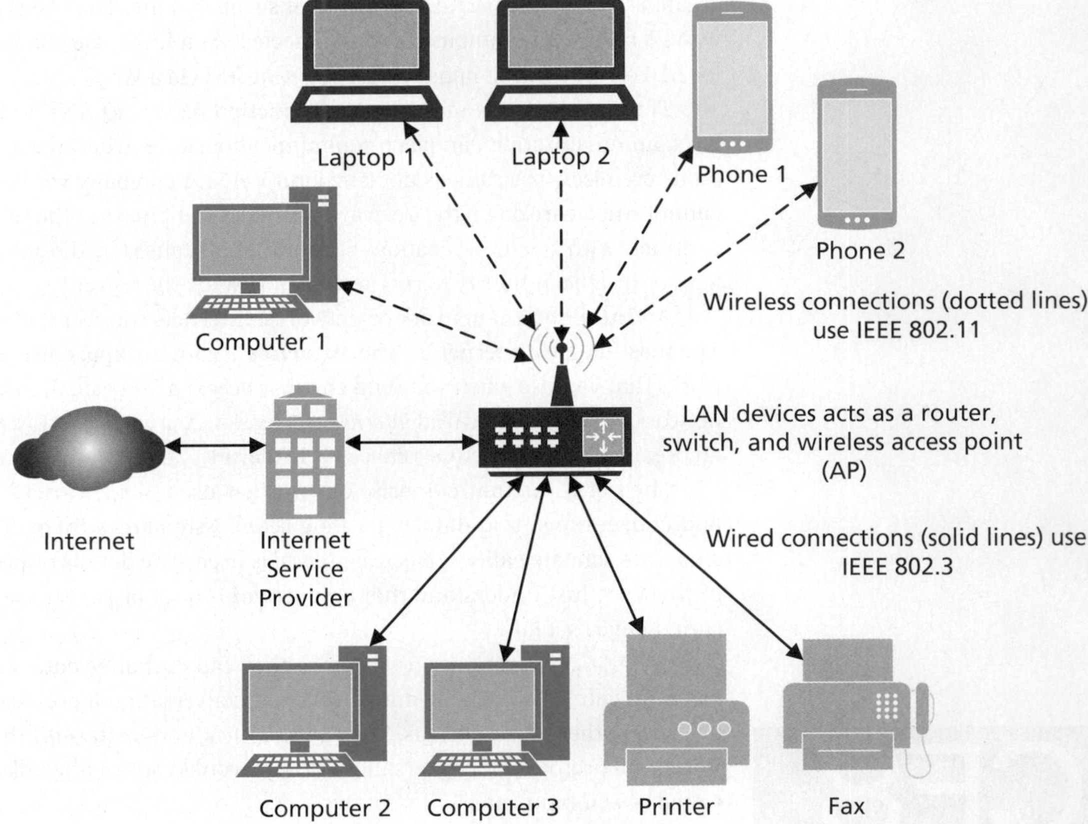

The computers and printers in Figure CE8-2 communicate via a mixture of wired and wireless connections. Some devices use wired connections, and others use wireless connections. The devices and protocols used differ for wired and wireless connectivity.

The Institute for Electrical and Electronics Engineers (IEEE, pronounced "I triple E") sponsors committees that create and publish protocols and other standards. The committee that addresses LAN standards is called the *IEEE 802 Committee*. Thus, IEEE LAN protocols always start with the numbers 802.

The **IEEE 802.3 protocol** is used for wired LAN connections. This protocol standard, also called the **Ethernet**, specifies hardware characteristics, such as which wire carries which signals. It also describes how messages are to be packaged and processed for wired transmission over the LAN.

Most personal computers today support what is called **10/100/1000 Ethernet**. These products conform to the 802.3 specification and allow for transmission at a rate of 10, 100, or 1,000 Mbps (megabits per second). Switches detect the speed that a given device can handle and communicate with it at that speed. If you check computer listings at Dell, Lenovo, and other manufacturers, you will see PCs advertised as having 10/100/1000 Ethernet. Today, speeds of up to 1 Gbps are possible on wired LANs.

By the way, the abbreviations used for communications speeds differ from those used for computer memory. For communications equipment, *K* stands for 1,000, not 1,024 as it does for memory. Similarly, *M* stands for 1,000,000, not 1,024 × 1,024; *G* stands for 1,000,000,000, not 1,024 × 1,024 × 1,024. Thus, 100 Mbps is 100,000,000 bits per second.

Also, communications speeds are expressed in *bits*, whereas memory sizes are expressed in *bytes*. These are different units of measurement. One byte consists of eight bits. This means a 1 MB file would consist of 8,388,608 bits. If you sent a 1 MB file over a 1 Mbps connection, it would take more than 8 seconds to send because your connection speed is measured in bits per second, not bytes per second.

Wireless LAN connections use the **IEEE 802.11 protocol**. Several versions of 802.11 exist, and as of 2015, the most current one is IEEE 802.11ac. The differences among these versions are beyond the scope of this discussion. Just note that the current standard, 802.11ac, allows speeds of up to 1.3Gps.

**Bluetooth** is another common wireless protocol used to make PAN connections. It is designed for transmitting data over short distances, replacing cables. Devices, such as wireless mice, keyboards, printers, and headphones, use Bluetooth to connect to desktop computers. Other devices like smartwatches and fitness trackers can use Bluetooth to connect to smartphones and send data over the Internet. More and more devices like clothing, automobiles, and sports equipment are becoming Bluetooth enabled.

## CONNECTING YOUR LAN TO THE INTERNET

Although you may not have realized it, when you connect your SOHO LAN, phone, iPad, or Kindle to the Internet, you are connecting to a WAN. You must do so because you are connecting to computers that are not physically located on your premises. You cannot start running wires down the street to plug in somewhere.

When you connect to the Internet, you are actually connecting to an **Internet service provider (ISP)**. An ISP has three important functions. First, it provides you with a legitimate Internet address. Second, it serves as your gateway to the Internet. The ISP receives the communications from your computer and passes them on to the Internet, and it receives communications from the Internet and passes them on to you. Finally, ISPs pay for the Internet. They collect money from their customers and pay access fees and other charges on your behalf.

Figure CE8-3 shows the three common alternatives for connecting to the Internet. Notice that we are discussing how your computer connects to the Internet via a WAN; we are not discussing the structure of the WAN itself. WAN architectures and their protocols are beyond the scope of this text. Search the Web for *leased lines* or *PSDN* if you want to learn more about WAN architectures.

| Type | Topology | Transmission Line | Transmission Speed | Equipment Used | Protocol Commonly Used | Remarks |
|---|---|---|---|---|---|---|
| Local area network | Local area network | UTP or optical fiber | Common: 10/100/1000 Mbps Possible: 1 Gbps | Switch NIC UTP or optical | IEEE 802.3 (Ethernet) | Switches connect devices, multiple switches on all but small LANs. |
| | Local area network with wireless | UTP or optical for non-wireless connections | Up to 600 Mbps | Wireless access point Wireless NIC | IEEE 802.11n (802.11ac not yet common) | Access point transforms wired LAN (802.3) to wireless LAN (802.11). |
| Connections to the Internet | DSL modem to ISP | DSL telephone | Personal: Upstream to 1 Mbps, downstream to 40 Mbps (max 10 likely in most areas) | DSL modem DSL-capable telephone line | DSL | Can have computer and phone use simultaneously. Always connected. |
| | Cable modem to ISP | Cable TV lines to optical cable | Upstream to 1 Mbps Downstream 300 Kbps to 10 Mbps | Cable modem Cable TV cable | Cable | Capacity is shared with other sites; performance varies depending on other's use. |
| | WAN wireless | Wireless connection to WAN | 500 Kbps to 1.7 Mbps | Wireless WAN modem | One of several wireless standards | Sophisticated protocol enables several devices to use the same wireless frequency. |

**Figure CE8-3**
Office (SOHO) LAN

SOHO LANs (such as that in Figure CE8-2) and individual home and office computers are commonly connected to an ISP in one of three ways: a special telephone line called a DSL line, a cable TV line, or a wireless-phone-like connection.

## Digital Subscriber Line (DSL)

A **digital subscriber line (DSL)** operates on the same lines as voice telephones, but it operates so it does not interfere with voice telephone service. Because DSL signals do not interfere with telephone signals, DSL data transmission and telephone conversations can occur simultaneously. A device at the telephone company separates the phone signals from the computer signals and sends the latter signal to the ISP. Digital subscriber lines use their own protocols for data transmission.

## Cable Line

A cable line is the second type of WAN connection. **Cable lines** provide high-speed data transmission using cable television lines. The cable company installs a fast, high-capacity optical fiber cable to a distribution center in each neighborhood it serves. At the distribution center, the optical fiber cable connects to regular cable-television cables that run to subscribers' homes or businesses. Cable signals do not interfere with TV signals.

Because up to 500 user sites can share these facilities, performance varies depending on how many other users are sending and receiving data. At the maximum, users can download data up to 50 Mbps and can upload data at 512 Kbps. Typically, performance is much lower than this. In most cases, the download speed of cable lines and DSL lines is about the same. Cable lines use their own protocols.

## WAN Wireless Connection

A third way you can connect your computer, mobile device, or other communicating device is via a **WAN wireless** connection. Amazon.com's Kindle, for example, uses a Sprint wireless network to provide wireless data connections. The iPhone uses a LAN-based wireless network if one is available and a WAN wireless network if not. The LAN-based network is preferred because performance is considerably higher. As of 2015, WAN wireless provides average performance of 1 Mbps, with peaks of up to 3.0 Mbps, as opposed to the typical 50 Mbps for LAN wireless.

# QCE8-3 HOW DOES THE INTERNET WORK?

The technology that underlies the Internet and the additional technology that enables the cloud to work are complicated. Here we will stay at a high level and help you learn overarching concepts and basic definitions. We begin with a simple example.

## AN INTERNET EXAMPLE

Figure CE8-4 illustrates one use of the Internet. Suppose you are sitting in snowbound Minneapolis, and you want to communicate with a hotel in sunny, tropical northern New Zealand. Maybe you are making a reservation using the hotel's Web site, or maybe you are sending an email to a reservations clerk inquiring about facilities or services.

To begin, note that this example is an internet because it is a network of networks. It consists of two LANs (yours and the hotel's) and four networks. (In truth, the real Internet consists of tens of thousands of networks, but to conserve paper we don't show all of them.) A **hop** is the movement from one network to another. As shown, in Figure CE8-4, the shortest path from you to the hotel's LAN consists of four hops. By the way, this term is frequently used by CDN vendors when they discuss provisioning servers to minimize the number of hops.

## CARRIERS AND NET NEUTRALITY

As your message, or **packet**, moves across the Internet, it passes through networks owned by large telecommunication providers known as **carriers**. Some of these large carriers include Sprint, AT&T, Verizon Business, and XO Communications. These large carriers exchange traffic freely via **peering** agreements without charging each other access fees. Carriers make revenue by collecting subscription fees from end users, but not peers.

The problem with peering is that some people use more bandwidth than others. Netflix, for example, accounts for about 33 percent of all Internet traffic in North America between 9:00 PM and 12:00 AM. Carriers argue that they should be able to charge varying rates based on content, application, or the user requesting the data.[1]

Netflix, eBay, Yahoo!, and Amazon.com say this could hurt consumers and innovation. They believe in the **net neutrality** principle where all data is treated equally. They argue that carriers should not be allowed to decide which sites load quickly, which apps are allowed on a network, and which content is acceptable.

In 2015, the Federal Communications Commission (FCC) approved new net neutrality regulations ensuring ISPs cannot discriminate between different types of Internet traffic. This means

**Figure CE8-4**
Using the Internet for a Hotel Reservation

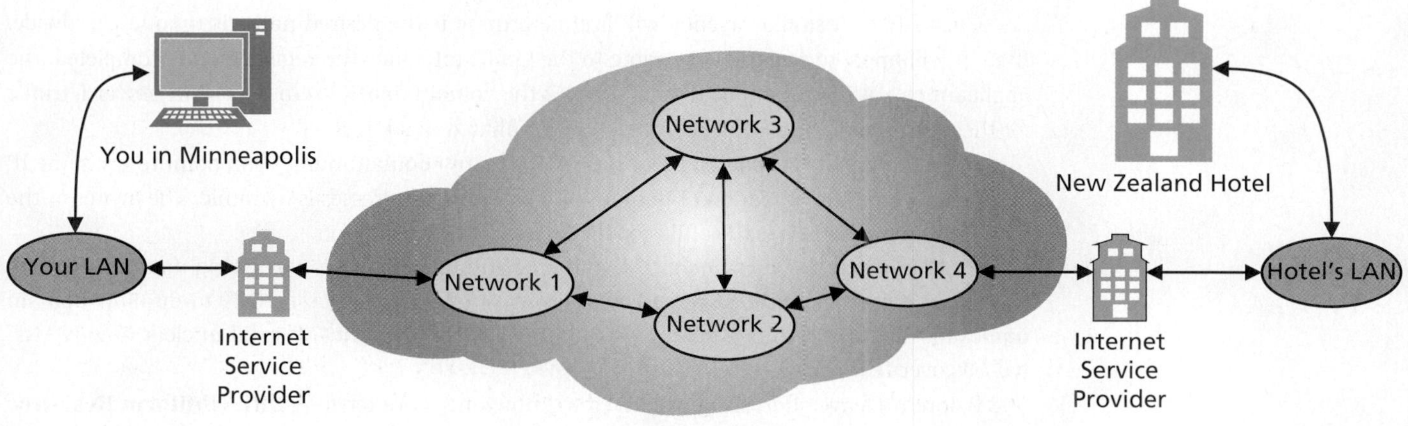

all consumers would have access to content on an equal basis. This ruling in many ways renders the Internet a utility like water or electricity that would be governed by comparable regulations. Several large carriers have already begun fighting these new regulations in court.

# INTERNET ADDRESSING

Just like regular surface mail, every location on the Internet needs an address. For reasons beyond this discussion, an Internet address is called an **IP address**, which is a number that identifies a particular device. **Public IP addresses** identify a particular device on the public Internet. In order to get on the Internet every device must have access to a public IP address. Because public IP addresses must be unique worldwide, their assignment is controlled by a public agency known as **ICANN (Internet Corporation for Assigned Names and Numbers)**.

**Private IP addresses** identify a particular device on a private network, usually on a LAN. Their assignment is controlled within the LAN, usually by the LAN device shown in Figure CE8-2. When you sign on to a LAN at a coffee shop, for example, the LAN device loans you a private IP address to use while you are connected to the LAN. When you leave the LAN, it reuses that address.

## Use of Private IP Addresses

When your computer accesses a public site, say, *www.pearsonhighered.com*, from within a LAN at a coffee shop, your traffic uses your private IP address until it gets to the LAN device. At that point, the LAN device substitutes your private IP address with its public IP address and sends your traffic out onto the public Internet.

This private/public IP address scheme has two major benefits. First, public IP addresses are conserved. All of the computers on the LAN use only one public IP address. Second, by using private IP addresses, you are protected from attackers directly attacking you because they cannot send attack packets to private IP addresses. They can only send packets to devices with public IP addresses.

## Public IP Addresses and Domain Names

IP addresses have two formats. The most common form, called **IPv4**, has a four-decimal dotted notation such as 165.193.123.253; the second, called **IPv6**, has a longer format and will not concern us here. In your browser, if you enter *http://165.193.140.14*, your browser will connect with the device on the public Internet that has been assigned to this address.

Nobody wants to type IP addresses such as *http://165.193.140.14* to find a particular site. Instead, we want to enter names such as *www.pandora.com* or *www.woot.com* or *www.pearsonhighered.com*. To facilitate that desire, ICANN administers a system for assigning names to IP addresses. First, a **domain name** is a worldwide-unique name that is affiliated with a public IP address. When an organization or individual wants to register a domain name, it goes to a company that applies to an ICANN-approved agency to do so. GoDaddy (*www.godaddy.com*) is an example of such a company (Figure CE8-5).

GoDaddy or a similar agency will first determine if the desired name is unique worldwide. If so, it will apply to register that name to the applicant. Once the registration is completed, the applicant can affiliate a public IP address with the domain name. From that point onward, traffic for the new domain name will be routed to the affiliated IP address.

Note two important points: First, several (or many) domain names can point to the same IP address. Second, the affiliation of domain names with IP addresses is dynamic. The owner of the domain name can change the affiliated IP addresses at its discretion.

In 2014, the U.S. Department of Commerce announced that it was giving up oversight over ICANN. Critics worry that less-free countries will now try to force ICANN to disallow domain names for dissident groups, thereby kicking them off the Internet. It's still unclear how ICANN will be governed.

Before we leave addressing, you need to know one more term. A **URL (Uniform Resource Locator)** is an address on the Internet. Commonly, it consists of a protocol (such as http:// or ftp://) followed by a domain name or public IP address. A URL is actually quite a bit more

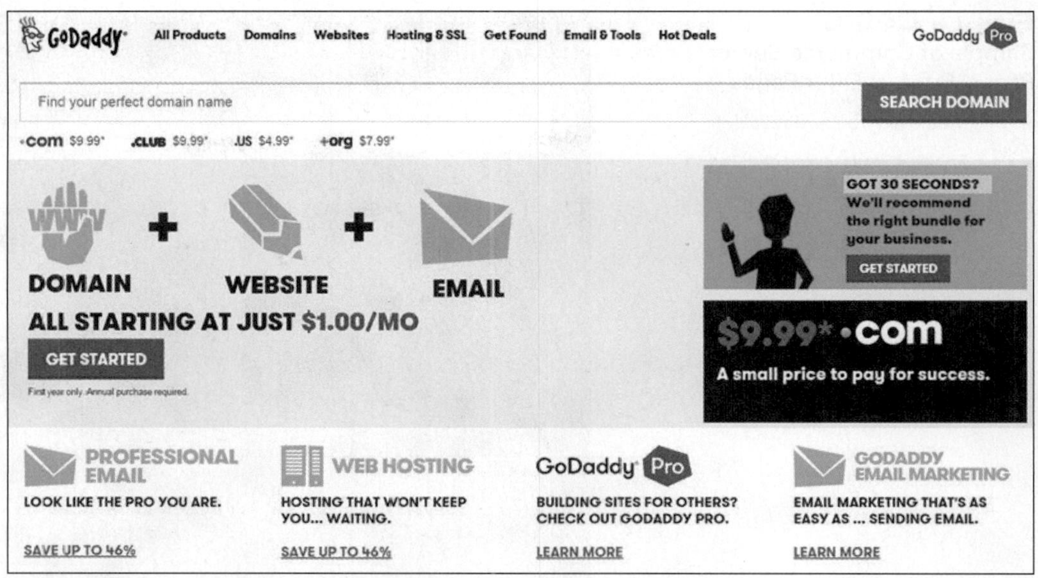


**Figure CE8-5**
GoDaddy Screenshot

*Source:* © 2015 GoDaddy Operating Company, LLC. All rights reserved.

complicated than this description, but that detailed knowledge is beyond the scope of this text, so we'll hurry along. The preferred pronunciation of URL is to say the letters *U, R, L.*

## PROCESSING ON A WEB SERVER

At this point, you know basic networking terms and have a high-level view of how the Internet works. To understand the value of the cloud, how it works, and how your organization can use it, you need to know a bit about the processing that occurs on a Web server. For this discussion, we will use the example of a Web storefront, which is a server on the Web from which you can buy products.

Suppose you want to buy an item from zulily, a private buyer's site that sells clothing. To do so, you go to *www.zulily.com* and navigate to the product(s) you want to buy (see Figure CE8-6). When you find something you want, you add it to your shopping cart and keep shopping. At some point, you check out by supplying credit card data. But what happens when your order data arrives at the server?

### Three-Tier Architecture

Almost all web applications use the **three-tier architecture**, which is a design of user computers and servers that consists of three categories, or tiers, as shown in Figure CE8-7. The **user tier** consists of computers, phones, and other mobile devices that have browsers that request and process Web pages. The **server tier** consists of computers that run Web servers and process application programs. The **database tier** consists of computers that run a DBMS that processes requests to retrieve and store data. Figure CE8-7 shows only one computer at the database tier. Some sites have multicomputer database tiers as well.

When you enter *www.zulily.com* in your browser, the browser sends a request that travels over the Internet to a computer in the server tier at the zulily site. In response to your request, a server-tier computer sends back a **Web page**, which is a document coded in, usually, html (and, as discussed in Chapter 4, probably includes css, JavaScript, and other data).

**Web servers** are programs that run on a server-tier computer and manage traffic by sending and receiving Web pages to and from clients. A **commerce server** is an application program that runs on a server-tier computer. Typical commerce server functions are to obtain product data from a database, manage the items in a shopping cart, and coordinate the checkout process. When a request comes to the server, the Web server examines it and sends it to the proper program for processing. Thus, the Web server passes e-commerce traffic to the commerce server.

**Figure CE8-6**
Sample of Commerce Server Pages; Product Offer Pages

*Source:* Retrieved from *www.zulily .com.*

It passes requests for other applications to those applications. In Figure CE8-7, the server-tier computers are running a Web server program, a commerce server application, and other applications having an unspecified purpose.

## QCE8-4 HOW DOES THE CLOUD WORK?

In Chapter 6, Mateo and Joni are flabbergasted at the low cost of the cloud. They doubt that it's real. They would be less cautious if they understood how the cloud operates. This section will give you the basic understanding that they lack and enable you to be an effective consumer of cloud services.

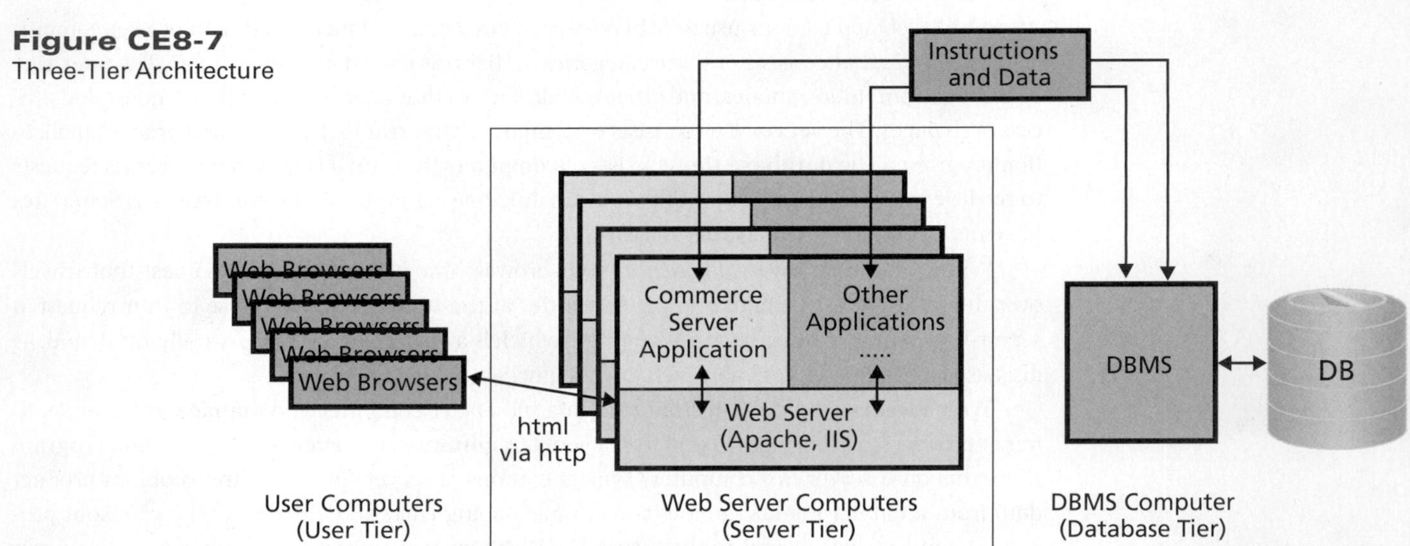


**Figure CE8-7**
Three-Tier Architecture

# SERVICE-ORIENTED ARCHITECTURE (SOA)

As stated in Chapter 6, the cloud would be impossible without a design philosophy called the **service-oriented architecture (SOA)**. According to this philosophy, all interactions among computing devices are defined as services in a formal, standardized way. This philosophy enables all the pieces of the cloud to fit together, as you will see. However, understanding SOA (pronounced "SO-ah") in depth requires you to learn more computer science than you need as a business professional. So, the best way for you to understand SOA is via a business analogy.

## A SOA Analogy

Figure CE8-8 shows an arrangement of departments at a hypothetical online bicycle part retailer named Best Bikes. The Sales Department receives orders and follows a process to have them approved for shipping. On request, the Credit Department verifies customer credit as needed to approve orders, and the Inventory Department verifies the availability of the inventory needed to fulfill an order.

In an informal, non-SOA-type organization, one salesperson would contact someone he or she knows in Credit and ask something like "Can you approve an allocation of $10,000 of credit to the ABC Bicycle Company?" In response, the credit person might say, "Sure," and the salesperson might note the name of the person who approved the amount. Some days, he or she might remember to record the date; other days, not so. Another salesperson might do something else, say, contact a different person whom he or she knows in Credit and ask something like, "I need $5,000 in credit for Order 12345," and that other person in Credit might say, "I don't know, send the order over, and if I can, I'll write 'Approved' on it." Other irregular but similar interactions could occur between the Sales and the Inventory departments.

Such operations are definitely *not* service-oriented. People are asking for credit verification in different ways and receiving responses in different ways. The process for approving an order varies from salesperson to salesperson and possibly from day to day with the same salesperson. The records of approvals are inconsistent. Such an organization will have varying levels of process quality and inconsistent results, and should the company decide to open a facility in another city, these operations cannot be readily duplicated, nor should they be.

Using SOA principles, each department would formally define the services it provides. Examples are:

For the Credit Department:

- CheckCustomerCredit
- ApproveCustomerCredit

**Figure CE8-8**
Approval Request Interactions Among Three Departments

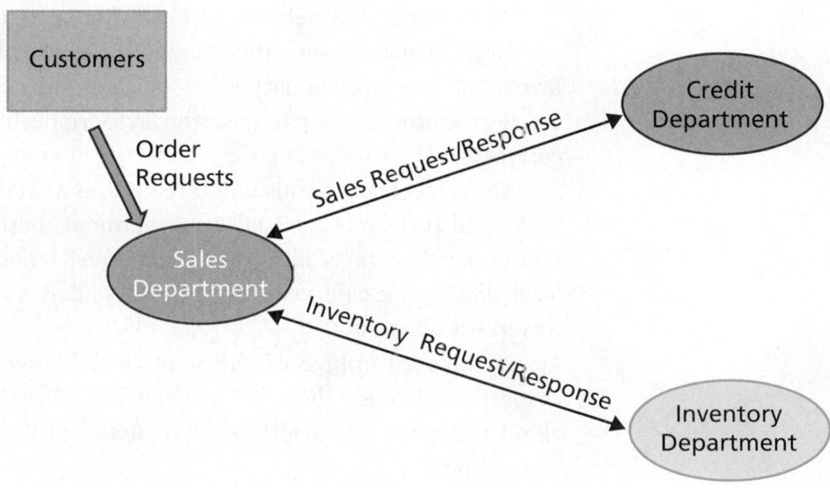

For the Inventory Department:

- VerifyInventoryAmount
- AllocateInventory
- ReleaseAllocatedInventory

Further, for each service, each department would formally state the data it expects to receive with the request and the data it promises to return in response. Every interaction is done exactly the same way. There is no personal contact between certain people in the departments; no salesperson need know who works in Credit or Inventory. Instead, requests are emailed to a generic email address in Credit or Inventory, and those departments decide who will process the request and how it will be processed. No department has or need have any knowledge of who works in another department, nor how the department accomplishes its work. Each department is free to change personnel task assignments and to change the way it performs its services, and no other department needs to know that a change occurred. In SOA terms, we would say the work of the department is **encapsulated** in the department.

With this organization, if Best Bikes wants to add another Inventory Department in another city, it can do so and no salesperson need change the way he or she sets up, submits, or receives responses to requests. Sales continues to send a VerifyInventoryAmount service request, formatted in the standard way, to the same email address.

With multiple sites, the Inventory function would change the way it implements service requests to first identify which of the several Inventory Departments should process the request. Sales would not know, nor need to know, this happened. Best Bikes could dynamically create 1,000 Inventory Departments and the Sales Department need not change anything it does. Later, it could reduce those 1,000 Inventory Departments to three and, again, Sales need not make any change.

## SOA for Three-Tier Architecture

From this discussion, you can see how SOA is used to enable cloud processing. The description and advantages and disadvantages of this analogy for SOA are the same for the cloud. Consider Figure CE8-9, which shows the three-tier architecture with SOA drawn in. In this case, the commerce server application formally defines services that browsers can request, the data they must provide with the request, and the data that each will receive in response to the request. Sample services are:

- ObtainPartData
- ObtainPartImages
- ObtainPartQuantityOnHand
- OrderPart

And so forth. Again each service also documents the data it expects and the data it will return.

Now, JavaScript (or other language) is written to invoke these services correctly. That JavaScript is included as part of the Web pages the server sends to the browsers, and when users employ the browsers to purchase, the JavaScript behind the Web page invokes the services in the correct way.

The server tier can consist of three servers at 3 AM, 3,000 servers at 11 AM, 6,000 servers at 6 PM, and 100 servers at 10 PM. Furthermore, those servers can move around the world; at one time of day they can be all located in the United States, and at another time of day, they can all be located in Europe, and so on. Nothing, absolutely nothing, in the browsers need change as these servers are adjusted.

To take advantage of the multiple Web servers, a load balancing program receives requests and sends them to an available server. The load balancing program keeps data about the speed and health of all its assigned Web servers and allocates work to maximize throughput.

**Figure CE8-9**
SOA Principles Applied to Three-Tier Architecture

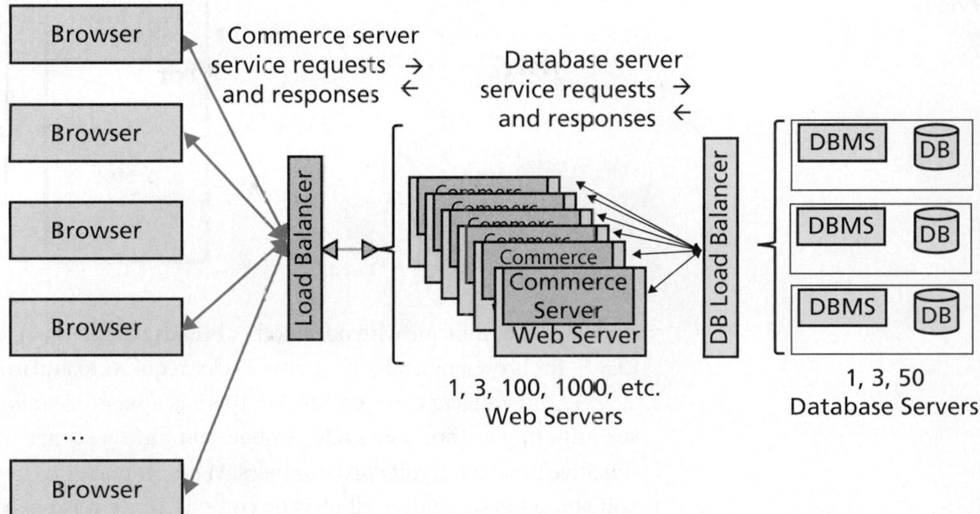


In addition, on the back end, SOA services are defined between the Web server and the database server. Accordingly, the database server need do nothing as the number and location of Web servers is adjusted. And that's a two-way street. Nothing in the Web servers need be changed if the number and location of database servers is adjusted. However, load balancing for database servers is considerably more complicated.

Do not infer from this discussion that SOA services and the cloud are only used for three-tier processing. Such services and the cloud are used for multitudes of applications across the Web. This three-tier application is just an example.

From this discussion, you can understand how cloud elasticity is possible. However, for many organizations to use the cloud and to be able to mix and match Web services, they need to agree on standard ways of formatting and processing service requests and data. That leads us to cloud standards and protocols. Again, we discuss these at a very high level.

## PROTOCOLS SUPPORTING WEB SERVICES

A protocol is a set of rules and data structures for organizing communication. Because the cloud's Web services use the Internet, the protocols that run the Internet also support cloud processing. We will start with them.

### TCP/IP Protocol Architecture

The basic plumbing of the Internet is governed by protocols that are defined according to an arrangement called the **TCP/IP Protocol architecture**. This architecture has five layers; one or more protocols are defined at each layer. Data communications and software vendors write computer programs that implement the rules of a particular protocol. (For protocols at the bottom layer, the physical layer, they build hardware devices that implement the protocol.)

### Internet Protocols: http, https, smtp, and ftp

The only Internet protocols that that you as a business professional are likely to encounter are those at the top, or application, layer of the TCP/IP architecture, shown in Figure CE8-10. **Hypertext Transport Protocol (http)** is the protocol used between browsers and Web servers. When you use a browser such as Microsoft Edge, Safari, or Chrome, you are using a program that implements the http protocol. At the other end, at the New Zealand hotel mentioned earlier, for example, there is a server that also processes http. Even though your browser and the server at the hotel have never "met" before,

**Figure CE8-10**
Protocols That Support Web Services

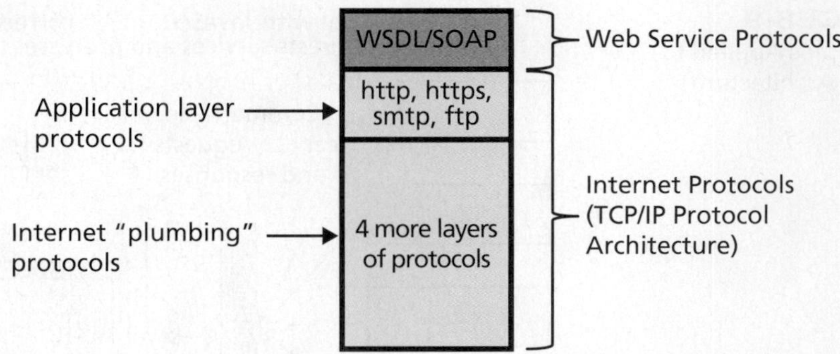


they can communicate with one another because they both follow the rules of http. Similarly, in Figure CE8-9, the browsers send and receive service requests to and from the commerce server using http.

As you will learn in Chapter 10, there is a secure version of http called **https**. Whenever you see *https* in your browser's address bar, you have a secure transmission, and you can safely send sensitive data like credit card numbers. When you are on the Internet, if you do not see *https*, then you should assume that all of your communication is open and could be published on the front page of your campus newspaper tomorrow morning. Hence, when you are using http, email, text messaging, chat, videoconferencing, or anything other than https, know that whatever you are typing or saying could be known by anyone else.

Two additional TCP/IP application-layer protocols are common. **Simple Mail Transfer Protocol, or smtp**, is used for email transmissions (along with other protocols). **File Transfer Protocol, or ftp**, is used to move files over the Internet. Google Drive and Microsoft OneDrive use ftp behind the scenes to transmit files to and from their cloud servers to your computer.

## WSDL, SOAP, XML, and JSON

To wrap up the discussion, we will briefly consider four standards used extensively for Web services and the cloud. Those standards and their purpose are as follows:

| | |
|---|---|
| **WSDL (Web Services Description Language)** | A standard for describing the services, inputs, outputs, and other data supported by a Web service. Documents coded according to this standard are machine readable and can be used by developer tools for creating programs to access the service. |
| **SOAP (no longer an acronym)** | A protocol for requesting Web services and for sending responses to Web service requests. |
| **XML (eXtensible Markup Language)** | A markup language used for transmitting documents. Contains much metadata that can be used to validate the format and completeness of the document, but includes considerable overhead (see Figure CE8-11a). |
| **JSON (JavaScript Object Notation)** | A markup language (such as html) used for transmitting documents. Contains little metadata and is preferred for transmitting volumes of data between servers and browsers. While the notation is the format of JavaScript objects, JSON documents can be processed by any language (see Figure CE8-11b). |

Service authors (computer programmers) create WSDL documents to describe the services they provide and the inputs and outputs required. These WSDL documents are seldom read by humans; instead, developer tools like Microsoft Visual Studio read the WSDL and configure the programming environment so that the service will be properly used by developers who write programs to access that service.

As shown in Figure CE8-10, SOAP, which is not an acronym although it looks like one, is a protocol that sits on top of http and the lower-level Internet protocols. *Sits on top of* means that it uses http to send and receive SOAP messages. (SOAP can also use smtp.) Programs that use Web services issue SOAP messages to request services; the Web service uses SOAP messages to return responses to service requests.

Finally, XML and JSON are ways of marking up documents so that both the service requestor and the service provider know what data they're processing. Figure CE8-11 shows a simple example of both. As you can see, XML documents contain as much metadata as they do application data. These metadata are used to ensure the document is complete and properly formatted. XML is used when relatively few messages are being transmitted and when ensuring a complete and correct document is crucial. Both WSDLs and SOAP messages are coded in XML.

As its name indicates, JSON uses the notation that JavaScript uses to format object data. It has much less metadata and is preferred for the transmission of voluminous application data. Web servers use JSON as their primary way of sending application data to browsers.

With this technical background, you should no longer be skeptical that the benefits of the cloud are real. They are. However, this fact does not mean that every organization uses the cloud well. That is where you can define your career.

**Figure CE8-11a**
Example XML Document

```
<person>
    <firstName>Kelly</firstName>
    <lastName>Summers</lastName>
    <dob>12/28/1985</dob>
    <address>
        <streetAddress>309 Elm Avenue</streetAddress>
        <city>San Diego</city>
        <state>CA</state>
        <postalCode>98225</postalCode>
    </address>
    <phoneNumbers>
        <phoneNumber type="home">685 555-1234</phoneNumber>
        <phoneNumber type="cell">685 555-5678</phoneNumber>
    </phoneNumbers>
</person>
```

**Figure CE8-11b**
Example JSON Document

```
{
  "firstName": "Kelly",
  "lastName": "Summers",
  "dob": "12/28/1985",
  "address": {
    "streetAddress": "309 Elm Avenue",
    "city": "San Diego",
    "state": "CA",
    "postalCode": "98225"
  },
  "phoneNumber": [
    {
      "type": "home",
      "number": "685 555-1234"
    },
    {
      "type": "cell",
      "number": "685 555-5678"
    }
  ]
}
```

# ACTIVE REVIEW

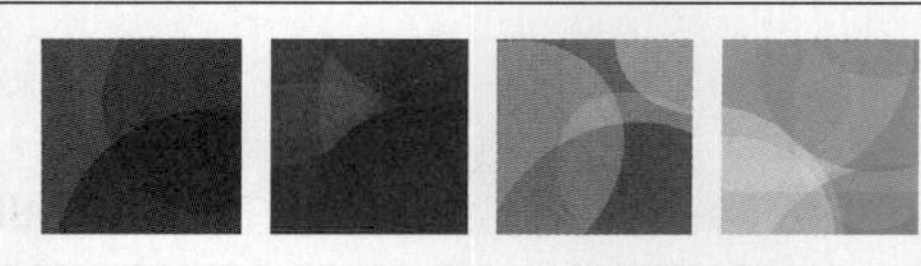

Use this Active Review to verify that you understand the ideas and concepts that answer this chapter extension's study questions.

## QCE8-1 WHAT IS A COMPUTER NETWORK?

Define *computer network*. Explain the differences among PANs, LANs, WANs, internets, intranets, and the Internet.

## QCE8-2 WHAT ARE THE COMPONENTS OF A LAN?

Define *protocol* and explain the purpose of protocols. Explain the key distinction of a LAN. Describe the purpose of each component in Figure CE8-2. Define *IEEE 802.3* and *802.11* and explain how they differ. List three ways of connecting a LAN or computer to the Internet. Explain the nature of each.

## QCE8-3 HOW DOES THE INTERNET WORK?

Explain the statement "The Internet is an internet." Define *IP address* and explain the different ways that public and private IP addresses are used. Describe the purpose of a domain name and explain how such names are associated with public IP addresses. Explain the role of agencies like GoDaddy. Define *URL*. Define *three-tier architecture* and name and describe the role of each tier. Explain the role of each tier in Figure CE8-7 in the way that the page in Figure CE8-6 is processed.

## QCE8-4 HOW DOES THE CLOUD WORK?

Using the department analogy, define *SOA* and explain why departments are encapsulated. Summarize the advantages of using SOA in the three-tier architecture. Define *TCP/IP protocol architecture* and explain, in general terms, the purpose of http, https, smtp, and ftp. Define the purposes and roles of WSDL, SOAP, XML, and JSON. State a key difference between XML and JSON.

## KEY TERMS AND CONCEPTS

10/100/1000 Ethernet 499
Bluetooth 499
Cable line 500
Carrier 501
Commerce server 503
Database tier 503
Digital subscriber line (DSL) 500
Domain name 502
Encapsulated 506
Ethernet 499
ftp (File Transfer Protocol) 508
Hop 501
http (Hypertext Transport Protocol) 507
https 508
ICANN (Internet Corporation for Assigned Names and Numbers) 502
IEEE 802.11 protocol 499
IEEE 802.3 protocol 499
Internet 497
Internet service provider (ISP) 499
Intranet 497
IP address 502
IPv4 502
IPv6 502
JSON (JavaScript Object Notation) 508
Local area network (LAN) 497
Net neutrality 501
Network 497
Packet 501
Personal area network (PAN) 497
Peering 501
Private IP address 502
Protocol 497
Public IP address 502
Server tier 503
Service-oriented architecture (SOA) 505
Small office/home office (SOHO) 498
smtp (Simple Mail Transfer Protocol) 508
SOAP 508
TCP/IP Protocol architecture 507
The Internet 497
Three-tier architecture 503
URL (Uniform Resource Locator) 502
User tier 503
WAN wireless 500
Web page 503
Web servers 503
WSDL (Web Services Description Language) 508
Wide area network (WAN) 497
XML (eXtensible Markup Language) 508

MyMISLab™

To complete the problems with the ✪, go to EOC Discussion Questions in the MyLab.

## USING YOUR KNOWLEDGE

✪ **CE8-1.** Suppose you manage a group of seven employees in a small business. Each of your employees wants to be connected to the Internet. Consider two alternatives:

**Alternative A:** Each employee has his or her own device and connects individually to the Internet.

**Alternative B:** The employees' computers are connected using a LAN, and the network uses a single device to connect to the Internet.

- **a.** Sketch the equipment and lines required for each alternative.
- **b.** Explain the actions you need to take to create each alternative.
- **c.** Which of these two alternatives do you recommend?

✪ **CE8-2.** Suppose that you have a consulting practice implementing LANs for fraternities and sororities on your campus.

- **a.** Consider a fraternity house. Explain how a LAN could be used to connect all of the computers in the house. Would you recommend an Ethernet LAN, an 802.11 LAN, or a combination? Justify your answer.
- **b.** This chapter extension did not provide enough information for you to determine how many switches the fraternity house might need. However, in general terms, describe how the fraternity could use a multiple-switch system.
- **c.** Considering the connection to the Internet, would you recommend that the fraternity house use a DSL modem, a cable modem, or WAN wireless? Although you can rule out at least one of these alternatives with the knowledge you already have, what additional information do you need in order to make a specific recommendation?
- **d.** Should you develop a standard package solution for each of your customers? What advantages accrue from a standard solution? What are the disadvantages?

✪ **CE8-3.** Suppose you own the business in question CE8-2 and you want to obtain a domain name. First, think of three suitable names for your business. Go to GoDaddy.com or another similar agency and determine if any of those names are still available. Choose other names if none of those are available and keep trying. Without buying anything, determine what is involved in obtaining that domain name. How much would it cost were you to do so?

MyMISLab™

Go to the Assignments section of your MyLab to complete these writing exercises.

**CE8-4.** Write a memo to Mateo and Joni at Falcon Security explaining SOA and the important Web service standards. In your memo, explain how the cloud would be impossible without SOA and the Web service standards. Describe a situation where Falcon Security could benefit from SOA.

**CE8-5.** Examine the documents at the end of QCE8-4. Summarize differences in the ways that XML and JSON represent content. Which of these two standards would result in the most reliable processing? Which would be faster to transmit? Describe one good application for each standard.

## ENDNOTE

1. Don Reisinger, "Netflix Gobbles a Third of Peak Internet Traffic in North America," *CNET*, November 7, 2012, accessed June 6, 2014, *www.cnet.com/news/netflix-gobbles-a-third-of-peak-internet-traffic-in-north-america*.

chapter extension **9**

**Chapter 7** provides the background for this extension.

# Enterprise Resource Planning (ERP) Systems

**STUDY QUESTIONS**

**QCE9-1** WHAT IS THE PURPOSE OF ERP SYSTEMS?

**QCE9-2** WHAT ARE THE ELEMENTS OF AN ERP SOLUTION?

**QCE9-3** HOW ARE ERP SYSTEMS IMPLEMENTED AND UPGRADED?

**QCE9-4** WHAT TYPES OF ORGANIZATIONS USE ERP?

**QCE9-5** HOW DO THE MAJOR ERP VENDORS COMPARE?

## QCE9-1 WHAT IS THE PURPOSE OF ERP SYSTEMS?

As stated in Chapter 7, **enterprise resource planning (ERP)** is a suite of applications, called **modules**; a database; and a set of inherent processes for consolidating business operations into a single, consistent computing platform. An **ERP system** is an information system based on ERP technology. ERP systems integrate all of an organization's purchasing, human resources, production, sales, and accounting data into a single system.

The primary purpose of an ERP system is integration; an ERP system allows the left hand of the organization to know what the right hand is doing. This integration allows real-time updates, globally, whenever and wherever a transaction takes place. Critical business decisions can then be made on a timely basis using the latest data.

To understand the utility of this integration, consider the pre-ERP systems shown in Figure CE9-1. This diagram of the processes used by a bicycle manufacturer includes five different databases, one each for vendors, raw materials, finished goods, manufacturing plan, and CRM. Consider the problems that appear with such separated data when the sales department closes a large order, say for 1,000 bicycles.

First, should the company take the order? Can it meet the schedule requirements for such a large order? Suppose one of the primary parts vendors recently lost capacity due to an earthquake, and the manufacturer cannot obtain parts for the order in time. If so, the order schedule ought not to be approved. However, with such separated systems, this situation is unknown.

Even if parts can be obtained, until the order is entered into the finished-goods database, purchasing is unaware of the need to buy new parts. The same comment applies to manufacturing. Until the new order is entered into the manufacturing plan, the production department doesn't know that it needs to increase manufacturing. And, as with parts, does the company have sufficient machine and floor capacity to fill the order on a timely basis? Does it have sufficient personnel with the correct skill sets? Should it be hiring? Can production meet the order schedule? No one knows before the order is approved.

Figure CE9-1 does not show accounting. We can assume, however, that the company has a separate accounting system that is similarly isolated. Eventually, records of business activity find their way to the accounting department and will be posted into the general ledger. With such a pre-ERP system, financial statements are always dated, becoming available several weeks after the close of the quarter or other accounting period.

Contrast this situation with the ERP system in Figure CE9-2. Here all activity is processed by ERP application programs (called *modules* in Figure CE9-2) and consolidated data are stored in a centralized ERP database. When sales is confronted with the opportunity to sell 1,000 bicycles, the information that it needs to confirm that the order, schedule, and terms are feasible can be obtained from the ERP system immediately. Once the order is accepted, all departments, including

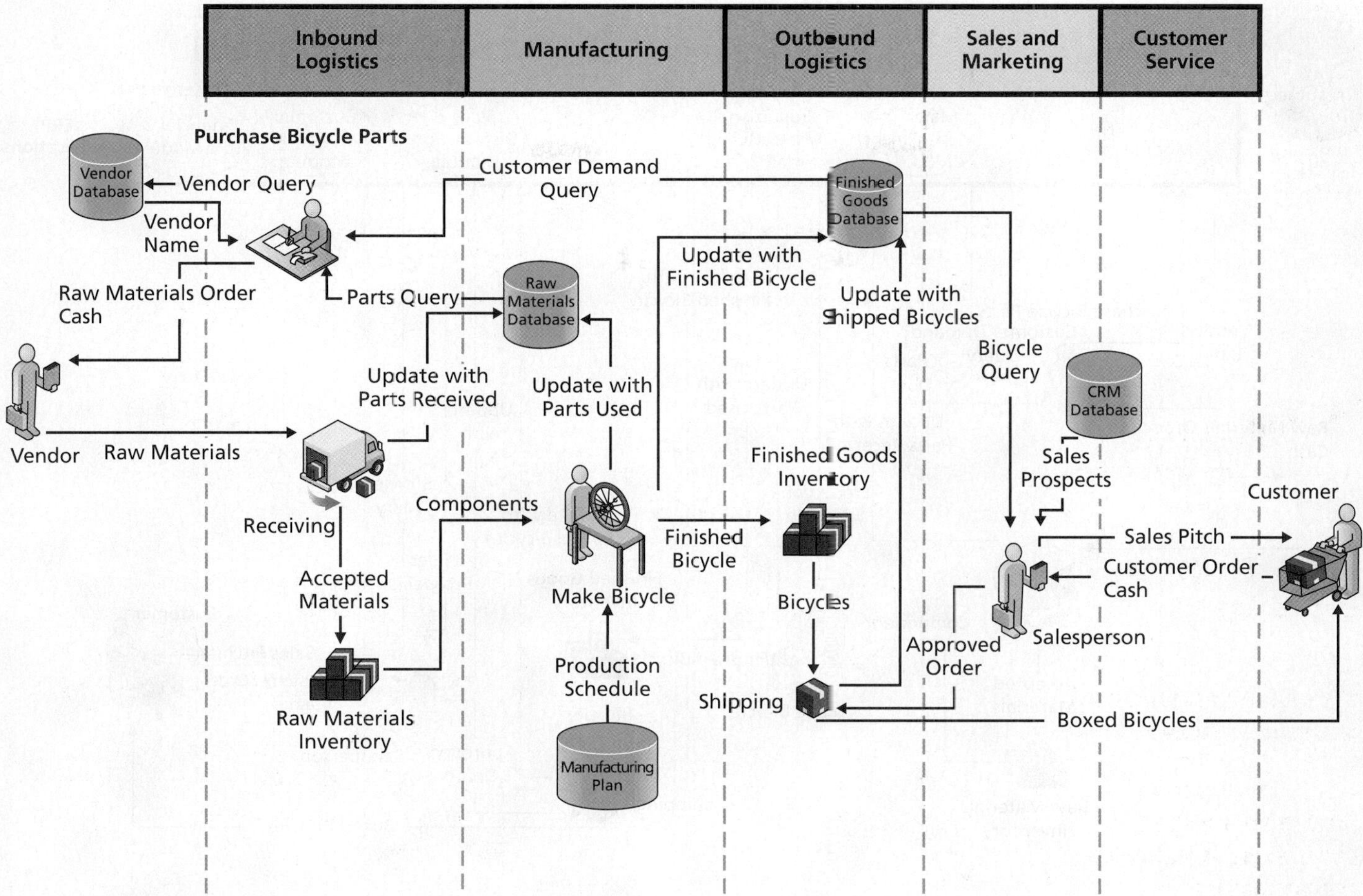


**Figure CE9-1**
Pre-ERP Information Systems

purchasing, manufacturing, human resources, and accounting, are notified. Further, transactions are posted to the ERP database as they occur; the result is that financial statements are available quickly, and in most cases correct financial statements can be produced in real time. With such integration, ERP systems can display the current status of critical business factors to managers and executives, as shown in the sales dashboard in Figure CE9-3.

Of course, the devil is in the details. It's one thing to draw a rectangle on a chart, label it "ERP Applications," and then assume that data integration takes all the problems away. It is far more difficult to write those application programs and to design the database to store that integrated data. Even more problematic, what procedures should employees and others use to process those application programs? For example, what actions should salespeople take before they approve a large order? The following are some of the questions that procedures need to answer or resolve:

- How does the sales department determine that an order is large? By dollars? By volume?
- Who approves customer credit (and how)?
- Who approves production capacity (and how)?
- Who approves schedule and terms (and how)?
- What actions need to be taken if the customer modifies the order?
- How does management obtain oversight on sales activity?

As you can imagine, many other questions must be answered as well.

In the late 1980s and early 1990s, some organizations attempted to develop their own ERP applications and procedures. The process was too difficult and expensive for most to succeed.

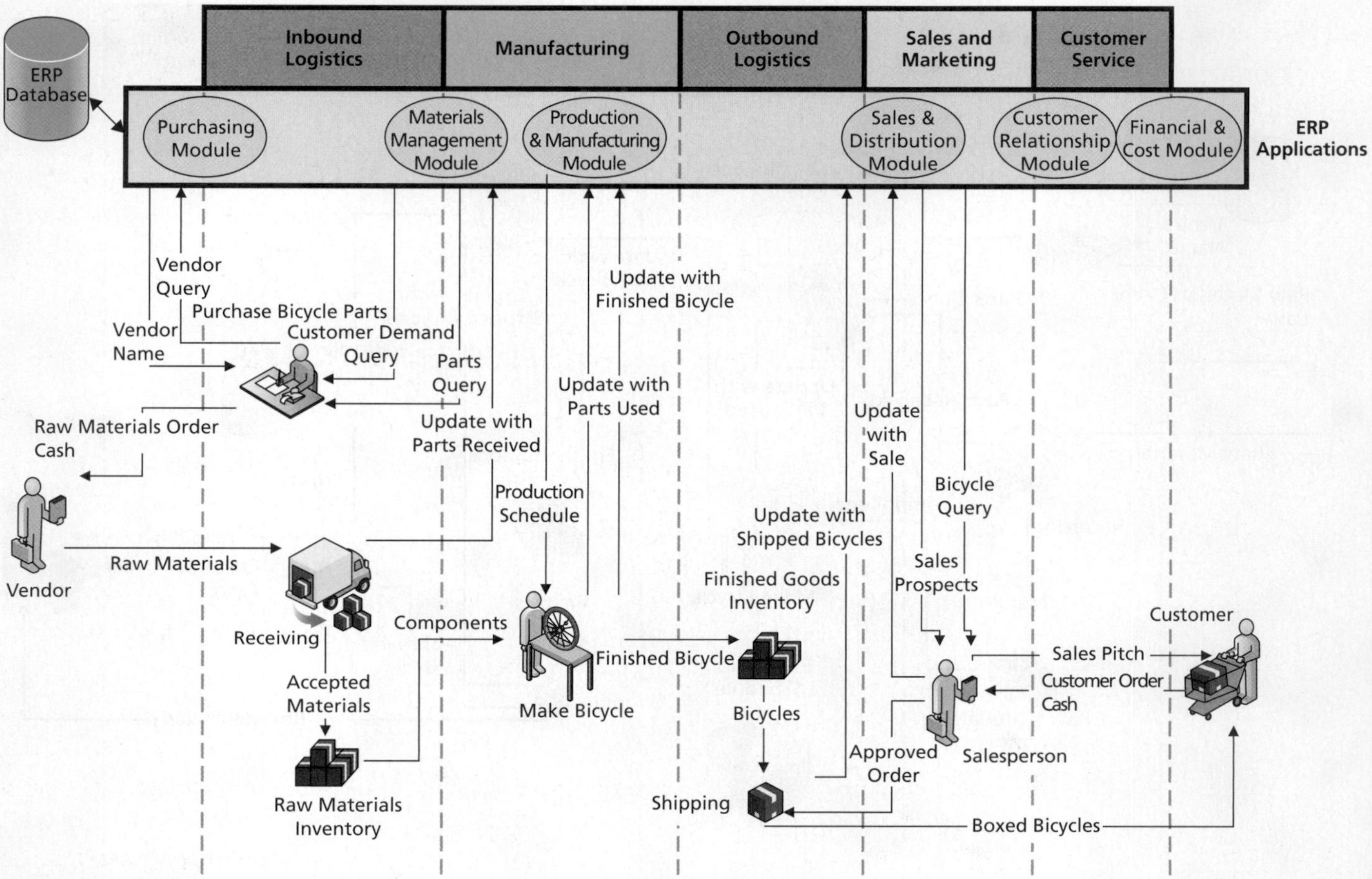

Inbound Logistics
Manufacturing
Outbound Logistics
Sales and Marketing
Customer Service
ERP Database
Purchasing Module
Materials Management Module
Production & Manufacturing Module
Sales & Distribution Module
Customer Relationship Module
Financial & Cost Module
ERP Applications
Vendor Query
Purchase Bicycle Parts
Vendor Name
Customer Demand Query
Parts Query
Update with Parts Received
Update with Parts Used
Update with Finished Bicycle
Raw Materials Order
Cash
Production Schedule
Update with Sale
Bicycle Query
Update with Shipped Bicycles
Sales Prospects
Vendor
Raw Materials
Receiving
Components
Finished Goods Inventory
Customer
Sales Pitch
Customer Order
Cash
Finished Bicycle
Make Bicycle
Accepted Materials
Bicycles
Salesperson
Approved Order
Raw Materials Inventory
Shipping
Boxed Bicycles

**Figure CE9-2**
ERP Information Systems

Microsoft Dynamics CRM
Dashboards
Workplace
Dashboard: Sales Performance w Map
Sales Pipeline
My Estimated vs. Actual Revenue by Salesperson_3D
Seattle
Bellevue
Kirkland
Redmond
Sammamish

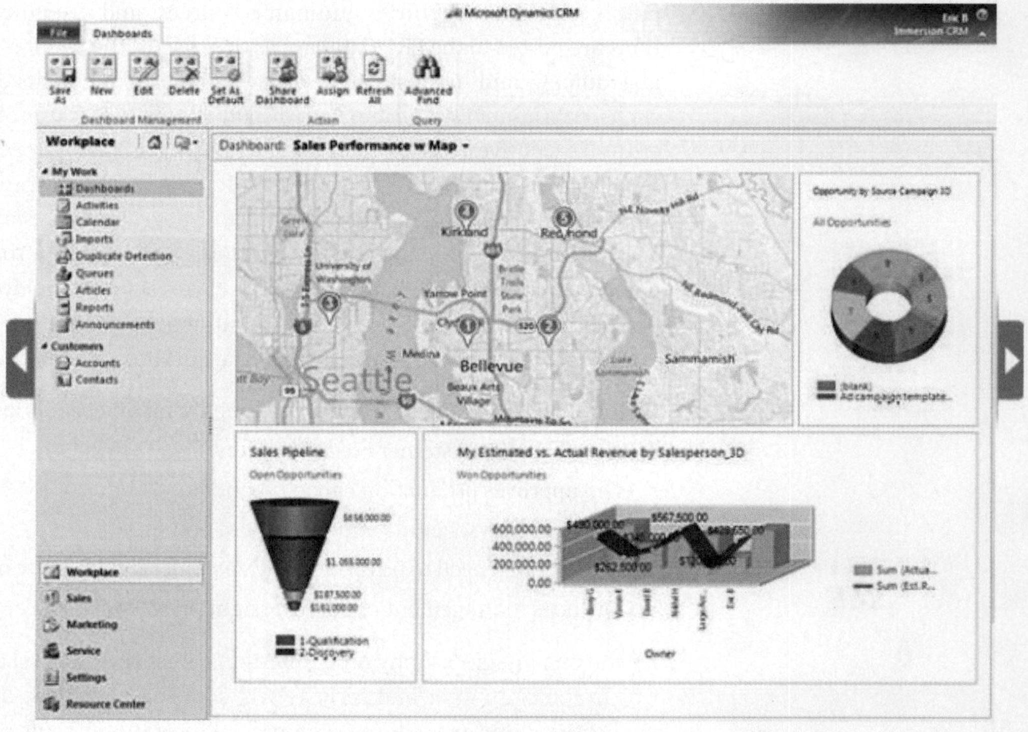

**Figure CE9-3**
Sales Dashboard

*Source:* Microsoft Corporation

SOURCE: Courtesy of Microsoft

During that era, ERP software vendors developed ERP applications that included program code, databases, and inherent processes that addressed issues such as those just listed. Today, almost no organization develops its own ERP software; such systems are licensed from vendors such as those described in QCE9-4.

Even with solutions provided by ERP vendors, however, the process of converting an organization from systems such as those in Figure CE9-1 to an ERP system such as the one in Figure CE9-2 is daunting and expensive. For most organizations, it is a multiyear project that involves millions of dollars and hundreds of employees, consultants, and vendor personnel.

## QCE9-2 WHAT ARE THE ELEMENTS OF AN ERP SOLUTION?

The term *ERP* has been applied to a wide array of application solutions. Some vendors have attempted to catch the buzz for ERP by misapplying the term to applications that are nothing more than one or two integrated functional applications.

The organization ERPSoftware360 publishes a wealth of information about ERP vendors, products, solutions, and applications. According to its Web site (*www.erpsoftware360.com/erp-101.htm*), for a product to be considered a true ERP product, it must include applications that integrate the following:

- Supply chain (procurement, sales order processing, inventory management, supplier management, and related activities)
- Manufacturing (scheduling, capacity planning, quality control, bill of materials, and related activities)
- CRM (sales prospecting, customer management, marketing, customer support, call center support)
- Human resources (payroll, time and attendance, HR management, commission calculations, benefits administration, and related activities)
- Accounting (general ledger, accounts receivable, accounts payable, cash management, fixed-asset accounting)

An ERP solution is an information system and as such has all five components. We consider each in turn.

### HARDWARE

Traditionally, organizations hosted ERP solutions on their own, in-house, networked server computers. Such hosting is still the case for many large ERP applications and for those ERP applications that were installed years ago and for which the hardware infrastructure is stable and well managed.

Increasingly, however, organizations are turning to cloud-based hosting in one of two modes:

- PaaS: Replace an organization's existing hardware infrastructure with hardware in the cloud. Install ERP software and databases on that leased cloud hardware. The using organization then manages the ERP software on the cloud hardware.
- SaaS: Acquire a cloud-based ERP solution. SAP, Oracle, Microsoft, and the other major ERP vendors offer their ERP Software as a Service. The vendor manages the ERP software and offers it to customers as a service.

The problem with cloud-based ERP hardware is that in some cases the law, industry practice, or other constraints require the organization to maintain physical control over its data, or at least substantial parts of it. In what is coming to be known as the **hybrid model**, many ERP customers will store most of their data on cloud servers managed by cloud vendors and store sensitive data on servers they manage themselves. Governmental agencies, financial analysts, and accountants will have defined standards against which organizations can be monitored for appropriate compliance. If you graduate as an accountant or financial analyst, this is interesting work in which you could be involved early in your career.

## SOFTWARE: ERP APPLICATION PROGRAMS

ERP vendors design application programs to be configurable so that development teams can alter them to meet customer requirements without changing program code. Accordingly, during the ERP development process, the development team sets configuration parameters that specify how ERP application programs will operate. For example, an hourly payroll application is configured to specify the number of hours in the standard work week, hourly wages for different job categories, wage adjustments for overtime and holiday work, and so forth. Deciding on the initial configuration values and adapting them to new requirements are challenging collaboration activities. More than 8,000 configuration decisions need to be made for the ERP product SAP. As an IS-knowledgeable business professional, you could well be involved in this activity yourself.

Of course, there are limits to how much configuration can be done. If a new ERP customer has requirements that cannot be met via program configuration, then it either needs to adapt its business to what the software can do or write (or pay another vendor to write) application code to meet its requirement. As stated in Chapter 4, such custom programming is expensive both initially and in long-term maintenance costs. Thus, choosing an ERP solution that has applications that function close to the organization's requirements is critically important to success.

## DATA: ERP DATABASES

An ERP solution includes a database design as well as initial configuration data. It does not, of course, contain the company's operational data. During development, the team must enter the initial values for that data as part of the development effort.

If your only experience with databases is creating a few tables in Microsoft Access, then you probably underestimate the value and importance of ERP database designs. SAP, the leading vendor of ERP solutions, provides ERP databases that contain more than 15,000 tables. The design includes the metadata for those tables, as well as their relationships to each other and rules and constraints about how the data in some tables must relate to data in other tables. As stated, the ERP solution also contains tables filled with initial configuration data.

Furthermore, although we did not discuss this database feature in Chapter 5, large organizational databases contain two types of program code. The first, called a **trigger**, is a computer program stored within the database that runs to keep the database consistent when certain conditions arise. The second, called a **stored procedure**, is a computer program stored in the database that is used to enforce business rules. An example of such a rule would be never to sell certain items at a discount. Triggers and stored procedures are also part of the ERP solution that developers and business users must configure.

Reflect on the difficulty of creating and validating data models and you will have some idea of the amount of intellectual capital invested in a database design of 15,000 tables. Also, consider the magnitude of the task of filling such a database with users' data!

## PROCEDURES: BUSINESS PROCESS PROCEDURES

The third component of an ERP solution is a set of inherent procedures that implement standard business processes. ERP vendors develop hundreds, or even thousands, of procedures that enable the ERP customer organization to accomplish its work using the applications provided by the vendor. Figure CE9-4 shows a part of the SAP ordering business process; this process implements

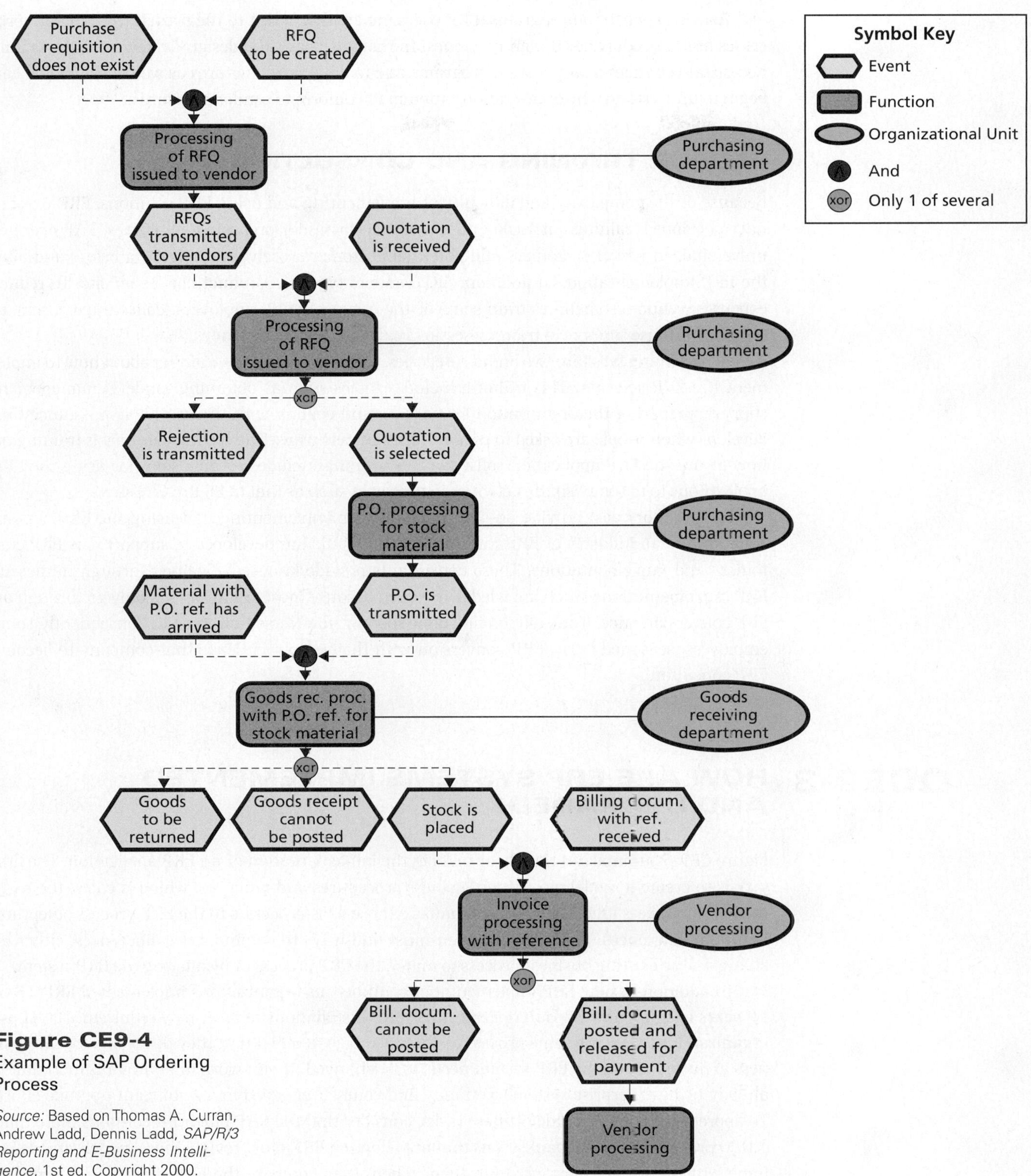


**Figure CE9-4**
Example of SAP Ordering Process

*Source:* Based on Thomas A. Curran, Andrew Ladd, Dennis Ladd, *SAP/R/3 Reporting and E-Business Intelligence*, 1st ed. Copyright 2000.

a portion of the activities shown on the left-hand side of Figure CE9-2. Some ERP vendors call the inherent processes that are defined in the ERP solution **process blueprints**.

Without delving into the details, you should be able to understand the flow of work outlined in this process. Every function (rounded rectangle) consists of a set of procedures for accomplishing that function. Typically, these procedures require an ERP user to use application menus, screens, and reports to accomplish the activity.

As with application programs, ERP users must either adapt to the predefined, inherent processes and procedures or design new ones. In the latter case, the design of new procedures may necessitate changes to application programs and to database structures as well. Perhaps you can begin to understand why organizations attempt to conform to vendor standards.

### PEOPLE: TRAINING AND CONSULTING

Because of the complexity and difficulty of implementing and using ERP solutions, ERP vendors have developed training curricula and numerous classes for preparing employees. SAP operates universities in which customers and potential customers receive training both before and after the ERP implementation. In addition, ERP vendors typically conduct classes on site. To reduce expenses, vendors sometimes train some of the organization's employees, called Super Users, to become in-house trainers in training sessions called **train the trainer**.

ERP training falls into two broad categories. The first category is training about how to implement the ERP solution. This training includes topics such as obtaining top-level management support, preparing the organization for change, and dealing with the inevitable resistance that develops when people are asked to perform work in new ways. The second category is training on how to use the ERP application software; this training includes specific steps for using the ERP applications to accomplish the activities in processes such as that in Figure CE9-4.

ERP vendors also provide on-site consulting for implementing and using the ERP system. Additionally, an industry of ERP third-party consultants has developed to support new ERP customers and implementations. These consultants provide knowledge gained through numerous ERP implementations. Such knowledge is valued because most organizations only go through an ERP conversion once. Ironically, having done so, they now know how to do it. Consequently, some employees, seasoned by an ERP conversion with their employer, leave that company to become ERP consultants.

## QCE9-3 HOW ARE ERP SYSTEMS IMPLEMENTED AND UPGRADED?

Figure CE9-5 summarizes the major tasks in the implementation of an ERP application. The first task is to create a model of current business procedures and practices, which is called the **as-is model**. Managers and analysts then compare those as-is processes to the ERP process blueprints and note differences. The company then must find ways to eliminate the differences, either by changing the existing business process to match the ERP process or by altering the ERP system.

In addition to new ERP implementations, numerous organizations implemented ERP 15 or 20 years ago and now need to upgrade their ERP installations to meet new requirements. Those organizations follow the same process as shown in Figure CE9-5, but they do so only for the business areas for which the ERP system needs to be changed. If you work in an organization that is already using enterprise systems, you may find yourself engaged in a significant upgrade effort. To appreciate the magnitude of these tasks, consider that the SAP blueprint contains more than 1,000 process models. Organizations that are adopting ERP must review those models and determine which ones are appropriate to them. Then, they compare the ERP models to the models developed based on their current practices. Inevitably, some current-practice models are incomplete, vague, or inaccurate, so the team must repeat the existing process models. In some cases, it is impossible to reconcile any existing system against the blueprint model. If so, the team must adapt, cope, and define new procedures, often to the confusion of current employees.

Once the differences between as-is processes and the blueprint have been reconciled, the next step is to implement the system. Before implementation starts, however, users must be trained on the new processes, procedures, and use of the ERP system's features and functions. Additionally,

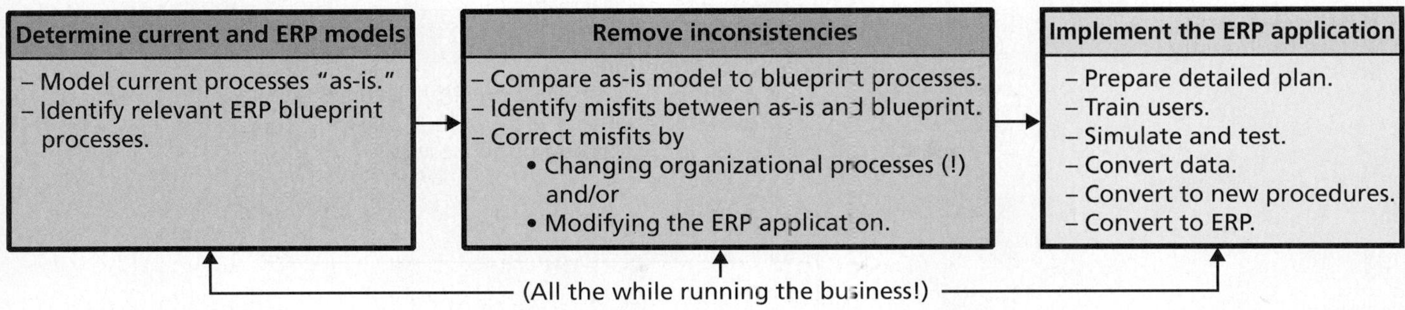


**Figure CE9-5**
ERP Implementation

the company needs to conduct a simulation test of the new system to identify problems. Then the organization must convert its data, procedures, and personnel to the new ERP system. All of this happens while the business continues to run on the old system.

As you'll learn in Chapter 12, plunging the organization into the new system is an invitation to disaster. Instead, a thorough and well-planned test of the new system is necessary, followed by a careful rollout of the new system in stages. Realize, too, that while the new ERP system is being installed normal business activity continues. Somehow the employees of the organization must continue to run the company while the rollout is underway. It is a difficult and challenging time for any organization that undergoes this process.

Implementing an ERP system is not for the faint of heart. Many ERP-implementation disasters have occurred. Recently, the U.S. Air Force gave up and canceled an ERP implementation in which it had already invested more than $1 billion.[1] In spite of this risk, however, more than 84 percent of organizations having between 100 and 1,000 employees have implemented ERP.[2]

Because of such risks and because so much organizational change is required, all ERP projects must have the full support of the CEO and executive staff. Like all cross-functional processes, ERP crosses departmental boundaries, and no single departmental manager has the authority to force an ERP implementation. Instead, full support for the task must come from the top of the organization. Even with such support there is bound to be concern and second-guessing.

## QCE9-4 WHAT TYPES OF ORGANIZATIONS USE ERP?

ERP originated as an outgrowth of MRP II manufacturing functional applications. ERP extended MRP II from just the planning and scheduling of manufacturing to include the planning and use of facilities, people, equipment, materials flow, orders, customers, and accounting, encompassing the scope described in QCE9-2.

### ERP BY INDUSTRY TYPE

Because of its origins, the first major ERP customers were large manufacturers. Manufacturers in the aerospace, automotive, and industrial equipment industries led the way. SAP, currently the market leader, spurred ERP growth by providing industry-specific implementations. For example, as SAP assisted one auto manufacturer in using its product, it learned process patterns that were typical of auto manufacturers. Over time, it constructed an auto-manufacturing-specific ERP solution as a product offering. These **industry-specific solutions** became popular, and today SAP and other ERP vendors offer dozens of them. SAP, for example, has 24 industry-specific versions of its ERP products.

Given their success with manufacturers it was natural for ERP vendors to go up the supply chain and sell ERP solutions to distributors, raw materials extractors and processors, and the petroleum industry. At the same time, health care was becoming more complex, and hospitals were changing from a service to a profit orientation. As you learned in Chapter 7, hospital systems

**Figure CE9-6**
ERP Use by Industry

- Manufacturing
- Distribution
- Mining, materials extraction, petroleum
- Medical care
- Government and public service
- Utilities
- Retail
- Education

are incredibly complex, and they were ripe candidates for ERP sales and solutions. Over time, ERP use spread to companies and organizations in other industries, as shown in Figure CE9-6.

## ERP BY ORGANIZATION SIZE

ERP, as stated, was initially adopted by large manufacturing organizations that had complex process problems that needed ERP solutions. Those large organizations also had the resources and skilled personnel needed to accomplish and manage an ERP implementation. Over time, ERP use spread downward from large companies with billions of dollars in sales to midsized companies with $100 million in sales. Today, ERP is used in small organizations with $5 million to $100 million in sales.

The value chains and basic business processes are similar for small and large organizations. The steps required to check credit, verify product availability, and approve terms are no different for order processing at *Amazon.com* than they are at Phil's Muffler Shop. They differ in scale but not in character.

However, companies of different sizes have one very important difference that has a major impact on ERP: the availability of skilled IT personnel. Small organizations employ only one or two IT specialists who not only manage the ERP system but the entire IS department as well (see Chapter 11 for a discussion of these responsibilities). They are spread very thin and often are in over their heads during an ERP implementation. Smaller, simpler ERP solutions are common among these companies, as discussed in QCE9-5.

Midsized organizations expand IT from one person to a small staff, but frequently this staff is isolated from senior management. Such isolation creates misunderstanding and distrust. As stated in QCE9-3, because of the expense, organizational disruption, and length of ERP projects, senior management must be committed to the ERP solution. When IT management is isolated, such commitment is difficult to obtain and may not be strong. This issue is so prevalent that many ERP consultants say the first step in moving toward ERP is to obtain deep senior-level management commitment to the project.

Large organizations have a full IT staff that is headed by the chief information officer (CIO), who is a business and IT professional who sits on the executive board and is an active participant in organizational strategic planning. ERP implementation will be part of that strategic process and, once begun, will have the full backing of the entire executive group. See *www.erpsoftware360.com/software-markets.htm* for more information about the role and use of ERP by size of business.

## INTERNATIONAL ERP

Another way that the ERP needs of large organizations differ from those of small organizations is international presence. Most billion-dollar companies operate in multiple countries, and the ERP application programs must be available in several languages. Inherent ERP procedures must be adaptable to different cultures. Some companies can declare a single "company language" and force all company business to be transacted in that language (usually English). Other companies must accommodate multiple languages in their ERP solution.

Once implemented, ERP can bring substantial benefits to multinational organizations. International ERP solutions are designed to support multiple currencies and languages, manage international transfers of goods in inventories, and work effectively with international supply chains. Even more important, ERP solutions provide a worldwide consolidation of financial statements on a timely basis. See *www.cio.com/article/694303/How_to_Achieve_Global_ERP* for more details on the advantages of ERP to international organizations. For some organizations, however, the advantages of one set of data, a single financial system, and worldwide process standards are outweighed by the cost of forcing disparate organizations to standardize. Some such organizations choose to implement a different ERP for each country, business unit, or region. We will discuss these issues and others associated with IS internationalization in Chapter Extension 18.

## QCE9-5 HOW DO THE MAJOR ERP VENDORS COMPARE?

Although more than 100 different companies advertise ERP products, not all of those products meet the minimal ERP criteria listed in QCE9-2. Even of those that do, the bulk of the market is held by the five vendors described in Figure CE9-7.

### ERP MARKET LEADERS

The ERP market is mature and, according to *Forbes*,[3] experienced only 3.8 percent growth to $25 billion in 2013. As the ERP market continues to mature, consolidation of vendors is likely, with smaller vendors falling out entirely. According to the same source, the top 10 vendors own 64 percent of the market share and the top five, listed in Figure CE9-7, own 55 percent.

The cloud is having a major impact on ERP vendors. Those with substantial resources (SAP) and deep technical talent (Oracle) are moving their product suites into some version of SaaS, PaaS, or IaaS. Others are unable to convert to the new technology and are gradually losing their customers to those who have converted or to new companies that have only ever offered cloud-based ERP solutions. Among organizations that use ERP, the movement from classical client/server ERP to the cloud will likely be a major business challenge during the early years of your career.

### ERP PRODUCTS

Figure CE9-8 shows how the ERP products from each of these companies relate to the size of their customers. Oracle and SAP serve the largest organizations. Infor, Sage, and Microsoft products primarily serve mid-sized to small companies.

**Figure CE9-7**
Characteristics of Top ERP Vendors

| Company | Market Share | Remarks |
|---|---|---|
| SAP | 25 percent | Market leader in client-server implementations. Expensive. Many consider it to be the gold standard of ERP. |
| Oracle | 13 percent | Intensely competitive company with strong technology base. Large customer base. Flexible SOA architecture. Leveraging technology base into innovative and effective cloud-based solutions. Strong challenge to SAP market leadership. Claims number 1 in CRM. |
| Sage | 6 percent | Sage adapted many of its legacy applications and solutions for the cloud and for mobile computing. Offers inexpensive, cloud-based solutions for startups and small businesses. Broad product suite. |
| Infor | 6 percent | Many solutions, not integrated, particularly specialized for manufacturing and supply chain management. Willl evolve with revolution in 3D manufacturing practices. |
| Microsoft | 5 percent | Microsoft AX, which is popular in Europe, is primarily used in manufacturing. Other products have smaller revenue. Dynamics CRM is offered as SaaS, but no full ERP solution is offered in the cloud. |

**Figure CE9-8**
Top ERP Vendors and Customer Size

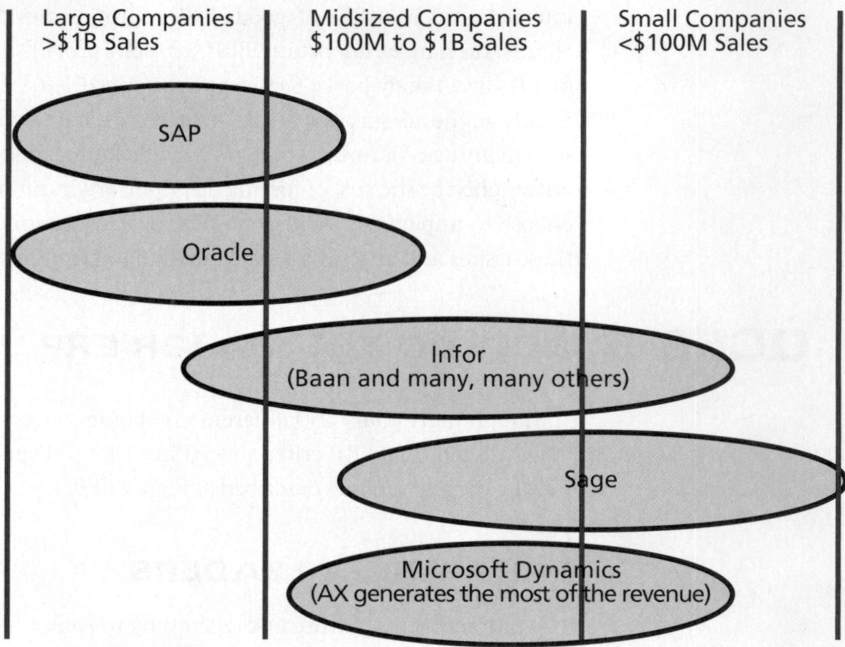


## SAP

SAP is the gold standard of ERP products. It steered the direction of the ERP industry in the 1990s and the first decade of the 21st century. SAP sells to the largest companies and offers the most expensive of the ERP products.

Ironically, SAP's past success creates problems today. Classic SAP uses thick-client, client/server architecture. Because of its installed base, SAP cannot dramatically move out of classic SAP to cloud-based solutions. Instead, it must focus resources and attention on the needs of its current customers (and the attendant large revenue stream from their maintenance contracts).

However, SAP cannot ignore the cloud and recently announced SAP HANNA, which is a PaaS ERP offering that serves as the foundation of their long-term cloud solution. SAP HANNA Enterprise Cloud can be used as an ERP solution by itself, or it can be integrated with existing, on-premises SAP installations.

SAP's biggest problem—and opportunity—is providing the benefits of the cloud to customers who want the economic benefits of the cloud on one hand, but don't want to disrupt their organization and go through the throes of a nearly new ERP installation on the other hand. SAP must meet these needs while maintaining its market share. It has many technical, marketing, sales, and customer support challenges ahead. Undoubtedly, many leaders within SAP wish the cloud had never come into existence. Situations like this often create employment opportunities for the ambitious, however.

## Oracle

Oracle is an intensely competitive company with a deep base of technology and high-quality technical staff. Oracle developed some of its ERP products in-house and complemented those products with the acquisition of PeopleSoft (high-quality HR products) and Siebel (high-quality CRM products).

Beginning with its first DMBS product release, Oracle has never been known to create easy-to-use products. It is known, however, for producing fully featured products with superior performance. They are also expensive.

Classic Oracle ERP products are designed according to SOA principles and hence are adaptable and customizable. In addition, Oracle offers ERP Cloud Service as SaaS; customers pay for what they use and need. ERP Services include financials, planning and budgeting, risk and controls management, procurement and sourcing, inventory and cost management, and others.[4] Oracle claims its products offer a modern user interface and a superior user experience on mobile devices.

Oracle's deep pool of technical talent will enable it to continue evolving its product suite into cloud-based services. Oracle is well positioned to use the cloud as a way to expand its market share.

### Infor

Infor was purchased in 2002 by private-equity investors, primarily Golden Gate Partners. The company then went on an acquisition binge, consolidating multiple product offerings under one sales and marketing organization. It purchased Baan, a well-known and successful ERP company, along with more than 20 other companies. Today, Infor sells many ERP products for many different industries.

As you might imagine, the products vary in purpose, scope, and quality. They span the midrange, serving higher-end small companies and lower-end large companies.

Recently, Infor began to offer the Infor Business Cloud, an ERP solution that can be used as a software service, can be installed on the customer's servers and managed by Infor personnel, or can be installed in a bare-bones way and offered as IaaS.

### Sage

Sage is an international company that began licensing accounting software in 1981. Via a process of acquisitions, Sage developed and now licenses enterprise applications, including CRM and ERP. It continues to offer numerous functional applications in finance as well. Today, Sage offers solutions primarily for the healthcare, construction, distribution, manufacturing, and retail industries.

### Microsoft Dynamics

Microsoft offers five ERP products, all obtained via acquisition: AX (pronounced "A and X," not "axe"), Nav, GP, Solomon, and Dynamics CRM. AX and Nav have the most capabilities; GP is more limited but is easier to use. The future of Solomon is uncertain; Microsoft supposedly outsources the maintenance of Solomon code to provide continuing support to existing customers. To add to the confusion, Dynamics CRM is primarily a CRM product, but it is extensible in ways that enable customers to use it for ERP as well as CRM.

Microsoft is in the process of consolidating its offerings. Most likely AX will continue going forward as a true ERP product for larger organizations. Dynamics CRM will serve as a CRM product as well as a platform for custom ERP solutions. GP, which is the easiest of the products to install, will continue as a general-ledger program that can also be used as a platform for simpler ERP solutions.

Microsoft relies heavily on its network of independent software vendors to create customer solutions using the Dynamics platform. These vendors take off-the-shelf Dynamics products and adapt and customize them for particular situations.

Microsoft offers its CRM product online as SaaS, but it has no full ERP implementation in the cloud.

## ERP IN THE FUTURE

Within the next 10 years, ERP vendors and customers will have sorted out the problems of cloud-based ERP using the hybrid model. Mobility, however, will still present problems. Within a few years, workers in the warehouse, loading dock, and shipping departments will all carry mobile devices that enable them to process ERP and other enterprise applications from wherever they happen to be. Managers, decision makers, and other knowledge workers will have similar applications on their own phones or other mobile devices—devices they can access from work, other offices, the street, or home.

However—and it's an enormous however—mobile devices are subject to severe security threats. It is one thing for criminals to steal data about the past. As we learned from the Sony Entertainment data loss in late 2014, data loss is aggravating and embarrassing and damages the innocent. No one on the outside knows for sure, but it appears that Sony paid the hackers handsomely to call off the data releases. So, that loss was expensive in direct payoff as well as in the disruption of business operations.

Consider, however, what would happen if some criminal, perhaps a malicious insider, infiltrated an ERP system. It would be possible to wreak havoc in, say, supply chain orders and inventories or in the operation of machinery on the factory floor. The hacked organization would have to shut down its ERP system, and thus its company, to sort out the mess. But allowing users mobile access to the ERP system will enable organizations to make significant improvements in process quality. So, in the next 10 years, organizations must engage in a delicate balancing act between risk of loss and improvement to processes. We discuss such trade-offs further in Chapter 10.

Consider also the effect of the Internet of Things. Future users of ERP systems will be not be just people, but also devices and machines. ERP vendors are adapting their software to the particular requirements of 3D printing. In the future, when a salesperson enters an order, he or she may be starting a machine to make that part on demand. In addition, factory automation will also add to process quality improvements. Inventory-picking robots are one example, but self-driving cars and trucks are likely to have an even larger effect. And within the next 10 years, machines will be able to employ the ERP system to schedule their own maintenance. For example, on the factory floor a milling machine will be able to order a replacement for a dull cutter, one that is possibly made by a 3D printer. Machines will schedule both routine and emergency maintenance for themselves, thus taking factory automation to a new level.

As we have stated many times, the future belongs not to those who specialize in existing methods, technology, and processes but rather to those who can find and implement innovative applications of emerging trends. Technology's effect on enterprise systems will be widespread because enterprise systems are widespread. Many opportunities will occur in the early years of your career.

# ACTIVE REVIEW

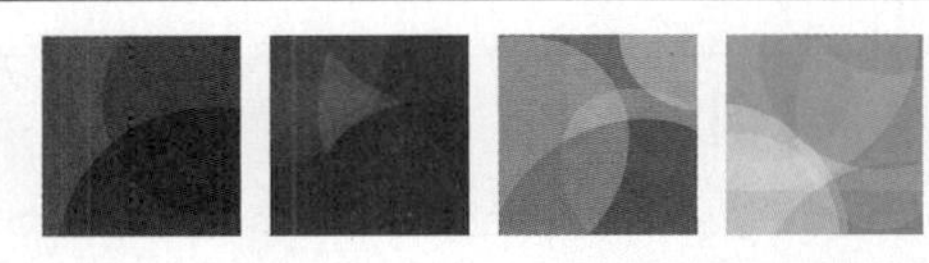

Use this Active Review to verify that you understand the ideas and concepts that answer this chapter extension's study questions.

## QCE9-1 WHAT IS THE PURPOSE OF ERP SYSTEMS?

Define *ERP* and *ERP system*. Identify the primary purpose of an ERP system. Summarize the problems that the bicycle manufacturer in Figure CE9-1 has. Explain how the ERP system in Figure CE9-2 overcomes those problems. Explain why "the devil is in the details." Describe the reasons that organizations find it next to impossible to create their own ERP solutions.

## QCE9-2 WHAT ARE THE ELEMENTS OF AN ERP SOLUTION?

List the requirements that a system must meet to be considered a legitimate ERP solution. Describe characteristics of the five components of an ERP system. Define the hybrid model. Explain how and why ERP applications are configurable. Describe the components of an ERP database design. Define *trigger* and *stored procedure.* How do such designs differ from the design of the typical Access database? Explain the importance of *process blueprints.* Interpret Figure CE9-4. Explain the term *train the trainer* and summarize two categories of training. Explain the role of consultants in ERP implementations.

## QCE9-3 HOW ARE ERP SYSTEMS IMPLEMENTED AND UPGRADED?

Summarize the process shown in Figure CE9-5. Explain why it is expensive and time consuming. Explain why it is necessary for the project to have the full support of senior management.

## QCE9-4 WHAT TYPES OF ORGANIZATIONS USE ERP?

Describe the origins of ERP and explain how those origins led to the initial ERP implementations in industry. Define *industry-specific solution.* Summarize the three categories of business size defined in this chapter extension. Explain how the fundamental ERP processes are the same for different-sized organizations and how the IT departments differ. Describe the value of ERP systems for international organizations.

## QCE9-5 HOW DO THE MAJOR ERP VENDORS COMPARE?

Name the five primary ERP vendors and rank them according to market size. Name and describe the primary product(s) of each of those five vendors. Explain how the vendors' products relate to customer size. Describe how each of the five vendors is responding to the opportunity of the cloud. Summarize important issues that will face ERP vendors and customers in the future.

## KEY TERMS AND CONCEPTS

MyMISLab™

To complete the problems with the ✪, go to EOC Discussion Questions in the MyLab.

## USING YOUR KNOWLEDGE

✪ **CE9-1.** Using the patient discharge process discussed in Chapter 7 (page 187), explain how the hospital benefits from an ERP solution. Describe why integration of patient records in one system is better than spreading patient records across separated databases. Explain the value of an industry-specific ERP solution to the hospital.

✪ **CE9-2.** In your own words, restate how ERP systems eliminate the problems of departmental information silos. Using your university as an example, describe silos that will exist if each college engages in its own procurement. Explain how an ERP system could eliminate such silos.

✪ **CE9-3.** Google or Bing each of the five ERP vendors discussed in this chapter extension. In what ways have their product offerings changed since this edition was written? Do those vendors have new products? Have they made important acquisitions? Have they been acquired? Have any new companies made important inroads into their market share?

MyMISLab™

Go to the Assignments section of your MyLab to complete these writing exercises.

**CE9-4.** Based on the discussion in QCE9-5, which of the leading ERP vendors is best suited to provide services for a rapidly growing 3D manufacturing company with $75M in sales? Justify your choice. Describe how a large vendor like SAP, which primarily services large companies, might expand its offerings to better service a smaller company like this 3D manufacturing company.

**CE9-5.** Go to *www.microsoft.com* and search for *Microsoft Dynamics*. Ignore Dynamics CRM. Have any important changes occurred in Microsoft's ERP product offerings since this edition was written? Has Microsoft brought a cloud-based ERP solution to market? Have any of the four ERP systems described in the chapter extension been better integrated with Office or the Microsoft Developer's platform? Using your knowledge guided by experience, what do you think are Microsoft's intentions with regard to ERP?

## ENDNOTES

1. Chris Kanaracus, "Air Force Scraps Massive ERP Project After Racking Up $1B in Costs," *Computerworld*, last modified November 14, 2012, *www.computerworld.com/s/article/9233651/Air_Force_scraps_massive_ERP_project_after_racking_up_1B_in_costs*.
2. Nick Castellina, "A Guide for a Successful ERP Strategy in the Midmarket," Aberdeen Group, last modified May 2012, *http://public.dhe.ibm.com/common/ssi/ecm/en/sml12349usen/SML12349USEN.pdf*.
3. Louis Columbus, "Gartner's ERP Market Share Update Shows The Future of Cloud ERP Is Now," *Forbes*, May 12, 2014, accessed April 9, 2015, *www.forbes.com/sites/louiscolumbus/2014/05/12/gartners-erp-market-share-update-shows-the-future-of-cloud-erp-is-now*.
4. "Oracle ERP Cloud Service," Oracle, accessed June 2013, *www.oracle.com/us/solutions/cloud/erp/overview/index.html*.

chapter extension **10**

**Chapter 7** provides the background for this extension.

# Supply Chain Management

STUDY QUESTIONS

**QCE10-1** WHAT ARE TYPICAL INTER-ENTERPRISE PROCESSES?

**QCE10-2** WHAT IS A SUPPLY CHAIN?

**QCE10-3** WHAT FACTORS AFFECT SUPPLY CHAIN PERFORMANCE?

**QCE10-4** HOW DOES SUPPLY CHAIN PROFITABILITY DIFFER FROM ORGANIZATIONAL PROFITABILITY?

**QCE10-5** WHAT IS THE BULLWHIP EFFECT?

**QCE10-6** HOW DO INFORMATION SYSTEMS AFFECT SUPPLY CHAIN PERFORMANCE?

## QCE10-1 WHAT ARE TYPICAL INTER-ENTERPRISE PROCESSES?

As stated in Chapter 7, an inter-enterprise system is an information system that is shared by two or more independent organizations. The PRIDE system is an inter-enterprise system shared by many organizations. Inter-enterprise system management is more difficult than management for other types of systems. As stated in Chapter 7, inter-enterprise cooperation is governed by negotiation and contract, and conflict resolution is done by negotiation, arbitration, and litigation.

Inter-enterprise IS vary in scope and complexity. An example of a simple inter-enterprise IS is a sales process at a small retailer in which the retailer processes customers' credit card transactions. The retailer, customer, and credit card company (and possibly the bank that issued the card) are all part of the business process that processes the payment. Such a process is common, standardized, and relatively simple; few businesses give it much thought. Processing of checks using the **Automated Clearing House (ACH)** system among banks is another example of a standardized inter-enterprise system, though one that is more complicated than that for processing credit card transactions.

At the other end of the spectrum are customized inter-enterprise systems among large companies. Consider, for example, the inter-enterprise IS that exists among Boeing, General Electric, and other companies for supplying engines to the 787 aircraft, whose production Boeing has largely outsourced. The complexity of the interactions among the supplying organizations, as well as the number of supplying organizations, meant that new, customized inter-enterprise processes had to be designed and agreed upon.

This chapter extension considers a sample inter-enterprise IS of supply chain management among distributors and retailers. We will consider supply chain management from a generic standpoint using examples that are much simpler than the Boeing/GE process. Understanding the principles in this chapter extension will serve as a good basis if you work in more complicated supply chain situations during your career.

## QCE10-2 WHAT IS A SUPPLY CHAIN?

A **supply chain** is a network of organizations and facilities that transforms raw materials into products delivered to customers. Figure CE10-1 shows a generic supply chain. Customers order from retailers, who, in turn, order from distributors, who, in turn, order from manufacturers, who, in turn, order from suppliers. In addition to the organizations shown here, the supply chain also includes transportation companies, warehouses, inventories, and some means for transmitting messages and information among the organizations involved.

**Figure CE10-1**
Supply Chain Relationships

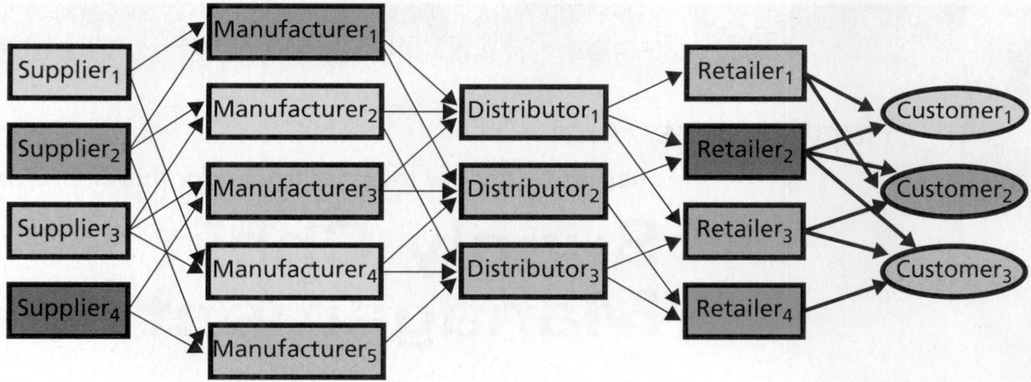


Because of disintermediation, not every supply chain has all of these organizations. Dell, for example, sells directly to the customer. Both the distributor and retailer organizations are omitted from its supply chain. In other supply chains, manufacturers sell directly to retailers and omit the distribution level.

The term *chain* is misleading. *Chain* implies that each organization is connected to just one company up (toward the supplier) and down (toward the customer) the chain. That is not the case. Instead, at each level, an organization can work with many organizations both up and down the supply chain. Thus, a supply chain and the processes that support it are networks.

To understand the operation of a supply chain, consider Figure CE10-2. Suppose you decide to take up cross-country skiing. You go to a recreation vendor such as REI (either by visiting one of its stores or its Web site) and purchase skis, bindings, boots, and poles. To fill your order, REI removes those items from its inventory of goods. Those goods have been purchased, in turn, from distributors. According to Figure CE10-2, REI purchases the skis, bindings, and poles from one distributor and boots from a second. The distributors, in turn, purchase the required items from the manufacturers, which, in turn, buy raw materials from their suppliers.

The only source of revenue in a supply chain is the customer. In the REI example, you spend your money on the ski equipment. From that point all the way back up the supply chain to the raw material suppliers, there is no further injection of cash. The money you spend on the ski equipment is passed back up the supply chain as payments for goods or raw materials. Again, the customer is the only source of revenue.

**Figure CE10-2**
Supply Chain Example

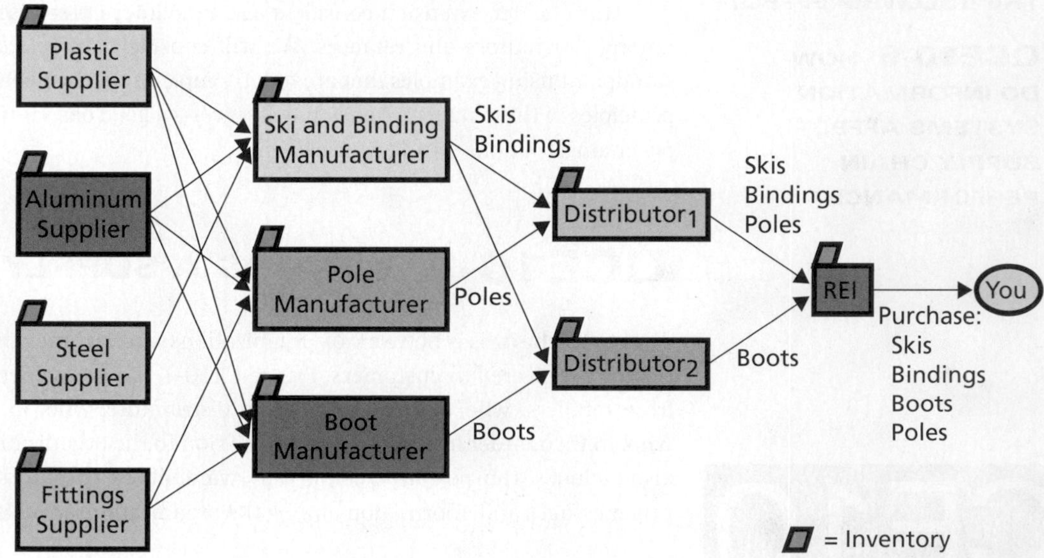

## QCE10-3 WHAT FACTORS AFFECT SUPPLY CHAIN PERFORMANCE?

Four major factors, or *drivers*, affect supply chain performance: facilities, inventory, transportation, and information.[1] Figure CE10-3 lists these drivers of supply chain performance. We will summarize the first three factors in this text and focus our attention on the fourth factor, information. (You can learn in detail about the first three factors in operations management classes.)

As Figure CE10-3 indicates, *facilities* concern the location, size, and operations methodology of the places where products are fabricated, assembled, or stored. The optimal design of facilities is a complicated subject. For example, given all of REI's stores and its e-commerce site, where should it locate its warehouses? How large should they be? How should items be stored and retrieved from the inventories? If one considers facilities for the entire supply chain, these decisions become even more complicated.

*Inventory* includes all of the materials in the supply chain, including raw materials, in-process work, and finished goods. Each company in Figure CE10-2 maintains one or more inventories. When you and others purchase items from REI, its inventory is reduced, and at some point REI reorders from its distributors. The distributors, in turn, maintain their inventories, and at some point they reorder from the manufacturers, and so forth.

Managing an inventory requires balancing between availability and cost. Inventory managers can increase product availability by increasing inventory size. Doing so, however, increases the cost of the inventory and, thus, reduces the company's profitability. However, decreasing the size of the inventory increases the odds that an item will be unavailable for purchase. If that happens, the customer may order from a different source, which will reduce the company's revenue and profit. Inventory management is always a balance between availability and cost.

Inventory management decisions include not only the size of the inventory, but also the frequency with which items are reordered and the size of reorders. For example, assume that REI determines that it needs an inventory of 1,000 boots per month. It can order the full 1,000 at the start of the month or it can order 250 four times per month. Decisions like this and other inventory management decisions have a major impact on supply chain performance.

*Transportation*, the third driver in Figure CE10-3, concerns the movement of materials in the supply chain. Some organizations have their own transportation facilities; others use outsourced vendors such as Roadway, UPS, and FedEx; still others use a combination. The transportation mode (such as surface versus air) influences both speed and cost. Routing decisions affect how goods are moved from stage to stage throughout the supply chain.

**Figure CE10-3**
Drivers of Supply Chain Performance

- **Facilities**
  – Location, size, operations methodology 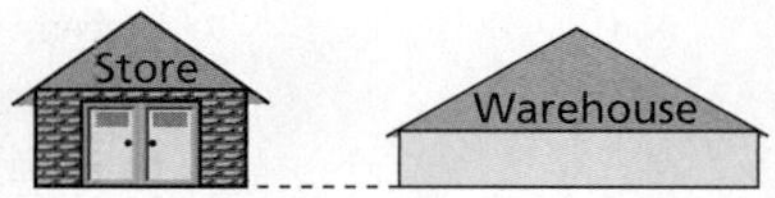
- **Inventory**
  – Size, inventory management 
- **Transportation**
  – In-house/outsourced, mode, routing 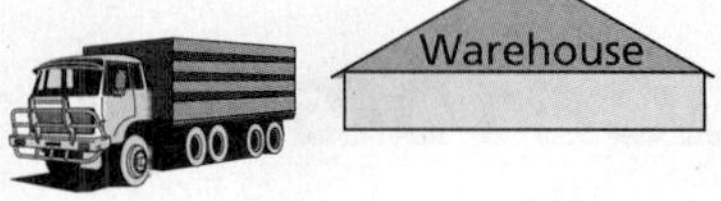
- **Information**
  – Purpose, availability, means

The fourth driver, *information*, is the factor that most concerns us. Information influences supply chain performance by affecting the ways that organizations in the supply chain make requests of one another, respond to one another, and share knowledge with one another. Figure CE10-3 lists three factors of information: purpose, availability, and means. The *purpose* of the information can be transactional, such as orders and order returns, or it can be informational, such as the sharing of inventory and customer order data. *Availability* refers to the ways in which organizations share their information; that is, which organizations have access to which information and when. Finally, *means* refers to the methods by which the information is transmitted. Modern organizations use some version of SOA and Web services for exchanging information.

We will expand on the role of information in the supply chain throughout this chapter extension. For now, however, we consider two of the ways that information can affect supply chain performance: supply chain profitability and the bullwhip effect.

## QCE10-4 HOW DOES SUPPLY CHAIN PROFITABILITY DIFFER FROM ORGANIZATIONAL PROFITABILITY?

Each of the organizations in Figures CE10-1 and Figure CE10-2 is an independent company, with its own goals and objectives. Each has a competitive strategy that may differ from the competitive strategies of the other organizations in the supply chain. Left alone, each organization will maximize its own profit, regardless of the consequences of its actions on the profitability of the others.

**Supply chain profitability** is the difference between the sum of the revenue generated by the supply chain and the sum of the costs that all organizations in the supply chain incur to obtain that revenue. In general, the maximum profit to the supply chain *will not* occur if each organization in the supply chain maximizes its own profits in isolation. Usually, the profitability of the supply chain increases if one or more of the organizations operates at less than its own maximum profitability.

To see why this is so, consider your purchase of the ski equipment from REI. Assume that you purchase either the complete package of skis, bindings, boots, and poles or you purchase nothing. For example, if you cannot obtain boots, the utility of skis, bindings, and poles is nil. In this situation, an outage of boots causes a loss of revenue not just for the boots, but also for the entire ski package.

According to Figure CE10-2, REI buys boots from distributor 2 and the rest of the package from distributor 1. If boots are unavailable, distributor 2 loses the revenue of selling boots, but does not suffer any of the revenue loss from the nonsale of skis, bindings, and poles. Thus, distributor 2 will carry an inventory of boots that is optimized considering only the loss of boot revenue—not considering the loss of revenue for the entire package. In this case, the profitability to the supply chain will increase if distributor 2 carries an inventory of boots that is larger than optimal for it.

In theory, the way to solve this problem is to use some form of transfer payment to induce distributor 2 to carry a larger boot inventory. For example, REI could pay distributor 2 a premium for the sale of boots in packages and recover a portion of this premium from distributor 1, who would recover a portion of it from the manufacturers, and so forth, up the supply chain. In truth, such a solution is difficult to implement. For higher-priced items or for items with very high volume, there can be an economic benefit for creating an information system to identify such a situation. If the dynamic is long-lasting, it might be worthwhile to negotiate the transfer-payment agreements. All of this would require a comprehensive supply-chain-wide information system.

## QCE10-5 WHAT IS THE BULLWHIP EFFECT?

The **bullwhip effect** is a phenomenon in which the variability in the size and timing of orders increases at each stage up the supply chain, from customer to supplier (in Figure CE10-2, from *You* all the way back to the suppliers). Figure CE10-4 summarizes the situation. In a famous study,[2] the bullwhip effect was observed in Procter & Gamble's supply chain for diapers.

**Figure CE10-4**
The Bullwhip Effect

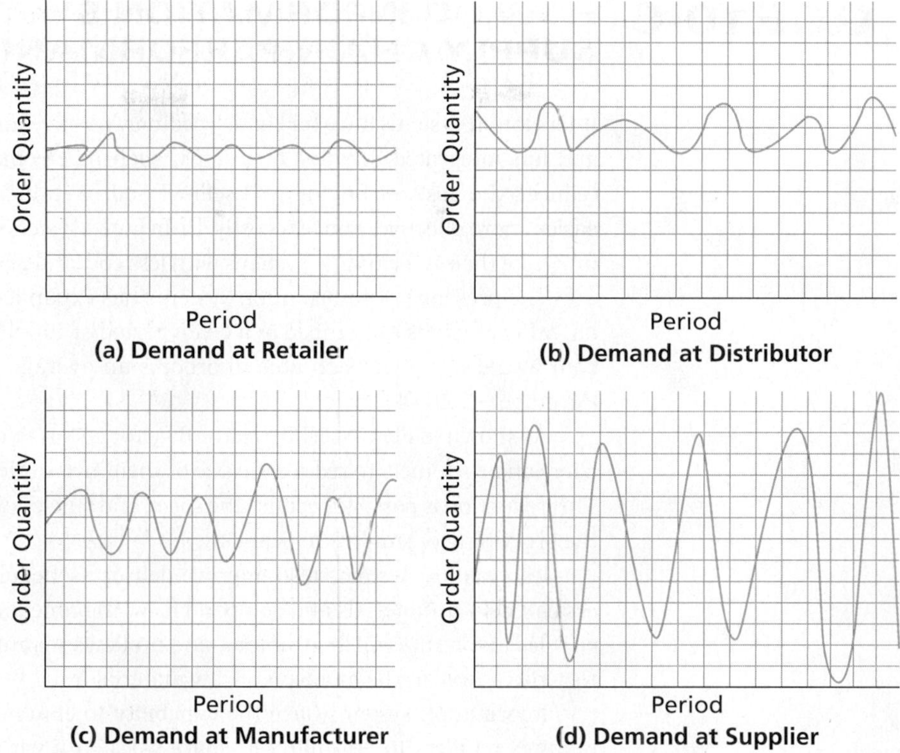


Except for random variation, diaper demand is constant. Diaper use is not seasonal; the requirement for diapers doesn't change with fashion or anything else. The number of babies determines diaper demand, and that number is constant or possibly slowly changing.

Retailers do not order from the distributor with the sale of every diaper package. The retailer waits until the diaper inventory falls below a certain level, called the *reorder quantity*. Then the retailer orders a supply of diapers, perhaps ordering a few more than it expects to sell to ensure that it does not have an outage.

The distributor receives the retailer's order and follows the same process. It waits until its supply falls below the reorder quantity, and then it reorders from the manufacturer, with perhaps an increased amount to prevent outages. The manufacturer, in turn, uses a similar process with the raw-materials suppliers.

Because of the nature of this process, small changes in demand at the retailer are amplified at each stage of the supply chain. As shown in Figure CE10-4, those small changes become quite large variations on the supplier end.

The bullwhip effect is a natural dynamic that occurs because of the multistage nature of the supply chain. It is not related to erratic consumer demand, as the study of diapers indicated. You may have seen a similar effect while driving on the freeway. One car slows down, the car just behind it slows down a bit more abruptly, which causes the third car in line to slow down even more abruptly, and so forth, until the thirtieth car or so is slamming on its brakes.

The large fluctuations of the bullwhip effect force distributors, manufacturers, and suppliers to carry larger inventories than should be necessary to meet the real consumer demand. Thus, the bullwhip effect reduces the overall profitability of the supply chain.

One way to eliminate the bullwhip effect is to give all participants in the supply chain access to consumer-demand information from the retailer. Each organization can plan its inventory or manufacturing based on the true demand (the demand from the only party that introduces money into the system) and not on the observed demand from the next organization up the supply chain. Of course, an *inter-enterprise information system* is necessary to share such data.

## QCE10-6 HOW DO INFORMATION SYSTEMS AFFECT SUPPLY CHAIN PERFORMANCE?

Information systems have had an exceedingly positive impact on supply chain performance. CRM and less-integrated functional systems, such as e-commerce sales systems, have dramatically reduced the costs of buying and selling. Sourcing, buying, and selling have all become faster, easier, more effective, and less costly. Distributed systems in the cloud have enabled businesses to integrate their information systems with less cost and greater speed and agility than ever before.

The presence of information systems has expanded supply chain **speed**, which is the dollar value of goods exchanged in a given period of time. Without information systems, Amazon.com would not have been able to process an average of 18 toys per second for 24 hours on December 1, 2014.

As shown in Figure CE10-5, a third factor is that information systems have enabled both suppliers and customers to reduce the size of their inventories and, thus, reduce their inventory costs. This reduction is possible because the speed and efficiency provided by information systems enable the processing of small orders quickly.

Information systems also improve delivery scheduling. Using information systems, suppliers can deliver materials and components at the time and in the sequence needed. Such delivery enables just-in-time (JIT) inventory, and it allows manufacturers to reduce raw materials inventory size as well as the handling of raw materials.

Information systems have the capability to eliminate the bullwhip effect, though doing so requires retailers to be willing to share sales data with the entire supply chain. Such sharing entails some risk, and many retailers refuse to release such data. Part of the problem is that the benefit of releasing such data accrues to the supply chain and not to the retailer. Although there is some possibility that eliminating the bullwhip effect will reduce prices, many retailers view it only as a *potential* possibility. In their view, it is more likely that the savings will be kept by upstream companies.

This doubt brings us to the last factor in Figure CE10-5. Information systems do not optimize supply chain profitability. They benefit the companies that actively participate in a particular information system. However, as noted, maximizing individual company profitability does not necessarily maximize supply chain profitability. Perhaps some system of transfer payments will someday be worked out.

**Figure CE10-5**
Benefits of Information Systems on Supply Chain Performance

- Reduce costs of buying and selling.
- Increase supply chain speed.
- Reduce size and cost of inventories.
- Improve delivery scheduling—enable JIT.
- Fix bullwhip effect.
- Do not optimize supply chain profitability.

# ACTIVE REVIEW

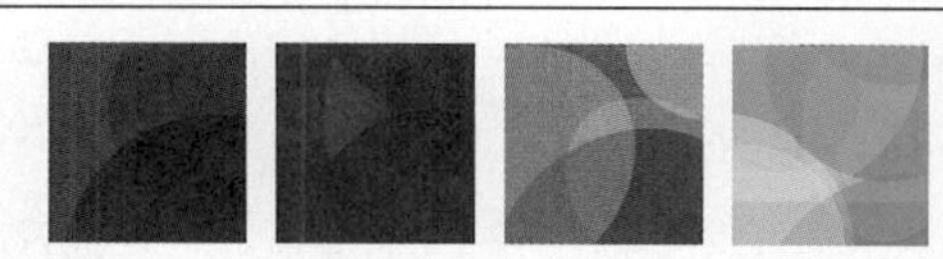

Use this Active Review to verify that you understand the ideas and concepts that answer this chapter extension's study questions.

## QCE10-1 WHAT ARE TYPICAL INTER-ENTERPRISE PROCESSES?

Define *inter-enterprise system* and explain why system management is more difficult for such processes than for functional or cross-functional processes. Give examples, other than ones in this book, of simple, standardized inter-enterprise processes and of complex, customized inter-enterprise processes.

## QCE10-2 WHAT IS A SUPPLY CHAIN?

Define *supply chain*. Explain how disintermediation affects supply chain structure. Explain why the term *chain* is misleading. Give an example of a supply chain different from the one in Figure CE10-2.

## QCE10-3 WHAT FACTORS AFFECT SUPPLY CHAIN PERFORMANCE?

Name the four factors that influence supply chain performance. Briefly explain each.

## QCE10-4 HOW DOES SUPPLY CHAIN PROFITABILITY DIFFER FROM ORGANIZATIONAL PROFITABILITY?

Explain the difference between supply chain profitability and organizational profitability. Give an example that demonstrates why maximizing organizational profitability does not necessarily lead to the maximization of supply chain profitability. Explain how, in theory, these two can be made the same.

## QCE10-5 WHAT IS THE BULLWHIP EFFECT?

Define the *bullwhip effect* and explain how it occurs. Describe why the bullwhip effect is undesirable. Explain how information systems can eliminate this effect.

## QCE10-6 HOW DO INFORMATION SYSTEMS AFFECT SUPPLY CHAIN PERFORMANCE?

List the ways in which inter-enterprise information systems affect supply chain performance. Define *speed* as it pertains to supply chains. Explain why information systems today cannot maximize supply chain profit.

# KEY TERMS AND CONCEPTS

MyMISLab™

To complete the problems with the ✪, go to EOC Discussion Questions in the MyLab.

## USING YOUR KNOWLEDGE

✪ **CE10-1.** Create a process diagram for the inter-enterprise process that exists to process debit card payments at a grocery store. Create separate swimlanes for the customer, the store, and the customer's bank. Make necessary assumptions and state them. Include sufficient detail so that your process includes the processing of a PIN.

✪ **CE10-2.** Consider the supply chain for Amazon.com. Assume that Amazon.com buys books directly from publishers and also buys from book distributors. Ignore used book sales.

**a.** Diagram this supply chain showing raw materials suppliers, manufacturers, distributors, Amazon, and customers. Because shippers are so important to Amazon.com, include them in your diagram as well.

**b.** Explain how the four factors described in QCE10-3 affect this supply chain's performance. Describe how these factors affect Amazon.com's profitability.

**c.** Do you think the bullwhip effect is a problem for this supply chain? Why or why not?

**d.** Explain how Amazon.com could use inter-enterprise information systems to obtain time and cost savings.

**CE10-3.** Search the Internet for the term *supply chain management in the cloud.* Look for at least one vendor that has a cloud-based software offering (IBM is one, but use another if you find it more interesting). Summarize the product offering. In what ways is it cloud based? In what ways will this offering appeal to multiple companies involved in a supply chain inter-enterprise IS?

MyMISLab™

Go to the Assignments section of your MyLab to complete these writing exercises.

**CE10-4.** Search the Internet for the term *supply chain management in the cloud*. Look for a case study about a company that has implemented a cloud-based supply chain system. From the case, summarize the ways that the system has resulted in the benefits listed in QCE10-6. Summarize benefits in that figure that have not been realized.

**CE10-5.** Consider the four major factors that affect supply chain performance discussed in QCE10-3. Describe how the development of self-driving cars and 3D printing (discussed in Chapter 4) will affect these four factors. How could self-driving cars and 3D printing minimize the bullwhip effect?

## ENDNOTES

1. Sunil Chopra and Peter Meindl, *Supply Chain Management*, 4th ed. (Upper Saddle River, NJ: Prentice Hall, 2004), pp. 41–43.
2. Hau L. Lee, V. Padmanabhan, and S. Whang, "The Bullwhip Effect in Supply Chains," *Sloan Management Review*, Spring 1997, pp. 93–102.

chapter extension **11**

**Chapter 8** provides the background for this extension.

# Enterprise Social Networks and Knowledge Management

STUDY QUESTIONS

**QCE11-1** HOW DO ORGANIZATIONS DEVELOP AN EFFECTIVE SMIS?

**QCE11-2** WHAT IS AN ENTERPRISE SOCIAL NETWORK (ESN)?

**QCE11-3** WHAT ARE THE BENEFITS OF KNOWLEDGE MANAGEMENT?

**QCE11-4** WHAT ARE EXPERT SYSTEMS?

**QCE11-5** WHAT ARE CONTENT MANAGEMENT SYSTEMS?

## QCE11-1 HOW DO ORGANIZATIONS DEVELOP AN EFFECTIVE SMIS?

In Chapter 8, you learned what a SMIS is, why it's important, and how it generates revenue. Now you need to know how to develop an effective SMIS that is strategically aligned with your organization's goals. You saw in Chapter 8 that SM can be used to benefit an organization, but how do you get to that point? We're not talking about a recipe for turning your organization into the next Facebook. Rather, the steps shown in Figure CE11-1 walk you through the process of developing a practical plan to effectively use existing social media platforms.

Many companies are still unsure how to use SM. They want to use it, but they're not quite sure how to do so in a way that facilitates their existing competitive strategy. Think back to Porter's model for competitive strategies from Chapter 3 (Figure 3-5). Such strategies can focus on being the cost leader or on differentiating one's products from one's competition. An organization can then employ this strategy across an entire industry, or it can focus on a particular segment within that industry. Depending on an organization's strategy, it will use different SM platforms in different ways. Again, the key is the premeditated alignment of the SMIS with the organization's chosen strategy.

Organizations know SM is popular and can be strategically beneficial. They hear about it constantly in the news, so it's not entirely their fault they want to jump on board. But social media is a relatively new development with a dizzying array of companies, platforms, and services that are constantly changing.

It's important to understand the SMIS development process outlined in Figure CE11-1 because you may be the "social media expert" at your future job. In this capacity, you may be called in to help develop the organization's SMIS. The following subsections take a closer look at each step in the development process.

### STEP 1: DEFINE YOUR GOALS

This may sound cliché, but the first step in developing an SMIS is to clearly define what the organization wants to achieve with SM. As previously mentioned, your goals must be clear, deliberate, and aligned with the organization's competitive strategy. Without clearly defined goals, you won't know whether your SM effort was successful.

As you learned in Chapter 3, the goals for each organization will be unique. For organizations that choose a differentiation strategy, goals for SM might include better employee recruiting, quicker product development, becoming an industry product leader, or increased customer

CE11

**Figure CE11-1**
Social Media Plan Development

loyalty. In general, most organizations will include increased brand awareness, conversion rates, Web site traffic, or user engagement as goals. Figure CE11-2 gives you examples of how these goals might manifest themselves in an organization's SM activities.

## STEP 2: IDENTIFY SUCCESS METRICS

After you know what you want to accomplish using SM, you then need to identify metrics that will indicate whether you've achieved your goals. These are referred to as **success metrics** or **key performance indicators (KPI)**. **Metrics** are simply measurements used to track performance. Every organization has different metrics for success. For example, a law firm may be interested in measuring billable hours, whereas a hospital may measure the number of patients seen or procedures performed. Similarly, manufacturers may look at units produced or operational efficiency.

The hard part in identifying success metrics is identifying the right ones. The right metrics help you make better decisions, while the wrong metrics are meaningless and don't affect your decision making. For instance, measuring the number of registered users on your site may be interesting, but it's not really meaningful. What *really* matters is the number of *active* users on your site each month. Twitter, for example, had 938 million total registered users in late 2014 but only 241 million monthly active users.[1] Metrics that sound good but don't improve your decision making are commonly referred to as **vanity metrics**.

Figure CE11-3 shows examples of possible success metrics for the goals mentioned in Figure CE11-2. Remember, however, that not all metrics are values you will want to increase. Whereas you may want to maximize a metric like **conversion rate**,[2] or the percent of people who achieve

**Figure CE11-2**
Common Social Media Strategic Goals

| Goal | Description | Example of SM Goal |
|---|---|---|
| Increased Brand Awareness | Increase the extent that users recognize a brand | Organization's brand is mentioned in more user tweets |
| Increased Conversion Rates | Increase the frequency that someone takes a desired action | More users like the organization's Facebook page |
| Increased Web Site Traffic | Increase the quantity, frequency, duration, and depth of visits to a Web site | A Google+ post helps increase traffic to an organization's site |
| Increased User Engagement | Increase the extent to which users interact with a site, application, or other media | Users comment more often on an organization's LinkedIn posts |

**Figure CE11-3**
Common Social Media Metrics

| Goal | Metrics |
|---|---|
| Increased Brand Awareness | Total Twitter followers; audience growth rate; brand mentions in SM; Klout or Kred score |
| Increased Conversion Rates | Click rate on SM content; assisted social conversions |
| Increased Web Site Traffic | Visitor frequency rate; referral traffic from SM |
| Increased User Engagement | Number of SM interactions; reshares of SM content |

a certain result, you will probably want to minimize other metrics like **bounce rate**, or the percent of people who visit your Web site and then immediately leave. As in sports, sometimes you want a high score (basketball), and other times you want a low score (golf). It just depends on what you're measuring.

## STEP 3: IDENTIFY THE TARGET AUDIENCE

The next step in creating an effective SMIS is to clearly identify your target audience. Chances are, it's not going to be everyone. For example, if you're Caterpillar Inc. and trying to use social media to sell more D11 dozers, your target audience probably won't include many teenagers. Organizations go to great lengths to identify their target audience because it helps them focus their marketing efforts.

Once you've identified your target audience, you need to find out which SM platforms audience members use. Certain social media platforms attract certain audiences. For example, about 70 percent of Pinterest users are women,[3] 46 percent of Tumblr users are between ages 16 and 24,[4] and 90 percent of Instagram users are under age 35.[5] Also, according to Quantcast, 84 percent of LinkedIn users are over age 25.[6] As these statistics illustrate, your target audience should certainly influence which SM platforms you use.

## STEP 4: DEFINE YOUR VALUE

After pinpointing your target audience, you'll need to define the value you'll provide to that audience. Why should these users listen to you, go to your Web site, like your posts, or tweet about your products? Are you providing news, entertainment, education, employee recruiting, or information? In essence, you need to define what you are going to give your audience in exchange for making a connection with you.

Shopping is a good metaphor to explain how you can do this. When you go shopping, you see something of value, then you exchange your *financial* capital (money) with the business for the item you value. The same is true of social media. Your audience is constantly browsing for things of value, and they have *social* capital to spend. They may eventually spend financial capital at your Web site, but with SM, it's the social capital that is most important. So, you need to define what you're going to offer users in exchange for their social capital.

Take LinkedIn as an example. LinkedIn builds social capital by helping people find jobs, build a professional network, join special interest groups, get introduced to prospective clients, and reconnect with past colleagues. From an organizational perspective, LinkedIn allows recruiters to quickly identify and contact potential hires from a large pool of candidates. This lowers hiring costs and improves the quality of new hires.

If you're unsure how your organization would add value to its social media offerings, start by performing a **competitive analysis** to identify the strengths and weaknesses in your competitor's use of social media. See what they're doing right and what they're doing wrong. Try to identify specifically how they provide value to their audience. Then consider whether a similar successful strategy would work for your organization.

### STEP 5: MAKE PERSONAL CONNECTIONS

The true value of social media can only be achieved when organizations use SM to interact with customers, employees, and partners in a more personal, humane, relationship-oriented way.

According to recent studies, younger users are more skeptical of organizational messages and may no longer listen to them. A 2014 CivicScience study found that 58 percent of younger consumers, ages 18 through 29, were more influenced by social media chatter than either TV ads or Internet ads.[7] Interestingly, the study also found that only 29 percent of consumers over the age of 55 thought social media chatter was more influential than TV or Internet advertising. Such skepticism by younger consumers is understandable. They grew up with more sources of information and feel comfortable using social media. Skepticism of organizational messages gives a competitive advantage to organizations that can make personal connections with users via social media.

Today, people want informed, useful interactions that help them solve particular problems and satisfy unique needs. They increasingly ignore prepackaged organizational messages that tout product benefits. To help ensure your organization's message isn't ignored, engage audience members, ask them questions, and respond to their posts. Avoid hard-selling products, overwhelming them with content, and contacting them too often.

A good example of how to make personal connections is the sales force in Apple stores that has been trained to act as customer problem-solving consultants and not as sellers of products. An organization's use of social media needs to mirror this behavior; otherwise, social media is nothing more than another channel for classic advertising.

### STEP 6: GATHER AND ANALYZE DATA

Finally, when creating a social media strategy, you need to gather the right amount of data necessary to make the most informed decision you can. You can use online analytical tools like Google Analytics, Facebook Page Insights, Clicky, or KISSmetrics to measure the success metrics you defined earlier. These tools will show you statistical information such as which tweets get the most attention, which posts generate the most traffic, and which SM platform generates the most referrals.

Then you can refine your use of social media based on the performance of your success metrics. Be sure to rely on analysis of hard data, not anecdotes from friends. Also, remember that the SM landscape is changing rapidly, and today's winners could be tomorrow's losers. MySpace, for example, was the top SM site in late 2007 valued at $65 billion, but then succumbed to Facebook's success and was sold for $35 million in 2011.[8] Users may shift away from current SM giants like Facebook toward a group of more customized applications like Instagram, Twitter, Snapchat, and WhatsApp.[9] Allow your use of social media to be flexible enough to change with the times.

**Much like organizations use social media to shape their brands, you can use social media to develop a personal brand. But what is a personal brand, and how does it help you engage with others? The Guide on pages 540–541 explores these questions.**

Senior managers need to see regular progress reports about how SM is affecting the organization. They also need to be educated about changes in the social media landscape. Watch for SM success stories and communicate them with upper management.

## QCE11-2 WHAT IS AN ENTERPRISE SOCIAL NETWORK (ESN)?

An **enterprise social network (ESN)** is a software platform that uses social media to facilitate cooperative work of people *within* an organization. Instead of using outward-facing SM platforms like Facebook and Twitter, ESNs use specialized enterprise social software designed to be employed inside the organization. These applications may incorporate the same functionality used by traditional social media, including blogs, microblogs, status updates, image and video sharing, personal sites, and wikis. The primary goal of ESNs is to improve communication, collaboration, knowledge sharing, problem solving, and decision making within organizations.

## ENTERPRISE 2.0

In 2006, Andrew McAfee wrote an article about how dynamic user-generated content systems, then termed **Web 2.0**, could be used in an enterprise setting. He described **Enterprise 2.0** as the use of emergent social software platforms within companies.[10] In other words, the term *Enterprise 2.0* refers to the *use* of enterprise social networks.

McAfee defined six characteristics that he refers to with the acronym **SLATES** (see Figure CE11-4).[11] First, workers want to be able to *search* for content inside the organization just like they do on the Web. Most workers find that searching is more effective than navigating content structures such as lists and tables of contents. Second, workers want to access organizational content via *links*, just as they do on the Web. They also want to *author* organizational content using blogs, wikis, discussion groups, published presentations, and so on.

According to McAfee, a fourth characteristic of ESNs is that their content is *tagged*, just like content on the Web, and these tags are organized into structures, as is done on the Web at sites like Delicious (*www.delicious.com*). These structures organize tags as a taxonomy does, but, unlike taxonomies, they are not preplanned; they emerge organically. In other words, ESNs employ a **folksonomy**, or a content structure that emerges from the processing of many user tags. Fifth, workers want applications that enable them to rate tagged content and to use the tags to predict content that will be of interest to them (as with Pandora), a process McAfee refers to as *extensions.* Finally, workers want relevant content pushed to them; or, in McAfee's terminology, they want to be *signaled* when something of interest to them happens in organizational content.

The potential problem with ESNs is the quality of their dynamic process. Because the benefits of an ESN result from emergence, there is no way to control for either effectiveness or efficiency. It's a messy process about which little can be predicted.

## CHANGING COMMUNICATION

The development of ESNs didn't happen overnight. Over the past 35 years advances in technology have progressively changed the way organizations communicate.

**Figure CE11-4**
McAfee's SLATES Model

| Enterprise 2.0 Component | Remarks |
|---|---|
| Search | People have more success searching than they do in finding from structured content. |
| Links | Links to enterprise resources (like on the Web). |
| Authoring | Create enterprise content via blogs, wikis, discussion groups, presentations, etc. |
| Tags | Flexible tagging (like Delicious) results in folksonomies of enterprise content. |
| Extensions | Using usage patterns to offer enterprise content via tag processing (like the style of Pandora). |
| Signals | Pushing enterprise content to users based on subscriptions and alerts. |

# Developing Your Personal Brand

The Guide in Chapter 8 (pages 236–237) discusses the need to protect your personal digital data from being exploited. Now, let's consider the other side of that coin. Instead of attempting to minimize the bad, suppose we ask: How can you use social media to maximize the good?

Leading professionals use social media to build their personal brand. You may be too young, too inexperienced, and not yet unique enough to have a personal brand, but, then again, maybe not. And even if now isn't the right time to build a personal brand, you will need to have, build, and maintain your personal brand at some point in the future if you want to be a business leader.

So, what is "building a personal brand"? It's not embarrassing self-promotion. It's not self-advertising, and it's not a resume of your recent experience. It is, instead, the means by which you conduct authentic relationships with the market for your talents and abilities. That market might be your professional colleagues, your employer, your fellow employees, your competition, or anyone else who cares about what you care about.

As a business professional, how do you create authentic relationships that are less transactional and more personal? You start by realizing that the people who consume your services are not just bosses and colleagues, but rather full-fledged human beings with the rich stew of complexity that all humans have. With this idea in mind, can you use social media to transform your relationships from being transactional in nature to more personal?

Such a transformation is difficult. You don't want to share every detail of your personal life on your professional blog; few readers will care about your vacation in the Bahamas. However, they might want to know what you read while lying on the beach, why you read it, and what you learned from it—or perhaps how disappointed you were about what you didn't learn. But your report has to be authentic. If you're reading Kierkegaard or Aristotle for the purpose of showing erudition on your personal blog, you missed the point. But if Kierkegaard has something interesting to say about the ethics of the latest business scandal that affects your professional interests, many readers who share those interests will want to know. And they will then have a way to approach you on a common interest. That common interest may lead to an exciting new job opportunity, or maybe it will lead to a fulfilling new relationship, or maybe it will go nowhere. You just don't know.

Be aware, however, that maintaining a professional brand can become all consuming. Just like personal Facebook use can suck up most of your free time, so, too, can maintaining your professional brand. To help avoid this situation, start modestly and work up from there.

When engaging in professional branding efforts, always be guided by your personal strategy. Consider Figure 3-9 again, in light of your personal competitive strategy. What is your personal competitive advantage? Why would someone choose you, your expertise, or your work products over others? Then, with answers to these questions in mind, start building your personal brand. Again, be sure your efforts focus on creating authentic relationships and not on shameless advertising.

Realize, too, that a strong personal brand is essential to some careers. For example, if you want to be an independent consultant, say, an expert on privacy and control for cloud data storage, you'll need to invest considerable time developing and maintaining your professional brand. But whether or not it's essential, having a strong personal brand is an asset in any field, in any job. And you can be sure that if you don't have a good personal brand, one of your competitors will.

## DISCUSSION QUESTIONS

**1.** Using your own words, define and describe a personal brand.

**2.** Describe how you could use social media to make an existing professional contact more personal in nature while still maintaining your privacy.

**3.** Pick a contemporary topic of interest in your major field of study. For example, if you're an operations major, pick something like *3D printing*. If you're an accounting major, choose something like *auditing in the cloud*. (Read question 4, however, before you pick.)

**a.** Search the Web for opinions about the realities, contemporary uses, big issues and problems, or other interesting dimensions of your topic.

**b.** Find two or three experts in that topic, and go to their professional brand sites. That brand might be a blog, a Web page, a collection of articles, an SM site on Facebook or LinkedIn, or some other public statement of their professionalism.

**c.** Which of the sites is the best? Explain why you think so.

**4.** Suppose you become an expert in the topic you used in your answer to question 3. Think about your experiences that relate to that topic. It could be experiences in class, out of class with fellow students, or in conversations with roommates. It could be something that happened at your job at McDonald's. Whatever.

**a.** Make a list of 10 such experiences. Go back in time as far as necessary to identify 10 experiences.

**b.** Describe how you could use social media, including blogs, to present five of the best of those 10 experiences in a way that helps build your professional brand.

**5.** Reflect on your answers to questions 1–4.

**a.** Do you think having a personal brand is important for you? Explain why or why not. (The answer to this question may not be *yes*, and for good reasons.)

**b.** What was the most difficult task for you when formulating your answers to question 4?

**c.** Summarize what you have learned from this exercise about how you might get more value from your college experiences.

*Source:* fergregory/Fotolia

Prior to 1980, communication in the United States was restricted to a few **communication channels**, or means of delivering messages. There were three major national TV networks and no more than a half-dozen major national newspapers. Consumers got their news twice a day: in the morning paper and the evening news. A small number of people decided which stories were told. You got what you were given with few alternatives.

Communication within organizations was similarly restricted. Employees could communicate with their immediate supervisor and coworkers in their vicinity. It was difficult for employees of large corporations to get private meetings with the CEO or to communicate with their counterparts in other countries. If an employee had a good idea, it was passed up through his or her boss to senior management. As a result, it was common for bosses to claim subordinates' ideas as their own.

In recent decades, the Internet, Web sites, social networking, email, cable TV, and smartphones have radically altered existing communication channels. At the societal level, you can now get your news instantly from hundreds of different sources. Traditional news outlets like newspapers have struggled to adapt to changes in traditional communication channels.

Communication channels within corporations have changed in equally dramatic ways. Using ESNs, employees can now bypass managers and post ideas directly for the CEO to read. They can also quickly identify internal subject matter experts to solve unforeseen problems. In addition, ESNs enable collaboration with teams dispersed across the globe.

To better understand the potential impacts of ESNs, let's consider an example. In 2012, Yammer (a Microsoft subsidiary) conducted a case study analyzing how restaurant chain Red Robin used an ESN to transform its business.[12] The CIO of Red Robin, Chris Laping, rolled out Yammer to Red Robin's 26,000 employees across 450 restaurants in an effort to give line employees a voice. This effort yielded more than just stronger employee engagement.

When Red Robin rolled out its new Pig Out burger, for instance, the customer response was disappointing. Employees used Yammer to give management immediate feedback about how the Pig Out recipe could be fixed. Within 4 months, the new and improved burger was ready to go. Here, using Yammer to improve internal communication resulted in an increase in organizational responsiveness. The result was a reduction in the amount of time needed to revamp the menu, from 12 to 18 months down to just 4 months.

In another example, Red Robin's CFO offered a $1,000 employee bonus for the best cost-saving idea. The winning idea was reusable kids' cups that saved hundreds of thousands of dollars. Laping attributes the cost savings to the ESN, stating, "I'm convinced that idea would never have surfaced if we didn't have a social network."

## DEPLOYING SUCCESSFUL ENTERPRISE SOCIAL NETWORKS

The use of ESNs in organizations is new, and organizations are still learning how to use ESNs successfully (which creates fascinating job opportunities for you, by the way.) Before deploying an ESN, organizations should develop a strategic plan for using SM *internally* using the same process they used for their *external* social media use. Once a strategic plan has been created, an ESN can then be implemented.

Deploying new systems—including ESNs—can be problematic, so the organization's strategic plan should be sure to address possible challenges, including the likelihood of employee resistance. Will employees adopt the new system? Not everyone uses social media platforms in their personal lives, so why should they use them at work?

In order to ensure successful implementation of an ESN, organizations can also follow industry **best practices**, or methods that have been shown to produce successful results in prior implementations. You'll learn more about systems implementation in Chapter 12. Figure CE11-5 shows a few best practices for implementing ESNs. Read through the 16 items and reflect on what you went through when you first started using SM. Think about how important your friends were in your decision to start. Having an internal champion, or defender of your internal ESN, is equally important.

**Figure CE11-5**
ESN Implementation Best Practices

| | ESN Deployment Best Practices |
|---|---|
| Strategy | 1. Define how the ESN supports the organization's existing goals and objectives.<br>2. Define success metrics.<br>3. Communicate the ESN strategy to all users.<br>4. Convey an expectation of organization-wide ESN adoption. |
| Sponsorship | 5. Identify an executive sponsor to promote the ESN.<br>6. Identify ESN champions within each organizational unit.<br>7. Encourage champions to recruit users.<br>8. Identify groups that would benefit most from the ESN. |
| Support | 9. Provide all users access to the ESN.<br>10. Mandate processes to be used within the ESN.<br>11. Provide incentives for ESN adoption and use.<br>12. Provide employee training and ESN demonstrations. |
| Success | 13. Measure ESN effectiveness via success metrics.<br>14. Evaluate how the ESN supports the organization's strategy.<br>15. Promote ESN success stories.<br>16. Continuously look for ways to use the ESN more effectively. |

## QCE11-3 WHAT ARE THE BENEFITS OF KNOWLEDGE MANAGEMENT?

Nothing is more frustrating for a manager to contemplate than the situation in which one employee struggles with a problem that another employee knows how to solve easily. Managers may be similarly troubled to learn that a large order has been returned because the customer could not perform a basic operation with the product that many employees (and other customers) can readily perform—or even worse, to learn that someone in the customer's organization knows how to use the product, but the people who bought the product weren't aware of this.

**Knowledge management (KM)** is the process of creating value from intellectual capital and sharing that knowledge with employees, managers, suppliers, customers, and others who need it. The goal of knowledge management is to prevent the kinds of problems just described.

KM existed in the days before social media, and we will discuss two such KM systems in QCE11-4 and QCE11-5. However, notice in the preceding paragraph that the scope of KM (employees, managers, suppliers, customers, and others) is similar to the scope of an ESN.

Before we turn to the specific technologies mentioned in QCE11-4 and QCE11-5, let's consider the overall goals and benefits of KM. KM benefits organizations in two fundamental ways:

- It improves process quality.
- It increases team strength.

As you know, process quality is measured by effectiveness and efficiency, and knowledge management can improve both. KM enables employees to share knowledge with each other and with customers and other partners. By doing so, it enables the employees in the organization to better achieve the organization's strategy. At the same time, sharing knowledge enables employees to solve problems more quickly and to accomplish work with less time and fewer resources, hence improving process efficiency.

Additionally, recall from the Chapter Extension 2 that successful teams not only accomplish their assigned tasks, but they also grow in capability—both as a team and as individuals. By sharing what they know through KM, team members learn from one another, avoid making repetitive mistakes, and grow as business professionals.

For example, consider the help desk at any organization, say, one that provides support for electronic components like iPhones. When a user has a problem with an iPhone, he or she might contact Apple support for help. The customer service department has, collectively, seen just about any problem that can ever occur with an iPhone. Thus, the organization as a whole knows how to solve the user's problem. However, that is no guarantee that a particular support representative knows how to solve that problem. The goal of KM is to enable employees to use knowledge possessed collectively by people in the organization, thus avoiding the situation in which any given support representative doesn't know how to answer a user's question. By preventing this from happening, KM improves both process quality and team capability.

## QCE11-4 WHAT ARE EXPERT SYSTEMS?

Organizations are inanimate; they themselves are not knowledgeable. Rather, it is the employees of organizations who possess knowledge. The earliest KM systems, called expert systems, attempted to directly capture employee expertise. These systems existed long before social media; in fact, they were in use well before the Internet.

**Expert systems** are rule-based systems that encode human knowledge in the form of **If/Then rules**. Such rules are statements specifying that if a particular condition exists, then some action should be taken. Figure CE11-6 shows an example of a few rules that could be part of a medical expert system for diagnosing heart disease. In this set of rules, the system examines various factors for heart disease and computes a *CardiacRiskFactor.* Depending on the value of that risk factor, other variables are given values. Unlike this example, real-world expert systems may consist of hundreds, if not thousands, of rules.

The programs that process a set of rules are called **expert systems shells**. Typically, the shell processes rules until no value changes. At that point, the values of all the variables are reported as results.

To create the system of rules, the expert system development team interviews human experts in the domain of interest. For example, the rules in Figure CE11-6 would have been obtained by interviewing cardiologists who are known to be particularly adept at diagnosing cardiac disease. The resulting system then encodes the knowledge of these highly skilled experts and makes it available to less-skilled or less-knowledgeable professionals.

Many expert systems were created in the late 1980s and early 1990s, but only a few have enjoyed success. The majority of these systems suffer from three major disadvantages. First, they are difficult and expensive to develop, in part because they require many labor hours from both experts in the domain under study and designers of expert systems. This expense is compounded by the high opportunity cost of tying up domain experts. Such experts are normally some of the most sought-after employees in an organization.

Second, expert systems are difficult to maintain. Because of the nature of rule-based systems, the introduction of a new rule in the middle of hundreds of others can have unexpected

**Figure CE11-6**
Example of If/Then Rules

```
Other rules here...

IF CardiacRiskFactor = 'Null' THEN Set CardiacRiskFactor = 0
IF PatientSex = 'Male' THEN Add 3 to CardiacRiskFactor
IF PatientAge >55 THEN Add 2 to CardiacRiskFactor
IF FamilyHeartHistory = 'True' THEN Add 5 to CardiacRiskFactor
IF CholesterolScore = 'Problematic' THEN Add 4 to CardiacRiskFactor
IF BloodPressure = 'Problematic' THEN Add 3 to CardiacRiskFactor
IF CardiacRiskFactor >15 THEN Set EchoCardiagramTest = 'Schedule'
...
Other rules here...
```

consequences. Even a small change can cause very different outcomes. Unfortunately, such side effects cannot be predicted or eliminated; they are the nature of complex rule-based systems.

Third, expert systems were unable to live up to the high expectations set by their name. Initially, proponents of expert systems hoped to be able to duplicate the performance of highly trained experts, like doctors. It turned out, however, that no expert system has the same diagnostic ability as knowledgeable, skilled, and experienced doctors. Even when expert systems were developed that came close in ability, changes in medical technology required constant changing of the expert systems, and the problems caused by unexpected consequences made such changes very expensive.

The few expert systems that have been successful have addressed more restricted tasks than duplicating a doctor's diagnostic ability. Such systems typically address problems such as checking for harmful prescription drug interactions or configuring products to meet customer specifications. These systems require many fewer rules and are therefore more manageable to maintain. However, unless expert systems technology gets a boost from massively parallel computing, their problems will cause them to fade from use.

## QCE11-5 WHAT ARE CONTENT MANAGEMENT SYSTEMS?

A **content management system (CMS)** is an information system that supports the management and delivery of documents and other expressions of employee knowledge. Typical users of content management systems are companies that sell complicated products and want to share their knowledge of those products with employees and customers.

Someone at Toyota, for example, knows how to change the timing belt on the four-cylinder 2015 Toyota Camry. Toyota wants to share that knowledge with car owners, mechanics, and Toyota employees. Similarly, Cisco wants to share with network administrators its knowledge about how to determine whether a Cisco router is malfunctioning. And Microsoft wants to share with the data miners of the world its knowledge about how to use its Data Transformation Services product to move data from an Oracle database into Excel.

### WHAT ARE THE CHALLENGES OF CONTENT MANAGEMENT?

Content management systems face serious challenges. First, most content databases are huge; some have thousands of individual documents, pages, and graphics. As an example, Figure CE11-7 shows the scale of the content management problem at Facebook (*www.facebook.com*).

A second challenge is that CMS content is dynamic. The size of the content store in Figure CE11-7 is impressive, but the more critical number is the amount of new or changed content per day: 500+ TB.[13] This includes billions of pieces of new content, 300 million photos, and 4.5 billion likes submitted by 802 million daily users *every day.*[14] Clearly, managing content versions is crucial to the success of Facebook—and all other CMSs as well.

**Figure CE11-7**
Document Management at Facebook.com

- 4.75 billion pieces of content per day
- 4.5 billion Like actions per day
- 300 million photos per day
- 1.28 billion monthly active users
- 802 million daily users
- 500+ TB of new data per day
- Scans 105 TB of data each half hour
- 100 PB of data in a single cluster

Still another complication for content management systems is that documents do not exist in isolation from each other. Documents refer to one another, and multiple documents may refer to the same product or procedure. Thus, when one of these documents changes, others must change as well. To manage these connections, content management systems must maintain linkages among documents so that content dependencies are known and used to maintain document consistency.

A fourth complication is that document contents are perishable. In other words, documents become obsolete and need to be altered, removed, or replaced. Consider, for example, what happens when a new product is announced. As of this writing, Microsoft is preparing to release Windows 10 (Windows Threshold) as a future product. The day it ships, however, all content referring to Windows 10 as a future product will be outdated. All of Microsoft's literature (including Web sites) will need to be altered to reflect that Windows 10 is available.

Finally, consider the content management problem for multinational companies. 3M, for example, has tens of thousands of products, some of which are harmful when used improperly. Therefore, 3M must publish product safety data for all such products in all languages. Every document, in whatever language it was authored, must be translated into all languages before it can be published on 3M's site. And when one of these data sheets changes, all of the translated versions must change as well.

## WHAT ARE CONTENT MANAGEMENT APPLICATION ALTERNATIVES?

Three common alternatives for content management applications are:

- In-house custom applications
- Off-the-shelf applications
- Public search engines

Let's take a closer look at each.

### In-house Custom Applications

In the past, organizations developed their own in-house content management applications. A customer support department, for example, might develop in-house database applications to track customer problems and their resolution. Similarly, operations might develop an in-house system to track machine maintenance procedures. Like all custom applications, however, custom content management applications are expensive to develop and maintain. Unless the domain of the content management is crucial to the organization's strategy and no off-the-shelf solution is available, most organizations today choose not to support a custom CMS application.

### Off-the-Shelf Applications

Because of the expense of custom applications, many organizations today use off-the-shelf software. Horizontal market products like Microsoft SharePoint provide generalized facilities to manage documents and other content types. As you learned in Chapter Extension 1, SharePoint supports document libraries and can track and manage document versions. Additionally, SharePoint provides workflows for automated document processing and also supports document search. Office 365 Professional provides SharePoint document processing and access in the cloud, using mobile devices when needed.

Some organizations choose vertical market off-the-shelf applications. An accounting firm, for example, may license a vertical market application to manage document flow for the processing of tax returns or the management of audit documents. Another example is law firms that use vertical applications to manage documents for court cases and other work.

Such off-the-shelf products have considerably more functionality than most in-house systems, and they are far less expensive to maintain. Keep in mind, however, that software is just one component of a content management system. Organizations need to develop data structures and procedures for managing their content, and they also need to train users.

## Public Search Engines

The largest collection of documents ever assembled exists on the Internet, and the world's best-known document search engine is Google. When you Google a term, you are tapping into the world's largest content management system. This system, however, was not designed for a particular KM purpose; it just emerged.

Because Google searches through all public sites of all organizations, Google is usually the fastest and easiest way to find a public document. This often is true even within an organization. It may be easier, for example, for a General Motors employee to find a General Motors document using Google than using an in-house search engine. Google will have crawled through the General Motors site and will have indexed all documents using its superior technology.

This is content management on the cheap. Just put documents on a public server and let Google or Bing do the rest! However, documents that reside behind a corporate firewall are not publicly accessible and will not be reachable by Google or other search engines. Organizations must index their own proprietary documents and provide their own search capability for them.

# ACTIVE REVIEW

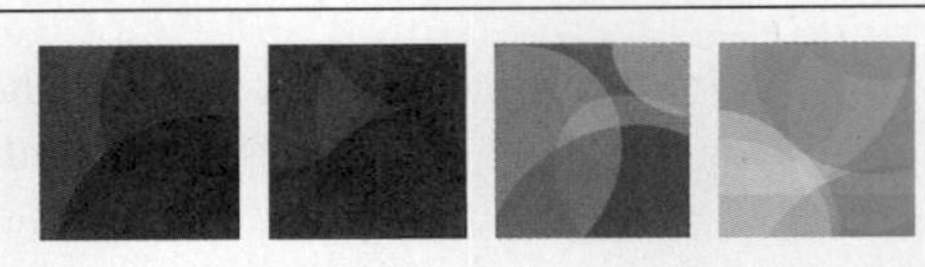

Use this Active Review to verify that you understand the ideas and concepts that answer this chapter extension's study questions.

## QCE11-1 HOW DO ORGANIZATIONS DEVELOP AN EFFECTIVE SMIS?

Discuss why aligning the development of an SMIS with the organization's strategy is important. Describe the process of developing an effective SMIS. List four common social media goals and describe why they are important. Define *metrics, success metrics,* and *vanity metrics* and give examples of metrics that could be measured for the four goals mentioned above. Describe the importance of making personal connections with users.

## QCE11-2 WHAT IS AN ENTERPRISE SOCIAL NETWORK (ESN)?

Define *enterprise social network (ESN)* and describe the primary goal of an ESN. Define *Web 2.0* and *Enterprise 2.0*. Explain each element of the SLATES model. Explain how changes in communication channels have changed the way organizations communicate with employees. Give an example of how an ESN could benefit an organization. Define *best practices* and explain how the ESN implementation best practices listed in Figure CE11-5 could improve adoption of the ESN.

## QCE11-3 WHAT ARE THE BENEFITS OF KNOWLEDGE MANAGEMENT?

Define *knowledge management (KM)*. Explain five key benefits of KM. Briefly describe three types of KM systems.

## QCE11-4 WHAT ARE EXPERT SYSTEMS?

Define *expert systems, If/Then rules,* and *expert systems shell.* Explain how expert system rules are created. Summarize the three major disadvantages of expert systems and assess the future of these systems.

## QCE11-5 WHAT ARE CONTENT MANAGEMENT SYSTEMS?

Define *content management system (CMS)*. Give two examples, other than those in this text, of the use of a CMS. Describe five challenges organizations face for managing content. Name three CMS application alternatives and explain the use of each.

## KEY TERMS AND CONCEPTS



MyMISLab™

To complete the problems with the ✪, go to EOC Discussion Questions in the MyLab.

## USING YOUR KNOWLEDGE

✪ **CE11-1.** Visit your university's public Web site. Describe how social media might be used to achieve your university's strategic goals. Explain how your university might benefit from an enterprise social network.

✪ **CE11-2.** Develop the If/Then rules for an expert system that determines whether a particular student can enroll in a class. For your system, is there a need for multiple passes through the rule set? How accurate do you think your system would be? Which of the disadvantages of expert systems described in the text apply to this system?

**CE11-3.** Consider the test bank that students in a fraternity, sorority, or other organization maintain. Is such a test bank an example of a content management system? Is it a computer-based system? Does it need to be computer-based to be considered a content management system? If it is not computer-based, describe advantages of having it be computer-based. What features and functions would you want in such a system? How could such a test bank be indexed? By professor? By class? What other dimensions might be used for indexing?

## MyMISLab™

Go to the Assignments section of your MyLab to complete these writing exercises.

**CE11-4.** Suppose you are hired by a local farming cooperative to develop its SMIS. The cooperative wants to promote eating healthy foods, increase awareness about its weekly farmer's market, increase traffic to its Web site, and sell more of its products directly to consumers. Which success metrics would indicate that the cooperative has achieved its goals? Who would be its target audience? What value would the cooperative's SMIS provide to its customers? How could the cooperative make personal connections with its customers? Which SM platform(s) would you recommend the cooperative use? Justify your recommendation.

**CE11-5.** Assume you developed the system in question CE11-3. Is it legal to use such a system? Is it ethical? Assume that your system is unavailable to all students. Is it unfair? How could you apply the skills and knowledge you obtained in developing such a system to your future career?

**CE11-6.** Explain how the challenges for content management systems described in this chapter extension would apply to the test bank system in your answer to question CE11-3.

## ENDNOTES

1. Jim Edwards, "Here's the Vast Number of People Who Abandon Twitter That Dick Costolo Refuses to Talk About," *Business Insider*, February 6, 2014, accessed May 5, 2015, *www.businessinsider.com/number-of-users-who-abandon-twitter-2014-2*.
2. While a *conversion* is having someone take a desired action, an *assisted social conversion* is when social media helps the conversion take place.
3. Sarah Perez, "Pinterest Goes After the Male Demographic with Debut of New Search Filters," *TechCrunch*, January 23, 2015, accessed May 7, 2015, *http://techcrunch.com/2015/01/23/pinterest-goes-after-the-male-demographic-with-debut-of-new-search-filters*.
4. Hilary Heino, "Social Media Demographics—Instagram, Tumblr, and Pinterest," Agile Impact, March 13, 2014, accessed May 7, 2015, *http://agileimpact.org/social-media-demographics-instagram-tumblr-and-pinterest*.
5. Cooper Smith, "LinkedIn May Not Be the Coolest Social Network, but It's Only Becoming More Valuable to Businesses," *Business Insider*, May 1, 2014, accessed June 25, 2014, *www.businessinsider.com/demographic-data-and-social-media-2014-2*.
6. Ibid.
7. CivicScience, "Social Media Now Equals TV Advertising in Influence Power on Consumption Decisions," *CivicScience.com*, September 2014, accessed May 5, 2015, *https://civicscience.com/library/insightreports/social-media-equals-tv-advertising-in-influence-power-on-consumption-decisions*.
8. Nicholas Jackson, "As MySpace Sells for $35 Million, a History of the Network's Valuation," *The Atlantic*, June 29, 2011, accessed June 18, 2015, *www.theatlantic.com/technology/archive/2011/06/as-myspace-sells-for-35-million-a-history-of-the-networks-valuation/241224/*.
9. Gene Marks, "Why Facebook Is in Decline," *Forbes*, August 19, 2013, accessed June 18, 2015, *www.forbes.com/sites/quickerbetter-tech/2013/08/19/why-facebook-is-in-decline/*.
10. Andrew McAfee, "Enterprise 2.0, Version 2.0," AndrewMcAfee.org, May 27, 2006, accessed June 18, 2015, *http://andrewmcafee.org/2006/05/enterprise_20_version_20/*.
11. Andrew McAfee, "Enterprise 2.0: The Dawn of Emergent Collaboration," *MIT Sloan Management Review*, Spring 2006, accessed June 18, 2015, *http://sloanreview.mit.edu/article/enterprise-the-dawn-of-emergent-collaboration*.
12. Yammer, "Empowering Employees for Improved Customer Service and a Better Bottom Line," Yammer.com, accessed June 25, 2014, *about.yammer.com/assets/Yammer-Case-Study-Red-Robin.pdf*.
13. Josh Constine, "How Big Is Facebook's Data? 2.5 Billion Pieces of Content and 500+ Terabytes Ingested Every Day," TechCrunch.com, August 22, 2012, accessed June 18, 2015, *http://techcrunch.com/2012/08/22/how-big-is-facebooks-data-2-5-billion-pieces-of-content-and-500-terabytes-ingested-every-day/*.
14. Dan Noyes, "The Top 20 Valuable Facebook Statistics—Updated May 2015," *Zephoria*, May 2015, accessed June 18, 2015, *http://zephoria.com/top-15-valuable-facebook-statistics*.

chapter extension **12**

**Chapter 9** provides the background for this extension.

# Database Marketing

STUDY QUESTIONS

**QCE12-1 WHAT IS A DATABASE MARKETING OPPORTUNITY?**

**QCE12-2 HOW DOES RFM ANALYSIS CLASSIFY CUSTOMERS?**

**QCE12-3 HOW DOES MARKET-BASKET ANALYSIS IDENTIFY CROSS-SELLING OPPORTUNITIES?**

**QCE12-4 HOW DO DECISION TREES IDENTIFY MARKET SEGMENTS?**

## QCE12-1 WHAT IS A DATABASE MARKETING OPPORTUNITY?

**Database marketing** is the application of business intelligence systems to the planning, execution, and assessment of marketing programs. The term is broader than it sounds. Databases are a key component of database marketing, but, as you'll see, data mining techniques are also very important. To understand the need for database marketing, consider the following scenario:

> Mary Keeling owns and operates Carbon Creek Gardens, a retailer of trees, garden plants, perennial and annual flowers, and bulbs. "The Gardens," as her customers call it, also sells bags of soil, fertilizer, small garden tools, and garden sculptures. Mary started the business 10 years ago when she bought a section of land that, because of water drainage, was unsuited for residential development. With hard work and perseverance, Mary has created a warm and inviting environment with a unique and carefully selected inventory of plants. The Gardens has become a favorite nursery for serious gardeners in her community.
>
> "The problem," she says, "is that I've grown so large, I've lost track of my customers. The other day, I ran into Tootsie Swan at the grocery store, and I realized I hadn't seen her in ages. I said something like, 'Hi, Tootsie, I haven't seen you for a while,' and that statement unleashed an angry torrent from her. It turns out that she'd been in over a year ago and wanted to return a plant. One of my part-time employees waited on her and had apparently insulted her or at least didn't give her the service she wanted. So she decided not to come back to The Gardens.
>
> "Tootsie was one of my best customers. I'd lost her, and I didn't even know it! That really frustrates me. Is it inevitable that as I get bigger, I lose track of my customers? I don't think so. Somehow, I have to find out when regular customers aren't coming around. Had I known Tootsie had stopped shopping with us, I'd have called her to see what was going on. I need customers like her.
>
> "I've got all sorts of data in my sales database. It seems like the information I need is in there, but how do I get it out?"

Mary needs database marketing.

## QCE12-2 HOW DOES RFM ANALYSIS CLASSIFY CUSTOMERS?

**RFM analysis** is a way of analyzing and ranking customers according to their purchasing patterns.[1] It is a simple technique that considers how *recently* (R) a customer has ordered, how *frequently* (F) a customer orders, and how much *money* (M) the customer spends per order. We consider this technique here because it is a useful analysis that can be easily implemented.

To produce an RFM score, the program first sorts customer purchase records by the date of most recent (R) purchase. In a common form of this analysis, the program then divides the customers into five groups and gives customers in each group a score of 1 to 5. Thus, the 20 percent of the customers having the most recent orders are given an **R score** of 1, the 20 percent of the

CE12

**Figure CE12-1**
Example of RFM Score Data

| Customer | RFM Score |
|---|---|
| Ajax | 1 1 3 |
| Bloominghams | 5 1 1 |
| Caruthers | 5 4 5 |
| Davidson | 3 3 3 |

customers having the next most recent orders are given an R score of 2, and so forth, down to the last 20 percent, who are given an R score of 5.

The program then re-sorts the customers on the basis of how frequently they order. The 20 percent of the customers who order most frequently are given an **F score** of 1, the next 20 percent of most frequently ordering customers are given a score of 2, and so forth, down to the least frequently ordering customers, who are given an F score of 5.

Finally, the program sorts the customers again according to the amount spent on their orders. The 20 percent who have ordered the most expensive items are given an **M score** of 1, the next 20 percent are given an M score of 2, and so forth, down to the 20 percent who spend the least, who are given an M score of 5.

Figure CE12-1 shows sample RFM data. The first customer, Ajax, has ordered recently and orders frequently. The company's M score of 3 indicates, however, that it does not order the most expensive goods. From these scores, the sales team members can surmise that Ajax is a good and regular customer but that they should attempt to up-sell more expensive goods to Ajax.

The second customer in Figure CE12-1 could be a problem. Bloominghams has not ordered in some time, but when it did order in the past, it ordered frequently, and its orders were of the highest monetary value. This data suggests that Bloominghams may have taken its business to another vendor. Someone from the sales team should contact this customer immediately.

No one on the sales team should be talking to the third customer, Caruthers. This company has not ordered for some time; it did not order frequently; and, when it did order, it bought the least-expensive items, and not many of them. The sales team should not waste any time on this customer; if Caruthers goes to the competition, the loss would be minimal.

The last customer, Davidson, is right in the middle. Davidson is an OK customer, but probably no one in sales should spend much time with it. Perhaps sales can set up an automated contact system or use the Davidson account as a training exercise for an eager departmental assistant or intern.

A reporting system can generate the RFM data and deliver it in many ways. For example, a report of RFM scores for all customers can be pushed to the vice president of sales; reports with scores for particular regions can be pushed to regional sales managers; and reports of scores for particular accounts can be pushed to the account salespeople. All of this reporting can be automated.

## QCE12-3 HOW DOES MARKET-BASKET ANALYSIS IDENTIFY CROSS-SELLING OPPORTUNITIES?

Suppose you run a dive shop, and one day you realize that one of your salespeople is much better at up-selling to your customers. Any of your sales associates can fill a customer's order, but this one salesperson is especially good at selling customers items *in addition to* those for which they ask. One day, you ask him how he does it.

"It's simple," he says. "I just ask myself what is the next product they would want to buy. If someone buys a dive computer, I don't try to sell her fins. If she's buying a dive computer, she's already a diver and she already has fins. But these dive computer displays are hard to read. A better mask makes it easier to read the display and get the full benefit from the dive computer."

A **market-basket analysis** is a data mining technique for determining sales patterns. A market-basket analysis shows the products that customers tend to buy together. In marketing transactions, the fact that customers who buy product *X* also buy product *Y* creates a **cross-selling** opportunity; that is, "If they're buying *X*, sell them *Y*" or "If they're buying *Y*, sell them *X*."

Figure CE12-2 shows hypothetical sales data from 400 sales transactions at a dive shop. The number on the diagonal (shaded) in the first set of rows is the total number of times an item was sold. For example, the 270 on the diagonal cell for *Mask* means that 270 of the 400 transactions included masks. The 120 in the diagonal cell for *Dive Computer* means that 120 of the 400 transactions included dive computers.

We can use the number of times an item sold to estimate the probability that a customer will purchase an item. Because 270 of the 400 transactions were masks, we can estimate the probability that a customer will buy a mask to be 270/400, or .675. Similarly, the probability of selling a dive computer is 120/400, or .3.

In market-basket terminology, **support** is the probability that two items will be purchased together. To estimate that probability, we examine sales transactions and count the number of times that two items occurred in the same transaction. For the data in Figure CE12-2, fins and masks appeared together 250 times, and thus the support for fins and a mask is 250/400, or .625. Similarly, the support for fins and weights is 20/400, or .05.

These data are interesting by themselves, but we can refine the analysis by taking another step and considering additional probabilities. For example, what proportion of the customers who

**Figure CE12-2**
Market-Basket Example

| | Mask | Tank | Fins | Weights | Dive Computer |
|---|---|---|---|---|---|
| Mask | 270 | 10 | 250 | 10 | 90 |
| Tank | 10 | 200 | 40 | 130 | 30 |
| Fins | 250 | 40 | 280 | 20 | 20 |
| Weights | 10 | 130 | 20 | 130 | 10 |
| Dive Computer | 90 | 30 | 20 | 10 | 120 |
| | | | | | |
| | Support | | | | |
| Num Trans | 400 | | | | |
| Mask | 0.675 | 0.025 | 0.625 | 0.025 | 0.225 |
| Tank | 0.025 | 0.5 | 0.1 | 0.325 | 0.075 |
| Fins | 0.625 | 0.1 | 0.7 | 0.05 | 0.05 |
| Weights | 0.025 | 0.325 | 0.05 | 0.325 | 0.025 |
| Dive Computer | 0.225 | 0.075 | 0.05 | 0.025 | 0.3 |
| | | | | | |
| | Confidence | | | | |
| Mask | 1 | 0.05 | 0.892857143 | 0.076923077 | 0.75 |
| Tank | 0.037037037 | 1 | 0.142857143 | 1 | 0.25 |
| Fins | 0.925925926 | 0.2 | 1 | 0.153846154 | 0.166666667 |
| Weights | 0.037037037 | 0.65 | 0.071428571 | 1 | 0.083333333 |
| Dive Computer | 0.333333333 | 0.15 | 0.071428571 | 0.076923077 | 1 |
| | | | | | |
| | Lift (Improvement) | | | | |
| Mask | | 0.074074074 | 1.322751323 | 0.113960114 | 1.111111111 |
| Tank | 0.074074074 | | 0.285714286 | 2 | 0.5 |
| Fins | 1.322751323 | 0.285714286 | | 0.21978022 | 0.238095238 |
| Weights | 0.113960114 | 2 | 0.21978022 | | 0.256410256 |
| Dive Computer | 1.111111111 | 0.5 | 0.238095238 | 0.256410256 | |

bought a mask also bought fins? Masks were purchased 270 times, and of those individuals who bought masks, 250 also bought fins. Thus, given that a customer bought a mask, we can estimate the probability that he or she will buy fins to be 250/270, or .926. In market-basket terminology, such a conditional probability estimate is called the **confidence**.

Reflect on the meaning of this confidence value. The likelihood of someone walking in the door and buying fins is 250/400, or .625. But the likelihood of someone buying fins, given that he or she bought a mask, is .926. Thus, if someone buys a mask, the likelihood that he or she will also buy fins increases substantially, from .625 to .926. Thus, all sales personnel should be trained to try to sell fins to anyone buying a mask.

Now consider dive computers and fins. Of the 400 transactions, fins were sold 280 times, so the probability that someone walks into the store and buys fins is .7. But of the 120 purchases of dive computers, only 20 appeared with fins. So the likelihood of someone buying fins, given he or she bought a dive computer, is 20/120 or .1666. Thus, when someone buys a dive computer, the likelihood that she will also buy fins falls from .625 to .1666.

The ratio of confidence to the base probability of buying an item is called **lift**. Lift shows how much the base probability increases or decreases when other products are purchased. The lift of fins and a mask is the confidence of fins given a mask, divided by the base probability of fins. In Figure CE12-2, the lift of fins and a mask is .926/.7, or 1.32. Thus, the likelihood that people buy fins when they buy a mask increases by 32 percent. Surprisingly, it turns out that the lift of fins and a mask is the same as the lift of a mask and fins. Both are 1.32.

We need to be careful here, though, because this analysis shows only shopping carts with two items. We cannot say from this data what the likelihood is that customers, given that they bought a mask, will buy both weights and fins. To assess that probability, we need to analyze shopping carts with three items. This statement illustrates, once again, that we need to know what problem we're solving before we start to build the information system to mine the data. The problem definition will help us decide if we need to analyze three-item, four-item, or some other sized shopping cart.

**Data mining and other business intelligence systems are useful, but they are not without their problems. But what does this mean to you as a business professional? The Guide on pages 556–557 considers this question.**

Many organizations are benefiting from market-basket analysis today. You can expect that this technique will become a standard CRM analysis during your career.

By the way, one famous market-basket analysis shows a high correlation of the purchase of beer and diapers.[2] That correlation was strongest on Thursdays. Interviews indicated that customers were buying goods for the weekend, goods which included both beer and diapers.

## QCE12-4 HOW DO DECISION TREES IDENTIFY MARKET SEGMENTS?

A **decision tree** is a hierarchical arrangement of criteria that predicts a classification or value. Here we will consider decision trees that predict classifications. Decision tree analyses are an unsupervised data mining technique: The analyst sets up the computer program and provides the data to analyze, and the decision tree program produces the tree.

### A DECISION TREE FOR STUDENT PERFORMANCE

The basic idea of a decision tree is to select attributes that are most useful for classifying entities on some criterion. Suppose, for example, that we want to classify students according to the grades they earn in the MIS class. To create a decision tree, we first gather data about grades and attributes of students in past classes.

We then input that data into the decision tree program. The program analyzes all of the attributes and selects an attribute that creates the most disparate groups. The logic is that the more different the groups, the better the classification will be. For example, if every student who lived off

**Figure CE12-3**
GPAs of Students from Past MIS Class (Hypothetical Data)

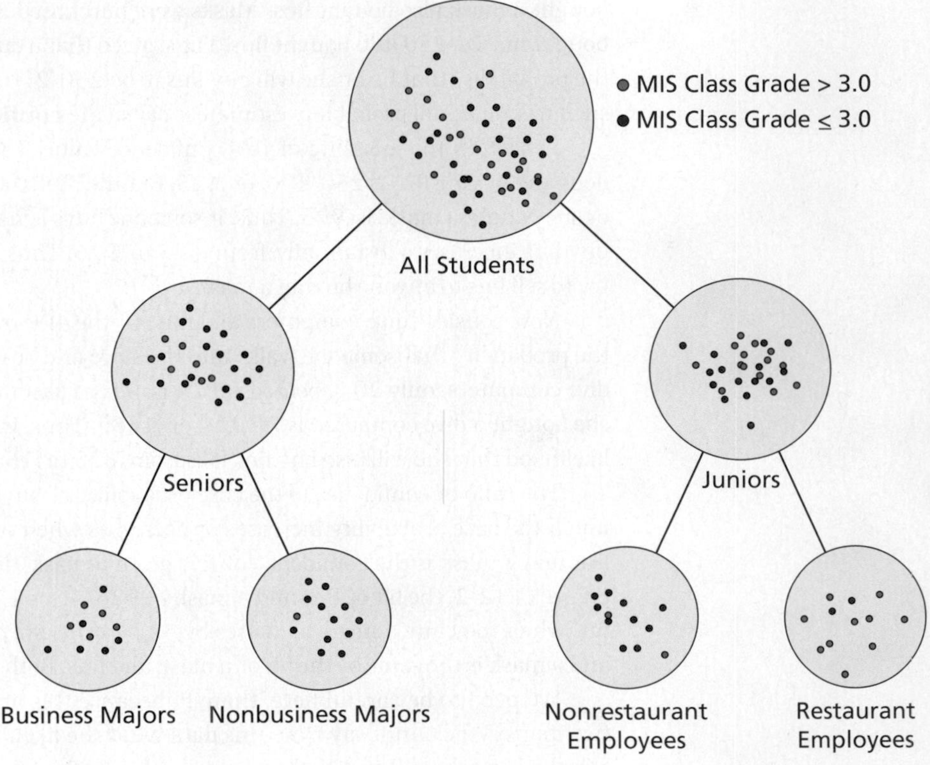


campus earned a grade higher than 3.0 and if every student who lived on campus earned a grade lower than 3.0, then the program would use the variable *live-off-campus* or *live-on-campus* to classify students. In this unrealistic example, the program would be a perfect classifier because each group is pure with no misclassifications.

More realistically, consider Figure CE12-3, which shows a hypothetical decision tree analysis of MIS class grades. Again, assume we are classifying students depending on whether their GPA was greater than 3.0 or less than or equal to 3.0.

The decision tree tool that created this tree examined students' characteristics, such as their class (junior or senior), their major, their employment, their age, their club affiliations, and other student characteristics. It then used values of those characteristics to create groups that were as different as possible on the classification GPA above or below 3.0.

For the results shown here, the decision tree program determined that the best first criterion is whether the students are juniors or seniors. In this case, the classification was imperfect, as shown by the fact that neither the senior nor the junior groups consisted of only students with GPAs above or below 3.0. Still, it did create groups that were less mixed than in the *All Students* group.

Next, the program examined other criteria to further subdivide *Seniors* and *Juniors* so as to create even more pure groups. The program divided the senior group into subgroups: those who are business majors and those who are not. The program's analysis of the junior data, however, determined that the difference between majors is not significant. Instead, the best classifier (the one that generated the most different groups) is whether the junior worked in a restaurant.

Examining these data, we see that junior restaurant employees do well in the class, but junior nonrestaurant employees and senior nonbusiness majors do poorly. Performance in the other senior group is mixed. (Remember, these data are hypothetical.)

A decision tree like the one in Figure CE12-3 can be transformed into a set of decision rules having the format If/Then. Decision rules for this example are:

- If student is a junior and works in a restaurant, then predict grade > 3.0.
- If student is a senior and is a nonbusiness major, then predict grade < 3.0.
- If student is a junior and does not work in a restaurant, then predict grade < 3.0.
- If student is a senior and is a business major, then make no prediction.[3]

As stated, decision tree algorithms create groups that are as pure as possible or, stated otherwise, as different from each other as possible. The algorithms use several metrics for measuring difference among groups. Further explanation of those techniques is beyond the scope of this textbook. For now, just be sure to understand that maximum difference among groups is used as the criterion for constructing the decision tree.

Let's now apply the decision tree technique to a business situation.

## A DECISION TREE FOR LOAN EVALUATION

A common business application of decision trees is to classify loans by likelihood of default. Organizations analyze data from past loans to produce a decision tree that can be converted to loan-decision rules. A financial institution could use such a tree to assess the default risk on a new loan. Sometimes, too, financial institutions sell a group of loans (called a *loan portfolio*) to one another. The results of a decision tree program can be used to evaluate the risk in a given portfolio.

Figure CE12-4 shows an example provided by Insightful Corporation, a vendor of business intelligence tools. This example was generated using its Insightful Miner product. This tool examined data from 3,485 loans. Of those loans, 72 percent had no default and 28 percent did default. To perform the analysis, the decision tree tool examined values of six different loan characteristics.

In this example, the decision tree program determined that the percentage of the loan that is past due (*PercPastDue*) is the best first criterion. Reading Figure CE12-4, you can see that of the

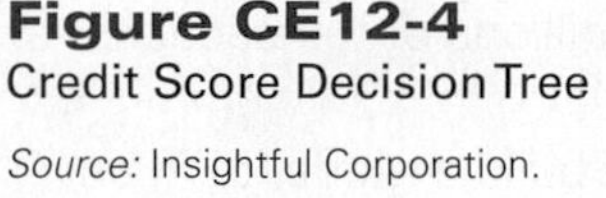
**Figure CE12-4**
Credit Score Decision Tree
*Source:* Insightful Corporation.

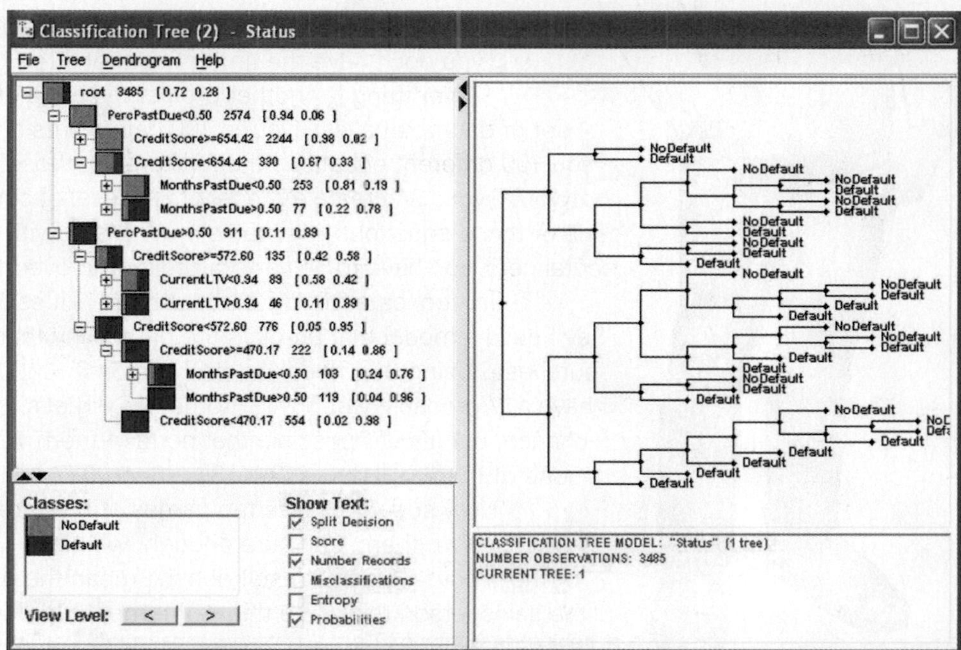

## Data Mining in the Real World

"I'm not really opposed to data mining. I believe in it. After all, it's my career. But data mining in the real world is a lot different from the way it's described in textbooks, for many reasons.

"One is that the data are always dirty, with missing values, values way out of the range of possibility, and time values that make no sense. Here's an example: Somebody sets the server system clock incorrectly and runs the server for a while with the wrong time. When they notice the mistake, they set the clock to the correct time. But all of the transactions that were running during that interval have an ending time before the starting time. When we run the data analysis and compute elapsed time, the results are negative for those transactions.

"Missing values are a similar problem. Consider the records of just 10 purchases. Suppose that two of the records are missing the customer number, and one is missing the year part of the transaction date. So you throw out three records, which is 30 percent of the data. You then notice that two more records have dirty data, and so you throw them out, too. Now you've lost half your data.

"Another problem is that you know the least when you start the study. So you work for a few months and learn that if you had another variable—say, the customer's ZIP code, or age, or something else—you could do a much better analysis. But those other data just aren't available. Or maybe they are available, but to get the data you have to reprocess millions of transactions, and you don't have the time or budget to do that.

"Overfitting is another problem, a huge one. I can build a model to fit any set of data you have. Give me 100 data points and in a few minutes, I can give you 100 different equations that will predict those 100 data points. With neural networks, you can create a model of any level of complexity you want, except that none of those equations will predict new cases with any accuracy at all. When using neural nets, you have to be very careful not to overfit the data.

"Then, too, data mining is about probabilities, not certainty. Bad luck happens. Say I build a model that predicts the probability that a customer will make a purchase. Using the model on new customer data, I find three customers who have a .7 probability of buying something. That's a good number, well over a 50–50 chance, but it's still possible that none of them will buy. In fact, the probability that none of them will buy is .3 × .3 × .3, or .027, which is 2.7 percent.

"Now suppose I give the names of the three customers to a salesperson who calls on them, and sure enough, we have a stream of bad luck and none of them buys. This bad result doesn't mean the model is wrong. But what does the salesperson think? He thinks the model is worthless, and he can do better on his own. He tells his manager who tells her associate, who tells everyone in the Northeast Region, and sure enough, the model has a bad reputation all across the company.

"Another problem is seasonality. Say all your training data are from the summer. Will your model be valid for the winter? Maybe, but maybe not. You might even know that it won't be valid for predicting winter sales, but if you don't have winter data, what do you do?

"When you start a data mining project, you never know how it will turn out. I worked on one project for 6 months, and when we finished, I didn't think our model was any good. We had too many problems with data: wrong, dirty, and missing. There was no way we could know ahead of time that it would happen, but it did.

"When the time came to present the results to senior management, what could we do? How could we say we took 6 months of our time and substantial computer resources to create a bad model? We had a model, but I just didn't think it would make accurate predictions. I was a junior member of the team, and it wasn't for me to decide. I kept my mouth shut, but I never felt good about it. Fortunately, the project was cancelled later for other reasons.

"However, I'm only talking about my bad experiences. Some of my projects have been excellent. On many, we found interesting and important patterns and information, and a few times I've created very accurate predictive models. It's not easy, though, and you have to be very careful. Also, lucky!"

## DISCUSSION QUESTIONS

**1.** Summarize the concerns expressed by this data analyst.

**2.** Do you think the concerns raised here are sufficient to avoid data mining projects altogether?

**3.** If you were a junior member of a data mining team and you thought that the model that had been developed was ineffective, maybe even wrong, what would you do? If your boss disagreed with your beliefs, would you go higher in the organization? What would be the risks of doing so? What else might you do?

*Source:* Paul Fleet/Fotolia

2,574 loans with a *PercPastDue* value of .5 or less (more than half paid off), 94 percent were not in default. Hence, any loan that is more than half paid off has little risk of default.

Reading down several lines in this tree, 911 loans had a value of *PercPastDue* greater than .5; of those loans, 89 percent were in default.

These two major categories are then further subdivided into three classifications: *CreditScore* is a creditworthiness score obtained from a credit agency; *MonthsPastDue* is the number of months since a payment; and *CurrentLTV* is the current ratio of outstanding balance of the loan to the value of the loan's collateral.

With a decision tree like this, the financial institution can structure a marketing program for "instant approval" refinancing. For example, from Figure CE12-4, the bank can deduce the following rules:

- If the loan is more than half paid, then accept the loan.
- If the loan is less than half paid and
  - If *CreditScore* is greater than 572.6 and
  - If *CurrentLTV* is less than .94, then accept the loan.
- Otherwise, reject the loan.

These rules identify loans the bank will approve, and they also specify characteristics that identify a particular market segment. On the basis of this analysis, the bank can structure a marketing campaign to appeal to that segment.

We have shown here how decision trees can identify a market segment, but realize that they can be used for numerous other classification and prediction problems as well. They are easy to understand and—even better—easy to implement using decision rules. They also can work with many types of variables, and they deal well with missing values. Organizations can use decision trees by themselves or combine them with other techniques. In some cases, organizations use decision trees to select variables that are then used by other types of data mining tools.

# ACTIVE REVIEW

  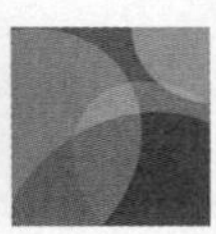 

Use this Active Review to verify that you understand the ideas and concepts that answer this chapter extension's study questions.

## QCE12-1 WHAT IS A DATABASE MARKETING OPPORTUNITY?

Define *database marketing.* Explain why the term is a misnomer. Give an example of the need for database marketing other than ones described in this chapter extension.

## QCE12-2 HOW DOES RFM ANALYSIS CLASSIFY CUSTOMERS?

Explain the meaning of *R, F,* and *M scores.* Describe how each score is computed. State the action(s) that should be taken for customers having the following RFM scores: [1, 1, 3], [5, 4, 5], [2, 2, 2], [3, 1, 1], [1, 3, 1], and [1, 1, 1].

## QCE12-3 HOW DOES MARKET-BASKET ANALYSIS IDENTIFY CROSS-SELLING OPPORTUNITIES?

Define *cross-selling.* Define *support, confidence,* and *lift.* In Figure CE12-2, state the probability that someone walks into the store and buys fins. Compute the support for fins and a dive computer. Explain what it means if the value of lift is greater than 1. Explain what it means if the value of lift is less than 1. Compute the lift for fins and a dive computer.

## QCE12-4 HOW DO DECISION TREES IDENTIFY MARKET SEGMENTS?

Define *decision tree* and explain the basic idea of decision trees. For the hypothetical data in Figure CE12-3, state the grade you would predict for senior nonbusiness students. State the grade you would predict for junior restaurant employees. State the grade you would predict for senior business majors. Explain how a decision tree could be used to identify a desirable market segment for loan refinancing.

## KEY TERMS AND CONCEPTS

Confidence 553
Cross-selling 552
Database marketing 550
Decision tree 553
F score 551
Lift 553
M score 551
Market-basket analysis 552
R score 550
RFM analysis 550
Support 552

MyMISLab™

To complete the problems with the ✪, go to EOC Discussion Questions in the MyLab.

## USING YOUR KNOWLEDGE

✪ **CE12-1.** Of the three database marketing techniques described in this chapter extension, which best solves the problem at Carbon Creek Gardens? Explain how Mary could have used that technique to identify Tootsie as a lost customer.

✪ **CE12-2.** Describe a use for RFM analysis at Costco. Explain what you would do for customers that have the following scores: [1, 1, 1], [3,1,1], [1, 4, 1], [3, 3, 1], and [1, 1, 3].

✪ **CE12-3.** Describe an application for market-basket analysis other than for a dive shop. Explain how you would use the knowledge that two products have a lift of 7. Explain how you would use the knowledge that two products have a lift of .003. If they have a lift of 1.03? If they have a lift of 2.1?

MyMISLab™

Go to the Assignments section of your MyLab to complete these writing exercises.

**CE12-4.** Describe an application for decision tree analysis for customer service and support at a computer vendor like Dell. Assume your decision tree analysis considered customer name, company, number of employees at that company, job title, and number and type of computer systems purchased. How could you use the results of your analysis to classify the knowledge and experience of your customers? How could you use those results to structure the buying experience for each of those customers? What other uses can you think of for the results of this decision tree analysis?

**CE12-5.** Suppose you work for an online sporting goods retailer. You've been hired as a business analyst with the task of increasing sales. Describe how you could use RFM and market-basket analysis to increase the sales of sporting goods. If used effectively, how could RFM and market-basket analysis affect customer satisfaction?

## ENDNOTES

1. Arthur Middleton Hughes, "Boosting Response with RFM," *Marketing Tools*, May 1996. See also *www.dbmarketing.com*.
2. Michael J. A. Berry and Gordon Linoff, *Data Mining Techniques for Marketing, Sales, and Customer Support* (New York: John Wiley, 1997).
3. Do not confuse these If/Then rules with those in expert systems. These rules are developed as a result of data mining via decision tree analysis. Typically, there are 10 or 12 such rules. Expert system rules are created by interviewing human experts. Typically, there are hundreds or even thousands of such rules.

chapter extension **13**

**Chapter 9** provides the background for this extension.

# Reporting Systems and OLAP

**STUDY QUESTIONS**

**QCE13-1** HOW DO REPORTING SYSTEMS ENABLE PEOPLE TO CREATE INFORMATION?

**QCE13-2** WHAT ARE THE COMPONENTS AND CHARACTERISTICS OF REPORTING SYSTEMS?

**QCE13-3** HOW ARE REPORTS AUTHORED, MANAGED, AND DELIVERED?

**QCE13-4** HOW ARE OLAP REPORTS DYNAMIC?

## QCE13-1 HOW DO REPORTING SYSTEMS ENABLE PEOPLE TO CREATE INFORMATION?

A **reporting system** is an information system that enables people to create information by processing data from disparate sources and delivering that information to the proper users on a timely basis. Chapter 1 discussed the difference between data and information. There we said that people conceive information from data. We also said that they do so by seeing data presented in a meaningful context. Reporting systems manipulate data into that meaningful context using four fundamental operations:

1. Filtering data
2. Sorting data
3. Grouping data
4. Making simple calculations on the data

Consider the sales data shown in Figure CE13-1. This list of raw data is hardly a meaningful context. It is just a list of data. We can create a meaningful context for this data by *sorting* by customer name, as shown in Figure CE13-2. In this format, we can see that some customers have ordered more than once, and we can readily find their orders.

This is a step forward, but we can produce more information by *grouping* the orders, as shown in Figure CE13-3 (page 563). Notice that the reporting tool not only grouped the orders, but it also *computed* the number of orders for each customer and the total purchase amount per customer.

Suppose we are interested in repeat customers. If so, we can *filter* the groups of orders to select only those customers that have two or more orders. The results of these operations are shown in Figure CE13-4 (page 563). The report in Figure CE13-4 not only has filtered the results, but it also has *formatted* them for easier understanding. Compare Figure CE13-4 to Figure CE13-1. If your goal is to identify your best customers, the report in Figure CE13-4 shows data in a far more useful context and will save you considerable work.

In the remainder of this chapter extension, we will consider the components and functions of these reporting systems as well as some examples.

## QCE13-2 WHAT ARE THE COMPONENTS AND CHARACTERISTICS OF REPORTING SYSTEMS?

Figure CE13-5 shows the major components of a reporting system. Data from disparate data sources are read and combined, using filtering, sorting, grouping, and simple calculating, to produce meaningful contexts. Figure CE13-5 combines data from an Oracle database, a SQL

**Figure CE13-1**
Raw Sales Data

*Source:* Microsoft Corporation

| ID | CustomerName | CustomerEmail | DateOfSale | Amount | Quarter |
|---|---|---|---|---|---|
| 1 | Ashley, Jane | JA@somewhere.com | 5/5/2014 | $110.00 | 2 |
| 2 | Corning,Sandra | KD@somewhereelse.co | 7/7/2014 | $375.00 | 3 |
| 3 | Ching, Kam Hoong | KHC@somewhere.com | 5/17/2014 | $55.00 | 2 |
| 4 | Rikki, Nicole | GC@righthere.com | 6/19/2012 | $155.00 | 2 |
| 5 | Corning,Sandra | SC@somewhereelse.coi | 2/4/2013 | $195.00 | 1 |
| 6 | Scott, Rex | RS@somewhere.com | 7/15/2014 | $56.00 | 3 |
| 7 | Corovic,Jose | JC@somewhere.com | 11/12/2014 | $55.00 | 4 |
| 8 | McGovern, Adrian | BL@righthere.com | 11/12/2012 | $47.00 | 4 |
| 9 | Wei, Guang | GW@ourcompany.com | 11/28/2013 | $385.00 | 4 |
| 10 | Dixon,Eleonor | ED@somewhere.com | 5/17/2014 | $108.00 | 2 |
| 11 | Lee,Brandon | BL@somewhereelse.coi | 5/5/2012 | $74.00 | 2 |
| 12 | Duong,Linda | LD@righthere.com | 5/17/2013 | $485.00 | 2 |
| 13 | Dixon, James T | JTD@somewhere.com | 4/3/2013 | $285.00 | 2 |
| 14 | La Pierre,Anna | SG@righthere.com | 9/22/2014 | $120.00 | 3 |
| 15 | La Pierre,Anna | WS@somewhere.com | 3/14/2014 | $47.50 | 1 |
| 16 | La Pierre,Anna | TR@righthere.com | 9/22/2014 | $580.00 | 3 |
| 17 | Ryan, Mark | MR@somewhereelse.cc | 11/3/2014 | $42.00 | 4 |
| 18 | Rikki, Nicole | MR@righthere.com | 3/14/2014 | $175.00 | 1 |
| 19 | Scott, Bryan | BS@somewhere.com | 3/17/2013 | $145.00 | 1 |
| 20 | Warrem, Jason | JW@ourcompany.com | 5/12/2014 | $160.00 | 2 |
| 21 | La Pierre,Anna | ALP@somewhereelse.cc | 3/15/2013 | $52.00 | 1 |
| 22 | Angel, Kathy | KA@righthere.com | 9/15/2014 | $195.00 | 3 |
| 23 | La Pierre,Anna | JQ@somewhere.com | 4/12/2014 | $44.00 | 2 |
| 24 | Casimiro, Amanda | AC@somewhere.com | 12/7/2013 | $52.00 | 4 |
| 25 | McGovern, Adrian | AM@ourcompany.com | 3/17/2013 | $52.00 | 1 |
| 26 | Menstell,Lori Lee | LLM@ourcompany.com | 10/18/2014 | $72.00 | 4 |
| 27 | La Pierre,Anna | DJ@righthere.com | 12/7/2013 | $175.00 | 4 |
| 28 | Nurul,Nicole | NN@somewhere.com | 10/12/2014 | $84.00 | 4 |
| 29 | Menstell,Lori Lee | VB@ourcompany.com | 9/24/2014 | $120.00 | 3 |
| 30 | Pham,Mary | MP@somewhere.com | 3/14/2014 | $38.00 | 1 |
| 31 | Redmond, Louise | LR@ourcompany.com | 1/3/2014 | $140.00 | 1 |
| 32 | Jordan, Matthew | MJ@righthere.com | 3/14/2013 | $645.00 | 1 |
| 33 | Drew, Richard | RD@righthere.com | 10/3/2013 | $42.00 | 4 |
| 34 | Adams, James | JA3@somewhere.com | 1/15/2014 | $145.00 | 1 |
| 35 | Garrett, James | JG@ourcompany.com | 3/14/2014 | $38.00 | 1 |
| 36 | Lunden,Haley | HL@somewhere.com | 11/17/2011 | $52.00 | 4 |
| 37 | UTran,Diem Thi | DTU@righthere.com | 5/3/2012 | $275.00 | 2 |
| 38 | Austin, James | JA7@somewhere.com | 1/15/2013 | $55.00 | 1 |
| 39 | Bernard, Steven | SB@ourcompany.com | 9/17/2014 | $78.00 | 3 |
| 40 | Daniel, James | JD@somewhere.com | 1/18/2014 | $52.00 | 1 |

**Figure CE13-2**
Sales Data Sorted by Customer Name

*Source:* Microsoft Corporation

| ID | CustomerName | CustomerEmail | DateOfSale | Amount | Quarter |
|---|---|---|---|---|---|
| 34 | Adams, James | JA3@somewhere.com | 1/15/2014 | $145.00 | 1 |
| 22 | Angel, Kathy | KA@righthere.com | 9/15/2014 | $195.00 | 3 |
| 1 | Ashley, Jane | JA@somewhere.com | 5/5/2014 | $110.00 | 2 |
| 38 | Austin, James | JA7@somewhere.com | 1/15/2013 | $55.00 | 1 |
| 39 | Bernard, Steven | SB@ourcompany.com | 9/17/2014 | $78.00 | 3 |
| 24 | Casimiro, Amanda | AC@somewhere.com | 12/7/2013 | $52.00 | 4 |
| 3 | Ching, Kam Hoong | KHC@somewhere.com | 5/17/2014 | $55.00 | 2 |
| 2 | Corning,Sandra | KD@somewhereelse.co | 7/7/2014 | $375.00 | 3 |
| 5 | Corning,Sandra | SC@somewhereelse.coi | 2/4/2013 | $195.00 | 1 |
| 7 | Corovic,Jose | JC@somewhere.com | 11/12/2014 | $55.00 | 4 |
| 40 | Daniel, James | JD@somewhere.com | 1/18/2014 | $52.00 | 1 |
| 13 | Dixon, James T | JTD@somewhere.com | 4/3/2013 | $285.00 | 2 |
| 10 | Dixon,Eleonor | ED@somewhere.com | 5/17/2014 | $108.00 | 2 |
| 33 | Drew, Richard | RD@righthere.com | 10/3/2013 | $42.00 | 4 |
| 12 | Duong,Linda | LD@righthere.com | 5/17/2013 | $485.00 | 2 |
| 35 | Garrett, James | JG@ourcompany.com | 3/14/2014 | $38.00 | 1 |
| 32 | Jordan, Matthew | MJ@righthere.com | 3/14/2013 | $645.00 | 1 |
| 27 | La Pierre,Anna | DJ@righthere.com | 12/7/2013 | $175.00 | 4 |
| 14 | La Pierre,Anna | SG@righthere.com | 9/22/2014 | $120.00 | 3 |
| 16 | La Pierre,Anna | TR@righthere.com | 9/22/2014 | $580.00 | 3 |
| 21 | La Pierre,Anna | ALP@somewhereelse.cc | 3/15/2013 | $52.00 | 1 |
| 23 | La Pierre,Anna | JQ@somewhere.com | 4/12/2014 | $44.00 | 2 |
| 15 | La Pierre,Anna | WS@somewhere.com | 3/14/2014 | $47.50 | 1 |
| 11 | Lee,Brandon | BL@somewhereelse.coi | 5/5/2012 | $74.00 | 2 |
| 36 | Lunden,Haley | HL@somewhere.com | 11/17/2011 | $52.00 | 4 |
| 8 | McGovern, Adrian | BL@righthere.com | 11/12/2012 | $47.00 | 4 |
| 25 | McGovern, Adrian | AM@ourcompany.com | 3/17/2013 | $52.00 | 1 |
| 26 | Menstell,Lori Lee | LLM@ourcompany.com | 10/18/2014 | $72.00 | 4 |
| 29 | Menstell,Lori Lee | VB@ourcompany.com | 9/24/2014 | $120.00 | 3 |
| 28 | Nurul,Nicole | NN@somewhere.com | 10/12/2014 | $84.00 | 4 |
| 30 | Pham,Mary | MP@somewhere.com | 3/14/2014 | $38.00 | 1 |
| 31 | Redmond, Louise | LR@ourcompany.com | 1/3/2014 | $140.00 | 1 |
| 4 | Rikki, Nicole | GC@righthere.com | 6/19/2012 | $155.00 | 2 |
| 18 | Rikki, Nicole | MR@righthere.com | 3/14/2014 | $175.00 | 1 |
| 17 | Ryan, Mark | MR@somewhereelse.cc | 11/3/2014 | $42.00 | 4 |
| 19 | Scott, Bryan | BS@somewhere.com | 3/17/2013 | $145.00 | 1 |
| 6 | Scott, Rex | RS@somewhere.com | 7/15/2014 | $56.00 | 3 |
| 37 | UTran,Diem Thi | DTU@righthere.com | 5/3/2012 | $275.00 | 2 |
| 20 | Warrem, Jason | JW@ourcompany.com | 5/12/2014 | $160.00 | 2 |
| 9 | Wei, Guang | GW@ourcompany.com | 11/28/2013 | $385.00 | 4 |

**Figure CE13-3**
Sales Data Sorted by Customer Name and Grouped by Number of Orders and Showing Total Purchases

*Source:* Microsoft Corporation

| CustomerName | NumOrders | TotalPurchases |
|---|---|---|
| Adams, James | 1 | $145.00 |
| Angel, Kathy | 1 | $195.00 |
| Ashley, Jane | 1 | $110.00 |
| Austin, James | 1 | $55.00 |
| Bernard, Steven | 1 | $78.00 |
| Casimiro, Amanda | 1 | $52.00 |
| Ching, Kam Hoong | 1 | $55.00 |
| Corning,Sandra | 2 | $570.00 |
| Corovic,Jose | 1 | $55.00 |
| Daniel, James | 1 | $52.00 |
| Dixon, James T | 1 | $285.00 |
| Dixon,Eleonor | 1 | $108.00 |
| Drew, Richard | 1 | $42.00 |
| Duong,Linda | 1 | $485.00 |
| Garrett, James | 1 | $38.00 |
| Jordan, Matthew | 1 | $645.00 |
| La Pierre,Anna | 6 | $1,018.50 |
| Lee,Brandon | 1 | $74.00 |
| Lunden,Haley | 1 | $52.00 |
| McGovern, Adrian | 2 | $99.00 |
| Menstell,Lori Lee | 2 | $192.00 |
| Nurul,Nicole | 1 | $84.00 |
| Pham,Mary | 1 | $38.00 |
| Redmond, Louise | 1 | $140.00 |
| Rikki, Nicole | 2 | $330.00 |
| Ryan, Mark | 1 | $42.00 |
| Scott, Bryan | 1 | $145.00 |
| Scott, Rex | 1 | $56.00 |
| UTran,Diem Thi | 1 | $275.00 |
| Warrem, Jason | 1 | $160.00 |
| Wei, Guang | 1 | $385.00 |

Server database, and other nondatabase data. Some data are generated within the organization, other data are obtained from public sources, and still other data may be purchased from data utilities.

A reporting system maintains a database of reporting metadata. The metadata describe reports, users, groups, roles, events, and other entities involved in the reporting activity. The reporting system uses the metadata to prepare and deliver reports to the proper users on a timely basis.

As shown in Figure CE13-5, organizations can prepare reports in a variety of formats. Figure CE13-6 lists report characteristics by type, media, and mode, which we discuss next.

**Figure CE13-4**
Sales Data Filtered to Show Repeat Customers

## Repeat Customers

| NumOrders | CustomerName | TotalPurchases |
|---|---|---|
| 6 | La Pierre,Anna | $1,018.50 |
| 2 | Corning,Sandra | $570.00 |
| 2 | Rikki, Nicole | $330.00 |
| 2 | Menstell,Lori Lee | $192.00 |
| 2 | McGovern, Adrian | $99.00 |

**Figure CE13-5**
Components of a Reporting System

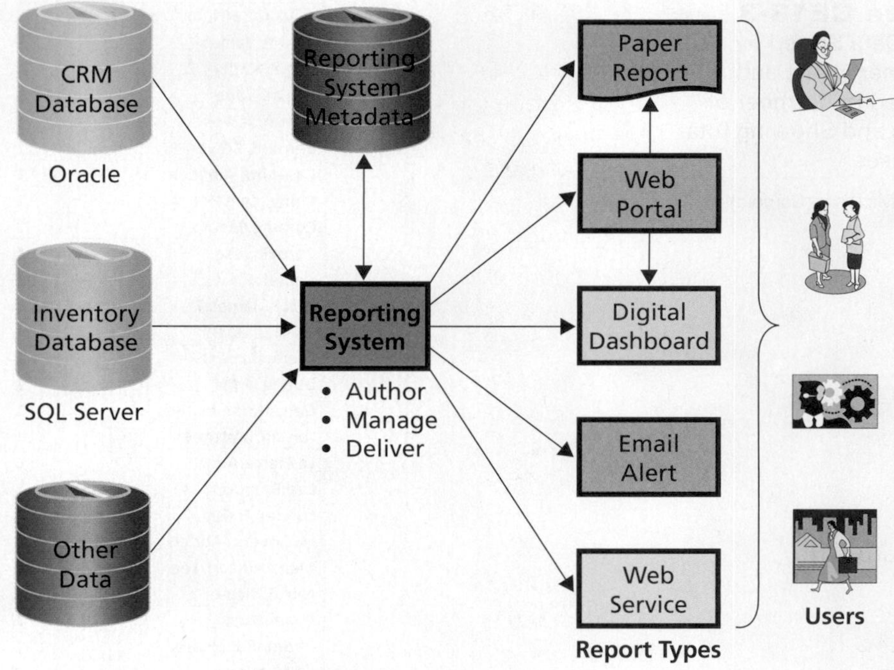


## REPORT TYPE

In terms of **report type,** reports can be *static* or *dynamic*. **Static reports** are prepared once from the underlying data, and they do not change. A report of past years' sales, for example, is a static report. Other reports are dynamic; at the time of creation, the reporting system reads the most current data and generates the report using that fresh data. A report on sales today and a report on current stock prices are both **dynamic reports.**

**Query reports** are prepared in response to data entered by users. Google provides a handy example of a query report: You enter the keywords you want to search, and the reporting system within Google searches its database and generates a response that is particular to your query. Within an organization, a query report could be generated to show current inventory levels. The user enters item numbers, and the reporting system responds with inventory levels of those items at various stores and warehouses.

*Online analytical processing* (*OLAP*) is a fourth type of report. OLAP reports allow the user to dynamically change the report grouping structures. OLAP reports are defined and illustrated in QCE13-4 of this chapter extension.

**Figure CE13-6**
Summary of Report Characteristics

| Type | Media | Mode |
|---|---|---|
| Static | Paper and PDF file | Push |
| Dynamic | Computer screen via application | Pull |
| Query | Web site | |
| Online analytical processing (OLAP) | Digital dashboard | |
| | Alerts via email or cell phone | |
| | Export to Excel, Quicken, TurboTax, QuickBooks, or other application | |
| | Web service | |

## REPORT MEDIA

Today, reports are delivered via many different **report media,** or channels. Some reports are printed on paper; others are created in formats, such as PDF, that can be printed or viewed electronically. Other reports are delivered to computer screens and mobile devices. Applications for CRM and ERP systems, for example, include dozens of different reports that users view online. Additionally, companies sometimes place reports on internal corporate Web sites for employees to access. For example, an organization might place a report of its latest sales on the sales department's Web site or a report on customers serviced on the customer service department's Web site.

Another report medium is a **digital dashboard,** which is an electronic display that is customized for a particular user. Vendors like Yahoo! and MSN provide common examples. Users of these services can define content they want—say, a local weather forecast, a list of stock prices, or a list of news sources—and the vendor constructs the display customized for each user. Figure CE13-7 shows an example.

Other dashboards are particular to an organization. Executives at a manufacturing organization, for example, might have a dashboard that shows up-to-the-minute production and sales activities.

**Alerts** are another form of report. Users can declare that they wish to receive notification of events, say, via email or on their cell phones. Of course, some cell phones are capable of displaying Web pages, and digital dashboards can be delivered to them as well.

Some reports are exported from the report generator to another program, such as Excel, Quicken, QuickBooks, and so forth. For example, application programs at many banks can export customer checking account transactions into Excel, Quicken, or Money.

Finally, reports can be published via a Web service. The Web service produces the report in response to requests from the service-consuming application. This style of reporting is particularly useful for inter-enterprise information systems like supply chain management.

## REPORT MODE

The final report characteristic in Figure CE13-6 is the **report mode,** a term that refers to the way a report is initiated. Organizations send a **push report** to users according to a preset schedule. Users receive the report without any activity on their part. In contrast, users must request a **pull report.** To obtain a pull report, a user goes to a Web portal or digital dashboard and clicks a link or button to cause the reporting system to produce and deliver the report.

**Figure CE13-7**
Digital Dashboard Example

*Source:* Microsoft Corporation

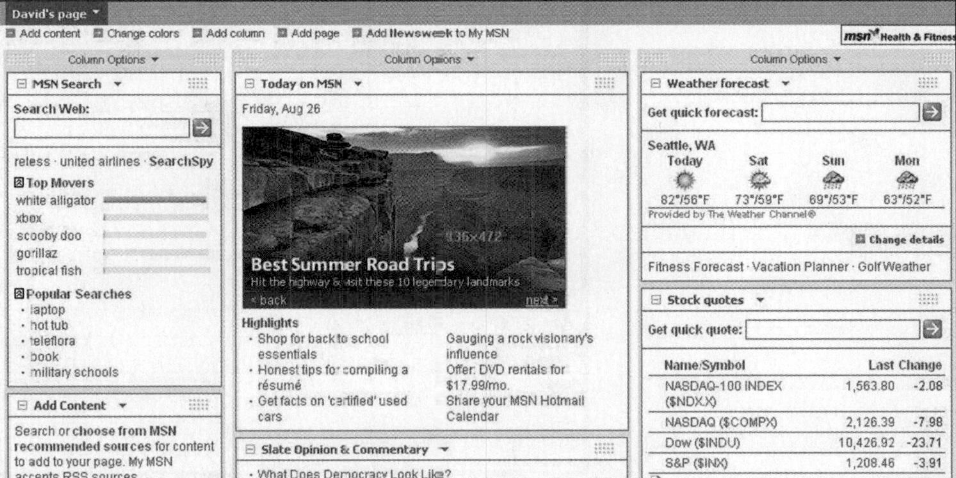

# QCE13-3 HOW ARE REPORTS AUTHORED, MANAGED, AND DELIVERED?

In the middle of Figure CE13-5, under the drawing of the reporting system, three functions of a reporting system are listed: author, manage, and deliver. Consider each.

## REPORT AUTHORING

**Report authoring** involves connecting to data sources, creating the report structure, and formatting the report. You can learn how to create a report for Microsoft Access in Chapter Extension 6, QCE6-5 (starting on page 462).

Of course, much organizational data resides in databases other than Access. One common way that developers author reports is to use tools such as Microsoft's Visual Studio that can connect to many different data sources. For example, in Figure CE13-8, a report author is using Visual Studio to connect to a database that contains source data and has just entered a SQL statement, shown in the lower center portion of this display, to generate a report. Visual Studio can be used to format the report as well.

## REPORT MANAGEMENT

The purpose of **report management** is to define who receives what reports, when, and by what means. Most report management systems allow the report administrator to define user accounts and user groups and to assign particular users to particular groups. For example, all of the salespeople would be assigned to the sales group, all of the executives assigned to the executive group, and so forth. All of these data are stored in the reporting system's metadata shown in Figure CE13-5 (page 564).

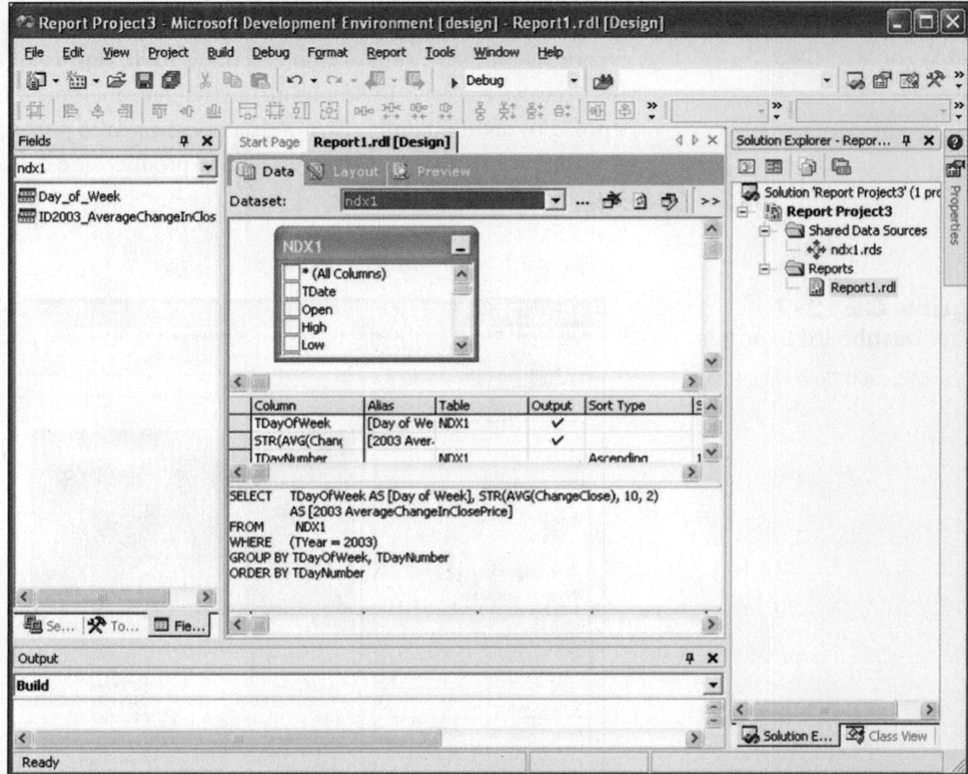


**Figure CE13-8**
Connecting to a Report Data Source Using Visual Studio
*Source:* Microsoft product screenshot reprinted with permission from Microsoft Corporation.

Reports that have been created using the report authoring system are assigned to groups and users. Assigning reports to groups saves the administrator work: When a report is created, changed, or removed, all the users that have been assigned to the report will inherit the changes. All of the users in the group will inherit the changes. Also, when someone is added to or removed from a group, report deliveries will be adjusted as necessary.

As stated, the report management metadata indicate which format of this report is to be sent to which user. The metadata also indicate what channel is to be used and whether the report is to be pushed or pulled. If the report is to be pushed, the administrator declares whether the report is to be generated on a regular schedule or as an alert.

## REPORT DELIVERY

The **report delivery** function of a reporting system pushes reports or allows them to be pulled according to report management metadata. Reports can be delivered via an email server, via a Web site, via SOA services, or by other program-specific means. The report delivery system uses the operating system and other program security components to ensure that only authorized users receive authorized reports. It also ensures that push reports are produced at appropriate times.

For query reports, the report delivery system serves as an intermediary between the user and the report generator. It receives user query data, such as the item numbers in an inventory query, passes the query data to the report generator, receives the resulting report, and delivers the report to the user.

# QCE13-4 HOW ARE OLAP REPORTS DYNAMIC?

**Online analytical processing (OLAP)** is a reporting technology that provides the ability to sum, count, average, and perform other simple arithmetic operations on groups of data. The remarkable characteristic of OLAP reports is that their format is dynamic. The viewer of the report can change the report's structure—hence the term *online.* OLAP reports have the same characteristics as Excel Pivot tables, so if you know how such tables work, you have the essence of the idea about OLAP. The major difference is that OLAP is designed to process tens and hundreds of thousands of records; such volume would be impossible in Excel.

An OLAP report has measures and dimensions. A **measure** is the data item of interest. It is the item that is to be summed or averaged or otherwise processed in the OLAP report. Total sales, average sales, and average cost are examples of measures. A **dimension** is a characteristic of a measure. Purchase date, customer type, customer location, and sales region are all examples of dimensions.

Figure CE13-9 shows a typical OLAP report. Here the measure is *Store Sales Net*, and the dimensions are *Product Family* and *Store Type.* This report shows how net store sales vary by product family and store type. Stores of type *Supermarket*, for example, sold a net of $36,189 worth of nonconsumable goods.

**Figure CE13-9**
OLAP Product Family by Store Type

*Source:* Microsoft Corporation

| | A | B | C | D | E | F | G |
|---|---|---|---|---|---|---|---|
| 1 | | | | | | | |
| 2 | | | | | | | |
| 3 | Store Sales Net | Store Type | | | | | |
| 4 | Product Family | Deluxe Supermarket | Gourmet Supermarket | Mid-Size Grocery | Small Grocery | Supermarket | Grand Total |
| 5 | Drink | $8,119.05 | $2,392.83 | $1,409.50 | $685.89 | $16,751.71 | $29,358.98 |
| 6 | Food | $70,276.11 | $20,026.18 | $10,392.19 | $6,109.72 | $138,960.67 | $245,764.87 |
| 7 | Nonconsumable | $18,884.24 | $5,064.79 | $2,813.73 | $1,534.90 | $36,189.40 | $64,487.05 |
| 8 | Grand Total | $97,279.40 | $27,483.80 | $14,615.42 | $8,330.51 | $191,901.77 | $339,610.90 |

A presentation of a measure with associated dimensions like that in Figure CE13-9 is often called an **OLAP cube** or sometimes simply a *cube*. The reason for this term is that some products show these displays using three axes, like a cube in geometry. The origin of the term is unimportant here, however. Just know that an *OLAP cube* and an *OLAP report* are the same thing.

The OLAP report in Figure CE13-9 was generated by SQL Server Analysis Services and is displayed in an Excel Pivot table. The data were taken from a sample instructional database, called Food Mart, that is provided with SQL Server. It is possible to display OLAP cubes in many ways besides with Excel. Some third-party vendors provide more extensive graphical displays. Possibly the easiest to use OLAP tool available is Tableau from Tableau Software. Visit *www.TableauSoftware.com* to see useful demos and tutorials.

As stated earlier, the distinguishing characteristic of an OLAP report is that the user can alter the format of the report. Figure CE13-10 shows such an alteration. Here the user added another dimension, *Store Country* and *Store State*, to the horizontal display. Product-family sales are now broken out by the location of the stores. Observe that the sample data include only stores in the United States and only in the western states of California, Oregon, and Washington.

With an OLAP report, it is possible to **drill down** into the data. This term means to further divide the data into more detail. In Figure CE13-11, for example, the user has drilled down into the stores located in California; the OLAP report now shows sales data for the four cities in California that have stores.

Notice another difference between Figures CE13-10 and CE13-11. The user has not only drilled down, but she has also changed the order of the dimensions. Figure CE13-10 shows *Product Family* and then store location within *Product Family*. Figure CE13-11 shows store location and then *Product Family* within store location.

Both displays are valid and useful, depending on the user's perspective. A product manager might like to see product families first and then store location data. A sales manager might like to see store locations first and then product data. OLAP reports provide both perspectives, and the user can switch between them while viewing the report.

Unfortunately, all of this flexibility comes at a cost. If the database is large, doing the necessary calculating, grouping, and sorting for such dynamic displays will require substantial

**Figure CE13-10**
OLAP Product Family and Store Location by Store Type
*Source:* Microsoft Corporation

| | A | B | C | D | E | F | G | H | I |
|---|---|---|---|---|---|---|---|---|---|
| 1 | | | | | | | | | |
| 2 | | | | | | | | | |
| 3 | Store Sales Net | | | Store Type | | | | | |
| 4 | Product Family | Store Country | Store State | Deluxe Supermarket | Gourmet Supermarket | Mid-Size Grocery | Small Grocery | Supermarket | Grand Total |
| 5 | Drink | USA | CA | | $2,392.83 | | $227.38 | $5,920.76 | $8,540.97 |
| 6 | | | OR | $4,438.49 | | | | $2,862.45 | $7,300.94 |
| 7 | | | WA | $3,680.56 | | $1,409.50 | $458.51 | $7,968.50 | $13,517.07 |
| 8 | | USA Total | | $8,119.05 | $2,392.83 | $1,409.50 | $685.89 | $16,751.71 | $29,358.98 |
| 9 | Drink Total | | | $8,119.05 | $2,392.83 | $1,409.50 | $685.89 | $16,751.71 | $29,358.98 |
| 10 | Food | USA | CA | | $20,026.18 | | $1,960.53 | $47,226.11 | $69,212.82 |
| 11 | | | OR | $37,778.35 | | | | $23,818.87 | $61,597.22 |
| 12 | | | WA | $32,497.76 | | $10,392.19 | $4,149.19 | $67,915.69 | $114,954.83 |
| 13 | | USA Total | | $70,276.11 | $20,026.18 | $10,392.19 | $6,109.72 | $138,960.67 | $245,764.87 |
| 14 | Food Total | | | $70,276.11 | $20,026.18 | $10,392.19 | $6,109.72 | $138,960.67 | $245,764.87 |
| 15 | Nonconsumable | USA | CA | | $5,064.79 | | $474.35 | $12,344.49 | $17,883.63 |
| 16 | | | OR | $10,177.89 | | | | $6,428.53 | $16,606.41 |
| 17 | | | WA | $8,706.36 | | $2,813.73 | $1,060.54 | $17,416.38 | $29,997.01 |
| 18 | | USA Total | | $18,884.24 | $5,064.79 | $2,813.73 | $1,534.90 | $36,189.40 | $64,487.05 |
| 19 | Nonconsumable Total | | | $18,884.24 | $5,064.79 | $2,813.73 | $1,534.90 | $36,189.40 | $64,487.05 |
| 20 | Grand Total | | | $97,279.40 | $27,483.80 | $14,615.42 | $8,330.51 | $191,901.77 | $339,610.90 |

| | A | B | C | D | E | F | G | H | I | J |
|---|---|---|---|---|---|---|---|---|---|---|
| 1 | | | | | | | | | | |
| 2 | | | | | | | | | | |
| 3 | Store Sales Net | | | | Store Type | | | | | |
| 4 | Store Country | Store Sta | Store City | Product Family | Deluxe Super | Gourmet Supermarket | Mid-Size Grocery | Small Grocery | Supermarket | Grand Total |
| 5 | USA | CA | Beverly Hills | Drink | | $2,392.83 | | | | $2,392.83 |
| 6 | | | | Food | | $20,026.18 | | | | $20,026.18 |
| 7 | | | | Nonconsumable | | $5,064.79 | | | | $5,064.79 |
| 8 | | | Beverly Hills Total | | | $27,483.80 | | | | $27,483.80 |
| 9 | | | Los Angeles | Drink | | | | | $2,870.33 | $2,870.33 |
| 10 | | | | Food | | | | | $23,598.28 | $23,598.28 |
| 11 | | | | Nonconsumable | | | | | $6,305.14 | $6,305.14 |
| 12 | | | Los Angeles Total | | | | | | $32,773.74 | $32,773.74 |
| 13 | | | San Diego | Drink | | | | | $3,050.43 | $3,050.43 |
| 14 | | | | Food | | | | | $23,627.83 | $23,627.83 |
| 15 | | | | Nonconsumable | | | | | $6,039.34 | $6,039.34 |
| 16 | | | San Diego Total | | | | | | $32,717.61 | $32,717.61 |
| 17 | | | San Francisco | Drink | | | | $227.38 | | $227.38 |
| 18 | | | | Food | | | | $1,960.53 | | $1,960.53 |
| 19 | | | | Nonconsumable | | | | $474.35 | | $474.35 |
| 20 | | | San Francisco Total | | | | | $2,662.26 | | $2,662.26 |
| 21 | | CA Total | | | | $27,483.80 | | $2,662.26 | $65,491.35 | $95,637.41 |
| 22 | | OR | | Drink | $4,438.49 | | | | $2,862.45 | $7,300.94 |
| 23 | | | | Food | $37,778.35 | | | | $23,818.87 | $61,597.22 |
| 24 | | | | Nonconsumable | $10,177.89 | | | | $6,428.53 | $16,606.41 |
| 25 | | OR Total | | | $52,394.72 | | | | $33,109.85 | $85,504.57 |
| 26 | | WA | | Drink | $3,680.56 | | $1,409.50 | $458.51 | $7,968.50 | $13,517.07 |
| 27 | | | | Food | $32,497.76 | | $10,392.19 | $4,149.19 | $67,915.69 | $114,954.83 |
| 28 | | | | Nonconsumable | $8,706.36 | | $2,813.73 | $1,060.54 | $17,416.38 | $29,997.01 |
| 29 | | WA Total | | | $44,884.68 | | $14,615.42 | $5,668.24 | $93,300.57 | $158,468.91 |
| 30 | USA Total | | | | $97,279.40 | $27,483.80 | $14,615.42 | $8,330.51 | $191,901.77 | $339,610.90 |
| 31 | Grand Total | | | | $97,279.40 | $27,483.80 | $14,615.42 | $8,330.51 | $191,901.77 | $339,610.90 |

**Figure CE13-11**
OLAP Product Family and Store Location by Store Type, Showing Sales Data for Four Cities

*Source:* Microsoft Corporation

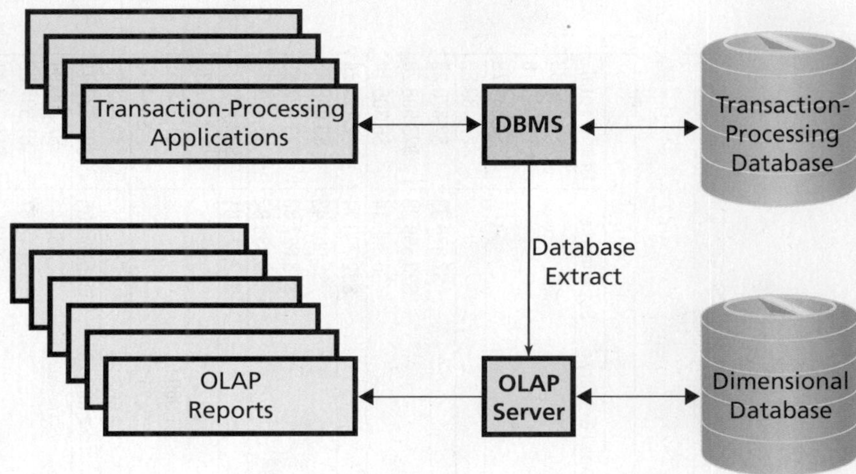


**Figure CE13-12**
Role of OLAP Server and Dimensional Database

computing power. Although standard, commercial DBMS products do have the features and functions required to create OLAP reports, they are not designed for such work. They are designed, instead, to provide rapid response to transaction processing applications, such as order entry or manufacturing operations.

Accordingly, special-purpose products called **OLAP servers** have been developed to perform OLAP analysis. As shown in Figure CE13-12, an OLAP server reads data from an operational database, performs preliminary calculations, and stores the results of those calculations in an OLAP database. (Databases that are structured to support OLAP processing are called **dimensional databases.**) Several different schemes are used for this storage, but the particulars of those schemes are beyond this discussion. Normally, for performance and security reasons, the OLAP server and the DBMS run on separate computers.

# ACTIVE REVIEW

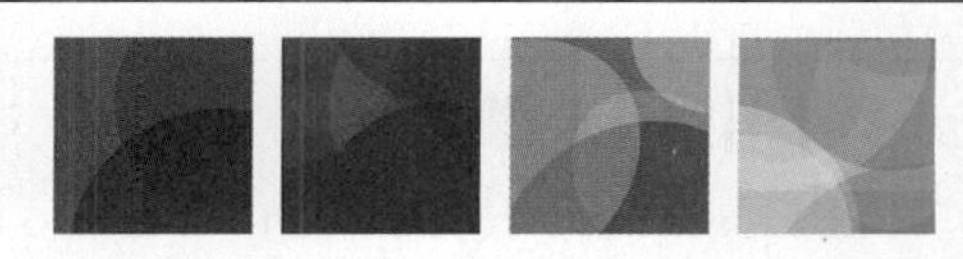

Use this Active Review to verify that you understand the ideas and concepts that answer this chapter extension's study questions.

## QCE13-1 HOW DO REPORTING SYSTEMS ENABLE PEOPLE TO CREATE INFORMATION?

Describe the purpose of a reporting system. Explain how reporting systems enable people to create information. List four basic reporting operations. Using Figures CE13-1 and CE13-4, explain how each context enables the creation of more information.

## QCE13-2 WHAT ARE THE COMPONENTS AND CHARACTERISTICS OF REPORTING SYSTEMS?

Describe the role of each of the components in Figure CE13-5. Explain what reporting metadata describes. Name four types of reports and give an example of each. Name seven different report media. Explain the difference between push and pull reports.

## QCE13-3 HOW ARE REPORTS AUTHORED, MANAGED, AND DELIVERED?

Name the three functions of report authoring. Explain the purpose of report management. Describe the role of metadata for report management. Describe the report delivery function. Explain the role of report delivery for security and for query reports.

## QCE13-4 HOW ARE OLAP REPORTS DYNAMIC?

Describe the basic operation of an OLAP report. Define *measure* and give an example. Define *dimension* and give at least two examples. Using hypothetical data and Figure CE13-9 as a guide, show how your measure and dimensions would appear in an OLAP report. Show how the structure of the report changes if you switch the two dimensions. Using your sample data, explain why OLAP reports are considered more dynamic than standard reports. Describe the circumstances under which an OLAP server is required.

## KEY TERMS AND CONCEPTS

MyMISLab™

To complete the problems with the ✪, go to EOC Discussion Questions in the MyLab.

## USING YOUR KNOWLEDGE

✪ **CE13-1.** Explain the difference in the following two expressions:

**a.** Reporting systems create information.

**b.** Reporting systems enable the creation of information.

✪ **CE13-2.** In your own words, explain the phrase *meaningful context*.

✪ **CE13-3.** Assume you are a buyer for a department at Home Depot and you are asked to describe the kind of report you want to help you negotiate with vendors. Describe (or sketch the outline of) a report that would give you a meaningful context about:

**a.** Popular products

**b.** Most profitable products

**c.** Lost revenue from products that are frequently out of stock

**d.** Products that sell unacceptably slowly

MyMISLab™

Go to the Assignments section of your MyLab to complete these writing exercises.

**CE13-4.** Suppose you're a buyer at an online sporting goods retailer and you'd like to evaluate vendors according to revenue, profitability, and performance (delivering the correct number of items with little damage). Describe (or sketch the outline of) a report that you need.

**CE13-5.** Assume you have the raw data shown in QCE13-1. Describe how filtering, sorting, grouping, and making simple calculations can help you determine which customers purchase items most frequently. Describe (or sketch the format of) a report that would help you understand which customers spend the most total money.

chapter extension **14**

**Chapter 10** provides the background for this extension.

# Data Breaches

**STUDY QUESTIONS**

**QCE14-1 WHAT IS A DATA BREACH?**

**QCE14-2 HOW DO DATA BREACHES HAPPEN?**

**QCE14-3 HOW SHOULD ORGANIZATIONS RESPOND TO DATA BREACHES?**

**QCE14-4 WHAT ARE THE LEGAL CONSEQUENCES OF A DATA BREACH?**

**QCE14-5 HOW CAN DATA BREACHES BE PREVENTED?**

## QCE14-1 WHAT IS A DATA BREACH?

A **data breach** happens when an unauthorized person views, alters, or steals secured data. Data breaches are particularly worrisome because of the amount of damage they can do to an organization. Verizon's latest data breach report estimates that more than 700 million people have been affected by data breaches in the past 11 years resulting in $400 million in direct financial losses.[1]

To give you an idea of how this affects organizations, Ponemon's *2015 Cost of Data Breach Study* notes that, on average, a single data breach costs an organization $3.8 million.[2] The average cost of losing a single record is $154.

Direct costs of handling a data breach include paying for:

- Notification
- Detection
- Escalation
- Remediation
- Legal fees and consultation

Ponemon also estimates that indirect costs related to loss of reputation, abnormal customer turnover, and increased customer acquisition activities averaged an *additional* $3.3 million per incident in the United States.

So, data breaches are costly. But what are the chances that your organization will be involved in a data breach? Based on actual responses from more than 1,600 organizations, Ponemon estimates that there is a 22 percent chance of losing 10,000 records over any given 24-month period.[3] The probability of losing 100,000 records over the same period is less than 1 percent. In other words, organizations are more likely to lose *smaller* amounts of data than *larger* amounts of data.

Take a minute to consider the costs and probabilities of a data breach at your organization. There is a one-in-five chance that your organization will lose 10,000 records in the next 2 years. Each of those records will cost on average $154. Is your organization financially, technically, and logistically prepared for such a breach?

Figure CE14-1 shows a small portion of the data breaches from the past few years. While Edward Snowden and Bradley Manning may have gotten more press because they stole classified documents, the data breaches shown in the figure directly affected the lives of hundreds of millions of people.

### WHY DO DATA BREACHES HAPPEN?

More than 67 percent of data breaches come from hackers trying to make money. Hackers are primarily looking for **personally identifiable information (PII)**, or data that can be used to identify a person. This includes names, addresses, dates of birth, Social Security numbers, credit card numbers, health records, bank account numbers, PINs, and email addresses.

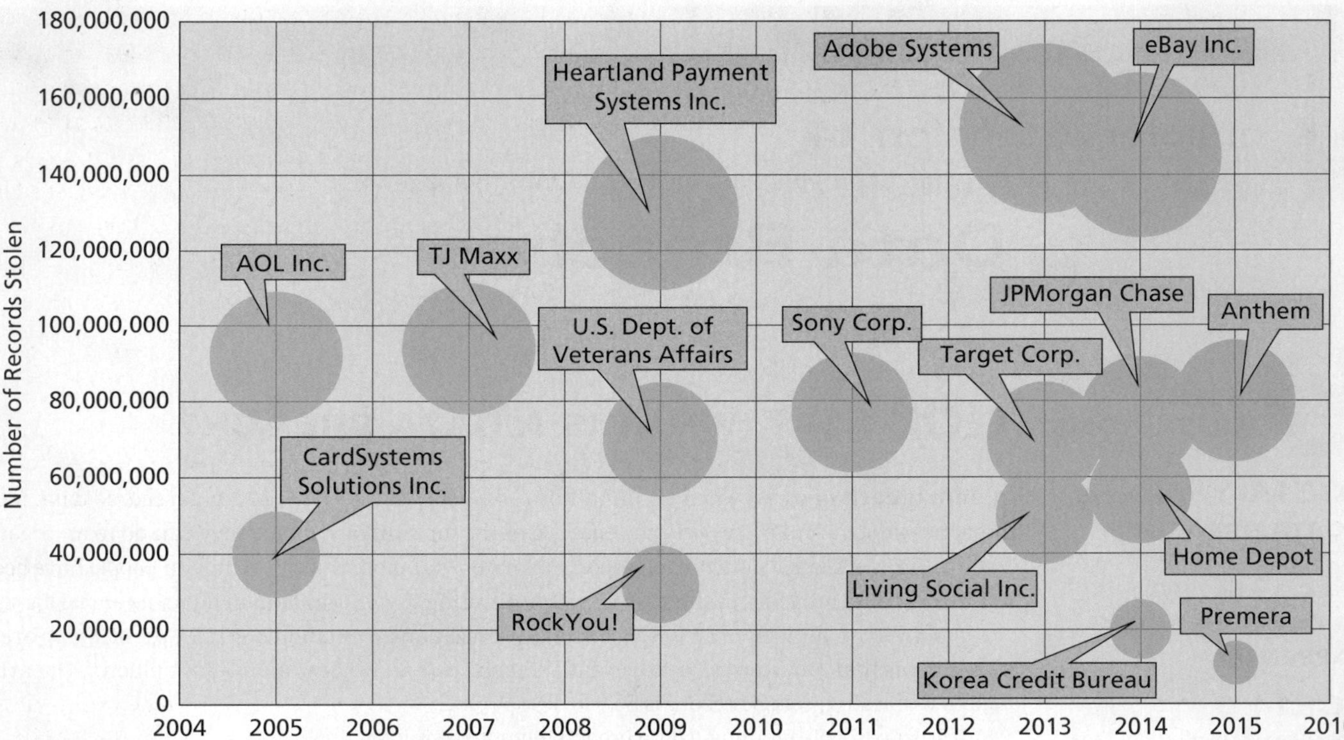


**Figure CE14-1**
Well-known Data Breaches

Stolen information is commonly used for credit card fraud. Stolen credit card information is validated through a process called **carding**, where a small charge is placed on the card to ensure it is working. Valid cards are then bundled and sold on the black market. The price of stolen credit cards can run from $2 to $45 per card depending on the type of account.[4] Interestingly, if a large number of credit card accounts are stolen and offered for sale at one time, the per-card price can drop as low as $0.75! This is exactly what happened after the Target data breach, which will be discussed later in this chapter extension.

Credit card fraud isn't the only way criminals make money from data breaches. Stolen data is commonly used for identity theft, extortion, and industrial espionage. Any organization with valuable data may be a targeted. For example, in 2014 a hacker group named Rex Mundi tried to extort €30,000 (about $40,500) from Domino's Pizza in France and Belgium by threatening to release the company's user account details (names, addresses, phone numbers, emails, passwords, and pizza preferences).[5] It's unknown if Domino's paid the hacker group.

Not all data breaches are the result of hackers in distant locales. Rogue internal employees can steal data even more easily than external hackers. In one stunning example, a 39-year-old technician working for the Korea Credit Bureau stole personal information for 104 million credit cards belonging to nearly 20 million people in South Korea.[6] This single data breach affected 40 percent of all South Koreans. The employee, identified only as Mr. Park, had been hired to improve the security of client data. He attempted to sell the stolen information to executives at a phone marketing company.

## QCE14-2 HOW DO DATA BREACHES HAPPEN?

The first step in protecting yourself from data breaches is understanding how they happen. Each one is different because hackers are continually developing new tools and techniques that enable them to steal more data. They experiment with new **attack vectors**, or ways of attacking a target. They might use a phishing scam one week in an effort to trick users into donating funds for a natural disaster. Then, the following week, they might develop an **exploit**, which is software used to take advantage of a newly discovered vulnerability in a target's application or operating system.

The following paragraphs detail the data breach at Target Corporation that happened in late 2013. While it's tempting to think less of Target because of the breach, it's not entirely fair to do so. Yes, there were missteps on Target's part, and we will discuss those. But Target has been extremely forthcoming with the details surrounding the data breach, and it has handled the fallout from the breach very well. Other companies involved in data breaches have not been as forthcoming. Ebay, for example, lost as many as 145 million customer accounts in 2014 and failed to notify users about the breach in a timely fashion.[7] It also provided few details about the attack in spite of multiple government investigations.

## HITTING TARGET

On December 18, 2013, Target Corporation announced that it had lost 40 million credit and debit card numbers to attackers. Less than a month later, Target announced an additional 70 million customer accounts were stolen, including names, emails, addresses, and phone numbers.

After accounting for some overlap between the two data losses, about 98 million customers were affected.[8] That's 31 percent of all 318 million people in the United States (including children and those without credit cards). This makes the Target data breach one of the largest in U.S. history.

Customer records were stolen from point-of-sale (POS) systems at Target retail stores during the holiday shopping season (November 27 to December 15, 2013). If you were shopping at a Target during this time, it's likely your data was lost.

## HOW DID THEY DO IT?

As shown in Figure CE14-2, the attackers first purchased malware designed specifically for the attacks they planned to carry out. They then used **spear phishing**, or a targeted phishing attack, to infect a Target third-party vendor named Fazio Mechanical Services (which provides

**Figure CE14-2**
Target Data Breach

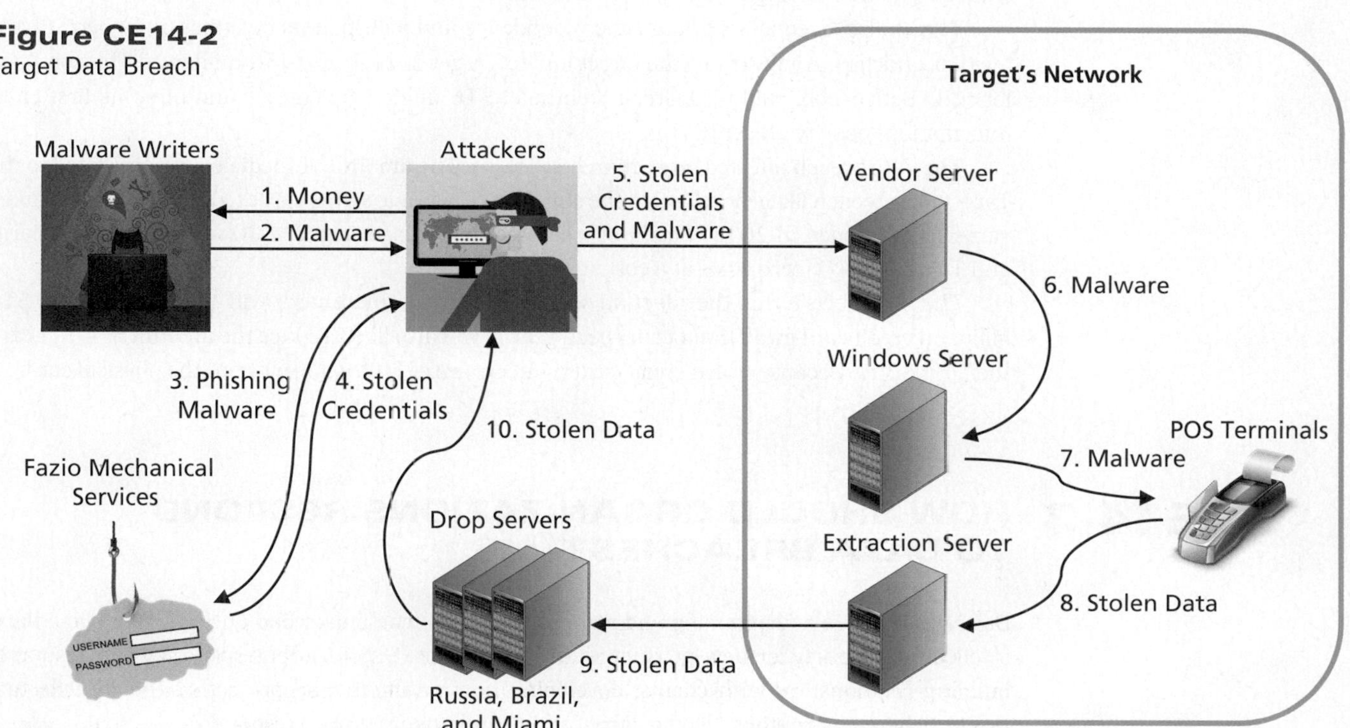

refrigeration and HVAC services).[9] Attackers placed a piece of malware called Citadel on Fazio's system to gather keystrokes, login credentials, and screenshots from Fazio users.[10] The attackers then used the stolen login credentials from Fazio to access a vendor portal (or server) on Target's network. The attackers escalated privileges on that server (i.e., took over the server) and gained access to Target's internal network.

Once inside Target's network, the attackers compromised an internal Windows file server. From this server, the attackers used malware named Trojan.POSRAM (a variant of BlackPOS) to extract customer data from POS terminals. BlackPOS was developed by a 17-year-old from St. Petersburg, Russia, and can be purchased from underground sites for about $2,000.[11]

Customer data was continuously sent from the POS terminals to an extraction server within Target's network. It was then funneled out of Target's network to drop servers in Russia, Brazil, and Miami. From there, the data was collected and sold on the black market.

## THE DAMAGE

For the attackers, the "damage" was substantial. It's estimated that the attackers sold about 2 million credit cards for about $26.85 each for a total profit of $53.7 million.[12] The prices for the remaining cards dropped due to the large supply available. The hackers could have chosen to hold back some of the stolen credit cards rather than flooding the market, but they had to sell them as quickly as possible because the stolen cards were being canceled and replaced by banks. The prices of stolen credit cards from Target, sold in batches of 100,000, dropped by 70 percent after 2 months.[13] This was likely due to a drop in credit card validity rates from nearly 100 percent to about 60 percent.

From the hackers' point of view, the operation was a spectacular success. The payoff was substantial for just a few weeks of work. Unfortunately, payoffs like these encourage even more data breaches.

Target, on the other hand, incurred much greater losses than the hackers' gains. It was forced to upgrade its payment terminals to support chip-and-PIN-enabled cards (to prevent cloning cards from stolen information), which cost more than $100 million. In 2015, Target lost a legal battle with banks over reimbursement of costs associated with the data breach, which could exceed $160 million. It also had to pay increased insurance premiums, pay legal fees, pay for consumer credit monitoring, and pay regulatory fines.

Target also faced a loss of customer confidence and a drop in its revenues (a 46 percent loss for that quarter). Analysts put the direct loss to Target as high as $450 million.[14] The company lost CIO Beth Jacob, paid CEO Gregg Steinhafel $16 million to leave,[15] and hired its first chief information security officer (CISO).[16]

The data breach affected more than just Target. The amount of media coverage related to the Target data breach likely accelerated the shift from magnetic swipe cards to EMV-compliant smart cards set to happen in 2015. This shift will force the replacement of 800 million payment cards and 14 million POS terminals at a cost of $7 billion.[17]

The good news is that the adoption of EMV-compliant smart cards will greatly reduce the $10 billion in credit card fraud that occurs each year. It will also likely reduce the amount of credit card theft by hackers because stolen credit card numbers are of little value without the physical card.

# QCE14-3 HOW SHOULD ORGANIZATIONS RESPOND TO DATA BREACHES?

Data breaches are embarrassing and demoralizing. It is crushing to find out that your client data, intellectual property, or new product plans were stolen. Organizations spend a lot of resources building relationships with clients, developing new products, and protecting their intellectual assets. When they're stolen, leaders are stunned and unsure how to respond.

Responses to data breaches need to be quick, preplanned, and honest. They also need to include a sincere apology to those affected. The following are a few guidelines to consider when responding to a data breach.

## RESPOND QUICKLY

Organizations need to respond to data breaches quickly for several reasons. First, by responding quickly an organization can stop hackers from doing more damage. Hackers can be prevented from accessing other internal systems, and affected systems can be patched and cleaned. Additionally, if organizations respond quickly enough, hackers may be prevented from **exfiltrating** (sometimes known as data extrusion), or illegally transferring, data out of the organization.

Second, responding quickly may mitigate the amount of damage hackers can do with the stolen data. If the affected users are notified immediately they can change their passwords, cancel their credit cards, and possibly activate credit monitoring services. Hackers will use any delay by the organization as a chance to convert the stolen data into money. Hackers know the value of stolen data drops quickly, so they will try to sell it as soon as possible.

Third, the longer organizations delay in notifying users, the more upset users become. Based on past data breaches, users are reasonably forgiving of organizations that quickly notify them about what happened and what steps are being taken to make things right. Users know hackers exist and that they steal things. Users have been forced to change their passwords before, and most consider it an understandable part of doing business. But mass user defection is often the result when organizations know users' data has been stolen and allow those users to be vulnerable for weeks or months.

## PLAN FOR A DATA BREACH

Like traffic accidents, data breaches aren't guaranteed to happen, but they are likely to happen. As a result, organizations need to plan for data breaches. They need to rehearse what they will do when a breach happens. Executives, managers, and systems personnel must perform a **walk-through** and discuss the specific steps each person will take after a breach occurs. This should done as part of a broader **business continuity planning** session that discusses how to return the organization to normal operations as quickly as possible.

As part of the planning process, organizations should form a **computer security incident response team (CSIRT)** consisting of staff from the legal and public relations departments as well as executives and systems administrators. Coordinated preplanning for an incident helps organizations avoid missteps like accidentally destroying evidence and issuing poorly worded data breach notices to users. After a data breach is discovered the clock starts ticking, tempers flare, law enforcement may become involved, and the ability to make effective decisions may be degraded. Decisions must be made before the incident, not while it's happening.

Finally, as part of the planning process, organizations need to identify additional technical and law enforcement professionals that may need to be brought in to help handle the data breach. Evidence of the breach must be preserved, and the extent of the damage needs to be accurately measured. Existing IT staff will likely know how to manage internal systems, but they probably won't have the necessary expertise to perform an effective forensic investigation.

## BE HONEST ABOUT THE BREACH

One of the most difficult parts of a data breach is managing the negative fallout. Users, vendors, credit processors, employees, managers, and executives will all be upset. The organization needs to work through the incident and get past it, and there are things that can be done to make the breach more manageable.

| Best Practice | The Right Way | The Wrong Way |
|---|---|---|
| 1. Be transparent in your activity and demonstrate that you are getting the word out. | Directly email every affected user with details about the data breach, and include a popup advisory on the company's most visited page. | Include a vague reference in a rarely read press release that includes plenty of technical jargon. |
| 2. Follow your normal media routine. | Notify local reporters that usually report on the organization, as well as issuing a typical press release. | Only send the notification to a small number of users. |
| 3. Avoid absolutes. | State that, so far, the data breach has affected a certain number of users but the investigation is still ongoing. | State that the breach affected only certain number of users and no more. |
| 4. Avoid misleading statements. | "We are investigating the possibility of lost credit card data." | "We don't have any evidence that credit cards have been compromised." But you've received notification from a credit processor that an investigation is underway. |
| 5. Don't attempt to withhold key details. | "It appears that at least 40% of user accounts were compromised." | "I can't comment on the number of accounts compromised at this time." |
| 6. Stay focused and concise. | Give a brief, concise, and factual statement about the data breach. | Provide extraneous details about failings of internal backup, offsite data policies, and unrelated criminal investigations. |

**Figure CE14-3**
Best Practices for Notifying Users of a Data Breach

Figure CE14-3 shows six best practices from Visa for merchants handling a data breach. It gives examples of the right and wrong ways of notifying users of the breach. Merchants regularly notify Visa of data breaches, so consider this advice carefully. Note that Visa recommends that organizations be open and honest about the data breach. It suggests giving users enough relevant details while avoiding extraneous details that may prolong an investigation.

Data breach notifications must include a sincere apology and an acceptance of responsibility for the incident. They should state that existing security policies and procedures were inadequate and that changes are being made to prevent similar breaches in the future.

## QCE14-4 WHAT ARE THE LEGAL CONSEQUENCES OF A DATA BREACH?

At the start of this chapter extension we looked at the costs organizations incur related to the handling of a data breach. These costs run about $154 per record lost, plus additional losses in reputation and customer turnover. In addition to these losses, organizations may also face lawsuits, fines from payment card issuers, insurance claims, and fines for violating industry regulations.

For example, in 2010, Genesco, a footwear company based in Tennessee, experienced a data breach. Visa collected $13.3 million in fines from Genesco for the breach.[18] Genesco subsequently sued Visa in 2013 claiming the fines were unjustified because Genesco was compliant with industry standards for securely storing payment card information, namely the **Payment Card Industry Data Security Standard (PCI DSS)** shown in Figure CE14-4.[19]

Genesco also noted that fines were applicable only if more than 10,000 records were stolen and demonstrable financial damage actually occurred. Genesco claimed that none of these factors was present in its case and the fines were unjustified. The case is still being litigated.

**Figure CE14-4**
PCI DSS Standards

| | PCI DSS Requirements |
|---|---|
| **Build and Maintain a Secure Network and Systems** | 1. Install and maintain a firewall configuration to protect cardholder data.<br>2. Do not use vendor-supplied defaults for system passwords and other security parameters. |
| **Protect Cardholder Data** | 3. Protect stored cardholder data.<br>4. Encrypt transmission of cardholder data across open, public networks. |
| **Maintain a Vulnerability Management Program** | 5. Protect all systems against malware, and regularly update anti-virus software or programs.<br>6. Develop and maintain secure systems and applications. |
| **Implement Strong Access Control Measures** | 7. Restrict access to cardholder data by businesses on a need-to-know basis.<br>8. Identify and authenticate access to system components.<br>9. Restrict physical access to cardholder data. |
| **Regularly Monitor and Test Networks** | 10. Track and monitor all access to network resources and cardholder data.<br>11. Regularly test security systems and processes. |
| **Maintain an Information Security Policy** | 12. Maintain a policy that addresses information security for all personnel. |

This example shows that regulatory fines imposed after a data breach can easily exceed the financial damage done during the data breach. Organizations need to understand the body of regulatory law relative to the *type* of information they store because they will be held accountable for implementing those standards. A few prominent regulatory laws govern the secure storage of data in certain industries. These include the following:

- The **Federal Information Security Management Act (FISMA)** requires security precautions for government agencies.
- The **Gramm-Leach-Bliley Act (GLBA)**, also known as the Financial Services Modernization Act, requires data protection for financial institutions.
- The **Health Information Portability and Accountability Act (HIPAA)** requires data protection for healthcare institutions.
- The Payment Card Industry Data Security Standard (PCI DSS), mentioned earlier, governs the secure storage of cardholder data.
- The **Family Educational Rights and Privacy Act (FERPA)** provides protection for student education records.

## QCE14-5 HOW CAN DATA BREACHES BE PREVENTED?

Can you prevent data breaches? Yes and no. Honestly, there is nothing you can do to make data breaches impossible. If a large government entity puts enough resources into getting your data, it will succeed. It has more money, manpower, and horsepower than you do. In addition, organizations can't afford to spend all of their resources fending off hackers. They need to advertise, sell products, serve clients, educate students, and treat patients. Hackers don't have to spend their time or money on any of those things.

That said, organizations can implement **countermeasures** that make data breaches *improbable*, or unlikely to occur. Countermeasures are software or procedures used to prevent an attack. Consider the Target example. At each step in the process, the hackers could have been detected and stopped by appropriate countermeasures. For example, better phishing detection software might have stopped the spear phishing attack on the third-party vendor. More secure authentication (i.e., multifactor authentication) might have prevented the hackers from using the vendor's credentials on Target's vendor portal. A **network intrusion detection system (NIDS)** used to examine traffic passing through Target's internal network might have identified possible attacks. Finally, **data loss prevention systems (DLP)**, which are designed to prevent sensitive data from being released to unauthorized persons, could have been used to stop the data from leaving the internal network.

Managers inevitably want a list that shows them exactly what to do to prevent a data breach. This is difficult to provide because data breaches happen in many different ways. For example, a simple SQL injection attack on a company's online store can't be stopped by additional user training, stronger vendor authentication, or an internal NIDS. Each attack is unique and requires its own set of countermeasures. A list of countermeasures to protect against many different types of attacks would be lengthy.

As a starting point, however, organizations should appoint a chief information security officer (CISO) to ensure sufficient executive support and resources are given to this process. Organizations then need to implement the security safeguards mentioned in Chapter 10 and appropriate data protections based on internal policies, like those shown in Figure CE14-5. In addition, special consideration should be given to regulatory requirements if the organization is storing certain types of sensitive data. Finally, organizations should form a CSIRT, have a business continuity plan in place, and rehearse their incident response plan.

**Figure CE14-5**
Suggestions for Preventing Data Loss

1. Don't collect more data than is necessary.
2. Permanently destroy old data.
3. Limit the number of places data is stored.
4. Limit employee access to data necessary to perform their job.
5. Document (log) access to critical data.
6. Develop effective termination procedures to prevent data theft.
7. Develop policies that govern offsite data storage and use.
8. Encrypt data when possible.
9. Provide training to users about data security standards.

# ACTIVE REVIEW

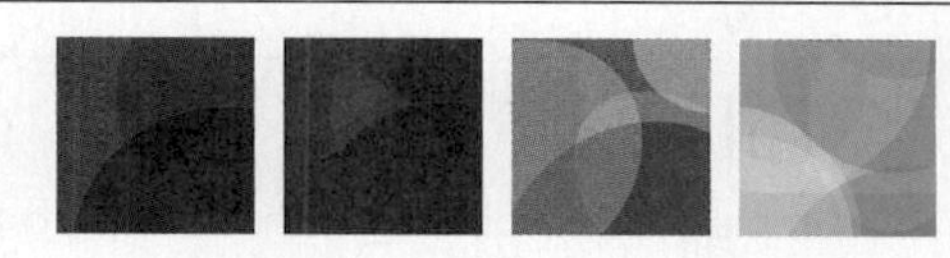

Use this Active Review to verify that you understand the ideas and concepts that answer this chapter extension's study questions.

## QCE14-1 WHAT IS A DATA BREACH?

Define *data breach, personally identifiable information (PII)*, and *carding*. List some of the direct and indirect costs related to data breaches. How likely is it that a data breach will occur? What motivates hackers to steal data? Explain how hackers can make money from stealing data.

## QCE14-2 HOW DO DATA BREACHES HAPPEN?

Define *attack vectors, exploit*, and *spear phishing*. Describe each step in the Target data breach. How did the hackers gain access to Target's internal network? Why did the hackers want to sell the stolen information as quickly as possible? Describe the damage caused by this data breach.

## QCE14-3 HOW SHOULD ORGANIZATIONS RESPOND TO DATA BREACHES?

Define *exfiltration, walkthrough, business continuity planning*, and *computer security incident response team (CSIRT)*. Why is it important to respond quickly to a data breach? Explain how planning for a data breach can mitigate the damage associated with a breach. List the six data breach best practices from Visa and explain how they could minimize the severity of a breach.

## QCE14-4 WHAT ARE THE LEGAL CONSEQUENCES OF A DATA BREACH?

Why should organizations be concerned with the legal consequences of a data breach? Explain why the payment card industry would want all merchants to be PCI DSS compliant. Why should merchants be concerned about the fines levied against Genesco? Define *PCI DSS, FISMA, GLBA, HIPAA*, and *FERPA*. Identify which industries are affected by each one.

## QCE14-5 HOW CAN DATA BREACHES BE PREVENTED?

Define *countermeasures, network intrusion detection system (NIDS)*, and *data loss prevention system (DLP)*. List two ways the Target data breach could have been prevented. Explain why there's nothing you can do to make data breaches impossible and how you can make them improbable. Describe what an organization should do to protect itself against data breaches.

## KEY TERMS AND CONCEPTS

Attack vectors 574
Business continuity planning 577
Carding 574
Computer security incident response team (CSIRT) 577
Countermeasures 579
Data breach 573
Data loss prevention system (DLP) 580
Exfiltration 577
Exploit 575
Family Educational Rights and Privacy Act (FERPA) 579
Federal Information Security Management Act (FISMA) 579
Gramm-Leach-Bliley Act (GLBA) 579
Health Information Portability and Accountability Act (HIPAA) 579
Network intrusion detection system (NIDS) 580
Payment Card Industry Data Security Standard (PCI DSS) 578
Personally identifiable information (PII) 573
Spear phishing 575
Walkthrough 577

MyMISLab™

To complete the problems with the ✪, go to EOC Discussion Questions in the MyLab.

## USING YOUR KNOWLEDGE

✪ **CE14-1.** Suppose you are a systems administrator for a small biotech startup that is developing a new medicated pain patch. You're concerned that the research staff are not adequately protecting sensitive data.

**a.** How would you help the researchers understand the potential for a serious data breach?

**b.** Why might a biotech startup be an attractive target for hackers?

**c.** How would hackers benefit financially from stealing data about the company's medicated pain patch?

✪ **CE14-2.** Suppose you are the CISO for a large aerospace contractor. You read about the Target data breach and are concerned that some of your vendors may fall prey to a similar spear phishing attack. You're also concerned about vendors accessing confidential systems through your vendor portal.

**a.** Explain how you could make your vendor portal more secure.

**b.** Describe how a data loss prevention system might be used to stop vendors from taking sensitive data.

**c.** What changes could you make to your internal security policies to mitigate these risks?

✪ **CE14-3.** Suppose you are the VP of Public Relations for an online retailer. The CIO just walked through your door and nervously announced that he believes at least half of all customer records, including credit card details, have been stolen. Explain in detail what you would say in the press release.

MyMISLab™

Go to the Assignments section of your MyLab to complete these writing exercises.

**CE14-4.** Suppose you were just notified that your company has experienced a major data breach. You've lost customer records, including usernames, email addresses, passwords, addresses, and phone numbers for all 500,000 of your customers. Estimate the direct costs for notification, detection, escalation, remediation, and legal fees. Suppose the attackers contact you and offer to destroy all records, tell no one about the data breach, and show you how to patch the security hole. The only problem is that they want to be hired as "consultants" and have $600,000 deposited into their European bank account. Would you pay the "consulting" fee? Justify your decision.

**CE14-5.** Considering the same data breach discussed in question CE14-3, describe how your company should respond based on the best practices for notifying users of a data breach discussed in QCE14-3. How might planning for a potential data breach help your company respond effectively?

## ENDNOTES


1. Verizon, "2015 Data Breach Investigations Report," April 13, 2015, accessed June 24, 2015, *www.verizonenterprise.com/DBIR/2015*.
2. Ponemon Institute, "2015 Cost of Data Breach Study," *IBM.com*, June 2015, accessed June 24, 2015, *www-03.ibm.com/security/data-breach*.
3. Ponemon Institute, "2014 Cost of Data Breach Study," *IBM.com*, May 2014, accessed July 21, 2014, *www-935.ibm.com/services/multimedia/SEL03027USEN_Poneman_2014_Cost_of_Data_Breach_Study.pdf*.
4. Jay McGregor, "Budget Crime: You Can Buy a Stolen Credit Card and Rent a Hacker for Under $20," *Forbes*, August 26, 2014, accessed June 24, 2015, *www.forbes.com/sites/jaymcgregor/2014/08/26/budget-crime-you-can-buy-a-stolen-credit-card-and-rent-a-hacker-for-under-20*.
5. Darren Pauli, "Give Us a Slice or We BLURT All Your Users' Topping Preferences to the WORLD," *The Register*, June 16, 2014, accessed June 24, 2015, *www.theregister.co.uk/2014/06/16/extortists_demand_dominos_dough_for_hacked_data/*.

6. Choe Sang-Hun, "Theft of Data Fuels Worries in South Korea," *The New York Times*, January 20, 2014, accessed July 22, 2014, *www.nytimes.com/2014/01/21/business/international/theft-of-data-fuels-worries-in-south-korea.html*.
7. Andy Greenberg, "EBay Demonstrates How Not to Respond to a Huge Data Breach," *Wired.com*, May 23, 2014, accessed July 22, 2014, *www.wired.com/2014/05/ebay-demonstrates-how-not-to-respond-to-a-huge-data-breach/*.
8. Ben Elgin, "Three New Details from Target's Credit Card Breach," *Bloomberg Business*, March 26, 2014, accessed July 22, 2014, *www.bloomberg.com/bw/articles/2014-03-26/three-new-details-from-targets-credit-card-breach*.
9. Brian Krebs, "Target Hackers Broke In via HVAC Company," KrebsonSecurity.com, February 5, 2014, accessed June 24, 2015, *http://krebsonsecurity.com/2014/02/target-hackers-broke-in-via-hvac-company*.
10. Chris Poulin, "What Retailers Need to Learn from the Target Data Breach to Protect Against Similar Attacks," Security Intelligence, January 31, 2014, accessed June 24, 2015, *http://securityintelligence.com/target-breach-protect-against-similar-attacks-retailers/#.VYngl_lVikr*.
11. Swati Khandelwal, "BlackPOS Malware Used in Target Data Breach Developed by 17-Year-Old Russian Hacker," *The Hacker News*, January 17, 2014, accessed June 24, 2015, *http://thehackernews.com/2014/01/BlackPOS-Malware-russian-hacker-Target.html*.
12. Brian Krebs, "The Target Breach, by the Numbers," KrebsonSecurity.com, May 6, 2014, accessed June 24, 2015, *http://krebsonsecurity.com/2014/05/the-target-breach-by-the-numbers*.
13. Brian Krebs, "Fire Sale on Cards Stolen in Target Breach," KrebsOnSecurity.com, February 19, 2014, accessed June 24, 2015, *http://krebsonsecurity.com/2014/02/fire-sale-on-cards-stolen-in-target-breach/*.
14. Bruce Horovitz, "Data Breach Takes Toll on Target Profit," *USA Today*, February 26, 2014, accessed June 24, 2015, *www.usatoday.com/story/money/business/2014/02/26/target-earnings/5829469*.
15. Fred Donovan, "Target Breach: A Timeline," *FierceITSecurity.com*, February 18, 2014, accessed June 24, 2015, *www.fierceitsecurity.com/story/target-breach-timeline/2014-02-18*.
16. Kristin Burnham, "Target Hires GM Exec as First CISO," *InformationWeek*, June 11, 2014, accessed June 24, 2015, *www.informationweek.com/strategic-cio/team-building-and-staffing/target-hires-gm-exec-as-first-ciso/d/d-id/1269600*.
17. Krebs, "The Target Breach, by the Numbers."
18. Jaikumar Vijayan, "Retailer Hauls Visa to Court over $13.3M Fine for Payment Card Data Breach," *Computerworld*, March 13, 2013, accessed June 24, 2015, *www.computerworld.com/s/article/9237588/Retailer_hauls_Visa_to_court_over_13.3M_fine_for_payment_card_data_breach*.
19. More information about the PCI DSS can be found at *www.pcisecuritystandards.org*.

chapter extension **15**

**Chapter 11** provides the background for this extension.

# International MIS

**STUDY QUESTIONS**

**QCE15-1** HOW DOES THE GLOBAL ECONOMY AFFECT ORGANIZATIONS AND PROCESSES?

**QCE15-2** WHAT ARE THE CHARACTERISTICS OF INTERNATIONAL IS COMPONENTS?

**QCE15-3** HOW DO INTER-ENTERPRISE IS FACILITATE GLOBALIZATION?

**QCE15-4** WHAT ARE THE SECURITY CHALLENGES OF INTERNATIONAL IS?

**QCE15-5** WHAT ARE THE CHALLENGES OF INTERNATIONAL IS MANAGEMENT?

## QCE15-1 HOW DOES THE GLOBAL ECONOMY AFFECT ORGANIZATIONS AND PROCESSES?

International business has been sharply increasing since the middle of the 20th century, and today's businesses compete in a global market. After World War II, the Japanese and other Asian economies exploded when those countries began manufacturing and selling goods to the West. The rise of the Japanese auto industry and the semiconductor industry in southeastern Asia greatly expanded international trade. At the same time, the economies of North America and Europe became more closely integrated.

Since then, a number of other factors have caused international business to mushroom. The fall of the Soviet Union opened the economies of Russia and Eastern Europe to the world market. Even more important, the telecommunications boom during the dot-com heyday caused the world to be encircled many times over by optical fiber that can be used for data and voice communications.

After the dot-com bust, optical fiber was largely underused and could be purchased for pennies on the dollar. Plentiful, cheap telecommunications enabled people worldwide to participate in the global economy. Before the advent of the Internet, if a young Indian professional wished to participate in the Western economy, he or she had to migrate to the West—a process that was politicized and limited. Today, that same young Indian professional can sell his or her goods or services over the Internet without leaving home. The Chinese economy has also benefited from plentiful, cheap telecommunications and has become more open to the world.

All of these developments led columnist and author Thomas Friedman to claim, now famously, that "the world is flat," implying seamless integration among the world's economies. That claim and the popular book[1] of the same name fit with the business press's biases and preconceptions and seemed to make intuitive sense. A general sense that the world's economies were integrated came to pervade most business thinking.

However, Harvard professor Pankaj Ghemawat decided to look deeper, and the data he found prompted him to write a *Foreign Policy* article titled "Why the World Isn't Flat." His article was published in 2007; the fact that it took such solid research more than 8 years to gain widespread attention is a testament to the power of bias and preconception.

Some of Ghemawat's data is summarized in Figure CE15-1. Even including cross-border Internet traffic, cross-border telecommunications average less than 17 percent. Even international commerce, which most people think is a large factor in all economies, is less than 23 percent, when corrected for double-counting.[2]

Does this mean that international business is not important to you? No, it does not. What it does mean, as Ghemawat points out, is that most of the opportunity of international commerce is ahead of us. The world is not (yet) flat. While information systems have already played a key role in international commerce, their effect in the future is likely to be larger. As Web services become more widespread, it becomes easier to link information systems together. As mobile devices

**Figure CE15-1**
Percent of Cross-Border Commerce

*Source:* Based on Pankaj Ghemawat and Steven Altman, *www.dhl.com/content/dam/Campaigns/gci2014/downloads/dhl_gci_2014_study_high.pdf.*

| Commerce Type | Cross-Border Percent |
|---|---|
| **Telecommunication** | Voice: 2 percent<br>Internet and voice: 17 percent |
| **Immigration** | 3 percent immigrants |
| **Investment** | 8 percent direct investment |
| **Exports** | 23 percent commerce |

continue their exploding growth in developing countries, even more users will enter the world economy via the Internet. And as collaboration tools become more powerful, it becomes possible to provide services as well as products on the international stage. Opportunities abound.

## HOW DOES THE GLOBAL ECONOMY CHANGE THE COMPETITIVE ENVIRONMENT?

To understand the effect of globalization, consider each of the elements in Figure CE15-2. The enlarging Internet-supported world economy has altered every one of the five competitive forces. Suppliers have to reach a wider range of customers, and customers can consider a wider range of vendors. Suppliers and customers benefit not just from the greater size of the economy, but also from the ease with which businesses can learn about each other using tools such as Google and Bing, as well as Baibu.com in China.

Because of the information available on the Internet, customers can more easily learn of substitutions. The Internet has enabled new market entrants, although not in all cases. Amazon.com, Yahoo!, and Google, for example, have garnered such a large market share that it would be difficult for any new entrant to challenge them. Still, in other industries the global economy facilitates new entrants. Finally, the global economy has intensified rivalry by increasing product and vendor choices and by accelerating the flow of information about price, product, availability, and service.

## HOW DOES THE EMERGING GLOBAL ECONOMY CHANGE COMPETITIVE STRATEGY?

The emerging global economy changes thinking about competitive strategies in two major ways. First, the sheer size and complexity of the global economy mean that any organization that chooses a strategy allowing it to compete industry-wide is taking a very big bite! Competing in many different countries, with products localized to the language and culture of those countries, is an enormous and expensive task.

**Figure CE15-2**
Organizational Strategy Determines Information Systems

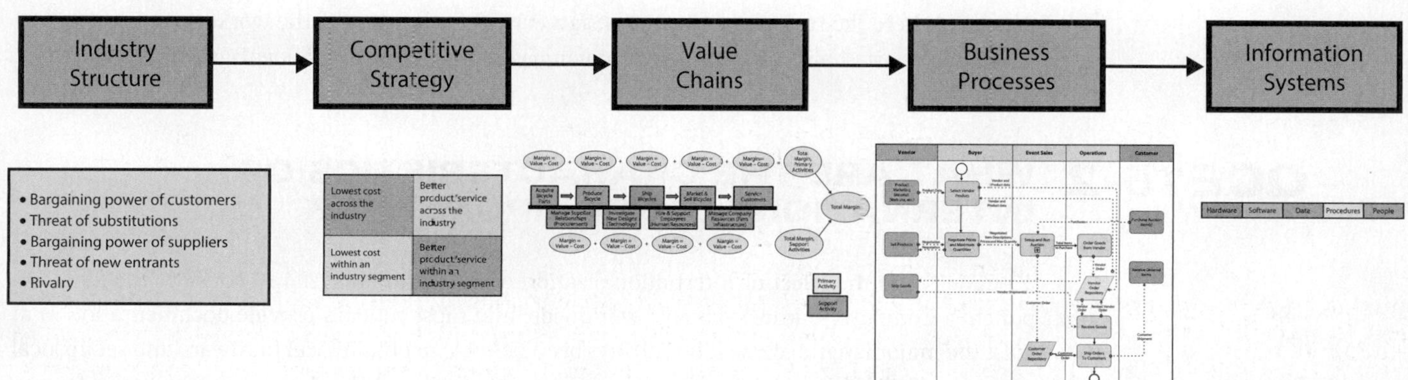

For example, to promote Windows worldwide, Microsoft must produce versions of Windows in dozens of different languages. Even in English, Microsoft produces a UK version, a U.S. version, an Australian version, and so forth. The problem for Microsoft is even greater because different countries use different character sets. In some languages, writing flows from left to right. In other languages, it flows from right to left. When Microsoft set out to sell Windows worldwide, it embarked on an enormous project.

The second major way today's world economy changes competitive strategies is that its size, combined with the Internet, enables unprecedented product differentiation. If you choose to produce the world's highest-quality and most exotic oatmeal—and if your production costs require you to sell that oatmeal for $350 a pound—your target market might contain only 200 people worldwide. The Internet allows you to find them—and them to find you.

The decision involving a global competitive strategy requires the consideration of these two changing factors.

### HOW DOES THE GLOBAL ECONOMY CHANGE VALUE CHAINS AND BUSINESS PROCESSES?

Because of information systems, any or all of the value chain activities in Figure CE15-2 can be performed anywhere in the world. An international company can conduct sales and marketing efforts locally, for every market in which it sells. 3M divisions, for example, sell in the United States with a U.S. sales force, in France with a French sales force, and in Argentina with an Argentinean sales force. Depending on local laws and customs, those sales offices may be owned by 3M, or they may be locally owned entities with which 3M contracts for sales and marketing services. 3M can coordinate all of the sales efforts of these entities using the same CRM system. When 3M managers need to roll up sales totals for a sales projection, they can do so using an integrated, worldwide system.

Manufacturing of a final product is frequently distributed throughout the world. Components of the Boeing 787 are manufactured in Italy, China, England, and numerous other countries and delivered to Washington and South Carolina for final assembly. Each manufacturing facility has its own inbound logistics, manufacturing, and outbound logistics activities, but those activities are linked together via information systems.

For example, Rolls-Royce manufactures an engine and delivers that engine to Boeing via its outbound logistics activity. Boeing receives the engine using its inbound logistics activity. All of this activity is coordinated via shared, inter-enterprise information systems. Rolls-Royce's CRM is connected with Boeing's supply processes, using techniques such as CRM and enterprise resource planning (ERP).

Because of the abundance of low-cost, well-educated, English-speaking professionals in India, many organizations have chosen to outsource their service and support functions to India. Some accounting functions are outsourced to India as well.

World time differences enable global virtual companies to operate 24/7. Boeing engineers in Los Angeles can develop a design for an engine support strut and send that design to Rolls-Royce in England at the end of their day. The design will be waiting for Rolls-Royce engineers at the start of their day. They review the design, make needed adjustments, and send it back to Boeing in Los Angeles, where the reviewed, adjusted design arrives at the start of the workday in Los Angeles. The ability to work around the clock by moving work into other time zones increases productivity.

## QCE15-2 WHAT ARE THE CHARACTERISTICS OF INTERNATIONAL IS COMPONENTS?

To understand the effect of internationalization on information systems, consider the five components. Computer hardware is sold worldwide, and most vendors provide documentation in at least the major languages, so it has always been possible to obtain local hardware and set up local networks. Today, however, the emergence of the international cloud makes it even easier for any company, anywhere in the world, to obtain the latest in server technology. Companies do need to know how to do so, however, pointing to a possible future role for you as an international IS major.

Regarding software, consider the user interface for an international information system. Does it include a local-language version of Windows? What about the software application itself? Does an inventory system used worldwide by Boeing suppose that each user speaks English? If so, at what level of proficiency? If not, what languages must the user interface support?

Next, consider the data component. Suppose that the inventory database has a table for parts data, and that table contains a column labeled Remarks. Suppose Boeing needs to integrate parts data from three different vendors: one in China, one in India, and one in Canada. What language is to be used for recording remarks? Does someone need to translate all of the remarks into one language? Into three languages?

The human components—procedures and people—are obviously affected by language and culture. As with business processes, information systems procedures need to reflect local cultural values and norms. For systems users, job descriptions and reporting relationships must be appropriate for the setting in which the system is used. We will say more about this in QCE15-5.

## WHAT'S REQUIRED TO LOCALIZE SOFTWARE?

The process of making a computer program work in a second language is called **localizing**. It turns out to be surprisingly hard to do. To localize a document or the content of a Web page, all you need to do is hire a translator to convert your document or page from one language to another. The situation is much more difficult for a computer program, however.

Consider a program you use frequently—say, Microsoft Word—and ask what would need to be done to translate it into a different language. The entire user interface would need to be translated. The menu bar and the commands on the menu bar would require translation. It is possible that some of the icons (the small graphics on a menu bar) would need to be changed because some graphic symbols that are harmless in one culture are confusing or offensive in another.

What about a CRM application program that includes forms, reports, and queries? The labels on each of these would need to be translated. Of course, not all labels translate into words of the same length, and so the forms and reports might need to be redesigned. The questions and prompts for queries, such as "Enter part number for back order," would also require translation.

All of the documentation would need to be translated. That should be just a matter of hiring a translator, except that all of the illustrations in the documentation would need to be redrawn in the second language.

Think, too, about error messages. When someone attempts to order more items than there are in inventory, the application produces an error message. All of those messages need to be translated. There are other issues as well. Sorting order is one. Spanish uses accents on certain letters, and it turns out that an accented *ó* will sort after *z* when you use the computer's default sort ordering. Figure CE15-3 summarizes the factors to address when localizing software.

**Figure CE15-3**
Factors to Address When Localizing a Computer Program

- Translate the user interface, including menu bars and commands.
- Translate, and possibly redesign, labels in forms, reports, and query prompts.
- Translate all documentation and help text.
- Redraw and translate diagrams and examples in help text.
- Translate all error messages.
- Translate text in all message boxes.
- Adjust sorting order for different character sets.
- Fix special problems in Asian character sets and in languages that read and write from right to left.

Programming techniques can be used to simplify and reduce the cost of localization. However, those techniques must be used in the beginning. For example, suppose that when a certain condition occurs, the program is to display the message "Insufficient quantity in stock." If the programmer codes all such messages into the computer program, then, to localize that program, a programmer will have to find every such message in the code and then ask a translator to change that code. A preferred technique is to give every error message a number and to place the number and text of the error message into a separate file. Then the code is written to display a particular error number from that file. During localization, translators simply translate the file of error messages into the second language.

The bottom line for you, as a future manager, is to understand two points: (1) Localizing computer programs is much more difficult, expensive, and time consuming than translating documents. (2) If a computer program is likely to be localized, then plan for that localization from the beginning. In addition, when considering the acquisition of a company in a foreign country, be sure to budget time and expense for the localization of information systems.

## IBM'S WATSON LEARNS JAPANESE

A good example of the inherent problems with localization can be seen in the recent partnership between IBM and the large Japanese telecommunications provider Softbank.[3] Softbank wants to use IBM's Watson, an artificial intelligence platform able to answer questions using a person's natural language, to improve customer service in their education, banking, healthcare, insurance, and retail sectors. In order to do this, Watson has started learning Japanese.

This is no easy task. The Japanese language uses different characters (kanji), doesn't use spaces between words, and, relative to English, can be contextually difficult to decipher. Watson uses an iterative process to learn Japanese. It processes some text in Japanese, gets feedback from humans that speak Japanese, and then processes more text. It continues this process until it learns how to speak Japanese.

The localization of IBM's Watson won't be easy, but the potential benefits are tremendous. Watson doesn't forget, sleep, or take vacations. It's continually learning and processing more information. It could potentially provide customer service to billions of customers worldwide across many different industries at the same time. And it could do it in the customer's native language, not a secondary language (Figure CE15-4).[4]

## WHAT ARE THE PROBLEMS AND ISSUES OF GLOBAL DATABASES?

When we discussed CRM and ERP in Chapter 7 and Chapter Extension 11, you learned of the advantage of having all data stored in a single database. In brief, a single database reduces data integrity problems and makes it possible to have an integrated view of the customer or the operations of the organization. International companies that have a single database must, however, declare a single language for the company. Every Remark or Comment or other text field needs to be in a single language. If not, the advantages of a single database disappear. This is not a problem for companies that commit to a single company language.

A single database is not possible, however, for companies that use multiple languages. Such companies often decide to give up on the benefits of a single database to let divisions in different countries use different databases, with data in local languages. For example, an international manufacturer might allow a component manufacturing division in South Korea to have a database in Korean and a final assembly division in Brazil to have a different database in Portuguese. In this scenario, the company needs applications to export and import data among the separated databases.

**Figure CE15-4**
Spoken World Languages

*Source:* Based on Statista Inc., "The Most Spoken Languages Worldwide," Statista.com, May 13, 2015, *http://www.statista.com/statistics/266808/the-most-spoken-languages-worldwide.*

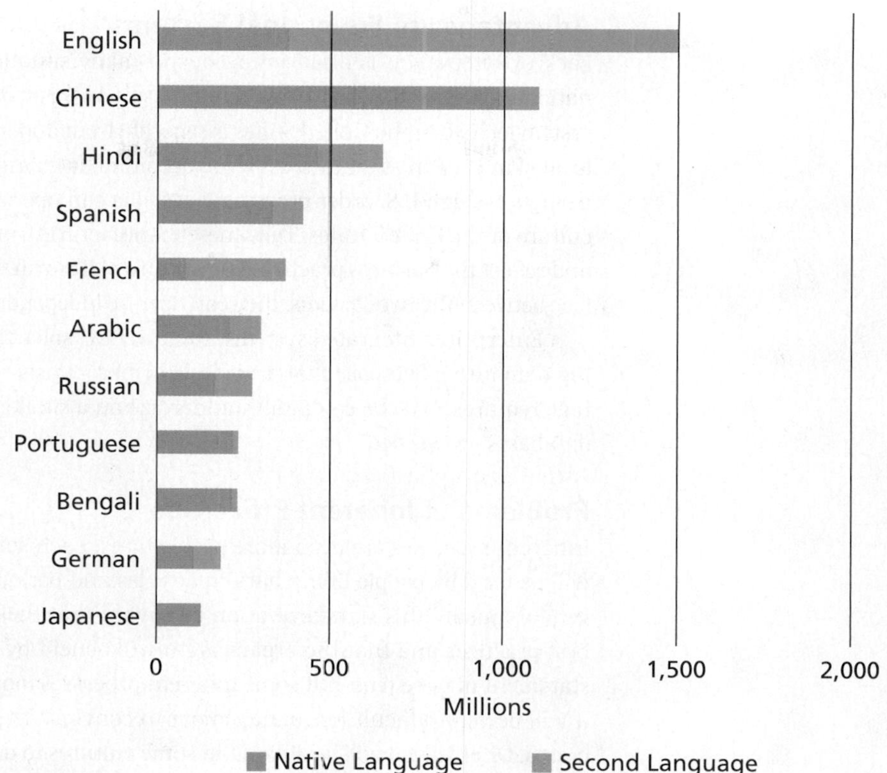


Besides language, performance is a second issue that confronts global databases. Oftentimes, data transmission speeds are too slow to process data from a single geographic location. If so, companies sometimes distribute their database in locations around the world.

**Distributed database processing** refers to the processing of a single database that resides in multiple locations. If the distributed database contains copies of the same data, it is called a **replicated database**. If the distributed database does not contain copies of the same data, but rather divides the database into nonoverlapping segments, it is called a **partitioned database**. In most cases, querying either type of distributed database can improve performance without too much development work. However, updating a replicated database so that changes are correctly made to all copies of the data is full of challenges that require highly skilled personnel to solve.

Companies like Amazon.com, which operates call centers in the United States, India, and Ireland, have invested in applications that are able to successfully update distributed databases worldwide. Given this infrastructure, Amazon then makes this distributed database technology available via its Web services. Thus, the cloud has made the international distribution of data much easier.

## WHAT ARE THE CHALLENGES OF INTERNATIONAL ENTERPRISE APPLICATIONS?

As you learned in Chapter 7, functional business processes and applications support particular activities within a single workgroup or department. Because the systems operate independently, the organization suffers from islands of automation. Sales and marketing data, for example, are not integrated with operations or manufacturing data.

You learned that many organizations eliminate the problems of information silos by creating enterprise systems. With international IS, however, such systems may not be worthwhile.

### Advantages of Functional Systems

Lack of integration is disadvantageous in many situations; it has *advantages*, however, for international organizations and international systems. For example, if an order-processing functional system located in the United States is separate from and independent of the manufacturing systems located in Taiwan, it is unnecessary to accommodate language, business, and cultural differences in a single system. U.S. order-processing systems can operate in English and reflect the practices and culture of the United States. Taiwanese manufacturing information systems can operate in Chinese and reflect the business practices and culture of Taiwan. As long as there is an adequate data interface between the two systems, they can operate independently, sharing data when necessary.

Enterprise, integrated systems, such as ERP, solve the problems of data isolation by integrating data into a database that provides a comprehensive and organization-wide view. That advantage requires that the company standardize on a single language. Otherwise, separate functional databases are needed.

### Problems of Inherent Processes

Inherent processes are even more problematic. Each software product assumes that the software will be used by people filling particular roles and performing their actions in a certain way. ERP vendors justify this standardization by saying that their procedures are based on industry-wide best practices and that the organization will benefit by following these standard processes. That statement may be true, but some inherent processes may conflict with cultural norms. If they do, it will be very difficult for management to convince the employees to follow those inherent processes. Or at least it will be difficult in some cultures to do so.

Differences in language, culture, norms, and expectations compound the difficulties of international process management. Just creating an accurate as-is model is difficult and expensive; developing alternative international processes and evaluating them can be incredibly challenging. With cultural differences, it can be difficult just to determine what criteria should be used for evaluating the alternatives, let alone performing the evaluation.

Because of these challenges, in the future it is likely that international business processes will be developed more like inter-enterprise business processes. A high-level process will be defined to document the service responsibilities of each international unit. Then the cloud and Web service standards will be used to connect those services into an integrated, enterprise, international system. The only obligation of an international unit will be to deliver its defined service. One service can be delivered using procedures based on autocratic management policies, and another can be delivered using procedures based on collaborative management policies. The differences will not matter to a cloud-based enterprise system.

## QCE15-3 HOW DO INTER-ENTERPRISE IS FACILITATE GLOBALIZATION?

As stated earlier, the Internet played a major role in facilitating international commerce. Along with the Internet, however, other major factors have contributed to the rise of international interorganizational systems. Two examples are supply chain and manufacturing systems, as we discuss next. At some point, social media systems may have a positive effect as well, although it is not yet clear how.

### HOW DO GLOBAL INFORMATION SYSTEMS AFFECT SUPPLY CHAIN PROFITABILITY?

In short, global information systems increase supply chain profitability. As you learned in Chapter Extension 10, supply chain performance is driven by four factors: facilities, inventories, transportation, and information. Every one of these drivers is positively affected by global information systems. Because of these systems, facilities can be located anywhere in the world. If Amazon.com finds it economically advantageous to warehouse books in Iceland, it can do so. If Rolls-Royce can manufacture its engine turbine blades more cheaply in Poland, it can do so.

Furthermore, information systems reduce inventories and hence save costs. They can be used to reduce or eliminate the **bullwhip effect**, a phenomenon in which the variability in the size and timing of orders increases at each stage of the supply chain. They also support just-in-time (JIT) inventory techniques worldwide. Using information systems, the order of a Dell computer from a user in Bolivia triggers a manufacturing system at Dell, which, in turn, triggers the order of a component from a warehouse in Taiwan—all automatically.

To underscore this point, consider the inventories that exist at this moment in time worldwide. Every component in one of those inventories represents a waste of the world's resources. Any product or component sitting on a shelf is not being used and is adding no value to the global economy. In the perfect world, a customer would think, "I want a new tablet," and that thought would trigger systems all over the world to produce and assemble necessary components instantly. Given that we live in a world bound by time and space, instantaneous production is unreachable. But the goal of worldwide information systems for supply chain inventory management is to come as close to instantaneous as possible.

Consider transportation, the third driver. When you order a book from Amazon.com, you are presented with at least four shipping options. You can choose the speed and attendant price that is appropriate for your needs. Similar systems for businesses allow them to choose the delivery option that optimizes the value they generate. Further, automated systems enable suppliers and customers to track the shipment's location, 24/7, worldwide.

Finally, global information systems produce comprehensive, accurate, and timely information. Information systems produce data at prodigious rates worldwide. That data facilitates operations as just discussed, but it also produces information for planning, organizing, deciding, and other analyses.

## WHAT IS THE ECONOMIC EFFECT OF GLOBAL MANUFACTURING?

Henry Ford pioneered modern manufacturing methods, and in the process he reduced the price of automobiles to the point where they were no longer the playthings of the very rich but were affordable to the general population. In 1914, Ford took the unprecedented step of unilaterally increasing his workers' pay from $2.50 per day for 10 hours' work to $5 per day for 8 hours' work. As a consequence, many of his workers could soon afford to purchase an automobile. By paying his workers more, Ford increased demand.

The increase in demand was not due only to purchases by his workers, of course. Because of what economists call the **accelerator effect**, a dollar spent will contribute 2 or 3 dollars of activity to the economy. Ford's workers spent their increased pay not just on autos, but also on goods and services in their local community, which benefited via the accelerator effect. That benefit enabled non–Ford workers to afford an auto as well. Further, because of the positive publicity he achieved with the pay increase, the community was strongly disposed to purchase a Ford automobile.

Consider those events in light of global manufacturing. For example, if Boeing manufactures airplanes entirely in the United States, the U.S. economy will be the sole beneficiary of that economic activity. If an Italian airline chooses to buy a Boeing plane, the transaction will be a cost to the Italian economy. There will be no accelerator effect, and the transaction will have no consequence on Italians' propensity to fly.

However, if Boeing purchases major components for its airplanes from Italian companies, those purchases then generate an accelerator effect for the Italian economy. By buying in Italy, Boeing contributes to Italy's economy and ultimately increases Italians' propensity to fly. That foreign-component purchase will, of course, reduce economic activity in the United States, but if it induces Italians to purchase sufficiently more Boeing airplanes, then it is possible that the loss will be compensated by the increase in airplane sales volume. That purchase will also benefit Boeing's image among Italians and increase the likelihood of sales to the Italian government.

The same phenomenon pertains to Dell computers, Cisco routers, and Microsoft Xboxes.

### HOW DOES SOCIAL MEDIA AFFECT INTERNATIONAL BUSINESS?

In truth, we do not yet know how social media affects international businsess, nor do we know the effectiveness of Enterprise 2.0 in multinational companies. It is possible that social media is so culturally biased that it works only in the culture in which it originates. A Facebook social graph of a young college woman in Japan is unlikely to connect in any meaningful way with a similar graph of a male business student in India. Each will have his or her own social network, but they will be domestic, not international.

Similar comments can be made about user-generated content. Teenagers in Chicago are unlikely to be influenced by user-generated tennis shoe designs that are popular in Hanover, Germany. Or are they? Is there a business opportunity for some innovative company to foster user-generated designs in one culture with the express purpose of marketing those designs in another culture? As of September 2015, we do not know.

Opportunities like this will exist for you and your classmates to explore early in your careers. As you use Facebook or Twitter and as you consume or create UGC, think about the international aspects of your activity. Both international social media and international Enterprise 2.0 seem to be ripe for innovation.

## QCE15-4 WHAT ARE THE SECURITY CHALLENGES OF INTERNATIONAL IS?

Managing international systems creates unique security challenges that derive from differences in legal systems, physical environments, and cultural norms. These security challenges represent very real threats to an organization's ability to operate in another country.

### LEGAL ENVIRONMENT

First, differences in legal environments between countries have a direct impact on the daily operation of information systems. The legal differences related to the use of encryption, distribution of content, and personal privacy protections can substantially affect international IS.

Most people are unaware that encryption is *illegal* or highly restricted in many countries. Yes, you read that correctly, illegal. In Russia and China, a license is required to import or export encryption products.[5] The use of any encryption product requires a license. Other countries like England, India, and Australia have laws that can force decryption. In fact, in 2015 British Prime Minister David Cameron suggested that back doors be placed in all software that would effectively circumvent all encryption. Companies that use encryption need to be aware that encryption laws differ between countries and may affect their ability to operate effectively.

Laws regarding the legality of the nature of the content stored in an organization's systems are also different between countries. For example, in 2010 Google moved its search engine service from China to Hong Kong over censorship problems. The People's Republic of China (PRC) regularly forced Google to remove content that the PRC found unacceptable. Google subsequently saw its search market share drop from 12 percent to about 1.7 percent in 2013.[6]

In fact, dozens of countries regularly block access to certain Internet companies. Iraq blocked Twitter, Facebook, and YouTube during a 2014 insurgency. Turkey's government blocked Twitter and YouTube once in 2014 to suppress an embarrassing video showing officials talking about starting a war and then again in 2015 to block a YouTube video of a prosecutor being held hostage.[7]

Variations in privacy laws can also affect the operation of an organization's international systems. For example, in parts of Europe employers cannot read their workers' emails, personal data cannot be collected without an individual's permission, organizations must provide individuals with the ability to correct inaccuracies in the data they collect, and personal data cannot be shared by companies without express permission. None of these apply to organizations in the United States.

Differences in privacy laws may become even more pronounced. In 2014, Google lost a legal battle and was forced to provide European users with the "right to be forgotten." Individuals can request references of them to be removed from search results. As of 2015, Google had received more than 250,000 removal requests for more than 920,000 URLs. It has removed 41.3 percent of the requested URLs.[8]

This ruling will likely be applied to other services providers like Bing, Yahoo!, and Ask.com as well. Unfortunately, none of these privacy protections apply to U.S. citizens. In fact, Google assembled its own panel of advisers, which recommended that the "right to be forgotten" rule not apply to any of Google's properties outside the EU. This means EU users can still see their removed URLs if they visit *www.google.com* rather than *www.google.co.uk*.

Organizations need to be aware that laws related to privacy, content, and encryption will affect the way they collect, process, and store data. Consider how these laws might affect organizations that use cloud-based services to store data. Organizations could operate in a country with loose content laws and then store all of their data and applications in another country with stricter privacy laws in order to protect their users. In other words, the intersection of international law and technology is forcing organizations to carefully evaluate how they manage their information systems, in particular, the location of their data.

## PHYSICAL SECURITY

Second, operating information systems internationally can be problematic because of different physical environments. This includes threats to infrastructure in the form of natural disasters, geopolitical risks, civil unrest, and terrorist attacks.

Place your data center in Kansas, and it's subject to tornados. Place your data center internationally, and it's potentially subject to typhoons/hurricanes, earthquakes, floods, volcanic eruptions, or mudslides. For example, the data centers in Japan survived the terrible effects of the 2011 earthquake, tsunami, and nuclear reactor meltdowns. They survived the shaking, flooding, and widespread power outages because they were housed in special facilities with shock-absorbing structures and had backup power generators.

An organization's physical infrastructure is also vulnerable to outright seizure. In 2011, the FBI seized several racks of servers from a data center in Reston, Virginia, that belonged to a Switzerland-based company named DigitalOne.[9] DigitalOne's owner, Sergej Ostroumow, said the seizure knocked several sites offline, but declined to say which one of his clients was being targeted.

Employees who run critical infrastructure can be targeted as well. In 2014, Russian president Vladimir Putin revoked visas for nearly 1,000 foreign workers when tensions flared between Russia and Western countries. Deloitte & Touche's local chief operating officer, Quentin O'Toole, was deported for his wife's speeding tickets.

## CULTURAL NORMS

Finally, cultural norms can affect the way organizations manage their international information systems. For example, bribery is generally considered unacceptable in the United States, but in other countries it is accepted as a normal way of doing business.

In 2012, Walmart became embroiled in a bribery scandal that showed that local Walmart executives in Mexico used bribes to get building permits and expedite its expansion in Mexico. The fallout from the scandal resulted in departures of several key executives and $439 million spent on investigations and a new compliance program. It's important to note that this is just one example. Graft is a worldwide problem. This example points out how differences in cultural norms can affect an organization's daily operations.

Apply these cultural differences to the management of international information systems. Can an organization depend on the control of separation of duties and authorities in a culture for which graft is an accepted norm? Could an organization lose valuable intellectual property in such an environment? Or what is the utility of a personal reference in a culture in which it is considered exceedingly rude to talk about someone when he or she is not present?

Organizations need to carefully examine how the deployment of international information systems might be affected by cultural norms. Because of differences in cultural norms, safeguards need to be chosen and evaluated on a culture-by-culture basis. Additional safeguards may be needed, but the technical and data safeguards described in Chapter 10 still apply to international systems.

## QCE15-5 WHAT ARE THE CHALLENGES OF INTERNATIONAL IS MANAGEMENT?

Size and complexity make international IS management challenging. International information systems are larger and more complex. Projects to develop them are larger and more complicated to manage. International IS departments are bigger and composed of people from many cultures with many different native languages. International organizations have more IS assets, and those assets are exposed to more risk and greater uncertainty. Because of the complexity of international law, security incidents are more complicated to investigate.

### WHY IS INTERNATIONAL INFORMATION SYSTEMS DEVELOPMENT MORE CHALLENGING?

The factors that affect international information systems development are more challenging than those that affect international software development. If the *system* is truly international, if many people from many different countries will be using the system, then the development project is exceedingly complicated.

To see why, consider the five components. Running hardware in different countries is not a problem, especially using the cloud, and localizing software is manageable, assuming programs were designed to be localized. Databases pose more difficulties. First, is a single database to be used, and if so, is it to be distributed? If so, how will updates be processed? Also, what language, currency, and units of measure will be used to store data? If multiple databases are to be used, how are data going to be transported among them? Some of these problems are difficult, but they are solvable and cloud-based databases make them more so.

The same cannot be said for the procedure and people components. An international system is used by people who live and work in cultures that are vastly different from one another. The way that customers are treated in Japan differs substantially from the way that customers are treated in Spain, which differs substantially from the way that customers are treated in the United States. The procedures for using a CRM will be correspondingly different.

Consider the phases of the SDLC as shown in Figure CE15-5. During system definition, we are supposed to determine the purpose and scope of the system. As you know by now, information systems should facilitate the organization's competitive strategy by supporting business processes. But what if the underlying processes differ? Again, customer support in Japan and customer support in Spain may involve completely different processes and activities.

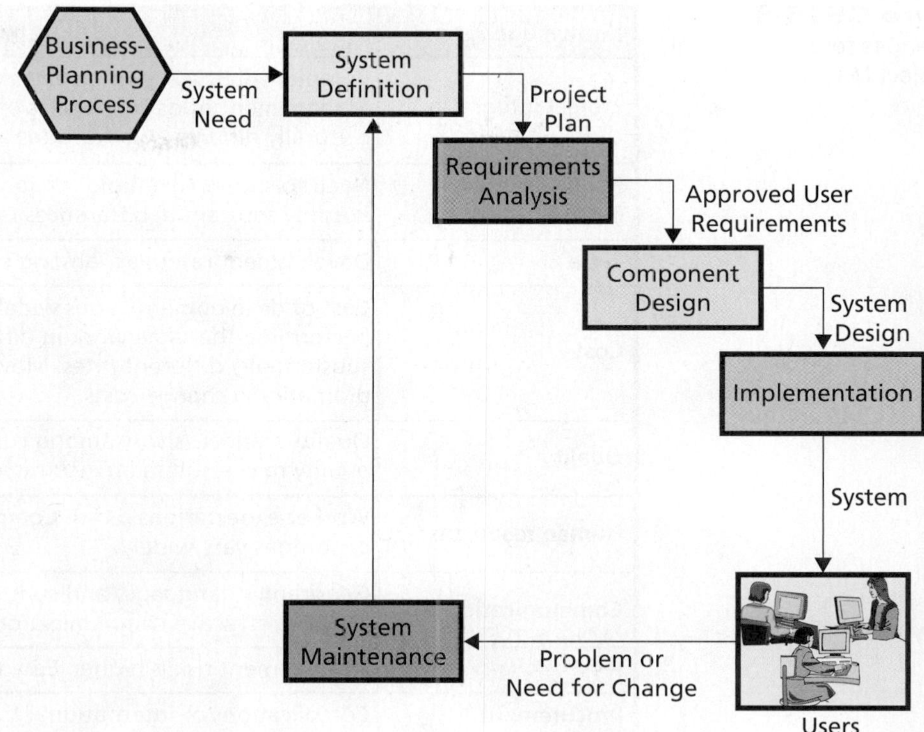


**Figure CE15-5**
Phases in the SDLC

Even if the purpose and scope can be defined in some unified way, how are requirements to be determined? Again, if the underlying business processes differ, then the specific requirements for the information system will differ. Managing requirements for a system in one culture is difficult, but managing requirements for international systems can be many times more difficult.

There are two responses to such challenges: (1) either define a set of standard business processes or (2) develop alternative versions of the system that support different processes in different countries. Both responses are problematic. The first response requires conversion of the organization to different work processes, and, as you learned in Chapter 7, such conversion can be exceedingly difficult. People resist change, and they will do so with vehemence if the change violates cultural norms.

The second response is easier to implement, but it creates system design challenges. It also means that, in truth, there is not one system, but many.

In spite of the problems, both responses are used. For example, SAP, Oracle, and other ERP vendors define standard business processes via the inherent procedures in their software products. Many organizations attempt to enforce those standard procedures. When it becomes organizationally infeasible to do so, organizations develop exceptions to those inherent procedures and develop programs to handle the exceptions. This choice means high maintenance expense.

## WHAT ARE THE CHALLENGES OF INTERNATIONAL PROJECT MANAGEMENT?

Managing a global information systems development project is difficult because of project size and complexity. Requirements are complex, many resources are required, and numerous people are involved. Team members speak different languages, live in different cultures, work in different time zones, and seldom meet face to face.

One way to understand how these factors affect global project management is to consider each of the project management knowledge areas as set out by the international Project Management Institute's document, the *PMBOK® Guide* (*http://marketplace.pmi.org/Pages/ProductDetail.aspx?GMProduct=00101095501*). Figure CE15-6 summarizes challenges for each

**Figure CE15-6**
Challenges for International IS Project Management

| Knowledge Areas | Challenge |
|---|---|
| **Project integration** | Complex integration of results from distributed workgroups. Management of dependencies of tasks from physically and culturally different workgroups. |
| **Requirements (Scope)** | Need to support multiple versions of underlying business processes. Possibly substantial differences in requirements and procedures. |
| **Time** | Development rates vary among cultures and countries. |
| **Cost** | Cost of development varies widely among countries. Two members performing the same work in different countries may be paid substantially different rates. Moving work among teams may dramatically change costs. |
| **Quality** | Quality standards vary among cultures. Different expectations of quality may result in an inconsistent system. |
| **Human resources** | Worker expectations differ. Compensation, rewards, work conditions vary widely. |
| **Communications** | Geographic, language, and cultural distance among team members impedes effective communication. |
| **Risk** | Development risk is higher. Easy to lose control. |
| **Procurement** | Complications of international trade. |

knowledge area. Project integration is more difficult because international development projects require the complex integration of results from distributed workgroups. Also, task dependencies can span teams working in different countries, increasing the difficulty of task management.

The scope and requirements definition for international IS is more difficult, as just discussed. Time management is more difficult because teams in different cultures and countries work at different rates. Some cultures have a 35-hour work week, and some have a 60-hour work week. Some cultures expect 6-week vacations, and some expect 2 weeks. Some cultures thrive on efficiency of labor, and others thrive on considerate working relationships. There is no standard rate of development for an international project.

In terms of cost, different countries and cultures pay vastly different labor rates. Using critical path analysis, managers may choose to move a task from one team to another. Doing so, however, may substantially increase costs. Thus, management may choose to accept a delay rather than move work to an available (but more expensive) team. The complex trade-offs that exist between time and cost become even more complex for international projects.

Quality and human resources are also more complicated for international projects. Quality standards vary among countries. The IT industry in some nations, like India, has invested heavily in development techniques that increase program quality. Other countries, like the United States, have been less willing to invest in quality. In any case, the integration of programs of varying quality results in an inconsistent system.

Worker expectations vary among cultures and nations. Compensation, rewards, and worker conditions vary, and these differences can lead to misunderstandings, poor morale, and project delays.

Because of these factors, effective team communication is exceedingly important for international projects, but because of language and culture differences and geographic separation, such communication is difficult. Effective communication is also more expensive. Consider, for example, just the additional expense of maintaining a team portal in three or four languages.

If you consider all of the factors in Figure CE15-6, it is easy to understand why project risk is high for international IS development projects. So many things can go wrong. Project integration is complex; requirements are difficult to determine; cost, time, and quality are difficult to manage; worker conditions vary widely; and communication is difficult. Finally, project procurement is complicated by the normal challenges of international commerce.

## WHAT ARE THE CHALLENGES OF INTERNATIONAL IS MANAGEMENT?

Chapter 11 defined the four primary responsibilities of the IS department: plan, operate, develop, and protect information systems and IT infrastructure. Each of these responsibilities becomes more challenging for international IS organizations.

Regarding planning, the principal task is to align IT and IS resources with the organization's competitive strategy. The task does not change character for international companies; it just becomes more complex and difficult. Multinational organizations and operations are complicated, and the business processes that support their competitive strategies tend also to be complicated. Further, changes in global economic factors can mean dramatic changes in processes and necessitate transformations in IS and IT support. Technology adoption can also cause remarkable change. The increasing use of cell phones in developing countries, for example, alters the requirements for local information systems. The rising price of oil will also change international business processes. Thus, planning tasks for international IS are larger and more complex.

Three factors create challenges for international IS operations. First, conducting operations in different countries, cultures, and languages adds complexity. Go to the Web site of any multinational corporation, say, *www.3m.com* or *www.dell.com*, and you'll be asked to click on the country in which you reside. When you click, you are likely to be directed to a Web server running in some other country. Those Web servers need to be managed consistently, even though they are operated by people living in different cultures and speaking different languages.

The second operational challenge of international IS is the integration of similar, but different, systems. Consider inventory. A multinational corporation might have dozens of different inventory systems in use throughout the world. To enable the movement of goods, many of these systems need to be coordinated and integrated.

Or consider customer support that operates from three different support centers in three different countries. Each support center may have its own information system, but the data among those systems will need to be exported or otherwise shared. If not, then a customer who contacts one center will be unknown to the others.

The third complication for operations is outsourcing. Many organizations have chosen to outsource customer support, training, logistics, and other backroom activities. International outsourcing is particularly advantageous for customer support and other functions that must be operational 24/7. Many companies outsource logistics to UPS because doing so offers comprehensive, worldwide shipping and logistical support. The organization's information systems usually need to be integrated with outsource vendors' information systems, and this may need to be done for different systems, all over the world.

The fourth IT department responsibility is protecting IS and IT infrastructure as was discussed in QCE15-4.

# ACTIVE REVIEW

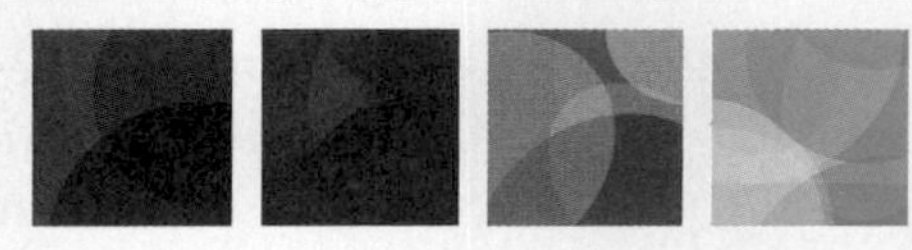

Use this Active Review to verify that you understand the ideas and concepts that answer this chapter extension's study questions.

## QCE15-1 HOW DOES THE GLOBAL ECONOMY AFFECT ORGANIZATIONS AND PROCESSES?

Describe how the global economy has changed since the mid-20th century. Explain how the dot-com bust influenced the global economy and changed the number of workers worldwide. Summarize why the idea that the world is flat gained momentum and why that notion is incorrect so far. State how that fact provides opportunities today. Summarize the ways in which today's global economy influences the five competitive forces. Explain how the global economy changes the way organizations assess industry structure. How does the global economy change competitive strategy? How do global information systems benefit the value chain? Using Figure 3-7 (page 65) as a guide, explain how each primary value chain activity can be performed anywhere in the world.

## QCE15-2 WHAT ARE THE CHARACTERISTICS OF INTERNATIONAL IS COMPONENTS?

Explain how internationalization affects the five components of an IS. What does it mean to localize software? Summarize the work required to localize a computer program. In your own words, explain why it is better to design a program to be localized rather than attempt to adapt an existing single-language program to a second language. Explain the problems of having a single database for an international IS. Define *distributed database, replicated database,* and *partitioned database.* State a source of problems for processing replicated databases.

Summarize the advantages of functional systems for international companies. Summarize the issues of inherent processes for multinational ERP. Explain how the cloud and Web service standards could be used to address the problems of international enterprise applications.

## QCE15-3 HOW DO INTER-ENTERPRISE IS FACILITATE GLOBALIZATION?

State the short answer to this question. Name the four drivers of supply chain profitability. Discuss how global information systems affect each driver. Explain how inventories represent waste. Summarize the effect that Henry Ford's act of increasing his workers' pay had on Ford auto sales. Explain how this same phenomenon pertains to Boeing acquiring major subsystems from manufacturers in Italy or to Toyota building autos in the United States. Explain how social media and Enterprise 2.0 affect international companies. Explain the meaning of the following sentence: "It's possible that social media technologies are so culturally biased that they work only in the culture in which they originate." Describe how this situation may create opportunities for businesses.

## QCE15-4 WHAT ARE THE SECURITY CHALLENGES OF INTERNATIONAL IS?

Explain legal differences between countries with respect to the use of encryption, distribution of content, and personal privacy protections. Describe how natural disasters, geopolitical risks, civil unrest, and terrorist attacks could threaten the physical security of international IS. Give an example of how differences in cultural norms may affect international IS.

## QCE15-5 WHAT ARE THE CHALLENGES OF INTERNATIONAL IS MANAGEMENT?

State the two characteristics that make international IS management challenging. Explain the difference between international systems development and international software development. Using the five-component framework, explain why international systems development is more difficult. Give an example of one complication for each knowledge area in Figure CE15-6. State the four responsibilities for IS departments. Explain how each of these responsibilities is more challenging for international IS organizations. Describe three factors that create challenges for international IS operations. Explain why international IT assets are subject to more threats. Give three examples. Explain why the likelihood of international threats is more difficult to determine.

## KEY TERMS AND CONCEPTS

Accelerator effect 591
Bullwhip effect 591
Distributed database processing 589
Localizing 587
Partitioned database 589
Replicated database 589

MyMISLab™

To complete the problems with the ✪, go to EOC Discussion Questions in the MyLab.

## USING YOUR KNOWLEDGE

✪ **CE15-1.** Suppose that you are about to have a job interview with a multinational company, such as 3M, Starbucks, or Coca-Cola. Further suppose that you wish to demonstrate an awareness of the changes that the Internet and modern information technology have made to international commerce. Using the information in QCE15-1, create a list of three questions that you could ask the interviewer regarding the company's use of IT in its international business.

✪ **CE15-2.** Suppose you work for a large business that is contemplating acquiring a company in Mexico. Assume you are a junior member of a team that is analyzing the desirability of this acquisition. Your boss, who is not technically savvy, has asked you to prepare a summary of the issues that she should be aware of regarding the merging of the two companies' information systems. She wants your summary to include a list of questions that she should ask of both your IS department and the IS department personnel in the prospective acquisition. Prepare that summary.

✪ **CE15-3.** Using the information in this chapter extension as well as in Chapter 7, summarize the strengths and weaknesses of functional systems, CRM, ERP, and EAI. How do the advantages and disadvantages of each change in an international setting? For your answer, create a table with strength and weakness columns and a row for each of the four system types.

MyMISLab™

Go to the Assignments section of your MyLab to complete these writing exercises.

**CE15-4.** Suppose you are a junior member of a newly formed international team that will meet regularly for the next year. You have team members in Europe, North and South America, Japan, Hong Kong, Singapore, Australia, and India. All of your team meetings will be virtual; some will be synchronous, but many will be asynchronous. The team leader has asked you to help prepare the environment for these meetings. In particular, he asked you to summarize the challenges that will occur in conducting these team meetings. He also wants you to assess the strengths and weaknesses of the three collaboration tool sets described in Chapter Extension 2. Use this chapter extension as well as information in Chapter Extensions 1 and 2 in your assessment.

**CE15-5.** Suppose you are working for a well-known social media company based in the United States. You've been placed in charge of expanding the company internationally. The first day on the job, the chief information security officer (CISO) informs you that there have been repeated intrusions into corporate servers located in Asia. The hackers targeted accounts of well-known political dissidents. And they continue to do so on a regular basis.

They make little effort to cover their tracks. The problem is that they're based in the country in which you're focusing your expansion efforts. Explain how different legal and cultural norms may hamper your expansion plans. Why might foreign government officials be hesitant to help you catch the hackers? Why types of concessions or changes might the foreign government ask you to make to your social media platform before you're given permission to operate in the country?

## ENDNOTES

1. Thomas L. Friedman, *The World Is Flat 3.0: A Brief History of the Twenty-First Century* (New York: Farrar, Strauss and Giroux, 2007).
2. Pankaj Ghemawat and Steven Altman, "DHL Global Connectedness Index 2014," DHL International GmbH, October 2014, accessed May 12, 2015, *www.dhl.com/content/dam/Campaigns/gci2014/downloads/dhl_gci_2014_study_high.pdf.*
3. IBM Corporation, "IBM, SoftBank Alliance to Bring Watson to All of Japan," February 10, 2015, IBM.com, accessed May 13, 2015, *www-03.ibm.com/press/us/en/pressrelease/46045.wss.*
4. Statistia Inc., "The Most Spoken Languages Worldwide," Statista.com, May 13, 2015, *www.statista.com/statistics/266808/the-most-spoken-languages-worldwide.*
5. Bert-Jaap Koops, "Crypto Law Survey," Cryptolaw.org, February 2013, *www.cryptolaw.org.*
6. Paul Carsten, "Microsoft Blocks Censorship of Skype in China: Advocacy Group," Reuters.com, November 27, 2013, accessed May 14, 2015, *www.reuters.com/article/2013/11/27/us-microsoft-china-censorship-idUSBRE9AQ0Q520131127.*
7. Raziye Akkoc, "Turkey Blocks Access to Social Media and YouTube over Hostage Photos," *The Telegraph*, April 6, 2015, accessed May 14, 2015, *www.telegraph.co.uk/news/worldnews/europe/turkey/11518004/Turkey-blocks-access-to-Facebook-Twitter-and-YouTube.html.*
8. Google Inc., "European Privacy Requests for Search Removals," Google .com, May 13, 2015, accessed August 10, 2015, *www.google.com/transparencyreport/removals/europeprivacy.*
9. Verne Kopytoff, "FBI Seizes Web Servers, Knocking Sites Offline," *The New York Times*, June 21, 2011, accessed June 27, 2014, *http://bits.blogs.nytimes.com/2011/06/21/f-b-i-seizes-web-servers-knocking-sites-offline/.*

chapter extension **16**

**Chapter 12** provides the background for this extension.

# Systems Development Project Management

**STUDY QUESTIONS**

**QCE16-1** WHY IS FORMALIZED PROJECT MANAGEMENT NECESSARY?

**QCE16-2** WHAT ARE THE TRADE-OFFS IN REQUIREMENTS, COST, AND TIME?

**QCE16-3** WHAT ARE THE DIMENSIONS OF PROJECT MANAGEMENT?

**QCE16-4** HOW DOES A WORK BREAKDOWN STRUCTURE DRIVE PROJECT MANAGEMENT?

**QCE16-5** WHAT IS THE BIGGEST CHALLENGE FOR PLANNING A SYSTEMS DEVELOPMENT PROJECT?

**QCE16-6** WHAT ARE THE BIGGEST CHALLENGES FOR MANAGING A SYSTEMS DEVELOPMENT PROJECT?

**QCE16-7** WHAT IS THE SINGLE MOST IMPORTANT TASK FOR USERS ON A SYSTEMS DEVELOPMENT PROJECT?

CE16

## QCE16-1 WHY IS FORMALIZED PROJECT MANAGEMENT NECESSARY?

Falcon Security is a small company, and it might be possible for it to apply the systems development life cycle (SDLC) without formalized project management. Small companies can sometimes get along by implementing small IS projects on an informal, catch-as-catch-can basis. Of course, good project management would be beneficial, but it might not be required. The situation is different for PRIDE, however, because the system development, even though relatively simple, may involve thousands of clients. PRIDE development will benefit from formal project management.

The situation is similar to that for PRIDE for projects at medium-sized and large companies. Here IS projects are large and complex, and strong, formalized project management is mandatory. Information systems at such companies have many features and functions. They require substantial computer resources and necessitate the creation of multifaceted, complicated computer programs. They process databases with hundreds of tables; dozens, possibly hundreds, of relationships; and terabytes of data. Such large-scale systems affect many business processes and support hundreds, possibly thousands, of concurrent users.

Because of their size, such systems require a large development team, often composed of 50 to 100 or more business and systems analysts, programmers, PQA engineers, and managers. To add further complexity, large-scale systems are often simultaneously developed at multiple sites. A project might involve teams in the United States, India, China, and other countries. Additionally, the development of large-scale systems can involve integrating products and services from different companies, as is done with PRIDE. In these larger development projects, some companies provide licensed software; others provide particular expertise, such as database design; and others provide development labor. Large-scale systems are frequently localized for different languages. Finally, large-scale systems development requires extended development intervals, sometimes as long as 5 or 6 years. Figure CE16-1 summarizes the characteristics of large-scale systems.

The Internal Revenue Service provides a good example of a large-scale IS project. The IRS employs more than 100,000 people in 1,000 different sites and processes more than 200 million tax returns a year. Starting in 1995, it set out to modernize the information systems for processing tax returns. Today, more than 20 years and several billion dollars later, it has not completed that project. In fairness, Congress keeps changing the tax law, sometimes in major ways, so the requirements are never stable—a common problem in IS development, as you'll learn.

Formalized project management is a necessity for such large-scale projects. Without it, millions, even billions, of dollars will be wasted, projects will run late, and team morale will be low. In this chapter extension, we will consider the major components of IS project management. We begin the discussion of IS project management by discussing project trade-offs.

**Fi…re C…-1**
Characteristics of Large-Scale Systems Development Projects

- Many features and functions
- Large, complex computer programs
- Databases with hundreds of tables, dozens to hundreds of relationships, and terabytes of data
- Affect many business processes
- Support hundreds or thousands of concurrent users
- Large development team
- Multiple sites
- International development
- Integration of work from several companies
- Localization necessary
- Extended development intervals

## QCE16-2 WHAT ARE THE TRADE-OFFS IN REQUIREMENTS, COST, AND TIME?

Systems development projects require the balancing of three critical drivers: **requirements** (scope)[1], **cost**, and **time**. To understand this balancing challenge, consider the construction of something relatively simple—say, a piece of jewelry, like a necklace, or the deck on the side of a house. The more elaborate the necklace or the deck, the more time it will take. The less elaborate, the less time it will take. Further, if we embellish the necklace with diamonds and precious gems, it will cost more. Similarly, if we construct the deck from old crates it will be cheaper than if we construct it of clear-grained, prime Port Orford cedar.

We can summarize this situation as shown in Figure CE16-2. We can *trade off* requirements against time and against cost. If we make the necklace simpler, it will take less time. If we eliminate the diamonds and gems, it will be cheaper. The same **trade-offs** exist in the construction of anything: houses, airplanes, buildings, ships, furniture, *and* information systems.

The relationship between time and cost is more complicated. Normally, we can reduce time by increasing cost, but *only to a point*. For example, we can reduce the time it takes to produce a deck by hiring more laborers. At some point, however, there will be so many laborers working on the deck that they will get in one another's way, and the time to finish the deck will actually increase. Thus, at some point, adding more people creates **diseconomies of scale** (recall Brooks' Law in Chapter 12).

In some projects, we can reduce costs by increasing time. If, for example, we are required to pay laborers time-and-a-half for overtime, we can reduce costs by eliminating overtime. If

**Figure CE16-2**
Primary Drivers of Systems Development

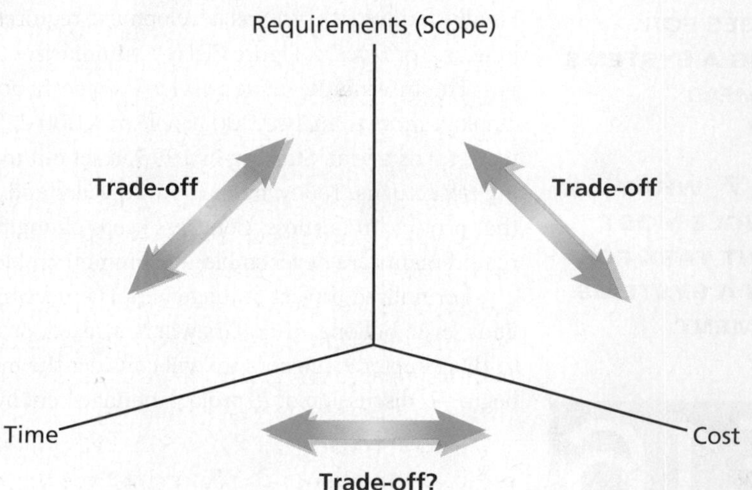

finishing the deck—by, say, Friday—requires overtime, then it may be cheaper to avoid overtime by completing the deck sometime the next week. This trade-off is not always true, however. By extending the project interval, we will need to pay labor and overhead for a longer period of time. Adding more time can increase cost.

Consider how these trade-offs pertain to information systems. We specify a set of requirements for the new information system, and we schedule labor over a period of time. Suppose the initial schedule indicates the system will be finished in 2 years. If business requirements necessitate the project be finished in 1 year, we must shorten the schedule. We can proceed in two ways: reduce the requirements or add labor. For the former, we eliminate functions and features. For the latter, we hire more staff or contract with other vendors for development services. Deciding which course to take will be difficult and risky.

Furthermore, in most projects, we cannot make these decisions once and for all. We begin with a plan, called the **baseline**. It stipulates the tasks to be accomplished, the labor and other resources assigned to those tasks, and the schedule for completion. However, nothing ever goes according to plan, and the larger the project and the longer the development interval, the more things will violate the plan. Critical people may leave the company; a hurricane may destroy an office; the company may have a bad quarter and freeze hiring just as the project is staffing up; technology will change; competitors may do something that makes the project more (or less) important; or the company may be sold and new management may change requirements and priorities. When these events occur, project managers must reassess the trade-offs between requirements, cost, and time. It is a balancing act undertaken in the presence of continual change and substantial risk and uncertainty.

## QCE16-3 WHAT ARE THE DIMENSIONS OF PROJECT MANAGEMENT?

Many methods exist for developing information systems. Chapter 12 described the SDLC, the workhorse of the industry for years. This technique stipulates phases and processes for constructing information systems, but it does not address the management of projects, particularly large-scale projects. The systems definition phase of the SDLC, for example, stipulates that the project should be planned, but it does not indicate how. It stipulates that components need to be designed, but it does not address the management of the design activity nor the communications among employees, groups, and sites. And so forth.

Large-scale projects require formalized project management. Although Mateo, the CEO at Falcon Security, can get by with informal meetings with Cam and her employees, Alaska Airlines cannot deliver mobile applications for reservations that way. A formalized project management process is needed.

Over the years, people have proposed dozens of different project management methodologies and processes. In recent years, the process promulgated by the **Project Management Institute (PMI)** has achieved prominence. PMI is an international organization focused on disseminating best practices in project management. Both the American National Standards Institute (ANSI) and International Standards Organization (ISO) have endorsed PMI's work.

PMI publishes project management documents and offers project management training. It also offers the **Project Management Professional (PMP)** certification. Professionals who have 4,500 hours of project work experience can earn the certification by passing PMI's examination. Once you have the required work experience, the PMP is a worthwhile certification for any professional involved in project management work of any type. (The PMP certification pertains to project management in general, not only to information systems project management. See *www.pmi.org* for more information.)

Since its origin in 1969, PMI has evaluated many project management concepts and techniques and brought the best of them together under the umbrella of a document titled the *Project Management Body of Knowledge (PMBOK®) Guide*. This document contains what many believe are the best project management processes, practices, and techniques. The document does not describe the details of each practice or technique but instead identifies those practices that are known to be effective for different situations and briefly describes their use. Versions of this document are denoted by the year in which they are published. As of 2015, the current version is *A Guide to the Project Management Body of Knowledge (PMBOK® Guide)*, Fifth Edition.

The *PMBOK® Guide* is organized according to the grid in Figure CE16-3, which shows five *process groups* and nine *knowledge areas*. The process groups refer to different stages in the life of a project; the nine knowledge areas refer to factors to be managed throughout the life of the project.

You can surmise the meanings of the process groups from their titles. The knowledge areas provide an excellent summary of project management dimensions. *Project integration* refers to the management of the overall project and the construction of the final product. We have already discussed the trade-offs among *requirements (scope)*, *time*, and *cost*. *Quality* management refers to quality assurance; for an IS project, it concerns planning and managing the product quality-assurance function.

The nature of *human resources* management is clear from its name. *Communications* management concerns the methods, media, and schedules for communicating with the project's sponsors, within the team itself, and with others having an interest in the progress of the project. The decision to use a team SharePoint site, for example, would be part of communications management. Risk is inherent in all projects, and especially so for projects that involve new technology or the innovative application of existing technology. The purpose of *risk* management is to ensure that managers understand project risks and balance risk factors—or that they take other appropriate actions to mitigate unwanted outcomes. Finally, *procurement* management concerns contracts with outside vendors for services, materials, and outsourcing of functions.

The *PMBOK® Guide* specifies practices, documents, techniques, and methods to be used for most of the cells of the grid in Figure CE16-3. For specific guidance on particular practices for process groups or knowledge areas, see the *PMBOK® Guide*. The particular contents of each cell are beyond the scope of this text; to learn more, take a project management class. However, you can consider the elements in Figure CE16-3 as a summary of the dimensions or factors that large-scale information systems development projects must address.

**Figure CE16-3**
Dimensions of Project Management

**Project Management Processes**

| Knowledge Areas | Initiating | Planning | Executing | Monitoring and Controlling | Closing |
|---|---|---|---|---|---|
| Project integration | | | | | |
| Requirements (Scope) | | | | | |
| Time | | | | | |
| Cost | | | | | |
| Quality | | | | | |
| Human resources | | | | | |
| Communications | | | | | |
| Risk | | | | | |
| Procurement | | | | | |

# QCE16-4 HOW DOES A WORK BREAKDOWN STRUCTURE DRIVE PROJECT MANAGEMENT?

The key strategy for large-scale systems development—and, indeed, the key strategy for any project—is to divide and conquer. Break up large tasks into smaller tasks and continue breaking up the tasks until they are small enough to manage, thus enabling you to estimate time and costs. Each task should culminate in one or more **deliverables**. Examples of deliverables are documents, designs, prototypes, data models, database designs, working data-entry screens, and the like. Without a deliverable, it is impossible to know if the task was accomplished.

A **work breakdown structure (WBS)** is a hierarchy of the tasks required to complete a project. The WBS for a large project is huge; it might entail hundreds or even thousands of tasks. Figure CE16-4 shows the WBS for the system definition phase of the operational PRIDE system. The overall task, *System definition,* is divided into *Define goals and scope, Assess feasibility, Plan project,* and *Form project team.* Each of those tasks is broken into smaller tasks, until the work has been divided into a number of small tasks that can be managed and estimated.

Again, note that the term **scope** is being used here in two different ways. As used in this WBS example, *scope* means to define the system boundaries, which is the sense in which it is used in the SDLC. As noted in QCE16-3, scope for the *PMBOK*® *Guide* means to define the requirements. That use of scope does not appear in Figure CE16-4.

Once the project is deconstructed into small tasks, the next step is to define task dependencies and to estimate task durations. Regarding dependencies, some tasks must begin at the same time, some tasks must end at the same time, and some tasks cannot start until other tasks have finished. Task dependencies are normally input to planning software such as Microsoft Project. Figure CE16-5 shows the WBS as input to Microsoft Project, with task dependencies and durations defined. The display on the right, called a **Gantt chart**, shows tasks, dates, and dependencies.

**Figure CE16-4**
Sample Work Breakdown Structure (WBS)

| | | | |
|---|---|---|---|
| System definition | | | |
| 1.1 | Define goals and scope | | |
| | 1.1.1 | Define goals | |
| | 1.1.2 | Define system boundaries | |
| | 1.1.3 | Review results | |
| | 1.1.4 | Document results | |
| 1.2 | Assess feasibility | | |
| | 1.2.1 | Cost | |
| | 1.2.2 | Schedule | |
| | 1.2.3 | Technical | |
| | 1.2.4 | Organizational | |
| | 1.2.5 | Document feasibility | |
| | 1.2.6 | Management review and go/no go decision | |
| 1.3 | Plan project | | |
| | 1.3.1 | Establish milestones | |
| | 1.3.2 | Create WBS | |
| | | 1.3.2.1 | Levels 1 and 2 |
| | | 1.3.2.2 | Levels 3+ |
| | 1.3.3 | Document WBS | |
| | | 1.3.3.1 | Create WBS baseline |
| | | 1.3.3.2 | Input to Project |
| | 1.3.4 | Determine resource requirements | |
| | | 1.3.4.1 | Personnel |
| | | 1.3.4.2 | Computing |
| | | 1.3.4.3 | Office space |
| | | 1.3.4.4 | Travel and Meeting Expense |
| | 1.3.5 | Management review | |
| | | 1.3.5.1 | Prepare presentation |
| | | 1.3.5.2 | Prepare background documents |
| | | 1.3.5.3 | Give presentation |
| | | 1.3.5.4 | Incorporate feedback into plan |
| | | 1.3.5.5 | Approve project |
| 1.4 | Form project team | | |
| | 1.4.1 | Meet with HR | |
| | 1.4.2 | Meet with IT Director | |
| | 1.4.3 | Develop job descriptions | |
| | 1.4.4 | Meet with available personnel | |
| | 1.4.5 | Hire personnel | |

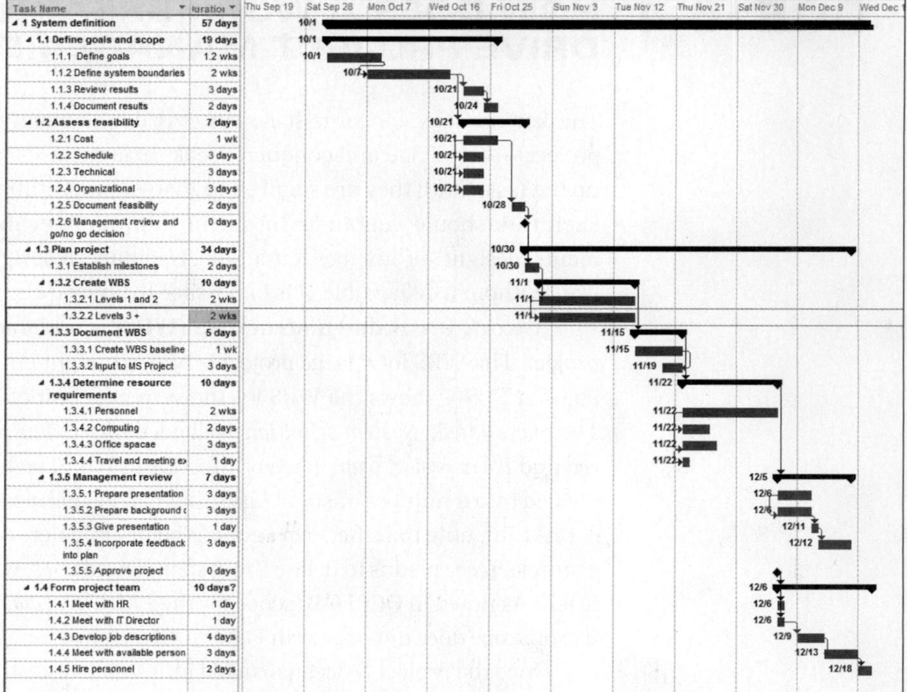


**Figure CE16-5**
Gantt Chart of WBS for Definition Phase of a Thin-Client System

*Source:* Microsoft Project 2013

All of the tasks from the WBS have been entered, and each task has been assigned a duration. Task dependencies have also been specified, although the means used to do so is beyond our discussion. The two red arrows emerging from task 1.1.2, *Define system boundaries*, indicate that neither the *Review results* task nor the *Assess feasibility* task can begin until *Define system boundaries* is completed. Other task dependencies are also shown; you can learn about them in a project management class.

The **critical path** is the sequence of activities that determine the earliest date by which the project can be completed. Reflect for a moment on that statement: The earliest date is the date determined by considering the *longest path* through the network of activities. Paying attention to task dependencies, the planner will compress the tasks as much as possible. Those tasks that cannot be further compressed lie on the critical path. Microsoft Project and other project-planning applications can readily identify critical path tasks.

Figure CE16-5 shows the tasks on the critical path in red. Consider the first part of the WBS. The project planner specified that task 1.1.2 cannot begin until 2 days before task 1.1.1 ends. (That's the meaning of the red arrow emerging from task 1.1.1.) Neither task 1.1.3 nor task 1.2 can begin until task 1.1.2 is completed. Task 1.2.1 will take longer than tasks 1.1.3 and 1.1.4, and so task 1.2—not tasks 1.1.3 or 1.1.4—is on the critical path. Thus, the critical path to this point is tasks 1.1.1, 1.1.2, and 1.2. You can trace the critical path through the rest of the WBS by following the tasks shown in red, though the entire WBS and critical path are not shown.

Using Microsoft Project or a similar product, it is possible to assign personnel to tasks and to stipulate the percentage of time that each person devotes to a task. Figure CE16-6 shows a Gantt chart for which this has been done. The notation means that Eleanore works only 25 percent of the time on task 1.1.1; Lynda and Richard work full time. Additionally, one can assign costs to personnel and compute a labor budget for each task and for the WBS overall. One can assign resources to tasks and use Microsoft Project to detect and prevent two tasks from using the same resources. Resource costs can be assigned and summed as well.

Managers can use the critical path to perform **critical path analysis**. First, note that if a task is on the critical path, and if that task runs late, the project will be late. Hence, tasks on the critical path cannot be allowed to run late if the project is to be delivered on time. Second, tasks not on the critical path can run late to the point at which they would become part of the critical path. Hence, up to a point, resources can be taken from noncritical path tasks to shorten tasks on

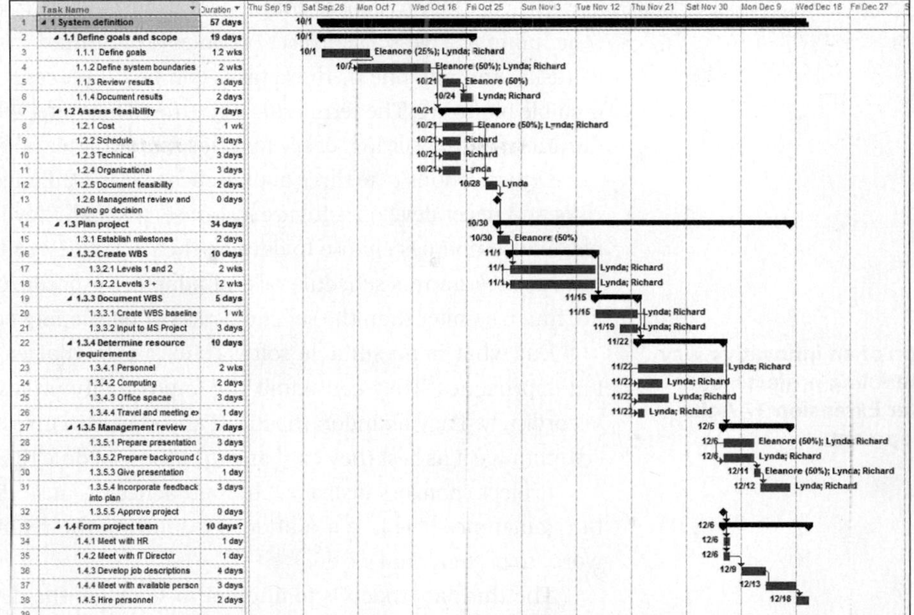


**Figure CE16-6**
Gantt Chart with Resources Assigned

*Source:* Microsoft Project 2013

the critical path. Using critical path analysis, managers can move resources among tasks so as to compress the schedule.

So far, we have discussed the role of the WBS for planning. It can be used for monitoring as well. The final WBS plan is denoted the **baseline WBS**. This baseline shows the planned tasks, dependencies, durations, and resource assignments. As the project proceeds, project managers can input actual dates, labor hours, and resource costs. At any point in time, Microsoft Project can report whether the project is ahead of or behind schedule and how the actual project costs compare with baseline costs.

As you can see, the WBS provides invaluable project management information. In fact, it is the single most important management tool for large-scale projects.

## QCE16-5 WHAT IS THE BIGGEST CHALLENGE FOR PLANNING A SYSTEMS DEVELOPMENT PROJECT?

As noted in Chapter 12, the biggest challenge in planning systems development is scheduling. How long does it take to develop a large data model? How long does it take to adapt that data model to the users' satisfaction? How long does it take to develop a computer program to process PRIDE privacy data on a cloud server if no one on the team has ever developed a cloud-based server application before?

Fred Brooks defined software as "logical poetry." It is pure thought-stuff. When pressed for a schedule, experienced software developers have been known to say, "What would Shakespeare have said if someone asked him how long it would take him to write *Hamlet?*" Another common rejoinder is "What would a fisherman say if you ask him how long it will take to catch three fish? He doesn't know, and neither do I."

No company should know better how to estimate software schedules than Microsoft. It has more experience developing software than any other company; it is loaded with smart, even brilliant, developers; it can draw from enormous financial resources; and it has strong incentives to schedule projects accurately. However, Microsoft Vista was delivered 2 years late. It was supposed to take 3 years, and it took 5. That's a 67 percent schedule overrun from the largest software developer in the world on what is arguably the world's most important computer program.

Part of the problem is that errors accumulate. If scheduling a single task is difficult, then scheduling a large-scale project becomes a nightmare. Suppose you have a WBS with thousands of tasks, and any one of those tasks can be 67 percent over schedule. It is impossible to do any credible planning. The term *critical path* loses meaning when there is that much doubt about task duration. In that setting, every task has some chance of being on the critical path.

Organizations take three approaches to this challenge. The first is to avoid the major schedule risks and never develop software in-house. Instead, they license software from vendors. For example, few companies choose to develop their own ERP or CRM software. ERP or CRM systems still have the substantial schedule risks of adapting procedures and training personnel, but those risks are much smaller than the schedule risks of developing complex software and databases.

**To learn of an innovative way of scheduling projects, see Chapter Extension 17, Agile Development.**

But what if no suitable software exists? In that case, companies take one of two remaining approaches. They can admit the impossibility of systems development scheduling and plan accordingly. They abandon the SDLC and decide to invest a certain level of resources into a project, manage it as best they can, and take the schedule that results.

Project sponsors dislike such approaches because they feel they are signing a blank check. But sometimes it is just a matter of admitting the reality that exists: "We don't know, and it's worse to pretend that we do."

The third approach is to attempt to schedule the development project in spite of all the difficulties. Several different estimation techniques can be used. If the project is similar to a past project, the schedule data from that past project can be used for planning. When such similar past projects exist, this technique can produce quality schedule estimates. If there is no such past project, managers can estimate the number of **lines of code** that will need to be written. Then they can use industry or company averages to estimate the time required. Another technique is to estimate the **function points** in a program, use each function point to determine the number of lines of code, and use that number to estimate schedules. A function point is simply a feature or function of the new program. Updating a customer record is an example. For more information on the use of lines of code and function points for software scheduling, visit *www.codeproject.com/Articles/9266/Software-Project-Cost-Estimates-Using-COCOMO-II-Mo*. Of course, lines of code and function point techniques estimate schedules only for software components. The schedules for creating databases and the other system components must be estimated using other techniques.

Chapter Extension 17 describes *agile* development techniques. Scrum, in particular, is good for schedule uncertainties because requirements are managed so as to fit within the time available. The result of a scrum project is a finished product that can be used; if there is insufficient time for complete development, some of the requirements will be unmet. But the final system will be a working version of at least some portion of the requirements.

During your career, be aware of the challenges and difficulties of scheduling large-scale information systems development. As a user or manager, do not take schedules as guarantees. Plan for schedule slippage, and if it does *not* occur, be pleasantly surprised.

## QCE16-6 WHAT ARE THE BIGGEST CHALLENGES FOR MANAGING A SYSTEMS DEVELOPMENT PROJECT?

The challenges of managing large-scale systems development projects arise from four different factors:

- Coordination
- Diseconomies of scale
- Configuration control
- Unexpected events

Larger IS development projects are usually organized into a variety of development groups that work independently. Coordinating the work of these independent groups can be difficult, particularly if the groups reside in different geographic locations or different countries. An accurate and complete WBS facilitates coordination, but no project ever proceeds exactly in accordance with the WBS. Delays occur, and unknown or unexpected dependencies develop among tasks.

The coordination problem is increased because software is pure thought-stuff. When constructing a new house, electricians install wiring in the walls as they exist; it is impossible to do otherwise. No electrician can install wiring in the wall as designed 6 months ago, before a change. In software, such physical constraints do not exist. It is entirely possible for a team to develop a set of application programs to process a database using an obsolete database design. When the database design was changed, all involved parties should have been notified, but this may not have occurred. Wasted hours, increased cost, and poor morale are the result.

As mentioned in Chapter 12, another problem is diseconomies of scale. Adding more people to a project increases coordination requirements. The number of possible interactions among team members rises exponentially with the number of team members. Ultimately, no matter how well managed a project is, diseconomies of scale will set in. According to Brooks' Law, adding more people to a late software project makes it later.

As the project proceeds, controlling the configuration of the work product becomes difficult. Consider requirements, for example. The development team produces an initial statement of requirements. Meetings with users produce an adjusted set of requirements. Suppose an event then occurs that necessitates a change to requirements. After deliberation, assume the team decides to ignore a large portion of the changes to the requirements resulting from the event. At this point, there are four different versions of the requirements. If the changes to requirements are not carefully managed, changes from the four versions will be mixed up, and confusion and disorder will result. No one will know which requirements are the correct, current requirements.

Similar problems occur with designs, program code, database data, and other system components. The term **configuration control** refers to a set of management policies, practices, and tools that developers use to maintain control over the project's resources. Such resources include documents, schedules, designs, program code, test suites, and any other shared resource needed to complete the project. Configuration control is vital; a loss of control over a project's configuration is so expensive and disruptive that it can result in termination for senior project managers.

The last major challenge to IS project management is unexpected events. The larger and longer the project, the greater the chance of disruption due to an unanticipated event. Critical people can change companies; even whole teams have been known to pack up and join a competitor. The organization can be acquired, and new management may have different priorities. Congress can change applicable laws; Sarbanes-Oxley is a good example of a law that affected not only financial systems but also other systems whose resources were taken to comply with the new law. Natural disasters such as hurricanes can destroy offices or significantly affect employees' lives.

Because software is thought-stuff, team morale is crucial. Author David Kroenke once managed two strong-headed software developers who engaged in a heated argument over the design of a program feature. The argument ended when one threw a chair at the other. The rest of the team divided its loyalties between the two developers, and work came to a standstill as subgroups sneered and argued with one another when they met in hallways or at the coffee pot. How do you schedule that event in your WBS? As a project manager, you never know what strange event is heading your way. Such unanticipated events make project management challenging, but also incredibly fascinating!

## QCE16-7 WHAT IS THE SINGLE MOST IMPORTANT TASK FOR USERS ON A SYSTEMS DEVELOPMENT PROJECT?

*Taking responsibility for requirements* is the single most important task you, a future user or manager of users, can perform for a large-scale development project. Taking responsibility goes beyond participating in requirements meetings and stating your opinion on how things should work. Taking responsibility means understanding that the information system is built for your business function and managing requirements accordingly. (See Case Study 12, pages 365–366.)

"There are no IT projects," says former Kaiser-Permanente CIO Cliff Dodd. Rather, he says, "Some business projects have an IT component."[2] Dodd is right. Information systems exist to help organizations achieve their goals and objectives. Information systems exist to facilitate business processes and to improve decision making. Every information system is simply a part of some larger business project.

When investigating the problems in the IRS modernization program, the IRS Oversight Board stated, "The IRS business units must take direct leadership and ownership of the Modernization program and its projects. In particular this must include defining the scope of each project, preparing realistic and attainable business cases, and controlling scope changes throughout each project's life cycle."[3]

Users cannot be passive recipients of the IS department's services. Instead, users are responsible for ensuring that requirements are complete and accurate. Users must ask only for what they need and must avoid creating requirements that cannot possibly be constructed within the available budget. Because users may not know what is difficult or unrealistic, requirements definition can occur only through an extended conversation among the users and the development team.

Once the requirements are known, the development team will create a project WBS and will initiate management activities for each of the nine knowledge areas in Figure CE16-3. It will fill staff positions, begin the design process, and, later, implement the stated requirements. If users subsequently change their minds about what is needed, considerable rework and waste will occur. **Requirements creep** is the process by which users agree to one set of requirements, then add a bit more ("It won't take too much extra work"), then add a bit more, and so forth. Over time, the requirements creep so much that they describe a completely new project, but the development team is left with the budget and plan of the original project.

Users must take responsibility for managing requirements changes and for avoiding requirements creep. Some amount of requirements change is inevitable; but if changes become extensive, if requirements creep cannot be avoided, start a new project. Don't try to turn a doghouse into a skyscraper, one small change at a time. In that course of action, disaster is the only outcome.

A final part of the users' responsibility for requirements concerns *testing*. You and those who work for you may be asked to help in several different ways. You may be asked to specify testing criteria. If so, you need to help define testable conditions that determine whether a feature or function is complete and operational. Testing may occur in several stages during the project. For example, you may be asked to test design components; evaluating a data model is a good example. Or you may be asked to provide sample data and sample scenarios for program and systems testing. You may be asked to participate in the testing of beta versions. Because only the users can know if a feature works correctly, testing is part of requirements management.

Once more: *Taking responsibility for system requirements is the single most important task you can perform on a large-scale development project!*

# ACTIVE REVIEW
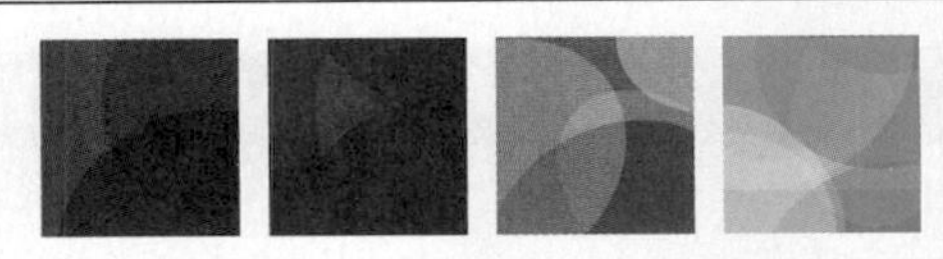

Use this Active Review to verify that you understand the ideas and concepts that answer this chapter extension's study questions.

## QCE16-1 WHY IS FORMALIZED PROJECT MANAGEMENT NECESSARY?

Summarize the characteristics of large-scale information systems development projects. Explain why these characteristics make large-scale projects hard to manage. Give two examples of large-scale systems development projects.

## QCE16-2 WHAT ARE THE TRADE-OFFS IN REQUIREMENTS, COST, AND TIME?

Describe two meanings for the term *scope*. Describe how requirements affect cost and time. Describe the trade-offs that exist between requirements and time. Explain the trade-offs that exist between time and cost. Describe circumstances in which increasing cost reduces time. Explain circumstances in which increasing cost increases time. Describe circumstances in which time extensions reduce costs.

## QCE16-3 WHAT ARE THE DIMENSIONS OF PROJECT MANAGEMENT?

Describe the difference between development processes such as the SDLC and project management. Summarize the activities of the PMI. Describe the contents of the *PMBOK® Guide*. Name the five process groups and the nine knowledge areas. Briefly explain the focus of each management area. Explain how you can use Figure CE16-3.

## QCE16-4 HOW DOES A WORK BREAKDOWN STRUCTURE DRIVE PROJECT MANAGEMENT?

State the key strategy for large-scale systems development. Explain why each task needs to produce one or more deliverables. Define *work breakdown structure* and give an example. In Figure CE16-4, explain the numeric notation under task 1.3. Define *Gantt chart* and describe its contents. Explain how task dependencies influence project work. Define *critical path analysis* and, using your own words, explain what it means. Describe two ways managers can use critical path analysis. Summarize how the WBS can be used to estimate costs. Define *baseline WBS* and explain how the baseline can be used to monitor a project.

## QCE16-5 WHAT IS THE BIGGEST CHALLENGE FOR PLANNING A SYSTEMS DEVELOPMENT PROJECT?

Name the biggest challenge for systems development planning. Explain why this is so. Describe how the logical-poetry nature of software development affects scheduling. Summarize the three approaches to the systems development scheduling challenge that organizations can take. Describe two ways of estimating time to write computer programs. Describe how you can use the knowledge about systems development scheduling that you have.

## QCE16-6 WHAT ARE THE BIGGEST CHALLENGES FOR MANAGING A SYSTEMS DEVELOPMENT PROJECT?

Name four factors that create challenges for managing systems development. Give an example of each factor. Define *configuration control*.

## QCE16-7 WHAT IS THE SINGLE MOST IMPORTANT TASK FOR USERS ON A SYSTEMS DEVELOPMENT PROJECT?

State and describe the single most important task for users on a systems development project. Explain why, as Dodd put it, there are no IT projects. Summarize user responsibilities for managing requirements. Define *requirements creep*. Describe the action that should occur if requirements creep cannot be stopped. Summarize the users' role for systems testing.

## KEY TERMS AND CONCEPTS

Baseline 603
Baseline WBS 607
Configuration control 609
Cost 602
Critical path 606
Critical path analysis 606
Deliverables 605
Diseconomies of scale 602
Function points 608
Gantt chart 605
Lines of code 608
Project Management Institute (PMI) 603
Project Management Professional (PMP) 603
Requirements 602
Requirements creep 610
Scope 605
Time 602
Trade-off 602
Work breakdown structure (WBS) 605

**MyMISLab™**

To complete the problems with the ✪, go to EOC Discussion Questions in the MyLab.

## USING YOUR KNOWLEDGE

✪ **CE16-1.** Consider two projects: one to track the assignment of people to one of 12 teams in a soccer league and the second to upgrade the reservations system for Alaska Airlines. Explain how the general characteristics of these two systems development projects differ.

✪ **CE16-2.** Consider the development of either the Amazon Fire phone or the Xbox application for PRIDE. Explain the trade-offs that can be made among requirements, cost, and schedule. For a given set of requirements, explain how cost and schedule can be traded off.

✪ **CE16-3.** Consider the process of an election campaign—say, a campaign to elect one of your fellow students for the position of student government president (or similar office at your university):

**a.** Develop a WBS for the election campaign.

**b.** Explain how knowledge of the critical path could help you plan the campaign.

**c.** Explain two ways you can use critical path analysis for planning the campaign.

**d.** Explain how you can use critical path analysis for executing and monitoring the campaign progress.

**e.** If you have access to Microsoft Project (or other planning software):

i. Input your WBS to Microsoft Project.
ii. Assign durations to tasks in your project.
iii. Specify task dependencies.
iv. Identify the critical path.

**MyMISLab™**

Go to the Assignments section of your MyLab to complete these writing exercises.

**CE16-4.** Suppose you have a computer virus that is so severe you must reformat your hard drive:

**a.** Develop a WBS for the process for recovering your computer.

**b.** Estimate the time it will take to perform each task.

**c.** Neither lines of code nor function point estimation pertains to this task. Explain one other way you can improve the quality of your estimate.

**d.** Suppose you suspect that your estimate for the time of recovery could be low by as much as 200 percent. How could you use this knowledge?

**CE16-5.** Suppose you work for a medium-sized oil and natural gas company as a systems developer. The CEO is interested in developing an application that will give him information about the amount of natural gas passing through pumping stations located around North America. He wants it to work on his desktop, iPad, and smartphone. The features he wants on the application seem to change every time you talk with him, and you're still in the planning phase. Now he's asked for a schedule. Why might it be difficult to develop a schedule for this project? How would you explain this to the CEO? Describe a metaphor you could use to explain how difficult it will be to accurately predict when the application will be completed.

## ENDNOTES

1. When we speak of information systems, we usually refer to the characteristics of the system to be constructed as *requirements*. The discipline of project management refers to those characteristics as project *scope*. If you read literature from the Project Management Institute, for example, it will use the term *scope* in the same sense that we use *requirements*. The SCLC uses the term *scope* to mean the broad outline of the project. Thus, you need to consider context when you see *scope* in this chapter extension.
2. Quoted in Steve Ulfelder, "How to Talk to Business," *Computerworld*, last modified March 13, 2006, *www.computerworld.com/managementtopics/management/story/0,10801,109403,00.html*.
3. "Independent Analysis of IRS Business Systems Modernization Special Report," *IRS Oversight Board*, accessed September 13, 2013, *www.irsoversightboard.treas.gov*.

chapter extension **17**

Chapter 12 provides the background for this extension.

# Agile Development

**STUDY QUESTIONS**

**QCE17-1 WHY IS THE SDLC LOSING CREDIBILITY?**

**QCE17-2 WHAT ARE THE PRINCIPLES OF AGILE DEVELOPMENT METHODOLOGIES?**

**QCE17-3 WHAT IS THE SCRUM PROCESS?**

**QCE17-4 HOW DO REQUIREMENTS DRIVE THE SCRUM PROCESS?**

## QCE17-1 WHY IS THE SDLC LOSING CREDIBILITY?

The systems development life cycle (SDLC) process that you learned about in Chapter 12 is falling out of favor in the systems development community, primarily for two reasons. First, the nature of the SDLC denies what every experienced developer knows is true: systems requirements are fuzzy and always changing. They change because they need to be corrected or more is known or users, once they see a part of the application, change their minds. Other reasons are that business needs change or technology offers other possibilities.

According to the SDLC, however, progress goes in a linear sequence from requirements to design to implementation. Sometimes this is called the **waterfall method** because the assumption is that once you've finished a phase, you never go back. Requirements are done. Then you do design. Design is done; then you implement. However, experience has shown that it just doesn't work that way.

The SDLC gained popularity when the U.S. Department of Defense stipulated that it would be used for all software development contracts. It did so because it had enjoyed success with a process like the SDLC for building physical things. If you're going to build a runway, for example, you specify how long it needs to be, how much weight the surface must withstand, and so forth. Then you design it, and next you build it. The waterfall model works.

However, software, information systems, and business processes are not physical; they're social. They're built for people to use to inform themselves and achieve their goals. People and social systems are incredibly malleable; they adapt. That characteristic enables humans to do many amazing things, but it also means that requirements change and the waterfall development process cannot work.

Also, as stated in Chapter 12, requirements change in response to new technology. While technology does change when building physical objects, the rate of change is much less than for information systems.

The second reason that the SDLC is falling out of favor is that it is very risky. The people for whom the system is being constructed cannot see what they have until the end. At that point, if something is wrong, all the money and time has already been spent. Furthermore, what if, as frequently happens, the project runs out of money or time before it is completed? The result is a form of management blackmail in which the developers say, "Well, it's not done yet, but give us another $100,000 or another 6 months, and *then* we'll have it done." If management declines, which it might because the time or money at that point is sunk, it is left not only with the loss but also with the unmet need that caused it to start the process in the first place.

In short, the SDLC assumes that requirements don't change, which everyone who has ever been within 10 feet of a development project knows is not true; it's very risky for the business that sponsors it as well.

## QCE17-2 WHAT ARE THE PRINCIPLES OF AGILE DEVELOPMENT METHODOLOGIES?

Over the past 40 years, numerous alternatives to the SDLC have been proposed, including *rapid application development*, the *unified process, extreme programming, scrum*, and others. All of these techniques addressed the problems of the SDLC, and by the turn of the century, their philosophy had coalesced into what has come to be known as **agile development**, which means a development process that conforms to the principles in Figure CE17-1.

The first principle is that the development process should expect, and even welcome, change. Given the nature of social systems, *expect* is not a surprise, but why *welcome*? Isn't welcoming requirements change a bit like welcoming a good case of the flu? No, because systems are created to help organizations and people achieve their strategies, and the more the requirements change, the closer they come to facilitating strategies. The result is better and more satisfying for both the users and the development team.[1]

Second, agile development processes are designed to frequently deliver a *working* version of the product. Frequently means something in the range of 1 to several weeks, sometimes as long as 8 weeks, but not longer. This frequency means that management is at risk only for whatever costs and time are used in that period. At its end, management will be able to use some product version that has some value to it.

Thus, unlike the SDLC, agile techniques deliver benefits early and often. The initial benefits might be small, but they are positive and increase throughout the process. With the SDLC, no value is generated until the very end. Considering the time value of money, this characteristic alone makes agile techniques more desirable.

The third principle in Figure CE17-1 is that the development team will work closely with the customer until the project ends. Someone who knows the business requirements must be made available to the development team and must be able and willing to clarify and elaborate on requirements. Also, customers need to be available to test the evolving work product and provide guidance on how well new features work.

The fourth principle is a tough one for many developers to accept. Rather than design the complete, overall system at the beginning, only those portions of the design that are needed to complete the current work are done. Sometimes this is called **just-in-time design**. Designing in this way means that the design is constantly changing, and existing designs may need to be revised, along with substantial revision to the work product produced so far. On the surface, it is inefficient. However, experience has shown that far too many teams have constructed elaborate, fanciful, and complete designs that turned out to be glamorous fiction as the requirements changed.

Test as you go, which is the next principle, is obvious if the team is going to be delivering working versions. Testing is initially conducted among members of the team but involves the business customer as well.

Development teams know how well they're doing. You could go into any development environment today and ask the team how it's doing, and once team members understood you were not about to inflict a new management program on them, you would find they know their

**Figure CE17-1**
Principles of Agile Development

- Expect, even welcome, changes in requirements.
- Frequently deliver *working* version of the product.
- Work closely with customer for the duration.
- Design as you go.
- Test as you go.
- Team knows best how it's doing/how to change.
- Can be used for applications, information systems, and business process development.

strengths, weaknesses, bottlenecks, and process problems quite well. That principle is part of agile development methodologies. At the end of every deliverable or some other (short) milestone, the team meets to assess how it's doing and how it can improve.

Finally, agile development methodologies are generic. They can be applied to the creation of applications, information systems, and business processes. They are applicable to other team projects as well, but that subject is beyond the scope of this text.

## QCE17-3 WHAT IS THE SCRUM PROCESS?

Scrum is an agile development methodology developed by Jeff Sutherland, Jeff McKenna, and John Scumniotales for a project at the Easel Corporation[2] and extended by others over the past 15 years. *Scrum* is a rugby term, first used for teamwork in a *Harvard Business Review* article written by Hirotaka Takeuchi and Ikujiro Nonaka.[3] In rugby, a *scrum* is a gathering of a team into a circle to restart play after a foul or other interruption. Think of it as a huddle in American football.

### SCRUM ESSENTIALS

Scrum is an agile development process that follows the principles shown in Figure CE17-2. First, the process is driven by a prioritized list of requirements created by the users and business sponsors of the new system. Work is divided into scrum work periods, which can be as short as a week but never longer than 8 weeks. From 2 to 4 weeks is recommended. Each work period, the team selects the top priority items that it will commit to delivering during that time. Each workday begins with a **stand-up**, which is a 15-minute meeting in which each team member[4] states:

- What he or she has done in the past day
- What he or she will do in the coming day
- Any factors that are blocking his or her progress

**Figure CE17-2**
Scrum Essentials

- **Requirements list drives process**
- **Each work period (1 to 4–8 weeks):**
  - Select requirements to consider
  - Determine tasks to perform—select requirements to deliver
  - Team meets daily for 15 min (stand-up)
    - What I did yesterday
    - What I'm going to do today
    - What's blocking me
  - Test frequently
  - Paired work possible
  - Minimal documentation
  - Deliver (something) that works
  - Evaluate team's work process at end of period (and say thanks)
- **Rinse and repeat until**
  - Customer says we're done
  - Out of time
  - Out of money
- **Three principal roles**
  - Product owner (business professional)
  - Scrum master
  - Team members (7 ± 2 people)

The purpose of the stand-up is to achieve accountability for team members' progress and to give a public forum for blocking factors. Often one team member will have expertise to help another blocked team member resolve the blocking issue.

Testing is done frequently, possibly many times per day. Sometimes the business owner of the project is involved in daily testing as well. In some cases, team members work in pairs; in **paired programming**, for example, two members share the same computer and write a computer program together. Sometimes, one programmer will provide a test, and the other will either demonstrate that the code passes that test or alter the code so that it will. Then the two members switch roles. Other types of paired work are possible as well.

Minimal documentation is prepared. The result of the team's work is not design or other documents, but rather a product that is a working version of the requirements that were selected at the start of the scrum period.

At the end of the scrum period, the working version of the product is delivered to the customer, who can, if desired, put it to work at that time, even in its not fully finished state. After the product is delivered, the team meets to evaluate its own process and to make changes as needed. Team members are given an opportunity to express thanks and receive recognition for superior work at these meetings. (Review the criteria for team success in Chapter Extension 1 and you will see how scrum adheres to the principles of a successful team.)

Figure CE17-3 summarizes the scrum process.

## WHEN ARE WE DONE?

Work continues in a repeating cycle of scrum periods until one of three conditions is met:

- The customer is satisfied with the product created and decides to accept the work product, even if some requirements are left unsatisfied.
- The project runs out of time.
- The project runs out of money.

Unlike the SDLC, if a scrum project terminates because of time or budget limitations, the customer will still have a useful, working result for the time and money expended. It may not be the fully functioning version that was desired, but it is something that, assuming requirements are defined and prioritized correctly, can generate value for the project sponsors.

**Figure CE17-3**
Scrum Process

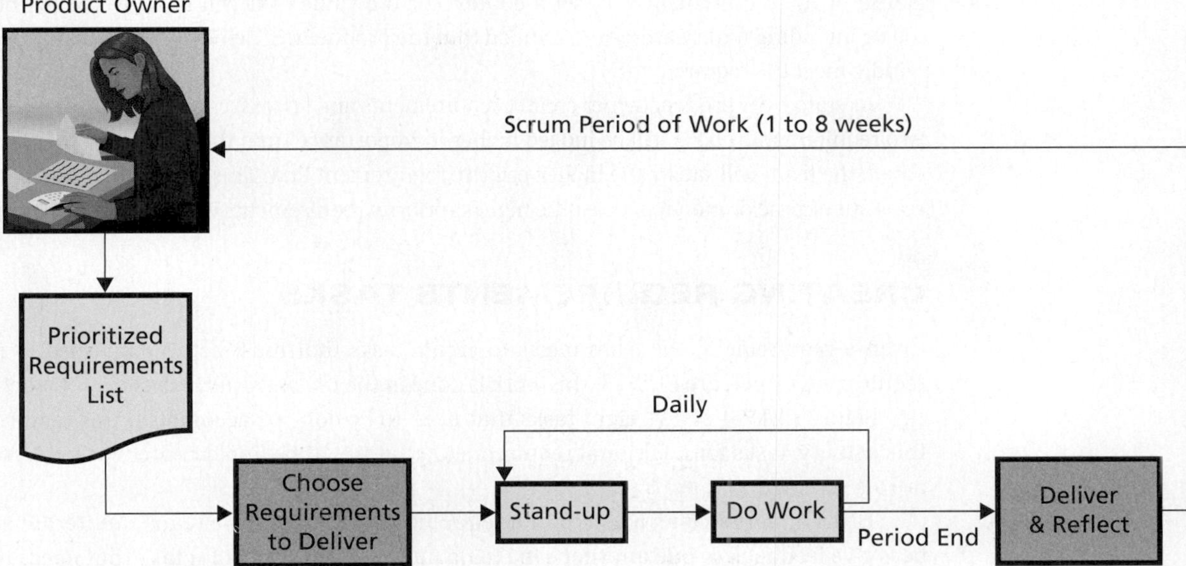

### KEY ROLES

Scrum defines three key roles. The **product owner** is the business professional who provides the requirements and is available for clarification and testing. The product owner is the only person on a scrum team who has the authority to add, delete, or change requirements and their priority.

A **scrum master** is an expert in scrum processes who helps to keep the process organized and operating. The scrum master is not the boss; he or she is more like a coach or even a referee. The scrum master steps in when meetings go too long, when team members are misusing meeting time, when the product sponsor isn't doing his or her job, and when other situations are not working. The scrum master is also the guardian of team members' time. If distractions occur, the scrum master steps in to eliminate them. If someone other than the product owner attempts to change requirements or priorities, the scrum master negates that attempt.

Finally, **team members** are the programmers, systems analysts, business analysts, database designers, cloud engineers, PQA testing personnel, and any other staff needed to build the work product. Scrum teams are small; five to nine team members are recommended. If work requires more personnel, then the work is reorganized to be accomplished by multiple scrum teams working in parallel. It's not clear that scrum works well for exceedingly large projects, but then again, it's not clear that any other development process works well for them, either.

## QCE17-4 HOW DO REQUIREMENTS DRIVE THE SCRUM PROCESS?

Scrum is distinguished from other agile development methodologies, in part, by the way that it uses requirements to drive planning and scheduling. First, requirements are specified in a particular manner. One common format is to express requirements in terms of *who* does *what* and *why*.

For example, in the PRIDE system, a requirement could be expressed as:

"As a personal trainer, I want to view the client's exercise records so I can make sure he is not doing too much."

Or

"As a personal trainer, I want to view the client's exercise records so I can make sure she is still actively involved in her exercise program."

Each of these requirements specifies who (the personal trainer) does what (view a client's exercise data) and why (make sure he is not doing too much.). It's not surprising that the requirement includes *who* and *what*, but the need for *why* may surprise you. The purpose of the why clause of the requirement is to set a context for the value that will be delivered by the requirement. Including it increases the likelihood that the product will deliver business value and not just blindly meet the requirement.

As stated, the product owner creates requirements and prioritizes them. For example, one of the two requirements above will be judged higher in importance than the other. All other things being equal, the team will satisfy the higher-priority requirement first. This means, too, that if the project runs out of time or money, at least the highest-priority requirements will have been completed.

### CREATING REQUIREMENTS TASKS

Given a requirement, the team meets to create tasks that must be accomplished to meet that requirement. In Figure CE17-3, this work is done in the *Choose requirements to deliver* activity.

Figure CE17-4 shows eight tasks that need to be done to accomplish this requirement. In this activity, tasks for additional requirements that might be implemented in this scrum period are also created.

Tasks are created as a group in a team meeting because the team can iterate and members give feedback to one another. One team member will think of a task that needs to be done

**Figure CE17-4**
Example Requirement and Tasks

**Requirement:**
"As a personal trainer, I want to view the client's exercise records so I can make sure she is still actively involved in her exercise program."

**Tasks:**

1. Authenticate the personal trainer.
2. Obtain client identifying data from the personal trainer.
3. Determine this personal trainer is authorized to view this client's records.
4. Read the database to obtain exercise records.
5. Read the database to obtain most recent record of most recent exercise program.
6. Format the data into a generic format.
7. Determine the type of mobile device the personal trainer is using.
8. Format the generic report into a report for that mobile device.

of which other members may not be aware. Or a member may realize that a particular task is incomplete or is doable in some other way.

## SCHEDULING TASKS

As described so far, scrum is a good idea, one of many agile processes that might be used. What makes scrum particularly innovative, however, is the way that tasks are scheduled.

Scrum methodology recognizes that developers are terrible, even wretched, at determining how long a task will take. However, developers are quite good at comparing how long something will take in comparison to something else. So, while a developer may be poor at estimating how long it will take to do, say, Task 2 in Figure CE17-4, he or she will likely be accurate when saying that Task 2 will take twice as long as Task 1 or determining some other ratio.

So, according to the scrum process, once the tasks are known for a given set of requirements, the next step is to assign each task a difficulty point score, called *points*. The easiest task has a point score of 1. A task that will take five times longer is given a point score of 5, and so on. For reasons that are beyond the scope of this discussion, points are expressed in values from a sequence of integers known as the Fibonacci sequence: {1, 2, 3, 5, 8, 13, 21, 34, 55, 89, 144, and ?}. The question mark is used because any number larger than 144 is meaningless. Most likely 89 and 144 are meaningless as well. Tasks with such point scores should be subdivided into multiple requirements. When all tasks have received points, the points are summed to a total for the requirement.

Scrum includes several different techniques for assigning points. Team estimation and planning poker are two. You can learn more about them in *The Elements of Scrum*.[5] The gist of these techniques is applying the team's expertise in an iterative, feedback-generating process to obtain team scores.

## COMMITTING TO FINISH TASKS

As teams work together, they will learn the total number of points of work they can accomplish each scrum period. That term is called the team's **velocity**. The team uses its velocity to determine how many requirements it can commit to accomplishing in the next scrum period. Of course, at first the team will not know its velocity. In that case, senior members will need to make a guess. That guess may be far off, but it will get better as the team gains experience. Unlike the SDLC, there is at least well-founded hope that over time, estimating will improve.

For example, suppose the five requirements on a team's prioritized requirements list total 125 points. If a team knows its velocity is 100 points per scrum period, they know they cannot do all

**Figure CE17-5**
Summary of Scrum Estimation Technique

1. Team assigns 1 point to simplest task.
2. Times to deliver working tasks are compared to each other and assigned points (Points are Fibonacci numbers.) Use:
   a. Team estimation
   b. Planning poker
   c. Other
3. Using past experience, team computes its velocity ... number of points it can accomplish per scrum period.
4. Working with product owner, team selects tasks for the upcoming scrum period, constrained by its velocity.

five. However, if the top four total, say, 80 points, they can commit to doing those four, plus something else. In this case, the team would go back to the product owner and ask if there is a requirement lower on the priority list that can be done for the available 20 points of capacity. The scrum estimation process is summarized in Figure CE17-5.

## HOCUS-POCUS?

If you haven't participated in software or systems development, this process may sound like so much hocus-pocus. However, it has two very important characteristics that make it not so. First, it is a methodology that incorporates team iteration and feedback for scheduling and tasking, which, as you know by now, is a way a team can create something together that far exceeds what each member can do individually. Second, it provides a framework for process learning. As a team works more scrum periods together, it learns how to assign points more accurately, and it increasingly learns what its true velocity is.

But scrum isn't a magic bullet. It can't guarantee that the project will produce a high quality product, on time, and under budget. But, as an alternative to the traditional SDLC, it can limit potential financial losses and produce substantial results in just a few weeks.

# ACTIVE REVIEW

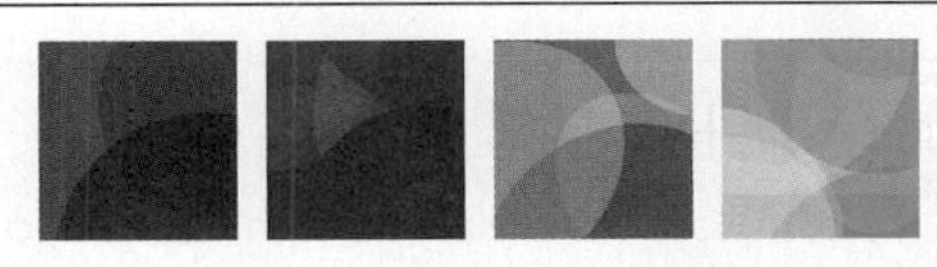

Use this Active Review to verify that you understand the ideas and concepts that answer this chapter extension's study questions.

## QCE17-1 WHY IS THE SDLC LOSING CREDIBILITY?

Summarize the two reasons that the SDLC is falling out of favor. Explain why the U.S. Department of Defense believed that it was a workable process. Explain the nature of social systems development. Explain what happens when an incomplete SDLC project runs out of time or money.

## QCE17-2 WHAT ARE THE PRINCIPLES OF AGILE DEVELOPMENT METHODOLOGIES?

Define *agile development*. In your own words, explain the benefits of each of the principles in Figure CE17-1. Explain why just-in-time design is difficult for some developers to accept. Describe the projects for which agile development is appropriate.

## QCE17-3 WHAT IS THE SCRUM PROCESS?

In sports, what is a scrum? Explain the origin of the term as it pertains to teamwork. In your own words, explain the benefits of the principles in Figure CE17-2. Define *scrum period* and state the recommended length for such periods. Define *stand-up* and explain what happens in a stand-up. Define *paired programming*. Explain the activities and flows in Figure CE17-3. State conditions that cause a scrum project to finish. Summarize the difference between an SDLC project that runs out of money and a scrum project that runs out of money. Name and define three key roles for scrum.

## QCE17-4 HOW DO REQUIREMENTS DRIVE THE SCRUM PROCESS?

Explain the format for stating requirements in scrum. Why is *why* needed? Give two examples of scrum-style requirements not in this text. Summarize the process for creating a task list for accomplishing a scrum requirement. Explain what scheduling activity developers do poorly and what scheduling activity they do well. Explain what points are and summarize how points are assigned to tasks and computed for requirements. Define *velocity* and explain how it is determined. Explain how velocity is used to plan work for a scrum period. In your own words, explain the meaning of "Unlike the SDLC, there is at least well-founded hope that over time, estimating will improve." Summarize the characteristics of scrum that make this statement true.

## KEY TERMS AND CONCEPTS

MyMISLab™

To complete the problems with the ✪, go to EOC Discussion Questions in the MyLab.

## USING YOUR KNOWLEDGE

✪ **CE17-1.** Read the criteria for team success in Chapter Extension 1. Explain scrum characteristics that support achieving team success.

✪ **CE17-2.** Read the opening to Chapter 12. Explain how PRIDE Systems could use a scrum process for managing the Xbox prototype. Describe how doing so would reduce the risk of failure.

✪ **CE17-3.** Suppose you suggest that an information system be developed for your department using scrum. Further suppose that your management is dubious. Write a one-page memo to justify using scrum.

MyMISLab™

Go to the Assignments section of your MyLab to complete these writing exercises.

**CE17-4.** Choose an important project type in a business discipline of interest to you. In accounting, it could be an audit; in marketing, it could be a plan for using social media; in operations, it could be a project of opening a new warehouse. Choose a major activity that is important and that you find interesting. Compare and contrast the use of a process such as the SDLC to a process such as scrum for your project. Which process would you recommend? Justify your recommendation.

**CE17-5.** The CEO of a medium-sized oil and natural gas company has approached you about developing a mobile application. He wants the application to give him data about the amount of natural gas passing through pumping stations located around North America. He is sure about some of the features he wants, but he keeps mentioning features that he wants to add. You're going to use scrum to develop the application. How would you explain to the CEO the importance of having a list of requirements before starting the project? Why do requirements drive the scrum process? What tasks might need to be created to satisfy the requirement that the application be able to monitor the flow of natural gas through the company's pipelines?

## ENDNOTES

1. Assuming those who are specifying requirements are competent and behave sanely. Alas, this is not always true, but we will leave that situation as an exception here.
2. Chris Sims and Hillary Louise Johnson, *The Elements of Scrum* (Foster City, CA: Dymaxicon, 2011), pp. 65, 66.
3. Hirotaka Takeuchi and Ikujiro Nonaka, "New New Product Development Game," *Harvard Business Review*, Jan. 1, 1986. Available for purchase at *http://hbr.org*.
4. Some scrum teams have the rule that only *pigs* can speak at stand-ups. The term comes from the joke about the difference between eggs and ham: the chicken is interested, but the pig is committed.
5. Chris Sims and Hillary Louise Johnson, *The Elements of Scrum* (Foster City, CA: Dymaxicon, 2011), pp. 125–133.

chapter extension **18**

**Chapter 12** provides the background for this extension.

# Business Process Management

**STUDY QUESTIONS**

**QCE18-1** WHY DO ORGANIZATIONS NEED TO MANAGE BUSINESS PROCESSES?

**QCE18-2** WHAT ARE THE STAGES OF BUSINESS PROCESS MANAGEMENT (BPM)?

**QCE18-3** HOW DO BUSINESS PROCESSES AND INFORMATION SYSTEMS RELATE?

**QCE18-4** WHICH COME FIRST: BUSINESS PROCESSES OR INFORMATION SYSTEMS?

**QCE18-5** HOW IS BPM PRACTICED IN THE REAL WORLD?

## QCE18-1 WHY DO ORGANIZATIONS NEED TO MANAGE BUSINESS PROCESSES?

As defined in Chapter 2, a *business process* is a network of activities, actors, roles, repositories, and data and sequence flows that interact to accomplish a business function. To review, activities are something that an actor takes to perform a part of the business function. Actors are either people or computer programs or both. You can think of roles as job titles. Example roles are *salesperson, credit manager, inventory supervisor*, and the like. Repositories are collections of something of value; for us, repositories are most often collections of data. Data flows represent the movement of data items among activities and repositories, and sequence flows depict the logical flow from one activity to another.

To set the stage for discussing business process management, consider a simple but representative example.

### A SAMPLE ORDERING BUSINESS PROCESS

Suppose that you work in sales for a company that sells equipment and supplies to the hotel industry. Your products include hotel furniture, cleaning equipment, and supplies, such as towels, linens, and staff uniforms. Processing an order involves the five steps shown in Figure CE18-1. You are one of many actors who perform the salesperson role.

As a salesperson, you do not perform all of the activities shown; rather, you orchestrate their performance. You are the customer's representative within the firm. You ensure that the operations department verifies that the product is available and can be delivered to the customer on the requested schedule. You check with Accounting to verify the credit required to process the order, and you check with your boss, a sales manager, to approve any special terms the customer might request (discounts, free shipping, extended return policy, and so forth). We will document this process further in QCE18-2.

### WHY DOES THIS PROCESS NEED MANAGEMENT?

When you joined the company, you were taught to follow this process, and you've been using it for 2 years. It seems to work, so why does it require management? The basic answer to this question is that processes are dynamic and often need to be changed. This need can arise because of a process quality problem, a change in technology, or a change in some business fundamental.

#### Improve Process Quality

As you learned in Chapter 2, process quality has two dimensions: efficiency (use of resources) and effectiveness (accomplish strategy). The most obvious reason for changing a process is that it has

CE18

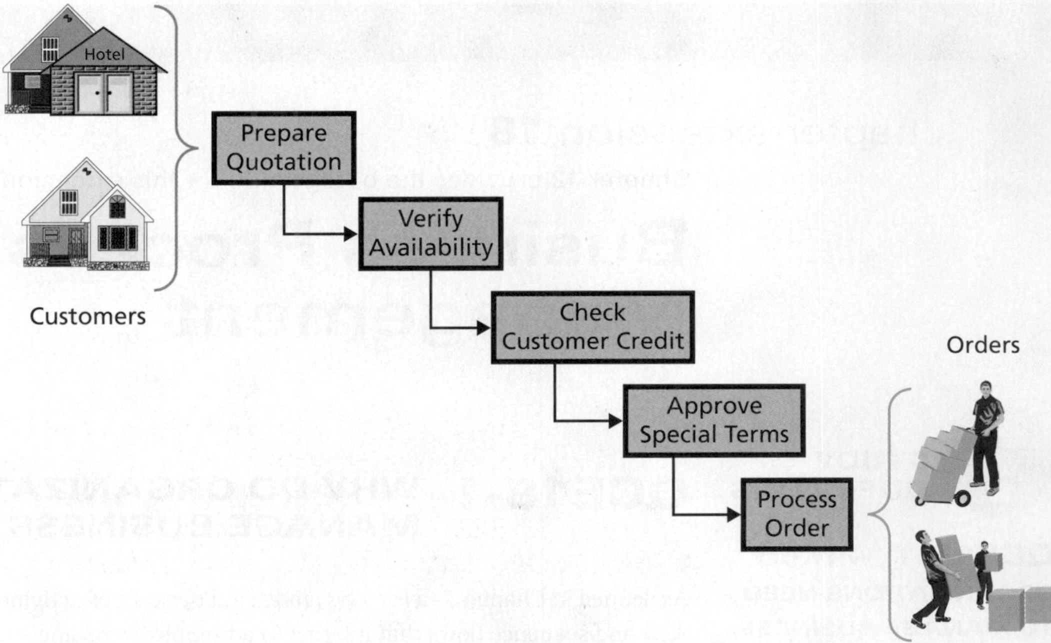


**Figure CE18-1**
Steps in Processing an Order

efficiency or effectiveness problems. Consider a sales process. If the organization's goal is to provide high-quality service, then if the process takes too long or if it rejects credit inappropriately, it is ineffective and needs to be changed.

With regard to efficiency, the process may use its resources poorly. For example, according to Figure CE18-1, salespeople verify product availability before checking customer credit. If checking availability means nothing more than querying an information system for inventory levels, that sequence makes sense. But suppose that checking availability means that someone in operations needs not only verify inventory levels, but also verify that the goods can be shipped to arrive on time. If the order delivery is complex, say, the order is for a large number of beds that have to be shipped from three different warehouses, an hour or two of labor may be required to verify shipping schedules.

After verifying shipping, the next step is to verify credit. If it turns out the customer has insufficient credit and the order is refused, the shipping-verification labor will have been wasted. So, it might make sense to check credit before checking availability.

Similarly, if the customer's request for special terms is disapproved, the cost of checking availability and credit is wasted. If the customer has requested special terms that are not normally approved, it might make sense to obtain approval of special terms before checking availability or credit. Your boss might not appreciate being asked to consider special terms for orders in which the items are not available or for customers with bad credit.

As you can see, it's not easy to determine what process structure is best. The need to monitor process quality and adjust process design, as appropriate, is one reason that processes need to be managed.

## Change in Technology

Changing technology is a second reason for managing processes. For example, suppose the company selling the goods in the process shown in Figure CE18-1 invests in new technology that enables it to provide next-day availability to customers. That capability will be of limited value, however, if the existing credit-checking process requires 2 days. "I can get the goods to you tomorrow, but I can't verify your credit until next Monday" will not be satisfying to either customers or salespeople.

Thus, when new technology changes any of a process's activities in a significant way, the entire process needs to be evaluated. That evaluation is another reason for managing processes.

### Change in Business Fundamentals

A third reason for managing business processes is a change in business fundamentals. A substantial change in any of the following factors might result in the need to modify business processes:

- Market (e.g., new customer category, change in customer characteristics)
- Product lines
- Supply chain
- Company policy
- Company organization (e.g., merger or acquisition)
- Internationalization
- Business environment

To understand the implications of such changes, consider just the sequence of verifying availability and checking credit in Figure CE18-1. A new category of customers could mean that the credit-check process needs to be modified; perhaps a certain category of customers is too risky to be extended credit. All sales to such customers must be cash. A change in product lines might require different ways of checking availability. A change in the supply chain might mean that the company no longer stocks some items in inventory but ships directly from the manufacturer instead.

Or the company might make broad changes to its credit policy. It might, for example, decide to accept more risk and sell to companies with lower credit scores. In this case, approval of special terms becomes more critical than checking credit, and the sequence of those two activities might need to be changed.

Of course, a merger or acquisition will mean substantial change in the organization and its products and markets, as will moving portions of the business offshore or engaging in international commerce. Finally, a substantial change in the business environment, say, the onset of a recession, might mean that credit checking becomes vitally important and needs to be moved to first place in this process.

## QCE18-2 WHAT ARE THE STAGES OF BUSINESS PROCESS MANAGEMENT (BPM)?

The factors just discussed will necessitate changes in business processes, whether the organization recognizes that need or not. Organizations can either plan to develop and modify business processes, or they can wait and let the need for change just happen to them. In the latter case, the business will continually be in crisis, dealing with one process emergency after another.

Figure CE18-2 shows the basic activities in **business process management (BPM)**, a cyclical process for systematically creating, assessing, and altering business processes. This cycle begins by creating models of business processes. The business users who have expertise and are involved in the particular process (this could be you!) adjust and evaluate those models. Usually teams build an **as-is model** that documents the current situation. Depending on the nature of the problem, new process models are then created, as we will discuss in QCE18-5.

Given the proposed model, the next step is to create process components. If the solution involves an information system, then it is created or adapted at this point. Finally, the new or changed business processes, along with any necessary IS, are implemented.

Well-managed organizations don't stop there. Instead, they create policy, procedures, and committees to continually assess business process effectiveness. The Information Systems Audit and Control Association has created a set of standard practices called **COBIT (Control Objectives for Information and related Technology)** that are often used in the assessment stage of the BPM cycle. Explaining these standards is beyond the scope of this discussion, but you should know that they exist. See *www.isaca.org/cobit* for more information.

**Figure CE18-2**
Stages in the BPM Cycle

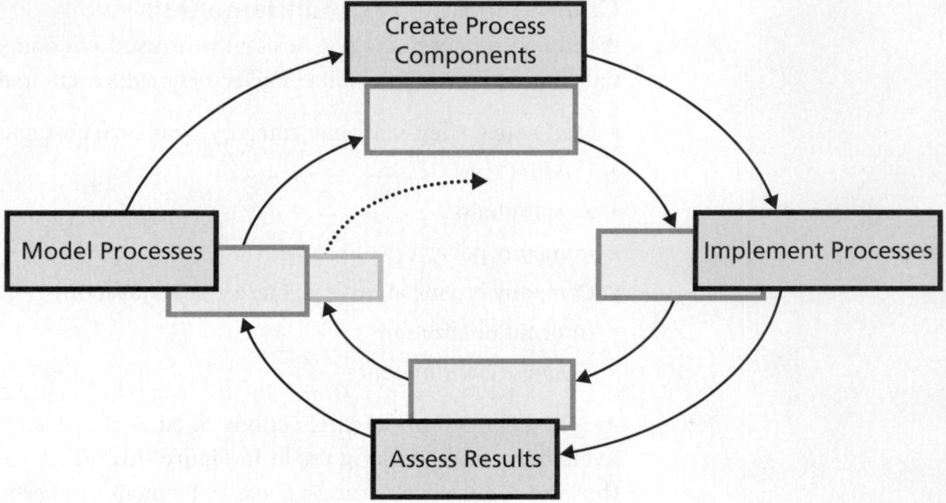


When the assessment process indicates that a significant need for change has arisen, the BPM cycle is repeated. Adjusted and new process models are developed, and components are created, implemented, and assessed.

Business process management has the same scope as discussed for information systems in Chapter 7: departmental, enterprise, and inter-enterprise. As shown in Figure CE18-3, BPM becomes more difficult as the scope of the underlying processes increases.

Finally, do not assume that business process management applies only to commercial, profit-making organizations. Nonprofit and government organizations have all three types of processes shown in Figure CE18-3, but most of these processes are service-oriented rather than revenue-oriented. Your state's Department of Labor, for example, has a need to manage its processes, as does the Girl Scouts of America. BPM applies to all types of organizations.

## QCE18-3 HOW DO BUSINESS PROCESSES AND INFORMATION SYSTEMS RELATE?

Before we address business process management in more detail, you need to understand that business processes and information systems are not the same thing. They overlap, but their purpose and their components are different. Information systems have the five components, as you know by now. Business processes have actors, roles, activities, and so on. The two relate to each other, but how?

**Figure CE18-3**
Scope of Business Process Management

| Scope | Description | Example | BPM Role |
|---|---|---|---|
| Departmental | Business process resides within a single business function. | Accounts payable | BPM authority belongs to a single departmental manager who has authority to resolve BPM issues. |
| Enterprise | Business process crosses into multiple departments within a single organization. | Customer relationship management (CRM); enterprise resource management (ERP) | BPM authority shared across several or many departments. Problem resolution via committee and policy. |
| Inter-enterprise | Business process crosses into multiple organizations. | Supply chain management (SCM) | BPM authority shared by multiple companies. Problem resolution via negotiation, contract, and litigation. |

To understand the relationship between business processes and information systems, examine Figure CE18-4, which is a slightly different version of Figure 2-4, the improved Best Bikes process we discussed in Chapter 2. In this figure, the generic repositories shown in Figure 2-4 have been replaced by databases, which are in red. Process activities that use those databases are shown in orange. These activities include procedures for using application programs that process the indicated databases.

By the way, be careful with the words *process* and *procedure*. They sound the same but are not. *Process* refers to the overall business process, like that in Figure CE18-4. A *procedure* is a component of an IS and is embedded within a process activity. Thus, in Figure CE18-4, a procedure for adding Vendor Orders to the Vendor Database is part of the Order Goods from Vendor activity, within the Best Bikes sales business process.

We can deduce three important principles from Figure CE18-4. First, information system elements are embedded within business processes, but some activities in business processes are not part of any information system. Again, business processes and information systems overlap, but they are different. Second, this business process uses two separate information systems, and, in general, a business process can use zero, one, or more information systems.

**Figure CE18-4**
Best Bikes Ordering Process

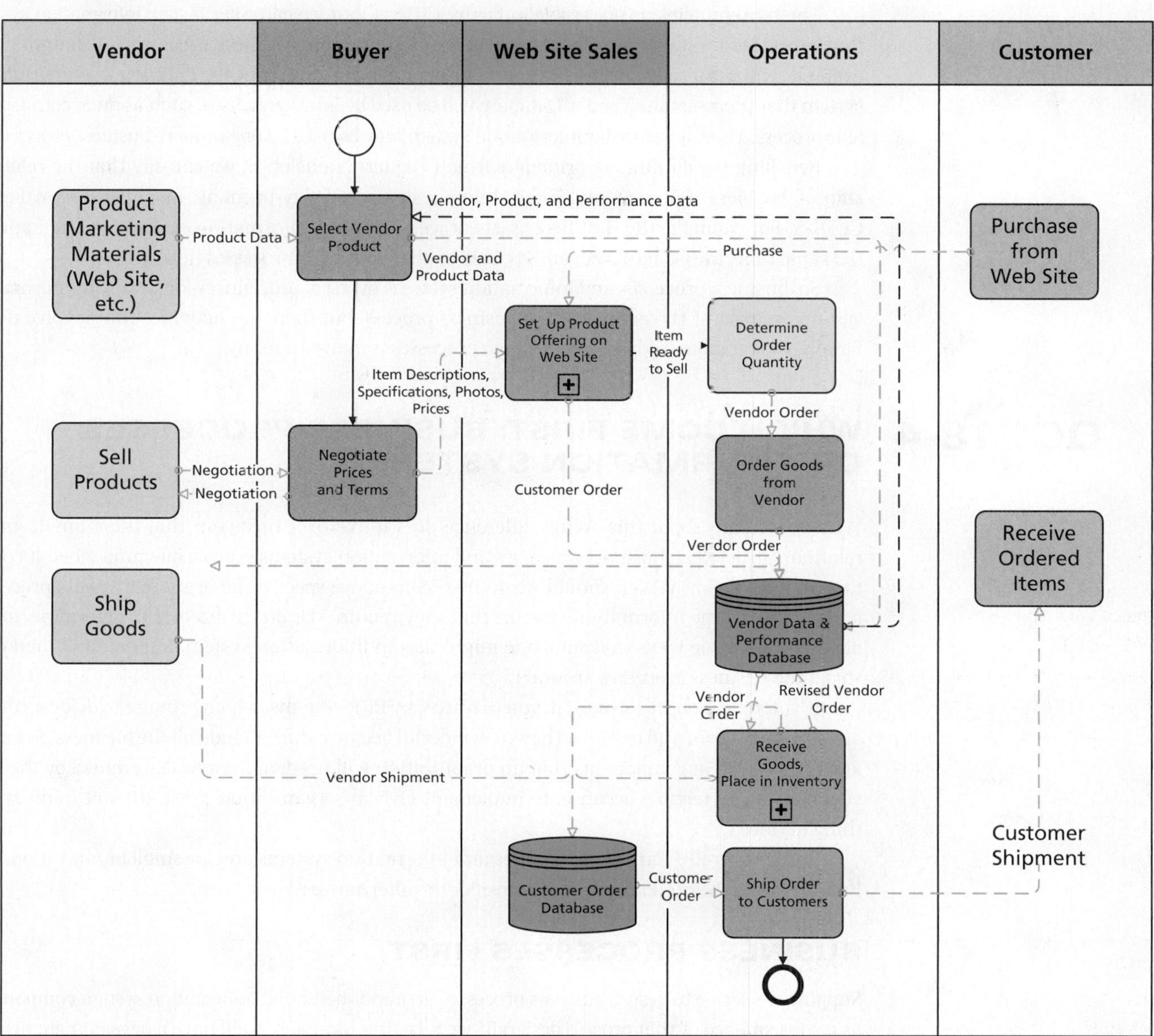

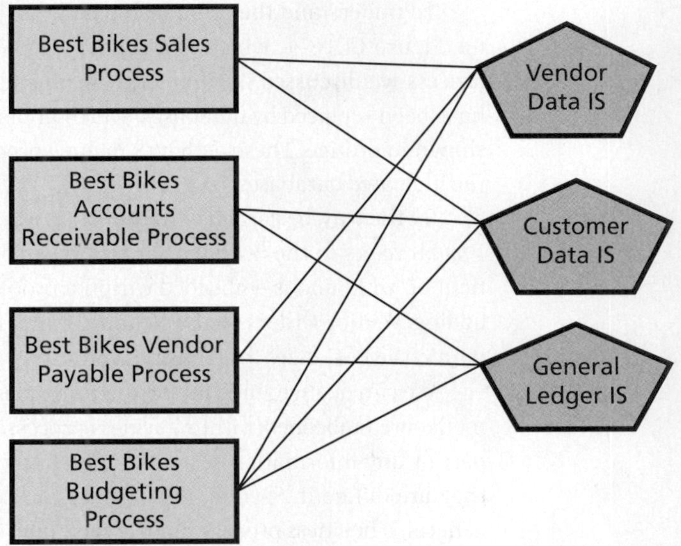


**Figure CE18-5**
Many-to-Many Relationship of Business Processes and Information Systems

The third principle is not visible in Figure CE18-4, but we can infer it. The information system that processes the Customer Database will be used by other business processes. Accounting, for example, will use it when billing customers or approving customer credit. Similarly, the information system that processes the Vendor Database will be used by other processes, such as an accounts payable process. Thus, a particular information system may be used by one or more business processes.

Recalling the cardinality principles from Chapter Extension 5, we can say that the relationship of business processes and information systems is many-to-many, as illustrated in Figure CE18-5. For example, the Best Bikes sales process uses two information systems (many), and, at the same time, the General Ledger IS is used by three different processes (also many).

So, business processes and information systems overlap; procedures for using an information system are part of the activities of a business process, but there are activities that involve no IS. Finally, the relationship between business processes is many-to-many.

## QCE18-4 WHICH COME FIRST: BUSINESS PROCESSES OR INFORMATION SYSTEMS?

Why do we care about this? What difference does it make? It turns out that the many-to-many relationship between business processes and information systems poses a dilemma when it comes time to build them. Which should we do first? Should we specify one or more business processes and then build the information systems that they require? Or do we attempt to determine, in the abstract, all of the ways that someone might use an information system, build it, and then construct the business processes around it?

If you reflect on this situation, you can see why ERP systems, which promise to do everything, are both wonderful and terrible. They're wonderful because they include all the business processes and all the system components that an organization will need, at least as determined by the ERP vendor. They're terrible because, to implement ERP, an organization must attempt to do everything at once.

But for non-ERP business processes and information systems and for small organizations like Best Bikes which should come first? Consider the alternatives.

### BUSINESS PROCESSES FIRST

Suppose we decide to design business processes first and then build information system components as a consequence of that process design. If we take this approach, we'll have a development process

**Figure CE18-6**
BPM and Systems Development

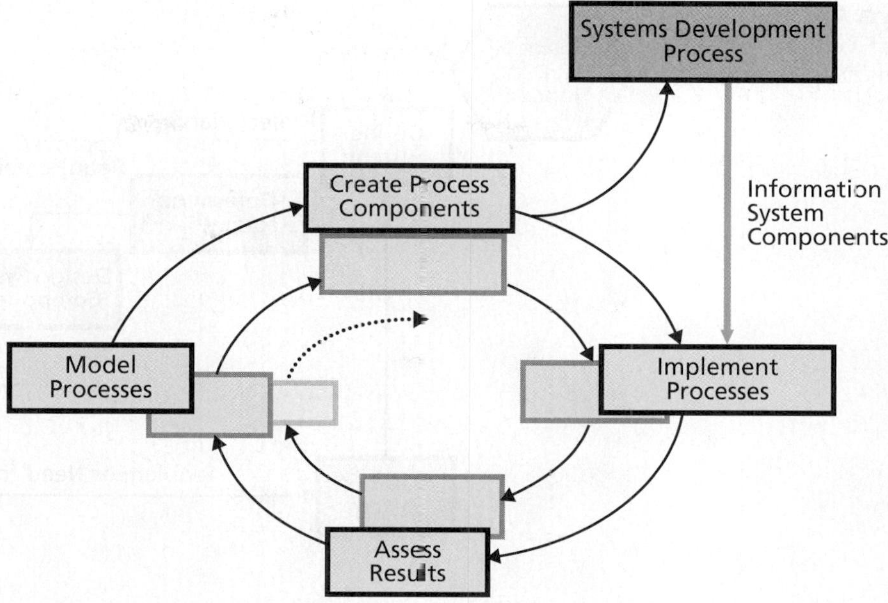


that looks like that in Figure CE18-6. The organization will engage in business process management and construct system components in the create process components stage of the BPM cycle.

This approach works well for the business processes that are being constructed, but what about others in the future? Suppose the Vendor Database information system is constructed to record vendor orders, shipments received, order shortages, and other data needed for this process. But what if Accounting wants to use this same information system to verify shipments received in an activity in its Accounts Payable process? Accounts Payable requirements were not part of the original requirements for the Vendor Database IS, and it will only be great fortune if that IS can support Accounting's needs for verification.

So, starting from processes and working toward information systems is likely to work well for the business processes under consideration but will cause problems later for other processes that use the same information systems. So, what if we start with the information system?

## INFORMATION SYSTEM FIRST

To start with systems first, a development team would talk with representative future users of the system and attempt to determine all of the needs that someone at Best Bikes might have for vendor data. In this case, business and systems analysts would meet with buyers, operations, accounting, and any other personnel who might have an interest in such data. From those requirements, they would then design components and construct the system.

Figure CE18-7 shows a modification to the SDLC that you studied in Chapter 12. As you can see, the processes that use this system are designed as part of Design System Components. This development process makes business processes a poor stepchild of the information systems development process. The focus is on hardware, software, data, procedures (for using the system only), and user training. Some aspects of business processes will be constructed as part of the system implementation; but, as you saw in Figure CE18-4, business processes can include many activities that are not part of the information system. Those activities are unlikely to be considered when the system is constructed.

## ANOTHER FACTOR: OFF-THE-SHELF SOFTWARE

A missing factor in this discussion is off-the-shelf software. Few organizations today can afford to create computer programs and design databases in-house. It is unlikely that Best Bikes, for

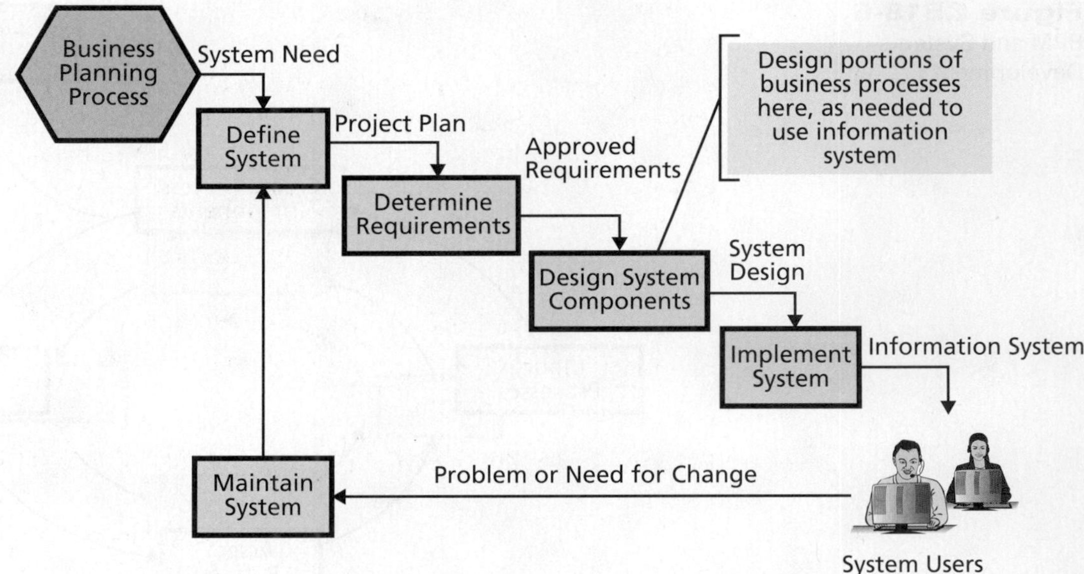


**Figure CE18-7**
Classic Five-Step Systems Development Life Cycle

example, will do so. Instead, most organizations attempt to license software off-the-shelf and adapt it to their needs or adapt their needs to it.

So, if an organization knows that it most likely will license off-the-shelf software, is it better to design processes first or to develop information systems first? Unfortunately, again, there is no demonstrably correct answer. If an organization starts with business processes first, it is likely to choose a package that will work well for the processes being developed, but that may not work well for other processes that may come along later (like Accounting wanting to use the Vendor Database to verify receipt of goods). However, if it starts with information systems and collects all the requirements, it is likely to find a package that will work better for all users, but, again, business processes will receive short shrift.

## AND THE ANSWER IS . . .

In theory, it is better to start with business processes. As discussed in Chapter 3, business processes are closer to the organization's competitive strategy and other goals and objectives. Starting with processes and working toward systems is more likely to result in processes and systems that are aligned with the organization's strategy and direction.

In practice, however, the answer is not clear. Organizations today take both approaches. Sometimes the same organization takes one approach with one set of processes and systems and a second approach with a different set.

The factor that overtakes all is off-the-shelf software. The vendor of the software knows the features that are most commonly needed by its customers. Therefore, if an organization starts with business processes and selects an application that works for those processes, it is likely that the application will also include features and functions that will be needed by other business processes to be designed in the future. At Best Bikes, an application that can be used to track vendor shipments is likely to be adaptable enough to also serve Accounting's need to verify goods received.

Usually, an application software vendor includes procedures for using that software as part of its offering. So, the procedure components in Figure CE18-4 (included in the orange activities) are most likely part of the package. However, the entire business process in Figure CE18-4 is unlikely to be part of the vendor's package.

Therefore, in most cases, if an organization is likely to license an application from a vendor, it is better to begin with processes. This rule is not ironclad, however. You should expect to find both approaches used in organizations during your career.

### Not Possible to Buy Processes or Systems Off-the-Shelf

Before we continue with systems development, do not be misled by the last few paragraphs. As stated in Chapter 12, it is possible to buy an off-the-shelf computer application, but the system that uses it is always in-house because the procedures and employees that use that application are in-house. Furthermore, even if the vendor of the application includes business processes as part of the package, as ERP vendors do, those business processes are not yours until you have integrated them into your business and trained your employees. Thus, neither information systems nor business processes can be purchased off-the-shelf.

Keep this in mind when you manage a department that is to receive a new information system or an upgrade. You need to allow time for such integration and training, and you should expect there will be mistakes and problems as the new application is first put into use.

## QCE18-5 HOW IS BPM PRACTICED IN THE REAL WORLD?

For the rest of the discussion in this chapter extension, we will assume that processes are to be created first, with systems developed during process creation, as shown in Figure CE18-6. Although the stages in Figure CE18-6 are known and accepted in industry, in the real world, things don't work out as neatly as they are diagrammed. We will consider some of the reasons in this question.

First, Figure CE18-6 implies that an organization has a group of business professionals who perpetually assess processes and wait to pounce on any process that is judged to need improvement. In some very large organizations that have fully endorsed COBIT or other similar alignment standards, it may work like that. But the reality for most organizations is that the need for process change comes from a problem or unmet need. Business requirements force the stages of the BPM cycle. In such organizations, no one thinks about a process until it's broken.

### DEFINING THE PROCESS PROBLEM

As stated in QCE18-1, process problems arise from process quality, from changes in technology, and from changes in the business fundamentals. For the first implementation of PRIDE, doctors couldn't give the quality care they wanted to give because they didn't have reliable patient exercise data (quality/effectiveness). In the PRIDE case, the solution only became possible because of new cloud technology, so PRIDE was partly the result of new technology as well as the effectiveness quality problem.

Whatever the source of the problem, the task of solving it is ideally given to a team of business analysts, professionals who specialize in business process management. Business analysts are well versed in Porter's models, organizational strategy, and systems alignment theory like COBIT. Business analysts understand the role of technology and information systems, though they are not technical experts. Business analysts may work in the IS Department, but they are equally likely to work in a business specialty such as operations or accounting. If the process problem involves information systems, the BPM team is augmented with systems analysts and technical personnel as they are needed. Figure CE18-8 shows the focus of these job categories.

Smaller companies may not employ any business analysts or, indeed, anyone with a background in process management. Instead, process problems are addressed by operational, usually nontechnical, business professionals. Often they are given the task of solving a process problem on a part-time, temporary basis.

As shown in Figure CE18-6, the first task is to assess the existing processes by creating an as-is model as described in QCE18-2 using Business Process Modeling Notation (BPMN). In practice, BPMN is used primarily by larger organizations that have professional and experienced business analysts. Other professionals who are filling the business analyst role for the purpose of a particular problem may not know about BPMN and how to use it, so they may draw less formal process schematics like that in Figure CE18-1.

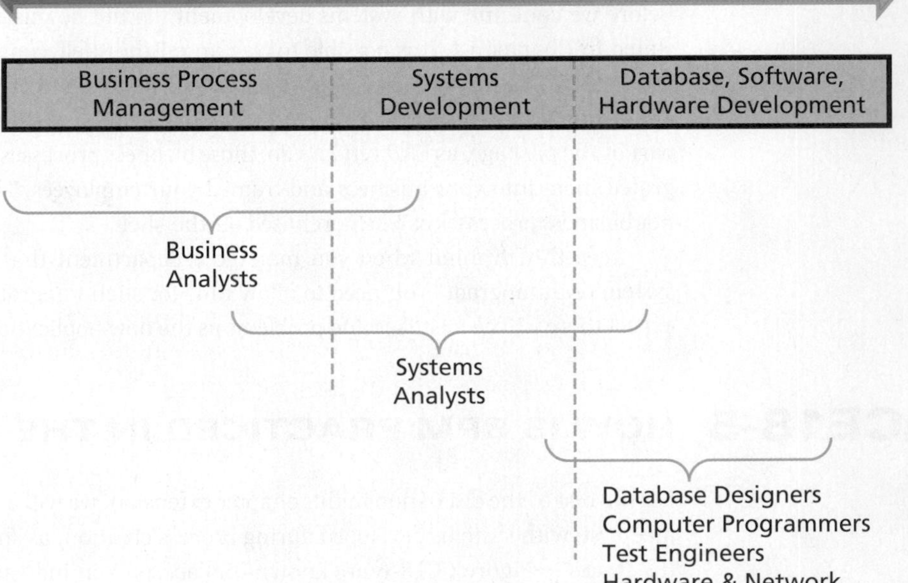


**Figure CE18-8** Focus of Personnel Involved in BPM and Systems Development

Depending on the sophistication of the organization, the difficulty of creating the as-is process diagram varies from easy to hard. An as-is diagram may already exist because it was produced when the existing process was created. On the other hand, the business process may have simply evolved, and it's possible that no one knows the entire process; they just know the particular part they play. This situation is typical in new ventures like those at Falcon Security.

Other complications include the fact that people disagree on what the existing process is, and sometimes, for a variety of reasons, people want to hide their portions of processes from others. One way or another, however, the job of the business analyst is to understand and document the existing business process. These real-world issues are summarized in Figure CE18-9.

**Figure CE18-9** Real-World BPM Issues

| Activity | Real-world Issues |
|---|---|
| Define Process Problem | Process change driven by problems and unmet needs.<br>Business analysts not available.<br>As-is process unknown, partially understood, viewed differently by different people, misunderstood, or hidden. |
| Designing the New Process | Simulations of alternatives expensive and often not worth it.<br>Best solution not obvious.<br>Undoing process changes difficult and expensive. |
| Create Process Components | Systems development risks:<br>Requirements difficult to specify or evolving.<br>Scheduling and budgeting difficulties.<br>Changing technology.<br>Diseconomies of scale. |
| Implement New Processes | Process migration awkward.<br>Resistance to change.<br>Lack of authority (enterprise and inter-enterprise). |

## DESIGNING THE NEW PROCESS

Given the as-is model, the next step is to specify alternatives for fixing the problem. As stated in Chapter 2, two fundamental actions are possible:

- Adjust role resources
- Change process structure

Of course, both can be done at the same time.

Regarding the resources assigned to roles, possibilities are to increase or decrease the number of employees performing a role, to move the role to employees in a different department, to hire employees with different skill sets, to give employees additional training, to change employee management, and so forth. Additionally, and of more relevance to MIS, information systems can be constructed to augment employee activity or even to replace employee activities with automation. If employees are already using an IS, another way of adjusting role resources is to improve the information system so as to facilitate the new process.

The second alternative is to change the process structure. Recall from Chapter 2 that the Best Bikes order process was changed to that in Figure CE18-4 in order to enable the the Select Vendor Product in response to a process problem that required the Select Vendor Product, the Order Goods from Vendor, and the Receive Goods activities to share the same database.

Given solution alternatives, the next task is to evaluate and select one. Sometimes the solution to a process problem is obvious, but more often, two or more alternatives are, at least in theory, good solutions. Consider the process in Figure CE18-1. What is the proper order for the middle three activities? Should credit or availability be checked first? In more sophisticated organizations, computer simulations using historical data are used to estimate the impact of different process alternatives. Simulations are expensive, however, and the simplified assumptions they necessitate make the results suspect.

In the real world, most companies form a team to develop and evaluate alternatives. The most promising alternative is chosen for implementation by discussion among the team members. Consideration of the four dimensions of feasibility used in the SDLC (cost, technical, schedule, and organizational) can help eliminate some alternatives. Qualified, talented business analysts are highly valued for this work because it is difficult and expensive to undo process changes that don't work. If processes interest you, becoming a business analyst can be a rewarding career choice.

## CREATE PROCESS COMPONENTS

Once one of the process alternatives is selected, the next step is to create components. Insofar as MIS is concerned, this means to create new, or adapt existing, information systems. The real-world risks that we discussed in Chapter 12 apply equally here: Requirements are difficult to specify and may change during the development process; schedules and budgets are difficult to estimate; technology can change while the project is under way; and if schedule delays occur, remedies are difficult because of diseconomies of scale. Refer to Chapter 12 and also Chapter Extension 17 for more on these risks.

## IMPLEMENT NEW PROCESSES

The problems of implementing a new or changed process are similar to the problems for implementing a new IS, but possibly greater. Migrating from an existing process to a new process is exceedingly awkward. Employees are unsure exactly what they are to do. "Are we using the new way or the old way on this one?" is a common question. Furthermore, old habits die hard. People in the organization who are not involved in the process change will be unaware of the new process and will attempt to do things the "old way." Similar comments pertain to customers, suppliers, and other partners.

As we discussed for ERP systems, some employees will actively resist change or comply but do so viciously. Some employees resist because they do not believe in the new process or because they are uncertain that they can succeed in it or because they do not understand it. Whatever the source of the resistance, it is a real factor when implementing process change. Finally, the resolution of implementation problems can be difficult for enterprise and inter-enterprise processes because there is no recognized authority, no boss, to enforce solutions. In the case of enterprise systems, the CEO or other senior executive does have such authority, but that person is seldom available to enforce low-level process solutions. With inter-enterprise processes, there is no such person; resolution occurs by agreement, negotiation, and even litigation. This authority problem is similar to that for enterprise and inter-enterprise IS.

None of this is to say, however, that business process management is too impractical to succeed. High-quality business processes are critical to the success of every organization. Somehow, one way or another, these challenges need to be overcome. It's just that in many situations it's more a matter of muddling through a messy situation than the diagram in Figure CE18-6 would lead you to believe.

# ACTIVE REVIEW

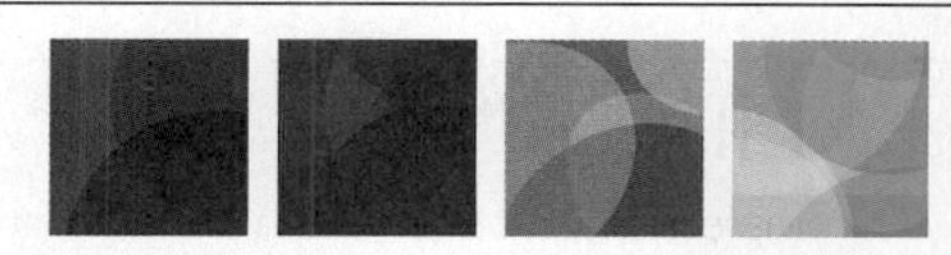

Use this Active Review to verify that you understand the ideas and concepts that answer this chapter extension's study questions.

## QCE18-1 WHY DO ORGANIZATIONS NEED TO MANAGE BUSINESS PROCESSES?

Define *business process.* Define *activities, roles, actors, repositories, data flows,* and *sequence flows.* Summarize three reasons that processes need to be changed and give an example of each.

## QCE18-2 WHAT ARE THE STAGES OF BUSINESS PROCESS MANAGEMENT (BPM)?

Describe the need for BPM and explain why it is a cycle. Name the four stages of the BPM process and summarize the activities in each. Explain the role of COBIT.

## QCE18-3 HOW DO BUSINESS PROCESSES AND INFORMATION SYSTEMS RELATE?

Explain how information systems and business processes differ. Give an example, other than one in this text, of a business process that uses two or more information systems. Give an example, other than one in this text, of an information system that is part of two or more business processes. Explain how the relationship of business processes and information systems is many-to-many.

## QCE18-4 WHICH COME FIRST: BUSINESS PROCESSES OR INFORMATION SYSTEMS?

Explain the problems that occur if business processes are developed first, with IS as a component. Explain the problems that occur if information systems are developed first, with business processes as a component. Explain the differences between Figures CE18-6 and CE18-7. Summarize the issues that must be addressed when determining which comes first. Explain why it is not possible to buy processes or systems off-the-shelf.

## QCE18-5 HOW IS BPM PRACTICED IN THE REAL WORLD?

Explain how the perpetual assessing of business processes is unrealistic. Name two factors that drive process change. Name and describe three factors that cause process problems. Define *business analyst,* describe the background of a business analyst, and differentiate business analysts from systems analysts. Summarize real-world issues for defining the process problem, designing the new process, creating process and system components, and implementing new processes.

# KEY TERMS AND CONCEPTS

MyMISLab™

To complete the problems with the ✪, go to EOC Discussion Questions in the MyLab.

## USING YOUR KNOWLEDGE

✪ **CE18-1.** Compare and contrast the initial Best Bikes process, shown in Q2-2 of Chapter 2, with the version shown in QCE18-3 of this chapter extension. (Treat the parallelograms in Figure 2-1 as databases.)

**a.** Summarize the problems that existed in the original process and explain how the adjusted process enables a solution to those problems.

**b.** Summarize the changes to information systems that will need to be made to implement the process change in QCE18-3. Consider each of the five information system components.

**c.** Which actors (employees) are the primary beneficiaries of the process change?

**d.** Suppose some employees who are not beneficiaries of a process change are required to do their work differently. Summarize management challenges you can expect. Describe how you would deal with those challenges.

✪ **CE18-2.** Suppose you are starting a business that is similar to Best Bikes.

**a.** Should you start with business processes first or information systems first? Defend your answer.

**b.** Most likely, you will obtain off-the-shelf software and alter it for your applications. How does this fact influence whether you start first with processes or IS?

**c.** Identify issues in QCE18-5 that apply to the Best Bikes situation. Explain the impact of those issues.

✪ **CE18-3.** Suppose you are starting a venture similar to PRIDE Systems.

**a.** Should you start with business processes first or information systems first? Defend your answer.

**b.** All of your mobile applications will be custom-developed. How does this fact influence whether you start first with processes or IS?

**c.** Identify issues in QCE18-3 that apply to the PRIDE Systems situation. Explain the impact of those issues.

MyMISLab™

Go to the Assignments section of your MyLab to complete these writing exercises.

**CE18-4.** As explained in Chapter Extension 5, Database Design, in order to represent a many-to-many relationship using the relational model, it is necessary to create an intersection table. If that table has nonkey data, that data represents something particular about the combination of one entity with another. For example, the relationship between Students and Classes is many-to-many, and Grade is an intersection table that represents the combination of a particular student with a particular class. What is the analog to the intersection table in the relationship between business processes and information systems? Where, for example, in the figure in QCE18-3 is there evidence of a particular IS application being used in a process?

**CE18-5.** Compare and contrast the advantages of specifying business processes first and then building the information systems versus building the information systems and then adapting business processes where necessary. What advantages does off-the-shelf software provide over these two options?

# APPLICATION EXERCISES

## PART 1

### CHAPTER 1: QUALITY OF INFORMATION WITH EXCEL

**1-1.** The spreadsheet in Microsoft Excel file **Ch01Ex01_E7e** contains records of employee activity on special projects. Open this workbook and examine the data that you find in the three spreadsheets it contains. Assess the accuracy, relevancy, and sufficiency of this data to the following people and problems.

**a.** You manage the Denver plant, and you want to know how much time your employees are spending on special projects.

**b.** You manage the Reno plant, and you want to know how much time your employees are spending on special projects.

**c.** You manage the Quota Computation project in Chicago, and you want to know how much time your employees have spent on that project.

**d.** You manage the Quota Computation project for all three plants, and you want to know the total time employees have spent on your project.

**e.** You manage the Quota Computation project for all three plants, and you want to know the total labor cost for all employees on your project.

**f.** You manage the Quota Computation project for all three plants, and you want to know how the labor-hour total for your project compares to the labor-hour totals for the other special projects.

**g.** What conclusions can you make from this exercise?

### CHAPTER 1: COMPARING INFORMATION FROM EXCEL AND ACCESS

**1-2.** The database in the Microsoft Access file **Ch01Ex02_E7e** contains the same records of employee activity on special projects as in Application Exercise 1-1. Before going any further, open that database and view the records in the Employee Hours table.

**a.** Eight queries have been created that process this data in different ways. Using the criteria of accuracy, relevancy, and sufficiency, select the one query that is most appropriate for the information requirements in Application Exercise 1-1, parts a–f. If no query meets the need, explain why.

**b.** What conclusions can you make from this exercise?

**c.** Comparing your experiences on these two projects, what are the advantages and disadvantages of spreadsheets and databases?

### CHAPTER 2: USE POWERPOINT TO DIAGRAM BUSINESS PROCESS

**2-1.** PowerPoint file **Ch02Ex01_E7e** contains a copy of Figure 2-4 as well as a collection of spare shapes. Using these shapes, create a business process for the Ship Order to Customers activity. Use your own knowledge and expertise to do this. Assume that the inputs to the activity are the Customer Order and items as well as a list of items from the Receive Goods Place in Inventory activity.

### CHAPTER 3: USE EXCEL TO COMPUTE INVENTORY VALUE

**3-1.** Figure AE-1 shows an Excel spreadsheet that the resort bicycle rental business uses to value and analyze its bicycle inventory. Examine Figure AE-1 to understand the meaning of the data. Now use Excel to create a similar spreadsheet. Note the following:

- The top heading is in 20-point Calibri font. It is centered in the spreadsheet. Cells A1 through H1 have been merged.
- The second heading, Bicycle Inventory Valuation, is in 18-point Calibri, italics. It is centered in cells A2 through H2, which have been merged.
- The column headings are set in 11-point Calibri, bold. They are centered in their cells, and the text wraps in the cells.

**a.** Make the first two rows of your spreadsheet similar to that in Figure AE-1. Choose your own colors for background and type, however.

**b.** Place the current date so that it is centered in cells C3, D3, and E3, which must be merged.

**Figure AE-1**
Worksheet

| | A | B | C | D | E | F | G | H |
|---|---|---|---|---|---|---|---|---|
| 1 | Resort Bicycle Rental | | | | | | | |
| 2 | Bicycle Inventory Valuation | | | | | | | |
| 3 | Saturday, May 27, 2017 | | | | | | | |
| 4 | Make of Bike | Bike Cost | Number on Hand | Cost of Current Inventory | Number of Rentals | Total Rental Revenue | Revenue per Bike | Revenue as Percent of Cost of Inventory |
| 5 | Wonder Bike | $325 | 12 | $3,900 | 85 | $6,375 | $531 | 163.5% |
| 6 | Wonder Bike II | $385 | 4 | $1,540 | 34 | $4,570 | $1,143 | 296.8% |
| 7 | Wonder Bike Supreme | $475 | 8 | $3,800 | 44 | $5,200 | $650 | 136.8% |
| 8 | LiteLift Pro | $655 | 8 | $5,240 | 25 | $2,480 | $310 | 47.3% |
| 9 | LiteLift Ladies | $655 | 4 | $2,620 | 40 | $6,710 | $1,678 | 256.1% |
| 10 | LiteLift Racer | $795 | 3 | $2,385 | 37 | $5,900 | $1,967 | 247.4% |

**c.** Outline the cells as shown in Figure AE-1.

**d.** Figure AE-1 uses the following formulas:

Cost of Current Inventory = Bike Cost × Number on Hand

Revenue per Bike = Total Rental Revenue/Number on Hand

Revenue as a Percent of Cost of Inventory = Total Rental Revenue/Cost of Current Inventory

Please use these formulas in your spreadsheet, as shown in Figure AE-1.

**e.** Format the cells in the columns, as shown.

**f.** Give three examples of decisions that management of the bike rental agency might make from this data.

**g.** What other calculation could you make from this data that would be useful to the bike rental management? Create a second version of this spreadsheet in your worksheet document that has this calculation.

## CHAPTER EXTENSION 1: MANAGERIAL DECISION MAKING WITH EXCEL

**CE1-1.** Suppose that you have been asked to assist in the managerial decision about how much to increase pay in the next year. Assume you are given a list of the departments in your company, along with the average salary for employees in those departments for major companies in your industry. Additionally, you are given the names and salaries of 10 people in each of three departments in your company.

- Assume you have been asked to create a spreadsheet that shows the names of the 10 employees in each department, their current salary, the difference between their current salary and the industry average salary for their department, and the percent their salary would need to be increased to meet the industry average. Your spreadsheet should also compute the average increase needed to meet the industry average for each department and the average increase, company-wide, to meet industry averages.

**a.** Use the data in the Word file **CE01Ex01_E7e** and create the spreadsheet.

**b.** How can you use this analysis to contribute to the employee salary decision? Based on this data, what conclusions can you make?

**c.** Suppose other team members want to use your spreadsheet. Name three ways you can share it with them and describe the advantages and disadvantages of each.

## CHAPTER EXTENSION 1: MANAGERIAL DECISION MAKING WITH ACCESS

**CE1-2.** Suppose that you have been asked to assist in the managerial decision about how much to increase pay in the next year. Specifically, you are tasked to determine if there are significant salary differences among departments in your company.

- You are given an Access database with a table of employee data with the following structure:
  - EMPLOYEE (Name, Department, Specialty, Salary)
  - Where *Name* is the name of an employee who works in a department, *Department* is the department name, *Specialty* is the name of the employee's primary skill, and *Salary* is the employee's current salary. Assume that no two employees have the same name. You have been asked to answer the following queries:

**(1)** List the names, department, and salary of all employees earning more than $100,000.

**(2)** List the names and specialties of all employees in the Marketing department.

**(3)** Compute the average, maximum, and minimum salary of employees in your company.

**(4)** Compute the average, minimum, and maximum salary of employees in the Marketing department.

**(5)** Compute the average, minimum, and maximum salary of employees in the Information Systems department.

**(6)** *Extra credit:* Compute the average salary for employees in every department. Use *Group By.*

**a.** Design and run Access queries to obtain the answers to these questions, using the data in the Access file **CE01Ex02_E7e.**

**b.** Explain how the data in your answer contributes to the salary increase decision.

**c.** Suppose other team members want to use your Access application. Name three ways you can share it with them, and describe the advantages and disadvantages of each.

## CHAPTER EXTENSION 2: FREE AND EASY COLLABORATION TOOLS

**CE2-1.** This exercise requires you to experiment with Google Drive. You will need two Google accounts to complete this exercise.

**a.** In a memo, explain the role of communication in collaboration. Go to *http://drive.google.com/* and sign in with one of your Google accounts. Upload your memo using Google Drive. Save your uploaded document and share it with the email in your second Google account. Sign out of your first Google account.

(If you have access to two computers situated close to each other, use both of them for this exercise. You will see more of the Google Drive functionality by using two computers. If you have two computers, do not sign out of your Google account. Perform step b and all actions for the second account on that second computer. If you are using two computers, ignore the instructions in the following steps to sign out of the Google accounts.)

**b.** Open a new window in your browser. Access *http://drive.google.com/* from that second window, and sign in using your second Google account. Open the document that you shared in step a.

**c.** Change the memo by adding a brief description of the need to manage the content in many collaboration projects. Save the document from your second account. If you are using just one computer, sign out from your second account.

**d.** Sign in on your first account. Open the most recent version of the memo and add a description of the role of version histories. Save the document. (If you are using two computers, notice how Google warns you that another user is editing the document at the same time. Click *Refresh* to see what happens.) If you are using just one computer, sign out from your first account.

**e.** Sign in on your second account. Reopen the shared document. From the File menu, save the document as a Word document. Describe how Google processed the changes to your document.

**CE2-2.** This exercise requires you to experiment with Microsoft OneDrive. You will need two Office Live IDs to complete this exercise. The easiest way to do this is to work with a classmate. If that is not possible, set up two Office Live accounts, using two different Hotmail addresses.

**a.** Go to *www.onedrive.com*, and sign in with one of your accounts. Create a memo about collaboration tools using the Word Web App. Save your memo. Share your document with the email in your second Office Live account. Sign out of your first account.

(If you have access to two computers situated close to each other, use both of them for this exercise. If you have two computers, do not sign out of your Office Live account. Perform step b and all actions for the second account on that second computer. If you are using two computers, ignore the instructions in the following steps to sign out of the Office Live accounts.)

**b.** Open a new window in your browser. Access *www.onedrive.com* from that second window, and sign in using your second Office Live account. Open the document that you shared in step a.

**c.** Change the memo by adding a brief description of content management. Do not save the document yet. If you are using just one computer, sign out from your second account.

**d.** Sign in on your first account. Attempt to open the memo and note what occurs. Sign out of your first account, and sign back in with your second account. Save the document. Now, sign out of your second account, and sign back in with the first account. Now attempt to open the memo. (If you are using two computers, perform these same actions on the two different computers.)

**e.** Sign in on your second account. Reopen the shared document. From the File menu, save the document as a Word document. Describe how OneDrive processed the changes to your document.

## PART 2

*Note: The exercises for the chapter extensions are basically tutorials. Therefore, they are presented first, followed by exercises for Chapters 4–6.*

## CHAPTER EXTENSION 4: LEARNING EXCEL

**CE4-1.** Complete Chapter Extension 4, CE4-1, page 434.

**CE4-2.** Complete Chapter Extension 4, CE4-2, page 434.

**CE4-3.** Complete Chapter Extension 4, CE4-3, page 434.

## CHAPTER EXTENSION 5: DATA MODELING WITH POWERPOINT

**CE5-1.** Complete Chapter Extension 5, CE5-2, page 448. Use PowerPoint to document your entity-relationship design.

**CE5-2.** Complete Chapter Extension 5, CE5-3, page 448. Use PowerPoint to document your entity-relationship design.

## CHAPTER EXTENSION 6: APPLY ACCESS SKILLS

**CE6-1.** Complete Chapter Extension 6, CE6-1, page 468. Requires you to complete CE5-1 first.

**CE6-2.** Complete Chapter Extension 6, CE6-2, page 468. Requires you to complete CE5-2 first.

## CHAPTER EXTENSION 7: GETTING THE BEST FEATURES FROM EXCEL AND ACCESS

**CE7-1.** Complete Chapter Extension 7, CE7-1, page 496.

**CE7-2.** Complete Chapter Extension 7, CE7-2 and CE7-3, page 496.

**CE7-3.** Complete Chapter Extension 7, CE7-4, page 496.

**CE7-4.** Complete Chapter Extension 7, CE7-5, page 496.

## CHAPTER 4: USING PARAMETERIZED QUERIES

**4-1.** In this exercise, you will learn how to create a query based on data that a user enters and how to use that query to create a data entry form.

**a.** Download the Microsoft Access file **Ch04Ex01_E7e**. Open the file and familiarize yourself with the data in the Customer table.

**b.** Click *Create* in the Access ribbon. Click the icon labeled *Query Design*. Select the Customer table as the basis for the query by clicking on *Customer*. Close the Show Table dialog. Drag CustomerName, CustomerEmail, DateOfLastRental, BikeLastRented, TotalNumberOfRentals, and TotalRentalRevenue into the columns of the query results pane (the table at the bottom of the query design window).

**c.** In the CustomerName column, in the row labeled Criteria, place the following text:

**[Enter Name of Customer:]**

Type this exactly as shown, including the square brackets. This notation tells Access to ask you for a customer name to query.

**d.** In the ribbon, click the red exclamation mark labeled *Run*. Access will display a dialog box with the text "Enter Name of Customer:" (the text you entered in the query Criteria row). Enter the value *Maple, Rex* and click OK.

**e.** Save your query with the name *Parameter Query*.

**f.** Click the Home tab on the ribbon and click the Design View (upper left-hand button on the Home ribbon). Replace the text in the Criteria row of the CustomerName column with the following text. Type it exactly as shown:

**Like "*" & [Enter part of Customer Name to search by:] & "*"**

**g.** Run the query by clicking *Run* in the ribbon. Enter *Maple* when prompted *Enter part of Customer Name to search by*. Notice that the two customers who have the name Maple are displayed. If you have any problems, ensure that you have typed the phrase previously shown *exactly* as shown into the Criteria row of the CustomerName column of your query.

**h.** Save your query again under the name *Parameter Query*. Close the query window.

**i.** Click *Create* in the Access ribbon. Under the Forms group, choose *Form Wizard*. In the dialog that opens, in the Tables/Queries box, click the down arrow. Select *Query: Parameter Query*. Click the double chevron (>>) symbol, and all of the columns in the query will move to the Selected Fields area.

**j.** Click *Next* two times. In the box under *What title do you want for your form?* enter *Customer Query Form* and click *Finish*.

**k.** Enter *Maple* in the dialog box that appears. Access will open a form with the values for Maple, Rex. At the bottom of the form, click the right-facing arrow and the data for the second customer named Maple will appear. What is that customer's first name?

**l.** Close the form. Select *Object Type* and *Forms* in the Access Navigation Pane. Double-click *Customer Query Form*, and enter the value *Amanda*. Access will display data for all three customers having the value Amanda in their name.

## CHAPTER 4: USING EXCEL AND ACCESS TO INFORM COMPUTER UPGRADE DECISIONS

**4-2.** You have been asked to help your department decide how to upgrade computers. Let's say, for example, that you want to upgrade all of the computers' operating systems to Windows 10. Furthermore, you want to first upgrade the computers that most need upgrading, but you have a limited budget. To address this situation, you would like to query the data in Figure AE-2, find all computers that do not have Windows 10, and then select those with slower CPUs or smaller memory as candidates for upgrading. To do this, you need to move the data from Excel and into Access.

- Once you have analyzed the data and determined the computers to upgrade, you want to produce a report. In that case, you may want to move the data from Access and back to Excel or perhaps into Word. In this exercise, you will learn how to perform these tasks.

**a.** To begin, download the Excel file **Ch04Ex02_E7e** from *www.pearsonhighered.com/kroenke* into one of your directories. We will import the data in this file into Access, but before we do so, familiarize yourself with the data by opening it in Excel. Notice that there are three worksheets in this workbook. Close the Excel file.

**b.** Create a blank Access database. Name the database *Ex21_Answer*. Place it in some directory; it may be the same directory into which you have placed the Excel file, but it need not be. Close the default table that Access creates and delete it.

**c.** Now we will import the data from the three worksheets in the Excel file **Ch04Ex02_E7e** into a single table in your Access database. On the ribbon, select *EXTERNAL DATA* and *Excel*. Start the import. For the first worksheet (Denver), you should select *Import the source data into a new table in the current database*. Ignore the warning about the first row by clicking OK. Be sure to click *First Row Contains Column Headings* when Access presents your data. You can use the default Field types and let Access add the primary key. Name your table *Employees* and click *Finish*. There is no need to save your import script.

For the second and third worksheets, again click *EXTERNAL DATA/Excel*, but this time select *Append a copy of the records to the table Employees*. Select the Miami worksheet and click *Finish*. Repeat to import the Boston office employees.

**d.** Open the *Employee* table, and examine the data. Notice that Access has erroneously imported a blank line and the *Primary Contact* data into rows at the end of each data set. This data is not part of the employee records, and you should delete it (in three places—once for each worksheet). The *Employee* table should have a total of 40 records.

**e.** Create a parameterized query on this data. Place all of the columns except *ID* into the query. In the OS column, set the criteria to select rows for which the value is not *Windows 10*. In the *CPU* (GHz) column, enter the criterion: <=*[Enter cutoff value for CPU]* and in the *Memory* (GB) column, enter the criterion: <=*[Enter cutoff value for Memory]*. Test your query. For example, run

**Figure AE-2**
Employee Computer Data

| | A | B | C | D | E | F | G | H |
|---|---|---|---|---|---|---|---|---|
| 1 | **EmpLastName** | **EmpFirstName** | **Plant** | **Computer Brand** | **CPU (GHz)** | **Memory (GB)** | **Disk (TB)** | **OS** |
| 2 | Ashley | Linda | Denver | Dell | 3 | 8 | 2 | Windows 8 |
| 3 | Davidson | Victor | Denver | Dell | 3 | 6 | 2 | Windows 8 |
| 4 | Ching | Diem Thi | Denver | HP | 3 | 6 | 2.5 | Windows 8 |
| 5 | Collins | James | Denver | Dell | 2.5 | 4 | 1 | Windows 7 |
| 6 | Corning | Haley | Denver | HP | 3 | 6 | 2 | Windows 8 |
| 7 | Scott | Richard | Denver | HP | 2.5 | 6 | 2.5 | Windows 8 |
| 8 | Corovic | Anna | Denver | Dell | 4 | 2 | 3 | Windows 10 |
| 9 | Lane | Kathy | Denver | Lenovo | 2.5 | 4 | 1 | Windows 7 |
| 10 | Wei | James | Denver | IBM | 3 | 8 | 2 | Windows 8 |
| 11 | Dixon | Mary | Denver | IBM | 2 | 4 | 1 | Windows 7 |
| 12 | Lee | Matthew | Denver | Dell | 2.5 | 4 | 1 | Windows 7 |
| 13 | Duong | Steven | Denver | Dell | 2 | 2 | 0.75 | Vista |
| 14 | Bosa | William | Denver | HP | 3 | 6 | 2.5 | Windows 8 |
| 15 | Drew | Tony | Denver | HP | 3 | 8 | 2 | Windows 8 |
| 16 | Adams | Mark | Denver | HP | 2.5 | 4 | 1 | Windows 7 |
| 17 | Lunden | Nicole | Denver | Lenovo | 4 | 2 | 3 | Windows 10 |
| 18 | Utran | Bryan | Denver | Dell | 3 | 6 | 2 | Windows 8 |
| 19 | | | | | | | | |
| 20 | | Primary Contact: | Kaye Davidson | | | | | |

your query and enter a value of 4 for both CPU and memory. Verify that the correct rows are produced.

f. Use your query to find values of CPU and memory that give you as close to a maximum of 15 computers to upgrade as possible.

g. When you have found values of CPU and memory that give you 15, or nearly 15, computers to upgrade, leave your query open. Now click *External data, Word*, and create a Word document that contains the results of your query. Adjust the column widths of the created table so that it fits on the page. Write a memo around this table explaining that these are the computers that you believe should be upgraded.

## CHAPTER 4: USING OPEN SOURCE SOFTWARE

**4-3.** As you read in Chapter 4, open source software is popular because it's stable, customizable, and free. But you may not have used open source software before. In this project, you will download an alternate to the Microsoft Office suite called LibreOffice. It has applications for making documents (Writer), spreadsheets (Calc), presentations (Impress), databases (Base), and graphics (Draw) similar to those in Microsoft Office.

If you're used to using Microsoft Office, it will take some time to become familiar with the LibreOffice interface. LibreOffice can do just about everything Microsoft Office can do, but it may do it in a slightly different way. The main benefit of using LibreOffice is that it's totally free. You can install it as many times as you'd like on as many computers as you'd like.

**a.** Browse to *www.libreoffice.org*.

**b.** Click on the Download menu and select LibreOffice Fresh.

**c.** Download and install the latest version of LibreOffice. (There are LibreOffice versions for Windows, Mac OS X, and Linux.)

**d.** Open LibreOffice Calc. (There will be a shortcut on your desktop.)

**e.** Enter your name, date, and time into the new spreadsheet in cells A1, A2, and A3 respectively.

**f.** Click Tools and Options.

**g.** Expand the Load/Save menu and click on General.

**h.** Change the "Always save as" dropdown from ODF Spreadsheet to Microsoft Excel 2007/2010/2013 XML and click OK. (You can do the same thing for documents and presentations.)

**i.** Click File, Save, and Save.

**j.** Take a screenshot with your name showing and paste it into your document. (You can take a screenshot by pressing Alt + Print Screen.)

**k.** Explain why more people don't use LibreOffice if it's free.

**l.** Explain why a systems administrator, who manages hundreds of servers (with Linux and Windows operating systems), might like using LibreOffice.

**m.** Explain why LibreOffice might be an important application for users or organizations in developing countries.

## CHAPTER 5: GRAPHING WITH EXCEL

**5-1.** As stated in Chapter Extension 7, a common scenario is to use Microsoft Access with Excel: Users process relational data with Access, import some of the data into Excel, and use Excel's tools for creating professional-looking charts and graphs. You will do exactly that in this exercise.

- Download the Access file **Ch05Ex01_E7e** from *www.pearsonhighered.com/kroenke*. Open the database; select *DATABASE TOOLS/Relationships*. As you can see, there are three tables: *Product*, *VendorProductInventory*, and *Vendor*. Open each table individually to familiarize yourself with the data.
- For this problem, we will define *InventoryCost* as the product of *IndustryStandardCost* and *QuantityOnHand*. The query *InventoryCost* computes these values for every item in inventory for every vendor. Open that query and view the data to be certain you understand this computation. Open the other queries as well so that you understand the data they produce.

**a.** Sum this data by vendor and display it in a pie chart. Proceed as follows:

**(1)** Open Excel and create a new spreadsheet.

**(2)** Click *DATA* on the ribbon, and select *From Access* in the *Get External Data* ribbon category.

**(3)** Navigate to the location in which you have stored the Access file **Ch05Ex01_7e**.

**(4)** Select the query that contains the data you need for this pie chart.

**(5)** Import the data into a worksheet.

**(6)** Format the appropriate data as currency.

**(7)** Select the range that contains the data, press the function key, and proceed from there to create the pie chart. Name the data and pie chart worksheets appropriately.

**b.** Follow a similar procedure to create a bar chart. Place the data and the chart in separate worksheets, and name them appropriately.

## CHAPTER 5: FIND THE PIANOS!

**5-2.** Read Case Study 5 on pages 147–151. A copy of Dean's database is stored in the Access file **Ch05Ex02_E7e.** Download a copy of this file and create queries to provide the following data:

**a.** Sort the pianos from high quality to low.

**b.** Sort the pianos from high quality to low and, within each quality, sort by Building and then by Location within that building.

**c.** List the pianos in the shed and sort the results by manufacturer.

**d.** List all of the pianos with a Type of 'Spinet.'

**e.** Count the pianos for each value of quality (ranging from 1 to 5).

**f.** Write a query to produce the report in Figure 5-24 on page 150.

## CHAPTER 5: USE ACCESS TO ALLOCATE COMPUTERS TO EMPLOYEES

**5-3.** In this exercise, you will create a two-table database, define relationships, create a form and a report, and use them to enter data and view results.

**a.** Download the Excel file **Ch05Ex03_E7e** from *www.pearsonhighered.com/kroenke*. Open the spreadsheet and review the data in the *Employee* and *Computer* worksheets.

**b.** Create a new Access database with the name *Ex5-3_Solution*. Close the table that Access automatically creates and Access will delete it.

**c.** Import the data from the Excel spreadsheet into your database. Import the *Employee* worksheet into a table named *Employee*. Be sure to check *First Row Contains Column Headings*. Select *Choose my own primary key* and use the ID field as that key.

**d.** Import the *Computer* worksheet into a table named *Computer*. Check *First Row Contains Column Headings*, but let Access create the primary key.

**e.** Open the relationships window and add both *Employee* and *Computer* to the design space. Drag ID from *Employee* and drop it on *EmployeeID* in *Computer*. Check *Enforce Referential Integrity* and the two checkmarks below. Be sure you know what these actions mean.

**f.** Open the Form Wizard dialog box (under *CREATE, Form Wizard*), and add all of the columns for each of your tables to your form. Select *View your data by Employee*. Title your form *Employee* and your subform *Computer*.

**g.** Open the *Computer* subform in design mode and delete *EmployeeID* and *ComputerID*. These values are maintained by Access, and it is just a distraction to keep them. Save your changes and open the Employee form in layout mode. Adjust the size of the subform until your form looks like that in Figure AE-3.

**h.** Use your form to add two new computers to *Michael Murphy*. Both computers are Dells, and both use Windows 10; one costs $1,750, and the other costs $1,400.

**Figure AE-3**
Employee Computer Assignment Form

Employee

FirstName: Michael
LastName: Murphy
Department: Marketing

Computer

| SerialNumber | Brand | PurchaseCost | OperatingSystem | EmployeeID |
|---|---|---|---|---|
| 100 | Dell | $1,750.00 | Windows 10 | 2 |
| 800 | HP | $750.00 | Windows 10 | 2 |
| * | | | | 2 |

Record: 3 of 3 No Filter Search

i. Delete the Lenovo computer for Hal Larsen.

j. Use the Report Wizard (under *Create*) to create a report having all data from both the *Employee* and *Computer* tables. Adjust the report design until you find a design you like. Correct the label alignment if you need to.

## CHAPTER 6: INTERNET SPEED: GETTING WHAT YOU PAY FOR?

**6-1.** Numerous Web sites are available that will test your Internet data communications speed. You can find a good one at *www.speedtest.net*. (If that site is no longer active, Google or Bing "What is my Internet speed?" to find another speed-testing site. Use it.)

**a.** While connected to your university's network, go to Speedtest.net and test your speed against servers in Seattle, New York City, and Atlanta. Compute your average upload and download speeds.

**b.** Run the Speedtest.net test again from your home or a public wireless site. Compute your average upload and download speeds. If you are performing this test at home, are you getting the performance you are paying for?

**c.** Contact a friend or relative in another state. Ask him or her to run the Speedtest.net test against those same three cities.

**d.** Compare the results in parts a, b, and c. What conclusion, if any, can you make from these tests?

## CHAPTER 6: ESTIMATING CLOUD COSTS WITH EXCEL

**6-2.** Assume you have been asked to create an Office application to estimate cloud computing costs. You decide to create a spreadsheet into which your customers can provide their cloud computing needs and which you can then import into an Access database, using queries to compute cloud computing costs.

Figure AE-4 shows the structure of the spreadsheet into which your customers will input their requirements. You can download this spreadsheet in the Excel file **Ch06Ex02_E7e**. Figure AE-5 shows an Access table that has costs corresponding to the requirements in Figure AE-4. You can download this database in the Access file **Ch06Ex02_E7e**.

**a.** Import the spreadsheet data into the Access database.

**Figure AE-4**
Spreadsheet with Cloud Computing Requirements

| | A | B | C | D | E | F | G |
|---|---|---|---|---|---|---|---|
| 1 | | Jan-17 | Feb-17 | Mar-17 | Apr-17 | May-17 | Jun-17 |
| 2 | **Compute requirements (hours):** | | | | | | |
| 3 | | | | | | | |
| 4 | Extra Small Instance | 1200 | 1200 | 1200 | 1200 | 1200 | 1200 |
| 5 | Small Instance | 2000 | 2000 | 2400 | 2400 | 0 | 3000 |
| 6 | Medium Instance | 900 | 1800 | 2700 | 3600 | 3600 | 3600 |
| 7 | Large Instance | 0 | 500 | 1000 | 1500 | 2000 | 2000 |
| 8 | Extra Large Instance | 0 | 0 | 0 | 1000 | 1500 | 2000 |
| 9 | | | | | | | |
| 10 | Storage requirements: | | | | | | |
| 11 | Storage Required (GB) | 30 | 35 | 40 | 45 | 50 | 55 |
| 12 | Storage Transactions (1000s) | 30 | 30 | 35 | 35 | 40 | 50 |
| 13 | | | | | | | |
| 14 | Database requirements (number of instances) | | | | | | |
| 15 | 10GB Database | 2 | 2 | 2 | 2 | 1 | 1 |
| 16 | 20GB Database | 0 | 3 | 3 | 3 | 3 | 3 |
| 17 | 30GB Database | | 4 | 5 | 6 | 6 | 7 |
| 18 | 40GB Database | 0 | 0 | 0 | 3 | 3 | 4 |
| 19 | 50GB Database | 0 | 0 | 2 | 2 | 3 | 0 |

**Figure AE-5**
Access Table Corresponding to Requirements in Figure AE-4

CloudCosts

| ID | Resource Name | Units | Cost |
|---|---|---|---|
| 1 | Extra Small Instance | Hours | $0.03 |
| 2 | Small Instance | Hours | $0.09 |
| 3 | Medium Instance | Hours | $0.12 |
| 4 | Large Instance | Hours | $0.37 |
| 5 | Extra Large Instance | Hours | $0.55 |
| 6 | StorageRequired | GB / month | $0.15 |
| 7 | StorageTransactions | 10,000 | $0.01 |
| 8 | 10GB Database | Each | $9.99 |
| 9 | 20GB Database | Each | $149.98 |
| 10 | 30GB Database | Each | $199.97 |
| 11 | 40GB Database | Each | $299.96 |
| 12 | 50GB Database | Each | $399.95 |

**b.** Write queries to compute the cost of each resource.

**c.** Create a report that shows the cost for each type of resource for each month. Show the total costs for the 6-month period for each resource as well. Include a grand total of all the costs.

**d.** Create a pie chart that breaks out the total costs by resource. *Hint:* You have to import the query data back into Excel.

**e.** Create a pie chart that breaks out the total costs by month. *Hint:* You have to import the query data back into Excel.

**f.** Assume that processing costs increase by 10 percent across the board. Repeat parts c, d, and e for the changed costs.

## CHAPTER 6: FILE COMPRESSION AND ENCRYPTION

**6-3.** There are a few problems with cloud-based storage. First, it seems like there's never enough of it. This is especially true if it's free. Second, you always wonder if it's really secure. Yes, your storage provider says your data is secure. But is it really? Is there some way to be sure?

In this project, you will learn how to use 7-Zip to solve both of these problems. You'll learn how to compress and encrypt important files and directories. If you are storing confidential data in the cloud, it's important to make sure it's encrypted—by you. Using a third-party encryption tool like 7-Zip means only *you* can access your data. Trusting your cloud providers isn't necessary. 7-Zip is also a very efficient file archiver that will save you a lot of space.

**a.** Browse to *www.7-zip.org*.

**b.** Click on Download and install the latest version of 7-Zip for your operating system. (There are 7-Zip versions for Windows, Mac OS X, Linux, BSD, and Unix.)

**c.** Go to your Downloads folder. (You can go to any folder that contains large files.)

**d.** Right-click on a large file.

**e.** Click 7-Zip and Add to archive.

**f.** Rename the file YourName.7z. (Replace "YourName" with your first and last names. If your name was John Doe, the file would be named JohnDoe.7z.)

**g.** In the Encryption section, enter a password—twice. (Choose a simple password you can remember.)

**h.** Take a screenshot and paste it into your document. (You can take a screenshot by pressing Alt + Print Screen.)

**i.** Click OK. (Notice that your original file remains unchanged.)

**j.** After your new YourName.7z file is compressed, right-click it and select 7-Zip and Extract to "YourName\".

**k.** Enter the password you set, and click OK. (Your file should start extracting.)

**l.** Explain why third-party encryption is important for highly confidential files.

**m.** Explain why compressing large files is important when using cloud-based storage.

# PART 3

## CHAPTER 7: PRODUCTION PLANNING WITH EXCEL

**7-1.** Suppose your manager asks you to create a spreadsheet to compute a production schedule. Your schedule should stipulate a production quantity for seven products that is based on sales projections made by three regional managers at your company's three sales regions.

**a.** Create a separate worksheet for each sales region. Use the data in the Word file **Ch07Ex01_E7e**, which you can download from the text's Web site. This file contains each manager's monthly sales projections for the past year, actual sales results for those same months, and projections for sales for each month in the coming quarter.

**b.** Create a separate worksheet for each region's data. Import the data from Word into Excel.

**c.** On each of the worksheets, use the data from the prior four quarters to compute the discrepancy between the actual sales and the sales projections. This discrepancy can be computed in several ways: You could calculate an overall average, or you could calculate an average per quarter or per month. You could also weight recent discrepancies more heavily than earlier ones. Choose a method that you think is most appropriate. Explain why you chose the method you did.

**d.** Modify your worksheets to use the discrepancy factors to compute an adjusted forecast for the coming quarter. Thus, each of your spreadsheets will show the raw forecast and the adjusted forecast for each month in the coming quarter.

**e.** Create a fourth worksheet that totals sales projections for all of the regions. Show both the unadjusted forecast and the adjusted forecast for each region and for the company overall. Show month and quarter totals.

**f.** Create a bar graph showing total monthly production. Display the unadjusted and adjusted forecasts using different colored bars.

## CHAPTER 8: TRACKING SOCIAL MEDIA

**8-1.** Suppose you are the manager of social media policy for an organization with 1,000 employees in seven different offices throughout North America. Further suppose that the CEO has requested a report showing a list of all of the employees' blogs, the employees' job titles and departments, and the purpose and URL of each blog. She doesn't want to control employees; she just wants to know where they are.

**a.** Explain the conditions under which using a spreadsheet to track this data would be appropriate.

**b.** Suppose employees can have more than one blog but that a blog is only supported by a single employee. Further suppose you decide that you need to track the dates on which a blog was first created and the date of the last posting if the blog is no longer active. Design a database for these requirements.

**c.** Fill your database with the sample data in the Word document **Ch08Ex01_E7e.docx**. EmployeeID is a unique identifier; a null value for EndDate means the blog is still active. Do not retype this data; import it instead. You can either import it several times, each time to a different table, or you can import it once and use queries to fill the tables.

**d.** Create a report that is suitable for the CEO's needs. Justify the content and structure of your report.

## CHAPTER 9: THIRD-PARTY COOKIES

**9-1.** Open your favorite browser. Go to the options that govern cookies. (On Microsoft Edge, go to Tools [the little wheel icon in the upper right-hand corner] / Internet Options / Privacy / Advanced.) If you use another browser and don't know where to go for the privacy settings, search the Internet for your browser name plus the words *disable third-party cookies.* Follow the instructions to find the options page.

**a.** Disable third-party cookies. Close your browser. Reopen your browser and visit at least five Web sites.

**b.** Enable third-party cookies. Close your browser. Reopen your browser and visit the same five Web sites.

**c.** Do you notice any difference in the way the sites you access or your browser behave between a and b? Describe any differences.

**d.** Go to the same privacy settings location in which you disabled third-party cookies, and select *prompt* rather than *block* third-party cookies. Go to any site you normally visit, or *www.msn.com* if you can't think of any others. Describe what happens.

**e.** Change your browser's privacy settings back to whatever level of third-party cookie blocking you had when you started this exercise.

**f.** Summarize your experiences in this exercise.

## CHAPTER EXTENSION 10: EVALUATE VENDORS WITH ACCESS

**CE10-1.** Assume that you have been given the task of compiling evaluations of vendors made by your company's purchasing agents. Each month, every purchasing agent evaluates all of the vendors that he or she has worked with in the past month on three factors: price, quality, and responsiveness. Assume the ratings are from 1 to 5, with 5 being the best. Because your company has hundreds of vendors and dozens of purchasing agents, you decide to use Access to compile the results.

**a.** Create a database with three tables: VENDOR (*VendorNumber, Name, Contact*), PURCHASER (*EmpNumber, Name, Email*), and RATING (*EmpNumber, VendorNumber, Month, Year, Price Rating, QualityRating, ResponsivenessRating*). Assume that *VendorNumber* and *EmpNumber* are the keys of VENDOR and PURCHASER, respectively. Decide what you think is the appropriate key for RATING.

**b.** Create appropriate relationships.

**c.** Go to this text's companion Web site and import the data in the Excel file **CE10Ex01_E7c**. Note that data for VENDOR, PURCHASER, and RATING are stored in three separate worksheets.

**d.** Create a query that shows the names of all vendors and their average scores.

**e.** Create a query that shows the names of all employees and their average scores. *Hint:* In this and in part f, you will need to use the *Group By* function in your query.

**f.** Create a parameterized query that you can use to obtain the minimum, maximum, and average ratings on each criterion for a particular vendor. Assume you will enter *VendorName* as the parameter.

**g.** Using the information created by your queries, what conclusions can you make about vendors or purchasers?

## CHAPTER EXTENSION 12: MAKE YOUR OWN MARKET-BASKET ANALYSIS WITH ACCESS

**CE12-1.** It is surprisingly easy to create a market-basket report using table data in Access. To do so, however, you will need to enter SQL expressions into the Access query builder. Here, you can just copy SQL statements or type them in. If you take a database class, you will learn how to code SQL statements like those you will use here.

**a.** Create an Access database with a table named *Order_Data* having columns *OrderNumber, ItemName*, and *Quantity*, with data types Number (*LongInteger*), Short Text (50), and Number (*LongInteger*), respectively. Define the key as the composite (*OrderNumber, ItemName*). (You can do this in the table designer by highlighting both columns and clicking the Primary Key icon.)

**b.** Import the data from the Excel file **CE12Ex01_E7e** into the *Order_Data* table.

**c.** Now, to perform the market-basket analysis, you will need to enter several SQL statements into Access. To do so, click *CREATE/Query Design*. Click *Close* when the Show Table dialog box appears. Right-click in the gray section above the grid in the *Select Query* window. Select *SQL View*. Enter the following expression exactly as it appears here:

```
SELECT  T1.ItemName as FirstItem,
        T2.ItemName as SecondItem
FROM    Order_Data T1, Order_Data T2
WHERE   T1.OrderNumber =
        T2.OrderNumber
AND     T1.ItemName <> T2.ItemName;
```

Click the red exclamation point in the toolbar to run the query. Correct any typing mistakes and, once it works, save the query using the name *TwoItemBasket*.

**d.** Now enter a second SQL statement. Again, click *CREATE/Query Design*. Click *Close* when the Show Table dialog box appears. Right-click in the gray section above the grid in the *Select Query* window.

Select *SQL View*. Enter the following expression exactly as it appears here:

```
SELECT     TwoItemBasket.FirstItem,
           TwoItemBasket.SecondItem,
           Count(*) AS SupportCount
FROM       TwoItemBasket
GROUP BY   TwoItemBasket.FirstItem,
           TwoItemBasket.SecondItem;
```

Correct any typing mistakes and, once it works, save the query using the name *SupportCount*.

**e.** Examine the results of the second query, and verify that the two query statements have correctly calculated the number of times that two items have appeared together. Explain further calculations you need to make to compute support.

**f.** Explain the calculations you need to make to compute lift. Although you can make those calculations using SQL, you need more SQL knowledge to do it, and we will skip that here.

**g.** Explain, in your own words, what the query in part c seems to be doing. What does the query in part d seem to be doing? Again, you will need to take a database class to learn how to code such expressions, but this exercise should give you a sense of the kinds of calculations that are possible with SQL.

## CHAPTER EXTENSION 13: REPORTING WITH ACCESS

**CE13-1.** In this exercise, you'll have an opportunity to practice creating reports in Access using the data shown in Figure CE13-1.

**a.** Open Access, create a new database, and import the data in the text file **CE13Ex01_E7e**. Notice that the data includes an identifier; the four fields in Figure CE13-1; and a sixth field, called Quarter, that represents the calendar quarter in which the sale was made.

**b.** Use Access to create a report that sorts the data and presents it as shown in Figure CE13-2, except exclude sales less than $75. To do so, first create a query that has this data and then create a report based on that query. Format your report professionally.

**c.** Modify your report in part b to include subtotals for each customer.

**d.** Create a query to present the data as shown in Figure CE13-3. Produce a professionally formatted report of this data.

**e.** Create a query to compute the average of Amount for each Quarter.

**f.** Create a second table named QUARTER_DATA with fields *QuarterNumber* and *Average_Amount*. Place four rows in this table, one for each quarter and average amount.

**g.** Create a report that lists the sale data in ascending order of *CustomerName*. In your report, include the date and amount of each sale, as well as the amount of the sale divided by the average amount of a sale for that quarter.

**h.** Explain how all of the work you have done has been the result of the simple operations of filtering, sorting, grouping, and calculating.

## CHAPTER EXTENSION 13: OLAP AND PIVOT WITH EXCEL

**CE13-2.** OLAP cubes are very similar to Microsoft Excel pivot tables. For this exercise, assume that your organization's purchasing agents rate vendors in the same way as the situation described in Application Exercise CE10-1.

**a.** Open the Excel file **CE13Ex02_E7e**, which you can find on the text's Web site. The spreadsheet has the following column names: *VendorName, EmployeeName, Date, Year*, and *Rating*.

**b.** Under the *INSERT* ribbon in Excel, click *Pivot Table*.

**c.** When asked to provide a data range, drag your mouse over the column names and data values so as to select all of the data. Excel will fill in the range values in the open dialog box. Place your pivot table in a new worksheet. Click OK.

**d.** Excel will create a field list on the right-hand side of your spreadsheet. Underneath it, a grid labeled *Drag fields between areas below:* should appear. Drag and drop the field named *VendorName* into the area named ROWS. Observe what happens in the pivot table to the left (in column A). Now drag and drop *EmployeeName* onto COLUMNS and *Rating* on to VALUES. Again observe the effect of these actions on the pivot table to the left. Voilà! You have a pivot table.

**e.** To see how the pivot table works, drag and drop more fields onto the grid in the bottom right-hand side of your screen. For example, drop *Year* just underneath *Employee*. Then move *Year* above *Employee*. Now move *Year* below *Vendor*. All of this action is just like an OLAP cube, and, in fact, OLAP cubes are readily displayed in Excel pivot tables. The major difference is that OLAP cubes are usually based on thousands or more rows of data.

# PART 4

## CHAPTER 10: ENABLING SECURE BROWSING

**10-1.** Most of the Web sites you visit are not secure. Anyone between you and the Web site you are visiting can see the contents of the packets you are sending. Hypertext Transfer Protocol Secure (https) provides secure communication between hosts. It encrypts the traffic between the two hosts and provides Web server authentication.

In this exercise, you will install HTTPS Everywhere®, an add-on from *www.EFF.org*. This add-on checks to see if the Web site you are visiting offers an https connection. Larger Web sites do offer https connections if requested.

**a.** Open your Firefox Web browser. (If you don't already have Firefox, it can be downloaded from *www.mozilla.org*.)

**b.** Browse to *www.wikipedia.org*. (Note that it does not use an encrypted connection.)

**c.** Browse to *https://www.eff.org/https-everywhere*.

**d.** Download and install HTTPS Everywhere for Firefox, and then restart your Web browser. (You should see an HTTPS Everywhere icon in the top right corner of your browser after it restarts.)

**e.** Browse to *www.wikipedia.org*. (Note that it is using an encrypted connection.)

**f.** Enter your name into the search box at the encrypted site.

**g.** Take a screenshot with your name showing and paste it into your document. (You can take a screenshot by pressing Alt + Print Screen.)

**h.** Explain why all Web sites don't offer https connections.

**i.** Explain why an employer might not like you using https connections.

**j.** Specify what would you need in order to start offering https on a Web site.

## CHAPTER 10: SAFE WEB BROWSING

**10-2.** Most users want an easy way to identify which Web sites are trustworthy and which Web sites they should avoid. Web of Trust® (WOT) provides a "scorecard" for each Web site you visit. This scorecard gives you a summary of four ratings: trustworthiness, vendor reliability, privacy, and child safety. The values shown on the scorecard are based on ratings from members of the WOT community who have contributed their evaluations of that Web site.

After installing WOT, you will notice a slight addition to the search results from major search engines (e.g., Google, Bing, and Yahoo!). You will see a WOT evaluation at the end of each search result. This evaluation provides a scorecard for each Web site displayed in the search results. The WOT evaluation can serve as a quick visual indicator of Web sites to avoid.

**a.** Open Firefox, click the Firefox menu, and click Add-ons.

**b.** Search for "WOT."

**c.** Click Install (WOT) and Restart now. (You should see a small flag in the navigation bar.)

**d.** Browse to *www.google.com* and search for your full name.

**e.** Take a screenshot of the results and paste it into your document. (You can take a screenshot by pressing Alt + Print Screen. Notice the WOT icons next to each of the search results.)

**f.** Click on the WOT icon for one of the search results. (This will show you the WOT scorecard for that specific Web site.)

**g.** Using Google, search for *warez keygen*. You should get a few Web sites with red circles, meaning they have a poor reputation.

**h.** Click on the WOT icon for WOT scorecard of one of the Web sites with a red circle.

**i.** Take a screenshot and paste it into your document.

**j.** Describe how WOT gets the values for its Web site scorecards.

**k.** Describe how you can evaluate Web sites using WOT.

**l.** Explain how WOT can protect users when they are surfing the Internet.

## CHAPTER 11: KEEPING TRACK OF REQUESTS

**11-1.** Tracking requests is a common need for both systems development projects and also for IS departments and, indeed, with any service department. With accurate request tracking, management can get involved when requests are repeatedly made for the same problem, when too many problems are being reported for the same facility or piece of equipment, or when too many problems are being reported by the same user.

- In this exercise, you will create such a system for an IS department that wants to track system problems and responses.
- Suppose an organization keeps the following data about requests:

  *Ticket#*
  *Date_Submitted*
  *Date_Opened*
  *Date_Closed*
  *Type (new or repeat)*
  *Reporting_ Employee_Name*
  *Reporting_Employee_Division*
  *Technician_Name Problem_System*
  *Problem_DescriptionONE*

- You can find sample ticket data in the Excel file **Ch11Ex01_E7e** on this text's Web site.
- However, managers often need more information. Among their needs are information that will help them learn who are their best- and worst-performing technicians, how different systems compare in terms of number of problems reported and the time required to fix those problems, how different divisions compare in terms of problems reported and the time required to fix them, which technicians are the best and worst at solving problems with particular systems, and which technicians are best and worst at solving problems from particular divisions.

**a.** Use either Access or Excel, or a combination of the two, to produce the information listed above from the data in the Excel file **Ch11Ex01_E7e**. In your answer, you may use queries, formulas, reports, forms, graphs, pivot tables, pivot charts, or any other type of Access or Excel display. Choose the best display for the type of information you are producing.

**b.** Explain how you would use these different types of information to manage your department.

**c.** Specify any additional information that you would like to have produced from this data to help you manage your department.

**d.** Use either Access or Excel or a combination to produce the information in part c.

## CHAPTER 12: PLANNING PROJECT COSTS WITH EXCEL

**12-1.** Suppose you are given the task of comparing labor costs of meetings for systems development projects to budgets. Download the Word file **Ch12Ex01_E7e.docx** and the Excel file with the same name. The Word file has records of meeting dates, times, and attendees. The document was created from informal notes taken at the meetings. The Excel file has the project budgets as well as labor costs for different categories of employees.

Assume your company uses the traditional SDLC and each step requires two types of meetings: working and review. *Working meetings* involve users, business analysts, systems analysts, programmers, and PQA test engineers. *Review meetings* involve all of those people, plus level-1 and level-2 managers of both user departments and the IS department.

**a.** Using either Access or Excel, whichever you think is better suited to the task, import the Word data to a work file and compute the total labor for each type of employee for each meeting.

**b.** Using the file you created in part a, compute the total labor for each type of employee for each phase of the project.

**c.** Combine your answer in part b with the data in the Excel file **Ch12Ex01_E7e.xlsx** to compute the total cost of meetings of each phase of the project.

**d.** Use a graphic chart of the type you think best to show the differences between meeting cost and budget.

**e.** Comment on your choice of Excel or Access for your work file. If you were to do this exercise over, would you use that same tool again? Why or why not?

## CHAPTER 12: TRACKING SYSTEMS FAILURES WITH ACCESS

**12-2.** Use Access to develop a failure-tracking database application. Use the sample data in the Excel file **Ch12Ex02_E7e** for this exercise. The file includes columns for the following:

*FailureNumber*
*DateReported*
*FailureDescription*
*ReportedBy (the name of the PQA engineer reporting the failure)*
*ReportedBy_email (the email address of the PQA engineer reporting the failure)*
*FixedBy (the name of the programmer who is assigned to fix the failure)*
*FixedBy_email (the email address of the programmer assigned to fix the failure)*
*DateFailureFixed*
*FixDescription*
*DateFixVerified*
*VerifiedBy (the name of the PQA engineer verifying the fix)*
*VerifiedBy_email (the email address of the PQA engineer verifying the fix)*

**a.** The data in the spreadsheet have not been normalized. When you enter (or, better, import) the data, normalize it by creating a Failure table, a PQA Engineer table, and a Developer table. Assume problems are reported and verified by PQA engineers and problems are fixed by developers. Add other appropriate columns to each table. Create appropriate relationships.

**b.** Create one or more forms that can be used to report a failure, to report a failure fix, and to report a failure verification. Create the form(s) so that the user can use a combo box to pull down the name of a PQA engineer or developer from the appropriate table to fill in the *ReportedBy*, *FixedBy*, and *VerifiedBy* fields.

**c.** Construct a report that shows all failures sorted by *ReportedBy* and then by *Date Reported.*

**d.** Construct a report that shows only fixed and verified failures.

**e.** Construct a report that shows only fixed but unverified failures.

## CHAPTER EXTENSION 18: PROCESS MODELING WITH VISIO

**CE18-1.** In this exercise, you will use Visio to create process diagrams in BPMN notation.

**a.** Download the Visio file **CE18Ex01_E7e** from this text's support site. Open the file and familiarize yourself with this diagram. Explain the major differences between the process documented in this file and that in Figure CE18-1.

**b.** Notice that Visio includes the BPMN shapes. Go to the Shape organizer to see other types of flowchart shapes that Visio supports.

**c.** Create a new Visio diagram. Add BPMN shapes that you may want to use.

**d.** Model the customer process Respond to Quotation. Make sure your process accepts the inputs shown in **CE18Ex01_E7e** and produces the outputs shown in that figure. Create your process so that your company checks prices and delivery dates and requests changes, if appropriate. Include other logic, if necessary.

**e.** Show your work by saving your document as a PDF file.

**10/100/1000 Ethernet** A type of Ethernet that conforms to the IEEE 802.3 protocol and allows for transmission at a rate of 10, 100, or 1,000 Mbps (megabits per second). 499

**Abstract reasoning** The ability to make and manipulate models. One of four key skills for nonroutine cognitive thinking. 10

**Accelerator effect** An economic phenomenon in which a dollar (or other currency) spent on a good or service can contribute 2 or 3 dollars of activity to the economy. 591

**Access** A popular personal and small workgroup DBMS product from Microsoft. 128

**ACID** An acronym standing for *atomic, consistent, isolated*, and *durable*. Used to describe the processing of transactions such that all of the transaction is processed or none of it is (atomic), transactions are processed in the same manner (consistent) whether processed alone or in the presence of millions of other transactions (isolated), and that once a transaction is stored it never goes away—even in the presence of failure (durable). 138

**Activity** A function in a business process that receives inputs and produces outputs. An activity can be performed by a human, by a computer system, or by both. 35

**Actor** In a business process, a person, group, department, organization, or information system. 35

**Ad-blocking software** Software that filters out advertising content. 226

**Advanced Persistent Threat (APT)** A sophisticated, possibly long-running computer hack that is perpetrated by large, well-funded organizations like governments. APTs are a means to engage in cyberwarfare. 283

**Adware** Programs installed on the user's computer without the user's knowledge or permission that reside in the background and, unknown to the user, observe the user's actions and keystrokes, modify computer activity, and report the user's activities to sponsoring organizations. Most adware is benign in that it does not perform malicious acts or steal data. It does, however, watch user activity and produce pop-up ads. 294

**Agile development** An adaptive project management process based on the principles listed in Figure CE17-1. Can be used for the management of many types of projects; in this text, it applies to the development of information systems. 615

**Alert** A form of report, often requested by recipients, that tells them some piece of usually time-related information, such as notification of the time for a meeting. 565

**Analysis paralysis** When so much time is spent documenting and revising project requirements that the project comes to a halt. 356

**Android** A mobile operating system that is a version of Linux. Android runs on the Google Nexus 7 and the Amazon Kindle Fire as well as many other mobile devices. 102

**Application software** Programs that perform a business function. Some application programs are general purpose, such as Excel or Word. Other application programs are specific to a business function, such as accounts payable. 105

**As-is model** A model that represents the current situation and processes. 518, 625

**Asymmetric encryption** An encryption method whereby different keys are used to encode and to decode the message; one key encodes the message, and the other key decodes the message. Asymmetric encryption is slower and more complicated than symmetric encryption. 291

**Asynchronous communication** Information exchange that occurs when all members of a work team do not meet at the same time, such as those who work different shifts. 382

**Attack vectors** Ways of attacking a target. 574

**Attribute** Characteristics of an entity. Example attributes of Order are *OrderNumber, OrderDate, SubTotal, Tax, Total*, and so forth. Example attributes of Salesperson are *SalespersonName, Email, Phone*, and so forth. 437

**Authentication** The process whereby an information system verifies (validates) a user. 290

**Automated Clearing House (ACH)** A network of information systems that provides for the interbank clearing of electronic payments. 527

**Baseline WBS** The final work breakdown structure that shows the planned tasks, dependencies, durations, and resource assignments. 607

**Baseline** An initial plan for the development of an information system. 603

**Bell's Law** A new computer class forms roughly each decade establishing a new industry. 5

**Best practices** Methods that have been shown to produce successful results in prior implementations. 542

**Beta testing** The process of allowing future system users to try out the new system on their own. Used to locate program failures just prior to program shipment. 353

**BI analysis** The process of creating business intelligence. The four fundamental categories of BI analysis are reporting, data mining, BigData, and knowledge management. 250

**BI application** The software component of a BI system. 247

**BI server** Web server application that is purpose-built for the publishing of business intelligence. 264

**BigData** A term used to describe data collections that are characterized by huge volume, rapid velocity, and great variety. 260

**Bigtable** A nonrelational data store developed by Google. 137

**Binary digits** See *bits*. 91

**Biometric authentication** The use of personal physical characteristics, such as fingerprints, facial features, and retinal scans, to authenticate users. 291

**Bits** The means by which computers represent data; also called binary digits. A bit is either a zero or a one. 91

**BlackBerry OS** One of the most successful early mobile operating systems; was primarily used by business users on BlackBerry devices. 102

**Bluetooth** A common wireless protocol designed for transmitting data over short distances, replacing cables. 499

**Bounce rate** Percent of people who visit your Web site and then immediately leave. 537

**Bring your own device (BYOD) policy** An official organizational policy that states employees' permissions and responsibilities when using personal mobile devices for organizational business. 413

**Brooks' Law** The adage that adding more people to a late project makes the project later. Brooks' Law is true not only because a larger staff requires increased coordination but also because new people need to be trained. The only people who can train the new employees are the existing team members, who are thus taken off productive tasks. The costs of training new people can overwhelm the benefit of their contributions. Named for Fred Brooks, author of *The Mythical-Man Month*. 344

**Brute force attack** A password-cracking program that tries every possible combination of characters. 286

**Bullwhip effect** A phenomenon in which the variability in the size and timing of orders increases at each stage up the supply chain, from customer to supplier. 530, 591

**Business analyst** A person who understands business strategies, goals, and objectives and who helps businesses develop and manage business processes and information systems. Compare to *systems analyst*. 347

**Business continuity planning** A planning session that discusses how to return the organization to normal operations as quickly as possible following a data breach. 577

**Business intelligence (BI)** The process of using operational and other data to create information that exposes patterns, relationships, and trends of importance to the organization. 247

**Business intelligence (BI) systems** Information systems that process operational and other source data to identify patterns, relationships, and trends and to make predictions. 247

**Business process** (1) A network of activities, repositories, roles, resources, and flows that interact to achieve some business function; sometimes called a business system. (2) A network of activities that generate value by transforming inputs into outputs. 34

**Business process management (BPM)** A cyclical process for systematically creating, assessing, and altering business processes. 625

**Business Process Modeling Notation (BPMN)** Standard set of terms and graphical notations for documenting business processes. 34

**Business process reengineering** The activity of altering existing and designing new business processes to take advantage of new information systems technology. 188

**Business-to-business (B2B)** Relationships through which businesses generate new retail leads. 218

**Business-to-consumer (B2C)** Relationships through which businesses market their products to end users. 218

**Bytes** (1) 8-bit chunks of data. (2) Characters of data. 91

**Cable line** Cable television lines that provide high-speed data transmission. 500

**Capital** Resources that are invested with the expectation of future gain. 220

**Carding** Validation process where a small charge is placed on a stolen credit card to ensure it is working. 574

**Carrier** A telecommunications company that provides voice and data transportation services. 501

**Cassandra** A durable, nonrelational data store that operates over hundreds or thousands of servers. Originally developed by Facebook but later turned over to the open source community; has become an Apache Top-Level Project (TLP). 137

**Cell** In a spreadsheet, the intersection of a row and a column. 417

**Central processing unit (CPU)** The portion of a computer that selects instructions, processes them, performs arithmetic and logical comparisons, and stores results of operations in memory. 89

**Charms** In Windows 10 applications, icons that slide in from the right of the display. 409

**Chief information officer (CIO)** The title of the principal manager of the IS department. Other common titles are vice president of information services, director of information services, and, less commonly, director of computer services. 316

**Chief information security officer (CISO)** The title of the person who manages security for the organization's information systems and information. 317

**Chief security officer (CSO)** The title of the person who manages security for all of the organization's assets: physical plant and equipment, employees, intellectual property, and digital. 316

**Chief technology officer (CTO)** The head of the technology group. The CTO filters new ideas and products to identify those most relevant to the organization. The CTO's job requires deep knowledge of information technology and the ability to envision how new IT could affect an organization over time. 316

**Chrome** Visual overhead, such as menus, status bars, and scroll bars, in a computer display. 408

**Client** PCs, tablets, and smartphones that access servers via the cloud. 90

**Closed source** Source code that is highly protected and only available to trusted employees and carefully vetted contractors. 108

**Cloud** A term that refers to elastic leasing of pooled computer resources over the Internet. 155

**Cluster analysis** An unsupervised data mining technique whereby statistical techniques are used to identify groups of entities that have similar characteristics. A common use for cluster analysis is to find groups of similar customers in data about customer orders and customer demographics. 260

**COBIT (Control Objectives for Information and related Technology)** A set of standard practices, created by the Information Systems Audit and Control Association, used in the assessment stage of the BPM cycle to determine how well an information system complies with an organization's strategy. 625

**Collaboration** The activity of two or more people working together to achieve a common goal via a process of feedback and iteration. One of four key skills for nonroutine cognitive thinking. 10

**Collaboration information system** An information system that supports collaboration. Also called a collaboration system. 375

**Collaboration system** See *collaboration information system*. 375

**Collaboration tool** The program component of a collaboration system. For the tool to be useful, it must be surrounded by the other four components of an information system. 376

**Collaboration** The activity of two or more people working together to achieve a common goal via a process of feedback and iteration. One of four key skills for nonroutine cognitive thinking. 367

**Columns** Also called fields, or groups of bytes. A database table has multiple columns that are used to represent the attributes of an entity. Examples are PartNumber, EmployeeName, and SalesDate. 125

**Comma-delimited file** An exported data file in which field values are separated by commas. 470

**Commerce server** An application program that runs on a server tier computer. A typical commerce server obtains product data from a database, manages items in users' shopping carts, and coordinates the checkout process. 503

**Communication channels** Means of delivering messages. 542

**Communities** See *communities of practice*. 211

**Communities of practice** Groups of people related by a common interest. Also called communities. 211

**Competitive analysis** An analysis performed to identify a competitor's strengths and weaknesses. 537

**Competitive strategy** The strategy an organization chooses as the way it will succeed. According to Michael Porter, there are four fundamental competitive strategies: cost leadership across an industry or within a particular industry segment and product or service differentiation across an industry or within a particular industry segment. 63

**Component design** The third phase in the SDLC, in which developers determine hardware and software specifications, design the database (if applicable), design procedures, and create job descriptions for users and operations personnel. 344

**Computer hardware** Electronic components and related gadgetry that input, process, output, store, and communicate data according to the instructions encoded in computer programs or software. One of the five fundamental components of an information system. 15, 89

**Computer security incident response team (CSIRT)** A team consisting of staff from the legal and public relations departments as well as executives and systems administrators. 577

**Computer-based information system** An information system that includes a computer. 15

**Confidence** In market-basket terminology, the probability estimate that two items will be purchased together. 553

**Configuration control** A set of management policies, practices, and tools that developers use to maintain control over the project's resources. 609

**Connection data** In social media systems, data about relationships. 215

**Content data** In social media systems, data and responses to data that are contributed by users and SM sponsors. 215

**Content delivery network (CDN)** An information system that serves content to Web pages over the Internet. To reduce wait time, data is typically stored and served from many geographic locations. 160

**Content management system (CMS)** An information system that supports the management and delivery of documentation, including reports, Web pages, and other expressions of employee knowledge. 545

**Context-sensitive chrome** Chrome that pops up in the display only when needed and appropriate. 408

**Conversion rate** Measures the frequency with which someone who clicks on an ad makes a purchase, "likes" a site, or takes some other action desired by the advertiser. 227

**Conversion rate** Measures the frequency with which someone who clicks on an ad makes a purchase, "likes" a site, or takes some other action desired by the advertiser. 536

**Cookie** A small file that is stored on the user's computer by a browser. Cookies can be used for authentication, for storing shopping cart contents and user preferences, and for other legitimate purposes. Cookies can also be used to implement spyware. 272, 287

**Cooperation** The process by which a group of people having the same skills work in parallel to shorten the time required to accomplish a job, for example, four painters each painting one wall of a room. 367

**Cost** The cost of a business process is equal to the cost of the inputs plus the cost of activities. 602

**Cost feasibility** An assessment of the cost of an information system development project that compares estimated costs the value delivered. Can also compare the estimated costs to the available budget. 346

**Countermeasures** Software or procedures used to prevent an attack. 579

**Critical path** The sequence of activities that determine the earliest date by which the project can be completed. 606

**Critical path analysis** The process by which project managers compress a schedule by moving resources, typically people, from noncritical path tasks to critical path tasks. 606

**Cross-selling** The sale of related products to customers based on salesperson knowledge, market-basket analysis, or both. 552

**Crowdsourcing** The dynamic social media process of employing users to participate in product design or redesign. 218

**Crow's feet** Lines on an entity-relationship diagram that indicate a 1:N relationship between two entities. 438

**Crow's-foot diagram** A type of entity-relationship diagram that uses a crow's foot symbol to designate a 1:N relationship. 439

**Custom-developed software** Software that is tailor-made for a particular organization's requirements. 106

**Customer life cycle** Taken as a whole, the processes of marketing, customer acquisition, relationship management, and loss/churn. The entire life cycle must be managed by CRM systems. 189

**Customer relationship management (CRM) system** A suite of applications, a database, and a set of inherent processes for managing all the interactions with the customer, from lead generation to customer service. 189

**Data** Recorded facts or figures. One of the five fundamental components of an information system. 15

**Data acquisition** In business intelligence systems, the process of obtaining, cleaning, organizing, relating, and cataloging source data. 249

**Data administration** An organization-wide function that develops and enforces data policies and standards. 295

**Data aggregator** See *data broker*. 266

**Data breach** When an unauthorized person views, alters, or steals secured data. 573

**Data broker** Also called data aggregator; a company that acquires and purchases consumer and other data from public records, retailers, Internet cookie vendors, social media trackers, and other sources and uses it to create business intelligence that it sells to companies and the government. 266

**Data flow** A BPMN symbol that documents the movement of data among activities and repositories in a business process. 36

**Data integrity** In a database or a collection of databases, the condition that exists when data values are consistent and in agreement with one another. 185

**Data integrity problem** In a database, the situation that exists when data item values disagree with one another. An example is two different names for the same customer. 440

**Data loss prevention system (DLP)** A system designed to prevent sensitive data from being released to unauthorized persons. 580

**Data mart** A data collection, smaller than the data warehouse, that addresses the needs of a particular department or functional area of the business. 258

**Data mining** The application of statistical techniques to find patterns and relationships among data for classification and prediction. 259

**Data model** A logical representation of the data in a database that describes the data and relationships that will be stored in the database. Akin to a blueprint. 436

**Data safeguards** Measures used to protect databases and other data assets from threats. Includes data rights and responsibilities, encryptions, backup and recovery, and physical security. 295

**Data warehouse** A facility for managing an organization's BI data. 255

**Database** A self-describing collection of integrated records. 125

**Database administration** A person or department that develops procedures and practices to ensure efficient and orderly multiuser processing of the database, to control changes to database structure, and to protect the database. 295

**Database application** A collection of forms, reports, queries, and application programs that facilitates users' processing of a database. A database can be processed by many different database applications. 131

**Database management system (DBMS)** A program for creating, processing, and administering a database. A DBMS is a large and complex program that is licensed like an operating system. Microsoft Access and Oracle Database are example DBMS products. 128

**Database marketing** The application of data business intelligence systems to the planning, execution, and assessment of marketing programs. 550

**Database tier** In the three-tier architecture, the tier that runs the DBMS and receives and processes requests to retrieve and store data. 503

**DB2** A popular, enterprise-class DBMS product from IBM. 128

**Decision support systems** An older term that is sometimes used as a synonym for decision-making BI systems. 248

**Decision tree** A hierarchical arrangement of criteria that predict a classification or a value. 553

**Deliverables** Measurable tasks in a development project. 605

**Denial of service (DoS)** Security problem in which users are not able to access an information system; can be caused by human errors, natural disaster, or malicious activity. 283

**Departmental information system** A workgroup information system that supports a particular department. 183

**Desktop virtualization** Also called client virtualization and PC virtualization. The process of storing a user's desktop on a remote server. It enables users to run their desktop from many different client computers. 104

**Digital dashboard** A Web page display customized for a particular user. 565

**Digital Revolution** The conversion from mechanical and analog devices to digital devices. 5

**Digital subscriber line (DSL)** A communications line that operates on the same lines as voice telephones, but does so in such a manner that its signals do not interfere with voice telephone service. 500

**Dimension** A characteristic of an OLAP measure. Purchase date, customer type, customer location, and sales region are examples of dimensions. 567

**Dimensional database** A database structured to support OLAP processing. 570

**Direct interaction** Driving application behavior by implementing obvious actions on user content; for example, clicking on an album to open the album's contents. 408

**Discussion forums** Forms of asynchronous communication in which one group member posts an entry and other group members respond. A better form of group communication than email because it is more difficult for one person to monopolize the discussion or for the discussion to go off track. 383

**Diseconomies of scale** A principle that states as teams become larger, the average contribution per worker decreases. See *Brooks' Law*. 602

**Distributed database processing** The processing of a single database that resides in multiple locations. 589

**Distributed systems** Systems in which application processing is distributed across multiple computing devices. 197

**Domain name** A worldwide unique name that is registered in the domain name system (DNS) and is affiliated with a public IP address. 502

**Drill down** With an OLAP report, the ability to further divide the data into more detail. 568

**Dual processor** A computer with two CPUs. 89

**Dynamic reports** Business intelligence documents that are updated at the time they are requested. 262, 564

**Dynamo** A nonrelational data store developed by Amazon .com. 137

**Effective business process** A business process that enables the organization to accomplish its strategy. 37

**Efficiency** The ratio of benefits to costs. 37

**Elastic** In cloud computing, the situation that exists when the amount of resource leased can be dynamically increased or decreased, programmatically, in a short span of time, and organizations pay for just the resources that they use. This term was first used in this way by Amazon.com. 155

**Email** A form of asynchronous communication in which participants send comments and attachments electronically. As a form of group communication, it can be disorganized, disconnected, and easy to hide from. 383

**Email spoofing** A synonym for phishing. A technique for obtaining unauthorized data that uses pretexting via email. The phisher pretends to be a legitimate company and sends email requests for confidential data, such as account numbers, Social Security numbers, account passwords, and so forth. Phishers direct traffic to their sites under the guise of a legitimate business. 282

**Encapsulated** A characteristic of systems design in which the details of a process are hidden from users of that process. A formal interface is defined for the process that specifies how the process is to be accessed, what data it requires, and the data that it will produce. The means by which that process creates those results are never exposed, nor do they need to be. 506

**Encryption** The process of transforming clear text into coded, unintelligible text for secure storage or communication. 291

**Encryption algorithms** Algorithms used to transform clear text into coded, unintelligible text for secure storage or communication. 291

**Enterprise 2.0** The use of emergent social software platforms within companies or between companies and their partners or customers. 539

**Enterprise application integration (EAI)** A suite of software applications that integrates existing systems by providing layers of software and metadata that connect applications together. 192

**Enterprise information system** Information systems that support cross-functional processes and activities in multiple departments. 184

**Enterprise resource planning (ERP)** A suite of applications called modules, a database, and a set of inherent processes for consolidating business operations into a single, consistent, computing platform. 192, 512

**Enterprise social network (ESN)** A software platform that uses social media to facilitate cooperative work of people within an organization. 538

**Entity** In the E-R data model, a representation of some thing that users want to track. Some entities represent a physical object; others represent a logical construct or transaction. 436

**Entity-relationship (E-R) data model** A tool for constructing data models that defines the entities stored in a database and the relationships among those entities. 436

**Entity-relationship (E-R) diagrams** A type of diagram used by database designers to document entities and their relationships to each other. 438

**ERP system** An information system based on ERP technology. 512

**Ethernet** Another name for the IEEE 802.3 protocol, Ethernet is a communications standard that specifies how messages are to be packaged, processed, and transmitted for wired transmission over a LAN. 499

**Exabyte (EB)** 1,024 PB. 91

**Exception reports** Reports produced when something out of predefined bounds occurs. 259

**Exfiltration** Illegally transferring data out of the organization (sometimes known as data extrusion). 577

**Experimentation** A careful and reasoned analysis of an opportunity, envisioning potential products or solutions or applications of technology and then developing those ideas that seem to have the most promise, consistent with the resources you have. One of four key skills for nonroutine cognitive thinking. 10

**Expert systems** Rule-based systems that encode human knowledge in the form of If/Then rules. 544

**Expert systems shells** A program in an expert system that processes a set of rules, typically many times, until the values of the variables no longer change, at which point the system reports the results. 544

**Exploit** Software used to take advantage of a newly discovered vulnerability in a target's application or operating system. 575

**F score** In RFM analysis, a number rating that indicates in which fifth a customer ranks in terms of ordering frequency. 551

**Family Educational Rights and Privacy Act (FERPA)** Regulation that provides protection for student education records. 579

**Federal Information Security Management Act (FISMA)** Regulation that requires security precautions for government agencies. 579

**Fields** Also called columns; groups of bytes in a database table. A database table has multiple columns that are used to represent the attributes of an entity. Examples are PartNumber, EmployeeName, and SalesDate. 125

**File** A group of similar rows or records. In a database, sometimes called a table. 125

**File server** A networked computer that stores files. 386

**Firewall** Computing devices located between public and private networks that prevent unauthorized access to or from the internal network. A firewall can be a special-purpose computer, or it can be a program on a general-purpose computer or on a router. 293

**Firmware** Computer software installed into devices such as printers, print services, and various types of communication devices. The software is coded just like other software, but it is installed into special, programmable memory of the printer or other device. 106

**Five forces model** Model, proposed by Michael Porter, that assesses industry characteristics and profitability by means of five competitive forces—threat of substitution, rivalry among firms, threat of new entrants, bargaining power of suppliers, and bargaining power of customers. 61

**Five-component framework** The five fundamental components of an information system—computer hardware, software, data, procedures, and people—present in every information system, from the simplest to the most complex. 15

**Folksonomy** A content structure that emerges from the activity and processing of many user tags. 539

**Foreign keys** A column or group of columns used to represent relationships. Values of the foreign key match values of the primary key in a different (foreign) table. 127

**Form** Data entry forms used to read, insert, modify, and delete database data. 131

**Freemium** A revenue model offering a basic service for free and then charging a premium for upgrades or advanced features. 226

**ftp (File Transfer Protocol)** A Layer-5 TCP/IP protocol used to copy files from one computer to another. In interorganizational transaction processing, ftp enables users to easily exchange large files. 508

**Function points** Estimating technique that attempts to schedule a development project by the number of function points in a project, using each function point to determine the number of lines of code and the time for the project. 608

**Functional information system** A workgroup information system that supports a particular business function. 183

**Gantt chart** A chart that shows tasks, dates, dependencies, and possibly resources. 605

**Gigabyte (GB)** 1,024 MB. 91

**GNU** A set of tools for creating and managing open source software. Originally created to develop an open source Unix-like operating system. 107

**GNU general public license (GPL) agreement** One of the standard license agreements for open source software. 107

**Google Docs** Web-based application software for processing documents, spreadsheets, presentations, drawings, and other types of data in a format that is proprietary to Google. Google Docs documents can be converted into Microsoft Office documents, and vice versa. 385

**Google Drive** A free, cloud-based server for sharing documents, spreadsheets, presentations, drawings, and other types of data. Provided by Google. Includes version tracking for Google Docs documents. 386

**Gramm-Leach-Bliley Act (GLBA)** Regulation also known as the Financial Services Modernization Act that requires data protection for financial institutions. 579

**Granularity** The level of detail in data. Customer name and account balance are large granularity data. Customer name, balance, and the order details and payment history of every customer order are smaller granularity. 257

**Graphical queries** Queries in which criteria are created when the user clicks on a graphic. 134

**Green computing** Environmentally conscious computing consisting of three major components: power management, virtualization, and e-waste management. 335

**Hacking** A form of computer crime in which a person gains unauthorized access to a computer system. Although some people hack for the sheer joy of doing it, other hackers invade systems for the malicious purpose of stealing or modifying data. 282

**Hadoop** An open source program supported by the Apache Foundation that manages thousands of computers and that implements MapReduce. 261

**Hardening** A term used to describe server operating systems that have been modified to make it especially difficult for them to be infiltrated by malware. 299

**Health Information Portability and Accountability Act (HIPAA)** Regulation that requires data protection for healthcare institutions. 579

**Hertz** Unit of measurement used to describe CPU speeds equal to a cycle per second. 92

**Honeypots** False targets for computer criminals to attack. To an intruder, a honeypot looks like a particularly valuable resource, such as an unprotected Web site, but in actuality the only site content is a program that determines the attacker's IP address. 301

**Hop** In an internet, the movement from one network to another. 501

**Horizontal-market application** Software that provides capabilities common across all organizations and industries; examples include word processors, graphics programs, spreadsheets, and presentation programs. 105

**Host operating system** In virtualization, the operating system that hosts the virtual operating systems. 103

**http (Hypertext Transport Protocol)** An application-layer protocol used between browsers and Web servers. 507

**https** An indication that a Web browser is using the SSL/TLS protocol to provide secure communications. 292, 508

**Human capital** The investment in human knowledge and skills with the expectation of future gain. 220

**Human safeguards** Steps taken to protect against security threats by establishing appropriate procedures for users to following during system use. 296

**Hybrid model** A systems architecture in which many ERP customers store most of their data on cloud servers managed by cloud vendors and store sensitive data on servers they manage themselves. 515

**ICANN (Internet Corporation for Assigned Names and Numbers)** The organization responsible for managing the assignment of public IP addresses and domain names for use on the Internet. Each public IP address is unique across all computers on the Internet. 502

**Identification** The process whereby an information system identifies a user by requiring the user to sign on with a username and password. 290

**Identifier** An attribute (or group of attributes) whose value is associated with one and only one entity instance. 437

**IEEE 802.3 protocol** A standard for packaging and managing traffic on wired local area networks. 499

**IEEE 802.11 protocol** A standard for packaging and managing traffic on wireless local area networks. 499

**If/Then rules** Statements specifying that if a particular condition exists, then a particular action should be taken. Used for both expert systems and decision trees. 544

**Implementation** In the context of the systems development life cycle, the phase following the design phase consisting of tasks to build, test, and convert users to the new system. 344

**Import/export** The process of transferring data from one computer application to another. 469

**In-memory DBMS** DBMS products that process databases stored in (very large) memories. Usually such DBMS utilize or extend the relational model. ACID support is common. 138

**Industry-specific solution** An ERP template designed to serve the needs of companies or organizations in specific industries. Such solutions save time and lower risk. The development of industry-specific solutions spurred ERP growth. 519

**Influencer** An individual in a social network whose opinion can force a change in others' behavior and beliefs. 222

**Information** (1) Knowledge derived from data, where data is defined as recorded facts or figures; (2) data presented in a meaningful context; (3) data processed by summing, ordering, averaging, grouping, comparing, or other similar operations; (4) a difference that makes a difference. 40

**Information Age** A period in history where the production, distribution, and control of information is the primary driver of the economy. 5

**Information silo** A condition that exists when data are isolated in separated information systems. Usually leads to data integrity problems. 184

**Information system (IS)** A group of hardware, software, data, procedure, and people components that interacts to produce information. 14

**Information technology (IT)** The products, methods, inventions, and standards used for the purpose of producing information. 14

**Infrastructure as a service (IaaS)** The cloud hosting of a bare server computer or data storage. 160

**Inherent processes** The procedures that must be followed to effectively use licensed software. For example, the processes inherent in ERP systems assume that certain users will take specified actions in a particular order. In most cases, the organization must conform to the processes inherent in the software. 189

**Inter-enterprise information system** An information system that supports one or more inter-enterprise processes. 184

**Internal firewalls** Firewalls that sit inside the organizational network. 293

**Internet** When spelled with a small i, as in internet, a private network of networks. When spelled with a capital I, as in Internet, the public internet known as the Internet. 497

**Internet of Things (IoT)** The idea that objects are becoming connected to the Internet so they can interact with other devices, applications, or services. 92

**Internet service provider (ISP)** An ISP provides a user with a legitimate Internet address; it serves as the user's gateway to the Internet; and it passes communications back and forth between the user and the Internet. ISPs also pay for the Internet. They collect money from their customers and pay access fees and other charges on the users' behalf. 499

**Intranet** A private internet (note small i) used within a corporation or other organization. 497

**Intrusion detection system (IDS)** A computer program that senses when another computer is attempting to scan the disk or otherwise access a computer. 286

**iOS** The operating system used on the iPhone, iPod Touch, and iPad. 102

**IP address** A series of dotted decimals in a format like 192.168.2.28 that identifies a unique device on a network or internet. 502

**IP spoofing** A type of spoofing whereby an intruder uses another site's IP address as if it were that other site. 282

**IPv4** The most commonly used Internet layer protocol; has a four-decimal dotted notation, such as 165.193.123.253. 502

**IPv6** An Internet layer protocol that uses 128-bit addresses and is gradually replacing IPv4. 502

**JSON (JavaScript Object Notation)** A markup language (such as html) used for transmitting documents. Contains little metadata and is preferred for transmitting volumes of data between servers and browsers. While the notation is the format of JavaScript objects, JSON documents can be processed by any language. 508

**Just-in-time data** Data delivered to the user at the time it is needed. 403

**Just-in-time design** Rather than design the complete, overall system at the beginning, only those portions of the design that are needed to complete the current work period are done. Common for agile development techniques such as scrum. 615

**Key** (1) A column or group of columns that identifies a unique row in a table. Also referred to as a primary key. (2) A string of bits used to encrypt data. The encryption algorithm applies the key to the original message to produce the coded message. Decoding (decrypting) a message is similar; a key is applied to the coded message to recover the original text. 127, 291

**Key escrow** A control procedure whereby a trusted party is given a copy of a key used to encrypt database data. 286

**Key logger** Malicious spyware that captures keystrokes without the user's knowledge. Used to steal usernames, passwords, account numbers, and other sensitive data. 294

**Key performance indicator (KPI)** See *success metrics*. 536

**Kilobyte (KB)** 1,024 bytes. 91

**Knowledge management (KM)** The process of creating value from intellectual capital and sharing that knowledge with employees, managers, suppliers, customers, and others who need it. 543

**Kryder's Law** The storage density on magnetic disks is increasing at an exponential rate. 7

**Libraries** In version-control collaboration systems, shared directories that allow access to various documents by means of permissions. 389

**License** A contract that stipulates how a program can be used. Most specify the number of computers on which the program can be installed; some specify the number of users that can connect to and use the program remotely. Such agreements also stipulate limitations on the liability of the software vendor for the consequences of errors in the software. 105

**Lift** In market-basket terminology, the ratio of confidence to the base probability of buying an item. Lift shows how much the base probability changes when other products are purchased. If the lift is greater than 1, the change is positive; if it is less than 1, the change is negative. 553

**Lines of code** Estimating technique that attempts to schedule a development project by the number of lines of code developers must write for the project. 608

**Linkages** In Michael Porter's model of business activities, interactions across value chain activities. 65

**Linux** A version of Unix developed by the open source community. The open source community owns Linux, and there is no fee to use it. Linux is a popular operating system for Web servers. 102

**Local area network (LAN)** A network that connects computers that reside in a single geographic location on the premises of the company that operates the LAN. The number of connected computers can range from two to several hundred. 497

**Localizing** The process of making a computer program work in more than one human language. 587

**Lost-update problem** A problem that exists in database applications in which two users update the same data item but only one of those changes is recorded in the data. Can be resolved using locking. 136

**M score** In RFM analysis, a number rating that indicates in which fifth a customer ranks in terms of amount spent per order. 551

**M-commerce** E-commerce transacted using mobile devices. 401

**Mac OS** An operating system developed by Apple Computer, Inc., for the Macintosh. The current version is Mac OS X El Capitan. Initially, Macintosh computers were used primarily by graphic artists and workers in the arts community, but today Macs are used more widely. 101

**Machine code** Code compiled from source code and ready to be processed by a computer. Cannot be understood by humans. 107

**Main memory** Memory that works in conjunction with the CPU. Stores data and instructions read by the CPU and stores the results of the CPU's computations. 89

**Maintenance** In the context of information systems, (1) to fix the system to do what it was supposed to do in the first place or (2) to adapt the system to a change in requirements. 344

**Malware** Viruses, worms, Trojan horses, spyware, adware, and ransomware. 293

**Malware definitions** Patterns that exist in malware code. Antimalware vendors update these definitions continuously and incorporate them into their products in order to better fight against malware. 294

**Management information systems (MIS)** The management and use of information systems that help organizations achieve their strategies. 14

**Managerial decisions** Decisions that concern the allocation and use of resources. 372

**Many-to-many (N:M) relationship** Relationships involving two entity types in which an instance of one type can relate to many instances of the second type and an instance of the second type can relate to many instances of the first. For example, the relationship between Student and Class is N:M. One student may enroll in many classes, and one class may have many students. Contrast with one-to-many relationship. 438

**MapReduce** A two-phase technique for harnessing the power of thousands of computers working in parallel. During the first phase, the Map phase, computers work on a task in parallel; during the second phase, the Reduce phase, the work of separate computers is combined, eventually obtaining a single result. 261

**Margin** The difference between the value that an activity generates and the cost of the activity. 64

**Market-basket analysis** A data mining technique for determining sales patterns. A market-basket analysis shows the products that customers tend to buy together. 552

**Maximum cardinality** The maximum number of entities that can be involved in a relationship. Common examples of maximum cardinality are 1:N, N:M, and 1:1. 439

**Measure** The data item of interest on an OLAP report. It is the item to be summed, averaged, or otherwise processed in the OLAP cube. Total sales, average sales, and average cost are examples of measures. 567

**Megabyte (MB)** 1,024 KB. 91

**Metadata** Data that describes data. 127

**Metcalfe's Law** The value of a network is equal to the square of the number of users connected to it. 7

**Metrics** Measurements used to track performance. 536

**Microsoft Office Online** Web-based applications for processing Microsoft Office documents. Provided with OneNote and SharePoint. 385

**Microsoft Windows** The most popular nonmobile client operating system. Also refers to Windows Server, a popular server operating system that competes with Linux. 100

**Minimum cardinality** The minimum number of entities that must be involved on one side of a relationship, typically zero or one. 439

**Mobile device** A small, lightweight, power-conserving, computing device that is capable of wireless access. 401

**Mobile device management (MDM) software** Products that install and update mobile-device software, back up and restore mobile devices, and wipe software and data from devices in the event that devices are lost or employees leave the company. Such products also report usage and provide other mobile device management data. 413

**Mobile systems** Information systems that support users in motion. 401

**Modern-style applications** Windows applications that are touch-screen oriented and provide context-sensitive, pop-up menus. 100

**Modules** A suite of applications in an ERP system. 512

**Monetize** A social media company's ability to make money from its application, service, or content. 225

**MongoDB** An open source, document-oriented, nonrelational DBMS. 136

**Moore's Law** A law, created by Gordon Moore, stating that the number of transistors per square inch on an integrated chip doubles every 18 months. Moore's prediction has proved generally accurate in the 40 years since it was made. Sometimes this law is stated that the performance of a computer doubles every 18 months. Although not strictly true, this version gives the gist of the idea. 6

**Multiuser processing** The situation that exists when multiple users process the database at the same time. 135

**MySQL** A popular open source DBMS product that is license-free for most applications. 128

**Named range** A subset of the cells in a worksheet that has a unique name. 485

**Native application** A software application that requires programs other than just the browser on a user's computer; that is, that requires code on both client and server computers. See also thick-client application. 100

**Net neutrality** The idea that all data should be treated equally as it passes between networks regardless of its type, source, or quantity. 501

**Network** A collection of computers that communicate with one another over transmission lines. 497

**Network intrusion detection system (NIDS)** An intrusion detection system that examines traffic passing within a network to identify possible attacks. 580

**NewSQL DBMS** Relational DBMS with ACID support that provide processing speeds equivalent to that of the NoSQL DBMS products. 138

**Nielsen's Law** Network connection speeds for high end users will increase by 50 percent per year. 7

**Nonvolatile** Memory that preserves data contents even when not powered (e.g., magnetic and optical disks). With such devices, you can turn the computer off and back on, and the contents will be unchanged. 92

**Normal forms** Definitions of table characteristics that identify various problems to which a table is subject. 441

**Normalization** The process of converting poorly structured tables into two or more better-structured tables. 440

**NoSQL DBMS** Nonrelational databases that support very high transaction rates processing relatively simple data structures, replicated on many servers in the cloud. No ACID support. 138

**Object-oriented** When referring to languages, ones that can be used to create difficult, complex applications and, if used properly, will result in high-performance code that is easy to alter when requirements change. 404

**Off-the-shelf software** Software that is used without making any changes. 106

**Off-the-shelf with alterations software** Software bought off the shelf but altered to fit an organization's specific needs. 106

**OLAP cube** A presentation of an OLAP measure with associated dimensions. The reason for this term is that some products show these displays using three axes, like a cube in geometry. Same as OLAP report. 568

**OLAP servers** Computer servers running software that performs OLAP analyses. An OLAP server reads data from an operational database, performs preliminary calculations, and stores the results of those calculations in an OLAP database. 570

**One-of-a-kind application** Software that is developed for a specific, unique need, usually for a single company's requirements. 105

**One-to-many (1:N) relationship** Relationships involving two entity types in which an instance of one type can relate to many instances of the second type, but an instance of the second type can relate to at most one instance of the first. For example, in most businesses, the relationship between Department and Employee is 1:N. A department may relate to many employees, but an employee relates to at most one department. Contrast with many-to-many relationship. 438

**OneDrive** A free, cloud-based server for sharing documents, spreadsheets, presentations, drawings, and other types of data. Provided by Microsoft. Includes version tracking for Office documents. 387

**Online analytical processing (OLAP)** A dynamic type of reporting system that provides the ability to sum, count, average, and perform other simple arithmetic operations on groups of data. Such reports are dynamic because users can change the format of the reports while viewing them. 567

**Open source** (1) Source code that is available for a community to access. (2) A collaborative effort by which software developers create a product such as Linux; the developers often volunteer their time. In most cases, the jointly developed product can be used without paying a license fee. 107

**Operating system (OS)** A computer program that controls the computer's resources: It manages the contents of main memory, processes keystrokes and mouse movements, sends signals to the display monitor, reads and writes disk files, and controls the processing of other programs. 99

**Operational decisions** Decisions that concern the day-to-day activities of an organization. 372

**Oracle Database** A popular, enterprise-class DBMS product from Oracle Corporation. 128

**Organizational feasibility** Whether an information system fits within an organization's customer, culture, and legal requirements. 346

**Outsourcing** The process of hiring another organization to perform a service. Outsourcing is done to save costs, gain expertise, and to free up management time. 320

**Over the Internet** When applied to cloud computing, the provisioning of worldwide servers over the Internet. 157

**Packet** A formatted message that passes through networks. 501

**Packet-filtering firewall** A firewall that examines each packet and determines whether to let the packet pass. To make this decision, it examines the source address, the destination addresses, and other data. 293

**Paired programming** The situation in which two computer programmers share the same computer and develop a computer program together. 617

**Parallel installation** A type of system conversion in which the new system runs in parallel with the old one and the results of the two are reconciled for consistency. Parallel installation is expensive because the organization incurs the costs of running both systems, but it is the safest form of installation. 353

**Partitioned database** A distributed database that divides the database into nonoverlapping segments. 589

**Patch** A group of fixes for high-priority failures that can be applied to existing copies of a particular product. Software vendors supply patches to fix security and other critical problems. 355

**Pay per click** Revenue model in which advertisers display ads to potential customers for free and pay only when the customer clicks. 225

**Payload** The program codes of a virus that causes unwanted or hurtful actions, such as deleting programs or data, or even worse, modifying data in ways that are undetected by the user. 294

**Payment Card Industry Data Security Standard (PCI DSS)** Standards governing the secure storage of cardholder data. 578

**PC virtualization** Synonym for desktop virtualization. 103

**Peering** Exchanging information between telecommunication providers without charging an access fee. 501

**People** As part of the five-component framework, one of the five fundamental components of an information system; includes those who operate and service the computers, those who maintain the data, those who support the networks, and those who use the system. Information exists only in the minds of people. 15

**Perimeter firewall** A firewall that sits outside the organizational network; it is the first device that Internet traffic encounters. 293

**Personal area network (PAN)** A network connecting devices located around a single person. 497

**Personal computers (PCs)** Classic computing devices that are used by individuals. Examples of PCs include laptop or desktop computers. 89

**Personal identification number (PIN)** A form of authentication whereby the user supplies a number that only he or she knows. 290

**Personal information system** An information system used by a single individual. 183

**Personally identifiable information (PII)** Information that can be used to identify a person. 573

**Petabyte (PB)** 1,024 TB. 91

**Phased installation** A type of system conversion in which the new system is installed in pieces across the organization(s). Once a given piece works, then the organization installs and tests another piece of the system until the entire system has been installed. 353

**Phisher** An individual or organization that spoofs legitimate companies in an attempt to illegally capture personal data, such as credit card numbers, email accounts, and driver's license numbers. 282

**Phishing** A technique for obtaining unauthorized data that uses pretexting via email. The phisher pretends to be a legitimate company and sends an email requesting confidential data, such as account numbers, Social Security numbers, account passwords, and so forth. 282

**Pig** Query language used with Hadoop. 262

**Pilot installation** A type of system conversion in which the organization implements the entire system on a limited portion of the business. The advantage of pilot implementation is that if the system fails, the failure is contained within a limited boundary. This reduces exposure of the business and also protects the new system from developing a negative reputation throughout the organization. 353

**PixelSense** The Microsoft product formerly known as Surface. It allows many users to process the same tabletop touch interface. Primarily used in hotels and entertainment centers. 116

**Platform as a service (PaaS)** Vendors provide hosted computers, an operating system, and possibly a DBMS. 160

**Plunge installation** A type of system conversion in which the organization shuts off the old system and starts the new system. If the new system fails, the organization is in trouble: Nothing can be done until either the new system is fixed or the old system is reinstalled. Because of the risk, organizations should avoid this conversion style if possible. Sometimes called direct installation. 353

**Pooled** The situation in which many different organizations use the same physical hardware. 156

**Power** The utility gained from a software product. 396

**Power curve** A graph that shows the relationship of the power (the utility that one gains from a software product) as a function of the time using that product. 396

**Pretexting** Deceiving someone over the Internet by pretending to be another person or organization. 282

**Primary activities** Activities that contribute directly to the production, sale, or service of a product; in Michael Porter's model, they are inbound logistics, operations/manufacturing, outbound logistics, sales and marketing, and customer service. 64

**Primary key** One or more columns in a relation whose values identify a unique row of that relation. Also known as a key. 127

**Private cloud** In-house hosting, delivered via Web service standards, which can be dynamically configured. 164

**Private IP address** A type of IP address used within private networks and internets. Private IP addresses are assigned and managed by the company that operates the private network or internet. 502

**Problem** A perceived difference between what is and what ought to be. 373

**Procedures** Instructions for humans. One of the five fundamental components of an information system. 15

**Process blueprints** In an ERP application, comprehensive sets of inherent processes for all organizational activities, each of which is documented with diagrams that use a set of standardized symbols. 517

**Product owner** On a scrum project, the business professional who provides the requirements and is available for clarification and testing. The only person on a scrum team who has the authority to add, delete, or change requirements and adjust their priorities. 618

**Product quality assurance (PQA)** The testing of a system. PQA personnel usually construct a test plan with the advice and assistance of users. PQA test engineers perform testing, and they also supervise user test activity. Many PQA professionals are programmers who write automated test programs. 352

**Project data** Data that is part of a collaboration's work product. 376

**Project Management Institute (PMI)** International organization focused on disseminating best practices in project management. 603

**Project Management Professional (PMP)** Certification awarded by the Project Management Institute to project management professionals who meet the organization's standards of practice and pass an examination. 603

**Project metadata** Data that is used to manage a project. Schedules, tasks, budgets, and other managerial data are examples. 376

**Protocol** A set of rules for packaging and processing traffic on a network. 497

**Public IP address** An IP address used to identify a particular device on the Internet. Such IP addresses are assigned to major institutions in blocks by the Internet Corporation for Assigned Names and Numbers (ICANN). Each IP address is unique across all computers on the Internet. 502

**Public key encryption** A special version of asymmetric encryption that is popular on the Internet. With this method, each site has a public key for encoding messages and a private key for decoding them. 291

**Publish results** The process of delivering business intelligence to the knowledge workers who need it. 250

**Pull data** Data that mobile or other computing devices request from the server. 411

**Pull publishing** In business intelligence (BI) systems, the mode whereby users must request BI results. 250

**Pull report** A report the user must request. To obtain a pull report, a user goes to a Web portal or digital dashboard and clicks a link or button to cause the reporting system to produce and deliver the report. 565

**Push data** Data that the server sends to or pushes onto mobile or other computing devices. 411

**Push publishing** In business intelligence (BI) systems, the mode whereby the BI system delivers business intelligence to users without any request from the users, according to a schedule, or as a result of an event or particular data condition. 250

**Push report** Reports sent to users according to a preset schedule. Users receive the report without any activity on their part. 565

**Quad processor** A computer with four CPUs. 89

**Query** A request for data from a database. 131

**Query report** Report prepared in response to data entered by users. 564

**R score** In RFM analysis, a number rating that indicates in which fifth a customer ranks in terms of most recent order. 550

**RAM** Random access memory. Another name for a computer's main memory. 89

**Ransomware** Malicious software that blocks access to a system or data until money is paid to the attacker. 294

**Records** Also called rows, groups of columns in a database table. 125

**Regression analysis** A type of supervised data mining that estimates the values of parameters in a linear equation. Used to determine the relative influence of variables on an outcome and also to predict future values of that outcome. 260

**Relation** The more formal name for a database table. 127

**Relational database** Database that stores data in the form of relations (tables with certain restrictions) and that represents record relationships using foreign keys. 127

**Relationships** Associations among entities or entity instances in an E-R model or an association among rows of a table in a relational database. 437

**Remote action system** An information system that provides action at a distance, such as telesurgery or telelaw enforcement. 168

**Replicated database** A distributed database that contains copies of the same data items. 589

**Report** A presentation of data in a structured, meaningful context. 131

**Report authoring** The process of connecting to data sources, creating the report structure, and formatting the report. 566

**Report delivery** The function of reporting systems that determines that reports are pushed or pulled in the right form and to the right people at the right time. 567

**Report management** The function of reporting systems that defines who receives what reports, when, and by what means. 566

**Report media** In reporting systems, the channels by which reports are delivered, such as in paper form or electronically. 565

**Report mode** In reporting systems, the categorization of reports into either push reports or pull reports. 565

**Report type** In reporting systems, the categorization of reports as either static or dynamic. 564

**Reporting analysis** The process of sorting, grouping, summing, filtering, and formatting structured data. 259

**Reporting system** An information system that enables people to create information by processing data from disparate sources and delivering that information to the proper users on a timely basis. 561

**Repository** In a business process model, a collection of something; for example, a database is a repository of data. 36

**Requirements** The features, functions, and characteristics of an information system; one of the critical drivers in large-scale IS development, which typically involves trade-offs with cost and time. 602

**Requirements analysis** The second phase in the SDLC, in which developers conduct user interviews; evaluate existing systems; determine new forms/reports/queries; identify new features and functions, including security; and create the data model. 344

**Requirements creep** The process in which users agree to one set of requirements and then add more complexity or more features over time. 610

**RFM analysis** A technique readily implemented with basic reporting operations to analyze and rank customers according to their purchasing patterns. 550

**Ribbon** The wide bar of tools and selections that appears just under the tabs in an Excel workbook. 419

**Roaming** Occurs when users move their activities, especially long-running transactions, across devices. 411

**Role** In a business process, a collection of activities. 35

**Rows** Also called records, groups of columns in a database table. 125

**Safeguard** Any action, device, procedure, technique, or other measure that reduces a system's vulnerability to a threat. 280

**Schedule feasibility** Whether an information system will be able to be developed on the timetable needed. 346

**Scope** (1) In the discipline of project management, the characteristics needed to be built into an information system; same as the term requirements. (2) In the systems development life cycle (SDLC), scope means to define the system boundaries. 605

**Screen-sharing applications** Applications that offer users the ability to view the same whiteboard, application, or other display over a network. 382

**Scrum master** An expert in scrum processes whose function is to keep the development process on track and to protect team members from external distractions and influences. 618

**Secure Sockets Layer (SSL)** A protocol that uses both asymmetric and symmetric encryption. When SSL is in use, the browser address will begin with https://. The most recent version of SSL is called TLS. 292

**Self-driving car** An autonomous, or driverless, car that uses a variety of sensors to navigate like a traditional car but without human intervention. 94

**Self-efficacy** A person's belief that he or she can successfully perform the tasks required in his or her job. 194

**Semantic security** Concerns the unintended release of protected data through the release of a combination of reports or documents that are not protected independently. 268

**Sequence flow** A BPMN symbol that documents the sequence of action among business process activities. 36

**Server** A computer that provides some type of service, such as hosting a database, running a blog, publishing a Web site, or selling goods. Server computers are faster, larger, and more powerful than client computers. 90

**Server farm** A large collection of server computers that is organized to share work and compensate for one another's failures. 90

**Server tier** In the three-tier architecture, the tier that consists of computers that run Web servers for generating Web pages and responding to requests from browsers. Web servers also process application programs. 503

**Server virtualization** The process of running two or more operating system instances on the same server. The host operating system runs virtual operating system instances as applications. 104

**Service pack** A large group of fixes that solve low-priority software problems. Users apply service packs in much the same way that they apply patches, except that service packs typically involve fixes to hundreds or thousands of problems. 355

**Service-oriented architecture (SOA)** A design philosophy that dictates that all interactions among computing devices are defined as services in a formal, standardized way. SOA makes the cloud possible. 157, 505

**Site license** A license purchased by an organization to equip all the computers on a site with certain software. 105

**SLATES** An acronym developed by Andrew McAfee that summarizes the key characteristics of Enterprise 2.0: search, links, author, tagged, extensions, signaled. 539

**Small office/home office (SOHO)** A business office with usually fewer than 10 employees, often located in the business professional's home. 498

**Smart cards** Plastic cards similar to credit cards that have microchips. The microchip, which holds much more data than a magnetic strip, is loaded with identifying data. Normally requires a PIN. 290

**Smart device** A device that has processing power, memory, network connectivity, and the ability to interconnect with other devices and applications. 93

**smtp (Simple Mail Transfer Protocol)** A TCP/IP protocol used for email transmission. 508

**Sniffing** A technique for intercepting computer communications. With wired networks, sniffing requires a physical connection to the network. With wireless networks, no such connection is required. 282

**SOAP** A protocol for requesting Web services and for sending responses to Web service requests. 508

**Social capital** The investment in social relations with expectation of future returns in the marketplace. 220

**Social CRM** CRM that includes social networking elements and gives the customer much more power and control in the customer/vendor relationship. 216

**Social media (SM)** The use of information technology to support the sharing of content among networks of users. 211

**Social media information system (SMIS)** An information system that supports the sharing of content among networks of users. 211

**Social media policy** A statement that delineates employees' rights and responsibilities when generating social media content. 228

**Social media providers** Companies that provide platforms that enable the creation of social networks. Facebook, Twitter, LinkedIn, and Google are all social media providers. 212

**Social networks** The social relationships among people with common interests. 212

**Software as a service (SaaS)** Leasing hardware infrastructure, operating systems, and application programs to another organization. 159

**Software** Instructions for computers. One of the five fundamental components of an information system. 15

**Source code** Computer code written by humans and understandable by humans. Source code must be translated into machine code before it can be processed. 107

**Spear phishing** A targeted phishing attack. 575

**Speed** The dollar-value rate at which goods are exchanged in a given period of time within a supply chain. 532

**Spoofing** When someone pretends to be someone else with the intent of obtaining unauthorized data. If you pretend to be your professor, you are spoofing your professor. 282

**Spreadsheet** A table of data having rows and columns. Computer-based spreadsheets, such as those processed by Excel, include formulas and sophisticated graphics and offer other capabilities. 417

**Spyware** Programs installed on the user's computer without the user's knowledge or permission that reside in the background and, unknown to the user, observe the user's actions and keystrokes, modify computer activity, and report the user's activities to sponsoring organizations. Malicious spyware captures keystrokes to obtain usernames, passwords, account numbers, and other sensitive information. Other spyware is used for marketing analyses, observing what users do, Web sites visited, products examined and purchased, and so forth. 294

**SQL injection attack** The situation that occurs when a user obtains unauthorized access to data by entering a SQL statement into a form in which one is supposed to enter a name or other data. If the program is improperly designed, it will accept this statement and make it part of the SQL command that it issues to the DBMS. 295

**SQL Server** A popular enterprise-class DBMS product licensed by Microsoft. 128

**Stand-up** In scrum, a 15-minute meeting in which each team member states what he or she has done in the past day, what he or she will do in the coming day, and any factors that are blocking his or her progress. 616

**Static reports** Business intelligence documents that are fixed at the time of creation and do not change. 262, 564

**Steering committee** A group of senior managers from a company's major business functions that works with the CIO to set the IS priorities and decide among major IS projects and alternatives. 320

**Storage hardware** Hardware that saves data and programs. Magnetic disks are by far the most common storage device, although optical disks, such as CDs and DVDs, also are popular. 89

**Stored procedure** A computer program stored in the database that is used to enforce business rules. 516

**Strategic decisions** Decisions that concern broad-scope, organizational issues. 372

**Strength of a relationship** In social media, the likelihood that a person or other organization in a relationship will do something that will benefit the organization. 223

**Strong password** A password with the following characteristics: at least 10 characters; does not contain the user's username, real name, or company name; does not contain a complete dictionary word in any language; is different from the user's previous passwords; and contains both upper and lowercase letters, numbers, and special characters. 17

**Structured data** Data in the form of rows and columns. 259

**Structured decision** A type of decision for which there is a formalized and accepted method for making the decision. 372

**Structured Query Language (SQL)** An international standard language for processing database data and metadata. 130

**Subscriptions** User requests for particular business intelligence results on a stated schedule or in response to particular events. 264

**Success metrics** Measures that indicate whether you've achieved a specific goal. Also called key performance indicators. 536

**SUM** A built-in arithmetic function in Excel that sums the values in a row or column. 429

**Supervised data mining** A form of data mining in which data miners develop a model prior to the analysis and apply statistical techniques to data to estimate values of the parameters of the model. 260

**Supply chain** A network for organizations and facilities that transforms raw materials into products delivered to customers. 527

**Supply chain profitability** The difference between the sum of the revenue generated by the supply chain and the sum of the costs that all organizations in the supply chain incur to obtain that revenue. 530

**Support activities** In Michael Porter's value chain model, the activities that contribute indirectly to value creation: procurement, technology, human resources, and the firm's infrastructure. 64

**Support** In market-basket terminology, the probability that two items will be purchased together. 552

**Swift** Apple's programming language for OS X and iOS applications. 404

**Swimlane format** A type of business process diagram. Like swim lanes in a swimming pool, each role is shown in its own horizontal rectangle. Swimlane format can be used to simplify process diagrams and to draw attention to interactions among components of the diagram. 34

**Switching costs** Business strategy of locking in customers by making it difficult or expensive to change to another product or supplier. 70

**Symbian** A mobile client operating system popular on phones in Europe and the Far East, but less so in North America. 102

**Symmetric encryption** An encryption method whereby the same key is used to encode and to decode the message. 291

**Synchronous communication** Information exchange that occurs when all members of a work team meet at the same time, such as face-to-face meetings or conference calls. 382

**System** A group of components that interacts to achieve some purpose. 15

**System conversion** The process of converting business activity from the old system to the new. 353

**System definition** The first phase in the SDLC, in which developers, with the help of eventual users, define the new system's goals and scope, assess its feasibility, form a project team, and plan the project. 344

**Systems analyst** IS professionals who understand both business and technology. They are active throughout the systems development process and play a key role in moving the project from conception to conversion and, ultimately, maintenance. Systems analysts integrate the work of programmers, testers, other team members, and users. Compare to *business analyst*. 347

**Systems development** The process of creating and maintaining information systems. It is sometimes called systems analysis and design. 341

**Systems development life cycle (SDLC)** The classical process used to develop information systems. The basic tasks of systems development are combined into the following phases: system definition, requirements analysis, component design, implementation, and system maintenance (fix or enhance). 344

**Systems thinking** The mental activity of making one or more models of the components of a system and connecting the inputs and outputs among those components into a sensible whole, one that explains the phenomenon observed. One of four key skills for nonroutine cognitive thinking. 10

**Tab-delimited file** An exported file in which data values are separated by tab characters. 470

**Table** Also called files, groups of similar rows or records in a database. 125

**Tablets** Computing device that allows interaction through a flat touch screen. 89

**Target** The asset that is desired by a security threat. 280

**TCP/IP protocol architecture** A protocol architecture having five layers and one or more protocols defined at each layer. Programs are written to implement the rules of a particular protocol. 507

**Team members** The programmers, systems analysts, business analysts, database designers, cloud engineers, PQA testing personnel, and any other staff needed to develop an information system. 618

**Team surveys** Forms of asynchronous communication in which one team member creates a list of questions and other team members respond. Microsoft SharePoint has built-in survey capability. 383

**Technical feasibility** Whether existing information technology will be able to meet the needs of a new information system. 346

**Technical safeguards** Procedures designed to protect the hardware and software components of an information system. Examples include identification and authorization, encryption, firewalls, malware protection, and application design. 290

**Telediagnosis** A remote access system used by healthcare professionals to provide expertise in rural or remote areas. 168

**Telelaw enforcement** A remote access system that provides law enforcement capability. 168

**Telesurgery** A remote access system that links surgeons to robotic equipment and patients at a distance. 168

**Terabyte (TB)** 1,024 GB. 91

**Test plan** Groups of action and usage sequences for validating the capability of new software. 352

**The Internet** The public collection of networks used for transmitting data worldwide. 497

**Thick-client application** A software application that requires programs other than just the browser on a user's computer; that is, that requires code on both client and server computers. See also *native application*. 100

**Thin-client application** A software application that requires nothing more than a browser. Also called a Web application. 100

**Third-party cookie** A cookie created by a site other than the one visited. 272

**Threat** A person or organization that seeks to obtain or alter data or other IS assets illegally, without the owner's permission and often without the owner's knowledge. 279

**Three-tier architecture** Architecture used by most e-commerce server applications. The tiers refer to three different classes of computers. The user tier consists of users' computers that have browsers that request and process Web pages. The server tier consists of computers that run Web servers and in the process generate Web pages and other data in response to requests from browsers. Web servers also process application programs. The third tier is the database tier, which runs the DBMS that processes the database. 503

**Time** In IS development projects, the duration from start to finish; one of the critical drivers in large-scale IS development, which typically involves trade-offs with cost and requirements. 602

**Trade-off** In project management, a balancing of three critical factors: requirements, cost, and time. 602

**Train the trainer** Training sessions in which vendors train the organization's employees, called Super Users, to become in-house trainers in order to improve training quality and reduce training expenses. 518

**Transport Layer Security (TLS)** The new name for a later version of Secure Sockets Layer (SSL). 292

**Trigger** A computer program stored within the database that is executed when certain conditions arise. Primarily used to maintain database consistency. 516

**Trojan horses** Viruses that masquerade as useful programs or files. A typical Trojan horse appears to be a computer game, an MP3 music file, or some other useful, innocuous program. 294

**Tunnel** A virtual, private pathway over a public or shared network from the VPN client to the VPN server. 163

**Unified Modeling Language (UML)** A series of diagramming techniques that facilitates OOP development. UML has dozens of different diagrams for all phases of system development. UML does not require or promote any particular development process. Generally less popular that the E-R model. 436

**Unix** An operating system developed at Bell Labs in the 1970s. It has been the workhorse of the scientific and engineering communities since then. 101

**Unstructured decision** A type of decision for which there is no agreed-on decision-making process. 372

**Unsupervised data mining** A form of data mining whereby the analysts do not create a model or hypothesis before running the analysis. Instead, they apply the data mining technique to the data and observe the results. With this method, analysts create hypotheses after the analysis to explain the patterns found. 260

**URL (Uniform Resource Locator)** An address on the Internet. Consists of a protocol followed by a domain name or public IP address. 502

**User experience (UX)** Not only the user interface (UI) but also the way the application affects the user's emotions and motivation to continue to use the interface. 408

**User interface (UI)** The presentation format of an application that consists of windows, menus, icons, dialog boxes, toolbars, and so on, as well as user content. 408

**User tier** In the three-tier architecture, the tier that consists of computers, phones, and other mobile devices that have browsers and request or process Web pages and other services. 503

**User-generated content (UGC)** Content on an organization's social media presence contributed by nonemployee users. 229

**Users** Individuals and organizations that use social media sites to build social relationships. 212

**Usurpation** Occurs when unauthorized programs invade a computer system and replace legitimate programs. Such unauthorized programs typically shut down the legitimate system and substitute their own processing to spy, steal and manipulate data, or achieve other purposes. 283

**Value chain** A network of value-creating activities. 64

**Value of social capital** Value of social network that is determined by the number of relationships in a social network, the strength of those relationships, and the resources controlled by those related. 221

**Value** As defined by Michael Porter, the amount of money that a customer is willing to pay for a resource, product, or service. 64

**Vanity metrics** Metrics that are interesting but don't improve your decision making. 536

**Velocity** In scrum, the total number of points of work that a team can accomplish in each scrum period. 619

**Version control** The process that occurs when the collaboration tool limits and sometimes even directs user activity. 388

**Version management** Tracking of changes to documents by means of features and functions that accommodate concurrent work. 386

**Vertical-market application** Software that serves the needs of a specific industry. Examples of such programs are those used by dental offices to schedule appointments and bill patients, those used by auto mechanics to keep track of customer data and customers' automobile repairs, and those used by parts warehouses to track inventory, purchases, and sales. 105

**Videoconferencing** Communication technology that enables online conferencing using video. 382

**Viral hook** An inducement that causes someone to share an ad, link, file, picture, movie, or other resource with friends and associates over the Internet. 213

**Virtual machines (vm)** Computer programs that present the appearance of an independent operating system within a second host operating system. The host can support multiple virtual machines, possibly running different operating system programs (Windows, Linux), each of which is assigned assets such as disk space, devices, and network connections over which it has control. 103

**Virtual meetings** Meetings in which participants do not meet in the same place and possibly not at the same time. 382

**Virtual private cloud (VPC)** A subset of a public cloud that has highly restricted, secure access. 165

**Virtual private network (VPN)** A WAN connection alternative that uses the Internet or a private internet to create the appearance of private point-to-point connections. In the IT world, the term *virtual* means something that appears to exist that does not exist in fact. Here a VPN uses the public Internet to create the appearance of a private connection. 163

**Virtualization** The process whereby multiple operating systems run as clients on a single host operating system. Gives the appearance of many computers running on a single computer. 103

**Virus** A computer program that replicates itself. 293

**Volatile** Data that will be lost when the computer or device is not powered. 92

**Vulnerability** An opportunity for threats to gain access to individual or organizational assets. Some vulnerabilities exist because there are no safeguards or because the existing safeguards are ineffective. 280

**Walkthrough** A meeting where participants discuss the specific steps each person will take after a data breach occurs. 577

**WAN wireless** A communications system that provides wireless connectivity to a wide area network. 500

**Wardriver** People who use computers with wireless connections to search for unprotected wireless networks. 294

**Waterfall** Used to describe the nature of the SDLC. Refers to the idea that, like a series of waterfalls, systems development operates in a sequence of nonrepetitive phases. 355

**Waterfall method** The assumption that one phase of the SDLC can be completed in its entirety and the project can progress, without any backtracking, to the next phase of the SDLC. Projects seldom are that simple; backtracking is normally required. 614

**Web 2.0** A dynamic system that uses user-generated content. 539

**Web application** See *thin-client application.* 100

**Web page** Document encoded in html that is created, transmitted, and consumed using the World Wide Web. 503

**Web servers** Programs that run on a server-tier computer and that manage http traffic by sending and receiving Web pages to and from clients and by processing client requests. 503

**Web service standards** Worldwide standards that programs use to declare what they do, the structure of the data they process, and the ways they will communicate. 157

**Web services** SOA-designed programs that comply with Web service standards. 157

**Webinar** A virtual meeting in which attendees can view a common presentation on one of the attendee's computer screens for formal and organized presentations. 382

**Wide area network (WAN)** A network that connects computers at different geographic locations. 508

**Windows 10 (mobile)** A Windows operating system designed for mobile devices. 103

**Windows Server** A version of Windows that has been specifically designed and configured for server use. It has much more stringent and restrictive security procedures than other versions of Windows and is popular on servers in organizations that have made a strong commitment to Microsoft. 103

**Work breakdown structure (WBS)** A hierarchy of the tasks required to complete a project; for a large project, it might involve hundreds or thousands of tasks. 605

**Workbook** In Microsoft Excel, one or more worksheets. 417

**Workflow control** Collaboration tool feature in which software manages the flow of documents, approvals, rejections, and other characteristics among a collaborating team. 390

**Workgroup information system** An information system that supports a particular department or workgroup. 183

**Worksheet** A spreadsheet in Microsoft Excel. 417

**Worm** A virus that propagates itself using the Internet or some other computer network. Worm code is written specifically to infect another computer as quickly as possible. 294

**WSDL (Web Services Description Language)** A standard for describing the services, inputs, outputs, and other data supported by a Web service. Documents coded according to this standard are machine readable and can be used by developer tools for creating programs to access the service. 497

**XML (eXtensible Markup Language)** A markup language used for transmitting documents. Contains much metadata that can be used to validate the format and completeness of the document, but includes considerable overhead. 508

**Zettabyte (ZB)** 1,024 EB. 91

*In this index, f represents figures, n represents notes, t represents table.*

## N

## T